National Audubon Society

W9-CLI-974

BIRDS

OF NORTH AMERICA

National Audubon Society

BIRDS

OF NORTH AMERICA

The complete guide to birding—
with full-color photographs,
updated range maps, and
authoritative notes on voice,
behavior, habitat, nesting, and
conservation status

Audubon

CONTENTS

GREATER SAGE-GROUSE

HOODED MERGANSER

BROWN-CAPPED ROSY-FINCH

About National Audubon Society

The National Audubon Society protects birds and the places they need, today and tomorrow. Audubon works throughout the Americas using science, advocacy, education, and on-the-ground conservation. State programs, nature centers, chapters, and partners give Audubon an unparalleled wingspan that reaches millions of people each year to inform, inspire, and unite diverse communities in conservation action. A nonprofit conservation organization since 1905, Audubon believes in a world in which people and wildlife thrive. The organization introduces nature lovers of all ages to the world around them, while Audubon experts, including scientists and researchers, guide lawmakers and agencies in developing conservation plans and policies. Audubon also works with several domestic and international partners, including BirdLife International, to identify and protect bird habitat. Audubon organizes the community science programs Christmas Bird Count every December, and Audubon's Climate Watch in winter and summer each year. The Audubon Bird Guide app is a free and complete field guide to more than 800 species of North American birds.

Bird Classification and Taxonomy

All birds belong to the kingdom Animalia, the phylum Chordata, and the class Aves. The class is further divided into various orders, the largest of which is Passeriformes, also known as Passerines, or perching birds. It may not seem necessary to think about the classification and taxonomy of birds as an amateur birdwatcher, but it does affect the order in which species are presented in a guide such as this one. Generally, species are arranged according to our understanding of birds' evolutionary history, with waterfowl and shorebirds positioned near the front, and Passerines (flycatchers, warblers, sparrows, finches, etc.) positioned at the end of the book. We followed the American Ornithological Society's *Checklist of North American Birds* when organizing this guide.

BLACK-CAPPED CHICKADEE

CERULEAN WARBLER

Bird Names

Each bird species has both a common or English name, such as Cerulean Warbler, and a scientific or Latin name, such as *Setophaga cerulea*. The common name is what we are generally most familiar with, and is what we use in everyday conversation. The scientific name is more precise for classification purposes and consists of the genus name and the species name. In *Setophaga cerulea*, the first part indicates this bird belongs to the wood warbler genus *Setophaga*, and the second part describes the specific species—in this case, a reference to the bird's color.

Size

It is helpful to note a bird's size when seeking an identification. The average length of each species, measured from the tip of the bill to the tip of the tail, is included in each species account. Keep this in mind when comparing species—for example, a Northern Mockingbird and a Blue-gray Gnatcatcher may both be grayish birds with relatively long tails, but one is the size of a robin and the other is scarcely larger than a hummingbird! You should also note the average wingspan of a species when comparing different types of hawks and other soaring birds.

Bird Habitats

Understanding bird habitat is one of the keys to being a good birder. Some birds prefer to live near the ocean and other aquatic habitats, some prefer woodland habitats, and others favor grasslands. Where a bird chooses to live is largely dependent on its nesting and eating habits. You'll find many species in forests, where food sources are plentiful. Birds use deciduous plants for breeding and nesting activities. Woody plants are also favored because they contain thousands of insects and provide other food sources like berries, nuts, seeds, sap, and nectar. Birds also use evergreen plants for food and shelter—

SAGE THRASHER

especially in the winter, when deciduous trees shed their leaves. Some birds, including American Goldfinches, Eastern Towhees, and Gray Catbirds, prefer overgrown habitat with tall natural grasses, weeds, and shrubbery. A backyard environment, with mowed grasslands and gardens, is suitable for birds such as American Robins, Mourning Doves, Northern Cardinals, and Northern Mockingbirds. Wetland birds such as Bald Eagles, herons, ducks, geese, Ospreys, and Roseate Spoonbills prefer rivers, lakes, ponds, swamps, and other types of waterways. Birds can also be found in deserts; certain owls and hawks, Cactus Wrens, and other species can be found eating desert-dwelling beetles, wasps, and reptiles. Some birds also favor urban and suburban environments, where food scraps left over by humans are plentiful. You can support your local birds and attract them to your yard by planting regionally native plants.

Ranges

Another consideration when looking for and identifying birds is the expected range of each species. A number of species are found only in western North America, for example, and would be considered quite rare if found east of the Mississippi. Pay close attention to each bird's range map when comparing various species in a guide such as this one. Although birds are known to venture outside their typical ranges, this is an exception to the rule; it is best to first consider the species common to your area at that particular time of year when attempting to identify an unknown bird. Keep in mind that a changing climate and human impact may be affecting the ranges of many species.

Most of the species accounts in this book include a map that shows the expected range of the bird at various seasons or during migration. Some species are found only irregularly in North America; these generally have no expected range within North America, although they can occur as vagrants and strays.

Migration

Birds migrate when resources become scarce. They travel to places where food sources are abundant and nesting habitats are favorable. At least 350 North American bird species, including many of our warblers and flycatchers, migrate long distances, but it's important to remember that some birds, such as cardinals and chickadees, don't migrate at all and are able to forage for food sources year-round in one environment. Others migrate short distances, traveling a few hundred miles or moving to higher or lower elevations. Short-distance migrants include waxwings and American Tree Sparrows. Some birds migrate when the weather turns cold, but some, including American Robins, are nomadic and move only when they run out of food.

Birds are born with an uncanny navigational system. They can remember where they were born and return to that location year after year. Some birds learn how to migrate from their parents. Scientists believe birds can also sense their way using the Earth's magnetic field, the sun, and the stars. Many migratory birds fly at night to take advantage of cooler temperatures and fewer predators. However, as they pass over cities, they can become disoriented by bright artificial lights, forcing them to waste energy and often causing them to collide with buildings or windows. Audubon's Lights Out program is an effort to reduce this problem by encouraging building owners to turn off excess lighting during the months migrating birds are flying overhead.

Migratory birds travel 15 to 55 miles per hour and cover at least 15 to 600 miles a day—or more. The Arctic Tern, which flies from the Arctic to the Antarctic, covers the longest known migratory route of any bird species, traveling 49,700 miles a year—roughly the equivalent of flying twice around the globe. Bar-tailed Godwits of Alaska also make remarkable journeys each year, flying more than 6000 miles over the ocean to Asia or Australia without stopping.

RED KNOT

Courtship, Breeding, and Nesting

The types of courtship rituals used by birds vary among species. While courting, male birds often sing songs, display attractive colors, and show off intricate dance moves to attract a mate and demonstrate to females that they are capable of producing healthy offspring. Courtship behaviors are a form of communication. Besides signaling willingness to mate, it also tells other birds that a territory is being occupied. Here are some common courtship behaviors:

Singing: Singing is one of the most common ways male birds attract mates. The variety of songs used advertises the male bird's intelligence and suitability to mate. Singing also signals to other birds that an area is being occupied. While males are more likely to sing than females, sometimes males and females sing together in a duet.

Plumage: Sometimes birds puff out their feathers and enhance their body shape as a way to show their strength and health. Peacocks are among the species best known for their vibrant color display, but many North American species also display using a colorful crest, tail, gorget, or various other feathers.

Dancing: Some male birds dance for the female by diving, flapping their wings, moving their head, and shrugging their shoulders. Sometimes the male dances alone. Other times males and females dance together.

Preening: This is where birds may groom each other or sit with their bodies touching to show that they are not intending to harm their partner.

Feeding: Some male birds offer food to demonstrate they are capable of providing for a female during egg incubation. Sometimes the male may bring food and leave it nearby for the female to eat, or the male may feed the female as they would with chicks.

The length of time birds remain together also varies by species. Most birds mate only once per season, but a small percentage will have multiple mates per season. Although rare, some birds mate for life. Geese, swans, and Bald Eagles remain together until one of them dies. Bald Eagles perform a risky ritual while courting where the male and female fly high in the air together and lock talons before falling through the air and letting go just before they hit the ground. This practice tests the strength of a mate. Once together, Bald Eagles stay together and raise their young.

House Wrens and hummingbirds, on the other hand, are known to have multiple mates. Male hummingbirds typically mate with multiple females during a breeding season; female hummingbirds raise their young alone. Meanwhile, male House Wrens build multiple nests and let the female choose which one she wants to nest in. Once a female chooses, the male will attract other females to other nests they've built and help raise multiple families at once.

If you notice any type of breeding or courtship behavior in the field, it's important to keep your distance and not to disturb the process.

Foraging

Birds spend most of their day foraging. Different species of birds gather food in different ways depending on their dietary needs and bill shapes, and many use a variety of feeding techniques, from picking food off a tree branch to catching food while in flight. Avian foraging methods have adapted

PINE GROSBEAK

WESTERN BLUEBIRD

AMERICAN DIPPER

to avoid predators and to take advantage of the food available in particular habitats. Some foraging behaviors to take note of include:

Scratching: Some birds use their feet to scratch on the ground or under piles of leaves or brush in search of seeds, bugs, or other food. Sparrows, grouse, towhees, and quail frequently use this foraging technique.

Gleaning: Oftentimes birds will pick food from surfaces and crevices such as tree bark, branches, grass, leaves, and even houses. Chickadees and titmice may glean from tree branches while warblers often glean from leaves.

Hawking: In this behavior, birds quickly grab food with their bills while flying and eat the prey without perching. This is the foraging method most commonly used by birds like swifts and swallows.

Sallying: Some birds catch insects in the air and carry them to eat on a perch. They may return to the same perch over and over as they feed, or carry the food to a new perch. Flycatchers commonly use this practice.

Scanning: Hawks and other raptors often soar or hover over an area and watch their prey before suddenly attacking it.

Probing: Some birds are equipped to dig their bills into the ground or other surfaces to find food such as worms. Woodpeckers probe trees, while hummingbirds probe flowers.

Lunging: This is where birds lunge after prey and strike rapidly. This is typically seen in roadrunners and herons.

Dabbling: Certain bird species, such as many ducks and geese, feel for food and submerge their head and neck under water. Green-winged Teals, Mallards, and Blue-winged Teals use this technique.

Dipping: Some birds see food and dip their bills completely or partly in the water as they feed. Gulls and American Dippers frequently use this method.

Diving: Birds that use this method dive and swim underwater to find food. Some species of ducks forage by diving, as do loons, Anhingas, penguins, and mergansers.

Plunge-Diving: Some birds dive into water while in flight and then capture prey with their feet or bill. Ospreys plunge-dive feet first while pelicans and gannets plunge-dive bill first.

Skimming: Some birds feel along the surface of the water to capture insects or fish and then scoop the prey in their lower bill to swallow it. Flamingos, Black Skimmers, and Roseate Spoonbills use this method.

Caching: Some species, such as woodpeckers and jays, gather food and hide it for future use. This is especially evident when food sources become scarce—especially in northern areas during the winter.

Trapping: Some birds use traps they or others built to catch prey. Hummingbirds, for example, can be seen eating insects from spider webs. Research shows that some birds will use bait to attract prey, such as when herons place insects on the surface of water to attract fish and other aquatic life before swallowing the prey whole.

Flight

Some birds don't fly, but for most species, flight is the primary way birds move around. Flying helps birds feed, avoid predators, and migrate. Flight is a complex form of locomotion, involving many intricate movements, from taking off to landing. How birds fly has been adapted through years of evolution. Flying is energetically taxing for birds, but everything about bird anatomy makes flight as efficient as possible. Birds hold most of their weight in their center of gravity, for example, which makes flying easier. Birds also have hollow bones, making them as lightweight as possible. Birds defecate as they need to, which helps them get rid of excess weight. They also eat foods high in calories, such as seeds, fruits, and meat to help them gain energy quickly.

The key to flying is in the wings. Wings contain tightly woven veins, providing strength needed to maintain flight. While in the air, wings act as an airfoil, allowing birds to use air pressure from slight curves in their wings to stay in the air. Birds gain power to fly during the downstroke of their wings.

KING EIDER

Bird Intelligence

Ornithologists are constantly studying birds and learning more about them and their behavior. Bird brains are much smaller than primate brains and structurally different, but studies have suggested that birds have a similar level of circuitry in their brains as some of the most advanced mammals. This may not be surprising—it's believed both birds and mammals descended from the same primitive reptiles that lived 300 million years ago.

What's known about bird intelligence today comes from controlled laboratory experiments by scientists as well as observations made in the field. Many scientists consider corvids—the family of birds that includes ravens, crows, jays, and magpies—to be the world's most intelligent birds. Ravens have been found to pre-plan tasks better than children and apes, for example, while both crows and ravens can learn how to use tools to hunt for food. Crows can even count up to five and remember human faces, studies have shown.

TAMAULIPAS CROW

Bird Communication

Birds communicate by voice and body language. Voice is often the most identifiable way birds communicate. You can hear birds sing, call, squeak, warble, rattle, howl, and make a number of other sounds. Birds also use their bodies to create certain visual displays.

Voice: Birds use their voices for a number of reasons—they may be claiming their territory, calling for each other, hunting for food, or seeking mates. Sometimes they use their voices to announce an intruder or the presence of a predator. Sometimes they sing with other birds in a duet. For many years, ornithologists believed that only male birds sang, but studies have shown some females sing as well. Female Bullock's Orioles, for example, sing while building a nest and sometimes sing more than the males. Other singing female birds include the House Finch and the Red-winged Blackbird. Male and female Northern Cardinals are known to sing together during courtship. Researchers believe they do this to claim their territory and alert other birds that a male and female are occupying a particular space.

Visual displays: Birds also communicate with their bodies. You may see birds puff out their feathers, flap their wings, lean forward, turn their head sideways, dance, and shrug. These displays are often used by males to attract females. Females are critical of males and search for those that will make the most eligible mates. Females look for males that sing well and have good plumage—signs of strength and health.

Identification of Birds

Correctly identifying birds requires carefully examining them in detail. As you learn to recognize species of birds, identifying them will become easier. Many experienced birders can identify birds with just a quick look. Next time you're birding, take the time to look closely at each part of a bird, noting any markings on their heads, tails, and wings; the length and color of their legs; the size of their feet; and the shapes and colors of their eyes. Taking the time to observe birds in detail will help you become a better birder. There are several visual keys that can help you:

Size: Although it can be difficult to judge from a distance, the length and overall size of a bird can be important identification clues. When measured from the tip of the bill to the tip of the tail, birds range in length from about 3 inches to 72 inches. Larger birds can also be identified by the size of the wingspan. In cases where you can't quite determine the size of a bird, consider using the shape of a bird as an identification tool.

Shape: The shape of the bird is one of the most important identifying characteristics. The shape of the body, neck, and legs differ between each species, and even more prominently among the various bird families.

Color and Pattern: The color and pattern is another important tool. Some birds have the same size and shape but differ slightly in color. Coloring can also indicate the age and sex of a bird.

Behavior: Knowing the way a bird flies, stands, and carries itself can help in identification. American Coots, for example, bob their heads while they swim, while many flycatchers flick their wings and tails while perched. Learning bird behavior takes time and practice, but it can be key in distinguishing one species from another.

Voice: Sometimes you won't see a bird, but you will hear it, and so it can be helpful to learn to identify birds by their voices. Most bird vocalizations can be placed in one of two categories: *songs* or *calls*. A bird's *song* is typically used to attract a mate or claim a territory, is generally more musical and complex, and is typically given only by adult males, although many female birds sing as well. Songs are used primarily during the breeding season. A bird's *call* is used for a variety of other communications, is generally shorter and less distinct than a song, and can be given by male and female birds of any age and at any time of year. You can use both calls and songs to identify birds, paying close attention to pitch, cadence, frequency, and length.

Habitat and Range: A bird's habitat is often a key part of its identity. For example, ducks and geese are usually found near water. Some birds prefer open meadows while others prefer forests. Certain birds are more likely than others to be found along beaches, near lakes, in dry areas, in suburban areas, or in cities. Different species have their own preferences for the areas in which they feed and breed, and understanding these preferences will greatly help you identify birds. A bird's range is important, too, as some species are common in one region but quite rare in another. Sometimes birds are found in places outside their expected habitat or geographic range; the more experienced you become as a birdwatcher, the more you'll come to know what birds to expect in certain habitats and regions.

Flight: Sometimes you can't see or hear a bird up close, but you can see them flying in the air. In these situations, birds can often be identified by their wings and flight pattern. You can learn the wing shape, wing markings, rhythm, and flight path of certain species and use that to identify them. Some questions to ask yourself while watching a flying bird are, how long and wide are the wings? Do the wings have distinct colors or markings?

WHITE-WINGED TERN

Taking the time to observe birds in detail will help you become a better birder.

IDENTIFICATION OF BIRDS

You can start your life list by simply paying attention to birds in your backyard. Visiting different habitats, including forests, farmlands, and wetlands, can also be a good way to find birds.

Is the bird soaring? Gliding? Flapping? What direction is the bird flying? Is the bird hovering? Circling? Observing these patterns about birds in the air can be a useful tool.

Finding Birds

Being good at finding birds takes practice. The key is knowing where to look and knowing enough about bird habitat and behavior to find them. All birds need to eat and drink, so identifying where these sources are most abundant will help you find the species you're looking for. The more you observe birds, the more you'll understand them.

Just as people live by daily schedules, birds have daily routines; there are certain times of day when you're more likely to see birds. Most birds are most active right after dawn and just before sunset, but some birds, such as owls, night-herons, and nightjars, are nocturnal. Learning these patterns of behavior can help birders determine the best time to see birds.

Birdwatchers should also consider the time of year. Birds are easiest to see during spring and fall migration when large numbers of species gather in large groups while they travel. Birds become more secretive and are less likely to be seen when they're nesting, but during courtship is when their plumage is brightest and their songs and calls are loudest. Knowing the difference between different bird songs will help you determine which species is near. Winter is usually a difficult time to see birds, but a lack of food sources and other factors can cause irruptions in many bird species, allowing observers to see birds outside their expected ranges.

Download the Audubon Bird Guide app to find where birds are being spotted near you. Local resources can also be helpful. Many states and government agencies have put together a list of popular birdwatching destinations. Local bird groups also often take field trips together and can help you learn about the native species in your region. Contact your local Audubon chapter to help get you started.

Remember to avoid sudden movements while watching birds, and to avoid getting too close and startling them. The closer you are, the more slowly and quietly you should move.

Life Lists and Record Keeping

A life list is a complete list of the birds a birdwatcher has identified in their lifetime. You can start your life list by simply paying attention to birds in your backyard. Visiting different habitats, including forests, farmlands, and wetlands, can also be a good way to find birds. To properly add a bird to your life list, the bird should be wild, free, and observed ethically. Here are some guidelines:

Identification: The birder should be able to positively identify a bird by looking at the markings, although other birders can help if needed.

Ethics: Violating any birdwatching ethics, including trespassing on private property to observe a bird, should make a sighting uncountable.

Must Be Alive: Dead birds and eggs can't be added to your life list.

Wild and Free: A bird must be observed in the wild to count on your list. Seeing birds at a zoo, at a wildlife rehabilitation center, or otherwise enclosed settings aren't acceptable sightings.

Habitat: Vagrant or accidental birds can be added to a life list as long as they arrived outside their normal range due to natural causes, without human assistance.

Building lists and understanding how to keep track of the birds you find is a hobby that can be shared with others over a lifetime.

SHARP-TAILED GROUSE

Optics and Photography

One of the great things about birdwatching is that you don't need a lot of fancy equipment—decent binoculars and a bird guide are generally all you need to find, identify, and enjoy birds. Most birders choose 8x42 or 10x42 binoculars, and many good options are available for a few hundred dollars or less. You may later decide to obtain a spotting scope as well, to help with viewing waterfowl or shorebirds at greater distances.

Many birders are also photographers. Photography can be a great way to keep a record of your sightings and to share the joy of birds with others. A telephoto lens or zoom lens is generally required for bird photography. Research the types of cameras and lenses available and talk with other nature photographers before investing in photography gear. Always practice good ethics when photographing birds: Do not approach too closely or disturb or harass birds in any way. Do not use drones to photograph birds.

Birdwatching Ethics

When finding, identifying, and enjoying birds, the animals' welfare must be top priority. Birdwatchers must be careful not to disturb a bird's vital habitat or do anything that would make them susceptible to predators. As you watch or photograph birds, you'll recognize that they're alarmed if they cock their head to the side, partially lift their wings, or freeze. If you notice any of these signs, back off slowly or keep still. Here are some tips to keep in mind while you're birdwatching:

1. Don't disturb a bird's habitat. Loud noises, barking dogs, and flashing cameras can scare some species of birds and could impact mating and breeding. In cold weather in particular, disturbing birds could cause them to use unnecessary energy at a time when food is hard to find and energy conservation is critical.

2. Respect private property. Never enter private lands without the landowner's permission. Public lands, such as parks and national wildlife refuges, offer plenty of great viewing opportunities.

3. Keep records of the species you see. Much of what's known about birds today comes from years of record keeping by professional naturalists and amateur wildlife watchers alike. You can help researchers by noting what you see while birding and sending records to your local bird recorder. You could also consider logging your sightings through the Audubon Bird Guide app or submitting them to the online database eBird. You can also participate in community science programs like Climate Watch, Christmas Bird Count, and Great Backyard Bird Count.

4. Be careful about rare birds. As you're out looking for birds, you may come across rare birds or accidental species that have traveled far from their region of origin. Be careful not to harass these birds and avoid traveling to see them or publicizing their whereabouts unless their breeding area or habitat is well-protected. Limit methods used to attract birds, especially in heavily birded areas or areas in which threatened or endangered species are known to exist. Also make sure you don't disturb nests as this could make birds at risk of predation.

5. Provide food and shelter. Many species can benefit from bird feeders, nest boxes, and other artificial structures for safety and survival. Make sure feeders are clean and bird roosts are in an area that's safe and far from predators and hazardous material. Baiting birds—especially owls—for photography is forbidden. Putting out bait for predatory birds is potentially dangerous to the animals due to the risks of disease and habituation to human interactions.

COMMON LOON

One of the great things about birdwatching is that you don't need a lot of fancy equipment—decent binoculars and a bird guide are generally all you need to find, identify, and enjoy birds.

BLACK-CHINNED HUMMINGBIRD

Birds at Home

Although birds don't need backyard bird feeders to survive, many will readily accept our offerings, providing a great way for us to see and enjoy birds up close and from the comfort of our own homes. What a bird prefers to eat depends on the size and shape of its bill. Birds that prefer seeds, such as finches and sparrows, have short, thick bills. Birds that eat a lot of insects, such as wrens and warblers, have longer, more pointy bills. Cardinals and grosbeaks, with large bills, are well-equipped to crush larger seeds such as striped sunflower. Hummingbirds, meanwhile, with their long, slender bills, feed on nectar. Audubon bird feeders and bird seed are reviewed by a team of scientists and designed with birds in mind. Here are some common types of foods you can offer wild birds:

Sunflower seeds: Finches, chickadees, nuthatches, cardinals, grosbeaks, and jays like all types of sunflower seeds. Sunflower seeds can also attract woodpeckers. Black oil sunflower is the best food you can offer to attract the widest variety of feeder birds.

Cracked corn: Cracked corn is enjoyed by a variety of ground-feeding birds, such as doves, towhees, blackbirds, quail, grouse, and ducks.

Fruit: Diced fresh fruit, including apples, melons, grapes, sliced oranges, and even dried fruit, can attract orioles, catbirds, and mockingbirds.

Mealworms: Mealworms are enjoyed by many birds, including bluebirds, mockingbirds, chickadees, wrens, and catbirds.

Millet: Millet provides magnesium, phosphorus, protein, and calcium. It's an attractive food source for many sparrow species.

Milo: Milo, a large, red seed, is enjoyed by doves, turkeys, and pheasants.

Nyjer: Nyjer, or thistle seed, is a favorite among birds with small bills, including goldfinches, siskins, redpolls, and chickadees.

Oats: Uncooked oatmeal can be sprinkled on the ground to attract birds of all kinds.

Peanuts: Many backyard birds enjoy peanuts. Whole peanuts will attract jays and woodpeckers, while shelled peanuts will attract chickadees, titmice, nuthatches, and a variety of other birds. Make sure to not feed birds flavored or salted peanuts as this could cause them to become ill. Also be aware that peanuts are a favorite among squirrels and chipmunks.

Safflower: Cardinals, jays, chickadees, nuthatches, grosbeaks, titmice, doves, and House Sparrows are some of the birds that love safflower.

Suet: Suet is a popular treat for woodpeckers, nuthatches, chickadees, jays, and starlings. Wrens, creepers, warblers, and kinglets will also feed on suet.

Sugar water: Make sure sugar water isn't too sweet. The best sugar-to-water ratio to attract hummingbirds is 1:4. Only use refined sugar. Do not add red food coloring to homemade nectar.

Keep in mind that birds don't chew their food. Rather, they swallow food whole and grind it in their gizzard. Because of this, birds can be found eating small pebbles and dirt to help with digestion. Eggshells and oyster shells are possible treats for birds that can help them digest food. When feeding backyard birds, avoid feeding them any salty items, moldy food, milk, and dried coconut as these foods could be fatal for birds.

Conservation

Birds face many threats, and the populations of many species are in serious decline due to a variety of factors, including habitat loss, cat predation, and glass collisions. Birdwatchers can help by planting native plants, not using pesticides, keeping cats indoors, taking steps to reduce window kills (screens or stickers on the outside of windows, for example, to break up the reflection of the surrounding habitat), and leading and supporting conservation initiatives. One of the best ways you can help birds as a birdwatcher is to share the joy of birds with others, especially young people. The more people value birds, the more likely they are to take action to protect them and their habitats.

Throughout this book, you will see references to the birds' conservation status as designated by the International Union for Conservation of Nature's Red List of Threatened Species. These designations, in order of severity, are denoted as follows:

 Least Concern   Critically Endangered

 Near Threatened   Extinct in the Wild

 Vulnerable   Extinct

 Endangered

CONNECTICUT WARBLER

In a widely publicized report in late 2019 titled *Survival by Degrees: 389 Bird Species on the Brink*, Audubon scientists published the sobering and alarming results of their efforts to model the future ranges of North America's native birds. This momentous report was the most comprehensive study of its kind to date, including more than 140 million bird records from more than 70 data sources and using the latest climate modeling methods.

The report found that two-thirds of North America's native species will be negatively impacted by a warming climate, placing 389 species at greater risk of extinction as their ranges and habitats contract or disappear entirely in a changing climate.

Birdwatchers can help by reducing their personal carbon emissions; supporting carbon-neutral policies and habitat conservation; voting for political candidates who pledge to address climate change; and talking to friends, family, and neighbors about their concerns.

By stabilizing carbon emissions and holding warming to 1.5°C above pre-industrial levels, 76 percent of vulnerable species will be better off, and nearly 150 species would no longer be vulnerable to extinction from climate change. The importance of enacting solutions to combat climate change cannot be overstated—for the sake of our birds and for many other forms of wildlife as well as for humans.

SCARLET TANAGER

Adaptations of Birds of Prey

The adaptations of birds of prey are truly amazing and vary greatly from one species to the next. Differences in their facial structure correspond with the way respective raptor species hunt and locate food. Wing and feather structures can help some soar slowly over great distances, while helping others to fly silently into the night. Even talons and feet have evolved to help birds become specialized hunters. All these adaptations and more are part of what makes looking for birds of prey so exciting.

The facial structure of birds of prey is one of the most interesting characteristics, with the greatest differences being seen between that of diurnal and nocturnal predators. These different configurations are due to the size and location of their eyes.

Owls, mostly nocturnal, have eyes so large in their skulls that they take up about half of the skull's cavity. They need to have such large apertures in order to see better at night. Although their eyes can do amazing things, they are also hindered by their relative size—the eyes are immobile, fixed in the eye sockets due to how much space they occupy. Owls have compensated for this by evolving extra vertebrae in their necks so they can swivel their heads 270 degrees around. Owls also have unbelievably good hearing due to their large ears and the satellite-disk shaped faces. Their ears are different from that of any other animal because of their location—rather than being of equal height on the sides of the skull, one ear is a little higher than the other. This adaptation assists in perfectly triangulating where a food source may be scurrying around, even under leaves or snow.

Diurnal raptors—hawks, eagles, and falcons—have striking differences to their skull structure and faces. Although their eyes are facing forward, they are positioned back along the sides of the head to help with a larger panoramic view of their landscape. Their eyes also have hoods above them, making them look almost angry; however, this is just to help block sunlight from getting into their eyes. Another fascinating adaptation with falcons in particular is the malar feathers, often dark, around their eyes. These feathers absorb light instead of reflecting it back into the bird's eyes. Many human athletes have adopted this same strategy by painting dark lines beneath their eyes.

BALD EAGLE

There are some birds of prey that are even able to see beyond the color spectrum into ultra-violet. They use this adaptation to search for the urine trails of small rodents, making hunting a little easier.

The feathers of birds of prey have some intriguing variations. Owls have soft, almost fuzzy feathers. The fuzziness helps to muffle the sound of their wings cutting through the air, allowing them to stay silent as they fly. Ridges on the edges of their flight feathers also help to muffle noise. This is important because many prey species have large, sensitive ears relative to their bodies; making noise as a nocturnal hunter could ruin the chances of seizing small forest critters. Although these adaptations help with their noise level, owls are not the most aerodynamic of birds, and they don't need to be if they stay quiet enough. Owl feathers are built for stealth.

Falcons, on the other hand, have slender, aerodynamic feathers evolved to achieve the highest speeds possible to hunt their prey. Falcon feathers are much smoother and much more flexible than those of owls. The flexibility helps falcons to make quick turns while flying at high speeds. Their wings are also tapered, allowing them to cut through the air to grab unsuspecting birds. Oftentimes a Peregrine Falcon will stoop (dive) at speeds of more than 200 mph (322 km/h) towards its prey, and rather than grabbing a bird with its talons, the falcon will hit and stun the bird with its enormous feet.

There are some birds of prey that are even able to see beyond the color spectrum into ultra-violet. They use this adaptation to search for the urine trails of small rodents, making hunting a little easier.

A bird of prey's feet are among its most important tools. Peregrines and other bird-eating birds have large feet relative to their size. These birds need this adaptation because of how fast they fly when hunting. Just as a baseball player uses a glove to catch a small ball, it is easier for a falcon or hawk to grab a smaller bird with its larger feet and longer toes. The longer toes also help when trying to grab a bird under its feathers. Bird-eating birds will also often have longer legs, void of any feathers for easy cleanup. Many owls, on the other hand, will have feathers growing all the way down to the talons, ensuring no noise is created in flight.

Owls also have a special adaptation shared with a few other birds, including the Osprey—zygodactyl toes. This means they are able to pivot one of their toes backwards so there are two in the front and two in the back. This adaptation helps them to hold branches, climb tree trunks when they are young, and grab difficult prey items.

The feet of Ospreys are unlike those of any other bird. Ospreys feed almost entirely on fish. This has led to some special adaptations to their talons and the bottoms of their feet. The bottoms of their feet have small ridges called spicules. The rough spicules allow Ospreys to more easily grab fish from the water, allowing the birds to get a good grip on the slimy scales when diving after prey. Osprey talons also have a tighter curve than those of other birds, which helps them hold onto slippery fish.

In contrast to Ospreys are caracaras—ground-dwelling raptors that rarely eat fish, instead preferring terrestrial prey such as lizards, snakes, and mice. These highly intelligent and socially sophisticated birds have short talons on long legs. The shorter talons allow them to run through grasses in search of quick-moving prey items. Although in the falcon family, caracaras are not agile fliers like their cousins; they are much better at using their brains than their brawn to hunt.

Birds of prey are amazing animals that are always exciting to watch. Just by knowing their adaptations, you can identify between a hawk and falcon in silhouette. These birds are so different, even though we tend to group them all together. They have finely specialized techniques and rely on their robust set of tools to be successful hunters. It is no wonder people become so captivated with these impressive birds.

■ *Michael Goldman*

Owl Hunting Techniques

Owls might be considered the tigers of the sky; they are among the most ferocious and strongest birds of prey in North America. Owls are the perfect nighttime predators, unmatched in their stealth and senses. With the ability to survive in almost any habitat, these wide-eyed creatures have people from all around the world spellbound.

Owls are not just predators—they are apex predators at the top of the food chain. Even much larger birds of prey, such as Bald Eagles, do not tangle with a Great Horned Owl, largely because of the owl's brute strength. Owls have the strongest grip strength of any bird in North America. They use this strength to grab prey much larger and heavier than themselves. Skunks are one of the favorite prey items for Great Horned Owls, even though skunks are much heavier than Great Horned Owls and they spray their infamous foul stench. Owls lack a sense of smell, allowing them to hunt for skunks without concern for getting sprayed.

Owls' hunting techniques are two-pronged: They rely on their enormous eyes as well as their relatively large ears. Owls may spend hours sitting in trees, perfectly camouflaged to their surroundings, listening. Their ears are huge, and take up a large amount of space on the sides of their heads. The ear placement is unlike that of any other animal. Whereas other birds have ears symmetrically positioned on each side of their head, owls have one ear a little higher and the other a little lower. By bobbing their heads around, owls are able to perfectly triangu-

Owls have the strongest grip strength of any bird in North America.

LONG-EARED OWL

late where small, unseen prey is scurrying. Great Gray Owls are able to hear so well that they can grab a vole from under several inches of snow without ever seeing it. Their facial feathers, which include special rigid feathers arranged like a satellite dish, help owls to pick up on even the tiniest amount of noise from great distances.

Owl eyes are extremely large relative to the size of their heads, allowing much more light to enter. (If humans' eyes were similarly proportioned, they would be the size of softballs.) Even when the moon is not out, owls are able to pick up on trace amounts of light. Their eyes also have binocular vision, allowing them to see tiny critters from far distances. With their silent flight they can close in without being noticed to seize mice and other rodents.

Owls enjoy a broad diet. Although many prefer small mammals, some owls such as screech-owls and Burrowing Owls prefer large insects such as grasshoppers or cockroaches. Some owls are also excellent at hunting aquatic creatures. Species like the Barred Owl prefer living near lakes and streams because they hunt for salamanders, frogs, and even crayfish. It is not uncommon for Barred Owls to swoop down on the water like an eagle to catch small fish and other small aquatic animals. Owls are also known to take other birds as prey. They have a distinct advantage at night while other birds are asleep, and will go for nesting birds. Large owls also see smaller owls as prey items; it is not uncommon for a Barred Owl to eat a screech-owl or for a Great Horned Owl to take a Barred Owl.

With their unmatched strength and senses, owls are the top predators. Not only can they see better than any other animal at night, but they can also hear better. Their silent flight allows them to travel undetected to seize unsuspecting prey. An important member of the food web, owls will eat just about any living creature that can fit into their massive talons.

■ *Michael Goldman*

Flycatching Habits, Adaptations, and Techniques

Insects are the most abundant animal food source on the planet, and there are many kinds of birds—indeed, whole phylogenetic groups—that are adapted in various ways to feeding largely or wholly upon flying insects. These orders and families of birds comprise the swifts, goatsuckers (nightjars), flycatchers, and swallows and martins, all represented in North America by multiple common species. Most of these birds are migratory and get to their breeding grounds as the insect supply is becoming plentiful, leaving in fall when that food supply diminishes or disappears.

Swifts are small, highly streamlined birds with long, pointed wings. They are unmistakably fashioned for the swift flight for which they are named. Indeed, swifts are among the fastest of the land birds. They feed upon relatively small insects from just above the treetops to tremendous heights above the ground. A swift's bill is short but its mouth gape is quite wide, allowing a foraging swift to gather scores of small insects and store them in the back of its mouth if it is gathering food for its young. Swifts likely spend more time in flight than any other land bird, giving them ample time to gather food.

The goatsuckers, which include nighthawks, whip-poor-wills, and other related species in the U.S. and Canada, are long-tailed, long-winged, large-eyed birds that fly about after their insect prey mainly at dawn and dusk. Their crepuscular feeding habits reduce competition with day-feeding and night-feeding species. Goatsuckers have extremely wide mouths, which allows them to feed on a wide range of insects, up to the size of silk moths.

New World flycatchers, also known as tyrant flycatchers, are the largest family of American birds, with hundreds of species inhabiting North and South America. One can imagine that such an enormous bird family must have a great spectrum of feeding habits—and it does. As it turns out, the flycatchers of Canada and the United States mainly forage by launching themselves from a perch, snatching at a passing insect above or below the canopy, and returning to the original or another perch to dispatch their prey. Kingbirds, wood-pewees, *Empidonax* flycatchers, and phoebes are among the flycatchers that feed this way.

WHITE-THROATED SWIFT

TREE SWALLOW

BROWN BOOBY

Swallows and martins are familiar, primarily open-country birds with slender bodies and long wings—adaptations for sustained, fast flight. The bill is small and broad, and the strong jaw muscles are arranged to allow the birds to open their mouths widely when catching insects in flight. Martins and swallows feed on a wide range of mostly medium-sized aerial insects. They seldom feed within woodlands but concentrate their efforts over fields, deserts, ponds, and other open areas where insects occur plentifully.

Beyond these distinct groups are dozens of species of North American birds that hunt, catch, and eat flying insects as part of their diet. There are gnatcatchers and warblers that actively leap from their perches and snatch small flying insects from the air with their small, pointed bills. Shrikes have larger, deeper, hooked-at-the-tip bills perfect for securing larger insects such as grasshoppers in a fast, direct flight. Waxwings commonly sally forth after all kinds of small to medium-sized flying insects, and hummingbirds specialize in small insects visiting the same flowers they haunt for nectar.

Larger birds, including Laughing Gulls and Black Terns, may also consume lots of flying insects such as grasshoppers and swarming, flying ants in their diets. Red-headed and Lewis's woodpeckers regularly catch insects in flight. Falcons, from Peregrines to kestrels, dash after dragonflies. The Aplomado Falcon of the southern U.S. border and southward is often seen cruising above grass fires, snatching large flying insects trying to escape the flames. Many species of owls have been seen flying after nocturnal insects. The Eastern Screech-Owl unfortunately regularly gets killed by traffic as it pursues moths that are attracted to car and truck lights.

■ *Brian Cassie*

Plunge-Diving Behavior in Seabirds

The world's oceans provide food for countless birds. Some of these birds feed at the tide's edge and some far out to sea. The Atlantic and Pacific Oceans off the eastern and western coasts of North America are home year-round to many species of so-called seabirds—namely, those groups of birds that spend much of their lives over the ocean, often far from shore. These include albatrosses, shearwaters, and other tube-nosed species; alcids, including puffins, murres, and auklets; skuas and jaegers; some pelagic terns and gulls; tropicbirds; pelicans; and boobies and gannets. Each group of birds has its special adaptations for procuring food. Some pick food from the surface. Some plunge shallowly from the surface and half submerge or barely submerge themselves, staying under water for a few seconds at most. Others have developed a most spectacular feeding behavior—that of plunge-diving.

Pelicans are undoubtedly the most well-known of the plunge-divers. The Brown Pelican, which occurs in southern California and from the Gulf States north to Virginia, can be seen diving from a significant height headfirst into the ocean. The technique employed is keeping a steady head, rotating and angling the wings and, just as the bill enters the water, pushing the wings and feet straight out behind. Below the surface, the pelican's bill opens, its throat pouch expands (to a capacity of about two-and-a-half gallons), and the upper mandible closes down. The Brown Pelican raises its bill and lets the seawater drain out while retaining whatever fishes may have been caught.

The tropicbirds are beautiful, buoyant fliers with long streaming tails. The White-tailed Tropicbird, known and beloved in Bermuda as the Longtail, is one of two tropicbirds that frequents, if just barely geographically, our southern shores. It hovers and then plunge-dives from 30 feet (9 m) or so above the surface. It is because tropicbirds are relatively lightweight that their plunges do not carry them far below the waves. They catch their prey in their long, slightly curved bills.

The final family of plunge divers is the family Sulidae, which includes the boobies and gannets. Boobies are tropical species and four of them occur rarely and sporadically in southern U.S. waters. The much larger and common Northern Gannet of temperate or sub-Arctic Atlantic waters is the other North American species in the family. All of the Sulidae have bodies evolved for blasting headfirst and very fast into the water. Their bills and tails are pointed and they possess an overall torpedo-like body.

Northern Gannets often plunge-dive communally, their brilliant white plumage letting other gannets know where the fishing may be particularly good. From up to 100 feet (30 m) above the ocean surface, the gannets dive, arrow-like, and enter the water at dazzling speed. The force of their dive, along with underwater wing movements, carries the birds up to 30 feet (9 m) below the surface. Subcutaneous air sacs help protect the bird's head from the surface impact and flaps of skin close the nostrils to keep seawater from entering. Gannets and boobies grab their prey with long, strong bills and swallow it while underwater.

■ *Brian Cassie*

Confusing Fall Warblers

For many birdwatchers, the American wood warblers are the glories of the spring. Their great variety of colors and patterns,

along with their varied but characteristic songs, make them arguably the most sought-after group of birds in April and May. On their return migrations, however, even the brilliant males have lost a lot of luster in their plumage, typically having molted into a less striking fall and winter plumage. Add to this the dull-colored females and immatures, which greatly outnumber the adult males, and the scene is set in autumn for confusion: What is this warbler? Is it even a warbler?

About 50 species of American wood warblers breed annually somewhere in the United States and Canada. That is a lot of small songbirds to sort through in the fall. One of the best things a birder can do is to learn which species typically occur in the spot where fall warbler watching is going on. Usually, the warblers that pass through in spring are the same species that come back through in the fall. "Birds have wings," as Roger Tory Peterson famously said, and a migratory bird of any species can show up almost anywhere. But, in reality, most of the warblers one finds will be the more common warblers, perhaps up to 20 species. The challenge is to learn their names, study the field guides, and then get into the field and apply your knowledge and enthusiasm to correctly identify the warblers.

After you have sorted out that the bird you have your binoculars fixed upon is actually a warbler, with its relatively small size, horizontal posture, and thin, pointed bill, here are the general field marks to look for:

Wing bars: A lot of warblers, including the Common Yellowthroat and Wilson's Warbler to name two common species, have plain wings. Many others, such as the Blackpoll Warbler and Yellow-rumped Warbler, show two faded to prominent, usu-

ORANGE-CROWNED WARBLER

Building a new set of feathers is energetically demanding, especially for small birds, which can double their metabolic rate as the cells in their follicles race to convert large quantities of dietary and body proteins into new feathers.

ally whitish, thin bars across their wings. Looking for wing bars will quickly separate the fall warblers into two workable groups: those with wing bars and those without.

Streaking: Unlike the lightly colored wing bars, streaking on warblers is dark. These markings can be subdued or quite prominent, depending on the species. The western Black-throated Gray Warbler and the eastern Blackburnian Warbler are two birds that sport easily visible streaks on their sides. The Hooded Warbler and Nashville Warbler are among the warblers with plain undersides. Streaking may also occur on the backs of warblers and so it is recommended to also check that area of the bird for markings.

Tail spots: Does your warbler in question have white oval spots on the underside of its tail? Many of the warblers with wing bars have these spots and this combination of light markings can help in field identification.

Tail wagging: A few warblers, including the common Palm Warbler and the rare and localized Kirtland's Warbler, habitually wag their tails up and down.

Yellow coloration: Warblers can have distinct areas of yellow coloration on their throat, face, belly, undertail coverts, and/or rump. The presence or absence of this yellowness is almost always a good field mark.

Facial patterns: If you are able to get a decent look at the head of the bird you are studying, check to see whether you notice a distinct eyeline, eye ring, or cheek patch that will help you determine the warbler's species.

One final and crucially important aid to identifying fall warblers (and all birds) is to always carry a field guide. Many good pocket-sized books and apps are available that are easy to take with you into the field. You may come across a group of warblers and find yourself sorting through a variety of species, and having a field guide handy for on-the-spot reference can be greatly helpful.

■ *Brian Cassie*

WESTERN TANAGER

Molt

Feathers are made of a protein similar to that in human hair, and like human hair, feathers become frayed and worn due to exposure to the elements. Thus, plumage must be renewed periodically in order to restore its function. However, unlike hair, which can be renewed continuously as new growth emerges from the follicle, a bird can only replace an old feather by dropping it from the follicle and then replacing it with an entirely new feather. In human terms, this is like trying to replace one's only pair of shoes and only set of clothes piece-by-piece, and while wearing them!

Molt—plumage renewal—is the only life history event common to every bird, every year. Building a new set of feathers is energetically demanding, especially for small birds, which can double their metabolic rate as the cells in their follicles race to convert large quantities of dietary and body proteins into new feathers. Once a feather has begun replacement the follicle works day and night, but because most birds do not eat at night, they must use protein stored in their tissues to produce new feathers overnight, and then forage to replenish their protein (and fat) stores the next day.

Successful molt is critical for future survival, because the plumage created in the current molt is typically used for the next 6–12 months in smaller birds, and some feathers are retained for up to three years in large birds. Because of the challenge and the necessity of producing a high-quality plumage, many North American birds dedicate months to molt—even more time than they spend nesting—and most birds separate molt from other energetically demanding events such as breeding and migration. Within this general pattern, however, a variety of strategies for successful molt have evolved among species according to their differing demands of time, food availability, and flight capabilities.

Passerines require about 10 days to produce one new inch of a given wing feather, but by simultaneously molting a few feathers symmetrically in each wing (plus a few in the tail and hundreds on the body), adults of most North American passerines are able to replace their entire plumage in 1–2 months. Eastern passerines typically molt on or near the breeding grounds in late summer, when food is abundant and the weather is benign, and the costs of missing feathers are relatively low. By contrast many western migratory passerines, such as the Western Tanager and the Ash-throated Flycatcher, move far south of their breeding grounds to molt in northwestern Mexico, coinciding with the onset of annual monsoon rains there. These "molt migrants" escape the dry summer conditions of the lowland west in favor of rainy, food-rich habitats to the south.

Large birds grow feathers more quickly (3–6 days per inch of feather) than small birds, but their proportionally greater total length of feathers means that if large birds only replaced a few feathers at a time, replacing all of the feathers would require many months, precluding activities like migration and breeding. Instead, waterfowl and loons shorten the process by molting all wing feathers simultaneously—becoming flightless—after migrating to special molting waters that provide both safety and food. Herons, seabirds, and raptors may replace only a subset of their feathers each year, retaining flight capabilities during molt, but resulting in a combination of fresh and heavily worn plumage over time, a phenomenon that can often be observed in the field and used as an indicator of age.

■ *Luke Butler*

BUFFLEHEAD

Sexual Dimorphism

Sexual dimorphism refers to the visual differences between males and females of the same species. These differences, typically in size or plumage, can be seen in some North American bird species.

The majority of North American birds, including loons, grebes, alcids, swans, geese, herons, gulls, most shorebirds, rails, swifts, corvids, flycatchers, and sparrows, exhibit little or no or sexual dimorphism, meaning the males and females are similarly-sized and similarly-plumaged. Some, such as jays and magpies, are brightly and colorfully plumaged year-round, but most are not.

Sexual dimorphism is evident in most birds of prey. Eagles, hawks, falcons, and owls are groups of birds in which the females are larger than the corresponding males. This difference in size is often quite noticeable in the field, where experienced birders can often identify male and female Sharp-shinned Hawks and Peregrine Falcons in flight.

The differences between males and females in raptor species allow them to use multiple food sources based on their size and weight. Females, by virtue of their larger size, are also better able to defend their nests while incubating or raising young birds.

Families and subfamilies of birds exhibiting differences in plumage between males and females are numerous. They include ducks, grouse, quails, woodpeckers, hummingbirds, kingfishers, kinglets, bluebirds, wood warblers, tanagers, orioles and blackbirds, grosbeaks, buntings, and finches. In these birds, the male is typically more brightly ornamented in some way than the female.

AMERICAN GOLDFINCH

The smooth, white brains of birds are capable of coordinating surprisingly sophisticated and complex behavior. Much of the cognitive processing in birds takes place in the pallium, a densely-packed array of cells that functionally resembles the mammalian cortex.

The most common form of sexual dimorphism is colorful plumage, which may occur all through the year, as in woodpeckers and the Northern Cardinal, or only in the breeding season, as in the Scarlet Tanager and most of the wood warblers. Bright and colorful plumages help males to attract females to breeding territories, while duller, more subtle plumages make nesting females in the woods or on the plains less conspicuous while they incubate and tend to young.

The female Belted Kingfisher is an unusual circumstance of a female being more brightly plumaged than the male, as she sports a rufous belly stripe missing in the male. Another unusual example of dimorphism occurs in the phalaropes. Phalaropes have the distinction among shorebirds of being sexually dimorphic both in size—with larger females—and in seasonal plumage, with females being the more colorful sex in spring and summer. It turns out that male phalaropes do all of the incubating and nest duties in this fascinating group of waders, and thus they have more cryptic plumage in the breeding season.

Another way in which birds show sexual dimorphism is in structural differences between the sexes. Around the world there are numerous examples of this, but in North America, the single species that exhibits this trait is the American Avocet, where the male has a longer and less curved bill than the female. This feature is readily observable in the field.

■ *Brian Cassie*

Avian Cognition, Memory, and Tool Use

Wild birds display their intelligence through their exploratory behavior, flexibility, boldness, and innovation. These traits all reflect inherent cognitive abilities—birds rely on their cognition to synthesize, integrate, and make predictions based on past experience. The essence of cognition is representation, which ties together the bird's behavior with its internal mental processing. Representations result from a transformation of the raw products of perception into algorithms that sketch out the features of the birds' environment. From the moment they hatch, birds begin the process of constructing the mental scaffolds that will serve them throughout life. As they mature, their behavior is increasingly guided by the preconceptions that they derive from their prior experiences with their physical and social world.

The smooth, white brains of birds are capable of coordinating surprisingly sophisticated and complex behavior. Much of the cognitive processing in birds takes place in the pallium, a densely-packed array of cells that functionally resembles the mammalian cortex. The pallium is a remarkably flexible processor—it forms associations between multiple sources of information, repurposes previously learned material, and it consolidates and stores long-term memories.

The sense organs of birds actively modify and reconfigure the signals they pass to the brain. Their eyes, for example, encode not just colored pixels, but also edges and surfaces; they send a partial impression of the physical structure of the external world to the brain. Incoming information from the sense organs is additionally massaged and filtered by the process of attention. Attention selects and enhances what the brain considers to be most important and begins to interpret the sensory information. After the attentional filter, incoming information is further modified in the brain—it is changed to fit into the bird's pre-existing view of how the world works. This process, called perception, generates an internal representation of the outside world. The internal representation gets channeled into a short-term buffer, otherwise known as working memory.

Avian cognition is grounded in memory, the imperfect faculty responsible for mental record-keeping. Memory, in birds as in people, is not a homogeneous process. Different kinds of memory rely on different sensory inputs—some respond to immediate sensations, some depend on previous processing, and some require multiple sensory dimensions. Working memory, for example, is always relational—it registers immediate perceptions from different sensory modalities and integrates them into representations of the flow of current events. The buffer is limited in size (there is only so much that can be stuffed into it), and it is volatile, lasting for only a brief period before it starts to

CALIFORNIA SCRUB-JAY

be overwritten by new content. This means that birds, like other animals, can easily be overwhelmed by too much information coming in too quickly. They require time to make sense of their surroundings. Working memory capacity is one of the primary bottlenecks in information processing, because it limits the number of representations that can be simultaneously interlinked.

The representation of a visual object in working memory is often called a "searching image." Searching images encode features of a target—a prey item, for example, or a cryptically colored seed—and they enhance the bird's ability to detect additional targets of the same appearance. Using searching images, birds such as Blue Jays and pigeons find cryptic food items with remarkable efficiency, and over time they only get faster and more accurate.

If working memory was all there was, then birds would treat every moment as if it were new. There would be no association between what's happening now and what happened on other occasions. But birds selectively convert some information from working memory into more permanent storage, called long-term memory, which is found in different specialized storage compartments in the bird's brain. One such compartment, called procedural memory, is located mainly in the cerebellum. Procedural memory encodes the actions required for particular physical tasks, such as building a nest or using a tool, into long-lasting sequences.

Another long-lasting storage compartment is called reference memory, which stores auditory and visual representations, such as calls, food items, other animals, and environmental features (like the image of a favorite roost tree). Reference memory also stores spatial representations, such as the location of a nest or a site with abundant insects. Reference memory even stores attributes of other individuals in a bird's social group—who is a relative, who's dominant, and who can be relied on as a guide to food.

One specialized kind of reference memory is called episodic memory, which links time, place, sound, and visual imagery together in a heterogeneous sensory experience. Episodic memory gives birds their excellent abilities to remember events—the full context of the what, when, where, and who. Corvids, for example, can recall the entire circumstances of a caching event: they know where they previously hid a food item, which kind of food it was, how long ago the event occurred, and which other individuals were present at the time. A single relevant environmental trigger can retrieve all of the dimensions of an episodic memory, pulling up a unified representation of a specific event that links its auditory, visual, and spatial information.

A major branch of research on avian cognition focuses on how objects or events in the environment are represented in a bird's mind. Cognitive representations direct the bird through an interlinked system of its memories and perceptions to guide its subsequent behavior. One of the best-established interlinked systems is a cognitive map, a representation of the surrounding space that allows a bird to get from one location to another without having to retrace its previous path. Instead of mindlessly flying to each of the locations visited earlier, birds can use their cognitive maps to determine more direct routes. In this way, displaced pigeons get back to their nest boxes efficiently, and Clark's Nutcrackers relocate cached food items even weeks after they hid them. In both cases, the birds use

Nuthatches and Green Jays pry up pieces of bark with a twig to search for prey underneath, Green Herons throw out leaves or cast feathers to bait small fish to come within reach, and ravens throw rocks at intruders near their nest.

their cognitive maps to navigate, orienting with a combination of internal compass guides, visible landmarks, and the position of the sun.

These map-like representations aren't limited to those with a spatial orientation. Birds can obtain new insights about relationships between individuals in their social group, using something akin to a representation of a social network. Highly social birds, such as Pinyon Jays and Common Ravens, form representations of dominance relationships and social attachments; they use these maps to track ongoing changes to the affiliations in their flock. They are even able to make transitive social inferences: they can predict how any two known individuals would interact, even if the observer has never previously seen them together. Similar information is acquired by territorial chickadees, who pay attention to conflicts between their neighbors and use this "eavesdropping" to determine how to interact with the other birds in the future.

Birds can also learn to recognize that certain objects or images share common characteristics—that they form a class with distinctive attributes. This ability is generally termed categorical discrimination, and it requires linking together disparate stimuli into a single representation that can be responded to as a unit. A classic example is the ability of pigeons to recognize the trees in photographic images as a class of objects, discriminating tree images from other kinds of pictures even when the trees are of different shapes and sizes. This suggests that birds are capable of forming a concept or category of "tree," a cognitive representation of a particular object class. Mistakes do occur, but they are frequently revealing, as when the birds incorrectly identify images of asparagus or broccoli as trees.

Tool use is a recognized feature of the foraging behavior of some bird species: African vultures drop stones on ostrich nests, and Galápagos Woodpecker Finches use cactus spines to extract insects from holes in trees. New Caledonian Crows are recognized as tool-use experts—they select particular leaves and stems from the pandanus tree, modify them by twisting, shaving, or shortening, and then they use them as probes and hooks to remove insect larvae from holes in tree bark. There are many other avian species that display behavior that is commonly considered tool use: nuthatches and Green Jays pry up pieces of

bark with a twig to search for prey underneath, Green Herons throw out leaves or cast feathers to bait small fish to come within reach, and ravens throw rocks at intruders near their nest.

These easily recognizable examples of tool use in birds occur alongside many kinds of behavior whose function is more obscure. Birds commonly manipulate a wide variety of natural items that have no evident function in foraging or nest-building. They pick up leaves, fiddle with twigs or fallen feathers, and poke at rocks and pebbles. Such exploration is common in juveniles that are still learning natural adult behavior patterns. Young Pinyon Jays, for example, often pick up leaves or twigs and carefully hide them under other litter, a suggestive precursor to the caching behavior they will later use in concealing pine nuts. Hawks and gulls will repeatedly pick up objects, carry them into the air, drop them, and then recapture them before they hit the ground.

Tool use, however, results from different cognitive processes than those that underlie other kinds of object manipulations. To be used as a tool, an object must be seen—even if only briefly—as a means to an end. Birds that use tools commonly have larger brains for their body size, and they show more diverse and complex behavior. To differentiate tool use, researchers have limited

CLIFF SWALLOW

the term to apply only to instances in which a bird manipulates one freely moveable object in order to attain a particular goal in reference to another. This definition excludes many otherwise ambiguous behaviors. Gulls that drop clams or sea urchins on a rocky shore wouldn't be included, since the rocks on the beach are not directly manipulated by the bird. But American Crows that hold rocks in their bills to hammer acorns open would fully qualify for tool use, because they move the rock with the intent of cracking open the acorn. American Crows are tool-use champions, and they have been recorded using at least half a dozen different tools.

Birds evolved from a group of dinosaurs, so one might expect them to have a rather reptilian intelligence. But birds evolved their own variety of sophisticated cognition over more than 60 million years as they diversified in their aerial world. In many respects, birds rival mammals for their cognitive capabilities— their social insight, their innovative approaches to foraging, and their willingness to learn from new situations.

■ *Judy Diamond and Alan B. Bond*

GREEN JAY

Corvid Intelligence

The sinister reputation, brash attitude, and aggressive demeanor of corvids—jays, crows, ravens, nutcrackers, and magpies— put many people off. But take a closer look and you will likely agree that they are wonderful birds worthy of the respect they garnered as gods and informants to Native Americans, the Norse, and people of the Far East. We are fortunate to share the United States and Canada with a rich diversity of corvids including 11 species of jay, four crows, two ravens, two magpies, and a nutcracker. Here are a few facts to guide your exploration of their world.

Watch jays at a backyard feeder and you may observe a scene like this: Three Steller's Jays hit the feeder with a *squak*. Quickly they swish their strong bills through the sunflower and millet to test and reap the handful of peanuts buried beneath the other seeds. By lifting and shaking each shell, the jays weigh the contents and select the heaviest. They communicate to one another not only with calls, but also by raising or lowering their crests. A fully raised crest is a signal of dominance and aggression. And they don't just talk to other jays—they frequently mimic the calls of hawks, which may flush other birds from bird feeders, enabling gluttony.

Corvids are songbirds, belonging to the order Passeriformes, and as such their vocal prowess is legendary. The Common Raven, the largest songbird in the world, can bark like a dog, crow like a rooster, or sound like dripping water. Crows, ravens,

COMMON RAVEN

The Common Raven, the largest songbird in the world, can bark like a dog, crow like a rooster, or sound like dripping water.

and magpies that are raised in captivity regularly pick up bits of human vocabulary. In the 1960s an American Crow was observed in Missoula, Montana, talking to dogs and luring them from their yards by commanding them to *come boy, here boy* just as their owners would do.

Ravens are also known as "wolf birds" because of their close association with wild canids. As wolves reclaim the West, watch how ravens follow them and flock to their kills. The abilities of crafty ravens to steal from wolves—one bird often distracts a lobo with the sharp yank of its tail while a second rushes in to grab a treat—is thought to be a major force shaping the pack life of wolves.

Magpies have a keen sense of smell, which is rare among birds, that allows them to sniff out and scavenge carrion. Their bulky, domed nests hide eggs and chicks from would-be predators. Some magpies move their eggs between alternative nests, perhaps to foil knowledgeable nest raiders.

Corvids mate for life, which can stretch across decades. The pair nesting high in your backyard tree can identify you by your face and remember if you have been naughty or nice. Experiments in Seattle demonstrate that a wronged crow will remember your face for 13 years (and counting!). Many people receive trinkets from their neighborhood crows. This apparent "gifting" follows kind acts, such as rescuing a trapped bird or feeding.

Clark's Nutcrackers, like all corvids, have large brains relative to their body size. These hoarders stash thousands of pine nuts in the ground each autumn and retrieve them throughout the year. The high fat and protein content of the seeds fuels the nutcracker's breeding and the energetic demands of remembering where it placed all the seeds. The part of its brain used to memorize cache locations grows each autumn and shrinks in spring and summer. Precise memory allows these birds to even dig through snow to recover a cache. Canada Jays avoid that necessity by caching on tree branches rather than in the soil. They have enlarged salivary glands that produce sticky spittle capable of gluing a mash of insects, meat, and pilfered sandwich to a branch.

Many corvids are on the increase throughout the United States. Their tolerance of people, understanding of our actions, and ability to exploit the landscapes we create enable these brainiacs to push beyond the city, ranch, and farm into wilder landscapes. There, they may challenge species less able to tolerate human presence, such as sage-grouse, Piping Plovers, Marbled Murrelets, and desert tortoises. By understanding how our activities increase corvid populations we might learn to modify lands less to their liking. Watching ravens, for example, can teach us to reduce road kill, restore the diversity of native predators, cover landfills, discourage nests on power transmission lines, and increase native plant cover on farmlands. Life-sustaining lessons flow from these powerful and knowledgeable birds.

■ *John Marzluff*

BLACK-BILLED MAGPIE

NORTHERN PINTAIL

Navigational Systems Used in Migration

Even with the advanced navigational technologies of the 21st century such as GPS, it is surprising that we still do not know how migrating animals find their way over global-scale distances. In order to accurately navigate from point to point, animals are thought to possess "map" and "compass" senses: a *map* to show the destination's direction, and a *compass* to find that direction or to remain oriented en route (or both). Birds are the most intensively studied far-traveled animals, and the domesticated homing pigeon is the preferred subject of study because it homes on demand from both familiar and unfamiliar release sites, rather than migrating every six months with the changing seasons. The "compass" senses of birds are relatively well known, but their "map" sense remains elusive and highly controversial. The primary "compass" used by birds is based on the sun's position and time of day indicated by their biological clock. They can also use the geomagnetic field or the apparent rotation of stars at night to orient themselves.

A bi-coordinate (latitude and longitude) mental "map" formed by gradients in the geomagnetic field (GMF) has been proposed to explain how birds determine their position. The GMF's inclination (angle of dip) and intensity change from equator to poles, becoming steeper and stronger, respectively. It has been suggested that the GMF's intensity gradient gives latitude, but areas of highly magnetic rocks commonly mask this weak poleward gradient. Moreover, there is no clear east-west gradient indicating longitude. Another problem with the magnetic "map" hypothesis is that experiments with pigeons carrying strong magnets that obscure the GMF are able to return home at normal rates and speeds on sunny days.

Another suggestion for the avian "map" is the olfactory hypothesis (sense of smell). Experiments by Italian scientists in the early 1970s showed that pigeons with an impaired sense of smell exhibited significant deficits in their homing ability. The scientists concluded that olfaction is important to avian navigation and that pigeons were possibly using gradients in atmospheric

Although birds' ears are too close together for them to identify the source direction of long-wavelength infrasonic signals, pigeons are known to circle at release sites before departing. By doing so they may be using Doppler shifts to determine when they are flying towards or away from an acoustic source.

odors to home. These results, however, have not been consistently reproduced at other experimental lofts. In addition, no particular odor or odors have been identified that birds might be using. An accurate navigational system that is based on passive odor gradients within a turbulent and rapidly changing atmosphere, especially over the great distances that birds migrate and forage, is difficult to imagine.

A third possibility for the avian "map" is natural atmospheric infrasound (low-frequency acoustic waves). In this case, the signals would act as "beacons" rather than as bi-coordinate gradient "maps." Because of their low frequencies (<15 Hz, the lower limit of human hearing), infrasound waves travel for great distances in the atmosphere—thousands of kilometers. Amazingly, pigeons in the laboratory can hear frequencies as low as 0.05 Hz. Continuously generated seismic energy from interfering deep-ocean waves causes the ground surface almost everywhere on Earth to oscillate ever so slightly at frequencies near 0.2 Hz. Birds might decipher the acoustic signatures of important topographic features produced by this movement and "hear" the landscape similar to the way we see it. Although birds' ears are too close together for them to identify the source direction of long-wavelength infrasonic signals, pigeons are known to circle at release sites before departing. By doing so they may be using Doppler shifts to determine when they are flying towards or away from an acoustic source. In flight, they could use their solar and/or magnetic compasses to stay on course.

The use of infrasonic signals by birds to navigate can explain a number of common experimental observations that the other two hypotheses cannot, including: (1) why pigeons are lost at some release sites—because these sites are in sound "shadows" relative to the loft area, (2) why birds depart sites in directions off the homeward bearing—because topographic features often deflect the homeward signals, and (3) why European pigeons home better during summer than winter—because the background noise of the atmosphere is louder in winter due to greater storm activity that generates higher amplitude deep-ocean waves.

Decades of contentious debate have not resolved the nature of the avian "map." Much work has yet to be done, but infrasonic "beacons" appear to be a promising solution to the problem. Radio beacons are commonly used in aeronautical navigation, and birds could possibly use natural infrasound, instead of artificial radio waves, to provide them with the necessary directional or "map" information.

■ *Jonathan T. Hagstrum*

PURPLE MARTIN

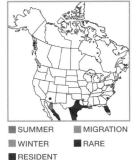

■ SUMMER   ■ MIGRATION
■ WINTER   ■ RARE
■ RESIDENT

These handsome, conspicuous birds often rest on large tree branches, stakes, or poles in the water or, less commonly, on the ground. They are easily domesticated and are quite tame even in the wild. Almost entirely herbivorous, they feed in shallow water on tubers and other aquatic vegetation, as well as in grain fields. Unlike many ducks, this species is largely nocturnal, migrating at night and resting and feeding during the day. It was formerly known as the "Black-bellied Tree Duck."

DESCRIPTION: 20–22" (51–56 cm). A tall, long-necked, long-legged duck. The body of the adult is mainly chestnut and black; its bill is red and its legs are pink. A large white wing patch is visible in flight. Immature is similar but much duller. Juveniles are paler with a gray bill.

VOICE: These noisy birds issue mellow whistles sometimes described as "wheezy." Their call is a high-pitched, four-note whistle, issued frequently in flight. May issue weak *yip* alarm calls when flushed.

NESTING: Often nests in colonies and may mate for life. The female places 12–16 white eggs in a tree cavity or human-provided nest box without a nest lining, or occasionally on the ground among reeds.

HABITAT: Wooded or tree-lined streams and ponds. Prefers shallow freshwater habitats, especially those with nearby trees for cover and nesting.

RANGE: Breeds in extreme southern Texas and Arizona; introduced birds have bred in southern Florida. Also found in American tropics. Not strongly migratory. Irregular summer wanderers occur throughout the Gulf states, occasionally straying even farther north and inland.

SIMILAR SPECIES: Adults are unmistakable. Fulvous Whistling-Duck is similar to a dark-billed immature, but much brighter; it lacks a white wing patch.

CONSERVATION: Human-provided nest boxes have helped these birds mount a recovery since the 1950s. It is now fairly common in southern Texas and naturalized in parts of Florida.

These long-legged, goose-like ducks frequent shallow wetlands and flooded rice fields. Although Fulvous Whistling-Ducks in North America breed only in California, Texas, Louisiana, and Florida, they sometimes wander. Small flocks have turned up as far away as British Columbia and Nova Scotia. They are widespread in the tropics of the Americas, Asia, and Africa. These long-legged ducks are often active at night and at twilight, feeding mostly on the seeds of aquatic plants and grasses, and they are often associated with rice fields in the United States. This species was formerly known as the "Fulvous Tree Duck." The name "fulvous" refers to its tawny color.

DESCRIPTION: 18–21" (46–53 cm). A long-legged, long-necked, goose-like duck. The body is mainly rich tawny, with a white stripe on the sides. The back and wings are dark; the rump and undertail coverts are white and conspicuous in flight.

VOICE: A hoarse whistle, *ka-wheee*. Males' voices are higher-pitched than females'.

NESTING: Mated pairs stay together for many years, possibly for life. Females lay 12–15 buff-white eggs in a shallow cup of grass or a well-woven basket of reeds in a marsh. Sometimes several females lay in the same nest.

HABITAT: Rice fields, freshwater marshes, wet meadows, and lagoons.

RANGE: Resident in southern California, coastal Texas and Louisiana, and southern Florida. Also in American tropics and Old World.

SIMILAR SPECIES: See immature Black-bellied Whistling-Duck.

CONSERVATION:

The species is nearly extirpated in the Southwest, and its numbers vary in the Southeast. Rice farming in the southeastern U.S. impacts this species by providing nesting sites and feeding grounds, but farmers do not always welcome their presence; it is unclear whether these ducks feed on the seeds of weeds that inhabit rice fields, or if they feed on (thus damage) the rice crops themselves.

■ SUMMER ■ MIGRATION
■ WINTER ■ RARE
■ RESIDENT

This small and stocky goose is uncommon and localized, frequenting tidewater marshes, reefs, sheltered lagoons, and coastal tundra in western Alaska and the Aleutian Islands. As with other tundra-dwelling birds, the head and neck of these geese take on a deep rust stain from the iron in stagnating waters, for they feed with head and neck submerged, plucking vegetation from the bottom. They also feed at mudflats exposed at low tides.

DESCRIPTION: 26–28" (66–71 cm). As large as Snow Goose or Greater White-fronted Goose. Its body and wings are silvery gray; black and white feather margins give it a scaled, bluish appearance. The head is white but often becomes stained orange or rust-colored in summer. The hindneck and tail are white. It sports a characteristic black throat and small, pinkish bill. Its legs and feet are bright orange. Juveniles are gray overall.

VOICE: Loud, musical notes, *kla-ha, kla-ha, kla-ha*. Its vocalizations have a tinny or nasal quality.

NESTING: Lays 3–8 creamy-white eggs in a down-lined nest placed on the ground on islets of marshy tundra or among driftwood on the coast.

HABITAT: Seacoasts, mudflats, and coastal tundra.

RANGE: Breeds on islands and marshy coasts of western Alaska. Winters mainly in the Aleutian Islands east to Kodiak Island.

SIMILAR SPECIES: The black pattern on the throat distinguishes this species from a blue-morph Snow Goose, which is relatively rare in Alaska.

CONSERVATION: NT

Hunting and oil pollution in the 70s and 80s are suspected in the sharp population declines witnessed in Emperor Geese during that time. The wild population is estimated at around 100,000 and appears to be stable or slightly increasing, but the species' restricted range and reliance on arctic and subarctic ecosystems leave it vulnerable to climate change.

■ SUMMER ■ MIGRATION
■ WINTER ■ RARE
■ RESIDENT

Snow Geese migrate long distances, sometimes flying so high that they can barely be seen. Even at this height, however, they can often be identified by the shifting curved lines and arcs they form as they fly. Hunters call these birds "Wavies," but not because of the shape of their flocks; the word is derived from *wewe*, the Chippewa name for the species. In the Far North fresh plant shoots are scarce in early spring, but the geese arrive with good fat reserves, built up from plants consumed on prairie marshes where they pause during their long spring migration. Snow Geese graze fields and marshes of Pacific coastal areas and the Southwest all winter. The largest concentrations are in California's Central Valley and along the Gulf Coast of Texas and Louisiana. As they do elsewhere, these birds spend the night resting on open water.

DESCRIPTION: 25–31" (64–79 cm). Smaller than the domestic goose. Snow Geese have pink legs and bills with black "lips" or "grin patches"—these structures, called tomia, act as cutting edges on the birds' mandibles. The "white-morph" Snow Goose is pure white with black wing tips. Young birds have a dark bill and are mottled with brownish gray above. A darker colored "blue-morph"—once considered a separate species called the "Blue Goose"—has bluish-gray upperparts, brownish underparts, and a white head and neck. Blue-morph birds have spread westward in recent decades and are now found locally throughout their winter range among the thousands of white Snow Geese.

VOICE: A high-pitched, barking *bow-wow!* or *howk-howk!*

NESTING: Snow Geese nest in colonies. They lay 4–8 white eggs—although the eggshells often become stained—in a nest sparsely lined with down on the tundra.

HABITAT: Breeds on the tundra and winters in salt marshes and marshy coastal bays; less commonly in freshwater marshes and adjacent grainfields.

RANGE: Breeds in Arctic regions of North America and extreme eastern Siberia. In the West, winters on the Pacific Coast from southern British Columbia south to Baja California; also the mid-Atlantic Coast and Gulf Coast from Mississippi to Texas. In smaller numbers in the interior.

SUBSPECIES: Snow Geese are separated into two subspecies. The larger Greater Snow Goose nests in the extreme north of eastern Canada and winters on the mid-Atlantic Coast; this subspecies is predominantly composed of white-morph individuals. The smaller Lesser Snow Goose subspecies is more widespread geographically and more prone to dark-morph individuals. Lesser Snow Goose winters in the interior United States, especially along the Gulf Coast and in the West and Southwest.

SIMILAR SPECIES: Ross's Goose is smaller with a shorter neck, stubbier bill, faster wingbeats, and more highly pitched call. Emperor Goose has dark tail coverts, scaly appearance, and lacks black "lips" on mandible; its range does not typically overlap that of the blue-phase Snow Goose with which it is most easily confused. Immature White-fronted Goose has a pink bill and orange feet.

CONSERVATION:

The population of Snow Geese has grown rapidly during the past few decades, to the point that hunting regulations have been relaxed in an effort to control the explosive growth rate. Ecologists worry that an overpopulation of Snow Geese may be degrading tundra and saltwater marsh breeding habitats critical to other wildlife, including other waterfowl species.

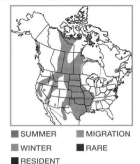

■ SUMMER   ■ MIGRATION
■ WINTER   ■ RARE
■ RESIDENT

This relatively rare bird is carefully monitored by both Canadian and United States game biologists, but some hunting is allowed on its winter grounds. The species' main population nests in the high arctic in Nanavut, Canada, and migrates in huge flocks to winter in California's Sacramento Valley. The population has increased in recent years, and there are now estimated to be more than 80,000 Ross's Geese, the great majority of which winter in California with the main population. Others are seen, less commonly, during migration and in winter in the interior United States, often mingling with other species.

DESCRIPTION: 24" (61 cm). A Mallard-sized edition of the Snow Goose. Ross's Goose has white wings, black wing tips, a stubby pink bill, and pink legs. It differs from Snow Goose in its smaller size, smaller bill, and rounder head. The two species are usually seen together and occasionally hybridize. The extremely rare blue-morph Ross's Goose looks like a smaller, darker version of a blue-morph Snow Goose.

VOICE: Soft cackling and grunting notes. Generally less vocal than Snow Goose.

NESTING: Lays 4 or 5 creamy-white eggs in a down-lined grass nest placed on a small island in a lake or river. Nests in loose colonies.

HABITAT: Arctic tundra in the breeding season, salt or freshwater marshes in the winter.

RANGE: Breeds in northeastern Mackenzie and on Southampton Island in Hudson Bay; winters mainly in California, but now occurs in increasing numbers in the lower Mississippi Valley and on the East Coast.

SIMILAR SPECIES: Similar to Snow Goose and often appear together; "Lesser" Snow Goose is larger and far more abundant. Compared to Ross's Goose, a Snow Goose has a longer bill and neck and a lower-pitched call.

CONSERVATION: LC
The population of Ross's Goose, although relatively small, appears to be growing steadily alongside that of Snow Goose.

■ SUMMER ■ MIGRATION
■ WINTER ■ RARE
■ RESIDENT

Greater White-fronted Goose is named for the white patch on its face at the base of the bill. Arctic breeders, these medium-sized geese often migrate in large flocks at night, when they can be identified by their distinctive call. Large wintering populations can be found in California's Sacramento Valley, the eastern Great Plains, and along the Gulf Coast in Louisiana and Texas.

DESCRIPTION: 27–30" (69–76 cm). A dusky-brown goose with conspicuous white belly and undertail coverts, a white patch on the front of the face, and underparts that are barred and flecked with black. Its legs are orange. The bill is usually pinkish or orange with a white tip. Birds from Greenland have orange bills. Young birds lack white face and black bars on underparts.

VOICE: A distinctive bark: *kla-ha!* or *kla-hah-luk!*

NESTING: Lays 5 or 6 cream-colored eggs in a down-lined grassy depression on the tundra.

HABITAT: Breeds on marshy tundra; winters on marshes and bays. Like other geese, they often leave the marshes to feed in nearby stubble fields, where they are frequently concealed from view unless flushed, when they rush noisily into the air.

RANGE: Breeds in Alaska, far-northern Canada, and Greenland. Winters from coastal British Columbia to California, in New Mexico, and along the Gulf Coast in Texas and Louisiana; more rarely on the East Coast and in the interior. It also breeds in northern Eurasia.

SUBSPECIES: The "Tule Goose" of the West Coast is considered a large race of the Greater White-fronted; its breeding grounds were unknown until 1979, when birds were found nesting near Anchorage, Alaska. These birds winter in central California marshes, mingled among other populations of Greater White-fronted Geese.

In addition, the subspecies that breeds in Greenland is distinct, and some argue it to be a separate species altogether called the Greenland White-fronted Goose. These birds differ from their mainland North American kin in appearance and behavior. They are rare strays in the Northeast in winter, usually migrating instead into Ireland and Scotland.

SIMILAR SPECIES: Immature blue-phase Snow Goose resembles immature White-front, but has a dark bill and feet; its paler blue-gray upperwing coverts are noticeable in flight.

In Alaska, the Bean Goose is larger and darker, especially on the head and neck; it lacks white on the face; has a larger black bill with an orange band; and lacks dark flecking on the belly.

Some similar dark geese are kept in captivity; escaped birds may be mistaken for White-fronts.

CONSERVATION:
Greater White-fronted Geese appear to have a large and stable population. The subspecies with limited numbers and restricted ranges are considered more vulnerable.

The Pink-footed Goose is a rare but regular vagrant to north-eastern North America in spring and fall, apparently because it occasionally migrates with a flock of geese of other species. As the population of Pink-footed Geese in their native range increases, more of them are turning up in unexpected places as well. Sightings have ranged from Newfoundland south to New England, and have been one or a few individuals in a flock of other geese.

DESCRIPTION: A small, Arctic-breeding goose (24–30", 60–75 cm), slightly smaller than the familiar Snow Goose. It is gray over most of the body and wings, with white scalloping. Its darker, brownish head and mostly dark bill help to distinguish this species.

VOICE: High-pitched honks.

NESTING: Lays 3 to 6 eggs in mid- to late May in nests formed on rocky crags and cliffs near glaciers.

HABITAT: Breeds in Arctic tundra, nesting in extremely inaccessible places such as rocky outcrops and crags, probably to protect its nest from ground-based predators. Winters in coastal estuaries and farm fields.

RANGE: Breeds in Greenland, Iceland, and Svalbard, and winters in northern British Isles and Netherlands.

SIMILAR SPECIES: Similar in appearance to the two forms of the very rare Bean Goose, except smaller and with pink legs and feet. Its dark head is quite noticeable.

CONSERVATION: LC
Pink-footed Goose populations are rising rapidly thanks to protection from hunting and ample food on farmland across its native wintering range in northern Europe. Its remote and inaccessible breeding grounds provide protection from both predators and human encroachment.

■ SUMMER ■ MIGRATION
■ WINTER ■ RARE
■ RESIDENT

These geese usually spend the winter in very large flocks, feeding on mudflats, constantly uttering their low, muttering calls. Migrating flocks can be identified at a great distance as they travel in erratic, constantly shifting bunches, unlike the V-shaped flocks of Canada Geese or the long curved lines of Snow Geese.

DESCRIPTION: 22–30" (56–76 cm). Similar to Canada Goose but smaller, shorter-necked, darker, and lacking the conspicuous white cheek patch. It is dark brown above with a black head and neck; and a white collar on the neck (less conspicuous in Atlantic birds, which have whitish bellies and flanks). West Coast birds have dark bellies and were formerly considered a separate species, the "Black Brant."

VOICE: A low, guttural *ruk-ruk*.

NESTING: Lays 3–5 dull-white eggs in a large mass of moss and down, placed on the tundra. Often nests in loose colonies.

HABITAT: Tundra and coastal islands in the Arctic; salt marshes and estuaries in winter.

RANGE: Breeds in coastal Alaska and Canadian Arctic. It winters along coasts south to California and the Carolinas. It is also found in Eurasia.

SUBSPECIES: This species is divided into several subspecies distinguished by geographic location and by the coloration of the belly and sides. The Black Brant, sometimes called the Pacific Brant, nests in the western Arctic and winters along the Pacific Coast. Its belly is the darkest of the subspecies, and its white neck patches are large and form a prominent collar.

The Pale-bellied Brant, sometimes called the Atlantic Brant, breeds in the eastern Arctic and winters along the Atlantic Coast. Its pale belly contrasts sharply with its dark neck and chest, and the white patches on each side of its neck are fainter and don't connect to one another.

The Dark-bellied Brant breeds in northeastern Arctic and winters in Europe, appearing in North America only as a rare vagrant

along the East Coast. Its coloration resembles that of a Black Brant but is not quite as dark.

A "Gray-bellied" form, sometimes considered a distinct fourth subspecies, breeds primarily on Melville Island in extreme north-central Arctic Canada and winters around Puget Sound. Its coloration is intermediate between the Pale-bellied and Dark-bellied subspecies.

SIMILAR SPECIES: Canada Goose is larger and longer-necked, with large white facial patches, a pale breast, and a larger bill. Barnacle Goose has a wholly white face, pure white underparts, and scalloped upperparts.

CONSERVATION: 🐦 **LC**
Today the Brant is locally common to abundant. In the 1930s a disease virtually wiped out eelgrass—until then the favorite food of the Brant—and numbers of this species declined sharply. The survivors switched to the seaweed called sea lettuce. Eelgrass is abundant again in coastal bays, and the numbers of Brant have risen; there are now more than 100,000 wintering on the East Coast, and more than 150,000 on the Pacific Coast. Although hunters take many Brant each year, the steady loss of winter habitats due to human encroachment represents a greater threat to the species.

BARNACLE GOOSE *Branta leucopsis*

SUMMER MIGRATION
WINTER RARE
RESIDENT

Few young waterfowl undergo the challenge faced by Barnacle Goose goslings that have to make their way from precipitous cliffs to the safety of water below in the first few hours after hatching. Females have actually been reported to carry the young to safety on their back or in their bill.

DESCRIPTION: 25–28" (63.5–71 cm). A small, white-faced goose. Its back is barred with black and gray; its crown, eye line, nape, neck, breast, bill, and legs are black. Its primaries are dark; its underparts are white.

VOICE: A short, hoarse barking note, sometimes rapidly repeated.

NESTING: Lays 4–6 gray-white eggs in down-lined nest placed on precipitous rock ledge, often far from salt water. Nests in small colonies.

HABITAT: Arctic rivers and marshlands; it winters in coastal marshes and grasslands.

RANGE: Breeds in Greenland and northern Eurasia. It winters in northern Europe and the British Isles. A rare vagrant in northeastern North America in winter, Barnacle Goose also is a popular bird in aviaries, thus many records pertain to escaped captive birds. When seen in North America, usually a single individual is found amid a flock of Canada Geese.

SIMILAR SPECIES: See Brant and Canada Goose.

CONSERVATION:
The Barnacle Goose population appears to be stable or increasing.

CACKLING GOOSE *Branta hutchinsii*

SUMMER MIGRATION
WINTER RARE
RESIDENT

Once considered a single species, scientists have determined that the four smallest (of eleven) subspecies of the Canada Goose are actually a distinct species—now called the Cackling Goose. Every characteristic and feature of this goose is critical in making a correct identification. These birds nest farther north and west than Canada Geese.

DESCRIPTION: Cackling and Canada Geese, male and female, are virtually identical in appearance. The primary differences are in size and proportion. Size is slightly more helpful in the east, where stray wintering Cackling Geese are noticeably dwarfed by the region's more typically giant form of Canada Geese. Flight is faster, somewhat like a Mallard Duck, and in flight, the wings can seem longer in proportion to the body. Cackling Geese also tend to have rounder heads, and shorter, stubbier bills than Canada Geese. Coloration varies among Cackling Geese, but they tend to be darker on the West Coast and lighter in the East. The head and neck are coal black with a white "chin strap" or band on the side of the face. The body overall is a gray-brown except for undertail coverts, which are white. The legs, feet, and bill are also black. Sizes among the four subspecies can range from 21 to 30" (53–76 cm) and from 2 to 6 lbs (1–3 kg). Beginning with the first autumn and winter, juveniles are similar to adults.

VOICE: Honking, high-pitched cackling, from which its common name is derived. Its higher-pitched call is a reliable differentiator from the otherwise similar Canada Goose with deeper-pitched honks.

NESTING: Only females incubate. Males protect and guard the nest. Nest material is limited in the arctic, so commonly available sedges, lichens, and mosses make up the structure that is then lined with feathers. The brooding hen incubates as few as 2 and as many as 8 white eggs. Goslings are precocial; they leave the nest within 24 hours and, although they stay with the adults, they can swim and feed on their own. They completely fledge at six to seven weeks, but migrate as a family group with their parents. The female selects the nest site and will usually choose a protected high spot on the shoreline or a small island or hummock in a pond. One subspecies, the Aleutian Cackling Goose, nests on grassy areas on the edge of steep coastal cliffs in the Aleutian Islands of Alaska.

HABITAT: Extreme northern tundra, always near bodies of water or coastal waterways from northern Hudson Bay west along the coast of Nunavut, north of Great Bear Lake on the Beaufort Sea, and all the way around coastal Alaska to the Aleutian Islands. Similar water-associated habitat is used in migration and on their wintering grounds. They also visit and reside on pasture, farmland, and urban parks with Canada Geese, where they are often considered a nuisance.

RANGE: Breeds in the Aleutians and coastal Alaska to Baffin Island. Winters on West Coast, and in areas of interior in California, the Southwest into Mexico, the southern Great Plains, and the Gulf Coast. May be seen in much of the West and interior in migration.

SUBSPECIES: Cackling Goose can be broken into a handful of subspecies, all of which are quite similar. The exact number and status of subspecies is complicated thanks to hybridization between subspecies within the Cackling–Canada Goose complex. Several isolated populations may be distinct.

The population of the Aleutian Cackling Goose (*B. h. leucopareia*) breeds on the Aleutian Islands off the western coast of Alaska, and migrates to wintering grounds in central California. This subspecies typically has a white neck ring that is only sometimes seen in other subspecies.

The Small Cackling Goose, or Pacific Cackling Goose (*B. h. minima*), is the smallest race, with dark coloration, a small bill, and a rounded head. It breeds in southwestern Alaska and winters along the West Coast.

Richardson's Cackling Goose (*B. h. hutchinsii*) is intermediate in size and is overall the palest of the Cackling Goose subspecies. It has a longer bill that rivals that of a Canada Goose. This subspecies breeds in Canada's Arctic Archipelago and spreads out to winter in the southern Great Plains and along the Gulf Coast, straying occasionally into the eastern United States.

SIMILAR SPECIES: Although the Cackling Goose is genetically distinct from the Canada Goose, there are many similarities to confuse the unwary birder. A generally smaller bird with a higher-pitched honking or "cackling" probably indicates a Cackling Goose, but natural size variations among Canada and Cackling Geese make identification by size alone difficult. Canada Goose generally has a somewhat longer neck and longer bill.

CONSERVATION: LC
The confusion surrounding species and subspecies classification in the Cackling–Canada Goose complex makes for a challenging conservation assessment. All subspecies are classed as game birds, and populations vary. At least two Cackling Goose subspecies are in need of monitoring. The Aleutian Cackling Goose was once thought to be extinct from predation by introduced arctic foxes, until biologists found a remnant population of 300 birds on a remote island in 1963. They were reestablished on other sites and have recovered enough to be removed from the Endangered Species List.

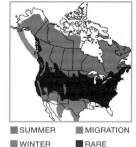

- ■ SUMMER ■ MIGRATION
- ■ WINTER ■ RARE
- ■ RESIDENT

Well known for their V-shaped migrating flocks and rich, sonorous honking, Canada Geese are among the most familiar of North America's waterfowl. Like other geese, these birds are chiefly grazers, feeding on stubble fields and eating marsh vegetation. Increasingly tolerant of humans, some Canadas even nest in city parks and suburbs. They are especially noticeable in late summer and early fall, when they form molting flocks on golf courses and large lawns; at such times, they have come to be regarded as pests.

DESCRIPTION: 35–45" (89–114 cm). A familiar and widespread large goose. Canada Goose has a brownish body with a black head, a long black neck, and conspicuous white cheek patch or "chin strap." Usually has a pale breast, although there are variations among geographical populations.

VOICE: Rich, musical honking.

NESTING: Lays 4–8 whitish eggs in a large mass of grass and moss lined with down; usually on the ground near water or on a muskrat lodge, but sometimes in a tree in an abandoned Osprey or Bald Eagle nest.

HABITAT: Lakes, bays, rivers, and marshes. Often feeds in open grasslands and stubble fields.

RANGE: Breeds from Alaska east to Baffin Island and south to California, Illinois, and Massachusetts. Winters south to northern Mexico and the Gulf Coast. Widespread as a semi-domesticated bird in city parks and on reservoirs.

SUBSPECIES: Ornithologists recognize more than a half-dozen subspecies of Canada Goose, mostly separated geographically. Generally, the subspecies tend to get darker the farther west they occur, and smaller the farther north they live, but this is a bit of an oversimplification, because there is plenty of overlap and hybridization among these populations. The most abundant race is the one that nests south of Hudson Bay, which numbers well over 1 million individuals.

SIMILAR SPECIES: The smaller Brant has a dark upper body that's almost black, a shorter neck, and a black head that lacks a white cheek patch; Brant is almost entirely confined to seacoasts.

Barnacle Goose has a wholly white face, black breast, and white belly and flanks.

The closely related Cackling Goose is smaller, darker, shorter-billed, and found mainly in the West.

CONSERVATION: LC
Canada Geese are abundant and widespread across nearly the entire continent. Some have taken so well to human-provided habitats such as parks, wildlife refuges, cultivated land, and suburban golf courses that they have ceased their usual migration pattern in favor of staying at these sites year-round. Sometimes these birds are considered nuisances. Hunters take millions of Canada Geese each year, but the species population continues to increase. Some localized populations may be vulnerable, however.

■ SUMMER   ■ MIGRATION
■ WINTER   ■ RARE
■ RESIDENT

With its wings arched over its back and its neck in a graceful S-curve, the male is extremely handsome on the water. Breeding pairs are highly aggressive and will defend the nest and young against all comers, using their powerful wings and strong bills to drive away other waterfowl and even humans.

DESCRIPTION: 58–60" (1.47–1.52 m) long with an average wingspan of 7–8' (2.1–2.4 m). Adults are all white; the bill is orange with a black knob at the base. Young birds are similar but dingy gray-brown, becoming whiter with age. The Mute Swan holds its neck in a graceful curve; native swans hold their necks straight up.

VOICE: Usually silent, but utters hissing and barking notes. A loud trumpeting call is rarely heard; wings make loud whirring sound in flight.

NESTING: Lays 4–6 gray or blue-green eggs in a huge mound-like nest lined with feathers and down, conspicuously placed at the edge of a pond or marsh.

HABITAT: Ponds, rivers, coastal lagoons, and bays.

RANGE: Introduced from Europe into northeastern United States; resident and most common in southern New England, southeastern New York, New Jersey, and Maryland; also established locally in Michigan.

SIMILAR SPECIES: See Tundra and Trumpeter swans.

CONVSERVATION:

Populations in North America are increasing explosively. Despite the swans' beauty and popularity in the court of public opinion, many wildlife management organizations consider Mute Swans a harmful invasive species that depletes native aquatic ecosystems and competes with native waterfowl. Many states are undertaking removal efforts to protect important ecosystems such as Chesapeake Bay and the Great Lakes, where Mute Swans have been recorded displacing or destroying nests of native Black Skimmers, Least Terns, Black Terns, and Trumpeter Swans.

SUMMER ■ MIGRATION
WINTER ■ RARE
■ RESIDENT

Trumpeter Swans are the largest native waterfowl in North America. Once threatened with extinction due to hunting and habitat loss, the recovery of this species is a true conservation success story. Today they are locally common breeders in pockets of the interior United States and Canada, and have reestablished in a broad stretch of Western Canada and Alaska.

DESCRIPTION: 60–72" (1.5–1.8 m). One of North America's largest birds. The adult is similar to a Tundra Swan but larger, with an all-black bill. Young birds are dusky gray-brown; the bill is pink with a black base and tip. Mute Swan, an introduced species, is smaller, with a black knob at the base of an orange bill; it holds its neck in a graceful curve.

VOICE: A bugling *ko-hoh*, lower-pitched than Tundra Swan's call.

NESTING: Lays 4–6 whitish eggs in a huge nest on a bulrush-covered island or a beaver lodge. Nesting pairs may use the same nest site for several years if undisturbed.

HABITAT: Marshes, lakes, or rivers with dense vegetation.

RANGE: Breeds in southern Alaska, northern British Columbia, western Alberta, Oregon, Idaho, Montana, and Wyoming. Winters in southeastern Alaska, western British Columbia, and on open water in its interior breeding range. Some reintroduced populations, especially in the interior United States, do not migrate.

SIMILAR SPECIES: Tundra Swan is smaller, with a yellow spot at the base of the bill, a more rounded head, and a shorter bill profile; it has a different call. Mute Swan is larger, "sails" on the water, and its calls are weaker. See Whooper Swan.

CONSERVATION: LC
Draining of marshes, widespread hunting, and other disturbances, along with a low rate of reproduction, brought the Trumpeter Swan close to extinction by the beginning of the 20th century. Conservation measures, including reintroductions and hunting bans, have allowed it to increase from a critically small number in the 1930s to tens of thousands today, with most of these in Alaska and Western Canada. The establishment of non-native Mute Swans around the Great Lakes has slowed Trumpeter's comeback in this portion of its former breeding range. Trumpeter Swans are extremely sensitive to nest site disturbance and may abandon nests and nestlings if threatened.

■ SUMMER   ■ MIGRATION
■ WINTER   ■ RARE
■ RESIDENT

Tundra Swan is the most numerous swan species on the continent, and the one with the widest range. A high-arctic breeder, its wintering grounds and migration routes cover most of the continent, making it possible to see Tundra Swans on open waters and croplands almost anywhere coast-to-coast. Tundra Swans tend to form large, gregarious flocks outside of the breeding season.

DESCRIPTION: 48–55" (1.2–1.4 m). The most common swan in the West and the only native swan in the East. Large and all white, it has a black bill, usually with a small yellow spot in front of the eye. The rarer Trumpeter Swan is larger and lacks yellow on the bill. It holds its neck straight up, unlike Mute Swan, which bends its neck in a graceful curve.

VOICE: Mellow bugling call, *hoo-ho-hoo*, usually heard from a flock of migrating birds.

NESTING: Lays 4–6 creamy-white eggs placed on a large mound of grass and moss on an island or beside a marshy tundra lake.

HABITAT: Arctic tundra; winters on marshy lakes and bays.

RANGE: Breeds in Alaska and far northern Canada east to Baffin Island. Winters from southern Alaska south to Nevada, Utah, and Baja California and on mid-Atlantic Coast; rare on Gulf Coast of Texas; occasional on Great Lakes.

SUBSPECIES: The nominate American subspecies is sometimes called "Whistling Swan." There is also a Eurasian subspecies called "Bewick's Swan," which rarely turns up as a North American visitor, usually found mixed among flocks of its American cousins.

SIMILAR SPECIES: Size, bill, and voice are useful in distinguishing this species.

Trumpeter Swan is larger. It lacks any yellow on the bill; the angle at the base of the bill is wider, encompassing the eye. In profile, the crown and forehead are long and flat, not rounded. Trumpters' call is low-pitched and trumpetlike.

A Eurasian relative, the Whooper Swan, is a possible vagrant in Alaska; it is larger with a conspicuous, broad yellow patch extending in a wedge from the base of the bill to beyond the nostrils.

Mute Swan has a different head and bill profile; its neck is generally curved, not straight; its orange bill has a black knob at the base. Its voice is much weaker and less frequently heard.

Snow and Ross's geese are smaller, with black primaries and a short pink bill.

CONSERVATION:
Tundra Swans are the most numerous swan species in North America; their population is large and stable enough to support a limited hunting season. Overhunting and lead poisoning from ingesting lead shot are two of this species' biggest threats. Because they breed in remote and little disturbed areas, Tundra Swans have so far escaped the fate of the closely related Trumpeter Swan of the West, which was reduced to near extinction by overhunting and habitat destruction.

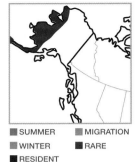

■ SUMMER   ■ MIGRATION
■ WINTER   ■ RARE
■ RESIDENT

The impressive Whooper Swan is widespread and familiar in many areas in Europe, both as a breeder and wintering species. In North America, however, it is seldom seen outside of Alaska's Aleutian Islands. Whooper Swans occurring elsewhere in North America are usually considered to be escaped captives since the species is regularly kept by collectors of exotic waterfowl.

DESCRIPTION: 56–70" (142–178 cm). A large swan, similar in size, shape, and head and bill profile to Trumpeter Swan. Its black bill has a broad yellow patch on the upper mandible extending from the base to beyond the nostril; it covers at least half of the bill. This swan often holds its head forward in a curved or kinked posture. Immatures are dusky; the bill is pinkish with a black tip.

VOICE: In flight, a low-pitched *whoop-whoop*; it also gives a single bugled note when alarmed.

NESTING: Lays 2–5 white eggs in large mound of reeds, sedges, and other plants, usually close to the water's edge.

HABITAT: Subarctic taiga or tundra; migrants and wintering birds occur on freshwater lakes and shallow salt water bays; regularly forages in meadows.

RANGE: Breeds mainly across northern Eurasia, including Iceland; uncommon but regular in winter on outer Aleutian Islands; very rare elsewhere in Alaska.

SIMILAR SPECIES: Adult Trumpeter and Tundra lack large yellow patch at base of bill. Immature Trumpeter in spring has solid dark bill. Rare "Bewick's" Swan is smaller and has half as much yellow on the bill; its call is different.

CONSERVATION: Least concern in its native range across Eurasia. Any Whooper seen in North America outside of Alaska is either a phenomenally rare vagrant or, more likely, an escaped captive bird.

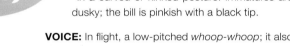

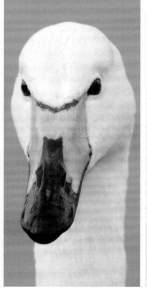

- ■ SUMMER
- ■ MIGRATION
- ■ WINTER
- ■ RARE
- ■ RESIDENT

Wild Muscovy Ducks are native to the American tropics and are sometimes found as far north as the Rio Grande in southernmost Texas. During breeding season they are found alone or in small groups; slightly larger groups (up to 16 individuals) are seen in the non-breeding season. Most sightings in North America are of domesticated, barnyard Muscovy Ducks, which are highly variable and turn up in parks and farms across much of the continent. The domestication of Muscovy Ducks predates European explorers: in the 1400s Christopher Columbus reported West Indian natives keeping waterfowl that were likely this species, and Spanish conquistadors in the 1500s saw wild-caught Muscovy Ducks being kept at Native American villages in Brazil.

DESCRIPTION: 25–34" (64–86 cm). Wild Muscovy Ducks are overall black in coloration with iridescent dorsal plumage and white wing patches. Distinctive, fleshy growths (caruncles) around the face and bill are especially noticeable on males. Plumage of domesticated Muscovies ranges from pure white through grays, browns, and blacks.

VOICE: Not often heard; quiet quacks and grunts.

NESTING: Nests (8–10 white eggs) located in naturally occurring hollow trees and stumps. Wild Muscovy Duck populations in Mexico are being managed through a nest box program.

HABITAT: Wetlands near forested areas; trees are used for roosting and nesting. These birds feed in shallow areas of flooded vegetation. Wild birds are wary, and spend considerable amounts of time in trees, often making them difficult to find and observe.

RANGE: Coastal Mexico, through Central America to South America, reaching Peru on the west and Uruguay and northern Argentina in the southeast. In the U.S., small numbers are resident in southern Texas, at the extreme northern edge of the species' range.

SIMILAR SPECIES: None, although distinguishing wild from feral individuals can be challenging.

CONSERVATION: LC
There are several feral populations of escaped domestic birds that have become established.

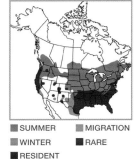

■ SUMMER   ■ MIGRATION
■ WINTER   ■ RARE
■ RESIDENT

One of the most beautiful of North American waterfowl, these colorful perching ducks are unusual in their affinity for trees. They are equipped with strong claws that allow them to grip onto tree bark and limbs. The Wood Duck's habit of nesting in cavities enables it to breed in areas lacking suitable ground cover. Males of this species are unmistakable. Successful conservation efforts have helped Wood Ducks tremendously, and today they are widespread and common around wooded swamps and ponds.

DESCRIPTION: 17–20" (43–51 cm). A beautiful, crested, multicolored duck. The distinctive male is patterned in iridescent greens, purples, and blues with a distinctive white chin patch and face stripes; its bill is mainly red; and it has a long tail. The female is grayish with a broad, white eye ring.

VOICE: Females give a loud *wooo-eeek!*; males issue a softer *jeee?* or *ter-weeeee?*

NESTING: Lays 9–12 whitish or tan eggs in a nest made of down in a natural tree cavity or artificial nest box, sometimes up to 50' (15 m) off the ground. The young leave the nest soon after hatching, jumping from the nesting cavity to the ground or water. Once out of the nest, they travel through wooded ponds with their mother. Snapping turtles take a heavy toll of the young.

HABITAT: Wooded rivers and ponds; wooded swamps. Visits freshwater marshes in late summer and fall.

RANGE: Breeds from British Columbia south to California, and from Montana east to Nova Scotia, and south to Texas and Florida; absent from the Rocky Mountains and Great Plains. Winters near Pacific Coast north to Washington, and to New Jersey in East, rarely farther north.

SIMILAR SPECIES: American Wigeon has large white speculum; lacks crest. Hooded Merganser has slender bill, white patches on wings, faster wingbeat, and more direct flight, often low over water.

CONSERVATION:

The Wood Duck was hunted nearly to extinction during the late 19th and early 20th centuries. In 1918 the hunting season was closed, and for the next two decades numbers rose steadily. There are now well over a million Wood Ducks in North America. Land conservation and the addition of artificial nest boxes around bodies of fresh water in public parks and on private lands have helped Wood Ducks in their recovery.

This Siberian species occasionally appears as a vagrant in Alaska, British Columbia, or the Pacific Northwest. Reports of this species require caution, because it is a spectacular bird common in zoos and private collections. Any report other than on the West Coast is almost certain to be an escaped captive, and even West Coast reports are likely to be captive birds.

DESCRIPTION: A small (15–17", 39–43 cm) dabbling duck, slightly larger than a Green-winged Teal. Breeding male is unmistakable, with elaborate facial pattern of swirled greens, blacks, and tans, and long, colorful scapular feathers. Female is similar to many other ducks in muted browns with a dark cap, distinguished from other teal by the light marking behind the bill. Juvenile and eclipse male resemble female, although juvenile has dark spotting on belly.

VOICE: The voice of both sexes is deep in pitch. Males call a multiple-note *wot-wot-wot*. Females issue a deep quack.

NESTING: Nests in the forested region of eastern Siberia. Lays 6–10 white or yellow-tinted eggs, which the female incubates alone.

HABITAT: In breeding season, the species can be found near the tundra line in forested swamplands. Wintering grounds include many types of freshwater.

RANGE: Breeds in Siberia, winters in Japan, China, and South Korea. A rare vagrant in Alaska, British Columbia, or the Pacific Northwest; most often North American sightings are of escaped captive birds.

SIMILAR SPECIES: Female Baikal Teal resembles a female Green-winged Teal. Green-winged has a shorter tail and lacks the Baikal's distinctive facial markings.

CONCERVATION:
Listed by the IUCN Red List as a species of "Least Concern," but Baikal Teals dipped into "Vulnerable" territory earlier in the 21st century due to pressures from hunting and habitat destruction. The species appears to be recovering in its native range.

■ SUMMER   ■ MIGRATION
■ WINTER   ■ RARE
■ RESIDENT

This Eurasian teal is sometimes found as a vagrant on freshwater lakes and marshes in North America. Garganey are rarely kept in captivity because they retain their colorful breeding plumage only briefly, so most reports in North America are thought to be true vagrants rather than escapees. A highly social and gregarious species, they migrate southward on a broad front beginning in late July and peaking in August-September. During the winter in Africa they wander in relation to seasonal flooding. Flocks of several thousand are common in Africa and Asiatic winter grounds. Northward migration begins in February, with birds beginning to arrive on the breeding grounds from March-May.

DESCRIPTION: A small dabbling duck, averaging 15.5" (39 cm) in length. The species is sexually dimorphic. The breeding male is unmistakable with a white band on the side of the head from eye to nape, contrasting with a dark reddish-brown head, neck, and breast. Pale gray flanks and breast and elongated black and white striped scapulars. Females and males in non-breeding plumage are more difficult to distinguish from other similar teals. Males resemble females from July through late winter except for more pronounced facial markings—a dark eyeline and a dark line below the eye. In flight the adult female is similar to a Green-winged Teal, but note the conspicuous white trailing edge of the wing. Males show a gray or silvery upper wing. These dabblers feed mainly by skimming rather than upending.

VOICE: Many of the calls are similar to Blue-winged Teal or Northern Shoveler. Males give an odd rattle-like call. Females emit a weak croak similar to a Green-winged Teal.

NESTING: Breeds in northern Eurasia, favoring meadows near lakes and marshes. Nests are usually within 100 feet of the shoreline and placed under the cover of tall grasses in a depression.

HABITAT: In North America, it is found mainly on freshwater lakes and marshes.

RANGE: Each year there are usually several scattered sightings of these vagrants across North America along the major waterfowl flyways, especially in the spring. Its normal range is extremely large, stretching across Eurasia during the breeding season and across southern Africa and Asia during the winter.

SIMILAR SPECIES: Female Blue-winged Teal usually has a less contrasting light-and-dark facial pattern with less obvious eyebrows; it has yellow legs and a darker bill. Female Green-winged Teal has a shorter bill, and lacks the facial pattern and grayish wing coverts. Female Cinnamon and Blue-winged teals have deeper, more clear-blue forewing.

CONSERVATION: ![LC]

Garganey is a widespread species globally. Although the population still appears to be healthy, it is gradually declining worldwide due to human encroachment and wetland drainage.

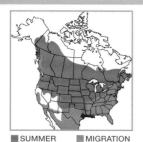

■ SUMMER ■ MIGRATION
■ WINTER ■ RARE
■ RESIDENT

Fast and wary, Blue-winged Teal fly in small groups or flocks, turning in unison and flashing the blue area of the wing. They arrive latest of all ducks at their breeding grounds and leave early in the fall. On low, marshy prairies in the central part of the continent, where this duck is most numerous, virtually every pond and pothole has a breeding pair. The male commonly "stands guard" on the pond while the female is incubating. Unlike other dabbling ducks that form pairs in the fall, this teal begins courting in the spring and often does not acquire the familiar breeding plumage until December or January. Like most ducks, it goes through an eclipse plumage and molts most of its feathers simultaneously, including the primaries, and so is flightless until new feathers grow in.

DESCRIPTION: 14–16" (36–41 cm). A small brown duck with pale blue shoulder patches. The male has a gray head and a white crescent in front of the eye. Females are mottled brown, similar to a female Cinnamon Teal but with obscure patterning on the face—and to a female Green-winged but grayer and larger-billed, with pale blue shoulder patches like the male.

VOICE: Soft lisping or peeping notes. The female utters a soft quack.

NESTING: Lays 9–12 dull white eggs in a down-lined hollow concealed in grass near water.

HABITAT: Marshes, shallow ponds, and lakes.

RANGE: Fairly common on lakes, ponds, and marshes across most of the continent, although less common along the West Coast. Breeds from southeastern Alaska and western Canada to Canadian Maritimes and south to northeastern California, New Mexico, and New York. Winters in southern California, the Gulf Coast, the Atlantic Coast to the Carolinas, and southward throughout tropical America.

SIMILAR SPECIES: See Green-winged and Cinnamon teals. Female Northern Shoveler can usually be distinguished even in flight by large, spoon-shaped bill.

CONSERVATION: LC

Blue-winged Teal are abundant, and populations appear to be stable. As early migrants, many of these birds have left before duck hunting season begins in many U.S. states. Poisoning from DDT and lead shot still threatens this species where these are still in use, notably in parts of Latin America.

SUMMER MIGRATION
WINTER RARE
RESIDENT

A western relative of the more widespread Blue-winged Teal, this is a sociable species that travels in small, fast flocks. Males of the two species look very different, but their close relationship is revealed by the females, which are similar and distinguishable only at close range and in good light. In fact, the two species are known to interbreed where their ranges overlap.

DESCRIPTION: 14–17" (36–43 cm). The male is bright rufous with pale blue shoulder patches. The female is a mottled sandy brown, dusky, with pale blue shoulder patches; its face is plainer than that of a female Blue-wing, but the two are often not distinguishable in the field.

VOICE: A soft quack; various chattering and clucking notes.

NESTING: Lays 9–12 pale buff or whitish eggs in a down-lined nest of grass concealed in vegetation, usually near water.

HABITAT: Marshes, ponds, and streams bordered with reeds.

RANGE: Primarily a western bird, it breeds in North America from southern British Columbia and Montana south to Texas. It winters in southern part of this breeding range and south to tropical America. Rare in East, usually found in flocks of Blue-winged Teal.

SUBSPECIES: Several subspecies occur in South America. Ours is the "Northern" subspecies of Cinnamon Teal.

SIMILAR SPECIES: Blue-winged Teal has a shorter, less spatulate bill; the breeding male has more waxy blue tone to the wing. The cheek and neck of a female Blue-winged is less tawny with a steeper forehead. Blue-winged eclipse male is less reddish, and lacks the orange eye of Cinnamon Teal.

Northern Shoveler has a larger, spatulate bill.

Ruddy Duck has a white face patch and a blue bill.

CONSERVATION: LC

This species is widespread and common, but scientists have placed it on a watch list of common birds experiencing steep declines. Although still numerous, hunting pressures and climate change appear to be taking a toll on this familiar dabbling duck.

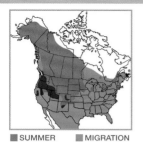

■ SUMMER ■ MIGRATION
■ WINTER ■ RARE
■ RESIDENT

The Northern Shoveler—a relative of the Blue-winged and Cinnamon teals—favors broad, shallow marshes where it can use the comb-like teeth along the edges of its large bill to strain aquatic animals, plants, and seeds from the water. Like the two teal, male shovelers wear eclipse plumage until February, much later than ducks whose courtship begins in the fall.

DESCRIPTION: 17–20" (43–51 cm). This duck has a large, shovel-shaped bill. The male has a green head, white body, and chestnut flanks. The female is streaked brown with pale blue shoulder patches.

VOICE: A low croak, cluck, or quack.

NESTING: Lays 8–12 pale buff or greenish eggs in a down-lined cup of grass concealed in vegetation, often some distance from water.

HABITAT: Marshes and prairie potholes. Sometimes found on salt or brackish marshes.

RANGE: Breeds from Alaska and northern Manitoba south to California, Nebraska, and Wisconsin; local and uncommon in the Great Lakes area and the Northeast. Winters from Oregon across the southern half of the U.S. to the Gulf Coast and north to New Jersey, south to Central America. Also found in the Old World.

SIMILAR SPECIES: Blue-winged Teal is smaller, with a smaller bill. Mallard drake has a smaller bill and lacks the alternating light-dark color pattern; female Mallard has a smaller bill and dark blue speculum.

CONSERVATION: Widespread and common. Although less numerous than in ancient times, the Northern Shoveler and other marsh ducks have lately become relatively abundant because game departments and private organizations in Canada, the United States, and Mexico have purchased wetland habitat to ensure their survival.

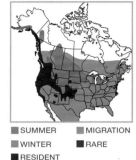

■ SUMMER   ■ MIGRATION
■ WINTER   ■ RARE
■ RESIDENT

This species has the widest range of any duck, breeding almost throughout the North Temperate Zone, and is abundant in winter in southern marshes. Often considered drab, the male Gadwall is a handsome duck clad in soft pastel grays and tans. This species is one of the dabbling ducks; it feeds by tipping forward so that the tail sticks up as it reaches for plants on the bottom.

DESCRIPTION: 18–21" (46–53 cm). The male is a medium-sized grayish duck with a white patch on the hind edge of the wing, a black rump, and a sandy brown head. The female is mottled brown, with a white patch on the hind edge of the wing.

VOICE: Utters a prototypical duck-like quack; also chatters and whistles.

NESTING: Lays 9–11 cream-white eggs in a down-lined nest of grass, usually hidden near water but sometimes in upland fields.

HABITAT: Freshwater marshes, ponds, and rivers; locally in salt marshes.

RANGE: Breeds from southern Alaska, British Columbia, and Minnesota south to California and western Texas; occasionally in the East. Winters in much of the United States. Also found in the Old World across much of Europe, Asia, and northern Africa.

SIMILAR SPECIES: American Widgeon has a white patch on the upperwing coverts. Female Mallard has a blue speculum and a wider, orange bill. American Black Duck is larger, dark, and lacks a white belly and speculum. Female Northern Pintail has a longer neck and bluish bill. Green-winged Teal is smaller, with a green speculum. In Alaska, see Falcated Duck.

CONSERVATION: LC

Hunters take many Gadwalls each year—perhaps upwards of 1 million birds annually—but their populations remain stable. Conservation efforts to save wetlands and upland nesting habitat in the Great Plains have benefited this species substantially since the 1960s, allowing Gadwall numbers to continue to grow.

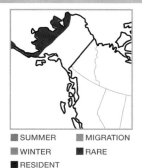

■ SUMMER ■ MIGRATION
■ WINTER ■ RARE
■ RESIDENT

This Asian species was formerly called Falcated Teal. Strays occur in western Alaska only rarely. Due to their attractive plumage, Falcated Ducks are often maintained in private waterfowl collections, which is likely the source of most of the North American records outside of Alaska.

DESCRIPTION: 19" (48.5 cm). A medium-sized duck resembling a Gadwall or wigeon. The male has a silver-gray back and sides; long, sickle-shaped inner flight feathers that overlap the base of the tail; underparts scalloped black and gray; and black undertail coverts. The male's crested head is colored chestnut and iridescent green, and its throat is white. The female is uniformly brown and mottled; the outer tail feathers are white; the speculum greenish, bordered front and back with white; the bill is gray and the legs blackish.

VOICE: Male utters low-pitched, trilled whistle; female quacks much like Gadwall.

NESTING: Lays 6–10 cream-white eggs in a down-lined grass nest placed in marshy ground near a river or wet mountain meadow.

HABITAT: Freshwater ponds, small lakes, and quiet rivers. Often forages and winters in rice fields or on shallow coastal bays.

RANGE: Breeds and winters in northeastern Asia and Japan. Rare to casual in the central and western Aleutian Islands and the Pribilofs.

SIMILAR SPECIES: Female Eurasian Wigeon differs subtly from female Falcated Duck with pinkish, unscaled sides and a white belly; a smaller, rounder head; and a smaller, delicate, bluish bill tipped with black. Female Gadwall has a white speculum, orange on the sides of the bill, and yellowish feet.

CONSERVATION: Near threatened in its native range; conservation efforts are under way, aimed at helping the species to recover, but overhunting and habitat loss continue to pressure the Falcated Duck population.

■ SUMMER ■ MIGRATION
■ WINTER ■ RARE
■ RESIDENT

This widespread Old World species is an uncommon-to-rare but regular stray into North America in winter, especially in the west. Confirmed records of individuals have occurred in nearly every state and province. The Eurasian Wigeon is usually found associating with flocks of its American counterpart. Like the American Wigeon, this species is unorthodox in its feeding habits: It spends much of its time grazing on land like a goose and also loiters around feeding flocks of diving ducks, snatching food from them when they bob back to the surface.

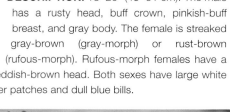

DESCRIPTION: 18–20" (46–51 cm). The male has a rusty head, buff crown, pinkish-buff breast, and gray body. The female is streaked gray-brown (gray-morph) or rust-brown (rufous-morph). Rufous-morph females have a reddish-brown head. Both sexes have large white shoulder patches and dull blue bills.

VOICE: Males give a piping, high-pitched, two-note whistle. A vocal species during the breeding season, its calls are seldom heard in North American wintering birds.

NESTING: Lays 7 or 8 cream-white eggs in a down-lined nest of grass, hidden in vegetation, often some distance from water.

HABITAT: Marshes, ponds, and lakes; tidal flats in nonbreeding season.

RANGE: Breeds in Eurasia; an uncommon but regular visitor to North America, mainly along the Atlantic and Pacific coasts.

SIMILAR SPECIES: Male American Wigeon has a brownish head, a white crown, and a green band sweeping back from the eye. Female American Wigeon is extremely difficult to distinguish from a gray-morph female Eurasian, but usually has a grayer head and pure white wing linings.

CONSERVATION: 🐦 LC

Although few details are known about the species' exact numbers, it is common and widespread in its native range. The increasing frequency of winter strays in the United States and Canada suggests a growing global population that is disbursing more widely, or potentially a yet-undiscovered established breeding site somewhere in North America.

- ■ SUMMER
- ■ MIGRATION
- ■ WINTER
- ■ RARE
- ■ RESIDENT

Known colloquially as a "Baldpate" in reference to the white stripe on its crown, the American Wigeon is a wary bird that takes flight readily if disturbed. Flocks rise straight up from the surface of the water, uttering their whistling calls. They are often seen on marshy ponds in the company of diving birds such as coots, Redheads, and Canvasbacks. Wigeons wait at the surface while the other birds dive, then snatch the food away when the birds reappear. They also visit grain fields and meadows to graze like geese on tender shoots. Unlike many dabbling ducks, these birds often spend the night on large open bays, sleeping in rafts well out from shore.

DESCRIPTION: 18–23" (46–58 cm). The breeding male is brownish with a conspicuous white crown, green ear patches, and bold white shoulder patches easily visible in flight. In eclipse plumage, the striking green and white marks on the male's head fade to a mottled gray. The female is mottled brown with a grayish head and whitish shoulder patches. The bill is pale blue in both sexes.

VOICE: A distinctive, whistled *whew-whee-whew*; it also quacks. This is a vocal species, often heard before it is seen.

NESTING: Lays 9–11 whitish or cream-colored eggs in a down-lined nest of grass, often several hundred yards from water.

HABITAT: Marshes, ponds, and shallow lakes in open or semi-open areas.

RANGE: Breeds from Alaska, northern Manitoba, and southern Quebec south to Nevada, the Dakotas, and the Great Lakes region; rarely farther east. It winters mainly along the Pacific, Atlantic, and Gulf coasts.

SIMILAR SPECIES: See Eurasian Wigeon and Gadwall. Female Mallard is larger than a female American Wigeon, and has a longer orange bill and blue speculum.

CONSERVATION:
American Wigeons are common birds, and although they have suffered steady declines, they appear to be gradually expanding their range eastward, with new breeding sites emerging in New England and eastern Canada. Hunting places some pressure on this species, and is managed carefully with bag limits based on the wigeon population size each year. Drought and wetland habitat loss also adversely affect the American Wigeon population.

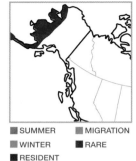

SUMMER ■ MIGRATION
■ WINTER ■ RARE
■ RESIDENT

This East Asian species is a rare, accidental visitor to North America, with a handful of records from Alaska's Aleutian Islands and Kodiak Island. The distinctive yellow tip of its bill is conspicuous, even from a distance.

DESCRIPTION: 24" (61 cm). Similar to an American Black Duck. Its bill is black with a yellow terminal band; the face and neck are pale gray. It has a distinct dark cap and eyeline. Its lower body is dark; its white tertials are conspicuous in flight.

VOICE: Similar to the common quack of a Mallard.

NESTING: Usually lays 8–10 grayish-white eggs in down-lined nest of grasses and rushes placed on ground near water.

HABITAT: Shallow freshwater lakes and marshes.

RANGE: Breeds in eastern Asia from Siberia south to India and Southeast Asia. It winters south to the Philippines.

SIMILAR SPECIES: Resembles a female Mallard or American Black Duck, but the bright yellow on the tip of its bill is distinctive.

CONSERVATION:
Least concern in its native range in Asia.

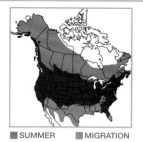

■ SUMMER ■ MIGRATION
■ WINTER ■ RARE
■ RESIDENT

The Mallard is undoubtedly the most abundant duck in North America. The ancestor of the common white domestic duck, Mallards frequently interbreed with domestic stock, producing a bewildering variety of patterns and colors. They also hybridize with wild species such as the closely related American Black Duck and even occasionally with Northern Pintails. Strong fliers, Mallards sometimes reach remote oceanic islands where isolated populations have evolved into new species. Like the Mottled Duck, these isolated populations often differ from the Mallard mainly in that they lack the colorful plumage of the male. Mallard courtship starts in the fall, and by midwinter pairs have formed. Mated pairs migrate northward together, heading for the female's place of origin. The male stays with the female until incubation is well under way, then leaves to join a flock of other males to begin the annual molt.

DESCRIPTION: 18–27" (46–69 cm). The male has a green head, white neck ring, chestnut breast, and grayish body; the inner feathers of the wing (speculum) are metallic purplish blue, bordered in front and back with white. The female is mottled brown with a white tail and purplish-blue speculum; it has a mottled orange and brown bill. The form in the Southwest ("Mexican Duck") is similar to a typical female Mallard but darker; its speculum is blue and there is no white in the tail; the bill of the male is yellow-green; the bill of the female is dusky orange.

VOICE: Males utter soft, reedy notes; females give a loud quack.

NESTING: Lays 8–10 light olive-green eggs in a down-lined nest often placed some distance from water, occasionally in a tree.

HABITAT: From ponds, lakes, and marshes to small river bends, bays, and even ditches and city ponds.

RANGE: Breeds from Alaska and Quebec south to southern California, Virginia, Texas, and northern Mexico. It winters throughout the United States and south to Central America and the West Indies. It is also found in Eurasia.

SIMILAR SPECIES: American Black Duck and Mottled Duck have sexes colored alike; both are similar to a female Mallard but darker, especially Black Duck. Mottled Duck is confined to states along the Gulf Coast (Louisiana, Alabama, and Texas) and Florida; Black Duck largely occurs east of the Great Plains.

CONSERVATION: 🐦

Mallards are the most abundant duck in North America, and probably the most abundant duck in the world—its expansive range covers most of North America, Europe, Asia, and beyond. The population of Mallards is large, and estimates fluctuate anywhere from around 5 million to upwards of 11 million birds. It is the most common species taken by duck hunters, and wildlife managers monitor the number of birds harvested each year.

SUMMER ■ MIGRATION
WINTER ■ RARE
■ RESIDENT

This eastern duck tends to be wary and shy, and it is a fast flier. American Black Ducks are often found in mixed groups with Mallards and can be difficult to distinguish from females of this related species. Widespread interbreeding between American Black Ducks and Mallards has resulted in recent years in a decrease of "pure" Blacks. Actually the bird is not black, but it appears so at a distance; it was formerly more aptly known as the "Dusky Duck."

DESCRIPTION: 19–22" (48–56 cm). Both sexes are similar. American Black Ducks are sooty brown with a paler head and conspicuous white wing linings and violet speculum. The bill is olive or dull yellow; females tend to have duller and darker bills.

VOICE: Issues a typical duck quack.

NESTING: Lays 9–12 greenish-buff eggs in a ground nest of feathers and down.

HABITAT: Marshes, woodland lakes and streams, coastal mudflats, and estuaries.

RANGE: Breeds in eastern and central North America, from Manitoba and Labrador to Texas and Florida. Winters from southern Minnesota and Nova Scotia south to southern Texas and central Florida.

SIMILAR SPECIES: A male Mallard has a green head, brown chest, and white belly and tail feathers. A female Mallard is lighter brown with a bill mottled with orange and black, and has whitish tail feathers and a speculum with a white border.

The sexes are also alike in Mottled Ducks but these are lighter than Black Duck; Mottled Ducks are restricted in range to the extreme southern United States, where Black Ducks seldom occur.

CONSERVATION: LC

Although the American Black Duck is still quite common and its range is large, the population's numbers have declined worryingly in recent decades, especially inland. Habitat loss due to urbanization and other human activity, water pollution, climate change, and hybridization and competition with a burgeoning population of Mallards all place pressure on this species.

■ SUMMER ■ MIGRATION
■ WINTER ■ RARE
■ RESIDENT

This southern dabbling duck is a close relative of both the American Black Duck and the widespread Mallard, but usually only shares its habitat in coastal marshes with the latter. Unlike its relatives, Mottled Ducks rarely travel in large, gregarious flocks, instead preferring to travel in pairs or small groups.

DESCRIPTION: 21" (53 cm). Both sexes are mottled dark brown and sandy. The boldly patterned body plumage is similar to that of a female Mallard, but Mottled Duck's bill is a bright yellow or orange-yellow, its throat is plain tawny, and its tail is dark rather than whitish.

VOICE: A loud quack, like that of a Mallard.

NESTING: Lays 9–13 pale greenish eggs in a down-lined nest of grass concealed in vegetation near a shore.

HABITAT: Coastal marshes and lagoons. Prefers open, treeless habitat.

RANGE: Resident in southern Florida and along the Gulf Coast of Louisiana and Texas. This species is generally nonmigratory, but may move from one local habitat to another.

SUBSPECIES: Resident populations along the Gulf of Mexico and in central-southern Florida may represent two distinct subspecies; their ranges do not overlap.

SIMILAR SPECIES: See American Black Duck and female Mallard.

CONSERVATION:

Mottled Ducks are still fairly common, but their range is limited and they have experienced steady declines since the 1960s. Climate change, coastal erosion, and wetland drainage—especially in Florida—threaten this species. Hybridization with introduced Mallards also places pressure on the wild population of Mottled Ducks. Although it is not yet threatened, its population is trending decidedly downward; it is a considered a priority species to monitor carefully.

SUMMER ■ MIGRATION
WINTER ■ RARE
■ RESIDENT

This bird of the Caribbean and South America occasionally turns up as a vagrant in southern Florida. A popular species in waterfowl collections, most sightings in North America outside of Florida and in Europe are escapees.

DESCRIPTION: 17" (43 cm). This duck is warm brown overall with a prominent white cheek and a red mark at the base of the bill. It has a pointed, buffy tail and a green speculum with buff-colored borders.

VOICE: The male gives a squeaky call, and the female gives a short quack.

NESTING: Breeding season is from February to June, but variable. The nest is a scrape concealed under a clump of vegetation, sometimes far from water. Females lay 5–12 light tan eggs.

HABITAT: Prefers waters with some degree of salinity, such as brackish lakes, estuaries, and mangrove swamps, but can also be found on freshwater marshes and ponds.

RANGE: A mostly sedentary duck of tropical America that rarely strays to southeastern North America, mostly Florida. Some North American sightings are probably escapees from captivity.

SUBSPECIES: There are three subspecies recognized. *A. b. bahamensis* is in the Caribbean, and a vagrant in the southeastern United States, *A. b. galapagensis* found on the Galápagos Islands, and *A. b. rubirostris* in South America is slightly larger and may be an austral migrant, breeding in Argentina and wintering farther north.

SIMILAR SPECIES: Northern Pintail and Gadwall are similar; both are much more common across North America.

CONSERVATION:
Least concern, but declining in some parts of its range, especially the Caribbean, mainly from overhunting.

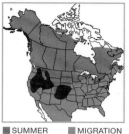

■ SUMMER ■ MIGRATION
■ WINTER ■ RARE
■ RESIDENT

Although not as numerous as the Mallard, this graceful dabbling duck is widespread and common, especially in the West. Winter flocks can be huge, numbering in the thousands. Seeds of aquatic plants are the Pintail's main food, but in winter it also eats small aquatic animals; when freshwater habitats freeze over, it resorts to tidal flats, where it feeds on snails and small crabs. Courting involves elaborate head gestures and paired flights. Male Northern Pintails are aggressive and often compete over females; some males will interbreed with other species.

DESCRIPTION: Males average 25–29" (64–74 cm) long; females average 21–23" (53–58 cm). A long-necked, slender duck. The male has a brown head; white underparts a neck with a white line extending onto the side of the head; a grayish back and sides; and long, black, pointed central tail feathers. The speculum is metallic brown and green with a white rear border that shows in flight. The female is mottled brown, similar to a female Mallard but paler, grayer, and more slender, with a brown speculum bordered with white at the rear edge only; the tail is more pointed than in a female Mallard. Both sexes have gray feet and legs.

VOICE: A distinctive two-tone buzzy whistle; females quack. Courting males issue a repeated high whistle.

NESTING: This species nests early in the spring, seeking out suitable breeding sites as a mated pair. The female creates the nest alone, laying 6–9 pale greenish-buff eggs in a shallow bowl of grass lined with down, often some distance from water. The female incubates alone, and leads the young from the nest within a few hours of hatching.

HABITAT: Marshes, prairie ponds, and tundra; sometimes salt marshes in winter. May take to agricultural fields where rice, wheat, corn, and barley are available.

RANGE: Breeds from Alaska and Labrador south to California, Nebraska, and Maine. Locally in East and occasionally elsewhere. Winters south to Central America and West Indies. Also in Eurasia.

SIMILAR SPECIES: Mallards are chunkier with a blue speculum and with a slower wingbeat. Gadwall has a grayish-white speculum. Blue-winged Teal is smaller with a blue shoulder patch.

CONSERVATION:

The population of Northern Pintails is large but has decreased steadily over many decades. Its numbers can vary considerably from year to year in response to droughts. The species is a popular game bird, and bag limits are put in place each year in the United States by the U.S. Fish & Wildlife Service in response to population estimates. Loss of wetland habitat and careless agricultural practices that destroy active nesting sites place additional stress on this species.

GREEN-WINGED TEAL *Anas crecca*

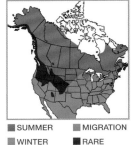

■ SUMMER ■ MIGRATION
■ WINTER ■ RARE
■ RESIDENT

A hardy species, Green-winged Teals are the smallest dabbling ducks in North America. They are among the last ducks to reach their winter habitat in fall and the first to depart in spring. Flocks of Green-winged Teal fly swiftly, executing sharp turns in unison like flocks of shorebirds. When the flock settles on water, the birds often separate into small groups consisting of one female courted by several males. Eventually the female chooses a mate, and the chosen male wards off other suitors. In spring the pair returns to the female's previous breeding place. Green-winged Teal often occur with other species, but are easy to distinguish because of their small size and short bills.

DESCRIPTION: 12–16" (30–41 cm). A small, dark duck. The male has a chestnut head, green ear patch, pale gray sides, and a pinkish breast with a vertical white stripe down the side. Female is dark brown without distinctive markings. Both sexes have bright green wing patches on the secondaries (speculum) that flash during flight.

VOICE: A clear, repeated whistle. Females quack.

NESTING: Lays 10–12 whitish or pale buff eggs in a down-lined cup in tall grass, often several hundred yards from water.

HABITAT: Marshes, ponds, and marshy lakes. Green-winged Teal may visit shallow water, including puddles, that are too small to attract other ducks.

RANGE: Breeds in northern Alaska, Manitoba, and Quebec south to California, Colorado, Nebraska, and New York. It winters in the southern states and along the coasts. It is also found in Eurasia.

SUBSPECIES: The North American and Eurasian forms were once considered distinct species. Each year a few males—and doubtless females—of the Eurasian form turn up in North America, giving rise to speculation that somewhere in North America a few of these so-called "Common Teal" may be breeding. Eurasian birds have a horizontal white stripe along the back instead of the vertical white shoulder stripe seen on American birds.

SIMILAR SPECIES: Blue-winged Teal has a conspicuous blue wing patch and dark belly; breeding-plumage males exhibit a gray-blue head with a contrasting white facial crescent.

CONSERVATION: Green-winged Teal are common and widespread, and their population has grown in recent decades. Their remote breeding grounds in Canada and Alaska have protected them from human encroachment, and bag limits have protected this species from overhunting.

■ SUMMER   ■ MIGRATION
■ WINTER   ■ RARE
■ RESIDENT

Inhabitants of large prairie marshes during the summer, these wary birds usually spend the winter on large lakes, bays, and estuaries. The Canvasback's scientific name is derived from *Vallisneria americana*, wild celery—a primary food source for these diving marshland birds. Canvasbacks have earned respect from hunters and birdwatchers alike for their elusiveness—they are wary and flush easily, and are fast, strong fliers. Their long, V-shaped flocks are a striking sight as they move from one feeding ground to another.

DESCRIPTION: 19–24" (48–61 cm). The male has a whitish body, black chest, and reddish head with low forehead. The female is light grayish with a sandy-brown head. The long bill gives the Canvasback's head a distinctive sloping profile in both sexes.

VOICE: Males grunt or croak; females quack.

NESTING: Lays 7–10 greenish eggs in a floating mass of reeds and grass anchored to stems of marsh plants.

HABITAT: Nests on marshes; winters on lakes, bays, and estuaries.

RANGE: Breeds from Alaska south and east to Nebraska and Minnesota. It winters in the coastal and interior West from British Columbia south and in the East from Massachusetts south to the Gulf Coast and in the Mississippi Valley.

SIMILAR SPECIES: At a distance, male Canvasbacks can be distinguished from similar Redheads by their white bodies, the male Redhead's body being largely gray. A Redhead male has a gray back, rounded head, and different bill shape and color.

Male Greater and Lesser scaup have grayer backs, black heads, and dark wings in flight with a white band at the trailing edge.

CONSERVATION:

Canvasback population numbers have fluctuated over the years, but draining of the large marshes they require to breed has caused Canvasback numbers to decline steadily over the past several decades. Loss of wild celery due to pollution and marshland habitat degradation can cause Canvasbacks to adjust their wintering sites and migration routes accordingly.

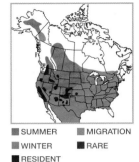

■ SUMMER ■ MIGRATION
■ WINTER ■ RARE
■ RESIDENT

Redheads do most of their feeding at night, spending the daylight hours resting on water. This medium-sized diving duck is best identified by its rounded, rufous-colored head and colorful bill, which ranges from pale blue to slate gray with a white ring and a black tip. The male's courtship display involves an odd-looking neck-stretching display and throwing its head back while issuing cat-like calls with a rising and falling pitch.

DESCRIPTION: 18–22" (46–56 cm). The male is gray with a brick-red head and black breast. The female is duller and browner, with a light area around the base of the bill and a pale stripe behind the eye. Both sexes have a pale gray wing stripe and a pale blue-gray bill (bluer in breeding males and slaty gray in females). Redheads have rounder heads than Ring-necked Ducks or Canvasbacks.

VOICE: Like the meow of a cat; also quacks. Both sexes issue a guttural call when threatened.

NESTING: Lays 10–16 buff eggs in a woven cup of reeds lined with white down and attached to marsh vegetation. Female Redheads regularly lay eggs in other nests, including those of other Redheads, other duck species, and a diverse array of unrelated waterbirds who happen to nest nearby.

HABITAT: Nests in marshes but at other times is found on open lakes and bays; often on salt water in winter.

RANGE: Breeds from Alaska and British Columbia east to Minnesota and south to California and Colorado. It winters in the southern half of the United States, the Mississippi Valley, and the Great Lakes region.

SIMILAR SPECIES: The similar Canvasback is larger and has a whiter body; its sloping forehead and bill appear wedge-shaped.

Male scaup have dark, iridescent heads and lighter gray backs; females are darker brown and lack the pale streak behind the eye.

The male Ring-necked Duck has a dark, puffy head and a black back; the female is darker brown.

CONSERVATION: LC
Formerly more abundant, this diving duck declined greatly in the mid-20th century due to the twin pressures of hunting and habitat destruction. In many areas the introduction of invasive carp from Eurasia has caused the destruction of the Redhead's aquatic food plants. Redhead populations have recovered from its lows thanks to stringent hunting restrictions and wetland conservation efforts.

This medium-sized diving duck might better be called the "Ring-billed Duck," because its chestnut neck ring is almost impossible to see except at close range, while the white ring on the bill is a prominent field mark. Ring-necked Ducks are more partial to acid ponds and lakes in wooded regions than are other diving ducks; there they eat the seeds of aquatic plants as well as snails and insects. Like other diving ducks, Ring-necks dive from the surface of the water in a graceful arc, propelling themselves downward with their feet to feed near the bottom. A fast flier, the Ring-neck undertakes longer migrations than most other diving ducks.

DESCRIPTION: 14–18" (36–46 cm). The male has a black back and breast, pale gray flanks, and a vertical white mark on the side of the breast; its angular head appears black with a purple gloss visible in favorable light. The female is brownish, and its face is lighter around the base of the bill, with a narrow white eye ring; the bill is pale gray with a white ring. The high angular shape of the head and white ring on the bill distinguish this bird from the scaup.

VOICE: Soft purring notes, but usually silent.

NESTING: Lays 8–12 buff or olive eggs in a down-lined cup concealed in vegetation near the edge of a pond.

HABITAT: Wooded lakes, ponds, and rivers; seldom on salt water except in the southern states. Frequents small and shallow wetlands, especially during migration.

RANGE: Breeds from Alaska, Manitoba, and Newfoundland south to California, Arizona, the Great Lakes, and Maine. It winters from Washington south along the Pacific Coast, east through the Southwest and Gulf Coast states, and north to New England. It is commonly seen in migration nearly anywhere in the interior of North America.

SIMILAR SPECIES: See Tufted Duck, Redhead, and Greater and Lesser scaup.

CONSERVATION:
The population of Ring-necked Ducks has enjoyed a general upward trend over the past several decades, although annual counts fluctuate widely, as they do in many duck species, based on the availability of food and healthy wetland ecosystems for breeding.

■ SUMMER ■ MIGRATION
■ WINTER ■ RARE
■ RESIDENT

This Old World bird is a counterpart of the Ring-necked Duck of North America. Fast-flying diving ducks, they may be found in the company of Ring-necked Ducks, Long-tailed Ducks, scaup, and goldeneyes, or by themselves on urban reservoirs. Some North American Tufted Ducks undoubtedly represent escaped captive birds, especially those seen near large cities in the Northeast.

DESCRIPTION: 17" (43 cm). The male is a stocky, blackish duck with white flanks and a wispy crest on the head. The female is warm brown, paler on the flanks, with a small white patch at the base of the bill and little or no crest.

VOICE: Various soft growling notes and low whistles.

NESTING: Lays 8–10 pale buff or greenish eggs in a down-lined bowl of grass concealed under a bush or tussock, usually near water.

HABITAT: Wooded lakes, streams, and marshes; in winter often in estuaries and shallow coastal bays.

RANGE: Breeds in northern Eurasia; casual in North America, chiefly along the coasts in Alaska, California, and the northeastern states. It is most often seen near urban areas.

SIMILAR SPECIES: Female Ring-necked Duck has peaked head shape, dark eyes, and white eye ring and eyeline. Female and juvenile Greater Scaup are similar to Tufted Duck, but generally paler above; its white wing stripe is shorter, less bold; the female has white feathering at the base of the bill; and the juvenile has no feathering and much less contrast between the back and flanks. Juvenile Lesser Scaup has a slightly more peaked head and a shorter wing stripe in flight. Both scaup have a narrower black tip to the bill and lack white undertail coverts.

CONSERVATION: 🐦 LC
Tufted Ducks are common in Eurasia, and their population is especially dense in the North European Plain and the United Kingdom, where they often occur year-round. Vagrants arrive rarely to both coasts of North America.

■ SUMMER ■ MIGRATION
■ WINTER ■ RARE
■ RESIDENT

Of North America's two extremely similar scaup species, the Greater Scaup is more likely to favor larger open lakes and salt water bays. Winter flocks on large lakes and along the coastal bays can contain thousands of individual birds. This scaup species nests farther north than its smaller cousins, mainly restricted to northern Canada and Alaska during the breeding season. Greater Scaup are strong divers that can delve more than 20' (6 m) below the surface to pick mollusks and other aquatic invertebrates out of the mud at the bottom of a lake or bay.

DESCRIPTION: 15–20" (38–51 cm). The breeding male has a light gray to whitish body, bookended by a black chest and rear, and a dark green-glossed head that may appear black depending on lighting. The female is a more uniform warm brown overall with a white patch at the base of the bill. Both sexes have a long, prominent white wing stripe. It is difficult to distinguish from the related Lesser Scaup.

VOICE: Usually silent; issues a series of discordant croaking calls on the breeding grounds.

NESTING: Lays 8–12 olive-buff eggs in a down-lined cup of grass concealed in a clump of grass on land or in marsh vegetation well out from shore.

HABITAT: Lakes, bays, and ponds; often on salt water in winter.

RANGE: Breeds in Alaska and northern Canada east to Hudson Bay and occasionally in the Maritime Provinces. Winters mainly along the Pacific, Gulf, and Atlantic coasts. Also found in Eurasia.

SIMILAR SPECIES: See Lesser Scaup—these two closely related species are difficult to distinguish. Greater Scaup tends to be larger with a wider and more smoothly rounded head. Lesser Scaup's voice is higher pitched.

Ring-necked Duck has a different head shape, darker mantle, a white blaze on its sides, and a markedly ringed bill. A female Ring-necked has a white eye ring and eyeline, and a different head profile.

Male Tufted Duck is black-backed with a distinctive head plume.

The female Redhead lacks distinct white patches about the bill and has a pale chin, a pale streak behind the eyes, and dark eyes.

CONSERVATION:
Although relatively common throughout their range, Greater Scaup are designated as a common bird in steep decline by Partners in Flight, denoting a population drop of more than 50% in the past 40 years. The exact reasons for the population losses aren't fully understood, but climate change, habitat degradation, coastal pollution, and hunting all likely contribute to a degree.

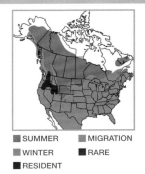

■ SUMMER ■ MIGRATION
■ WINTER ■ RARE
■ RESIDENT

Both the Lesser and Greater scaup are colloquially called "bluebills"; they are notoriously difficult to tell apart. Lesser Scaup tend to prefer smaller bodies of fresh water compared to Greater Scaup, but the two often occur together in winter. Lesser Scaup are more common in the interior of the continent; most scaup found on small interior lakes and ponds are Lessers. Both species can form huge winter flocks; when they share a habitat, each scaup species tends to stick with their own kind. Lesser Scaup flocks tend to be denser as the birds stick more closely together.

DESCRIPTION: 15–18" (38–46 cm). The male has a light gray to whitish body, a blackish chest, and a dark head that usually appears black, similar to Greater Scaup. Ideal light conditions reveal a subtle purple gloss to the dark head, compared to the green gloss of Greater Scaup. The female is dark brown with a small white face patch; not easily distinguishable from female Greater Scaup. Lesser Scaup's crown is higher and forehead steeper, giving the head a more angular appearance. In flight, the Lesser's white wing stripe is shorter than that of the Greater Scaup, which extends three-fourths of the wing's length.

VOICE: Seldom heard, but issues sharp whistles and guttural scolding notes.

NESTING: Usually lays 9–12 dark olive-buff eggs in a down-lined cup of grass hidden in vegetation, often located some distance from the edge of the water.

HABITAT: Ponds and marshes; during migration and in winter it occurs on lakes, rivers, and ponds, and in the southern states on salt water.

RANGE: Breeds from interior Alaska and northern Canada south to Colorado and Iowa; occasionally farther east. Winters regularly along the coasts south from British Columbia and Massachusetts to the Gulf of Mexico; also inland south of Colorado and the Great Lakes.

SIMILAR SPECIES: The male Greater Scaup is larger, usually has unmarked white flanks, and has a more rounded, wider head with a greenish gloss visible only under ideal lighting conditions. Greater's bill is wider with a longer nail. The female Greater has more extensive white feathering at the base of the bill, and may appear slightly rust-brown. Both sexes of Greater have a white wing stripe that extends through the speculum and most of the primaries.

The Ring-necked Duck has a more exaggerated profile, a darker mantle, a white ring on the bill, and a white blaze on the flank. Female Ring-neckeds have a white eye ring and eyeline, and a different profile.

Female Redheads lack white patches about the bill; and have a pale streak behind the eye, a pale chin, and dark eyes.

CONSERVATION:
Lesser Scaup are the most abundant diving duck in North America, and although their populations have been gradually declining for many decades, they remain a common sight throughout the continent. Like their relatives the Greater Scaup, the exact causes of the Lesser Scaup's population declines are poorly understood.

■ SUMMER   ■ MIGRATION
■ WINTER   ■ RARE
■ RESIDENT

Our smallest eider, this fast-flying, beautiful sea duck is most frequently seen on coasts and on open ocean in the Bering Sea. It is a social bird, often staying in dense flocks that migrate and forage in close proximity; flocks may even dive synchronously in search of food. It spends most of the year foraging at sea, where it dives for crustaceans, insect larvae, and even aquatic plants and their seeds. Birds resting on the water often hold the tail at an angle above the surface.

DESCRIPTION: 17–18½" (43–47 cm). A small eider the size of a goldeneye. The male is pale chestnut below, boldly black and white above; its head is white with a black ring around the eye and a small black and green crest on the nape. The female is rich mottled brown like other eiders, but with a smaller head. Both sexes have a speculum like that of a Mallard—purple, bordered in the front and back with white.

VOICE: The male has a weak moan similar to Common Eider's; the female makes low growling notes.

NESTING: Lays 6–10 yellowish or greenish eggs in a down-lined depression in moss on tundra.

HABITAT: Tundra pools and adjacent coastal waters.

RANGE: Breeds on the northern and western coasts of Alaska in low-lying tundra. Winters on the southern coast of Alaska and the Aleutians.

SIMILAR SPECIES: The male Steller's Eider is unmistakable. All other female eiders are larger, have clearly barred, paler plumage, feathering extending down on the bill, and more rounded heads; they also lack a purple speculum. Female scoters are blackish.

CONSERVATION:
Its limited range and small population make Steller's Eider a vulnerable species. It is on the U.S. Endangered Species List and is classified as threatened in Alaska. As an arctic breeder, climate change poses an enhanced risk to the survival of the species.

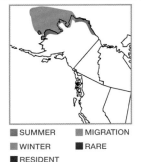

SUMMER ■ MIGRATION
WINTER ■ RARE
RESIDENT

During the winter the Spectacled Eider's diet consists largely of mussels and other mollusks, which it captures in deep dives over submerged ledges and reefs. On its tundra breeding grounds this duck feeds mainly on aquatic insects, crustaceans, and the seeds of water plants. This uncommon sea duck is local and declining in Alaska.

DESCRIPTION: 20½–22" (52–56 cm). The breeding male has a white neck, back, and shoulders, with a black breast and belly; its head is light olive green with large, white, black-rimmed "spectacles" around the eye. The female is mottled buff, with pale buff "spectacles" and a large bill that's feathered at the base.

VOICE: Usually silent; a soft *ah-hoo!*

NESTING: Lays 4–9 greenish or olive-buff eggs in a down-lined depression in the tundra near fresh or brackish water.

HABITAT: Coastal tundra during breeding season; inshore waters during most of the year.

RANGE: Breeds along the northern and western coasts of Alaska. Winters off the Alaska Peninsula and eastern Aleutians, in the Bering Sea.

SIMILAR SPECIES: Male Common Eider is larger with a white breast and a paler face and nape. Female Common and King eiders are less tawny, lack spectacles, and show more of their bills below the feathering. First-year male Common and King eiders show head and bill patterns suggesting adults'.

CONSERVATION: EN
The Spectacled Eider is on the U.S. Endangered Species List; it is classified as endangered in Alaska. Its population suffered devastating losses at one of its former major breeding sites in the Yukon-Kuskokwim delta, where roughly ⅓ of the world's Spectacled Eiders once nested—by the mid-1990s, this nesting population had declined by 96%. Habitat loss due to climate change and oil and gas exploration in their Arctic range is the biggest threat to this species.

■ SUMMER ■ MIGRATION
■ WINTER ■ RARE
■ RESIDENT

Although the world population of the King Eider is large, the birds are seldom seen in North America except in the extreme north and out to sea; most winter farther north and favor deeper water than the Common Eider. They can dive quite deeply in search of food, having been recorded swimming at depths of up to 150 feet (50 meters). Like the Common Eider, they take large numbers of mussels and other shellfish but vary their diet with small fish, squid, sand dollars, and sea urchins. The migrations of the King Eider are spectacular, with huge flocks traveling in long lines along the coast, heading to or from their breeding or wintering grounds.

DESCRIPTION: 18–25" (46–64 cm). A large sea duck. Similar to the Common Eider, but the male has a black back, a conspicuous orange-yellow bill, and a "shield" on the forehead. The female is similar to a female Common Eider, but the bill is shorter, not extending as far back toward the eye, and lacks the distinctive sloping profile; its flanks are marked with black crescents, not bars. King Eider usually holds its bill more horizontal to the surface of the water than does Common Eider.

VOICE: A guttural croaking. The male's song is a short series of deep cooing notes, *croo-croo-croo*.

NESTING: Lays 4–7 buff-olive eggs in a down-lined depression on rocky tundra, often some distance from the edge of the water.

HABITAT: Rocky coasts and islands, on the surface of deep waters and the open ocean.

RANGE: A circumpolar species found throughout the Arctic. Breeds in freshwater ponds and lakes in Alaska and Arctic islands of Canada, south locally to Hudson Bay. Its migration routes tend to go around land masses rather than over them. It winters along the coasts south to southern Alaska and from Labrador to New Jersey; strays are rarely found farther south and on the Great Lakes.

SIMILAR SPECIES: The adult male is unmistakable. An immature male usually has an orange bill, which is useful for identification of Atlantic Coast birds, but may not separate immature male King Eiders from immature male Common Eiders of the Pacific race. The slightly concave profile of the bill, "bumped" front, and rounded crown are the most useful diagnostic characteristics. The head of both sexes are generally held higher than a Common Eider's. The female Common Eider has linear streaks on the flanks.

Black Duck lacks flank marks and has a different head shape.

See female Steller's Eider.

CONSERVATION: ![LC]
Abundant within its limited circumpolar range. These birds nest in remote regions of the Arctic, where they have suffered little disturbance from human activity. Their reliance on Arctic habitat, however, makes them particularly vulnerable to the effects of climate change.

■ SUMMER ■ MIGRATION
■ WINTER ■ RARE
■ RESIDENT

A large, stocky, and highly social sea duck found on northern coastlines, often in large flocks. Only eiders in the Arctic are strongly migratory; in the warmer parts of their range they may remain near the breeding grounds all year. Their principal foods are mussels and other shellfish; the birds gather in huge rafts where these are available.

DESCRIPTION: 23–27" (58–69 cm). The largest North American duck. The male has black underparts, a white back, white head and breast, a dark crown, and a a greenish tinge on the back of the head. The female is mottled brown with barred flanks. Common Eider's long, sloping bill gives the bird a distinctive profile. It usually holds its bill pointing slightly down toward the surface of the water, whereas the King Eider tends to hold its bill more upright and parallel to the water.

VOICE: During courtship the male gives a hollow moan and various cooing notes, sometimes written as *rah-ool*. The female quacks.

NESTING: Lays 4–7 olive or buff eggs in a substantial mass of grass thickly lined with down. Often several pairs form a loose colony.

HABITAT: Rocky coasts and coastal tundra.

RANGE: Breeds on the Arctic coasts of Alaska and Canada and south from the Maritimes to Massachusetts. It winters south along the Pacific Coast from Alaska to Washington and along the Atlantic Coast to Long Island, occasionally farther. It is also found in northern Eurasia.

SUBSPECIES: There are four subspecies in North America that differ mainly in bill color and shape, and female plumage coloration. Females of Eastern (subsp. *dresseri*) and Hudson Bay (subsp. *sedentaria*) eiders are rusty reddish-brown, whereas Northern (subsp. *borealis*) and Pacific (subsp. *v-nigrum*) forms are grayer. Eastern eiders in the Atlantic have a greenish-yellow bill; the more northerly subspecies have muted yellowish bills. The Pacific form is genetically distinct and may be a separate species—it has a thin but distinctive black V on its throat and a bright orange-yellow bill.

SIMILAR SPECIES: Female and immature King Eiders have steeper forehead, shorter bill, and usually hold bill parallel to water; females have crescent-shaped marks on flanks. American Black Duck has a different bill shape, white wing linings, and lacks barring on flanks. In Alaska, see Spectacled Eider.

CONSERVATION: NT

Until the end of the 19th century, eiders were heavily hunted for their down—specifically the soft breast feathers of the females. For hundreds of years eiderdown has been gathered from nests and used to line pillows, quilts, and parkas. Today this practice is rare and is performed more sustainably, as eiderdown has gradually been replaced by farm-raised goose feathers and by synthetic materials. Since the widespread overhunting practices ended, Common Eiders have enjoyed a spectacular increase in numbers along the Maine coast, and they are once again nesting there in large numbers.

■ SUMMER   ■ MIGRATION
■ WINTER   ■ RARE
■ RESIDENT

These small sea ducks are surprisingly strong swimmers, able to navigate rough waters eschewed by many other ducks. During breeding season, the Harlequin Duck is a bird of swift mountain streams, where it catches the nymphs of stoneflies, caddisflies, and other aquatic insects. In the fall the birds move to the coast, where they thrive in the rough surf in toward rocky cliffs, wrenching mussels, chitons, barnacles, and other attached animals from the surface and diving for crabs and other crustaceans. These intrepid ducks may be seen swimming against fast-flowing currents and clambering over rough coastal cliff faces.

DESCRIPTION: 14–20" (36–51 cm). A small, dark duck marked with striking plumage. The male is blue-gray (appearing black at a distance), with chestnut flanks and distinctive white patches on the head and body. The female is dusky brown with 2 or 3 whitish patches on the sides of the face. In flight, this species lacks large white patches on the wings.

VOICE: A mouse-like squeak and various low whistles. Its squeaky calls have earned it the nickname "sea mouse."

NESTING: Lays 6–8 pale buff or cream-colored eggs in a mass of down concealed in a crevice in rocks along a stream.

HABITAT: Swift-moving streams in summer; rocky, wave-lashed coasts and jetties in winter.

RANGE: Breeds from Alaska and Yukon south to Wyoming and the Sierra Nevada of California, and from southern Baffin Island south to Labrador and the Gaspé Peninsula. It winters along the coasts south to central California and Long Island. It is also found in Eurasia.

SIMILAR SPECIES: Female Bufflehead is plumper with a single, elongated white mark behind the eye and a white wing patch visible in flight.

Female and immature Surf Scoters are larger, with a different profile; their facial spots are larger, less circular, and less sharply defined.

The female Long-tailed Duck has more white on the face.

CONSERVATION:  LC
Although still common in most of its range, this species has declined from its historical population numbers, but may be increasing today. Harlequin Duck populations appear to be stable in the Northwest, but their decline in eastern North America has caused the species to be listed as endangered in Canada and threatened in Maine.

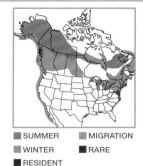

■ SUMMER　■ MIGRATION
■ WINTER　■ RARE
■ RESIDENT

Nicknamed "skunk-head" for the white patch on its head, the Surf Scoter is the only scoter species confined to the New World. It is common on both coasts in winter, and especially so on the Pacific Coast, where it sometimes feeds quite close to rocky headlands and in shallow inlets. These birds are similar in their habits to the other scoters but are more often seen diving for mollusks and crustaceans along the line of breaking surf. The bold white patches on the male's head are used in displays; a bird may threaten a rival simply by turning its head and presenting its white nape. These scoters depart for breeding grounds in early spring, but a few—usually young males—may spend their second summer on the wintering grounds.

DESCRIPTION: 17–21" (43–53 cm). The male is black with prominent white patches on the crown and nape. The bill is colorful and swells at the base, bearing a large black spot. The female is brownish black, with two whitish patches on the cheek. Both sexes lack a white wing patch.

VOICE: Usually silent, but females make a low, guttural croaking. Males may issue a short gurgling or a louder *puk-puk* call. The male's wings can produce a low whistling in flight.

NESTING: Lays 5–8 pinkish-buff eggs in a down-lined depression hidden under bushes or in marsh vegetation, not necessarily near water.

HABITAT: Breeds on northern freshwater lakes; winters almost entirely on the ocean and in large coastal bays.

RANGE: Breeds in Alaska and across northern Canada to Labrador. It winters mainly along both coasts, from Alaska south to California and from Newfoundland south to Florida and rarely to Texas.

SIMILAR SPECIES: See White-winged Scoter. In Surf Scoters, both sexes lack the white wing patch seen on White-wingeds in flight.

CONSERVATION: 🐦 LC
Although little is known of the population of Surf Scoters, they remain common and widespread, and their numbers appear to be stable.

Melanitta deglandi **WHITE-WINGED SCOTER**

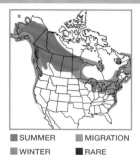

■ SUMMER ■ MIGRATION
■ WINTER ■ RARE
■ RESIDENT

White-winged Scoters are named for the prominent white patches on the wings of both sexes, which are visible in flight. Our largest scoter, White-wingeds often fly in long, irregular lines consisting of thousands of individuals, just offshore and only a few feet above the waves. The most abundant and widespread of the scoters—there are more than a million individuals in North America—these sociable birds gather in large flocks or rafts to feed and to sleep. This species feeds chiefly on mollusks, which it collects from mussel beds at depths of 15 to 40 feet (5 to 12 meters). They also feed on crabs, starfish, sea urchins, and some fish.

DESCRIPTION: 19–24" (48–61 cm). The male is black with bold white wing patches, white crescents around the eyes, and a yellow bill with a black knob at the base. Females are dull brown, with two whitish facial spots and white wing patches. For both sexes, the white wing patches on the secondaries are prominent during flight.

VOICE: Usually silent. During displays, males make soft whistles both vocally and with their wings. Both sexes issue brief, guttural croaks.

NESTING: Lays 5–17 (usually 9 or 10) buff or pink eggs in a hollow lined with sticks and down, under a bush, or in a crevice near water, often on an island in a lake.

HABITAT: Breeds on large lakes; winters mainly on the ocean and on large coastal bays, but a few remain on lakes in the interior.

RANGE: Breeds in Alaska and much of western and central Canada. Winters along both coasts, from Alaska south to California and from Newfoundland south to Carolinas, rarely to Florida and Texas. Also in Eurasia.

SUBSPECIES: Formerly considered a subspecies of White-winged Scoter, its close Eurasian cousin Stejneger's Scoter (*M. stejnegeri*) is a casual stray to western Alaska. These birds have darker flanks and a different bill with a more prominent nasal "hook."

SIMILAR SPECIES: Male Surf Scoters have obvious white front and nape patches and a more prominent bill. Female Surfs generally, but not always, have more prominent white facial patches than female White-wings; adult female Surfs have a dull whitish nape patch, which is not easily seen. Surf's head profile is flatter, less concave; the bill appears swollen at the base, extending farther onto the face.

Male Black Scoters are smaller, have a bright orange bill process, and lack any white on the head. Black Scoters carry their bills parallel to the surface of the water.

In flight, White-winged Scoters show a white speculum, whereas other scoters' wings are dark.

CONSERVATION: LC
Widespread and common. Like all birds that dive and rest on the sea, White-winged Scoters are vulnerable to oil spills and other coastal and ocean pollution.

BLACK SCOTER *Melanitta americana*

■ SUMMER   ■ MIGRATION
■ WINTER   ■ RARE
■ RESIDENT

Scoters are gregarious, and the three species often feed together, gathering over submerged reefs where mollusks, barnacles, chitons, and limpets abound. Black Scoters often swim with their tails cocked upward, usually swimming and taking flight in tightly packed groups. Newly hatched young remain on fresh water for several days, feeding on small freshwater mussels and the larvae of aquatic insects before moving to salt water.

DESCRIPTION: 17–21" (43–53 cm). The male is black, with a bill black with a large yellow knob at the base. The female is duller, with pale cheeks and an all-dark bill. Both sexes show silvery wing linings in flight.

VOICE: In spring, males issue a soft, musical, whistled *cour-loo*. Females make a nasal call that is described as sounding like a creaking door hinge. It is much more vocal than other scoter species.

NESTING: Lays 5–8 pale buff eggs in a down-lined cup of grass hidden in a rock crevice or clump of grass near edge of water.

HABITAT: Breeds on ponds in boreal forests; winters on oceans and in large saltwater bays.

RANGE: Breeds in western Alaska, Labrador, and Newfoundland. It winters along the coasts from Alaska south to California, from Newfoundland south to the Carolinas, along portions of the Gulf Coast, and on the Great Lakes. Also found in Eurasia.

SUBSPECIES: A European cousin, the Common Scoter, is considered a subspecies of Black Scoter by some and a full, distinct species by others. These birds have a dark bill with a yellow stripe and a dark knob at the base.

SIMILAR SPECIES: See White-winged Scoter.

A winter Ruddy Duck—sometimes confused with a female Black Scoter—has pale flanks and brighter cheek patches; the female Ruddy has a dark stripe across the cheek, and generally occupies freshwater habitat.

CONSERVATION: NT

The Black Scoter is the least common of the three scoters in North America, numbering perhaps 500,000 individuals. Its population is poorly understood, and its remote nesting sites are rarely discovered. Although still a regular sight on coastal waters, its population is widely believed to be declining.

SUMMER ■ MIGRATION
WINTER ■ RARE
RESIDENT

The Long-tailed Duck is a distinctive cold-water sea duck known for its showy plumage and unmistakable vocalizations. In midwinter Long-tailed Ducks begin their courtship displays. Several males gather around a single female and utter their mellow, barking, far-carrying call. Although courtship lasts until after the birds have returned to their nesting grounds, most birds are paired when they arrive in the North. In winter these diving ducks feed mainly on mollusks, shrimps, and crabs, but when nesting they switch to roots, buds, and seeds; the ducklings feed mainly on insect larvae. While most diving ducks paddle with their webbed feet, the Long-tailed Duck uses its partially folded wings to propel itself underwater. It is one of the deepest-diving ducks, known to reach depths of 200 feet (60 meters) below the surface.

DESCRIPTION: Males reach 19–22" (48–56 cm) long, and females are typically around 15–17" (38–43 cm) in length. The male is boldly patterned in black and white—more white in winter and more black in summer—with the species' namesake long, slender central tail feathers. Females are duller and lack the long tail feathers. A series of multiple molts per year produces a complex set of seasonal plumages in both sexes, but a dark breast and white belly remain at all times of year. Both sexes show all-dark, unpatterned wings in flight.

VOICE: Various clucking and growling notes. The male's courtship call is a loud, musical *ow-owdle-ow, ow-owdle-ow*, frequently repeated. These vocalizations can carry for great distances.

NESTING: Lays 5–11 yellowish or cream-colored eggs in a down-lined cup of grass concealed on tundra near water.

HABITAT: Breeds on tundra; winters on open bays and inshore waters.

RANGE: Breeds in Alaska and Arctic Canada. Winters along the coasts from the Bering Sea south to California, from Labrador south to the Carolinas, along portions of the Gulf Coast, and on the Great Lakes. Also found in Eurasia.

SIMILAR SPECIES: This species is distinctive in its habits, plumages, and vocalizations. Its closest living relatives are the goldeneyes, which are easily distinguished.

CONSERVATION: VU
The Long-tailed Duck is classified as a common bird in steep decline and is listed as Vulnerable on the IUCN Red List of Threatened Species. Its offshore, often deep-water winter habitat makes it difficult to get an accurate population count, and makes the species particularly vulnerable to oil spills and entanglement in commercial fishing nets.

■ SUMMER ■ MIGRATION
■ WINTER ■ RARE
■ RESIDENT

A relative of the goldeneyes, the Bufflehead is one of our smallest ducks. Named for their unusually bulbous head shape, these beautiful ducks are cavity nesters that often take up residence in old woodpecker holes and even artificial nest boxes. Less social than other ducks, they tend to travel in smaller flocks than goldeneyes and often feed closer to shore. When a flock is diving for food, at least one bird in the group usually remains on the surface watching for danger. These fast fliers usually fly close to the water but make no whistling sound in flight.

DESCRIPTION: 13–15" (33–38 cm). A small, chubby duck. The male is largely white with a black back, a black head with greenish and purplish gloss, and a large white patch from behind the eye to the top and back of the head. The female is all dark, with a single whitish patch on the cheek. These ducks are fast fliers with a rapid wingbeat.

VOICE: The male has a squeaky whistle; the female, a soft, hoarse quack.

NESTING: Lays 6–12 pale buff or ivory eggs in a mass of down placed in a tree cavity, often using an old woodpecker hole up to 20' (6 m) off the ground.

HABITAT: Breeds on wooded lakes and ponds; winters mainly on saltwater bays and estuaries.

RANGE: Breeds in Alaska and in Canada east to western Quebec, and south in the mountains to Washington and Montana. It winters along the Atlantic to northern Florida and across the southern United States, south to Mexico and the Gulf Coast.

SIMILAR SPECIES: The male Bufflehead is unmistakable.

A female Harlequin Duck has three rounded white face patches, whereas a female Bufflehead has a single, elongated white face patch.

The male Hooded Merganser has a somewhat similar face pattern, but has a longer bill and brownish flanks.

See Common Goldeneye.

CONSERVATION: LC

Bufflehead populations appear to be stable. Overhunting in the early 20th century reduced the population from its historical numbers, and although still considered a game bird, more sustainable hunting practices and bag limits have allowed the species to recover. Today, habitat degradation and the effects of climate change are its biggest threats. Providing nest boxes with small openings—2.5 inches (6.5 cm) in diameter—near wooded lakes and ponds in the bird's breeding range can help, as these are one of few cavity nesting ducks that will accept artificial nest boxes.

Bucephala clangula **COMMON GOLDENEYE**

■ SUMMER ■ MIGRATION
■ WINTER ■ RARE
■ RESIDENT

Common Goldeneyes are the more populous of our two goldeneye species. Its wings produce a loud whistling sound in flight, easily identified even when the birds cannot be seen; hunters call this species the "Whistler." Goldeneyes can dive to depths of 20 feet (6 meters) or more, but generally limit themselves to about 10 feet (3 meters). In winter, goldeneyes feed mainly on mollusks; in summer, their diet shifts to aquatic plants and insects. Pair formation begins in midwinter, and until then the two sexes often form separate flocks—male Common Goldeneyes tend to winter farther north than do the females. During its courtship display, the male stretches its head forward along the water and then snaps it rapidly upward over the back, bill pointed skyward, while uttering a shrill, two-note call. Then it swings its orange feet forward, sending up a small shower in front of it.

DESCRIPTION: 16–20" (41–51 cm). The male has a white body and a black back. Its head appears black but is actually glossy greenish when seen in the proper light conditions; it bears a large, round white spot in front of its namesake golden-yellow eyes. The female is grayish, with a warm brown head, white neck ring, and a dark bill. Both sexes have a distinctive puffy head shape and a large white wing patch that is conspicuous in flight. See Barrow's Goldeneye.

VOICE: The male's courtship call is a high-pitched *jeee-ep!* Females utter a low quack.

NESTING: This species prefers large cavities for nesting, especially natural tree cavities and old woodpecker holes, and sometimes abandoned buildings or artificial nest boxes. The nests may be located as much as 60 feet (18 meters) above the ground. The female lays 8–12 pale green eggs in a mass of down inside the nest cavity. Some females will return to use the same successful nest site year after year.

HABITAT: Breeds on wooded lakes and ponds; winters mainly on coastal bays and estuaries.

RANGE: Breeds in Alaska and across Canada to Newfoundland and Maritime Provinces, south to mountains of Montana and Great Lakes. Winters in much of the United States, wherever water is open. Also found in Eurasia.

SIMILAR SPECIES: The similar Barrow's Goldeneye has a more elongated head and a smaller, stubbier bill. The male Barrow's Goldeneye has a purplish head and a crescent-shaped white facial spot, along with a smaller white wing patch and more black on the sides. The female Barrow's is darker overall, with a chocolate-brown head, a darker breast band, and less white visible on the folded wing. Juveniles of the two species are nearly identical.

Bufflehead is smaller; the male has a large white patch on a puffy, rounded head; the female has an elongated white facial mark.

Mergansers are more elongated with slender bills.

CONSERVATION:
Common Goldeneye populations are large and stable overall. These birds depend on dead trees for natural nest cavities, and may decline where human development causes these trees to be removed. Some, however, will use artificial nest boxes where suitable natural sites are scarce.

BARROW'S GOLDENEYE *Bucephala islandica*

SUMMER ■ MIGRATION
WINTER ■ RARE
■ RESIDENT

Barrow's Goldeneye favors alpine lakes, often breeding at elevations of 10,000 feet (3000 meters) or more. It is usually found in smaller flocks than the Common Goldeneye. It feeds almost entirely on mollusks obtained by diving, but also takes an occasional snail, urchin, or marine worm. Named for a population described in Iceland, Barrow's Goldeneye is more commonly a bird of the Pacific Northwest, with population pockets occurring in the Northeast. These birds also make casual appearances around the Great Lakes and elsewhere in the interior of the continent, although rarely. Its patchy distribution suggests that it is an ancient species that was once more widespread. In the East, it is greatly outnumbered by the Common Goldeneye, but may occur in flocks of hundreds in the Canadian Maritimes.

DESCRIPTION: 16½–20" (42–51 cm). The male has white body and black back. Its head appears black, but its glossy purple sheen becomes visible in ideal light conditions. The female is gray with a brown head, white collar, and usually an orange-yellow bill. Both sexes differ from Common Goldeneye in having a steeper forehead and smaller white wing patches.

VOICE: Soft grunts and croaks during courtship; otherwise usually silent.

NESTING: Lays 5–15 pale green eggs on a bed of down in a hollow tree. In treeless areas, these birds may nest in a crevice among rocks, in burrows, or under bushes.

HABITAT: Breeds on forested lakes and rivers; winters mainly on open bays and estuaries along coast.

RANGE: Breeds in the mountains from Alaska south to central California and Wyoming, and in northern Quebec and Labrador. Winters along the Pacific Coast from Alaska south to California and in smaller numbers along the Atlantic from the Maritime Provinces south to Long Island. It also breeds in western Greenland and Iceland.

SIMILAR SPECIES: A male Barrow's Goldeneye resembles a male Common Goldeneye, but has more black on the sides, a stubbier bill, and a crescent-shaped (rather than round) white spot in front of the eye.

CONSERVATION: LC
Although less numerous than Common Goldeneyes, Barrow's Goldeneye populations are stable to increasing.

In North America, the Smew occurs only as a rare but regular migrant in the Aleutian Islands; very rare along Pacific Coast. Reports of this species elsewhere in North America are often suspected of being escaped captives since the species is kept and bred in captivity.

DESCRIPTION: 14–16" (35.5–40.5 cm). A small white merganser. The male has a whitish body, a black back and face with a black bill, and a V-shaped black patch on the nape of the neck. Its flanks are marked with vertical black bars. The female has a grayish body, white throat and lower face, and a reddish head and nape.

VOICE: Generally silent.

NESTING: Lays 6–9 white eggs in tree cavity near water.

HABITAT: Breeds in taiga; prefers lakes, ponds, bays, and rivers. It tends to prefer covered areas, such as under small trees.

RANGE: Breeds in northern Eurasia. It winters from Iceland to Russia and Kamchatka, south to northwestern Africa, the Mediterranean Sea, eastern China, and Japan.

SIMILAR SPECIES: Males are distinctive. The female Smew resembles other female mergansers. Note the bright white throat and short, dark bill that distinguish it from its North American cousins.

CONSERVATION: **LC** Least concern in its native range, it is a rare vagrant in Alaska.

HOODED MERGANSER *Lophodytes cucullatus*

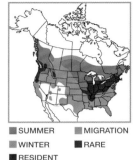

■ SUMMER ■ MIGRATION
■ WINTER ■ RARE
■ RESIDENT

These birds are aptly named for the prominent crest atop the heads of both sexes. The smallest of our mergansers, Hoodeds are most often seen along rivers and in estuaries during the fall and winter. They are usually found in pairs or in flocks of up to a dozen; when startled, they are among the fastest-flying of our ducks. Males perform a beautiful courtship display and, once mated, swim energetically around the female in further ritual displays. Hooded Mergansers feed chiefly on small fish, which they pursue in long, rapid, underwater dives; they also take small frogs, newts, tadpoles, and aquatic insects.

DESCRIPTION: 16–19" (41–48 cm). A small duck with a slender, pointed bill. The male has a white, fan-shaped, black-bordered crest, along with a blackish body with dull rusty flanks and a white breast with two black stripes down the side. The female is dull gray-brown, with a warmer brown head and crest. Both sexes show a white wing patch in flight.

VOICE: Hoarse grunts and chatters. Males make a popping note followed by a low, gurgling growl.

NESTING: Lays 8–12 white eggs in a down-lined cup in a natural tree cavity or sometimes in a fallen hollow log. It sometimes uses artificial nest boxes intended for Wood Ducks.

HABITAT: Breeds on wooded ponds, lakes, and rivers; winters in coastal marshes and inlets.

RANGE: Breeds from southern Alaska south to Oregon and Montana, and from Manitoba and Nova Scotia south to Arkansas and northern Alabama. Winters near the coast from British Columbia south to California and from New England south to Florida and Texas.

SIMILAR SPECIES: Female Wood Duck has a bold, elongated eye ring and shows an iridescent blue inner wing in flight.

See Bufflehead.

CONSERVATION:  LC
Hooded Mergansers are common in much of the East, uncommon in the West. Their numbers are stable, and possibly increasing with the help of artificial nest boxes. Forest destruction and clearing reduced the availability of nesting sites for these and many other cavity nesters during the 20th century. Responsible management of wooded habitat and the preservation of mature trees help to ensure suitable nesting sites for these ducks.

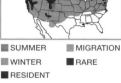

■ SUMMER ■ MIGRATION
■ WINTER ■ RARE
■ RESIDENT

These large-bodied diving birds are the expected merganser on interior freshwater lakes in North America, often seen submerging in pursuit of food. Although they prefer to feed on lakes, cold weather sometimes drives Common Mergansers to brackish water or rivers, where they are found in flocks of 10 to 20 birds, all facing upstream and diving in pursuit of fish. The bird's specialized bill—narrow, with a hooked upper mandible and fine, saw-like teeth along the edges—is adapted to catching slippery fish in addition to a variety of aquatic invertebrates. Pairs are formed in late winter, and until then these birds often form single-sex flocks. In summer it is not uncommon to see a female with a large group of ducklings in tow.

DESCRIPTION: 22–27" (56–69 cm). The male has crisp white sides, a white breast, and a dark green head. Sometimes the male's white plumage is tinged with pink. The female has a gray body and sides and a reddish-brown, crested head that contrasts sharply from a white throat. Both sexes have a long, thin, red bill with a hooked tip.

VOICE: Low, rasping croaks. The female quacks, most often in flight.

NESTING: Lays 9–12 pale buff or ivory eggs in a down-lined tree cavity or sometimes on the ground or in an artificial nest box. Usually nests near water. The young stay with the female for several weeks.

HABITAT: Breeds on wooded rivers and ponds; winters mainly on lakes and rivers, occasionally on salt water.

RANGE: Breeds across Canada from eastern Alaska, Manitoba, and Newfoundland south in the mountains to California, northern New Mexico, the Great Lakes, and northern New England. It winters south to northern Mexico, the Gulf Coast states, and Georgia (rarely farther). It is also found in Eurasia, where the species is called "Goosander."

SIMILAR SPECIES: Red-breasted Merganser is similar. The male Red-breasted is darker, with gray sides and a rust-colored breast, and a shaggy crest not seen in Common males. In flight, the Red-breasted appears dark-chested, with two dark bars separating the white inner wing. Male Red-breasted Mergansers also have bright red eyes and a white neck ring. The female Red-breasted lacks the sharply defined white chin—instead, the reddish brown of the head blends into the gray of the neck. Female Red-breasted Merganser may appear double-crested; in flight, it has a smaller speculum with a dark bar. In both sexes, the Red-breasted's bill is slenderer and thinner at the base; the nostril is closer to the base.

CONSERVATION: LC
Common Merganser populations appear to be stable in North America, although they have declined gradually since the middle of the 20th century. Mergansers are at the top of the aquatic food chain, and many environmentalists look to them as an indicator species to measure the health of local habitat. Their fish-heavy diets make them more susceptible to pesticide and heavy metal pollution that can accumulate in and degrade their aquatic habitats.

RED-BREASTED MERGANSER *Mergus serrator*

SUMMER ■ MIGRATION
WINTER ■ RARE
■ RESIDENT

The Red-breasted Merganser breeds farther north than its relatives and is also the most common winter merganser on salt water, especially where rocky coves provide good fishing. It is a common sight on the coasts, often found near the shore foraging alone or in small groups. Like the other two merganser species, it captures fish in swift underwater dives, aided by its long, pointed bill lined with sharp, tooth-like projections. These birds may also gather into large flocks where fish are abundant, and have even been observed hunting cooperatively by "herding" fish into shallower water.

DESCRIPTION: 19–26" (48–66 cm). The male has a green head with a wispy crest, gray sides, a white neck ring, and a rusty streaked breast. The female is grayish, with a reddish-brown head shading gradually into the gray of the neck. Both sexes have shaggy crests and thin, red bills.

VOICE: Usually silent; various croaking and grunting notes during courtship.

NESTING: Lays 8–10 olive-buff eggs in a down-lined depression concealed under a bush or in a brush pile.

HABITAT: Breeds on wooded lakes and tundra ponds; winters mainly on salt water.

RANGE: Breeds in Alaska and across northern Canada to Newfoundland and south to the Great Lakes. It winters chiefly along the coasts from Alaska south to California, from the Maritime Provinces south to Florida, and along the Gulf Coast. Also found in Eurasia.

SIMILAR SPECIES: See Common Merganser. When observed together in mixed flocks, Common Mergansers appear generally larger and have a thicker bill.

CONVERSATION:

Red-breasted Mergansers are common, and their populations are stable. Their far-north breeding habitat makes them vulnerable to the effects of climate change. These birds tend to aggregate in large concentrations at migration stopover sites, such as the Great Lakes—disturbance or habitat destruction at these sites could have an outsized impact on this species.

SUMMER ■ MIGRATION
WINTER ■ RARE
RESIDENT

This tropical, stiff-tailed duck is a rare and irregular visitor to southern Texas and Florida, usually with only a few confirmed records each year. These birds seem to wander nomadically rather than following an established migration path. A relative of the Ruddy Duck, the Masked Duck is highly secretive and difficult to spot, spending most of its time hidden in marsh vegetation, where it dives for food and paddles away quickly at the first sign of danger. It flies readily and swiftly, however, and can take flight directly from the surface of the water. It seems to be more willing to fly than the Ruddy, and is most active at dusk and at dawn.

DESCRIPTION: 12–14" (30–36 cm). A small brown duck with a white speculum. The breeding male is mainly reddish brown with a black face and crown and a pale blue bill. Females and winter males are brown, marked with blackish bars or spots, a blackish line through the eye, and a dark line across the cheek.

VOICE: Usually silent; low grunts and whistling calls. Also produces a low puffing or popping sound.

NESTING: Lays 4–6 buff eggs on a large mass of marsh vegetation concealed near shore.

HABITAT: Freshwater marshes, rice fields, and weedy ponds and lake margins.

RANGE: Breeds irregularly on the Gulf Coast in Texas; a few winter in southern Florida. Also found in the American tropics.

SIMILAR SPECIES: See Ruddy Duck.

CONSERVATION:
The Masked Duck enjoys a wide range in the American tropics but isn't especially numerous within this range. Its highly secretive nature and irregular wandering make it difficult for conservationists to accurately measure the species' population.

■ SUMMER　■ MIGRATION
■ WINTER　■ RARE
■ RESIDENT

This stiff-tailed duck is one of the most aquatic members of the family and, like a grebe, can sink slowly out of sight. Although it can avoid danger by diving or by hiding in marsh vegetation, it is a strong flier and undertakes long migrations to and from its nesting places. Largely a vegetarian, Ruddy Duck favors pondweed and the seeds of other aquatic plants, but also consumes large numbers of midge larvae during the breeding season. These compact birds often swim with their long tails raised. The male's courtship display involves rapidly slapping its bill against its breast to create a soft clapping noise.

DESCRIPTION: 14–16" (36–41 cm). A small, chunky duck with a long tail that is often held straight up. The male in breeding plumage has a chestnut body, black crown, and white cheeks. Female and winter males are dusky brown, with the whitish cheeks of the female crossed by a dark stripe. The male's bill is blue in breeding season and black at other times of year.

VOICE: Usually silent. A courting male produces ticking and clapping sounds by pressing its bill against its breast and produces an odd sputtering call.

NESTING: Lays 6–20 white or cream-colored eggs in a floating nest of dry stems lined with down, concealed among reeds or bulrushes in a marsh.

HABITAT: Breeds on freshwater marshes, marshy lakes, and ponds; winters on marshes and in shallow coastal bays.

RANGE: Breeds from British Columbia, Mackenzie, and Quebec south to California, southern New Mexico, and southern Texas, with occasional breeding farther east. Winters on the coasts north to British Columbia and Massachusetts and as far inland as Missouri.

SIMILAR SPECIES: The Masked Duck (rare and local in Texas and Florida) is similar in shape but smaller; it shows a white patch in the secondaries in flight; the breeding-plumage male has a black mask on the face and forecrown, and heavy spotting on sides. Females and nonbreeding males and immatures have a blackish crown, a buff eyebrow, a dark eyeline, and a dark horizontal stripe across the cheek below the eye.

A female Black Scoter resembles a winter-plumage male Ruddy Duck, but is larger and darker-bodied with a proportionately smaller bill.

CONSERVATION: LC
Ruddy Duck populations appear to be stable. Wetlands in North America's prairie pothole region are important to this species; efforts to restore and protect this habitat from livestock grazing and wetland drainage benefit Ruddy Duck and many other species.

■ SUMMER   ■ MIGRATION
■ WINTER   ■ RARE
■ RESIDENT

These noisy, gregarious birds are a feature of the Rio Grande delta and locally common in the Santa Ana National Wildlife Refuge, where they have become remarkably unwary of humans. Although primarily arboreal in habits, they often come to the ground to feed on leaves, buds, berries, nuts, and insects. Historically, these chicken-like birds were hunted as game.

DESCRIPTION: 18–21" (46–53 cm). Wingspan 26" (66 cm). About the size of a large crow or pheasant. These birds are olive-brown with a long tail glossed with green and tipped with white. They have a small crest atop their heads, with patches of bare, pinkish-red skin at the sides of the throat.

VOICE: Loud, raucous *cha-cha-lac*, often given by a group in chorus at dawn and dusk. The male's calls are lower pitched than the female's.

NESTING: Usually lays 3 dull-white eggs in a stick nest lined with leaves and moss, usually on a low tree limb. Downy young are able to leave the nest and follow the mother shortly after hatching.

HABITAT: Riverside woodlands and thickets.

RANGE: Resident from extreme southern Texas to Nicaragua.

SUBSPECIES: There are several subspecies recognized in Mexico and Central America.

SIMILAR SPECIES: Female Wild Turkey is a much larger, ground-dwelling bird that lacks white tail tips.

Greater Roadrunner has a distinctive shape, with long legs, neck and tail.

CONSERVATION: LC
Plain Chachalaca is common throughout its range. It seems remarkably adaptable to human activity, taking to orchards, parks, gardens, and other human-populated areas as long as suitable wooded habitats remain.

■ SUMMER ■ MIGRATION
■ WINTER ■ RARE
■ RESIDENT

This is the largest quail in North America. Mountain Quail "migrates" on foot from its high-elevation breeding territory to protected valleys, where it winters in coveys of 6 to 12 birds. These secretive birds usually stay hidden in dense brush, dashing around on the ground with surprising speed, rarely straying from cover. They often freeze in place rather than flush when approached, making them difficult to spot. For the best chance to see these birds, search for family groups in summer that often appear along streams, springs, and remote roads, especially early in the day.

DESCRIPTION: 10½–11½" (27–29 cm). A large quail with long, slender, straight head plumes atop the heads of birds of both sexes. The male is brown above with a gray head, neck, and breast; a chestnut throat; and chestnut flanks with bold white bars. The female has a similar plumage pattern, but the coloration is duller.

VOICE: Its frequent call is a loud, echoing *kyork* or *woook.* Other notes include soft whistles.

NESTING: Lays 8–12 light reddish eggs in a depression lined with dry grass and leaves, hidden among protective rocks, logs, or thick vegetation.

HABITAT: Dry mountains, brushy wooded areas, and chaparral.

RANGE: Resident in Washington, Idaho, Oregon, and California.

SIMILAR SPECIES: See Gambel's and California quails. The long, slender, straight head plume and prominent white barring on the flanks of the Mountain Quail are distinctive. Usually, range and habitat are enough to distinguish Mountain Quail from its relatives.

CONSERVATION: 🐦 **LC**
Mountain Quail is common across most of its range, and its populations appear to be stable. Its reliance on mountainous chaparral habitat west of the Rocky Mountains makes it vulnerable to habitat loss.

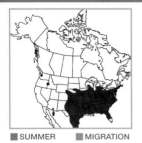

■ SUMMER   ■ MIGRATION
■ WINTER   ■ RARE
■ RESIDENT

The Northern Bobwhite is the only quail native to the eastern United States. It can be found in farmlands, open woodlands, and brushland throughout the Midwest and Eastern U.S., as well as south into Mexico and west to the foothills of the southern Rocky Mountains. After the breeding period, these birds live together in a covey, huddling together at night and in cold weather. When danger threatens, they fly out noisily in every direction, startling the would-be predator, which often catches none of them. Northern Bobwhites are also known to perform a "broken wing" display, in which the bird drags its wing along the ground in an effort to draw a predator's attention. A bobwhite behaving this way may appear to be injured, but is most likely protecting eggs or young hidden nearby.

DESCRIPTION: 8–11" (20–28 cm). A small, chunky, brown bird; its underparts are pale and streaked; the face is patterned in black and white in males, buff and white in females. It is usually seen in groups called coveys.

VOICE: Its song is a clear, two- or three-note whistle with an emphasis on the last syllable: *bob-WHITE!* or *poor-bob-WHITE!*

NESTING: Both parents construct the nest, which is a scrape in the ground lined with grass, which the birds often obscure from view by weaving surrounding grasses and weeds to cover it. The female usually lays 12–16 white or cream-colored eggs per clutch. Downy young leave the nest shortly after hatching and follow the parents in a family group for several weeks.

HABITAT: Brushy pastures, grassy roadsides, farmlands, and open woodlands.

RANGE: Permanent resident from Kansas, Iowa, Pennsylvania, and Cape Cod southward. Fluctuating populations occur farther north and west. It has been introduced locally elsewhere.

SUBSPECIES: There are almost two dozen regional subspecies recognized, each with variations in size, coloration, and patterns that are most obvious in the males—the females of all subspecies look similar.

SIMILAR SPECIES: No other quail overlaps the present range of Bobwhite. Gray Partridge has a bright rusty tail, and occurs in open agricultural land.

CONSERVATION: Northern Bobwhite was once much more numerous, and is listed as a common bird in steep decline. The reasons for its disappearance—most notably in the northerly part of its range—are poorly understood. Urbanization and habitat loss may be contributing to the decline. Widespread pesticide and herbicide usage on agricultural land may be reducing available food supplies. Fire suppression practices and the gradual replacement of old pastures with dense stands of young trees may be reducing the availability of ideal bobwhite habitat.

SCALED QUAIL   *Callipepla squamata*

■ SUMMER   ■ MIGRATION
■ WINTER   ■ RARE
■ RESIDENT

Scaled Quails are characteristic birds of the drier desert grassland areas of the Southwest. They are colloquially called "Cotton Tops" and "Blue Quail" for their white-tipped crest and bluish-gray plumage, respectively. They seldom fly, preferring to run when disturbed. Although they are birds of arid habitat, Scaled Quail must visit water holes regularly. They nest in the rainy season, when moisture produces some vegetation, and do not breed during extremely dry summers. They spend most of the year in small flocks, breaking up into pairs at the beginning of the breeding season.

DESCRIPTION: 10–12" (25–30 cm). A small, stocky quail, Scaled Quail is gray-brown above with a buff-white crest. Bluish-gray feathers on its breast and mantle have black semicircular edges, creating a scaled effect; the belly also has brown "scales." Both sexes look alike; the female tends to be more of a pale gray with less of a bluish hue.

VOICE: Its song is a high, sharp note. Its calls are a low nasal *pe-cos* and harsh clucking. In spring, males sometimes emerge from cover to deliver their songs from prominent perches.

NESTING: Both sexes construct the nest in dense vegetation. Lays 12–14 pale buff eggs, evenly spotted with reddish brown, in a grass-lined hollow. Downy young hatch alert and ready to follow the parents out of the nest.

HABITAT: Dry grasslands and brushy deserts.

RANGE: Resident in Arizona, Colorado, western Kansas, and western Oklahoma south to central Mexico.

SUBSPECIES: Several subspecies display regional differences in coloration.

SIMILAR SPECIES: Gambel's Quail and California Quail have rounded heads with a long, dark, forward-curved head crest. Compare this to the Scaled Quail's short, backward-facing, peaked crest tipped with white. As its name suggests, Scaled Quail is the only quail with a "scaled" pattern covering its entire upper body, including the belly, chest, and neck.

CONSERVATION: ![LC]

Scaled Quail numbers fluctuate markedly from year to year, because the birds are sensitive to both drought and heavy rains. Overall the population has been in steady decline for several decades. Hunting appears to have only a modest impact on this species' numbers; of greater concern is the overgrazing of pasturelands that reduces the available food and cover for these birds.

This plump, attractive quail is the state bird of California, where it is common in parks and suburban gardens and yards. A little birdseed spread on the ground near cover is enough to attract them into view at backyard feeding stations. The bird's range covers most of the western United States and spills into southern British Columbia, where it can be found in a variety of habitats including weedy thickets, woodland edges, chaparral, coastal sage scrub, semi-arid high desert, and foothills at lower elevations west of the Rocky Mountains. Perched on a tree or a fence post, the male California Quail claims territory by cackling and posturing. The entire family takes to trees for roosting as well as for safety. After the breeding season, these birds become gregarious, gathering in large coveys.

DESCRIPTION: 9–11" (23–28 cm). A stocky, mainly gray quail with a curved black head plume. Similar to Gambel's Quail, but its crown is brown, not chestnut; its forehead is buff, not black; and its belly is scaled, lacking a black patch in the center. The female is less boldly marked than the male.

VOICE: Loud, distinctive, squeaky calls—*ka-kah-ko* or *Chi-ca-go*—with emphasis on the second note.

NESTING: Lays 12–16 cream- or buff-colored eggs, blotched and dotted with brown, in a shallow depression lined with grass. Downy young leave the nest shortly after hatching and follow both parents.

HABITAT: Brushy chaparral foothills and live-oak canyons; also adjacent desert and suburbs.

RANGE: Originally resident from southern Oregon south to Baja California. Introduced to Pacific Northwest, Idaho, and other inland states.

SIMILAR SPECIES: Male Gambel's Quail has a plain buff-white belly with a dark spot, a richer rusty brown crown, and a black forehead; it is paler above. Female Gambel's has chestnut on the flanks and a buff-white belly with fine streaks.

Mountain Quail has a chestnut throat, black-and-white bars on chestnut flanks, and a long, straight plume (spike).

CONSERVATION: The population seems to be gradually increasing, except in the coastal areas where the heaviest development and urbanization have taken place. California Quail seems to adapt reasonably well to human proximity.

GAMBEL'S QUAIL *Callipepla gambelii*

■ SUMMER ■ MIGRATION
■ WINTER ■ RARE
■ RESIDENT

These desert-dwelling quail are attracted to sources of water and gather in large numbers—often representing several coveys—at streams and water holes, as well as artificial water sources such as backyard water features or stock tanks maintained for cattle. The ringing call of the male, heard even in the heat of day, is one of the characteristic sounds of the Desert Southwest. Gambel's Quail have adapted to human settlement, often coming to backyards to partake in birdseed and water that are offered on the ground.

DESCRIPTION: 10–11½" (25–29 cm). A stocky, mainly gray quail with a curved, black head plume. The male has a bold black face and throat, a chestnut crown, rusty sides with diagonal stripes, and an unscaled, buff-white belly with a black patch in the center. The female is similar to the male but with a shorter head plume and without the distinct facial pattern. See California Quail.

VOICE: A ringing *puk-kwaw-cah*, with the second syllable highest in pitch. During the breeding season, the male issues strident calls from a prominent perch.

NESTING: Lays 10–20 buff-colored eggs, spotted with brown, in a depression lined with grass and twigs at base of tall shrub or mesquite.

HABITAT: Desert thickets and arid country. These birds may congregate in large numbers near sources of water.

RANGE: Resident in southwestern deserts from California east to Texas. Introduced in Idaho and western New Mexico.

SUBSPECIES: Gambel's Quail is known to hybridize with Scaled Quail where their ranges overlap. The resulting offspring have a "scaled" plumage pattern with a curved, brownish head plume.

SIMILAR SPECIES: In southern California, occurs sympatrically with California and Mountain quails. The Gambel's Quail's plain buff belly with a dark patch is a useful diagnostic field mark. California Quail's belly appears scaled and heavily patterned. Mountain Quail has a chestnut throat and a long, narrow plume; its belly is dark and lacks a central spot.

CONSERVATION:  LC

Gambel's Quail populations experience boom-and-bust cycles, with dry years yielding fewer young. The population generally appears healthy and stable overall.

■ SUMMER ■ MIGRATION
■ WINTER ■ RARE
■ RESIDENT

Found in the United States in southern Arizona, New Mexico, and west Texas, Montezuma Quail is an uncommon bird found primarily in the mountainous regions of Mexico. These birds occur locally in upland areas of grassy, scattered woodlands and tend to travel in pairs or small family groups rather than in large coveys. At the approach of danger, this secretive quail often crouches and freezes, only flushing in an explosive burst of flight when it's practically underfoot. It may sometimes be seen creeping stealthily away, looking more like a rodent than a bird. This omnivore relishes berries and acorns as well as tubers and bulbs in winter, which it scratches out with its sturdy feet. By summertime, following the rainy season, insect food is abundant for breeding birds and their newly hatched offspring.

DESCRIPTION: 8–9½" (20–24 cm). A stocky quail with a particularly round body shape and a complex face pattern. These birds have a short neck, short tail, plump body, and rounded head. The male has striking black-and-white face markings, a rounded buff crest, and bold white spots on the sides and flanks. The female is duller with a less distinct head pattern.

VOICE: The male's song is a loud, quavering, descending whistle. Both sexes give a variety of low, piping calls to locate one other and to assemble their coveys.

NESTING: Lays 8–14 white eggs in a grass-lined depression concealed in dense grass. Downy young leave the nest shortly after hatching and accompany both parents, travelling in small family groups.

HABITAT: Grassy and brush-covered ground in pine-oak woodlands.

RANGE: Resident from southern Arizona to western Texas and southward into Mexico.

SIMILAR SPECIES: The intricate facial pattern of the male is unique, and usually no other quail is found sharing its range and habitat.

Female Northern Bobwhite has a pale, buff-colored throat and thick stripe over the eye, compared to a female Montezuma Quail's facial pattern of indistinct brown-and-white spots and streaks.

Male "Masked" Northern Bobwhites that also occur in the Southwest have an all-black head and rufous undersides that lack the Montezuma Quail's intricate pattern of white spots.

CONSERVATION: LC
Montezuma Quail populations appear to be stable, although the bird's secretive nature makes getting an accurate count difficult. These quail are hunted as popular game birds, which has a modest impact on their numbers, mostly in Mexico. Habitat loss caused by livestock overgrazing appears to be a more systemic threat to the species' long-term wellbeing.

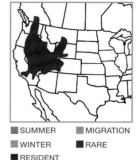

■ SUMMER   ■ MIGRATION
■ WINTER   ■ RARE
■ RESIDENT

Best known for its loud call, the Chukar has successfully established itself in the arid plains, rocky canyon slopes, and high deserts of the West. Introduced as a game bird from the dry Mediterranean area of southern Europe, the Chukar is a hardy bird and a surprisingly agile runner over steep terrain. Released or escaped captive Chukar, still widely used for sport hunting, may sometimes appear elsewhere in North America. Where the species has established breeding populations, especially in the Great Basin in the West, it has become quite common. Outside of the breeding season, these birds travel in coveys of up to 40 individuals, which may congregate near sources of water.

DESCRIPTION: 13–15½" (33–39 cm). Chukar is similar in size and shape to Gray Partridge. Its white cheeks and throat are framed by a broad, black band. It has bold chestnut and black diagonal striping on the flanks, and bright rufous outer tail feathers. It has a light brown back and wings; a creamy-white belly; and gray-tinged cap, breast, and rump. Its bill and legs are orange-red. Both sexes are similar.

VOICE: Males issue a loud, fast *chuck-chuck-chuck*. These birds make various cackling calls.

NESTING: Lays 8–15 whitish eggs, spotted with brown, in a nest lined with grass and feathers in the shelter of rocks or brush.

HABITAT: Rocky, arid hillsides and canyons.

RANGE: Resident from British Columbia and Alberta south to California and Colorado. It is native to Eurasia.

SIMILAR SPECIES: See Northern Bobwhite and Gray Partridge. Chukar is larger than most quail.

CONSERVATION:
Chukar is widespread in Eurasia. It is non-native in North America but has firmly established itself in arid parts of the West.

Formerly called "Black Partridge," these birds native to India and the Middle East are occasionally seen in North America as either escaped captives or deliberately released birds. These beautiful partridges are fairly common in aviaries, and an escaped bird can survive through the winter anywhere the climate is not too cold. Attempts in the 1950s and 1960s to release these birds in the southeastern United States for hunting purposes resulted in small, isolated colonies that persisted in Florida and Louisiana until the 1980s. An established, introduced population in Hawaii is regularly hunted.

DESCRIPTION: Similar in size to a Gray Partridge (13–15", 33–36 cm). The male is distinctive, with a black face, white patch below the eye, chestnut collar, and black chest. The female has paler and more uniform plumage, brown with darker and lighter barring. The female's wings are darker than the body, and has two notable markings: a white throat and a chestnut patch on the back of the neck. Juveniles are generally similar to adult females.

VOICE: Creaking sound, loud during the breeding season.

NESTING: Lays 4–10 eggs in a simple scrape in the ground, sometimes lined with vegetation.

HABITAT: Thick vegetation, brushy areas, and tall grasslands; generally near water. Inhabits "mosaic" areas where forests and cultivated lands meet, but is not an interior forest bird. More closely associated with water than many other partridges.

RANGE: Southern Asia from the Middle East to India. Historically also found in Southern Europe, but extirpated from there by overhunting and habitat destruction. Reintroduced in central Italy after extirpation. Introduced to Hawaii and, less successfully, in the southeastern United States.

SIMILAR SPECIES: Northern Bobwhite is much smaller and has dark legs.

CONSERVATION: LC
In its expansive native range, this bird's population appears to be quite large and stable. The species is non-native in North America; the introduced colonies in the southern United States appear to have died out.

HIMALAYAN SNOWCOCK *Tetraogallus himalayensis*

■ SUMMER ■ MIGRATION
■ WINTER ■ RARE
■ RESIDENT

Himalayan Snowcock—a large Asian pheasant species of montane habitats—was introduced in Nevada's Ruby Mountains as an exotic game bird and became established as a breeding species there by the early 1980s. Its remote mountainous habitat, elusive nature, and large size have made it a trophy game bird for hunters, but also a destination species for bird watchers hoping to add this exotic pheasant to their life lists. A few hundred snowcocks persist in Nevada's mountains, especially in the Ruby Dome/Thomas Peak area, where intrepid birders hoping to see this species must travel into its remote, roadless territory on foot, by horseback, or even by helicopter.

DESCRIPTION: 22–29" (55–74 cm). A large and stocky bird with a relatively short tail. It is gray-brown overall with lighter streaks on the back and wings. Its whitish face and throat include prominent brown stripes. Its wings appear mostly white in flight. Both sexes are similar, but the female is slightly smaller and the coloration is grayer around the forehead and eyes.

VOICE: Displaying male gives loud, fluting whistle; also various chuckling clucks.

NESTING: Its ground nests are located along steep slopes with rocky outcrops, often under rock or shrub overhangs, grass thickets, or in shallow depressions. The female lays 5–12 pale yellowish to gray-buff eggs with small brownish blotches, especially at the smaller end.

HABITAT: High alpine meadows surrounded by steep mountain peaks, cliffs, and steep slopes with large expanses of rocky outcrops; often near lower boundaries of perpetual snow fields.

RANGE: Native to mountain ranges of northern and eastern Afghanistan, northern Pakistan, and India (southeast to western Nepal), and from Central Asia through western and west-central China. Successfully introduced during the early 1970s into the Ruby Mountains of northeast Nevada.

SIMILAR SPECIES: Given the considerable effort necessary to reach its remote habitat above the tree line in Nevada's mountains, this bird is unlikely to be mistaken for any other species.

CONSERVATION: LC
Considered a species of least concern by the IUCN in its native range; its population appears to be stable. The introduced colony in Nevada seems to fluctuate between 200 and 500 individuals; its inaccessible location protects this population from much human disturbance.

■ SUMMER ■ MIGRATION
■ WINTER ■ RARE
■ RESIDENT

Introduced as a game bird from its native range across Eurasia in the 19th and early 20th centuries, Gray Partridge has become solidly established in North America, especially across the northern tier of the contiguous United States and southern Canada. Also called the "Hungarian Partridge," this bird is well adapted to areas of intensive agriculture, a habitat claimed by no native game bird. It forms coveys outside the breeding season, like the Northern Bobwhite, but does not defend a territory. In spring, the flocks break up into pairs.

DESCRIPTION: 12–14" (30–36 cm). A small, stocky, chicken-like bird. It is largely gray with a black U-shaped mark on the underparts and bright rust-colored tail, most evident when it flies.

VOICE: Hoarse *kee-ah*; when flushed, a rapid cackle.

NESTING: The female lays 10–20 unmarked olive eggs in a shallow depression lined with grass and concealed in vegetation. The female incubates the eggs alone. All the eggs tend to hatch on the same day, and the large group of downy young follows both parents from the nest. The family group stays together through the young's first winter.

HABITAT: Grainfields, agricultural grasslands, northern prairies.

RANGE: Introduced and locally established in Nova Scotia, New Brunswick, northern New York, Ontario, Ohio, Indiana, southern Michigan, Iowa, Minnesota, and across northern part of western United States to British Columbia. Introduction in the West has been much more successful than in the East. Native to Eurasia.

SIMILAR SPECIES: See Northern Bobwhite.

Chukar has a white face and throat with a black border, and lacks the dark belly spot; Chukar also occurs in rocky, steep terrain rather than grassy fields and agricultural lands.

CONSERVATION: LC
In its native range across a wide swath of Eurasia, the Gray Partridge is a common bird experiencing a steady decline. Efforts are under way to protect this species from further declines in parts of Europe where development has diminished the availability of food and breeding habitat. In North America, the Gray Partridge's high reproductive rate enables it to withstand the heavy annual toll taken by hunting, predators, and cold northern winters. Although its population is lower than it was in the 1950s, it is still widespread and common in many areas.

RING-NECKED PHEASANT *Phasianus colchicus*

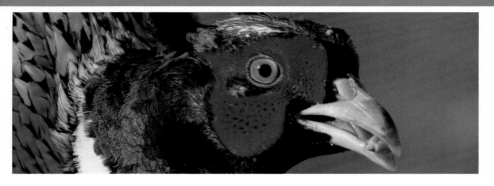

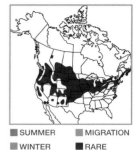

■ SUMMER   ■ MIGRATION
■ WINTER   ■ RARE
■ RESIDENT

The North American birds of this species are descended from stock brought from several different parts of the Old World and thus are somewhat variable. They are typically tolerant of humans and can get by with a minimum of cover; they often nest on the outskirts of large cities. Although successful in most grassland habitats, this species has its North American head-quarters in the central plains. Single-sex flocks form in winter, which break up as the breeding season begins, at which point males establish large territories and mate with several females. Young chicks feed largely on insects but soon shift to the adult diet of ber-ries, seeds, buds, and leaves.

DESCRIPTION: 30–36" (76–91 cm). This pheasant is larger than a chicken, with a long pointed tail. The male has a red patch of facial skin surrounding the eye, a brilliant green head, and (usually) a white neck ring; the body is patterned in soft brown and iri-descent russet. The female is mottled sandy brown, with a pale head and a pointed tail.

VOICE: Loud, crowing *caw-cawk!* followed by a resonant beat-ing of the wings. When alarmed, it flies off with a loud cackle.

NESTING: Lays 6–15 buff-olive eggs in a grass-lined depres-sion concealed in dense grass or weeds.

HABITAT: Farmlands, pastures, and grassy woodland edges.

RANGE: Introduced widely across North America, from British Columbia, Alberta, Minnesota, Ontario, and the Maritime Prov-inces south to central California, Oklahoma, and Maryland. It is native to Asia.

SUBSPECIES: Several regional populations exist across North America that show differences in coloration and patterns. Released or escaped game and farm-raised pheasants have hybridized with the wild-living populations to create further local variability.

SIMILAR SPECIES: Sharp-tailed Grouse is similar to the female but has shorter tail with white outer tail feathers.

CONSERVATION:
Ring-necked Pheasants are generally common throughout their range, although some populations are declining. Some of the introduced populations in North America do not appear to be self-sustaining, but their numbers are regularly bolstered by the release of farm-raised game birds. These birds—particularly the colorful males—are widely hunted. Game managers often stock these popular game birds, which are relatively easy to breed in captivity.

■ SUMMER   ■ MIGRATION
■ WINTER   ■ RARE
■ RESIDENT

Ruffed Grouse is a variable, crested chicken-like bird of deciduous and mixed forests that prefers denser undergrowth than most other grouse species. This uncommon, secretive grouse is easiest to find in winter, when snow covers the ground and the birds fly up into the bare treetops to feed on buds and catkins. Their summer diet, which is much more varied, consists of insects, seeds, fruits, and even an occasional small snake or frog. Around sunrise in the spring, listen for their muffled drumming, which males create by beating their wings against the air with increasing speed.

DESCRIPTION: 16–19" (41–48 cm). A brown or gray-brown chicken-like bird with a slight crest; a fan-shaped, black-banded tail; barred flanks; and black "ruffs" on the sides of the neck. These birds can range from a dark gray morph to a rufous morph and countless intermediate variations in between. Bold barring on the flanks and a dark-banded tail help to distinguish Ruffed Grouse from its relatives.

VOICE: The female gives soft, hen-like clucks. Both sexes cluck and squeal when alarmed.

Although not a vocalization, in spring, the displaying male sits on a log and beats the air with its wings, creating a low drumming sound that increases rapidly in tempo. This low, reverberating drumming may be felt rather than heard, and usually takes place in the early morning just before and after sunrise.

NESTING: Lays 9–12 pinkish-buff eggs, plain or spotted with dull brown, in a shallow depression lined with leaves and concealed under a bush.

HABITAT: Deciduous and mixed forests, especially those with scattered clearings and dense undergrowth, and overgrown pastures.

RANGE: Resident from the tree line in Alaska and northern Canada south to California, Wyoming, Minnesota, Missouri, and Carolinas, and in Appalachians to Georgia.

SUBSPECIES: Multiple subspecies of Ruffed Grouse are recognized.

SIMILAR SPECIES: Sharp-tailed Grouse is chunkier, generally lighter brown, with a pointed tail; it lives in more open cover.

Spruce Grouse is generally darker, with a prominent rust-colored or yellowish band on the tip of the tail; it seldom occurs in hardwoods, but may occur with Ruffed Grouse in northern coniferous forests.

Adult Dusky and Sooty grouse are larger and darker; juvenile Dusky Grouse in the Rocky Mountains resemble Ruffed Grouse but lack the subterminal tail band.

CONSERVATION: LC
Although somewhat uncommon, these birds are widespread. Ruffed Grouse populations seem to go through roughly decade-long cycles of high and low numbers that may be linked to natural predator populations. Long one of the most highly esteemed game birds in North America, the Ruffed Grouse can withstand hunting pressure as long as suitable habitat exists. These birds thrive in the undergrowth of early successional forest; where forests are left to mature, the grouse seem to lose out to reintroduced Wild Turkeys.

GREATER SAGE-GROUSE *Centrocercus urophasianus*

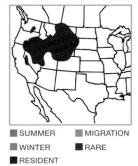

■ SUMMER　■ MIGRATION
■ WINTER　■ RARE
■ RESIDENT

The Greater Sage-Grouse is well named, for it is found only in the sagebrush (*Artemesia* spp.) ecosystems of western North America, especially grassy sagebrush plains. In the fall and winter, the leathery leaves of sagebrush are one of its only foods, and during the rest of the year, sagebrush provides it with cover. Each spring the males gather on a traditional display ground, called a lek, to court the females. The dominant males jostle for position at the center of the lek, fanning their tails and inflating air sacs on their chests using a lunging motion, while making burbling calls. Dozens of birds may be involved in these elaborate displays. Once a female has mated, the bird leaves to raise a family alone.

DESCRIPTION: Males average 26–30" (66–76 cm) long; females average 22–23" (56–58 cm). Both sexes are mottled gray-brown above with a black belly. The male has a long pointed tail, black throat, and white breast, with elongated neck plumes flanking the breast. A displaying male fans the tail and tilts it forward, and inflates a pair of yellowish-green air sacs in the neck and breast. The female's head, back, and breast are uniformly barred.

VOICE: When flushed, a chicken-like cackling call. Males make a bubbling sound during courtship.

NESTING: Lays 6–9 olive-green eggs, lightly spotted with brown, in a well-concealed grass-lined depression.

HABITAT: Open country and sagebrush plains.

RANGE: Resident from southern Alberta and Saskatchewan south to eastern California, Nevada, Colorado, and South Dakota.

SIMILAR SPECIES: All other North American grouse are substantially smaller than a male Greater Sage-Grouse.

Dusky and Sooty grouse males are similar in size to a female Greater Sage-Grouse, but are slate- to blue-gray with square tail feathers, and have red-yellow eye stripes and white rosettes (not easily seen except in breeding season) around yellow to crimson air sacs. Female Dusky and Sooty grouse are smaller and browner with more black-barred feathers.

Sharp-tailed Grouse is much smaller. They have shorter, square-tipped central tail feathers, purple to crimson air sacs, and white spotting on the wings and upper back; white underparts show clearly in flight.

CONSERVATION:  **NT**

The Greater Sage-Grouse is declining, having disappeared from much of its former range. These birds require large patches of undisturbed sagebrush habitat and freedom of movement to collect into large groups for lekking in order to breed. The loss or fragmentation of its habitat due to farming activity, energy development, and invasive plants reduce sage-grouse reproductive rates and population sizes.

■ SUMMER ■ MIGRATION
■ WINTER ■ RARE
■ RESIDENT

Gunnison Sage-Grouse was long considered a subspecies of Greater Sage-Grouse, but in 2000 it was determined to be a separate species. This highly localized bird is only found in specific sagebrush habitats in western Colorado and in one county in southeastern Utah. Like Greater Sage-Grouse, large groups of these birds gather in leks to undertake elaborate courtship displays and mate selection. Because these birds are endangered and extremely sensitive to disturbance, most known lek sites are closed to public viewing.

DESCRIPTION: Male 22" (56 cm), female 18" (46 cm). This species is distinguished from Greater Sage-Grouse by geographic range and by its smaller size and prominent white bars on the tail. The displaying male has a prominent recurved crest (filoplumes) on the head.

VOICE: Displaying male gives 9 or 10 hooting gobbles on one low pitch, interspersed with 3 wing noises; quite different from the display of Greater Sage-Grouse.

NESTING: Nests on the ground in grassy or brushy areas, especially in dense patches of big sagebrush (*Artemisia tridentata*). The female assumes all nest-building, incubation, and chick-rearing duties. An average clutch contains 6–10 olive-buff eggs with brown spots. Downy young leave the nest to follow the female shortly after hatching; they are precocious and able to feed themselves.

HABITAT: These birds rely on different types of sagebrush in different seasons, usually at elevations above 7000 feet (2133 meters). In winter they prefer locations with big sagebrush, black sagebrush, and low sagebrush as well as deciduous shrubs for cover. Leks occur in clearings such as on ridgetops, in dried lakebeds, and in swales or recent burn sites. Nesting requires dense expanses of big sagebrush. Females with young chicks in tow often forage in moist areas such as irrigated pastures and wet meadows in addition to various sagebrush habitats.

RANGE: Restricted to the sagebrush steppe of the western United States. Small numbers remain in southeastern Utah and southwestern Colorado, with the largest group found in Colorado's Gunnison Basin.

SIMILAR SPECIES: Greater Sage-Grouse is larger and lacks pale white barring on the tail. The ranges of the two species do not overlap.

CONSERVATION: Gunnison Sage-Grouse is a rare and endangered species, with a total population of around 4000–5000. Only one group remains in Utah and six in Colorado, the largest numbering about 3000 birds in Colorado's Gunnison Basin. This species depends on large areas of big sagebrush (*Artemisia tridentata*) for survival. Loss and degradation of sagebrush lands as well as disturbance from human activity and development continue to endanger the survival of the species.

SPRUCE GROUSE *Falcipennis canadensis*

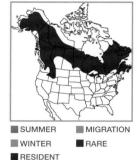

■ SUMMER　■ MIGRATION
■ WINTER　　■ RARE
■ RESIDENT

Spruce Grouse is a bird of the conifer forests of the Far North. This northern grouse is extraordinarily unwary; explorers reported being able to approach the birds to within an arm's length, earning it the colloquial nickname "Fool Hen." It is generally a quiet bird, thinly distributed in its habitat and easy to overlook. Its principal foods are the needles and buds of evergreens, although young birds consume large quantities of insects. A male performs an energetic courtship display in the presence of a female by puffing up, raising the bright red combs above the eyes, and posturing and marching while swishing and fanning the tail. Spruce Grouse are generally found singly or in small family groups, quietly picking their way over the forest floor or sitting in dense conifers.

DESCRIPTION: 15–17" (38–43 cm). A dark, chicken-like bird with a fan-shaped tail. The male is dusky gray-brown, with a red comb over the eye, a black throat and upper breast, white-spotted sides, and a chestnut-tipped tail. Birds in northern Rockies and Cascades (a subspecies *franklinii*, known as "Franklin's Grouse") have white tips on the upper tail coverts and lack the chestnut tail tip. Females of both forms are browner; their underparts are barred with brown.

VOICE: Males give a low *krrrrk, krrrk, krrk, krrk, krrk,* said to be the lowest-pitched vocal sound of any North American bird. Females produce low clucking notes.

NESTING: Lays 8–11 buff eggs, plain or spotted with brown, in a hollow lined with grass and leaves concealed on the ground under low branches of a young spruce.

HABITAT: Found in coniferous forests—especially those with a mixture of spruce and pine—and at the edges of deep forests and bogs.

RANGE: Resident from Alaska, northern Manitoba, Quebec, and Nova Scotia south to Washington, Wyoming, central Manitoba, Michigan, and northern New England.

SUBSPECIES: Subspecies of Spruce Grouse are generally separated into two groups that differ in male plumage and display. There is some debate over whether these two groups represent distinct species, although they intergrade in central British Columbia where their ranges overlap.

In the northern Rockies and Cascade Mountains, the "Franklin's Grouse" group's display involves a lengthy glide of several hundred feet from a perch, followed by two loud wing claps that resemble gunshots. The male's fanned tail has square-tipped, all-black feathers with white tips on the upper tail coverts.

In the Far North, the "Taiga" subspecies group's display involves gliding from a height of 10–20 feet (3–6 meters), then turning and hovering to the ground. The male's fanned tail has rounded feathers with pale rufous tips.

SIMILAR SPECIES: Ruffed Grouse occasionally acts as tame, but it is spotted rather than barred, with a dark band near the tip of the tail and contrasting ruff feathers on the sides of the neck.

Female Dusky and Sooty grouse are similar but larger, with black tails (usually with a grayish terminal band visible).

CONSERVATION: ![LC]
Spruce Grouse is common in much of its range, and overall its population is increasing. The population seems to be shifting farther north, as it is declining at the southern edge of its range and booming in the Far North. It is listed as endangered or threatened in several U.S. states at the southern edge of its range. Local populations fluctuate. Hunting pressure and fire suppression may be responsible for the changes observed in this species' range.

■ SUMMER ■ MIGRATION
■ WINTER ■ RARE
■ RESIDENT

The largest and most widespread ptarmigan of the Far North, Willow Ptarmigan is associated with wet thickets of dwarf willow on the tundra, generally north of the timberline, and sometimes occurs in brushy openings in the northern coniferous forests. Unlike any other grouse species, the male Willow Ptarmigan guards a territory around the female while she incubates eggs on the nest. When the chicks grow up, several families gather in large flocks and often migrate southward together when winter arrives. In summer, ptarmigans feed on green shoots, buds, flowers, and insects; in winter, they take mainly twigs and buds of willows and alders.

DESCRIPTION: 15–17" (38–43 cm). A grouse of the tundra with a red comb over each eye. In winter, these birds are entirely white except for a black tail and have thick white feathers on the feet. In summer, the male is rusty red with white wings and belly; the female is mottled and barred with brown except for the white wings. This species molts twice per year; spring and fall molting plumages show a variety of checkered patterns.

VOICE: In flight, courting males have a loud, staccato *go-back, go-back, go-back*, and other guttural calls. Both sexes give clucking notes.

NESTING: Lays 7–10 yellowish eggs, blotched with brown, in a scrape lined with grass and feathers, often sheltered by vegetation, rocks, or logs. Young hatch fully covered in thick down and leave the nest within 12 hours of hatching.

HABITAT: Tundra; also thickets in valleys and foothills; muskeg.

RANGE: Breeds from Alaska east to Labrador, and south to central British Columbia, northern Ontario, and central Quebec. Winters south to forested regions of central Canada. It is also found in Eurasia.

SUBSPECIES: Several subspecies are found around the world; most look similar. The "Red Grouse" in Britain and Ireland is a subspecies of Willow Ptarmigan that retains its mottled reddish-brown plumage year-round.

SIMILAR SPECIES: The summer males of other ptarmigan species are more grayish.

Rock Ptarmigan is slightly smaller, with a much smaller bill. It has a black eyestripe in winter and is brown rather than rust-colored in summer plumage. A winter Rock Ptarmigan has a distinctive black eyestripe.

White-tailed Ptarmigan is smaller, with a smaller bill and white tail feathers. White-tailed Ptarmigan has an entirely white tail.

CONVERSATION:

Although this species is prone to cycles of population booms and busts—becoming abundant in some years and scarcer in others—overall the population is large and appears to be healthy. Its global range in the Far North isolates it from much human disturbance and development.

ROCK PTARMIGAN *Lagopus muta*

SUMMER MIGRATION
WINTER RARE
RESIDENT

Like other ptarmigan species, these birds undergo two molts per year in order to blend in with their barren tundra habitat, becoming mottled gray-brown in summer and white in winter. Male Rock Ptarmigans, however, delay their spring molt until after courtship, retaining conspicuous white plumage even after the snow melts, well into the breeding season. Pairs of Rock Ptarmigans remain together until midway through incubation, when the male deserts its mate. The female raises the chicks, which move about on the tundra in search of insects, buds, and berries, becoming independent at about three months old. The white winter plumage of ptarmigans provides both good camouflage and protection against the cold, because white feathers have empty cells filled with air that help in insulation, whereas colored feathers contain pigment.

DESCRIPTION: 13–14" (33–36 cm). In winter, Rock Ptarmigan are entirely white except for a black tail and, in males and most females, a distinctive black eyestripe. In summer, the male is flecked with dark gray-brown, and the wings and belly are white. The female is paler with gray, yellowish, and brown on most feathers.

VOICE: Courting male gives a snoring *kurr-kurr*. Female has clucking and purring notes.

NESTING: Lays 6–9 buff eggs, spotted with dark brown, in a sheltered hollow lined with grass and moss.

HABITAT: Upland tundra with thickets of willows and heaths.

RANGE: Breeds in Alaska and northern Canada. It winters south to the tree line.

SIMILAR SPECIES: See Willow and White-tailed ptarmigans. Rock Ptarmigan's black eyestripe in winter is distinctive.

Willow Ptarmigan is larger with a larger bill.

White-tailed Ptarmigan looks similar except its tail is entirely white with no black outer tail feathers.

CONSERVATION: LC
Common and widespread in the vast Far North wilderness away from human settlements, where it remains largely isolated from disturbance.

WHITE-TAILED PTARMIGAN
Lagopus leucura

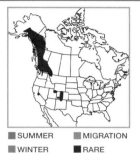

White-tailed Ptarmigan is the smallest of the ptarmigans, the only one with an all-white tail, and the only one whose range extends south into the alpine tundra of the western United States. This elusive, mountain-dwelling ground bird moves little in winter, often roosting in snow banks to stay hidden and conserve energy. It engages in short migrations of only a few miles, moving down to the edge of the forest in the fall and back onto the alpine tundra in spring. The two sexes often winter separately, with females gathering in larger flocks than males.

DESCRIPTION: 12–13" (30–33 cm). In winter, White-tailed Ptarmigan is pure white except for a black bill and eyes. In summer, it is mottled and barred with brown on the head, breast, and back, with white wings, belly, and tail. A thin, red comb above the eye is largest in spring males.

VOICE: High-pitched "creaking" notes and soft, low clucks.

NESTING: Lays 6–8 buff eggs faintly spotted with brown in a hollow sparsely lined with grass, leaves, and feathers.

HABITAT: Alpine meadows and open rocky areas above the timberline.

RANGE: Resident in the Rocky Mountains from Alaska south to New Mexico, and coastal ranges south to Washington; introduced in the Sierra Nevada of California.

SIMILAR SPECIES: Rock and Willow ptarmigans have white wings and black tails. In late summer, male Rock and White-tailed ptarmigans are similar except for tail color and bill size. Females and winter birds are quite similar but lack the white tail.

Male Rock Ptarmigan remains white until after the peak of breeding.

Breeding male Willow Ptarmigan has a rusty head and neck.

CONSERVATION:
Although White-tailed Ptarmigan numbers have declined slightly over the decades, the species is considered of low conservation concern. It remains an uncommon to locally common bird, thinly populating its range. Its remote habitat isolates it from most human disturbance. The species has been successfully introduced in several high-altitude western sites in California, Colorado, New Mexico, Oregon, and Utah.

DUSKY GROUSE *Dendragapus obscurus*

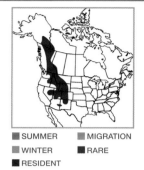

■ SUMMER   ■ MIGRATION
■ WINTER   ■ RARE
■ RESIDENT

The Dusky Grouse can be even harder to locate than the closely related Sooty Grouse, because the male's call is both softer and even lower pitched. The search is worth the effort, however, to observe the male's striking displays. The displaying male struts around a patch of open ground and issues a series of low-pitched hoots while fanning the tail over the back, spreading the feathers on the neck to reveal the patch of brightly colored skin, and erecting the combs over the eyes. In winter, this grouse feeds exclusively on conifer needles; its summer diet consists of insects, seeds, and berries.

DESCRIPTION: 15½–21" (39–53 cm). A large grouse. The male is dusky gray or bluish gray, with an orange-yellow or red comb over the eye, some mottling on the wings, and a blackish tail with a pale gray terminal band. Birds in the Rocky Mountains lack this terminal tail band. In display, the male shows a patch of reddish or purplish skin on the neck surrounded by a rosette of white feathers. Females and immatures are mottled gray-brown with a dark tail.

VOICE: The male gives a series of deep hoots—*whoop, whoop, whoop, whoop, whoop*—increasing in tempo and volume. Both sexes make soft clucking or barking sounds.

NESTING: Lays 5–10 cream-colored eggs lightly spotted with brown in a scrape lined with pine needles and grass, usually sheltered by a stump or rock.

HABITAT: Burned areas, brush in coastal rainforest; montane forests, slashes, and subalpine forest clearings.

RANGE: Resident inland from southern Yukon and Northwest Territories south to California, Arizona, Colorado, and New Mexico. Birds found along the Pacific Coast from southeast Alaska and British Columbia to central California are the closely related Sooty Grouse.

SIMILAR SPECIES: Dusky Grouse and Sooty Grouse were formerly considered the same species, called Blue Grouse. Sooty Grouse has less white on the neck and averages darker overall, although both species are variable. Sooty Grouse has a different courtship display, during which it shows a bumpy yellowish patch of skin on the neck rather than the darker, reddish-purple skin of the Dusky Grouse's neck patch. Females are not reliably distinguishable between these two species.

CONSERVATION: ![LC]
Dusky Grouse is fairly common, and its population has remained stable for many decades. Hunting and forest management practices can impact these birds locally. They flourish amid early successional forests following clear-cuts or fires, and do not take easily to even-aged tree farms or old-growth forests.

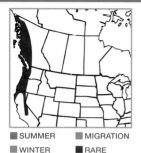

■ SUMMER ■ MIGRATION
■ WINTER ■ RARE
■ RESIDENT

A close relative of the Dusky Grouse, the Sooty Grouse is an inconspicuous, subtly plumaged bird of western coastal forests and the Sierra Nevada in California. These slow-moving birds forage mostly on the ground, especially in the summer, where they eat a diet of conifer needles, leaves, flowers, buds, berries, and insects. In the spring, males generally perform their courtship displays from a perch in a tree, often high up in a dense conifer, issuing a series of pulsing hoots that rise and fall in pitch.

DESCRIPTION: 20" (51 cm). A large grouse; its plumage is similar to that of Dusky Grouse. The male is sooty gray or bluish gray, with an orange-yellow to orange-red comb over the eye. In display, the male shows a patch of yellowish or orange skin on the neck surrounded by a rosette of white feathers. The white border on the neck may be somewhat thinner than that of a Dusky Grouse. Females and immatures are mottled gray-brown with a dark tail.

VOICE: Displaying male gives a low, owl-like hooting, sounding like air blown across the top of a jug. These vocalizations can often be heard at great distances, unlike the softer, lower calls of Dusky Grouse. Both sexes make soft clucking or barking sounds.

NESTING: Lays 5–10 eggs in a shallow scrape on the ground lined with dead vegetation, usually with at least slight overhead cover or at the base of a large tree. Eggs are light beige and splotched with brown.

HABITAT: Found in forests dominated by Douglas fir and true firs or western hemlock with mixtures of western red cedar and Sitka spruce; populations on clear-cuts decline as second-growth canopies close. Winters in semi-open conifer forests, where conifer needles comprise most of its diet.

RANGE: Southeastern Alaska to California between the coast and western slopes of the Cascades and Sierra Nevada; also in the Sierra Nevada of California.

SIMILAR SPECIES: Sooty Grouse and Dusky Grouse were formerly considered the same species, called Blue Grouse. Dusky Grouse averages paler overall and is generally found farther inland. Dusky Grouse has a different courtship display and shows a smoother, dark reddish-purple skin patch on the neck, compared to the yellowish skin on the Sooty Grouse's neck patch. Females are not reliably distinguishable between these two species.

CONSERVATION:
Sooty Grouse is still fairly common, but the slow, steady decline of its population over many decades causes conservationists some concern. Hunting, grazing, and forest management practices all add pressure to these birds. Like Dusky Grouse, Sooty Grouse flourish amid early successional forests following clear-cuts or fires, and do not take easily to even-aged tree farms or even to mature, old-growth forests.

SHARP-TAILED GROUSE *Tympanuchus phasianellus*

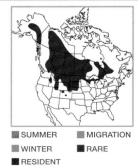

■ SUMMER   ■ MIGRATION
■ WINTER   ■ RARE
■ RESIDENT

The habitat requirements of this grouse are not as specialized as those of the prairie-chickens, and so this species has a wider range and has managed to survive in much larger numbers. The cutting of large areas of northern coniferous forest, which has created vast tracts of brushland, has helped the Sharp-tail. Sharp-tails, like prairie-chickens and Sage Grouse, perform elaborate displays on communal mating grounds called leks, to which they return faithfully every year. In one case a homestead was built over a lek, and the grouse displayed on the farmhouse roof the following spring. The Sharp-tailed Grouse's lek sites are so reliable that many local bird clubs or companies schedule group tours that allow visitors to view these spectacular early morning displays with minimal disturbance to the birds.

DESCRIPTION: 15–20" (38–51 cm). Resembles, but is slightly smaller than, a female pheasant. It is mottled with buff, slightly paler below. Its tail is short and pointed, with white outer tail feathers. The male has a purple neck patch and yellow combs over the eyes; its tail is longer than that of a female. Similar prairie-chickens are barred, not mottled, and show no white in the tail.

VOICE: During courtship, a low single or double cooing note.

NESTING: Lays 10–13 buff-brown eggs in a grass-lined depression in tall grass or brush.

HABITAT: Grasslands, scrub forest, and arid sagebrush.

RANGE: Resident from Alaska east to Hudson Bay and south to Utah, northeastern New Mexico, and Michigan.

SUBSPECIES: Several subspecies are recognized. In general, the birds that live in Alaska and northern Canada are darker than the birds that live in the plains of the United States.

This species is known to interbreed with Greater Prairie-Chickens and Dusky Grouse where their ranges overlap, creating rare—often confusing—intermediate hybrids.

SIMILAR SPECIES: Greater and Lesser prairie-chickens—the only other grouse associated with prairies—have short, rounded, dark brown tails.

Ruffed Grouse and Spruce Grouse also have different tail pattern. No other grouse has Sharp-tailed's frosty-looking wings.

CONSERVATION: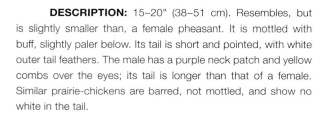

Sharp-tailed Grouse have been eliminated from much of their former range, and some of its subspecies are threatened. Overall, these birds are uncommon and local. Fragmentation and loss of their prairie habitat is the main threat to this species. Since the 1980s, the Conservation Reserve Program in the United States—which pays farmers to take a portion of their croplands out of production and convert them to vegetative cover for wildlife—has benefited this and other prairie wildlife species.

Tympanuchus cupido GREATER PRAIRIE-CHICKEN

■ SUMMER ■ MIGRATION
■ WINTER ■ RARE
■ RESIDENT

Where they still survive, Greater Prairie-Chickens perform striking courtship dances on communal display grounds (leks), sometimes called "booming grounds" for these birds on account of the deep cooing calls produced by displaying males. The males strut and stamp their feet, with "horns" erect and yellow-orange sacs of skin inflated on the sides of the neck, while uttering their unforgettable deep cooing or "booming" call that can carry as far as a mile. Males on the lek compete for position; they leap and whirl in the air, and threaten each other by short runs with tail raised, head down, and horns erect. Females visit the booming grounds, survey the field of prospective partners, and select one male with which to mate. "Ancestral" booming grounds—known lek sites that are used every year—make for popular bird-watching destinations; annual prairie-chicken festivals occur in several Plains states to celebrate and observe these iconic birds.

DESCRIPTION: 16–18" (41–46 cm). A chicken-like bird, heavily barred above and below with grayish brown, with a short black tail. The male has yellow-orange air sacs inflated during courtship display, and long black feathers on sides of neck erected into "horns" during courtship; horns of the female are shorter. Males also have bright orange combs over the eyes, which are raised during courtship. See Lesser Prairie-Chicken.

VOICE: Hollow "booming" call during display; also cackles and clucks.

NESTING: Lays 8–12 olive eggs finely spotted and blotched with brown in a well-concealed, grass-lined depression in the ground.

HABITAT: Undisturbed native tall-grass prairie.

RANGE: Resident locally in Wisconsin, Illinois, and Michigan, and from Manitoba south through the Great Plains to Oklahoma; Attwater's is found on the coastal prairies of Texas.

SUBSPECIES: The critically endangered Attwater's Prairie-Chicken (*T. c. attwateri*) is restricted to grasslands along the Gulf Coast in southeastern Texas.

SIMILAR SPECIES: See Lesser Prairie-Chicken and Sharp-tailed Grouse.

CONSERVATION: VU
Once widespread, today the Greater Prairie-Chicken is rare and local, classified as vulnerable, and occupies only a small fraction of its historic range. Its population has declined due primarily to habitat loss and fragmentation, and the species is susceptible to heavy population losses during spring flooding events. The East Coast subspecies, the Heath Hen, became extinct in the early part of the 20th century due to overhunting. The coastal Texas subspecies, Attwater's Prairie-Chicken, is critically endangered and at high risk of extinction, with its wild population having dipped into the low double digits.

LESSER PRAIRIE-CHICKEN *Tympanuchus pallidicinctus*

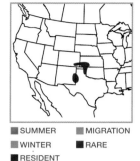

■ SUMMER ■ MIGRATION
■ WINTER ■ RARE
■ RESIDENT

A slightly smaller, paler cousin of the Greater Prairie-Chicken, the Lesser Prairie-Chicken prefers higher, arid short-grass prairies where stands of scrub oaks are common. Here, males gather and engage in their communal courtship displays in which the birds dance about with the colorful air sacs on their necks inflated, uttering low cooing or "booming" notes.

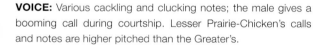

DESCRIPTION: 16" (41 cm). A chicken-like bird, barred above and below with grayish brown, with a short black tail. The courting male has long black feathers on the sides of the neck that form erect "horns"; it inflates reddish-purple air sacs during its courtship display. Horns of the female are shorter. Greater Prairie-Chicken of the plains farther east is similar but larger and more strongly barred, with yellow-orange air sacs.

VOICE: Various cackling and clucking notes; the male gives a booming call during courtship. Lesser Prairie-Chicken's calls and notes are higher pitched than the Greater's.

NESTING: Lays 11–13 creamy or buff-colored eggs in a grass-lined depression, usually under a low bush or shrub.

HABITAT: Dry grasslands with shrubs and short trees.

RANGE: Resident in southern Colorado and Kansas, south locally in western Oklahoma, Texas, and eastern New Mexico. This species replaces the Greater Prairie-Chicken in higher, drier grasslands.

SIMILAR SPECIES: Greater Prairie-Chicken is slightly larger, darker, and more strongly barred. Its air sacs are larger and bright yellow-orange; its call is a deeper booming. It is more closely associated with prairie and low plains farther east and north.

See Sharp-tailed Grouse.

CONSERVATION: VU

Once abundant, today Lesser Prairie-Chicken is uncommon to rare and local, and is classified as vulnerable in the United States. Its place on the Federal List of Endangered and Threatened Wildlife in the United States—which would afford the species protections under the Endangered Species Act—is the subject of legal and political debate. Regardless of its legal status, the species has unquestionably suffered significant declines since the 19th century. Habitat loss has been the main culprit, as natural prairies have been converted into agricultural land.

■ SUMMER ■ MIGRATION
■ WINTER ■ RARE
■ RESIDENT

Unlike the barnyard variety of domestic turkeys, wild turkeys are swift runners and quite wary. They often roost over water because of the added protection that this location offers. Turkeys spend most of their time foraging on the ground and are especially active in the early morning and at dusk. They are strong fliers and typically roost overnight in trees, often in groups settled high in the treetops. These birds are polygamous, and the male gobbles and struts with the tail fanned to attract and maintain a harem. Turkeys can be attracted to backyards with seed or corn spread on the ground.

DESCRIPTION: Males average 48" (1.2 m); females average 36" (0.91 m). This large, familiar ground bird is unmistakable. It is dusky brown and barred with black; its feathers have an iridescent bronze sheen. Its head and neck are naked, with bluish and reddish wattles. The tail is fan-shaped with chestnut, buff, or white tail tips. The male has spurs on its lower legs and a long "beard" on the breast. The female is smaller, lacks spurs, and usually does not have a "beard." Domestic turkeys are similar, but usually tamer and stockier.

VOICE: Familiar gobbling calls similar to those of the domestic turkey.

NESTING: Lays 8–15 buff-colored eggs, spotted with brown, in a shallow depression lined with grass and leaves.

HABITAT: Oak woodlands and pine-oak forests.

RANGE: Resident in much of the southern United States from Arizona east, as far north as New England. Introduced to many western states, including California.

CONSERVATION:

By the end of the 19th century, the Wild Turkey had been hunted almost to extinction in much of its original range. Now, with protection, restocking programs, and the return of the mature forests that turkeys favor, this species is making a marked comeback. It is now common in areas where it was totally absent a few decades ago. Its population is increasing in many regions, and wild turkeys are becoming more common at the edges of suburban settings in many eastern states, where they may be attracted to backyard feeding stations.

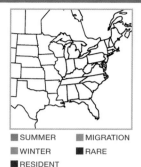

■ SUMMER ■ MIGRATION
■ WINTER   ■ RARE
■ RESIDENT

American Flamingo was once treated as a subspecies of the Greater Flamingo—a widespread native to Africa, India, the Middle East, and southern Europe—but today is considered a distinct species. These birds were formerly more numerous and probably bred at one time along the coast of Florida. Flamingos are extremely sensitive to disturbance and today nest only in a few isolated localities. The birds use their curiously shaped bills to strain small animals from the mud. Occasional wanderers from colonies in the Bahamas make their way to Florida Bay, and flamingos from Yucatán Peninsula colonies may wander rarely into coastal Texas, but most other sightings in the United States are probably escapees from captivity. Flamingo-like birds, known today only by fossil records, once lived in western North America 50 million years ago.

DESCRIPTION: 48" (1.2 m) long with an average wingspan of 4'7" (1.4 m). Unmistakable. A tall, long-legged, long-necked pink bird with a short, down-curved bill tipped with black. The wings have black tips and trailing edges. Immature birds are gray. These gregarious birds usually live and feed in large flocks that include many adults and young.

VOICE: Goose-like honking and cackling notes.

NESTING: Lays 1 white egg on a low mound of mud on a mudflat. Nests in dense colonies.

HABITAT: Shallow coastal lagoons and mudflats.

RANGE: Resident in the Bahamas, West Indies, Yucatán, northern South America, and Galápagos Islands. A casual visitor to the U.S. coast from Carolinas to Texas.

SIMILAR SPECIES: Roseate Spoonbill is also large and pink, but has a long, spatulate bill and shorter neck.

CONSERVATION:
Despite their slow reproduction rate—each female produces only a single egg each year—American Flamingos are a species of low concern, and their population is gradually increasing. The rebound of flamingos in the Bahamas since the 1950s is one of the great conservation success stories of the Caribbean.

This tropical diving bird is the smallest of North America's grebes. Southern Texas represents the extreme northernmost tip of its range, which expands south throughout the American tropics. These birds may inhabit a variety of permanent or temporary wetlands, but are easy to overlook. They feed mainly on aquatic insects on or below the water's surface, and on small fish by diving and swimming in pursuit of prey. They have also been known to feed on algae and aquatic vegetation. Least Grebes seldom fly, and they rarely leave the immediate vicinity of their nesting places. When not nesting, they are often found in small flocks.

DESCRIPTION: 8–10" (20–25 cm). Robin-sized. Similar to Pied-billed Grebe, but smaller, with a more slender bill. These birds are brownish gray overall with golden orange-yellow eyes and a small, dark bill. White wing feathers are visible in flight. Winter birds have a white throat and a paler bill.

VOICE: This vocal bird makes a loud *peek!* and several other calls year-round. Mated pairs communicate back and forth with metallic trilling or chatter calls.

NESTING: Lays 3–6 bluish-white eggs that become stained with brown, in a floating nest of aquatic vegetation usually anchored to reeds or other emergent plants.

HABITAT: Dense floating vegetation on quiet ponds and slow-moving streams.

RANGE: Resident in southern Texas and the West Indies to South America.

SUBSPECIES: The Least Grebes that range into North America, *T. d. brachypterus*, are representatives of only one out of several subspecies that are each distinguished by geographic range, size, and coloration.

SIMILAR SPECIES: See Pied-billed and Eared grebes.

CONSERVATION: Least Grebes are uncommon and local, and their numbers in the United States vary. Inclement winter weather in southern Texas can decimate the bird's northernmost populations. Little is known about the species' overall numbers, but it continues to be hunted in much of its range.

PIED-BILLED GREBE *Podilymbus podiceps*

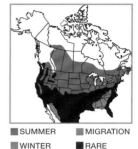

■ SUMMER ■ MIGRATION
■ WINTER ■ RARE
■ RESIDENT

On ponds and marshes where it breeds, the Pied-billed Grebe advertises its presence with loud, barking calls. It eats small fish, crustaceans, and aquatic insects, but is especially fond of cray-fish, which it crushes easily with its stout bill. When alarmed, this grebe often sinks slowly into the water, resurfacing out of sight among the reeds. It can also dive with amazing speed, propel-ling itself underwater using its feet, which are set far back on its body. Pied-billed Grebes go by many colloquial nicknames, including "hell-diver" and "dabchick." They are wide-spread across the continent and the most com-mon nesting grebes in the East.

DESCRIPTION: 12–15" (30–38 cm). Pigeon-sized. A stocky, uniformly brownish water bird, with a stout whitish bill that has a black ring around it during breeding season. Pied-billed Grebes have dark eyes and a relatively short neck. Breeding adults have a black chin and throat, which fade to a white chin and pale rufous throat in winter birds. In flight, almost no white can be seen on the wings except for a faint, pale trail-ing edge—quite different than the white flight feathers found on other North American grebes.

VOICE: A series of hollow cuckoo-like notes that slows down at the end: *cow-cow-cow-cow, cow, cow, cowp, cowp, cowp*; various clucking sounds.

NESTING: Lays 5–7 whitish eggs, often stained brown, in a well-hidden floating mass of dead marsh vegetation anchored to adjacent plants.

HABITAT: Marshes and ponds; salt water in winter if freshwa-ter habitats freeze.

RANGE: Breeds from British Columbia, southern Mackenzie, and Nova Scotia southward. Winters in the southern states or wherever water remains open.

SIMILAR SPECIES: Other grebes have proportionally thinner bills. Least Grebe is smaller and darker with a thinner bill and yellow or orange eyes.

CONVERSATION: Pied-billed Grebes are common and widespread. Although their populations appear to be stable overall, they are declining for unknown reasons in New England, where several states have granted them threatened or endangered status. Loss of its wet-land habitat appears to be the species' biggest threat.

■ SUMMER ■ MIGRATION
■ WINTER ■ RARE
■ RESIDENT

These small grebes are only occasionally seen in flight; they migrate almost entirely at night over much of the interior of the continent. They seldom fly once on the wintering grounds. Birds of fresh water during the nesting season, Horned Grebes migrate to salt water for the winter, and therefore are thought of as saltwater birds, but some can be found on open water in the interior of California and other western states. Horned Grebes are named for the conspicuous buff to golden yellow ear tufts, or "horns," seen on these birds in their breeding plumage, which they can raise erect. Like other grebes, the young can swim and dive immediately after hatching but are often seen riding on the parents' backs. These adept divers forage by diving from the surface and swimming underwater, propelled by their feet. Horned Grebes are generally more solitary than other grebes, but occasionally forage cooperatively.

DESCRIPTION: 12–15" (30–38 cm). A small, slender-necked grebe with a short, sharply pointed bill with a whitish tip. In breeding plumage, both sexes have a dark body that appears scaled on the back, and a rufous neck and flanks; the head is blackish with conspicuous buff to yellow ear tufts ("horns"). In winter it adopts its familiar black-and-white plumage; the upperparts are dark, and the chin and foreneck are white. This is the most common grebe found on salt water in the East.

VOICE: Usually silent. On breeding grounds, pairs make a duet of a variety of croaks, shrieks, and chatters.

NESTING: Lays 4–7 bluish-white eggs, stained buff, on nest of floating vegetation anchored to marsh plants.

HABITAT: Breeds on marshes and lakes; winters mainly on salt water, but also on lakes and rivers where the water does not freeze.

RANGE: Breeds from Alaska and northern Canada south to Washington and Oregon, the Dakotas, and the northern Great Lakes, and rarely to Wisconsin. Winters in the Aleutians and south along the Pacific Coast to southern California, and along the Atlantic and Gulf coasts to Texas. Also occurs in Eurasia, where it is known as Slavonian Grebe.

SIMILAR SPECIES: Red-necked Grebe in breeding plumage has a whitish throat and cheeks.

A winter-plumage Red-necked Grebe is larger, with a less extensive white facial area, a heavier and longer gray neck, and a dull yellow bill.

Eared Grebes have a black neck and crown, with ear tufts extending well below the eyeline in breeding plumage; they have a gray neck and cheeks in winter. Eared Grebes have a slightly upturned bill.

CONSERVATION: VU
Horned Grebes are widespread but listed as vulnerable on the IUCN Red List after decades of population declines. Evidence suggests that their breeding range in western Canada and Alaska—as well as globally—is contracting due to human disturbance, habitat loss, and possibly the effects of climate change, but more solid data is needed to confirm these suspicions.

RED-NECKED GREBE *Podiceps grisegena*

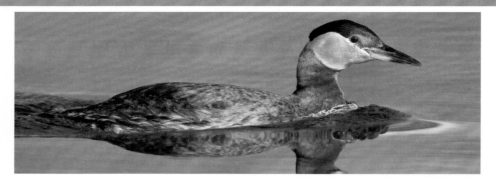

■ SUMMER   ■ MIGRATION
■ WINTER   ■ RARE
■ RESIDENT

Highly aquatic, grebes can swim with only their heads above water, concealing themselves in low pond vegetation. The young, handsomely striped in black and white, are often seen riding on the parents' backs. Like loons, grebes are expert divers, propelling themselves with their lobed toes as they pursue fish, crustaceans, and aquatic insects.

DESCRIPTION: 18–20" (46–51 cm). A slender bird and the largest regularly occurring grebe in the East. In breeding plumage, it has a rufous neck; a black cap; whitish cheeks; and a long, pointed, yellowish bill. In winter, it is mainly gray with paler cheeks and a pale—not necessarily yellow—bill. In flight, Red-necked Grebes can be distinguished from loons by their smaller size and white wing patches.

VOICE: Usually silent. On breeding grounds, a variety of squeaks, growls, and wailing calls.

NESTING: Lays 4 or 5 bluish-white eggs, stained brown, on a floating mass of dead reeds and grass in reedy lakes. Rarely nests in colonies.

HABITAT: Ponds and lakes in summer; large lakes, coastal bays, and estuaries during winter and migration.

RANGE: Breeds from Alaska and northern Canada south to Oregon, Idaho, Ontario, and southern Minnesota; rarely east to southern Quebec. Winters south along coasts to southern California and Georgia, rarely to Florida. Also in Eurasia.

SIMILAR SPECIES: See Eared, Horned, and Western grebes.

CONSERVATION: ![LC]
Red-necked Grebes are common and widespread. Their populations aren't well understood but appear to be stable to slightly declining. Degradation of wetlands by human disturbance—especially at the southern edge of their breeding range in the northern U.S. and southern Canada—and pollution in coastal wintering areas are the biggest threats to this species.

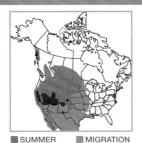

■ SUMMER ■ MIGRATION
■ WINTER ■ RARE
■ RESIDENT

This small diver is a common grebe of freshwater lakes in western North America. In the fall, most Eared Grebes migrate southwestward to the Pacific, but the species also winters on open water in the Southwest and as far east as Texas, and a few turn up each year on the East Coast. Unlike the Horned Grebe, which supplements its diet with small fish, the Eared Grebe feeds almost exclusively on aquatic insects and small crustaceans. These birds are highly gregarious, not only nesting in large, dense, and noisy colonies, but also assembling in large flocks in winter. Eared Grebes' complex courtship displays involve an elaborate dance between the male and female that includes loud advertising calls, a series of dives and posturing, and culminates in the pair rearing up out of the water and "running" together along its surface.

DESCRIPTION: 12–14" (30–36 cm). A small, slender-necked, slender-billed grebe. In breeding plumage, it has a black head and back; wispy, golden ear tufts; and a black crest. In winter plumage, it is dark gray above and white below with a dusky-colored neck. It is similar in winter to Horned Grebe, but chunkier, and its bill appears slightly upturned; the sides of Eared Grebe's face are smudged with gray and it has a whitish patch behind the ear.

VOICE: On breeding grounds, frog-like cheeping notes—breeding colonies can sound like a frog chorus. Generally quiet outside of the breeding season.

NESTING: Lays 3–5 bluish-white eggs, often stained brown, on a floating mass of vegetation in a marsh. Usually nests in dense colonies.

HABITAT: Marshy lakes and ponds; open bays and ocean in winter.

RANGE: Breeds from British Columbia, southern Manitoba, and the Dakotas south to California and New Mexico. Winters on the Pacific, Gulf, and (rarely) Atlantic coasts, occasionally on open water in the interior Southwest and Texas. Also occurs in Eurasia, where it is known as the Black-necked Grebe.

SIMILAR SPECIES: Horned Grebes in winter plumage have a white cheek, neck, and breast and a flatter crown; they have a rufous neck and breast in breeding plumage.

Winter-plumage Red-necked Grebes are larger with a heavier head; a longer neck; and a larger, dull yellow bill.

CONSERVATION: Eared Grebes are common and the population is usually stable, but at some seasons the species is reliant on a few major sites including the Great Salt Lake, Mono Lake, and the Salton Sea. These gregarious birds' tendency to form huge flocks makes them vulnerable to localized events; mass die-offs involving tens or hundreds of thousands of individuals have been recorded following outbreaks of disease, severe weather, and oil spills.

WESTERN GREBE *Aechmophorus occidentalis*

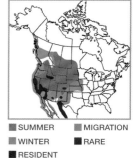

■ SUMMER ■ MIGRATION
■ WINTER ■ RARE
■ RESIDENT

North America's largest grebe is striking with its bold black-and-white coloration and its long bill and neck. The mating display of the Western Grebe is spectacular, with both members of a pair paddling vigorously and churning across the surface of the water in an upright posture. Sometimes many pairs in a colony display simultaneously. During migration, Western Grebes fly in loose flocks but spread out to feed during the day. Western Grebe and Clark's Grebe (*A. clarkii*) were formerly considered one species—understandable considering the two species hold much of their range, habitat, appearance, and habits in common, and often occur together. Western Grebes generally outnumber Clark's Grebes.

DESCRIPTION: 22–29" (56–74 cm). A large, slender grebe with a long neck. It is blackish above with the black of its cap extending below its eyes, which contrasts sharply with white below and on the front of the neck. Its bill is long, straight, slender, and dull olive greenish to yellow. Long white wing stripes show in flight. See Clark's Grebe.

VOICE: Western Grebes' voice is thin and reedy, used to make mechanical-sounding trills and chattering. Makes a rolling *kr-r-rick, kr-r-rick!* sound most often on the breeding grounds but sometimes also in winter.

NESTING: Lays 3 or 4 bluish-white eggs, stained brown or buff, on a floating nest anchored to reeds. It nests in dense, noisy colonies.

HABITAT: Breeds on large lakes with tules or rushes; winters mainly on shallow coastal bays and estuaries.

RANGE: Breeds from British Columbia, Saskatchewan, and Minnesota south to southern California; sparsely in Arizona, New Mexico, and Colorado. Winters along the Pacific Coast from southeastern Alaska to California, on the Gulf Coast of Louisiana and Texas, and on large river systems in the West.

SIMILAR SPECIES: Closely resembles Clark's Grebe. Clark's Grebes average slightly smaller and slightly paler, and the bill is often more brightly yellow or yellow-orange. Intermediates occur regularly and cannot be identified reliably.

Winter-plumage Red-necked Grebe has shorter neck and bill, and a dull gray neck. Winter-plumage loons are larger, with shorter necks.

CONSERVATION: LC

Western Grebes have mounted a comeback after being overhunted in the early 1900s for their silky white breast feathers, used to make clothing and hats. Their numbers may be on the decline once again, however. On their coastal wintering grounds, these birds often fall victim to oil spills; fishing lines and gill nets; and insecticides that accumulate in their food, build up in their bodies, and reduce their breeding success. Careless boaters who approach a group nesting site can flush the entire colony.

■ SUMMER   ■ MIGRATION
■ WINTER   ■ RARE
■ RESIDENT

First described in 1858, at the same time as the Western Grebe (*A. occidentalis*), Clark's Grebe was originally regarded as a distinct species. In the early 20th century, it came to be considered merely a color morph of the Western Grebe, until the species were once again split in 1985 after studies found that they nest side by side with little interbreeding and make different calls—subsequent genetic evidence further supports the split. In most outward respects, the two species are alike. Clark's Grebe is usually outnumbered by Western Grebes, but is more common in the southern portions of the two species' combined range; it is relatively rare in the northern part of the range. Clark's Grebe's courtship display is similar to that of the Western Grebe, involving an elaborate dance between the male and female that includes the pair rearing up out of the water and "running" together along its surface.

DESCRIPTION: 22–29" (56–74 cm). A large, slender grebe with a long neck and a bright yellow or orange-yellow bill. Nearly identical to the Western Grebe: blackish above with a black cap, and white below and on the front of the neck. Its bill is long, straight, slender, and bright yellow to yellow-orange. Extensive white wing stripes show in flight.

VOICE: A loud *kr-r-rick*, not doubled as in Western Grebe; heard most often on breeding grounds.

NESTING: Lays 3 or 4 bluish-white eggs, stained brown or buff, on a floating nest anchored to reeds. Like Western Grebes, Clark's Grebes nest in dense, noisy colonies.

HABITAT: Breeds on large lakes with tules or rushes; winters mainly on shallow coastal bays and estuaries.

RANGE: Breeding range broadly overlaps that of Western Grebe, from British Columbia, Saskatchewan, and Minnesota south to southern California, and sparsely to Arizona, New Mexico, and Colorado. It winters along the coast from southeastern Alaska to California, along the Gulf Coast, and on large river systems in the West.

SIMILAR SPECIES: Extremely similar to Western Grebe in all seasons, but especially in winter. In breeding plumage, the black on the Western Grebe's head extends down over the eyes, giving it a black "hood," whereas the Clark's Grebe has black only on the cap, leaving the face around the eyes largely white. This distinction, however, all but fades away in the winter plumage of these two species, leaving bill color as an imperfect but best-available field mark for distinguishing them outside of the breeding season. Western Grebe's bill ranges from a dull olive green to yellow; that of Clark's is bright yellow to yellow-orange.

CONVERSATION: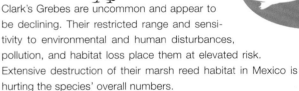
Clark's Grebes are uncommon and appear to be declining. Their restricted range and sensitivity to environmental and human disturbances, pollution, and habitat loss place them at elevated risk. Extensive destruction of their marsh reed habitat in Mexico is hurting the species' overall numbers.

ROCK PIGEON *Columba livia*

■ SUMMER　■ MIGRATION
■ WINTER　■ RARE
■ RESIDENT

Most everyone recognizes Rock Pigeons. In their ancestral range in Europe, North Africa, and India, Rock Pigeons nest on cliff ledges or high among rocks. European settlers introduced these birds to North America in the 1600s, whereupon they spread prolifically, sustaining themselves in the wild in close association with human settlements. Today they are a common sight in virtually all North American cities, and are also common in suburbs and farmland across the continent. Pigeons have become a signature bird of big cities, living amid the bustling humans on streets and parking lots, feeding on food scraps and nesting on buildings and window ledges. Over the centuries, many strains and color varieties have been developed in captivity through selective breeding.

DESCRIPTION: 13½" (34 cm). The common pigeon of towns and cities; it is a large and chunky pigeon with a short, rounded tail. In its "natural" plumage, which most resembles its ancestral wild form, it is bluish-gray with a darker head; two narrow, black wing bands and a broad black terminal tail band; a white rump; and iridescent feathers on the neck. There are many color variants, ranging from all white through rusty to all black.

VOICE: Soft, guttural cooing.

NESTING: Lays 2 white eggs in a crude nest lined with sticks and debris, placed on a window ledge, building, bridge, or cliff.

HABITAT: City parks, suburban gardens, and farmlands.

RANGE: Native to the Old World. Introduced and established in most of North America from central Canada southward.

SIMILAR SPECIES: White-crowned Pigeon is all dark with a white crown. Band-tailed Pigeon has a pale gray tail tip and dark wing linings. Red-billed Pigeon is all dark with a red-and-white bill. White-winged Dove has bold, white patches on the wings and tail. Other town-dwelling doves are smaller and browner or paler, with narrower or more pointed tails.

CONSERVATION:

Rock Pigeons are abundant and widespread. Rock Pigeons' apparent comfort around humans has allowed them to be adaptable to urban environments and facilitated their spread around the world. Although their populations have declined since the 1960s, they are still quite numerous, with an estimated global breeding population topping 120 million. Numerous unsuccessful efforts to eradicate pigeons from cities have demonstrated these birds' resilience.

■ SUMMER   ■ MIGRATION
■ WINTER   ■ RARE
■ RESIDENT

In the United States, the White-crowned Pigeon breeds only in the mangrove swamps of the Florida Keys and, to a lesser extent, among the gumbo-limbo and mahogany trees of the adjacent mainland. In former years—before protective laws were passed in 1913—great numbers of White-crowned Pigeons were shot for food, and they became quite wary. They are strong and fast fliers, known to travel as many as 30 miles (50 km) on the wing each day, island-hopping between feeding and nesting sites. They eat mainly fruits of hardwood trees, but also some insects and seeds.

DESCRIPTION: 13" (33 cm). Slightly larger than a Rock Pigeon with a longer neck and tail. It is uniformly dark slate-gray, almost black, with a conspicuous white crown and white iris, and a red bill with a pale tip.

VOICE: An owl-like *coo-coo-co-wooo*.

NESTING: Lays 1 or 2 white eggs in a grass-lined stick nest placed in a tree or bush; often nests in colonies.

HABITAT: Mangrove swamps and tropical hardwood hammocks.

RANGE: Breeds in the Florida Keys and West Indies. Most winter farther south.

SIMILAR SPECIES: Rock Pigeon is paler with white rump and two parallel black bars on wings; not generally found in same range. Darker Rock Pigeons have shorter tails and white rather than blackish wing linings.

CONSERVATION: Uncommon and decreasing. On many Caribbean islands these birds are threatened by hunting and habitat loss. The total population in Florida is only around 7500 breeding pairs. They are a protected species in Florida, and all the mangrove forests in which they breed are within national parks and refuges. Hurricanes, however, can disrupt or destroy substantial portions of this critical habitat.

RED-BILLED PIGEON *Patagioenas flavirostris*

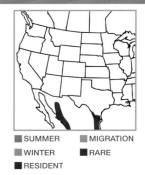

SUMMER ■ MIGRATION
WINTER ■ RARE
■ RESIDENT

This tropical pigeon is found in the densely wooded bottomlands near the U.S.-Mexico border and occasionally in more open country around clearings in the forest, or in groves of large trees along rivers. It feeds in the crowns of tall trees on wild figs, other fruits, various nuts, and seeds. These birds are usually shy and wary and seldom come to the ground except to drink. Like many other pigeons, it makes a series of cooing calls and a loud clapping noise with its wings as it rises in flight.

DESCRIPTION: 14" (36 cm). A large pigeon, it is deep maroon and dark gray without distinctive markings. Its short bill is red with a pale yellowish tip. Adults have a reddish wash on the neck.

VOICE: Loud, clear, high-pitched coo, followed by a three-syllable coo repeated 3 times.

NESTING: Lays 1 white egg in a nest of sticks, lined with grass or fibers and placed in a bush or tree.

HABITAT: Thick forests and woodland borders, often near water.

RANGE: Breeds in the lower Rio Grande Valley of Texas to Costa Rica. Most winter farther south.

SIMILAR SPECIES: No other Texas dove or pigeon is normally all dark. See Rock Pigeon and Band-tailed Pigeon.

CONSERVATION: LC

Uncommon and local in Texas; rare in winter. Red-billed Pigeons are common in dry woods in Mexico and Central America. They are not considered threatened, but their population is decreasing and they are vulnerable to overhunting in most of their range. Although protected from hunting in the United States, these birds have declined in Texas due to native habitat loss.

■ SUMMER ■ MIGRATION
■ WINTER ■ RARE
■ RESIDENT

This shy forest pigeon is adapting to parks and gardens along the Pacific Coast, where it feeds on lawns and ornamental berries, especially holly. Already a city bird in the Northwest, it has spread from natural redwood pockets to conifer plantings in suburbs of Santa Barbara and other California towns. These native western pigeons may visit backyard feeding stations for seeds, and they are attracted to berry bushes and fruit trees. In fall, Band-tailed Pigeons gorge themselves on acorns. These gregarious birds are often seen flying swiftly overhead or foraging in large flocks, and may nest in small colonies.

DESCRIPTION: 14–15½" (36–39 cm). Larger than a Rock Pigeon. It is dark gray above with a pale gray terminal band on the tail. The head and underparts are a purplish plum, whitening toward the extreme lower belly. Adults have a narrow, crescent-shaped white collar on the neck, easily visible on perched birds. They have yellow legs and a yellow bill tipped with black.

VOICE: A deep, owl-like *whoo-hoo*.

NESTING: Lays 1 white egg in a loosely constructed platform nest of twigs in a tree.

HABITAT: Coniferous forests along northwestern Pacific Coast; in southwestern part of range, it prefers oak or pine-oak woodlands, where it can feed on acorns.

RANGE: Breeds from southeastern Alaska south along coast through California, and from Utah and Colorado south into Mexico. Winters north to California, New Mexico, and western Texas.

SIMILAR SPECIES: Rock Pigeon usually has a white rump patch, and red feet and bill; its overall plumage is frequently multicolored. In Texas, see Red-billed Pigeon.

Mourning Dove is smaller and brown to blue-gray with a pointed tail.

White-winged Dove is smaller with large white wing patches and a white-tipped tail.

All other doves in North America are either smaller, browner, more scaled in appearance, or more noticeably white in flight.

CONSERVATION: LC

Band-tailed Pigeons are common within their range, but their populations are declining. At one time these birds were heavily hunted, driving their populations to historic lows, but they became federally protected in the United States in the aftermath of the much-publicized extinction of the Passenger Pigeon in the early 1900s. Under this protection, the species rebounded enough that the federal protection was lifted, and several states allowed hunting to resume (with harvest limits) by the middle of the 20th century. Conservationists today are concerned at the cumulative, steady decline of the species over the past several decades, perhaps due to hunting pressure combined with changing land use and environmental factors.

ORIENTAL TURTLE-DOVE *Streptopelia orientalis*

This is a common dove throughout most of Asia, and individual strays occasionally appear as rarities in Alaska and elsewhere along the Pacific Coast. Oriental Turtle-Doves are also widely kept in captivity, so most other sightings may pertain to escaped captives, especially away from the West Coast.

DESCRIPTION: A stocky, medium to large dove (13–14", 33–35 cm), approximately the size of a Rock Pigeon. Its wing coverts and secondaries have black centers and chestnut edges, giving the wings a prominent scalloped pattern. It has a black and gray lined neck patch. The chest and belly are pink to rufous; its head is grayish, blending gradually into the surrounding rufous wash.

VOICE: A multisyllable coo: *Goo, goo-goo, goo, goo.*

NESTING: Not known to breed in North America. In Asia, these birds nest in trees in the mid-canopy, building a simple platform nest out of sticks lined with leaves and grass, typical of other pigeons and doves. The female lays 2 white eggs per clutch, and the pair may raise multiple broods per season.

HABITAT: The Oriental Turtle-Dove is a generalist in its Asian home range, with habitats ranging from boreal zones to tropical forest. Adapts well to human habitation, using farm fields and field edges as well as tree-lined streets. Found from sea level to as high as 13,000 feet (4000 meters).

RANGE: Native across Asia from Siberia in the north to Vietnam in the south, and west through China, India, and Russia almost to the Ural Mountains. Vagrant to Europe and the West Coast of North America.

SIMILAR SPECIES: Similar in size to the highly variable and ubiquitous Rock Pigeon, but its scalloped wing pattern and neck patch are distinctive.

CONSERVATION:
Least concern in its wide native range in Asia.

■ SUMMER ■ MIGRATION
■ WINTER ■ RARE
■ RESIDENT

Originally a Mideastern species, the Eurasian Collared-Dove has extended its range dramatically into western Europe since about 1930. It was inadvertently released in the Bahamas in the 1970s then spread to South Florida, probably by natural means, in the late 1970s or early 1980s. Its range has exploded north and west since then, now encompassing most of the United States and parts of southernmost Canada. Both in Europe and in North America, these birds have adapted to the agricultural and urban environments associated with human settlement. They are usually seen solitarily in areas with little vegetation, often calling from prominent perches such as utility wires, fence-posts, and rooftops. Eurasian Collared-Dove forages mostly at ground level and readily comes to backyard feeders for seed and especially millet.

DESCRIPTION: 13–14" (31–34 cm) long with an average wing-span of 25–28" (63–70 cm). Larger than a Mourning Dove. It is generally gray-brown with a subtle pink flush, especially on the chest. It is named for the distinctive black collar marking on the nape—the collar has white edges that are not always visible in the field. It has dark eyes and a dark bill. Dark primaries and a pale gray-brown mantle are separated by a silvery patch on the wing wrist. Its underwings are white, and its legs are red. The tail is banded white below, dark near the rump, and not sharply pointed as it is in a Mourning Dove.

VOICE: Its call is a deep, repeated *kuk-kooooo-kuk*, accented on the middle syllable. It also has a harsh, mewing, nasal call note, reminiscent to many observers of a loud Gray Catbird call.

NESTING: Lays 2 white eggs in nest on tree or building ledge. Its nesting period is variable across its range, and may be essentially continuous in warmer habitats.

HABITAT: Adaptable to human settlement; suburbs, small towns, and agricultural areas.

RANGE: Broadly distributed in Eurasia. North American populations, originating in southern Florida, have rapidly expanded to the north and west to cover most of the United States except the Northeast.

SIMILAR SPECIES: Mourning Doves are smaller and richer brown, with no collar on the neck. The Eurasian Collared-Dove's mournful call is shorter and given more frequently than the familiar call of the Mourning Dove.

CONSERVATION: LC
Eurasian Collared-Doves have vastly expanded their range, and their populations appear to be booming on multiple continents. Unlike many other introduced species, Eurasian Collared-Doves don't appear to have any obvious harmful effects on native North American bird populations, although possible interactions with native flora and fauna are not yet fully understood.

SPOTTED DOVE   *Streptopelia chinensis*

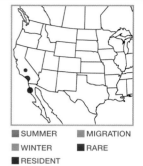

■ SUMMER   ■ MIGRATION
■ WINTER   ■ RARE
■ RESIDENT

Spotted Doves were introduced from Asia to the Los Angeles, California, area in the early 1900s and became firmly established, spreading gradually to other residential areas in southern California, from San Diego to Santa Barbara. This dove seems to be a harmless addition to the southern California garden avifauna, feeding on seeds and nesting quite secretively. It seems unwary of humans and comfortable foraging in suburban lawns and gardens. The courting male may be observed bowing rhythmically, then flying up with tail spread wide. Flushed Spotted Doves take off almost straight up with their wings flapping noisily.

DESCRIPTION: 13" (33 cm). Larger and stockier than Mourning Dove. Spotted Dove is dark cinnamon-gray above and buffy below, with a light gray head. It is named for the wide black collar with white spots on the back of the neck. In flight, its long, blunt tail looks black with flashy white corners. Juveniles lack the collar on the hindneck but are otherwise similar to the adults.

VOICE: A three-syllable, rolling *coo-coo-cooooo*.

NESTING: Lays 2 white eggs in a flimsy stick platform in a tree.

HABITAT: Suburban areas and gardens.

RANGE: Asian native, introduced in coastal southern California.

SIMILAR SPECIES: See White-winged and Mourning doves and Eurasian Collared-Dove.

CONSERVATION: LC

In recent years, the introduced population in Southern California has declined quite sharply. It remains common in its native range in Asia, and introduced populations have become established in several areas worldwide.

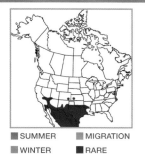

■ SUMMER ■ MIGRATION
■ WINTER ■ RARE
■ RESIDENT

This tiny dove is shaped much like a Common Ground Dove except for its longer tail. They show little fear of humans; these birds frequently nest in city parks and gardens, and are often found around human dwellings. Its range has expanded north from Mexico into the growing human settlements in the Southwest. These ground foragers are drawn to backyard ground and platform feeders, and are especially attracted to well-watered landscapes in otherwise arid environments.

DESCRIPTION: 8" (20 cm). This tiny, slender, long-tailed dove appears scaly and pale gray overall with contrasting rufous in the primary wing feathers, most visible in flight when the wings are outstretched. Dark edges of the bird's pale gray body feathers produce a "scaly" or "scalloped" appearance.

VOICE: A high, whistled two-note call, *COO-coop* or *no-hope*, often repeated.

NESTING: Lays 2 white eggs in a frail nest, usually of small twigs, placed low in a tree or bush. Incubation is performed by both parents.

HABITAT: Mesquite thickets or cacti in semiarid country; also parks, yards, and ranches.

RANGE: Resident in southeastern California, Arizona, New Mexico, and southern Texas. It is also found in the tropics.

SIMILAR SPECIES: Mourning Dove is larger, browner, not scaly, and has a pointed tail; it has different calls.

Common Ground Dove is rounder, stockier, and darker; its tail is shorter with much more black on the outer edges and white only on the outer tips.

White-tipped Dove is much larger; it is dusty gray-brown above and paler below, with no dark scaling.

CONSERVATION:
Inca Doves are abundant, and their range continues to expand north.

COMMON GROUND DOVE *Columbina passerina*

This is a tiny, unobtrusive, ground-dwelling dove that is quiet and easy to overlook. The Common Ground Dove flies fast and low, with its short wings beating rapidly, almost like those of a quail. In flight, these birds' wings make a faint whirring or rattling sound. When it walks, it nods like a pigeon. It searches for seeds on the ground but requires low brush for nesting and roosting. Most courtship behavior takes place on the ground, with the male pursuing the female, bobbing its expanded neck in rhythm with its repetitious cooing.

DESCRIPTION: 6½" (17 cm). A sparrow-sized, short-tailed brown dove. It has rusty-red underwings that flash in flight. When its wings are folded, dark spots on the wing coverts give the wings a freckled look. Its tail is dark with white corners. The neck and breast feathers have a scaled appearance, although the pattern may be faint on some birds, especially in lighter females of the paler Western race.

VOICE: A soft, repeated string of simple cooing notes, each with rising inflection—*coo-oo, coo-oo, coo-oo*.

NESTING: Lays 2 white eggs in a nest on or close to the ground, often hidden in a tuft of grass or among weeds.

HABITAT: Open areas such as fields, gardens, farmlands, and roadsides.

RANGE: Resident in southern parts of California, Arizona, and Texas, and east to southern North Carolina.

SUBSPECIES: Experts recognize multiple subspecies of Common Ground Doves throughout their range, but the two subspecies that occur in the United States are characterized simply as Eastern (the nominate race, *C. p. passerina*) and Western (*C. p. pallescens*).

Eastern birds are found in southeastern Texas and in the Gulf states, and typically forage on open ground. The western subspecies resides in central Texas and the Southwest; it forages in brushy rangeland. Western males tend to be paler than their Eastern counterparts, and females have more white on the belly.

SIMILAR SPECIES: Inca Dove has scaly back and long gray tail with white margin. White-tipped Dove much larger, lacks black spots on back and upper wings.

CONSERVATION: LC
Common Ground Doves are widespread and common throughout their range. The population in the United States, however, has declined markedly with the loss of scrub habitat to human development, especially in the Southeast.

■ SUMMER ■ MIGRATION
■ WINTER ■ RARE
■ RESIDENT

Widespread in Latin America, the Ruddy Ground Dove appears to have extended its range in northwestern Mexico as arid scrub is cleared to make way for agriculture, including ranch yards with shade trees. Whether because of this change in distribution or because of improved field birding coverage, the number of reported vagrancies in the southwestern United States has increased. They are most often reported in the U.S. in the fall and often stay through the winter. It is still a rare visitor from Mexico, and care should be taken when identifying this species; it closely resembles Common Ground Dove.

DESCRIPTION: 6½–7" (17–18 cm) long with an average wingspan of 16½–18" (42–45 cm). A small, short-tailed dove with prominent rufous primaries visible in flight. Generally difficult to distinguish from Common Ground Dove; rosy body color is not a sufficient field mark, since many Ruddy Ground Doves in the U.S. belong to a relatively pale race (*C. t. eluta*). Ruddy Ground Dove is best distinguished by its plain gray-brown head, neck, and breast (sometimes with a pinkish hue, especially in the male) that lacks the dark scaling pattern seen in Common Ground Dove. Ruddy's bill is uniformly dark. Its tail is slightly longer and darker than a Common Ground Dove, and the corners of the tail are buffy or rusty colored rather than white. Its scapulars are marked with black streaks (unmarked in Common), its wing coverts are lightly marked (heavily marked in Common), and its axillaries are black (chestnut in Common).

VOICE: Variously described as *kitty-woo*, *per-whoop* and *p-ter-woo*; slightly lower and more complex than the simple, repetitious *coo-oo* notes of Common Ground Dove.

NESTING: Lays 2 white eggs placed in a nest in a tree or shrub. It is known to use old nests of other birds.

HABITAT: Sandy savannas, open or semi-open habitats including villages, clearings, and forest edge; it prefers humid areas, and may congregate at ground feeding sites where seeds are available. U.S. vagrants appear in widely varying habitats, including lawns, desert oases, ranches, etc.

RANGE: Mexico to Peru and Argentina; a rare but regular vagrant to the southern U.S. states bordering Mexico.

SUBSPECIES: Most U.S. records are of the West Mexican subspecies *C. t. eluta*, which tends to be paler overall. The East Mexican subspecies, *C. t. rufipennis*, accounts for a few records in Texas; this subspecies has a richer cinnamon-colored body.

SIMILAR SPECIES: Common Ground Dove is similar. Common's head, neck and breast show dark scaling; its bill is bi-colored with a dark tip and red or pink at the base. Common Ground Dove has a slightly shorter tail with less black, and with white corners rather than buff or chestnut. Common Ground Doves have unmarked scapulars, compared to Ruddy's scapulars marked with dark streaks.

CONSERVATION:
Ruddy Ground Dove is widespread and common in the tropics, and its numbers appear to be increasing. It takes well to cultivated and urban landscapes.

This round-bodied dove of tropical America and the Caribbean islands occasionally strays to southern Florida or Texas. The handful of accepted sightings, almost all of which were in southern Florida, appear to have been of wild birds that had strayed north of their native range. In the tropics, these shy birds spend most of their time on the forest floor foraging for seeds and small invertebrates.

DESCRIPTION: A small- to medium-sized dove (8–11", 21–28 cm), intermediate in size between an Inca Dove and a Mourning Dove. The predominant color is the deep chestnut of the wings and back, which has a purple iridescence, especially on the back of the neck. The underparts are tan, with a whitish throat and a tan stripe below the eye. The chestnut and tan color scheme is distinctive from any other dove likely to be found in North America, and the dark head distinguishes this bird from the White-tipped Dove, the only other species with dark brown wings.

VOICE: Long coos: *whoooo, oooooo*.

NESTING: Does not nest in North America. In the tropics, it lays 2 buffy eggs in a flimsy platform nest either in a shrub or on the ground.

HABITAT: Unbroken wet, tropical forests and woodlands. Also found in coffee plantations and other second-growth shrublands.

RANGE: Both coasts of central and southern Mexico, south through Central America and much of tropical South America. Also found on most larger Caribbean islands.

SIMILAR SPECIES: Not easily mistaken for any native North American dove.

CONSERVATION:
Ruddy Quail-Dove is widespread in tropical forests and woodland habitats. These birds appear to be sensitive to forest fragmentation, however, as they tend to disappear from small patches of forest.

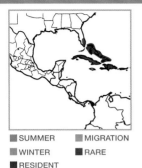

■ SUMMER ■ MIGRATION
■ WINTER ■ RARE
■ RESIDENT

First discovered on the Florida Keys, the Key West Quail-Dove was extirpated from Florida as a breeding bird by the mid-19th century. Today, occasional vagrants in the Keys or southernmost mainland Florida are the only remnant of this species in our range, although it is not uncommon on nearby Caribbean islands. Quail-doves are named for their resemblance to quail, both in their shape and their preference for foraging on the ground. Key West Quail-Dove is no exception; these solitary birds spend most of their time on the ground foraging for seeds and fruits amid dense cover, making them easy to miss.

DESCRIPTION: Slightly smaller than a Mourning Dove (11–12", 27–31 cm), this attractive, chunky dove is chestnut brown above and light grayish below. Green to bronze iridescence from crown to nape of neck, becoming purple along the back. The males are noticeably more iridescent than the females, and juveniles nearly lack iridescence altogether. Both sexes are whitish on the underbelly and have a prominent white stripe under the eye.

VOICE: Deep, hollow cooing: *ooo-wooooo*.

NESTING: Historically nested in Key West, Florida, but extirpated there by the mid-1800s; it no longer breeds in the United States. On many Caribbean islands, Key West Quail-Doves nest on the ground or in a low shrub, laying 2 buff-colored eggs in a flimsy platform nest.

HABITAT: Dry woodlands and scrublands, also wetter montane forests.

RANGE: Most northern Caribbean islands, north as far as the Bahamas and south to Puerto Rico.

SIMILAR SPECIES: Ruddy Quail-Dove, also a rare visitor to southern Florida, is smaller and rusty colored above with cinnamon-buff underparts.

CONSERVATION: ![LC]

Fairly common in its native range. Key West Quail-Dove's numbers appear to be stable, but its overall population size has not been officially quantified.

WHITE-TIPPED DOVE *Leptotila verreauxi*

■ SUMMER ■ MIGRATION
■ WINTER ■ RARE
■ RESIDENT

Uncommon and local along the U.S.-Mexico border, the White-tipped Dove is primarily a forest species that feeds mainly on the ground amid dense low growth, but also flies with surprising speed. When flushed, the bird makes a whistling sound with its sickle-shaped outermost primaries. The species is named for the white tips of its tail feathers, which the bird puts on full display by raising its tail when alarmed. It feeds on various seeds and nuts, and occasionally on small fruits such as wild figs, palm fruit, and various berries.

DESCRIPTION: 12" (30 cm). A stocky dove with dark brown wings and upperparts that contrast with a pale belly and whitish face. It has a red orbital ring around the eyes and red legs. White tips of the tail feathers can be seen in flight or when the bird raises its tail when alarmed. Chestnut underwing coverts are visible in flight.

VOICE: Deep, drawn-out, descending coo, often described as a hollow moan, lower pitched than most of our pigeons and doves.

NESTING: Lays 2 white eggs in a stick nest lined with plant fibers and placed in a dense bush, vine, or tree.

HABITAT: Dense, moist woodlands and thickets.

RANGE: Resident in southernmost Texas. It is also found in the American tropics.

SIMILAR SPECIES: See Common Ground Dove and Mourning, Inca, and White-winged doves.

CONSERVATION: Although it faces some hunting pressure in parts of its range, the White-tipped Dove population appears to be stable or even increasing in Central and South America. A stable population remains in undisturbed habitats in southernmost Texas.

■ SUMMER ■ MIGRATION
■ WINTER ■ RARE
■ RESIDENT

During the midday heat of long summer days in the southwestern desert, often the only sound heard is the monotonous, repetitious *who-cooks-for-you* of the White-winged Dove. In flight or perched, this big, heavy, grayish-brown dove clearly shows large, white areas on the wing and tail. This species is abundant in desert habitats including agricultural areas, riparian woodlands, residential areas, and canyons of lower mountain elevations. In the desert its main seasonal food is the fruit of cacti; elsewhere it supplements its seed diet with berries. White-winged Doves frequently feed on the tops of flowering cacti. They are seen in large flocks in agricultural areas, often with Mourning Doves, from midsummer into fall. The flight is direct, with deep, consistent beats and occasional glides, with the wings often bent back at an angle.

DESCRIPTION: 12" (30 cm). A brownish-gray dove with blackish wings that have a broad diagonal white bar; its rounded tail has whitish corners noticeable in flight. The overall body shape and coloration suggest a large, heavy Mourning Dove, but the White-winged Dove has white greater and median coverts that form conspicuous patches on the blackish wings. The broad, long, slightly fan-shaped tail has rectangular white patches on the end of the outer tail feathers. The rest of the body is grayish-brown to sandy-buff, paler on the lower belly and becoming darker on the upperparts. There is a small black spot on the side of the head, and a purplish sheen on the crown and nape. The iris is red.

VOICE: A drawn-out *hooo-hooo-ho-hooo* or *who-cooks-for-you*. The first two syllables are separated from the second two by a slight pause. Also a mellower *hoo-hoot-who-who-hooo*. In general, the first note is somewhat rough.

NESTING: Lays 2 cream-buff eggs in a frail platform of loose twigs in low bushes.

HABITAT: Open country with dense thickets of shrubs and low trees; also in suburban and agricultural areas.

RANGE: Breeds in southwestern United States and southern Texas. Winters south of United States; small numbers on Gulf Coast east to Florida. Also in American tropics.

SIMILAR SPECIES: Other pigeons and large doves lack black wings with bold white patches.

CONSERVATION:
White-winged Doves declined in the early 20th century but have since been recovering and expanding their range northward. They are once again abundant, having adapted well to landscapes altered by human development.

ZENAIDA DOVE *Zenaida aurita*

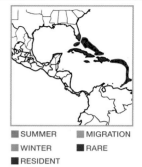

■ SUMMER   ■ MIGRATION
■ WINTER   ■ RARE
■ RESIDENT

Zenaida Dove is a rare, casual visitor in southern Florida, primarily in fall and winter. Take extra care when identifying this species: Anywhere in North America a vagrant Zenaida Dove might appear, the Mourning Dove is a common year-round resident. The two species are difficult to distinguish, and photos documenting a Zenaida Dove sighting will need to clearly show a distinguishing field mark.

DESCRIPTION: 11–12" (28–30 cm). Similar in appearance to the closely related and much more common Mourning Dove. This species is slightly smaller, and slightly darker and redder than a Mourning Dove. It has a shorter, more rounded tail, and its wings have a white trailing edge in flight, which the Mourning Dove does not. Zenaida Dove lacks gray on the nape of the neck seen in Mourning Doves.

VOICE: Quite similar to a Mourning Dove, but faster and with the first note less modulated.

NESTING: Zenaida Doves once bred on the Florida Keys, but are now found only as vagrants there and in southernmost mainland Florida.

HABITAT: A wide variety of lowland habitats, from cultivated fields to shrublands and open woodlands.

RANGE: Caribbean islands from the Bahamas south to Grenada, also the Yucatán Peninsula of Mexico. It is a vagrant to South Florida and the Keys.

SIMILAR SPECIES: Difficult to distinguish from the common Mourning Dove, which is slightly larger and lighter tan-colored with a longer tail and with no white on the wings.

Distinguished from White-winged Dove by the prominent white patch on the wing coverts; Zenaida Dove has a small patch of white only on the tips of the outer secondaries.

CONSERVATION: LC
Zenaida Doves are abundant in much of their breeding range in the Caribbean islands.

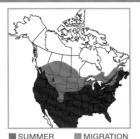

■ SUMMER ■ MIGRATION
■ WINTER ■ RARE
■ RESIDENT

The Mourning Dove is one of the most abundant and wide-spread birds native to North America. It is found in almost every available habitat, except densely forested regions. The Mourning Dove is common in rural areas in all parts of the United States, as well as city parks and suburban feeders. Its species name, *macroura*, is Greek for "long-tailed." Its mournful call is well known in most residential areas throughout its range. This species can often be seen in large flocks, especially in the south, in agricultural areas and near water in arid regions. The Mourning Dove calls before first light and flies directly and rapidly on stiff wingbeats well before dawn; it is often the first diurnal bird detected. The wingbeats make a considerable whistling noise upon takeoff that decreases but persists in flight. During the courtship display, the male performs a steep, climbing flight, which terminates in a series of circular glides on stiffly spread wings.

DESCRIPTION: 12" (30 cm). This rather elongated, soft brown dove has a rounded body topped by a slim neck and small head. The tail is long and tapered, narrowly bordered by white on the periphery. The underparts are gray, washed with pinkish-buff to cinnamon. The upperparts are darker brown, and the wings are dark gray-brown, blackish at the tips, with indistinct blackish spotting on the scapulars and tertials. There is a blackish spot on the side of the head, and purplish iridescence—more notice-able on the male—on the nape and sides of the neck.

VOICE: Low, mournful (hence its name) *coo-ah, coo, coo, coo*.

NESTING: Lays 2 white eggs in a loosely made nest of sticks and twigs placed in low bushes and tall trees, more rarely on the ground. The young are fed regurgitated, partially digested food known as pigeon milk.

HABITAT: Open fields, parks, and lawns with many trees and shrubs.

RANGE: Breeds from southeastern Alaska, Saskatche-wan, Ontario, Quebec, and New Brunswick south-ward to Mexico and Panama. Winters north to the northern United States.

SIMILAR SPECIES: See Band-tailed Pigeon, and White-winged and Inca doves. Ringed Turtle-Dove and Spotted Dove are stouter, with square-tipped tails; Ringed Turtle-Dove has a nar-row black collar.

CONSERVATION:
Mourning Doves are common continent-wide and have adapted well to human-made habitats. This abundant bird has increased with the cutting of forests and burning off of grass. In some states it is hunted as a game bird, while in others it is protected as a songbird.

SMOOTH-BILLED ANI *Crotophaga ani*

■ SUMMER ■ MIGRATION
■ WINTER ■ RARE
■ RESIDENT

This long-tailed, heavy-billed, sociable bird once occurred regularly in southern Florida in dense brush or hedgerows near fields or marshes. Originally a tropical bird of the Caribbean and South America, Smooth-billed Anis may have begun nesting in North America as recently as the 1930s. Although it became an uncommon resident in Florida for many decades, its numbers there appear to have dropped off sharply again, to the point where it is now only a very rare visitor, with a few individuals seen each year. These birds have some peculiar traits. They often live in small groups of several breeding pairs, defending a single territory and sharing a single nest, with the female depositing eggs in layers separated by leaves or grass. Up to 30 eggs have been found in one nest; those at the bottom do not hatch. Anis prefer cultivated country and rangelands, where they often alight on the backs of cattle to feed on ticks.

DESCRIPTION: 14" (36 cm). A dark, pigeon-sized bird with a long tail. The adult is mostly black with bronze-brown edgings on the head and nape; the scapulars, back, and lesser wing coverts have crescents of iridescent green. Its flight feathers and tail are glossed with purple. Immatures are slightly browner, especially on the wings and tail. Its bill is thick, with an arched ridge and no grooves—hence "smooth-billed."

VOICE: Slurred double note with a rising inflection that has a whining, metallic quality; quite different from that of the Groove-billed Ani.

NESTING: Each female lays 3–5 blue-green (often stained) eggs in a bulky stick nest in dense vegetation. Multiple females lay eggs in communal nests, which may contain dozens of eggs. All the adults in the group help to incubate and raise the young.

HABITAT: Open agricultural country, often near cattle or other livestock; also found in scrub and thickets.

RANGE: Formerly resident in southern Florida, now may be only a rare visitor. Also occurs in the American tropics.

SIMILAR SPECIES: See Groove-billed Ani and Boat-tailed Grackle.

CONSERVATION: LC

Globally this is a species of least concern, although its population has decreased somewhat. The conversion of forest to open habitat in the American tropics may be helping this species, which prefers agricultural and scrub lands to unbroken forests. Smooth-billed Ani may be disappearing from Florida, perhaps reverting to its historic range.

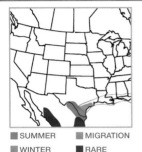

■ SUMMER ■ MIGRATION
■ WINTER ■ RARE
■ RESIDENT

Like the Smooth-billed Ani, this species is a sociable black cuckoo. In flight, both anis flap their wings loosely, alternating with short glides. The long tail, which appears as if on a hinge, swings up and down and from side to side like a pendulum, and looks as though it might drop off. Both anis feed largely on a mixed diet of insects, seeds, and fruits. They feed mostly on the ground, hopping in a clumsy, loose-jointed manner, and are often found with livestock, which stir insects from the grass. These birds fly with several rapid flaps and then an unsteady, stiff-winged glide. In the United States, the ranges of the two anis do not overlap; the Groove-billed occupies semi-open country in southern Texas.

DESCRIPTION: 12" (30 cm). Jay-sized, with a long tail half the length of the bird. This species is mainly black, with a purplish gloss on the wings and tail and greenish edgings on the head and upperparts. Young birds are similar but browner. Its bill is thick with an arched ridge, and features narrow grooves on the sides of the upper mandible in most adults—but these may be lacking in some adults and many immatures.

VOICE: Soft, liquid, gurgling notes and, if alarmed, rather loud harsh calls. Also a rollicking *wee-cup*.

NESTING: Lays 3 or 4 pale blue eggs in a huge stick nest, often situated in thorny scrub. Multiple females lay eggs in communal nests, which may contain dozens of eggs. All the adults in the group help to incubate and raise the young.

HABITAT: Arid agricultural land, especially where there are cattle.

RANGE: Resident in lower Rio Grande Valley. Small numbers migrate north and east along the Gulf Coast in winter. Also occurs in the American tropics.

SIMILAR SPECIES: Smooth-billed Ani lacks grooves on the bill and does not occur in Texas, although both species wander widely. Smooth-billed is slightly larger, thicker-necked, and seems to hold its head higher in flight. The feathers of the nape are edged with bronze-brown, not greenish.

See Great-tailed Grackle.

CONSERVATION:
Groove-billed Anis are common and widespread in the tropics, and although their global population may be decreasing somewhat, they are adaptable to land converted to agricultural use; they prefer open habitats to unbroken forests. The North American population appears stable.

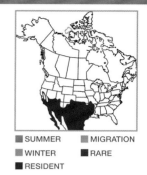

SUMMER   MIGRATION
WINTER   RARE
RESIDENT

The Greater Roadrunner is a huge, ground-dwelling, crested cuckoo that escapes predation and pursues its prey of lizards, mice, small snakes, birds, and invertebrates by running swiftly on long, sturdy legs. Typically associated with a desert landscape, the Greater Roadrunner is also found in chaparral, grasslands, open woodlands, agricultural areas, and even moist woodlands of eastern Texas. It is characteristically seen running with its long neck outstretched and tail held parallel to the ground. It may stop suddenly to raise its head, cocking it sideways or erecting its bushy crest; then pumping its tail. The Roadrunner usually holds its crest down while running; with each stop, the bird appears to swell in size as it opens its wings slightly and erects its tail, crest, and body feathers. Occasionally, Roadrunners fly short distances on rounded wings, then glide into a landing. Tracks left by the bird's stout feet demonstrate that two toes face forward and two backward.

DESCRIPTION: 24" (61 cm). The Greater Roadrunner is a large bird with a long tail and neck and a bushy crest. It has a large, long, pointed bill. At a distance, the Roadrunner appears mostly grayish, heavily streaked with dark on the neck, breast, back, and wings. Closer observation reveals iridescent blue-greens and bronze on the upperparts and on the long, white-tipped, otherwise dark tail. The rest of the underparts are off-white. There is a bright blue-and-red elongated patch behind the eye, absent from juveniles. Its blue-gray legs are long and sturdy. In flight, the rounded wings display a white crescent.

VOICE: Clucks, crows, dove-like coos, dog-like whines, and hoarse guttural notes.

NESTING: Lays 3–5 ivory-colored eggs in a flat stick nest lined with grass, usually in a thick shrub or cactus not far above ground.

HABITAT: Open arid country with scattered thickets.

RANGE: Resident from northern California, Nevada, Utah, Colorado, Kansas, Oklahoma, Arkansas, and Louisiana southward into Mexico.

SIMILAR SPECIES: Greater Roadrunner is unmistakable.

CONSERVATION:
Greater Roadrunners are numerous and their population overall is stable, although they have experienced long-term declines in southern California where habitat loss due to human development has fragmented its natural habitats and reduced the availability of nesting sites and prey.

This Old World cuckoo is dissimilar to North American cuckoos; its shape and coloration suggest a small hawk or falcon. It is a casual visitor from northern Eurasia, with rare but regular occurrences on the western Alaskan islands in late spring and early summer. Although famous for its *cuck-oo* call, after which cuckoo clock chimes are modeled, this call is made on its breeding grounds in Europe and Asia and generally not uttered by North American strays.

DESCRIPTION: A medium-sized (13–14", 32–33 cm), slender, long-tailed gray bird with a yellow eye ring and a black and white barred chest. The male has a light gray throat and breast, while the female has a reddish tinge in those areas. There is also a rufous morph (female only), where the ash-gray wings and back are replaced by rust color scalloped with black. The back of the head in a rufous bird is also rust and black, fading to a black and white scalloping on the throat, chest, and belly.

VOICE: Males give the famous *cuck-oo* of cuckoo clocks. Females call *kwik-kwik-kwik*.

NESTING: Unlike the three North American cuckoo species, the Common Cuckoo is an obligate brood parasite, always laying its eggs in another bird's nest. The cuckoo chick then removes all other nestlings, ensuring that it receives all the food its surrogate parents can provide. In at least some populations, the cuckoo chick has evolved to mimic the feeding calls of an entire brood of host nestlings.

HABITAT: In its native range, the Common Cuckoo is a generalist, largely of forested and wooded areas, but found in meadows and wetlands as well.

RANGE: Breeds throughout Europe and Asia, winters in India, southeast Asia, and southern Africa. It is a regular vagrant to Alaska and the Bering Sea islands, accidental on the East Coast of the United States.

CONSERVATION: Least Concern in its wide Old World range.

YELLOW-BILLED CUCKOO *Coccyzus americanus*

■ SUMMER ■ MIGRATION
■ WINTER ■ RARE
■ RESIDENT

This widespread bird's tendency to utter its distinctive call at the approach of a storm has earned it the nickname "Rain Crow." Both the Yellow-billed and Black-billed cuckoos are fond of hairy caterpillars and are valuable during outbreaks of tent caterpillars in helping to keep these creatures in check. Usually shy and elusive, these birds are easy to overlook.

DESCRIPTION: 10½–12½" (27–32 cm). Jay-sized. A slender, long-tailed bird, brown above and white below, with large white spots on the underside of the tail and a flash of rufous in the wings. Its bill is slightly curved, with a yellow lower mandible.

VOICE: A rapid, harsh, rattling *ka-ka-ka-ka-ka-ka-kow-kow-kowp, kowp, kowp, kowp,* slowing down at the end.

NESTING: Lays 2–4 pale blue-green eggs in a flimsy saucer of twigs placed in a bush or small sapling.

HABITAT: Moist thickets, willows, overgrown pastures, and orchards.

RANGE: Breeds from central California, Minnesota, and southern New Brunswick southward. Winters in South America.

SIMILAR SPECIES: See Black-billed and Mangrove cuckoos. Black-billed Cuckoo is similar, but has little rufous in the wings and smaller white spots on the tail.

CONVERSATION: Yellow-billed Cuckoos are listed as a common bird in steep decline. They are vulnerable to the loss of their riparian habitat to urbanization and agriculture, and they have disappeared entirely from large areas of the western United States and British Columbia.

■ SUMMER ■ MIGRATION
■ WINTER ■ RARE
■ RESIDENT

In North America, this species is found only in the Florida Keys and on the adjacent Gulf Coast of Florida as far north as Tampa Bay. It is difficult to observe, remaining hidden in dense thickets much of the time. Strictly insectivorous, it feeds on hairy caterpillars, grasshoppers, moths, larvae, and spiders.

DESCRIPTION: 12" (30 cm). Brown above, rich buff or tawny below, with a black facial mask. The upper mandible of its curved bill is black; the lower mandible is yellow. Its tail is long and graduated with large black-and-white spots at the tip.

VOICE: Low guttural *gaw-gaw-gaw-gaw-gaw*, almost like a soft bark or the scolding of a squirrel.

NESTING: Lays 2 or 3 pale greenish-blue eggs in a stick nest in a low shrub.

HABITAT: Mangrove swamps.

RANGE: Breeds in southern Florida. A few remain during winter, but most leave for the tropics.

SIMILAR SPECIES: See Black-billed Cuckoo. Yellow-billed Cuckoo has rufous in its primaries, especially visible in flight, and lacks the black ear patch.

CONSERVATION: LC
Although Mangrove Cuckoo is still common where it occurs, its restricted range and reliance on mangrove habitat puts it at risk. It is uncommon and declining in Florida as its habitat is lost to human development.

■ SUMMER ■ MIGRATION
■ WINTER ■ RARE
■ RESIDENT

Both of North America's widespread cuckoos—the Black-billed and the Yellow-billed—are adept at hiding and skulking in dense vegetation and are more often heard than seen. Their distinctive notes, repeated over and over, are reminiscent of those of grebes and doves, but deeper in tone and more repetitive. When tracked down, the birds slip away to another location and repeat the call. Cuckoos are extremely beneficial to the farmer and horticulturist, consuming enormous quantities of destructive hairy caterpillars, especially gypsy moth and tent caterpillars. They are most numerous in years of tent caterpillar infestations.

DESCRIPTION: 12" (30 cm). Brown above and white below; its tail feathers are graduated with small white tips; its primaries have little or no rufous. Its bill is black and slightly decurved, sometimes with a dusky gray base. Adults have a narrow, red eye ring; that of immatures is a dull yellow-green.

VOICE: Its song is a series of soft staccato *cu-cu-cu-cu* notes issued in repeating patterns of 2–5 notes, often triplets, all on the same pitch. Calls include a rolling, guttural croak.

NESTING: Lays 2–4 blue-green eggs in a flimsy shallow nest of twigs lined with grass and plant down, placed within a few feet of the ground in a dense thicket.

HABITAT: Moist thickets in low, overgrown pastures and orchards; also occurs in thicker undergrowth and sparse woodlands.

RANGE: Breeds from Alberta and Montana east to the Maritime Provinces, and south to northern Texas, Arkansas, and South Carolina. Winters in South America.

SIMILAR SPECIES: See Yellow-billed and Mangrove cuckoos. Similar to Yellow-billed Cuckoo, but its bill is entirely black, and it has small, distinct white spots at the tips of the tail feathers.

CONSERVATION: Uncommon and declining. Black-billed Cuckoo populations naturally fluctuate and move from year to year to coincide with caterpillar and cicada outbreaks. Habitat loss—especially in their tropical winter grounds—and efforts to control destructive caterpillars using pesticides may have had a negative impact on these birds, as their populations have declined overall throughout their range since the 1970s.

■ SUMMER ■ MIGRATION
■ WINTER ■ RARE
■ RESIDENT

The Lesser Nighthawk is associated with arid lowlands and southerly desert regions. With relatively large, long wings and a rather long, fuselage-shaped body, the Lesser Nighthawk flies with deep wingbeats leading to a bounding flight that is suddenly checked by erratic fluttering. This low-flying aerial forager is most easily seen in the evenings and early mornings and less frequently during the day, especially during migration. Usually solitary, large numbers of these birds can often be found skimming low just over riparian vegetation and adjacent water where there is a high concentration of insects. Dispersed groups are found in desert and other open habitats in the Southwest. During courtship flight display, the male pursues the female close to the ground, flashing its white throat as it calls.

DESCRIPTION: 8–9" (20–23 cm). Similar to Common Nighthawk but smaller, with a white wing patch (buff in female) nearer the tip of the wing, which is visible in flight. Like the Common Nighthawk, this species has a short bill; long, pointed wings; and a long, notched, rectangular tail. It is mottled above and below with buff, brown, gray, and white. Both sexes have a buffy cast to the underparts. The male's throat is white; the female's is buff. Whereas Common Nighthawk hunts and calls from high up, Lesser Nighthawk flies low and utters no loud aerial calls.

VOICE: A soft, sustained, tremolo whirring; often difficult to locate. Its call is a low, soft *chuck* note.

NESTING: Lays 2 spotted, light gray eggs on open ground.

HABITAT: Open dry scrublands, desert valleys, prairies and pastures.

RANGE: Breeds from central California, Arizona, and parts of Nevada, Utah, New Mexico, and Texas southward. Winters in the tropics.

SIMILAR SPECIES: Common Nighthawk has a longer tail. It flies with slower, deeper wingbeats and has a less fluttery flight. Its wings are longer in proportion and more sharply pointed; the patch on the primaries is midway between the bend of the wing and the tip. Its underparts show more contrast, and its undertail coverts are white or whitish. It also has a different call.

See Antillean Nighthawk, found in the Florida Keys.

CONSERVATION: Lesser Nighthawks are a species of low conservation concern, and their population appears to be stable or possibly increasing. Their nocturnal nature makes Lesser Nighthawks difficult to survey accurately.

SUMMER ■ MIGRATION
WINTER ■ RARE
■ RESIDENT

Common Nighthawks are widespread and found in many habitats across North America, including forests, sagebrush plains, and meadows. They have also adapted to human settlements, where flat roofs provide abundant nest sites, and railroad yards, vacant lots, and sports fields offer good feeding opportunities. Common Nighthawks feed primarily in the evening and at night, but can be seen airborne any time of day, particularly during migration, when they congregate in flocks. After darkness sets in, the only clue to the presence of foraging birds high in the night sky is a buzzy, nasal *peent* call. The birds can, however, be seen foraging near bright lights in residential areas, catching flying insects on the wing. Common Nighthawks consume large numbers of flying insects—including moths, beetles, grasshoppers, and several pest species including mosquitoes, winged ants, and termites—and may take several hundred in a single evening. During most daylight hours, Common Nighthawks can be found perched motionless, lengthwise on tree limbs, fence posts, rocky outcroppings, or rooftops, with their eyes squeezed shut.

DESCRIPTION: 10" (25 cm). A jay-sized bird, mottled brownish-black above and below, perfectly matching the ground. It has a long, notched or square-tipped tail and long, pointed wings with a broad white wing bar. The male has a white throat patch and white subterminal tail bar. The female has a buff throat patch and no tail bar. This species' flight is high and fluttery.

VOICE: A loud nasal call, *peent* or *pee-yah*, heard primarily at dusk.

NESTING: Lays 2 creamy or olive-gray, finely and densely speckled eggs on the ground or a graveled roof.

HABITAT: Open woodlands, clearings, or fields; towns with roosting trees or fence posts.

RANGE: Breeds from central Canada southward to Nova Scotia and through most of United States. Winters in the American tropics.

SIMILAR SPECIES: See Lesser Nighthawk. Other nightjars have rounded, blunt-tipped wings and tails, and (except Pauraques) lack white wing patches and contrasting, even barring on the underparts of the nighthawk. Lesser Nighthawks' flight is more fluttery or moth-like, with foraging occurring nearer to or on the ground.

CONSERVATION: Common Nighthawk is a common bird in steep decline in many parts of North America. Widespread pesticide use to control insects such as mosquitoes has impacted the food supply for these birds. Habitat-loss threats include both the loss of natural open spaces to development and the replacement of flat gravel rooftops in urban settings, which Common Nighthawks often use as nesting sites.

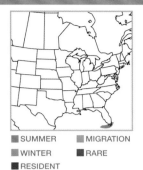

■ SUMMER ■ MIGRATION
■ WINTER ■ RARE
■ RESIDENT

Originally considered a subspecies of the Common Nighthawk, this West Indian species is a common nesting bird on the Caribbean islands and locally uncommon in the Florida Keys.

DESCRIPTION: 9½" (24 cm). A jay-sized bird, mottled grayish-black above and whitish below, heavily barred with black. It has a long, slightly notched tail and long, pointed wings with a broad white wing bar. It closely resembles Common Nighthawk, although slightly smaller and paler, and is best distinguished by voice.

VOICE: A dry *killy-ka-dick*, often repeated.

NESTING: Lays 2 whitish to olive eggs with dark blotches on the bare ground.

HABITAT: Open country.

RANGE: Breeds in the Florida Keys, wandering to southern peninsular Florida in summer. Probably winters in South America. Also found in the West Indies.

SIMILAR SPECIES: See Lesser and Common nighthawks. Antillean Nighthawk is reliably distinguished in the field from Common Nighthawk only by voice.

CONSERVATION:
Antillean Nighthawk is a local, uncommon breeder on the Florida Keys. Its population on the Keys increased as parts of the islands were cleared for development, but in recent years it has declined there. Globally, the species' population appears to be stable.

COMMON PAURAQUE *Nyctidromus albicollis*

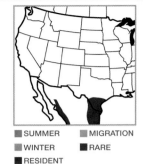

■ SUMMER   ■ MIGRATION
■ WINTER   ■ RARE
■ RESIDENT

Pauraques are virtually impossible to see on the ground in daylight because they match dead leaves and twigs almost perfectly. But when one is flushed from the side of the road by car headlights, the white wing patch, like that of a nighthawk, may be seen distinctly, and the eyes shine a brilliant red. Like other nightjars, Pauraques have an enormously wide gape that enables them to catch large moths, beetles, crickets, and fireflies on the wing at night.

DESCRIPTION: 12" (30 cm). Larger than a Whippoor-will. The Common Pauraque is finely patterned in shades of brown and gray. In good light, one can see its fairly plain, gray crown (with a few darker streaks), chestnut ear patch, white area on the lower throat, and large black spots on the scapulars. The male's white bar across the primaries is conspicuous in flight; when the tail is spread, a long, white stripe is visible near each outer edge. In the female, the white is less extensive and may be tinged with buff. This species is identified in the field mainly by voice.

VOICE: A burry *pur-wheeer*, slurred downward and uttered at night. Issues various low throaty sounds when disturbed or while foraging.

NESTING: Lays 2 pinkish-buff, brown-blotched eggs on bare ground near a bush or a tree.

HABITAT: Semi-open scrub country with thickets, and light woodland clearings.

RANGE: Resident in extreme southern Texas. Also in the American tropics.

SIMILAR SPECIES: In flight, the white bar across the primaries rules out confusion with all other rounded-winged nightjars. When Common Pauraque is perched, its tail looks proportionately much longer than that of its cousins. Nighthawks also have white in primaries but angular, pointed wings, and less substantial tails without longitudinal white stripes.

CONSERVATION:
Common Pauraque is common and widespread in Central America. Southern Texas represents the far northern limit of this species' range; it is locally common where suitable habitat exists.

■ SUMMER ■ MIGRATION
■ WINTER ■ RARE
■ RESIDENT

The Common Poorwill is a common resident of dry, low, brushy areas in western North America, where its characteristic name-sake call is heard at twilight and, less frequently, during the night. Widely distributed from lowlands to mountain slopes, the Common Poorwill inhabits a variety of arid upland areas. It has been discovered hibernating in the desert in California, surviving long cold spells in a torpid condition without food and with its body temperature lowered almost to that of its surroundings—this adaptation is unique among birds. It chases insect prey by fluttering up from the ground like a big moth. These nightjars are seen most often sitting on roads at night.

DESCRIPTION: 7–8½" (18–22 cm). Our smallest nightjar. It is mottled gray-brown with no white marks on the wings. A whitish collar separates a black throat from its mottled underparts. Dark outer tail feathers are tipped with white, more conspicuously in the male. The tail is rounded.

VOICE: A mellow *poor-will* call, from which the bird's name is derived, includes a long first syllable and accent on the second. At close range, a soft third note can be heard. When disturbed, these birds may give a *kweep-kweep* in flight.

NESTING: Lays 2 pinkish-white eggs on bare ground.

HABITAT: Desert, chaparral, sagebrush, and other arid uplands.

RANGE: Breeds from southeastern British Columbia, Alberta, and Montana south throughout western United States. Winters in southwestern states and Mexico.

SIMILAR SPECIES: Lesser Nighthawk forages in the air; it has long, pointed wings. Female and juvenile Lesser Nighthawks lack the white patch on the wing or have only an incon-spicuous one; they are frequently misidentified as Common Poorwills. Whip-poor-will has a longer tail and generally darker coloration.

CONSERVATION: Common Poorwill is widespread and common, and its population is stable or increasing. Urbanization that results in habitat loss can drive local populations down, and vehicle strikes pose a danger where dirt roads create enticing habitats for these birds.

■ SUMMER   ■ MIGRATION
■ WINTER   ■ RARE
■ RESIDENT

Although large and locally common, the "Chuck" is nocturnal and rarely seen during the day. When flushed, it flies off a short distance, then drops to the ground again. These birds hunt close to the ground, catching flying insects such as moths, beetles, and winged ants and termites. They have occasionally been reported to prey on bats and small birds such as hummingbirds, warblers, and sparrows. Its small bill belies a large mouth that can open widely, which Chuck-will's-widow uses to capture prey on the wing and swallow whole.

DESCRIPTION: 12" (30 cm). Pigeon-sized, larger than a Whip-poor-will. The Chuck-will's-widow has reddish-brown plumage mottled with black spots and streaks. The bird's chin is brown, and the overall plumage has a brown tone, its cryptic pattern providing excellent camouflage against a backdrop of dead leaves on the forest floor. The male shows restricted areas of white on the outer tail feathers and has a narrow white throat patch. The female has an entirely brown tail and a buff throat patch.

VOICE: A mellow, four-note *chuck-will's-widow*, repeated in a long series; the first note is deep and low, and the rest of the call is whistled. Also utters a low, single *chuck* note.

NESTING: Lays 2 creamy-white eggs, with purple and brown markings, on bare ground or dead leaves.

HABITAT: Open woodlands and clearings near agricultural country.

RANGE: Breeds from Kansas, Indiana, and Long Island south to the Gulf Coast states. Winters chiefly in the tropics, but a few winter in Florida and along the Gulf Coast.

SIMILAR SPECIES: Whip-poor-will is smaller and has a blackish chin and overall gray tone to its plumage; its call is quite different.

Nighthawks have narrow, pointed wings with white on primaries; their tails and underparts are barred.

CONSERVATION: NT

Chuck-will's-widow is a common species that has undergone steep decline and is now listed as near threatened. The species' nocturnal nature makes its numbers difficult to survey with certainty. Habitat loss, pesticide usage, and disturbance of nesting sites are all suspected in contributing to the Chuck-will's-widow's decline.

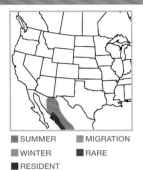

■ SUMMER   ■ MIGRATION
■ WINTER   ■ RARE
■ RESIDENT

This little-known nightjar is a rare summer visitor to the Southwest, where it has been found in arid rocky washes and canyons. It is much more common in varied habitats south of U.S.-Mexico border.

DESCRIPTION: 9" (23 cm). Buff-collared Nightjar is mottled dark gray and brown, and paler below with fine barring. Its complete buff or rust-colored collar is diagnostic but hard to see. Its flight feathers have some rust or buff. Its tail is long and barred with buff and dark gray; the male's has white patches at the outer corners.

VOICE: A staccato *cu-cu-cu-cuc-cuc-cuc-uh-chee-ah*, heard at night.

NESTING: This nightjar's nesting habits are poorly understood. It does not appear to build nests; instead, it lays a pair of eggs directly on the ground or atop a few leaves. Only a few such sites have been discovered.

HABITAT: Dry canyons and rocky streambeds.

RANGE: Resident in southeastern Arizona and southwestern New Mexico.

SIMILAR SPECIES: Other nightjars lack full buff or rust collar, and have different calls.

CONSERVATION:
Buff-collared Nightjar is uncommon and local where it occurs in the southwestern United States. It is widespread and common in Mexico and into parts of Central America, although its global population is decreasing.

EASTERN WHIP-POOR-WILL *Antrostomus vociferus*

■ SUMMER ■ MIGRATION
■ WINTER ■ RARE
■ RESIDENT

The common, widespread Eastern Whip-poor-will is nocturnal and feeds on flying insects that it captures on the wing. This cryptically colored species inhabits deciduous woodlands and forest edges, where it roosts during the day on the ground or with the body positioned lengthwise on a horizontal limb. At night, its eyes reflect ruby red. It and the virtually identical Mexican Whip-poor-will once comprised a single species known simply as "Whip-poor-will" in older guides.

DESCRIPTION: 10" (25 cm). Robin-sized. This strictly nocturnal bird is mottled grayish-brown with black spots and streaks and a blackish chin; there is an overall grayish tone to the plumage. The male has a narrow, white throat patch and prominent white outer tail feathers that are visible in flight; the female has a buff throat patch and no white in the tail.

VOICE: A loud, rhythmic *whip-poor-will*, repeated in a long series at night.

NESTING: Lays 2 white eggs, scrawled with gray and brown, placed on the ground among dead leaves.

HABITAT: Deciduous or mixed woodlands.

RANGE: Breeds from Saskatchewan and the Maritime Provinces south to Kansas, northern Louisiana, and northern Georgia. It winters from Florida and the Gulf Coast southward. Whip-poor-will sightings in eastern Texas could be either the Eastern or the Mexican species. The boundary between the two species' ranges is a subject of active study, and caution should be exercised in the area where the ranges could overlap.

SIMILAR SPECIES: Mexican Whip-poor-will is visually nearly indistinguishable, best separated by voice and range.

See Chuck-will's-widow and Buff-collared Nightjar. Chuck-will's-widow is larger and more buff-colored.

Nighthawks have barred tails and underparts, and narrow, pointed wings with white bars across the primaries.

CONSERVATION: Eastern Whip-poor-wills are declining and are now listed as near threatened. Threats to the species include human development/urbanization, forest disturbance, and the widespread use of pesticides that eliminate moths and other flying insects upon which these birds rely for food.

Antrostomus arizonae **MEXICAN WHIP-POOR-WILL**

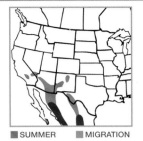

■ SUMMER ■ MIGRATION
■ WINTER ■ RARE
■ RESIDENT

The Mexican Whip-poor-will is rarely seen because it sleeps by day on the forest floor, its coloration matching the dead leaves. At night, its eyes reflect ruby red. It is most often identified by voice when it issues its loud whip-poor-will song at night. Mexican Whip-poor-will is almost identical to the Eastern Whip-poor-will, and until recently the two were considered a single species. Usually the two species can be separated based on their range; only in parts of Texas are they likely to overlap. There, careful observers can use their slightly different songs to tell the two species apart.

DESCRIPTION: 10" (25 cm). Robin-sized. A leaf-brown, strictly nocturnal bird with a black throat. The male has broad white tips on the outer tail feathers that are visible in flight. The female has an all-brown tail.

VOICE: A loud, rhythmic *whip-poor-will*, repeated in a long series at night; slightly rougher and lower-pitched than the song of the Eastern Whip-poor-will, and sung at a different cadence.

NESTING: Lays 2 white eggs, scrawled with gray and brown, placed on the ground among dead leaves.

HABITAT: Dry, open woodlands and canyons, mountain forests.

RANGE: Breeds in west Texas, Arizona, New Mexico, and southern California. Winters in central and western Mexico. Note that birds migrating through east Texas or wintering along Mexico's Caribbean coast are likely to be Eastern Whip-poor-wills. The precise range of each of the two species is still under scientific investigation, and caution should be used in identifying whip-poor-wills anywhere that both species might be found.

SIMILAR SPECIES: Eastern Whip-poor-will is visually nearly indistinguishable, best separated by voice and range.

See Chuck-will's-widow and Buff-collared Nightjar. Chuck-will's-widow is larger and more buff-colored.

Nighthawks have barred tails and underparts, and narrow, pointed wings with white bars across the primaries.

CONSERVATION: LC
Mexican Whip-poor-will populations are not well documented. They remain common locally in their limited U.S. range and are considered a species of least concern.

BLACK SWIFT *Cypseloides niger*

■ SUMMER   ■ MIGRATION
■ WINTER   ■ RARE
■ RESIDENT

The largest of our North American swifts, the Black Swift is a widespread but patchily distributed summer resident in the western United States. Its larger size, uniform sooty-black color, and longer, slightly forked tail serve immediately to distinguish it from all other swifts. Although its flight may appear slow and erratic with its stiff, shallow wingbeats, the Black Swift is a strong flier. Foraging high in the air, it ranges widely from its unique nest and roost sites behind mountain waterfalls, on damp coastal cliffs, and in seacoast caves. Black Swifts are most commonly seen in migration or during overcast weather, when flocks can be found foraging at low elevations, frequently over bodies of water or in company with other swifts or swallows.

DESCRIPTION: 7–7½" (18–19 cm). Black Swift is the size of a large swallow but has longer, sickle-shaped wings. It is all black except for some frosted white edgings to the feathers of the forehead, apparent at close range. Its broad, longish tail is slightly forked and often held fanned out. Feathers of immatures are edged with white.

VOICE: Less vocal than other swifts, rarely heard away from roost or nest sites. Gives soft, high-pitched twitter: *twit-twit-twit-twit*.

NESTING: Lays 1 white egg in a moss, grass, and algae nest well hidden under a waterfall, on a protected sea cliff ledge, or on a canyon wall. Nests in colonies.

HABITAT: Mountains and coastal cliffs; most frequently seen in the open sky.

RANGE: Breeds from southern Alaska south to southern California, Montana, and Colorado. Winters in tropics.

SIMILAR SPECIES: The male Purple Martin has broader wings and slower flight, and perches frequently; Purple Martins occur away from typical Black Swift habitat and frequently in association with humans.

CONSERVATION: VU
Uncommon and extremely local, Black Swifts are declining at an alarming pace. Unfortunately so little is known about this species that the causes for its decline are poorly understood. Fewer than 200 nesting sites have been discovered in North America, and the species' winter range is only partially known thanks to recent studies using geolocators. The global breeding population is estimated to be between 150,000–200,000.

This species is a rare to accidental vagrant from the Neotropics that may stray through much of the southern United States. Multiple records have come from along the Gulf Coast, especially in Texas and Florida, and other widely scattered sightings have been recorded as far north as New Jersey and Michigan.

DESCRIPTION: A huge, blackish swift that is much larger than any native swift, 8–8½" (20–21.5 cm) long with a wingspan of almost 20" (50 cm). Adults have a conspicuous white collar around the neck that may be absent or reduced in juveniles. The tail is long, wide, and somewhat forked. It may show white on the forehead. Its flight is like that of other swifts, but its wingbeats are somewhat slowed by its large size. For a swift, it has a chunky build and broad wings.

VOICE: Twittering, scratchy *chee, chee, chee.*

NESTING: Does not nest in North America. In its native range in the American tropics, White-collared Swift nests in colonies along cliff ledges or in caves. The female lays 2 eggs in a cup nest constructed of mud and moss.

HABITAT: Moist to wet tropical forests and shrublands, from sea level to above 14,000 ft (4350 m). Less abundant to absent in dry habitats. This is one of the swift species that often nests behind waterfalls, similar to the Black Swift native to our range.

RANGE: Native from southeastern Mexico and various Caribbean islands south through much of South America. Scattered distribution, especially in South America.

SIMILAR SPECIES: Although smaller than a White-collared, Black Swift is our largest native swift; both are mostly dark. Black Swift lacks the conspicuous white collar; it occurs in the West, mainly around its nest sites.

CONSERVATION:  White-collared Swift is widespread and common in its native range in the American tropics.

CHIMNEY SWIFT *Chaetura pelagica*

■ SUMMER ■ MIGRATION
■ WINTER ■ RARE
■ RESIDENT

These gregarious birds fly rapidly on narrow, swept-back wings, alternating bouts of shallow wingbeats with gliding. Chimney Swifts are among the fastest fliers in the bird world. They spend all of their daylight hours on the wing and come to rest only in the evening to roost overnight. They feed exclusively on flying insects, and they drink and bathe by dipping into a pond or river as they fly over it. These swifts gather in communal roosts in air shafts or large chimneys, often whirling in a huge circle as they funnel down for the night.

Chimney Swifts may roost or nest inside uncapped traditional brick chimneys. If you wish to welcome these birds to visit your unused chimney in the summer, keep the damper closed for the season, and schedule a chimney cleaning after the breeding season ends (never during). Capping your chimney will exclude the swifts.

DESCRIPTION: 4¾–5½" (12–14 cm). Nearly uniform gray-brown, slightly darker above and on the wings. In fresh plumage, it shows a greenish gloss on the wings and mantle. It is light below, palest on the upper breast and throat. Its tail is stiff and slightly rounded when fanned, with spines at the tips of the feathers.

VOICE: Loud, chattering twitters.

NESTING: Lays 4 or 5 white eggs in a nest made of twigs cemented together with saliva and fastened to the inner wall of a chimney or similar structure. Natural nesting sites are inside large, hollow trees, but today these birds almost always nest in artificial structures.

HABITAT: Breeds and roosts in chimneys; feeds entirely on the wing over forests, open country, and towns.

RANGE: Breeds from southeastern Saskatchewan, southern Manitoba, central Ontario, southern Quebec, and Nova Scotia south to the Gulf Coast states. Winters in the tropics.

SIMILAR SPECIES: The narrow wings and rapid, erratic flight easily distinguish Chimney Swift form any similar-sized swallows.

Vaux's Swift is similar but slightly smaller and less uniformly gray-brown, with a lighter throat and breast.

CONSERVATION: VU

Chimney Swifts became common and widespread as their numbers increased dramatically after European settlers constructed countless brick chimneys as they spread out across the continent. Unfortunately, in recent years the species has declined in many areas, and today is listed as vulnerable. Modern chimney designs and capped traditional chimneys tend to exclude these birds, denying them the nesting sites upon which they have come to depend. The clearing of old-growth forests has reduced the availability of natural nesting and roosting sites, leaving the species almost entirely reliant on human-provided structures.

- ■ SUMMER   ■ MIGRATION
- ■ WINTER   ■ RARE
- ■ RESIDENT

The better-known eastern Chimney Swift now uses chimneys for nesting, whereas the Vaux's is still mainly a forest dweller. These swifts have stubby tails, each feather ending in a naked shaft with a hard spine that helps to support the bird as it clings to vertical surfaces, such as its nesting cavity walls. Its fast flight is characterized by sailing glides between spurts of rapid flapping.

DESCRIPTION: 4–4½" (10–11 cm). A tiny swift, it is dark overall with dingy, lighter underparts, especially pale on the throat and upper breast. Its wings are long, stiff, and gently curved; the tail is slightly rounded. See Chimney Swift.

VOICE: A bat-like chipping. Usually silent on migration.

NESTING: Lays 3–5 white eggs in a nest of small sticks cemented together with saliva and attached to the inside surface of a hollow tree.

HABITAT: Forests and woodlands.

RANGE: Breeds from southeastern Alaska and Montana to central California. Winters in tropics.

SIMILAR SPECIES: Chimney Swift is slightly larger, usually more uniformly brown; Vaux's is lighter grayish-brown on the belly, distinctly paler on the upper breast and throat, contrasting with a darker crown. Identification of the two species in areas of sympatry should be made with care. Vocal and behavioral differences may prove more reliable in the field.

CONSERVATION:

The population of Vaux's Swift appears to be stable, although declines have occurred locally in Oregon and Washington. The clearing of old-growth forests in the Pacific Northwest has limited the availability of the nesting habitats these swifts require. Unlike the Chimney Swift, Vaux's Swifts are not as widely adapted to nesting in human structures, and rely instead on large mature trees and snags typical of old-growth forests.

■ SUMMER ■ MIGRATION
■ WINTER ■ RARE
■ RESIDENT

This boldly patterned, black-and-white bird is familiar in the West, where it frequents the rocky cliffs of mountain or desert canyons. These common swifts are often seen in the vicinity of steep cliffs, where they may fly in small groups, chattering constantly. Like some other swifts, they mate in flight, gyrating earthward in a free fall, separating only when about to hit the ground.

DESCRIPTION: 6–7" (15–18 cm). The size of a Barn Swallow, but with the typical stiff, fast wingbeats of a swift. It has a striking piebald appearance in the air; seen from below, its wings, flanks, and tail are black, the rest is white. Seen more closely, one can see its prominent white throat and upper breast with a white midline streak extending to the lower belly. It has two bold white patches on the flanks and prominent, broad white terminal edges on the secondaries. Its tail is long and slightly forked, with no terminal spines.

VOICE: A prolonged series of grating notes, *jee-jee-jee-jee-jee*.

NESTING: Lays 3–6 white eggs in a nest of feathers glued together with saliva built in a cleft of a sea or mountain cliff. Nests in colonies.

HABITAT: Arid mountains or other rocky areas.

RANGE: Breeds from British Columbia through the Rocky Mountains and in the Southwest, including California. It winters from central California and the Southwest to Central America.

SIMILAR SPECIES: Vaux's and Chimney swifts are more uniformly colored and smaller. Black Swift is larger and blackish. See Violet-green Swallow.

CONSERVATION: Common and widespread, White-throated Swift numbers remain stable or may be declining slightly. Widespread pesticide use to control insects places pressure on White-throated Swifts and many other aerial insectivores, but this species' population appears to be enduring.

■ SUMMER   ■ MIGRATION
■ WINTER   ■ RARE
■ RESIDENT

A rare but annual visitor from Mexico, Mexican Violetear is the only mostly green hummingbird with a decurved bill likely to visit hummingbird feeders. This species has reached many midwestern and eastern states and even Alberta, mostly in summer. The reasons for this sharp increase in extralimital records are not known. The species was formerly known as Green Violetear.

DESCRIPTION: 4¾" (12 cm) long with a wingspan of 7" (18 cm). An entirely iridescent bronze-green hummingbird with large bluish-violet patches on the lores, ear coverts, and the center of the breast. The bill is relatively short and slightly decurved. Adult birds have a green throat and crown. At all ages these birds have banded, bluish tails. Its undertail coverts are dark gray; younger birds often have paler undertail coverts. Females are similar but slightly duller than males. Immatures have feathers edged with gray.

VOICE: Call is a dry *tchap*.

NESTING: Lays 2 small white eggs inside a small, sturdy cup nest woven from spider webbing, down, and plant materials.

HABITAT: Clearings and forest edges in the mountainous highlands of the American tropics. Wanderers into North America may appear at hummingbird feeders.

RANGE: Native to the Neotropics, as far as central Mexico. It is casual in central and southern Texas; rarely an individual may stray as far north as Canada.

SIMILAR SPECIES: The much rarer Green-breasted Mango, recorded in Texas and North Carolina, has violet in the tail, and young birds and females have white streaks from throat to belly.

CONSERVATION: Mexican Violetear is a common bird in its native range in the American tropics, although much remains unknown about its population trends and seasonal movements.

This striking hummingbird is casual visitor that has appeared in southern Texas at least a couple dozen times, usually in fall and winter. Most of the vagrants are young birds. It has been recorded elsewhere in the United States on very rare occasions, including single records in Georgia, North Carolina, and Wisconsin.

DESCRIPTION: Large by hummingbird standards at 4½–5" (11–12 cm), the Green-breasted Mango is one of the few primarily dark hummingbirds that could be present in our range. The male is primarily various shades of green, with a large black throat and chin patch bordered in blue. The female is green above, and has a prominent bluish black stripe running from chin to belly through the white underparts. The female's stripe is unmistakable. Both sexes have a downward-curving black bill.

VOICE: A high-pitched *tsup* call and a buzzy, multisyllabic song.

NESTING: Lays 2 white eggs in a small cup nest made of lichen and plant materials, usually constructed on a high, thin branch.

HABITAT: Grassy or shrubby areas, including shade-grown coffee plantations, at low elevations from sea level to 3900 ft (1200 m). Uses manmade habitats ranging from coffee plantations to urban parks, and may grow more common with certain types of development.

RANGE: Central Mexico to northern South America, primarily near the coasts.

SIMILAR SPECIES: Male Broad-billed Hummingbird is a locally common native hummingbird that is green below like the male Mango. It has a blue throat and a red bill.

CONSERVATION:

Little is known about this species' overall population, but it is widespread and believed to be of low conservation concern in its native range.

■ SUMMER ■ MIGRATION
■ WINTER ■ RARE
■ RESIDENT

The Rivoli's Hummingbird (formerly called Magnificent Humming-bird) is an uncommon to somewhat common summer resident in its limited U.S. range in the high mountain pine-oak woods, meadows, and canyons of the Southwest. It flies more slowly than the smaller hummers, sometimes sailing on set wings. It is more of an insect gleaner than the other species, though it takes its share of nectar from flowers and feeders.

DESCRIPTION: 4½–5½" (11–14 cm). A large, long-tailed hummingbird. The male is deep green above and black below, with an iridescent purple forehead and crown and metallic-green gorget. The female is olive green above and gray below, with a lightly streaked throat and pearly gray tips on the outer tail feathers. Immature males are heavily flecked with irides-cent green below.

VOICE: A high-pitched *teek*, not as drawn out as the call of the Blue-throated Mountain-gem.

NESTING: Lays 2 white eggs in a tiny nest of lichen and plant down placed on a horizontal limb.

HABITAT: Canyons, deciduous and pine-clad slopes, and streamsides.

RANGE: Breeds in the mountains of southeastern Arizona, south-western New Mexico, and western Texas. It winters in Mexico.

SIMILAR SPECIES: The adult male is unmistakable.

Female Blue-throated Mountain-gem has a more substantial blue-black tail with large, white corners, more distinct striping on the face, and more smoothly gray underparts.

Female Rivoli's might also be confused with some other female hummingbirds, like Anna's Hum-mingbird, which is grayish below and moder-ately bulky. However, with a good view, Rivoli's larger size, flat forehead, and very long bill should be obvious.

See also White-eared Hummingbird.

CONSERVATION:

Little is known about the population trends of Rivoli's Humming-bird. Flowers and backyard feeders help to sustain a healthy population where they occur in the Southwest. The species may be vulnerable to habitat loss in Mexico and Central America, which account for most of the species' range.

PLAIN-CAPPED STARTHROAT *Heliomaster constantii*

The Plain-capped Starthroat is a rare but regular vagrant to southern Arizona. Native as far north as northwestern Mexico, Plain-capped Starthroats visit southern Arizona in summer and early fall almost annually, often reported at feeders. Plain-capped Starthroats prey more heavily on small flying insects than do most other hummingbirds, but they also consume plenty of nectar from feeders and flowers.

DESCRIPTION: A large hummingbird, 4½–5" (11.5–12.5 cm), with an extremely long, straight black bill. It has duller coloration than many other hummingbirds: green to bronze above and gray below. A distinctive white rump patch and two bold white facial stripes distinguish this species from any native hummingbird. Its throat is flecked with blackish and iridescent red, visible only in ideal light conditions. Both sexes are similar.

VOICE: Strong, sharp chipping calls. Its song is a series of chips interspersed with an occasional two-syllable *pi-chip*.

NESTING: This bird's nest is a shallow cup of plant material camouflaged with bark and lichen, often constructed at the tip of a high branch of a tree. The species' reproductive habits are not well understood. The population in western Mexico is reported to nest from January to June, while Costa Rican populations nest from October to January.

HABITAT: Dry forests, shrublands, and artificial equivalents such as coffee plantations. Low to mid altitudes (to 5000 ft, 1500 m).

RANGE: Pacific-slope lowlands and foothills of Mexico and Central America, from northern Mexico to southern Costa Rica. Locally to Caribbean slope in some parts of Central America, where conditions are dry enough.

SIMILAR SPECIES: White rump patch and white facial stripes are distinctive.

CONSERVATION: Least concern in its native range; its population appears to be stable.

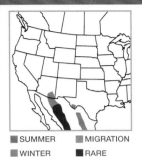

■ SUMMER ■ MIGRATION
■ WINTER ■ RARE
■ RESIDENT

Formerly called Blue-throated Hummingbird. Found along the United States-Mexico border, this unmistakable large hummingbird is especially common at nectar feeders in the Huachuca and Chiricahua mountains of Arizona. Blue-throated Mountaingem's large size and long wings make the wingbeats nearly discernible; its wingbeats may even make an audible humming sound. Uncharacteristic of hummingbirds, this species often locks its wings stiffly and glides over short distances. The loud, high, *seeep* song is diagnostic. This species inhabits canyons of higher southwestern mountains, usually in the vicinity of flowing water. They take both nectar and insects. This bird is notable for its aggressiveness, often dominating other hummingbirds and chasing them away from its preferred food sources, or mobbing much larger birds to drive them away.

DESCRIPTION: 4½–5" (11–13 cm). A large hummingbird. The male is dark metallic green above, dusky gray below, with an iridescent, bright blue gorget. It has a blue-black tail with broad white corners on the outer tail feathers. Both sexes have a white stripe above the eyes and a thinner white "whisker" stripe below the eyes. Females lack the blue throat and show less definition in the whisker mark.

VOICE: A high-pitched, loud *seeep* or *seeek*, often strongest at end of note, given at intervals in flight. Males give the same note from their territorial perch, usually near running water. In this case, the song is a repetitious *seeek, seeek, seeek* at rapid intervals.

NESTING: Lays 2 white eggs in a large cup nest with green mosses woven into the outside wall, fastened to a vertical plant stalk, occasionally in the shelter of cabins or on electrical wires; usually over or near water. Studies in Mexico show that their nests are typically sheltered from rain and sun and located near water, where flowering vegetation abounds. The Blue-throated returns to such a site year after year.

HABITAT: Streamside growth in canyons.

RANGE: Breeds in southeastern Arizona, southwestern New Mexico, and western Texas. Winters in Mexico.

SIMILAR SPECIES: Rivoli's Hummingbird is the only other large hummingbird in the same range; its tail is more slender, with distinct green tones and much less white, and it lacks the conspicuous whisker mark.

CONSERVATION:

Blue-throated Mountain-gem is common in its range, most of which is in Mexico. Its specific and limited range north of the border makes it vulnerable to any habitat changes at a handful of important sites, but its range may have expanded slightly in the U.S. in recent years.

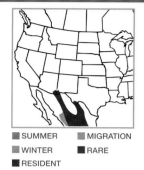

■ SUMMER   ■ MIGRATION
■ WINTER   ■ RARE
■ RESIDENT

The Lucifer Hummingbird, a common bird of Mexico's central plateau that is uncommon and local in North America, is closely associated with the century plant (agave) that is found in arid mesas and foothills in western Texas. The male Lucifer's outer tail feathers are hard and narrow, and hum loudly during aerial displays. It performs a zigzagging dance to attract females and repel other males. In Latin, lucifer means "light-bearing" and was applied in Old English to the morning star. Thus, when William Swainson named this bird in 1827, he might have been thinking of the luminous glow of its colors.

DESCRIPTION: 3¾" (10 cm). A small hummingbird with a slightly decurved bill. The male is iridescent green, with a green crown and long purple gorget; it is white below with buff on the flanks. The male has a deeply forked tail that is usually held closed, giving it a pointed look. The female lacks the colorful gorget and is buff below, with a more rounded tail.

VOICE: A shrill shriek. Also light, high-pitched chipping notes.

NESTING: Lays 2 white eggs in a small cup nest of downy plant fibers, cobwebs, and lichens, usually near the ground in agave and other vegetation.

HABITAT: Open arid country; desert vegetation, especially agaves.

RANGE: Breeds in Chisos Mountains of western Texas. Accidental summer visitor to extreme southeastern Arizona. Found throughout central and northern Mexico.

SIMILAR SPECIES: Male Costa's Hummingbird has violet on the crown as well as the gorget, and lacks rich buff on the sides; it has a straight bill.

Other female hummers that share the Lucifer's range lack extensive buff across the underparts; those that show much buff or rust on the sides and flanks (*Selasphorus* spp.) have shorter, straighter bills. Female Black-chinned has a slight decurvature to the bill, but the buff coloration is limited to an inconspicuous spot on the flanks.

CONSERVATION:

Classified as a species of least concern throughout Mexico, although little information is known about this bird's population trends. Its restricted range and specific habitat requirements in the U.S. make it vulnerable to habitat loss or disturbance in critical areas, although its range north of the U.S.-Mexico border may be gradually expanding.

■ SUMMER ■ MIGRATION
■ WINTER ■ RARE
■ RESIDENT

The only hummer occurring throughout most of eastern North America, the Ruby-throated Hummingbird possesses the typical hummingbird characteristics of small size, rapid wingbeats, and nectar-feeding habits. It occupies woodlands, parks, and gardens where flowers are plentiful. These diminutive birds are particularly attracted to tubular red flowers such as salvia and trumpet creeper, as well as bee balm, petunia, jewelweed, and thistle. Hummers are also attracted to artificial feeders—red glass tubes filled with sweet liquid. During courtship, the female sits quietly on a perch while the male displays in a pendulum dance, swinging in a wide arc and buzzing loudly with each dip.

DESCRIPTION: 3½" (9 cm). A tiny hummingbird with a needle-like bill. It is metallic green above and white below; the male has a brilliant, iridescent red throat. Immature males lack the red throat. The female is green above, with a white throat and breast, buff sides, and white-tipped outer tail feathers.

VOICE: Mouse-like, twittering squeaks.

NESTING: Lays 2 white eggs in a woven nest of plant down held together with spider silk and covered with lichens. Nest is saddled to the branch of a tree, usually in a forest clearing.

HABITAT: Suburban gardens, parks, and woodlands.

RANGE: The only hummingbird that breeds east of the Mississippi River. Breeds from southern Canada to Gulf Coast. Winters mainly in tropics, rarely on Gulf Coast.

SIMILAR SPECIES: The male of the closely related Black-chinned Hummingbird has a black-and-purple gorget, a more distinct white collar between the gorget and olive sides, and a less deeply forked tail. Female Black-chinned is not safely distinguished from a female Ruby-throat in the field. Rufous Hummingbird is the only other likely hummer in the East; it shows extensive rufous or deep buff in all plumages. Male Broad-tailed Hummingbird has a rosier gorget, rufous edges to the rectrices, and a loud, musical wing trill in flight.

CONSERVATION: Ruby-throated Hummingbirds are common and widespread, and the population is stable to increasing.

BLACK-CHINNED HUMMINGBIRD *Archilochus alexandri*

SUMMER ■ MIGRATION
WINTER ■ RARE
■ RESIDENT

The Black-chinned Hummingbird, the western counterpart of the Ruby-throated Hummingbird, commonly nests in the oak and riparian woodlands of canyons and lowlands. There, females build their nests in sycamores or other broadleaf trees. Flying males are often located by the dry buzz made by their wings; they can be observed in their woodland habitat, where they maintain a mating and feeding territory in spring. Courting males perform a dazzling, shallow-arc pendulum display. When mating interest wanes, the male often takes up residence elsewhere, near a good food supply. Later, when plant blooming and insect swarming subside, the birds move south.

DESCRIPTION: 3¼–3¾" (8–10 cm). A small hummingbird. Males have dark green upperparts and a black chin bordered below by an iridescent purple-violet band. This dark gorget, not elongated on the sides, is set off from the olive-tinged underparts by a distinct white collar. The dark tail is shallowly notched. Females are green above and whitish below, with an immaculate throat and a slight tinge of buff on the flanks. The bill is moderately long and slightly decurved. Both sexes show a small white spot behind the eye.

VOICE: A low *tup*.

NESTING: Lays 2 white eggs in a nest of fluffy plant wool and lichens woven together with spider webs, placed in a shrub or low tree.

HABITAT: Mountain and alpine meadows, woodlands, canyons with thickets, chaparral, and orchards.

RANGE: Breeds from British Columbia south throughout West to Mexico and central Texas. Winters in Mexico.

SIMILAR SPECIES: See Ruby-throated Hummingbird. In the East, females of the two species are not distinguishable in the field.

Female Anna's Hummingbird is slightly larger than the female Black-chinned; Anna's has grayer underparts and some red spotting on the throat.

Female Costa's Hummingbird is closely similar to the female Black-chinned but with a shorter bill, a thin whitish line behind the eye rather than a white spot, no buff on the flanks, and a different voice.

CONSERVATION:
Black-chinned Hummingbirds are common and widespread, and the population is stable to increasing. In the arid West, these birds depend on streamside habitats and disappear from areas in which these ecosystems are disturbed.

■ SUMMER   ■ MIGRATION
■ WINTER   ■ RARE
■ RESIDENT

A rare vagrant to southern Florida, although it is possible that a tiny bird like this is more frequent than is generally realized. In its native Bahamas, the Bahama Woodstar breeds year-round.

DESCRIPTION: The Bahama Woodstar is a small hummingbird, 3½" (9 cm) long, slightly smaller than a Ruby-throated. Both sexes are green above with a white chest and a cinnamon-colored belly (some green feathers on the belly). Breeding male has a brilliant purple chin and throat.

VOICE: Sharp chipping noises, *tit* or *tit-it*; a dry song, *pritithidee*.

NESTING: Lays 2 white eggs in a small, woven cup nest made of plant materials and down.

HABITAT: Found in all habitats on the Bahamas and nearby islands, which have comparatively little geographic diversity (notably very little elevation change).

RANGE: Bahamas and Turks and Caicos; it is a rare vagrant to south Florida.

SIMILAR SPECIES: The only hummingbird native to Florida, where the Bahama Woodstar is a vagrant, is the Ruby-throated, which has no cinnamon or orange on the belly. No other hummingbird reported from Florida combines green upperparts with a cinnamon or rufous belly.

CONSERVATION: Least concern in its native range in the Bahamas—the population appears to be stable.

ANNA'S HUMMINGBIRD   *Calypte anna*

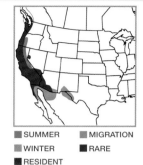

■ SUMMER   ■ MIGRATION
■ WINTER   ■ RARE
■ RESIDENT

Slightly larger than other West Coast hummingbirds, Anna's Hummingbird is an abundant resident of California parks, gardens, chaparral, and woodlands; it is the only hummer to remain commonly throughout most of the West Coast in winter. The rose iridescence on both the throat and the crown of the male is unique. Males are often spotted "singing" from a conspicuous perch or giving spectacular displays that combine a long, steep dive with a loud, explosive popping sound given at the bottom. Anna's and other hummingbirds vigorously defend their feeding territories which, although often as small as a few clumps of fuchsias, provide adequate nectar and small nectar-feeding insects. From July to late fall, however, transient and juvenile birds disregard territorial claims, and competition at feeders increases greatly.

DESCRIPTION: 3½–4" (9–10 cm). A medium-sized hummingbird. Both sexes are metallic green above; the male has a dark rose-red crown and gorget, and a grayish chest. The female has a spotted throat with a central patch of red spots, grayish-white underparts, and white-tipped outer tail feathers. The throats of juveniles are frequently unmarked.

VOICE: A sharp chip and a rapid *chee-chee-chee-chee-chee*.

NESTING: Lays 2 white eggs in a tiny woven cup of small twigs and lichen fastened onto a sheltered horizontal limb.

HABITAT: Chaparral, brushy oak woodlands, and gardens.

RANGE: Resident from northern California southward. Winters regularly from British Columbia south to Arizona.

SIMILAR SPECIES: No other hummer in North America shows rose-red on the crown.

Male Costa's has a blue-violet iridescence to the crown and to its elongated gorget. Female Black-chinned and Costa's are similar to a female Anna's but are slightly smaller and whiter below with unmarked or finely spotted throats. A juvenile Anna's with a plain throat closely resembles Black-chinned and Costa's hummingbirds, but is grayer below, is slightly larger, and has different calls.

See Rivoli's Hummingbird.

CONVSERVATION: Anna's Hummingbird has expanded its range north and east in recent decades and has adapted to suburban habitats and backyard feeders. It has become very common in its range and is of low conservation concern.

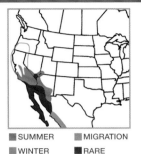

■ SUMMER ■ MIGRATION
■ WINTER ■ RARE
■ RESIDENT

Costa's Hummingbird is a small hummer of the southwestern deserts that frequents arid washes and hillsides, dry chaparral, and suburban areas where exotic plants have been introduced. Territorial males often perch conspicuously on the stalks of yucca, ocotillo, and other shrubs, displaying a distinctive violet-blue crown and elongated gorget. Like other hummingbirds, they feed on both insects and nectar. In southern and central California, Costa's feeds extensively on the red penstemon. Since this plant is found mainly in habitats where Costa's is the only resident hummingbird, these birds serve as a key pollinator for red penstemon.

DESCRIPTION: 3–3½" (8–9 cm). A tiny hummingbird. The male is green above and white below with an olive tinge to the sides. The crown and gorget of the male are iridescent violet to violet-blue; the gorget is greatly elongated on the sides. Females are gray-green on the upperparts and white on the underparts, including the unmarked throat. Females show a thin, white line behind the eye and white spots on the tail corners. The bill is relatively short in both sexes. Costa's preference for more arid terrain and its habit of soaring between flower clusters are helpful in identifying it.

VOICE: A light *chip* and high, tinkling notes.

NESTING: Lays 2 white eggs in a delicately woven cup, with leaves or lichens fastened to the outside, built low on a protected branch of a bush or small tree.

HABITAT: Low desert; in California, chaparral.

RANGE: Breeds from central California, southern Nevada, and southwestern Utah southward. It winters in southern California and Mexico.

SIMILAR SPECIES: See male Anna's and Lucifer hummingbirds. Female Anna's Hummingbird is larger than the female Costa's, with gray underparts and red spotting on the throat.

The male Costa's violet-purple crown and elongated gorget distinguish it from Black-chinned Hummingbird. The female Costa's Hummingbird is difficult to distinguish from a female Black-chinned except by their vocalizations. Female Black-chinned is slightly longer-billed than a female Costa's, with buff spot on the flanks.

CONSERVATION: Costa's Hummingbird is common in its range, and its population is stable or decreasing slightly. The species' biggest threat is the clearing of desert scrub habitat for development, although some Costa's Hummingbirds, their diets supplemented by hummingbird feeders, are adapting to life in suburban environments.

BUMBLEBEE HUMMINGBIRD *Atthis heloisa*

This very rare visitor to southern Arizona flies so much like an insect that larger hummingbirds seem to accept that it is one. Rather than establishing territories of its own, it forages in other hummers' territory, going unnoticed as an "insect."

DESCRIPTION: Among the smallest birds in the world measuring 2¾–3" (7–7.5 cm) long, the Bumblebee Hummingbird is more likely to be mistaken for a large insect than for another bird. It has a short tail and a delicate, short, straight bill. Its wings, back, and nape are green, sometimes with a bronze wash. Its underparts are whitish, with some chestnut on the flanks. The male has a brilliant pink to purple gorget.

VOICE: Gives a chipping call and a low song: *sssssssiu.*

HABITAT: Mid- to upper-elevation (5000–10,000 ft; 1500–3000 m) forest edges, clearings, and open woodlands.

RANGE: Mountains of central and southern Mexico.

SIMILAR SPECIES: Calliope Hummingbird is another very small hummingbird—it is much more common in North America and has a much wider, more northerly range. Use care when trying to positively identify a Bumblebee Hummingbird, as its presence in North America is an extreme rarity. Male Bumblebee Hummingbird's gorget is solid, not striped as in the Calliope. Females of the two species are not safely distinguishable in the field, but the female Bumblebee has buff tips to the outer tail feathers as opposed to whitish in the Calliope.

CONSERVATION: Least concern in its native range; its population appears to be stable.

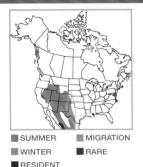

■ SUMMER ■ MIGRATION
■ WINTER ■ RARE
■ RESIDENT

A montane hummingbird of the Rockies and the Great Basin, this species occurs commonly around meadows and patches of flowers within pine, fir, and aspen forests. Male Broad-tailed Hummingbirds are easily recognized by the loud, musical, cricket-like trilling produced by their wings in flight. These males are the only western hummers with a green crown and rose gorget. Accounts of this species mention that it nests in the same tree or bush year after year—a phenomenon known as philopatry. It will return to the same branch and even build a new nest atop an old one.

DESCRIPTION: 4–4½" (10–11 cm). The male is metallic green above and mostly white below, with a bright rose-red gorget, a green crown, and a broad tail with little rufous. The female lacks the iridescent gorget and has a wash of rich buff on the sides, resembling female Rufous and Allen's hummingbirds, but has green central tail feathers; the outer tail feathers are rust-colored at the base, black in the middle, and white on the outer tips. The tail is relatively broad in both sexes.

VOICE: Call is a sharp *chick*. Adult males also make a cricket-like wing trill, except when in molt.

NESTING: Lays 2 white eggs in a woven cup nest of lichen and plant down.

HABITAT: Mountain meadows, pinyon-juniper woodlands, dry ponderosa pines, fir or mixed forests, and canyon vegetation.

RANGE: Breeds in the mountains from eastern California and northern Wyoming south through the Great Basin and Rocky Mountain states to southern Arizona and western Texas. Winters in Mexico.

SIMILAR SPECIES: Female Calliope Hummingbird is smaller and shorter-billed than the female Broad-tailed. Female and juvenile Rufous and Allen's hummingbirds are similar to corresponding Broad-taileds but smaller with a richer buff or rust wash on the sides, more extensive rufous in the tail, and a more golden-green (less emerald) sheen to the upperparts.

See Ruby-throated Hummingbird.

CONSERVATION: While showing a slow decline in some surveys in the past few decades, Broad-billed Hummingbirds remain widespread and common, with no specific conservation concerns.

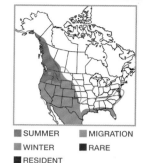

■ SUMMER   ■ MIGRATION
■ WINTER   ■ RARE
■ RESIDENT

This small, pugnacious western hummingbird differs from most other North American hummers in having extensively orange-rufous plumage. The buzzing of the males' wings may be heard in northwestern gardens, parks, and woodlands during the breeding season and through much of the Pacific lowlands in spring. Large numbers occur around mountain meadows during the southward migration. This species and Allen's are early migrants, moving north as early as February and south by August. In the East, Rufous Hummingbirds are known as a scarce migrant and winter visitor to the Gulf states, where these birds feed at hummingbird feeders and at hibiscus and salvia flowers, which often bloom all winter long; a few birds generally spend the winter, but may disappear abruptly when the first severe cold spell occurs.

DESCRIPTION: 3½–4" (9–10 cm). Adult males are almost entirely orange-rufous above and on the tail; they have an iridescent orange-red gorget (appearing golden-green in some light) and an extensive orange-rufous wash on the sides. The female is green above, with a rufous tinge on the rump and flanks, and much rufous in the tail. Females lack the iridescent gorget; instead they have small red to golden-green spots on the throat.

VOICE: An abrupt, high-pitched *zeee*; various thin squealing notes.

NESTING: Lays 2 white eggs in a lichen-covered cup of plant down and spider web attached to a horizontal branch.

HABITAT: Mountain meadows, forest edges; on migration and in winter, it frequents gardens with hummingbird feeding stations.

RANGE: Breeds from southeastern Alaska, British Columbia, southwestern Alberta, and western Montana south to Washington, Oregon, Idaho, and northern California. Winters mainly in Mexico. Occurs in small numbers along the Gulf Coast and occasionally farther inland in the Southeast during migration and in winter.

SIMILAR SPECIES: See female Calliope and Broad-tailed hummingbirds.

Allen's Hummingbird is almost identical in all corresponding plumages and should be identified with caution. The adult male Allen's Hummingbird has a green crown and back; the female and immature Allen's are not safely separable from Rufous in the field, but have narrower outer tail feathers.

Female Ruby-throated and Black-chinned are similar, but lack rufous on the rump and flanks.

CONSERVATION: NT

Although widespread and still common, the Rufous Hummingbird is listed as a Near Threatened species. Its numbers have declined across its range over many decades and continue to decrease. Habitat fragmentation and loss, altered bloom times of food sources due to climate change, and insecticides may all be playing a role in its decline.

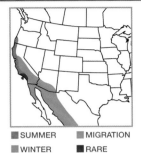

SUMMER ■ MIGRATION
WINTER ■ RARE
RESIDENT

This coastal hummingbird often nests in loose colonies and is quite aggressive in defending its nesting territory from other hummers. Territorial battles are most common in early morning, when intruders are more likely to appear. At this time of day, the birds tend to feed around the edges of their territories. Nearly identical to the Rufous Hummingbird in appearance and behavior, Allen's occurs in Pacific Coast parks and woods.

DESCRIPTION: 3–3½" (8–9 cm). A very small hummingbird. The male has an iridescent green crown and back, and a rufous rump and tail. Males have a bright, iridescent copper-red gorget (appears dark when not in direct sunlight), a white breast, and rufous sides. The female is bronze-green above, including the central tail feathers, with white-tipped rufous outer tail feathers, a flecked throat, and white underparts with a rust-colored tinge on the flanks. See Rufous Hummingbird.

VOICE: A low *chup*, and an excited *zeeee chuppity-chup*.

NESTING: Lays 2 white eggs in a tiny, tightly woven cup placed on a sheltered branch.

HABITAT: Coastal chaparral, brushland, and edges of redwood forests.

RANGE: Breeds along the Pacific Coast from southern Oregon to southern California. Resident in southern California. Also winters in Mexico.

SUBSPECIES: There are two subspecies of Allen's Hummingbird. The subspecies that makes up most of the population, *S. s. sasin*, is migratory and spends winters in Mexico. The other subspecies, *S. s. sedentarius*, consists of a nonmigratory population that resides in southern California year-round.

SIMILAR SPECIES: See Rufous Hummingbird; these two species are nearly identical and difficult to distinguish where their ranges overlap.

CONSERVATION: Although common in its range and listed as a species of least concern, Allen's Hummingbird numbers declined enough in some surveys in the late 20th century to put conservationists on alert. Non-migrating subspecies are increasing in winter counts, and it appears as though its decades-long decline may be slowing. Human development of this bird's coastal habitat is placing pressure on the species and forcing parts of the population to adapt to suburban environments. Hummingbird feeders and non-native flowering plants may be providing additional food sources to help offset some of the development pressure.

CALLIOPE HUMMINGBIRD *Selasphorus calliope*

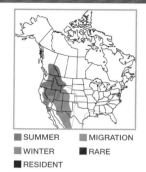

■ SUMMER ■ MIGRATION
■ WINTER ■ RARE
■ RESIDENT

The Calliope Hummingbird frequents meadows, riparian thickets, and other brushy areas within the coniferous forests of western mountains. Tiny even for a hummingbird, the Calliope is further distinguished by its relatively short bill; the male has a distinctive pattern of iridescent rays on the gorget. As in most hummers, this species' bill, forehead, and chin are often discolored by pollen.

DESCRIPTION: 2¾–3¼" (7–8 cm). The smallest North American hummingbird. The male is metallic green above and has a white gorget with purple-violet rays, which can be raised to give a whiskered effect. (All other North American hummers have solid-colored gorgets.) The female is green above and white below, with dark streaks on the throat, buffy flanks, and white-tipped tail corners. Female Calliope resembles the female Rufous Hummingbird, but smaller, with a smaller bill, paler flanks, and less rufous at the base of the tail.

VOICE: A high-pitched *tsew*.

NESTING: Lays 2 bean-sized white eggs—surprisingly large for such a tiny bird—in a small lichen-and-moss nest covered with cobwebs, placed on a limb of a bush or well-protected small tree.

HABITAT: Montane and subalpine forest clearings, brushy edges, and alpine meadows.

RANGE: Breeds in mountains from interior and southern coastal British Columbia south through the Pacific states and east to Colorado. Winters in Mexico.

SIMILAR SPECIES: Female and especially juvenile Rufous and Allen's hummingbirds closely resemble female Calliope, but are slightly larger and longer-billed, and show darker and more extensive buff on the sides and more rust in the rectrices. Female Broad-tailed is considerably larger and longer-billed.

CONSERVATION: ![LC]
Calliope Hummingbirds are fairly common and their populations appear stable, although they may be locally vulnerable to habitat loss.

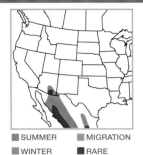

■ SUMMER   ■ MIGRATION
■ WINTER   ■ RARE
■ RESIDENT

The Broad-billed Hummingbird is said to be quieter and less active than most hummers, often sitting on a high perch for long periods. However, its flight is more irregular and jerky than that of others in the same habitat.

DESCRIPTION: 3¼–4" (8–10 cm). The male is dark green above and below, with a bright metallic-blue gorget (throat patch), and a bright red-orange bill with a black tip. The female's unmarked gray throat and underparts and red-orange bill distinguish it from other female hummers of the same size.

VOICE: A rapid, scratching *chi-dit*, like the note of a Ruby-crowned Kinglet.

NESTING: Lays 2 white eggs in a rough, loosely woven cup nest on a vertical branch of a streamside tree.

HABITAT: Desert canyons; mesquite and other thickets in arid country.

RANGE: Breeds in southern Arizona, southwestern New Mexico, and western Texas. Winters south of U.S.-Mexico border.

SIMILAR SPECIES: See White-eared Hummingbird.

CONSERVATION:
Broad-billed Hummingbirds are quite common in their limited range north of Mexico. Overall the species population appears to be stable to increasing.

BERYLLINE HUMMINGBIRD *Amazilia beryllina*

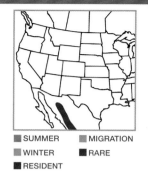

■ SUMMER ■ MIGRATION
■ WINTER ■ RARE
■ RESIDENT

The Berylline Hummingbird is among the rarer of southeastern Arizona's hummingbird strays, and is much sought after by visiting birders. Common and widespread in Mexico, the colorful strays are most likely to be seen in the United States in the summer at hummingbird feeders in wooded mountain canyons, such as Madera Canyon or in the Huachuca or Chiricahua mountains.

DESCRIPTION: 3½–4¼" (9.5–11 cm). Iridescent green above and below, with deep chestnut wings, tail, and rump. The belly is chestnut on males and grayish on females. Females and immature birds look like males, but tend to be duller, with more extensively gray underparts. The bill has a black tip, and the base of the lower mandible is red. Its relatively long wings occasionally beat with a discernible stroke. The tail is wide and slightly fan-shaped.

VOICE: Song a series of repeated buzzy twitters, *dzzzir* or *dzzzzrrt*.

NESTING: Lays 2 eggs in a nest of plant down and fibers, lichen and spider web, placed on a thin branch of a deciduous tree or shrub. It has bred and nested in southeastern Arizona during the summer rainy season; most nesting occurs in Mexico.

HABITAT: Oak and pine woodlands and edges, oak scrub and clearings, plantations; in the U.S., it uses forested canyons of desert mountains.

RANGE: Endemic of southern and western Mexican foothills and highlands; seen in southeastern Arizona as a stray, occasionally breeds.

SIMILAR SPECIES: Buff-bellied Hummingbird is pale buff rather than grayish below; its tail is noticeably forked.

CONSERVATION: This hummingbird is common in Mexico and considered a species of least concern, although its population trends are poorly understood.

■ SUMMER ■ MIGRATION
■ WINTER ■ RARE
■ RESIDENT

This mainly Mexican species may be found among dense tangled thickets and vines in light, open woodlands. It also feeds on flowers in gardens and suburban areas. It usually leaves the Rio Grande area in winter and retires southward into adjacent Mexico until the following spring. A few move north and east along the Gulf Coast each year and winter in coastal Texas or Louisiana.

DESCRIPTION: 4½" (11 cm). Green above with a glittering green throat, brown tail, and tawny or rich buff belly. Its bill is long and thin, and bright orange-red with a black tip. Unlike most other hummers north of Mexico, the sexes are alike in color.

VOICE: Shrill squeaks.

NESTING: Lays 2 white eggs in woven nest of plant fibers decorated with lichens, saddled to the limb of a tree or shrub.

HABITAT: Woodland borders and thickets.

RANGE: Breeds in the lower Rio Grande Valley of Texas. Rare in winter there and elsewhere along the Gulf Coast.

SIMILAR SPECIES: In Arizona, see Berylline Hummingbird.

CONSERVATION:
The Buff-bellied Hummingbird population appears to be stable to increasing. Land development along the Gulf Coast may reduce the availability of winter habitat.

VIOLET-CROWNED HUMMINGBIRD *Amazilia violiceps*

- ■ SUMMER ■ MIGRATION
- ■ WINTER ■ RARE
- ■ RESIDENT

Although rare in its very limited range in southeastern Arizona, the Violet-crowned Hummingbird is common in Mexico. It is a conspicuous bird and behaves aggressively toward other hummers.

DESCRIPTION: 3¾–4½" (10–11 cm). Sexes appear similar. This species is bronze above and white below, including the throat—no colorful gorget. The crown is violet-blue; its bill is red with a dark tip.

VOICE: A loud chatter.

NESTING: Lays 2 white eggs in a downy, lichen-covered nest on a horizontal branch.

HABITAT: Canyons and streamside growth.

RANGE: Breeds in southeastern Arizona and southwestern New Mexico. Winters in Mexico.

SIMILAR SPECIES: Unmistakable. Its violet-blue crown with immaculate white underparts and a bright red bill are unlike any other hummingbird in North America.

CONSERVATION: First recorded in the U.S. in 1959, the species has since become a regular visitor in southeastern Arizona. Its numbers and range seem to be gradually increasing, although overall population trends aren't fully understood.

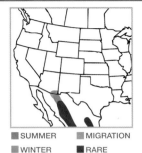

■ SUMMER ■ MIGRATION
■ WINTER ■ RARE
■ RESIDENT

This tiny hummingbird is a resident of middle- and high-elevation mountain forests in Mexico and Central America. It is an uncommon to rare visitor to the extreme southwestern United States. Individual strays irregularly appear in the canyons of southern Arizona and may stay for several weeks.

DESCRIPTION: 3½" (9 cm). A small hummingbird. Both sexes have a long, broad white stripe behind the eye and a red bill with dark tip. The male is green above and below, with a purple crown and iridescent blue-green chin; the female lacks the bright crown and chin and is whitish below with green spotting and barring on the throat and sides.

VOICE: Breeding male utters a long, monotonous clinking sound: *tink-tink-tink*.

NESTING: Lays 2 white eggs in a moss nest interwoven with needles, lichens, and twigs, placed in a small tree. Early in the year, male White-eared Hummingbirds establish individual feeding territories. As the breeding season approaches, several males gather in an area where they court vigorously. Females with a nest visit these groups and return to their nesting area with a male.

HABITAT: Mountain woodlands.

RANGE: Irregular summer visitor to extreme southeastern Arizona; rare in New Mexico and Texas.

SIMILAR SPECIES: Female Broad-billed is uniformly grayish on the underparts, with little or no green blotching and spotting; it has a whitish ear patch bordered below by a dark area, but it is much less extensive, less defined, and straighter (not sharply angled). Female Rivoli's Hummingbird is often confused with White-eared but is much larger, with a much longer, all-dark bill, and a poorly defined eyestripe. White-eared's call note is unique.

CONSERVATION: Widespread and common in Mexico, it is a species of least conservation concern. Although complete data on overall population trends is lacking, its numbers appear to be stable. This species is vulnerable to widespread clearing of high-mountain forests in Mexico.

XANTUS'S HUMMINGBIRD *Hylocharis xantusii*

Xantus's Hummingbird is endemic to southern Baja California. The fact that this species has been reported as a vagrant in southern California is perhaps unsurprising, given that it is native within a few hundred miles of the U.S.-Mexico border. The well-documented vagrant that spent the winter of 1997–1998 in southern British Columbia is much harder to explain, especially given that it was not sighted between Mexico and Canada.

DESCRIPTION: A small- to medium-sized hummingbird, 3¼–3¾" (8–9 cm) long. Both sexes have an orangish chest and belly, a green nape and back, purplish-brown wings, and a white stripe above and behind the eye. The male has a bluish-black head with a bright green throat, while the female has duller coloration around the head, with a chestnut throat and a mix of green and chestnut atop the head. The combination of the bold facial pattern and overall color scheme make Xantus's easy to distinguish from other hummingbirds.

VOICE: A low, fast rattle; also high chips, which seem to be a territorial warning.

NESTING: Nests only in Baja California.

HABITAT: In dry, semidesert forests and scrublands at a wide range of elevations. Often found near water and avoids the driest areas at low elevation. Uses human-created open woodlands such as orchards and irrigated shrubs.

RANGE: Fairly common in, and endemic to, southern Baja California.

SIMILAR SPECIES: Resembles the closely related White-eared Hummingbird. Location is usually enough to determine between the species, but in the case of out-of-range vagrants, Xantus's orange to cinnamon brown underparts help to distinguish it.

CONVERSATION: Classified as Least Concern by the IUCN Red List of Threatened Species despite its limited range. The populations in Baja are stable.

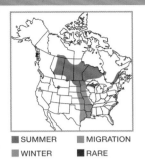

■ SUMMER ■ MIGRATION
■ WINTER ■ RARE
■ RESIDENT

Most rails live in dense marsh vegetation and are difficult to observe or even flush, but this tiny rail is especially secretive. Usually easy to hear but quite difficult to see, it is primarily active at night, when its rhythmic pattern of ticking notes can go on endlessly. It is seldom seen even by active and experienced bird-watchers. It can conceal itself in short grass and is seldom induced to fly, preferring to sneak mouse-like through the reeds. The best way to see one is to follow a mowing machine in a damp meadow in the Deep South during September or October. When the uncut grass is reduced to a small patch, one or more birds may flush into view, fly weakly away, and disappear into the nearest patch of tall grass. This species migrates through the interior of the continent at night, where it is rarely detected at stopovers.

DESCRIPTION: 6–8" (15–20 cm). A sparrow-sized rail, it is brownish buff, with a short yellow bill and yellow feet. Its white wing patches show in flight but are often only visible in good light.

VOICE: Makes 2 or 3 clicks, sounding like pebbles being tapped together, repeated in a long series. Usually heard at night.

NESTING: Lays 7–10 buff eggs, with a ring of dark spots around larger end, in a firm cup of grass well concealed in a grassy marsh. Little is known about this secretive bird's behavior, but it is known that incubation is done by the female alone, and that the female continues to add material to the nest until the eggs are hatched. The young—clad in black down like the young of other rails—leave the nest and follow the female about in search of food.

HABITAT: Grassy marshes and wet meadows.

RANGE: Breeds from northern Alberta east to Quebec and New Brunswick, and south to North Dakota, northern Michigan, and Maine. Winters from Carolinas south to Florida and along Gulf Coast; rarely in southern California.

SIMILAR SPECIES: Immature Sora is larger and darker, with a solid brown back and a white patch under the tail; it lacks a white wing patch.

CONSERVATION:
Officially a species of least concern, several states and provinces list the Yellow Rail as threatened or endangered locally. They can be surprisingly common in some locations, especially in wet years, only to disappear in drier years. Surveys of this secretive species involve a degree of uncertainty, but the population appears to be stable. The southern end of its breeding range may be shrinking, primarily due to habitat loss from development, changes to water levels, and invasive plant species.

BLACK RAIL *Laterallus jamaicensis*

■ SUMMER ■ MIGRATION
■ WINTER ■ RARE
■ RESIDENT

The Black Rail is a rare, little-known, and secretive wetland species. Its numbers are dwindling because of destruction of its habitat. The birds spend much of their time creeping about under mats of dead marsh grass or through thick stands of marsh plants such as salicornia. The best way to detect them is to enter a salt marsh after dark during the breeding season and listen for the male's high-pitched, piping call notes, which carry as far as a mile on a still night. These birds respond to an imitation of their call and may sometimes be lured within range of a flashlight—please observe the American Birding Association's Code of Birding Ethics when using audio lures.

DESCRIPTION: 5–6" (13–15 cm). A sparrow-sized, secretive rail. It is black with a rusty nape and white flecks on the back. It has red eyes, a black bill, and greenish legs and feet. It can be confused with the downy black young of larger rails.

VOICE: A piping *ki-ki-doo*, the last note lower in pitch.

NESTING: Lays 6–8 pale buff eggs, lightly spotted with brown, in a loose cup of grass, usually concealed under a mat of dead marsh vegetation.

HABITAT: Coastal salt marshes; more rarely, inland freshwater marshes.

RANGE: Breeds along the Pacific and Atlantic coasts from San Francisco Bay and Long Island southward, and locally in the midwestern interior and along the lower Colorado River. Winters north to the Gulf Coast and Florida and in its breeding range in the West.

SIMILAR SPECIES: Chicks of other rails have glossy black down, but lack bars on the flanks.

CONSERVATION:

The Black Rail is in decline; the North American Waterbird Conservation Plan lists the Black Rail as a Species of Highest Concern. Its population has decreased sharply in the upper Midwest, and it is considered Endangered in Arizona and Threatened in California. Loss of habitat to agriculture and aquaculture, invasive plant species, dams, and variable water levels from droughts and floods all threaten the wetlands where they breed.

Corn Crake sightings, never common in North America, almost entirely ceased as the breeding population in Western Europe declined precipitously in the 20th century. The Corn Crake was negatively affected by changes in agricultural practices in Western Europe, and was a focus of grassland habitat conservation efforts in its native range.

DESCRIPTION: A medium-sized rail (11–12", 27–30 cm), larger than a Virginia Rail but much smaller than a King Rail. It is primarily tan, brown, or chestnut above, with prominent dark spots on the wings and back. The breast and belly are brownish-orange with white scalloping. The face and throat are gray, with a brownish stripe through the eye and a pink to orange bill. The only native rail with a gray throat is the Sora, which has a bright yellow bill.

VOICE: An extremely unmusical, rasping *crex, crex*.

NESTING: Nests in Eurasia; does not nest in North America.

HABITAT: Unlike any North American rail, the Corn Crake is an upland bird, found in meadows and farm fields as well as brushy areas. It avoids the standing water and deep marshes that typify the habitat of our native rails. Their habitat is more similar to that of North American meadowlarks and bobolinks than to our rails.

RANGE: Breeds across northern and central Europe into western and central Asia. It winters in southeastern Africa. It is a very rare vagrant to the East Coast of North America.

CONSERVATION:
This species declined sharply in its breeding range in Europe and Asia in the late 20th century. The population has stabilized and may have begun to recover in recent decades. Accidental in North America.

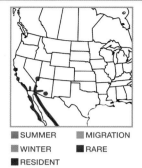

■ SUMMER ■ MIGRATION
■ WINTER ■ RARE
■ RESIDENT

Ridgway's Rail is quite similar to the eastern Clapper Rail, and until 2014 was considered the same species. These secretive birds are uncommon and extremely local in coastal California salt marshes and in freshwater marshes along the lower Colorado River. Its small numbers and limited habitat make this species a high conservation priority.

DESCRIPTION: 14–16" (36–41 cm). A long-billed, chicken-sized rail primarily of salt marshes. Like Clapper Rails, Ridgway's Rails have black-and-white barred flanks. They have rusty underparts similar to a King Rail. Unlike other rails in its range, it has a rusty orange face.

VOICE: Harsh clattering *kek-kek-kek-kek-kek*.

NESTING: Lays 9–12 buff eggs, spotted or blotched with brown, in a shallow saucer or deep bowl of dead marsh grasses, often domed.

HABITAT: Salt marshes and some freshwater marshes.

RANGE: Found year-round along the Pacific Coast from central California southward and around San Francisco Bay. Also found inland on the Salton Sea and lower Colorado River. It may be found upstream on the Colorado and on the Gila River, especially in summer.

SUBSPECIES: The species is further broken geographically into four subspecies.

SIMILAR SPECIES: Virginia Rail is much smaller, with strongly contrasting gray cheeks and a rust breast. See Black Rail.

CONSERVATION: NT

Near Threatened and decreasing. All three subspecies that occur in the United States are on the U.S. Endangered Species List. The nominate race along with the "Light-footed Rail" (*R. o. levipes*) are classified as endangered in California, and the "Yuma Rail" (*R. o. yumanensis*) is classified as endangered in both California and Arizona.

■ SUMMER   ■ MIGRATION
■ WINTER   ■ RARE
■ RESIDENT

The rattling call of the Clapper Rail is one of the most familiar sounds in the salt marshes in summer. Generally secretive, the birds are sometimes forced into view by high tides, when they may be seen along roads in the marsh or standing on floating boards. Otherwise they are most often glimpsed as they dart across tidal creeks between sheltering grasses. This species may be confused with the rustier King Rail when the latter enters the salt meadows for the winter.

DESCRIPTION: 14–16" (36–41 cm). A long-billed, chicken-sized rail of salt marshes. Clapper Rails have black-and-white barred flanks. East Coast populations are grayish brown without the rusty underparts of the similar King Rail. Birds on the Gulf Coast are rustier and more like the King Rail, but do not show rust on the shoulders or the sides of the face.

VOICE: Harsh clattering *kek-kek-kek-kek-kek*.

NESTING: Lays 9–12 buff eggs, spotted or blotched with brown, in a shallow saucer or deep bowl of dead marsh grasses, often domed.

HABITAT: Salt marshes.

RANGE: Breeds along the Atlantic Coast from Massachusetts southward and all along the Gulf Coast. Winters north to New Jersey, rarely farther north.

SUBSPECIES: The Atlantic subspecies is generally duller and grayer overall, making it easier to distinguish from other rails. The Gulf Coast subspecies is brighter and has more rusty tones, making it more likely to be confused with King or Virginia rails.

SIMILAR SPECIES: King Rail is larger and more richly colored, with rust-colored shoulders and cheeks; it is usually found in freshwater or brackish habitats. Virginia Rail is much smaller, with strongly contrasting gray cheeks and a rust breast. See Black Rail.

CONSERVATION: LC
Clapper Rails are common but secretive and difficult to survey accurately. They are believed to be decreasing due to habitat loss and degradation, but they remain fairly numerous and are listed as a species of Least Concern by the IUCN Red List.

KING RAIL *Rallus elegans*

SUMMER ■ MIGRATION
WINTER ■ RARE
■ RESIDENT

This large eastern rail is common in the larger freshwater marshes of the interior. Although difficult to see, it has a loud call that often reveals its presence. It occasionally hybridizes with the similar Clapper Rail where freshwater and salt marshes occur together; the two species are closely related, and differences between the two are subtle.

DESCRIPTION: 15–19" (38–48 cm). Similar to the Clapper Rail of salt marshes but its head, neck, shoulders, and underparts are rusty. Rust-colored shoulders and bright rust-colored breast help to distinguish it from similar rails. It lacks contrast between the cheek and the side of the neck. Its flanks are barred with black and white.

VOICE: A harsh, clattering *kek-kek-kek-kek-kek*, almost identical to that of Clapper Rail.

NESTING: Lays 8–11 buff eggs, spotted with brown, in a deep bowl of grass, often with surrounding marsh grass pulled down and woven into a dome.

HABITAT: Freshwater marshes and roadside ditches; wanders to salt marshes in fall and winter.

RANGE: Breeds from North Dakota east to Massachusetts, and south to Florida and Texas. Winters regularly along Gulf Coast, in Mississippi Valley, and rarely northward to southern New England.

SIMILAR SPECIES: See Clapper and Virginia rails. Virginia Rail is smaller, with a gray patch on the face.

CONCERVATION: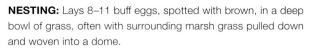

Once far more common throughout its range, King Rails have lost wetland habitat to development and agriculture-based run-off. The species is classified as Near Threatened and may still be declining, but some estimates suggest the population may have reached a smaller but stable equilibrium.

■ SUMMER ■ MIGRATION
■ WINTER ■ RARE
■ RESIDENT

This common but elusive marsh bird is most often detected by its call. Like other rails, the Virginia Rail prefers to escape intruders by running through protective marsh vegetation rather than by flying. When it does take wing, it often flies only a few yards before slipping back out of sight into the marsh. Despite its apparently weak flight, it migrates long distances each year and has been recorded as far out of its normal range as Bermuda and Greenland. Superficially, this species looks like a miniature version of a King Rail.

DESCRIPTION: 9–11" (23–28 cm). A small rail with a long reddish bill, a rusty breast, strongly barred black-and-white flanks, and a streaked olive back. Its gray face and cheeks contrast with its rusty-colored neck. The coloration of adults is similar to a King Rail, but Virginia Rail is much smaller. Young juveniles are black; late-summer young birds are similar to adults, but have blackish breasts and dark bills.

VOICE: A far-carrying *ticket, ticket, ticket, ticket*; various grunting notes.

NESTING: Lays 5–12 pale buff eggs, spotted with brown, in a shallow and loosely constructed saucer, often woven into surrounding marsh vegetation.

HABITAT: Freshwater and brackish marshes; may visit salt marshes in winter.

RANGE: Breeds from British Columbia east to Maritime Provinces and south to southern California, Oklahoma, and Virginia. Winters regularly on coasts north to Washington and Virginia, occasionally farther north.

SIMILAR SPECIES: Other small rails have short bills. The much larger King Rail has a dark bill and buff or rusty cheeks. Clapper Rail is larger and usually paler, with olive-brown shoulders.

CONSERVATION:  While populations have declined in some areas as marshes have been drained for development, these birds are still common throughout their range. Their overall population appears to be stable or possibly increasing, but their secretive nature makes getting an accurate count difficult.

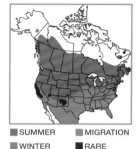

■ SUMMER ■ MIGRATION
■ WINTER ■ RARE
■ RESIDENT

The Sora is a common rail throughout its nesting area, its whinnying call familiar to anyone who has watched birds in a marsh. It is seldom seen, however, except by birders who wait patiently beside an opening in the reeds or who wade quietly through the cattails. These birds are especially numerous in fall and winter in southern marshes and rice fields, where they are primarily seed eaters.

DESCRIPTION: 8–10" (20–25 cm). A quail-sized rail with a short yellow bill, gray breast, and black face. It is a plump bird with heavily barred flanks. Its upperparts are mottled brown; its lower abdomen is banded with black and white. Young birds in fall lack the black face and have a buff breast.

VOICE: Its most familiar call is a musical series of piping notes rapidly descending the scale; also a repeated *ker-wee*, with rising inflection. Near the nest, birds utter an explosive *keek!* Startled birds may give a whinnying call.

NESTING: Lays 6–15 pale yellow-buff eggs, spotted with brown, in a cup of cattails and dead leaves, usually placed in a clump of reeds in an open part of the marsh.

HABITAT: Freshwater marshes and marshy ponds; rice fields and salt marshes in winter.

RANGE: Breeds from British Columbia east through Mackenzie to Maritime Provinces and south to Pennsylvania, Oklahoma, Arizona, and central California; winters mainly along coasts north to California and Virginia.

SIMILAR SPECIES: Yellow Rail is smaller and has a buff back streaked and checkered with dark markings; in flight, it shows white patches on the secondaries. Virginia Rail has brighter plumage and a long, thin bill.

CONSERVATION: LC

Sora are widespread and remain the most abundant rail species in North America despite pressure from hunting, habitat loss, and migration hazards. Sora hunting is still legal in most states and provinces, but the practice of hunting these elusive birds has become less popular. The greatest threat to the species is the destruction of the freshwater marshes where they breed: Sora have consequently become scarce in heavily populated areas.

■ SUMMER ■ MIGRATION
■ WINTER ■ RARE
■ RESIDENT

This colorful bird is often seen walking on lily pads, supporting its weight on its long toes, and may even sometimes be seen climbing up into low bushes in search of food. When walking or swimming, it constantly jerks its head and tail. Its flight is slow and weak, but this has not prevented individual birds from traveling far out of their normal range; they have turned up in California, southern Canada, Bermuda, and even South Africa. The Purple Gallinule associates freely with American Coots and Common Gallinules, but is more apt to stay in cover than these species.

DESCRIPTION: 11–13" (28–33 cm). A strikingly colored, chicken-sized marsh bird. It is purplish blue with green upperparts, white undertail coverts, yellowish-green legs, a red-and-yellow bill, and a light blue frontal shield on the face. Immatures are buff-brown, with greenish wings and a dark bill.

VOICE: Squawking and cackling; also guttural grunts.

NESTING: Lays 6–10 pinkish-buff eggs with fine dark spots in a nest of dead stems and leaves of water plants, placed on a floating tussock or in a clump of sawgrass or thicket over water.

HABITAT: Freshwater marshes with lily pads, pickerelweed, and other aquatic vegetation.

RANGE: Breeds from southern Texas, Arkansas, and Carolinas south to Florida and the Gulf Coast. Winters along the Gulf Coast in Texas, Louisiana, and Florida.

SIMILAR SPECIES: Adult and immature Common Gallinule have a brown back, white side stripes, greenish legs, and a black central division of the white undertail coverts. Immature American Coot has a grayish back, a white or grayish-white bill, gray legs, and a black central division of the white undertail coverts.

CONSERVATION:

Populations have declined significantly over the past 50 years, but these birds remain common in appropriate habitat. Hunting, wetland habitat loss, and changes in agricultural practices may threaten them in some areas. New rice cultivars, for example, are ready for harvest sooner, giving birds less time to raise their broods.

■ SUMMER ■ MIGRATION
■ WINTER ■ RARE
■ RESIDENT

Like coots, Common Gallinules are rails that often swim in open water, bobbing their heads as they cross a pond or pool. This bird owes its wide distribution to its choice of a common habitat and a varied diet. Almost any open water fringed by marsh plants will do, and these birds eat mosquitoes, spiders, tadpoles, insect larvae, fruits, and seeds. Their long toes enable them to swim in water or walk on floating marsh vegetation with equal ease. Males build several nests on the pair's territory; once the young have hatched and left their original nests to wander through the marsh, they use these extra nests as places to spend the night.

DESCRIPTION: 13" (33 cm). A duck-like swimming bird that constantly bobs its head while moving. The adult is slate-gray with a conspicuous red frontal shield on the face and a red bill with a yellow tip. It has a distinctive white stripe on the flanks and white undertail coverts. Young birds are similar but duller, with drab gray underparts, and without the colorful bill.

VOICE: Squawking and croaking notes similar to those of coots.

NESTING: Lays 7–14 cinnamon or buff eggs, lightly spotted with brown, on a shallow platform of dead cattails, rushes, and other marsh plants, usually a few inches above the water level.

HABITAT: Freshwater marshes and ponds with cattails and other aquatic vegetation.

RANGE: Breeds in California, Nevada, Arizona, and New Mexico, and from Minnesota east to New Brunswick and south to the Gulf Coast and Florida. Winters in California, Arizona, and along the Atlantic and Gulf coasts from Virginia to Texas. Also found in the American tropics and in the Old World.

SIMILAR SPECIES: A solitary Purple Gallinule may appear alongside a loose group of Common Gallinules; it has colorful purple, blue, and green plumage on the back and wings, and lacks the white stripe on the flank.

Common Gallinules often forage alongside larger flocks of American Coots, which have white bills and lack the white flank stripe.

CONSERVATION: LC

Common Gallinules are common and widespread. This adaptable species has maintained a more stable population than other members of this family in light of wetland habitat loss by using human-created marshy habitats such as rice fields and retention ponds.

- SUMMER
- MIGRATION
- WINTER
- RARE
- RESIDENT

Coots are the most aquatic members of their family, moving on open water like ducks and often feeding with them. Coots feed in many ways: by diving to the bottom, dabbling at the surface, grazing on land near shore, and stealing food from other diving birds. They are expert swimmers, propelled by wide lobes on their toes, but they are also heavy birds that must patter over the water before becoming airborne.

DESCRIPTION: 15" (38 cm). A dark gray, duck-like bird with a white bill and frontal shield; the frontal shield has a red swelling at the upper edge that's visible at close range. This bird's white undertail coverts appear as a small white patch on the tail while it's swimming or flying. Its legs range from greenish gray in juveniles to bright yellow in adults, and it has lobed toes. Immatures are similar but paler, with a duller bill and grayish underparts.

VOICE: A variety of clucks, cackles, grunts, and other harsh notes.

NESTING: Lays 8–10 pinkish eggs, spotted with brown, on a shallow platform of dead leaves and stems, usually on water but anchored to a clump of reeds.

HABITAT: Open ponds and marshes; in winter, also on coastal bays and inlets.

RANGE: Breeds from British Columbia, western Canada, and New York locally southward. Winters north to British Columbia, Kansas, Illinois, and Massachusetts. Also in the American tropics.

SIMILAR SPECIES: See Purple Gallinule and Common Gallinule. Of these species, American Coot is the most widespread and the most likely to congregate in large flocks. All three may be seen together in suitable ponds and marshes. Adult American Coots have a distinctive white bill.

CONSERVATION: LC
American Coots are widespread and common to abundant. The population is stable or slightly decreasing (especially in the East). American Coots are an indicator species that conservationists can use to monitor the health of aquatic ecosystems.

■ SUMMER ■ MIGRATION
■ WINTER ■ RARE
■ RESIDENT

Related to cranes and rails, the Limpkin is active mainly at night. For food, it depends chiefly on apple snails (*Pomacea* spp.) but also takes frogs, tadpoles, and aquatic insects. Its loud, strident, eerie call—familiar at night in the Florida marshes—sounds like a human in distress, so the Limpkin is known locally as the "Crying Bird."

DESCRIPTION: 25–28" (64–71 cm). A long-legged, long-necked, goose-sized marsh bird. It is grayish brown with white spots and streaks with a long, slender, slightly down-curved bill. In flight, its wings have a rapid upstroke and slower downstroke. It walks with a slow gait on long legs and large, webless feet.

VOICE: A loud, wailing *krrr-eeeow*, given primarily at night.

NESTING: Lays 5–8 buff eggs, with dark brown spots and blotches, in a shallow nest of marsh vegetation just above the water; more rarely in a stick nest in low trees or bushes.

HABITAT: Wooded swamps and marshes.

RANGE: Resident locally in southern Georgia and Florida. Also in American tropics.

SIMILAR SPECIES: Immature night-herons have much shorter legs and necks, and shorter, stouter, straight bills. Immature Glossy Ibis and White Ibis are slightly smaller, lack white spots and streaks in brown plumage, and have more strongly decurved bills.

CONSERVATION: LC
Uncommon and local. Although populations were hunted nearly to extinction by the early 20th century, legal protections and conservation efforts have helped the population to rebound and stabilize. Although much less abundant in Florida than it was historically, today Limpkin is no longer a species of high concern. Wetland restoration efforts in Florida stand to benefit this marsh- and swamp-dependent species.

■ SUMMER   ■ MIGRATION
■ WINTER   ■ RARE
■ RESIDENT

These cranes migrate in great flocks and assemble in vast numbers at places like the Platte River in Nebraska. Here it is possible to see what must have been a common sight when the species bred over most of the interior United States. The mating dance of the Sandhill Crane is spectacular. Facing each other, members of a pair leap into the air with wings extended and feet thrown forward. Then they bow to each other and repeat the performance, uttering loud croaking calls. Courting birds also run about with their wings outstretched and toss tufts of grass in the air.

DESCRIPTION: A tall bird, 34–48" (86–122 cm) long with a 6'8" (2 m) wingspan, with a long neck and long legs. It is largely gray with a red forehead; immatures are browner with no red on the head. Its plumage often appears rusty because of iron stains from the water of tundra ponds.

VOICE: A loud rattling *kar-r-r-r-o-o-o*.

NESTING: Lays 2 buff eggs, spotted with brown, in a large mound of grass and aquatic plants in an undisturbed marsh.

HABITAT: Large freshwater marshes, prairie ponds, and marshy tundra; also on prairies and grainfields during migration and in winter.

RANGE: Breeds from Siberia and Alaska east across Arctic Canada to Hudson Bay and south to western Ontario, with isolated populations in Rocky Mountains, northern prairies, and Great Lakes region, and in Mississippi, Georgia, and Florida. Winters in California's Central Valley, and across southern states from Arizona to Florida. Also found in Cuba.

SUBSPECIES: Several subspecies vary in size and migratory habits. The southernmost subspecies, Greater Sandhill Crane (*A. c. tabida*) is the largest, and the northernmost (nominate) subspecies is the smallest. The Greater and Lesser subspecies are migratory; other subspecies are resident within restricted ranges in Mississippi, Florida, and Cuba.

SIMILAR SPECIES: See Whooping Crane. Distinguished from Great Blue Heron by neck shape and voice; Sandhill Cranes also forage in large flocks, whereas Great Blue Herons tend to be solitary except when roosting or in migration.

CONSERVATION: Sandhill Cranes generally are numerous, and their numbers are stable. Protection of their habitat at key migratory stopover sites is critical to the continued survival of the migratory populations. The Mississippi Sandhill Crane (*A. c. pulla*), a localized subspecies, is on the U.S. Endangered Species List; it is classified as endangered in Mississippi.

This is the most common crane across Europe and Asia, but is strictly a vagrant in North America, seen among flocks of native Sandhill Cranes. Ecologically, it is the Old World equivalent of our Sandhill Crane. It is a rare visitor, with only about one record occurring in North America per year. It is most often found amid a migrating flock of Sandhill Cranes on the Great Plains.

DESCRIPTION: A huge wading bird the size of a Sandhill Crane or a Great Blue Heron, 43" (115 cm) long. It is primarily gray, with a black throat and head, a red cap, and a white stripe running from directly behind the eye down the nape of the neck.

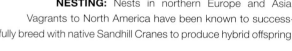

VOICE: Loud, trumpeting call similar to a Sandhill Crane.

NESTING: Nests in northern Europe and Asia. Vagrants to North America have been known to successfully breed with native Sandhill Cranes to produce hybrid offspring.

HABITAT: Breeds in shallow wetland areas, especially with open ponds or small lakes. Needs nest sites inaccessible to land-based predators. Winters feeding in agricultural fields, roosting in shallow waters nearby.

RANGE: Breeds across northern Europe and Asia, from Scandinavia to Siberia. Winters in southern Europe, southern Asia, and North Africa.

SIMILAR SPECIES: There are only three other wading birds of similar size in North America, and all are easily distinguished. The Great Blue Heron is also mainly gray, but has white markings on top of the head and behind the bill, and a black stripe above and behind the eye. The heron's throat is gray, whereas the Common Crane's is black. A vagrant Common Crane is likely to be seen interspersed with a flock of native Sandhill Cranes, which are almost entirely gray, lacking the black markings of the Common Crane. Finally, the Whooping Crane is primarily bright white.

CONSERVATION: Overall the Common Crane population is large and increasing in its native range. It has been extirpated from a number of locations within its historic range due to human encroachment.

■ SUMMER   ■ MIGRATION
■ WINTER   ■ RARE
■ RESIDENT

One of our most spectacular birds, the Whooping Crane stands nearly 5 feet (1.5 meters) tall and has a wingspan of more than 7 feet (2.1 meters). The only self-sustaining wild population of this magnificent bird is a single flock of around 300 individuals that migrates between Canada's Wood Buffalo National Park and Aransas National Wildlife Refuge in Texas. It nests in impenetrable muskeg wilderness and winters in salt marshes, traveling 2500 miles (4000 km) each way between its nesting and wintering grounds. Smaller populations have been reintroduced from captive-bred birds.

DESCRIPTION: North America's tallest bird at 45–50" (1.1–1.3 m) long with a 7'6" (2.3 m) wingspan. A distinctive large crane, pure white with black wing tips, with red on the forehead and cheeks. Young birds are similar but strongly tinged with brown.

VOICE: A trumpet-like call that can be heard for several miles.

NESTING: Lays 2 buff eggs, blotched with brown, on a mound of marsh vegetation.

HABITAT: Breeds in northern freshwater bogs; winters on coastal prairies.

RANGE: Breeds in Wood Buffalo National Park in northeastern Alberta. Winters on the Gulf Coast of Texas at Aransas National Wildlife Refuge. A few winter at Bosque del Apache National Wildlife Refuge in New Mexico. An eastern migratory population, which migrates between Wisconsin and Florida, has been reestablished. Small resident populations have been reintroduced in Florida and Louisiana.

SIMILAR SPECIES: Sandhill Crane has a similar flight profile, with neck and legs fully extended; however, a gray Sandhill is easily distinguished from a white Whooper in good light.

CONSERVATION: **EN**

The Whooping Crane is on the U.S. Endangered Species List and was nearly brought to extinction by the 1940s due to agriculture and hunting. Today the threats to these birds include collisions with utility lines, severe weather and contaminant spills on the Gulf Coast, and occasional shooting by hunters mistaking them for Sandhill Cranes. The total wild population is estimated at less than 500 individuals. Numbers are increasing moderately with intensive conservation efforts since the late 20th century. Nonmigratory flocks reintroduced in the 1990s into Florida and Louisiana are sustained using captive-bred birds, but hold promise of becoming self-sustaining. It appears as though Whooping Cranes learn their migration paths by following those of previous generations, so these reintroduced populations do not migrate. More recently, conservationists have successfully reintroduced a migratory population in the eastern United States. This involved releasing captive-bred chicks into Wisconsin and teaching the first-generation birds a migration path to Florida following an ultralight aircraft.

BLACK-NECKED STILT *Himantopus mexicanus*

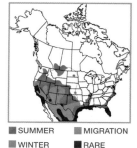

■ SUMMER   ■ MIGRATION
■ WINTER   ■ RARE
■ RESIDENT

Noisy and conspicuous, Black-necked Stilts are lanky wading birds of shallow wetlands. Their long and thin legs, wings, and bills give them a "delicate" appearance. In the nesting season, they are particularly aggressive and will often fly low over an intruder—their long red legs trailing behind them—uttering a sharp alarm call.

DESCRIPTION: 13–16" (33–41 cm). A slender, long-legged shorebird. It is black above and white below, and its head is patterned in black and white. It has a long neck and its bill is long and thin. Its pink-red legs are quite long and slender. The female has a brown back.

VOICE: A sharp *kip-kip-kip-kip*.

NESTING: Lays 3 or 4 buff eggs, spotted with brown, in a shallow depression lined with grass or shell fragments in a marsh. Nests in loose colonies.

HABITAT: Salt marshes, shallow coastal bays, and freshwater marshes.

RANGE: Breeds along coasts from Oregon and Delaware southward, and locally in western interior states east to Idaho, Kansas, and Texas. Winters along Pacific Coast north to central California; also in Florida and other Gulf Coast states.

SUBSPECIES: Some sources consider this bird a subspecies of the widespread Black-winged Stilt (*Himantopus himantopus*) found in Eurasia and Africa, but official checklists in North America designate the Black-necked Stilt as its own full species. A distinctive endemic Hawaiian subspecies is known as the Hawaiian Stilt (*H. m. knudseni*) or the Ae'o in the Hawaiian language.

SIMILAR SPECIES: American Avocet is somewhat larger with a long, upturned bill and pale bluish-gray legs. American Avocets have a white patch on the wing compared to the solid black wings of the Black-necked Stilt. Breeding adult avocets have a rusty-brown head and neck.

CONSERVATION: LC

Black-necked Stilts have declined from their historic numbers due to hunting and habitat destruction, but today they are a species of least concern. The species' population is increasing and its breeding range is expanding farther north. The Hawaiian Stilt subspecies (*H. m. knudseni*) is federally endangered due mainly to invasive predators.

■ SUMMER ■ MIGRATION
■ WINTER ■ RARE
■ RESIDENT

Avocets feed much like spoonbills, sweeping their bills from side to side along the surface of the water to pick up crustaceans, aquatic insects, and floating seeds. They often feed in flocks of several dozen individuals, a line of birds advancing abreast, sometimes entirely submerging their heads as they sweep the water for food. During their southward migration every fall, an increasing number of American Avocets stray eastward to the Atlantic Coast, where migrants or wintering birds may be seen singly or in small flocks on shallow lagoons and coastal ponds.

DESCRIPTION: 16–20" (41–51 cm). A large, long-legged shorebird with a slender, upturned bill. Its upperparts and wings are patterned in black and white, and its underparts are white. Its long legs are a pale blue or bluish-gray. The head and neck of breeding adults are rust-colored in summer, and white in winter.

VOICE: A loud, repeated *wheep*.

NESTING: Lays 4 olive-buff eggs, spotted with brown and black, in a shallow depression sparsely lined with grass on a beach or mudflat. Often nests in loose colonies.

HABITAT: Freshwater marshes and shallow marshy lakes; breeds locally in salt or brackish marshes. Many move to the coasts in winter.

RANGE: Breeds from interior Washington, Saskatchewan, and Minnesota south to California and Texas. Winters on the West Coast north to California, on the Gulf Coast, and in Florida. An increasingly regular visitor on the Atlantic Coast in fall and winter.

SIMILAR SPECIES: In distant flight, American Avocets may be confused with Willet or winter Hudsonian and Black-tailed godwits, but these lack black stripes down the back and across the inner wing; Black-tailed Godwits are extremely rare in the range of American Avocet. Both godwits have a black tail band, and Hudsonian Godwit has black wing linings.

CONSERVATION:

American Avocet is common and its populations are stable, with more avocets occurring in the East in recent decades as migrants and wintering birds. In the 19th and 20th centuries, small breeding populations have occurred along the Atlantic Coast as far north as southern New Jersey, but hunting and the degradation and draining of wetlands caused them to largely disappear as breeders in the East. It is a species of least concern, although it is vulnerable to the loss of healthy wetlands, especially in its remaining breeding range in the West.

AMERICAN OYSTERCATCHER *Haematopus palliatus*

■ SUMMER ■ MIGRATION
■ WINTER ■ RARE
■ RESIDENT

American Oystercatchers are large, conspicuous shorebirds seen on Atlantic and Gulf Coast beaches. Oystercatchers insert their long, blade-like bills into mussels and other bivalves, severing the powerful adductor muscles before the shells can close. They also feed on barnacles and snails. Although they do not breed in colonies, these birds gather in large flocks during migration and in winter.

DESCRIPTION: 17–21" (43–53 cm). A large, stocky shorebird, boldly patterned in blackish brown and white. Its bill is long and red; its legs and feet are pink. It shows a bold white wing patch in flight.

VOICE: A piercing *kleep!* and a plover-like *cle-ar*.

NESTING: Lays 2–4 buff eggs, sparsely marked with brown, in a shallow depression lined with shell fragments.

HABITAT: Sandy and pebbly beaches, mudflats, and borders of salt marshes.

RANGE: Breeds along coasts from Baja California and New England southward. Winters from New Jersey southward.

SUBSPECIES: The West Mexican subspecies of Baja California—a casual stray up the Pacific Coast to southern California—shows less white on the wings and tail.

SIMILAR SPECIES: Black Oystercatcher has entirely dark plumage.

CONSERVATION: LC

These oystercatchers were hunted to near-extinction along the Atlantic Coast in the 19th century, but given legal protection in the 20th century, they have once again become numerous and now nest in numbers as far north as New England and Cape Sable Island, Nova Scotia. Restricted to specific intertidal and coastal beach habitats, the species has adjusted to the influx of human beachgoers by beginning to use dredge spoil islands for nesting. Never a particularly numerous species, today the population appears stable.

■ SUMMER ■ MIGRATION
■ WINTER ■ RARE
■ RESIDENT

The Black Oystercatcher is a widespread species found along the length of the Pacific Coast. It is only rarely found on sandy beaches—the normal habitat of the American Oystercatcher—and instead favors rocky coasts. It can be hard to see against a background of wet, seaweed-encrusted rocks and usually forages alone or in small groups. It feeds on a variety of marine life, specializing in creatures that cling to rocks below the high-tide line.

DESCRIPTION: 17–17½" (43–44 cm). A large, stocky shorebird, Black Oystercatcher is dark brownish-black, without a white wing stripe. Its bill is long, stout, and bright orange-red. Its stocky legs and feet are dull pink, and its eyes are yellow. Juveniles are somewhat browner than adults and have dusky bills that are orange at the base.

VOICE: A whistled *wheeee-whee-whee-whee*.

NESTING: Lays 2 or 3 olive-buff eggs, with brownish-black blotches, among pebbles in a shallow rocky depression or in a hollow on a beach.

HABITAT: Rocky seacoasts.

RANGE: Resident from Aleutian Islands southward along Pacific Coast to Baja California.

SIMILAR SPECIES: American Oystercatcher occurs in Baja California and casually north to southern California; it has white underparts and a broad white wing stripe; it prefers sandy beaches. Other rock-inhabiting shorebirds are much smaller, have paler upperparts and light underparts, and most have conspicuous wing stripes or a white rump.

CONSERVATION: Although widespread along the Pacific Coast and locally common, this species is particularly sensitive to oil spills and other pollution, and to nest site disturbance. Its small global population size and restricted habitat make it a priority species that conservationists monitor closely.

NORTHERN LAPWING *Vanellus vanellus*

■ SUMMER ■ MIGRATION
■ WINTER ■ RARE
■ RESIDENT

This widespread Old World plover is best known in North America as a late fall and winter stray following severe storms originating in the eastern Atlantic Ocean, although there are records for other times of the year as well. Presumably lapwings are wind-assisted to eastern Canada and the northeastern United States during such events. Usually only a single stray occurs, but occasionally small groups of lapwings find themselves on our continent following a major winter storm. The species has also occurred in Bermuda, the Bahamas, Puerto Rico, and Barbados.

DESCRIPTION: 12" (30.5 cm). A large, upland shorebird. Its upperparts are dark and glossed with greenish; its underparts are white with a broad black breast band. Its head has a black crown and long, wispy crest. In flight, it has broad rounded wings with white tips and wing linings.

VOICE: Flight note is a thin, whistled *pee-wit*.

NESTING: Lays 4 pale brown eggs blotched with black in a grass-lined scrape on the ground in a pasture or wet meadow.

HABITAT: Open fields, pastures, and grassy banks of ponds and lakes; also cultivated fields, seacoasts, and mudflats during migration and winter.

RANGE: Widespread breeder in Eurasia. Winters from British Isles west across Europe to Japan, south to northern Africa, Southeast Asia, and Formosa. Casual to accidental in North America.

SIMILAR SPECIES: Unmistakable for any North American plover.

CONSERVATION: NT
Although still numerous in its native range, Northern Lapwings are classified as Near Threatened and decreasing at a concerning rate. The decline is mainly driven by changes in land use and by intensive agriculture.

■ SUMMER ■ MIGRATION
■ WINTER ■ RARE
■ RESIDENT

Most of us see the Black-bellied Plover during the winter or in migration, when it may lack its bold black underparts but is nonetheless conspicuous among its usual companions—the smaller plovers, turnstones, and sandpipers. It is one of the shyer species, usually the first to take flight when a flock of shorebirds is approached. When disturbed, it commonly flies out over water, circles, and lands again behind the observer. It is one of the familiar winter shorebirds along the Atlantic Coast, and a few—mostly fledged the previous summer—spend the summer south of the breeding range. Its principal foods are small crabs and sandworms. Its plaintive call is a characteristic winter sound on mudflats and beaches.

DESCRIPTION: 10–13" (25–33 cm). A quail-sized plover. Breeding adults are gray with flecks of light and dark above, black on the face and breast, and white on the belly. Winter adults are similar, but the face and breast are white like the belly. Young birds have upperparts flecked with yellow, and a breast and belly that are finely streaked. In all plumages, Black-bellied Plovers have a bold white wing stripe, a white rump, and a black patch under the wing.

VOICE: A clear whistled *pee-a-wee*.

NESTING: Lays 3 or 4 buff eggs, spotted with brown, in a shallow depression lined with moss, lichens, and grass.

HABITAT: Breeds on tundra; winters on beaches, mudflats, and coastal marshes, less commonly on inland marshes, lakeshores, and plowed fields.

RANGE: Breeds in northwestern Alaska and Arctic Canada. Winters mainly along the coasts from British Columbia and Massachusetts southward. Also found in Eurasia, where it is commonly called Grey Plover.

SIMILAR SPECIES: Nonbreeding American and Pacific golden-plovers show more contrast between their pale eyebrows and dark crowns, and have proportionately smaller bills; in breeding plumage, both golden-plovers have black underparts extending to the tail, with their upperparts spotted with golden-yellow. In flight, the golden-plovers show only a faint white wing stripe, pale axillaries, and dark rump; Black-bellied Plover has a prominent white wing stripe, black axillaries, and a white rump.

Nonbreeding Red Knot is smaller, with a proportionately longer and more slender bill, and uniform grayish upperparts. It holds its body more horizontally, not in the erect posture typical of plovers.

CONSERVATION:
Little is known about the population trends for this species, but its numbers appear to be stable. Its remote high-Arctic breeding territory makes getting accurate counts difficult.

■ SUMMER ■ MIGRATION
■ WINTER ■ RARE
■ RESIDENT

The American Golden-Plover annually performs one of the longest migrations of any North American bird. In late summer, birds from the Arctic gather in eastern Canada, where they fatten on insects, crowberries, and other small fruits before beginning their nonstop flight over the Atlantic Ocean to the northern coast of South America—a journey of some 2500 miles (4000 kilometers). Smaller numbers move southward in the fall across the Great Plains. Once in South America, they make another long flight across the vast Amazon Basin, finally arriving at their principal wintering grounds on the pampas of central Argentina and in Patagonia and Tierra del Fuego. Historically these birds gathered there in enormous numbers, but heavy hunting in both North and South America during the 19th century took a serious toll from which the species has not fully recovered. In spring, the birds return to the Arctic, moving north by way of the Great Plains.

DESCRIPTION: 9–11" (23–28 cm). A quail-sized plover. In breeding plumage, it is dull golden-brown above, with black throat, breast, flanks, belly, and undertail coverts. A bold white stripe runs from the forehead, over the eye, and down the side of the neck and breast. In winter, it has a bold whitish eyebrow and grayish-white underparts. It lacks the white wing stripe, white rump, and black patch under the wing of the larger and paler Black-bellied Plover. See Pacific Golden-Plover.

VOICE: A mellow *quee-lee-la*.

NESTING: Lays 3 or 4 buff eggs spotted with brown in a shallow depression lined with reindeer moss, usually on a ridge or other elevated spot in the tundra.

HABITAT: Breeds on tundra; during migration found on coastal beaches and mudflats, and inland on prairies and plowed fields.

RANGE: Breeds from Alaska east to Baffin Island. In migration, most birds travel south over the Atlantic Ocean from the Canadian Maritimes to South America and return northward in spring over the Great Plains, but some winter on islands in the Pacific and appear along the West Coast during migration.

SIMILAR SPECIES: Pacific Golden-Plover is nearly identical, but has slightly more yellow in its plumage and larger spots. In breeding plumage, Pacific Golden-Plover has white on the flanks and undertail coverts.

Black-bellied Plover is larger and paler, with a prominent white wing stripe, white rump, and a black patch under the wing.

CONSERVATION: LC
Widespread overhunting in the 19th century significantly reduced the population of American Golden-Plovers. The population rebounded somewhat after market hunting ceased, but the species today is declining slowly once again due to habitat loss, especially in this bird's South American wintering range.

- ■ SUMMER
- ■ WINTER
- ■ RESIDENT
- ■ MIGRATION
- ■ RARE

The Pacific Golden-Plover is a long-distance migrant like the American Golden-Plover. Although some winter along the California coast, most migrate to islands in the South Pacific. The two birds were considered races of a single species until 1993, however they do not interbreed even where their breeding ranges overlap in western Alaska. It is easy to see why these species were combined for so long—they share similar habits and habitats and can be difficult to distinguish visually when they occur together.

DESCRIPTION: 9–11" (23–28 cm). A quail-sized plover. It is similar to American Golden-Plover but more slender. In breeding plumage, it has a narrow white stripe along the flanks and mottled black and white undertail coverts (American usually has all-black flanks and mainly black undertail coverts). In winter plumage, it has a buff (not white) eyebrow, warmer brown upperparts, and yellow-buff (not grayish) underparts. Juveniles are similar to American Golden-Plovers but buffier, with buff eyebrows.

VOICE: A mellow *quee-lee-lee*.

NESTING: Lays 3 or 4 buff eggs, spotted with brown, in a shallow depression lined with reindeer moss, usually on a ridge or other elevated spot in the tundra.

HABITAT: Breeds on tundra; in migration, it is found on coastal beaches and mudflats.

RANGE: Breeds along the coast of the Bering Sea in Alaska. Winters locally along the Pacific Coast; most winter on islands in the Pacific, with some continuing to Australia and New Zealand. Also occurs in Asia.

SIMILAR SPECIES: Almost identical to American Golden-Plover. American Golden-Plovers tend more toward gray coloration, especially in nonbreeding adults and juveniles. In breeding plumage, American Golden-Plover is more solidly black underneath, with much less white on the flanks and black undertail coverts. In flight, American Golden-Plovers show a dark tail and rump and a gray underwing.

CONSERVATION: Pacific Golden-Plover is a species of least concern, although its wintering grounds on Pacific islands may be threatened by rising sea levels caused by climate change. Its population trends are not well studied, but it is thought to be decreasing.

EURASIAN DOTTEREL *Charadrius morinellus*

■ SUMMER ■ MIGRATION
■ WINTER ■ RARE
■ RESIDENT

The Eurasian Dotterel, a familiar bird in northern Europe, is only a rarity in Alaska. This tundra-dwelling bird has nested a few times in western Alaska, and strays occur rarely along the Pacific Coast in fall. It usually occurs in North America singly or in pairs.

DESCRIPTION: 8–9" (20–23 cm). A chunky Arctic plover. The breeding adult is brown above, with a bold white eyebrow, a white band across the breast, and a russet breast. Winter adults and immatures are duller, with buff eyebrows and a vague breast band.

VOICE: A soft *pip-pip* or *pip-pip-pip*.

NESTING: Lays 2 or 3 buff, yellowish, or greenish eggs, spotted with blackish-brown, in a shallow depression in tundra vegetation.

HABITAT: Alpine tundra.

RANGE: Breeds in northwestern Alaska on Seward Peninsula and on nearby Saint Lawrence Island. Winters in Old World. Also in Eurasia.

SIMILAR SPECIES: Juvenile Pacfic Golden-Plover has less distinct eyestripes that do not meet at the nape, and lacks a breast band; the tips as well as the sides of all its tail feathers are marked in beige. It also has a different calls.

CONSERVATION: ![LC]
Least concern in its native range, although its numbers are decreasing in parts of its range, especially in Europe.

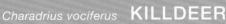

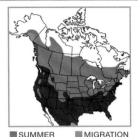

■ SUMMER ■ MIGRATION
■ WINTER ■ RARE
■ RESIDENT

This noisy plover is probably our best-known shorebird. Few golf courses or extensive vacant lots are without their breeding pair of Killdeer. Because of their abundance and proximity to people, Killdeer are notorious for fooling humans with their "broken wing" display. Near a nest, a Killdeer may meet an intruder with a conspicuous distraction display, fluttering and dragging itself as though seriously injured, often hopping on one foot, bending a wing as though it's broken, and fanning its rusty tail. This feigning of injury is often effective in luring predators away from eggs or young, at which point the parent bird "recovers" and flies off, calling loudly.

DESCRIPTION: 9–11" (23–28 cm). Our largest "ringed" plover, it is brown above and white below, with two black bands across the breast. It has long legs and a relatively long tail. In flight, it shows rusty uppertail coverts and rump.

VOICE: A shrill *kill-deee*, *fill-deee* or *killdeer, killdeer*. Also *dee-dee-dee*.

NESTING: Lays 4 pale buff eggs, spotted with blackish brown, in a shallow depression lined with grass on bare ground.

HABITAT: Open country including plowed fields, golf courses, and short-grass prairies.

RANGE: Breeds from Alaska east across continent to Newfoundland and southward. Winters north to British Columbia, Utah, Ohio Valley, and Massachusetts. Also in South America.

SIMILAR SPECIES: Wilson's Plover is smaller; it has a proportionately longer, heavier bill and one broad breast band. Its short white eyebrow extends back from the forehead. See Semipalmated Plover.

CONSERVATION:  Although Killdeer populations have decreased, they remain widespread and abundant throughout their range. These birds seem adaptable to human-modified habitats, often found on open ground ranging from golf courses to pastures.

COMMON RINGED PLOVER *Charadrius hiaticula*

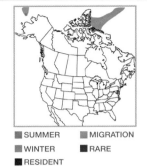

■ SUMMER ■ MIGRATION
■ WINTER ■ RARE
■ RESIDENT

The Common Ringed Plover is widespread across Europe, Asia, and Africa, and its range wraps around the globe to the western tip of Alaska and the eastern high-Arctic Canadian islands. In the Old World, this species fills the ecological niche that its close cousin, the Semipalmated Plover, holds across most of North America. The Common Ringed Plover is one of the most difficult shorebirds to identify in North America, even in regions where it is known to occur regularly. Were it not for the species' distinctive call notes, undoubtedly many individuals would go unnoticed, mistaken for its widespread and common cousins.

DESCRIPTION: 7" (19 cm). Nearly identical to the Semipalmated Plover. Black breast band usually wider in center; white eyebrow often more extensive, especially in male; bill slightly longer; webbing between toes less extensive.

VOICE: A soft, 2-syllable *too-ip* or *too-eep* with slightly rising inflection.

NESTING: Lays 4 buff eggs, spotted with brown or black, placed in a scrape lined with shell fragments, small stones, and bits of driftwood, usually on the sand of a beach above the high-water mark.

HABITAT: Breeds on sandy areas or grassy tundra with scattered low vegetation; in migration and winter occurs on mudflats, beaches, and shores of lakes, ponds, and rivers.

RANGE: Breeds in Bering Strait area, rarely in western Alaska, and islands in eastern Canadian Arctic; also in northern Eurasia. Winters in the Old World.

SIMILAR SPECIES: Nearly identical to Semipalmated Plover, from which it is best distinguished by call.

CONSERVATION: **LC**
Common Ringed Plover is a globally widespread species of low concern, although its population trends show a slow decline.

■ SUMMER   ■ MIGRATION
■ WINTER   ■ RARE
■ RESIDENT

Semipalmated Plovers are usually the most common plovers seen in migration in North America. Like other plovers, the Semipalmated forages in short bursts—a quick run followed by a stop—during which it scans the sand or mud in front of it for any sign of life before running on. It does not probe like its usual associates, the longer-billed sandpipers. Taking most of their food right from the surface, Semipalmated Plovers prey mainly on small crustaceans and mollusks.

DESCRIPTION: 6–8" (15–20 cm). A brown-backed plover with white underparts and a single black breast band. Its bill is stubby and yellow-orange with a dark tip. Immatures have an all-black bill and a brownish breast band.

VOICE: A plaintive two-note whistle, *tu-wee*. Also a soft, rather musical rattle.

NESTING: Lays 4 buff eggs, spotted with dark brown and black, placed in a shallow depression sparsely lined with shell fragments, pebbles, and bits of vegetation on the tundra.

HABITAT: Breeds on sandy or mossy tundra; during migration found on beaches, mudflats, shallow pools in salt marshes, and lakeshores.

RANGE: Breeds from Alaska east to Newfoundland and Nova Scotia. Winters regularly along the Gulf Coast, the Pacific Coast in California, and the Atlantic Coast to the Carolinas, rarely farther north.

SIMILAR SPECIES: Piping Plover is much paler above, with a white rump.

Wilson's Plover is somewhat paler above with longer, flesh-colored legs; a much longer, heavier, black bill; and a broad breast band.

Killdeer is much larger with longer legs; it has two breast bands (except when very young), a long black bill, and a long tail with a rusty base.

Common Ringed Plover usually has a breast band that's wider overall, widest at the center; the white spot behind the eye is larger and usually more clearly defined.

CONSERVATION:
Semipalmated Plovers are widespread and common. Overhunting in the 19th century severely reduced their numbers, but the species has since rebounded. The population today is healthy and appears to be stable or slightly increasing.

PIPING PLOVER *Charadrius melodus*

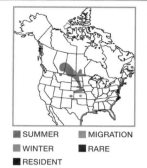

■ SUMMER   ■ MIGRATION
■ WINTER   ■ RARE
■ RESIDENT

Piping Plover is found on sandy beaches, where it nests above the high-water line or on sandy flats among the dunes, where vegetation is sparse. The color of dry sand, the Piping Plover is difficult to see on the beach, but its frequent vocalizing often makes its presence known. The eggs and downy chicks also blend in with the sand. The Piping Plover arrives much earlier in spring and departs for the South much earlier in fall than does the Semipalmated Plover.

DESCRIPTION: 6–7" (15–18 cm). A stocky, small, pale plover with sand-colored upperparts. It has a narrow, incomplete black breast band; a short, stubby bill with an orange base; and yellowish legs. Young birds are similar, with a black bill and a broken gray breast band.

VOICE: Vocalizations include a repeated, melodious, plaintive *peep*; a clear, whistled *peep-lo*; a *pee-a-weet*; and a flat *per-uee*.

NESTING: Lays 4 buff-white eggs, evenly marked with small dark spots, in a depression in the sand lined with pebbles and bits of shells.

HABITAT: Bare, dry, sandy areas, both inland and on the coast.

RANGE: Breeds along the Atlantic Coast from Quebec and Newfoundland south to North Carolina, and locally from Alberta east to Minnesota and the Great Lakes. Winters on the Atlantic and Gulf coasts, north regularly to the Carolinas.

SIMILAR SPECIES: See Semipalmated and Snowy plovers. Snowy Plover has a thin black bill and black legs. Semipalmated Plover has much darker upperparts.

CONSERVATION: NT

These rare shorebirds have been seriously impacted by human activity on beaches and rivers in the continent's interior. The Piping Plover is on the U.S. Endangered Species List and classified as Near Threatened by the IUCN Red List. It is classified as endangered in the Great Lakes watershed in the states of Illinois, Indiana, Michigan, Minnesota, New York, Ohio, Pennsylvania, and Wisconsin; it's listed as threatened in other parts of these states and in all other U.S. states within its range. It is thought to be extirpated from a swath of its historic range in central Canada. Extensive conservation effort has yielded an increase in Piping Plover numbers in recent years; conservation actions focus on predator control, restoring breeding habitat, and restricting human activity on beaches near breeding sites.

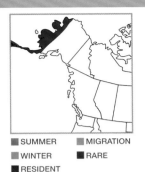

■ SUMMER   ■ MIGRATION
■ WINTER   ■ RARE
■ RESIDENT

Like several other Asian shorebirds, Lesser Sand-Plovers occur annually in the western Aleutian Islands, on islands in the Bering Sea, and in western mainland Alaska. More rarely they appear as accidental strays elsewhere on the Pacific Coast of North America; there are also records for Alberta, Ontario, Louisiana, and New Jersey. These strays are usually single birds found associating with Semipalmated Plovers. The bright pattern of the breeding adults is hard to miss.

DESCRIPTION: 8" (20.5 cm). Slightly larger than a Semipalmated Plover, with warm brown upperparts and a bright cinnamon-rufous crown, neck collar, and breast band. It has a black mask and stripe over its white forehead and contrasting white throat. It has white underparts, a blackish bill, and dark gray legs. Juveniles and winter adults lack the cinnamon-rufous breast, and instead have white underparts with buffy or grayish patches at the sides of the breast.

VOICE: A short, soft, low-pitched *crrik* or *crrik-crrik*.

NESTING: Lays 3 cinnamon-buff eggs, evenly spotted with dark brown and black, in dried stem-lined scrape often placed close to water.

HABITAT: Breeds on barren flats along stony banks of rivers, lakes, and ponds; during migration found on mudflats, beaches, and lakeshores.

RANGE: Breeds in Asia; also rarely in northern and western Alaska. Winters in Old World from the Red Sea east to southeastern China and the Philippines south to southern Africa, New Guinea, and Australia.

SIMILAR SPECIES: Other banded plovers have black or dark brown breast bands.

CONSERVATION: 🐦 Although population trends for Lesser Sand-Plovers are unknown, they are widespread and numerous in their native range.

SUMMER · MIGRATION · WINTER · RARE · RESIDENT

The long, stout, black bill that makes this bird easy to distinguish from other plovers also enables it to partake of a more varied diet than its relatives. In addition to the usual fare of crustaceans, worms, and small mollusks, it also takes hard-shelled crabs, including fiddler crabs. Wilson's Plover feeds both day and night. Nesting pairs alternate between feeding and incubating; males tend to feed during the day and then incubate the eggs at night while the females take their turn foraging.

DESCRIPTION: 7–8" (18–20 cm). The upperparts of Wilson's Plover are the color of the wet sand it lives on, and it is white below with a broad black eye patch. Its most distinctive feature is its heavy black bill, more than half as long as its head. Breeding adults have a single black breast band. Both sexes are similar except the female is slightly drabber. The breast band is often incomplete in juveniles.

VOICE: A clear, whistled *queet* or *quit-keet*, but usually silent.

NESTING: Lays 3 or 4 buff eggs with small, blackish spots and blotches, placed in a slight depression on open, level sand or occasionally in dunes. Sometimes nests in loose colonies.

HABITAT: Sandy beaches and mudflats.

RANGE: Breeds on Atlantic and Gulf coasts from southern New Jersey (rare) and Maryland to Florida and Texas. Winters chiefly along Gulf Coast and in Florida.

SIMILAR SPECIES: See Semipalmated Plover and Killdeer.

CONSERVATION: LC

Uncommon and local, Wilson's Plover populations are declining gradually. The species' range has contracted southward down the Atlantic Coast in recent decades, causing it to be listed as threatened or endangered in some states.

■ SUMMER ■ MIGRATION
■ WINTER   ■ RARE
■ RESIDENT

This plover is poorly named, since it generally avoids mountainous areas. It favors instead arid plains and short-grass prairies of western valleys and hills, usually far from water. With its range centered on the short-grass prairie—a region subject to heavy grazing and cultivation—the Mountain Plover's numbers have sharply declined since the middle of the 20th century. It feeds singly or in small flocks, mostly on insects. In winter, larger concentrations can be seen in a variety of open arid habitats, as well as in fields.

DESCRIPTION: 8–9½" (20–24 cm). A long-legged, sandy-brown plover. The breeding adult has a black forecrown, white forehead, and thin black eyeline. Nonbreeding adults and young birds have dark eyes that contrast conspicuously against a plain face. In all plumages, Mountain plovers have a whitish wing stripe, whitish wing linings, and a black band near the tail tip.

VOICE: A harsh single note, *krrrp*.

NESTING: Lays 3 dark olive eggs, heavily spotted with brown, in a shallow depression on the ground, sometimes lined with bits of cow dung, twigs, or grass.

HABITAT: Arid plains, short-grass prairies, and fields.

RANGE: Breeds in Montana, Wyoming, Colorado, New Mexico, and the Texas Panhandle east to Nebraska. Winters from central California and southern Arizona southward into Mexico.

SIMILAR SPECIES: Winter-plumage and juvenile Black-bellied Plovers are larger and grayer, with mottled or spotted upperparts and much white in the rump, tail, and wings; they show black axillaries in flight. American Golden-Plover is spotted with buff or gold above, has a spotted or finely streaked breast, lacks a prominent wing stripe, and lacks the overall sandy color of Mountain Plover. Other plovers in the same range have distinct breast and head markings.

CONSERVATION: Mountain Plover populations have decreased significantly in step with decreases in prairie habitat, as much of this land has been converted for agricultural uses. It is listed as near threatened, although populations may be starting to stabilize.

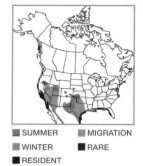

■ SUMMER　　■ MIGRATION
■ WINTER　　　■ RARE
■ RESIDENT

The Snowy Plover's patchy distribution, not only in North America but elsewhere in the world, is due to its specialized habitat requirements. Keeping to large, flat expanses of sand, it avoids competition for food in a habitat in which few other birds can exist. Here these plovers, with their pale coloration, are difficult to see even when they run. As soon as the plover stops running it seems to disappear, blending into its surroundings. The eggs also blend with dry sand or salty barren soil and are almost impossible to find once the incubating bird slips off them. Inland, these birds feed mainly on insects, but along the coast they also take crustaceans, worms, and other small marine creatures.

DESCRIPTION: 5–7" (13–18 cm). Our smallest plover, it is whitish with pale brown upperparts, black legs, a slender black bill, and a small black mark on each side of the breast. Juveniles have paler ear coverts and breast patches, the same color as that of the upperparts.

VOICE: A plaintive *chu-we* or *o-wee-ah.*

NESTING: Lays 2 or 3 buff eggs, spotted with black, in a sandy depression lined with a few shell fragments or bits of grass.

HABITAT: Flat sandy beaches, salt flats, and sandy areas with little vegetation.

RANGE: Resident along the Pacific Coast from British Columbia to Mexico, and along the Gulf Coast from Texas to the Florida Panhandle. Also breeds locally in the interior from California and Nevada east to Oklahoma and Texas. Also in the Old World.

SUBSPECIES: Geographically divided into subspecies: Western (*C. n. nivosus*) and Gulf Coast (*C. n. tenuirostris*). Gulf Coast birds are paler.

SIMILAR SPECIES: Piping Plover is larger and paler with shorter, orange or yellow legs (often dull in winter), and a much shorter bill that has an orange base in breeding birds. It has pale ear coverts and a white rump. In breeding plumage, a dark bar behind the forehead separates the forehead from the eyebrow.

CONSERVATION:

Globally the Snowy Plover is considered to be near threatened, primarily due to human disturbances of beaches. The Western Snowy Plover subspecies is on the U.S. Endangered Species List and classified as threatened in California, Oregon, and Washington, within 50 miles of the Pacific Ocean. The Gulf Coast subspecies is uncommon and declining.

■ SUMMER ■ MIGRATION
■ WINTER ■ RARE
■ RESIDENT

This tropical marsh bird wanders occasionally to southern Texas, especially when consecutive wet seasons with plentiful rain have created an abundance of suitable habitat. With their strikingly long toes, Northern Jacanas are adept at balancing on floating plants and are therefore able to exploit a habitat available to few other birds. They are quarrelsome and often engage in combat with one another, using sharp spurs on the bend of the wing. Females are somewhat larger than males and defend a large territory in which several males build nests and care for the eggs and young.

DESCRIPTION: 8–9" (20–23 cm). A dark, robin-sized marsh bird with very long toes. Its head and neck are black; its body and folded wings are dark rufous. Large, pale green wing patches are visible in flight. It has a colorful yellow bill with a white base and a distinctive bright yellow frontal shield on the face.

VOICE: Various high-pitched squeaking and bickering notes.

NESTING: Lays 4 pale buff eggs, heavily scrawled with black, in a loose cup of leaves and stems placed in the open on floating vegetation.

HABITAT: Marshes and ponds with heavy growth of lily pads and other floating plants.

RANGE: Rare wanderer and occasional breeder in southern Texas; also in American tropics.

SIMILAR SPECIES: Distinctive. Immatures, which have white undersides, might momentarily be mistaken for Wilson's Phalarope or a similar shorebird.

CONSERVATION:  Common within its range, with stable populations.

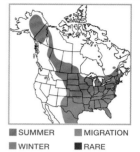

■ SUMMER ■ MIGRATION
■ WINTER ■ RARE
■ RESIDENT

Formerly abundant, this attractive bird of open grasslands was shot in such large numbers for food and sport that it became very scarce. Now given complete protection, it has increased once again; its principal danger is now habitat destruction. The Upland Sandpiper often flies with wings held stiffly in a downward curve, like a Spotted Sandpiper, especially on its nesting grounds. When alighting, Upland Sandpiper holds its wings over its back before folding them down in a resting position. In old books this bird is called the "Upland Plover," and it was known colloquially to hunters as the "Grass Plover."

DESCRIPTION: 11–12½" (28–32 cm). A sandpiper of open meadows with long yellowish legs, a slender neck and small head, and a short bill. Its upperparts are brown and scaly; its underparts are streaked and barred. The ends of the wings are dark in flight, and the tail is long and wedge-shaped. It often holds its wings upward briefly on alighting, exposing black-and-white barring on the underwing.

VOICE: Alarm call a mellow *quip-ip-ip-ip*. On breeding grounds and at night during migration, it gives a long, mournful, rolling whistle.

NESTING: Lays 4 pinkish-buff eggs, with brown spots, in a grass-lined nest in a hollow on the ground.

HABITAT: Breeds in open grasslands, prairies, and hayfields, also grassy airfields; generally frequents open country during migration.

RANGE: Breeds from Alaska east to New Brunswick and south to northeastern Oregon, Oklahoma, and Virginia. Winters in southern South America.

SIMILAR SPECIES: Buff-breasted Sandpiper is smaller, with a proportionately larger head, thicker neck, and shorter tail; it lacks strong bars or streaks on its buff underparts.

CONSERVATION: Once an abundant species, this bird was widely hunted commercially in the 1800s, causing a sharp drop in their numbers. Today it is a species of least concern and its overall numbers are stable or increasing, although dozens of states and provinces list Upland Sandpiper as a species of concern locally due to declining populations, often caused by habitat loss or changing agricultural practices.

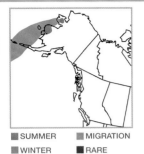

■ SUMMER ■ MIGRATION
■ WINTER ■ RARE
■ RESIDENT

The first nest of this little-known shorebird was discovered in 1948 on the lower Yukon River in Alaska. The species is known to nest only in a few remote hilly areas in western Alaska. Its population is small, and although it is not yet threatened on its breeding grounds, its Pacific island wintering grounds are becoming increasingly settled.

DESCRIPTION: 17" (43 cm). A large shorebird with a down-curved bill. Similar to Whimbrel but tinged buff, especially on the breast, with a pale rufous tail. The base of its bill is pale.

VOICE: A plaintive drawn-out whistle, *too-lee*.

NESTING: Lays 4 greenish eggs, spotted with brown, in a depression lined with tundra mosses.

HABITAT: Mountain tundra in summer; island beaches in winter.

RANGE: Breeds in small area of western Alaska; winters in Hawaii and other Pacific island groups.

SIMILAR SPECIES: Whimbrel is much grayer brown, and lacks the rufous rump and tail; its call also differs.

CONSERVATION: Rare and vulnerable. These birds are most vulnerable to hunting and introduced predators on their remote Pacific-island wintering grounds, when they become flightless during a period of their molt. Populations also may be losing wintering habitat due to rising sea levels.

■ SUMMER ■ MIGRATION
■ WINTER ■ RARE
■ RESIDENT

The Whimbrel is found along both coasts, as well as in the interior of the continent. It is still numerous because of its wary behavior and the remoteness of its nesting grounds on the Arctic tundra. They tend to concentrate in large flocks at favored sites during migration. Like many other tundra breeders, those in the East fly offshore over the Atlantic during their autumn migration to South America, returning in spring mainly along an interior route.

DESCRIPTION: 17" (43 cm). This curlew is a large brown shorebird with a long, somewhat thick, down-curved bill (2¾–4", 7–10 cm). It is mottled brown or gray-brown above, with bold head stripes and long legs. The legs are a dark blue-gray.

VOICE: A series of 5–7 loud, clear, whistled notes: *pip-pip-pip-pip-pip*.

NESTING: Lays 4 olive eggs, heavily marked with brown, in a depression in moss or in a sedge clump on the ground.

HABITAT: Breeds on the Arctic tundra, especially near the coast; coastal salt meadows, mudflats, and grassy shoreline slopes during migration.

RANGE: Breeds in Arctic Alaska and Canada. Winters in southern California, the Gulf Coast, and the Atlantic Coast north to Virginia. Also found in Eurasia.

SIMILAR SPECIES: Long-billed Curlew usually has a much longer bill (5–7", 13–18 cm), lacks head stripes, and is much warmer brown, with bright cinnamon wing linings.

Godwits' bills are also very long but slightly upturned.

Bristle-thighed Curlew (restricted to Alaska and Hawaii) is warmer brown with a light reddish-brown tail and rump.

CONSERVATION: Widespread. Overhunting seriously reduced the population in the 19th century and early 20th century, but the species recovered thanks to hunting restrictions. More recently, populations have shown a new downward trend, possibly due to degradation of key migration stopover habitats, but it remains a species of low concern.

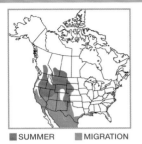

■ SUMMER ■ MIGRATION
■ WINTER ■ RARE
■ RESIDENT

Our largest shorebird, the "Sicklebill" was once a plentiful game bird of the Great Plains and the formerly extensive prairies to the east. Its prolonged, musical whistles carry far, signaling the birds' arrival in spring. On grasslands, they consume grasshoppers, crickets, and beetles; on shores and beaches during migration, they feast on small crustaceans and mollusks or on berries and seeds. While they incubate eggs, their warm colors blend with the brown grass, making them difficult to detect. Curlews are sociable birds when feeding, roosting, and migrating. The bill of this species looks almost as long as the body, whereas in the smaller Whimbrel the bill is only about the length of the head and neck.

DESCRIPTION: 23" (58 cm). This is an extremely large shorebird with a long neck and a spectacular, sickle-shaped bill that may reach 5–7" (13–18 cm) long when fully developed in adults; young birds have shorter bills. The warm brownish plumage is mottled on the wings and back; the belly is unmarked buff, and there are no head stripes. Cinnamon wing linings are conspicuous in flight. The neck is rather long, and the crown is unstriped.

VOICE: A clear *curleee*; a sharp *whit-whit, whit, whit, whit, whit*.

NESTING: Lays 4 olive-buff eggs, spotted with brown, in a grass-lined nest in a hollow on the ground.

HABITAT: Breeds on plains and prairies; on migration, it frequents lake and river shores, mudflats, salt marshes, and sandy beaches.

RANGE: Breeds from southern Canada to northern California, Utah, northern New Mexico, and Texas. Winters from California, Texas, Louisiana, South Carolina, and Florida southward.

SIMILAR SPECIES: Whimbrel has prominent crown stripes, lacks bright cinnamon wing linings, and usually has a much shorter bill; its plumage is not as warm in tone.

Godwits' bills are very long but slightly upturned. Marbled Godwit is quite similar; the difference in its bill shape may not be discernible at a distance.

CONSERVATION:  Long-billed Curlew is a species of least concern, although populations have decreased significantly due to loss of grasslands used for breeding and wetlands used for wintering habitat. Once a widespread and common species before overhunting and agricultural development in the 1800s depleted their numbers, today Long-billed Curlews are uncommon.

Accidental in North America. One of two large Old World curlews that occasionally visit North America, the Eurasian Curlew is a rare visitor to the Atlantic Coast, while the similar but even larger Far Eastern Curlew is a rare visitor to the Aleutian Islands, and extremely rarely seen in mainland Alaska or western Canada.

DESCRIPTION: A large curlew, 20–24" (50–60 cm) long, similar to the native Long-billed Curlew, but pale brown overall with a white lower back and rump. Its underparts are much more heavily spotted and much grayer than in the Long-billed. Eurasian Curlew's size and long, downturned bill distinguish this vagrant species from almost any native shorebird.

VOICE: *Curloo-oo*—the call from which the name "curlew" is derived.

NESTING: Not known to nest in North America.

HABITAT: Breeds primarily in freshwater wetlands, but also in wet grasslands and meadows. Winters mostly in coastal wetlands, but also in mudflats on lake and river shores. Uses agricultural fields as a migratory stopover, along with naturally occurring grasslands.

RANGE: Breeds across northern Europe and Asia, from Norway to Siberia. Winters along coasts of Africa, the Middle East, and South Asia.

SIMILAR SPECIES: Similar in size to the Long-billed Curlew native to North America. Long-billed Curlew is plain buffy underneath.

CONSERVATION: NT
Near Threatened and decreasing in its native range.

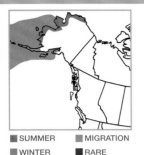

■ SUMMER   ■ MIGRATION
■ WINTER   ■ RARE
■ RESIDENT

This widespread Eurasian godwit is found in summer across northern Europe and Asia, with a small portion of its population crossing into western Alaska to breed. These large, noisy, and colorful birds are easy to detect in the low tundra where they nest. They have relatively short legs for a godwit, and they wade in open water and probe deeply for worms and crustaceans.

DESCRIPTION: 15–18" (38–46 cm). A large, slender shorebird with a long, slightly upturned bill. The breeding adult has barred chestnut underparts and mottled brown upperparts. Fall birds are grayish above and whitish below. Similar to Hudsonian Godwit but larger, with barred tail, no white wing stripe, and brown wing linings with white barring.

VOICE: A loud *kew-wew* and various other notes.

NESTING: Lays 4 greenish eggs with small brownish spots in a shallow depression lined with lichens, moss, or grass.

HABITAT: Tundra marshes in summer; estuarine mudflats and lake edges in winter and during migration.

RANGE: Breeds in northwestern Alaska. Winters largely in Old World. A casual visitor to Pacific and Atlantic coasts.

SUBSPECIES: Globally this species is broken into three subspecies and several subpopulations, each of which uses different migratory flyways. The Alaska breeding population belongs to the largest subspecies (*baueri*), which rarely appears as strays along the Pacific Coast. Occasionally a stray member of the smaller European subspecies (*lapponica*) will stray to the East Coast; these birds have a white rump and white underwings.

SIMILAR SPECIES: Marbled Godwit is much larger, with proportionately longer bill and legs; it has cinnamon wing linings and much cinnamon in the wings and tail.

Hudsonian and Black-tailed godwits are smaller than the Pacific subspecies, but closer in size to the European strays that occasionally appear in the East. Hudsonian and Black-tailed godwits have proportionally longer legs, a bold wing stripe, a white-and-black tail, and black or white wing linings.

CONSERVATION: NT
Most of this species' population lives in the Old World, where its numbers are decreasing rapidly. The decline is especially severe for populations whose migratory paths take them to the Yellow Sea between China and the Korean Peninsula, where habitat is being lost at an alarming rate. The population that breeds in Alaska is among the birds that use this key migratory flyway.

BLACK-TAILED GODWIT *Limosa limosa*

■ SUMMER ■ MIGRATION
■ WINTER ■ RARE
■ RESIDENT

Black-tailed Godwit is a casual spring migrant in the Aleutian Islands, Pribilofs, St. Lawrence Island, and Little Diomede Island; it also appears rarely as a stray on the Atlantic Coast of North America. This species replaces the Hudsonian Godwit in Eurasia.

DESCRIPTION: 12–15" (30.5–38 cm). It is similar to Hudsonian Godwit, except its wing linings and wing stripe are extensively white. The breeding adult has a rich orange head, neck, and breast; its sides and flanks are variably barred with black. Its tail is black with broad white uppertail coverts. Its long, bicolored bill is only slightly recurved. Winter birds are gray above and whitish below.

VOICE: A loud *quee-quee-quee*; often silent.

NESTING: Lays 3–4 olive-green eggs, usually blotched and spotted dark-brown, in shallow grass-lined scrape in short vegetation on ground.

HABITAT: Breeds in marshy grasslands, wet meadows, and moorlands; flooded fields, beaches, and mudflats in winter.

RANGE: Breeds in Iceland and northern Eurasia. Winters from British Isles and Mediterranean region east to China and the Philippines south to east-central Africa, the East Indies, Australia, and Tasmania.

SUBSPECIES: Western Alaska records are of the *melanuroides* subspecies found across northern China, Mongolia, Siberia, and eastern Russia. East Coast records are of the *islandica* subspecies, which breeds primarily in Iceland.

SIMILAR SPECIES: See Hudsonian Godwit; no other shorebird has a similar tail pattern.

CONSERVATION: NT
Although widespread, this species is Near Threatened and decreasing mainly due to human development, wetland drainage, and changes in agricultural practices throughout its range.

■ SUMMER   ■ MIGRATION
■ WINTER   ■ RARE
■ RESIDENT

Never common, unrestricted hunting caused the Hudsonian Godwit to become quite scarce. Now protected, it has rebounded from its historic lows. It is uncommon and local in North America; during migration to and from the Southern Hemisphere, the Hudsonian Godwit engages in long flights, traveling nonstop between James Bay, Canada, and the Gulf Coast, and thus bypasses most observers. On the coastal mudflats of the northeastern states, this large shorebird can be seen in flocks of up to several dozen during fall passage.

DESCRIPTION: 15" (38 cm). A large, slender shorebird with a long, slightly upturned bill. The breeding adult has barred chestnut underparts and mottled brown upperparts. Fall birds are grayish above and whitish below. All plumages have a black and white tail, a broad white wing stripe, and black wing linings.

VOICE: A loud *kerreck* or *god-wit* call, similar to call of Marbled Godwit but higher pitched. Usually silent.

NESTING: Lays 4 olive-buff eggs, spotted with brown and black, in a shallow grass-lined hollow on the ground.

HABITAT: Breeds on tundra; mainly mudflats during migration.

RANGE: Breeds in Alaska, Mackenzie, northwestern British Columbia, and around Hudson Bay. Winters in southern South America.

SIMILAR SPECIES: See Willet.

Black-tailed Godwit (rare) has white uppertail coverts and wing linings; a longer, wider wing stripe; and a straight bill. Marbled Godwit is larger, tawny below, lacks a wing stripe and contrasting tail pattern, and has cinnamon wing linings. The rare Bar-tailed Godwit has a barred tail, brownish wing linings, and shorter legs.

CONSERVATION:
Long migration flights and remote breeding habitat leave the status and population trends of these birds poorly understood due to the difficulty of monitoring them. The species' small population appears to be stable or slightly decreasing.

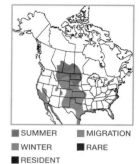

■ SUMMER   ■ MIGRATION
■ WINTER   ■ RARE
■ RESIDENT

In spring on the Great Plains, the aerial displays and noisy calls of Marbled Godwits are conspicuous. Males chase one another and perform figure-eight flights. The birds nest in loose colonies, and although the female alone incubates the eggs, both parents guard the young birds as they feed. These birds may occur in large flocks, often associating loosely with other shorebirds. Like the Long-billed Curlew, it is a rich buff color, blending perfectly with the brown grass of the plains.

DESCRIPTION: 18" (46 cm). A crow-sized shorebird, dark and mottled above, cinnamon-buff below, with a long, pinkish, upturned bill. It is distinguished from other godwits by its cinnamon wing linings, inner primaries, and secondaries, giving its underwing a clean orange or cinnamon appearance in flight. The outer wing is dark toward the tip; blackish primary coverts form a dark wing patch. It has dark legs.

VOICE: A loud *kerreck* or *god-wit*, usually heard on breeding grounds.

NESTING: Lays 4 olive-buff eggs blotched with brown in a slight depression lined with grass on the ground.

HABITAT: Breeds on grassy plains; visits salt marshes, tidal creeks, mudflats, and sea beaches on migration.

RANGE: Breeds on the central plains from Saskatchewan to Minnesota. Winters on the coasts from California and Virginia southward and along the Gulf Coast.

SIMILAR SPECIES: See Black-tailed, Hudsonian, and Bar-tailed godwits. Long-billed Curlew is larger with an especially long decurved bill.

CONSERVATION: 🐦 LC
Marbled Godwits are common with stable or slightly decreasing populations. Habitat loss is the biggest threat to the species as more prairie is converted to farmland and coastal wintering habitats are degraded.

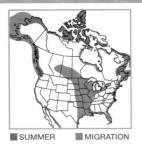

■ SUMMER ■ MIGRATION
■ WINTER ■ RARE
■ RESIDENT

In their nesting territories, neighboring turnstones display head to head, the harlequin pattern of the face and black-and-white fanned tail serving as colorful banners. Turnstones are named for their method of feeding, in which they walk along the beach, deftly overturning small stones and pebbles and seizing the animals hiding underneath. They also dig holes in the sand, often larger than themselves, in pursuit of burrowing crustaceans. Although Ruddy Turnstones are usually encountered only in small groups, they are quite common; during the winter they scatter over a huge area, regularly occurring as far south as Australia, New Zealand, southern Africa, and South America, as well as on remote islands in the South Pacific, where they sometimes prey on nesting terns' eggs.

DESCRIPTION: 8–10" (20–25 cm). A stocky shorebird with orange legs. Its upperparts are mainly rusty red in summer and brown in winter. In all plumages, its underparts are plain white. Its face and breast have conspicuous black markings that are duller but still visible in winter. Its bold pattern of black and white is visible in flight.

VOICE: A metallic but musical *netticut* or *kek-kek*.

NESTING: Lays 4 (sometimes 2–3) olive-green to olive-buff eggs blotched with dark brown.

HABITAT: Breeds on coastal tundra; winters on rocky, pebbly, and sandy coasts and beaches.

RANGE: Breeds in northwestern Alaska and the islands of the Canadian Arctic. Winters on the coasts from Oregon and Connecticut southward and along the Gulf. Also in Eurasia.

SIMILAR SPECIES: Black Turnstone lacks rust in any plumage, is black and white in summer, and is somewhat more slate-colored in winter. The head and breast are almost entirely black; the legs are dark reddish-brown.

CONSERVATION: LC

Common and widespread with relatively stable numbers that may be decreasing slightly—exact population trends for this species are difficult to gauge.

BLACK TURNSTONE *Arenaria melanocephala*

■ SUMMER　■ MIGRATION
■ WINTER　■ RARE
■ RESIDENT

Unlike the widespread Ruddy Turnstone, the Black Turnstone is partial to rocky coasts and almost never seen far from salt water. Turnstones are aggressive; a wintering bird that has found a good foraging spot will hotly defend it against other turnstones.

DESCRIPTION: 9" (23 cm). Resembles Ruddy Turnstone in general patterns. In breeding plumage, it has black upperparts, head, and breast; a large white spot in front of the eye and a white line above eye; fine white spotting from the nape across the side of the breast; and a white belly. In winter plumage, it is dusky black with an unstreaked white belly. Its legs are dark, and its bill is short and slightly upturned. In flight, it shows a striking black-and-white pattern.

VOICE: A grating rattle similar to that of Ruddy Turnstone.

NESTING: Lays 4 yellowish-olive eggs, with darker olive and brown markings, in an unlined depression on an open, pebbly ridge or a gravel bar in wet tundra.

HABITAT: Breeds in marshy coastal tundra; seaweed-covered rocky shores in fall and winter.

RANGE: Breeds on western and southern coasts of Alaska. Winters all along the West Coast from Alaska south to Baja California and Sonora, Mexico.

SIMILAR SPECIES: Nonbreeding Ruddy Turnstone is browner overall, with paler cheeks and throat, a patchier dark coloration to the breast, and bright orange legs. Some dark juvenile Ruddies are almost as dark as Blacks.

Surfbird is larger, grayer overall in winter, with a dark lower back, less white in the wing, a yellow or orange-yellow base to the bill, and greenish-yellow legs.

CONSERVATION: LC

Black Turnstone is common and its overall population is stable, although it may be declining slightly in some areas where ecosystems are degraded.

■ SUMMER   ■ MIGRATION
■ WINTER   ■ RARE
■ RESIDENT

In breeding plumage, with their rich rufous underparts, set off by marbled gray backs, Red Knots are among the handsomest of shorebirds. Those that winter in southern South America may make a round trip of nearly 20,000 miles (32,000 km) each year. These birds congregate in enormous, dense flocks at key stopover sites during migration.

DESCRIPTION: 10.5" (27 cm). A robin-sized shorebird. Breeding adults have a pinkish-rufous face and underparts, and dark brown upperparts with pale feather edgings. Fall birds are gray above and whitish below. Its rump is dark. It has a faint wing stripe, a straight and slightly tapered bill, and greenish legs.

VOICE: A soft *quer-wer*; also a soft *knut*.

NESTING: Lays 4 olive-buff eggs, spotted with brown, in a slight depression lined with lichens, often among rocks.

HABITAT: Breeds on tundra; during migration, on tidal flats, rocky shores, and beaches.

RANGE: Breeds on islands in the high Arctic of Canada and in northernmost Alaska. Winters on coasts from California and Massachusetts southward to southern South America. Also in Eurasia.

SUBSPECIES: Six geographically distinct subspecies around the globe vary slightly in size. The largest subspecies *roselaari* breeds in Alaska and migrates through western North America; the *rufa* subspecies is second largest, breeds in the Canadian high Arctic, and migrates through eastern North America. A third subspecies, *islandica*, breeds in the extreme northeastern tip of the Canadian high Arctic and in Greenland; this subspecies migrates to Europe.

SIMILAR SPECIES: Nonbreeding Black-bellied Plovers are somewhat similar to winter and juvenile Red Knots, but are larger with a short, stout bill, spotted upperparts, and a more erect posture; the two species are often found together. Breeding-plumage Curlew Sandpiper is smaller and darker rufous, with a bolder wing stripe and a drooped or decurved bill.

CONSERVATION:  NT

All three North American subspecies of Red Knot have shown declining populations, and the species is listed as near threatened. The *rufa* subspecies is listed as federally Threatened in the United States. This subpopulation relies heavily on the eggs of horseshoe crabs in Delaware Bay as food during a stopover on their long migration; commercial overharvesting of these crabs has decreased the available food for these birds and hurt their numbers dramatically.

■ SUMMER　■ MIGRATION
■ WINTER　■ RARE
■ RESIDENT

Surfbird breeds in rocky alpine areas in Alaska, but is named for its preferred habitat in migration and winter along the rocky Pacific Coast, often on rocks amid the pounding surf. This species is found in small or medium-sized flocks during the nonbreeding season, often in mixed groups with tattlers and turnstones. Its short, thick-based bill is almost plover-like. That two such distantly related shorebirds as the Surfbird and Black Turnstone have similar plumage is attributed to a similar need for camouflage in the same environment. The bright wing stripe is a signal, perhaps helping to keep the flying flock in formation.

DESCRIPTION: 10" (25 cm). A stocky, rock-dwelling shorebird, slightly larger than Black Turnstone. Breeding adults have blackish upperparts spotted with white and chestnut, and whitish underparts barred with black. Winter birds are dark gray above and on the breast. All plumages have a bold white wing stripe and white rump.

VOICE: A shrill *kee-wee* in flight.

NESTING: Lays 4 buff eggs, spotted with various colors, on bare ground among rocks.

HABITAT: Breeds above the timberline in Arctic mountains; winters on rocky shores, headlands, and islets.

RANGE: Breeds on mountain tundra of Alaska. Winters along Pacific Coast from southern Alaska southward to Baja California.

SIMILAR SPECIES: Wandering Tattler is uniformly dark gray above with no white markings and has a longer bill.

Black Turnstone is smaller and darker, and has more white in the upperparts visible in flight on the lower back and wings.

Rock Sandpiper is smaller and longer-billed, and has a vertical black bar across the rump.

CONSERVATION: LC
Surfbird populations are not well studied; their numbers appear to be small but stable.

■ SUMMER   ■ MIGRATION
■ WINTER   ■ RARE
■ RESIDENT

A native Eurasian shorebird, this species is a rare but regular migrant to western Alaska, both coasts, and the Great Lakes region, and casual elsewhere in North America. The Ruff is one of the most remarkable of all shorebirds. It is one of the few waders in which the two sexes are dramatically different in color, pattern, and size during the breeding season. The males also form leks, or display grounds, and engage in courting. After mating, the females build their nests away from the courtship area.

DESCRIPTION: 11" (28 cm). A stocky shorebird with a short tapered bill. Breeding males have extraordinarily variable plumage, showing ear tufts, ruffs, and gorgets in any combination of black, white, chestnut, gray, buff, etc. Females (called "Reeves") and winter males are much duller-gray or brown above with a pale spot at the base of the bill, white below. Leg color varies from yellow to green, brown, and red. In flight, two oval white patches are visible at the sides of the rump. In all seasons, the male is noticeably larger than female.

VOICE: Usually silent, but occasionally a soft *tu-whit* when flushed.

NESTING: Lays 4 gray, green, or buff eggs, heavily marked with deep brown blotches, in a grass-lined depression in a meadow or marsh.

HABITAT: Short grassy meadows and marshy ponds.

RANGE: Breeds in northern Eurasia. A rare migrant in Western Alaska, along the Pacific and Atlantic coasts, and on the Great Lakes.

SIMILAR SPECIES: Smaller Pectoral Sandpiper always has breast streaks terminating evenly across the lower breast. Both yellowlegs are slimmer with streaked breasts and bright yellow legs, and show dark, unstriped wings in flight. Winter-plumage Red Knot is shorter-legged; has a white breast and dark lores; and shows a soft wing stripe, grayish-white rump, and tail in flight. See Sharp-tailed Sandpiper.

CONSERVATION: LC
Least concern but decreasing in its native range.

SHARP-TAILED SANDPIPER *Calidris acuminata*

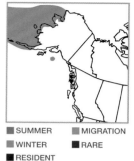

■ SUMMER ■ MIGRATION
■ WINTER ■ RARE
■ RESIDENT

An Asian species closely related to our Pectoral Sandpiper, Sharp-tailed Sandpiper appears in North America mainly after the end of the nesting season. A few wander to Alaska and the Pacific Northwest each year from September to November. Most of the birds recorded in North America are the young of the year.

DESCRIPTION: 8½" (22 cm). Similar to Pectoral Sandpiper in size and behavior. Brownish overall but more rusty than Pectoral, with a redder cap and broader eyebrow. Its breast is paler, more of a buff color, with faint streaking limited to the sides in immatures; the breast pattern is less sharply contrasted with a white belly than in Pectoral Sandpiper.

VOICE: A sharp *whit-whit*.

NESTING: Lays 4 buff eggs, spotted with brown, in a nest of grass on the ground.

HABITAT: Grassy areas of coastal marshes and tidal flats.

RANGE: Breeds in Siberia. Appears in small numbers along the West Coast in fall, less often inland and on the East Coast.

SIMILAR SPECIES: Pectoral Sandpiper always has breast streaking terminating in a well-defined line across the lower breast. Juvenile Ruff has a non-contrasting buff eyebrow, a dark brown cap, and longer legs. Juvenile Dunlin is much smaller, with a decurved bill.

CONSERVATION: LC
The population in its native range appears to be stable.

■ SUMMER ■ MIGRATION
■ WINTER ■ RARE
■ RESIDENT

Often associated with dowitchers and yellowlegs, Stilt Sand-pipers resemble both species and appear to be intermediate between the two. Yellowlegs move about continually in nervous, jerky motions, and dowitchers feed slowly, probing deep into the mud. Stilt Sandpipers move like yellowlegs but cover more ground, while feeding deliberately like dowitchers.

DESCRIPTION: 8½" (22 cm). A starling-sized sandpiper with long, greenish legs and a long bill, slightly down-curved at the tip. Its wings lack a stripe. The breeding adult has chestnut head stripes and barring below. Nonbreeding birds have much paler plumage and a white line over the eye.

VOICE: Simple *tu-tu*, similar to the call of Lesser Yellowlegs.

NESTING: Lays 4 pale buff eggs, marked with brown, on open ground in a grass tussock near water.

HABITAT: Grassy pools and shores of ponds and lakes.

RANGE: Breeds in northern Alaska and northern Canada east to Hudson Bay. Winters in small numbers in southern California's Salton Sea, Gulf Coast, and Florida.

SIMILAR SPECIES: Winter-plumage small dowitchers and Lesser Yellowlegs are similar to a winter-plumage Stilt Sandpiper. Dowitchers are much heavier-bodied, longer-billed, and distinctly different in flight, with white lower backs. Lesser Yellowlegs are slightly larger with a straight bill, bright yellow legs, an indistinct whitish eyebrow, and a different manner of feeding. Juvenile Curlew Sandpiper is quite similar to a juvenile Stilt Sandpiper, but has a bill tapering to a fine tip; its legs are much shorter; its legs and feet are black; and it has a bold, white wing stripe visible in flight. Curlew Sandpiper also has a sooty gray tail and gives a different flight call.

CONSERVATION:
There is little information on Stilt Sandpiper population trends and counts seem to show considerable variability in their numbers. Overall these birds are numerous and occur throughout a wide range. Populations may be increasing in North America according to some surveys.

CURLEW SANDPIPER *Calidris ferruginea*

■ SUMMER ■ MIGRATION
■ WINTER   ■ RARE
■ RESIDENT

Except for a small area on the Arctic coast of Alaska, where it is a rarity, this Old World species breeds solely in northern Siberia. During spring migration the adults are in their bright chestnut breeding plumage and are easily distinguished in the field from their usual associates—Red Knots and Dunlins—by their curved bills and white rumps. In fall migration in their dull winter plumage, however, they are much more difficult to spot among the hordes of other shorebirds.

DESCRIPTION: 8" (20 cm). Similar in size and shape to Dunlin, but its entire bill is noticeably curved. Summer adults are rich cinnamon or chestnut. Winter birds are gray above and white below. Immatures have a buff breast and upperparts marked with buff scaling. Its white rump is visible in flight.

VOICE: A soft, dry *chirrip*.

NESTING: Lays 4 yellow-buff eggs, with dark brown spots, in a depression on the ground in tundra.

HABITAT: Breeds on tundra; chiefly coastal mudflats on migration.

RANGE: Breeds in Eurasia and very rarely in northern Alaska. A rare but regular migrant to the East Coast, less common on the West Coast. Winters mainly in Old World.

SIMILAR SPECIES: Dunlin in winter plumage has darker streaking below; it is best distinguished from a winter Curlew Sandpiper by its dark rump. Differing proportions are only apparent in direct comparison.

Juvenile Stilt Sandpiper is quite similar to juvenile Curlew Sandpiper, but has a blunt-tipped bill. Its legs are much longer; its legs and feet are grayish-green or yellowish. Its white wing stripe is short and narrow, its tail is grayish-white, and its flight call is dissimilar.

Fall White-rumped Sandpiper is smaller than Curlew Sandpiper and more heavily marked below; its bill is nearly straight.

CONSERVATION: NT
Population trends are difficult to determine for this species. It is thought to be decreasing in its native range.

This Eurasian species occasionally visits Alaska or the northwest coast of North America (only as far south as Washington State). Temminck's Stint falls into the category of small sandpipers many birders refer to as "peeps." Peeps are difficult to identify, and there are several native species that are far more likely in North America. The most reliable ways to distinguish Temminck's Stint are its call and the white sides of its tail.

DESCRIPTION: A tiny sandpiper, 5–6" (13–15 cm) long, Temminck's Stint is only slightly larger than the Least Sandpiper, the smallest of all shorebirds. It has more extensive white underneath—especially on the rump and underside of the tail—than Least, Semipalmated, and Western sandpipers, all of which are native sandpipers of similar size. In breeding plumage, it is mainly white below, and gray to olive brown with darker spots above. In nonbreeding plumage, it is plain dark gray above and on the throat, and white below.

VOICE: A high, cricket-like trill, distinctive from other tiny sandpipers.

NESTING: Nests in Eurasia. Lays 3–4 eggs in a scrape in the ground.

HABITAT: Breeds in Arctic tundra vegetation, preferring shrubby areas and avoiding severe Arctic conditions without plants. Winters in various wetland types, preferring freshwater wetlands (occasionally salt or tidal marshes) and avoiding open coast.

RANGE: Breeds across northern Europe and Asia, from Scandinavia to the Russian Far East. Winters in West and Central Africa, the Middle East, India, and Southeast Asia. Very rare visitor to the northwest coast of North America.

SIMILAR SPECIES: Similar to several of our native peeps; best distinguished by its call. Vagrants are generally solitary rather than among a flock of other peeps.

CONSERVATION:
Least concern in its native range, although its global population trends are poorly understood. The European population is believed to be stable.

RED-NECKED STINT *Calidris ruficollis*

SUMMER ■ MIGRATION
WINTER ■ RARE
■ RESIDENT

With the rise in popularity of bird watching, we have learned that this Asian species is more numerous in North America than was previously thought. Once considered a rarity confined to Alaska—where it is known to nest in small numbers each year—it is now known that each year a few strays tend to migrate south through the Americas, with a few turning up occasionally on either coast and rarely in the interior of the continent. Many of these strays are seen migrating in July, still wearing their distinctive breeding plumage; also, since juveniles scarcely differ from juvenile Semipalmated Sandpipers, it is possible that young Red-necked Stints may go undetected.

DESCRIPTION: 6½" (17 cm). A small sandpiper. In breeding plumage, its face, neck, and upper breast are rufous, with a white chin spot, and the rest of the underparts are white; the upperparts are rufous and brown with black blotches. Fall birds lack the rufous tone and closely resemble Semipalmated Sandpipers but have thinner bills. The rump is dark, the bill and feet are black, and it has a white wing stripe.

VOICE: A thin *chit-chit*.

NESTING: Lays 4 cream-colored eggs, marked with brown, on dry willow leaves in a depression on the tundra. Both parents may tend to the young for a period, but the female often leaves the young to be tended by the male shortly after hatching.

HABITAT: Breeds on marshy tundra; frequents mudflats and ponds in winter and on migration.

RANGE: Breeds in Siberian Asia and northwestern Alaska. A rare migrant outside of Alaska. Winters chiefly in the Old World.

SIMILAR SPECIES: See Sanderling and Semipalmated Sandpiper.

CONSERVATION: NT

Near Threatened and declining significantly in recent years. The global Red-necked Stint population relies on the East Asian-Australasian flyway, where degradation and loss of habitat at key stopover sites in the Yellow Sea region threaten this and many other species of migratory birds.

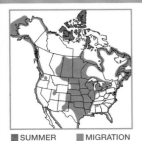

■ SUMMER ■ MIGRATION
■ WINTER ■ RARE
■ RESIDENT

The Sanderling is a great introduction to sandpiper identification. These small, plump, active shorebirds are widespread and common, and easy to identify at sandy beaches from fall through spring. They are best known for chasing receding waves, scurrying up and down the beach on their small legs. As a wave comes roaring in, the birds run up on the beach just ahead of the breaker, then sprint after the retreating water to feed on the tiny crustaceans and mollusks exposed by the tide.

DESCRIPTION: 8" (20 cm). A starling-sized shorebird with a conspicuous white wing stripe. Summer adults have a rufous head and breast, and a white belly. In winter, the rufous areas are replaced by a pale gray, and the birds look almost white. The bill and legs are black in all seasons.

VOICE: A sharp *kip*. Conversational chatter while feeding.

NESTING: Lays 4 olive eggs, spotted with brown, placed in a hollow on the ground lined with grasses and lichens.

HABITAT: Breeds on tundra; winters on ocean beaches, sandbars, mudflats, and lake and river shores.

RANGE: Breeds in high Arctic tundra from Alaska eastward to Baffin Island. Winters along coasts from British Columbia and Massachusetts southward to southern South America. Also in Eurasia.

SIMILAR SPECIES: Rufous-necked Stint is similar to a fading adult Sanderling, but Rufous-necked and other peeps are smaller and browner, with proportionately slimmer bills; peeps lack the bold white wing stripe. Winter-plumage Sanderling is paler gray than any sandpiper of similar size. Sanderling in breeding plumage in sometimes mistaken for Baird's Sandpiper, but Baird's is slimmer and longer-winged, with a thinner bill and no conspicuous wing stripe.

CONSERVATION:

This species has a wide range, and it is one of the most common shorebirds in North America. Its population trends are difficult to survey, but some surveys suggest these common birds may be in steep decline. Sanderlings rely on a few key staging areas in their long-distance migration, making large segments of the population vulnerable to the destruction or degradation of those stopover sites.

DUNLIN *Calidris alpina*

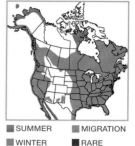

■ SUMMER ■ MIGRATION
■ WINTER ■ RARE
■ RESIDENT

These handsome birds, once known as "Red-backed Sand-pipers," are among the hardiest of shorebirds. They are often among the last shorebirds to migrate in the fall, and thousands sometimes spend the winter months on sandbars or inlets along the coast as far north as southeastern Alaska and southern New England, where they feed on mollusks, crustaceans, and marine worms.

DESCRIPTION: 8½" (22 cm). A starling-sized shore-bird. Its bill is fairly long with distinct droop at the tip. Breeding adults have a reddish back, whitish underparts, and a distinctive black patch in the center of the belly. Winter birds are dull gray and paler below.

VOICE: A soft *cheerp* or *chit-lit*.

NESTING: Lays 4 olive eggs, blotched with brown, in a grass clump on a dry hummock on the open tundra.

HABITAT: Nests on tundra; winters on beaches, mudflats, sand flats, and inland lake and river shores.

RANGE: Breeds from western and northern Alaska east to Hudson Bay. Winters along coasts from southern Alaska and Massachusetts southward. Also in Eurasia.

SUBSPECIES: Several subspecies differ in size, bill length, and breeding plumage. Pacific birds (subsp. *pacifica* and *articola*) tend to have a paler head and breast than their cousins in the East (subsp. *hudsonia*). Subspecies that breed in Greenland (subsp. *arctica* and *schinzii*) may occasionally wander to the East Coast; these birds are smaller and drabber, and have shorter bills than other Dunlins in North America.

SIMILAR SPECIES: Rock Sandpiper in breeding plumage has a smudge on the underparts that is usually less solidly black and on the lower breast rather than the belly.

Sanderling is much paler than a winter-plumage Dunlin, with a shorter, straight bill.

Winter-plumage Purple Sandpiper is slightly darker above and below with shorter, orange-yellow legs, feet, and base of the bill; it has streaked flanks and undertail coverts.

Western Sandpiper is smaller, paler in winter, and lacks the belly patch in summer.

Curlew Sandpiper in winter plumage has paler streaking below; it is best distinguished from a winter Dunlin by the white rump with no median line.

Differing proportions among these related species are only apparent in direct comparison.

CONSERVATION: LC

Although Dunlin populations have decreased during the past several decades, they remain widespread and abundant. Reasons for the dip in this species' numbers are not well known, but their decline has been noticeable in some coastal areas where numbers of these birds historically have wintered.

■ SUMMER ■ MIGRATION
■ WINTER ■ RARE
■ RESIDENT

This stocky shorebird replaces the Purple Sandpiper on the Pacific Coast up to western Alaska. It shows a great deal of variability in its size and color patterns. Along rocky coastlines, dark gray birds feeding in loose flocks at the waterline or on exposed, seaweed-covered rocks may be Rock Sandpipers, Black Turnstones, or Surfbirds. All are similarly camouflaged to match dark, wet rocks. In flight, the three are easily distinguished: The Rock Sandpiper has a dark tail, the Surfbird has a white tail terminating in a black triangle, and the Black Turnstone has a checkered black and white pattern on the back.

DESCRIPTION: 8–9" (20–23 cm). A small, rock-dwelling sandpiper. Winter birds are plain slate-gray on the head, breast, and upperparts; its dark bill has a pale base. Breeding birds are rusty above, with a pale head and dark ear patch, and a black patch on the lower breast (not on the belly as in Dunlin). Its legs are greenish yellow.

VOICE: Usually silent; low whistled notes sometimes heard in winter.

NESTING: Lays 4 buff-olive eggs, spotted with brown, in a mossy depression on the tundra.

HABITAT: Breeds on upland tundra; rocky shores in winter.

RANGE: Breeds along the coast of western Alaska. Winters from the Aleutians south along the Pacific Coast to Washington, rarely farther south.

SUBSPECIES: The nominate *ptilocnemis* subpopulation breeds on the Pribilof Islands and migrates down Alaska's Pacific Coast; it is larger and paler with more chestnut hues on the upperparts. The Aleutian population (subsp. *couesi*) is resident on the Aleutian Island chain and the Alaskan Peninsula; they are smaller and darker. Several intermediate variations are not safely distinguished in the field. Birds wintering south of Alaska to California likely belong to the Bering Sea population (*tschuktschorum*).

SIMILAR SPECIES: Dunlin in breeding plumage (found occasionally on rocky shores) has a more distinct black patch on the belly (not on the lower breast) and dark legs. Surfbird is larger; Surfbird and Black Turnstone both have a shorter, stouter bill and white rump and tail base. It is indistinguishable from Purple Sandpiper in winter, but the normal ranges of these two species do not overlap.

CONSERVATION: Rock Sandpiper is a species of low conservation concern, although it is uncommon. Its population trends are poorly understood, and its numbers appear to be gradually decreasing.

PURPLE SANDPIPER *Calidris maritima*

■ SUMMER   ■ MIGRATION
■ WINTER   ■ RARE
■ RESIDENT

These hardy birds remain through the coldest winters on rocks along the ocean front. Sometimes flocks of as many as 50 or more may be found on stone jetties. In recent years, these birds have been found lingering later in spring, and a few nonbreeding birds have been reported even in summer as far south as Long Island. Their food consists of small crustaceans and mollusks such as periwinkles and other marine snails.

DESCRIPTION: 9" (23 cm). A stocky sandpiper of wave-lashed rocks. Breeding birds are finely streaked with brown and black on the head and neck, and heavily spotted on breast. Winter adults are mainly dark slate, with a whitish spot in front of the eye, and with yellow legs. The bill is dull orange with a black tip.

VOICE: A single or double *twit* or *twit-twit*.

NESTING: Lays 4 buff eggs, spotted with brown, in a depression lined with grass and leaves on the ground.

HABITAT: Breeds on tundra; rocky coasts and promontories in winter.

RANGE: Breeds on islands in the High Arctic of Canada. Winters along the East Coast from Newfoundland to Virginia. Also found in Eurasia.

SIMILAR SPECIES: See Rock Sandpiper and winter Dunlin.

CONSERVATION:

This species has a large range and breeds in remote Arctic areas, making accurate counts difficult to collect. The species is considered one of least concern, although its numbers appear to be slowly declining in recent decades.

■ SUMMER   ■ MIGRATION
■ WINTER   ■ RARE
■ RESIDENT

Research shows that in the fall adult Baird's Sandpipers fly rapidly along a narrow route through the Great Plains of North America, while young birds migrate over a broad front, and regularly appear on both Pacific and Atlantic coasts. It is suspected that they may cover up to 4000 miles (6400 kilometers) nonstop. The species is named in honor of American naturalist Spencer Fullerton Baird (1823–1887), who served as a longtime Secretary of the Smithsonian Institution.

DESCRIPTION: 7½" (19 cm). A slender "peep" with a short straight bill. It is larger than Least, Semipalmated, and Western sandpipers; about the same size as White-rumped. Its wing tips extend beyond the end of the tail, giving the bird's rear a "pointed" look. Breeding adults have a buff tinge on the face and a splotchy pattern on the upperparts. Juveniles have a buff face and breast, and bold white scaling on the upperparts.

VOICE: A soft *krrrrt*; also a loud trill similar to that of other "peeps."

NESTING: Lays 4 tawny eggs, spotted with brown, in a dry depression on the ground, often among rocks.

HABITAT: Breeds on tundra; frequents grassy pools, wet meadows, and lake and river shores on migration.

RANGE: Breeds in northern Alaska and Canadian Arctic. Migrates mainly through Great Plains and along Pacific Coast in fall, through Great Plains in spring. Regular in small numbers on East Coast in fall. Winters in South America.

SIMILAR SPECIES: White-rumped Sandpiper (*C. fuscicollis*), an Alaska breeder that migrates east of the Rockies, is similar but lacks the scaly pattern above and has a bold white rump.

Juvenile Semipalmated Sandpiper in fresh plumage is noticeably smaller, with a scaled pattern on the back; its upper breast is buff with thin dark streaks, but the face and foreneck are white; its wing tips do not extend beyond the end of the tail at rest.

CONSERVATION: LC
Baird's Sandpipers are common and have maintained a stable population. Climate-related impacts on its Arctic breeding grounds could pose a threat in the future.

LITTLE STINT *Calidris minuta*

■ SUMMER　　■ MIGRATION
■ WINTER　　■ RARE
■ RESIDENT

Sightings of this common, difficult-to-identify Eurasian arctic breeder weren't confirmed in North America until the 1970s. It is rare and accidental in western Alaska, along the Pacific Coast, and in the Northeast. Populations of Little Stint appear to be regulated indirectly by lemming populations. During summers when lemming numbers are low, predatory species such as skuas and snowy owls turn their attention to these small shore-birds as a source of food.

DESCRIPTION: Similar in size to Least Sand-piper, about 6" (15 cm) long, this small sand-piper has a fine, short bill that droops slightly. The breeding adult has rust-orange tertials and coverts, a white throat, and a pale orange face. The breast is speckled with an orange wash, and the back shows a well-defined white V pattern. Identification of juveniles and winter-plumage adults is exceptionally difficult, as this species closely resembles several of North America's native sandpipers.

VOICE: Its call is a sharp, high *stit* in a short series.

NESTING: Lays 3–5 eggs in a scrape on bare ground. It is polyg-amous, and male and female may incubate separate clutches.

HABITAT: Favors more open habitats than the similar Least Sandpiper.

RANGE: Breeds in Arctic Eurasia and winters in Africa and southern Asia. Rarely seen in the Aleutian Islands and other Ber-ing Sea islands. It is a vagrant among other sandpipers along the coasts of North America. Spring and early summer vagrants are adults, while all records after August have been juveniles.

SIMILAR SPECIES: Least Sandpiper, Semipalmated Sand-piper, and other *Calidris* species. In all plumages it closely resembles Red-necked Stint.

CONSERVATION: LC
Little Stint is common in the Old World and its numbers appear to be increasing.

 SUMMER  MIGRATION
WINTER RARE
RESIDENT

Our smallest "peep," the Least Sandpiper is a common bird on inland mudflats and wet grassy areas. With their yellowish legs, they look like miniature Pectoral Sandpipers; like Pectorals, they prefer grassy areas to the more open flats frequented by most shorebirds. As might be expected of an inland bird, it feeds heavily on insects, but when it feeds along the coast its diet is like that of the other "peeps"—the Western, Semipalmated, White-rumped, and Baird's sandpipers—and includes crustaceans, mollusks, and marine worms.

DESCRIPTION: 6" (15 cm). The smallest of North America's shorebirds. It is brownish above with yellowish or greenish legs; a short, thin bill; and a streaked breast. It is grayer in winter plumage. Its bill is shorter, thinner, and more pointed than in Semipalmated or Western sandpipers.

VOICE: A clear *treep*; when feeding, a soft chuckle.

NESTING: Lays 4 pinkish-buff eggs, spotted with brown, in a nest lined with moss and grass placed on a dry hummock in a depression on boggy tundra.

HABITAT: Grassy pools, bogs, and marshes with open areas; also flooded fields and mudflats.

RANGE: Breeds from Alaska east across northern Canada to Newfoundland and Nova Scotia. Winters along coasts from northern California and North Carolina southward; also in Southwest and Southeast.

SIMILAR SPECIES: Other peeps are larger with paler mantles, less finely tapered bills, distinctly different voices, and black legs and feet (but beware birds foraging in dark mud or viewed in midday sunlight). Semipalmated and Western sandpipers are not as warmly colored, appear larger-headed, and crouch much less often.

CONVERSATION: LC
Widespread and common. Least Sandpiper's use of a wide variety of wetland habitats has helped keep this large population stable, although it has declined in the East in recent decades.

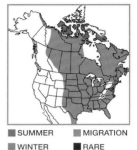

■ SUMMER ■ MIGRATION
■ WINTER ■ RARE
■ RESIDENT

A long-distance flier, the White-rumped Sandpiper performs annual migrations between the Arctic and the subantarctic region. On its wintering grounds in Argentina, this is the most common of the smaller sandpipers. With its conspicuous white rump, this species is the easiest of the "peeps" to identify.

DESCRIPTION: 7½" (19 cm). A slender "peep" (small sandpiper) with a short, straight bill and a white rump. About the same size as Baird's Sandpiper; it is larger than Least, Semipalmated, and Western sandpipers. Its wing tips extend beyond the end of the tail, giving the bird a "pointed" look behind. Breeding adults have a tinge of rusty color on the crown and ear coverts, and dark brown streaks or spots on the flanks. Fall adults have gray upperparts and a gray wash on the breast, and a narrow, pale eyebrow. Young birds are brighter, with the feathers of the upperparts edged with rufous.

VOICE: A high-pitched *tzeet*; also a swallow-like twitter.

NESTING: Lays 4 olive eggs, spotted with brown, in a grass-lined nest in a slight depression on the ground.

HABITAT: Breeds on tundra; flats, grassy pools, wet meadows, and shores during migration.

RANGE: Breeds in northern Alaska and the Canadian Arctic. Migrates mainly through the eastern and central United States. Winters in South America.

SIMILAR SPECIES: Standing White-rumpeds usually exhibit their rumps only when preening. Breeding Western Sandpiper is far more colorful above. Winter-plumage Semipalmated and Western sandpipers are quite similar, have broader whitish eyebrows and largely white foreparts; their wing tips do not extend beyond the end of the tail. Baird's Sandpiper in fresh plumage has a bright buff foreneck and upper breast, but also has a clearly defined scaled pattern to the back; it also has a different flight call. Curlew and Stilt sandpipers also have white rumps but are larger with proportionately longer bills, necks, and legs.

CONSERVATION: LC
A species of least concern, although its use of select migration stops during its long flights makes it susceptible to any loss or degradation of that habitat.

- ■ SUMMER
- ■ WINTER
- ■ RESIDENT
- ■ MIGRATION
- ■ RARE

This species looks like a small, buffy edition of the Upland Sandpiper, at times its grassland associate. It is slow to flush, and when approached it often runs through the short grass instead of flying off. Like the American Golden-Plover, it undertakes an amazing migration in both spring and fall. After the nesting season in the far Northwest, it migrates southward on a broad front, eventually ending up on the Argentine pampas, where it spends the winter. On the return passage in spring, its movements are much more confined, carrying it chiefly up the Mississippi Valley and to the West, but ultimately back to the Arctic shores of Alaska and Canada.

DESCRIPTION: 8" (20 cm). A starling-sized sandpiper with a small head. Its underparts and face are buff, and its legs are dull orange-yellow. The bill is short and straight.

VOICE: A low *tik-tik-tik*.

NESTING: Lays 4 pale buff, brown-blotched eggs in a grass-lined nest on the Arctic tundra.

HABITAT: Breeds on dry tundra; visits short-grass prairies, fields, and meadows on migration.

RANGE: Breeds in northernmost Alaska and Canada. Migrates mainly through the Great Plains, but small numbers appear on the East Coast and smaller numbers on the West Coast. Winters in South America.

SIMILAR SPECIES: The larger Upland Sandpiper has a small, bony head; a thin neck; and a long tail. Its face is finely streaked, its underparts are streaked and barred, and its underwing is barred. See juvenile Baird's Sandpiper.

CONSERVATION: NT
Once hunted widely, this species is now dealing with the loss of migration stopover prairie habitat to agriculture. This once abundant species is listed as Near Threatened.

PECTORAL SANDPIPER *Calidris melanotos*

■ SUMMER ■ MIGRATION
■ WINTER ■ RARE
■ RESIDENT

In the days when shorebirds were shot as game, hunters called this species the "Grass Snipe"—referring to its liking for grassy meadows—or "Krieker" because of its grating, snipe-like flight call. During the short Arctic breeding season, food—insects, especially flies and their larvae—is at a premium. To ensure an adequate supply for the young, male Pectoral Sandpipers depart for the south before the eggs hatch, so they don't compete for food with the mothers and their chicks. Then the adult females leave, too, and in the last few weeks of summer the young have the tundra to themselves.

DESCRIPTION: 9" (23 cm). A chunky, somewhat short-legged sandpiper with a heavily streaked breast sharply delineated from an unmarked white belly. It has yellow legs. In flight, it shows dark wings with no prominent stripe. Birds in breeding plumage have largely sooty brown upperparts, with chestnut and buff edges to the feathers; the dense, dark brown streaking on the throat and upper breast terminates abruptly in a clean-cut line across the lower breast, contrasting with the white belly, flanks, and undertail coverts. Birds in winter plumage are similar to breeding-plumage adults but are duller.

VOICE: A dull *krrrrp*.

NESTING: Lays 4 buff-white eggs, marked with brown, in a slight depression in boggy tundra.

HABITAT: Breeds on tundra; during migration, it visits moist grassy places, grass-lined pools, golf courses and airports after heavy rains, and salt creeks and meadows.

RANGE: Breeds on the Arctic coasts from Alaska east to Hudson Bay. Migrates along the Atlantic and Pacific coasts and through the interior. Winters in southern South America.

SIMILAR SPECIES: Sharp-tailed Sandpiper in breeding plumage resembles a juvenile Pectoral but lacks the incomplete V mark on the back; in flight, all plumages of Sharp-tailed show a different pattern of streaking on the underparts. Least Sandpiper is somewhat similar in all plumages, but much smaller.

CONSERVATION: Once widespread in North America, overhunting seriously hurt Pectoral Sandpiper numbers in the 19th century. Its population has stabilized in recent decades.

Calidris pusilla SEMIPALMATED SANDPIPER

■ SUMMER   ■ MIGRATION
■ WINTER   ■ RARE
■ RESIDENT

These small, plain-looking sandpipers are numerous and found across North America, sometimes occurring by the thousands during migration. Often they are seen on mudflats feeding together with their close relatives, the Least and Western sandpipers. The word "Semipalmated" means "half-webbed," referring to the birds' toes. In fact, the toes are only slightly lobed at their bases, but they do help the birds to walk on mud without sinking.

DESCRIPTION: 5½–6¾" (14–17 cm). Slightly larger than a Least Sandpiper. In all plumages, it is grayer above with a less-streaked breast than other "peeps." Its feet are black. The bill is black and short, drooping slightly at the tip, and noticeably stouter than the bill of a Least Sandpiper.

VOICE: A sharp *cheh* or *churk*, not as drawn out as the notes of the Least and Western sandpipers.

NESTING: Lays 4 buff eggs, marked with brown, in a depression on the ground.

HABITAT: Breeds on tundra; winters on and migrates along coastal beaches, lake and river shores, mudflats, and pools in salt marshes.

RANGE: Breeds in northern Alaska and Canada south to Hudson Bay. Migrates commonly through Canada and the eastern and central United States, rarely but regularly in the West. Winters in South America.

SIMILAR SPECIES: Western Sandpipers' longer, dropped bill often is cited as the best field mark to distinguish Western and Semipalmated, but Semipalmateds in the west tend to show longer bills than eastern birds. Many female Semipalmateds from eastern Canada have bills overlapping in size with those of male Westerns. Where these species mix in migration, only birds with very short or very long bills can be identified by bill length alone. Breeding-plumage birds are distinctive; more rapidly molting adult Westerns show some rusty scapular feathers

and streaks on the flanks into August. Juvenile Westerns have brighter, more rusty-edged scapulars and tertials than juvenile Semipalmateds, but also molt earlier. The best characteristic for distinguishing these species is voice, but recognizing different calls takes practice, and individual calls are often difficult to pick out.

Also see Red-necked Stint and Least and Baird's sandpipers.

CONSERVATION:

Once among the most abundant shorebirds on the continent, even into the 21st century, Semipalmated Sandpiper populations have been in steep decline in recent years, especially the eastern population. The species was listed as Near Threatened in 2012 by the IUCN Red List. Semipalmated Sandpipers depend heavily on key migratory stopover sites, many of which have been turned into wildlife reserves as conservationists look to protect key habitats for this species and other migratory shorebirds.

WESTERN SANDPIPER *Calidris mauri*

■ SUMMER ■ MIGRATION
■ WINTER ■ RARE
■ RESIDENT

This species often associates with the slightly smaller Semipalmated Sandpipers. Western Sandpipers usually feed in deeper water than the other "peeps" (small sandpipers) and sometimes immerse their bills completely. In all other respects, these sandpipers are much alike in their behavior and are difficult to distinguish in the field. The flocks of these "peeps" that spread out on mudflats during fall and winter take flight readily when threatened. When the tide covers their shallow feeding grounds, the flocks move to higher ground; there they preen themselves, rest, and wait for the next low tide, when they can resume feeding.

DESCRIPTION: 6½" (17 cm). Similar to Semipalmated Sandpiper and not always easy to distinguish, but its bill tends to be longer, with a more evident droop at the tip. In summer, its crown and upper back are rusty; in winter, the crown and upper back are dull gray.

VOICE: A soft *cheep* or *kreep*, higher and thinner than that of Semipalmated.

NESTING: Lays 4 creamy eggs, with red-brown spots, in a grass-lined depression on either wet or dry tundra.

HABITAT: Shores, mudflats, grassy pools, and wet meadows.

RANGE: Breeds in northern and western Alaska. Winters mainly along the coasts from California and Virginia southward to South America.

SIMILAR SPECIES: See Semipalmated, Least, and White-rumped sandpipers, Red-necked Stint, and Dunlin.

CONSERVATION: 🐦

One of the most abundant species of shorebirds in North America. Populations are decreasing slightly, but they remain a species of least concern.

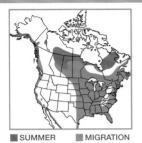

■ SUMMER ■ MIGRATION
■ WINTER ■ RARE
■ RESIDENT

These are among the first shorebirds to migrate south, with adult Short-billed Dowitchers leaving as early as July and the young following in August. Dowitchers often occur in large flocks—sometimes in the thousands—on coastal flats during migrations, remaining well bunched whether in flight or feeding on a mudflat. They probe deeply with their long bills, with rapid up-and-down movements like sewing machines, seeking marine worms, snails, tiny crustaceans, and aquatic larvae.

DESCRIPTION: 12" (30 cm). A snipe-like, long-billed shorebird with a white lower back and rump, black-and-white checkered tail, dark bill, and green legs. Summer adults have rusty underparts (the belly is often whitish) with variable spotting on the breast and sides, barred flanks, and reddish edges on the feathers of the upperparts. Winter birds are gray overall, with a pale eyebrow and a white lower back and rump. See Long-billed Dowitcher.

VOICE: A soft *tu-tu-tu*, quite unlike call of Long-billed Dowitcher.

NESTING: Lays 4 greenish eggs, spotted with brown, in a nest lined with grass and moss in a depression on the ground.

HABITAT: Breeds on moist tundra or beside forest pools; visits mudflats, creeks, salt marshes, and tidal estuaries during migration and in winter.

RANGE: Breeds in southern Alaska, central interior Canada, and northern Quebec. Winters along the coasts from California and Virginia southward.

SUBSPECIES: Three populations of Short-billed Dowitchers are divided by range. The Atlantic and Pacific populations are similar to one another: darker overall, with dense spotting on the neck and breast and more white on the belly. The Central population is brighter and tends more toward having clean orange underparts and almost no white on the belly.

SIMILAR SPECIES: See Long-billed Dowitcher and Stilt Sandpiper. Common Snipe has shorter legs, a median crown stripe, and facial and back stripes; it lacks a white wedge up the back and the barred tail.

CONSERVATION:
Although still numerous, conservationists are monitoring Short-billed Dowitchers because of their decreasing population. Habitat loss from development and climate change are placing pressure on this species.

LONG-BILLED DOWITCHER *Limnodromus scolopaceus*

■ SUMMER ■ MIGRATION
■ WINTER ■ RARE
■ RESIDENT

Dowitchers are most often seen during migration. This species favors freshwater habitats, while the Short-billed Dowitcher is more partial to salt water. The main fall migration of Long-bills takes place in September and October, after most of the Short-bills have already departed.

DESCRIPTION: 12" (30 cm). A snipe-like, long-billed shorebird with a white lower back and rump, black-and-white checkered tail, dark bill, and green legs. Summer adults have rusty reddish underparts (including the belly) with barring on the breast, sides, and flanks, and reddish edges on the feathers of the upperparts. Winter birds are gray overall, with a pale eyebrow and a white lower back and rump. See Short-billed Dowitcher.

VOICE: A high sharp *keek*, quite unlike call of Short-billed Dowitcher.

NESTING: Lays 4 olive eggs, spotted with brown, in a grass and moss-lined nest on the ground.

HABITAT: Breeds in muskeg; found on mudflats, marshy pools, and margins of freshwater ponds during migration and in winter.

RANGE: Breeds in western Alaska and extreme northwestern Mackenzie. Winters mainly along the coasts from Washington and Virginia southward.

SIMILAR SPECIES: Breeding Short-billed Dowitcher either has a white belly or lacks the densely spotted throat and bars on the sides of the upper breast. The light bars on its tail feathers are usually broader. The juvenile's upperparts are broadly edged with rust or buff with conspicuous internal markings; the breast speckled or streaked. The difference in call is diagnostic. Common Snipe has shorter legs, a median crown stripe, and facial and back stripes; it lacks the white wedge up the back and barred tail.

CONSERVATION: LC
Widespread and common. Although the species' population trends are unclear, some surveys suggest the breeding population may be increasing.

■ SUMMER ■ MIGRATION
■ WINTER ■ RARE
■ RESIDENT

The American Woodcock is seldom seen, for its protective coloring renders it virtually invisible against a background of dried leaves. When flushed, it zigzags off through the brush with a whistling of wings. Those fortunate enough to live near their breeding grounds may see woodcocks perform their courtship flight in early spring each year. In these spectacular aerial displays, the male spirals up to a considerable height, circles, then plummets down to the ground, twittering during the descent. Woodcocks subsist chiefly on earthworms, which they extract with their long bills; the tip of the upper mandible is flexible so that they can grasp a worm while probing in mud without opening the bill. Insect larvae and occasionally vegetable matter are also eaten.

DESCRIPTION: 11" (28 cm). A chunky, quail-sized bird with a long bill and rounded wings. It is rufous below with a "dead leaf" pattern above, giving the bird superb camouflage. It has transverse black bands on the head. Its eyes are large, bulging, and located close to the back of the head.

VOICE: A loud, buzzy *bzeep!* similar to the call of a nighthawk and often repeated on the ground about every two seconds during courtship.

NESTING: Lays 4 buff eggs, spotted with brown, in a hollow among dead leaves or under a bush.

HABITAT: Moist woodlands and thickets near open fields.

RANGE: Breeds from southern Manitoba and Newfoundland south to Texas, Gulf Coast states, and central Florida. Winters in southeastern states.

SIMILAR SPECIES: Common Snipe has a striped head and back, and pointed wings; it usually calls when flushed.

CONSERVATION:
Common, although difficult to locate and count with much accuracy. American populations are declining, but Canadian numbers are increasing as harvested forests give way to thickets, which these birds use. American Woodcocks are still hunted in the U.S., although the overall decrease in population is not strongly tied to hunting.

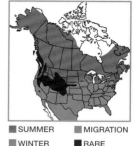

■ SUMMER ■ MIGRATION
■ WINTER ■ RARE
■ RESIDENT

This species, an upland bird, is one of the few shorebirds that can still be hunted legally. It stays well hidden in ground cover, flushes abruptly, and zigzags sharply in flight, all habits that make it difficult to shoot and therefore a favorite among hunters. In addition to the alarm note described in the Voice section, these birds have a variety of calls heard only on the breeding ground, and they perform a spectacular aerial territorial display in which the feathers of the tail produce an eerie whistling sound. Although the Wilson's Snipe generally migrates in flocks at night, during the day the birds scatter and usually feed alone. They seek food early in the morning and in late afternoon, and seem to be more active on cloudy days. They use their long bills to probe deeply in the mud to find small animals.

DESCRIPTION: 10½" (27 cm). A long-billed, brownish shorebird with a striped head and back, white belly, and rusty tail. It is usually seen when flushed from the edge of a marsh or a pond. Its flight is fast and erratic.

VOICE: A sharp rasping *scaip!* when flushed.

NESTING: Lays 4 pale olive-brown eggs, spotted with black, concealed in a grass-lined depression in a grass tussock in a marsh.

HABITAT: Freshwater marshes, ponds, flooded meadows, and fields; more rarely in salt marshes.

RANGE: Breeds from northern Alaska and Canada south to California, southwestern states, and New Jersey. Winters north from tropical America to British Columbia, northern Gulf Coast states, and Virginia.

SIMILAR SPECIES: Dowitchers lack stripes on the head, have a white wedge up the back, and a barred tail; they are rusty below in breeding plumage and grayish in winter plumage.

Wilson's Snipe is similar to the Common Snipe (*G. gallinago*), a mainly Eurasian species that occurs in North America only rarely. Common Snipe is best distinguished by white wing bars on the underwing, visible in flight.

CONSERVATION: 🐦 Widespread and common but inconspicuous, Wilson's Snipe populations are relatively stable or perhaps declining slightly. Draining of wetlands and collisions with human structures and vehicles pose the greatest threats to these birds.

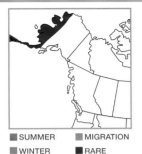

■ SUMMER ■ MIGRATION
■ WINTER ■ RARE
■ RESIDENT

A rare Eurasian migrant on the western Aleutian Islands, Pribilofs, St. Lawrence Island, and southern coast of Alaska; there are also several records for the Pacific Coast of the United States and one from Massachusetts.

DESCRIPTION: 10" (25.5 cm). A medium-size shorebird with a long, upturned, pale-based, dark bill. It has short orange-yellow legs. Its upperparts are gray-brown, contrasting with black scapular lines. In flight, it shows dark leading edge of the wing in contrast with a white trailing edge of the inner wing.

VOICE: A rolling series of shrill whistles.

NESTING: Lays 4 pale buff eggs, spotted and blotched with black-brown, in shallow vegetation-lined cup on the ground.

HABITAT: River meadows, marshes, vegetated banks of lakes, ponds, and streams; in winter, it is found in mudflats and shallow estuaries.

RANGE: Breeds in central and eastern Eurasia. Winters from the Persian Gulf, Southeast Asia, and Hainan south to South Africa, India, the East Indies, New Guinea, and Australia.

SIMILAR SPECIES: The upturned bill is distinctive. Lesser Yellowlegs is larger with longer legs. Solitary Sandpiper is smaller with olive-colored legs.

CONSERVATION: Least concern but decreasing in its native range.

COMMON SANDPIPER *Actitis hypoleucos*

■ SUMMER ■ MIGRATION
■ WINTER ■ RARE
■ RESIDENT

Like a number of Eurasian shorebird species, Common Sandpiper occurs as a rare migrant on the western Aleutian Islands, Pribilofs, and St. Lawrence Island. This bird is abundant in Eurasia and resembles its common North American cousin, the Spotted Sandpiper.

DESCRIPTION: 8" (20.5 cm). Breeding adult resembles Spotted Sandpiper in non-breeding plumage. The upperparts are brown, barred, and lightly streaked with dark. The upper breast is finely streaked, and the underparts are white. Its longer tail and more white in the wing help to distinguish juvenile and winter adults from Spotted Sandpipers.

VOICE: A high-pitched, piping *twee-wee-wee*.

NESTING: Lays 4 buff eggs, spotted, speckled, and streaked with red-brown, in substantial cup lined with vegetation, usually near water.

HABITAT: Margins of streams, ponds, lakes, and seacoasts.

RANGE: Breeds in Eurasia from British Isles to northern Siberia south to Mediterranean region and Japan. Winters from southern Europe to Japan south to southern Africa, Australia, and islands of the western Pacific.

SIMILAR SPECIES: See Spotted Sandpiper.

CONSERVATION:  Common but decreasing in its native range.

Actitis macularius # SPOTTED SANDPIPER

■ SUMMER ■ MIGRATION
■ WINTER ■ RARE
■ RESIDENT

This is one of the best known of American shorebirds. Its habit of endlessly bobbing the rear part of its body up and down has earned it the colloquial name "Teeter-tail." When flushed from the margin of a pond or stream, it is easily identified by its distinctive flight—short bursts of rapidly vibrating wingbeats alternating with brief glides. Most of our shorebirds breed in the Far North; this is one of the few that nests in the United States as well as subarctic and continental Canada.

DESCRIPTION: 7½" (19 cm). A starling-sized shorebird that bobs its tail almost constantly. Breeding adults are brown above with a bold white wing stripe, and white below with bold black spots on the breast and belly. Fall birds lack black spots below and have a brownish smudge at the sides of the breast.

VOICE: A clear *peet-weet*; also a soft trill.

NESTING: Lays 4 buff eggs, spotted with brown, in a nest lined with grass or moss in a slight depression on the ground.

HABITAT: Ponds, streams, and other waterways, both inland and along the shore.

RANGE: Breeds from northern Alaska and Canada across most of the continent to the southern United States. Winters along the Pacific Coast south from British Columbia and across the southern states south to South America.

SIMILAR SPECIES: See Solitary Sandpiper.

Common Sandpiper is a rare migrant in North America. It has a longer tail; longer, more prominent wing stripes and trailing edges; streaked breast patches; a dark-brown bill with a pale base; and pale greenish legs all year. It lacks spots in breeding plumage; winter birds and juveniles are browner, less gray, with less conspicuous barring on the wing coverts.

CONSERVATION: LC
Although its numbers have decreased in recent decades, Spotted Sandpiper remains one of our most common and widespread shorebird species.

SOLITARY SANDPIPER *Tringa solitaria*

■ SUMMER   ■ MIGRATION
■ WINTER   ■ RARE
■ RESIDENT

The well-named Solitary Sandpiper usually migrates alone rather than in flocks. It feeds along the margin of a wooded pond or stream and, in the West, along the edges of irrigation canals and small ponds, especially where cattle are watered. When disturbed, it bobs its head and flies up, uttering its ringing note call. Unlike other North American shorebirds, which generally nest on the ground, Solitary Sandpiper reuses abandoned songbird nests placed high in the trees surrounding northern spruce bogs and ponds.

DESCRIPTION: 8½" (22 cm). A small, dark sandpiper with dark olive legs, speckled upperparts, a white tail barred with black, and prominent eye rings. Its flight is swallow-like. It has no white wing stripe, as is seen in Spotted Sandpiper.

VOICE: A high-pitched *peet-weet* or *peet-weet-weet*, more shrill than the call of Spotted Sandpiper.

NESTING: Lays 4 pale green or buff eggs, thickly spotted with gray and brown, in deserted tree nests of thrushes, jays, or blackbirds.

HABITAT: Ponds, bogs, wet swampy places, and woodland streams.

RANGE: Breeds in Alaska and across Canada to Labrador, south to northeastern Minnesota. Winters in the American tropics.

SIMILAR SPECIES: See Lesser Yellowlegs. Wood Sandpiper is similar, but the species' ranges overlap only minutely. Spotted Sandpiper has a white wing stripe and trailing edge, unspotted upperparts, heavily spotted underparts in breeding plumage, and rapid, stiff, shallow wingbeats.

CONSERVATION:
Solitary Sandpipers are fairly common but their numbers are declining due to habitat loss and degradation. Exact counts for this widely dispersed species are difficult to collect.

■ SUMMER   ■ MIGRATION
■ WINTER   ■ RARE
■ RESIDENT

A relatively little known species, the Gray-tailed Tattler occurs as a rare but regular spring and fall migrant on the outer Aleutian Islands, Pribilofs, and St. Lawrence Island, and casually on the Alaska coast north to Point Barrow; there are also single records from Washington and California.

DESCRIPTION: 10" (25.5 cm). Similar to Wandering Tattler, except its ventral barring is finer and confined to the breast and flanks; the midbreast, belly, and undertail coverts are nearly pure white; and its distinct white eyebrows meet on the forehead. Winter birds and juveniles are best distinguished by voice.

VOICE: A mellow, whistled, up-slurred *too-weet*.

NESTING: Lays 4 greenish eggs, heavily blotched and spotted with brown, in a shallow scrape on a stony river bank; also in used nests of thrushes several feet above the ground.

HABITAT: Breeds along streams in stony or mossy situations in mountainous or hilly regions. Winters and in migration on rocky seacoasts and islets; also on sandy beaches on oceanic islands.

RANGE: An annual migrant in the western Aleutians; casual farther east in the Aleutians, on the Alaska islands of the Bering Sea, and on the Alaska coast north to Point Barrow. Native to eastern Asia.

SIMILAR SPECIES: See Wandering Tattler.

CONSERVATION: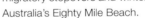
Gray-tailed Tattler is decreasing. Threats to the species include loss and degradation of wetlands, hunting, and disturbance at key migratory stopovers and wintering sites such as Australia's Eighty Mile Beach.

■ SUMMER ■ MIGRATION
■ WINTER ■ RARE
■ RESIDENT

The Wandering Tattler breeds above the timberline in Alaska's rugged mountains and frequents rocky shores along the Pacific Coast for much of the rest of the year. It is seen only rarely on sandy beaches and mud flats. A medium-sized shorebird, this species is immediately distinguished by its uniform dark gray upperparts. It has relatively long wings and pumps the rear part of its body when it walks. Usually seen singly or in small groups, it is regularly found among flocks of other shorebirds on rocky coastlines.

DESCRIPTION: 11" (28 cm). A medium-sized sandpiper, uniform gray above with a whitish eyebrow, dark rump and tail, and greenish-yellow legs. Breeding birds have heavily barred underparts. Winter birds are whitish below, with a gray wash on the sides and flanks. It has a straight, medium-length bill.

VOICE: A series of 3 or 4 clear whistles, given in flight. It is named for its loud alarm call, which alerts other birds to the presence of danger.

NESTING: Lays 4 greenish eggs, marked with dark brown, in a finely built nest of roots, twigs, and dry leaves on a gravel bar in a mountain stream above the timberline.

HABITAT: Mountain streams in summer; coastal rocks, shell beaches, and rocky coves in fall and winter.

RANGE: Breeds in mountain areas of south-central Alaska and northwestern British Columbia. Winters on the Pacific Coast from central California southward.

SIMILAR SPECIES: Gray-tailed Tattler is slightly paler above; barring on the underparts is limited to the breast, sides, and flanks, and the bars are narrower and paler, especially on the flanks; adults may have a broader white eyebrow. Juveniles and non-breeding adults are distinguishable only by call. Other shorebirds lack the combination of uniform slate-gray upperparts and a straight, medium-length bill.

CONSERVATION:
The small population of this widespread species appears to be stable.

■ SUMMER   ■ MIGRATION
■ WINTER   ■ RARE
■ RESIDENT

The smaller of the two yellowlegs shares most of the habits of its larger relative but is considerably more gregarious, often feeding in large, loose flocks of several dozen or even hundreds of birds. Both yellowlegs species pick and jab at their food, but the Lesser lacks the sweeping technique for catching fish. The Lesser is more apt than the Greater to avoid open beaches, often inhabits smaller ponds, and is typically more approachable. Both species of yellowlegs bob their heads up and down when watching an intruder.

DESCRIPTION: 10½" (27 cm). A slender, gray-streaked wader with a conspicuous white rump and long bright yellow legs. It appears to be a smaller, more slender edition of the Greater Yellowlegs, with a proportionately shorter, straighter, more slender bill.

VOICE: A flat *tu-tu*, less musical than call of Greater Yellowlegs.

NESTING: Lays 4 buff eggs, blotched with brown, in a slight depression on the open ground near water.

HABITAT: Breeds in northern bogs; frequents marshy ponds, lake and river shores, and mudflats during migration.

RANGE: Breeds from Alaska to Hudson Bay. Winters on coasts from southern California and Virginia southward, and along the Gulf Coast.

SIMILAR SPECIES: See Greater Yellowlegs. The Lesser Yellowlegs is so similar to the Greater Yellowlegs that identification of a solitary, silent bird is often difficult. Bill length is the best clue; the bill of Lesser Yellowlegs is about the length of the head, whereas the bill of Greater Yellowlegs is much longer than the head and may be slightly upturned.

Solitary Sandpiper is smaller, dark brown above with a brown rump, a largely dark tail, and much shorter, dull green legs.

CONSERVATION: Lesser Yellowlegs was formerly a favorite game bird but is now fully protected. Today it is a common bird but its numbers are decreasing.

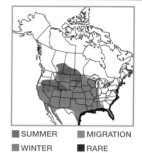

■ SUMMER   ■ MIGRATION
■ WINTER   ■ RARE
■ RESIDENT

Willets look quite nondescript on the ground and superficially resemble yellowlegs, but in flight or with wings spread, they are distinguished by their striking black-and-white color pattern. They separate when feeding but remain in loose contact. If one bird takes flight, all the others will join it; the birds usually fly together, calling back and forth, before dropping down farther along the beach.

DESCRIPTION: 15" (38 cm). A large, gray-brown shorebird with a long, straight bill. It is best identified in flight by its flashy black-and-white wing pattern. Its gray legs and thicker bill distinguish it from Greater Yellowlegs.

VOICE: A loud, ringing *pill-will-willet* and a quieter *kuk-kuk-kuk-kuk-kuk*.

NESTING: Lays 4 olive-buff eggs, spotted with brown, in a nest lined with weeds or bits of shell placed in a depression on open ground or in a grass clump.

HABITAT: Coastal beaches, freshwater and salt marshes, lakeshores, and wet prairies.

RANGE: Breeds from central Canada to northeastern California and Nevada; also along the Atlantic and Gulf coasts south from Nova Scotia. Winters along the coasts from Oregon and the Carolinas southward.

SUBSPECIES: There are two distinct Willet populations in North America. The Eastern group is a coastal population year-round, nesting in salt marshes along the Atlantic and Gulf coasts. Eastern Willets have stouter bills and are more heavily barred. The Western population breeds in inland prairie marshes in the West and migrates to winter on both coasts. Western Willets tend to be larger and paler gray. There is a slight difference in the pitch of their calls, with the Western birds' voices being subtly lower-pitched.

SIMILAR SPECIES: A winter-plumage Hudsonian Godwit has a longer, tapered, upturned bill that is always pink at the base; less white on the wing; and a broad, black tail band. See Greater Yellowlegs.

CONSERVATION: 
Willets are common and their populations have stabilized after hunting and habitat loss reduced their numbers from historic levels.

■ SUMMER ■ MIGRATION
■ WINTER ■ RARE
■ RESIDENT

The Spotted Redshank is a rare spring and fall visitor to the Aleutian Islands and Pribilofs. It is accidental outside of Alaska on both coasts; records of strays have been confirmed far inland in North America.

DESCRIPTION: 12" (30.5 cm). A slim, yellowlegs-like shorebird. Its bill is long and slender with a droop at the tip and a red lower mandible. Its legs are orange or orange-red. The breeding adult has black underparts and upperparts spotted with white. Its wing linings, upper rump, and back all show white in flight. Adults in winter are uniformly gray above and white below; juveniles are similar except for warm brownish-gray barring on the underparts.

VOICE: A clear *chew-whit*, with rising inflection.

NESTING: Lays 4 pale green eggs, spotted and blotched with dark brown, in a shallow scrape lined with a small quantity of stems, leaves, and a few feathers and placed in the open.

HABITAT: Breeds in marshy sites in bushy tundra and taiga edge; frequents marshes, ponds, wet meadows, and mudflats during migration and winter.

RANGE: Breeds in northern Eurasia. Winters from the Mediterranean region to eastern China south to equatorial Africa and Southeast Asia.

SIMILAR SPECIES: Unique in spring plumage. In fall, it is distinguishable from other *Tringa* species in Alaska by its size, the orange or red base of its straight bill, a white back and rump, and its deep red or orange-red legs.

Greater Yellowlegs is nearly the same size but shorter-billed; in fall, it appears darker above.

Ruff is smaller, stockier, with a shorter bill; it lacks a white rump.

CONSERVATION: LC
Widespread in Eurasia, the Spotted Redshank population appears to be stable.

COMMON GREENSHANK *Tringa nebularia*

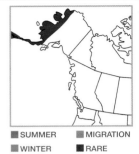

■ SUMMER ■ MIGRATION
■ WINTER ■ RARE
■ RESIDENT

In North America, the Common Greenshank occurs as a regular spring migrant in the Aleutian Islands and casually in the Pribilofs, with a few records of strays along the East Coast. This species fills the same ecological niche as our Greater Yellowlegs, and the two species closely resemble one another in voice and appearance.

DESCRIPTION: 12" (30.5 cm). A large shorebird, quite similar to Greater Yellowlegs, except its legs are greenish, its lower back and rump are white, its tail is barred with gray, and its long bill has a distinct upward sweep.

VOICE: A sharp *tew-tew-tew*, all on the same pitch.

NESTING: Lays 4 off-white eggs, heavily blotched, streaked, and speckled with varying shades of red and chocolate brown, with surface markings of gray, violet, and lavender, in a grass-lined scrape, often near a rock or piece of wood.

HABITAT: Breeds in taiga marshes, bogs, and wet meadows; frequents marshes, ponds, lakeshores, and mudflats during migration and winter.

RANGE: Breeds in northern Eurasia. Winters from the Mediterranean region east to eastern China, south to southern Africa, New Guinea, and Australia.

SIMILAR SPECIES: Greater Yellowlegs is darker above and below, with bright yellow legs; white is confined to the rump, lower belly, and undertail coverts.

CONSERVATION:
Widespread in Eurasia, the Common Greenshank population appears to be stable.

■ SUMMER ■ MIGRATION
■ WINTER ■ RARE
■ RESIDENT

The larger of the two yellowlegs is a noisy and conspicuous bird. It is also more wary than its smaller relative and flushes at a greater distance. It often runs about wildly in shallow water or wades up to its belly and occasionally even swims. With its long legs, it easily obtains food in pools. The bill, slightly upturned, is used to skim small animals from the surface of the water as the bird swings it from side to side. This behavior, seldom seen in the Lesser Yellowlegs, makes a Greater Yellowlegs recognizable at a long distance.

DESCRIPTION: 14" (36 cm). A slender, gray-streaked wader with a conspicuous white rump and long yellow legs. Lesser Yellowlegs is similar but smaller, with a shorter, straighter, and more slender bill and a different call.

VOICE: A series of musical whistled notes: *whew-whew-whew*.

NESTING: Lays 4 tawny eggs, heavily marked with brown, in a slight depression on the ground in a damp open spot.

HABITAT: Breeds on tundra and marshy ground; frequents pools, lakeshores, and tidal mudflats on migration.

RANGE: Breeds from south-central Alaska eastward across central Canada to the Maritime Provinces and Newfoundland. Winters mainly along coasts from Washington State and Virginia southward, and along the Gulf Coast.

SIMILAR SPECIES: Lesser Yellowlegs is smaller; has a fine, straight, proportionally shorter black bill; has a white belly in breeding plumage, and a gray breast in juvenal plumage; and has a different call.

Willet has blue-gray legs, a heavier bill, and a bold black-and-white pattern to the wings.

CONSERVATION: Common and widespread. Although population trends for this far-north breeder are difficult to assess, its overall numbers appear to be stable.

WOOD SANDPIPER *Tringa glareola*

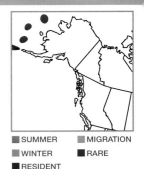

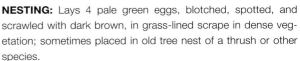

The Wood Sandpiper is a fairly common spring migrant and an occasional breeder in the western Aleutian Islands; less frequent, but regular, on the Pribilofs and St. Lawrence Island. It makes casual appearances in northern and western Alaska, as well as stray occurrences in New York and Barbados.

DESCRIPTION: 8–9" (20.5–23 cm). Resembles a chunky Lesser Yellowlegs. Its upperparts are dark and heavily spotted with white. It has a prominent whitish eyebrow, grayish-white underparts, a relatively short bill, and greenish legs. Pale wing linings, the lack of a wing stripe, its white rump, and densely barred tail show in flight.

VOICE: A loud, sharp whistled *fee-fee-fee-fee-fee*, or *chip-ip-ip-ip*.

NESTING: Lays 4 pale green eggs, blotched, spotted, and scrawled with dark brown, in grass-lined scrape in dense vegetation; sometimes placed in old tree nest of a thrush or other species.

HABITAT: Breeds near taiga pond edges. Frequents pond and lakeshores, bogs and shallow pools, and wet meadows during migration and winter.

RANGE: Breeds in northern Eurasia. Winters from Mediterranean region east to southern China, south to southern Africa, the Malay Peninsula, East Indies, and Australia.

SIMILAR SPECIES: Solitary Sandpiper and Lesser Yellowlegs are similar but rarely overlap.

CONSERVATION: Abundant and widespread throughout the Old World.

■ SUMMER ■ MIGRATION
■ WINTER ■ RARE
■ RESIDENT

Among phalaropes, the female is larger and has brighter plumage, and the male incubates the eggs and cares for the young. These active sandpipers float buoyantly, picking small creatures from the surface of the water with rapid jabs of the bill, often while swimming in tight circles to stir up the water and raise food items to the surface. Wilson's is larger than the Red and Red-necked phalaropes and has a much longer, thinner bill. Unlike the others, this species does not have fully lobed toes and so rarely swims, spending no time at sea. When it does feed in water, however, it spins in circles more rapidly than the other two. It is limited to the Western Hemisphere and breeds much farther south than the other phalaropes.

DESCRIPTION: 9" (23 cm). A strikingly patterned shorebird with a needle-like bill, pearl-gray head and back, white underparts, a black stripe through the eye and down the neck, and chestnut markings on the breast and back. In fall plumage, it is pale gray above and white below; in this plumage, its pale color, more terrestrial habits, and slender bill distinguish it from other phalaropes. Females are more boldly patterned than males.

VOICE: A soft *quoit-quoit-quoit*.

NESTING: Lays 4 pale buff eggs, spotted with brown, in a grass-lined nest placed in a slight depression on the ground near water.

HABITAT: Prairie pools and marshes, lake and river shores, and marshy pools along the coast.

RANGE: Breeds from southern Yukon and Minnesota south to California and Kansas; also in the Great Lakes region and in Massachusetts. Winters mainly in the American tropics; a few birds winter in California and Texas.

SIMILAR SPECIES: Both other phalaropes have a shorter bill and legs, a white wing stripe, a dark-centered rump, a dark crown and nape in breeding plumage, and a black mask in winter plumage.

Lesser Yellowlegs has finely spotted upperparts and dark streaks or a gray wash on the throat and upper breast.

Stilt Sandpiper has a longer, heavier bill, drooping near the tip.

CONSERVATION: LC
Wilson's Phalaropes are numerous and their populations are stable to increasing. Heavy reliance on saline or alkaline lakes for migration—such as Utah's Great Salt Lake and Mono Lake and the Salton Sea in California—makes them vulnerable to alterations in these areas.

RED-NECKED PHALAROPE *Phalaropus lobatus*

■ SUMMER ■ MIGRATION
■ WINTER ■ RARE
■ RESIDENT

Male and female Red-necked Phalaropes are unmistakable in breeding plumage; winter-plumage birds, on the other hand, are much more nondescript and less easy to identify. During migration and in winter, Red-necked and Red phalaropes occur on the ocean, where they are sometimes seen in large flocks. This species' flight is erratic and darting. Red-necked Phalaropes, like Red Phalaropes but unlike other shorebirds, prefer to swim rather than wade, a habit that enables them to spend the winter on the high seas, although on occasion they wade in pools and feed on mudflats with many other shorebirds.

DESCRIPTION: 7" (18 cm). A sparrow-sized swimming shorebird with a conspicuous wing stripe. Breeding adults have a dark head and back, a white chin and belly are separated by a chestnut upper breast and sides of the neck. Females are more boldly patterned than males. In winter, it is darker above, with a dark line through the eye and usually with a dark crown, and entirely white below. Its bill is thin.

VOICE: A sharp *twit* or *whit*.

NESTING: Lays 4 olive eggs, spotted with brown, in a slight hollow on the ground in marshy tundra.

HABITAT: Breeds on tundra pools; visits open ocean, beaches, flats, and lake and river shores during migration.

RANGE: Breeds in Alaska and across northern Canada. Migrates along both coasts, more rarely in the interior, and winters mainly at sea in the Southern Hemisphere. Also found in the Old World.

SIMILAR SPECIES: Red Phalarope is larger with a stouter bill and more robust appearance, and a less contrasting white wing stripe; its streaks on the back are less obvious in breeding plumage and absent in winter.

Wilson's Phalarope has a longer, thinner bill and no white wing stripe.

Winter-plumage Sanderling has less erratic flight and lacks the head pattern and streaks on the back.

CONSERVATION: LC

Red-necked Phalaropes are numerous globally and may be common locally, but its populations have shifted in recent decades, perhaps in response to loss of zooplankton in cool waters used for breeding. Because of these shifts, it is difficult to state North American population trends with certainty, but they are believed to be decreasing. The declines have been steepest at some migration sites in eastern Canada; a huge population that once gathered by the millions each fall at Canada's Bay of Fundy has dropped sharply and all but disappeared.

■ SUMMER ■ MIGRATION
■ WINTER ■ RARE
■ RESIDENT

Hundreds of these shorebirds may be seen from fishing boats far at sea; bobbing like corks, they look like miniature gulls riding the waves. While they are at sea, the greater part of their diet is made up of tiny marine organisms known as plankton. On land, they forage around tundra pools for the aquatic larvae of mosquitoes, midges, and beetles. As in other phalaropes, after the female completes egg-laying, the male takes over the duties of incubating the eggs and rearing the young.

DESCRIPTION: 8" (20 cm). A starling-sized swimming shorebird with a conspicuous wing stripe and a short yellow bill with a black tip. Breeding adults are rich chestnut, with a dark crown and white face. Females are more boldly patterned than males. In winter, it is gray above and white below, with a pale crown, a dark line through the eye, and a dark bill.

VOICE: Sharp metallic *kreeep*.

NESTING: Lays 4 olive eggs, speckled with brown, placed in a grass-lined depression on an elevated spot in low marshy tundra.

HABITAT: Breeds on tundra; found on open ocean, bays, inlets, lakes, shores, and coasts during migration.

RANGE: Breeds in Alaska and northern Canada. Migrates off both coasts, very rarely in the interior. Winters mainly at sea in the Southern Hemisphere; irregular along the Pacific Coast. Also found in the Old World.

SIMILAR SPECIES: See Wilson's and Red-necked phalaropes. Winter-plumage Sanderling has less erratic flight, darker wings with a more contrasting white wing stripe, and shows no patterning on head.

CONSERVATION: It is difficult to estimate Red Phalarope numbers and population trends because they breed in remote sites in the Arctic and winter out at sea, usually far from land. Climate change could affect their Arctic breeding habitat and, as surface feeders on open ocean waters in winter, they are vulnerable to oil spills and plastic pollution.

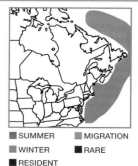

■ SUMMER ■ MIGRATION
■ WINTER ■ RARE
■ RESIDENT

Great Skuas occur off the shores of the Northern Hemisphere most often in winter, where they are common on the fishing banks off Newfoundland. They feed on a variety of shrimp, fish, and rodents, and on the eggs and young of colonial seabirds. They are vigorous in the defense of their nests, diving boldly at human intruders.

DESCRIPTION: 23" (58 cm). A large, dark, bulky, gull-like bird. It is mottled gray-brown with conspicuous white patches on the outer wing. It has a warm brown or reddish-brown color with streaks and blotches that are only visible in good light at fairly close range. Its tail is short and blunt, its wings are broad, and its posture may appear hunched.

VOICE: A harsh *hah-hah-hah-hah*; various quacking and croaking notes. Generally silent away from the breeding grounds.

NESTING: Lays 2 olive-brown eggs, with dark brown spots, in a grass-lined nest on the ground. Often nests in loose colonies.

HABITAT: Breeds on open bare ground near the sea; at other times, ranges over the ocean.

RANGE: Nests in Iceland and on islands north of Britain. Winters off the Atlantic Coast south to Maryland.

SIMILAR SPECIES: South Polar Skua is basically gray, lacks the streaked or mottled look; light phase has an obvious pale area on the nape and looks two-toned. Intermediate phase shows a uniformly pale but less prominent area on the nape. Dark phase is uniformly dark, including the nape. Immatures of larger gulls lack prominent white wing patches.

CONSERVATION: LC
Populations appear to be stable overall.

SUMMER ■ MIGRATION
WINTER ■ RARE
RESIDENT

This Antarctic seabird is a rare spring and fall visitor to the far-offshore waters off both coasts; it can be found in much smaller numbers in summer. Like its relatives the jaegers, it is both a predator and scavenger. At sea, it eats fish and carrion, and often gathers around groups of other seabirds to pirate food.

DESCRIPTION: 21" (53 cm). A large, dark, heavy-bodied, gull-like bird, most often uniform gray with conspicuous white patches on the outer wing. Its tail is short and blunt. South Polar Skuas have two color phases, light and dark, with intermediate variations. Light phase birds have an obvious pale area on the nape and looks two-toned, with whitish streaks. Intermediate phase shows a uniformly pale but less prominent area on the nape. Dark phase is uniformly dark, including the nape.

VOICE: Usually silent away from the breeding grounds.

NESTING: Lays 1 or 2 olive-brown eggs, with dark brown spots, in a depression on the ground. Often nests in colonies.

HABITAT: Open ocean.

RANGE: Breeds in Southern Hemisphere; rare summer visitor off Pacific and Atlantic coasts.

SIMILAR SPECIES: Similar to Great Skua, but typically more uniformly gray, not mottled. Immatures of larger gulls are similar, but lack white wing patches.

CONSERVATION: Global populations appear stable. Its remote Antarctic breeding sites encounter few human interactions and disturbances.

POMARINE JAEGER *Stercorarius pomarinus*

■ SUMMER ■ MIGRATION
■ WINTER ■ RARE
■ RESIDENT

The largest of our jaegers, the Pomarine preys on birds up to the size of terns and small gulls, as well as on lemmings, carrion, and the eggs and young of colonial seabirds. Like the Parasitic Jaeger, at sea it also pursues gulls and terns, forcing them to disgorge their food, which it snatches up in midair. Although it can be spotted from land at times, it is much more often seen far offshore.

DESCRIPTION: 22" (56 cm). Larger and stockier than the Parasitic Jaeger, with a more extensive white flash on the outer wing. Its central tail feathers are twisted and blunt or spoon-shaped, rather than pointed. The Pomarine Jaeger's normal flight is powerful, steady, purposeful, and slow, with relatively shallow wingbeats. This species' wings are broad at the base; the bird does not seem to rise and fall with each wingbeat. Dark-phase and light-phase color morphs occur, as well as intermediate morphs, creating considerable variability in the colors and patterns exhibited by this species.

VOICE: Harsh chattering calls; a harsh *which-yew*.

NESTING: Lays 2 olive-brown eggs, with darker brown spots, in a grass-lined depression on the ground.

HABITAT: Breeds on swampy tundra; migrates and winters over ocean.

RANGE: Breeds above the Arctic Circle in Alaska and across northern Canada. Winters at sea as far north as California and North Carolina. Very rare in migration on the Great Lakes. Also found in Eurasia.

SIMILAR SPECIES: See Parasitic and Long-tailed jaegers; Parasitic is usually seen closer to shore. Pomarine's bill is heavier, its wings are broader at the base, and its flight is more direct.

Great and South Polar skuas are larger and bulkier, with broader wings.

CONSERVATION:
Breeding populations rely on lemmings for food, leading to large fluctuations from year to year, and making it difficult to determine long-term changes. Although uncommonly seen, they are listed as a species of least concern.

■ SUMMER   ■ MIGRATION
■ WINTER   ■ RARE
■ RESIDENT

This is the most familiar of our jaegers since it comes more readily into bays and estuaries and often feeds closer to shore. It is named for its habit of stealing food from other birds; like the other jaegers, it relentlessly harries smaller gulls and terns and forces them to drop their food.

DESCRIPTION: 21" (53 cm). A fast-flying, gull-like seabird. Typical adults are brown above, white or light dusky below, with an incomplete gray-brown band across the breast; a dark, almost black, crown; and short (up to 3–4", 8–10 cm), pointed central tail feathers. Dark-phase birds are uniform dusky brown with a darker cap; intermediates between the two color phases occur. Often seen harrying gulls and terns.

VOICE: Usually silent; a variety of mewing and wailing notes on breeding grounds.

NESTING: Lays 2 olive-brown eggs, with darker brown spots, in a grass-lined depression on the ground or among rocks.

HABITAT: Breeds on grassy tundra and stony ground near inland lakes; at other times on the ocean.

RANGE: Breeds in Alaska and northern Canada. Winters in warm waters in the Southern Hemisphere. Also found in northern Eurasia.

SIMILAR SPECIES: See Pomarine and Long-tailed jaegers.

CONSERVATION: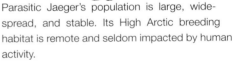
Parasitic Jaeger's population is large, widespread, and stable. Its High Arctic breeding habitat is remote and seldom impacted by human activity.

LONG-TAILED JAEGER *Stercorarius longicaudus*

■ SUMMER ■ MIGRATION
■ WINTER ■ RARE
■ RESIDENT

The smallest of the three jaegers, the Long-tailed is rarely seen because it migrates chiefly far offshore over open ocean. Although it sometimes steals food from other seabirds as do the other jaegers, it feeds mainly by catching its own fish, taking flying insects in the air, and sometimes preying on small birds. On the breeding grounds, lemmings and berries are its staple foods.

DESCRIPTION: 21" (53 cm). The adult is similar to a light-phase Parasitic Jaeger but smaller, more graceful, and with long central tail feathers (up to 6", 15 cm). Its upperparts are paler than in other jaegers, and its blackish cap is smaller and more sharply defined. Its flight is more buoyant. Juveniles have variable morphs (light, dark, and intermediate) like other jaegers, but the adults are consistently lighter, with no dark morph.

VOICE: A harsh *kreeah*; other yelping and rattling notes on breeding grounds.

NESTING: Lays 2 olive-brown eggs with brown spots in a grass-lined nest placed either on bare ground or among rocks.

HABITAT: Breeds on tundra and stony hillsides; at other times, it ranges over open ocean.

RANGE: Breeds in Alaska and Canada north of the Arctic Circle; winters far offshore in both the Atlantic and Pacific oceans.

SIMILAR SPECIES: See Pomarine and Parasitic jaegers.

CONSERVATION: LC

Long-tailed Jaeger populations fluctuate with Arctic prey populations, but have remained stable over the long term.

■ SUMMER　■ MIGRATION
■ WINTER　　■ RARE
■ RESIDENT

The Dovekie, the smallest of the Atlantic alcids, numbers in the millions in cold Arctic regions and is among the world's most abundant birds. Great flocks move south during severe cold spells, but the vast majority winter far out at sea. During migration in November, powerful easterly gales occasionally blow numbers of them great distances inland. Dovekies eat phytoplankton, krill, small fish, and crustaceans.

DESCRIPTION: 8" (20 cm). A starling-sized alcid. It appears chunky, black above and white below, with a short, stubby bill. Breeding adults have a black head; winter birds have a black crown and white cheeks.

VOICE: Squeaking notes. Its call is a high trill that rises and falls. It is generally silent at sea.

NESTING: Lays 1 bluish-white egg in a rock crevice. Nests in the High Arctic south to Greenland.

HABITAT: Breeds on rocky cliffs; winters chiefly at sea.

RANGE: Breeds in eastern Arctic Canada. Winters south to New Jersey. Also found in northern Europe.

SIMILAR SPECIES: In summer, it may be confused with juvenile Razorbills and Thick-billed Murres that have left nesting ledges and are on the water. Dovekies always distinguishable by their short, stubby bill. In Alaska, no other small alcid is so sharply black-and-white with a completely black head and neck.

CONSERVATION: 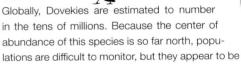 Globally, Dovekies are estimated to number in the tens of millions. Because the center of abundance of this species is so far north, populations are difficult to monitor, but they appear to be stable to slightly decreasing.

COMMON MURRE *Uria aalge*

SUMMER MIGRATION
WINTER RARE
RESIDENT

The murres, like all alcids, use their wings for swimming and diving, and seem to fly through the water. This species is more abundant on the Pacific Coast of the United States than on the Atlantic, where it is outnumbered by the Thick-billed Murre. In the Arctic, however, it nests in huge colonies, with incubating birds standing side by side on long narrow ledges. When half grown, young murres jump 30 to 50 feet (9 to 15 meters) into the sea, and accompany their parents, first swimming, then flying, often for hundreds of miles to their wintering areas. Apart from having their nests plundered for the eggs in the 19th century, murres of the Pacific Coast have long been safe from human intrusion, but oil spills now pose a threat to whole colonies.

DESCRIPTION: 17" (43 cm). Crow-sized. Common Murre's head and upperparts are brownish black, and it is white below. Its bill is long and pointed. Winter birds have extensive white on the face, with a dark line behind the eye. See Thick-billed Murre.

VOICE: Purring or murmuring, hence the name "murre." Also a guttural croak and higher-pitched bleat.

NESTING: Lays 1 blue-green egg, with black marks, on a bare rock ledge.

HABITAT: Rocky coasts.

RANGE: Breeds along the Arctic and subarctic coasts south to central California and the Gulf of Saint Lawrence. It winters south to southern California and Massachusetts. Also found in Eurasia.

SIMILAR SPECIES: Razorbill is blacker above, with a heavier head and bill; it often holds its tail cocked.

Thick-billed Murre has a shorter, thicker bill with an evenly decurved culmen; its upperparts are blacker and its head shape is less attenuated; its face is darker with the white restricted to the lower cheek in winter plumage.

CONSERVATION:

Common Murres are numerous and their North American population appears to be increasing, although a large population in Iceland is in steep decline. These birds are frequently the victims of oil spills and pollution.

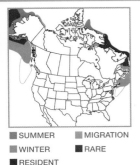

■ SUMMER ■ MIGRATION
■ WINTER ■ RARE
■ RESIDENT

One of the most abundant seabirds in the Northern Hemisphere, the Thick-billed Murre generally has a more northerly distribution than the Common Murre. Murres are among the chief prey of the large northerly falcons, the Gyrfalcons and Peregrines. In turn, murres feed on fish, squid, and various crustaceans. They are expert swimmers, capable of diving to depths of more than 500 feet (150 meters) and staying submerged for more than three minutes. In the air, they fly with fast wingbeats on a steady course but alight with a "stall" and an ungraceful splash. They take off by plunging from a cliff or, on water, by pattering over the surface like heavy ducks.

DESCRIPTION: 18" (46 cm). Similar to Common Murre, but blacker above with a shorter, thicker bill. In breeding plumage, the Thick-billed has a starkly black back and head and a white mark on the gape of the upper mandible that is visible only at close range. The white breast angles sharply into the dark neck, forming an inverted V. In winter plumage, the Thick-billed appears dark-headed—the face is mainly black, with white only on cheeks and throat.

VOICE: Similar to Common Murre: low, purring *murrrr*; also croaks and growls on breeding grounds.

NESTING: Lays 1 large bluish-green egg, scrawled with brown, on a narrow ledge. Nests in dense colonies.

HABITAT: Rocky coasts.

RANGE: Breeds on the Arctic and subarctic coasts south to southern Alaska and the Gulf of Saint Lawrence. It winters on the coasts south to southern Alaska and New Jersey. Also found in Eurasia.

SIMILAR SPECIES: See Common Murre. Razorbill has a bulky head with a more massive, blunt bill, and often seen with its tail raised; it also has a white ear crescent in winter plumage.

CONSERVATION: LC

Thick-billed Murres have a large and stable population, but groups are vulnerable to oil spills.

RAZORBILL *Alca torda*

■ SUMMER   ■ MIGRATION
■ WINTER   ■ RARE
■ RESIDENT

These birds often can be recognized at a distance on the water by their large heads, stout bills, and upward-pointed tails. As with many alcids, Razorbills migrate southward after severe cold spells and visit our shores in the midst of winter. They are hardy birds, spending most of their time at sea and approaching land only after strong easterly gales. During the breeding season, they prefer rocky coasts, where they lay their eggs and raise their young. Razorbills feed mostly on fish, shrimp, and squid. They are adept at diving and have been caught in gill nets as deep as 60 feet (18 meters).

DESCRIPTION: 17" (43 cm). A crow-sized diving bird. Black above and on the head, and white below. The deep, laterally compressed bill has white bands in adults. Winter birds have white on the throat and cheeks, and behind the eye. Immatures have smaller, unmarked bills.

VOICE: Low croaks and growls.

NESTING: Lays 1 brown-spotted, bluish egg on or under rocks.

HABITAT: Coastal waters.

RANGE: Breeds from Arctic south to Maine. Winters south to New Jersey, rarely to Carolinas. Also in Europe.

SIMILAR SPECIES: See Thick-billed and Common Murres.

CONSERVATION: 🐦 NT

Although the North American population is increasing, more than half of the world's Razorbills occur in Iceland, where they are experiencing a steep, rapid decline. The species has been listed as Near Threatened due to this alarming population crash, which may be linked to the crash in sandeel populations around Iceland. Because they live near shore, these birds are susceptible to oil spills and other pollution in the North Atlantic.

■ SUMMER ■ MIGRATION
■ WINTER ■ RARE
■ RESIDENT

In summer plumage, these jet-black seabirds with large white wing patches and bright red feet are conspicuous, especially when in flight. A characteristic field mark is their habit of dipping their bills into the water. Guillemots are hardy birds, rarely migrating even in subzero weather. Their diet consists primarily of small fish, crustaceans, mollusks, and marine worms.

DESCRIPTION: 13" (33 cm). Pigeon-sized. In summer, it is all black with a large white wing patch; in winter, the black is largely replaced by white. It has bright red feet and a pointed bill. Murres are larger.

VOICE: Shrill, mouse-like squeaks.

NESTING: Lays 2 whitish eggs, with dark brown blotches, placed under rocks either on a bare surface or on loose pebbles.

HABITAT: Rocky coasts, even in winter.

RANGE: Breeds from Arctic Alaska and Canada south along the Atlantic Coast to Maine. Winters south to the Bering Sea and Long Island (rarely). Also found in northern Europe.

SUBSPECIES: Juveniles and nonbreeding adults of the East Coast race (*C. g. arcticus*) are darker than those of the high Arctic race (*C. g. mandtii*), which tend to be mostly white.

SIMILAR SPECIES: Adult Pigeon Guillemot has a distinctive dark wedge intruding into its white wing patch; its wing linings are silver-gray or even blackish.

CONSERVATION:

Although many threats have had effects on the population—including oil spills, pollution, and introduced predators at nesting sites—the wide range of this species and its scattered nest sites have helped to keep its overall numbers strong. Global trends are difficult to assess due to scattered data and the species' fluctuating range.

PIGEON GUILLEMOT *Cepphus columba*

■ SUMMER ■ MIGRATION
■ WINTER ■ RARE
■ RESIDENT

Found along the Pacific Coast, Pigeon Guillemots appear to be the least social of all the alcids. Where coastal cliffs allow only one nesting cavity, only one pair will occupy it. Elsewhere, territories are laid out like beads on a string. These birds feed by diving, taking mostly small fish.

DESCRIPTION: 12–14" (30–36 cm). Pigeon-sized. In breeding plumage, it is black with a large, white wing patch interrupted by two black stripes. In winter, its head and upperparts lighten slightly, giving a dusky mottled effect; the underparts are white with buff-colored barring on the flanks and dusky wing linings. In all seasons, the feet and bill lining are brilliant red.

VOICE: High, thin whistles and squeaks.

NESTING: Lays 1 or 2 whitish or greenish, dark-spotted eggs in a crevice or burrow.

HABITAT: Rocky coasts.

RANGE: Breeds on coasts and islands from southern Alaska south to southern California. Winters far offshore.

SIMILAR SPECIES: Winter murrelets are much smaller and shorter-billed; they have darker heads and backs and whiter underparts. See Black Guillemot.

CONSERVATION: Little is known about Pigeon Guillemot population trends. Human disturbance, oil spills, and other pollution all place pressure on these birds. Higher water temperatures in summer may decrease the available food and nesting success for this species, making climate change a potential threat as well.

Long-billed Murrelet, recognized as a separate species from Marbled Murrelet based on genetic criteria in the late 90s, breeds only in northeastern Asia. Long-billed Murrelet is more prone to vagrancy than Marbled Murrelet; it has an extensive record of vagrancy into the interior and even to the Atlantic Coast from October to December. Look for these vagrants especially at inland reservoirs and lakes; in the Pacific Northwest, look for Long-billed on the ocean in August and September.

DESCRIPTION: 10" (25 cm). A small seabird, closely related to the Marbled Murrelet. It is chunky with a short neck and tail. In summer it is brown above, marbled with light brown and gray below. In winter it is black above, white below, with a white wing patch, and has a white throat and dark nape (no collar).

VOICE: Its call is a distinct, incisive *keer*, higher and noticeably shorter than Marbled Murrelet. Usually silent at sea.

NESTING: Nests in trees found in coastal, older forests; nest heights range from 8–23 feet (2.5–7 m) above ground. Some nests are placed on the ground on rock scree slopes, cliffs, or boulder fields near the ocean. A small depression in soil or on tree limb (covered with lichen, twigs, needles, and dry deciduous leaves) holds a single pale olive egg marked with darker spots.

HABITAT: Breeds in mature and old-growth coniferous forests with multilayered canopies and on sea-facing talus slopes or cliffs; nesting sites may occur as far as 25 miles (40 km) inland. This small seabird's breeding habitat usually includes large trees with large limbs or platforms created by damage, disease, mistletoe, or other factors, covered by moss or other nesting substrate. It mainly forages throughout the year in relatively shallow salt water less than 200 feet (60 meters) deep found in bays, inlets, fjords, and open ocean within 3 miles (5 km) of shore.

RANGE: Breeds from the Kamchatka Peninsula in Russia southward to Hokkaido Island, Japan, and south and east along the coast of Primorski Krai, Russia, and the Sea of Japan to Vladivostok. Vagrant to North America and Europe.

SIMILAR SPECIES: See Marbled Murrelet.

CONSERVATION:
Near Threatened and decreasing in its native range.

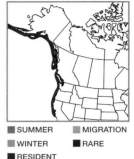

■ SUMMER ■ MIGRATION
■ WINTER ■ RARE
■ RESIDENT

Most alcids use burrows or ledges on coastal cliffs, but Marbled Murrelets' nests eluded scientists for nearly two centuries. The birds were observed taking off from the sea at twilight, burdened with fish, and disappearing inland. Some weeks later, feathered young would appear, bobbing on the water. Only in 1974 was a nest discovered in a Douglas fir in the Santa Cruz Mountains of California, about 135 feet (41 meters) above the ground. It is now known that these birds nest high up in trees, sometimes up to 45 miles (70 km) inland. On the water, Marbled Murrelets move about in small groups; they dive for fish and other aquatic animals.

DESCRIPTION: 9½–10" (24–25 cm). A chubby, robin-sized seabird, with a short neck and tail. In summer, it is brown above, marbled with light brown and gray below. In winter, it is black above, white below, with a white wing patch and an incomplete white collar.

VOICE: A plaintive *keer, keer, keer*. Vocal in flight both at sea and near the nest site.

NESTING: Lays 1 olive or yellowish egg, spotted with brown, black, and lavender, in a platform of moss placed high in a forest tree.

HABITAT: Breeds in coastal rainforests; inshore waters at other times.

RANGE: Breeds from the Aleutian Islands south to central California. It is mostly resident near its breeding areas, but small numbers may push farther south along the California coast in winter.

SIMILAR SPECIES: Kittlitz's Murrelet is lighter brown, and much more finely mottled over the entire body; it has a much shorter bill. In winter, the white face of Kittlitz's extends to above the eye. Ancient Murrelet lacks white scapulars, and shows distinct contrast between its blackish cap and grayer back. See Scripps's and Guadalupe murrelets.

CONSERVATION: EN

The Marbled Murrelet is classified as Endangered due to steep, ongoing population declines, especially in the southern part of its range. It has been federally protected in the United States and Canada since the early 90s. It is classified as state-endangered in California and Washington, and threatened in Oregon. This species' unique nesting habits make it vulnerable to habitat threats both on land and at sea, including logging and other disturbance of old-growth forests in the Northwest, oil spills, and overfishing of the murrelet's preferred prey.

Brachyramphus brevirostris KITTLITZ'S MURRELET

SUMMER ■ MIGRATION
WINTER ■ RARE
RESIDENT

Kittlitz's Murrelet is among the most mysterious and poorly understood of North American birds. Few of their nests have ever been found. It is not known whether both sexes incubate the single egg, or for how long; neither is it known how long it takes the young to fledge. It is closely related to Marbled Murrelet but breeds farther north, mainly in Alaska.

DESCRIPTION: 7½–9" (19–23 cm). A small, chubby seabird. In summer, it is dusky above with buff marbling; its foreparts are buff with dark barring, and its belly is whitish. In winter, it is white below and slate-gray above and on the top of the head, with a white face. A white patch on its dark wings is sometimes visible on swimming birds and always visible in flight. Its bill is short and stubby.

VOICE: A low-pitched groaning call.

NESTING: Lays a single olive egg with heavy markings on a mountain slope among rocks. Details of its nesting and incubation habits are little known.

HABITAT: Nests on talus slopes of high mountains; winters on ocean waters and glacier bays.

RANGE: Breeds on coasts of the Bering Sea, Aleutians, and southeastern Alaska. Rarely farther south in winter. Also in Asia.

SIMILAR SPECIES: See Marbled Murrelet. In winter, Ancient Murrelet lacks the white scapular stripe and has a longer bill; it has a distinct contrast between its blackish cap and grayer back.

CONSERVATION:

The Kittlitz's Murrelet population is difficult to monitor due to its remote breeding areas. The species was listed as critically endangered until 2014 when new surveys suggested its rate of decline was not as severe as once feared. It is still, however, listed as Near Threatened and decreasing. Aside from danger from oil spills and commercial fishing, these birds feed near glaciers, and many of those glaciers are in retreat as a result of climate change.

■ SUMMER ■ MIGRATION
■ WINTER ■ RARE
■ RESIDENT

Formerly considered the same species as Guadalupe Murrelet, called Xantus's Murrelet. This species spends most of its time in warm, southerly climates. During the breeding season, the entire Scripps's Murrelet population is concentrated within a fairly small region off the coasts of southern California and Mexico. The birds disperse after breeding, sometimes as far north as British Columbia. More than 80 percent of the U.S. breeding population of Scripps's Murrelets (about a third of the world's population) occurs on the Channel Islands, which is the only breeding ground north of Mexico. The Mexican population nests primarily on the Baja California islands of San Benito, Coronado, and San Jeronimo.

DESCRIPTION: 9½–10½" (24–27 cm). It is robin-sized but slender, resembling a tiny murre. It is black above with no distinctive pattern; it has white eye arcs above and below the eyes, and white cheeks, throat, and underparts. The underwing coverts are white. Its bill is thin and narrow, slightly shorter and thicker than that of the closely related Guadalupe Murrelet. It shows no seasonal change in plumage.

VOICE: High, thin whistles, usually in a quick series.

NESTING: Lays 1 or 2 buff-colored eggs with brown markings among boulders or in crevices off island beaches.

HABITAT: Ocean; nests in colonies on rocky sea islands.

RANGE: Breeds on offshore islands of Baja and southern California; occasionally wanders northward as far as Vancouver Island, British Columbia, but usually far offshore in warm waters.

SIMILAR SPECIES: See Guadalupe Murrelet.

CONSERVATION: VU
Uncommon. The small population of Scripps's Murrelet is declining moderately and is listed as Vulnerable by the IUCN. These birds are highly susceptible to nest predation from introduced species such as deer mice on their island breeding grounds. Introduced predators have extirpated a number of colonies.

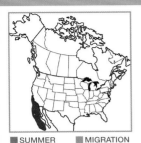

■ SUMMER　■ MIGRATION
■ WINTER　■ RARE
■ RESIDENT

Formerly considered the same species as Scripps's Murrelet, called Xantus's Murrelet. At sea these birds are often seen in pairs. Guadalupe Murrelets feed by diving and swimming underwater in pursuit of small fish and crustaceans. Interestingly, they are nearly always observed feeding in pairs rather than in flocks. Adults are active at the colony only at night. This curious feeding strategy takes place year-round, including during the breeding season. Since one member of each breeding pair is at the nest throughout the breeding season, unrelated birds may pair up to feed cooperatively.

DESCRIPTION: 9½–10½" (24–27 cm). A robin-sized but slender seabird that resembles a tiny murre. It is black above, with no distinctive pattern; it has white cheeks, throat, and underparts. A white patch on the neck extends to just above the eyes. Its underwing coverts are white. This species' white eye arcs are not as distinctive as those of the closely related Scripps's Murrelet. Its bill is thin and narrow, slightly longer and thinner than that of Scripps's Murrelet. It shows no seasonal change in plumage.

VOICE: A rattling trilled call that is much different than Scripps's Murrelet.

NESTING: Lays 1 or 2 buff-colored eggs, with brown markings, among boulders or in crevices off island beaches.

HABITAT: Ocean; nests in colonies on rocky sea islands.

RANGE: Breeds on offshore islands from Guadalupe Island south to the San Benito Islands. After breeding season ends, they disperse out to sea. Rarely seen north of central California.

SIMILAR SPECIES: See Scripps's Murrelet.

CONSERVATION:
Endangered and decreasing. The few known islet and island colonies have been threatened or extirpated by introduced mammalian predators. The eradication of introduced house rats and cats from Guadalupe Island and other breeding sites may be the cornerstone of efforts to preserve the remaining population.

CRAVERI'S MURRELET *Synthliboramphus craveri*

■ SUMMER ■ MIGRATION
■ WINTER ■ RARE
■ RESIDENT

As with many other species that nest in the Gulf of California, Craveri's Murrelet wanders northward in fall to feeding grounds in the California Current. Its habits are similar to those of Scripps's and Guadalupe murrelets.

DESCRIPTION: 8½–10" (22–25 cm). It is black above and white below, with black extending down the neck to form a partial collar. Its underwing is grayish. The black on the face extends below the bill on Craveri's Murrelet but not on Scripps's.

VOICE: In breeding season, a trilling whistle heard near the colony at sea.

NESTING: Lays 2 white eggs in a rock crevice or under a boulder.

HABITAT: Rocky cliffs and offshore waters.

RANGE: Breeds on islands in the Gulf of California and off Baja California north to San Benito Islands. After breeding, it wanders to the southern California coast, occasionally farther north.

SIMILAR SPECIES: See Scripps's, Guadalupe, Marbled, Kittlitz's, and Ancient murrelets.

CONSERVATION: VU

As with other alcid species nesting off the coast of California and Mexico, introduced mammalian predators have decreased populations through nest predation. Conservation measures include efforts to eradicate invasive predators from breeding islands.

■ SUMMER   ■ MIGRATION
■ WINTER   ■ RARE
■ RESIDENT

This bird's name is derived from the white plumes above the eyes, which resemble an old man's white locks. It is often seen in pairs or in small groups at sea, occasionally forming flocks of several dozen birds. By moving to and from land at twilight, these birds avoid most predators, with the exception of Peregrine Falcons. Ancient Murrelets are not strong fliers, but heavy storms may rarely carry them as far inland as the Great Lakes and the Atlantic Coast.

DESCRIPTION: 9½–10½" (24–27 cm). A quail-sized seabird. It has a black head and gray back. It is white below, has white plumes over the eyes, and has a small white-barred area at the side of the neck. It has a pale or white bill. In winter, it has a wide white area on the throat and face, and its back is a solid slate-gray; the similar Marbled Murrelet has a white patch on the flanks and a dark bill.

VOICE: Low, shrill whistling notes.

NESTING: Lays 2 brown to green eggs, spotted with brown and lavender, in a burrow dug by the adults.

HABITAT: Open ocean; nests on oceanic islets with enough soil for a burrow, often under heavy timber.

RANGE: Breeds on offshore islets of North Pacific and mainland shores south to central British Columbia. Winters south to southern California. Also in Asia.

SIMILAR SPECIES: See Marbled, Kittlitz's, Scripps's, Guadalupe, and Craveri's murrelets.

CONSERVATION:  Although this species is still numerous, its numbers are declining, mostly due to predation from foxes, rats, and raccoons.

CASSIN'S AUKLET   *Ptychoramphus aleuticus*

■ SUMMER   ■ MIGRATION
■ WINTER   ■ RARE
■ RESIDENT

Adult Cassin's Auklets take 24-hour watches while incubating the chick. During the nesting season, they grow a pouch under the tongue and fill it with food. These island birds fly to sea long before dawn to avoid Western Gulls and other predators. They feed on shrimp and plankton by day and approach the colony only after dark.

DESCRIPTION: 8–9" (20–23 cm). A dark, stocky, robin-sized seabird. It is slate-gray above and lighter gray below, with a white belly. Its eyes are dark brown during its first year, lightening to white in breeding adults. Its stubby bill has a white spot at the base of each side of the lower mandible. It shows no seasonal change in plumage.

VOICE: Weak croaking calls given at night.

NESTING: Lays 1 white egg, usually placed in a burrow but also in a cavity among rocks. Nests in colonies.

HABITAT: Open ocean. Nests on cliffs and isolated headlands.

RANGE: Breeds from Aleutians to central Baja California. Winters in waters off southern part of breeding range.

SIMILAR SPECIES: Parakeet Auklet has white underparts extending higher into the lower breast, sides, and flanks. All other auklets in breeding plumage, including Parakeet, have a brightly colored bill and white facial stripes. Young Crested and Whiskered auklets have dark bellies.

CONSERVATION:
Although numerous, Cassin's Auklet is listed as Near Threatened and is decreasing due to introduced mammalian predation (foxes and rats), although populations have rebounded following predator control efforts.

■ SUMMER ■ MIGRATION
■ WINTER ■ RARE
■ RESIDENT

This auklet, common on its Alaskan home grounds, does not form large colonies but mainly nests scattered among the puffins and Pigeon Guillemots that prefer the same habitat. Adults sit high up on the cliffs, each on watch near its nesting cavity while its mate is incubating or tending the young. In the morning or afternoon, it leaves the cliff to feed, diving for krill, which it captures near the sea bottom.

DESCRIPTION: 10" (25 cm). A robin-sized auklet whose short tail and chubby body make it look larger. It is sooty black above and white below. In summer, a white, mustache-like plume extends from below the eye to the lower neck. It has a stubby, upturned red bill. In winter, it lacks the white plume, its throat and underparts are white, and its bill is duskier.

VOICE: Generally silent; clear whistles in breeding colonies.

NESTING: Lays 1 white oval egg in a cliff crevice or among boulders.

HABITAT: Open ocean; nests on coastal or island cliffs.

RANGE: Breeds on Bering Sea islands and nearby coasts. Winters offshore, very rarely south to California.

SIMILAR SPECIES: Cassin's Auklet is smaller with a darker bill, and no white in the breast, sides, or flanks. Breeding Rhinoceros Auklet is much larger, with two white plumes on the face and a longer, slimmer bill with a pale knob on the upper mandible.

CONSERVATION: Although still numerous, its large population is decreasing.

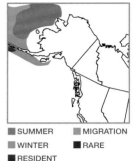

■ SUMMER ■ MIGRATION
■ WINTER ■ RARE
■ RESIDENT

In winter, vast numbers of Least Auklets leave their Arctic breeding islands before the sea freezes, and they return in June when the slopes are still snow-clad. These tiny alcids are extremely gregarious, with some colonies numbering more than a million birds. It nests in the rock crevices of talus slopes and on grass-covered lava flows, often in the company of other auklets. Like Crested Auklets, Least Auklets return to their colony en masse at dusk from offshore foraging areas and usually remain quite vocal until dark.

DESCRIPTION: 6" (15 cm). Our smallest alcid, only about the size of a sparrow. It is black above and white below. In summer, it has a white plume behind the eye, dark markings on the sides and breast (often forming a breast band), and a white throat; its bill is orange with a yellow tip. In winter, its plume is smaller, it is unmarked white below, its bill is dark, and it shows a white patch on the wing.

VOICE: Various twittering notes around breeding colonies.

NESTING: Lays 1 white egg in a small crevice. Nests in huge colonies on rocky slopes.

HABITAT: Rocky coasts and open ocean.

RANGE: Breeds on the Aleutians and islands of the Bering Sea. Winters offshore near breeding range.

SIMILAR SPECIES: Whiskered Auklet is much grayer and has a crest on the forehead. See Cassin's Auklet.

CONSERVATION: 🐦 LC
This species is common, but its large population is decreasing.

■ SUMMER ■ MIGRATION
■ WINTER ■ RARE
■ RESIDENT

The most restricted and rarest of the auklets found in Alaska, the Whiskered resembles the larger Crested Auklet in appearance and habits.

DESCRIPTION: 7–7½" (18–19 cm). Sparrow-sized. In all plumages, it is dusky gray above and lighter gray below. Adults have a forward-curling, quail-like gray topknot and three white ornamental plumes projecting backward from the face like long mustaches. Its short bill is red during summer and brown in winter. Immatures are dark with traces of the three white head stripes.

VOICE: A whining *me-ow*.

NESTING: Lays 1 white egg in rock crevices; nests in colonies.

HABITAT: Nests on rock slides and cliffs; inshore waters for feeding.

RANGE: Breeds and winters in the Aleutian Islands. Also in Asia.

SIMILAR SPECIES: See Cassin's Auklet and Least Auklet. Crested Auklet is larger with a single facial stripe and larger, orange bill; its crest is usually fuller.

CONSERVATION: LC
The population is declining slowly, likely due to predation by introduced predators and habitat loss.

CRESTED AUKLET *Aethia cristatella*

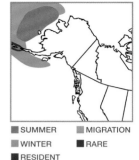

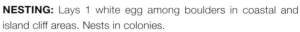

■ SUMMER ■ MIGRATION
■ WINTER ■ RARE
■ RESIDENT

Like other auklets, the Crested feeds on planktonic crustaceans, filling a special pouch under its tongue with food for its single chick. At dusk, these common seabirds of the Alaska islands return to the colony in beelike swarms, performing spectacular aerial displays.

DESCRIPTION: 9½–10½" (24–27 cm). A chubby seabird without much visible tail. It is slate-black above and brownish gray below. In breeding season, it has a white plume behind its white eye and a prominent, forward-curving black crest. It has a red bill with an extra red plate on the side of the face. In winter, the crest is shorter and the bill is brown. Juveniles lack a crest.

VOICE: A variety of loud honking and grunting notes on breeding grounds; otherwise silent.

NESTING: Lays 1 white egg among boulders in coastal and island cliff areas. Nests in colonies.

HABITAT: Nests on island coasts where sliding rocks form a talus slope, with the largest boulders at the bottom and bare cliff at the top, near the sea for feeding.

RANGE: Breeds in the Aleutians and other islands and coasts around the Bering Sea. Winters in nearby ocean waters.

SIMILAR SPECIES: See Cassin's and Whiskered auklets.

CONSERVATION:
This species is common and breeds over a wide range, but like other alcids it is vulnerable to invasive fox and rat predation, habitat disturbance, and pollution.

■ SUMMER ■ MIGRATION
■ WINTER ■ RARE
■ RESIDENT

This bird's common name is a misnomer; it is more closely related to puffins than to the small, plankton-feeding alcids we commonly call "auklets." Rhinoceros Auklets feed on the open sea during the day but may be seen at sunset in summer among inlets and islands. They swim and bob with a bill full of fish, waiting for nightfall before venturing ashore to feed their young.

DESCRIPTION: 14½–15½" (37–39 cm). A pigeon-sized seabird. It is dark above with a lighter gray throat and breast, and with white underparts. It has a slender, pale yellow bill and white eyes. In breeding plumage, it develops a short, upright "horn" at the base of the bill, with white drooping "whiskers" at either side and white plumes above the eyes. Immatures are dark gray above and light below with a duller, smaller bill and dark eyes.

VOICE: Low growling notes.

NESTING: Lays 1 white egg, often spotted, in a burrow. Nests in colonies, sometimes in large numbers.

HABITAT: Feeds on fish offshore; digs deep burrows in grassy or timbered headlands.

RANGE: Breeds from the Aleutians south to central California. Winters off the breeding grounds and south to southern California. Also found in Asia.

SIMILAR SPECIES: Immature Tufted Puffin is darker, has a deeper bill, and shows a broad gray stripe behind the eye; it may occur farther offshore.

CONSERVATION: Widespread and still numerous despite modest declines overall and the near complete losses of some colonies to predation by introduced mammals, and loss of nest burrows to rabbits.

■ SUMMER   ■ MIGRATION
■ WINTER   ■ RARE
■ RESIDENT

Puffins are sometimes affectionately called "clowns of the sea" on account of their gaudy bill, red-rimmed yellow eyes, and habit of waddling around and hopping actively from rock to rock. Atlantic Puffin nests in much smaller colonies than do most other alcids. Puffins hunt small fish, shellfish, and shrimp in rocky coastal waters and also at sea. They are excellent swimmers and divers. Project Puffin, an effort led by the National Audubon Society to reintroduce puffins on former nesting islands off the coast of Maine, has been a major conservation success story.

DESCRIPTION: 12" (30 cm). A short, stocky bird. It is black above and white below, with a white face and red legs; its remarkable triangular bill is brilliant red and yellow. In fall, the colorful outer covering of the bill is shed, leaving it smaller and duller.

VOICE: Deep throaty purrs and croaks.

NESTING: Lays 1 white egg in a burrow in soft soil or a rock crevice; nest cavity is lined with grass. Nests in colonies.

HABITAT: Chiefly rocky coasts.

RANGE: Breeds from Canadian Maritimes south to Maine. Winters offshore near nesting colonies, rarely south to Long Island. Also in northern Europe.

SIMILAR SPECIES: Razorbills and murres have an elongated flight profile, and have a puffy white area on the sides of the rump. Immature Razorbill is larger, not so stubby in appearance, with an elongated head and an entirely white cheek and throat.

CONSERVATION: VU

Despite its large numbers, the species is listed as vulnerable because it is in rapid decline. Invasive species and pollution have hurt populations and eliminated puffins from some former nesting islands, and food shortages in warm-water years have hurt nesting success.

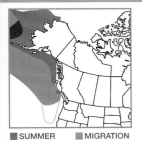

■ SUMMER ■ MIGRATION
■ WINTER ■ RARE
■ RESIDENT

The Horned Puffin's relatively huge bill is useful in catching and holding small fish, enabling parents to bring three or four fish at a time to their young. It is also used to signal to a mate or neighbor, especially during breeding time in crowded colonies. The colonies may contain thousands of these birds, yet in the Aleutians and on other islands where they nest among Tufted Puffins, Horned Puffins are lost among the throngs of other species.

DESCRIPTION: 14½" (37 cm). A pigeon-sized, chunky seabird. It is black above and white below. Its white face makes its head appear large; it has a colorful, bright yellow, parrot-like bill with a red tip. Its red eyelids and small, black, upturned "horns" above the eyes are visible at close range. In winter, its face is darker, its feathers are brownish, and its bill is smaller with a dusky base. Young birds have a darker face and narrow, sooty-brown bills.

VOICE: Usually silent but utters harsh notes from its burrow.

NESTING: Lays 1 whitish egg with small dark spots in a crevice or in a deep hole among boulders. Nests in colonies.

HABITAT: Cold ocean waters, sea cliffs, and rocky or grass-covered islets and rocks.

RANGE: Breeds from northern Alaska south to British Columbia border. Winters at sea south to Washington, rarely to California. Also found in Asia.

SIMILAR SPECIES: See Tufted Puffin.

CONSERVATION:

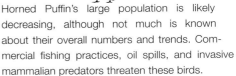

Horned Puffin's large population is likely decreasing, although not much is known about their overall numbers and trends. Commercial fishing practices, oil spills, and invasive mammalian predators threaten these birds.

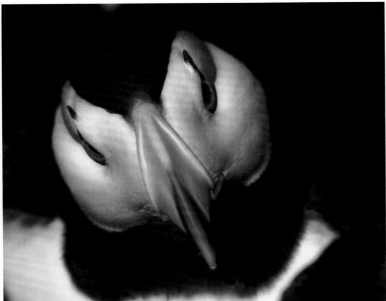

TUFTED PUFFIN *Fratercula cirrhata*

SUMMER ■ MIGRATION
■ WINTER ■ RARE
■ RESIDENT

In most mixed seabird colonies, a strict social order prevails within and between species. Each seems to have adapted to a specific niche, which includes occupying the terrain in a manner most suited to it. This reduces competition between species, but sharpens it within each species. The Tufted Puffin has adapted a burrowing strategy for nesting. It typically digs a tunnel from 2 to 9 feet (0.5 to 3 meters) into a turf-covered slope, then lays its single egg at the end of the burrow. Many other alcids place their eggs on cliff ledges.

DESCRIPTION: 14½–15½" (37–39 cm). A pigeon-sized puffin, mostly seen sitting upright on a sea cliff. In breeding plumage, its stubby body is black, its face is white with down-curved yellowish tufts hanging behind the eyes, and its parrot-like bill is enlarged and bright orange-red. In winter, the birds molt their colorful bill plates, leaving the bill smaller and duller; the face turns dusky and the tufts disappear. Immatures are dusky above and light gray below, with a small bill. In flight, the large, webbed red feet are conspicuous.

VOICE: Silent except for occasional growling notes uttered around the nest site.

NESTING: Lays 1 white egg, often spotted, in a burrow on an island or coastal cliff. Nests in colonies.

HABITAT: Nests on vertical sea cliffs, in colonies or singly. Feeds at sea.

RANGE: Breeds from northern Alaska south to northern California. Winters at sea off the breeding grounds. Also found in Asia.

SIMILAR SPECIES: See Rhinoceros Auklet. Winter-plumage and immature Horned Puffins have a dusky face and white underparts.

CONSERVATION: LC

As with other puffins, drift-net fishing was once a greater threat, but restrictions on commercial fishing practices have helped the North American populations to rebound in recent decades. Invasive mammalian predators and high sea surface temperatures remain as threats to this species, but its population remains large.

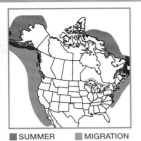

SUMMER MIGRATION
WINTER RARE
RESIDENT

This common gull is not often seen from shore; it generally spends the entire winter on the open ocean, where it feeds on small fish and plankton. Quick, short wingbeats give kittiwakes a buoyant, distinctive flight that allows experienced observers to identify them from a distance. Kittiwakes bank and glide more easily in strong winds than other gulls; they are like fulmars and other tubenoses in this foul-weather adaptation. This is the only gull that dives and swims underwater to capture food.

DESCRIPTION: 16–18" (41–46 cm). A small seagoing gull. The adult is white with a pale gray back and wings; it has a sharply defined black wing tip, as if dipped in black ink. It has black feet, a yellow bill, and a slightly forked tail. The winter adult has a dusky gray patch on the nape. Young birds have a dusky band on the nape, a dark diagonal wing band, and a black-tipped tail. See Red-legged Kittiwake.

VOICE: Variety of loud harsh notes. Very noisy on breeding grounds. With a little imagination, its common call can seem to resemble its name: *kittiwake*.

NESTING: Lays 2 pinkish-buff spotted eggs in a well-made cup of mosses and seaweed at the top of a cliff or on a ledge. Nests in colonies.

HABITAT: Cliffs and seacoasts in the Arctic; winters at sea.

RANGE: Breeds in the North Pacific, Arctic Ocean, and Atlantic south to the Gulf of Saint Lawrence. Winters from the edge of sea ice southward, rarely to the Gulf of Mexico. Also in Eurasia.

SIMILAR SPECIES: Red-legged Kittiwake is smaller, more compact, with a rounder head, shorter bill, and darker mantle; the black on the wing tips is more extensive and less sharply defined; its feet and legs are bright red.

Adult Mew Gull is similar in size and mantle shade, but the black on the wing tip is more extensive, irregularly shaped, and has a white spot; summer Kittiwakes with unmarked heads may appear similar to a Mew Gull when the two species float on the water.

Immature Sabine's Gull is more cleanly marked.

CONERVATION:  Listed as vulnerable, this species has likely declined due to lost food resources, oil spills, and avian influenza. Narrow habitat needs in polar conditions imply that climate change could significantly impact this species.

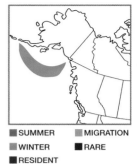

■ SUMMER   ■ MIGRATION
■ WINTER   ■ RARE
■ RESIDENT

This bird has one of the most limited distributions of any species in the West, but the Pribilof Islands colony is perhaps the most spectacular seabird colony in the world; every ledge is packed with tens of thousands of kittiwakes, murres, fulmars, and other seabirds.

DESCRIPTION: 14–15½" (36–39 cm). A small, seagoing gull. The adult is white with a pale gray back and wings and sharply defined black wing tips. It is similar to Black-legged Kittiwake but smaller, darker above, with more extensive black at the wing tips, and red legs and feet.

VOICE: Less vocal than Black-legged Kittiwake; its calls are higher pitched.

NESTING: Lays 2 buff or creamy eggs, marked with brown, in a grass and mud nest placed on a ledge.

HABITAT: Open ocean; nests on ledges of sea cliffs.

RANGE: Breeds in Alaska in the Aleutian Islands, the Commander Islands, and the Pribilof Islands. Winters in North Pacific Ocean.

SIMILAR SPECIES: See Black-legged Kittiwake. Sabine's Gull has a more sharply marked white triangle on the wing, a black triangle on the primaries, and a browner mantle.

CONSERVATION: VU
Vulnerable and decreasing. This bird's limited breeding range and narrow variety of prey fish species make it susceptible to environmental changes.

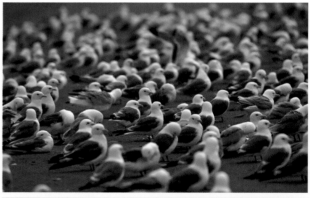

■ SUMMER ■ MIGRATION
■ WINTER ■ RARE
■ RESIDENT

The circumpolar Ivory Gull shares the realm of the Inuit and the polar bear. Indeed, it follows these hunters in quest of food, for it is largely a scavenger, feeding on the remains of their kills— mainly seals. It also eats wolf and fox dung, whale blubber, lemmings, crustaceans, and insects.

DESCRIPTION: 17" (43 cm). A rather small, short-legged gull; adults are pure white with a yellowish bill and legs; immatures (more often seen in southern latitudes) are similar, but with black bars and spots in varying quantities.

VOICE: A harsh *eeeer*.

NESTING: Lays 2 buff-olive eggs, marked with dark blotches, in a nest lined with moss, lichens, and seaweed, placed on bare ground among rocks or on gravel-covered polar ice.

HABITAT: Breeds on rocky cliffs or stony ground; winters at edge of the pack ice in Arctic seas.

RANGE: Known to breed in New World only on Somerset and Ellesmere islands in Canadian Arctic; more common in Eurasia. Winters in the Arctic Ocean, appearing rarely farther south.

SIMILAR SPECIES: A pale Iceland Gull is similar at a distance but is much larger.

CONSERVATION:
This species breeds in a small range and uses circumpolar habitat outside of the breeding season—both habits put it at risk in the face of climate change.

SABINE'S GULL *Xema sabini*

SUMMER ■ MIGRATION
■ WINTER ■ RARE
■ RESIDENT

This delicate gull is almost exclusively oceanic and is seldom seen outside the breeding season. On the tundra coastline it gracefully plucks small crustaceans and insects from the surface of the water like a tern. It also takes eggs from nesting colonies of Arctic Terns. The best way to see this oceanic species is to take a boat trip off the Pacific Coast.

DESCRIPTION: 13–14" (33–36 cm). A small, fork-tailed gull with black primaries and a triangular white patch on the rear edge of the wing. It has a dark hood in breeding plumage. Its bill is black with a yellow tip. Immatures lack the dark hood but can be distinguished by their forked tail and striking wing pattern.

VOICE: High-pitched grating or squeaking notes.

NESTING: Lays 3 or 4 olive-brown eggs, spotted with darker brown, placed in a grass-lined depression on the ground. Nests in small colonies.

HABITAT: Tundra ponds in summer; open ocean on migration and in winter.

RANGE: Breeds on coastal tundra around the shores of the Arctic Ocean, farther inland in Alaska. Migrates mainly at sea. Winter range is not fully known; some birds winter off the Pacific Coast of northern South America.

SIMILAR SPECIES: Bonaparte's and Common Black-headed gulls have a white triangular patch on wing tips. Juvenile Black-legged Kittiwake shows a narrow M on the back and mantle; it lacks the juvenile Sabine's considerable gray-brown coloring on the head and sides of the breast; it has a dark bar from the wrist to the tertials, and does not have a triangular patched wing pattern.

CONSERVATION: LC
The large Sabine's Gull population is stable; it breeds and winters in remote areas away from most human disturbance.

Chroicocephalus philadelphia **BONAPARTE'S GULL**

- ■ SUMMER
- ■ MIGRATION
- ■ WINTER
- ■ RARE
- ■ RESIDENT

Because they breed in the Far North, these beautiful gulls are most often seen on lakes and rivers during migration or along the coast in winter. They keep to themselves, seldom joining groups of larger gulls at garbage dumps. They feed in tidal inlets and at sewage outlets, picking scraps of food from the water. During spring migration, they may often be seen flying northward along large rivers such as the Hudson and the Mississippi. The species is named for Charles Lucien Bonaparte (a nephew of Napoleon), who was a leading ornithologist in the 1800s in the U.S. and Europe.

DESCRIPTION: 12–14" (30–36 cm). A small, delicate gull, it is silvery gray above, with conspicuous white, wedge-shaped patches on the leading edge of the outer wing. The head is black in breeding adults and white in winter with a dark spot behind the eye. Its bill is black. Young birds have dark markings on the upper surface of the wing and a black tail band.

VOICE: Rasping *tee-ar*; soft, nasal snarling note.

NESTING: Lays 2–4 olive or buff, spotted eggs in a well-made cup of grass, moss, and twigs placed in a spruce or fir tree near a lake or river.

HABITAT: Forested lakes and rivers; winters along coasts, in estuaries, and at the mouths of large rivers.

RANGE: Breeds in Alaska and interior northwestern Canada east to James Bay. Winters along both coasts, on Pacific from Washington southward, on Atlantic from southern New England southward.

SIMILAR SPECIES: See Little Gull and Franklin's Gull. Common Black-headed Gull is similar but larger, with a red bill and dark wing linings.

CONSERVATION: LC
Bonaparte's Gull numbers are stable to slightly increasing.

BLACK-HEADED GULL *Chroicocephalus ridibundus*

SUMMER ■ MIGRATION
WINTER ■ RARE
RESIDENT

Although this Old World gull is rare in North America, it may be seen regularly in small numbers in northeastern coastal waters. In Europe it is one of the most familiar gulls. Like that of the Bonaparte's Gull, with which it is almost always found in America, the flight of the Common Black-headed Gull is light and buoyant. In the air it resembles a tern more than a gull.

DESCRIPTION: 15" (38 cm). A small gull with a gray back and inner wings and flashing white primaries. In breeding plumage, it has a dark brown hood; in winter, its head becomes white. It has a red bill and legs. The immature is darker above, but shows some white in the primaries and has a narrow black tip to the tail. In all plumages, the under-surface of primaries is blackish.

VOICE: A harsh *kwup*; various squealing notes.

NESTING: Lays 3 buff-brown eggs, with black blotches, in a nest lined with grass, sticks, and seaweed placed in trees, bushes, on rocks, or on the ground. Nesting colonies located on sand dunes, beaches, marshes, and in open fields.

HABITAT: Bays and estuaries.

RANGE: Breeds in northern portions of Europe and Asia south to their southern parts; it winters from the southern portions of the breeding range south to Africa and southern Asia. It is an uncommon to rare but regular winter visitor to the North American Pacific Coast, and also in the East and the Great Lakes (rare).

SIMILAR SPECIES: Bonaparte's Gull is notably smaller; it has a white underwing narrowly bordered with black (only the primaries on adults; the entire trailing edge on immatures). The bill is smaller, and all or mostly black. The breeding adult's head is black with more prominent white eye crescents. The immature's upperwing has black-edged outer primary coverts and a narrow, neat, black trailing edge with most primaries and secondaries showing white tips when new. See Little Gull.

CONSERVATION:
Black-headed Gull's large and increasing global population now includes a few North American colonies in Newfoundland.

■ SUMMER ■ MIGRATION
■ WINTER ■ RARE
■ RESIDENT

This tiny gull was known for decades as a rare winter visitor to the Northeast before it was found nesting in Ontario. Today it is known to be an irregular breeder on the Great Lakes and farther north. Its flight is rather buoyant and tern-like, and it often plucks food from the surface while on the wing or dives from the air after minnows and aquatic insects. It often consorts with Bonaparte's Gulls.

DESCRIPTION: 11" (28 cm). The smallest gull. Summer adult has a pale gray back and wings, white underparts, a black hood, and blackish underwings. Winter plumage is similar, but the head is white with a partial gray cap and a dark spot behind the eye. It has a dark red bill and legs. Immatures have a narrow black tail tip, a diagonal dark bar on the forewing, and dark primaries.

VOICE: A soft *kek-kek-kek-kek*.

NESTING: Lays 3 olive-brown eggs, with dark spots, in a nest lined with grass and leaves, placed among marsh vegetation.

HABITAT: Inland marshes, meadows, lakes, and rivers; also coastal bays, flats, harbors, and estuaries.

RANGE: Central Europe east to southern Siberia. Breeds locally in Ontario and Wisconsin; winters regularly in small numbers in eastern North America, especially along the coast from New Brunswick to New Jersey and on the Great Lakes.

SIMILAR SPECIES: Bonaparte's Gull is slightly larger; breeding adults have dark wing tips; winter birds lack the partial gray crown.

CONSERVATION: Global numbers are increasing while European populations are in decline.

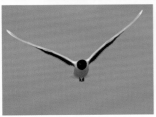

■ SUMMER ■ MIGRATION
■ WINTER ■ RARE
■ RESIDENT

This beautiful Old World gull winters mainly above the Arctic Circle, only rarely visiting places where it can be seen by most birders. The appearance of a Ross's Gull in settled areas often makes headlines and attracts many eager observers.

DESCRIPTION: 12–14" (30–36 cm). A rare visitor from the Arctic. Breeding adults have a narrow black collar; pale gray back and wings, including underwings; pinkish tinge on underparts; and wedge-shaped tail. Winter adults lack collar and pinkish tinge. Its flight is graceful and tern-like.

VOICE: A harsh *miaw*; usually silent in winter.

NESTING: Lays 2 or 3 deep olive eggs, spotted with brown, in a grass-lined depression.

HABITAT: Breeds on swampy tundra; winters near pack ice. Rarely visits river mouths and coastal beaches.

RANGE: Breeds mainly in Old World Arctic, but a few nest in Canada. Appears as migrant off northern Alaska. Winters rarely south to British Columbia and mid-Atlantic Coast. Also in Eurasia.

SIMILAR SPECIES: See Little and Bonaparte's gulls; Ross's Gull has a smaller bill than either and has uniformly pale gray wings.

CONSERVATION:
This species' remote breeding habitat makes it difficult to monitor populations accurately. Its small global population is the greatest concern for this species.

■ SUMMER ■ MIGRATION
■ WINTER ■ RARE
■ RESIDENT

A common summer gull along the Atlantic and Gulf coasts, this noisy species' namesake call is distinctive. Agile on the wing, they forage on beaches and in harbors feeding chiefly on small fish, and sometimes hawk insects. They may also steal the eggs of nesting terns.

DESCRIPTION: 15–17" (38–43 cm). A slender, medium-sized gull with a black hood in breeding plumage. In summer, the adult's back and wings are dark gray; the trailing edge of the wing is white, and the wing tip is black, without white spots. In winter, it lacks a hood. Young birds are dark brown with a contrasting rump and a broad black tail band.

VOICE: Loud, high-pitched *ha-ha-ha-ha-haah-haah-haah-haah-haah*.

NESTING: Lays 3 olive-brown eggs, with dark blotches, in a ground nest lined with grass and weed stems placed on sand or in a salt marsh. Nests in colonies.

HABITAT: Mainly salt marshes and lagoons in West.

RANGE: Breeds from Nova Scotia to the Caribbean; in summer and fall, it regularly visits the Salton Sea in southern California. It winters regularly north to Virginia, and in smaller numbers farther north.

SIMILAR SPECIES: See Franklin's Gull. Juvenile Herring Gull is much larger and heavier than a juvenile Laughing Gull; it has brown underparts, rump, and base of the tail, and pale inner primaries.

CONSERVATION: Once impacted by the feather trade, this species has recovered well and is widespread and increasing, although some colonies face competition from larger gulls.

■ SUMMER ■ MIGRATION
■ WINTER ■ RARE
■ RESIDENT

A freshwater version of the Laughing Gull, Franklin's Gull breeds in large colonies and thus is sensitive to habitat destruction. When agriculture encroaches on a nesting marsh and it becomes too small for a large colony, the birds move elsewhere. These gulls of the Great Plains are less numerous than in the past, but migrating flocks of these "Prairie Doves" are still a familiar sight in spring on the southern plains.

DESCRIPTION: 13–15" (33–38 cm). A slender gull with a black hood in breeding plumage, similar to a Laughing Gull but smaller and paler. In summer, the adult has a dark gray back and wings; the trailing edge of the wing is white, and the wing tips are black, separated from the gray by white spots. It has a smudgy half-hood in winter. Young birds are dark brown with a contrasting white rump and a broad black tail band.

VOICE: A strident *ha-ha-ha-ha-ha-ha*, similar to Laughing Gull's but higher pitched.

NESTING: Lays 3 buff-brown eggs, spotted with brown, on a loose platform in a marsh. Nests in large, noisy colonies.

HABITAT: Prairie marshes and sloughs. Often feeds in plowed fields.

RANGE: Breeds on prairie marshes from southern Canada to South Dakota and Iowa; also in scattered marshes in West. Migrates to southeast and winters mainly along the west coast of South America.

SIMILAR SPECIES: Laughing Gulls are larger and less chunky, with relatively longer wings, bills, and legs. Adults lack the white bar across the wing tip and gray in the tail; the white primary tips are much less prominent on the folded wing, and the outer wing is much more extensively black below. Nonbreeding Laughing Gull's head is pale, with indistinct markings; the eye crescents are not joined at the rear and are less conspicuous. A first-year's tail band is complete; its breast and flanks are gray; the inner primaries are dark.

Bonaparte's Gull is smaller, with a paler mantle; adults have a white wedge on the primaries; immatures have a strongly patterned mantle and inconspicuous eye crescents.

CONSERVATION: 🐦 LC

Local numbers and breeding sites change from year to year based on rainfall amounts and marsh conditions. Franklin's Gulls are numerous and their population is stable to slightly increasing.

This common species from the west coast of South America has been reported in California and Florida as an accidental vagrant. The Florida records may pertain to Olrog's Gull, a threatened species from the east coast of South America that was previously considered the same species as Belcher's before being split into a distinct species.

DESCRIPTION: Belcher's Gull is a medium-sized gull (19–21", 48–52 cm), about the size of the familiar Ring-billed Gull. Its blackish mantle distinguishes this species from any native gull of similar size. It has a black tail with a white terminal band, all-black primaries, and a gray band at the nape of the neck. It has a yellow bill with a red tip and black ring, and yellow feet. In nonbreeding plumage, it has a dark hood (white in breeding plumage).

VOICE: Typical raucous gull cry, lower-pitched than a Ring-billed Gull.

HABITAT: Rocky shores and small rocky islands.

RANGE: West coast of South America from northern Peru to central Chile (nonmigratory).

SIMILAR SPECIES: Larger Western and Yellow-footed gulls have a white tail and significant areas of white on the primaries, and lack the black on the bill and the gray nape.

CONSERVATION: Belcher's Gulls are thought to be increasing in their native range.

BLACK-TAILED GULL *Larus crassirostris*

■ SUMMER ■ MIGRATION
■ WINTER ■ RARE
■ RESIDENT

This East Asian native is recorded almost annually in North America, with most of the records coming from western Alaska and the coasts. They appear to arrive in the east via a northern route across Canada.

DESCRIPTION: 18" (46 cm). Similar in size to a Ring-billed Gull, but appears to be longer winged and darker above. Adult plumage is attained in four years. In flight, the jet black tail band is diagnostic. Black-tailed Gulls have yellow legs and a long yellow bill with a black ring and cherry red tip. In subadult plumages, they have distinct white eye crescents, which are lacking in other similar North American gulls.

VOICE: Seldom vocalizes as a vagrant. Gives a *kaoo-kaoo* call.

NESTING: A colonial nester, with colonies forming in April. It lays 2–3 eggs by early June. Incubation lasts approximately 24 days.

HABITAT: Maritime shorelines and bays. Sometimes found on large inland lakes as a vagrant in North America.

RANGE: A common gull of eastern Asia with a range centered on coastal China and Japan. It is migratory with birds found as far south as Hong Kong. It is a regular vagrant in Alaska and on the east coast more than the west coast of North America.

SIMILAR SPECIES: See Laughing Gull and Ring-billed Gull.

CONSERVATION:
The current population trends aren't well known, but the species' numbers are thought to be stable.

■ SUMMER ■ MIGRATION
■ WINTER ■ RARE
■ RESIDENT

This gull demonstrates that all migration in the Northern Hemisphere is not necessarily southward in fall and northward in spring. On its breeding grounds and in migration, Heermann's Gulls commonly follow Brown Pelicans, stealing fish from them as the pelicans surface with a catch. Farther north, they scavenge along beaches and feed on herring eggs.

DESCRIPTION: 18–21" (46–53 cm). A predominantly dark gull with a red bill. Its snow-white head blends into gray on the neck, back, and rump; it has slate-black wings and tail, with a white terminal band on the tail and secondaries. Juveniles are dusky with a lighter throat, a tail trimmed in white, and a dark bill.

VOICE: A high *see-whee*. Also a low-pitched *kuk-kuk-kuk*.

NESTING: Lays 2 or 3 eggs in a scrape; nests in large colonies on offshore islands.

HABITAT: Coastal waters, islands, and beaches.

RANGE: Breeds on islands in the Gulf of California and on the San Benito Islands off the west coast of Baja California. Some migrate northward from July to October, spending winter on the Pacific Coast north to Vancouver Island; others migrate southward as far as Panama. Nonbreeders are found year-round on the coast of California; adults leave by January.

SIMILAR SPECIES: Dark first-year immatures of California Gull and other gulls are much more mottled on the mantle and underparts.

CONSERVATION: NT
Heermann's Gull numbers have undergone significant fluctuations over the past several decades. More than 90 percent of the world's breeding Heermann's Gulls nest on Isla Rasa, Mexico, in the Gulf of California. The island became a wildlife sanctuary in the 1960s, limiting the impact of human disturbance.

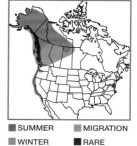

■ SUMMER ■ MIGRATION
■ WINTER ■ RARE
■ RESIDENT

This small gull is as versatile a feeder as the larger species of gulls, but its egg-stealing in seabird colonies is less destructive. It often catches insects, sometimes from swarms in the air.

DESCRIPTION: 16–18" (41–46 cm). White with gray mantle, black wing tips, and greenish-yellow legs. Its bill is small compared to those of larger gulls and is unmarked greenish-yellow in adults. Juveniles are similar to young Ring-billed Gulls, but generally darker with a less crisply marked tail band.

VOICE: A high, mewing *kee-yer*.

NESTING: Lays 2 or 3 olive eggs, with brown or black blotches and scrawls, in a grass nest placed on a beach or riverbank, or in a treetop, on a stump, or on pilings. Almost always nests in colonies, often among other gulls.

HABITAT: Nests along rivers and lakeshores as well as seacoasts.

RANGE: Breeds from Alaska east to central Mackenzie and south to northern Saskatchewan and along the coast to southern British Columbia. Winters on the Pacific Coast. Also found along the boreal forest belt of Eurasia.

SUBSPECIES: Our native Mew Gulls are of the "Short-billed" or "American" subspecies (*L. c. brachyrhynchus*). Rarely a member of the nominate European subspecies (*L. c. canus*), also called "Common Gull," wanders across the Atlantic Ocean to the East Coast. A few are seen each year, usually in winter, from Newfoundland to Massachusetts. Mew Gulls from northeast Asia of the Siberian subspecies (*L. c. kamtschatschensis*), called the "Kamchatka Gull," occur annually in western Alaska in spring and summer.

SIMILAR SPECIES: This bird's fine bill and small size are distinctive in all plumages.

First-winter Ring-billed Gull is similar, but its underparts are whiter and more heavily spotted, its wing and tail patterns are more distinct, and its bill is stouter. (Note that European Mew Gulls—which occur casually on the East Coast—have slightly larger, stouter bills and thus more closely resemble Ring-bills.) Second-winter and adult Ring-billed Gulls have a paler gray mantle, pale eyes, and a distinct black band on a pale bill.

California Gull and Herring Gull are much larger, with longer, heavier bills.

Immature "Thayer's" Iceland Gull is larger with paler wing tips; first-winter Thayer's bill is entirely black.

CONSERVATION:
Mew Gull's large, globally distributed population appears to be stable, although population trends are difficult to determine.

 SUMMER MIGRATION
WINTER RARE
RESIDENT

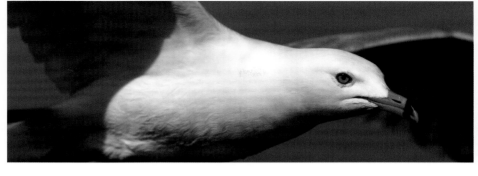

The Ring-billed is a common, medium-sized gull that can be found at various seasons over much of the United States and southern portions of Canada. It is well adapted to humans, often feeding on scraps in parking lots, landfills, and agricultural fields. It nests in large colonies; as many as 85,000 pairs nest on a single island in Lake Ontario. By contrast, colonies of Herring Gulls seldom number more than a few score pairs. Mischaracterized as a "seagull," this bird is regularly found inland, nesting around bodies of fresh water as readily as on seacoasts.

DESCRIPTION: 18–20" (46–51 cm). The adult is silvery gray on the back and white on the head, tail, and underparts. It is similar to Herring Gull but smaller, with greenish-yellow feet and a narrow black ring around the bill. Young birds are mottled brown, paler than young Herring Gulls, with a blackish tail band and flesh-colored legs. It acquires adult plumage in three years.

VOICE: Loud, raucous mewing cry, like that of Herring Gull but higher pitched.

NESTING: Lays 2–4 spotted buff or olive eggs in a hollow in the ground, sometimes lined with grass or debris. In the North, they sometimes nest in low trees. Nests in colonies, often with other gulls or terns, usually on islands in lakes.

HABITAT: Lakes and rivers; many move to salt water in winter.

RANGE: Breeds in the Northwest (locally south to California), northern Great Plains, and southern prairie provinces of Canada; also in the Great Lakes region, Canadian Maritimes, and northern New England. Winters on coasts, rivers, and lakes from southern New England south to Cuba, from the Great Lakes to the Gulf Coast, and from British Columbia to southern Mexico.

SIMILAR SPECIES: Mew Gull has a much finer bill; first-winter birds have darker, less heavily spotted underparts; its wing and tail patterns are less distinct; second-winter and adult birds have a darker gray mantle and dark eyes; the adult also has an unmarked bill.

See California Gull and immature Herring Gull. Also compare second-year with adult Black-legged Kittiwake.

CONSERVATION:
Although seriously impacted by human activity in the 19th century, these birds have mounted a strong comeback and are now among our most common and widespread gulls. Their numbers continue to increase as these adaptable birds readily feed on scraps from parking lots, landfills, beaches, and farmlands throughout the continent. Ring-billed Gull's booming population represents a threat to other birds such as smaller gulls and terns, with which they often compete for food and nest sites.

■ SUMMER ■ MIGRATION
■ WINTER ■ RARE
■ RESIDENT

The Western Gull is a large, common gull found in marine habitats along the Pacific Coast from around Vancouver Island south to Baja California. The Western is the only widespread, large, dark-mantled gull on the West Coast. It breeds on offshore islands and protected islets along the coast, rarely venturing far inland. The large gulls of the Pacific Coast have a common ancestor but evolved separately in isolation. The Glaucous-winged Gull resembles the Western Gull in size and habits, but its coloration is extremely light. The two species regularly hybridize in the Pacific Northwest.

DESCRIPTION: 24–27" (61–69 cm). It is snow white with a dark slate-colored back and wings. It has yellow eyes and a yellow bill; the breeding adult's bill has a red dot near the tip of the lower mandible. It has pinkish or flesh-colored feet. In winter, the head and nape are faintly dusky. First-year birds are dark gray-brown with dark, almost black primaries, contrasting with lighter areas on the nape and rump; these immature birds have a dark bill.

VOICE: Squeals and raucous notes.

NESTING: Lays 3 light buff, blotched eggs in a grass or seaweed nest in a depression, protected and slightly isolated by broken terrain. Nests in colonies on rocky headlands, islands, or dikes.

HABITAT: Coastal waterways, beaches, harbors, and dumps; open ocean.

RANGE: Breeds on the Pacific Coast from Washington to Baja California. In winter, it regularly occurs north to British Columbia.

SUBSPECIES: "Northern" Western Gulls (subsp. *occidentalis*) are paler and have darker eyes on average; "Southern" Western Gulls (subsp. *wymani*) have a darker mantle and their eyes tend toward a pale yellow. Intergrades between the two occur in central California.

SIMILAR SPECIES: Glaucous-winged Gull is similar in all plumages but paler than even northern Westerns; their wing tips are never blackish; and adults show more mottling on the head, neck, and chest in winter. Hybrids between Western and Glaucous-winged gulls are numerous in the Pacific Northwest.

Adult Herring Gull has more contrast between the mantle and black wing tips, a less bulbous bill, and a pale yellow eye; immature Herrings have paler wings and a slimmer bill.

Yellow-footed Gull has bright yellow legs and feet, a darker mantle, and a deeper bill; first-years are whiter below; second-winter birds are similar to third-winter Westerns, but with yellow legs and a black tail band.

See Great Black-backed Gull. Slaty-backed Gull, accidental in British Columbia, is larger with a darker mantle.

CONSERVATION:
Western Gull numbers are stable to slightly increasing, with local habitat disturbances negatively affecting some nesting colonies. This species' limited range and small overall numbers merit observation, but the population appears healthy.

■ SUMMER ■ MIGRATION
■ WINTER ■ RARE
■ RESIDENT

Long considered a subspecies of the more widespread Western Gull, the Yellow-footed Gull nests only in the Gulf of California. It is a regular visitor to extreme southern California, usually after the end of its breeding season. A strictly coastal species, visiting birds favor the immediate shoreline at the Salton Sea.

DESCRIPTION: 21–23" (53–58 cm). Similar to Western Gull, but with yellow legs. First-winter birds have pink legs like Westerns but are paler, with a contrasting white belly.

VOICE: Similar to the calls of Western Gull, but deeper.

NESTING: Lays 3 light buff, blotched eggs in a grass or seaweed nest placed in a depression, on rocky headlands or islands.

HABITAT: Beaches, harbors, and dumps; open ocean.

RANGE: Resident in the Gulf of California; visits the Salton Sea and San Diego area mainly in summer and fall.

SIMILAR SPECIES: Western Gull has pink legs and feet, and usually has a paler mantle; its bill is less deep. First-winter Westerns are darker and more uniform gray-brown below, without the strongly contrasting whitish belly of the juvenile Yellow-footed Gull. A third-winter Western resembles a second-winter Yellow-footed but has pink legs.

Other than Western Gull, no large, dark mantled gulls normally occur in the range of Yellow-footed. See Lesser Black-backed Gull.

CONSERVATION: LC
The Yellow-footed Gull population appears to be stable. Its extremely limited range makes the species more vulnerable to overfishing and pollution in the Gulf of California.

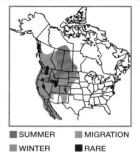

■ SUMMER ■ MIGRATION
■ WINTER ■ RARE
■ RESIDENT

This common western gull breeds in colonies on the islands and shores of interior lakes, and winters in large flocks along the Pacific Coast. Foraging birds range widely from coastal and interior valleys to urban centers, seacoasts, and offshore waters. The California Gull attained fame when it arrived in great numbers at a colony of Mormon pioneers near Great Salt Lake and devoured an insect swarm that threatened the settlers' crops. A statue in Salt Lake City commemorates the event, known as the "Miracle of the Gulls," and the California Gull became the state bird of Utah thanks to its role in the settlers' early history.

DESCRIPTION: 20–23" (51–58 cm). A common inland gull, similar to Herring Gull but smaller, with a darker gray mantle, a dark eye, a reddish eye ring, and greenish legs. The bill of the breeding adult has a red spot overlapped by black. Winter and immature birds have a black subterminal bar on the bill and lack the red eye ring of adults.

VOICE: A repetitive *kee-yah*.

NESTING: Lays 2 or 3 heavily blotched, buff-olive eggs in a nest made of grass, dead weeds, and sticks. Large colonies are found on islands in shallow inland lakes, often together with Ring-billed Gulls, though each species remains with its own kind.

HABITAT: In breeding season, on interior lakes and marshes; in winter, mostly on seacoasts.

RANGE: Breeds in northern prairie provinces east to North Dakota, south to northwestern Wyoming and Utah, west to northeastern California. Winters mainly on the coast from Oregon southward, and in lesser numbers inland.

SIMILAR SPECIES: Ring-billed Gull is slightly smaller and shorter-billed. Adult Ring-billed is paler gray on the mantle, with white eyes and a black bill ring. A first-winter Ring-billed is whiter below than a same-age California; it shows pale gray on the back and tail with a thinner, dark subterminal band. Third-winter California Gulls may show a distinct black ring on the bill, but have darker mantles than Ring-bills and never have pale eyes.

Herring Gull is larger with a stouter bill; the adult is paler on the mantle, with pink legs and a light eye.

Mew Gull is much smaller, with a shorter, slimmer bill.

First-winter Heermann's Gull is similar to a juvenile California Gull, but has dark undertail coverts and black legs.

CONSERVATION:
Common throughout its range, California Gull populations have been largely stable in recent decades with only a small decline over the past 40 years.

SUMMER MIGRATION
WINTER RARE
RESIDENT

In most of North America, this is the most common gull inland and along the East Coast. In recent decades, it has become abundant thanks to broad conservation efforts and the availability of food around landfills and fishing vessels, and has extended its range southward along the Atlantic Coast, often to the detriment of colonial birds such as terns and Laughing Gulls. Although a scavenger, it also eats large numbers of aquatic and marine animals and feeds on berries. It often drops clams and other shellfish on exposed rocks or parking lots in order to break the shells and get at the soft interior.

DESCRIPTION: 23–26" (58–66 cm). A large gull. The adult is white with a light gray back and wings; the wing tip is black with white spots; it has a yellow bill with a red spot on the lower mandible. Its feet are pink or flesh colored. It acquires full adult plumage in four years; first- and second-year birds are brownish. See California Gull.

VOICE: Loud rollicking call, *kuk-kuk-kuk*, *yucca-yucca-yucca*, and other raucous cries.

NESTING: Lays 2–4 heavily spotted, olive-brown eggs in a mass of seaweed or dead grass on the ground or a cliff; most often on islands. Nests in colonies.

HABITAT: Lakes, rivers, estuaries, and beaches; common in all aquatic habitats.

RANGE: Breeds from Alaska east across northern Canada to the Maritime Provinces, south to British Columbia, north-central Canada, and the Great Lakes, and along the Atlantic Coast to North Carolina. Winters in all but the northernmost breeding areas; also along coasts, rivers, and lakes both in the Southeast and in the West from southern Alaska south to Baja California. Also found in Eurasia.

SUBSPECIES: Most Herring Gulls in North America are the "American" group (subsp. *smithsonianus*), sometimes called Arctic Herring Gull or Smithsonian Gull. Siberian Herring Gulls

(subsp. *vegae*), also called Vega Gulls, are rare but regular visitors to western Alaska. European Herring Gulls (subsp. *argenteus*) rarely wander to Newfoundland and farther south along the Atlantic Coast. The taxonomy of this group of birds is complicated and unsettled, with some authorities regarding European Herring Gull and American/Arctic Herring Gull as separate species.

SIMILAR SPECIES: See Ring-billed, California, Thayer's, and immature Lesser and Great Black-backed gulls.

CONSERVATION: LC
Hunted for feathers and eggs in the 19th century, the species recovered mightily once protections and market demand made such practices both illegal and unprofitable. Although still widespread and abundant, Herring Gull numbers are decreasing due to overfishing, pollution, and deliberate control measures.

YELLOW-LEGGED GULL *Larus michahellis*

This large Old World gull is a casual winter visitor to the northeastern Atlantic Coast. The Yellow-legged Gull is part of the complex group of gulls related to the Herring Gull, which it closely resembles and which is much more common and widespread in North America.

DESCRIPTION: 25" (64 cm). A large gull, similar to Herring Gull. The adult is white with a gray back and wings (darker than Herring Gull, but lighter than Lesser Black-backed Gull). It has a bold, broad black area at the end of the wing, with limited white spotting toward the tip of the wing. Its bill is bright yellow with a red spot on the lower mandible (sometimes extending onto maxilla). Its legs and feet are yellow. Acquires adult plumage in three years.

VOICE: A deep, strident *kyow*.

NESTING: Similar to Herring Gull.

HABITAT: Beaches and shorelines.

RANGE: Eurasia; infrequent visitor to Atlantic Coast, recorded from Newfoundland to North Carolina.

SIMILAR SPECIES: See Herring Gull, which is much more common in North America.

CONSERVATION: LC

The Yellow-legged Gull is a common and widespread species in Europe, the Mediterranean, and North Africa with a large range and population size. The overall population is increasing.

■ SUMMER ■ MIGRATION
■ WINTER ■ RARE
■ RESIDENT

Both this species and the Glaucous Gull, being relatively scarce, are eagerly sought by birders—but present an identification challenge because typical adults of the two species differ only in size. The habits of these two "white-winged" gulls are similar, but the smaller Iceland Gull is more buoyant and graceful on the wing. It is also more of a scavenger and much less predatory. In addition to landfills and sewage outlets, this species frequents places where fish are being cleaned.

DESCRIPTION: 23" (58 cm). A smaller version of the Glaucous Gull, with a relatively smaller bill and rounded head. Adults are pearl-gray above, and white on the head and below. Their feet are pinkish and darker than those of a Herring Gull. Canada-breeding subspecies usually have darker gray or black markings at the wing tips. Immatures are creamy buff; they have a dark bill in first winter.

VOICE: Like Herring Gull, a variety of croaks, squeaks, and screams.

NESTING: Lays 2 or 3 light brown eggs, with darker blotches, in a nest lined with grass, moss, and seaweed placed either on a cliff or a sandy shore.

HABITAT: Lake and river shores, ocean beaches, sewer outlets, and refuse dumps.

RANGE: Breeds on eastern Baffin Island and coastal Greenland. It winters in eastern North America south to New Jersey and the Great Lakes. Also found in Eurasia. "Thayer's" form breeds in the Canadian high Arctic and winters chiefly on the Pacific Coast south to Baja California; it is a very rare winter visitor to Maritime Canada and the northeastern United States.

SUBSPECIES: "Thayer's" Gull (subsp. *thayeri*), primarily a Western bird, was formerly considered a separate species. Paler Thayer's are not always separable from darker adults of the main species, but usually has more black in the upperwing tips; the mantle is sometimes darker and the eyes may be lighter brown or dark yellow. "Kumlien's" Iceland Gull (subsp. *kumlieni*) breeds on the eastern part of Baffin Island and has wing tips with variable gray marks, and a few are pure white. The nominate race of Greenland breeders (subsp. *glaucoides*) are slightly smaller and paler than the other subspecies.

SIMILAR SPECIES: First-winter Glaucous Gull has a pink bill with a sharply defined black tip. Glaucous at other ages is distinguished by its larger size, but this is often difficult to determine—smaller Glaucous Gulls overlap the larger Herring Gulls in overall size, and larger Iceland Gulls overlap smaller Herring Gulls. Size is best judged in the bulk of the bill, head, and neck. Wing tips of Glaucous Gulls at rest can extend beyond the tail a distance no greater than the bill length; Iceland's wing tips extend beyond the tail a distance greater than the bill length. Glaucous sometimes has a flatter, less rounded head profile.

Glaucous-winged Gull, a Pacific Coast species, is similar, but has a stouter bill.

CONSERVATION: The Iceland Gull is a widespread species with a stable, possibly increasing population. The numbers of Iceland Gulls wintering in New England have increased over the past century. Their remote breeding habitat in the Far North protects these birds from human encroachment but also makes assessing their population trends difficult.

■ SUMMER ■ MIGRATION
■ WINTER ■ RARE
■ RESIDENT

Although this Old World species was once rare on this side of the Atlantic, Lesser Black-backed Gulls have become common visitors in North America as both their breeding and wintering ranges have expanded. It can be found in and around larger cities along the Atlantic Coast and in the Great Lakes region, especially in winter; it has become common in Florida and regular along the Gulf Coast. During the colder months, it may be found at landfills, fishing harbors, reservoirs, and other such sources of food.

DESCRIPTION: 23" (58 cm). Slightly smaller than the Herring Gull. The adult has yellow legs and a dark slate-gray back and wings. Immatures of this species and Herring Gull are similar and hard to distinguish.

VOICE: A strident *kyow*; deeper than that of Herring Gull.

NESTING: Lays 3 pale-green eggs, spotted with brown, in a nest sparsely lined with grass or laden with debris, placed on open ground or on rocky islets. Usually nests in colonies.

HABITAT: Nearly all types of open country—coasts, islands, fields, lakes, airports, landfills, etc.

RANGE: Breeds in northern Europe; newer breeding populations have become established in Iceland and Greenland. An increasingly regular visitor to eastern North America; rarer inland and in the West.

SUBSPECIES: Most North American records are of the subspecies that breeds in Britain and Iceland (subsp. *graellsii*); a few records in the East may pertain to the subspecies found in Denmark (subsp. *intermedius*), which has a darker mantle and more closely resembles Great Black-backed Gull.

SIMILAR SPECIES: Herring Gull is larger with pink legs and a shorter-winged appearance when at rest. Adult and subadult Herring Gulls have a light gray mantle; immatures have pale inner primaries and greater secondary coverts.

Great Black-backed Gull is much larger, and has pink legs and a black mantle; its head is unstreaked in winter.

Darker Western Gulls have pink legs and amber-yellow eyes. Western and Yellow-footed gulls (which have lemon-yellow eyes) have larger bodies and unstreaked heads in winter. Their longer and much stouter bills have tips that are bulbous above and sharply angled below.

CONSERVATION:
The Lesser Black-backed Gull appears to be expanding both its wintering and breeding ranges. It is a species of low concern as its population booms.

■ SUMMER ■ MIGRATION
■ WINTER ■ RARE
■ RESIDENT

Slaty-backed Gulls appear regularly in small numbers in Western Alaska during the summer, and rarely as a stray inland elsewhere in North America. Its similarity to several other species make it potentially easy to overlook outside of its traditional habitat in western Alaska, but like many other gulls, the species is known to wander widely.

DESCRIPTION: 27" (68.5 cm). Resembles an oversized Western Gull. Its head, underparts, and tail are pure white; its back and wings are dark slaty-gray with a broad white trailing edge. Its legs are bright pink, its bill is yellow with an orange spot, and its eyes are creamy-yellow. Immature plumages are similar to those of Great Black-backed Gull but paler.

VOICE: Similar to that of Herring Gull, but deeper and more guttural.

NESTING: Lays 3 olive-buff, brown-spotted eggs, in a seaweed-built nest placed on a rock; occasionally on a sandy beach.

HABITAT: Breeds on sea cliffs and rocky islands; forages on mudflats.

RANGE: Breeds in northeastern Eurasia. Winters from the Bering Sea and Kamchatka south to Japan and the coast of eastern China. Regularly wanders to the Aleutian Islands and the coast of western Alaska; strays rarely to widely scattered locations in the continental interior.

SIMILAR SPECIES: See Herring and Western Gulls.

CONSERVATION:
The Slaty-backed Gull is listed as a species of least concern in its native range, although little is known about its overall population trends.

Glaucous-winged Gull is common along the northern Pacific Coast and rarely seen away from salt water. Like other large gulls, this species feeds mainly along the shore. Over water, it picks up edibles such as dead or dying fish and squid; on the beach, it feeds on dead seabirds, seals, whales, starfish, clams, and mussels. In harbors and towns, it scavenges garbage. It is a paler northern relative of the Western Gull, with which it frequently hybridizes.

DESCRIPTION: 24–27" (61–69 cm). A large white gull with a pearly gray mantle and wings. Gray primaries show a white "window" near the tip of each feather; the bill is yellow with a red spot on the lower mandible. Its eyes are light brown or silvery, and its feet are pink. In winter, the red spot on the bill becomes a diffuse black; the head and nape look dusky. Juveniles are similar to Western Gull juveniles, but much paler. First-year birds are gray-brown overall, with wing tips the same color as the mantle. It has a black bill and dark eyes and feet. Second-year birds acquire more gray and are generally paler.

VOICE: A raucous series of similar notes on one pitch; also soft *ga-ga* notes when an intruder approaches.

NESTING: Lays 2 or 3 light olive-brown eggs, with dark speckles, in a grass or seaweed nest placed in a depression on remote islets or headlands. Nests in colonies.

HABITAT: Rocky or sandy beaches, harbors, and dumps; open ocean.

RANGE: Resident from the Aleutians and western and southern coasts of Alaska south to northwestern Washington. It winters south along the coast to southern California.

SIMILAR SPECIES: Western Gull has a darker mantle and primaries. Frequent Western x Glaucous-winged hybrids in the Northwest may be superficially similar to Herring Gull, but Herring has a thinner bill, a pale yellow eye, and sharply contrasting black wing tips.

"Thayer's" Iceland Gull is usually smaller, with a smaller, thinner bill and slightly darker wing tips; however, Glaucous-winged hybrids have darker primaries like Thayer's. Immature Glaucous-winged looks more smudged overall than Thayer's; at rest, its primaries are the same color as or slightly paler than the rest of the wing, not slightly darker as in Thayer's.

Glaucous Gull is heavier, and has whiter primaries; the immature Glaucous has a black bill tip sharply cut off from the basal two-thirds of the bill, which is pinkish to flesh-colored.

CONSERVATION:

The Glaucous-winged Gull is a common species that has been steadily increasing in recent decades. Their growing numbers may present a concern for other coastal birds due to this gull's predation of eggs and young.

■ SUMMER ■ MIGRATION
■ WINTER ■ RARE
■ RESIDENT

This is one of our largest and palest gulls. The Glaucous Gull is a bird of the high Arctic that sometimes moves far to the south in the winter. Uncommon south of Canada; it is usually found with flocks of other gulls when it visits the United States, occasionally as far south as California, Texas, and Florida. This is one of the most predatory of gulls, capturing and eating auks, plovers, small ducks, ptarmigans, and songbirds as well as lemmings and fish. It is also a scavenger, feeding on garbage, dead animal matter, and even bird droppings.

DESCRIPTION: 28" (71 cm). A large gull. Adults are pearl-gray above, with no black in the wing tips, and white on the head and underparts. Its bill is yellowish and its feet are pinkish. Immatures are creamy buff with a pinkish, dark-tipped bill. See Glaucous-winged Gull.

VOICE: Hoarse croaks and screams.

NESTING: Lays 3 light brown eggs, with dark chocolate blotches, placed in a cliff nest lined with moss and grass.

HABITAT: Shores of lakes, rivers, and seacoast; it also frequents refuse dumps and sewage outflows.

RANGE: Breeds in Alaska and northern Canada. Winters along the coast south to California (rarely) and Virginia; rare in the Great Lakes and on the Gulf Coast. Also found in Eurasia.

SIMILAR SPECIES: Iceland Gull is similar but has a much smaller bill and often more gray markings in the primaries. Iceland is smaller, but this difference is sometimes difficult to determine; size is best judged in the bulk of the bill, head, and neck. First-winter Iceland has a bill that's all or mostly dark.

Adult Glaucous-winged Gull has extensive gray in the primaries, and a somewhat shorter and more bulbous bill; immatures may be quite pale—particularly in worn plumage at end of the first and second winters—but their bills are entirely black, or extensively and irregularly tipped in black.

Albinos of other large, pink-legged gulls (Herring, Western) are occasionally observed; they lack the regular gray-buff mottling of a young Glaucous and do not show the Glaucous' bill pattern. Other gulls in worn summer plumage may be mistaken for Glaucous.

CONSERVATION: LC
Glaucous Gull is a widespread species in the Far North around the world, and its global population is quite large and stable. This species is not greatly affected by human activity due to the remoteness of most of its range. These adaptable birds may be better able to weather the effects of climate change than many other Arctic species thanks to their highly variable diet.

■ SUMMER ■ MIGRATION
■ WINTER ■ RARE
■ RESIDENT

Our largest gull, this coastal species accompanies the ever-present Herring Gull at all times of the year, even during the summer, when they nest together in mixed colonies. The Great Black-backed, however, typically asserts dominance over its smaller relative. It preys on almost anything smaller than itself, including Dovekies, small ducks, petrels, fish, and shellfish, as well as the eggs and young of other gulls. It is also highly opportunistic, scavenging at landfills and docks.

DESCRIPTION: 30" (76 cm). A large gull. The adult has a black back and wings; the rest of the plumage is white. It has a yellow bill and pinkish legs. The immature is mottled with brown and is paler on the head and breast, with a black tail tip and a dark bill.

VOICE: Similar to that of Herring Gull, but deeper and more guttural, a deep *keeow*.

NESTING: Lays 3 olive eggs, with dark brown blotches, placed in a ground nest lined with grass.

HABITAT: Coastal beaches, estuaries, and lagoons; also at refuse dumps. Less commonly on inland lakes and rivers.

RANGE: Breeds from Labrador south to the Carolinas, rarely farther; also on the Great Lakes. Winters south to Florida. Also found in Eurasia.

SIMILAR SPECIES: See immature Herring Gull and Lesser Black-backed Gull.

CONSERVATION:
Egg collectors and feather hunters in the 19th century nearly wiped out the Great Black-backed Gull, but legal protection in the early 20th century allowed the species to make a full recovery. They continue to increase in number and expand their range southward along the eastern seaboard and inland to the Great Lakes. Unfortunately, this species often displaces other gulls, terns, and puffins from their breeding habitats, leading wildlife officials to try to control Great Black-backed Gull breeding populations at important sites for these other birds.

Kelp Gulls are widespread in the Southern Hemisphere, and have rarely appeared in the Gulf of Mexico and farther north. An influx of Kelp Gulls arrived on the Chandeleur Islands in the Gulf of Mexico off the Louisiana coast in the late 1980s and early 1990s, with a few pairs nesting there and several others hybridizing with the local Herring Gulls. Kelp Gulls are opportunistic feeders, preying on and scavenging everything from fish to even their own chicks and eggs. They will eat scraps scavenged from petrels and will frequently raid penguin colonies. In Argentina they have been observed feeding on live right whales using their powerful bill to peck into the skin and blubber, often leaving the whales with large open sores.

DESCRIPTION: A large gull, 23" (58 cm) long. Once thought to be subspecies of Lesser Black-backed Gull, it is heavier bodied and billed, has duller legs and is darker above. It is similar to Western Gull subspecies *wymani*, but its legs are a dull yellowish green. Adults have black upperparts and wings. The head, underparts, tail, and the small areas of the wing tips are white. The bill is yellow with a red spot, and the legs are greenish-yellow and become brighter and more yellow during the breeding season. Juveniles have dull legs, a black bill, a dark tail band, and an overall gray-brown plumage densely edged in whitish, but they quickly change into a pale base to the bill and largely white head and underparts. They take three or four years to attain adult plumage.

VOICE: The call is a strident *ki-och*.

NESTING: Nests in loose colonies or scattered single pairs on offshore islands, laying 2–3 mottled eggs in a well-made bowl or loose pile of plants and seaweed on the ground, near rocks or vegetation. Both adults build the nest, incubate the eggs, and feed the young. Eggs hatch in 23 to 30 days and the young fledge in 45 to 60 days. Most Kelp Gulls return to the colonies where they were born.

HABITAT: Maritime coasts, bays, inlets, and estuaries. Fond of landfills.

RANGE: Found along coasts and islands through much of the Southern Hemisphere, but has nested on islands off Louisiana in Gulf of Mexico where it hybridizes with Herring Gulls.

SIMILAR SPECIES: Mostly closely related to Herring Gull but it is slightly slimmer with a larger bill.

Kelp Gull's dark mantle is even darker than that of Great Black-backed Gull. Immatures of the two species may be indistinguishable in the field.

Western Gull is similar in size and shape, but its legs are pale pinkish rather than yellowish-green.

CONSERVATION: LC
The Kelp Gull is common in the Southern Hemisphere and its overall population trend is increasing.

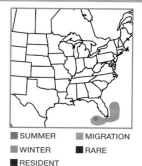

■ SUMMER　■ MIGRATION
■ WINTER　■ RARE
■ RESIDENT

These dark brown terns with light caps commonly associate with Sooty Terns, at least at breeding colonies. Unlike them, however, the Noddy does not wander northward after the nesting season; as a result, few are reported in our area north of southern Florida. They catch their food, primarily small fish, by pouncing on them at the water's surface rather than diving as most terns do. These oceangoing terns are fond of perching on floating pieces of driftwood, and they occasionally alight on the water and float.

DESCRIPTION: 15" (38 cm). It is dark sooty brown with a pale grayish-white crown, a wedge-shaped tail, and a slender black bill.

VOICE: Low *cah*, similar to the call of a young crow.

NESTING: Lays 1 buff egg spotted with lilac and brown in a stick nest lined with seaweed and often bits of shell and coral, placed on rocks, in trees or bushes, or on exposed coral reefs.

HABITAT: Coastal and oceanic islands during the breeding season; open ocean at other times.

RANGE: Breeds on Dry Tortugas, Florida. Found nearly throughout warmer ocean regions of the world.

SIMILAR SPECIES: Black Noddy is smaller and has a slenderer bill, blacker plumage throughout (visible only in good light), and a more sharply defined white cap.

CONSERVATION: 🐦 LC

Common in the tropics worldwide, the Brown Noddy population appears stable. Egg collectors in the 19th century may have displaced these birds from the Dry Tortugas in Florida; today one colony of around 4500 noddies breeds in Dry Tortugas National Park.

■ SUMMER ■ MIGRATION
■ WINTER ■ RARE
■ RESIDENT

This pantropical tern is of extremely local occurrence in North America, but in most years since 1960 these dark brownish-black birds have been found among nesting Brown Noddies in the Dry Tortugas. Although seen there regularly, the Black Noddy has not yet been known to nest there.

DESCRIPTION: 12" (30 cm). Smaller and darker than Brown Noddy, with a more extensive pure white cap. The rest of its plumage is dark brownish black. Its feet are brownish black. Its bill is long, thin, straight, and black. It has a wedge-shaped tail.

VOICE: A sharp *kit, kit*.

NESTING: Lays 1 whitish egg spotted with brown in a stick nest lined with grass or seaweed, placed in a tree or bush.

HABITAT: Small oceanic and coastal islands in breeding season; otherwise wanders at sea.

RANGE: Tropical portions of Atlantic, Pacific, and Indian oceans. In North America, found only in Dry Tortugas, Florida (rare).

SIMILAR SPECIES: See Brown Noddy.

CONSERVATION:
Globally, the Black Noddy is listed as a species of least concern and its population appears stable. It is widespread throughout the tropics.

SOOTY TERN *Onychoprion fuscatus*

SUMMER ■ MIGRATION
■ WINTER ■ RARE
■ RESIDENT

Sooty Terns are notorious wanderers; when not nesting they range far and wide over the seas. Perhaps this is why they are so often blown inland, sometimes many hundreds of miles, by hurricanes and tropical storms. These birds have a remarkable homing ability. When individuals marked with dye were released along the coasts of North Carolina and Texas, all returned to their Dry Tortugas breeding grounds within a week. Sooty Terns feed largely at dusk and at night. Unlike most other terns, they do not dive but pluck small fish and squid from the surface of the water. They spend most of their time in the air, almost never perching or alighting on the water.

DESCRIPTION: 16" (41 cm). The adult is black above with a white forehead; it is white below. It has a deeply forked tail and a thin black bill. Immature birds are dark brown, and finely spotted with white on the back and wings.

VOICE: Harsh squeaky notes and croaks.

NESTING: Lays 1 white egg with reddish brown blotches in a hollow in the sand; occasionally nests on rocks or ledges. Almost always nests in large colonies.

HABITAT: Coastal and oceanic islands during breeding season; open ocean at other times.

RANGE: Tropical seas; in North America, it breeds only on Dry Tortugas, Florida.

SIMILAR SPECIES: Bridled Tern is paler above, with a complete white collar; its white eyebrow extends rearward; its outer tail feathers are white, and the central part of the tail is gray. Immatures have a white head, nape, and underparts. Bridled's flight is slightly faster, with shallower wingbeats.

CONSERVATION: LC

The Sooty Tern has a large population and an extremely large range. Its overall population trends are unknown; some subpopulations have increased and others have decreased. Climate change and the variation in sea-surface temperatures in some areas has had a negative impact on foraging in breeding colonies and on reproductive success.

■ SUMMER   ■ MIGRATION
■ WINTER   ■ RARE
■ RESIDENT

This bird was long thought to be a casual visitor to the North American coast, but as more birders travel out to the Gulf Stream, it has become evident that the species is fairly common 20 or 30 miles (30 to 50 km) offshore.

DESCRIPTION: 14–15" (36–38 cm). A stocky oceanic tern, it is dark gray above and white below, with a black cap. It has a white forehead and eyebrow, and a conspicuous white collar, or "bridle," on the hindneck. Sooty Tern is similar, but lacks the collar and is blacker on the upperparts.

VOICE: Usually silent; various high-pitched barking notes on breeding grounds.

NESTING: Lays 1 white egg spotted with brown in a shallow depression among rocks on an island. Nests in colonies.

HABITAT: Open ocean; breeds on rocky or sandy islands.

RANGE: Breeds in the tropical Atlantic, Indian, and Pacific oceans; in nonbreeding season, it ranges to offshore Gulf Stream waters from the Carolinas to Florida.

SIMILAR SPECIES: See Sooty and Black terns.

CONSERVATION:
The Bridled Tern is a common species with a large range throughout the tropics. Although not a significant threat to the global population, human disturbance such as visitation and egg harvesting may severely disrupt breeding colonies.

ALEUTIAN TERN *Onychoprion aleuticus*

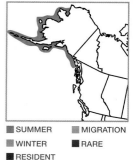

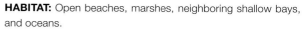

■ SUMMER   ■ MIGRATION
■ WINTER   ■ RARE
■ RESIDENT

The poorly studied, uncommon Aleutian Tern nests in coastal Alaska, usually among Arctic Terns, which are notoriously aggressive in defense of their nests. The Aleutians seem to take advantage of their neighbors' behavior, making little attempt to defend their own nests.

DESCRIPTION: 13½–15" (34–38 cm). This tern's mantle and wings are dark gray; its cap is black but its forehead is white; and its underparts are grayish. It has a forked, white tail.

VOICE: A musical *whee-hee-hee*; chirping notes like those of House Sparrow.

NESTING: Lays 2 olive or buff eggs placed in a depression above high-tide line on small offshore islands and in coastal meadows. Nests in colonies.

HABITAT: Open beaches, marshes, neighboring shallow bays, and oceans.

RANGE: Breeds in coastal Alaska. It winters off the coast of Indonesia and Malaysia.

SIMILAR SPECIES: Common and Arctic terns are paler gray above and below.

CONSERVATION:  VU
This uncommon bird's numbers continue to decline. Larger colonies are showing steeper declines than smaller colonies. Aleutian Terns are sensitive to human disturbance and mammalian predation, which can contribute to population decline and permanent colony abandonment.

■ SUMMER ■ MIGRATION
■ WINTER ■ RARE
■ RESIDENT

Our smallest tern. Most often seen hovering over the water, the Least Tern peers downward in search of small minnows and other marine or freshwater organisms.

DESCRIPTION: 8–10" (20–25 cm). A small tern with a black-tipped yellow bill and a fast, shallow wingbeat. It is white with a black cap, pale gray back and wings, a forked tail, and a white forehead. It has a conspicuous black wedge or M shape on the outer primaries.

VOICE: Sharp *killick* or *kip-kip-kip-kiddeek*.

NESTING: Lays 2 or 3 buff, lightly spotted eggs in an unlined scrape on a sand spit or gravel beach. Nests in colonies.

HABITAT: Sandy and pebbly beaches along the coast; sandbars in large rivers. Often on landfills.

RANGE: Breeds along the California coast, along rivers in the Mississippi Valley, and coastally from Maine south to Florida. Winters from Southern Mexico and the Caribbean south to the coast of South America.

SIMILAR SPECIES: Common and Forster's terns are larger and bulkier with broader wings.

CONScRVATION: LC

The Least Tern is a widespread species that has undergone a serious decrease. Although listed as a species of least concern by the IUCN, the interior population is on the U.S. Endangered Species List and Least Terns are given protection as a threatened or endangered species in most U.S. states. The species is vulnerable to human disturbance and loss of nesting sites due to development, recreation, and water diversion activities.

LARGE-BILLED TERN *Phaetusa simplex*

This common South American inland tern is strictly an accidental visitor to eastern North America, with only a few records widely scattered in space and time.

DESCRIPTION: A large tern (15", 38 cm) with a distinctive wing pattern and a large, heavy yellow bill, the Large-billed Tern is unlikely to be confused with any species native to North America. The Large-billed Tern's wings are dark gray to black at the tips, white along the secondaries, and lighter gray at the roots. The black hood has distinctive "ear-flaps" that reach down to the eyes.

VOICE: A gooselike honk.

NESTING: Does not nest in North America.

HABITAT: Breeds on the sandy shores of major rivers and lakes, only rarely on the coast. Outside of breeding season, it uses both its breeding habitat and coastal habitats including beaches and mangrove swamps.

RANGE: Eastern South America, north to Venezuela and south to northern Argentina.

SIMILAR SPECIES: The only native tern in our area with a yellow bill is the much smaller and more delicate Least Tern, which lacks the wing pattern of the Large-billed Tern. Any native tern close to this size would have an orange or black bill.

CONSERVATION: LC
The Large-billed Tern population is stable in its native range.

■ SUMMER　■ MIGRATION
■ WINTER　■ RARE
■ RESIDENT

In addition to the usual tern diet of fish and crustaceans, this bird catches insects in flight and pursues them on the ground in plowed fields or croplands. Although not numerous, it is widespread, breeding in scattered colonies. In America, it was one of the species hardest hit by the millinery trade and has never recovered its former numbers, although recently it has slowly extended its range northward.

DESCRIPTION: 13–15" (33–38 cm). A pigeon-sized tern. It is pale with almost white back and wings, a black cap, and a stout black bill. Its tail is not as deeply forked as in other terns. Winter birds lack the black cap.

VOICE: Rasping *katy-did*, similar to the sound made by that insect.

NESTING: Lays 2 or 3 spotted buff eggs in a shell-lined shallow depression (occasionally a well-made cup of dead marsh grasses) on a sandy island in a salt marsh. Nests in colonies and often breeds with other species of terns.

HABITAT: Coastal marshes and sandy beaches.

RANGE: Breeds from Long Island south to the Gulf of Mexico and West Indies; also locally at Salton Sea, California. It winters north to the Gulf Coast. Also in Eurasia, Africa, and Australia.

SIMILAR SPECIES: Sandwich Tern has a longer and thinner bill with a yellow tip; it has a shaggy black crest.

CONSERVATION:

The Gull-billed Tern population is decreasing due to human disturbance and loss of breeding habitat. It is listed as a species of special concern in California, where the small population that colonized there has declined sharply in recent decades.

■ SUMMER   ■ MIGRATION
■ WINTER   ■ RARE
■ RESIDENT

Much less gregarious than other terns, Caspians usually feed singly. Pairs nest by themselves or in small colonies or may attach themselves to colonies of other birds such as the Ring-billed Gull. Caspians are more predatory than most other terns, readily taking small birds or the eggs and young of other terns.

DESCRIPTION: 19–23" (48–58 cm). Our largest tern. It is largely white, with a black cap, a slight crest, pale gray back and wings, and dusky underwing. It has a heavy, bright red bill. Royal Tern is similar, but has an orange-red bill, a more obvious crest, and paler underwing; it is almost never seen away from the coast.

VOICE: Low harsh *kraa*. Also a shorter *kow*.

NESTING: Lays 2 or 3 spotted buff eggs in a shallow depression or a well-made cup of dead grass, most often on a sandy or rocky island. Solitary or in small colonies.

HABITAT: Sandy or pebbly shores of lakes and large rivers and along seacoasts.

RANGE: Breeds in scattered colonies from Mackenzie, the Great Lakes, and Newfoundland south to the Gulf Coast and Baja California. Winters north to California and North Carolina. Also breeds in Eurasia, Africa, and Australia.

SIMILAR SPECIES: Royal Tern is smaller and slimmer. It has narrower wings, a more slender, yellow-orange to orange-red bill, and a prominent crest on the back of the head. Its tail is more deeply forked and its flight is more buoyant. The underside of Royal Tern's primaries is white to gray with a narrow black border; its forehead is white except at the onset of the breeding season.

CONSERVATION: LC

The Caspian Tern is common with a large global range and an increasing population.

■ SUMMER   ■ MIGRATION
■ WINTER   ■ RARE
■ RESIDENT

This tern usually nests in small groups and in shallow water. The nests are sometimes conspicuous; perhaps this is why the young often leave the nest at the first sign of an intruder, swimming quietly away to hide in the surrounding marsh vegetation. It is not unusual to visit an active colony and find all the nests empty. Unlike other terns, these birds frequently fly over land areas as they hawk for insects. Black Terns also eat small fish and crustaceans, which they pick from the water.

DESCRIPTION: 9–10" (23–25 cm). A medium-sized tern with a solid black head and underparts, gray wings, and moderately forked gray tail. In fall and winter, its head and underparts are white with dusky smudging around the eyes and the back of the neck.

VOICE: Sharp *kick*; also a shrill *kreek* when disturbed.

NESTING: Lays 2 spotted, olive-buff eggs placed in a hollow on a mass of floating marsh vegetation or in a well-made cup of dead grass. Nests in colonies.

HABITAT: Freshwater marshes and marshy lakes in summer; sandy coasts on migration and in winter.

RANGE: Breeds from British Columbia east to New Brunswick and south to central California and New York. Winters south of U.S.-Mexico border, rarely in California. Also found in Eurasia.

SIMILAR SPECIES: White-winged Tern has a shorter bill; in breeding plumage it has white wings, a white tail, black wing linings, and a red bill and legs. In fall, it has much less black on the head, a white rump, and no breast patches.

Bridled Tern is much larger with a long, deeply forked tail.

Larger terns in winter plumage are much less uniform above, and have clearly forked tails.

CONSERVATION:

The Black Tern is a common and widespread species that has experienced a small decline in population during the past 40 years. Wetland drainage and agricultural runoff are contributing to impacts on breeding habitats. The species is hard to monitor due to annual changes in nesting locations from changing water levels.

WHITE-WINGED TERN *Chlidonias leucopterus*

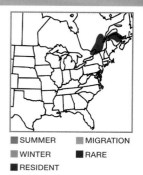

SUMMER   MIGRATION
WINTER   RARE
RESIDENT

This rare Eurasian vagrant attracts numerous birders whenever it appears in our area, usually during fall migration. Care is required to separate it from its close relative, the Black Tern, in their different respective plumages. These two species are quite closely related and often associate with one another; there are a few records of a White-winged Tern pairing and nesting with a Black Tern, producing hybrid offspring.

DESCRIPTION: A small tern 9½" (24 cm) long with a wingspan of 25–27" (63–67 cm). It resembles a Black Tern, but it has a shorter bill and a shorter, less notched tail. In breeding plumage, White-winged has a red bill, a white tail and rump, whitish upperwing coverts, and black underwing linings; its outermost flight feathers on the upperwing are black. In molt, its body plumage is patchy black-and-white, and its rump and tail are whitish (versus dark gray in Black Tern). Its bill is black.

VOICE: Call is a loud, harsh *kwek* or *creek*; also *kvrr-kak*.

NESTING: Generally similar to Black Tern, although they sometimes use drier, less permanent marshlands; its eggs are placed on a mat of floating marsh vegetation or dead grass.

HABITAT: Breeds in freshwater marshes and grassy lakes; in migration, frequently visits coastal marshes; winters along the coast.

RANGE: A Eurasian species, it is a casual vagrant to the U.S. East Coast, accidental inland, in Texas, and on the western Aleutian Islands. Winters in Africa, southeast Asia, and Australia.

SIMILAR SPECIES: See Black Tern.

CONSERVATION: LC
The White-winged Tern is a common, widespread species in the Old World with an extremely large, stable population. The European population may fluctuate.

SUMMER **MIGRATION**
WINTER **RARE**
RESIDENT

The Roseate Tern is much less numerous than other terns of similar size, and its patchy distribution around the world suggests that it is an old species, perhaps more abundant and widespread ages ago. It frequently nests in colonies of Common Terns, occupying less favorable, marginal sites. Roseate Terns have short wings and fly with snappy wingbeats; Roseates in flight can often be recognized by this field mark alone.

DESCRIPTION: 14–17" (36–43 cm). White with a black cap and pale gray back and wings. It has a long, notably slender bill; short wings; and long, white tail feathers that extend well beyond the ends of the wings when the bird is at rest. The wings are pale, with a narrow blackness to the leading edge on the outermost primary. It is similar to Common, Arctic, and Forster's terns, but its bill is usually solid black, its upperparts are paler, and the tail is longer and more deeply forked.

VOICE: Loud, harsh *zaap*, likened to the sound of tearing cloth. Also a softer *chew-wick*.

NESTING: Lays 2 or 3 spotted buff or olive eggs in a hollow in the ground, sometimes lined with dead grass; may be located in the open but more often concealed in vegetation or among rocks. Nests in colonies, often with other species of terns.

HABITAT: Coastal beaches, islands, and inshore waters.

RANGE: Breeds along the Atlantic Coast from Nova Scotia to Long Island. Winters in the tropics. Also found in Eurasia, East Africa, and southwest Pacific.

SIMILAR SPECIES: See Common Tern. Upon arrival in spring, the proximal half of Common Tern's bill is red earlier; its back is darker and the outer tail feathers are short and black-edged; its voice also is distinctive. In winter plumage, these species are nearly indistinguishable and can best be identified by call. The lighter back of the Roseate, when seen in good light and in direct comparison with Common, may aid in identifying winter birds.

CONSERVATION:

Widespread globally, but the subspecies of Roseate Tern that lives in North America, *Sterna dougallii dougallii*, is on the U.S. Endangered Species List, with an estimated 16,000 breeding birds left on the continent at only a few key nesting sites in the northeast and Florida. Some of the species' historic breeding islands were overrun by Herring Gulls in the mid-20th century.

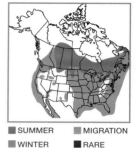

■ SUMMER ■ MIGRATION
■ WINTER ■ RARE
■ RESIDENT

Common Tern is usually the most numerous tern in the East and in the Old World (it is outnumbered by Forster's Tern in the West). It is a familiar sight on almost all large bodies of water where protected nesting sites exist. This bird flies gracefully over the water with deliberate wingbeats, its head turned down at a right angle to the body. When it sees a fish or tadpole, it dives much like a booby to catch its aquatic prey. These birds aggressively defend their nesting sites and will attack human intruders in the nesting colonies, often striking them on the head with their bills.

DESCRIPTION: 13–16" (33–41 cm). Adults in breeding plumage have a black cap, a pale gray back and wings, and red legs and feet; they are washed with gray below (usually darker than Roseate or Forster's). The tail is deeply forked; the tail feathers are black along the outer edge and do not reach beyond the ends of the folded wings. The upperwings have a dark wedge on the primaries; a broad, dark trailing edge is visible from below. It shows little or no translucence to the wings. In spring, the bill is red on the basal half with a black tip; it may become entirely red. Winter adults lose their black cap, retain their dark nape, and have a dark bar at the bend of the wing; their legs, feet, and bill become black.

VOICE: *Kip-kip-kip*; also a drawn-out *tee-aar*.

NESTING: Lays 2 or 3 spotted olive-buff eggs in a depression in sand or in a shallow cup of dead grass, located on sandy or pebbly beaches or open rocky places. Nests in colonies, most often on islands or isolated peninsulas.

HABITAT: Lakes, ponds, rivers, coastal beaches, and islands.

RANGE: Breeds in scattered colonies from Alberta and Labrador south to Montana, the Great Lakes, and the Caribbean. A common migrant along the Pacific Coast. Winters from Florida to southern South America. Also widespread in Eurasia.

SUBSPECIES: The Siberian population of Common Terns sometimes crosses into western Alaska; these birds are similar to their North American counterparts except the breeding adults are darker gray on the back and wings, with dark legs and an almost all-black bill.

SIMILAR SPECIES: Forster's Tern has a silvery-white surface on the upper primaries, a paler gray mantle, and a gray tail; its underparts are always white. The breeding adult has orange legs and an orange, black-tipped bill; the winter adult has a gray to blackish nape, and a pale hind crown. The immature has no dark bar across the inner wing.

See Arctic and Roseate terns.

CONSERVATION:  LC

Common Terns have recovered from earlier declines driven by human interactions—primarily feather and egg collection—but still face threats on breeding grounds from human disturbance, now in the form of motorboats, dogs, and off-road vehicles. Sensitive to disturbance during the breeding season, whole colonies often fail to breed successfully because of human disruption. Despite these threats, and despite predation from larger gulls, Common Terns have a large, widespread population.

■ SUMMER ■ MIGRATION
■ WINTER ■ RARE
■ RESIDENT

These terns annually perform spectacular migrations, every fall heading eastward across the Atlantic and down the west coasts of Europe and Africa to winter in the Antarctic Ocean. In spring they return north, following the east coast of South and North America, a round-trip that can total 22,000 miles (35,000 kilometers). They migrate over oceans and are rarely seen from land outside of the breeding grounds. These birds see more daylight than any other living creature because they are in the Arctic and the Antarctic during the periods of the longest days at each pole. During the northern winter, this species is more truly oceanic than its close relatives, feeding chiefly on small seagoing shrimp and other planktonic animals. The Arctic Tern's harsh, rasping, high-pitched cry makes a colony a noisy place. All members assemble to mob an intruder. The nests and eggs left unattended during an attack are so well camouflaged that a predator is not likely to find them. These terns attack so fiercely that human observers have to protect their heads.

DESCRIPTION: 14–17" (36–43 cm). These terns have a short neck, a short and deep bill, a rounded head profile, and a deeply forked tail. In flight, it can almost seem to lack a neck, with its small head barely projecting beyond the wing tips; this feature distinguishes Arctic from other similar terns (Common, Roseate, and Forster's). Its upperwings are plain, unmarked gray; from below, a translucent area on the flight feathers is visible; this area and a well-defined dark trailing edge of the primaries are good field marks. It is gray below, darker than other similar terns. Its undertail coverts and long tail streamers are white. Breeding adults have a black cap with a pale streak just below it; the bill, feet, and legs are blood-red. Winter adults and immatures have a white forehead, a black nape, a dark bill, white underparts, and a short tail; these somewhat resemble Aleutian Tern.

VOICE: Harsh *tee-ar* or *kip-kip-kip-tee-ar*, higher pitched than the call of a Common Tern.

NESTING: Lays 2 spotted olive-buff eggs in a shallow depression in the ground, sometimes lined with grass or shells. Nests in colonies, usually on islands or protected sand spits.

HABITAT: Coastal islands and beaches; also on tundra in summer.

RANGE: Breeds from the Aleutians, northern Alaska, and northern Canada east to Ellesmere Island and Newfoundland, and south to northern British Columbia, northern Manitoba, Quebec, and Massachusetts. Winters at sea in the Southern Hemisphere. Also breeds in northern Eurasia.

SIMILAR SPECIES: Common Tern is more heavily built, longer-legged, with a stouter bill; it has a dark wedge in outer primaries and a broader, less crisply defined trailing edge on the primaries. Only its inner primaries, not all flight feathers, are translucent. Immature Common usually has some orange at the base of the bill.

Forster's Tern has no translucence in flight feathers, and lacks a dark trailing edge. Its bill is larger and orange; it has a paler gray nape and a different shape overall.

CONSERVATION:
Arctic Tern colonies are often predated by mink, and efforts have been made to remove mink from breeding sites. Additionally, these birds are vulnerable to human disturbance and habitat degradation at nesting colonies and to reduced food availability caused by overfishing. It remains a species of least concern, owing to its large, widespread population.

FORSTER'S TERN *Sterna forsteri*

- ■ SUMMER   ■ MIGRATION
- ■ WINTER   ■ RARE
- ■ RESIDENT

One of the few exclusively New World terns, Forster's is so similar to the Common Tern that it was not recognized as a distinct species until 1831. Its preference for marshes enables it to avoid competition with the Common Tern, which favors sandy or pebbly beaches and rocky islands. It was named after Johann Reinhold Forster (1729–1798), a German pastor-naturalist who accompanied Captain Cook around the world in 1772.

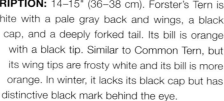

DESCRIPTION: 14–15" (36–38 cm). Forster's Tern is white with a pale gray back and wings, a black cap, and a deeply forked tail. Its bill is orange with a black tip. Similar to Common Tern, but its wing tips are frosty white and its bill is more orange. In winter, it lacks its black cap but has distinctive black mark behind the eye.

VOICE: A harsh, nasal *beep*.

NESTING: Lays 3 or 4 buff, spotted eggs on a large platform of dead grass lined with finer grasses, usually placed on masses of dead marsh vegetation. Nests in colonies.

HABITAT: Freshwater marshes in West; salt marshes in East.

RANGE: Breeds along the Atlantic Coast from Massachusetts to Texas and in the interior from Alberta and California east to the Great Lakes. Winters along the coasts from California and Virginia southward. It is a common resident along much of the Gulf Coast.

SIMILAR SPECIES: Roseate Tern has a long, deeply forked white tail, a dark or basally scarlet bill, and coral-red legs. Their voices are diagnostic.

Gull-billed Tern has a heavy black bill and shallowly forked tail.

See Common and Arctic terns.

CONSERVATION: ⬤LC

Forster's Tern populations have been stable to increasing during the past 50 years.

■ SUMMER ■ MIGRATION
■ WINTER ■ RARE
■ RESIDENT

The Royal Tern breeds in large, dense colonies. Nests are sometimes washed away by storm tides, but the birds usually make a second attempt, often at a new location. This bird has fewer young than other terns but maintains its numbers wherever it has protection from disturbance. It feeds almost entirely on small fish, rather than on the crustaceans and insects taken by most other terns.

DESCRIPTION: 18–21" (46–53 cm). A large, crow-sized tern with a long, heavy, yellow-orange to orange-red bill. It has a black cap, a wispy crest, pale gray back and wings, and a white forehead. Its tail is moderately forked. Similar Caspian Tern has blood-red bill, darker forehead and underwing, and shorter tail.

VOICE: Harsh *kee-rare*, like Caspian Tern but higher pitched.

NESTING: Lays usually 1 buff, spotted egg in a sand scrape on an island or a sheltered peninsula.

HABITAT: Sandy beaches.

RANGE: Breeds along the Atlantic and Gulf coasts from Maryland to Texas, wandering regularly farther north in summer. Winters from North Carolina, the Gulf Coast, and southern California southward into South America. Also found in west Africa.

SIMILAR SPECIES: See Caspian Tern.

Elegant Tern in southern California is smaller; it has a longer, slimmer, slightly downcurved, orange-yellow to yellow bill. It also has a longer, shaggier black crest on the back of the head. The bill in immatures is yellowish. At rest, its wing tips extend to or beyond the tip of the tail. The white forehead of nonbreeding adults does not extend to the eye.

CONSERVATION:

Populations have been fairly stable during the past 50 years. Future concerns include erosion of coastal islands used for nesting, human disturbance, and disturbance from tropical storms, which have been increasing in intensity. West Coast populations have declined in step with sardine populations.

SANDWICH TERN *Thalasseus sandvicensis*

SUMMER MIGRATION
WINTER RARE
RESIDENT

The Sandwich Tern is a fairly large, uncommon white tern native to both the New and Old Worlds. It is one of three crested terns occurring along North America's coasts. Like the Royal Tern, with which it frequently associates, this species is restricted to saltwater areas. Its flight is strong and swift. Most frequently found along beaches, inlets, estuaries, and bays, it may also forage far offshore. It feeds primarily by diving for fish, shrimp, and squid; inshore they have been reported to eat marine worms as well.

DESCRIPTION: 16" (41 cm). A large, slender tern. Adults at the beginning of the breeding season have a black cap with a shaggy crest on the back of the head. During the nesting season, the adults acquire a white forehead. The mantle is pearl-gray and the remainder of the plumage is white; the tail is forked. The long, slender bill is black with a yellow tip, and the feet are black. The immature has a white forehead and underparts, a mottled brown and gray mantle, and a dark tail. This species is intermediate in size between the Forster's and Royal terns; it is the only native tern with a long, black, yellow-tipped bill.

VOICE: Loud harsh *curr-it*.

NESTING: Lays 2 greenish, black-marked eggs on bare sand; usually nests with Royal Terns.

HABITAT: Coastal beaches and islands.

RANGE: Breeds locally on the Atlantic and Gulf coasts from Virginia to Florida and Texas. Winters in the tropics. Also found in Eurasia.

SIMILAR SPECIES: Gull-billed Tern has a shorter, deeper bill.

CONSERVATION: LC

Sandwich Tern populations are not large, but have been stable in the past 50 years. Egg and feather collection significantly reduced their numbers in the 19th century; hunting remains a locally significant threat in some areas today. This tern is highly vulnerable to human encroachment and has been known to abandon eggs en masse if a nesting colony is disturbed.

- ■ SUMMER ■ MIGRATION
- ■ WINTER ■ RARE
- ■ RESIDENT

This is the Pacific Coast counterpart of the Sandwich Tern. Historically the nesting of the Elegant Tern was restricted mostly to Isla Rasa, a small flat island in the northern part of the Gulf of California, where several colonies would include hundreds of crowded nests. Increasingly these birds are being pushed northward, with more nesting along the southern California coast.

DESCRIPTION: 16–17" (41–43 cm). A large tern with a long orange or yellow bill. It is white with a gray mantle and wings, a black cap ending in a shaggy crest, and a deeply forked tail. In nonbreeding plumage, its forehead becomes white but the crown, crest, and region around the eye remain black.

VOICE: A loud, grating *kar-eek*.

NESTING: Lays 1 egg, often buff-colored (but the color is variable), placed in a depression on a sandy beach, usually on an island. Nests in colonies.

HABITAT: Lagoons and beaches.

RANGE: Breeds in the Gulf of California and at San Diego. Winters to south and north; some to South America, others regularly visiting the northern California coast.

SIMILAR SPECIES: Royal Tern is larger with a stouter bill much thicker at the base and deeper orange; nonbreeding Royals on the West Coast have eyes surrounded by white and a much shorter black crest. Sandwich Tern (accidental on the West Coast) has a black bill with a yellow tip.

CONSERVATION: NT

Elegant Tern populations are thought to fluctuate but seem fairly stable over the long term. Their limited nesting sites and periodic population swings earn them a listing as a near-threatened species. Until 2000, most Elegant Terns returned annually to nest on Isla Rasa in western Mexico, but the population has scattered in some years following fluctuations in food availability due to commercial fishing and sea surface temperature anomalies. More of these terns are choosing nesting sites in California, including near populated areas in San Diego, where they face increased threats from feral animals and human disturbance.

BLACK SKIMMER *Rynchops niger*

■ SUMMER ■ MIGRATION
■ WINTER ■ RARE
■ RESIDENT

This extraordinary bird impresses even the most casual observer, especially when in flight. Usually only one or two are seen as they gracefully skim the surface for fish, with the tip of the elongated lower mandible cutting through the water. They also wade in shallow water, jabbing at the fish scattering before them. Compact flocks may be seen flying in unison, wheeling in one direction and then another—showing first the jet black of the long wings, then the gleaming white of the underparts. They are especially attracted to the sand fill of newly dredged areas; such places sometimes contain colonies of up to 200 pairs. These sites are usually temporary, abandoned as soon as too much grass appears.

DESCRIPTION: 18" (46 cm). Black Skimmers are black above and white below, with short red legs. Its long bill is red with a black tip, laterally compressed and blade-like. It is unique among birds in having a lower mandible much longer (about one-third) than the upper. Immature is mottled above, with a shorter bill.

VOICE: Distinctive short barking notes.

NESTING: Lays 3 or 4 brown-blotched buff eggs on bare sand, usually among shell fragments and scattered grass clumps.

HABITAT: Breeds chiefly on sandbars and beaches; feeds in shallow bays, inlets, and estuaries.

RANGE: Breeds along the Atlantic and Gulf coasts from Massachusetts and Long Island to Florida and Texas. Winters north to southern California and Virginia. Also in the American tropics.

SIMILAR SPECIES: Its black and white plumage and unusual, bicolored bill distinguish Black Skimmer from large terns and gulls.

CONSERVATION: LC

Although Black Skimmer numbers have recovered strongly since egg and feather hunters decimated eastern populations in the 19th century, these birds are once again declining. These birds are highly sensitive to disturbance during the nesting season and prefer the kinds of sandy beaches frequented by human vacationers and beachgoers. Because they nest close to the water and often on populated beaches, skimmer nests can be destroyed by unrestrained dogs, vehicles driven on the beach, storms, high tides, or oil spills.

■ SUMMER ■ MIGRATION
■ WINTER ■ RARE
■ RESIDENT

These tropical birds are rare but regular visitors to warm ocean waters far offshore. They are most often seen around Hawaii and Dry Tortugas, Florida, but also regularly enter the Gulf Stream off the East Coast in summer months. In pursuit of fish and squid, tropicbirds engage in graceful dives from the air. They fly with rapid wingbeats and glide occasionally. Tropicbirds forage far from land, sometimes following ships. After the breeding season, many gather in the Sargasso Sea, in the middle of the Atlantic Ocean.

DESCRIPTION: 32" (81 cm) with a wingspan of 3'1" (94 cm). The adult is a white, pigeon-sized seabird with extraordinary, long central tail feathers, bold black wing markings, and a yellow bill. Young birds lack the long tail feathers and are white, with fine black barring above.

VOICE: A piping *keck-keck-keck* and other tern-like calls, given in flight.

NESTING: Lays 1 pinkish egg, speckled with brown, on bare soil or a rock or in a crevice among rocks on an island.

HABITAT: Tropical oceans.

RANGE: Breeds on Bermuda and the Bahamas, and on other islands in the tropical Atlantic, Indian, and Pacific oceans. A rare visitor off the coasts of Florida and the Carolinas.

SIMILAR SPECIES: Adult Red-billed Tropicbird lacks the broad, black bands across the tertials and secondary coverts; its wings are broader at the base; its wingbeat rhythm is slower; and the adult has a larger, red bill. Red-billed Tropicbirds have a finely barred back at all ages, appearing gray or dusky at a distance; the broadly spaced barring of an immature White-tailed is visible at a greater distance.

CONSERVATION: LC
Widespread globally, this species is declining due to human disturbance, periodic loss of nesting habitat from tropical storms, and predation by invasive species.

RED-BILLED TROPICBIRD *Phaethon aethereus*

■ SUMMER ■ MIGRATION
■ WINTER ■ RARE
■ RESIDENT

This bird may rarely be seen far out to sea off the southern California coast, and extremely rarely in the Gulf of Mexico or off the Atlantic Coast to the Carolinas. With their mainly white plumage and long central tail feathers, tropicbirds are unmistakable in flight. Near breeding colonies they habitually display in the air with tail and feet spread, soaring and circling up and down. They have very short legs and are rarely seen at rest on land except on cliffs and at burrow entrances.

DESCRIPTION: 40" (1 m) long, including tail feathers, with a wingspan of 3'8" (1.1 m). The adult is a large, white seabird with long central tail feathers, fine black bars on the back and upper surface of the wings, and a red bill. Young birds are similar, but lack the long tail streamers.

VOICE: A loud rattling call given in flight.

NESTING: Lays 1 reddish or buff egg spotted or blotched with brown, placed in a burrow or in a cavity on a cliff.

HABITAT: Open ocean.

RANGE: Breeds on rocky islands in tropical seas. A rare visitor in summer and fall to the Pacific Coast, irregularly north to Washington.

SIMILAR SPECIES: Adult White-tailed is smaller, lacks fine barring on the back, and has broad black bands across the tertials and secondary coverts. White-tailed has narrower wings and a faster wingbeat; its bill is smaller; and it generally lacks the strong, black eyeline. Juvenile White-tailed has broader, more distinct barring on the back, which does not appear gray at a distance.

CONSERVATION:
Although listed as a species of least concern, Red-billed Tropicbird's small population is declining. Some nesting sites in Brazil have been decimated by invasive rats, and human settlement and development have reduced the availability of suitable nesting habitat.

An extremely rare visitor from the central Pacific, Red-Tailed Tropicbird has been seen well off the California coast and more regularly around Hawaii. The Red-tailed may engage in courtship "bicycling flight," where one bird hovers above the other, then shifts position with the other. With its somewhat stockier build, the Red-tailed appears more ponderous in flight, and seems more prone to wandering than other tropicbirds.

DESCRIPTION: 30–37" (76–94 cm) long, including the tail, with a wingspan of 41" (104 cm). Adults have deep red bills, mostly white body plumage, a dark eye patch, and thin red tail streamers (often difficult to see in the field). The juvenile lacks tail streamers, and has a black bill and barred upperparts. When approaching maturity, the juvenile's bill changes from black to yellow, then to red; during this transition, it may be confused with White-tailed Tropicbird.

VOICE: Usually silent at sea.

NESTING: Nesting period for various populations at tropical sites extends through the year; it lays 1 egg on hard rock or in a crevice.

HABITAT: Highly pelagic; seldom seen anywhere near shore in our area.

RANGE: Breeds on tropical islands of the Indian and Pacific oceans. Disperses widely after breeding. Occurs in North American waters as an accidental off southern California.

SIMILAR SPECIES: Juveniles may be difficult to distinguish from Red-billed and White-tailed tropicbirds. Unlike other tropicbirds, at all ages its flight feathers are mostly white.

CONSERVATION:
Like many island-nesting birds, Red-tailed Tropicbirds have been impacted by rat predation, but many of their nesting islands remain free from these introduced predators, and the species has benefited from rat eradication efforts. Its numbers appear to be stable.

SUMMER   MIGRATION
WINTER   RARE
RESIDENT

The attractive breeding plumage of this loon is seldom seen in temperate latitudes, because the birds molt just before they depart for their nesting grounds. Although not as social as Pacific Loons, wintering Red-throated Loons may gather in large numbers where food is abundant. They are common on salt water of all depths but frequently forage in shallow bays and estuaries rather than far out at sea. Because their legs are located so far back, loons have difficulty walking on land and are rarely found far from water. Most loons must paddle furiously across the surface of the water before becoming airborne, but the small Red-throated can practically spring directly into the air from land—a useful ability on its tundra breeding grounds.

DESCRIPTION: 24–27" (61–69 cm). This small loon is seldom seen far from salt water. In breeding plumage, it has a gray head and neck, a rusty throat, and a black back spotted with white. In winter, it is similar to Common Loon but smaller and paler, with a thinner bill appearing slightly upturned. Red-throated Loon often holds its head tilted up.

VOICE: Its call, rarely sounded away from the breeding grounds, is a series of high-pitched wails and shrieks.

NESTING: Lays 2 brownish-olive, usually spotted eggs in a nest of aquatic vegetation floating in or beside water.

HABITAT: Coastal and tundra ponds during summer; large lakes, bays, estuaries, and ocean in migration and winter.

RANGE: Breeds in the Aleutian Islands, Alaska, and Canadian Arctic south to British Columbia, northern Manitoba, and Newfoundland. Winters south along the Pacific Coast to southern California and along the Gulf Coast and both coasts of Florida. Also found in northern Eurasia.

SIMILAR SPECIES: See Arctic Loon. Yellow-billed Loon is much larger and darker, and has a much heavier, uptilted bill with a yellow cast. Grebes are slenderer, with long, thinner necks; most are smaller or show white wing patches in flight.

CONSERVATION:
Red-throated Loons experienced declines in the late 20th century, possibly due to lake acidification, but populations are now stable. Climate change poses a future threat from loss of breeding habitat, and this species is susceptible to human disturbances ranging from collisions with wind turbines to oil spills.

SUMMER   MIGRATION
WINTER   RARE
RESIDENT

Since the Arctic and Pacific Loons were split in 1985, field observers have sought reliable means of separating the two species, especially in winter plumage. The challenge of identifying winter Arctics remains formidable. Migrants are seen in coastal western Alaska and vagrants appear rarely on the West Coast. Like its North American counterpart, the Arctic Loon feeds on fish, mollusks, crustaceans, and some amphibians and aquatic vegetation.

DESCRIPTION: 23–28" (58–73 cm), wingspan 43–51" (110–130 cm). Similar to Pacific Loon; the Arctic is slightly larger and longer-necked; it has a white flank patch before the tail that is visible at the waterline and in flight. The striped patch on the side of the neck in breeding plumage is more conspicuous than the Pacific's (frequently visible at some distance and in flight); the nape and hindneck are darker. Breeding Arctic Loon has a dark throat patch with green iridescence visible only at close range.

VOICE: Similar to Pacific Loon, a harsh *kok-kok-kok-kok*. Adults on nesting ground issue an eerie, long-carrying moan or wail.

NESTING: Lays 1–3 brownish eggs with scattered markings on a mass of mud and aquatic vegetation at the edge of shallow water.

HABITAT: Tundra and taiga lakes and marshy inlets; coastal areas and open ocean in winter.

RANGE: Primarily an Old World species, breeds in North America only at isolated sites in western Alaska; possible along either coast in winter.

SUBSPECIES: The Arctic Loons that breed in Alaska are of the Siberian subspecies (*G. a. viridugularis*). European Arctic Loons (*G. a. arctica*), not known to occur in North America, are similar except their throat patch is typically iridescent purple like that of Pacific Loon.

SIMILAR SPECIES: Pacific Loon is highly similar, especially difficult to distinguish in winter; breeding Pacific Loon's throat patch is iridescent purple rather than green.

Red-throated Loon in winter plumage is pale and its patterns are less contrasting; it carries its bill tilted upward.

Common Loon is larger, with more white around the eye, less sharp definition between the dark and light areas on the head and neck; often with the suggestion of a collar on the sides of the neck and a steeper forehead profile.

Murres are smaller and stockier.

CONSERVATION: As with most loons, Arctic Loons are susceptible to oil spills and bycatch from commercial fishing. Their populations are nonetheless fairly stable, and widespread in the Old World.

■ SUMMER ■ MIGRATION
■ WINTER ■ RARE
■ RESIDENT

The Pacific Loon is so named because nearly all of these birds winter along the Pacific Coast. In the East, it is the rarest and least known of the three loons found there. More social than other loons, this species frequently gathers in large flocks. On the northern breeding grounds across the northern tier of Canada, adults often fly many miles between their nesting ponds and suitable feeding areas. It usually feeds closer to shore than other loons; its diet consists mainly of fish, but on the breeding grounds it also takes crustaceans.

DESCRIPTION: 24" (61 cm). A small loon with a straight, slender bill. In breeding plumage, its head is pale gray; its neck and back are black with white stripes; its throat is black with a purple iridescence best visible in good light on birds swimming on the water. In winter plumage, it is blackish above, white below; it often shows thin, dark "chin straps."

VOICE: A harsh *kok-kok-kok-kok*; wailing notes on breeding grounds.

NESTING: Lays 2 spotted olive-brown eggs, usually in a slight depression lined with aquatic vegetation (sometimes on bare ground) at the edge of water.

HABITAT: Breeds on lakes and ponds in tundra and northern forests; winters on coastal bays and inlets and on the ocean.

RANGE: Breeds from Alaska east to Hudson Bay, and south to northern British Columbia, Manitoba, and Ontario. Winters chiefly along the Pacific Coast; rare inland in the West and increasingly rare to the East Coast.

SIMILAR SPECIES: Red-throated Loon in winter is paler, with less contrast between the dark crown and hindneck and the white throat, and with a slightly upturned bill.

Common Loon is larger, with a stouter bill.

CONSERVATION: This is an abundant North American loon, and its numbers are stable to increasing.

■ SUMMER ■ MIGRATION
■ WINTER ■ RARE
■ RESIDENT

The naturalist John Muir, who knew the Common Loon during his early years in Wisconsin, described its call as "one of the wildest and most striking of all the wilderness sounds, a strange, sad, mournful, unearthly cry, half laughing, half wailing." These birds are expert divers; their eyes can focus both in air and under the water, and their nearly solid bones make them heavier than many other birds. They are able to concentrate oxygen in their leg muscles to sustain them during the strenuous paddling that can take them as far as 200 feet (60 meters) below the surface. Their principal food is fish, but they also eat shellfish, frogs, and aquatic insects.

DESCRIPTION: 28–36" (71–91 cm). A large, heavy-bodied loon with a thick, pointed, usually black or dark gray bill held horizontally. In breeding plumage, its head and neck are black with white bands on the neck; it has a black back with white spots. In winter, the crown, hindneck, and upperparts are dark grayish; its throat and underparts are white.

VOICE: Its best-known call is a loud, wailing laugh, also a mournful yodeled *oo-AH-ho* with middle note higher, and a loud ringing *kee-a-ree, kee-a-ree* with middle note lower. Often calls at night and sometimes on migration.

NESTING: Lays 2 olive-brown or greenish, lightly spotted eggs in a bulky mass of vegetation near water's edge, usually on an island.

HABITAT: Nests on forested lakes and rivers; winters mainly on coastal bays and ocean.

RANGE: Breeds from Aleutian Islands, Alaska, and northern Canada south to California, Montana, and Massachusetts. Winters along the Great Lakes, Gulf Coast, and Atlantic and Pacific coasts. Also breeds in Greenland and Iceland.

SIMILAR SPECIES: Winter Yellow-billed Loon is browner above, and whiter on the face; its heavy, consistently uptilted bill has a yellow cast.

Arctic Loon is smaller, with sharply marked black-and-white contrast on the head and neck, no trace of a collar, and a more sloping forehead profile.

The feet of Red-throated and Arctic loons are smaller and less conspicuous in flight.

CONSERVATION: LC

The Common Loon's population is large, widespread, and stable, although its breeding range has contracted slightly in the last few decades as deep forested lakes in the interior United States have been compromised by pollution and vacationers. Common Loons have disappeared from former breeding areas in the Midwest, but intense conservation efforts in the Northeast have helped to protect this species.

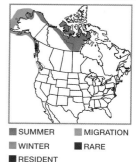

■ SUMMER ■ MIGRATION
■ WINTER ■ RARE
■ RESIDENT

This large loon, closely related to the Common Loon, nests in a relatively small part of the Arctic, and is probably the least abundant of the five loons that nest regularly in North America. A winter visitor to the West Coast, it is rare enough to attract crowds of birders whenever it appears.

DESCRIPTION: 33–38" (84–97 cm). Breeding and winter plumages are similar to those of Common Loon, but its bill is an ivory-yellow and appears upturned. In winter plumage, it has more white on the face and typically shows a dark spot behind the eyes.

VOICE: Yodeling calls are similar to those of Common Loon but louder and harsher; this species is generally less vocal.

NESTING: Lays 2 brownish eggs placed in a grass-lined depression, usually on an island at the water's edge.

HABITAT: Tundra lakes and ponds in summer; inshore coastal waters in winter.

RANGE: Breeds from northern Alaska and northern Canada east nearly to Hudson Bay. Winters along the coast from Alaska south to British Columbia, and occasionally to California. Also found in northern Eurasia.

SIMILAR SPECIES: See Common Loon. Red-throated Loon is much smaller, paler, and grayer.

CONSERVATION: NT
Yellow-billed Loon populations are difficult to calculate, but are certainly small, with a total global population that may be as low as 10,000–20,000. Threats to this small population include subsistence hunting of these birds in Alaska, heavy metal contamination and other pollution, and loss of breeding habitat due to climate change.

■ SUMMER ■ MIGRATION
■ WINTER ■ RARE
■ RESIDENT

This and the slightly larger Black-browed Albatross are the only recorded albatross species in the North Atlantic, and both are extremely rare visitors to North America's Atlantic Coast. Because they are long-lived, it is possible that some albatross sightings may actually refer to the same individual for many years in succession. Yellow-nosed Albatrosses feed mainly on squid and fish.

DESCRIPTION: Relatively small for an albatross at 29–34" (73.5–86.5 cm) long with a wingspan between 6'4"–6'11" (193–211 cm). This large, black-and-white seabird has long, slim wings and a short, rounded tail. Its back, upperwings, and tail are blackish; the rest of the body is white (except some individuals have pale gray on the head and neck visible at close range). The underwing is white with a narrow, dark trailing edge and a broader dark leading edge. Its dark bill is slender and hooked, and has a thin yellow stripe on the culmen. Juveniles have a black bill and no gray on head.

VOICE: Generally silent at sea.

NESTING: Lays 1 white egg, finely spotted with reddish, in a truncated mud cone placed on a cliff ledge, slope, or plateau. Nests are solitary, but some birds also breed in colonies of hundreds of pairs.

HABITAT: Open ocean; rarely seen from shore.

RANGE: Breeds in southern Atlantic Ocean, ranging west to southern South America and east to South Africa. Accidental off the Atlantic and Gulf coasts of North America.

SIMILAR SPECIES: Black-browed Albatross is similar but slightly larger, with an orange bill in adults and a dusky bill in juveniles.

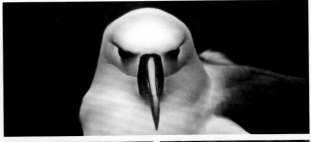

CONSERVATION: [EN] Endangered and decreasing. The species' breeding numbers at a handful of known colony sites on islands in the South Atlantic are closely monitored each year.

■ SUMMER   ■ MIGRATION
■ WINTER   ■ RARE
■ RESIDENT

Although the Laysan Albatross occurs off the West Coast less frequently than the Black-footed Albatross, the Laysan is regularly observed from Alaska to northern California. Unlike the Black-footed Albatross, it pays little attention to refuse from ships, but feeds mainly on squid. Albatrosses are known colloquially as "Gooney Birds," but they are impressive, long-lived birds that spend most of their lives at sea.

DESCRIPTION: 32" (81 cm) long with an average wingspan of 6'6" (2 m). A large, black and white seabird with long wings and a short tail. Its back, wings, and tail are dark gray or blackish; the head, neck, and underparts are white; the underwing is white with black edging and irregular black patches. Its bill is thick, hooked, and either yellow with a gray tip or solid gray. A conspicuous dark patch around the eye is visible at close range.

VOICE: Silent at sea, except for grunting calls when squabbling over food.

NESTING: Lays 1 buff-white egg in a shallow sandy depression on an offshore island. Nests in colonies.

HABITAT: Open ocean, usually well offshore.

RANGE: Breeds on mid-Pacific islands, chiefly in the Hawaiian chain. A rare visitor to offshore waters of the North Pacific and the Gulf of Alaska.

SIMILAR SPECIES: Short-tailed Albatross, a rare visitor over open ocean in the Pacific, is larger and heavier, with a massive pink bill. The adult has a yellow wash on the head, a white back, and the basal half of the upperwing is white. The subadult has a mottled brown back and a dark hood on the back of the head and neck, and white patches on the upperwing.

Shy Albatross (extremely rare) is larger and heavier than Laysan, with a mostly clean white underwing.

CONSERVATION: NT
This species faces many threats, from commercial fishing and mammalian predation to pollution and climate-related habitat loss. Because they use low-lying islands such as atolls for breeding, sea level rise poses a significant threat for these birds. Efforts to remove invasive predators such as mice and feral cats from these islands has significantly increased nesting success in some cases.

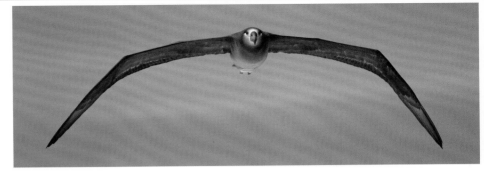

- ■ SUMMER
- ■ WINTER
- ■ RESIDENT
- ■ MIGRATION
- ■ RARE

The only albatross that commonly visits the West Coast, the Black-footed is most commonly seen in North America during the summer. Its primary diet consists of fish and squid, which it catches mainly at night; it can be found following shrimp or fishing boats to feed on refuse in their wake. Once these birds leave their nesting islands, young albatross do not return for six or seven years. Aside from humans, they face few natural predators and may live for many years. Marked birds recaptured on Midway have reached 25 years of age or more.

DESCRIPTION: A large, long-winged seabird, 28–36" (71–91 cm) long with a wingspan of up to 7' (2.1 m). It is mainly blackish brown, with white on the face and a dark bill. The amount of white increases as birds age. Its conspicuous white primary shafts show in flight. Some adults have white undertail coverts. This bird glides like a shearwater, with stiff wingbeats.

VOICE: Shrieks and squeals during fights over food; on nesting grounds, it makes a variety of bill-clapping sounds, quacks, and whistles.

NESTING: Lays 1 dull-white egg spotted with reddish brown in a shallow depression on the ground. Nests on islands in loose colonies.

HABITAT: Open ocean, rarely seen from shore.

RANGE: Breeds on islands in the mid-Pacific Ocean. It is a nonbreeding visitor along the entire Pacific Coast of North America.

SIMILAR SPECIES: Juvenile Short-tailed Albatross is larger and stockier, with a pink bill and feet and no white in its plumage. Old Black-footeds may resemble a subadult Short-tailed, but the Short-tailed has a black hood and throat, white patches on upperwings, and dark undertail coverts and underside of the tail.

Dark shearwaters are much smaller.

CONSERVATION:

Black-footed Albatross numbers have been stable or slightly increasing in recent decades, but major threats to the species include longline fishing, disruption of breeding habitat by storm surges, and the loss of island breeding habitat caused by rising sea levels.

WILSON'S STORM-PETREL *Oceanites oceanicus*

■ SUMMER ■ MIGRATION
■ WINTER ■ RARE
■ RESIDENT

Among the most abundant birds in the world, this species nests in countless millions on islands in the Southern Hemisphere and visits the Northern Hemisphere during our summer months, where it is much rarer in the North Pacific than it is in the North Atlantic. Wilson's Storm-Petrel often hovers at the surface of the water, its wings held over its back and its feet gently touching the water. Although normally a bird of the open ocean, it sometimes enters bays and estuaries, and often follows ships. This bird is named after American ornithologist Alexander Wilson (1766–1813).

DESCRIPTION: 7" (18 cm). A small seabird that darts and skims over the waves like a swallow. It is black with a white rump, and a square-tipped or rounded tail. It has longer legs than other western storm-petrels, with yellow webs between the toes.

VOICE: A soft peeping, heard at close range when birds are feeding.

NESTING: Lays 1 white egg placed in a crevice among rocks or in a burrow in soft earth.

HABITAT: Open ocean.

RANGE: Breeds on islands in Antarctic and sub-Antarctic seas; in nonbreeding season, it ranges northward over the Atlantic, Pacific, and Indian oceans; in the eastern Pacific, it travels rarely north to Monterey Bay.

SIMILAR SPECIES: Leach's Storm-Petrel is similar, but has a notched tail and flies like a nighthawk. See Band-rumped Storm-Petrel.

CONSERVATION: ■ LC
This species' nesting grounds are susceptible to predation by invasive mammals, pollution, and degradation of habitat in the Antarctic, but it retains a large, stable population.

This highly pelagic storm-petrel in the western North Atlantic is a rare visitor from its breeding grounds in the eastern Atlantic, usually in late summer, sometimes appearing to North American birders far off the coasts from Massachusetts to North Carolina. When feeding, it gives the appearance of using both feet to push off the water in one direction, then another, in a distinctive pendulum motion.

DESCRIPTION: 8" (20.5 cm). A grayish-backed storm-petrel with a gray rump, white underparts, and a white face with a distinct dark line running through the eye. It has white underwings with a broad, dark trailing edge. Its long legs and yellow-webbed feet extend beyond its square tail. It swings erratically from side to side during its gliding flight.

VOICE: Generally silent at sea.

NESTING: Lays 1 white egg speckled with brown around the large end, placed in a burrow. Nests in colonies.

HABITAT: Open ocean; possibly most frequent along the continental shelf break in areas of submarine upwelling.

RANGE: Breeds mainly in east-central Atlantic; a rare vagrant to western North Atlantic waters in late summer and fall.

SIMILAR SPECIES: White-faced Storm-Petrels' size and distinctive head pattern may suggest a phalarope, but the tail and head shapes of these types of birds are different.

CONSERVATION:
Egg predation by introduced mammals is the greatest threat to this species at present. It also has among the highest rates of plastic intake of any seabird, which could have a negative impact on feeding behaviors. The population is large but declining.

FORK-TAILED STORM-PETREL *Hydrobates furcata*

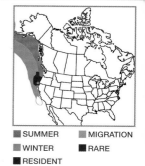

■ SUMMER ■ MIGRATION
■ WINTER ■ RARE
■ RESIDENT

Fork-tailed Storm-Petrels use their nesting burrows year after year, the male and female often spending many days in the burrow together before the single egg is laid. Once they have an egg, they incubate it irregularly, often leaving it for several days at a time. The chick inside thus grows slowly, taking as long as 68 days to hatch. These storm-petrels spend the day feeding at sea and approach their nesting islands at dusk. Birds still on the sea at night are attracted by lights and often gather near vessels.

DESCRIPTION: 8–9" (20–23 cm). A gray storm-petrel, somewhat darker above than below, with a forked tail but without a white rump. All other Pacific storm-petrels are blackish. It flies with deep, regular wingbeats.

VOICE: Twittering and squeaking notes given near nest.

NESTING: Lays 1 white egg, with a ring of black or purplish spots around large end, placed in a burrow or crevice. Nests in colonies.

HABITAT: Open ocean; nests in colonies on rocky islands.

RANGE: Breeds on islands from southern Alaska south to northern California. Also on the Pacific coast of Asia.

SUBSPECIES: The paler and larger Aleutian population (subsp. *furcata*) is found along the Pacific Coast from Alaska's Aleutian Islands to northern California. The Southern group (subsp. *plumbea*) breeds farther south and is smaller and darker.

SIMILAR SPECIES: All other storm-petrels are much darker above.

CONSERVATION:

The population is widespread and stable or increasing. Like other storm-petrels, this species does face risks from oil spills and other pollution, as well as nest predation by introduced rats, but the population appears to remain healthy despite these threats.

■ SUMMER   ■ MIGRATION
■ WINTER   ■ RARE
■ RESIDENT

Even near their nesting islands, Leach's Storm-Petrels are seldom seen because they feed far out at sea and visit their burrows only at night. The presence of the birds is not difficult to detect, however; their burrows have an unmistakable musky odor—produced by an oily orange liquid that the birds emit when disturbed—and at night the air is filled with their eerie calls. Like other storm-petrels, they feed mainly on small shrimp and other planktonic animals, which they pluck deftly from the surface of the water.

DESCRIPTION: 8–9" (20–23 cm). A black storm-petrel with a shallowly forked tail and a white rump with a dark center; south of central California, the birds lack the white rump. It flies like a nighthawk, with much bounding and veering. This species seldom follows boats.

VOICE: A variety of trills, screams, and cooing notes.

NESTING: Lays 1 white egg placed in a shallow burrow in the ground or hidden under a log. Nests in colonies. Both parents incubate the egg, changing places roughly every three days. The egg hatches in about six weeks, and the young bird leaves its burrow after about 10 weeks.

HABITAT: Open ocean; nests on spruce-covered islands and rocky coasts.

RANGE: Breeds on coasts and offshore islands from the Aleutians south to Baja California. Also breeds in the western Pacific and North Atlantic from Labrador south to Maine and Massachusetts. Winters mainly in tropical seas.

SUBSPECIES: Northern birds in both the Atlantic and Pacific (subsp. *leucorhoa*) are larger and show the most white on the rump. Chapman's (subsp. *chapmani*) seen from central California and southward usually have an all-dark rump.

SIMILAR SPECIES: See Wilson's and Band-rumped storm-petrels.

The endangered Townsend's Storm-Petrel (*H. socorroensis*) was formerly considered a subspecies of Leach's Storm-Petrel. It is sometimes seen in waters off the coast of southern California.

CONSERVATION: VU
Leach's Storm-Petrels are still quite numerous, with global populations in the millions, but they have declined sharply in recent decades for reasons that are not yet fully understood. These birds are vulnerable to predatory gulls as well as many terrestrial predators. Nest predation from introduced predators such as foxes, mice, rats, and feral cats may represent the greatest cause of their decline.

ASHY STORM-PETREL *Hydrobates homochroa*

■ SUMMER ■ MIGRATION
■ WINTER ■ RARE
■ RESIDENT

This endangered seabird nests on only a few islands off the West Coast, usually in colonies of several hundred or a few thousand pairs. Its best known colony is about 2000 pairs that nest on the Farallon Islands off the coast of San Francisco. Like other storm-petrels, the Ashy ejects a musky orange oil when disturbed. Its favorite food, at least in southern California, is the larvae of one of the spiny lobsters; it is also known to feed on plankton and algae.

DESCRIPTION: 7½" (19 cm). An all-black storm-petrel with a shallowly forked tail and somewhat rounded wings. The ashy color of its head and neck and light mottling on the undersides of the wings may be visible at close range. It flies with shallow wingbeats.

VOICE: Twittering and squeaking notes given near nest burrow.

NESTING: Lays 1 white egg, sometimes with a ring of fine red speckling, in a crevice in a rock slide or in a burrow.

HABITAT: Open ocean; nests on rocky islands.

RANGE: Breeds on islands from northern California south to northern Baja California.

SIMILAR SPECIES: Other dark-rumped storm-petrels may be distinguished by comparative size and flight characteristics. The similar Black Storm-Petrel is larger, with longer wings and more leisurely flight style. Dark- or white-rumped Leach's Storm-Petrel has pointier wings and flies like a nighthawk.

CONSERVATION: EN
Endangered and decreasing, the world population of this small seabird is thought to be below 10,000. Most of the world's population concentrates on Monterey Bay in the fall, putting the species at risk from an ill-timed oil spill or severe weather event. This species has many protections in place, but faces threats from human disturbance in its low lying nesting habitat, predation by owls, chemical pollution, and the risk of nest sites flooding with sea level rise.

■ SUMMER ■ MIGRATION
■ WINTER ■ RARE
■ RESIDENT

This species was not considered a native to North American waters until the 1980s, when pelagic bird expeditions ventured into deeper Gulf Stream waters off North Carolina; it is now seen annually in this area. The flight pattern of Band-rumped differs both from the swooping, swallow-like flight of Wilson's Storm-Petrel and from the buoyant, nighthawk-like flight of Leach's; Band-rumped flies with alternating quick wingbeats and long, horizontal zig-zag glides, reminiscent of a shearwater. It commonly feeds with its wings held horizontally, and seldom follows ships.

DESCRIPTION: 7½–9" (19–23 cm) long with an average wingspan of 16½–18" (42–45 cm). Intermediate in many respects between Wilson's and Leach's storm-petrels and often difficult to identify reliably at sea. It is blackish-brown overall with pale wing bars and a clear, curved white band across the rump. The white on the rump is more extensive than on Leach's but less than on Wilson's (on which the white extends fully onto the undertail coverts). Its tail is slightly forked, but this feature is difficult to discern at sea. Its legs do not extend beyond the tail in flight. Its wings are thinner and more angular than Wilson's, but thicker and less angular than Leach's. It tends to be larger than Wilson's.

VOICE: Usually silent at sea.

NESTING: Lays 1 blunt oval egg, flat white with occasional pale red spots, in burrows on tropical islands. To maximize the use of scarce nesting sites, some populations breed in sequential cycles, making alternate use of the same burrows. Breeding occurs throughout the year in various populations.

HABITAT: Open oceans in our area, especially in warm water currents such as the Gulf Stream, well offshore.

RANGE: Breeds on tropical islands in the Atlantic and Pacific oceans, including Hawaii, Galápagos, Cape Verde, Ascension, St. Helena, and Madeira. It has a fairly wide pelagic dispersal in the Atlantic; in North America, it is seen most regularly in the Gulf Stream off North Carolina.

SIMILAR SPECIES: Difficult to identify reliably at sea. See Wilson's and Leach's storm-petrels.

CONSERVATION: Band-rumped Storm-Petrels have a large, widespread population. Throughout its range it faces threats from nest predators, as do all members of this genus. Its inaccessible nesting sites provide at least some protection.

This bird wanders widely in the eastern Pacific and has been recorded a few times off the coast of California between August and January.

DESCRIPTION: 6" (15 cm). A tiny, compact dark brown storm-petrel of South American islands. Extensive white uppertail coverts almost reach the tip of its short tail. Its overall shape and wingbeats resemble Least Storm-petrel.

VOICE: Makes sharp, squeaky notes at sea that are rarely heard. At breeding colonies it makes twittering and purring notes.

NESTING: Nests in natural crevices among rocks often more than a half meter deep.

HABITAT: Pelagic. Only comes to land to breed.

RANGE: A bird of South American islands, it breeds in the Galápagos Islands and on the coast of Peru. A rare or casual visitor to California waters during the nonbreeding season (August to January).

SUBSPECIES: Two subspecies are recognized, *O. t. tethys,* which breeds in the Galápagos Islands, and the much lesser known *O. t. kelsalli,* which breeds on islands off the coast of Peru.

SIMILAR SPECIES: See Least Storm-Petrel, Black Storm-Petrel, Ashy Storm-Petrel, and Wilson's Storm-Petrel.

CONSERVATION:
This species is widespread and populous enough to be a species of least concern, although its numbers are declining over the long term. Competition with other seabirds for nest sites and natural predation by owls appear to be drivers of the decline.

■ SUMMER   ■ MIGRATION
■ WINTER   ■ RARE
■ RESIDENT

This is the largest and most commonly seen of the all-dark storm-petrels in California. It is also the species most likely to enter bays and estuaries in search of its food, which consists of the larvae of spiny lobsters and other small marine animals. The Black Storm-Petrel often gathers in feeding flocks and follows ships.

DESCRIPTION: 9" (23 cm). A large, all-dark storm-petrel with long, pointed wings and a forked tail. Its flight is smoother and more languid, with deeper and more graceful wingbeats, than that of other storm-petrels. Other all-dark storm-petrels are smaller, with different flight styles.

VOICE: A loud *tuck-a-roo*, given at nesting colonies.

NESTING: Lays 1 white egg placed in a crevice or in the abandoned burrow of another seabird. Nests in colonies.

HABITAT: Open ocean; nests on rocky islands.

RANGE: Breeds on islands off both coasts of Baja California. Ranges from the coast of northern California to South America.

SIMILAR SPECIES: Ashy Storm-Petrel is smaller and flies with shallow wingbeats. Least Storm-Petrel is much smaller and has a short tail and more rapid wing-beats. See Leach's Storm-Petrel.

CONSERVATION:
This species is relatively numerous but declining. Cats and rats introduced on breeding islands pose the greatest threat to this species.

LEAST STORM-PETREL *Hydrobates microsoma*

■ SUMMER ■ MIGRATION
■ WINTER ■ RARE
■ RESIDENT

Our smallest storm-petrel. Birders in southern California face the problem of distinguishing several all-dark and dark-rumped storm-petrels. The Least is the smallest of these; its size is a key field mark. Its small size and rapid wingbeats are often more readily perceived than its short, wedge-shaped tail and short wings.

DESCRIPTION: 6" (15 cm). The smallest storm-petrel on the West Coast. An all-dark bird with short wings. Its tail is short and wedge-shaped rather than forked; it often appears tailless at a distance. Its flight is swift and low, with rapid wingbeats.

VOICE: Twittering and squeaking notes at nesting colonies.

NESTING: Lays 1 white egg placed in a crevice among rocks. Nests in colonies.

HABITAT: Open ocean.

RANGE: Breeds on islands off both coasts of Baja California. In summer and fall, it ranges northward to San Diego County, California.

SIMILAR SPECIES: See Ashy, Black, and Leach's storm-petrels.

CONSERVATION: LC
Sustained efforts to remove mammalian predators from breeding islands have helped to stabilize populations. Future predation from introduced predators as well as overfishing and pollution continue to put pressure on this small seabird.

■ SUMMER ■ MIGRATION
■ WINTER ■ RARE
■ RESIDENT

The Northern Fulmar feeds on fish, squid, shrimp, and the refuse cast overboard by fishing boats. The expansion of commercial fishing in the 20th century caused a great increase in the population of this species, especially in the North Atlantic.

DESCRIPTION: 18" (46 cm). A stocky gull-like seabird, seldom seen from shore. Two color phases are common: one pale gray on the back and wings, and white elsewhere—the phase most common in the East—and the other uniformly dark gray. Intermediates, as well as nearly all-white birds, also occur. Its bill is yellow, short, and thick, with nostril tubes. It is easily distinguished from a gull by its flight: several fast, shallow wingbeats followed by a stiff-winged glide.

VOICE: Chuckling and grunting notes when feeding; various guttural calls during breeding season.

NESTING: Lays 1 white egg placed on a bare rock or in a shallow depression or hollow lined with fresh vegetation.

HABITAT: Open ocean; nests on cliffs and rocky islands, often in colonies of many thousands of birds.

RANGE: Breeds in Aleutians and on coasts and islands of Alaska and Canadian Arctic. Winters at sea, in Pacific Ocean south to California and in Atlantic south to North Carolina. Also in northern Eurasia.

SIMILAR SPECIES: Gulls have longer necks and slimmer bills without nostril tubes; they leap from the water into more agile flight. Shearwaters of similar size are typically more slender, with thinner bills held more horizontally; their wings are narrower, more tapered, and more flexed in flight.

CONSERVATION: 🐦 LC

Northern Fulmar populations have increased over time in conjunction with commercial fishing, and these birds often feed on refuse around human activities. Likely in part because of this habit, Northern Fulmars have been susceptible to ingesting plastic.

MURPHY'S PETREL *Pterodroma ultima*

■ SUMMER ■ MIGRATION
■ WINTER ■ RARE
■ RESIDENT

Most North American sightings of this seabird are off the West Coast, dozens of miles offshore. Although rats have been eradicated from the largest breeding colonies on some South Pacific islands where it breeds, this species remains near threatened as the population continues to slowly decline within its moderately small range.

DESCRIPTION: 15.5" (39 cm) long. Generally pearl-gray in color with its plumage becoming browner as it becomes worn. It is pale on the chin and face around the base of the bill. It has pale primary feathers that may flash in flight depending on lighting conditions. Its relatively large head and delicate bill are noticeable. Its tail often appears wedge-shaped. It has a black bill and black legs and eyes.

VOICE: Generally silent at sea. Its sounds include accelerating *boo* or *hoo* calls similar to a Boreal Owl; a gull-like cry; and long, undulating hoots.

NESTING: Nesting colonies are found on rocky islets and cliffs. Individual nests are a simple ground scrape under the shade of a Heliotrope tree close to neighbors. Eggs hatch in late July–August, followed by a nestling period of around 100 days.

HABITAT: A pelagic species that only comes ashore to breed on small, rocky islands.

RANGE: Found breeding in the South Pacific in the Pitcairn Islands, Tuamotu Archipelago, Austral Islands, Gambier Islands, and perhaps in the Cook Islands. Non-breeding dispersal is poorly known but mostly north as far as the Hawaiian Islands in the west. It's frequently seen in the eastern tropical Pacific as far as the Californian current. In North America, it is mostly observed during spring in deep waters off the California coast and sometimes as far north as Washington.

SIMILAR SPECIES: Compare to dark shearwaters, Northern Fulmar, jaegers, and other Pacific petrels.

CONSERVATION: NT

Numbers of these remote-island breeders were in decline before efforts were made to remove Polynesian rats from breeding grounds. Unfortunately, even after these invasive rats were eradicated, the Murphy's Petrel numbers have continued to slowly decline.

■ SUMMER   ■ MIGRATION
■ WINTER   ■ RARE
■ RESIDENT

A rare visitor to the waters offshore in the north Pacific. At sea, the Mottled Petrel flies rapidly, darting and gliding up and down over the waves more quickly than a shearwater, searching for fish and squid. This petrel does not follow ships and usually remains far from land.

DESCRIPTION: 14" (36 cm). A small petrel with a distinctively short, heavy bill. It is gray above, with dark bars on the upper surfaces of the wings forming a flattened M shape; it is darker gray on the breast and belly. The undersides of the wings show broad, sharply defined black bands.

VOICE: Usually silent at sea.

NESTING: Lays 1 white egg placed in a burrow in a cliff or in a rock crevice.

HABITAT: Open ocean.

RANGE: Breeds on islands off New Zealand. It is a spring and summer visitor to the Bering Sea and cool northeastern Pacific waters; it rarely appears south to Oregon and California.

SIMILAR SPECIES: See Cook's Petrel.

CONSERVATION: NT
More data collection is needed, but this species, which breeds only on a few islands near New Zealand, is thought to be declining in the face of several threats. In years with higher surface ocean temperatures, large numbers of birds have washed ashore. The species is also threatened by nest predation from introduced rats, and from the recently introduced Weka (*Gallirallus australis*), a flightless bird in the rail family.

BLACK-CAPPED PETREL *Pterodroma hasitata*

■ SUMMER　■ MIGRATION
■ WINTER　■ RARE
■ RESIDENT

The endangered Black-capped Petrel is a rare seabird that visits its Caribbean nesting colonies only at night, which are concentrated on a heavily deforested mountain in southern Haiti. The total population is small, a handful drift northward along the Gulf Stream in summer and fall each year, after the breeding season. There they feed chiefly on squid, which they snatch from the surface of the water.

DESCRIPTION: 14–18" (36–46 cm). A long-winged, long-tailed petrel that's dark above with a black cap. It has a white collar and rump (lacking in Manx and Audubon's shearwaters) and white underparts. Viewed from below, its wings have broad, dark margins.

VOICE: Usually silent at sea.

NESTING: Lays 1 white egg in a burrow or rocky crevice on an isolated mountain ridge.

HABITAT: Open ocean, especially Gulf Stream waters.

RANGE: Breeds on larger islands in the West Indies; visits the Gulf Stream regularly as far north as the Carolinas.

SIMILAR SPECIES: See Great Shearwater, Bermuda Petrel.

CONSERVATION: EN

Black-capped Petrels were once abundant in the Caribbean, but nest predation by invasive mammals and human disturbance have brought their estimated global numbers down to below 2000. In addition to predation by introduced mongoose, rats, and cats, humans hunting these birds for food has contributed to their decline, and may be continuing in some locations.

■ SUMMER ■ MIGRATION
■ WINTER ■ RARE
■ RESIDENT

Populations may be improving following the recent eradication of Pacific Rats and feral cats at the largest breeding colony on Little Barrier Island in New Zealand. Although a few birds may still occur on Great Barrier Island, this bird may have been effectively extinct as a reproductively viable population there for several decades now.

DESCRIPTION: 11". This species is much smaller than other North American gadfly petrels. It is pale gray above with a dark M pattern on the wing. Its gray uppertail coverts contrast with black tips of the central retrices; the outer retrices are white. It has a distinct, dark eye patch. The underwings are nearly entirely white.

VOICE: Generally silent at sea. On breeding grounds, it gives a series of high pitched notes similar to Mottled Petrel but even higher pitched.

NESTING: Nests in burrows on forested ridges and steep slopes; ideal breeding habitat is unmodified forest close to ridgetops with a low and open canopy and many large stems. It formerly bred in suitable habitat throughout New Zealand.

HABITAT: Highly pelagic, rarely approaching land except to breed.

RANGE: Endemic to New Zealand where it breeds on Little Barrier, Great Barrier, and Codfish Islands. It is found in the Pacific Ocean from New Zealand north to the Aleutian Islands. It sometimes can be seen well off the west coast of the United States and well off the west coast of tropical South America in the non-breeding season (May-October).

SIMILAR SPECIES: The rare oceanic Stejneger's Petrel (*P. longirostris*), found far offshore in the Pacific Ocean, has a blackish cap extending to the eyes. It has black outer retrices (white in Cook's).

CONSERVATION: VU
Cook's Petrel numbers are increasing following the eradication of Pacific Rats at the largest breeding colony on Little Barrier Island, New Zealand. Fledging success there increased from only 5 percent to 70 percent. Feral cats were removed in 1980. Continued conservation efforts focus on controlling multiple invasive species on breeding islands.

CORY'S SHEARWATER *Calonectris diomedea*

■ SUMMER   ■ MIGRATION
■ WINTER   ■ RARE
■ RESIDENT

This is the only large shearwater found off the East Coast that breeds in the Northern Hemisphere. At sea off North American coasts, these birds forage at night, feeding on squid and crustaceans; they also follow schools of mackerel and other large fish, catching smaller fish driven close to the surface. Unlike many shearwaters, they seldom follow ships in search of food.

DESCRIPTION: 20–22" (51–56 cm). A large, stocky shearwater, dull gray-brown above and whitish below. Its bill is pale, usually yellow, sometimes marked with a dusky color. It is similar to Great Shearwater, but the dull gray crown of Cory's blends evenly with the white sides of the face, without the abruptly contrasting "cap" seen in Great Shearwater.

VOICE: Howling, gurgling calls heard only on breeding grounds.

NESTING: Lays 1 white egg in a rock crevice or on open ground on an island, occasionally in a cave or burrow. Nests in colonies.

HABITAT: Open ocean.

RANGE: Breeds in the eastern Atlantic and Mediterranean; in late spring, summer, and fall, it frequents the East Coast of North America.

SUBSPECIES: Most of these birds seen in North America are of the larger *borealis* subspecies that breeds in the eastern Atlantic. The *diomedea* subspecies that breeds in the Mediterranean also occurs more rarely—it is slightly smaller and the underside of the primaries is paler.

SIMILAR SPECIES: Great Shearwater has faster, stiffer wingbeats, although differing wind conditions may make comparisons difficult. Great is darker above with scaly-looking upperparts, a more distinct dark cap, more white on the nape, a dusky belly with a dark belly smudge (usually), more splotching on the underwing, and a black bill.

CONSERVATION: LC

This species is widespread in the Atlantic and its numbers appear to be stable. The primary threats facing these birds are interaction with commercial fisheries—it is among the birds most commonly caught as incidental bycatch by longline fishing practices—and nest predation from a range of introduced species.

■ SUMMER ■ MIGRATION
■ WINTER ■ RARE
■ RESIDENT

A very rare visitor to the waters off the coast of California from the subtropical Pacific. The Wedge-tailed Shearwater is a long-lived seabird, with the oldest known bird at 29 years old. They feed on larval forms of fish and squid, mostly during the day in association with skipjack tuna and other predatory fish. Schools of tuna often force smaller fish and squid to the surface of the ocean. Experienced fishers know that where many shearwaters are feeding, there might be a school of tuna nearby.

DESCRIPTION: 16" (40 cm) long. Its common name is derived from the large wedge-shaped tail, which is usually held closed, making its shape difficult to see. Its long tail and wings give this medium-sized shearwater a distinctive shape in flight. There are two color morphs—dark and pale. Pale predominates in the North Pacific, but both exist in all populations. The pale morph has gray-brown plumage on the back, head, and upperwing, and whiter plumage below. The darker morph has the same dark gray-brown plumage over the whole body. This bird has a slender gray bill and flesh-colored legs and feet.

VOICE: Generally silent at sea. Courting birds emit a variety of rising and falling moaning and wheezing sounds. The wailing sound made by these birds at their burrows at night inspired the Hawaiian name, 'Ua'u kani, which means "moaning petrel." Their call is sometimes likened to a crying child.

NESTING: Breeding colonies are typically low, flat islands and sand spits with little or no vegetation. They breed from February to November. Breeding pairs lay a single white egg in a burrow on the ground or in natural crevices. Incubation averages 53 days. Both sexes incubate for shifts up to 12 days. Adults leave the breeding colony to feed before sunrise and return after sunset. By late November, both adults and fledglings leave and are believed to migrate to the open ocean in the eastern Pacific. Adults usually return to the same nest site each year.

HABITAT: Pelagic. Only comes to land to breed.

RANGE: Extremely large range. Breeds in the Hawaiian Archipelago from Kure Atoll in the north to the offshore islets of Maui in the south, off the west coast of Mexico, on Johnston Atoll and Christmas Island, on islands in the west and south Pacific, off the eastern and western coasts of Australia, and in the Indian Ocean. Both morphs have been recorded more than a dozen times off the coast of California.

SIMILAR SPECIES: Pink-footed Shearwater is slightly larger and heavier and has a pink bill in adults.

CONVERSATION:
Although the species has declined somewhat, these birds are widespread and number around 5 million individuals. Competition with commercial fisheries, especially tuna fisheries, have had a negative impact on the birds' food supply.

- ■ SUMMER ■ MIGRATION
- ■ WINTER ■ RARE
- ■ RESIDENT

An uncommon visitor to the waters off the West Coast, irregularly appearing in September or October during its southward migration. This distinctive shearwater doesn't follow ships, but searches for squid and crustaceans on its own. Its flight, more languid and graceful than that of most other shearwaters, is characterized by less frequent wing flapping and longer glides with wings arched. Buller's Shearwater is not a common bird in our waters, but is likely to be seen in pure flocks where its food is plentiful.

DESCRIPTION: 16½–18" (42–46 cm). A small shearwater with a blackish, wedge-shaped tail. It is gray above with a distinct blackish cap; it has pure white underparts and wing linings. In flight, the dark bar on the upper surface of the wings and lower back forms an M-shaped pattern.

VOICE: Silent at sea.

NESTING: Lays 1 white egg in a burrow; nests in colonies.

HABITAT: Open ocean.

RANGE: Breeds on islands near New Zealand. It is a summer visitor to the North Pacific, appearing off the West Coast from the Aleutian Islands south to California.

SIMILAR SPECIES: The smaller Mottled Petrel also has a dark "M" mark on the upperwing but is less cleanly patterned above and lacks the black cap. It has a dark gray patch on the breast and belly and a heavy black bar under the secondary coverts. In flight, it arcs up much higher and zooms down faster, often tilting past vertical at the top of the arc.

See Pink-footed Shearwater.

CONSERVATION: Although numerous, this species' limited breeding range and ongoing and future threats account for its listing as a vulnerable species. Bycatch from various fishing methods, nest predation, and disturbance of nesting habitat by climate change and invasive species are all factors. Removal of pigs from some islands has improved nesting success enough to stabilize populations.

■ SUMMER　　■ MIGRATION
■ WINTER　　■ RARE
■ RESIDENT

This species, abundant near its breeding grounds, is called the "Mutton Bird" in Tasmania and Australia, where the young are taken for food. In the Bass Strait, which separates Tasmania from mainland Australia, an observer once saw a flock he estimated to contain 150 million birds. After the breeding season, this species migrates in a great figure eight: first northward toward Japan, then on to the waters around Alaska, then southward along the Pacific Coast of the United States, and then southwestward across its earlier flight path to Australia.

DESCRIPTION: 13–14" (33–36 cm). A dark shearwater, with a dark bill and feet. Distinguished from Sooty Shearwater by its slightly smaller size, dull gray (rather than whitish) wing linings, shorter tail and bill, and slightly faster wingbeats.

VOICE: Silent at sea.

NESTING: Lays 1 white egg in a burrow in a nesting colony.

HABITAT: Open ocean.

RANGE: Breeds on coasts and islands of southeastern Australia. A summer visitor to the Pacific Coast of North America, from the Bering Sea and Aleutian Islands south to California; rare south of British Columbia.

SIMILAR SPECIES: See Sooty Shearwater.

Flesh-footed Shearwater is larger and more uniformly dark, with a larger pinkish bill and broader wings; it soars more frequently.

CONSERVATION: This species is widespread and abundant. Populations in North America are stable, although global populations may be declining due to bycatch by commercial fisheries.

SUMMER · MIGRATION
WINTER · RARE
RESIDENT

These common visitors to both coasts of our continent are the most likely shearwater to be seen from land. Near shore and at the edge of the continental shelf, flocks of hundreds of thousands may be found at good feeding places. These flocks are worth inspecting closely because they often contain other, less common shearwaters. Sooty Shearwaters seen off the West Coast breed mainly on islands in the cool southwestern part of the Pacific Ocean. They raise their single chicks there and then migrate northward to spend the Southern Hemisphere winter on the warm seas of the North. Most that appear off the East Coast breed around Tierra del Fuego. After breeding, they begin a great circular migration around the Atlantic Ocean, arriving off the East Coast of North America in May, continuing on to Europe, then down the west coast of Africa, and returning to their nesting islands in November.

DESCRIPTION: 16–18" (41–46 cm). A large shearwater. It is uniformly dark sooty brown above and below, with silvery whitish wing linings—it is the only shearwater In the Atlantic with this coloration. Its bill and feet are dark. This slender, narrow-winged seabird skims on stiff wings over the waves, alternately gliding and flapping.

VOICE: Silent at sea; a variety of cooing and croaking notes on breeding grounds.

NESTING: Lays 1 white egg in a burrow. Nests in colonies.

HABITAT: Open ocean.

RANGE: Breeds on islands in cold southern oceans. Spends Northern Hemisphere summer in North Pacific and North Atlantic.

SIMILAR SPECIES: See Northern Fulmar and Flesh-footed and Short-tailed shearwaters. Manx Shearwater is smaller with white underparts.

CONSERVATION:
Once among the most abundant birds in the world, Sooty Shearwater is still rather numerous; threats from human interactions play a major role in this species being listed as Near Threatened. Fisheries catch many of the birds in nets, overfishing reduces prey populations, and the birds are regularly hunted on their breeding islands near New Zealand. Climate change has also disrupted feeding habitat and timing, although these effects are more difficult to quantify.

■ SUMMER　　■ MIGRATION
■ WINTER　　　■ RARE
■ RESIDENT

Adept divers, Great Shearwaters feed mainly on small fish and squid, which they pursue underwater with partially open wings and paddling feet.

DESCRIPTION: 18–20" (46–51 cm). A large shearwater, more slender than Cory's, it is dull brown above with pale scaling and white below with a dusky belly. It has a dark cap that contrasts with its white face, and its bill is black. It may show white at the base of the tail.

VOICE: Usually silent at sea, but birds resting on water have a low nasal, squealing call.

NESTING: Lays 1 white egg in a burrow on a grassy slope. It nests in large, dense colonies.

HABITAT: Open ocean.

RANGE: Breeds on islands of Tristan de Cunha in the South Atlantic. It spends the northern summer, from May to early November, as a nonbreeding visitor to the North Atlantic. At the end of the breeding season in the Southern Hemisphere, Great Shearwaters follow a "Great Circle" route around the Atlantic, appearing in North American waters as early as May, then moving on to the eastern Atlantic by late summer.

SIMILAR SPECIES: Cory's Shearwater upperparts are more uniformly gray-brown, and do not appear scaly. It lacks a dark belly smudge and has a larger, paler yellowish bill (sometimes dark-tipped). It lacks the contrast between the crown and face. Cory's flight is usually slower, with less stiff, deeper wingbeats, but this distinction requires some experience.

Sooty Shearwater is slimmer and appears all dark.

Black-capped Petrel has more dashing flight, with more soaring and swooping. It generally has more pronounced white on the nape and rump, it lacks the scaly appearance on the upperparts and upperwing, its bill is shorter and stouter, and it lacks the dark belly smudge.

CONSERVATION:  Despite facing many of the same threats common to other shearwaters (hunting and bycatch, especially), this species has a large and widespread population that has not shown signs of significant declines.

PINK-FOOTED SHEARWATER *Ardenna creatopus*

■ SUMMER ■ MIGRATION
■ WINTER ■ RARE
■ RESIDENT

This pale-bellied shearwater usually stays far offshore, but when it comes within sight of land, it is often seen foraging with flocks of smaller Sooty Shearwaters. At such times thousands may gather at places such as Monterey Bay or just outside San Francisco's Golden Gate strait. The Sooties often dive for food, but the Pink-footed Shearwater seldom does. A broad-winged species, it soars more frequently and for longer periods than other shearwaters.

DESCRIPTION: 20" (51 cm). A gull-sized shearwater, dark gray-brown above and whitish below; the undersides of the wings are white with dark borders. Its bill is pinkish with a dark tip; its feet are pale pink.

VOICE: Silent at sea.

NESTING: Lays 1 white egg placed in a burrow on an island.

HABITAT: Open ocean; seldom seen from shore.

RANGE: Breeds on islands off the coast of Chile. A nonbreeding visitor in summer to waters off California and Oregon, rarely as far north as southeastern Alaska.

SIMILAR SPECIES: Black-vented Shearwater is smaller, with sharper contrast between the dark upperparts and white underparts; its wingbeats are much faster.

Buller's Shearwater has a much "cleaner" pattern.

Streaked Shearwater (*Calonectris leucomelas*), a very rare visitor from the western Pacific, is larger, lighter brown above, and pure white below; its whitish head has dark streaks visible at close range. A light band across the uppertail coverts may be visible.

CONSERVATION: VU

Further research is needed on this species' population trends, but their numbers appear to be stable. Longline commercial fishing activities impact this species in both its breeding and nonbreeding ranges. Bycatch by small, poorly regulated longline fishing vessels in South America may have a greater impact than large-scale fishing operations. Harvesting of nestlings on the breeding islands and nest predation from introduced predators have been addressed in recent years, but remain as ongoing threats to these birds.

■ SUMMER ■ MIGRATION
■ WINTER ■ RARE
■ RESIDENT

This dark shearwater is most often found in feeding flocks of Sooty Shearwaters, where its larger size attracts attention. Its normal diet consists of fish and squid, but it has developed a habit of taking bait from fishing lines. Near its nesting grounds in the Southern Hemisphere it is often seen to dive, but seldom does so in northern waters.

DESCRIPTION: The largest and heaviest of the dark-bodied shearwaters in the North Pacific, 19½" (50 cm) long with a wingspan of 3'3" (1 m). It is sooty black above, below, and on the wing linings. It has a heavy pinkish or yellowish bill with a dark tip, and pale pink feet. Its wingbeats are slower than those of other shearwaters.

VOICE: Usually silent at sea.

NESTING: Lays 1 white egg in a burrow. Nests in colonies.

HABITAT: Open ocean.

RANGE: Breeds on islands off western Australia, on Lord Howe Island east of Australia, and in New Zealand. Summer visitor to North Pacific south to British Columbia and more rarely to California.

SIMILAR SPECIES: See Sooty and Short-tailed Shearwaters, which have noticeably faster wingbeats. Sooty Shearwater has whitish wing linings, a dark bill, and dark feet.

Dark-phase Northern Fulmar is smaller, stubbier, and paler, with a different flight and posture.

CONSERVATION: Flesh-footed Shearwater is frequently found caught in various forms of commercial fishing nets throughout its range; despite many efforts to reduce bycatch, it remains the greatest threat to the species. These birds also face nest predation from foxes and rats, and have had lower fledgling success due to increasing rates of plastic ingestion.

■ SUMMER ■ MIGRATION
■ WINTER ■ RARE
■ RESIDENT

Unlike the large shearwaters of the western Atlantic, the Manx Shearwater seldom follows ships and is usually seen skimming past them at some distance. A few Manx Shearwaters are known to breed in North America, but because they visit their nesting islands only at night, they may be breeding more frequently and in more places on our shores than is presently known. These birds are great travelers whose movements are poorly understood; one bird banded in Britain was later recovered off Australia.

DESCRIPTION: 12½–15" (32–38 cm). A small shearwater, uniform blackish above and white below with a sharp contrast between the black and white. The underwing is white, often narrowly margined in black; the flanks may show some mottling. Manx Shearwater flies in bursts of stiff wingbeats alternating with periods of gliding and banking.

VOICE: Cooing and clucking notes heard at night in breeding colonies.

NESTING: Lays 1 white egg in a burrow or rock crevice on an island. Nests in colonies.

HABITAT: Open ocean.

RANGE: Breeds mainly in the eastern Atlantic, but also on islands off Newfoundland, and in Massachusetts (one record). An uncommon but increasingly regular visitor off the East Coast. Rare off the West Coast.

SIMILAR SPECIES: See Audubon's, Sooty, Great, and Cory's shearwaters. Great Shearwater is larger, with pale scaling on brown upperparts, a distinct blackish cap—darker than the back—and usually a distinct white patch at the base of the tail. Audubon's Shearwater is similar, but has a longer tail and dark undertail coverts (white in Manx).

CONSERVATION: ![LC]
Predation by domestic pigs, rats, and feral cats as well as human exploitation on nesting grounds have impacted this species, but its widespread population has weathered these threats. Other threats including habitat destruction, longline fishing bycatch, and oil spills and other marine pollution have also impacted these birds.

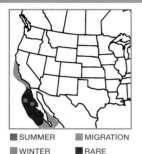

■ SUMMER ■ MIGRATION
■ WINTER ■ RARE
■ RESIDENT

This bird flies close to the waves, its flight more fluttery than that of other shearwaters. It rarely follows ships, but feeds by snatching food from the water's surface and sometimes by diving. This shearwater even swims beneath the surface, aided by its wings. Its diet includes small fish and crustaceans.

DESCRIPTION: 12½–15" (32–38 cm). The smallest shearwater that regularly visits the West Coast. It is blackish-brown above with contrasting white underparts and wing linings. It has a black bill and pink feet. Its flight is rapid, with much flapping and little gliding. The form that visits California waters has dark undertail coverts.

VOICE: Usually silent at sea.

NESTING: Lays 1 white egg placed in a burrow or a crevice. Nests in colonies.

HABITAT: Open ocean; often seen from shore.

RANGE: Breeds on islands off Baja California. A year-round visitor to waters off southern California, most common in late fall and winter.

SIMILAR SPECIES: Manx Shearwater has white undertail coverts. Pink-footed Shearwater is much larger, with heavier flight, darker wing linings, and a grayish back.

CONSERVATION:
Feral cats introduced on the breeding islands reduced populations significantly, although this threat has been removed. Populations have since stabilized, raising hopes for a recovery.

AUDUBON'S SHEARWATER *Puffinus lherminieri*

■ SUMMER   ■ MIGRATION
■ WINTER   ■ RARE
■ RESIDENT

Similar to the Manx Shearwater, this tropical species appears regularly on the Gulf Stream during the summer, sometimes in large numbers. The short-winged, long-tailed shearwater is a small, active bird that flies with rapid, fluttery wingbeats and short glides, often using its tail as a rudder. It is prone to quicker turns and changes of direction than the Manx.

DESCRIPTION: 11–12" (28–30 cm). A small shearwater, brownish-black above and white below except for dark undertail coverts. It is half the size of a Great Shearwater. In flight, its flesh-colored legs may be visible against the dark brown undertail coverts but do not extend beyond the tail. There are often dark smudges on the sides of the breast.

VOICE: Twittering calls and mewing notes heard at night in breeding colonies.

NESTING: Lays 1 white egg in a burrow or rock crevice on an island. Nests in colonies.

HABITAT: Open ocean.

RANGE: Breeds on islands in tropical seas around the world. Wanders northward along the Gulf Stream from the Caribbean and Bermuda as far as the Carolinas and, rarely, New England.

SIMILAR SPECIES: Manx has slower wingbeats, and it glides and banks more often; it has a shorter tail and white undertail coverts; in good light it appears darker above.

CONSERVATION: LC

Nesting sites in the Caribbean have declined, especially on the larger islands, due to disturbance from tourism and population growth in the region. Invasive rats also pose a threat to nesting grounds.

SUMMER | MIGRATION
WINTER | RARE
RESIDENT

The largest flying bird in the Americas, this dramatic, improbable-looking species is related to the Old World storks, a status it shares in North America only with the Wood Stork. Jabirus fly with slow, methodical wingbeats as they patrol wetlands, often in flocks, looking for prey, which consists mostly of fish, amphibians, reptiles, insects, and small mammals.

DESCRIPTION: 51–60" (129–153 cm). Huge, much larger than a Wood Stork. The adult's wings and body are all-white. Its naked head; massive, slightly upcurving bill; and long legs are all solid black. It has a conspicuous red throat patch. Immature is mottled gray-brown, with a blackish head.

VOICE: Normally silent.

NESTING: Lays 2–4 whitish eggs in stick nest set high in trees, often atop a palm; sometimes in loose colonies. Seasonal timing is irregular.

HABITAT: Tropical and semi-tropical llanos and savannas with scattered trees and wetlands; also rice fields and wet woods; vagrants in U.S. may associate with Wood Storks.

RANGE: Resident from southeastern Mexico through Central and South America to northern Argentina and Uruguay; accidental stray in North America to Texas.

SIMILAR SPECIES: Wood Stork is smaller, without the red throat patch; its bill is downcurved rather than upturned.

CONSERVATION: This rare visitor to the U.S. is fairly widespread in its usual range in Central and South America.

■ SUMMER   ■ MIGRATION
■ WINTER   ■ RARE
■ RESIDENT

This is North America's only native stork, found primarily in the Southeast. It is easily distinguished from white herons by its large size, upright posture, featherless dark head and neck, and heavy bill with a downward curve at the tip. These birds perch motionless on a bare branch or slowly stalk through marshes in search of food. They obtain food—mainly fish and snakes—by probing the water with their bills, locating prey by sense of touch.

Experts at soaring, they are sometimes seen circling high in the air on rising air currents. They nest in enormous colonies numbering up to 10,000 pairs.

DESCRIPTION: A large wader, 40–44" (1–1.1 m) long with a wingspan of 5'6" (1.7 m). It is white with a black tail and flight feathers. Its head and neck are bare and dark gray. The bill is long, stout, and slightly curved; it is black in adults and dull yellow in immatures. Unlike herons, storks fly with the neck extended.

VOICE: A dull croak. Usually silent except around a nest. Young make clattering noises with their bills.

NESTING: Lays 2 or 3 white eggs on a huge stick platform in a tree. Nests in colonies.

HABITAT: On or near the coast, breeding chiefly in cypress swamps; also in mangroves.

RANGE: Breeds in Florida and Georgia; rarely elsewhere along the coast from South Carolina to Texas. Outside the breeding season, it wanders as far as California and Massachusetts (rarely). Also breeds in tropical America.

SIMILAR SPECIES: White Ibis is much smaller, with thinner, decurved bill, and black only on tips of outer primaries.

High-soaring White Pelican has similar wing pattern, but has a white tail and short legs; it lacks a long neck.

See Whooping Crane.

CONSERVATION: LC

After decades of severe population declines, the Wood Stork was on the U.S. Endangered Species List until being delisted in 2014. Conservation efforts since the late 20th century allowed these birds to rebound and expand their range. Estimates of current population numbers vary. Florida populations remain vulnerable to changes in water levels caused by low rainfall or by water management practices.

■ SUMMER   ■ MIGRATION
■ WINTER   ■ RARE
■ RESIDENT

Frigatebirds are among the most agile of birds on the wing. They have the largest wingspan in proportion to weight of any bird. In addition to stealing fish from other seabirds—their most famous method of obtaining food—they can soar for hours and often dip down to the surface to pick fish and other marine animals from the water, or skim past a breeding colony of boobies to snatch young birds from their nests. Frigatebirds never alight on the ground or water; their short legs and narrow wings make it difficult for them to take off except from a height, such as the limb of a tree or a rock. Magnificent Frigatebirds are most commonly seen in Florida and along the Gulf Coast; those on the Pacific Coast that wander northward to California (and casually to southern Alaska) probably come from colonies on islands off the western coast of Mexico.

DESCRIPTION: 38–40" (97–102 cm) long with an average wingspan of 7'6" (2.3 m). It is black with long, narrow, pointed wings; a deeply forked tail; and a long, hooked bill. The male has a brilliant red throat pouch in the breeding season, which it inflates to a huge size during courtship. The female has a white breast. Young have white heads and underparts.

VOICE: Usually silent at sea; harsh guttural calls during courtship.

NESTING: Lays 1 white egg placed in a flimsy nest of sticks in bushes or trees or on rocks.

HABITAT: Open ocean and inshore waters. Nests on mangrove islands.

RANGE: In the United States, it breeds locally on mangrove islands in Florida Bay; also in the tropical Atlantic, Gulf of Mexico, and eastern Pacific. A rare but regular visitor to the West Coast, wandering to northern California, the Salton Sea, and the lower Colorado River in summer.

SIMILAR SPECIES: The white on the breast of females and the head and underparts of immatures can cause confusion with a Swallow-tailed Kite at a distance. Swallow-tailed Kite is much smaller with a much shorter bill, with much more extensive white on the underwings in addition to the head and breast.

CONSERVATION:
Global populations are difficult to monitor, but these birds are increasing in North America.

- ■ SUMMER
- ■ WINTER
- ■ RESIDENT
- ■ MIGRATION
- ■ RARE

This is the large, white booby of tropical waters; its name derives from its dark facial pattern. The Masked is the largest of the boobies and may be confused with the Northern Gannet, which it resembles in size and adult and juvenal plumages. Boobies obtain their prey in spectacular plunges from the air into the sea. Principal foods include flying fish and squid; boobies are seldom found in areas where these marine creatures are not plentiful.

DESCRIPTION: 32" (81 cm). A stocky white seabird with a black tail, black tips and trailing edges to the wings, and stout pinkish or orange bill. In breeding season, these birds have a patch of bare, bluish skin at the base of the bill. Northern Gannet is similar but larger, with only the wing tips being black.

VOICE: Usually silent; a variety of hissing and quacking notes on breeding grounds.

NESTING: Lays 2 chalky, pale blue eggs in a shallow depression on the ground. Nests in colonies.

HABITAT: Tropical seas.

RANGE: Breeds in the Bahamas and West Indies, and on other islands in the tropical Atlantic, Indian, and Pacific oceans. A rare visitor to coasts of Florida, Louisiana, and Texas, and in the Gulf Stream to the Carolinas.

SIMILAR SPECIES: Adult Northern Gannet lacks dark secondaries and a dark tail. A first-year gannet is entirely dark; it may show a combination of a light head and dark mantle, in contrast to a first-year Masked Booby's dark head and back separated by a white collar. From a distance, however, first-year birds must be carefully distinguished, especially off the Florida coast and in the Gulf of Mexico.

Adult white-morph Red-footed Booby is smaller, with light inner secondaries and sometimes a light tail; it has no dark patches. First-year Red-footed is smaller, appearing all-dark and often with a discernible dusky breast band.

First-year Brown Booby appears all dark with the suggestion of the adult's breast demarcation line.

CONSERVATION: 🐦
The Masked Booby is a rare visitor to the North Atlantic, but widespread in the tropics. It is fairly common but may be declining slightly due to unsustainable hunting and egg collection and invasive predators at breeding colonies.

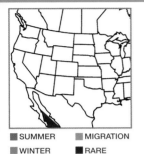

- ■ SUMMER
- ■ WINTER
- ■ RESIDENT
- ■ MIGRATION
- ■ RARE

Boobies fly fairly high over the ocean with steady, rapid, even strokes, followed by a short glide. When fishing, Blue-footed Boobies plunge headlong into the water with wings partly folded; they sometimes snatch flying fish out of the air.

DESCRIPTION: 32–34" (81–86 cm). A large seabird with long pointed bill, wings, and tail. Its head and neck are pale and streaked with brown. Its wings, back, and tail are dark brown; it has white patches on the nape and rump; and its underparts are white. Its legs and feet are bright blue. The back and rump of immatures are slightly mottled.

VOICE: Usually silent; trumpeting and whistling noises on breeding grounds.

NESTING: Lays 2 or 3 chalky pale blue or green eggs on the ground. Usually nests in colonies on islands or isolated cliffs.

HABITAT: Open sea.

RANGE: Breeds from Gulf of California south to Peru. In summer, a few stray to the Salton Sea in southeastern California or, infrequently, to the southern California coast.

SIMILAR SPECIES: Brown Booby lacks white patches on the nape and rump; its feet are yellow or greenish yellow.

CONSERVATION: Breeding populations on the Galápagos Islands appear to be suffering from a food shortage as their preferred prey fish species have declined, causing delayed breeding and nesting failure. Although the global population seems to be stable, conservationists are closely monitoring this species, concerned about a potential crash if the new generation fails to breed.

BROWN BOOBY *Sula leucogaster*

■ SUMMER   ■ MIGRATION
■ WINTER   ■ RARE
■ RESIDENT

Of the boobies seen off the beaches of the Gulf of Mexico, this species is by far the most plentiful. Like the Northern Gannet, Brown Booby dives for fish by plunging into the sea, but it also skims the surface to catch flying fish that leap clear of the surf. Frigatebirds often harass boobies, chasing them and forcing them to disgorge their prey, which the agile frigatebird then catches in midair. When on the wing but not fishing, boobies often flap and glide in lines close to the surface of the waves and may resemble shearwaters. On land, these birds are dependent on a strong wind for takeoff from a tree or other elevated perch. On calm days they rest in vegetation or on the ground.

DESCRIPTION: 30" (76 cm). The adult has a dark brown head, upperparts, and breast, with a sharply contrasting white belly and white underwing coverts. The immature is gray-brown above and below; it is darker on the head, wings, and tail.

VOICE: Usually silent, but gives a variety of quacking, grunting, and screeching calls on the breeding grounds.

NESTING: Lays 1–3 pale blue or green eggs on bare ground in a slight mound of broken shells and scattered vegetation, usually at the edge of a cliff.

HABITAT: Tropical and subtropical seas; breeds on coastal islands.

RANGE: Worldwide in tropical seas. Summer visitor to the Gulf Coast and Caribbean Sea; casually farther north in the western Atlantic; occasionally seen in southern California's Salton Sea; accidental along the Pacific Coast.

SUBSPECIES: Pacific and Atlantic subspecies are most reliably distinguished in adult males. Adult males of the Pacific (subsp. *brewsteri*) have pale white to frosty gray on the head and neck. Adult males of the Atlantic (subsp. *leucogaster*) share the dark brown head and neck typical of females and juveniles of the species.

SIMILAR SPECIES: Adult Brown Booby is unmistakable. First-year Northern Gannet is larger than a first-year Brown Booby; until the head and underparts of Northern Gannet become paler with age, it may be difficult to distinguish at a distance.

First-year Blue-footed Booby is smaller with white patches on the nape and rump contrasting with a dark back.

First-year Masked Booby has a white patch on the nape between its dark head and dark mantle, and an inverted U- or V-shaped (not straight and horizontal) line dividing its dark upper breast from the paler lower breast and belly.

First-year Red-footed Booby is smaller, with narrower wings and a faster wingbeat; it usually has an indistinct band of dark feathering on the breast.

CONSERVATION: LC

The Brown Booby is sensitive to human disturbance, with birds abandoning nests after close human approach. It is widespread and nests in many tropical areas worldwide, but its numbers are declining due to disturbance and unsustainable hunting in some parts of its range.

■ SUMMER ■ MIGRATION
■ WINTER ■ RARE
■ RESIDENT

A pantropical species, the Red-footed Booby's lifestyle is adapted to the relatively nutrient-poor waters in which it hunts for fish and squid. These birds engage in a "sky pointing" display similar to other sulids, but it is performed in trees. When feeding young, it engages in long foraging flights, at times exceeding 90 miles (150 km). It flies quickly and gracefully, and plunge-dives or snatches flying fish in mid-air. Its nocturnal habits discourage piracy by frigatebirds. Local populations may crash with the cyclical loss of food species, or with deforestation of tropical islands.

DESCRIPTION: Smallest of the sulids at 26–30" (66–77 cm) long with a wingspan of 36–40" (91–101 cm). The plumage in this species is highly variable; there are multiple adult color morphs in any given geographic population. White morph adults are all white with dark flight feathers, have a dark carpal patch on the underwing, and a variable golden-yellow wash; white-tailed brown morph is all brown with white rump and tail; the white-headed brown morph resembles the white-tailed, but the head and neck are also white (Pacific only). All have straight, pale blue bills, bright red feet, and bare pink facial skin at the base of the bill. Juveniles and subadults are pale brown with drab yellowish-gray feet and a blackish-brown bill. Juveniles mature over 2–3 years.

VOICE: Usually silent at sea.

NESTING: Lays 1 large egg with a long incubation period; the young develop slowly. Nests colonially in tree cavities on tropical islands; nesting dates vary with location and conditions.

HABITAT: Open oceans and subtropical islands (e.g., Dry Tortugas).

RANGE: Breeds on tropical islands worldwide, including the Caribbean, Galápagos, and Indian Ocean; strays to Dry Tortugas off Florida, accidental off the Gulf and California coasts.

SIMILAR SPECIES: First-year Northern Gannet is much larger, all-dark, and has heavier flight. Second- and third-year birds have a light head, dark back, and white underparts. The adult resembles a white-morph Red-footed, but is larger and has white inner and outer secondaries.

First-year Masked Booby is larger and usually has a white nape patch and inverted U-shaped line separating its dark upper breast and the white lower breast and belly. The adult has dark inner and outer secondaries and a dark tail.

Blue-footed Booby has 2–3 white patches above and bright blue feet.

First-year Brown Booby is larger. It appears all-dark at a distance, but at close range, a dim breast line and broad underwing margins can be seen.

CONSERVATION:
Numbers of Red-footed Booby are declining due to poaching in parts of its range, predation by invasive mammals, and habitat loss. Nest trees have been cleared for firewood or for development.

■ SUMMER   ■ MIGRATION
■ WINTER   ■ RARE
■ RESIDENT

The only northern member of the booby family, the Northern Gannet is one of the most spectacular sea birds. During migrations, gannets may be observed offshore, either gliding above the water or diving into the sea after fish, sometimes plunging headlong from heights as great as 50 feet (15 meters) or more. An intricate system of air sacs under the skin of the breast cushions the impact when a bird strikes the water. Gannets, like boobies, engage in an elaborate series of breeding displays. When one bird returns to a nest site, it is greeted by its mate. Both birds raise their heads and cross bills, which they clash together like swords, then bow to each other with wings and tails raised. This is followed by mutual preening of the head and neck. Usually the bird who has been relieved at the nest will pick up sticks or seaweed to present to its mate. Finally, the departing bird stands with head and neck extended straight up and wings raised over the back, then launches itself into the air.

DESCRIPTION: 35–40" (89–102 cm). The adult is white with black wing tips, its head tinged with orange-buff. It has a long, pointed tail and wings. The immature is dark gray, variously speckled and patterned with white, depending on age. Northern Gannet alternately flaps and glides in flight; it plunge-dives when feeding. The gleaming white of the adult is visible at great distances.

VOICE: A guttural croak or grunt, heard only on breeding islands.

NESTING: Lays 1 bluish-white egg that soon changes to brown in a shallow nest of dried seaweed high on a precipitous cliff or along the top of a bluff. Nests in colonies, with nests close together.

HABITAT: Open seas. Nests on northern rocky sea cliffs.

RANGE: Breeds on a few isolated islands off Newfoundland, in the Gulf of Saint Lawrence, and off Nova Scotia. Winters in coastal waters south to Florida and occasionally to Texas; also on the northwest coast of Europe.

SIMILAR SPECIES: See Masked Booby.

Adult white-morph Red-footed is much smaller, with dark outer secondaries, red feet, and pink and pale blue facial skin.

First-year Brown Booby is smaller and shows a semblance of the adult's breast demarcation line.

First-year Blue-footed Booby is much smaller, often with a dark breast band.

CONSERVATION: ![LC]

Widespread and numerous. Global Northern Gannet populations appear to be increasing despite regular loss of these birds to commercial fishing bycatch.

■ SUMMER   ■ MIGRATION
■ WINTER   ■ RARE
■ RESIDENT

Brandt's Cormorants often gather in flocks of several hundred and fly to feeding grounds in long straggling lines. This species and the Pelagic Cormorant frequently nest on the same cliffs, with Brandt's forming colonies on level ground at the top of the cliff and the Pelagic choosing inaccessible ledges. Nest robbing by Western Gulls is such a serious problem that nests are rarely left unguarded.

DESCRIPTION: 33–35" (84–89 cm). A solidly built cormorant, thick-necked and large-headed. Its plumage is black with little gloss. Breeding birds have a bright cobalt-blue throat pouch bordered with yellow, and slender white plumes on the face and back. Young birds are duller and buff colored on the breast.

VOICE: Croaks and grunts.

NESTING: Lays 3–6 chalky bluish eggs in a large nest of seaweed or other debris. Nests in colonies on cliffs and rocky islands.

HABITAT: Coastal or offshore rocks and waters near shore.

RANGE: Resident along Pacific Coast from southeastern Alaska south to Baja California.

SIMILAR SPECIES: Pelagic Cormorant is smaller, longer-tailed, slenderer, with a thinner neck and bill. Its smaller head is not distinctly thicker than the neck. In flight, Pelagic holds its neck out straight, without a slight bend at the base, so that the centerline of the neck and body is parallel to the water. Adult Pelagic shows much more iridescence; in breeding plumage, it has large, white flank patches, and at close range it shows a small, red throat pouch. Juvenile Pelagic is darker and more uniform.

Double-crested Cormorant is longer-tailed and flies with a distinct crook in the neck, with its head held above the centerline of its body. At close range, it shows a bright yellow, unfeathered throat pouch with no blue. Juvenile Double-crested has varying amounts of whitish on the underparts.

CONSERVATION:
This species has undergone a significant decline in recent decades. Human disturbance from recreational activities at or near its nesting sites can reduce colony attendance. Its breeding success seems particularly sensitive to water temperature variations and thus may be particularly vulnerable to the effects of climate change.

SUMMER MIGRATION
WINTER RARE
RESIDENT

Primarily a tropical species, the Neotropic Cormorant is most likely to be seen along the Gulf Coast, where it is the smallest of the three cormorants in the East, but a few individuals live near Elephant Butte, on the Rio Grande in New Mexico. It often perches on utility wires, where it can be seen spreading its wings to dry. When alarmed, it is more apt to escape by flying than by diving, as its larger relatives do. These birds sometimes engage in communal fishing, lining up across a stream and moving forward with flailing wings to drive fish into shallow water. It was formerly called Olivaceous Cormorant.

DESCRIPTION: 25" (64 cm). This is a small, delicate-looking cormorant of southern lagoons and marshes. It is black glossed with olive-brown, with an orange throat pouch narrowly bordered with white. Immatures are dull grayish-brown, a bit paler below, the throat and breast fading to buff or even whitish.

VOICE: Soft grunts.

NESTING: Lays 2–6 chalky blue eggs, often stained with brown, in a shallow nest of sticks lined with grass. Nests in trees or bushes in small colonies.

HABITAT: Brackish and fresh water.

RANGE: Resident along the Gulf Coast of Louisiana and Texas, in southern New Mexico, and south to southern South America.

SIMILAR SPECIES: In North America, this cormorant overlaps only with Double-crested Cormorant, and must be carefully distinguished from that species. Double-crested Cormorant is larger, lacks a white border on the throat pouch, has a shorter tail, and flies with a crook in its neck. The white border to the throat pouch of a breeding Neotropic Cormorant is diagnostic, but some Double-cresteds—especially in several western populations—have noticeable white plumes elsewhere on the head in breeding season. With experience, Neotropic may be identified by its slimmer neck, smaller head, and thinner bill. At close range, note the tips of the scapulars are bluntly pointed in Neotropic, and rounded in Double-crested.

CONSERVATION: LC
This species is widespread, and its population is increasing and spreading north inland in the southwestern United States and into the southern Great Plains.

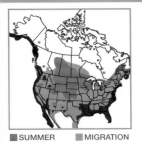

■ SUMMER ■ MIGRATION
■ WINTER ■ RARE
■ RESIDENT

Double-crested Cormorant is the most generally distributed cormorant in North America, and the one most likely to live and nest inland on most of the continent. Along the Pacific Coast, where it nests on cliffs, it is usually outnumbered by Brandt's Cormorant. It takes some practice to pick out the crook in the neck of a Double-crested, but once this field mark is spotted, distinguishing the two is easy. Double-crested Cormorants often take shortcuts over land, whereas both Brandt's and the smaller Pelagic Cormorant nearly always fly over water. Like geese, cormorants migrate in large arcs or in wedge-shaped flocks, but are silent when flying.

DESCRIPTION: 30–35" (76–89 cm). A solidly built black cormorant with an orange throat pouch and long neck. Its long, hooked bill is tilted upward when the bird swims. Adults have a short tuft of feathers over each eye during the breeding season. Young birds are browner, and whitish or buffy on the breast, upper belly, and neck. In flight, the neck shows a slight crook, not seen in the similar Brandt's Cormorant, the larger Great Cormorant, or the smaller Neotropic Cormorant.

VOICE: Deep guttural grunts.

NESTING: Lays 3–5 chalky, pale blue-green eggs in a well-made platform of sticks, or of seaweed on the coast, placed in a tree or on a cliff or rocky island. Nests in colonies.

HABITAT: Lakes, rivers, swamps, and coasts.

RANGE: Breeds locally in the interior from Alaska, Manitoba, and Newfoundland south to Mexico and Bahamas. Winters mainly on the coasts, north to Alaska and southern New England.

SIMILAR SPECIES: See Great, Neotropic, and Red-faced cormorants.

Brandt's Cormorant has a shorter tail, and it flies with its neck straight or very slightly kinked. Juvenile and nonbreeding Brandt's may have extensive tan feathers bordering the throat pouch, but not the bright yellow unfeathered throat pouch of Double-crested.

Pelagic Cormorant is small with a much thinner neck, head, and bill; it flies with its neck held straight out.

CONSERVATION: LC
Despite years of persecution by fishers who viewed it as a competitor, the species is currently increasing in number and expanding its range.

GREAT CORMORANT *Phalacrocorax carbo*

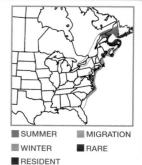

SUMMER ■ MIGRATION
■ WINTER ■ RARE
■ RESIDENT

The largest member of its family, the well-named Great Cormorant is widespread in the Old World but nests only along the eastern coast of Canada in the New World. The Great Cormorant has increased in numbers in recent decades, and dozens may now be observed in winter on offshore rocks where a single bird would have been a real find just a few years ago. The word "cormorant" is derived, through French, from the Latin *corvus marinus*, or "sea crow." Members of this long-lived species were once kept as captive birds trained to help catch fish in a practice dating back to the 5th century in the Far East.

DESCRIPTION: 35–40" (89–102 cm). A large, thick-necked cormorant. The adult is black with a white throat and yellow chin pouch; in breeding plumage, it has white flank patches. The immature is dull brown, with a dusky neck and white on the belly.

VOICE: Deep guttural grunts.

NESTING: Lays 3 or 4 chalky, pale blue-green eggs in a nest of sticks lined with seaweed, placed on isolated cliffs or rocky islands.

HABITAT: Sea cliffs, rocky coasts, and inshore waters.

RANGE: Breeds from Newfoundland and the Gulf of St. Lawrence south to Nova Scotia, Bay of Fundy, and Maine. Winters south to Virginia and the Carolinas, uncommonly to Florida. Also found in the Old World.

SIMILAR SPECIES: Double-crested Cormorant is the only species with an overlapping range; it is smaller and slimmer, with a slenderer head and bill profile, an orange-yellow throat pouch, and no white flank patches. Immature Double-crested is variable, but usually has a paler neck and chest and a brown belly—the reverse of an immature Great Cormorant.

CONSERVATION: LC

Historically, all cormorants have faced persecution from humans because of perceived competition for fish, although cormorants generally prey on fish species of little commercial or recreational value. Great Cormorants have increased in North America in recent decades, expanding their range farther south along the Atlantic Coast.

■ SUMMER ■ MIGRATION
■ WINTER ■ RARE
■ RESIDENT

The Red-faced Cormorant is one of several seabirds confined to the northernmost parts of the Pacific Ocean. Based on its appearance and its courtship displays, it seems most closely related to the Pelagic Cormorant. The Red-faced is more social than the Pelagic, however, and nests on the open tops of cliffs—areas the Pelagic normally avoids.

DESCRIPTION: 28–30" (71–76 cm). A medium-sized cormorant similar to Pelagic Cormorant but larger, with a brighter red throat pouch extending onto the face, and a pale bill. The bright red patch of bare skin on its face becomes duller in winter. Young birds are dull brown but still have a red face and pale bill.

VOICE: A low *korr*. Hoarse croaking notes at breeding colonies.

NESTING: Lays 3 or 4 chalky bluish eggs in a large nest of seaweed or grass. Nests in colonies.

HABITAT: Open ocean; nests on sea cliffs.

RANGE: Resident in Alaska, from the Aleutian and Pribilof islands east and south to Kodiak Island and Prince William Sound. Also found in northeastern Asia.

SIMILAR SPECIES: Pelagic Cormorant is smaller, with a thinner, more serpentine neck and with a thinner, blackish bill; a thicker, paler bill will distinguish Red-faced from Pelagic in all plumages in flight. Pelagic has dark red facial skin that does not extend to the forehead; the brilliant scarlet or orange-red facial skin of Red-faced can be seen a great distance, whereas Pelagic's black bill and dark red facial skin looks completely dark-headed at a distance. Juveniles of these two species can be distinguished by size and by the thickness and color of the bill.

See Double-crested Cormorant and Brandt's Cormorant.

CONSERVATION: LC
This species has declined in recent decades. The primary factors appear to be nest predation by foxes, and poor nesting success at colonies hit by tropical storms.

■ SUMMER ■ MIGRATION
■ WINTER ■ RARE
■ RESIDENT

The Pelagic Cormorant feeds mainly on fish, which it pursues both close to shore and far out at sea. It also takes crabs and other crustaceans. To catch this prey it dives deeply; birds have been recorded at depths of 180 feet (55 meters). This species' small size enables it to spring directly from the water, rather than paddling along the surface as other cormorants do.

DESCRIPTION: 25–30" (64–76 cm). The smallest and most delicate of the Pacific cormorants. It is glossy black with a dark bill, a long, slender neck held out straight in flight, a head no wider than its neck, and a red throat pouch. Breeding birds have a bold white spot on each flank. At close range two crests—fore and aft—are visible. Immature birds are dark brown, with the same proportions as adults. Other coastal cormorants are bulkier with slower wingbeats.

VOICE: Groaning and hissing calls around breeding colonies.

NESTING: Lays 3–7 chalky bluish eggs in a nest of seaweed, feathers, and other debris. Nests are used year after year and may grow quite large.

HABITAT: Offshore and inshore waters. Nests on sea cliffs and rocky islands.

RANGE: Breeds from the Bering Sea south to northern Baja California. Winters south from southern Alaska. Also found in northeastern Asia.

SIMILAR SPECIES: Red-faced Cormorant (Alaska only) is larger, with a thicker, pale bill.

Brandt's Cormorant is larger, shorter-tailed, more robust, with a head distinctly thicker than its neck; Brandt's flies with its neck held straight out but often bent, with its head below the centerline of its body.

Double-crested Cormorant is larger, with a larger head and stockier neck; it flies with a distinct crook in the neck and its head held above the centerline of the body.

CONSERVATION: LC

The population of this species hasn't been fully assessed. Although they are fairly widespread on both sides of the Pacific Ocean, climate fluctuations seem to acutely impact Pelagic Cormorant breeding success. El Niño events in the past 50 years have resulted in years of near-zero breeding success; food shortages resulting from these climatic events cause these birds to leave nests exposed or abandon nests entirely—a cause for concern among researchers as climate change strengthens El Niño patterns.

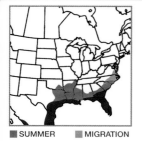

■ SUMMER ■ MIGRATION
■ WINTER ■ RARE
■ RESIDENT

Known colloquially as the "Snakebird" for its long, serpentine neck, the Anhinga often swims with its body submerged and only its head and long, slender neck visible above the water. Its long, dagger-shaped, serrated bill is ideally suited for catching fish, which it stabs and then flips into the air and gulps down headfirst. Cormorants and Anhingas lack oil glands with which to preen and so must perch with their wings half open to dry them in the sun. Anhingas often soar in circles high overhead.

DESCRIPTION: 34–36" (86–91 cm). A blackish bird of southern swamps, shaped like a cormorant but with a long, slender, S-shaped neck. It has a long, spear-like bill and a long, fan-shaped tail. The male's plumage has a greenish iridescence; the upper surface of the wings are silvery gray. The female has a tawny-brown neck and breast, sharply set off from a black belly. Immatures resemble adult females; the sexes look alike until their third winter.

VOICE: Low grunts like those of cormorants.

NESTING: Lays 3–5 chalky blue eggs in a nest of sticks lined with fresh green leaves and built in trees. Often nests in colonies of Double-crested Cormorants.

HABITAT: Freshwater ponds and swamps with thick vegetation, especially where there are large trees.

RANGE: Breeds near Atlantic and Gulf coasts from North Carolina to Texas, in Florida, and in Mississippi Valley north to southern Missouri and Kentucky. Winters along Gulf Coast north to South Carolina. Also in tropical America.

SIMILAR SPECIES: Cormorants have a hooked tip of the bill and a much shorter neck and tail; they lack white dorsal plumes.

CONSERVATION: LC

Uncommon and declining globally. Anhinga breeding locations are difficult to access, making it hard to assess the population, but North American numbers may be stable to increasing. Declines do not seem to be large enough to warrant a listing as vulnerable. Discarded fishing lines, with which these birds may become entangled, and loss of wetland habitat are among the main conservation threats to this species.

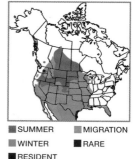

■ SUMMER ■ MIGRATION
■ WINTER ■ RARE
■ RESIDENT

American White Pelicans are gregarious birds, often associated with Double-crested Cormorants. A flock of migrating American White Pelicans is a majestic sight—a long line of ponderous birds, flapping and coasting. Each bird seems to take its cue from the one in front of it, beginning to flap and starting a glide when its predecessor does. These birds ride rising air currents to great heights, where they soar slowly and gracefully in circles. These birds are more buoyant than Brown Pelicans and do not dive for their food. They cooperate to surround fish in shallow water, scooping them into their pouches. They take in both water and fish, and then hold their bills vertically to drain out the water before swallowing the food.

DESCRIPTION: A huge white bird, 55–70" (1.4–1.8 m) long with a wingspan of 8'–9' (2.4–2.7 m). It has a long, flat distinctive orange to yellow bill with an extendable pouch used to scoop fish from the water. It has black primaries and outer secondaries. In breeding season, it has a short yellowish crest on the back of the head and a horny plate on the upper mandible. Young birds are duskier than adults.

VOICE: Usually silent; grunts or croaks on nesting grounds.

NESTING: Lays 1–6 whitish eggs on a low mound of earth and debris on a marshy island; occasionally on rocky islands in desert lakes. Nests in colonies.

HABITAT: Shallow lakes and coastal lagoons.

RANGE: Breeds from British Columbia and Mackenzie south to northern California, Utah, and Manitoba; also along the Texas Gulf Coast. Winters from central California, the Gulf Coast, and Florida south to Panama.

SIMILAR SPECIES: Wood Storks also soar in flocks and have a similar wing pattern, but have black inner secondaries, tail, and head; its long legs always trail beyond the tail. Otherwise, American White Pelican should be unmistakable; note that from a distance, a worn adult Brown Pelican can look surprisingly pale, with dark flight feathers.

CONSERVATION:

American White Pelicans declined in the 20th century from pesticides, habitat loss, and hunting, but they have rebounded since, with populations increasing steadily since the 1970s. As with other species of fish-eating birds, they are sometimes targeted by those with fishing interests, although it has been shown that their primary food sources are fish of little commercial value.

■ SUMMER ■ MIGRATION
■ WINTER ■ RARE
■ RESIDENT

These social birds fly in single file low over the water; upon sighting prey they plunge with their wings half-folded from heights of up to 50 feet (15 meters), surfacing to drain water from their bills before swallowing the fish. Unlike its larger white relative, the Brown Pelican seldom soars. Around waterfronts and marinas individual birds may act quite tame, taking fish offered them by humans.

DESCRIPTION: A large, stocky bird 45–54" (1.1–1.4 m) long with a wingspan of 7'6" (2.3 m). It has a dark brown body and a long, flat bill with a huge throat pouch. The head is whitish in adults, with dark brown on the hindneck during the breeding season. Both sexes are alike. Young birds have a dark brown head and whitish bellies.

VOICE: Usually silent, but utters low grunts on nesting grounds.

NESTING: Lays 2 or 3 chalky white eggs in a nest of sticks, straw, or other debris, usually on a rocky island near the coast. Nests in colonies.

HABITAT: Sandy coastal beaches and lagoons, waterfronts and pilings, and rocky cliffs.

RANGE: Resident of the Pacific Coast from southern California south to Chile, dispersing northward as far as southern British Columbia after nesting season. Also on the Atlantic Coast from North Carolina south to Venezuela.

SUBSPECIES: Brown Pelicans of the Pacific Coast (subsp. *californicus*) have a bright red gular pouch during the breeding season. The Eastern populations on the Atlantic and Gulf coasts (subsp. *carolinensis*) have a grayish gular pouch and average slightly smaller than their western cousins.

SIMILAR SPECIES: White Pelican is white in all plumages with black primaries and some black secondaries.

CONSERVATION:

The Brown Pelican is a conservation success story—it was initially protected by a predecessor to the U.S. Endangered Species Act in 1970, and was one of the species protected when the current Endangered Species Act was passed in 1973. Brown Pelicans and several other large predatory birds were a major impetus behind the ban on general use of the pesticide DDT in the United States in 1972. Following the ban, eggshell thickness, productivity, and population sizes of these and many other birds rapidly improved. By 2009, the population of Brown Pelicans had recovered to or beyond historical levels, and the bird was removed from the Endangered Species list, although it is still protected by the Migratory Bird Treaty Act.

AMERICAN BITTERN *Botaurus lentiginosus*

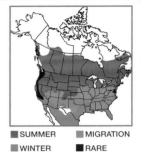

■ SUMMER   ■ MIGRATION
■ WINTER   ■ RARE
■ RESIDENT

The American Bittern has a remarkable, though rarely seen, courtship display. The male arches its back, exposing whitish plumes, shortens its neck, dips the breast forward, and "booms" at the female. Both members of the pair engage in a complicated aerial display flight. Bitterns spend most of their lives in concealment, stepping slowly and methodically through the reeds in search of food. When approached, it prefers to freeze and trust its concealing coloration rather than flush like other herons. When an observer is nearby, it will often stretch its neck up, point its bill skyward, and sway slowly from side to side, as if imitating waving reeds. If this doesn't fool the intruder, the bittern will fly off, uttering a low barking call.

DESCRIPTION: 23–34" (58–86 cm). A secretive, medium-sized, streaked brown heron. The outer wing appears blackish brown in flight, contrasting with the lighter brown of the inner wing and body. At close range adults show a long black stripe down the side of the throat. Young night-herons are similar but stockier, with shorter necks and more rounded wings without dark tips; they lack the secretive habits of bitterns.

VOICE: On breeding grounds, it makes a loud pumping sound, *oong-KA-chunk!* repeated a few times and often audible for half a mile (nearly a kilometer). Its light call is a low *kok-kok-kok*.

NESTING: Lays 2–6 buff or olive-buff eggs placed on a platform of reeds concealed in a marsh. Does not nest in colonies.

HABITAT: Freshwater and brackish marshes and marshy lakeshores; regular in salt marshes during migration and winter.

RANGE: Breeds from southeastern Alaska, Manitoba, and Newfoundland south to California, New Mexico, Arkansas, and Carolinas. Winters from coastal British Columbia, Southwest, Illinois, and along Atlantic Coast to Long Island (occasionally farther north), and south to Costa Rica (rarely) and Greater Antilles.

SIMILAR SPECIES: Immature night-herons are darker, lack contrast between the dark wing tips and the rest of the upperparts, and have no black neck patch. The flight of a night-heron is slower, usually higher, and not as steady.

Green Heron is smaller, with bright yellow legs; it lacks a black neck stripe. Other herons readily perch in trees; bitterns rarely do so.

CONSERVATION: Bitterns are widespread but secretive, making it a challenge to monitor their numbers. They appear to be declining as wetlands are degraded or developed, especially in the southern part of their breeding range.

■ SUMMER   ■ MIGRATION
■ WINTER   ■ RARE
■ RESIDENT

Although this heron is common in suitable habitat, it takes luck or patience to see one. Even more furtive than the American Bittern, this species relies on its cryptic coloration to escape detection and seldom flies, and then does so only for a few seconds before it drops out of sight. It spends most of its time picking its way quietly through the densest marshes, looking for frogs, crayfish, and other small aquatic creatures. It is a skilled climber and can be found several feet above the water, holding onto the swaying reeds with its long toes.

DESCRIPTION: 11–14" (28–36 cm). A tiny, secretive heron with a blackish back and conspicuous buff wing patches and underparts. Females and young are similar but duller and more buffy.

VOICE: A soft *coo-coo-coo*, easily overlooked.

NESTING: Lays 2–7 pale blue or green eggs placed on a flimsy platform of dead cattails or reeds, usually about a foot above the water.

HABITAT: Freshwater marshes where cattails and reeds predominate.

RANGE: Breeds locally in Oregon, California, and Southwest, and from Manitoba and Texas east to the Atlantic Coast. Winters from southern California, the lower Colorado River, and the Gulf Coast southward. Also found in South America.

SUBSPECIES: The extremely rare dark rufous form, once thought to be a separate species, is called "Cory's Least Bittern." Only a handful of records have been documented since the mid-20th century.

SIMILAR SPECIES: Unmistakable. Green Heron is much larger, with completely dark wings. Rails lack the buff wing patches.

CONSERVATION: Although many of the wetlands used for breeding have been degraded or developed, Least Bitterns have also been able to use smaller artificial wetlands, and their numbers have remained relatively stable.

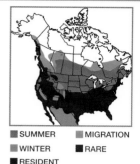

■ SUMMER ■ MIGRATION
■ WINTER ■ RARE
■ RESIDENT

An adaptable bird whose large size enables it to feed on a variety of prey—from large fish and frogs to mice, small birds, and insects—the Great Blue has one of the widest ranges of any North American heron. This wide choice of food enables it to remain farther north during the winter than other species, wherever there is open water, although such lingering birds may fall victim to severe weather. Most Great Blues nest in colonies in tall trees; their presence is often unsuspected until the leaves fall and the groups of saucer-shaped nests are exposed to view. In late summer young herons disperse widely and may be encountered at small ponds, in mountain waters, or even in backyard pools—wherever fish are plentiful.

DESCRIPTION: A common, large heron 39–52" (99–132 cm) long with a wingspan of 5'10" (1.8 m). It is a mainly grayish heron with a pale or yellowish bill. Foraging birds stand upright and nearly motionless. This species may be mistaken for a Sandhill Crane, but these big herons fly with their necks folded or "tucked in," not extended like that of a crane.

VOICE: A harsh squawk.

NESTING: Lays 3–7 pale greenish-blue eggs placed on a shallow platform of sticks lined with finer material, usually in a tree but sometimes on the ground or concealed in a reedbed. Nests in colonies.

HABITAT: Lakes, ponds, rivers, and marshes.

RANGE: Breeds locally from coastal Alaska, south-central Canada, and Nova Scotia south to Mexico and the West Indies. Winters as far north as southern Alaska, the central United States, and southern New England. Also found in the Galápagos Islands.

SUBSPECIES: In southern Florida an all-white form, "Great White Heron," is common on the Florida Keys; an intermediate form known as "Wurdemann's Heron," with an all-white head and light neck, is uncommon, chiefly found in the Florida Keys as well. These birds resemble a Great Egret but are larger, with greenish-yellow rather than black legs.

SIMILAR SPECIES: Other dark herons are smaller, and lack the black-and-white head and yellow bill. Great Egret is smaller, with a less massive bill and black legs and feet.

Sandhill Crane has its entire plumage rather uniform gray or gray-brown, and has black bill; it flies with its neck fully extended.

CONSERVATION: LC

Widespread and abundant. Local colonies are vulnerable to disruption from human disturbance, or from predation from Bald Eagles, which will take herons at any stage of their life cycle. They also suffer reduced nesting success in instances where pollutants such as mercury and DDT are present at high levels.

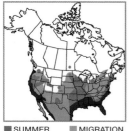

■ SUMMER   ■ MIGRATION
■ WINTER   ■ RARE
■ RESIDENT

Formerly known by many names including "American Egret," "Common Egret," "Large Egret," "White Egret," and "Great White Egret," this bird's official name in North America is now Great Egret. One of the most magnificent of our herons, it has fortunately recovered from historic persecution by plume hunters. Like the Great Blue Heron, it usually feeds alone, stalking fish, frogs, snakes, and crayfish in shallow water. Each summer, many individuals—especially young ones—wander far north of the breeding grounds.

DESCRIPTION: 35–41" (89–104 cm) long with an average wingspan of 4'7" (1.4 m). A large, all-white heron with a yellow bill and black legs. In breeding plumage, it has long, lacy plumes on the back. In most areas it is the largest all-white heron, and has a very long, thin neck without shaggy plumes.

VOICE: A guttural croak. Also loud squawks at nesting colonies.

NESTING: Lays 3–5 pale blue-green eggs placed on a platform of sticks in a tree or bush. Nests in colonies, often with other species of herons.

HABITAT: Fresh and salt marshes, marshy ponds, and tidal flats.

RANGE: Breeds locally from Oregon south to western Mexico, and from Minnesota to the Mississippi Valley and the Southeast, and along the Atlantic Coast north to southern New England. Winters regularly from Oregon south through Southwest, Texas, and the Gulf Coast states to Mexico, and on the Atlantic Coast north to New Jersey. Also found in tropical America and warmer parts of the Old World.

SIMILAR SPECIES: In southern Florida, the white-morph Great Blue Heron is larger, with a massive yellow bill and greenish yellowish legs.

White-morph Reddish Egret is smaller, with a flesh-colored, black-tipped bill and bluish legs.

Immature Little Blue Heron is smaller, with a bluish, dark-tipped bill and greenish legs.

Snowy Egret is much smaller and more slender, with a slender black bill, black legs, and yellow feet.

Immature Cattle Egret may have a yellow bill and black feet, but is much smaller, with yellow legs.

CONSERVATION:

Great Egrets were nearly wiped out by feather hunters in the 1800s continuing to 1910. Populations quickly recovered once protections were enacted. In recent years the breeding range of these widespread birds has been shifting northward. The destruction of wetlands—especially in the West where colonies are fewer and widely scattered, as well as in the southern part of its range—reduces the available habitat to support these majestic birds.

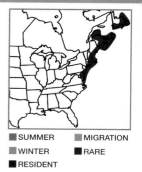

■ SUMMER ■ MIGRATION
■ WINTER ■ RARE
■ RESIDENT

The only record of Little Egret in the New World before 1980 was on Barbados in April 1954. Since then it has occurred as a casual spring and summer visitor several times along the East Coast. Individuals are seen with increasing regularity as far south as Brazil and northward along the Atlantic Coast to Newfoundland. Many European breeders migrate south across the Sahara to winter in equatorial Africa. Birds seen in North America might have strayed to the Caribbean and South America and are following their "normal" migration pattern northward in the spring and summer months, except they are now in the Western Hemisphere.

DESCRIPTION: A small egret, 25" (63 cm) long. Compared to the similar Snowy Egret, it has a longer and heavier bill, thicker legs, slate gray lores, and an overall larger size. Breeding individuals have two long head plumes and elongated breast feathers.

VOICE: Usually silent. Some calls are similar to Snowy Egret. Breeding individuals give rapid gobbling sounds.

NESTING: Colonies of nests made of platforms of sticks in trees or shrubs, often with other wading birds. In Cape Verde Islands, it nests on cliffs. Pairs will defend a small territory immediately around the nest site. The female lays 3 to 5 five blue-green eggs, which both parents incubate.

HABITAT: Large coastal and inland wetlands.

RANGE: A rare visitor to the Atlantic Coast originally from Eurasia and Africa.

SIMILAR SPECIES: This species is the Old World equivalent to the Snowy Egret, which it closely resembles. Breeding Snowy Egret lacks the two long head plumes; an immature Snowy is slightly smaller with lighter yellow legs.

CONSERVATION:

This rare North American visitor has a large, widespread Old World population that appears to be increasing.

This heron of coastal West Africa has been sighted a few times up and down the Atlantic Coast of North America from New Jersey to Newfoundland. Numerous sightings from 2005 to 2007 may have been of a single individual. This species is taxonomically complex, having often been included in a single species along with the Little Egret, and sometimes even with the North American Snowy Egret.

DESCRIPTION: The Western Reef-Heron is a small heron, 23–25" (58–62 cm) long, closely related to the Little Egret. It is uniformly dark gray, generally with a light or white throat and bright yellow feet.

VOICE: Squawk similar to many related species.

NESTING: Nests in single pairs or small colonies on the ground or in reedbeds, bushes or mangrove trees.

HABITAT: Coastal habitats, especially rocky or sandy shores and reefs.

RANGE: Coastal west Africa, accidental vagrant to the East Coast of North America.

SIMILAR SPECIES: Little Blue Heron is similar but lacks the white chin and bright yellow feet; its foraging movements are much slower and less active.

CONSERVATION: This species is hunted in some parts of Africa, but its numbers remain stable.

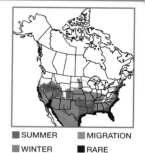

■ SUMMER ■ MIGRATION
■ WINTER ■ RARE
■ RESIDENT

These delicate, agile birds often feed by sprinting rapidly through shallow water, chasing schools of minnows and shrimp. This habit makes them easy to identify without seeing their bills and feet. Often several Snowies will be found feeding together, and it is thought that their white color, visible at great distances, lets other birds know where the feeding is good; the sprinting behavior also attracts other birds that then join in the feast. There is evidence that members of a pair of Snowy Egrets, like other large waders, cannot recognize one another except at the nest. Even there, a bird arriving to relieve its mate must perform an elaborate greeting ceremony in order to avoid being attacked as an intruder. During this display the plumes on the head are raised and the incoming bird bows to the one that is sitting. Appeased by this display, the sitting bird leaves and the other takes over.

DESCRIPTION: A small, delicate, all-white heron, 20–27" (51–69 cm) long with a wingspan of 3'2" (97 cm). It has a slender black bill, black legs, and yellow feet. In breeding season, it has long, lacy plumes on its head, neck, and back. Immature is similar to the adult, but it lacks the long plumes and has a yellow stripe up the back of the leg.

VOICE: A harsh squawk.

NESTING: Lays 3–5 pale blue-green eggs placed on a platform of sticks in a bush or reedbed or on the ground. Nests in colonies, often with other species of herons.

HABITAT: Marshes, ponds, swamps, and mudflats.

RANGE: Breeds locally from Oregon and California east to New England, mainly along the coasts but also at scattered localities inland. Winters regularly from California, Arizona, and Virginia south to the West Indies and South America. Also resident in tropical America.

SIMILAR SPECIES: Snowy has a more slender head, neck, and body than other all-white herons.

White-morph Reddish Egret is larger and stockier, with a flesh-colored, black-tipped bill.

Adult Cattle Egret has a pale bill, legs, and feet; immature has a dark bill, legs, and feet.

Much larger Great Egret has a yellow bill and black legs and feet.

Immature Little Blue Heron has a larger body with a bluish, dark-tipped bill, dark lores, and greenish legs.

CONSERVATION:
Reduced by plume hunters in the 19th and early 20th century, Snowy Egrets have since been protected, and both the size and range of their populations have grown.

■ SUMMER   ■ MIGRATION
■ WINTER   ■ RARE
■ RESIDENT

A common heron in the Southeast, Little Blue Herons may be observed in large mixed concentrations of herons and egrets. It eats more insects than the larger herons and is sometimes seen following a plow to pick up exposed insect larvae. Adults usually forage alone, stalking the marshes for prey, but immatures tend to feed in groups, their white plumage serving as a signal, drawing distant birds together at good foraging places. Unlike the egrets, it has no fancy plumes and was thus spared by plume hunters in the 19th century.

DESCRIPTION: A small heron, 25–30" (64–76 cm) long with a wingspan of 3'5" (1 m). The adult is slate blue with a maroon neck. Its bill is grayish with a black tip; its legs are greenish. The immature is white, usually with dusky tips on the primaries. Young birds acquiring adult plumage usually have a piebald appearance.

VOICE: Usually silent; squawks when alarmed. Various croaks and screams at nesting colonies.

NESTING: Lays 3–5 pale blue-green eggs placed in a nest of sticks in a small tree or bush. Nests in colonies.

HABITAT: Freshwater swamps and lagoons in the South; coastal thickets on islands in the North.

RANGE: Breeds from southern California (rare), southern New Mexico, Texas, and Oklahoma east to southern Missouri and southern New England, and south to Gulf Coast; more common along the coast. Winters along the Gulf Coast, in Florida, and on the Atlantic Coast north to New Jersey. Also in tropical America.

SIMILAR SPECIES: Reddish Egret is larger with a thicker, shaggy neck and a flesh-colored, black-tipped bill, bluish legs; neck and head of dark-phase Reddish Egret rusty, not purplish.

Snowy Egret is somewhat smaller, all white, and has a slender black bill, yellow lores, black legs; it feeds much more actively.

Tricolored Heron is dark, with a contrasting white belly.

CONSERVATION: LC

The short, dark plumes of the Little Blue Heron were not as prized by feather hunters, which protected this species from the declines faced by many other herons and egrets in the 19th century. Habitat loss has reduced their numbers modestly over the past 50 years.

■ SUMMER ■ MIGRATION
■ WINTER ■ RARE
■ RESIDENT

Formerly called the "Louisiana Heron," this is a heron primarily of the Deep South, although in the West it nests in southern New Mexico, and it is liable to turn up in late summer as far away as Arizona, California, Oregon, Colorado, and even Manitoba. The Tricolored Heron is extremely slender and moves gracefully as it searches about for frogs or fish. Despite its relatively small size, it forages in deep water; often its legs are completely underwater, and the bird appears to be swimming.

DESCRIPTION: A smallish, slender heron, 25–30" (64–76 cm) long with a wingspan of 3'2" (97 cm). It is gray-blue with a rufous neck, white underwing coverts, and a clean white belly. There are maroon feathers at the base of its dark neck (and at the base of the back plumes during breeding season). The distal portion of the plumes is buff to cinnamon. A white stripe extends along the length of the neck from the base of the bill to the breast.

VOICE: Guttural croaks and squawks.

NESTING: Lays 3 or 4 blue-green eggs in a nest of sticks placed in a tree or reedbed, or on the ground.

HABITAT: Swamps, bayous, coastal ponds, salt marshes, mangrove islands, mudflats, and lagoons.

RANGE: Breeds on the Gulf Coast, along the Atlantic Coast north to southern Maine (rare), and in southeastern New Mexico and Texas. Winters along the coast from Texas and New Jersey south to northern South America and the West Indies. Also resident in tropical America.

SIMILAR SPECIES: Little Blue Heron is smaller with a dark blue-gray belly.

Reddish Egret lacks the white belly; its neck is more rusty colored or pale reddish and lacks a white stripe.

CONSERVATION: LC

Tricolored Heron numbers are largely stable, although local populations have undergone steep declines in response to habitat degradation and development. The species has been reported nesting farther north and inland in recent decades.

■ SUMMER   ■ MIGRATION
■ WINTER   ■ RARE
■ RESIDENT

The Reddish Egret forages by rushing rapidly about in shallow salt water with its wings raised, chasing down fish, frogs, and crustaceans. It also brings its wings forward in front of its body, creating a "canopy" of shade from which it spots its prey more easily. Mated pairs may be of the same or different color morphs. During its courtship display, this species erects the shaggy plumes on its head, neck, and back.

DESCRIPTION: A medium-sized heron, 30" (76 cm) long with a wingspan of 3'10" (1.2 m). The species has two color morphs. The predominant dark morph is slate-gray with a shaggy, pale rufous head and neck, bluish legs, and a pink bill with a dark tip. White morph adult has bluish legs and a pink bill with dark tip. Both color morphs may be seen on the Gulf Coast, the dark one predominating in Florida waters, the white more numerous in Texas. Juveniles begin to show their color morph beginning with the downy stage in the nest; either or both morphs may arise in a single brood. In either color morph, the immature resembles the adult but duller, with a dark bill.

VOICE: Squawks and croaks.

NESTING: Lays 3 or 4 pale blue-green eggs in a nest of sticks placed in mangroves or low bushes, or on the ground.

HABITAT: Salt and brackish waters, breeding in shallow bays and lagoons; in mangroves (Florida); among cacti, willows, and other shrubs (Texas).

RANGE: Locally resident in extreme southern Florida and along the Gulf Coast of Texas and Louisiana. Also found in Mexico and the West Indies.

SIMILAR SPECIES: Adult Little Blue Heron is darker, without shaggy neck, and with a grayish (not pink) bill.

CONSERVATION: NT
Plume hunters decimated the Reddish Egret population in the late 19th and early 20th centuries. The white plumes of the white-morph birds were especially prized, and to this day white-morph Reddish Egrets are seen far less frequently in most areas. Protections have allowed the birds' numbers to recover gradually, and they may still be increasing, but they remain uncommon in a limited range. Their total population in North America is estimated at around 10,000 mature individuals.

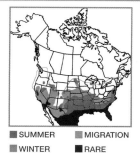

SUMMER   MIGRATION
WINTER   RARE
RESIDENT

Originating in the Old World, the Cattle Egret crossed the Atlantic, probably flying from Africa to South America, where this species was first reported in the late 19th and early 20th centuries. The birds gradually spread northward through the West Indies and into Florida, then northward and westward. As in the Old World, Cattle Egrets in North America follow large grazing animals to feed on the insects they disturb and can often be seen perched on the backs of livestock. At some airports, especially those near salt marshes, these small herons wait at the edge of runways for passing airplanes to blow insects out of the grass. Unlike other egrets, this species rarely takes fish, although it is known to capture an occasional frog or toad.

DESCRIPTION: 20" (51 cm). A small, stocky white heron with buff on the crown, breast, and back during breeding season. Adults have pale yellow or orange legs; the legs may be blackish in some immatures. Its bill is short and yellow or orange, and dark in juveniles. No other small white heron has a yellow bill.

VOICE: Hoarse croaks.

NESTING: Lays 3–5 pale blue eggs placed in a nest of sticks in a bush or tree. Usually nests in colonies with other herons in a marsh.

HABITAT: Forages mainly alongside livestock in open fields and pastures, but breeds near water with other herons.

RANGE: Breeds locally from California and most western states east to the Great Lakes and Maine, and southward to the Gulf Coast. Also found in the American tropics and the Old World.

SIMILAR SPECIES: Great Egret is much larger, with long black legs. All other white herons are larger, with longer necks and different colored bills.

CONSERVATION: LC

Abundant over much of the continent. Cattle Egrets have continued to expand their range, although this trend has slowed from the initial decades following its spread into North America. Officials in some urban areas try to prevent the formation of (or remove) colonies of these birds, which may be considered a public nuisance in large numbers. Their impact on native wildlife is minimal except in the north, where they may compete for nesting sites and crowd out native herons or egrets.

■ SUMMER ■ MIGRATION
■ WINTER ■ RARE
■ RESIDENT

The Green Heron is rather solitary, feeding alone or in pairs. A wary bird, it erects its short crest, straightens its neck, and nervously flicks its short tail when alarmed. It is often first noticed when it flushes unexpectedly from the edge of the water and flies off uttering its sharp call. Our smallest heron except for the diminutive Least Bittern, the Green Heron preys on a wide variety of insects, frogs, and small fish; its broad diet enables it to breed on small inland ponds and marshes that won't support other herons. It stretches its neck and bill forward as if taking aim, and, after a few elaborately cautious steps, seizes its prey with a jab of its bill.

DESCRIPTION: 16–22" (41–56 cm). A dark, crow-sized heron. Its crown is black, and its back and wings appear dark gray-green or gray-blue (depending on lighting). Its neck is chestnut colored, its bill is dark, and its legs are bright orange. Immatures have streaks on the neck, breast, and sides.

VOICE: Call is a sharp *kyowk!* or *skyow!*

NESTING: Lays 3–6 pale green or pale blue eggs in a loose nest of sticks built in a tree or dense thicket.

HABITAT: Breeds mainly in freshwater or brackish marshes with clumps of trees. Feeds along the margin of any body of water.

RANGE: Breeds over a wide region from Canadian border to the Gulf of Mexico, west to the Great Plains, western Texas, and southwestern New Mexico; in the West from the Fraser River delta of British Columbia south to California and Arizona. Winters from coastal California south to southern Arizona and Texas, along the Gulf Coast, and along the Atlantic Coast north to South Carolina.

SUBSPECIES: There are several subspecies among the larger complex of related herons sometimes lumped together as "Green-backed Heron." Species and subspecies delineation among these birds is unsettled. Among North America's Green Herons, some treat the resident populations in the southern U.S. as a separate subspecies from the migratory birds that breed farther north.

SIMILAR SPECIES: Little Blue Heron is larger and lacks bright yellow legs.

American Bittern is larger, longer-winged, and browner. It has prominent black neck stripes.

Least Bittern is much smaller, with buff wing patches.

CONSERVATION:  LC
Despite threats from habitat destruction and human disturbance, Green Heron populations have been stable or slightly declining. As with other species of herons and egrets, they have shown a slow range expansion northward in recent decades.

BLACK-CROWNED NIGHT-HERON *Nycticorax nycticorax*

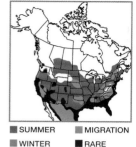

■ SUMMER　■ MIGRATION
■ WINTER　■ RARE
■ RESIDENT

As its name implies, this noisy bird is largely nocturnal, beginning to forage at dusk, when other herons are on their way to roosts. Night-herons are less likely to nest in mixed colonies than other herons; when they do, they often keep to themselves in a separate corner. These birds are sluggish hunters, standing quietly for long periods of time waiting for a frog or fish to pass by. They also plunder the nests of other herons and make regular nighttime visits to colonies of terns or Franklin's Gulls, where they sometimes take large numbers of chicks. Night-herons also stalk in grasslands in places where meadow voles are abundant, preying on these small rodents.

DESCRIPTION: A medium-sized, stocky heron, 23–28" (58–71 cm) long with a wingspan of 3'8" (1.1 m). It has a rather short neck, a black crown and back, gray wings, and white underparts. Its bill is short and black, and its legs are pinkish or yellowish. In breeding season it has two or more long white plumes on the back of the head. Young birds are dull gray-brown, lightly spotted with white.

VOICE: Loud, barking *kwok!* or *quawk!* often heard at night or at dusk. Utters a variety of croaks, barks, and other harsh calls in nesting colonies.

NESTING: Lays 3–5 pale blue-green eggs in a shallow saucer of sticks or reeds in a thicket or reedbed; occasionally in tall trees. Nests in colonies, sometimes with other species of herons.

HABITAT: Marshes, swamps, and wooded streams.

RANGE: Breeds throughout the United States and the southern tier of Canada (except in the Rocky Mountain region), from Washington, Saskatchewan, Minnesota, and New Brunswick to southern South America. Winters in the southern half of the United States. Also occurs in much of the Old World.

SIMILAR SPECIES: Immature Yellow-crowned Night-Heron is a grayer slate-brown with fine, light spots on the upperparts. Young Yellow-crowned Night-Herons have stouter bills and longer legs; in flight, the entire foot projects well beyond the tail (this characteristic alone can distinguish the two species).

American Bittern lacks pale spots on the upperparts; it has blackish primaries and secondaries, and a different shape and flight.

CONSERVATION:
Black-crowned Night-Herons are widespread and common but have declined since the mid-20th century. Habitat loss caused by draining and development of wetlands, and water pollution are their biggest threats. These birds are susceptible to pollutants that accumulate in wildlife such as persistent organochlorine pesticides, PCBs, and heavy metals.

SUMMER ■ MIGRATION
WINTER ■ RARE
RESIDENT

The Yellow-crowned Night-Heron is similar in size, shape, and posture to the Black-crowned Night-Heron, but is somewhat less common and a bit more active during the day. Unlike the Black-crowned, the Yellow-crowned preys chiefly on crabs and crayfish, which it crushes with its short, powerful bill. In flight, it looks more like a miniature Great Blue Heron than like a Black-crowned. It is found in a wide range of saltwater and fresh-water habitats; like other herons with a southerly distribution, this species has increased and expanded its range northward in recent decades.

DESCRIPTION: A medium-sized heron, 22–27" (56–69 cm) long with a wingspan of 3'8" (1.1 m). The adult is slate-gray with a black head, white cheeks, yellowish crown and plumes, a black bill, and yellow or orange legs. In flight, its feet and part of the legs extend beyond the tail. The immature is grayish brown, finely speckled with white above.

VOICE: A loud *quawk!* that is higher pitched than that of Black-crowned Night-Heron.

NESTING: Lays 3–5 blue-green eggs in a nest of sticks in a tree or occasionally on the ground. Nests singly or in small colonies, occasionally with other herons.

HABITAT: Wooded swamps and coastal thickets.

RANGE: Breeds from southern New England to Florida and west to Texas, mainly near coasts, but also found in the interior north to Minnesota and along the Mississippi River and its larger tributaries. It ranges more widely after nesting season. Winters along the Gulf Coast and on the Atlantic Coast north to South Carolina. Also found in tropical America.

SIMILAR SPECIES: Black-crowned Night-Heron has a bill that is less deep at the base. The immature is simi-lar to Black-crowned but browner, and less finely spotted on the upperparts. In flight, both the adults' and immatures' wings are less strongly two-toned; only the toes (not entire foot) pro-ject beyond tail.

CONSERVATION:

Although populations of these nocturnal birds are dif-ficult to monitor, Yellow-crowned Night-Heron numbers appear to be stable. As with many other herons, it appears to be expanding its breeding range northward.

SUMMER MIGRATION
WINTER RARE
RESIDENT

The White Ibis is a highly gregarious species that congregates in flocks that fly in long lines or V formations. White Ibises inhabit lagoons, swamp forests, and mudflats along much of the Atlantic and Gulf coasts. Around their colonies, ibises eat crabs and crayfish, which in turn devour quantities of fish eggs. By keeping down the numbers of crayfish, the birds help increase fish populations. In addition, their droppings fertilize the water, greatly increasing the growth of plankton, the basic food of all marsh life. White Ibises gather at dusk in spectacular roosts, long lines of birds streaming in from all directions.

DESCRIPTION: 23–27" (58–69 cm) long with a wingspan of 3'2" (97 cm). The adult is white with black wing tips (usually hidden when the bird is at rest); a red, down-curved bill and a red patch of bare facial skin in the breeding season. Its legs are red in the breeding season, and otherwise slate gray. Immatures are brown above and white below, with a brown bill and legs.

VOICE: Grunts and growls.

NESTING: Lays 3 or 4 greenish-white eggs with dark spots or blotches in a stick nest in trees over water. Nests in colonies.

HABITAT: Marshes, mudflats, lagoons, and swampy forests.

RANGE: Coastal resident from North Carolina to Florida and Texas. Also found in the American tropics.

SIMILAR SPECIES: Adult White Ibis is unmistakable. Immature Glossy Ibis is wholly brown, lacking white on the rump and belly present in White Ibis. Limpkin is brown with white spots and streaks.

CONSERVATION: LC

Locally common to abundant, the overall White Ibis population is stable. The species has lost some breeding habitat to development, but has adapted to urbanization in some areas, using artificial wetlands as long as there are sufficient prey populations.

■ SUMMER ■ MIGRATION
■ WINTER ■ RARE
■ RESIDENT

The Glossy Ibis probably crossed the Atlantic from Africa to northern South America in the 19th century, dispersing northward into the eastern United States by way of the Caribbean region. In recent years it has expanded its range considerably and is now a common breeder in areas where it was formerly rare or absent. Away from salt water it frequently eats crayfish, but along the coast it feeds mostly on fiddler crabs. It also eats insects and snakes, including the poisonous water moccasin.

DESCRIPTION: A large, all-dark marsh bird, 22–25" (56–64 cm) long with a wingspan of 3'1" (94 cm). It has a long, light brownish, down-curved bill. Its plumage is a rich chestnut in the breeding season; its wings are glossy greenish and its eyes are brown. The dark patch of bare facial skin is outlined by a thin line of white. Breeding White-faced Ibis is similar, but it has red eyes, all-red legs, and a broader band of white feathers around its bare face. Outside the breeding season, both species have streaks on the head and neck and brown eyes, and are difficult to distinguish.

VOICE: Low grunts and higher-pitched bleats.

NESTING: Lays 3 or 4 pale blue-green eggs in a stick nest in a bush or tree, rarely on the ground. Nests in colonies, often along with herons.

HABITAT: Marshes, swamps, flooded fields, coastal bays, and estuaries.

RANGE: Breeds on or near the coast, chiefly from Maine to Florida and Texas. Resident and found in winter along the Gulf Coast and on the Atlantic Coast south from the Carolinas. Also found in the Old World.

SIMILAR SPECIES: White-faced Ibis is similar, but in breeding plumage it has a prominent border of white feathers around the face; maroon facial skin, bill, and legs; and red eyes. Winter adults are distinguishable only by iris color; juveniles are indistinguishable.

Curlews are much smaller and paler.

CONSERVATION: 🐦 LC

The Glossy Ibis is increasing and expanding its range in North America. Globally the species is on the decline, largely due to habitat degradation. Many areas in the tropics have adopted aggressive mosquito control measures that involve the draining of marshes, which has had an adverse effect on these birds.

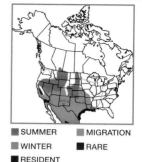

■ SUMMER ■ MIGRATION
■ WINTER ■ RARE
■ RESIDENT

This western counterpart to the Glossy Ibis is believed to have derived from a common ancestor that long ago colonized the New World and evolved in isolation into a separate species. The only ibis in the West, the White-faced overlaps with other ibises only in coastal Texas and Louisiana, where most dark ibises can be assumed to be White-faced. Its diet is diverse, consisting of insects, salamanders, crustaceans, and small fish and shellfish.

DESCRIPTION: A large marsh bird, 22–25" (56–64 cm) long with a wingspan of 3'1" (94 cm). It is chestnut-bronze with a long, down-curved bill. It is similar to the Glossy Ibis of the East, but with a band of white feathers around its bare face, and red eyes and legs. Glossy Ibis has brown eyes, gray legs, and a narrow band of white skin around the edge of its bare face. In winter, White-faced Ibis has streaks on the head and neck, and brown eyes; it is then virtually impossible to distinguish the two species.

VOICE: Low croaks and grunts.

NESTING: Lays 3 or 4 pale blue-green eggs in a shallow cup of reeds lined with grass in low bushes in a marsh.

HABITAT: Salt and fresh marshes in the West, and coastal marshes and brushy islands in Louisiana and Texas.

RANGE: Breeds from Oregon sporadically east to Minnesota and south to southeastern New Mexico and Texas, and east to coastal Louisiana. Winters from southern California and the Gulf Coast of Texas and Louisiana to El Salvador.

SIMILAR SPECIES: See Glossy Ibis. A red iris distinguishes an adult White-faced, but juvenile Glossy and White-faced ibises are indistinguishable in the field.

CONSERVATION: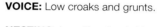
These birds have increased in recent decades and have gradually expanded their range, mainly to the east and somewhat farther north. The species was once severely depleted because of pesticide usage, but this striking marsh bird is now making a comeback in much of its range.

■ SUMMER   ■ MIGRATION
■ WINTER   ■ RARE
■ RESIDENT

The Roseate Spoonbill is a medium-sized, bright pink wader with an unusual spatulate bill. These birds spend much time feeding in the shallow waters of Florida Bay and the Gulf of Mexico on shrimp, small fish, snails, and aquatic insects, which they detect by their sense of touch as they rhythmically sweep their "spoon-shaped" bills from side to side.

DESCRIPTION: A medium-sized, long-legged wading bird, 30–32" (76–81 cm) long with a wingspan of 4'5" (1.3 m). Its distinctive bill is long and straight with broad spatulate tip, from which the bird gets its name. It is mainly white with brilliant pink wings and flanks, and an orange tail; its shoulder is rich crimson. The immature is pale pink and white.

VOICE: Low croaks and clucking sounds.

NESTING: Lays 2 or 3 dull-white eggs, with dark spots and blotches, in a bulky nest of sticks built in a low bush or tree. Nests in colonies.

HABITAT: Mangroves and saltwater lagoons.

RANGE: Resident locally on coasts of Texas, Louisiana (rare), and southern Florida. Also in American tropics.

SIMILAR SPECIES: Flamingos are also large pink wading birds, but have a shorter, sharply hooked bill with a black tip, and a longer neck.

CONSERVATION:

Although U.S. populations are well below historic highs, the numbers of these birds are relatively stable now, with a wide range of breeding habitat. Plume hunters severely reduced populations in the 19th century before protections were put in place in the 1910s.

BLACK VULTURE *Coragyps atratus*

■ SUMMER ■ MIGRATION
■ WINTER ■ RARE
■ RESIDENT

Black Vultures are scavengers that feed on carrion, but they also take weak, sick, or unprotected young birds and mammals. They soar in a group, alternately flapping and gliding, until one of them discovers carrion, whereupon all the others converge on the find. They are smaller but more aggressive than Turkey Vultures and will drive the latter from a carcass. Both species are often found perched in trees, on fence posts, and on the ground, or flying high overhead, especially on windy days, taking advantage of thermals or updrafts. Unlike Turkey Vultures, Black Vultures depend on their vision to find food.

DESCRIPTION: A broad-winged vulture, 22–24" (56–61 cm) long with a wingspan of 4'6" (1.4 m). It is black, with a white patch near each wing tip that is conspicuous in flight. Its head is bare with grayish skin. Its feet extend beyond the short tail. Black Vulture flaps its shorter and rounder wings more often and more rapidly than a Turkey Vulture.

VOICE: Hisses or grunts; seldom heard.

NESTING: Lays 2 white or gray-green eggs blotched with brown under a bush, in a hollow log, under large rocks, or in a cave.

HABITAT: Open country, but breeds in light woodlands and thickets.

RANGE: Resident from western Texas and Arkansas north and east to southern New England—increasingly seen northward to Vermont and Maine as its range expands—and south to Florida. Also found in the American tropics.

SIMILAR SPECIES: See Turkey Vulture. Eagles soar on flat wings.

CONSERVATION: LC

The Black Vulture population has increased during the past 50 years. Its numbers have declined in parts of the southeastern United States from the loss of breeding trees, but these birds have expanded their range northward during that time.

■ SUMMER ■ MIGRATION
■ WINTER ■ RARE
■ RESIDENT

The most common and widespread of the New World vultures, this species nests throughout all of the United States except northern New England. Turkey Vultures are valuable to the ecosystem as part of nature's cleanup crew, feeding on carrion. Soaring for hours over woodland and nearby open country, the Turkey Vulture searches for carcasses, locating them at least partly by means of its acute sense of smell. As they soar, these "buzzards" ride on rising columns of warm air called thermals to save energy as they cover miles of territory. The importance of this energy saving is clear from the fact that we seldom see a Turkey Vulture on a windless day, when thermals do not form. At night they often gather in large roosts.

DESCRIPTION: An eagle-sized blackish bird, 25–32" (64–81 cm) long with a 6-foot (1.8-meter) wingspan. Turkey Vultures are often seen soaring high over the countryside. In flight, the long wings are held upward in a wide, shallow V; its flight feathers are silvery below and its tail is long. Its head is small, bare, and reddish (gray in immatures). It resembles a Black Vulture, but its wings are narrower; it flaps its wings less frequently and often seems to rock or sway from side to side when soaring.

VOICE: Usually silent; hisses or grunts when feeding or at nest.

NESTING: Lays 2 whitish eggs, heavily marked with dark brown, placed without nest or lining in a crevice in rocks, in a hollow tree, or in a fallen hollow log.

HABITAT: Mainly deciduous forests and woodlands; often seen over adjacent farmlands.

RANGE: Breeds from southern British Columbia, central Saskatchewan, the Great Lakes, and New Hampshire southward. Winters in the Southwest, and in the East northward to southern New England.

SIMILAR SPECIES: Black Vulture is chunkier, with a stubby tail, shorter wings, and white patches at the base of the primaries; it flies with flatter wings and faster, shallower wingbeats. Black Vultures soar in tighter circles and, when in groups, generally fly closer together than Turkey Vultures. Immature Turkey Vulture has a gray head like a Black Vulture, but its flight posture is different.

Bald and Golden eagles hold their wings horizontally, not in a V. Osprey has a kink in its wings when soaring.

In the Southwest, see Zone-tailed Hawk.

CONSERVATION: 🐦 LC
The Turkey Vulture declined in the 20th century with widespread DDT use and the use of lead shot, which these scavengers will consume along with carrion left by hunters. Populations have been stable in recent decades with changes in farming and hunting practices.

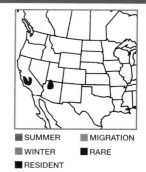

SUMMER   MIGRATION
WINTER   RARE
RESIDENT

The California Condor can be instantly identified based on size alone: its wingspan is twice that of the Turkey Vulture. Condors were once seen soaring around mountain and ridgetops or coasting high over intervening valleys in the rugged chaparral- and pine-covered mountains in central and southern California. They nested in caves or on rocky cliff ledges, and rarely in large hollow trees. California Condors take five to seven years to reach breeding age, and in the wild females lay only a single egg every other year. These birds are very sensitive to human disturbance.

DESCRIPTION: The largest flying bird in North America at 45–55" (1.1–1.4 m) long, with a wingspan of more than 9' (2.75 m). It is black with a bare head—reddish orange in adults, blackish in young—a black ruff, conspicuous white wing linings, and pale feet.

VOICE: Usually silent.

NESTING: Lays 1 white egg placed in an inaccessible cave or cavity on a cliff. They are monogamous and pair for life. Condors normally breed once every two years. If the egg is lost, they can lay another. The parents care for the young condor for nearly a year and a half after hatching.

HABITAT: Mountains and surrounding open, sparsely covered brush country where it can easily detect and safely approach carrion.

RANGE: Reintroduced populations survive in western Monterey County, eastern San Luis Obispo County, and eastern Santa Barbara County in California, and near the Grand Canyon in Arizona.

SIMILAR SPECIES: Golden Eagle and Turkey Vulture are smaller, with pale areas on different parts of the underwings. Golden Eagle has a proportionately larger head and slimmer body. Turkey Vulture has a decidedly more buoyant, tilting flight. Both have proportionately longer, slimmer tails.

CONSERVATION: CR

The California Condor is on the U.S. Endangered Species List. The wild population dipped so low in the mid-1980s that the decision was made to capture all remaining wild birds and bring them to captive breeding programs. By 1987, the California Condor was extinct in the wild—only 22 birds remained in human care. In 1992, enough chicks had been born in captivity that releases to the wild could begin. The first chick born to released parents hatched in 2003. The species now numbers more than 500, with nearly half of those in the wild. Many condors released to the wild die of lead poisoning from ammunition in carcasses upon which they feed. The wild population is not capable of sustaining itself without continued releases of captive-reared birds, and scientists are not hopeful about a self-sustaining wild population until mortality from lead poisoning can be reduced. Although heroic efforts have saved this majestic bird from certain extinction, it remains critically endangered and dependent on human efforts for its survival.

SUMMER   MIGRATION
WINTER   RARE
RESIDENT

Also known as a "fish hawk," Ospreys are distinctive birds of prey that search for fish by flying and hovering over the water, watching the surface below. When prey is sighted, an Osprey dives steeply, its talons outspread, and splashes into the water. It quickly resurfaces and, if it has made a catch, flies off, adjusting the fish in its claws so that the head is pointed forward. Ospreys declined drastically because of pesticides during the 1950s and 1960s, but since then they have made a comeback and are nesting again in areas from which they had disappeared.

DESCRIPTION: A large, long-winged raptor, 21–24" (53–61 cm) long with a wingspan up to 6' (1.8 m). It is brown above and white below; its head is white with a dark line through the eye and on the side of the face. Its wing shows a distinctive bend at the "wrist" in flight. At a distance, it can resemble a gull.

VOICE: Loud musical chirping.

NESTING: Lays 2–4 white, pink, or buff eggs blotched with brown in a bulky mass of sticks and debris placed in a tree, on a utility pole, on rocks, or on flat ground.

HABITAT: Lakes, rivers, and seacoasts.

RANGE: Breeds from Alaska, north-central Canada, and Newfoundland south to Arizona and New Mexico; also along the Gulf Coast and Atlantic Coast south to Florida. Winters regularly in North America north to the Gulf Coast and California. Also found in South America and in the Old World.

SIMILAR SPECIES: Subadult Bald Eagle is similar in some plumages, but is larger and splotchier; it lacks a definite crook in the wings in flight.

CONSERVATION: About 90 percent of breeding pairs that lived on the East Coast of North America between NYC and Boston disappeared between 1950 and 1970 due to pesticide use, but Osprey numbers have increased dramatically in the last half-century thanks to conservation efforts and pesticide bans. Artificial nesting sites have also played a role in this bird's resurgence, helping to offset natural habitat lost to residential development.

■ SUMMER   ■ MIGRATION
■ WINTER   ■ RARE
■ RESIDENT

The elegant White-tailed Kite was formerly shot in large numbers by farmers who thought it threatened their chickens, although these birds feed almost entirely on insects and a few small rodents. The North American population was rare and endangered into the 1940s; thankfully, White-tailed Kites have since made a spectacular comeback in California and Texas and are now common in suitable lowland habitats. Like other kites, they are sociable outside the breeding season, congregating at roosts in groups of a dozen or more. They feed mainly on small rodents and insects, which they locate by hovering kestrel-like high in the air. These kites prefer to rest on treetops or other high lookouts.

DESCRIPTION: A delicate, graceful, gull-like bird of prey, 15–16" (38–41 cm) long with a wingspan of 3'4" (1 m). It is largely white, with a gray back, a black patch on the shoulder and the undersurface of its pointed wings, and a white tail. The back and breast of young birds are streaked with warm brown. It often dangles its feet in flight.

VOICE: A whistled *keep-keep-keep*; also a longer, plaintive *kreep*.

NESTING: Lays 4 or 5 white eggs, heavily spotted with brown, in a nest of sticks and twigs lined with grass and placed in a tall tree, usually near water.

HABITAT: Open country and farmlands with scattered trees or fencerows; mesquite grasslands.

RANGE: Resident in coastal and interior California, Arizona, and southern Texas. Also in American tropics.

SIMILAR SPECIES: Swallow-tailed and Mississippi kites in flight show a black tail. Swallow-tailed Kite's tail is deeply forked and it has darker black wings.

CONSERVATION:
White-tailed Kites are common and increasing. Urban and suburban growth impact nesting sites, as do modern farming practices. In response to these pressures, White-tailed Kites have moved into new areas, including places in the American tropics where forests have been cleared.

■ SUMMER ■ MIGRATION
■ WINTER   ■ RARE
■ RESIDENT

A tropical species that enters the United States only along the Rio Grande, the Hooked-billed Kite feeds mainly on tree snails, which it deftly extracts from their shells with its long, hooked bill. This bird often has a favorite feeding perch, marked by a pile of empty snail shells on the ground below. As it flies through the dense mesquites, this kite flaps its short wings several times and then glides unsteadily.

DESCRIPTION: 15–17" (38–43 cm) long with a wingspan of 33" (84 cm). A small bird of prey with a long, hooked bill; short, rounded wings; and a tail boldly banded with black and white. The male is slate-gray above, and barred below with gray. The female is brown on the back with a rufous collar, and with rufous barring on the underparts.

VOICE: Musical whistles; harsh chattering during courtship or when disturbed.

NESTING: Lays 2 white eggs in a nest of twigs placed in a tree.

HABITAT: Mesquite woods along rivers and streams.

RANGE: Resident in extreme southern Texas. Also found in the American tropics.

SIMILAR SPECIES: Gray Hawk has a smaller bill, dark eyes, and a different flight silhouette; it lacks bold barring on the outer primaries. Cooper's, Sharp-shinned, Red-shouldered, and Broad-winged hawks also have reddish barring on the underparts but have different flight silhouettes.

CONSERVATION: Hook-billed Kites have historically been natives of Mexico and areas in Central America, but have taken up regular residence in southern Texas since the mid-1970s. It is believed that these birds have been driven north due to tropical deforestation; their numbers are decreasing globally.

SWALLOW-TAILED KITE   *Elanoides forficatus*

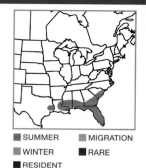

■ SUMMER ■ MIGRATION
■ WINTER ■ RARE
■ RESIDENT

The Swallow-tailed Kite is the most aerial of our birds of prey. It catches much of its insect food on the wing, snatches lizards from the trunks of trees, eats what it has caught while flying, drinks by skimming the surface of ponds and marshes, and even gathers nesting material by breaking dead twigs from the tops of trees as it flies past. Formerly more abundant, this distinctive bird nested as far north as Minnesota and Illinois, but habitat destruction and indiscriminate shooting reduced it to its present range.

DESCRIPTION: 22–24" (56–61 cm) long with a wingspan of 4'2" (1.3 m). A graceful bird of prey with long, pointed wings and a deeply forked tail. Its head and underparts are white; its back, wings, and tail are black.

VOICE: A shrill *klee-klee-klee*.

NESTING: Lays 2–4 creamy-white eggs, boldly marked with brown, in a stick nest often lined with Spanish moss and usually in a tall tree.

HABITAT: Swamps, marshes, river bottoms, and glades in open forests.

RANGE: Breeds mainly on or near coasts from Texas east to Florida, and north to South Carolina; local farther inland in Gulf states. Winters in American tropics. Also breeds in tropics.

SIMILAR SPECIES: White-tailed Kite also has a white head and underparts but is bulkier and has light gray on the back instead of black. Is white tail lacks the distinctive, deeply forked shape.

CONSERVATION:
Although Swallow-tailed Kites are currently increasing, these birds have severely declined since the mid-20th century. At one time their breeding range included at least 16 U.S. states, as far north as Minnesota, but they are currently only regular in seven southeastern states, with most of their remaining breeding sites found in Florida.

■ SUMMER ■ MIGRATION
■ WINTER ■ RARE
■ RESIDENT

Common in much of the West, these majestic eagles prey mainly on jackrabbits and large rodents but will also feed on carrion. In some parts of their range, Golden Eagles are not migratory but remain in their territories all year. The Golden Eagle is more scarce in eastern North America; after long persecution, only a few breeding pairs remain in the eastern part of its range.

DESCRIPTION: 30–41" (76–104 cm) long with a wingspan of 6'6" (2 m). A large, all-dark eagle with a pale golden nape. Its bill is smaller and darker than that of a Bald Eagle. In young birds, the tail is white at the base and black at the tip; immatures also have white patches on the undersides of the wings.

VOICE: A high-pitched *kee-kee-kee*; also a high scream or squeal, but usually silent.

NESTING: Lays 1–4 whitish eggs, unmarked or lightly speckled with dark brown, in a large mass of sticks placed on a rocky ledge or in a tall tree.

HABITAT: Mountain forests and open grasslands; some winter on salt marshes in the East, found in any habitat during migration.

RANGE: Breeds from Alaska east across northern Canada south to Mexico, the Canadian prairie provinces, and Labrador. Winters in the southern part of its breeding range and in much of the United States, except in the Southeast. Also found in Eurasia.

SIMILAR SPECIES: Immature Bald Eagle has a larger bill and broader wings; it often shows much white blotching on the back and underparts.

See Turkey Vulture, Black Vulture.

CONSERVATION: 🐦 LC
Populations of this raptor have remained stable since the middle of the 1900s, in large part thanks to the U.S. Bald and Golden Eagle Protection Act passed in 1962. Still, it is estimated that nearly three-quarters of Golden Eagle deaths are directly or indirectly caused by humans. Golden Eagles sometimes collide with power lines and wind turbines; some farmers with small livestock deliberately trap, poison, or shoot Golden Eagles despite the laws protecting them; and these birds are known to consume poisoned bait left out for coyotes and lead ammunition left in hunter-shot prey. Because Golden Eagles eat mammals instead of fish, however, they were not as strongly impacted as were other raptors by the use of DDT and other pesticides associated with farm runoff.

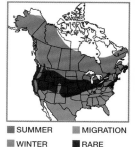

- ■ SUMMER
- ■ WINTER
- ■ RESIDENT
- ■ MIGRATION
- ■ RARE

This is the only North American member of a group of hawks known as harriers. All harriers hunt by flying close to the ground and taking small animals by surprise. They seldom pursue their prey in the air or watch quietly from an exposed perch, as do other birds of prey. Harriers have keener hearing than other hawks; their disk-shaped faces, not unlike those of owls, enable them to amplify sound. This species is also known as the Marsh Hawk.

DESCRIPTION: 16–24" (41–61 cm) long with a wingspan of 3'6" (1.1 m). A long-winged, long-tailed hawk with a white rump, usually seen gliding unsteadily over marshes with its wings held in a shallow V. The male has a pale gray back, head, and breast; its wing tips are black. The female and young are brown above and streaked below; young birds have a rusty tone on the underside.

VOICE: At the nest it utters a *kee-kee-kee-kee* or a sharp whistle, but usually silent.

NESTING: Lays 4 or 5 pale blue or white eggs, unmarked or with light brown spots, on a mound of dead reeds and grass in a marsh or shrubby meadow.

HABITAT: Marshes and open grasslands.

RANGE: Breeds from Alaska, northern Canada, and the Maritime Provinces south to southern California, Arizona, Kansas, and Virginia. Winters from South America north to British Columbia, the Great Lakes, and New Brunswick. Also found in Eurasia.

SIMILAR SPECIES: Red-tailed and Rough-legged hawks are larger, and have broader wings and proportionately shorter tails.

CONSERVATION:

This raptor has declined slowly but steadily over the past several decades due to habitat and prey loss, and due to poisoning caused by pesticide buildup and by eating poisoned animals. Known as mouse hunters, they are usually welcomed by farmers.

Accipiter striatus **SHARP-SHINNED HAWK**

■ SUMMER   ■ MIGRATION
■ WINTER   ■ RARE
■ RESIDENT

The smallest and most numerous of the accipiters, the Sharp-shinned Hawk feeds mainly on birds, which it catches in sudden and swift attacks. Its rounded wings and long, narrow tail enable it to pursue birds through the woods, making sharp turns to avoid branches. In the East, this species seems to be undergoing a decrease in number, perhaps because some of its prey species are also declining. Nonetheless, it is still one of the most common species at hawk migration lookouts in both the East and the West.

DESCRIPTION: Jay-sized, 10–14" (25–36 cm) long with a 21" (53 cm) wingspan. This is a fast-flying hawk with a long, narrow, square-tipped tail and short, rounded wings. The adult is slate-gray above and pale below, with fine rust-colored barring. Immature birds are brown above with whitish spots, creamy white below with streaks on the breast, and have barring on the flanks. Cooper's Hawk is bigger, with a proportionately larger head and a more rounded tail tip; it flies with slower wingbeats.

VOICE: Sharp *kik-kik-kik-kik*; also a shrill squeal.

NESTING: Lays 4 or 5 whitish eggs, marked with brown, on a shallow, well-made platform of twigs concealed in a dense conifer.

HABITAT: Breeds in dense coniferous forests, less often in deciduous forests. During migration and in winter, may be seen in almost any habitat.

RANGE: Breeds from Alaska through Mackenzie to Newfoundland, and south to California, New Mexico, the northern Gulf Coast states, and the Carolinas. Winters across the United States north to British Columbia and the Canadian Maritimes.

SIMILAR SPECIES: See Cooper's Hawk and Northern Goshawk. Of the three closely related accipiters, Sharp-shinned Hawks are the most buoyant fliers and flap their wings the fastest. Cooper's Hawk is intermediate in this respect; Goshawks, with the highest wing loading, flap most slowly and appear heaviest in flight. Accipiters exhibit a number of subtle differences among the species; although these are variable and show some overlap, they can often provide confirmation of identification under good viewing conditions.

CONSERVATION: Sharp-shinned Hawks nest in remote, deep-forest habitats, making nesting success difficult to estimate, but statistics gained from migration counts imply that numbers are on the rise. These raptors prey on small birds, thus the increase in popularity of backyard bird feeders may have indirectly helped this species as well.

COOPER'S HAWK *Accipiter cooperii*

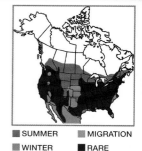

■ SUMMER   ■ MIGRATION
■ WINTER   ■ RARE
■ RESIDENT

Like its smaller look-alike the Sharp-shinned Hawk, Cooper's Hawk feeds mainly on birds, which it chases relentlessly through the woods. It also takes small mammals and, in the West, lizards and snakes. During incubation and the early stages of brooding the young, the male bird does all the hunting, bringing food to both its mate and the nestlings. Cooper's Hawks mature rapidly for birds their size; a full 25 percent of young birds breed the year after they are hatched, and the rest the year after that.

DESCRIPTION: Crow-sized, 14–20" (36–51 cm) long with a 28" (71 cm) wingspan. A medium-sized accipiter with a long tail and short, rounded wings. The adult is slate-gray above, with a dark cap, and finely rust-barred below. The immature is brown above, and whitish below with fine streaks. Its tail tip is rounded, not squared-off. See Sharp-shinned Hawk.

VOICE: Loud *cack-cack-cack-cack*.

NESTING: Lays 4 or 5 dull-white eggs spotted with brown on a bulky platform of sticks and twigs, usually more than 20' (6 m) above the ground.

HABITAT: Deciduous and, less often, coniferous forests, especially those interrupted by meadows and clearings.

RANGE: Breeds from British Columbia east to Manitoba and the Canadian Maritimes, and south to Mexico, the Gulf Coast, and northern Florida; absent or local throughout much of the Great Plains. Winters from Central America north to British Columbia and southern New England.

SIMILAR SPECIES: Sharp-shinned Hawk has proportionately longer wings and appears shorter, with a smaller head; in flight, the head appears even with, or behind, the leading edge of the wings. The male Sharp-shinned's tail is more notched or square; the female's is slightly more rounded but not as obviously so as Cooper's. Immature Sharp-shinned and immature Northern Goshawk are more heavily streaked below; they appear darker at a distance.

CONSERVATION: Cooper's Hawk numbers have remained stable for the last several decades, and are increasing. Like most raptors, these birds declined due to shooting and widespread pesticide use until the mid-20th century, but their population has since recovered.

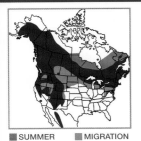

- ■ SUMMER   ■ MIGRATION
- ■ WINTER   ■ RARE
- ■ RESIDENT

This big raptor is mainly a resident of mountainside coniferous forests. It is fearless in defense of its nest and will boldly attack anyone who ventures too close. It has recently begun extending its range to the South and now breeds in small numbers in deciduous forests.

DESCRIPTION: 20–26" (51–66 cm) long with a wingspan of 3'6" (1.1 m). A robust hawk with a long narrow tail, short rounded wings, and a bold white eyebrow. Adults are blue-gray above with a black crown; their pale underparts are finely barred with gray. The immature is similar in size and shape, but is brown above and streaked below.

VOICE: A loud *kak-kak-kak-kak-kak* when disturbed.

NESTING: Lays 3 or 4 white or pale bluish eggs in a large mass of sticks lined with fresh sprigs of evergreen and placed in a tree.

HABITAT: Breeds in coniferous forests; winters in farmlands, woodland edges, and open country.

RANGE: Breeds from Alaska east through Mackenzie and northern Quebec to Newfoundland, and south to New Mexico, the Great Lakes, and New England; also southward to the northern Appalachians. Winters south to Virginia and the Southwest.

SIMILAR SPECIES: Cooper's Hawk is usually smaller and has a proportionately longer, more rounded tail; the tail's terminal band is wider, and the dark barring of the tail is more even. Its undertail coverts lack spotting or streaking. The adult lacks a white eyebrow. See Sharp-shinned Hawk.

CONSERVATION: LC

Widespread but uncommon to rare, these secretive birds are difficult to observe and to survey, favoring large tracts of forests with mature trees for nesting and foraging. This habitat preference makes them sensitive to logging activities. Populations are thought to have declined since the mid-1900s but appear to be more stable today.

BALD EAGLE *Haliaeetus leucocephalus*

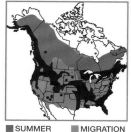

■ SUMMER   ■ MIGRATION
■ WINTER   ■ RARE
■ RESIDENT

The Bald Eagle is primarily a fish-eating bird of impressive size with long, broad wings and a large, strong bill. During the breeding season, it is closely associated with large bodies of water, which provide an abundant source of food. This species' large stick nests are typically built in tall trees, but in areas where suitable trees are scarce, the nests are placed on ridges, cliffs, and sea stacks. Bald Eagles usually hunt from perches adjacent to the water but are also known to pursue their prey in flight. During the winter, major concentrations of these birds occur near dams and other areas with ice-free water. The Bald Eagle also sometimes scavenges on carrion or crippled waterfowl. Hunting, poaching, human encroachment, and pesticide accumulation reduced its population drastically, but, thanks to conservation actions, this majestic bird has staged a comeback.

DESCRIPTION: 30–31" (76–79 cm) long with a wingspan from 6'–7'6" (1.8–2.3 m). A large, blackish eagle with a distinct white head and tail and heavy yellow bill. Young birds lack the white head and tail, and resemble adult Golden Eagles, but are variably marked with white and have a more massive, black bill.

VOICE: Squeaky cackling and thin squeals.

NESTING: Lays 2 or 3 white eggs in a massive nest of sticks in a tall tree or, less frequently, on top of a cliff.

HABITAT: Lakes, rivers, marshes, and seacoasts.

RANGE: Breeds from Alaska east to Newfoundland and south locally to California, the Great Lakes, and Virginia; also in Arizona, along the Gulf Coast, and in Florida. Formerly more widespread. Winters along the coasts and large rivers in much of the United States.

SIMILAR SPECIES: Juvenile Golden Eagles have well-defined areas of white on the tail and wings, lack white or silver in the wing linings, and have a smaller bill.

CONSERVATION: LC

Trapping, shooting, poisoning, and pesticide-related illnesses (especially thinned eggshells related to DDT) caused Bald Eagles to seriously decline in the late 19th and early 20th centuries, but conservation efforts have helped these birds make a strong comeback in the last several decades. The Bald Eagle was listed for protection under the Endangered Species Act in 1978 and was further listed as threatened on the U.S. Endangered Species list in every state except Alaska. By the late 90s, breeding pairs could again be found across North America, and its numbers continue to rise to this day. The species' recovering populations are one of the major success stories of the Endangered Species Act and conservation efforts, allowing the Bald Eagle to be removed from the endangered species list in 2007.

- ■ SUMMER
- ■ WINTER
- ■ RESIDENT
- ■ MIGRATION
- ■ RARE

One of the largest eagles in the world, this spectacular East Asian species is a casual visitor to Alaska. It is named for the noted 18th-century zoologist Georg Wilhelm Steller.

DESCRIPTION: A large eagle, 34–36" (86.5–91.5 cm) long with an average wingspan of 80–95" (203–241 cm). It has conspicuous white shoulder patches and white thighs; a massive, orange-yellow bill at all ages; a wedge-shaped, white tail, and white undertail coverts. The immature is similar to a subadult Bald Eagle, but has broad, white, squarish patches on the underwing extending from the inner primaries to the bases of the outer primaries.

VOICE: Deep-toned barking *ra-ra-ra-rau-rau*.

NESTING: Lays 1–3 greenish-white eggs in a massive stick nest placed in a large tree or, rarely, on a rocky crag.

HABITAT: Seacoasts and lower portions of coastal rivers.

RANGE: Mainly resident in northeastern Asia. It winters from the breeding range south to Korea and Japan. Accidental to casual in the Aleutian Islands and western Alaska.

SIMILAR SPECIES: Similar to Golden and Bald eagles, especially immatures that have streaks of white on the underwing. Steller's Sea-Eagle shows a white shoulder and white leading edge of the wing, paired with a massive yellow bill, at all ages.

White-tailed Sea-Eagle (*H. albicilla*), a rare visitor to the Aleutian Islands, has a pale head and a smaller bill.

CONSERVATION: VU
These birds are declining, threatened by residential and commercial development in coastal areas in northeast Asia.

SUMMER   MIGRATION
WINTER   RARE
RESIDENT

This graceful, buoyant kite is a marvelous flier and spends hours in the air. It is quite gregarious, often seen in flocks and even nesting in loose colonies. Although chiefly insectivorous, feeding largely on grasshoppers and dragonflies, it occasionally takes small snakes and frogs.

DESCRIPTION: 12–14" (30–36 cm) long with an average wingspan of 3' (91 cm). A small bird of prey with narrow, pointed wings. The adult is gray, paler below and on the head. It has a black tail and outer flight feathers in the wings; the inner flight feathers are whitish. Young birds are streaked below, with a banded tail.

VOICE: Gives 2 or 3 high, clear whistles, but is seldom heard.

NESTING: Lays 2 or 3 white eggs in a stick nest placed in a tree.

HABITAT: Open woodlands and thickets, usually near water.

RANGE: Breeds from Arizona and the southern Great Plains east to the Carolinas and south to the Gulf Coast. Its range has expanded somewhat in recent years; it increasingly wanders north to southern New England in the spring. Winters in the tropics.

SIMILAR SPECIES: A soaring Peregrine Falcon has a similar flight silhouette, but falcons lack an all-black tail and a whitish patch on the upper side of the secondaries.

Female and immature Merlin and Peregrine Falcon have patterned faces and barring on the underside of the primaries and secondaries.

CONSERVATION: LC

Mississippi Kites have increased in the past half-century. Historically found in the southeast and Great Plains areas, they have expanded their territory north and west, and now appear in new areas of the southwestern United States. Logging and forest clearing for development have created more open areas that this species finds ideal for foraging.

■ SUMMER　■ MIGRATION
■ WINTER　■ RARE
■ RESIDENT

This round-winged kite feeds exclusively on apple snails of the genus *Pomacea*, found in shallow ponds and swampy places. The kite's slender, sharply hooked bill easily extracts the snails from their unbroken shells.

DESCRIPTION: 16–18" (41–46 cm) long with an average wingspan of 3'8" (1.1 m). A crow-sized bird of prey with a long, thin, strongly hooked bill; broad, rounded wings; and a dark tail with a white base. The male is dark slate in color, with reddish feet, face, and base of the bill. Females and immatures have brown upperparts and a heavily streaked breast; the base of the bill is yellowish and their feet are dull orange or pinkish.

VOICE: Low cackles and chatters when disturbed.

NESTING: Lays 2–5 white eggs, heavily spotted and blotched with brown, in a stick nest placed in low bushes or in marsh grasses.

HABITAT: Freshwater marshes and lakes.

RANGE: Resident mainly on Lake Okeechobee and in the Everglades in southern Florida. Widespread in the American tropics.

SIMILAR SPECIES: Female and immature Northern Harriers are more slender; they have longer, narrower, pointed wings; a white patch on the rump, not on the tail; and their flight is more direct, with wings held in a shallow V.

CONSERVATION: 🐦LC

Snail Kites are believed to be increasing. The Everglades Snail Kite (*R. s. plumbeous*), the subspecies of the Snail Kite that occurs in the United States, is on the U.S. Endangered Species List, classified as Endangered in Florida. Apple snails—upon which this species depends for food—are strongly affected by water levels. Draining of Florida wetlands has hurt the local populations of snail and kite alike.

COMMON BLACK HAWK *Buteogallus anthracinus*

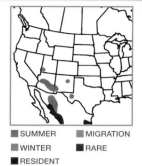

■ SUMMER ■ MIGRATION
■ WINTER ■ RARE
■ RESIDENT

More common in Mexico and Central America, a few hundred pairs of Common Black Hawk nest in the southwestern United States. These bulky birds feed mainly on aquatic creatures such as frogs, small fish, crabs, and crayfish. They often perch for long periods on a branch over water, waiting for their prey to appear. This species is vulnerable to disturbance near its nesting sites, vigorously sounding alarm calls at an intruder's approach and sometimes abandoning nesting areas following repeated disturbance.

DESCRIPTION: 20–23" (51–58 cm). A stocky, black bird of prey with broad wings and a broad white band across the tail. The fleshy ridge at the base of the bill (the cere) is yellow. Its legs are yellow and usually visible in flight. When soaring, it holds its wings flat and somewhat resembles a Black Vulture; a light, comma-shaped spot is visible on the underwing at the base of the primaries. Immatures are similar in size and shape but dark brown with tawny barring above and pale buff with streaks below; they have a dark tail with several pale bands.

VOICE: Shrill, whistled screams.

NESTING: Lays 1 or 2 white eggs, lightly spotted with brown, in a bulky nest of sticks lined with green leaves and grass.

HABITAT: Wooded canyons and riverside woodlands.

RANGE: Breeds from southernmost Utah south through Arizona and southwestern New Mexico, and in southwestern Texas. Most winter south of the United States. Also found in the American tropics.

SIMILAR SPECIES: A perched adult Zone-tailed Hawk shows a tail crossed by several black and white bands of relatively even width, not a single wide white band; light bands on the upper surface of the tail appear gray rather than white. In flight, its wings are held at an angle, and they are clearly two-toned with dark linings and lighter flight feathers; its wings and tail are longer and narrower.

Adult Harris's Hawk appears dark at a distance, but the chestnut color on the wings and legs is usually visible. It has a white band on the long, narrow base of the tail, including white undertail and uppertail coverts. Zone-tailed and Harris's hawks also have narrow white tips to the tail, visible from both sides.

CONSERVATION: LC
Although still numerous, Common Black Hawks are declining due to habitat loss throughout their range.

■ SUMMER   ■ MIGRATION
■ WINTER   ■ RARE
■ RESIDENT

This strikingly marked hawk of the Southwest is often seen perched on utility poles or giant cacti, or flying slowly along searching for rabbits, quail, lizards, or snakes. Members of a pair or family group hunt cooperatively and share food. Harris's Hawk is occasionally observed on the ground feeding on carrion with vultures. This hawk's social nature and relative comfort around humans has made it popular among falconers, and illegal capturing threatened its numbers in some areas.

DESCRIPTION: 18–23" (46–76 cm) long with an average wingspan of 3'7" (1.1 m). A black, crow-sized hawk with chestnut shoulders and thighs, white on rump and the base of the tail, and a white tail tip. Immatures are similar but more streaked.

VOICE: A low, harsh hissing sound.

NESTING: Lays 2–4 dull-white eggs faintly spotted with brown in a stick nest lined with grass, usually placed low in scrubby brush, cacti, or small trees.

HABITAT: Semiarid regions in scrub with mesquite, cacti, and yucca.

RANGE: Resident in southern Arizona, southeastern New Mexico, and southern Texas. Also in American tropics.

SIMILAR SPECIES: See Common Black Hawk and Zone-tailed Hawk.

Immature Red-shouldered Hawk (not generally found in the same habitat) is streaked above as well as below, and generally is lighter in overall appearance, with fewer bars on the tail.

CONSERVATION:

Harris's Hawk numbers are declining due to habitat being lost to urbanization and oil and gas development. Human encroachment reduces natural habitat quality and prey populations. Mesquite habitat is sometimes targeted for elimination by brush control programs.

WHITE-TAILED HAWK *Buteo albicaudatus*

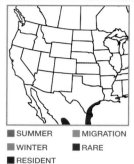

■ SUMMER   ■ MIGRATION
■ WINTER   ■ RARE
■ RESIDENT

This handsome and conspicuous hawk is a common sight in south Texas, where it is usually seen perched along highways on utility poles, fence posts, or dead trees. It mainly preys on rabbits, but this bird is an opportunist, gathering in flocks with other hawks at brush fires to feed on rodents, rabbits, lizards, and insects driven out by the flames. Like related hawks, it rides the air currents on motionless wings, often soaring to great heights.

DESCRIPTION: 21–23" (53–58 cm) long with an average wingspan of 4' (1.2 m). A large, stocky hawk. The adult is gray above and white below, with a narrow but conspicuous black band on its short white tail, and a rufous shoulder patch. Immature birds are dark with a gray tail.

VOICE: A musical *ke-ke-ke-ke-ke* or *cutta-cutta-cutta-cutta*.

NESTING: Lays 2 dull-white or pale bluish eggs, unmarked or lightly spotted with brown, in a grass-lined nest of sticks in a low bush, cactus, or small tree.

HABITAT: Coastal prairies, grasslands, and semiarid scrub.

RANGE: Resident in southern Texas. Also in American tropics.

SIMILAR SPECIES: Immatures might be confused with either dark buteos having pale tails. The dark "Harlan's" form of Red-tailed Hawk is the most similar, but its tail feathers are mottled and streaked lengthwise with darker gray; it soars with its wings held more horizontally. Dark-morph Rough-legged Hawk is slimmer, and its tail is longer with a dark band at the tip, and it has more contrast on the underwing. Dark-morph Ferruginous Hawk is longer-winged and longer-tailed, has more contrast on the underwing, with its secondaries usually whitish; its body is more uniformly maroon-brown. Dark-morph Swainson's Hawk has a darker, more strongly banded tail.

CONSERVATION:

White-tailed Hawks are fairly common in coastal and southeastern Texas, and their numbers are increasing. They are sensitive to nest disturbances, but their greatest threats are overgrazing, cultivation, and development of nesting habitats, including deforestation of tropical forests.

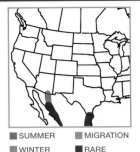

■ SUMMER   ■ MIGRATION
■ WINTER   ■ RARE
■ RESIDENT

A tropical hawk that nests locally in southeastern Arizona and occurs as a rare year-round resident in the lower Rio Grande Valley in southern Texas. Like many birds of prey living in deciduous woods, these hawks often line their nests with fresh leafy branches. These are plucked from the vicinity of the nest at first, but the male brings in fresh branches even after the nest is finished and incubation is underway. Gray Hawks feed mainly on lizards, dropping on them from a perch.

DESCRIPTION: 16–18" (41–46 cm) long with an average wingspan of 3' (91 cm). A small, compact hawk with a yellow cere (the fleshy ridge at the base of the bill). It is pale gray above with white underparts finely barred with gray, and with bold white bands on the tail. Immatures have streaked brown upperparts, pale underparts blotched with dark brown, and a narrowly banded tail.

VOICE: A clear whistle, *who-fleeer*.

NESTING: Lays usually 2 whitish eggs in a small nest of sticks lined with fresh green sprigs placed in a tall tree.

HABITAT: Riverside woodlands of cottonwoods, willows, and sycamores.

RANGE: Breeds in southeastern Arizona and southwestern New Mexico. Most migrate south in winter. Also in American tropics.

SIMILAR SPECIES: Immature Gray and Broad-winged hawks are distinguishable only with care. Generally, Gray Hawk shows finely barred thighs; immature Broad-winged usually (but not always) has bolder dark markings on the thighs and usually has paler, finer markings on the underparts. Most immature Gray Hawks have rust-colored or dark rufous streaking and blotching on the upperparts; immature Broad-winged lacks a rusty tone. Gray Hawk also usually has bolder malar stripes. Immature Broad-winged has brown crown finely streaked with white; Gray Hawk's crown is irregularly streaked with buff or rust. Broad-winged has a yellowish eye; Gray Hawk's is brownish.

CONSERVATION: Gray Hawks are widespread throughout the American tropics. They were common in Arizona in the 19th century, but as settlers moved westward, the mesquite and cottonwood forests were cleared for farmland. Populations have increased in the past few decades as the land recovers after a reduction in deforestation and overgrazing.

RED-SHOULDERED HAWK *Buteo lineatus*

■ SUMMER ■ MIGRATION
■ WINTER ■ RARE
■ RESIDENT

The Red-shouldered Hawk prefers lowlands, especially swampy woods and bogs. There it hunts by watching quietly from a low perch, dropping down to capture snakes and frogs. It also eats insects and small mammals. Normally shy, these birds become less wary if they are not persecuted and in some places may nest in suburban areas. During courtship a pair can be quite noisy, wheeling in the sky above their nesting territory and uttering their distinctive whistled scream.

DESCRIPTION: 16–24" (41–61 cm) long with an average wingspan of 3'4" (1 m). A large, long-winged hawk with white barring on dark wings, rusty shoulders, pale underparts barred with rust, and a narrowly banded tail. In flight it shows a translucent area near the tip of the wing, visible from below. Young birds are streaked below; they are best distinguished from young Red-tailed Hawks by their somewhat smaller size, narrower tail, longer and narrower wings, and the absence of a white chest.

VOICE: Shrill scream, *kee-yeeear*, with a downward inflection.

NESTING: Lays 2 or 3 white eggs, spotted with brown, in a large mass of leaves and twigs placed 20–60' (6–18 m) up in a forest tree.

HABITAT: Deciduous woodlands, especially where there is standing water.

RANGE: Breeds from Minnesota east to New Brunswick and south to the Gulf Coast and Florida, and on the Pacific Coast in California. Winters in breeding range north to southern New England.

SUBSPECIES: Red-shouldered Hawk is divided into five subspecies distinguished by geography, size, and coloration. The widespread nominate eastern race *lineatus* is the largest. The West Coast subspecies *elegans* is more rufous-orange below, sometimes appearing solidly orange or rust colored across the breast. The southeastern subspecies *alleni* is smaller, has more gray on the head and usually lacks breast streaks. The central Texas subspecies *texanus* is similar to the southeastern birds but with more rufous below than eastern birds. The South Florida subspecies *extimus* is the smallest and palest, with a gray head and only faint barring on the breast.

SIMILAR SPECIES: Broad-winged Hawk is plumper with shorter wings; it has cream-colored to white wing linings, and lacks a white crescent-shaped patch at the base of the primaries. Immature Broad-winged tends to be paler below, with finer streaks. See Northern Goshawk and Red-tailed Hawk.

CONSERVATION:

Populations of these raptors have steadily increased over the past half-century. Their biggest conservation threat is the continued clearing of their woodland habitat.

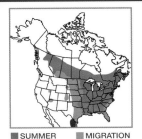

■ SUMMER　■ MIGRATION
■ WINTER　■ RARE
■ RESIDENT

The Broad-winged Hawk is mostly an eastern species, best known for its spectacular migrations; often thousands of birds travel together, with single flocks numbering up to several hundred individuals. Great numbers migrate along the eastern ridges in mid-September; more than 19,000 were counted in one day as they passed over the lookout at Hawk Mountain, Pennsylvania. During the breeding season, this hawk becomes more inconspicuous; it lives mainly in the woods, beneath the canopy or hidden among the foliage. Often an observer is made aware of its presence only through its call. Its diet consists mainly of snakes, mice, frogs, and insects.

DESCRIPTION: 13–15" (33–38 cm) long with an average wingspan of 33" (84 cm). A stocky, pigeon-sized hawk. The adult is plain brown above and barred with rusty color below, with broad black-and-white tail bands. Immatures are similar, but sparsely spotted or blotched below, and with less distinct tail bands. A rare dark-morph occurs on the western edge of the species' range. Dark-morph birds are solid dark brown above and below with white only in the underwings and on the tail bands.

VOICE: A thin whistle, *pe-heeeeeeeee?* Blue Jays are known to mimic the call.

NESTING: Lays 3 or 4 white eggs, with irregular brown spots, in a nest of sticks lined with green leaves placed in the crotch of a tree.

HABITAT: Breeds mainly in deciduous woodlands.

RANGE: Breeds from Alberta east to Manitoba and Nova Scotia, south to the Gulf Coast and Florida. Winters from southern Florida southward into the tropics.

SIMILAR SPECIES: A narrow, dark, straight trailing edge of the wing in the adult Broad-winged Hawk is distinctive. Cooper's Hawk has a proportionately much longer tail. See Red-shouldered, Gray, and Red-tailed hawks.

CONSERVATION:

The Broad-winged Hawk population is large and increasing. Large numbers of Broad-Winged Hawks were shot when they concentrated during migration until conservation laws were passed in the early 1900s. Today, habitat destruction is the biggest threat to these hawks, particularly in the tropics where they winter.

SHORT-TAILED HAWK   *Buteo brachyurus*

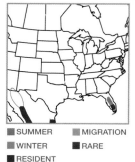

■ SUMMER   ■ MIGRATION
■ WINTER   ■ RARE
■ RESIDENT

This rare, tropical hawk is found in Florida, although strays from Mexico rarely wander to southeast Arizona and Texas. The species is easily identified in either of its two color morphs, because it is the only hawk in the area that is either pure black or pure white below. It often perches low on poles or trees near swampy areas and darts out after birds, rodents, lizards, or insects. It also hunts from high in the air, obtaining its prey in deep and swift dives from great heights.

DESCRIPTION: 13–14" (33–36 cm) long with an average wingspan of 35" (89 cm). A stocky, pigeon-sized hawk with two color morphs. The light morph is dark above and white below; the dark morph (more common in Florida) is black above and below except for the light bases of the primaries. Both morphs have a banded black-and-white tail, a yellow cere (the fleshy ridge at the base of the bill), and yellow legs and feet. Immatures are like adults, but with more numerous tail bands.

VOICE: A high-pitched squeal, *kleeeea*, dropping in pitch at the end; it is usually silent away from the nest.

NESTING: Lays 2 white eggs, sometimes spotted or blotched with brown, in a stick nest lined with leaves and sometimes decorated with Spanish moss, placed in a tree.

HABITAT: Open woodlands of pine and oak, cypress swamps, and mangroves.

RANGE: Local resident in southern Florida. Also in tropical America.

SIMILAR SPECIES: In Florida, the adult Red-shouldered and Broad-winged hawks have different colors and patterns of the breast and belly, and they are much darker, with more numerous tail bands. Immature Red-shouldered and Broad-winged show varying amounts of dark streaking on the underparts, unlike the unstreaked light-morph immature Short-tailed. Both Red-shouldered and Broad-winged soar with flat wing tips. Behavior, size, and tail patterns should distinguish a Short-tailed.

CONSERVATION:

Rare and local in Florida, it is estimated that there are only around 500 of these birds living there. Numbers of Short-tailed Hawks are on the rise in the tropics and in coastal Mexico, resulting in more frequent strays into the southwestern United States.

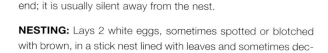

■ SUMMER   ■ MIGRATION
■ WINTER   ■ RARE
■ RESIDENT

Named after the English naturalist William Swainson (1789–1855), this species is highly gregarious, often migrating in great soaring flocks of thousands of birds. Its migrations are longer than those of other species; most individuals go all the way to Argentina to spend the winter, making a round trip of as much as 17,000 miles (27,000 kilometers). On its breeding grounds on the Great Plains, this hawk preys mainly on rodents and huge numbers of grasshoppers.

DESCRIPTION: 18–22" (46–56 cm) long with an average wingspan of 4'1" (1.2 m). A large, slender hawk with several color morphs. Most Swainson's Hawks are of the light morph; these birds are uniformly brown above and white below, with a warm-brown breast. Its tail is dark brown and indistinctly banded. It soars with its wings held in a shallow V, and it has longer, more pointed wings than a Red-tailed Hawk. The immature is similar to an immature Red-tail, but tends to have darker markings on the breast, whereas young Red-tails are more heavily marked on the flanks and belly. Rare all-dark and rufous color morphs also occur, as well as many intermediate color morphs; these various color morphs combined represent about 10 percent of Swainson's Hawks, and are more prevalent in the far West.

VOICE: Long, plaintive, whistled *kreee*.

NESTING: Lays 2–4 white eggs, unmarked or lightly spotted with brown or black, in a large nest of sticks, often placed conspicuously in an isolated tree.

HABITAT: Open plains, grasslands, and prairies.

RANGE: Breeds across much of the western United States south to northern Mexico and Texas; locally in Alaska, Yukon, and Mackenzie. Winters chiefly in the tropics, but small numbers winter in Florida.

SIMILAR SPECIES: All other melanistic buteos (Red-tailed, Rough-legged, Ferruginous, and Broad-winged hawks) lack buff undertail coverts and have white or light gray flight feathers. Red-tailed has a larger bill and a different look to the head.

CONSERVATION: Swainson's Hawk populations have remained stable since the mid-1900s, although they seem to have been driven from the westernmost part of their range. There were periods of time when these birds faced extreme challenges from hunters and pesticides, but conservation efforts have been successful in stabilizing their numbers.

ZONE-TAILED HAWK *Buteo albonotatus*

■ SUMMER ■ MIGRATION
■ WINTER ■ RARE
■ RESIDENT

Zone-tailed Hawks are fairly common but local in canyons and wooded river bottoms of the Southwest. Except for its tail bands, this long-winged black hawk bears a superficial resemblance to the larger Turkey Vulture, with which it often associates. It soars similar to a Turkey Vulture and holds its wings in a similar V shape. This resemblance is thought to deceive small lizards, mammals, and birds, which mistake it for a nonthreatening scavenger. The hawk makes a close approach, ignored as a harmless "vulture," and then makes its catch with a direct and powerful strike.

DESCRIPTION: 18½–21½" (47–55 cm) long with an average wingspan of 4' (1.2 m). A mainly black hawk with long, narrow wings held in a shallow V like those of a Turkey Vulture. Adults have 3 or 4 pale bands in the tail. Immatures have several light, narrow tail bands; a wide, dark terminal tail band; and fine white spotting on a black breast.

VOICE: A loud scream falling in pitch at the end.

NESTING: Lays 2 or 3 white eggs, often lightly marked with brown, in a large nest of sticks and green branches in a tall tree or cliff.

HABITAT: Forested canyons and riverside woodlands.

RANGE: Breeds in southern Arizona, southern New Mexico, and western Texas. Winters south of the United States.

SIMILAR SPECIES: Turkey Vulture has a naked, reddish head; its tail is wider and lacks pale bands.

Blackish dark-morph Swainson's Hawk resembles an immature Zone-tailed and often holds its wings in a slight dihedral, but its wings and tail are wider, giving it a more typical buteo shape. The upper surface of its tail is dark brownish, with blackish barring above, usually with buff or rust markings on the upperparts and wing linings.

The dark-morph of "Harlan's" Red-tailed Hawk is similar to an immature Zone-tailed but is conspicuously spotted with white on the upperparts and wing linings, has a broader tail and wings, and does not carry its wings at an angle. Its tail generally is not as evenly barred, being more or less whitish, with a dark subterminal band.

See Common Black Hawk.

CONSERVATION: 🐦 LC

The Zone-tailed Hawk is widespread throughout Mexico and into South America, and its population is increasing. Habitat loss represents the main threat to these birds, as residential development and landscape modifications have altered nesting and foraging grounds, and these hawks have disappeared from some former nesting areas.

The Red-tailed Hawk is the most common and widespread North American member of the genus *Buteo*, which also includes the Red-shouldered, Swainson's, and Gray hawks, among others. It soars over open country in search of its prey like other hawks of this group, but just as often it perches in a tree at the edge of a meadow, watching for the slightest movement in the grass below. Although historically persecuted by farmers, Red-tailed Hawk rarely takes poultry, feeding mainly on small rodents.

DESCRIPTION: 18–25" (46–64 cm) long with an average wingspan of 4' (1.2 m). A large, stocky hawk. Adults have a distinctive rufous-red tail. Typical light-phase birds have whitish breast and rust-colored tail. Young birds are duller and more streaked, lacking the rust-colored tail of the adult; they are distinguished from Red-shouldered and Swainson's hawks by their stocky build, broader and more rounded wings, and white chest. This species is quite variable in color, especially in the West, where blackish individuals occur; these usually retain the rusty tail. Dark and intermediate morphs represent about 10 to 20 percent of western birds, with only a few occurrences of these darker morphs in eastern North America.

VOICE: High-pitched, descending scream with a hoarse quality: *keeeeer*.

NESTING: Lays 2 or 3 white eggs, spotted with brown, in a bulky nest of sticks lined with shreds of bark and bits of fresh green vegetation, placed in a tall tree or on a rock ledge.

HABITAT: Deciduous forests and open country of various kinds, including tundra, plains, and farmlands.

RANGE: Breeds throughout North America, from Alaska east to Nova Scotia and southward. Winters across the United States north to southern British Columbia and the Maritime Provinces. *(continued on next page)*

SUBSPECIES: Some sources recognize more than a dozen subspecies, but not all authorities accept all of these classifications, and many intergrades exist that blend adjacent subspecies where their ranges meet. Eastern populations (subsp. *borealis*) have slightly shorter wings, a white throat, white breast, and a well-defined band across the belly. Western birds (subsp. *calurus*) are the most variable, ranging from light to dark plumages. Another western subspecies (subsp. *harlani*) was formerly considered a separate species called "Harlan's Hawk"; these birds have a grayish, faintly streaked or mottled tail, and also have a rare light morph and a typical dark morph. Southwestern populations (subsp. *fuertesi*) resemble the Western group but with fainter streaks on the belly and a paler tail. A scarce Great Plains population (subsp. *krideri*), called "Krider's Red-tailed Hawk," is pale with white underparts and barely a hint of a belly band; it has white on the upperparts and head, and a much lighter tail.

SIMILAR SPECIES: Swainson's Hawk lacks a belly band, has a dark bib in the adult and some immatures, and has pale wing linings and dark flight feathers. A dark-morph Swainson's has buffy tail coverts, and dark flight feathers below.

Ferruginous Hawk is larger; adults are clean white below, with rusty brown legs and a whitish tail; immatures are nearly clean white below, with white on the basal half of the tail.

Rough-legged Hawk has a large, dark wrist patch and white at the base of the tail. A dark-morph Rough-legged is discernibly darker with a wrist patch on the underwing; its tail is dark, sometimes with one to three white tail bands.

Red-shouldered Hawk is smaller; in flight it shows a white crescent-shaped wing patch on the outer primaries; adults have four to seven white bands in the tail.

Broad-winged Hawk is noticeably smaller, with no distinguishing marks on the underwing. It lacks a belly band, and adults have two white bands in the tail.

See also White-tailed Hawk.

CONSERVATION: LC

Red-tailed Hawk is the most common and widespread hawk in North America. Their numbers have been on the rise for several decades, and they appear to be adapting to life near human development. They readily nest on artificial structures, with some pairs nesting in cities on skyscrapers and utility towers.

■ SUMMER   ■ MIGRATION
■ WINTER   ■ RARE
■ RESIDENT

This large hawk often hovers above its prey like a kestrel. Lemmings, other rodents, and birds are its main sources of food during the breeding season. The number of eggs laid by the Rough-legged Hawk, like the Snowy Owl, depends on the food supply, with larger clutches occurring in years when lemmings are abundant. On the wintering grounds, where it takes larger rodents and upland birds, it can be found in a variety of open habitats. At a distance, this hawk can be identified by its habit of hovering and by the way it perches—balancing precariously on the most slender twigs at the top of a tree. The species is named for its feathered legs.

DESCRIPTION: 19–24" (48–61 cm) long with an average wingspan of 4'4" (1.3 m). A large, long-winged hawk that often hovers. Its tail is white at the base with a dark terminal band. It has distinct light and dark morphs. A light-morph adult has a sandy-brown head and neck, a blackish belly, and dark "wrist" marks on the underside of the wing. All-dark forms can usually be identified by the underwing and tail pattern. Dark morphs are more common in the East, and there are few intermediate plumages.

VOICE: Loud or soft whistles, often in a descending scale.

NESTING: Lays 2–7 white eggs, speckled with brown and black, in a nest of moss and sticks placed on a cliff or rocky outcropping on the tundra.

HABITAT: Tundra; winters on open plains, agricultural areas, and marshes.

RANGE: Breeds in the Aleutians and northern Alaska east to Baffin Island, and south to northern Manitoba and Newfoundland. Winters from southern Canada and across the United States irregularly south to California, Texas, and Virginia. Also found in Eurasia.

SIMILAR SPECIES: See dark-morph Red-tailed, Ferruginous, and Swainson's hawks.

Red-tailed Hawk is broader-winged and stockier, with a white rump patch that is smaller than the white base of a Rough-legged's tail.

Ferruginous Hawk lacks a black belly.

CONSERVATION: 🦅 **LC**

Until the 1930s, farmers hunted Rough-legged Hawks, believing them to be a threat to their poultry. Once this practice ended, the hawk's numbers stabilized. Although population trends are difficult to monitor due to the Rough-legged Hawk's remote nesting grounds, local populations are known to fluctuate with prey availability; overall the species is stable and its numbers appear healthy.

FERRUGINOUS HAWK *Buteo regalis*

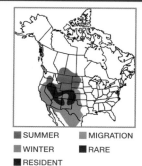

■ SUMMER ■ MIGRATION
■ WINTER ■ RARE
■ RESIDENT

The largest of the North American buteos, the Ferruginous Hawk is a long-winged, pale-headed bird that inhabits unbroken terrain in the Great Plains and arid intermountain regions of western Canada and the United States. Ferruginous Hawks, which feed mainly on prairie dogs and ground squirrels, lay more eggs when prey abounds, and fewer eggs in years when rodent populations decrease. They also take grasshoppers, birds, and lizards.

DESCRIPTION: 22½–25" (57–64 cm) long with an average wingspan of 4'8" (1.4 m). A large hawk. Light-morph adult is rufous above, mainly whitish below, with a rufous "wrist" patch and leg feathers, and black primary tips. The rare dark morph is deep rufous above and below, with a whitish tail. Its legs and feet are feathered down to the talons. Immatures resemble light-morph adults but with few or no rufous markings.

VOICE: A loud, descending *kree-e-ah*.

NESTING: Lays 3–5 white eggs, blotched or spotted with brown, in a nest of roots, sticks, sagebrush, cow dung, or even old cattle bones, placed in a tree or bush, or on a rocky hillside.

HABITAT: Prairies, brushy open country, and badlands.

RANGE: Breeds from Canadian prairie provinces south to eastern Oregon, Nevada, Arizona, New Mexico, and western Oklahoma. Winters in the southern half of the breeding range and in the southwestern states from central California to southwestern Texas into Mexico.

SIMILAR SPECIES: Pale Red-tailed Hawks are stockier, broader-winged, and lack chestnut-brown thighs. Light-morph Rough-legged Hawk has a dark belly and bold black wrist marks, and lacks chestnut-brown thighs. See also dark-morph Red-tailed, Swainson's, and Rough-legged hawks.

CONSERVATION: LC
Ferruginous Hawks are rebounding after a serious decline in the 20th century. These birds have benefited from modern conservation efforts, including sustainable ranching practices that maintain prairie-dog towns, and the introduction of artificial nesting platforms. Current threats to their habitats include urbanization, agriculture, grazing, small mammal control, mining, and wildfires.

■ SUMMER   ■ MIGRATION
■ WINTER   ■ RARE
■ RESIDENT

The distinctive Barn Owl is widespread and commonly found in open habitats such as prairie, farmland, savanna, marshland, and desert; it also occupies residential and urban areas. This nocturnal ghost of a bird frequents such places as belfries, deserted buildings, and hollow trees. A Barn Owl's diet consists mainly of rodents, especially voles; these birds are effective mousers and take many mice and rats. Owls do not digest fur and bone but periodically rid themselves of these in the form of regurgitated pellets. Barn Owl pellets are easily collected from roosts and can be a useful source of information about the small mammals in an area. Their large eyes give them especially good night vision, but Barn Owls depend more on their keen hearing to locate their prey.

DESCRIPTION: 18" (46 cm) long with an average wingspan of 3'8" (1.1 m). This crow-sized owl is buff-brown above and white below, with a heart-shaped face and numerous fine, dark dots on the white underparts. Its eyes are dark and it has long legs.

VOICE: Hissing notes, screams, guttural grunts, and bill snapping. Young give rapid grackle-like clicks.

NESTING: Lays 5–10 white eggs on bare wood or stone in buildings, hollow trees, caves, or even in burrows. When food is scarce, they lay fewer eggs or may not breed at all.

HABITAT: Open country, forest edges and clearings, cultivated areas, and cities.

RANGE: Resident from southern British Columbia, Dakotas, Michigan, and southern New England southward. Also in South America and Old World.

SIMILAR SPECIES: In the glare of a flashlight or headlights at night, a flying Barn Owl looks snow white and may be mistaken for a Snowy Owl.

CONVERSATION:

Barn Owls are uncommon but found on every continent except Antarctica. The fact that they are both nocturnal and reclusive makes it difficult to estimate their numbers accurately. Populations seem to have remained stable or slightly increased during the past few decades. They currently face habitat loss as rural areas undergo urban and suburban development.

FLAMMULATED OWL *Psiloscops flammeolus*

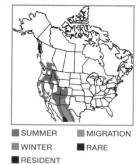

■ SUMMER　　■ MIGRATION
■ WINTER　　　■ RARE
■ RESIDENT

This small owl breeds in forests of the western mountains, especially ponderosa pine, where it may be locally common. This species is notoriously difficult to detect—by day, its cryptic coloration gives it exceptional camouflage, and its continuous, soft, low-pitched hooting call at night is deceptively tricky to pinpoint. As with other owls, during the breeding season the male Flammulated supplies food and protection, while the female is the chief nest-tender. Mice and similar prey are usually decapitated, the male feeding on the head, the female and young getting the softer body. Later the female leaves the nestlings and shares hunting duties with its mate.

DESCRIPTION: 6–7" (15–18 cm). Slightly larger than a sparrow; similar to but smaller than a Western Screech-Owl, with small indistinct ear tufts, rufous edges on the facial disks, and dark eyes rather than yellow. Most are grayish above, light below, with variegated black, white, and rust-colored markings; some birds exhibit a red morph with more extensive rusty reddish coloration. Both sexes look similar, but the female is larger than the male.

VOICE: A monotonous low hoot, single or double, repeated almost endlessly. These birds may sing nonstop for hours at a time from May to July.

NESTING: Lays 3 or 4 white eggs in a tree hollow or deserted woodpecker hole.

HABITAT: Coniferous woodlands and forest edges in the Northwest; dry ponderosa pine woods in the Southwest.

RANGE: Breeds in southern British Columbia south to southern California, Arizona, New Mexico, and western Texas. Winters south of the United States.

SIMILAR SPECIES: Western Screech-Owl and Whiskered Screech-Owl are larger with yellow eyes; both lack rufous scapular stripe and rufous on facial disk.

CONSERVATION: LC

There is little historical data on Flammulated Owl populations, but numbers appear to be in decline. As insect hunters, they are sensitive to pesticide use, and are also threatened by logging and other forms of habitat loss.

■ SUMMER   ■ MIGRATION
■ WINTER   ■ RARE
■ RESIDENT

This common owl favors oak and riparian woodlands of the West. The distinctive "bouncing ball" song is given by both sexes. Western Screech-Owls incubate each egg as it is laid— thus the eggs hatch in sequence and the young within a brood vary widely in size and age. This allows the parents to raise all their young if food is plentiful, or only the first few if food is scarce. This pattern is widespread among owls and birds of prey that feed on mice and meadow moles, whose populations fluctuate widely.

DESCRIPTION: 7–10" (18–25 cm). A small, mottled gray owl with ear tufts. Populations of Western Screech-Owl show clinal variation: birds from dry southwestern areas are usually pale gray; those from the humid coastal northwest are browner. Its eyes are yellow.

VOICE: An accelerating "bouncing ball" series of 6–8 low whistles, often dropping in pitch toward the end. Also gives a quick series on one pitch.

NESTING: Lays 4 or 5 white eggs in a natural cavity, a woodpecker's hole, or an artificial nest box.

HABITAT: Woodlands, coastal areas, orchards, and parks and yards with many trees.

RANGE: Resident from southeastern Alaska and British Columbia southward into Mexico and east throughout the U.S. Rockies.

SIMILAR SPECIES: See Flammulated Owl, Eastern and Whiskered screech-owls. Western Screech-Owl is nearly identical to the Eastern Screech-Owl of the East, and the two species overlap in a small part of western Texas and the Great Plains. The gray morph of the Eastern is almost identical to the Western but has a different call: a tremulous, descending wail.

CONSERVATION: Though Western Screech-Owls are widespread and common, they have experienced significant declines in the past few decades due to habitat loss. Their natural habitats tend to be prime real estate sites for residential development.

EASTERN SCREECH-OWL *Megascops asio*

■ SUMMER   ■ MIGRATION
■ WINTER   ■ RARE
■ RESIDENT

These common owls are fearless in defense of their nests and will often strike unsuspecting humans on the head as they pass nearby at night. When discovered during the day, they often freeze in an upright position, depending on their cryptic coloration to escape detection. The two color morphs, which vary in their relative numbers according to geography, are not based on age, sex, or season.

DESCRIPTION: 10" (25 cm). A small, mottled owl with prominent ear tufts and yellow eyes. Populations of Eastern Screech-Owl show clinal variation: northern birds tend to be larger and paler than their southern counterparts. Both rufous and gray color morphs occur, as well as brownish intermediates. Rufous-morph individuals are most common in the mid-Atlantic U.S. states and rare farther south and west.

VOICE: A tremulous, descending wail; soft purrs and trills.

NESTING: Lays 3–8 white eggs placed without a nest lining in a cavity in a tree or in a nest box.

HABITAT: Open deciduous woods, woodlots, suburban areas, lakeshores, and old orchards.

RANGE: Resident from Canada's southern prairie provinces east to southern Maine, and south to the Gulf of Mexico and Florida.

SIMILAR SPECIES: Western Screech-Owl occupies a mostly non-overlapping range and has almost no red morphs. In the tiny zone of overlap (Texas/southern Great Plains), voice is the only way to distinguish the gray forms of these two species.

CONSERVATION: Common and increasing, thanks in part to the bird's ability to adapt to the presence of humans. As a generalist, it is not picky about its food choices or nest sites. It readily accepts artificial nest boxes and can thrive in suburban settings where prey is plentiful and predators are few.

■ SUMMER ■ MIGRATION
■ WINTER ■ RARE
■ RESIDENT

This common owl of the oak canyons of southeastern Arizona is virtually indistinguishable from the Western Screech-Owl, except at night when its distinctive voice identifies it. Birders in the Tucson area make night trips to find this and many other species of owls in the nearby canyons and mountains. This species tends to prefer higher elevations than other screech-owls.

DESCRIPTION: 6½–8" (17–20 cm). Almost identical to Western Screech-Owl, but with longer bristles at the base of the bill, larger white spots on the upperparts, and heavier streaking on the breast. It is best identified by voice.

VOICE: A series of low whistles in a distinctive Morse code-like pattern: *hoo-hoo hooo hoo, hoo-hoo hooo hoo*, and so on. Also a rapid *hoohoohoohoo*.

NESTING: Lays 3 or 4 white spherical eggs in a deep tree cavity or a flicker hole.

HABITAT: Pine-oak woods, oaks, and sycamores.

RANGE: Resident in southern Arizona and southwestern New Mexico. Also in Central America.

SIMILAR SPECIES: See Flammulated Owl. Western Screech-Owl has a different voice.

CONSERVATION:  Although they have only a limited range in North America, their numbers are increasing.

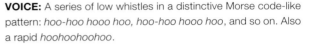

GREAT HORNED OWL *Bubo virginianus*

■ SUMMER ■ MIGRATION
■ WINTER ■ RARE
■ RESIDENT

The largest of American "eared" owls, the Great Horned is exceeded in size only by the rare Great Gray Owl. The Great Horned Owl preys on a wide variety of creatures, including grouse and rabbits as well as beetles, lizards, frogs, and birds, including crows, ducks, and other owls. On occasion, it even captures skunks. It is the largest and best known of the common owls. It is one of the first birds to nest, laying its eggs as early as late January, even when there is still snow on the ground.

DESCRIPTION: 25" (64 cm) long with an average wingspan of 4'7" (1.4 m). A large owl, varying in color from nearly white (in the Arctic) to dark brown and gray. It is mottled and streaked below, setting off the white throat; it has prominent, widely spaced ear tufts and yellow eyes.

VOICE: Series of low, sonorous, far-carrying hoots: *hoo, hoo-hoo, hoo, hoo*, with the second and third notes shorter than the others.

NESTING: Lays 2 or 3 white eggs on the bare surface of a cliff or cave or even on the ground; in the East it most often appropriates the unused stick nest of a heron, hawk, or crow.

HABITAT: Forests, deserts, open country, swamps, and even city parks.

RANGE: Resident throughout North America south of tree line.

SIMILAR SPECIES: Barred, Spotted, Great Gray, and Snowy owls all lack ear tufts. Long-eared Owl is much smaller; its ear tufts are set closer together, and the facial disks are deep chestnut-orange; and it has more boldly patterned belly markings.

CONSERVATION:
The Great Horned Owl population is stable. These adaptable birds take a wide variety of prey and can pose a threat to other species of concern, including other owls. Great Horned Owls were heavily hunted until the mid-20th century, and some illegal hunting persists. Pesticides and other toxic substances eaten by their prey can inadvertently poison these owls.

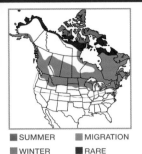

■ SUMMER ■ MIGRATION
■ WINTER   ■ RARE
■ RESIDENT

This great white owl is a beautiful sight perched upright or in flight. Strictly a bird of open country, it is practically never seen in a tree; it sits on the ground, a low perch, a rooftop, or other exposed resting place. In the Far North where it breeds, Snowy Owls depend largely on lemmings for food. The size of the lemming population periodically changes (due to population booms and subsequent crashes), and when lemming numbers decrease the owls wander farther southward in search of food. In southern latitudes, the owls prey on rabbits, rodents, and waterfowl, and sometimes on fish or carrion.

DESCRIPTION: 24" (61 cm) long with an average wingspan of 4'7" (1.4 m). A big, round-headed owl, ranging in color from pure white to white with dark spotting or barring. The female is larger and more heavily marked than the male, but the markings are variable enough that some birds are difficult to sex. Immature birds are the most heavily marked and the most likely to participate in these birds' periodic southward irruptions. Older adult males may be pure white.

VOICE: Usually silent; gives a hoarse croak and shrill whistle on breeding grounds.

NESTING: Lays 5–8 white eggs with a lining of feathers, mosses, and lichens placed on open tundra. It lays fewer eggs when food is scarce.

HABITAT: Open country: tundra, dunes, marshes, fields, plains, and airports in winter.

RANGE: Breeds in northern Alaska and in northernmost Canada. Winters south throughout Canada into the northern United States, irregularly farther south. Also found in Eurasia.

SIMILAR SPECIES: White-morph Gyrfalcon is slimmer, with a longer tail and more pointed wings.

Barn Owl is almost pure white below, but it has a heart-shaped facial disk and mottled golden-brown upperparts.

The arctic population of Great Horned Owl is whitish but has ear tufts and a bulkier body shape.

CONSERVATION: VU
The Snowy Owl is declining; some fluctuation of its population is natural, tied to lemming population cycles. Climate change, however, impacts their arctic habitat as well as the availability of their prey. Their breeding areas are remote from direct human contact, and they are protected from trapping and hunting when they winter closer to populated areas.

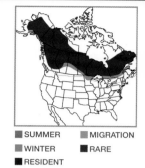

SUMMER ■ MIGRATION
WINTER ■ RARE
■ RESIDENT

In the northern domain of this fast-flying owl, the sun seldom sets during the summer half of the year. Adapted to these conditions, this is the most diurnal of all North American owls. It feeds on rodents—including mice and lemmings—that are active throughout the 24-hour day. In winter, when rodent runways are deep beneath the snow, it eats more birds, including grouse, than mammals. Because it does not depend on any one source of food, it is seldom subject to forced population shifts like other northern predators. Occasional winter wanderers may reach the northern tier of the United States and may stay for several weeks.

DESCRIPTION: 15–17" (38–43 cm) long with an average wingspan of 33" (84 cm). Smaller than a crow. A long-tailed, day-flying owl that behaves more like a hawk. It has a barred breast, and its facial disks have bold black borders.

VOICE: Whistling *ki-ki-ki-ki-ki-ki*, similar to call of a kestrel.

NESTING: Lays 3–7 white eggs in a tree cavity, in an abandoned bird's nest, or (rarely) on a cliff.

HABITAT: Clearings in boreal coniferous forest and muskeg.

RANGE: Resident from Alaska east to Labrador and south to British Columbia, Newfoundland, and the Gaspé Peninsula. May wander farther south in winter. Also found in Eurasia.

SIMILAR SPECIES: See Boreal Owl and Northern Goshawk.

CONSERVATION: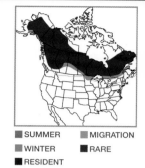

The Northern Hawk Owl population is widespread and stable, fluctuating somewhat with the boom-and-bust cycles of northern small mammal prey. Found in remote Arctic regions, this species rarely encounters human disturbance, but unsustainable logging of boreal forests can reduce available nesting sites and hunting perches.

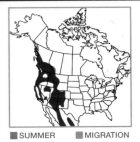

■ SUMMER ■ MIGRATION
■ WINTER ■ RARE
■ RESIDENT

This small owl sometimes hunts by day, attacking birds even larger than itself. In spring the male is conspicuous, uttering a staccato whistle every few seconds while flicking its long tail upward and sideways. In response, the small forest birds sound an excited alarm, scolding and mobbing this tiny owl, just as they would any larger owl.

DESCRIPTION: 7–7½" (18–19 cm). A sparrow-sized owl. It has a small, round head and a long, finely barred tail that is often held to one side. It is varying shades of brown with fine buff spotting above, and buff-white with bolder brown streaks below. Its eyes, bill, and feet are yellow. The back of the neck sports two false eyespots—white-edged black spots that suggest eyes in the back of its head. Regional populations vary slightly in color; Pacific birds are darker and more brown than Rocky Mountain birds of the interior West.

VOICE: A series of mellow whistles on one pitch. Also a thin rattle around the nest. Northern Pygmy-Owls from different regions give their calls in different rhythms, with Pacific birds usually giving single notes, Rocky Mountain birds mixing in a few paired notes, and Mexican populations (found in southeastern Arizona) giving mostly double notes.

NESTING: Lays 3–6 white eggs in an abandoned woodpecker hole.

HABITAT: Open coniferous forests or mixed aspen and oak woods; dense canyon growth.

RANGE: Resident from southeastern Alaska southward throughout most of the West.

SIMILAR SPECIES: See Ferruginous Pygmy-Owl. No other small, "earless," yellow-eyed owl has black nape patches, spotted upperparts, and a long, white-barred tail.

Flammulated Owl has dark eyes and a short tail.

Elf Owl has a short tail and indistinct streaking on the underparts; it lacks black nape patches.

Screech-owls are larger, stockier, short-tailed, and eared.

CONSERVATION: LC
Northern Pygmy-Owl is uncommon but increasing. Its biggest threats are the loss of dead trees in which to nest, and declines in western woodpecker populations, because the Northern Pygmy-Owl relies on woodpeckers to bore holes in trees for their nests.

FERRUGINOUS PYGMY-OWL *Glaucidium brasilianum*

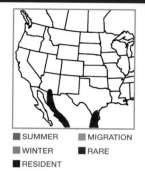

■ SUMMER   ■ MIGRATION
■ WINTER   ■ RARE
■ RESIDENT

The male Ferruginous calls incessantly in spring, at a rate of 90 to 150 times a minute. One is reported to have called for three solid hours. This tiny tropical owl is rare and local in the United States, and the small population around Tucson, Arizona, is a great attraction to bird watchers. Like the Northern Pygmy-Owl, the Ferruginous is both nocturnal and diurnal. It flies low to the ground and directly over short distances, with quick beats of its short wings. Upon landing, the bird often cocks its tail.

DESCRIPTION: 6½–7" (17–18 cm). Resembles the Northern Pygmy-Owl, but it is more rust-colored, with a rusty, faintly cross-barred tail and streaked flanks. Its crown is streaked with white, and its underparts are streaked with red-brown. It has false eyespots typical of pygmy-owls—white-bordered black patches on each side of nape that look like rear-facing "eyes."

VOICE: Monotonous, repeated, harsh *poip*; also whistles.

NESTING: Lays 3 or 4 white eggs in a hole in a saguaro cactus or a tree.

HABITAT: Saguaro desert; mesquite or dense streamside growth.

RANGE: Resident in southern Arizona and along the lower Rio Grande Valley of Texas. Also found in the American tropics.

SIMILAR SPECIES: Northern Pygmy-Owl has white lines on the tail, white spotting on the sides, and a different call. It generally does not overlap in range; in Arizona, Northern Pygmy-Owl is found primarily in mountain forests, and Ferruginous is found in lowland desert.

Elf Owl has a short tail and lacks nape patches.

CONSERVATION: LC

Widely distributed in Central and South America, but its numbers are decreasing. The Cactus Ferruginous Pygmy-Owl (subsp. *cactorum*) is on the U.S. Endangered Species List. It is classified as endangered in Arizona. Destruction of its habitat—by residential and industrial development, farming practices, livestock grazing, wood cutting, and other human practices—has been the greatest threat to this species. it is very rare in southern Arizona; greater numbers are found in Texas and Mexico.

■ SUMMER ■ MIGRATION
■ WINTER ■ RARE
■ RESIDENT

Elf Owl is the smallest owl species in the world. These wide-spread owls live in deserts, riparian areas, and oak and pine-oak woodlands near the Mexico border. It feeds almost exclusively on insects, catching them in the air or on the ground, but also takes mice and lizards. Hunting only at dusk or at night, Elf Owl hunts from a perch and swoops down onto prey to capture it with its feet.

DESCRIPTION: 5½" (14 cm). A tiny owl with a short tail, no ear tufts, and bright yellow eyes. It is grayish-brown above with buff mottling; its wings are grayish-brown with buff spots. Its scapulars form rows of large, whitish spots. It is whitish below with indistinct buff-brown streaking; the facial disks are pale reddish-brown or buff. White eyebrows extend to form whiskers.

VOICE: A rapid series of high-pitched notes, higher in the middle. The males sing loudly to establish breeding territories and attract females.

NESTING: Lays 3 white eggs in a deserted woodpecker hole in a cactus or an oak, pine, or other tree.

HABITAT: Deserts, dry open woodlands, and streamside thickets with trees.

RANGE: Breeds in southeastern California, southern Arizona, southwestern New Mexico, and the Rio Grande Valley of Texas. Winters in Mexico.

SIMILAR SPECIES: See Northern and Ferruginous pygmy-owls, Saw-whet Owl, and screech-owls; Flammulated Owl has dark eyes.

CONSERVATION:

Elf Owl numbers are decreasing along the North American southwest. Loss of habitat is considered the biggest threat to these birds, especially along the lower Colorado River and into south Texas.

BURROWING OWL *Athene cunicularia*

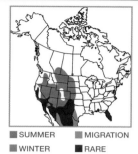

■ SUMMER   ■ MIGRATION
■ WINTER   ■ RARE
■ RESIDENT

This endearing bird is one of the most diurnal of all owls. It often perches on the ground near its hole; when approached too closely, it will bob up and down and finally dive into its burrow rather than take flight. It usually claims burrows that have been abandoned by prairie dogs or pocket gophers but is quite capable of digging its own.

DESCRIPTION: 9" (23 cm). A robin-sized terrestrial owl, short-tailed and long-legged. It has yellow eyes, no ear tufts, and a face framed in white, with a blackish collar. Both sexes are sandy-colored over the head, back, and wings, with barring on the breast and belly. Its exposed, sparsely feathered legs appear extremely long. Females are larger and usually appear darker than the males in the summer.

VOICE: Liquid cackling; also a mellow *coo-coooo*, repeated twice.

NESTING: Lays 7–10 white eggs in a long underground burrow lined with grasses, roots, and dung.

HABITAT: Plains, deserts, fields, and airports.

RANGE: Breeds from Canada's southern prairie provinces south throughout the western United States to southern California and Texas. Winters in the southwestern states. Resident in central and southern Florida. Also found in tropical America.

SUBSPECIES: The Florida population (subsp. *floridana*) is darker above with a narrower band of white on the face compared to Western Burrowing Owls (subsp. *hypugaea*).

SIMILAR SPECIES: Unmistakable. Most other owls are closely associated with trees, whereas Burrowing Owls are terrestrial, found in open, treeless expanses such as grasslands, prairies, deserts, and farmland.

CONSERVATION: 🦉 LC

Although still numerous, the Burrowing Owl population is decreasing. Their greatest threats are habitat loss and control programs that reduce populations of burrowing animals such as prairie dogs, gophers, and ground squirrels, which create the burrows in which these owls nest. These birds face other human-made hazards such as vehicle strikes, pesticides, and domestic cats and dogs.

- ■ SUMMER
- ■ WINTER
- ■ RESIDENT
- ■ MIGRATION
- ■ RARE

This large and secretive rodent eater, rare in much of the West, lives in dense stands of mature forests. The cutting of old-growth forest has been followed by the disappearance of the Spotted Owl, and the conflict between conservationists and the timber industry in the Pacific Northwest has become a political flashpoint.

DESCRIPTION: 16½–19" (42–48 cm). A medium-sized owl with a rounded head without ear tufts. Its upperparts are dark brown with white spots; its underparts are white and heavily barred with brown; it has dark eyes.

VOICE: Gives 2 or 3 short barking hoots followed by a louder, more prolonged *hooo-ah*.

NESTING: Lays 2 or 3 white eggs, usually in a natural tree or canyon wall cavity or an abandoned hawk's nest.

HABITAT: Old-growth coniferous forests, densely wooded canyons.

RANGE: Resident from southwestern British Columbia to southern California; also in the mountains of Utah and Colorado south to Arizona, New Mexico, and western Texas.

SUBSPECIES: Northern Spotted Owl (subsp. *caurina*) in the Pacific Northwest is the largest and darkest of these owls, with smaller white spots. It and the California Spotted Owl (subsp. *occidentalis*), which occurs farther south along the West Coast, frequent old-growth conifer forests including redwoods and Douglas-firs. The Mexican Spotted Owl (subsp. *lucida*) found in the interior West tends to favor oak and conifer forests in canyons in the shade of rocky cliffs.

SIMILAR SPECIES: Barred Owl is paler and grayer, with streaks (not bars) on breast and belly.

CONSERVATION: NT

Declining as a result of habitat loss; this species requires undisturbed, old-growth forest. Spotted Owls may reoccupy forests that are selectively logged—leaving behind large trees with cavities, snags, and woody debris—only after several decades. Unfortunately for the owls, these mature old-growth forests tend to have a high commercial value for residential development and for the logging and mining industries. Spotted Owls also may be displaced by or hybridize with Barred Owls, and are preyed upon by large raptors including Northern Goshawks and Great Horned Owls. Two of the three subspecies of Spotted Owl occurring in the U.S.—the Northern Spotted Owl and the Mexican Spotted Owl—are on the U.S. Endangered Species List. The Northern Spotted Owl is classified as threatened in California, Oregon, and Washington.

■ SUMMER ■ MIGRATION
■ WINTER ■ RARE
■ RESIDENT

This owl is most often seen by those who seek it out in its dark retreat, usually a thick grove of trees in lowland forest. There it rests quietly during the day. It sometimes calls in the daytime and if disturbed will fly easily from one grove of trees to another. It emerges at night to feed on rodents, birds, frogs, and crayfish. In recent years, this owl has been expanding its range in the Northwest.

DESCRIPTION: 20" (51 cm) long with an average wingspan of 3'8" (1.1 m). A large, stocky, dark-eyed owl. It is gray-brown with cross-barring on the neck and breast, and has vertical streaks on the belly. It lacks ear tufts. Barred Owls have short, broad wings and move easily through the forest on slow wingbeats.

VOICE: A loud barking *hoo, hoo, hoo-hoo; hoo, hoo; hoo, hooo-aw!* and a variety of other barking calls and screams.

NESTING: Lays 2–4 white eggs in an unlined cavity in a hollow tree or (rarely) an abandoned building; sometimes in an old crow's nest.

HABITAT: Low, wet woods and swampy forests.

RANGE: Breeds from British Columbia, Alberta, Quebec, and Nova Scotia south to northern California and throughout the East to Texas and Florida.

SIMILAR SPECIES: Great Gray Owl is larger and has yellow eyes and a prominent white "mustache."

Spotted Owl is darker and richer brown, with a spotted belly.

CONSERVATION: LC

Barred Owl numbers are increasing as they expand their range from the East Coast to the Pacific Northwest, where they compete with the Spotted Owl. These birds prefer old-growth forest with large, dead trees for nesting, which leaves them sensitive to deforestation.

■ SUMMER ■ MIGRATION
■ WINTER ■ RARE
■ RESIDENT

North America's largest owl. Like other owls of the Far North, this species hunts during the day, often watching for prey from a low perch. Because it spends much of its time in dense conifers, it is often overlooked. One of the most elusive of birds, European explorers discovered the Great Gray in America before they realized that the species also occurs in Europe.

DESCRIPTION: 24–33" (61–84 cm) long with an average wingspan of 5' (1.5 m). It is a huge, dusky gray owl with yellow eyes, large facial disks, and no ear tufts. It has a distinctive black chin spot bordered by white patches that resembles a bowtie. Barred and Spotted owls are smaller, stockier, and browner, with dark eyes.

VOICE: Deep, booming *whoo*, repeated 10 times or more, and gradually descending the scale.

NESTING: Lays 2–5 white eggs in a bulky nest of sticks in a dense conifer.

HABITAT: Coniferous forests and muskeg.

RANGE: Resident from Alaska and across interior Canada south to northern California, northern Wyoming, Minnesota, and Quebec. In winter it wanders rarely southward into northern New England and the Great Lakes region. Also found in Eurasia.

SIMILAR SPECIES: Barred and Spotted owls also large and "earless," but have dark eyes, are smaller, and lack the white "bowtie."

CONSERVATION:

Uncommon to rare. As residents of remote northern sections of Canada and the Arctic region, the Great Gray Owl numbers are increasing. The primary threats to these owls are human disturbance and loss of habitat to development.

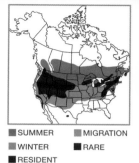

■ SUMMER ■ MIGRATION
■ WINTER ■ RARE
■ RESIDENT

Although these woodland owls are gregarious in winter, they are so quiet during the day that up to a dozen may inhabit a dense evergreen grove without being detected. They have a tendency to roost near the trunk of a tree, and because they elongate themselves by compressing their feathers, they resemble part of the trunk itself. Only by peering intently upward can one detect the round face and telltale long ear tufts. A good way to locate an owl roost is to search in pine woods for groups of pellets on the ground. These regurgitated bundles of undigested fur and bones provide an excellent indication of the bird's food habits.

DESCRIPTION: 15" (38 cm) long with an average wingspan of 3'3" (1 m). A slender, crow-sized owl with long ear tufts set close together. It is heavily mottled brown with chestnut facial disks. The boldly patterned belly feathers are cross-hatched and have conspicuous, dark vertical markings. The flanks and wing linings are tawny, as are the bases to most feathers. Its eyes are orange. Its buoyant, erratic flight is somewhat like that of a moth or butterfly.

VOICE: Soft low hoots; also whistles, whines, shrieks, and cat-like meows. Seldom heard except during breeding time.

NESTING: Lays 4 or 5 white eggs in a deserted crow, hawk, or squirrel nest.

HABITAT: Deciduous and coniferous forests.

RANGE: Breeds from central British Columbia, southern Mackenzie, and Quebec south to California, Arkansas, and Virginia. Winters in the southern part of the breeding range and in the southern tier of the United States. Also found in Eurasia.

SIMILAR SPECIES: Great Horned Owl is much larger with a white throat patch and widely spaced ear tufts.

Screech-owls are smaller and chunkier.

In flight, Short-eared Owl has a pale band on the trailing edge of the flight feathers and a buff patch at the base of the primaries; it lacks the prominent ear tufts.

CONSERVATION: LC

Although still fairly common across North America, the Long-eared Owl is believed to be decreasing slightly; populations fluctuate locally and are difficult to monitor because of their nomadic movements and secretive nature. Habitat loss is considered their biggest threat, especially the loss of riparian, grassland, and other open habitats to development.

■ SUMMER   ■ MIGRATION
■ WINTER   ■ RARE
■ RESIDENT

This owl is most commonly seen late in the afternoon as it begins to move about in preparation for a night of hunting. It can often be identified at a great distance by its habit of hovering; its flight is erratic and bounding. Occasionally several birds may be seen at once, an indication that small rodents are especially numerous.

DESCRIPTION: 16" (41 cm). A crow-sized, long-winged owl of open country. Its short ear tufts are rarely visible. The relatively small facial disks and short, thick neck give this species a stout, blunt-headed look. The dark brown upperparts are heavily mottled with buff spots and bars; the neck and upper breast are streaked with dark brown. The belly and flanks are buff with distinct, neat, dark stripes. The tawny facial disks have dark centers surrounding the bright yellow eyes. A prominent pale buff patch contrasts with the dark upperwing. The best characteristic in flight is the pale band that extends along the trailing edge of all but the outermost flight feathers. In its buoyant, loose flight, the Short-eared Owl bounds from side to side with frequent glides on wings angled forward, slightly ahead of the body.

VOICE: Usually silent; on nesting grounds, a variety of barks, hisses, and squeals.

NESTING: Lays 5–7 white eggs in a grass-lined depression on the ground, often concealed in weeds or beneath a bush.

HABITAT: Freshwater and salt marshes; open grasslands, prairies, and dunes; open country generally during migration.

RANGE: Breeds from Alaska across Canada south locally to California, Kansas, and New Jersey. Winters in the southern part of the breeding range and south throughout the United States to Central America. Also found in South America and most of the Old World.

SUBSPECIES: Short-eared Owls seen in the Florida Keys and Dry Tortugas are likely the West Indian subspecies, the Caribbean Short-eared Owl (*A. f. domingensis*). These owls

are smaller than their northern kin, with darker scapulars, dark uppertail coverts rather than pale, and finer streaks below.

SIMILAR SPECIES: Barn Owl is paler, with unstreaked lower parts and a white, heart-shaped face.

Long-eared Owl in flight has dark, grayer upperwings that lack a pale trailing edge; the orangish patch at the base of the primaries is less conspicuous than in Short-eared Owl. Its ear tufts are much longer and more prominent, and its underside is more mottled and cross-barred rather than vertically streaked.

CONSERVATION:
Although fairly common, the Short-eared Owl population is declining, especially in the southern regions of North America. The cause for their decreasing numbers is thought to be loss of habitat as development, agriculture, livestock grazing, and other factors have fragmented the long stretches of open grassland these owls require.

BOREAL OWL *Aegolius funereus*

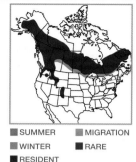

■ SUMMER ■ MIGRATION
■ WINTER ■ RARE
■ RESIDENT

This small, secretive owl is considered one of the rarest winter visitors from the North. Normally a bird of boreal forests, it irregularly irrupts south of its normal range in response to prey scarcity. Its retiring habits cause it to be overlooked, and it is easily confused with its more common relative, the Northern Saw-whet Owl. It is entirely nocturnal, spending the day concealed in dense spruce or a hollow tree. It preys mainly on rodents.

DESCRIPTION: 9–12" (23–30 cm) long with an average wingspan of 24" (61 cm). A rare, robin-sized owl without ear tufts. It is brown with white spots above, and rust-streaked below. It is similar to Northern Saw-whet Owl but larger, with dark borders on the facial disks, more spotting on the upperparts, a spotted (not streaked) forehead, and a yellow (not dark) bill.

VOICE: Rapid series of whistled notes.

NESTING: Lays 4–6 white eggs placed in a woodpecker hole or other tree cavity or in the abandoned nest of another bird.

HABITAT: Boreal coniferous forests and muskeg.

RANGE: Breeds in Alaska, Yukon, Saskatchewan, Manitoba, Quebec, Labrador, and Newfoundland south to northern British Columbia, Colorado (in the Rocky Mountains), southern Manitoba, Ontario, and New Brunswick. In winter it wanders rarely south to the northern tier of the United States. Also found in Eurasia.

SIMILAR SPECIES: Northern Saw-whet Owl is somewhat smaller, and lacks an obvious dark frame around the face; it has a rounder head and a darker bill.

Screech-owls also have black facial frames; with their ear tufts flattened, they may resemble Boreal.

Northern Hawk Owl has a similar face pattern but is larger, with heavy barring below.

CONSERVATION: LC

Although its secretive nature and boreal range make surveys difficult, the Boreal Owl population is believed to be stable, especially in the northern part of its range across Canada.

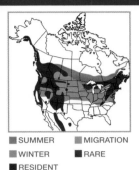

- ■ SUMMER ■ MIGRATION
- ■ WINTER ■ RARE
- ■ RESIDENT

A common resident of boreal and montane forests, Northern Saw-whet Owls are almost entirely nocturnal, spending the day roosting quietly in dense foliage. At such times, they are extraordinarily patient and allow for prolonged viewing, but they are small and difficult to see. In winter, it will roost for days at a time at the same location. At night, this tiny owl becomes a rapacious hunter, preying on large insects, mice, and other small rodents. Although widespread in Canada and all of the northern and western United States, its distribution is spotty. This pattern may be attributable to uneven or inadequate food supplies in areas with severe winter conditions.

DESCRIPTION: 7" (18 cm). A small, yellow-eyed owl with no ear tufts. It is brown above, with white streaks on the forehead, a dark bill, and a short tail. Juveniles are chocolate-brown above, buff below, with a white triangle on the forehead extending between the eyes. See Boreal Owl.

VOICE: Usually silent; in late winter and spring, it utters a monotonous series of tooting whistles. The bird gets its name from its song, which settlers likened to a whetstone sharpening a saw.

NESTING: Lays 5 or 6 white eggs placed without a nest lining in a deserted woodpecker hole or natural cavity.

HABITAT: Coniferous woodlands; in winter, also in evergreen thickets in parks, gardens, and estates; also isolated pines.

RANGE: Breeds from southeastern Alaska, Manitoba, and Nova Scotia south to southern California, Arizona, Illinois, North Carolina (in mountains), and Connecticut. Winters in breeding range and south to Arkansas and North Carolina.

SUBSPECIES: A distinctive subspecies, *A. a. brooksi*, lives on Haida Gwaii (formerly Queen Charlotte Islands) off the north Pacific coast of Canada. These birds are much darker than the mainland population, with a buffy wash on the underparts and face and white only above the eyes.

SIMILAR SPECIES: See Boreal Owl.

Flammulated Owl has dark eyes.

Elf Owl is smaller.

Northern and Ferruginous pygmy-owls also have smaller heads and less obvious facial disks.

CONVERSATION: LC
Although widespread and common, this species has declined slightly in recent decades. Habitat loss is the main threat to the Northern Saw-whet Owl, as mature forests with dead wood are lost to logging and development. These owls can breed successfully in many forest types, and have shown a willingness to accept artificial nest boxes, which can help with conservation efforts. Climate change also may negatively affect these birds, especially in the southern part of their range.

ELEGANT TROGON *Trogon elegans*

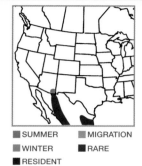

■ SUMMER ■ MIGRATION
■ WINTER ■ RARE
■ RESIDENT

The Elegant Trogon is the only member of its family that regularly occurs north of Mexico. In southeastern Arizona, it is found in oak or pine-oak-covered mountain canyons and in sycamore, walnut, and cottonwood trees along canyon streams. Finding the Elegant Trogon is a rare treat for birders that have long been drawn to southeastern Arizona by the chance to glimpse this rare, exotic-looking, tropical bird whose range barely extends into the United States. Trogons are insectivorous, but their diet also includes small fruits.

DESCRIPTION: 11–12" (28–30 cm). Unmistakable. A jay-sized bird with a stout yellow bill, upright posture, and a long, square-cut tail. The male has glossy, dark emerald-green upperparts, head, and upper breast; a white breast band; and a crimson belly and undertail coverts. Its copper-red tail has a black terminal band, but viewed from below it is gray with broad white bars. The female is plain brown where the male is green, with a white patch on the cheek; she is pink where the male is crimson, with white and light coffee-colored bands on the breast.

VOICE: A loud but hard-to-locate *ko-ah ko-ah ko-ah* or *kum! kum! kum!*

NESTING: Lays 3 or 4 white eggs in an unlined woodpecker hole, termite nest, or other cavity.

HABITAT: Thick deciduous mountain growth; sycamore canyons.

RANGE: Breeds in southeastern Arizona. A few winter there, but most cross into Mexico. Also found in Central America.

SIMILAR SPECIES: Eared Quetzal (extremely rare in Arizona) is larger, has a black bill, and lacks a white collar. Its tail is blue rather than coppery, and the underside of its tail is not vermiculated, but rather mostly white.

CONSERVATION: The Elegant Trogon's population status is difficult to determine, although they may have increased slightly in southeastern Arizona. They remain rare there, with perhaps a few dozen nesting pairs north of Mexico. Throughout its range, loss of habitat due to destruction of riparian forests can lead to fewer nesting sites for these tropical birds.

This rare vagrant to southeastern Arizona tends to forage more actively and higher in trees than Elegant Trogon; in fall, it is especially attracted to fruiting madrone trees. Its "ears" are wispy plumes behind the eyes, difficult to see in the field.

DESCRIPTION: 14" (36 cm) long with an average wingspan of 24" (61 cm). The male has a rich green head, neck, shoulders, and upper breast. The female's head and breast are mostly brownish. Both have a vivid rose-red belly and a broad tail with a mostly white underside. This species is noticeably larger than the Elegant Trogon, with a thicker body.

VOICE: Its song is a series of tremulous whistles, increasing in volume. Calls include a squeaky, tenuous, rising *weee* or *suwee*, usually closing with a sharp *KT!*; a high, quavering Blue Jay-like *kee-yah*, repeated in rapid series on one pitch; and a harsh, rattling, descending *krr-krr-krr*.

NESTING: Nests in tree cavities in pine-oak forests.

HABITAT: Montane pine forests.

RANGE: The Eared Quetzal range runs primarily along the mountainous regions of Mexico. Casual in southeastern Arizona, especially in the Huachuca Mountains.

SIMILAR SPECIES: See Elegant Trogon.

CONSERVATION: Eared Quetzal numbers are stable in their native range in Mexico.

RINGED KINGFISHER *Megaceryle torquata*

SUMMER · MIGRATION
WINTER · RARE
RESIDENT

The Ringed Kingfisher is the largest of the three species of king-fishers in North America, where it is found only on the lower Rio Grande in Texas. Its habits are like those of the widespread Belted Kingfisher.

DESCRIPTION: 13" (33 cm). Pigeon-sized. It is similar to Belted Kingfisher but larger, and with more chestnut on the belly. It has a bushy crest and a large, dagger-shaped bill. It is blue-gray above and chestnut below with a white collar. The female is similar but has a gray band across the upper breast.

VOICE: A harsh rattle, louder than that of Belted Kingfisher. Also a loud *kleck*.

NESTING: Lays 5–7 white eggs in a burrow in a sandbank.

HABITAT: Tree-lined rivers, streams, and lakes.

RANGE: Resident from extreme southern Texas to southern South America.

SIMILAR SPECIES: See Belted Kingfisher.

CONSERVATION: LC
Tropical birds found along coastal areas of Mexico and into South America, Ringed Kingfishers are increasing and their range has extended into Texas.

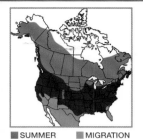

■ SUMMER ■ MIGRATION
■ WINTER ■ RARE
■ RESIDENT

While searching for fish, the familiar Belted Kingfisher perches conspicuously on a limb over a river or lake. Upon sighting a fish, it flies from its post and hovers like a tern over the water before plunging after its prey. In addition to fish, it may eat crabs, crayfish, salamanders, lizards, mice, and insects. Often a kingfisher patrols a regular beat along a stream or lakeshore, stopping at favorite exposed perches along the way. When flying from one perch to another, often a good distance apart, it utters its loud rattling call.

DESCRIPTION: 13" (33 cm). A dove-sized bird, blue-gray above, white below, with a bushy crest and a dagger-like bill. The male has a blue-gray breast band; the female is similar but also has a chestnut belly band.

VOICE: A loud, penetrating rattle, given on the wing and when perched.

NESTING: Lays 5–8 white eggs in an unlined chamber at the end of a tunnel up to 8' (2.5 m) long, dug in a sand or gravel bank.

HABITAT: Rivers, lakes, and saltwater estuaries.

RANGE: Breeds from Alaska eastward across southern Canada and south throughout most of the United States. It winters on the Pacific Coast north to southeastern Alaska, and throughout the South north to the Great Lakes and along the Atlantic Coast to New England.

SIMILAR SPECIES: Near the Mexican border, see Green Kingfisher.

Ringed Kingfisher is much larger and mostly rufous below; it shows a more conspicuous white collar.

CONSERVATION:
Widespread throughout North America, Belted Kingfisher numbers are stable. Because they nest in earthen banks, human-made sand and gravel pits provide additional nesting sites, but they may abandon territories following repeated human disturbance.

GREEN KINGFISHER *Chloroceryle americana*

■ SUMMER ■ MIGRATION
■ WINTER ■ RARE
■ RESIDENT

The smallest of the three kingfisher species found in North America, these birds may be observed in southern Texas and southeastern Arizona near shaded, forest-fringed pools and streams of clear water, where they sit for long periods on a low limb overhanging water until they spot a minnow or other small fish. They then plunge into the water after their prey. At other times, when at a considerable distance from water, they feed on small lizards or grasshoppers.

DESCRIPTION: 8" (20 cm). A starling-sized kingfisher with a long, dagger-like bill. It is dark glossy green above and white below. The male has a broad rufous breast band; the female has a green breast band. Both sexes have a white collar.

VOICE: An insect-like buzz; also low clicking notes.

NESTING: Lays 4–6 white eggs in a cavity at the end of a burrow dug in a sandy bank.

HABITAT: Woodland streams and pools.

RANGE: Resident from extreme southern Texas south into the tropics. Straggles to western Texas and southern Arizona, where it may nest locally.

SIMILAR SPECIES: Belted Kingfisher is larger, blue-gray above, and conspicuously crested; it lacks the white outer tail feathers that flash in flight.

CONSERVATION: Green Kingfishers are increasing and their range is expanding north out of Mexico into southern Arizona. Their numbers may be declining in parts of southern Texas with the loss of streamside habitats.

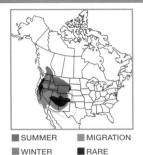

■ SUMMER ■ MIGRATION
■ WINTER ■ RARE
■ RESIDENT

Unlike most woodpeckers, Lewis's does not peck at wood for food and is seen more often on top of a fence post than clinging to it vertically. As with the Acorn Woodpecker, one of its methods of getting food is catching flying insects; both species also store acorns and other nuts for winter, and sometimes damage fruit orchards. Lewis's is the common woodpecker of mountain ranchlands, and some ranchers call it the "Crow Woodpecker" because of its dark color, large size, and slow flight.

DESCRIPTION: 10½–11½" (27–29 cm). Smaller than a flicker. It is metallic greenish black above; it has a gray collar and breast, a pinkish-red belly, and a dark red face framed with greenish black. The sexes are alike. Its flight is crow-like, not undulating.

VOICE: Usually silent, but occasionally gives a low churring note.

NESTING: Lays 6–8 white eggs in a cavity in a dead stump or tree limb, often at a considerable height. Nests in loose colonies.

HABITAT: Open pine-oak woodlands, oak or cottonwood groves in grasslands, and ponderosa pine country.

RANGE: Breeds from southern British Columbia and Alberta south to central California, northern Arizona, and northern New Mexico. Winters from southern British Columbia and Oregon to Colorado and south to northern Mexico; wanders east to the Great Plains.

SIMILAR SPECIES: Adults are unmistakable. Immature sapsuckers and Red-headed Woodpeckers lack reddish coloring on the belly; they have white patches or marks on the upperparts and wings.

CONSERVATION: Lewis's Woodpecker numbers have decreased somewhat as a result of changes to North America's western forests—notably the reduction in dead or decaying trees available for nesting—resulting from fire suppression efforts, logging, grazing, and climate change.

RED-HEADED WOODPECKER *Melanerpes erythrocephalus*

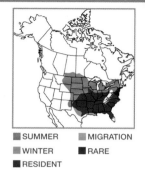

■ SUMMER ■ MIGRATION
■ WINTER ■ RARE
■ RESIDENT

These woodpeckers are fond of open agricultural country with groves of dead and dying trees, particularly orchards. They often flycatch, swooping low across a highway or along the shoulder of a road after flying insects. They store nuts and acorns, hiding them in holes and crevices. Red-headed Woodpeckers frequently are driven off by aggressive European Starlings, which occupy their nest holes, and by the removal of dead trees.

DESCRIPTION: 10" (25 cm). This woodpecker's whole head is red. Its wings and tail are bluish black, with a large white patch on each wing; it has white underparts and shows a conspicuous white rump in flight. The immature resembles an adult, but has a brown head and two dark bars across the white wing patch.

VOICE: A loud *churr-churr* and *yarrow-yarrow-yarrow*.

NESTING: Lays 5 white eggs placed without nest lining in a cavity in a tree, utility pole, or fence post.

HABITAT: Open country, farms, rural roads, open park-like woodlands, and golf courses.

RANGE: Breeds from Saskatchewan, Manitoba, and Quebec south to Florida and the Gulf Coast. It formerly bred in the northeastern United States but now is scarce there, appearing as a fall vagrant. Winters in the southern part of its breeding range.

SIMILAR SPECIES: Adults are unmistakable. Immatures resemble young sapsuckers, but have a white patch on the rear of the wings, and a contrasting brown upper breast and whitish lower breast.

CONSERVATION: LC

The Red-headed Woodpecker population is decreasing across its range. They are vulnerable to loss of habitat as dead wood and nut-producing trees become less available. Competition with aggressive, introduced European Starlings for nest holes has also contributed to their decline. Because they forage for flying insects by swooping into road clearings, these woodpeckers are often struck by vehicles.

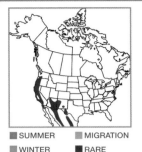

■ SUMMER ■ MIGRATION
■ WINTER ■ RARE
■ RESIDENT

This well-named woodpecker harvests acorns and, in agricultural or suburban areas, almonds and walnuts as well. In fall, the birds store their crop of nuts tightly in individual holes so that no squirrel can pry them out. The storage trees are usually mature or dead pines or Douglas-firs with thick, soft bark, but dead oak branches and fence posts are also used. The holes made by a colony are used year after year. Acorns seem to be emergency provisions; on mild winter days these birds catch flying insects.

DESCRIPTION: 8–9½" (20–24 cm). The male has a yellowish-white forecrown; a red crown; light eyes; and a black nape, back, wings, and tail. Its chin is black and the throat and sides of the head are yellowish white. The breast and flanks are whitish with heavy dark streaking, and it has a white belly, wing patches, and rump. The female has a black forecrown and is otherwise identical to the male.

VOICE: A loud *ja-cob, ja-cob* or *wake-up, wake-up*.

NESTING: Lays 4 or 5 white eggs in a hole in a tree. Nests in colonies, with all members of the colony sharing in excavating holes—mostly in dead oak branches—feeding young, and possibly incubating.

HABITAT: Open oak and pine-oak forests.

RANGE: Resident from southern Oregon south through California, and in Arizona, New Mexico, and western Texas. Also found in the American tropics.

SIMILAR SPECIES: Red-headed and White-headed woodpeckers are similar but have red and white heads, respectively. Pileated Woodpecker is larger, with a striped face and red crest on the head.

CONSERVATION:

Acorn Woodpeckers are common and slightly increasing across the California coast and the Southwest in suitable habitat. Although loss of oak and pine-oak habitat—especially due to overgrazing and development—is a threat to these birds, they are adaptable and may colonize residential areas, roosting and storing acorns in artificial structures. Introduced European Starlings have been known to take over these woodpeckers' nests.

GILA WOODPECKER *Melanerpes uropygialis*

■ SUMMER ■ MIGRATION
■ WINTER ■ RARE
■ RESIDENT

The Gila Woodpecker is a characteristic bird of the Sonoran Desert—the Southwestern counterpart of the closely related Golden-fronted and Red-bellied woodpeckers. Like the Elf Owl and the Gilded Flicker, it nests in holes in giant saguaro cacti. It feeds in trees, cacti, and bushes, as well as on the ground and at feeders, eating all manner of insects, worms, and fruit; it will also feed on lizards and the eggs of other birds. This species excavates nesting and roosting holes in cacti and various trees. Vocal and conspicuous, Gila Woodpeckers are often seen in the open, perching on cacti and trees, or flying in the open with an undulating flight. This bird frequently gives a bowing display with accompanying calls.

DESCRIPTION: 8–10" (20–25 cm). The larger, longer-billed male has a red patch on the crown not seen in the female. Both sexes have a pale forehead; the rest of the head and most of the underparts are an unpatterned gray-tan. The belly is golden-yellow, and the flanks are barred. The upperparts are barred with black and buff-white or white, including most of the wings and the center of the tail; the outer tail feathers and most of the primaries are black, with a small white wing patch visible in flight. Immatures are duller but recognizable as Gila Woodpeckers.

VOICE: A rolling *churrr*.

NESTING: Lays 3–5 white eggs in a hole in a giant saguaro or a tree.

HABITAT: Low desert scrub with saguaro or mesquite trees for nesting.

RANGE: Resident in southeastern California, southern Nevada, Arizona, and New Mexico.

SIMILAR SPECIES: Ladder-backed Woodpecker has a black-and-white striped face and streaky underparts. Flickers are brown- and black-barred above with spotted underparts and a different head pattern. Both lack Gila's wing patch.

The ranges of the similar Golden-fronted and Red-bellied woodpeckers do not overlap with Gila Woodpecker.

CONSERVATION: LC
Gila Woodpecker numbers remain stable in Arizona and across most of its southwestern range, although it has declined in California. The biggest threats to these birds are habitat loss, especially from development in the Sonoran Desert, and European Starling nest invasions.

■ SUMMER ■ MIGRATION
■ WINTER ■ RARE
■ RESIDENT

This familiar woodpecker is common in the parks and shade trees of Texas towns and cities. Conspicuous and vocal, it feeds on a great array of fruits, berries, seeds, corn, nuts (including acorns), and various insects that it sometimes takes by flycatching. Its other habits are similar to those of the closely related Red-bellied and Gila woodpeckers. The species name *aurifrons* is Latin for "gold-fronted"—a reference to the golden tinge on the belly that is difficult to see in the field.

DESCRIPTION: 9½" (24 cm). Gold or orange on the nape with a gold nasal patch, the Golden-fronted Woodpecker is barred with black and white on the back, wings, and central tail. The face and underparts are tan-gray with a buffy belly tinged with gold (difficult to see in the field) and some barring on the flanks and belly. The rump and a small wing patch are white. Males have a rectangular red crown patch that is lacking in females. Immatures sufficiently resemble the adults to be recognizable as Golden-fronteds.

VOICE: Loud *churrrr*. Its call is a burry *chuck-chuck-chuck*.

NESTING: Lays 4 or 5 white eggs in holes in mesquite trees, poles, and posts.

HABITAT: Open woods in dry country and river bottoms with trees.

RANGE: Resident in southwestern Oklahoma and central Texas.

SIMILAR SPECIES: In Texas and Oklahoma where its range overlaps that of Golden-fronted, Red-bellied Woodpecker is distinguished by its red nape; Golden-fronted's gold belly, if visible, is a useful trait, as is the yellow patch at the base of the bill.

CONSERVATION: Once persecuted as pests for their tendency to drill into utility poles, Golden-fronted Woodpecker numbers declined in the 20th century but are now stable.

RED-BELLIED WOODPECKER *Melanerpes carolinus*

SUMMER ▪ MIGRATION
WINTER ▪ RARE
RESIDENT

A common woodpecker over much of the eastern United States. The Red-bellied Woodpecker is a vocal, conspicuous bird often seen at bird-feeding stations and in various wooded areas, especially wet woodlands, pinewoods, parks, orchards, and gardens. Like most woodpeckers, it is beneficial, consuming large numbers of wood-boring beetles as well as grasshoppers, ants, and other insect pests. It also feeds on acorns, beechnuts, and wild fruits. It is one of the woodpeckers that habitually stores food.

DESCRIPTION: 10" (25 cm). It is barred black and white above, and pale buff below and on the face. The sexes are similar except that the male has a red crown and nape, and the female has a red nape only. The reddish patch on the lower abdomen for which it is named is seldom visible in the field.

VOICE: *Chuck-chuck-chuck*, descending in pitch. Also a loud, often repeated *churrrr*.

NESTING: Lays 4 or 5 white eggs in a tree cavity, often at the edge of woodlands.

HABITAT: Open and swampy woodlands; comes into parks during migration and to feeders in winter.

RANGE: Breeds from South Dakota, the Great Lakes, and southern New England south to the Gulf Coast and Florida. These birds are mostly resident, but local populations move around in response to the availability of food.

SIMILAR SPECIES: In most of its range, a barred back distinguishes the Red-bellied from other woodpeckers. Red-cockaded and Ladder-backed woodpeckers have facial markings and side spotting; they lack the white rump, white wing patch, and red belly. Golden-fronted Woodpecker also occurs in central Texas; it has a gold or orange nape and hindcrown, gold nasal tufts, and a gold belly.

CONSERVATION: LC

Red-bellied Woodpeckers have increased in both numbers and range in recent decades. Northern populations had declined in the early 1900s, but these common woodpeckers have slowly repopulated the north.

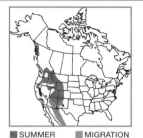

- ■ SUMMER   ■ MIGRATION
- ■ WINTER   ■ RARE
- ■ RESIDENT

In most North American woodpecker species, there is little—if any—difference in plumage between the male and the female, but the sexes of the Williamson's Sapsucker are so different in pattern that they were once described as separate species. This bird's habits are like those of the Yellow-bellied and Red-breasted sapsuckers; however, its diet includes more ants. Williamson's Sapsucker frequents spruce, fir, and pine forests, wintering more commonly in pine and pine-oak woodlands adjacent to its breeding range. In southern areas the cool climates it prefers occur at high elevations, whereas in northern latitudes such conditions occur closer to sea level.

DESCRIPTION: 9½" (24 cm). Male has a black head, breast, and back; white facial stripes; a bright red throat; and large white wing and rump patches. Its lemon-yellow belly is bordered with black and white barred flanks. The female is starkly different with a brown head; dark brown and white zebra stripes above and on the flanks; a large, dark bib; and a smaller, less brilliant yellow area on the belly.

VOICE: A soft nasal *churrr*, descending in pitch.

NESTING: Lays 3–7 white eggs, usually in pine or fir snags; it may reuse a nesting tree but it chisels a new hole each time.

HABITAT: Ponderosa pine forests and open coniferous forests; subalpine forests in the Southwest.

RANGE: Breeds from southern British Columbia south to southern California, central Arizona, and central New Mexico. Winters in southern part of breeding range and in Southwest.

SIMILAR SPECIES: Males are distinctive, with red throats as adults and white throats as immatures. Females on the ground may resemble flickers, but have an unspotted yellow belly and a browner, less patterned head. Immature Yellow-bellied Sapsuckers can be differentiated from female Williamson's Sapsucker by its mottling and less clear barring on and about the sides; immature Yellow-bellies have facial stripes and show a white wing patch when perched.

CONSERVATION: Williamson's Sapsuckers are fairly common and their numbers are stable. The northern tip of the species' breeding range extends into southern British Columbia, and there it is listed as Endangered because of the loss of old-growth western larch to timber harvesting.

YELLOW-BELLIED SAPSUCKER *Sphyrapicus varius*

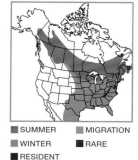

■ SUMMER　　■ MIGRATION
■ WINTER　　■ RARE
■ RESIDENT

This species, at least on migration, is the quietest of the wood-peckers; aside from a few squeaks and whines, it is mainly silent. It is also the least conspicuous, hitching around to the opposite side of the tree trunk when approached. Sapsuckers get their name from their habit of boring holes into the cambium layer or inner bark, letting the sap exude and run down the trunk. The birds lick up the oozing sap with their brush-like tongues and also consume insects attracted to the sap. They return again and again to the same tree, and hummingbirds and other sap-loving wildlife may be drawn to the sapwells. Unfortunately, sapsucker holes may damage trees and sometimes provide points of entry for fungus and other tree diseases.

DESCRIPTION: 8½" (22 cm). A furtive wood-pecker, mottled with off-white and black. The male has a red crown and throat; the female has red only on the crown. Both sexes are dull yellowish below. Immatures are dull brown. In all plumages, a distinctive mark is the conspic-uous white wing stripe, visible both at rest and in flight. It is

similar to Red-naped Sapsucker, but the male lacks a red nape patch, and its red throat is enclosed by black; the throat of the female is all white. This species hybridizes with Red-naped Sap-sucker in the Rocky Mountains, where puzzling intermediates can be found.

VOICE: Mewing and whining notes.

NESTING: Lays 5 or 6 white eggs in a tree cavity excavated by both members of the pair.

HABITAT: Young, open deciduous or mixed forests with clear-ings; on migration it visits parks, yards, and gardens.

RANGE: Breeds from central Canada to Newfoundland, south to British Columbia, North Dakota, Missouri, and central New England, and in the mountains to North Carolina. Winters from Missouri east to New Jersey and south to Florida and Texas; also in tropical America.

SIMILAR SPECIES: Other pied, striped-face woodpeckers lack the black breast patch and red patch on the forehead-crown.

The closely related Red-breasted Sapsucker of the West Coast has all-red hood broken by a white malar stripe.

Immature Red-headed Woodpecker is similar to the immature Yellow-bellied, but it is dull white below, the border of the hood is sharply defined on the breast, and it has a large white wing patch on the secondaries.

Female Williamson's Sapsucker also resembles an immature Yellow-bellied, but it lacks white on the face and is sharply barred on the back and sides.

CONSERVATION:

Although numerous and widespread, Yellow-bellied Sapsucker has disappeared from parts of its historic breeding range. These birds prefer the early successional forests that result from refor-estation efforts.

■ SUMMER   ■ MIGRATION
■ WINTER   ■ RARE
■ RESIDENT

The Red-naped Sapsucker is the common member of the sapsucker group in the Rocky Mountains. It interbreeds with the Yellow-bellied at the eastern edge of its breeding range and with the Red-breasted to the West. The resulting hybrids can be difficult to identify. All three birds were formerly considered a single species.

DESCRIPTION: 8–9" (20–23 cm). A furtive woodpecker mottled with off-white and black. The male has a red crown, nape patch, and throat; its throat patch is incompletely enclosed by black. The female has a white chin and red throat, and lacks the red nape patch. Both sexes are dull yellowish below. Immatures are dull brown. All plumages have a conspicuous white wing patch, visible both at rest and in flight.

VOICE: A soft, slurred *whee-ur* or *mew*.

NESTING: Lays 4–6 white eggs in a cavity drilled in a tree.

HABITAT: Edges of coniferous forests, woodlands, and groves of aspen and alder.

RANGE: Breeds in the Rocky Mountains from British Columbia and Alberta south to east-central California, central Arizona, and southern New Mexico. Winters north to southern California, central Arizona, and central New Mexico.

SIMILAR SPECIES: The closely related Yellow-bellied Sapsucker can be difficult to distinguish where the two species occur together. Telling the species apart requires a good look at the nape of the neck (usually red in Red-naped) or at the throat (Yellow-bellied male's red throat is enclosed by a complete black border; the throat of the female is all white).

CONSERVATION: Red-naped Sapsuckers have experienced some loss of habitat in the last several decades, but they are still common in their range. Populations increased slightly from the 1960s to the 2010s, but according to the IUCN Red List, its numbers are currently thought to be in decline.

RED-BREASTED SAPSUCKER *Sphyrapicus ruber*

SUMMER MIGRATION
WINTER RARE
RESIDENT

This mainly coastal sapsucker has habits similar to those of the Red-naped and Yellow-bellied sapsuckers. In drilling holes for sap, the Red-breasted will work around a tree trunk in horizontal lines or a checkerboard pattern. It hybridizes with the Red-naped Sapsucker in California and British Columbia.

DESCRIPTION: 8–9" (20–23 cm). Smaller than a flicker. A shy woodpecker with a long white wing patch, a barred back, and a white rump. In adults, the entire head, throat, and breast are bright red, and the belly is yellow. Immatures are dusky brown with light spots above, lighter below, with black-and-white checkered wings and tail.

VOICE: Soft, slurred *whee-ur* or *mew*, like the call of Red-naped Sapsucker.

NESTING: Lays 4–6 white eggs in a cavity drilled in a tree.

HABITAT: Woodlands and their edges, groves of aspen and alder.

RANGE: Breeds from southeastern Alaska and British Columbia south to coastal California. Winters in most of the breeding range except interior British Columbia.

SUBSPECIES: Two subspecies are divided sharply in southern Oregon. Northern Red-breasted Sapsuckers (subsp. *ruber*) have a brighter red head that ends in a cleaner edge along the yellow belly. These birds show little white on the head. Southern Red-breasted Sapsuckers (subsp. *daggetti*) have duller red heads and duller yellow bellies; these birds have more white on the head, including a more extensive white "mustache" and sometimes a thin white stripe behind the eye.

SIMILAR SPECIES: Nearly all-red hood is diagnostic—the Red-breasted's range does not overlap that of the Red-headed Woodpecker.

CONSERVATION: Red-breasted Sapsuckers are numerous but may be declining due to habitat loss. They were once considered to be orchard pests and exterminated, but they have since become protected by law and have rebounded.

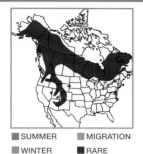

■ SUMMER ■ MIGRATION
■ WINTER ■ RARE
■ RESIDENT

This species inhabits coniferous forests, especially spruce and flr, and is attracted to burned areas and swampy forests with dead trees. It is broadly sympatric with the Black-backed Woodpecker, but one species is usually rare and the other more common in any given area. The Three-toed prefers denser conifers in mountains at higher elevations. In the southern and eastern portions of its range, the American Three-toed Woodpecker is less numerous than the Black-backed, but its range extends farther south in the Rockies. It is also more sedentary, rarely moving far from its home range.

DESCRIPTION: 8½" (22 cm). A robin-sized woodpecker. Similar to Black-backed Woodpecker, but smaller; its bill is shorter, and its back is variably barred black and white. The male has a yellow crown; the female has a solid black crown.

VOICE: A soft *pik*, similar to call of Downy Woodpecker.

NESTING: Lays 4 white eggs in a tree hole that is beveled on the lower side of the entrance to form a sort of doorstep for the birds.

HABITAT: Coniferous forests in the boreal zone, especially where burned, logged, or swampy.

RANGE: Resident in Alaska and east across Canada to extreme northern United States and south in West to mountains of Arizona and New Mexico.

SUBSPECIES: The nominate Rocky Mountain race (subsp. *dorsalis*) has an almost entirely white back with irregular barring. East Taiga birds (subsp. *bacatus*) are almost entirely black on the back with only faint white barring. West Taiga birds (subsp. *fasciatus*) are intermediate with a moderate amount of black-and-white barring on the back.

SIMILAR SPECIES: Black-backed Woodpecker lacks barring on the back and outer tail feathers; even very black eastern Three-toeds usually show some white on the back.

Downy and Hairy woodpeckers have a white back; they are buff to grayish-white or white below. Males have a red nape patch. Downy's flanks and sides are unmarked. Hairy has little or no black barring on the outer tail feathers.

CONSERVATION:

Local numbers of American Three-toed Woodpeckers vary considerably in their remote range, making population trends difficult to assess, but these birds' overall numbers are thought to be stable. These birds are sensitive to forest fragmentation from timber harvesting and pesticides used to kill bark beetles during outbreaks. Their northern forest habitat may be at risk from the effects of climate change.

BLACK-BACKED WOODPECKER *Picoides arcticus*

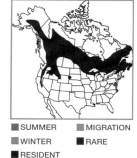

SUMMER ■ MIGRATION
■ WINTER ■ RARE
■ RESIDENT

The Black-backed Woodpecker occupies the northern and montane western coniferous forests, often in the same geographic areas as American Three-toed Woodpecker. The two look much alike, but their behavior and calls differ markedly and they rarely occur together. The Black-backed is vocally active and aggressive; it is often seen low in conifers or in the open in dead trees. Dead conifers with large areas of peeled bark generally indicate the presence of this uncommon woodpecker. When alarmed, it quickly sidles to the far side of the tree and reappears cautiously. If frightened, the bird flies away, often calling sharply. Like American Three-toed Woodpeckers, this species has only three toes on each foot.

DESCRIPTION: 9" (23 cm). This robin-sized woodpecker has a solid black back and barred flanks, and is white below. The male has a yellow crown; the female has a solid black crown.

VOICE: A sharp, fast *kyik* and a scolding rattle.

NESTING: Lays 4 white eggs in a cavity excavated in a tree, often rather close to ground.

HABITAT: Coniferous forests in the boreal zone, especially where burned, logged, or swampy.

RANGE: Resident from Alaska east across Canada to the northernmost United States and south to the mountains of California, Wyoming, and South Dakota in the West.

SIMILAR SPECIES: The all-black back and barred sides of Black-backed Woodpecker are diagnostic; the yellow crown patch of males is even more so. Its call also is distinctive.

Western American Three-toed Woodpecker has a barred back; the blacker eastern form has barred outer tail feathers and dusky nasal tufts; it always shows contrast between the head and back and has some white on the back.

Female Hairy Woodpecker has a white or buff-white back and a paler face than a female Black-backed.

CONSERVATION: LC

Local populations of these birds fluctuate with food availability, but overall their numbers are thought to be stable. Forestry management practices and the effects of climate change are the biggest risks facing these coniferous forest dwellers.

- ■ SUMMER
- ■ WINTER
- ■ RESIDENT
- ■ MIGRATION
- ■ RARE

The Downy is a familiar bird in its range, especially in winter, when many move into the suburbs and feed on suet at bird feeders. It is often seen in the mixed flocks of chickadees, nuthatches, creepers, and kinglets that gather in the woods during migration and winter. As with other woodpeckers, the male is larger than the female and chisels deep into wood with its longer, stronger bill, whereas the female pries under the bark with its shorter bill. Thus a pair is able to share the food resources without competing with one another.

DESCRIPTION: 6" (15 cm). A sparrow-sized, black-and-white woodpecker. Males have a small red patch on the nape. The back is white; the underparts are white or gray-white and usually unmarked. The white outer tail feathers have two or more black bars, and the wings are barred black-and-white. It is similar to Hairy Woodpecker but smaller and with a short, stubby bill.

VOICE: A quiet *pik*. Also a descending rattle.

NESTING: Lays 4 or 5 white eggs in a hole in a tree.

HABITAT: Woodlands, parks, and gardens.

RANGE: Resident from Alaska across Canada, south throughout the United States except in parts of the Southwest.

SUBSPECIES: Varies geographically; several subspecies are recognized. Western birds usually show some white on the wing coverts and tertials. Birds of the Rocky Mountains have less white spotting on the wings. Pacific Northwest birds have a pale gray-brown back and underparts.

SIMILAR SPECIES: See Hairy Woodpecker. Other small black-and-white woodpeckers do not have an unbarred white back.

CONSERVATION:

Downy Woodpeckers are common in their natural habitats, and populations have remained stable for the past several decades. The clearing and thinning of trees in older forest areas plays to this species' preference for young forests for nesting.

HAIRY WOODPECKER *Dryobates villosus*

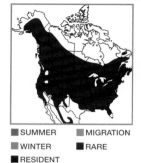

■ SUMMER ■ MIGRATION
■ WINTER ■ RARE
■ RESIDENT

The Hairy Woodpecker is more a forest bird and is shyer than its smaller relative, the Downy Woodpecker. The Hairy Woodpecker feeds on many harmful insects, such as wood-boring beetles, which it extracts from holes with its barbed tongue. Like other woodpeckers, it drums on a dead limb as part of its courtship ceremony and to proclaim its territory.

DESCRIPTION: 9" (23 cm). A robin-sized woodpecker. It is black and white, with an unspotted white back and a long bill; the male has a red head patch. Like most woodpeckers, it has an undulating flight. See Downy Woodpecker.

VOICE: A sharp, distinctive *peek*, louder than that of Downy Woodpecker; also a loud rattle on one pitch.

NESTING: Lays 4 white eggs in a hole in a tree.

HABITAT: Deciduous forest; more widespread in winter and during migration.

RANGE: Resident from Alaska and across Canada south throughout the United States to the Gulf of Mexico. Some northern birds migrate south for winter.

SUBSPECIES: Varies geographically; several subspecies are recognized. Most of these geographical variations parallel those of Downy Woodpecker. Western birds are darkest, with mostly black wings. Birds of the Rocky Mountains are a bit paler. A subpopulation in Arizona has a dark strip on the flanks and appears more brown than black on the back. Juveniles in some populations in the Canadian Maritime Provinces may have barred backs and flanks.

SIMILAR SPECIES: Hairy Woodpecker is easily confused with the smaller Downy Woodpecker. Downy has a much shorter bill and white outer tail feathers with two or more black bars; its calls differ, as does its general behavior. Hairy is shyer, flies more readily, and taps more loudly and vigorously.

Most black-and-white or brown-and-white woodpeckers (Arizona, White-headed, Nuttall's, Red-cockaded) do not have an unbarred white back; Arizona and Nuttall's woodpeckers are also spotted or barred below.

Sapsuckers are much less conspicuous; they have a patterned back and underparts.

Female Black-backed and American Three-toed woodpeckers have barred sides and a solid black or barred back.

Northern Flicker has a barred outer tail.

CONSERVATION: 🐦 LC
Common and widespread, populations of Hairy Woodpeckers are thought to have increased since the mid-1900s. Fragmentation of forests into smaller parcels and competition for nesting sites from European Starlings and House Sparrows negatively impact their numbers.

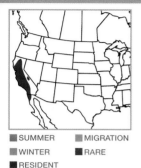

■ SUMMER ■ MIGRATION
■ WINTER ■ RARE
■ RESIDENT

A small and retiring woodpecker, Nuttall's is often hidden in foliage and may be heard before it is seen. It eats mainly insects, foraging by gleaning the bark, sometimes tapping and drilling, and occasionally flycatching. Nuttall's Woodpecker is a small, barred-backed species that lives in the chaparral, oakwoods, and streamside trees of the Far West. Only at the southern edge of its range does it meet another barred species, the closely related Ladder-backed Woodpecker.

DESCRIPTION: 7–7½" (18–19 cm). Black-and-white barred above, with a conspicuous unbarred black area on the upper back, Nuttall's Woodpeckers have mainly white outer tail feathers crossed with a few small bar marks. The face is black-and-white striped with a broad black eyeline and mustache extending to the black back and wings. The top of the head is black and variably spotted with white; males have a red nape patch, but this is lacking in females. The nasal tufts are white. The underparts are white with a slight grayish cast on the sides in fresh plumage. The sides are checked with black, and the flanks are barred. It is similar to Ladder-backed Woodpecker, but with black cheeks and wider black bars on the back; the black and white areas more sharply contrasting. Where its range overlaps that of Ladder-backed, it can be distinguished by its call.

VOICE: A rolling call, *prreep*; a sharp *pit-it*.

NESTING: Lays 3–6 white eggs in a hole excavated in a thin dead branch of an oak or cottonwood, or even a large, thick-stemmed elderberry bush.

HABITAT: Canyon scrub oaks, oak woodlands, and streamside growth.

RANGE: Resident from northern California to Baja California.

SIMILAR SPECIES: Ladder-backed Woodpecker is not as black, with its upper back barred rather than black and with less-sharply contrasting black-and-white markings; it has dusky nasal tufts and a large white patch on the cheeks. Male Nuttall's has less red on the head, but worn Ladder-backs may appear similar. Their calls also differ.

Sympatric Downy and Hairy woodpeckers are not barred on the back.

Immature Yellow-billed Sapsucker has a mottled, not clearly barred back; it also has mottled underparts and a white wing patch.

CONSERVATION: Nuttall's Woodpecker numbers are increasing. Although not currently a species of concern, its limited range and reliance entirely on oak forests for nesting leave it vulnerable to disruption of these forests in California.

LADDER-BACKED WOODPECKER *Dryobates scalaris*

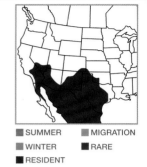

■ SUMMER   ■ MIGRATION
■ WINTER   ■ RARE
■ RESIDENT

Desert scrub and streamside trees are the habitat of this small woodpecker. This species feeds in trees, bushes, and yuccas, often wandering into parks and suburban gardens. Paired birds call frequently and can be seen in undulating flight between trees or cacti. Within most of its range, the Ladder-backed is the only small woodpecker so marked. The most numerous member of its family in Texas, it replaces the Downy Woodpecker in more arid areas. It is closely related to Nuttall's Woodpecker of California.

DESCRIPTION: 7" (18 cm). As its name implies, the Ladder-backed Woodpecker is barred with black and white above, including the wings and outer tail feathers. Its underparts are buff-white with fine streaks on the sides and bars on the flanks. There is a black eyestripe connecting on the neck with a partial mustache—the mustache is checked with white near the bill. The nasal tufts are dusky. The larger, longer-billed males have red from the crown to the forehead and white spots on the forehead, but the red wears off the forehead by spring or summer in some individuals. Females have no red on a white-spotted, black crown.

VOICE: A sharp *pik*, similar to that of Downy Woodpecker; also a descending whinny.

NESTING: Lays 4 or 5 white eggs in a hole in a tree, cactus, pole, or post.

HABITAT: Arid areas with thickets and trees.

RANGE: Resident in the southwestern United States from California, Nevada, Utah, Colorado, Oklahoma, and Texas south into the tropics.

SIMILAR SPECIES: Sympatric Gila Woodpeckers are larger with a white patch on the rump and wings; they lack facial stripes.

Ladder-backed marginally overlaps with Hairy, Downy, Arizona, and Nuttall's woodpeckers at the edges of its range; its barred back distinguishes it from all but Nuttall's. Nuttall's is less dingy, more sharply black-and-white, with its outer tail less fully barred; the black bars on its back are broader than the white bars. Its face is black-and-white striped, with more black in the face, and its underparts are whitish. Nuttall's call is a double *pit-it*. The two species hybridize in southern California.

CONSERVATION: LC
Ladder-backed Woodpeckers are widespread and common, and their numbers have remained stable during the past several decades.

Dryobates borealis RED-COCKADED WOODPECKER

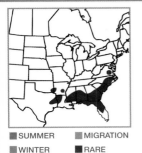

SUMMER ■ MIGRATION
■ WINTER ■ RARE
■ RESIDENT

Once widespread and common in the Southeast, the Red-cockaded Woodpecker has become a rare and local species due to a steep population decline. It is restricted to mature pine woods that contain trees whose heartwood has been softened by fungus, where the bird digs its nest cavity. Much less noisy and conspicuous than other woodpeckers and therefore seldom noticed, it travels in family groups of four to six. This woodpecker also has the peculiar trait of digging holes in trees adjacent to its nest, allowing pine gum or resin to ooze from the holes. Such signs of pitch may be evidence of its presence.

DESCRIPTION: 8" (20 cm). This woodpecker has a black cap and nape, with a large white cheek patch. Its back is barred black and white; it is white below with black spots on the sides and flanks. The male has a small, hard-to-see red spot behind the eye.

VOICE: A nuthatch-like *yank-yank*. Also a rattling scold note.

NESTING: Lays 4 white eggs in a tree cavity, usually in a live tree with decayed heartwood.

HABITAT: Pine forests, especially yellow and longleaf pines.

RANGE: Historically, resident from southeastern Oklahoma and Maryland to the Gulf Coast and central Florida. It has disappeared from many parts of its range, with spotty distribution remaining mainly in the Southeast.

SIMILAR SPECIES: See Yellow-bellied Sapsucker, Downy and Hairy woodpeckers.

CONSERVATION: NT

The Red-cockaded Woodpecker is on the U.S. Endangered Species List, and it is classified as endangered in states throughout its range due to its small population size (perhaps 10,000 individuals) and the significant decline it has shown since the 1970s. These woodpeckers were once common in the Southeast but are now mostly rare and local. The species depends on old-growth southern pine and appears uniquely susceptible to poor forest management practices—clearcutting, forest fragmentation, conversion of longleaf pine forest to slash pine forest, and fire suppression efforts have reduced its habitat and fragmented its range, resulting in its extirpation from several states.

WHITE-HEADED WOODPECKER *Dryobates albolarvatus*

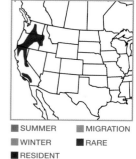

■ SUMMER   ■ MIGRATION
■ WINTER   ■ RARE
■ RESIDENT

The White-headed Woodpecker inhabits far-western pine forests. An inconspicuous bird, hard to find due to its silent habits, the White-headed Woodpecker rarely taps or drums, vocalizing only around the nest. It feeds by scaling bark off trees to reach the insects underneath. Although its bold black-and-white pattern is striking in flight, it provides excellent camouflage when the bird perches in a shady forest.

DESCRIPTION: 9" (23 cm). This woodpecker is almost entirely black except for a white head, throat, and wing patch. The male has a red patch on the nape; the female lacks a red patch. Males are heavier and longer-billed than females.

VOICE: Usually silent. A sharp *pee-dink* and a more prolonged *pee-dee-dee-dink*.

NESTING: Lays 3–5 white eggs in a nest cavity in a pine stub or snag, often close to the ground.

HABITAT: Ponderosa pine belts of the mountains; also in subalpine belts of firs.

RANGE: Resident from extreme south-central British Columbia, northeastern Washington, and Idaho, south to southern California and western Nevada. Some birds move down mountain slopes in winter.

SIMILAR SPECIES: A mainly white head and wing patches on a black body is distinctive among woodpeckers; it is not readily confused with other species. Acorn and Hairy woodpeckers are a similar size but have extensive white on the underparts and distinctly different facial patterns.

CONSERVATION: LC

White-headed Woodpecker populations are difficult to monitor due to their silent and secretive nature, but they are relatively common and their numbers are believed to be stable.

■ SUMMER ■ MIGRATION
■ WINTER ■ RARE
■ RESIDENT

The Arizona Woodpecker is a shy bird that frequents oak and pine-oak woodland on the mountain slopes of southeastern Arizona. It works at the bark, excavating it with almost as much vigor and noise as the Hairy Woodpecker and using angled blows to strip the bark from dead trees to get at underlying insects. It is usually found below habitats occupied by the Hairy Woodpecker and above the desert scrub frequented by the Ladder-backed Woodpecker; however, it overlaps somewhat with both. Like other woodpeckers, it lays white eggs in a cavity without making a nest. Other hole-nesters such as chickadees and some flycatchers, which build nests and lay patterned eggs, have probably evolved the hole-breeding habit more recently.

DESCRIPTION: 7–8" (18–20 cm). An unstreaked, brown-backed woodpecker, with a brown crown and brown ear patch on a white face. Its underparts are spotted and barred with brown. The male is distinguished by a red nape.

VOICE: Call is a sharp *peek!* or a rasping *jee-jee-jee.*

NESTING: Lays 3 or 4 white eggs in a cavity in a dead branch of a live tree.

HABITAT: Dry live-oak and pine-oak woodlands.

RANGE: Resident in mountains of southeastern Arizona and locally in southwestern New Mexico. Also in Mexico.

SIMILAR SPECIES: Ladder-backed Woodpeckers are similar but have a barred black-and-white back, compared to Arizona Woodpecker's solid brown back.

CONSERVATION:

Predominantly a native of Mexico, Arizona Wood-peckers are increasing. Habitat loss and fragmentation due to overharvesting of forests, especially in Mexico, are the main conservation concerns for this species. In Arizona, groundwater removal and grazing can reduce the numbers of Arizona sycamore, upon which Arizona Woodpecker relies.

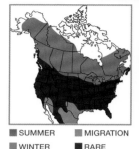

■ SUMMER   ■ MIGRATION
■ WINTER   ■ RARE
■ RESIDENT

Northern Flickers occur in two color forms: the "Red-shafted" in the West and the "Yellow-shafted" east of the Rocky Mountains. The ice ages separated the ancestral flickers, keeping them scattered in several refugia for thousands of years. Today those barriers are gone. The related Gilded Flicker has become adapted to the desert, whereas the two northern populations of Northern Flicker inhabit the same type of woodland habitat, with only the treeless Great Plains keeping them somewhat apart. All three forms interbreed where their ranges come together, and numerous confusing intermediates and hybrids can be found. In the East, flickers are the only brown-backed woodpeckers, and the only woodpeckers in North America that commonly feed on the ground, searching for ants and beetle larvae.

DESCRIPTION: 12" (30 cm). A large, brownish woodpecker. It has a brown back with dark bars and spots; and is whitish or buff below with black spots. It has a black crescent on the breast, and a white rump visible in flight. Eastern birds ("Yellow-shafted Flickers") have a red patch on the nape and yellow wing linings; the male has a black "mustache." Western birds ("Red-shafted Flickers") lack the nape patch and have salmon-pink wing linings; males have a red "mustache."

VOICE: A loud, repeated flicker or *wicka-wicka-wicka*; also a loud *kleeer*.

NESTING: Lays 6–8 white eggs in a tree cavity, utility pole, or birdhouse.

HABITAT: Open country with trees; parks and large gardens.

RANGE: Resident from Alaska east through Manitoba to Newfoundland and south throughout the United States. Northernmost birds are migratory.

SIMILAR SPECIES: In most of North America, Northern Flicker is only woodpecker apt to feed on open ground; its brown color, barred back, white rump, and yellow to orange wing linings and undertail surface are all distinctive. The Gilded Flicker, found in the Sonoran Desert of the Southwest, was once considered the same species; it combines the gray face and red malar stripe typical of a Red-shafted Northern Flicker with the yellow underwings and undertail of the Yellow-shafted form; its calls are higher pitched.

CONSERVATION: LC
Although its numbers are perhaps half of what they used to be in the mid-1900s, Northern Flickers remain common and are easily found in their native habitats. Their numbers are gradually decreasing, however, due in large part to competition for nesting sites with introduced European Starlings.

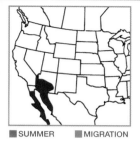

- ■ SUMMER
- ■ WINTER
- ■ RESIDENT
- ■ MIGRATION
- ■ RARE

The Gilded Flicker was once considered a subspecies of the widespread Northern Flicker, and it's easy to see why—the bird resembles a mix between the "Red-shafted" western Northern Flicker and its "Yellow-shafted" eastern form. What's more, its habits resemble those of Northern Flicker and the two species freely interbreed where their ranges overlap, producing hybrids that further confuse identification. Gilded Flicker, however, is smaller than its Northern cousins and is adapted to the saguaro deserts of the Southwest, where it eats mainly ants as well as beetles, termites, caterpillars, and other insects, along with many fruits and sometimes seeds and nuts.

DESCRIPTION: 12" (30 cm). A large, brownish woodpecker. It has a brown back with dark bars and spots. It is whitish or buff below with black spots, and has a black crescent on the breast; its white rump and yellow underwings are visible in flight. It has a cinnamon-brown crown and forehead, and its face and throat are pale gray; the male has a red "mustache."

VOICE: A loud, repeated *woika*; also a loud series of *kee* notes.

NESTING: Lays 6–8 white eggs in a tree or cactus cavity, utility pole, or artificial nestbox.

HABITAT: Saguaro deserts, cottonwood-lined streams, towns.

RANGE: Resident from southeastern California and central Arizona south into Mexico.

SIMILAR SPECIES: See Northern Flicker.

CONSERVATION:
Gilded Flickers are fairly common in their limited range, but their numbers have dipped significantly in the past several decades due to habitat loss.

PILEATED WOODPECKER *Dryocopus pileatus*

■ SUMMER　　■ MIGRATION
■ WINTER　　　■ RARE
■ RESIDENT

This is the largest woodpecker in North America (except possibly for the Ivory-billed Woodpecker, which is thought to be extinct). Despite its size, this elegant woodpecker is often shy and hard to observe. Obtaining a close view of one usually requires careful stalking. Although primarily a forest bird, the species has recently become adapted to civilization and has become relatively numerous even on the outskirts of large cities, where its presence is most easily detected by its loud, ringing call and by its large, characteristically rectangular excavations in trees. Its staple food consists of carpenter ants living in fallen timber, dead roots, and stumps. The woodpecker excavates fist-sized rectangular cavities, then uses its enormously long, sticky tongue to reach the ant burrows.

DESCRIPTION: 17" (43 cm). A crow-sized woodpecker with a long neck and prominent red crest. It is black with white neck stripes and conspicuous white wing linings. The male has a red "mustache"; the female's is black.

VOICE: A loud, flicker-like *cuk-cuk-cuk-cuk-cuk*, rising and then falling in pitch and volume.

NESTING: Lays 4 white eggs in a tree cavity.

HABITAT: Mature forests and borders.

RANGE: Resident from British Columbia east across southern Canada to Nova Scotia, south to northern California, southern Idaho, eastern North Dakota, central Texas, and Florida.

SIMILAR SPECIES: Its size, coloration, and shape are distinctive in North America. See the discussion of the Ivory-billed Woodpecker.

CONSERVATION: LC

Pileated Woodpeckers are common in the Southeast and uncommon elsewhere, but its numbers are increasing. As European settlers cleared northern woods in the 18th and 19th centuries, these birds suffered sharp losses, but their numbers stabilized and started to grow again at the beginning of the 20th century as the birds adapted to second-growth woods and proximity to human activity.

Campephilus principalis IVORY-BILLED WOODPECKER

This majestic woodpecker was a resident of southeastern forests through early colonial times. Its numbers declined rapidly through the 18th and 19th centuries, largely because it was shot for food, novelties, and specimens, and because old-growth lowland forests were felled for timber. The last unquestioned photographic images of the species were taken in northern Louisiana in 1935. Occasional sight reports have persisted until modern times. Because most sightings of this species pertain in fact to the similar and widespread Pileated Woodpecker, observers should take care to document and photograph all suspected Ivory-billeds.

DESCRIPTION: 19" (48 cm). The adult male has a red hindcrest covered by a black forecrest; females and immatures have an all-black crest. This species has a long, heavy, pale yellow to ivory white bill and a black chin. The white secondaries and inner primaries form a white "shield" on the back.

VOICE: Call a nasal *kent*, given in irregular series and likened to calls of Red-breasted Nuthatch; also gives a territorial double-rap: two knocks in quick succession.

NESTING: Lays 2 to 5 eggs in a large cavity with an oval to rectangular opening excavated in a dead or dying tree.

HABITAT: Old-growth lowland forests.

RANGE: Formerly found in the southeastern United States.

SIMILAR SPECIES: Pileated Woodpecker has a dark bill, a red or black mustache, a white throat, a white stripe from the bill across the cheek, and a white patch only on the forward two-thirds of the wing lining. Its call is different.

CONSERVATION: CR

Ivory-billed Woodpeckers were never especially common, and deforestation of their mature, old-growth forest habitat in the southeastern U.S. had rendered them quite rare by the 1880s. Whether the Ivory-billed Woodpecker is extinct in the wild today is the subject of some debate in the birding community. A handful of reports in the early and mid-2000s provided a glimmer of hope for this bird, but no confirmed sightings have been recorded since, despite an extensive search. Contemporary reports of Ivory-bills are treated with skepticism—especially considering their similarity to the fairly common Pileated Woodpecker in the same range. Officially the species is listed as Critically Endangered by the IUCN Red List, but without indisputable evidence to the contrary, most experts concede the species is probably extinct.

CRESTED CARACARA *Caracara cheriway*

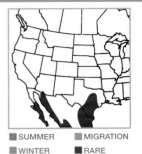

■ SUMMER ■ MIGRATION
■ WINTER ■ RARE
■ RESIDENT

The national bird of Mexico, this scavenger has probably the most varied diet of any bird of prey. It often accompanies and dominates vultures at fresh kills or carrion and also eats small animals. It is primarily a ground-inhabiting falcon of open prairies, with long legs that enable it to walk and run with ease.

DESCRIPTION: 20–22" (51–56 cm) long with an average wingspan of 4' (1.2 m). It is a large, long-legged, hawk-like bird with rounded wings. It is dark brown with a black cap and a bare red face; the throat, neck, and base of the tail are white; the tip of the tail has a black band. In flight, it shows large white patches near the wing tips. It is often seen on the ground.

VOICE: A high, harsh cackle.

NESTING: Lays 2 or 3 white eggs with heavy brown spots and blotches in a nest of twigs, grasses, weeds, and briars lined with leaves and moss; usually in palmettos or live oaks, rarely on the ground.

HABITAT: Prairies, savannas, desert scrub, and seashores.

RANGE: Resident in southern Arizona, southern Texas, southwestern Louisiana (rare), and central and southern Florida. Also in American tropics.

SIMILAR SPECIES: See Black and Turkey vultures, both of which have bare heads. All three species eat carrion; Crested Caracara often drives other vultures away from food.

CONSERVATION:

Increasing throughout its range in Mexico and the American tropics. The "Audubon's" Crested Caracara, a subpopulation of the Crested Caracara, is on the U.S. Endangered Species List and classified as threatened in Florida.

Although only rarely seen in North America, Eurasian Kestrel is the most common diurnal raptor in Great Britain and many other parts of its range. This kestrel feeds primarily on small mammals, including mice, voles, and shrews. Although this species was long thought to be closely related to the American Kestrel, recent genetic studies have shown the several species of Old World kestrels to be closely related to each other, but that the American Kestrel is a more distant relative.

DESCRIPTION: 11–13" (29–32 cm), wingspan 26–32" (65–82 cm). This accidental visitor to North America is larger than an American Kestrel and is longer-winged than the similarly-sized Merlin. Both sexes have rufous wings that are spotted with black, and with dark tips. It has much less gray on the wings than any native falcon. The male has a distinctive, entirely gray head and a primarily gray tail with a black bar. The female resembles a female American Kestrel but is significantly larger and lacks the distinctive head pattern.

VOICE: Shrill *kee-kee-kee* scream, similar to other falcons.

NESTING: Lays 3–7 eggs in a variety of nesting sites in the Old World.

HABITAT: In its native Eurasia, highly adaptable to most open or semi-wooded terrain. The few Eastern North American records have been in coastal grasslands, which would be consistent with a bird that may have "hitched a ride" on a ship.

RANGE: Common and wide-ranging in Europe and Asia, accidental vagrant to the East and West coasts of North America, rare but regular in the Aleutian Islands and Bering Sea area.

SIMILAR SPECIES: Resembles American Kestrel but is much larger and has a plain head, lacking the American kestrel's distinctive, bold head pattern.

CONSERVATION: Numerous but decreasing in its large Old World range.

AMERICAN KESTREL *Falco sparverius*

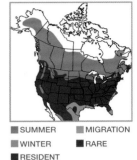

■ SUMMER ■ MIGRATION
■ WINTER ■ RARE
■ RESIDENT

Unlike larger falcons, the "Sparrow Hawk" has adapted to humans and nests even in our largest cities, where it preys chiefly on House Sparrows. In the countryside, it takes insects, small birds, and rodents, capturing its prey on the ground rather than in midair like other falcons. The female does most of the incubating and is fed by the male. The male calls as it nears the nest with food; the female flies up, receives the food, and returns to the nest. After the eggs hatch, the male continues to bring most of the food. The young stay with the adults for a time after fledging, and it is not uncommon to see family parties in late summer.

DESCRIPTION: 9–12" (23–30 cm) long with an average wingspan of 21" (53 cm). A small, jay-sized falcon with pointed wings, often seen hovering. It is recognizable in all plumages by its rusty tail and back. The adult male has slate-blue wings. The female has rusty wings and back, and narrow bands on the tail. Both sexes have two bold, black stripes on face.

VOICE: Shrill *killy-killy-killy*.

NESTING: Lays 4 or 5 white or pinkish eggs blotched with brown, placed without nest or lining in a natural or artificial cavity.

HABITAT: Towns and cities, parks, farmlands, and open country.

RANGE: Breeds from Alaska and the Northwest Territories east through the Maritime Provinces and south throughout the continent. Winters north to British Columbia, the Great Lakes, and New England. Also found throughout much of Central and South America.

SIMILAR SPECIES: Merlin is larger and stockier, and lacks the bold stripes on the face. Sharp-shinned Hawk has broader wings, a darker back, heavier markings underneath, and a thicker build.

CONSERVATION: 🐦 LC

Although their numbers have declined in recent decades, they now appear to be stable. American Kestrels remain among the most common and widespread of North America's falcon species. Loss of nesting sites and prey sources due to agricultural practices, pesticides, and pollution are their primary threats.

■ SUMMER   ■ MIGRATION
■ WINTER   ■ RARE
■ RESIDENT

The so-called "Pigeon Hawk" is most abundant during the migrations of smaller birds, on which it feeds. It is swift and aggressive, regularly harassing larger hawks and gulls and attacking intruders at its nest. As with other falcons, the female begins incubating as soon as the first egg is laid so the young hatch at intervals; when food is scarce, the larger young are fed first, the smaller ones sometimes dying of starvation. This practice ensures that some young will be raised successfully even in hard times.

DESCRIPTION: 10–14" (25–36 cm) long with an average wingspan of 23" (58 cm). A jay-sized falcon, stockier than American Kestrel. It is slate colored (males) or brownish (females) above, and light and streaked below, except in Pacific coast birds, which are darker underneath. Its long tail is boldly banded. It lacks the facial stripes of most other falcons.

VOICE: A high, loud cackle, also *klee-klee-klee* like an American Kestrel, but usually silent.

NESTING: Lays 5 or 6 buff eggs, stippled with purple and brown, placed in a tree cavity without a nest or lining, on a rocky ledge, or in an abandoned crow's nest.

HABITAT: Coniferous forests; more widespread in winter.

RANGE: Breeds from Alaska east through Mackenzie to Newfoundland and south to Wyoming, Montana, and northeastern Maine. Winters mainly in southern United States north along the West Coast to British Columbia and on the East Coast to southern New England; locally elsewhere north to southern Canada. Also found in tropical America and Eurasia.

SUBSPECIES: North America's Merlins are divided into three subspecies. The most widespread of these are the nominate birds (subsp. *columbarius*) that breed in the eastern taiga region. Prairie birds of the Great Plains (subsp. *richardsonii*) are lighter with less extensive marking underneath. Pacific coast birds (subsp. *suckleyi*), sometimes called "Black Merlin," are similar to eastern birds but even darker. Intermediates occur where the ranges of these subpopulations meet.

SIMILAR SPECIES: See American Kestrel, Peregrine Falcon, and Sharp-shinned Hawk.

CONSERVATION:

Pesticide contamination led to widespread decline in the mid-1900s, but conservation efforts have helped Merlin populations to stabilize. Their numbers have increased in the last several decades, and the birds have expanded their breeding range deeper into New England, to New York, Vermont, New Hampshire, and Maine. They seem tolerant around human activity and have adapted to urban settings.

The Eurasian Hobby is a fast, powerful flier, even by falcon standards. This sleek bird can give the impression of an oversized swift when catching insects (a primary food source) on the wing. This species is a long-distance migrant, breeding across Europe and Asia, wintering on the Indian Subcontinent and in southern Africa. The vagrants seen in North America are primarily during migration, mostly in Alaska; on rarer occasions, they have been seen in Washington state and Massachusetts.

DESCRIPTION: Merlin-sized, 11–14" (28–36 cm) long with an average wingspan of 28–33" (69–84 cm). A dark falcon of Europe and Asia that occasionally visits Alaska and has been seen a few times on both the East and West coasts of North America. Its wings and back are darker than most Merlins. Its chest and belly are whitish or buff with dense, dark streaking. It has red-orange thighs and undertail area. Its pale to white throat and facial area contrast with the rest of the generally dark bird.

VOICE: Shrill scream *keer-keer-keer*.

NESTING: Lays 2–4 eggs in the old nests of crows and other birds.

HABITAT: In its native habitat, open wooded areas, woodland edges and fields. Prefers semi-open areas with sufficient trees or shrubs for perching. In North America, most often seen near coasts in summer.

RANGE: Across most of Europe and Asia in summer, wintering in Southern Africa and the Indian Subcontinent; a resident population lives in southern China. A vagrant to North America, primarily in Alaska, there have been confirmed individual sightings in Washington State, Massachusetts, and Newfoundland.

SIMILAR SPECIES: A dark Merlin will lack the red on the thighs and tail, and the pale facial markings.

CONSERVATION:
A species of least concern, although their numbers are decreasing in their native range.

■ SUMMER ■ MIGRATION
■ WINTER ■ RARE
■ RESIDENT

This striking falcon was once common in dry grasslands of the southwestern United States, but now is rare and endangered in North America. It is usually found perched on a tall cactus or utility pole. When it flies off in alarm or in pursuit of prey, it often dips down and courses low over the ground. Most of its diet consists of small birds, but it also takes reptiles and large insects. It is most active at dawn and dusk.

DESCRIPTION: 15–18" (38–45.5 cm) long with an average wingspan of 40–48" (102–122 cm). Resembles a small, long-tailed, boldly patterned Peregrine Falcon. The adult is blue-gray above, with a bold "mustache" on the face, a white eyebrow, and a black stripe through the eye. Its nape is rusty and its throat is white. Its upper breast is buff with heavy streaks, the lower breast and flanks are black, and the thighs and belly are cinnamon. Young birds are brown above, streaked on the breast, and plain brown on the flanks.

VOICE: A rapid *kak-kak-kak-kak*.

NESTING: Lays 3–4 white or pinkish eggs spotted with brown in a deserted nest of a raven or other large bird.

HABITAT: Open arid country, grasslands, deserts, and savannas.

RANGE: Formerly ranged from southeastern Arizona to southern Texas southward to Argentina. Small numbers have reappeared in New Mexico and southern Texas.

SIMILAR SPECIES: Prairie Falcon can have black axillars that extend to the belly, but it is paler, stockier, and shorter-tailed; it lacks pronounced patterning. Peregrine Falcon is larger and stockier, without the light eyestripe; its underparts lack bold contrast between the belly and breast.

CONSERVATION:
A species of least concern globally, but its numbers are decreasing. The Northern Aplomado Falcon (*F. f. septentrionalis*), the population of the Aplomado Falcon that occurs in the United States and northern Mexico, is on the U.S. Endangered Species List. It is classified as endangered in Texas, where conservationists are trying to reintroduce the species to areas where it formerly occurred in the wild. Its population appears to be increasing in the U.S. thanks to these efforts.

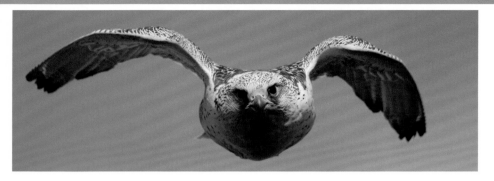

■ SUMMER ■ MIGRATION
■ WINTER ■ RARE
■ RESIDENT

Gyrfalcon is the largest falcon in the world, and many adults are year-round residents in the high Arctic, above the Arctic Circle. Juveniles and some adults move south in winter into populated parts of the continent; it is a memorable occasion for bird watchers when a Gyrfalcon is sighted on a coastal salt marsh or over open country inland. In the Far North it feeds mainly on ptarmigans, but during the summer months it also takes shorebirds, eiders, and gulls, and makes frequent raids on the great colonies of murres and Dovekies.

DESCRIPTION: 22" (56 cm) long with an average wingspan of 4' (1.2 m). The largest of the true falcons. This falcon's broader, less pointed wings and longer tail resemble those of an accipiter. These birds have highly variable plumage, and three color morphs occur: blackish, white, and gray-brown. Intermediate gray or brownish-gray morphs are the most common. Juveniles are typically more heavily streaked below than adults. All morphs are more uniformly colored than Peregrine Falcon, which has bold dark "mustaches" and hood and a proportionately larger head.

VOICE: A chattering scream, *kak-kak-kak-kak*.

NESTING: Usually 4 whitish or buff eggs, finely spotted with reddish brown, on a rock ledge or in the abandoned nest of a Rough-legged Hawk or Common Raven.

HABITAT: Arctic tundra and rocky cliffs, usually near water. Each winter a few move south to coastal beaches and marshes.

RANGE: Breeds on tundra of northern Alaska and northern Canada. Winters in breeding range and also rarely but regularly south to northern tier of states, especially along the coasts.

SIMILAR SPECIES: See Peregrine Falcon and Northern Goshawk. An occasional albino or partial albino Red-tailed Hawk may be mistaken for a white-morph Gyrfalcon.

CONSERVATION: 🐦 **LC**

North American populations are considered stable, but threats in Europe include the eggs and young being taken from the nest for falconry, and habitat modification. The Gyrfalcon's remote breeding range keeps them safe from most human activity in Canada and the U.S., but this habitat may be vulnerable to a warming climate.

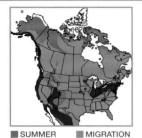

■ SUMMER ■ MIGRATION
■ WINTER ■ RARE
■ RESIDENT

Following an alarming decline during the 1950s and 1960s, this spectacular falcon, also called the "Duck Hawk," has rebounded now that pesticides that caused thinning of eggshells have been banned. After an intensive program of rearing birds in captivity and releasing them in the wild, this large falcon is reclaiming nesting grounds from which it disappeared a few decades ago. A favorite nesting site nowadays is a tall building or bridge in a city; these urban Peregrines subsist mainly on pigeons. Peregrine Falcons may be the fastest animals on Earth, capable of reaching speeds of 200 mph (320 km/h) during their spectacular dives after prey.

DESCRIPTION: 15–21" (38–53 cm) long with an average wingspan of 3'4" (1 m). A large, robust falcon with a black hood and wide black "mustaches." Adults are slate-gray above and pale below, with fine black bars and spots. Young birds are brown or brownish slate above, and heavily streaked below.

VOICE: Rasping *kack-kack-kack-kack*, usually heard at nest; otherwise generally silent.

NESTING: Lays 2–4 cream or buff eggs spotted with reddish brown, placed in a scrape with little lining on a cliff or building ledge or in an abandoned bird's nest.

HABITAT: Open country, especially along rivers; also near lakes, along coasts, and in cities. Migrates chiefly along the coasts.

RANGE: Breeds from Alaska and the Canadian Arctic south locally through the mountainous West, and sparingly in the East. Winters coastally, north to British Columbia and Massachusetts. Also found in southern South America and in the Old World.

SUBSPECIES: The tundra-breeding population (subsp. *tundrius*) is the most widespread in migration and in winter; these birds are the palest among the Peregrines. Birds of the northern Pacific coast and islands (subsp. *pealei*, also called "Peale's Peregrine Falcon") are the largest and darkest; because many birds released through reintroduction efforts resemble these dark birds, individuals resembling Pacific birds can appear elsewhere in North America. Intermediate birds (subsp. *anatum*) once ranged across much of the interior of the continent, but are now mainly found in the Rocky Mountains and West; these individuals have a thicker "mustache" and often show buff or rufous underparts.

SIMILAR SPECIES: Merlin is much smaller and usually darker; it lacks the distinctive mustache. Prairie Falcon has dark wing linings and axillars. Gyrfalcon has longer wings, somewhat broader at the base, and a longer tail; its undersides and back usually show less contrast. Other falcons lack Peregrine's bold facial markings.

CONSERVATION:
Peregrine Falcons suffered huge losses in the middle of the 20th century due to DDT poisoning; as a result, they were listed as an Endangered Species. In the past several decades, Peregrine numbers have recovered thanks to conservation efforts, reintroduction programs, and pesticide restrictions, and today their population is stable to increasing.

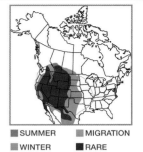

■ SUMMER   ■ MIGRATION
■ WINTER   ■ RARE
■ RESIDENT

The Prairie Falcon is usually found in places far from water, while the Peregrine is nearly always found near a river or lake. The Prairie Falcon's diet consists mainly of small mammals as well as birds, which it pursues on the wing but usually captures on or near the ground. Where elevated perches are available, the Prairie Falcon will spend a considerable amount of time watching for prey. In open country without high perches, its style of hunting is to fly low above the ground and flush prey.

DESCRIPTION: 17–20" (43–51 cm) long with an average wingspan of 3'6" (1.1 m). A large falcon, it is sandy brown above, whitish or pale buff below with fine spots and streaks, with a narrow brown "mustache" stripe and dark wing linings.

VOICE: A loud *kree-kree-kree*, most often heard near nest.

NESTING: Lays 4 or 5 white or pinkish eggs blotched with brown, placed without a nest on a cliff ledge or in the abandoned nest of another large bird.

HABITAT: Barren mountains, dry plains, and prairies.

RANGE: Breeds from British Columbia and the Canadian prairie provinces south to Mexico and northern Texas. Winters in the breeding range and sparingly farther east.

SIMILAR SPECIES: Peregrine Falcon is slightly larger and darker, with bolder facial markings.

CONSERVATION: 🐦 LC

Widespread and difficult to count accurately, it is believed that Prairie Falcons are increasing. Their populations dipped dramatically in the mid-1900s due to DDT poisoning, but after laws were passed banning the pesticide, Prairie Falcon numbers began rising again. Today, their main threats are illegal shooting and development that destroys habitat or interferes with local populations of ground squirrels, which are a primary food source.

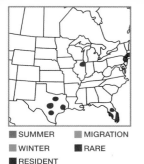

■ SUMMER   ■ MIGRATION
■ WINTER   ■ RARE
■ RESIDENT

This noisy but attractive parrot was first reported in the wild in the late 1960s, presumably having escaped from a shipment at New York's Kennedy Airport. Since that time, it has spread to surrounding regions. Populations descended from escaped or released captive birds can be found in several other metropolitan areas including Chicago, Providence, Miami, Phoenix, Dallas, and New Orleans. Its huge stick nests, used both for breeding and roosting, are conspicuous and may contain from one to as many as six pairs of birds.

DESCRIPTION: 11" (28 cm). It is bright green above and pale gray below, with scalloping on the throat; it has dark blue primaries; its tail is long and pointed.

VOICE: Loud, harsh, screeching *eeeh-eeeh*.

NESTING: Lays 5 or 6 white eggs in a huge, bulky stick nest, placed in a tree or on top of a utility pole, or attached to a building wall. The nest is domed and has entrances to egg chambers on the sides and bottom.

HABITAT: City parks, suburban yards, and semi-open country.

RANGE: Introduced from southern South America, and now established in pockets in the northeastern and southern United States.

CONSERVATION:
These birds remain plentiful in their original South American range.

GREEN PARAKEET *Psittacara holochlorus*

■ SUMMER   ■ MIGRATION
■ WINTER   ■ RARE
■ RESIDENT

Found in urban groves and gardens, Green Parakeet is a common resident of southernmost Texas. Its population is probably a mix of escaped captives and wild colonists from northeastern Mexico. Feral Green Parakeets are also widespread in Florida and California, along with other mostly greenish parakeets native to Central and South America (sometimes called conures); some have established small local populations.

DESCRIPTION: 12½" (32 cm). It is a large, uniformly bright green parakeet with a pale bill; some individuals have red flecks on the head or throat. It is stocky and has a relatively short tail.

VOICE: A rolling, grating, high-pitched chatter.

NESTING: Lays 3–4 eggs in a tree cavity or in crevices on cliff faces.

HABITAT: Native populations occur in tropical and subtropical woodlands, farmlands, and plantations; feral U.S. populations occur near populated areas in the Rio Grande Valley of southern Texas.

RANGE: Mexico, from southwestern Chihuahua and southern Nuevo Leon south into Veracruz to northern Nicaragua; Rio Grande Valley of southern Texas.

CONSERVATION: LC
The historical range of these birds extends from the U.S.-Mexico border through Mexico and into northern Central America; their numbers are declining, but recently, these birds have expanded their range into the lower Rio Grande Valley in southern Texas, where a significant naturalized population seems to have become established.

Originally natives of the foothills on the eastern side of the Andes in South America—Peru, eastern Bolivia, and northwestern Argentina. Escaped pets have now established feral flocks in Los Angeles and San Francisco, and also in southeastern Florida. They frequent areas that are extensively planted with exotic plant species, such as suburbs and parks, rather than occupying native North American habitat. Like other parrots and parakeets, they eat seeds, nuts, and fruits.

DESCRIPTION: 15" (38 cm). Typical of the genus, the adult is mainly green. Its forehead is brownish-red with bright scattered red feathers on the cheeks, sides of the neck, and nape. It has bare white eye rings and gray feet. Juveniles show little or no red plumage.

VOICE: In flight, it produces a high ringing *kerEET*. Its call has been described as a harsh *weee weee* or *cheeah cheeah*.

NESTING: Not much is known. It breeds in cliff colonies. In Argentina, 2–3 broad, oval eggs are sometimes laid in tree hollows lined with pieces of decayed wood; 3–4 eggs are reported in captivity. Eggs hatch in 23 days.

HABITAT: Subtropical or tropical forests and shrubland ecosystems. Its natural habitats are deciduous forests, humid woodland, and associated habitats at altitudes of 3300–11,150 ft. (1–3.5 km). The introduced population in California primarily occurs in urban parks and residential areas.

RANGE: In the U.S., introduced populations are found mainly in Florida, California, and Hawaii.

CONSERVATION: Its population is thought to be stable but patchily distributed in its native range. This species is heavily captured for the international pet trade.

THICK-BILLED PARROT *Rhynchopsitta pachyrhyncha*

■ SUMMER ■ MIGRATION
■ WINTER ■ RARE
■ RESIDENT

Once an irregular visitor to forests of southern Arizona and New Mexico, sightings of Thick-billed Parrots in the U.S. ceased by 1938. A reintroduction program in the Chiricahua Mountains, Arizona, in the 1980s and 90s was not successful in establishing a viable population.

DESCRIPTION: 16" (40 cm) long with an average wingspan of 33" (83 cm). Its plumage is predominantly green, with red in the leading edge of the wings; it has a red forehead that extends back as a superciliary stripe. It has a black bill. The underwing bar is yellow, and the bird's long, pointed tail and pointed wings are visible in flight.

VOICE: A gentle, talkative *ahhr* and *a-ha-ha-ha*, soft for a parrot.

NESTING: Nests in tree cavities, including abandoned large woodpecker holes. Nest site availability likely has been impacted by the decline and probable extinction of Mexico's large Imperial Woodpecker (*Campephilus imperialis*).

HABITAT: Temperate conifer, pine, and mature pine-oak and fir forests.

RANGE: Restricted mainly to the Sierra Madre Occidental in Chihuahua and Durango, Mexico.

CONSERVATION: EN

Thick-billed Parrots are endangered and, according to the IUCN Red List, their numbers continue to decline rapidly due to habitat loss, poaching for the pet trade, and predators such as hawks and owls.

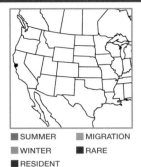

■ SUMMER ■ MIGRATION
■ WINTER ■ RARE
■ RESIDENT

This boldly marked parakeet frequently escapes domestic confinement and can be seen occasionally in the heart of large cities like New York and San Francisco; it nests successfully in California and Florida.

DESCRIPTION: 9" (23 cm). A small, stocky green parakeet with a pointed tail and a flash of yellow and white in the wing.

VOICE: A rapid series of shrill metallic notes.

NESTING: Lays 5 white eggs placed in a natural cavity or in a dense cluster of dead palm fronds.

HABITAT: Suburban areas, parks, and gardens.

RANGE: Native to tropical America. Introduced and established in southern California and southern Florida.

CONSERVATION: Its numbers are stable in its native range. Popular in the pet trade, large numbers of these birds escaped captivity and established feral populations in southern Florida in the 1960s and 1970s. Some escaped birds have also thrived in California as well.

Captive-bred Yellow-headed Parrots are popular pets, as these colorful, long-lived birds can be trained to mimic human speech. Unfortunately, their capture for the pet trade has endangered this species in the wild, as poaching persists even with laws governing the sale and international trade of captive-bred birds. Escaped cage birds have established small feral flocks around Los Angeles and San Diego, California, and locally in southern Florida and southern Texas.

DESCRIPTION: 15" (38 cm). A large, chunky parrot with extensive yellow on the head and a pale bill. Immatures show less yellow on the head.

VOICE: Generally a mellow *herra* or a long descending *yadadadada*, also makes low-pitched screams; usually flies silently. These birds' calls sound almost human and they are excellent mimics; in captivity they can be taught to mimic human speech.

NESTING: Nests in a cavity in a tree or palm. It usually lays 2–3 eggs per clutch.

HABITAT: Tropical semi-deciduous, deciduous, and riparian forests (including clearings). It can be found in various moist and dense forests, pine savannas, mangroves, coastal shrubs, and cultivated areas with trees.

RANGE: Formerly widespread in Mexico and northern Central America, it has drastically declined in the wild. What remains is patchy distribution in southern and eastern Mexico and in Belize, also in Guatemala and Honduras. In the U.S., introduced populations are resident in southern California and southern Florida; a few occur in southern Texas.

CONVERSATION: **EN**

Endangered and decreasing mainly due to poaching for the pet trade. Importing/exporting and sales of captive-bred birds are regulated by international law, but their popularity as cage birds and high price tag continue to drive poaching from the endangered wild population.

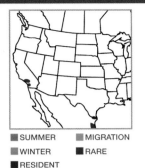

■ SUMMER   ■ MIGRATION
■ WINTER   ■ RARE
■ RESIDENT

A native of Mexico, Red-crowned Parrot inhabits urban, agri-cultural, and forested areas. Naturalized populations are found in the U.S. in southern California, Texas, and Florida. Only the Monk Parakeet compares in its success as a feral psittacine in North America. These parrots are highly gregarious, flying between communal roosts and feeding areas and delivering raucous calls in early morning and late afternoon. At other times of day, the species is less conspicuous as it feeds or rests within foliage.

DESCRIPTION: 12" (30 cm). This is a large, stocky parrot with a blocky body and head, broad wings, and a short, squared-off tail with a yellow tip. Bright green overall, adult birds have a red crown; young birds have only a red forehead.

VOICE: Gives various talkative, grating calls when perched; in flight, it gives a piercing, high-pitched call followed by 3 or 4 much lower, abrupt *klaak!* calls.

NESTING: Red-crowned Parrots occupy existing cavities created by large woodpeckers or natural decay processes. Clutches are 2–5 white eggs, similar in size and shape to those of a Rock Pigeon; incubation is completed by the female alone.

HABITAT: In Mexico, sub-deciduous tropical forests and Tamau-lipan scrub. Introduced populations in the U.S. occur in urban settings where large trees provide food and nesting sites.

RANGE: Resident (but endangered) in a limited area of north-eastern Mexico (eastern Nuevo Leon, southern Tamaulipas, eastern San Luis Potosí, and northeast Veracruz). Feral popula-tions are established in southern California, Texas, Puerto Rico, Hawaii, and Florida; some suggest that birds in Texas represent a natural range expansion forced by habitat modification and severe frosts in Mexico.

CONSERVATION: EN

In its native range, the Red-crowned Parrot is endangered due to habitat loss and depreda-tion of nests to supply birds for a lucrative pet trade. Escapees and birds "released" during illegal transit have resulted in the establish-ment of feral populations in the U.S., which number hundreds if not thousands of birds—these naturalized populations may, in fact, outnumber the birds remaining in the species' native range.

LILAC-CROWNED PARROT *Amazona finschi*

These chunky parrots are native to western Mexico, and they are often kept in captivity. Escaped birds may survive for many years around southern cities. Lilac-crowned Parrots are seen regularly in cities of coastal southern California, especially around Los Angeles. Other sightings come from around cities in southeastern Florida. In small feral flocks, they often mix with related species such as Red-crowned Parrot and Yellow-headed Parrot (*A. oratrix*).

DESCRIPTION: 13" (33 cm). Lime green overall, lighter on the breast and abdomen. It has a distinct band of deep red-maroon across the forehead between the eyes. It is lilac-blue across the top of the head, over the nape, and on the sides of the neck. Its legs and feet are blue-gray. It may be confused in mixed flocks with the similar Red-crowned Parrot. The end of the tail is noticeably longer than in similar species, but is squared off, not as pointed as in similar species.

VOICE: Contrasting to the down-slurred whistle of the Red-crowned Parrot, the Lilac-crowned gives a squeaky, up-slurred *kree, kree*; a rolling *krreeeih*; and a raven-like croak.

NESTING: Pacific coastal forests in humid valleys at elevations of 2000–3300 ft. (600–1000 m) are its optimal nesting habitat, providing important food resources during the dry season.

HABITAT: Deciduous and semi-deciduous forests along the Mexican coast, as well as pine-oak forests. Escaped or released birds and their descendants occur in residential and suburban areas in California, sometimes in native oaks. It has nested in native coniferous forest in the San Gabriel Mountains. Also found in Florida. It is not abundant in any of these areas.

RANGE: Native to the Pacific coast of western Mexico from southeastern Sonora to southern Oaxaca. Feral U.S. populations are found mainly in the San Gabriel Valley, Los Angeles, and Orange counties. Birds have also been sighted in Riverside County and a small population documented in Santa Barbara County.

CONSERVATION: EN

Endangered and decreasing in its native range in Mexico. Native populations are seriously diminished due to deforestation and the pet trade, and it is estimated that only 7000 to 10,000 individuals survive. Adults are easily netted in large numbers because of their habit of gathering in large communal roosts, and chicks are poached from nests. The bird's preferred nesting habitat in the Pacific coastal forest is being lost at a greater rate than any other forest type in Mexico.

In southern California and southern Texas, birds escaped from captivity are often seen in mixed flocks of other feral parrots, including Red-crowned and Yellow-headed parrots.

DESCRIPTION: 13" (33 cm). This parrot is mostly green with a red forehead, blue crown and, in some subspecies, yellow cheeks. Males and females appear the same. Juveniles are similar but noticeably green on the head. Dark edging on the feathers of the crown and breast create a slightly scalloped effect. Its gray bill graduates to pale yellow at the base of the upper mandible. It has a white eye ring around a yellow to orange eye.

VOICE: Produces a wide variety of sounds, from high-pitched trilling to loud, metallic scolding.

NESTING: Lays 3–4 white eggs in a tree cavity. Eggs require a 26-day incubation, and chicks fledge about 60 days after hatching.

HABITAT: Wide range of habitats including tropical rainforest, wet woodlands, cultivated areas with trees, and plantations; mostly occurs below 2,500 ft. (762 m).

RANGE: Native from eastern Mexico south to Ecuador. Despite its becoming rare in the wild, in parts of Mexico and Venezuela it has shown a remarkable adaptability to developed areas.

CONSERVATION:
Popular in the pet trade, Red-lored Parrot numbers in the wild are declining. Its adaptability and its large natural range may help to counteract these losses.

MEALY PARROT *Amazona farinosa*

Also called Mealy Amazon, this is one of the many exotic parrot species introduced in Florida.

DESCRIPTION: 16" (41 cm). One of the largest of the Amazons, this dull, all-green parrot is characterized by its two-toned tail, darker green at the base and bright green at the tip, and its obvious white eye ring (orbital). A "chalky" appearance on the feathers makes it appear dusty or "mealy," as if covered in a faint layer of flour. Its bill is a yellow-horn color at the base, darkening at the tip. The iris is orange-red to red. Its feet are light gray. Subspecies may display a spattering of yellow feathers, or a blue/violet tinge, on the crown.

VOICE: Less raucous and quieter than other Amazons, and its voice is deeper, perhaps because of its larger size. It issues a variety of screeches and multisyllabic notes in flight.

NESTING: Breeding occurs from November to March, and the female lays 3 eggs on average, incubating them for about 4 weeks. Like many parrots, the young stay with their parents for a considerable time—about 2 months—before establishing their independence.

HABITAT: Humid to semi-humid forest and plantations. Absent in open or dry habitats.

RANGE: Tropical Central and South America.

CONSERVATION: NT

Like others in this family, Mealy Parrot appears to be in decline for many of the same reasons: habitat loss and capture by humans for food, as a crop pest, and for the pet trade.

Yellow-naped Parrot is popular as a cage bird. Escapees or released birds may be seen free-flying in southern cities of the U.S., often associating with flocks of other feral parrots. It is related to the Yellow-headed Parrot and the Yellow-crowned Parrot (*A. ochrocephala*), and—being similar in appearance—is sometimes difficult to accurately identify. If you are observing a juvenile of any of these species, and their plumage is still developing, it may be confusing.

DESCRIPTION: 14" (35 cm). The adult Yellow-naped may be identified by the distinct yellow patch or band across the back of the neck. The rest of the head is typically green—the occasional individual may have a bit of yellow on its forehead. Its dark gray bill becomes a lighter gray color towards the base of the upper mandible. Its feet are dark gray, and its eyes are orange to red. Males and females have the same coloring.

VOICE: Gives noisy calls early in the morning and again at sunset.

NESTING: Lays 3–4 eggs, which are incubated for 26–28 days. The young fledge at 8–12 weeks.

HABITAT: Tropical woodlands and forests. This habitat provides its main food sources—fruits, seeds, nuts, blossoms, and leafy buds of foliage—similar to many parrots of the region.

RANGE: It is found along the Pacific Coast from southern Mexico south to northern Costa Rica.

CONSERVATION:
Endangered and decreasing in its native range. It is threatened by habitat loss and poaching for the local and international pet trade.

Native to southern Asia and central Africa, this big, long-tailed parakeet has been popular as a cage bird for centuries around the world. Escaped birds have established stable feral populations in many regions, most of these centered around large cities. In the U.S., there are wild flocks around Los Angeles and Bakersfield, California, and around Naples, Florida, with scattered sightings elsewhere.

DESCRIPTION: 16" (40 cm) long including the tail. This all-green to yellow-green parakeet is sexually dimorphic. The male has a red "necklace," while females and juveniles show a faint hint of a gray neck ring or none at all. A pink to red bill is a striking contrast against the vivid green plumage. It has a dark/black "mustache" and chin. Various shades of blue may be apparent as undertones in the low light of cloudy days. The long, pointed tails may be nearly half the birds' length, up to 7" (18 cm). The two longest tail feathers are blue. Because this bird has been kept as a pet since ancient Roman and Greek times, there are aviculture-produced color mutations that are blue or yellow and without the neck ring.

VOICE: A noisy, loud, screechy descending *kee-ak . . . kee-ak . . . kee-ak*. As hundreds of birds may congregate in flight and evening roosts, this is a considerable aural experience.

NESTING: Lays 2–5 eggs in the cavity of a mature tree with little additional nesting material.

HABITAT: Adaptable to disturbed habitats. Established feral colonies inhabit several urban areas around the world.

RANGE: In their native ranges they are common in forests and arid environments.

CONSERVATION:

These birds are adaptable and increasing, and they have colonized urban and deforested areas in Florida and California, as well as many other sites globally. In many such places there are no natural predators to check their numbers, and some perceive these non-native colonies as a threat to the native ecology and/or a serious crop pest.

A small parrot native to Australia. This familiar cage bird, which occurs in a variety of colors besides those of the wild type described here, escapes so frequently that they may be seen almost anywhere in North America. Escapees have been known to nest successfully in Florida.

DESCRIPTION: 7" (18 cm). The typical adult is barred above with black and yellow; its rump and underparts are green (occasionally blue). Its tail is long, pointed, and green. White-winged Parakeet is slightly larger. Its plumage is entirely green except for yellow-and-white patches on the wings; it has a much larger bill.

VOICE: A chattering warble, interspersed with screeching notes.

NESTING: Lays 4–7 white eggs in a natural cavity or birdhouse.

HABITAT: Suburbs, parks, and gardens.

RANGE: Introduced from Australia and established in west-central Florida and elsewhere in the state. Escapees may be seen continentwide.

CONSERVATION: Least concern and increasing in its native range in Australia.

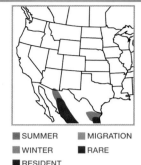

■ SUMMER ■ MIGRATION
■ WINTER ■ RARE
■ RESIDENT

This quiet, unobtrusive tropical bird spends most of its time foraging in tall trees and is therefore difficult to find. It is adept at catching flying insects, like its relatives the flycatchers, and also feeds on berries. The northern limit of its range is just within the southern U.S. border, but it is common nowhere in our area.

DESCRIPTION: 6½" (17 cm). Sparrow-sized. The male is gray above, with a black cap and a pale rose-red throat; it is whitish below. The female is brown, paler below, with a dusky grayish cap.

VOICE: A high-pitched whistle, *seeeeooo*; various chattering notes.

NESTING: Lays 2 or 3 brown-speckled white eggs in a globular nest of plant fibers with a side entrance.

HABITAT: Thick woodlands along streams and wooded canyons.

RANGE: Breeds from southeastern Arizona and the Rio Grande Valley of Texas southward. Winters south of the U.S.-Mexico border.

SUBSPECIES: In the subspecies found in western Mexico and in Arizona (*P. a. albiventris*), males are all gray with a dark crown and the females are browner on the back. The larger subspecies (*P. a. gravis*) is found in eastern Mexico and may casually occur along the lower Rio Grande in Texas, usually in winter; males in this population are darker, and the females are more rufous compared to their western counterparts.

SIMILAR SPECIES: Black Phoebe and Say's Phoebe are both common, grayish flycatchers with dark heads, but neither has the plain gray belly of the male Rose-throated Becard or the plain brown/rufous belly of the female. Phoebe bills are thinner and needle-like.

CONSERVATION:

This species is more common and widespread in Mexico and Central America, where its numbers are stable. Its occurrence in Arizona may have increased slightly in recent decades, although it is still rare and local.

NORTHERN BEARDLESS-TYRANNULET
Camptostoma imberbe

■ SUMMER ■ MIGRATION
■ WINTER ■ RARE
■ RESIDENT

This tiny bird, the smallest flycatcher in the United States, lacks the stout bristles at the base of the bill that are present in most members of its family, hence its name. Instead of flycatching on the wing, it looks and acts like a Verdin, kinglet, or small vireo, hopping among twigs and branches in search of insects. Because it is small, nondescript, and inhabits thickets, it is most often identified by its distinctive calls.

DESCRIPTION: 4" (10 cm). A nondescript, dull-colored bird with a tiny bill. It is olive-gray above with pale buff wing bars; it is whitish below with a dusky throat and breast.

VOICE: A thin *tee-tee-tee-tee-tee*, loudest in the middle. Also give three long notes followed by a trill.

NESTING: Lays 3 brown-spotted buff eggs in a twig nest lined with lichens, mosses, and grasses, placed near the end of a branch among the foliage well up in an evergreen tree.

HABITAT: Low thorn scrub, especially mesquite thickets and woodland borders.

RANGE: Breeds in southeastern Arizona and southernmost Texas. Many birds migrate to Mexico for the winter. Also found in the tropics.

SIMILAR SPECIES: See immature Verdin, *Empidonax* flycatchers, and vireos.

CONSERVATION: Its numbers in North America are increasing. It is widespread in Mexico and Central America south to Costa Rica.

SUMMER ■ MIGRATION
WINTER ■ RARE
RESIDENT

All flycatchers in the genus *Myiarchus* are similar in appearance. They may be identified by their habitats and, where habitats overlap, by voice. Though fairly common in suitable habitats, this bird is more often heard than seen; in this respect it is like the more widespread Great Crested Flycatcher of eastern woodlands, whose general habits it shares. Small groups of Dusky-capped Flycatchers have been observed "sunning" face down, with wings and tails spread wide, on the steep, bare slope of an arroyo, or dry wash.

DESCRIPTION: 6½–7" (17–18 cm). A small *Myiarchus* flycatcher, with much brown, but no rufous on the tail. It is pale olive-brown above, with a grayish throat and breast, and a pale yellow belly. Its bill is relatively long and black.

VOICE: A plaintive *pee-ur*, rising and then falling in pitch, followed by a soft *huit*. Its call note is a soft *huit*.

NESTING: Lays 4 or 5 brown-spotted, creamy-white eggs in a nest lined with vegetable fibers in a tree or a cactus hole.

HABITAT: Scrub oak thickets and canyon growth.

RANGE: Breeds in southeastern Arizona and southwestern New Mexico. Winters south of the U.S.-Mexico border. Also found in the tropics.

SIMILAR SPECIES: Great Crested, Brown-crested, and Ash-throated flycatchers are larger and have conspicuous cinnamon-rufous in the tail; their calls are also quite different.

CONSERVATION:
This species' numbers in Arizona and New Mexico fluctuate annually; globally they are declining due to habitat loss in the American tropics.

Myiarchus cinerascens **ASH-THROATED FLYCATCHER**

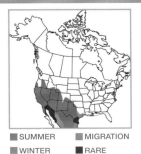

■ SUMMER ■ MIGRATION
■ WINTER ■ RARE
■ RESIDENT

The Ash-throated Flycatcher lives in the hottest, driest parts of the West, but is also found farther north in dry, shady, open woodlands. These birds launch their pursuit of insects from the dead upper branches of mature trees at the edges of woods. Trunk rot in these trees creates cavities useful as nesting sites. Open nests would be too exposed in the sparse foliage of this dry habitat, transitional between woodland and open range. Although this flycatcher has become a hole-breeder, it still builds a nest and has streaked, camouflaged eggs like its open-nesting ancestors.

DESCRIPTION: 8" (20 cm). It is dull olive above and yellowish below. It is similar to Brown-crested Flycatcher (and to Great Crested Flycatcher of the East) but smaller and less colorful; its back is browner, and its throat and breast are grayish white. Its bill is black.

VOICE: *Purreeeer*, similar to call of Brown-crested Flycatcher but softer. Also a soft *ka-brick*.

NESTING: Lays 2–7 eggs in a cup-shaped nest built inside a cavity. Ash-throated Flycatchers are secondary cavity nesters, reusing holes originally made by woodpeckers or other species, or using naturally occurring cavities in dead trees or cacti. They also use many types of artificial cavities ranging from nest boxes to fence posts to mailboxes and other structures.

HABITAT: Deserts with cactus and mesquite thickets; also dry woods.

RANGE: Breeds from Washington and Wyoming south to the southwestern United States, and east to Texas. It is rare on the Atlantic Coast in late fall, when it is the only *Myiarchus* likely to occur. It winters in southern California and Arizona southward.

SIMILAR SPECIES: Identification is most reliable when based on voice. Great Crested Flycatcher has substantially darker throat and breast, a brighter yellow belly, a more olive back, and a paler bill.

Brown-crested Flycatcher is slightly larger, darker above and on the throat; its belly is slightly brighter; the rufous in its tail extends to the tip.

Dusky-capped Flycatcher is slightly smaller and somewhat darker throughout; it lacks conspicuous rufous in the tail.

CONSERVATION:
Ash-throated Flycatchers are common throughout the arid West, and their numbers have increased slightly in recent decades.

This tropical flycatcher is an accidental vagrant to the south-western United States, from Arizona and possibly New Mexico to California. Although there are only a few records, some of the birds to visit our range have remained for a significant period of time, often in a single location, making it easier to spot than vagrants that visit more briefly. Any possible location for a Nutting's Flycatcher could also host a similar Ash-throated Flycatcher. Fortunately, Nutting's Flycatcher calls outside of the breeding season, and its call is quite distinct.

DESCRIPTION: 7–7½" (18–19 cm). A typical *Myiarchus* flycatcher, it is extremely difficult to distinguish from Ash-throated in the field. Its call is distinctly different from that of Ash-throated and other similar species. Its yellow secondary edges (which are white in adult Ash-throated) are a possible visual cue.

VOICE: Its sharp *wheep* or *wheek* is the best way to identify this species.

NESTING: Lays 5 or 6 creamy-white, brown-spotted eggs in tree cavities or artificial nest boxes. The bulky nest may be lined with all sorts of items—plastic, snakeskins, string, rags, etc.

HABITAT: Forests and shrublands, generally in drier areas.

RANGE: Western Mexico and Central America, from southern Sonora, Mexico to Costa Rica.

SIMILAR SPECIES: Best distinguished from more common Ash-throated Flycatcher by its call.

CONSERVATION: Nutting's Flycatcher numbers are stable in the bird's native range.

Myiarchus crinitus **GREAT CRESTED FLYCATCHER**

■ SUMMER ■ MIGRATION
■ WINTER ■ RARE
■ RESIDENT

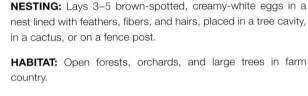

This common eastern flycatcher is noisy, aggressive, and colorful. Living mostly under the forest canopy, however, it is much more often heard than seen. While searching for food or in encounters with other birds, the Great Crested typically erects its crown feathers, peers about with an outstretched head and neck, and slowly bobs its head in a deliberate fashion. The Great Crested is the only eastern flycatcher that nests in holes. It has a curious habit of using shed snakeskins in its nest lining. Whether this is intended to frighten off predators or merely decorate the nest is not known.

DESCRIPTION: 9" (23 cm). It is slightly crested, brown above, with a gray throat, yellow belly, rufous wings and tail, and pale brown at the base of the lower mandible.

VOICE: A loud, whistled, slightly buzzy *wheep*, sometimes repeated. Also a raucous *whit-whit-whit-whit*.

NESTING: Lays 3–5 brown-spotted, creamy-white eggs in a nest lined with feathers, fibers, and hairs, placed in a tree cavity, in a cactus, or on a fence post.

HABITAT: Open forests, orchards, and large trees in farm country.

RANGE: Breeds from south-central and southeastern Canada to Gulf Coast. Winters in southern Florida; also in tropics.

SIMILAR SPECIES: See Brown-crested and Ash-throated flycatchers.

CONSERVATION:  Great Crested Flycatcher numbers have been stable over the past several decades. Local declines may result from a shortage of nest cavities where dead snags are cleared; these birds will accept artificial nest boxes.

■ SUMMER   ■ MIGRATION
■ WINTER   ■ RARE
■ RESIDENT

A conspicuous and noisy summer resident of open cactus and deciduous woodlands of the southwestern United States, the Brown-crested Flycatcher shares its habitat with the similar Ash-throated Flycatcher. The Brown-crested is virtually identical in general appearance and habits to the more widespread Great Crested Flycatcher, which migrates through the Brown-crested's range in southern Texas. This bird's former name, "Wied's Crested Flycatcher," was in honor of Prince Maximilian of Wied, a German naturalist and traveler in early 19th-century America.

DESCRIPTION: 9½" (24 cm). A large flycatcher, olive above and yellow below, with cinnamon in the wings and tail. Its larger size, black bill, and brighter sulphur-yellow belly distinguish it from Ash-throated Flycatcher. Great Crested Flycatcher has brighter underparts and a brown, not blackish, lower mandible; it is best distinguished by voice.

VOICE: A burry *purreeeer*, a sharp *wit!*, or *way-burg*.

NESTING: Lays 3–6 eggs, usually 4–5, in a cavity nest built either in a natural cavity such as an old woodpecker hole or in an artificial site such as a bird house or hollow fence post. Both parents build the nest, bringing material such as grass, weed, bark, feathers, and other debris usually including a piece of snakeskin or a piece of clear plastic.

HABITAT: Arid lands in areas with cacti or large trees.

RANGE: Breeds from southern California, southern Nevada, central Arizona, and southern Texas southward. Winters mainly south of U.S.-Mexico border, but a few winter in southern Florida.

SUBSPECIES: Western populations (subsp. *magister*) in the Southwest average larger with a larger bill than the Eastern populations (subsp. *cooperi*) that occur in Texas.

SIMILAR SPECIES: Age and seasonal variation make identification difficult without recourse to voice. Great Crested Flycatcher is olive-brown above, has a slightly darker throat and breast, a somewhat brighter yellow belly, and a paler lower mandible. See Ash-throated and Dusky-capped flycatchers.

CONSERVATION: LC

Widespread in the American tropics; its numbers in its limited U.S. range are stable to increasing.

Myiarchus sagrae LA SAGRA'S FLYCATCHER

- ■ SUMMER
- ■ MIGRATION
- ■ WINTER
- ■ RARE
- ■ RESIDENT

La Sagra's Flycatcher is a nearly annual vagrant in Florida, with accidental sightings elsewhere in the Southeast. It is a rare visitor from the Bahamas, with one or two recorded each year in brushy woods of hardwood trees and shrubs in southeastern Florida.

DESCRIPTION: 7½–9" (19–22 cm). A medium-sized, drab *Myiarchus* flycatcher. It is large-billed and flat-headed. It has almost no yellow or sulphur color on the breast or belly—it is the grayest among *Myiarchus* species in North America. *Myiarchus* is one of the most difficult of all avian genera to identify, and La Sagra's best distinguishing mark is its drabness.

VOICE: *Wheet-ze-wheet* and buzzy *brrr*. It does not have a long, pure whistle without a buzzy interruption.

NESTING: Lays 4 creamy-white, brown-spotted eggs in a bulky, domed stick nest with the entrance at the side, often in a thorn tree or bush.

HABITAT: Forests, woodlands, scrublands, and thickets. Because it nests in tree cavities and broken branches, La Sagra's needs some trees large enough to provide such holes.

RANGE: Cuba, the Bahamas, and other northern Caribbean islands.

SIMILAR SPECIES: Ash-throated Flycatcher has a somewhat shorter bill and considerably more rufous on the outer tail.

CONSERVATION: Although this species' numbers aren't well documented, it is considered to be fairly common in its native range. Its numbers are believed to be decreasing due to ongoing habitat loss.

GREAT KISKADEE *Pitangus sulphuratus*

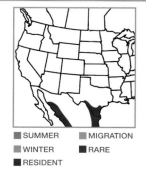

■ SUMMER ■ MIGRATION
■ WINTER ■ RARE
■ RESIDENT

This large and striking bird, named for its call, is common throughout Latin America. In addition to insects, it eats small fruits and even fish, diving straight into the water like a kingfisher, although not as deeply.

DESCRIPTION: 10½" (27 cm). A stocky, robin-sized flycatcher. It has a broad, black bill; a black-and-white striped head; a rufous-brown back; bright yellow underparts; and rufous wings. Its rufous tail is conspicuous in flight.

VOICE: Loud, piercing *kis-ka-dee*; also an incessant, shrill chattering.

NESTING: Lays 3–5 white or buff eggs, with spots and blotches, in a nest in a tree cavity.

HABITAT: Rivers, streams, and lakes bordered with dense vegetation; also found in more open country and in parks in most of its range.

RANGE: Resident from extreme southern Texas (lower Rio Grande Valley) southward.

SIMILAR SPECIES: Tropical, Couch's and Western kingbirds all have gray heads and lack the bold black-and-white head pattern; they also lack the rich reddish-brown color on the back and tail.

CONSERVATION: LC

Widespread and common in Central and South America, Great Kiskadee numbers are increasing. Its numbers in its limited North American range may also be increasing.

■ SUMMER　　■ MIGRATION
■ WINTER　　■ RARE
■ RESIDENT

These loud, vividly marked birds are easily detected when they sally forth from high treetop perches in pursuit of flying prey, but when sitting still they are well camouflaged and inconspicuous. Like the closely related kingbirds, they have a brightly colored crest, but it is hidden among their crown feathers.

DESCRIPTION: 7½–8½" (19–22 cm). A large, heavily streaked flycatcher. Its upperparts are buff-brown with brown streaks; its underparts are yellow with blackish streaks. It has a dark line across the eye and a dark "mustache." Its tail and rump are rufous.

VOICE: Loud, shrill *peet-chee* calls, sounding like a squeaking hinge or wheel, uttered by a single bird or pair in duet. The male has a soft *tre-le-re-re* song.

NESTING: Lays 3–4 white to pale buff eggs, heavily spotted with reddish brown. In Arizona, it prefers to nest in large natural cavities of sycamore trees that are 20–50' (6–15 m) above the ground. These birds are aggressive during the nesting season, and pairs of Sulphur-bellies may compete for choice sites with other cavity-nesting birds considerably larger than themselves.

HABITAT: Wooded canyons; prefers sycamores.

RANGE: Breeds from southeastern Arizona southward. Occurs casually in coastal California and along the Gulf Coast. Winters in the tropics.

SIMILAR SPECIES: Heavy, dark streaking above and below and a yellow breast makes Sulphur-bellied Flycatcher difficult to mistake for any other native flycatcher. *Myiarchus* flycatchers generally have gray throats and pale yellow bellies with no streaks; Great Kiskadee has a clean, bright yellow breast without streaking.

CONSERVATION:
In recent years, the Sulphur-bellied Flycatcher's numbers have been steady—if not increasing—throughout its range, including in its limited range in North America.

Piratic Flycatcher is an accidental vagrant across the southern tier of the United States from Florida to New Mexico. Outside of southern Arizona, where the Sulphur-bellied Flycatcher is native, any streak-bellied flycatcher is unexpected in North America. The three possible species are distinguished by size and pattern. Piratic Flycatcher's name comes from its habit of using other small birds' nests, evicting the owner if necessary.

DESCRIPTION: 5¾–6½" (14.5–17 cm). A smallish flycatcher whose best distinguishing mark is its breast marked with blurry streaks. It has a dark, unstreaked back and an all-dark tail. Its head is boldly striped with black and white, and includes a dark mask that extends below the eye.

VOICE: Whistled *whee-whee*. Reportedly silent when encountered outside of its native range.

NESTING: Lays 2–4 brown eggs streaked with black in a nest appropriated from another bird, often a domed or enclosed nest of a larger species. Piratic Flycatchers drive off the nest's owner and remove the eggs before laying their own.

HABITAT: Forests and woodland, clearings with some tall trees still present.

RANGE: Breeds from east-central Mexico south to southern Brazil and northern Argentina, winters in northern and central South America. Both the northernmost and southernmost breeding populations appear to migrate closer to the central part of the range.

SIMILAR SPECIES: This species is much smaller than the Sulphur-bellied, the only native flycatcher with a streaked breast, and is somewhat smaller than the Variegated Flycatcher, another vagrant to consider.

CONSERVATION:

Piratic Flycatcher is widespread in the American tropics, where its population is large and stable.

This South American flycatcher has been sighted across the United States and into Canada, seemingly with little pattern. Less than 10 North American records have included sightings in Maine, Tennessee, Washington State, and Ontario. Despite the distance from its native range, this species seems more likely to appear accidentally in northern North America than the similar Sulphur-bellied Flycatcher.

DESCRIPTION: 7–7½" (18–19 cm). A fairly large flycatcher, the Variegated's streaked breast is unlike any native North American species except for the Sulphur-bellied of southern Arizona. It is streaked and dark above, and pale yellow below with dark blurry streaks. It has two bold, dark facial lines and rufous-edged tail feathers.

VOICE: *Chee-chee-chu*, also a high-pitched buzz *zeeeeete*.

NESTING: Lays 3–5 spotted, buff-colored eggs in a cup nest on a horizontal branch.

HABITAT: Forest edges, openings, and shrublands.

RANGE: Northern South America, east of the Andes. One sub-species is a long-distance migrant, which occasionally seems to migrate past its usual range.

SIMILAR SPECIES: Resembles a small Sulphur-bellied Flycatcher. Sulphur-bellied is more boldly streaked on the back and underside, and is normally found in southeastern Arizona (casually along the California and Gulf coasts).

Piratic Flycatcher, another vagrant to North America, is similar but quite a bit smaller with no rufous on the tail.

CONVERSATION:

The Variegated Flycatcher is considered fairly common and its population is thought to be stable throughout South America, although its numbers are not well documented.

TROPICAL KINGBIRD *Tyrannus melancholicus*

■ SUMMER ■ MIGRATION
■ WINTER ■ RARE
■ RESIDENT

This species is one of a group of Mexican birds that make a post-breeding reverse migration in the late summer and fall northward along the Pacific Coast. It is quiet, inconspicuous, and less gregarious than other kingbirds and visually resembles other kingbird species. It and the similar Couch's Kingbird, found in southern Texas, were once considered the same species and are extremely difficult to distinguish from one another in the field where their ranges overlap. In recent decades, the Tropical Kingbird has become a rare visitor to the Rio Grande Valley, posing a challenge to local birders.

DESCRIPTION: 8–9½" (20–24 cm). Resembles the more widespread Western Kingbird, and is almost identical to Couch's Kingbird. It has a gray head; an olive back; and a brown, notched tail with no white. It has a white throat and a bright yellow upper breast, belly, and undertail coverts.

VOICE: Twittering trills.

NESTING: Lays 3 or 4 pinkish, brown-spotted eggs in a stick nest lined with grass and moss in a tree.

HABITAT: Woodland borders, savannas, and riverside groves.

RANGE: Breeds in southeastern Arizona, uncommonly in southern Texas, and throughout the American tropics. Winters mostly south of the U.S.-Mexico border, but also wanders widely, rarely to the Pacific Coast.

SIMILAR SPECIES: Couch's and Tropical kingbirds are normally distinguished in the U.S. by range and by voice, but vagrant individuals seldom call. Any fall bird on the Pacific Coast is probably a Tropical Kingbird. Farther east, wandering Couch's confirmed at least in western Texas and southern Louisiana, but Tropical could easily occur in these areas. Minor visual differences are useless in sightings of lone wanderers. Immatures wander most often and may be impossible to distinguish from species in the field.

See Western, Cassin's, and immature Thick-billed kingbirds.

CONSERVATION: LC

The Tropical Kingbird population is increasing due to rainforest being cleared and turned into open habitat that this species prefers. Its numbers in the United States may also be increasing slowly.

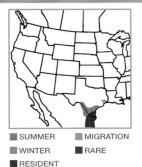

■ SUMMER ■ MIGRATION
■ WINTER ■ RARE
■ RESIDENT

In summer, Couch's Kingbird may be fairly common in southern Texas, where it frequents the borders of woods and river-edge brush. Couch's Kingbird and Tropical Kingbird were once considered the same species, but the voices of the two differ consistently, and they do not interbreed where they live together in eastern Mexico.

DESCRIPTION: 8½" (22 cm). It has bright yellow underparts, an olive back, and a dark patch through the eye. It has a slightly forked brown tail without white edges. Tropical Kingbird, rare in southern Texas, is essentially identical in appearance but has distinctive twittering calls.

VOICE: A series of *breer* notes, followed by *puit-puwit-puwit-pawitcheew*. Its call is a short *kip*.

NESTING: Lays 3–5 white, spotted eggs in a bulky nest lined with twigs, grass, or animal hair, placed on a horizontal limb, well hidden.

HABITAT: Borders of woodlands and brushy streamside thickets.

RANGE: Resident in extreme southern Texas. Casual on the Gulf Coast in fall and winter.

SIMILAR SPECIES: See Tropical and Western kingbirds and *Myiarchus* flycatchers.

CONSERVATION:

Couch's Kingbird numbers are increasing in the northern part of its range in northern Mexico and Texas. In its central range through eastern Mexico, its number may increase with partial forest clearing, but total clearing of the forest drives these birds out.

■ SUMMER   ■ MIGRATION
■ WINTER   ■ RARE
■ RESIDENT

Cassin's Kingbird breeds from desert riparian areas into the southwestern mountains, where it may be found in pinyon-yucca, pine-oak, and even open pine forests; in western California, it inhabits open valley woodlands and foothill grassland communities. Cassin's Kingbird is often found high on a tree, where it sits more quietly than a Western Kingbird.

DESCRIPTION: 8–9" (20–23 cm). Similar to Western Kingbird but darker, with a more olive-gray back, and a black tail lightly white-tipped but lacking white margins. Its darker gray breast makes its white throat patch appear smaller and more clearly defined than that of a Western Kingbird.

VOICE: A loud *chi-beer!* and a rapid *chi-beer, ch-beer-beer-beer-r-r.*

NESTING: Lays 3 or 4 white eggs, spotted with brown, in a cup of twigs and weed stems in a sycamore or cottonwood.

HABITAT: Savannas, rangelands, pinyon-juniper woodlands.

RANGE: Breeds in southern California and from Montana south to southern Utah and Southwest. Winters in southern California.

SIMILAR SPECIES: Worn or molting Western Kingbird occasionally shows little or no white on the tail, but still appears much paler on the upperparts and breast.

Tropical and Couch's kingbirds are pale greenish-gray on the upper breast. They have a larger, longer bill; a green back; and a brownish, deeply forked tail. Worn kingbirds in early fall present the greatest identification difficulty.

CONSERVATION: ![LC]
The widespread and common Cassin's Kingbird is stable throughout its range, which is expanding northward into Wyoming and Colorado. The success of the species is higher where it does not overlap with the Western Kingbird.

■ SUMMER ■ MIGRATION
■ WINTER ■ RARE
■ RESIDENT

The Thick-billed Kingbird is one of the Mexican species that regularly cross the border and make southeastern Arizona so fascinating for birders. Within its limited North American range, this species often frequents large territories and commonly flies great distances between perches. These birds are easiest to locate early in the season, in May and June, and early in the morning. They perch high in trees and prey on flying insects. These kingbirds react to predators with loud cries, calls, and attacks.

DESCRIPTION: 9" (23 cm). This flycatcher is brownish above, with a darker brown head. Its tail is uniformly gray-brown. Its throat and breast are whitish, and it has a pale yellow tinge on the lower belly. It has a stocky neck and a large, black bill that is especially thick at the base.

VOICE: A loud *kiterreer* and a high-pitched *bur-ree*.

NESTING: Lays 4 creamy-white eggs in a stick nest lined with plant fibers and placed in a tree or bush.

HABITAT: Streamside growth and sycamore canyons.

RANGE: Breeds extremely locally in southeastern Arizona and adjacent New Mexico. Winters south of the U.S.-Mexico border.

SIMILAR SPECIES: Other North American kingbirds have more extensive yellow on the underparts, a yellow or gray breast, and gray or green upperparts.

Tropical Kingbird is similar to immature Thick-billed but has a smaller bill, a pale head, and pale edgings to the wing coverts.

Myiarchus flycatchers in worn plumage (especially Brown-crested) may look similar but show reddish in the tail and wings; they lack the especially dark head and white throat, and their bills are less triangular.

CONSERVATION:
The Thick-billed Kingbird population seems to have increased throughout its steadily expanding range since its first documented appearance in the United States in the mid-1950s.

■ SUMMER　　■ MIGRATION
■ WINTER　　　■ RARE
■ RESIDENT

The Western Kingbird is found on almost every ranch in the West, where alfalfa and livestock pastures provide many of the flying insects that make up the bulk of its diet. Like the Horned Lark, the Western Kingbird has benefited from the cutting of forests; the species has moved eastward in recent decades. After the young fledge it is not uncommon to see half a dozen or more kingbirds sally from the dry upper branches of shade trees to capture insects. When it has a nest full of young to defend, the Western Kingbird will attack crows and other larger birds. In the Southwest, especially in arid regions, there are two other kingbirds, Cassin's and Tropical, that look like the Western; however, the Western is distinguished by white feathers on the sides of the black tail.

DESCRIPTION: 8–9" (20–23 cm). This common flycatcher is olive-brown above and yellow below, with a gray head and a lighter grayish throat and upper breast. It has darker, dusky wings and a blackish tail with white margins. A red-orange crown stripe is usually concealed and rarely visible. Immatures are more olive on the back and have a brownish tinge on the breast and tail margins.

VOICE: A loud, sharp *kit* and various chattering notes.

NESTING: Lays 3–5 spotted white eggs in a large bulky nest consisting of heaps of twigs, straw, and twine lined with hair and rootlets; built on horizontal limb of a tree, often near water.

HABITAT: Open country; ranches, roadsides, streams, and ponds with trees.

RANGE: Breeds throughout the West from southern Canada south to Mexico, east to the Great Plains. It is a regular fall stray on the Atlantic Coast. Winters in the tropics to Central America; a small number winter in central and southern Florida.

SIMILAR SPECIES: See Cassin's Kingbird.

Tropical and Couch's kingbirds have a forked brown tail.

Gray Kingbird is larger, lacks yellow on the underparts, and has a forked tail.

Immature Scissor-tailed Flycatcher has a whiter head and chest, and orange-pink tinged underparts.

CONSERVATION: LC

The Western Kingbird is common in the open country of the West, and its population is growing steadily and expanding eastward and northward. The species is taking advantage of human activities by using utility poles and landscaping for nesting and hunting perches as well as land-clearing activities to further foraging.

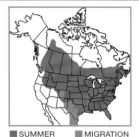

■ SUMMER ■ MIGRATION
■ WINTER ■ RARE
■ RESIDENT

This conspicuous and widespread bird is familiar along rural roadsides, water courses, or woodland edges, and in almost any open environment with suitable perches for flycatching. When another bird flies into its territory—even one much larger than itself—it attacks fiercely, uttering a piercing cry. When one of a pair starts the battle, the other usually joins in. Its aggressive and territorial behavior has earned this bird its common and Latin names. In late summer and early fall they often flock for migration, and large numbers pursue flying insects; they also feed on wild berries, which they deftly pluck while on the wing. It flies with shallow, quivering wingbeats and calls frequently.

DESCRIPTION: 8–9" (20–23 cm). Eastern Kingbird has a blackish head, a blue-black mantle and wings, and a black tail with white terminal band. It is white below with a faint gray breast band. Red feathers in the middle of the crown are usually concealed. Its long crown feathers and upright posture give it a distinctive silhouette.

VOICE: A sharp *dzee* or *dzeet*. Also a series of harsh, rapid calls: *kit* and *kitter*.

NESTING: Lays 3 pinkish eggs, blotched with brown, in a grass-lined stick nest placed in a mangrove thicket, usually over or near salt water.

HABITAT: Savannas, rangelands, forest edges, riverside groves, and even city parks and roadsides.

RANGE: Breeds from British Columbia across interior Canada to Maritime Provinces and south to northern California, central Texas, Gulf Coast, and Florida. Winters in tropics.

SIMILAR SPECIES: Eastern Phoebe is smaller with a paler gray back. Black Phoebe is also smaller and has a dark breast rather than white.

In Florida, see Gray and Loggerhead kingbirds; both of these have longer bills. Gray Kingbird has a lighter gray crown. Loggerhead Kingbird, a rare stray in extreme southern Florida, has a bushy black crest.

CONSERVATION:  LC
Although still widespread and common, the Eastern Kingbird population has been gradually declining since at least the 1960s. The decrease may be due to habitat loss and the decline of small farmsteads.

GRAY KINGBIRD *Tyrannus dominicensis*

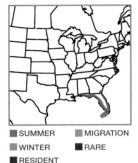

■ SUMMER   ■ MIGRATION
■ WINTER   ■ RARE
■ RESIDENT

This flycatcher is common to the coastal zone, primarily in Florida. It is found in mangroves, marsh edges, shrubs, and suburbs. Like other kingbirds, this species is fearless, even chasing hawks and crows. Noisy and belligerent, it frequently emits harsh notes as it sits on exposed perches, ready to dart after flying insects.

DESCRIPTION: 9" (23 cm). This is a stocky, large-headed, pale gray flycatcher of coastal habitats. Its underparts are whitish and its tail is notched and without white edges. It has a dusky blackish patch through the eye, and its bill is relatively long and heavy.

VOICE: A shrill, buzzy *pe-cheer-y*.

NESTING: Lays 3–5 pink eggs spotted with brown in flimsy nest of coarse twigs, lined with grasses, and placed in small tree or shrub, sometimes over water.

HABITAT: Coastal, in mangrove thickets, on utility wires, and in small groves of palms and oaks.

RANGE: Breeds in coastal regions of South Carolina, Georgia, Florida, and the northern Gulf Coast. Winters in the American tropics.

SIMILAR SPECIES: See Eastern, Western, and Loggerhead kingbirds.

CONSERVATION:

The Gray Kingbird is showing a stable population throughout its Caribbean range as it adapts to human disturbance and development. In the northern edge of its range in the southeastern United States, its numbers have declined slightly, but it is still locally common.

■ SUMMER ■ MIGRATION
■ WINTER ■ RARE
■ RESIDENT

This rare vagrant to Florida from the West Indies has a heavier bill than its smaller relative, the Eastern Kingbird. It is also more partial to wooded habitats.

DESCRIPTION: 9" (23 cm). This flycatcher has a blackish head with a bushy crest, which contrasts with a grayish-olive back. It has a long and thick bill. Its underparts are whitish, and its belly and undertail coverts are washed with pale yellowish. Its wing coverts are edged with whitish and its tail is tipped with buffy-white.

VOICE: A chattering, rolled *teeerrp*.

NESTING: Lays 5 creamy, brown-spotted eggs in a bulky stick nest lined with soft fibrous material and placed in an isolated tree.

HABITAT: Open woodlands; less often in open situations.

RANGE: Resident in the northern Bahama Islands and the Greater Antilles; a rare vagrant to southern Florida.

SIMILAR SPECIES: Closely resembles Gray Kingbird, which has a paler gray head and no shaggy crest.

CONSERVATION: ![LC]
The Loggerhead Kingbird's population is believed to be stable in its native range.

SCISSOR-TAILED FLYCATCHER *Tyrannus forficatus*

■ SUMMER ■ MIGRATION
■ WINTER ■ RARE
■ RESIDENT

The Scissor-tail is often seen perching on fences or wires with its extraordinarily long tail held out in a horizontal position. Like a kingbird, it erects its crest, emits harsh cries, and fiercely attacks hawks, crows, or other large birds that invade its nest area. In spring, they put on a wonderful aerial courtship display. With their long scissor-like tail, they can maneuver and "sky-dance" gracefully. Nearly all of their food is captured on the wing; included in their diet are many insects harmful to agriculture.

DESCRIPTION: 14" (36 cm). The adult of this distinctive bird has bright salmon-pink sides and belly; and a pale grayish-white head, upper back, and breast. More than half its length is the conspicuously long and deeply forked black-and-white tail. Young birds are similar but have a shorter tail and lack bright pink on the sides and belly.

VOICE: A harsh *kee-kee-kee-kee*. Also chattering notes like those of Eastern Kingbird.

NESTING: Lays 2–5 eggs in a cup nest of twigs, fibers, and grass. No U.S. breeding records.

HABITAT: Open country along roadsides and on ranches with scattered trees and bushes; also fence wires and posts.

RANGE: Breeds from eastern Colorado and Nebraska south to Texas and western Louisiana. Winters south of the U.S.-Mexico border; a few in southern Florida.

SIMILAR SPECIES: Compare immature Scissor-tailed to Western Kingbird.

CONSERVATION:

Scissor-tailed Flycatcher is common but decreasing globally, although its numbers may fluctuate locally. The species may be expanding its range due to forest clearing limiting available nesting sites. Planting shelterbelt trees or leaving intact patches or strips of brush when clearing can provide suitable perches and nesting habitat for these birds.

Tyrannus savana FORK-TAILED FLYCATCHER

■ SUMMER ■ MIGRATION
■ WINTER ■ RARE
■ RESIDENT

The Fork-tailed Flycatcher is a tropical species that strays regularly to the United States and Canada. Many are thought to be migratory "overshoots" of South American individuals (including young birds) moving northward after the breeding season in southern South America. Most records in North America are in fall, but strays have also been recorded in spring and winter. Although it occurs most frequently along the Atlantic Coast and in Texas, individuals have also appeared unpredictably throughout the continent, including in California, Ontario, and in the Southwest. Like other flycatchers, this species often perches on roadside wires or fences.

DESCRIPTION: 10–16" (25–41 cm). A black cap, white underparts, and white wing linings all separate this species from the Scissor-tailed Flycatcher. The yellow crown patch in the adult is usually concealed. The extremely long black tail of the adult flutters in flight. Juveniles are similar to adults, but the tail is much shorter.

VOICE: A buzzy chattering song; call note a sharp *sick* or *plik*.

NESTING: Lays 4 or 5 white eggs spotted with brown in a chamber in a globular nest of grass and plant fibers suspended from the tip of a drooping branch.

HABITAT: Savannas and open scrubby habitat; usually found on or near the ground; North American vagrants are typically found in coastal scrub and fields.

RANGE: Southern Mexico to Argentina; strays to the eastern seaboard and irregularly elsewhere in North America.

SIMILAR SPECIES: See Scissor-tailed Flycatcher.

Eastern Kingbird is similar to the shorter-tailed immature, but its tail is not forked.

CONSERVATION: LC
The Fork-tailed Flycatcher population is stable throughout its primary range of South and Central America.

OLIVE-SIDED FLYCATCHER *Contopus cooperi*

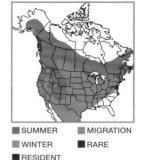

■ SUMMER ■ MIGRATION
■ WINTER ■ RARE
■ RESIDENT

A large, dark, big-headed flycatcher of northern and montane coniferous forests, the Olive-sided Flycatcher almost always perches on dead branches in an exposed position at or near the tops of the tallest trees. Even in migration, it almost invariably chooses such high, conspicuous perches, more so than any other flycatcher; a flycatcher seen high on a dead snag will often turn out to be an Olive-sided. It feeds almost entirely on winged insects; it is not known to take spiders, caterpillars, or other larvae.

DESCRIPTION: 7½" (19 cm). A large-billed and heavy-headed bird, it is deep olive-brown, with dark sides of the breast and flanks separated by a white patch down the center of the breast. White feather tufts protrude from the lower back at the base of the tail; its tail is broad and prominently notched.

VOICE: Song is a distinctive and emphatic *quick-three-beers*; call a loud *pip-pip-pip*.

NESTING: Lays 3 or 4 dull-white, spotted eggs in a compact, woven, grass-lined cup nest high in the prong of a horizontal limb, secured with cobwebs and camouflaged outside.

HABITAT: Boreal spruce and fir forests, usually near openings, burns, ponds, and bogs.

RANGE: Breeds in Alaska, east across Canada to northern New England, and south to the mountains of California, Arizona, and New Mexico, and in northern New York and New England. Winters in the American tropics.

SIMILAR SPECIES: Greater Pewee is the same size, shape, and overall color, but it lacks the "vested" appearance. Wood-pewees can have similar underparts but are smaller with more prominent wing bars.

CONSERVATION: NT

In the past several decades, numbers of Olive-sided Flycatchers have declined significantly. Loss of wintering habitat is thought to be a major factor impacting these birds, and the availability of insect prey on the breeding grounds may affect this and other flycatcher species.

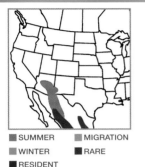

■ SUMMER ■ MIGRATION
■ WINTER ■ RARE
■ RESIDENT

Like other flycatchers, Greater Pewees sit upright on prominent posts, watching for insects. When they spot prey, they dart out, catch it in flight, and return in an arc-shaped flight to the same or a nearby perch. This species has a loud and distinctive call that is often heard on the soundtracks of Westerns.

DESCRIPTION: 7–7¾" (18–20 cm). A large-headed flycatcher with a slight crest. It is olive-brown above and slightly lighter below. It has a small, light gray throat patch, a yellow lower mandible, and indistinct wing bars.

VOICE: Song is a plaintive *Jo-se-Ma-ri-a*. Call note a repeated *pwit*.

NESTING: Lays 3 or 4 white eggs spotted with brown in a shallow saucer of grass fastened to a horizontal branch.

HABITAT: Highland coniferous forests, especially pine and pine-oak.

RANGE: Breeds from central Arizona and southwestern New Mexico southward. Winters mainly south of the U.S.-Mexico border.

SIMILAR SPECIES: Olive-sided Flycatcher is similar, but has olive-brown flanks, giving it a "vested" appearance. Wood-pewees are smaller and lack the slight crest.

CONSERVATION:

Although there is little historical data on population trends for these birds, their numbers appear to be stable. Conservation efforts aimed at protecting the pine-oak forest habitats of the Spotted Owl and Northern Goshawk are likely to benefit the Greater Pewee as well.

WESTERN WOOD-PEWEE *Contopus sordidulus*

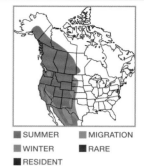

SUMMER ■ MIGRATION
WINTER ■ RARE
■ RESIDENT

This species is generally found in more open, park-like woodlands than the Eastern Wood-Pewee and is thus more readily observed. In a few areas along the western edge of the Great Plains the two pewees occur together without interbreeding— conclusive evidence that despite their great similarity, they are distinct species.

DESCRIPTION: 6½" (17 cm). A sparrow-sized flycatcher, dull olive-gray above, slightly paler below, with 2 whitish wing bars. Eastern Wood-Pewee of the East is extremely similar, but generally less dark below; the two species are best distinguished by voice. *Empidonax* flycatchers are smaller and usually have noticeable eye ring.

VOICE: A harsh nasal *pee-eeer*, quite different from the sweet *peee-ah weee* of the Eastern Wood-Pewee.

NESTING: Lays 3 or 4 creamy-white, brown-dotted eggs in finely woven, cup-shaped nest made of vegetable fiber and covered with lichens, saddled to a horizontal limb and blending in with the branch.

HABITAT: Open woodland and woodland edges; orchards.

RANGE: Breeds from eastern Alaska, Mackenzie, and Manitoba south through the western United States. Winters in South America.

SIMILAR SPECIES: Eastern Wood-Pewee is best distinguished by range and voice.

Most *Empidonax* flycatchers have prominent white eye rings; Willow Flycatcher is more brownish above and paler below; and its lower mandible is brighter orange-yellow.

See Olive-sided Flycatcher and Greater Pewee.

CONSERVATION: LC

Western Wood-Pewees remain common but are gradually declining due to riparian habitat loss in North America and, most likely, to additional habitat loss along their migration route and in their winter range.

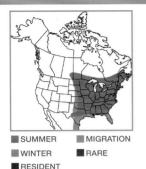

■ SUMMER ■ MIGRATION
■ WINTER ■ RARE
■ RESIDENT

Eastern Wood-Pewees are more often heard than seen because of their dull coloration and because they frequent the dense upper canopy of the forest. They are widespread in the East in deciduous and mixed woodlands and in shade trees; they arrive late in spring.

DESCRIPTION: 6½" (17 cm). A sparrow-sized flycatcher, dull olive-gray above, slightly paler below, with two whitish wing bars (these bars are buff in first-winter birds). There is no conspicuous eye ring, although fall birds may have a slight suggestion of one. The underparts are whitish, washed with olive-gray on the sides of the breast; this wash may appear as a band across the breast. The lower mandible is paler than the upper, and the tail is uniformly dark.

VOICE: A plaintive *pee-ah-weee* or *pee-weee*, falling in pitch on the last note.

NESTING: Lays 2–4 (usually 3) whitish eggs with brown and purple blotches often concentrated toward the larger end in a small cup nest made of woven grass and supplemented with weeds, wool, bark strips, twigs, roots, mosses, pine needles, or leaves. The outside of the nest is covered with lichens for camouflage.

HABITAT: Forests, open woodlands, orchards, and shade trees in parks and along roadsides.

RANGE: Breeds from south-central and southeastern Canada to the Gulf Coast and central Florida. Winters in the American tropics.

SIMILAR SPECIES: See Western Wood-Pewee, Olive-sided Flycatcher, and Eastern Phoebe.

Western Wood-Pewee is extremely similar, but is generally darker below; the two species are best distinguished by voice.

Empidonax flycatchers are smaller and usually have a noticeable eye ring.

CONSERVATION:
Eastern Wood-Pewees are widespread and common. Their numbers have declined slightly in the past few decades for reasons that are not fully understood.

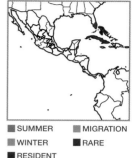

■ SUMMER ■ MIGRATION
■ WINTER ■ RARE
■ RESIDENT

Cuban Pewee is native to the Bahamas and Cuba and has only been seen a few times in wooded areas in South Florida. Many tyrant flycatchers are extremely difficult to identify, and any record of this species will require extensive documentation due to its similarity to the common, native Eastern Wood-Pewee.

DESCRIPTION: 6–6½" (15–16.5 cm). Very similar to the Eastern Wood-Pewee, which is native anywhere a Cuban Pewee might be found. It is differentiated by a white crescent behind the eye, very short primaries making it appear smaller-winged than the Eastern Wood-Pewee, and voice.

VOICE: Descending *weeeeooooo*, a variety of *weet*-like notes; it does not have the *pee-a-wee* song of Eastern Wood-Pewee.

NESTING: Lays 3 or 4 whitish eggs with brown spots in a nest of moss and rootlets on the ground.

HABITAT: Forests, woodlands, and wetlands.

RANGE: Cuba and Bahamas.

SIMILAR SPECIES: See Eastern Wood-Pewee.

CONSERVATION: LC

A single Cuban Pewee's appearance in Florida in 1995 was the first accepted record of this species in North America. It has since been recorded a few times in southeastern Florida. It is a common bird in its native range and its population is believed to be stable.

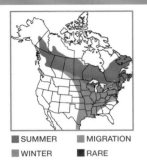

■ SUMMER ■ MIGRATION
■ WINTER ■ RARE
■ RESIDENT

This retiring little flycatcher spends most of its time on migration in dense thickets and so is easily overlooked. With its yellowish throat, underparts, and eye ring, it is the easiest of the eastern *Empidonax* flycatchers to identify.

DESCRIPTION: 5½" (14 cm). A small flycatcher, olive-green above, yellowish below (including on the throat), with two white wing bars and a yellowish eye ring. Other flycatchers of the genus *Empidonax* (Acadian, Alder, Willow, and Least flycatchers) have more whitish throats, underparts, and eye rings.

VOICE: On breeding grounds, a flat *chilk* or *killic*; also a rising two-note whistle, *per-wee?*

NESTING: Lays 3 or 4 brown-spotted buff eggs in a woven nest of plant fibers in a bush or tree, usually over a stream.

HABITAT: Bogs and moist thickets in northern coniferous forests; on migration, it may be found in second-growth woodlands.

RANGE: Breeds from central Canada and Newfoundland south to the Great Lakes region, northern New York, northern New England, and the Maritime Provinces. Winters from Mexico to Panama.

SIMILAR SPECIES: Voice is often the most helpful feature in distinguishing among *Empidonax*.

In migration, Yellow-bellied can overlap Acadian Flycatcher's range and habitat; in fall, immature Acadian is also yellowish below and greenish above, but tends to have a whiter throat.

Yellow-bellied is casual in the West, so a yellowish *Empidonax* there is more likely to be a Pacific-slope Flycatcher or Cordilleran Flycatcher, or an immature Hammond's Flycatcher. Hammond's tends to be less yellow on the throat. Pacific-slope and Cordilleran flycatchers are not as bright on the back and lack the yellow on the throat; many lack bright yellow underparts. Their greater wing coverts and the bases of the flight feathers are not as dark. Also, these western flycatchers flick their wings and tail simultaneously, while Yellow-bellied normally only flicks its tail.

CONSERVATION:
Due to extensive forest loss in Canada before the 1960s, populations of Yellow-bellied Flycatchers had decreased dramatically, but since then their numbers have risen steadily.

ACADIAN FLYCATCHER *Empidonax virescens*

SUMMER | MIGRATION
WINTER | RARE
RESIDENT

The Acadian Flycatcher and its relatives in the genus *Empidonax* are difficult to distinguish visually, but the Acadian is the only breeding species in much of the Southeast; between June and August, any *Empidonax* seen in the lowlands south of New Jersey and Missouri can safely be called an Acadian.

DESCRIPTION: 6" (15 cm). This flycatcher is olive-green above and whitish or sometimes yellow below (especially on the flanks and belly), with a distinct white eye ring. It is identified chiefly by voice and habitat. The juvenile is similar to the adult, but its wing bars are buffy and its body feathers have buffy edges.

VOICE: An emphatic two-note *flee-see!* or *peet-seet!* with the second syllable accented and higher pitched, uttered on the breeding grounds and occasionally on migration.

NESTING: Lays 3 or 4 white eggs, finely speckled with brown, in a loose cup of grass with little or no plant down, placed in a low bush or sapling.

HABITAT: Beech and maple or hemlock forests, usually under the canopy but also in clearings; often in wooded ravines.

RANGE: Breeds from southern Minnesota east through southern New England, south to the Gulf Coast and central Florida. Winters in the American tropics.

SIMILAR SPECIES: See Yellow-bellied Flycatcher.

Willow Flycatcher has a more brownish-green back and no obvious eye ring.

Alder Flycatcher also has a less obvious eye ring.

Least Flycatcher sometimes shares the same breeding habitat; it is usually not distinguishable except by voice, but tends to have a more grayish-green back.

CONSERVATION:
The population of these common birds is stable. They are, however, vulnerable to forest fragmentation, loss of wintering habitat, and nest parasitism by Brown-headed Cowbirds.

■ SUMMER ■ MIGRATION
■ WINTER ■ RARE
■ RESIDENT

These birds hunt in the airspace below the canopy of tall alders in swamps or along creeks. They sit erect on a twig, then dart out after flying insects. This species has a more northerly distribution than its close relative the Willow Flycatcher. The two species were once lumped together, but studies revealed that their song patterns and breeding habits differed; in the fall, when they do not sing, they are indistinguishable.

DESCRIPTION: 5–6" (13–15 cm). Slightly smaller than a House Sparrow. It is dull gray-green above and whitish below, with two dull white wing bars and a narrow white eye ring (often not noticeable). It is indistinguishable in appearance from Willow Flycatcher, and is best identified by its voice, breeding habitat, and nest.

VOICE: A burry *fee-bee-o*, rather different from the wheezy *fitz-bew* of the Willow Flycatcher.

NESTING: Lays 3 or 4 creamy-white eggs, with fine brown speckling, in a neat, compact cup of plant down and fibers placed in a low bush or sapling.

HABITAT: Alder swamps, streamside and lakeside thickets, and second-growth forests.

RANGE: Breeds from Alaska east through Manitoba to Newfoundland and south to British Columbia, the Great Lakes region, and southern New England, southward through the Appalachian Mountains. Winters in the American tropics.

SIMILAR SPECIES: Least and Acadian flycatchers have more obvious eye ring. See Willow Flycatcher and Eastern Wood-Pewee.

CONSERVATION: With most of its breeding grounds in remote northern areas with little human disturbance, Alder Flycatcher populations are large and stable.

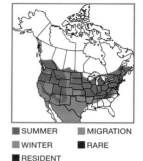

■ SUMMER　　■ MIGRATION
■ WINTER　　■ RARE
■ RESIDENT

The species of the genus *Empidonax* are so similar in appearance that only an expert can tell them apart by sight alone. The Alder and Willow were once considered a single species ("Traill's Flycatcher"). During the breeding season each species lives in its characteristic habitat, but during migration birders may encounter birds of different species in a habitat in which they are not usually found. Thus, the only sure way to identify breeding males is by their voices, which are different in each species. In other seasons when males do not sing, all that can readily be told is that they are *Empidonax* flycatchers.

DESCRIPTION: 6" (15 cm). Slightly smaller than a House Sparrow. It is dull gray-green above, whitish below, with two dull white wing bars and a narrow white eye ring (often not noticeable). It is distinguishable from Alder Flycatcher only by voice, breeding habitat, and nest. Other western *Empidonax* flycatchers have a more conspicuous eye ring or are grayer above.

VOICE: A wheezy *fitz-bew* or *pit-speer*. The song of the Alder Flycatcher is a burry *fee-bee-o*, descending more abruptly in pitch.

NESTING: Lays 4 cream-white eggs in a finely woven, cup-shaped nest made of vegetable fibers and lined with grass and feathers, firmly wedged in the fork of a tree.

HABITAT: Swampy thickets, upland pastures, and old abandoned orchards; Alder Flycatchers occur along wooded lakeshores and streams.

RANGE: Breeds from southern British Columbia, Alberta, North Dakota, New York, and Maine south to central California, Nevada, Southwest, Arkansas, and Virginia. Winters in the American tropics.

SUBSPECIES: The species is divided into four geographic populations. The nominate Eastern subspecies, *E. t. traillii*, has a pale gray head and more greenish back. The Northwestern subspecies, *E. t. brewsteri*, has a dark head and more brown tones on the back, and duller wing bars. The Great Plain subspecies, *E. t. adastus*, is similar to *brewsteri* but paler; the Southwestern subspecies, *E. t. extimus*, is paler still.

SIMILAR SPECIES: Alder Flycatcher tends to have a greener back. Where the two species breed together, Willow usually prefers smaller, brushier, sometimes drier, more open thickets; Alder usually prefers wet alder swamps or thickets among larger trees like aspens. Willow and Alder flycatchers are best distinguished by voice.

All other *Empidonax* flycatchers except Alder have obvious eye rings. Also see Western and Eastern wood-pewees.

CONSERVATION: Although still common in most of its range, Willow Flycatcher numbers have gradually declined in some areas due to habitat loss. The Southwestern Willow Flycatcher (*E. t. extimus*) that nests along streams in the Southwest is on the U.S. Endangered Species List. It is classified as endangered in Arizona, California, Colorado, New Mexico, Texas, and Utah.

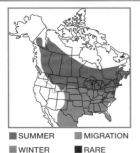

■ SUMMER ■ MIGRATION
■ WINTER ■ RARE
■ RESIDENT

The Least Flycatcher is widespread in deciduous forests, open woodlands, farm groves, and towns. It is one of the most vocal *Empidonax* flycatchers and it is smaller and stubbier-billed than most other members of its genus. In the East, this is the empid most often identified in migration, and is the only one likely to be found anywhere except the Gulf Coast after early October.

DESCRIPTION: 5¼" (13 cm). This small flycatcher is dull olive-gray above, whitish below, with two whitish wing bars and a conspicuous white eye ring. It is best distinguished by voice and breeding habitat.

VOICE: Dry, insect-like *che-bec*, snapped out and accented on the second syllable, and uttered incessantly through the hottest days of summer.

NESTING: Lays 3 or 4 white eggs, occasionally spotted, in a well-built cup nest saddled on a branch 15–60' (4.5–18 m) high in a coniferous tree.

HABITAT: Widely distributed in open country, nesting in shade trees and orchards in villages and city parks, and along rural roadsides and woodland borders.

RANGE: Breeds from southern Yukon east to central Quebec and Maritime Provinces, and south to Wyoming, Indiana, and New Jersey, and south in mountains to North Carolina. Winters in tropics.

SIMILAR SPECIES: Alder and Willow flycatchers can share Least's breeding habitat, but lack the obvious eye ring; Alder generally has greener back.

Least Flycatcher is rare in the West during migration, but probably not separable from Dusky Flycatcher there. Hammond's Flycatcher tends to be darker below, especially on the throat, with a slight "vested" appearance; it often flicks its wings and tail simultaneously (Least only flicks its tail upward). Fall birds showing a whitish outer web of the outer rectrix are most likely Dusky or Hammond's flycatchers.

Gray Flycatcher is paler gray above; it flicks its tail downward, not up.

Acadian Flycatcher shares Least's habitat where their ranges overlap; these two species are probably only distinguishable by voice.

CONSERVATION: LC
Least Flycatchers are widespread and common but in decline, especially in the southern part of their range. They may be sensitive to forest disturbances that create openings in unbroken forests or change the understory, such as logging and heavy browsing by deer.

HAMMOND'S FLYCATCHER *Empidonax hammondii*

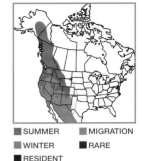

SUMMER ■ MIGRATION
WINTER ■ RARE
RESIDENT

Hammond's Flycatcher inhabits tall, moist, closed-canopy montane conifer forests, sometimes those with a broadleaf understory; in the Far North, this species prefers deciduous forests. Because climatic conditions at sea level in the North are similar to those at higher elevations farther south, this flycatcher is able to nest in boreal forest on the low plains of Alaska as well as in subalpine forest at elevations around 10,000' (3 km) in the southern Rocky Mountains. Hammond's forages among the branches, often high in the trees, in shade. Among western empids, it is distinguished by its small bill, proportionally long wings, short tail, and typically dusky or ashy coloration. When perched and while foraging, it characteristically flicks its wings and tail simultaneously.

DESCRIPTION: 5–5½" (13–14 cm). This small western flycatcher is olive-gray above; it has a light throat, a gray breast, and a pale yellow belly. It shows a conspicuous white eye ring and white wing bars. It flicks wings and tail more vigorously than other similar species. Field identification among Empidonax flycatchers is notoriously difficult and best determined by voice.

VOICE: Song is *seweep-tsurp-seep*, the last part rising. Calls are a high peep (like the note of a Pygmy Nuthatch) and a soft *wit*.

NESTING: Lays 3 or 4 white eggs in a grass-woven cup nest placed low in sagebrush or a small tree.

HABITAT: Mature coniferous forests at high altitudes.

RANGE: Breeds from eastern Alaska south to northern California and northern New Mexico. Winters in Mexico and Central America, rarely in southeastern Arizona.

SIMILAR SPECIES: Hammond's has burriest song of forest *Empidonax*; this feature is helpful in identification. It has limited breeding habitat overlap with Dusky, Pacific-slope, and Cordilleran flycatchers, none with other empids. Dusky Flycatcher has a longer tail and shorter wings; it seldom wing-flicks when perched silently and undisturbed; the tip of its tail is usually double-rounded. Dusky is also longer-billed; appears to be smaller-headed; and is paler, with less contrast, but these differences are slight and overlapping.

Least Flycatcher has lighter underparts; its bill has obvious yellow-orange on the lower mandible. Least usually shows a greater degree of contrast in the wing pattern, and its call is different.

See also Gray, Pacific-slope, and Cordilleran flycatchers.

CONVERSATION:
Widespread and common, numbers of Hammond's Flycatchers have grown modestly since the mid-20th century. They prefer to live in mature forests, making them sensitive to logging practices.

■ SUMMER ■ MIGRATION
■ WINTER ■ RARE
■ RESIDENT

This flycatcher lacks the olive and yellow tinges on the back and underparts that mark the other *Empidonax* flycatchers. Its color blends with the blue-gray hues of sagebrush and helps conceal it from predators.

DESCRIPTION: 5½" (14 cm). Similar to other *Empidonax* flycatchers, but it is gray above, and whitish below. It has a long bill and its lower mandible is pinkish-orange. Its eye ring is not prominent. When perched, this species slowly bobs its tail downward—a behavior that helps to distinguish it from similar species.

VOICE: Its song is in two parts, rising in tone: *chiwip* (or *chi-bit*) cheep. Call is a soft *whit*.

NESTING: Lays 3–5 white eggs in a neat twiggy cup set low in the crotch of a shrub or small tree.

HABITAT: Sagebrush and pinyon-juniper woodlands.

RANGE: Breeds from southern Washington and southwestern Wyoming south to eastern California, central Arizona, and central New Mexico. Winters in southern California and southern Arizona south into Mexico.

SIMILAR SPECIES: All other empids flick their tail rapidly upward. Breeding habitat and foraging style provide helpful clues for identification.

Gray Flycatcher's song is less varied than Dusky or Hammond's, and without burry notes.

Dusky Flycatcher is typically darker, with more pattern contrast, shorter wings and bill, and often a plumper head and body; the edge of the tail is grayish-white in fresh plumage, not pure white.

Hammond's Flycatcher flicks its wings and tail; it has a darker, more contrasting plumage pattern, a short bill, and a short tail with a pale gray edge; its head and body are plumper, and its tail is often held vertically.

Least Flycatcher lacks the white edge to the tail; it has a short bill and short tail; its head is proportionally larger; it has a more contrasting wing pattern and eye ring.

Willow Flycatcher is much browner above; it has a wider bill that is entirely light on the lower mandible; its tail lacks a white edge; its wing bars are dull.

CONSERVATION: Gray Flycatchers are widespread, common, and increasing. Its biggest threat is the loss of sagebrush habitat, especially to industrial development and to invasive cheatgrass in the Great Plains.

■ SUMMER　■ MIGRATION
■ WINTER　■ RARE
■ RESIDENT

Hammond's and Dusky flycatchers are closely related, similar in appearance and voice, and difficult to distinguish. The species probably derive from a common ancestor whose populations were separated when the ice fields of the North advanced and the forests were divided into western and eastern refuges. When the flycatchers returned to the newly forested northern half of the continent, each had developed differing habitat needs, allowing them to coexist without competing for nesting sites and food. The Dusky usually nests in the lower ranges of the forest, preferring chaparral; the Hammond's chooses higher levels of tall fir trees.

DESCRIPTION: 5¼–6" (13–15 cm). Dusky Flycatcher has a gray back with a slight olive tinge, a buffy breast and a pale yellow belly, with a light throat. It has a narrow white eye ring and white wing bars, and a long tail.

VOICE: Its song is similar to that of Hammond's Flycatcher: a staccato series of chirps, transcribed as *se-lip, churp, treep*. Its call is a sharp *whit*.

NESTING: Lays 3 or 4 white eggs spotted with brown in a moss-lined cup nest of small twigs and rootlets. The nest is set in a deciduous shrub or tree (sometimes a conifer), placed in a fork several feet off the ground, usually near areas with plenty of dense undergrowth.

HABITAT: Woodlands containing tall trees and tall undergrowth, mountain chaparral, and open, brushy coniferous forests.

RANGE: Breeds from British Columbia and western South Dakota south to southern California, central Arizona, and northern New Mexico. It winters throughout much of Mexico and Guatemala, and infrequently in suitable habitat on the U.S. side of the border with Mexico, from California to western Texas.

SIMILAR SPECIES: Dusky Flycatcher's song has some clearer notes than Hammond's Flycatcher, and is burrier and more varied than Gray's Flycatcher. Breeding habitat and foraging style provide useful clues for distinction.

Hammond's tends to migrate earlier in spring and later in fall; it has a relatively short tail and long wings that it usually flicks consistently; it is also shorter, shorter-billed, chunkier, and ashier, with slightly more contrast in the face, however these differences are slight and all overlap. Hammond's holds its tail vertically more often; its tail has little contrast to the outer web, and its tip is forked.

Least Flycatcher is whiter below, including the throat; it lacks the distinctive pale outer edge to its shorter tail. It usually has a shorter bill.

See Willow and Gray flycatchers.

CONSERVATION:
Dusky Flycatchers are widespread and still fairly common, although their numbers have declined slightly in recent years. Dusky Flycatchers benefit from some types of habitat disturbances that increase shrubby undergrowth, but decline wherever shrublands are degraded or removed, and where stream corridors are cleared.

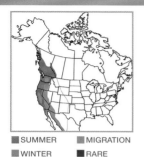

■ SUMMER ■ MIGRATION
■ WINTER ■ RARE
■ RESIDENT

The Pacific-slope Flycatcher forages in the shade between the tangled ground cover of huckleberry and salmonberry and the low branches of towering Douglas firs, cedars, or redwoods. It is the most frequently observed *Empidonax* in California. Formerly lumped with the closely related Cordilleran Flycatcher; together they were collectively called "Western Flycatcher."

DESCRIPTION: 5½–6" (14–15 cm). It is olive-brown above, with a yellow throat and belly separated by a dusky olive breast. It has an elongated white eye ring and light wing bars. Fall birds may be duller. Its bill is long and wide, and its lower mandible is bright yellow.

VOICE: Quite distinct, rising *pseet-ptsick-seet*. The first part alone is often used as a call, or is repeated on a drawn-out, almost sibilant high pitch. The second part is rapid and louder. Its call note is a sharp *pit-peet*.

NESTING: Lays 3 or 4 white eggs spotted with brown in a moss-lined cup nest of small twigs and rootlets.

HABITAT: Moist, shaded coniferous or mixed forests; canyons.

RANGE: Breeds from Alaska south along the Pacific Coast to Baja California. Winters south of the U.S.-Mexico border.

SUBSPECIES: A subspecies (*E.d. insulicola*) on the Channel Islands off the California coast is slightly more drab and gray than mainland birds, and its call is a rising *tsweep*.

SIMILAR SPECIES: Cordilleran Flycatcher looks almost identical and is best distinguished by voice and range.

All other western empids have burry, rough, or lower notes in songs. They lack the almond-shaped eye ring and strongly yellowish throat. Hammond's, Dusky, and Gray flycatchers all have a narrow bill with a dark-tipped lower mandible.

Hammond's has the most similar habitat; foraging and wing-flicking behavior; tail coloration; and proportions of the head, body, tail, and wings. It is easily distinguishable, however, by its song, its bill, the shape of its eye ring, and its whitish throat.

See Yellow-bellied and Acadian flycatchers.

CONSERVATION:
Although widespread and common, Pacific-slope Flycatchers have undergone a small decline in recent years. Their main threat is the loss of forest habitat in the Northwest.

CORDILLERAN FLYCATCHER *Empidonax occidentalis*

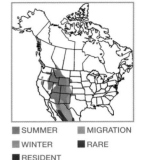

■ SUMMER ■ MIGRATION
■ WINTER ■ RARE
■ RESIDENT

The Cordilleran Flycatcher is the common, yellow-bellied *Empidonax* flycatcher in the mountains of the western interior. Like the Pacific-slope Flycatcher of the West Coast, it has a large, tear-shaped eye ring.

DESCRIPTION: 5½–6" (14–15 cm). This flycatcher is olive-brown above, with a yellow throat and belly separated by a dusky olive breast; it has an elongated white eye ring and light wing bars. Fall birds may be duller. Its bill is long and wide, and the lower mandible is bright yellow. This species is identical in appearance to Pacific-slope Flycatcher; the two are distinguishable only by voice and range.

VOICE: Its song is a thin, high *whee-seet*.

NESTING: Lays 3 or 4 creamy-white eggs in a well-camouflaged nest saddled at the base of a horizontal branch.

HABITAT: Mountain forests and wooded canyons.

RANGE: Breeds from Alberta south through Nevada and the Rocky Mountains to southeastern Arizona, southern New Mexico, and western Texas. Winters south of the U.S.-Mexico border.

SIMILAR SPECIES: Nearly identical to Pacific-slope Flycatcher, best distinguished by range and voice.

CONSERVATION: Cordilleran Flycatcher is widespread and common but has undergone a slight decline in recent years. Logging of western forests may be affecting the population's numbers.

Empidonax fulvifrons BUFF-BREASTED FLYCATCHER

- ■ SUMMER
- ■ MIGRATION
- ■ WINTER
- ■ RARE
- ■ RESIDENT

Buff-breasted Flycatcher is scarce and extremely local in the southwestern United States, found nesting in a few canyons in the Huachuca Mountains and Chiricahua Mountains of Arizona and casually in New Mexico; within its limited range, it establishes loose little breeding "colonies" in open, transition-zone pine and pine-oak woodlands. This bird characteristically hunts from a low perch, often launching its pursuit from the top of a weed. However, it can also be seen hovering over a pine branch, picking insects from among the needles. It is one of the few *Empidonax* flycatchers that are easily distinguished by its coloration.

DESCRIPTION: 4½–5" (11–13 cm). This small flycatcher is olive above with rich buffy underparts, especially on the breast and lighter on the throat and belly. Adults in worn summer plumage may appear grayer. It has a white eye ring and white wing bars. It has a rounded head and a short tail.

VOICE: Song is a quick *chicky-whew*. Call is a dull *pit*.

NESTING: Lays 3–6 white eggs with a few faint speckles in a mud, moss, and grass nest lined with soft material—often feathers or hair—built directly under an overhanging branch or group of leaves, or among hanging roots near the top of an embankment close to water.

HABITAT: Open canyon growth and pine-oak forests.

RANGE: Breeds locally in southeastern Arizona. It was once more widespread as a breeder in the Southwest. It winters in Mexico.

SIMILAR SPECIES: Pacific-slope and Cordilleran flycatchers are larger, with distinctly green upperparts and strongly yellow on underparts. They have teardrop-shaped eye rings. Their songs are high, thin whistles, much different from that of Buff-breasted.

Other western *Empidonax* flycatchers usually have a grayish or olive wash across the breast, and different call notes and songs.

CONSERVATION: Although its numbers are declining due to habitat loss, the small Arizona population may be increasing. Buff-breasted Flycatcher used to be more widespread in the southwestern United States, but its numbers reached a record low in the 1960s and only a small population remains north of Mexico—perhaps a few dozen pairs. It is recognized as a state-endangered species in Arizona.

■ SUMMER　■ MIGRATION
■ WINTER　■ RARE
■ RESIDENT

Black Phoebes are territorial and solitary nesters, often remaining year-round in an established territory. They are usually associated with water, especially in drier regions; they are common at moderate and lower elevations. The wanderers found in atypical winter habitats (chaparral or grassland) are thought to be first-year, nonbreeding birds.

DESCRIPTION: 6–7" (15–18 cm). Black Phoebe is slate-black except for white on the belly, undertail coverts, and outer tail feathers. Its tail wagging, erect posture, and insectivorous feeding habits are helpful in field identification. Juveniles are similar but browner.

VOICE: Song is a thin, buzzy *pi-tsee*, usually repeated. Call is a sharp, down-slurred *chip*.

NESTING: Lays 4 or 5 white eggs in a mud-and-grass nest lined with moss and hair and attached to a ledge of a building, bridge, cliff, or quarry, or among the roots of a fallen tree.

HABITAT: Shady areas near water, streams, and pond and lake banks; in winter, city parks and open chaparral.

RANGE: Resident from southwest Oregon south and east to western Texas. Also found in the tropics.

SIMILAR SPECIES: Eastern Phoebe is not as dark on the back and has much more white underneath, extending to the breast and throat.

Some color forms of Dark-eyed Junco may show a similar pattern of a slate-gray head and back with a white belly, but these birds have a pale, triangular bill used for eating seeds and berries as well as insects.

CONSERVATION:

Thanks in part to the popularity of artificial ponds in their traditional nesting habitats, Black Phoebe numbers are on the rise. Other human-made structures such as culverts, bridges, and some buildings can create suitable nesting sites as well. Their need for clean water sources makes water quality an issue for these birds.

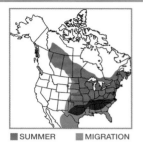

- ■ SUMMER
- ■ MIGRATION
- ■ WINTER
- ■ RARE
- ■ RESIDENT

This medium-sized eastern flycatcher is easily identified by its persistent habit of tail-pumping. Almost always found near fresh running water, especially when breeding, the Eastern Phoebe is often detected year-round by its clear, sweet call note; in the breeding season its *fee-bee* song is distinctive. In its call note and behavior, it resembles the Black Phoebe. The Eastern Phoebe arrives early in spring and departs late in fall, sometimes even staying through the winter in the northern states. In the absence of insects, its winter food is berries. The Eastern Phoebe was probably the first bird ever banded, as John James Audubon marked one with a silver wire on the leg in 1804 and recorded its return the following year.

DESCRIPTION: 7" (18 cm). The Eastern Phoebe is grayish-black above; the head, wings, and tail are slightly darker than the back. This flycatcher has an all-black bill and no eye ring. Adults lack distinct wing bars. The underparts are whitish with a subtle, pale yellowish wash. Immatures may have a slightly more evident wing bar and a more prominent yellowish wash below. The tail is rather long, giving the bird an elongated appearance; it often wags its tail.

VOICE: Clear *fee-bee*, repeated many times; the second syllable is alternately higher or lower than the first. Its call note is a distinctive, short *chip*.

NESTING: Lays 4 or 5 white eggs in a nest of grass and wool in a sheltered, elevated, dry site on a ledge, rock wall, or building.

HABITAT: Open woodlands near streams; cliffs, bridges, and buildings with ledges.

RANGE: Breeds in Canada and United States east of the Rockies, south to the northern edge of the Gulf states. Winters from Virginia, the Gulf Coast, and Florida southward.

SIMILAR SPECIES: Pewees and much smaller *Empidonax* flycatchers have wing bars, light-colored lower mandibles, and proportionately shorter tails. Most *Empidonax* flycatchers have an eye ring.

CONSERVATION: LC

Eastern Phoebe's range has expanded with human development, because landscapes and structures such as bridges and buildings create new potential nesting sites. They are a popular backyard bird and will often nest where they can be easily observed. Their numbers have risen steadily during the past few decades and continue to rise.

SAY'S PHOEBE *Sayornis saya*

■ SUMMER ■ MIGRATION
■ WINTER ■ RARE
■ RESIDENT

This highly migratory species is fairly common in the open country of the West in areas with warm temperatures, a lack of dense vegetation, and little rain. Although primarily insect eaters (as are all flycatchers), Say's Phoebes will eat other foods—such as berries—during long spells of cold or inclement weather, when insects are unavailable, or during migration.

DESCRIPTION: 7–8" (18–20 cm). This flycatcher has a dusky head, breast, and back, with darker wings and a black tail. It has a light rust-colored belly and undertail coverts.

VOICE: A mellow, whistled *pee-ur* with a plaintive quality.

NESTING: Lays 3 creamy-white eggs with dark brown spots in a well-made nest of fibers, feathers, and spider web lined with bits of lichen, placed on a horizontal branch.

HABITAT: Plains; sparsely vegetated countryside; dry, sunny locations; often near ranch houses, barns, and other buildings.

RANGE: Breeds from central Alaska, Yukon, and northern Mackenzie south through the western mountains to Mexico; it is not present west of the Cascades and Sierra Nevada except locally in south-central California and western Oregon. Winters in California and in the Southwest southward.

SIMILAR SPECIES: See female Vermilion Flycatcher.

CONSERVATION: LC

Say's Phoebe numbers have increased modestly in the past few decades, as these birds benefit from human structures in arid regions. Their numbers continue to rise.

■ SUMMER ■ MIGRATION
■ WINTER ■ RARE
■ RESIDENT

This species is unusual among flycatchers in that the sexes are differently colored. In southern Texas it is conspicuous, often nesting near houses and farmyards. The bright colors of the male have earned it the nickname *brasita de fuego* in Mexico, or "little fire." Despite its brilliant color, the Vermilion Flycatcher is hard to detect in cottonwoods, willows, or mesquite, since it hunts from the highest canopy and generally remains well concealed. In sparsely vegetated areas, however, it may descend to the ground after insect prey. The male defends its territory with a prominent aerial display; it flies up singing, its red underparts and cap contrasting with the blue sky. When trying to attract a female, the male sings even at night.

DESCRIPTION: 6" (15 cm). The male has a brilliant scarlet crown and underparts with a dark brown back, wings, and tail. The female is similar to the male above but is white below with dark streaks. The bellies of females and immatures vary from pink to yellow to white.

VOICE: Call is *peet-peet* or *peet-a-weet*. Also has a soft, tinkling flight song.

NESTING: Lays 4 or 5 creamy-white, finely marked eggs in a tree cavity.

HABITAT: Trees and shrubs along rivers and roadsides.

RANGE: Breeds from southeastern California east to western Texas and south into the tropics. Winters in the southern part of its breeding range, but wanders as far east as the Gulf Coast.

SIMILAR SPECIES: Immature Say's Phoebe may show relatively indistinct streaking and a yellowish wash, but it is longer-tailed, larger, and never as white on the breast as female and immature Vermilion Flycatchers.

CONSERVATION:

This species is numerous and widespread in Central and South America, but decreasing in North America. Its numbers have dropped dramatically in the lower Colorado River Valley due to water use and land development, and surveys show a decline in the breeding population in Texas. Habitat loss is the most likely culprit behind the declines.

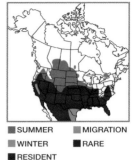

■ SUMMER   ■ MIGRATION
■ WINTER   ■ RARE
■ RESIDENT

In the southern half of North America this species is the counterpart of the Northern Shrike of the boreal regions of Alaska and Canada. In behavior and choice of habitat the two species are essentially similar, although the Loggerhead feeds mainly on large insects such as locusts. In cold weather, when insects are hard to find, it will hunt small birds or mice. The Loggerhead sometimes impales its prey—usually a small bird, mouse, or insect—on a thorn or barbed-wire fence to be eaten later, earning it the nickname "Butcher Bird."

DESCRIPTION: 8–10" (20–25 cm). This shrike is bluish-gray above with white underparts and a broad black mask across the face. It is slightly smaller than Northern Shrike, and slightly darker gray above, with its black face mask extending over its short, slightly hooked bill. The immature is paler and finely barred overall.

VOICE: A variety of harsh and musical notes and trills; a thrasher-like series of double phrases.

NESTING: Lays 4–6 white eggs, spotted with gray and brown, in a bulky mass of twigs and grass lined with plant down and feathers and set in a thorny shrub or tree.

HABITAT: Grasslands, orchards, and open areas with scattered trees; open grassy woodlands; deserts in the West.

RANGE: Breeds from southern British Columbia, central Alberta, central Saskatchewan, southern Manitoba, southern Ontario, and southern Quebec, south throughout the United States. Winters in the southern half of its breeding range.

SUBSPECIES: An endangered subspecies (*L. l. mearnsi*) is endemic to San Clemente Island off southern California.

SIMILAR SPECIES: Northern Shrike is larger, and appears paler gray above; its upperparts are finely barred. It has a narrower mask that stops at the bill; a whitish line over the mask and bill; and a longer, more powerful-looking, less conical and more hooked bill. Immatures are brownish overall.

Northern Mockingbird is longer, thinner, lacks the black mask, and has larger white wing patches. It has more leisurely flight with slower wingbeats.

CONSERVATION: NT

The Loggerhead Shrike population has declined significantly in recent decades in North America. The reasons for the decline require further study, but conservationists suspect increased pesticide use, habitat disruption, and changing land use to be primary factors. Once much more common and widespread, the species is now classified as Near-Threatened. Although still fairly common in the South and West, it has become an uncommon to rare sight in the Northeast and upper Midwest.

The San Clemente Loggerhead Shrike is on the U.S. Endangered Species List and is classified as endangered in California.

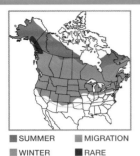

■ SUMMER ■ MIGRATION
■ WINTER ■ RARE
■ RESIDENT

Known as the Great Grey Shrike or Northern Grey Shrike in Europe, the Northern Shrike sits quietly, often in the top of a tree, before swooping down after insects, mice, and small birds. It kills more than it can eat, impaling its prey on a thorn or wedging it in a forked twig. On lean days it feeds from its larder. Like other northern birds that depend on rodent populations, the Northern Shrike's movements are cyclical, becoming more abundant farther south when northern rodent populations are low. Sometimes they hunt from an open perch, where they sit motionless until prey appears; at other times, they hover in the air, ready to pounce on anything that moves.

DESCRIPTION: 9–10½" (23–27 cm). A robin-sized shrike, usually seen perched atop a tree in the open. It is pale gray above, white below, with faint barring on the underparts, and a bold black mask ending at the bill. It has a black tail with white edges. It has a stout, distinctly hooked bill. The immature is browner.

VOICE: A mixture of warbles and harsh tones with a robin-like quality.

NESTING: Lays 4–6 pale gray eggs, spotted with dark gray and brown. Its nest is a large mass of twigs, lichens, moss, and feathers, usually in a dense conifer.

HABITAT: Open woodlands and brushy swamps in summer; open grasslands with fence posts and scattered trees in winter.

RANGE: Breeds from Alaska across northern Canada to Labrador, south to northern British Columbia. Winters irregularly across the northern tier of the United States south to northern California, Kansas, and Pennsylvania. Also found in the Old World.

SIMILAR SPECIES: Loggerhead Shrike is smaller and shorter-billed, with a wider black mask that crosses its forehead.

CONSERVATION: 🐦 LC

The Northern Shrike's population is considered stable throughout its range. The species' numbers are difficult to assess because of its cyclical movements, its solitary nature, and the remoteness of its breeding grounds. The negative population trends among other types of shrikes, however, suggest the need to monitor the health of this species closely.

■ SUMMER ■ MIGRATION
■ WINTER ■ RARE
■ RESIDENT

This little vireo, with its restricted range, differs from most vireos in being rather nervous and active—more like a warbler in its behavior. It is a tireless singer but is often difficult to find in the dense oak scrub. It has a titmouse-like habit of hanging upside down while foraging among twigs.

DESCRIPTION: 4½–4¾" (11–12 cm). Smaller than a sparrow. It is olive green above and white below. The crown and sides of the male's head are glossy black. The female and immature males are similar, but the crown and sides of the head are slate-gray. Immature females are buffier. Both sexes have white "spectacles" around the eyes.

VOICE: Harsh and varied phrases, sometimes musical. Its common call is a *chidit*; also a scolding *tchee*.

NESTING: Lays 4 unspotted white eggs in a well-made pendant cup of plant fibers and bark strips decorated with lichens and concealed in a shrub or bush.

HABITAT: Dense oak scrub and juniper thickets.

RANGE: Breeds from Kansas south through Oklahoma to central Texas. Winters in Mexico.

SIMILAR SPECIES: See Plumbeous, Blue-headed, and Cassin's vireos; other vireos lack white spectacles on a dark face.

CONSERVATION: VU

The Black-capped Vireo population is currently decreasing, although it has made a significant comeback since the mid-1980s when it was added to the U.S. Endangered Species List. It was delisted in 2018, and today the breeding population is estimated in the low tens of thousands. Especially vulnerable to parasitism by Brown-headed Cowbirds and to habitat loss, the species suffered major declines and had disappeared from much of its historic range by the late 20th century. Intensive conservation and recovery efforts that involved cooperation between federal agencies, state programs, and private landowners helped to reverse some of these declines, but the species remains a high conservation concern that will likely require ongoing habitat maintenance and continued management to ensure its survival.

■ SUMMER ■ MIGRATION
■ WINTER ■ RARE
■ RESIDENT

While most vireos inhabit tall trees, this species is usually found in thickets, where its presence is most easily detected by its loud and distinctive song. A patient observer can usually get a good look at one by standing quietly and waiting for the bird's curiosity to bring it into view. Its diet consists mainly of insects, but in winter it also eats a variety of small fruits. The Brown-headed Cowbird favors this vireo's nest for its own eggs.

DESCRIPTION: 5" (13 cm). Warbler-sized. It is olive green above and white below with yellow flanks and white wing bars. It has yellow "spectacles" around the eyes. The adult's eyes have a distinctive white iris that's visible at close range; immatures have dark gray or brown eyes.

VOICE: Loud, explosive series of notes, *chip-a-wheeoo-chip* or *Quick, give me a rain check!*

NESTING: Lays 4 brown-dotted white eggs in a purse-shaped nest of bark strips and grass, lined with spider silk, moss, and lichens, and set from 3 to 6' (1 to 2 m) up in thick undergrowth.

HABITAT: Dense swampy thickets and hillsides with blackberry and briar tangles.

RANGE: Breeds from Nebraska, Illinois, Ohio, southeastern New York, and central New England south to eastern Texas and southern Florida. Winters from the Gulf Coast and Florida southward.

SUBSPECIES: The nominate race that occupies most of the species' North American range is the largest and is fully migratory. A resident population found on the Florida Keys (subsp. *maynardi*) is grayer above with less yellow on the flanks. A resident South Texas population (subsp. *micrus*) is similarly colored and smaller.

SIMILAR SPECIES: All other vireos have dark eyes and lack yellow on the forehead. Cassin's and Blue-headed vireos have white spectacles. Bell's Vireo has an inconspicuous white spectacle or broken eye ring; it has duller wing bars and less yellow on the sides. Yellow-throated Vireo has a bright yellow chin and throat.

CONSERVATION: This species is common and its population is increasing. The northern limit of its range tends to fluctuate naturally, but typically reaches as far as Massachusetts and Michigan.

BELL'S VIREO *Vireo bellii*

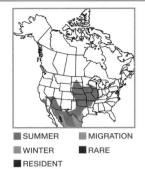

■ SUMMER ■ MIGRATION
■ WINTER ■ RARE
■ RESIDENT

John James Audubon named this species for John G. Bell (1812–1899), a New York taxidermist who accompanied him on his trip up the Missouri River in the 1840s. The bird's strong, somewhat curved bill with a slight hook at the end, like a miniature of a shrike's bill, reminds the observer that these tiny birds are determined predators. They feed on caterpillars, aphids, various larvae, and spiders. The species has become less common in many areas in recent years.

DESCRIPTION: 4¾–5" (12–13 cm). This small, stout vireo shows a great deal of geographical variation. It is dull olive-gray above and whitish below, with a faint white eye ring and fainter wing bars. Midwestern populations are short-tailed, while birds from the Southwest have comparatively long tails.

VOICE: A fast, warbled *tweedle-deedle-dum? tweedle-deedle-dee!* with the first phrase ascending and the second phrase descending.

NESTING: Lays 3–5 white eggs, sparsely marked with brown, in a well-made pendant cup of plant down and bark strips, placed in a dense tree or shrub.

HABITAT: Dense bottomland thickets, willow scrub, and mesquite.

RANGE: Breeds from southern California, Colorado, the Dakotas, and Indiana southward. Absent from the eastern third of the United States. Winters in the tropics.

SUBSPECIES: This species shows considerable geographical variation. Eastern birds (*V. b. bellii*) are more greenish above and yellower below, and these birds bob their tails. Western birds are divided into three populations: an Arizona subspecies (*V. b. arizonae*), a West Texas group (*V. b. medius*), and an endangered West Coast subspecies (*V. b. pusillus*) commonly called the California or Least Bell's Vireo. These western populations tend to flick their tails up and sideways more like gnatcatchers.

SIMILAR SPECIES: Warbling Vireo has longer proportions; a longer bill; and a longer, generally more conspicuous eyebrow. The two species' calls are distinctly different.

White-eyed Vireo has a white iris, yellow lores, and often yellow on the forehead.

Gray Vireo is larger and more pure gray, with different calls and habitat.

CONCERVATION:  **LC**

The Bell's Vireo population is large overall and increasing slowly, but its breeding numbers in parts of the Midwest and in California have declined markedly. The Least Bell's Vireo (*V. b. pusillus*) is on the U.S. Endangered Species List and is state-endangered in California. The species is threatened by habitat loss and frequent cowbird parasitism.

■ SUMMER ■ MIGRATION
■ WINTER ■ RARE
■ RESIDENT

This bird's overall gray blends with the blue-gray of the junipers. Even the bunchgrass and sagebrush have the same pale grayish color, a feature of the vegetation widespread on the arid mesas, slopes, and plateaus of the West. The Gray Vireo needs this camouflage when it searches for food near the top of the low cover it prefers.

DESCRIPTION: 5–5¾" (13–15 cm). This vireo is gray above and whitish below, with a faint white eye ring and lores; it has a single, indistinct wing bar. The sideways twitching of its tail is unusual among vireos and is reminiscent of that of gnatcatchers.

VOICE: Song is a series of 4–6 phrases with a pause between each phrase and a much longer pause between stanzas: *cheerio . . . che-whew . . . chireep? . . . cheerio.*

NESTING: Lays 3 or 4 white eggs lightly spotted with brown in a nest hung from a forked branch in a bush.

HABITAT: Dry brush, especially juniper in the pinyon- and juniper-covered slopes of the southwestern mountains; scrub oak and other types of chaparral.

RANGE: Breeds from southern California east to Utah, south to western Texas and Baja California. Winters south of the U.S.-Mexico border.

SIMILAR SPECIES: See Cassin's, Blue-headed, Plumbeous, Bell's, and Hutton's vireos.

CONSERVATION: LC
The Gray Vireo population is small and poorly studied, but appears to be stable or perhaps increasing. It is, however, limited to a restricted range and has specific habitat needs. Climate change threatens its breeding habitat of pinyon-juniper forests with rising temperatures and the risk of wildfires.

■ SUMMER ■ MIGRATION
■ WINTER ■ RARE
■ RESIDENT

This bird moves slowly, almost sluggishly through the canopy, halting after every move to forage for insects among the foliage. During winter, Hutton's Vireo may join a mixed flock, where it is easily confused with the smaller Ruby-crowned Kinglet.

DESCRIPTION: 4¼–4¾" (11–12 cm). A small, grayish-olive vireo with a partial white eye ring below, incomplete "spectacles," and two white wing bars separated by a dark patch. Its tail and bluish legs are short. Its bill is stout with a pale base, and the upper mandible is subtly hooked.

VOICE: Loud, short whistles and chatter. A monotonous two-part phrase, either up-slurred or down-slurred: *chu-whe, chu-wee* or *che-eer, che-eer*. Its call is a harsh *chit-chit*.

NESTING: Lays 3 or 4 white eggs with scattered brown spots in a hanging cup nest lined with feathers and moss suspended from a shrub branch or young tree.

HABITAT: Deciduous and mixed forests, primarily oak woodlands; also, live-oak tangles in canyons of the Southwest.

RANGE: Resident in southwestern British Columbia south to southern California, central Arizona, southwestern New Mexico, and western Texas.

SUBSPECIES: The species has two distinct populations. Birds of the Interior Southwest and Mexico (subsp. *stephensi*) are slightly larger and grayer with more distinct white wing bars and eye rings than the Pacific Coast population (subsp. *huttoni*).

SIMILAR SPECIES: Ruby-crowned Kinglet is smaller with a tiny black bill, a smaller head and tail, and a tapered body. Its darkest area is a patch behind the second wing bar.

CONSERVATION:
Hutton's Vireo is fairly common in its range and its population is considered stable. These birds are threatened by logging and habitat degradation as well as by the spread of the fungal disease called sudden oak death in California and Oregon, which can devastate forests of oaks and other tree species. Given that this species does not migrate, there is some concern that these birds will be affected by climate change as suitable winter temperature zones shift.

Vireo flavifrons YELLOW-THROATED VIREO

■ SUMMER   ■ MIGRATION
■ WINTER   ■ RARE
■ RESIDENT

These handsome vireos are found mainly in open groves of tall hardwood trees. This rather uncommon eastern vireo frequents mature, moist, semi-open forest. It often sings from high in the deciduous canopy.

DESCRIPTION: 6" (15 cm). A stocky, sparrow-sized vireo. It has a bright yellow throat, breast, and "spectacles" around the eyes. It has two conspicuous white wing bars, an olive green head and back, a gray rump, and a white belly.

VOICE: Similar to the song of Red-eyed and Blue-headed vireos, but lower in pitch and with a husky or burry quality to the phrases.

NESTING: Lays 4 brown-blotched, pinkish eggs in a cup-shaped nest of lichens, mosses, and grasses decorated and lined with spider silk and egg cases, and set in a forked branch well up in a tree.

HABITAT: Tall deciduous trees at the edge of forests, along streams, roadsides, orchards, and parks.

RANGE: Breeds from Manitoba, Minnesota, Ontario, and central New England south to the Gulf Coast states. Winters in the American tropics, with a few in southern Florida.

SIMILAR SPECIES: See Pine Warbler and Yellow-breasted Chat.

CONSERVATION:

Yellow-throated Vireo numbers are increasing slightly, especially in the Midwest. These birds declined in the northeastern United States in the early 20th century, possibly due to a shortage of nesting habitat or due to the widespread use of insecticides such as DDT.

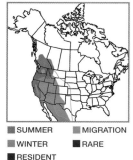

SUMMER — MIGRATION
WINTER — RARE
RESIDENT

Ornithologists split the bird formerly known as the Solitary Vireo into three separate species: Cassin's, Plumbeous, and Blue-headed vireos. Cassin's Vireo occupies the westernmost part of the former Solitary Vireo's range.

DESCRIPTION: 5–6" (13–15 cm). This western vireo is similar to its close relatives, the Blue-headed and Plumbeous vireos. It is duller and grayer overall than Blue-headed but shares that species' yellow sides and flanks, olive back, white wing bars, and bold white "spectacles."

VOICE: Its song is a series of phrases; intermediate between the clear notes of Blue-headed Vireo and the rough, husky notes of Plumbeous Vireo. Its call is a husky chatter.

NESTING: Lays 3–5 white eggs, lightly spotted with brown, in a pendant cup of bark strips and down, placed in a forked twig of a small forest tree.

HABITAT: Coniferous and mixed forests.

RANGE: Breeds from British Columbia and southwestern Alberta south to central Idaho and along the West Coast to southern California. Most leave the U.S. for Mexico in the fall, but a small number overwinter in southeastern Arizona.

SIMILAR SPECIES: Closely similar to both Blue-headed Vireo and Plumbeous Vireos, with plumage roughly intermediate between the two.

Hutton's Vireo is smaller and lacks the clean white spectacles and underparts.

CONSERVATION:
Cassin's Vireo is common in its range, where its numbers are slightly increasing.

- ■ SUMMER
- ■ WINTER
- ■ RESIDENT
- ■ MIGRATION
- ■ RARE

The Blue-headed Vireo is handsome and distinctively patterned. It is known as a fairly common migrant in most of North America, usually arriving somewhat earlier in the spring than other vireos. It and the White-eyed Vireo are the only two eastern vireos that remain in the southeastern United States in winter. Like other vireos, it moves slowly and deliberately through the trees, peering with its head cocked to one side in search of insects. This species, Plumbeous Vireo, and Cassin's Vireo were formerly considered a single species known as the Solitary Vireo.

DESCRIPTION: 5–6" (13–15 cm). It has a blue-gray crown, nape, and face; an olive-green back; and a white throat and underparts. It has two broad, white wing bars and large white "spectacles," and yellow flanks and sides. Females and immatures are grayer on the head.

VOICE: Its song is a rather slow series of sweet, slurred phrases like that of Red-eyed Vireo, but slower and more musical. Call is a husky chatter.

NESTING: Lays 3–5 white eggs lightly spotted with brown in a pendant cup of bark strips and down, placed in a forked twig of a small forest tree.

HABITAT: Coniferous and mixed forests.

RANGE: Breeds from northeastern British Columbia across central interior Canada to Newfoundland and south through the Great Lakes region, southern New England, and in the Appalachians to North Carolina. Winters from the Carolinas to Texas and south to Costa Rica.

SUBSPECIES: The subpopulation of Appalachian breeders (subsp. *alticola*) is slightly larger, darker, grayer, and thicker-billed than Northern birds (subsp. *solitarius*).

SIMILAR SPECIES: See Plumbeous Vireo and Cassin's Vireo.

CONVERSATION:
The Blue-headed Vireo population is increasing, and it has been expanding its breeding range farther southward in recent decades.

PLUMBEOUS VIREO *Vireo plumbeus*

■ SUMMER ■ MIGRATION
■ WINTER ■ RARE
■ RESIDENT

The Plumbeous Vireo is a common and widespread summer bird in much of the West. In migration and winter, when it occurs with its sibling, Cassin's Vireo, care should be taken to differentiate the two species, which can look much alike even under good viewing conditions. This species, Cassin's Vireo, and Blue-headed Vireo were formerly considered a single species known as the Solitary Vireo; Plumbeous Vireo averages the largest and darkest of the trio.

DESCRIPTION: 5–6" (13–15 cm). This bird has a gray crown, nape, face, and back; a white throat and underparts; white wing bars and flight feather edges; and large, white "spectacles." The sides of the breast are olive-gray, and its flanks sometimes have a yellowish tinge.

VOICE: Its song is a rather slow series of burry phrases, slower and rougher than that of Cassin's Vireo. Its call is a husky chatter.

NESTING: Lays 3–5 white eggs lightly spotted with brown in a pendant cup of bark strips and down, placed in a forked twig of a small forest tree.

HABITAT: Coniferous and mixed forests.

RANGE: A breeding bird of the Great Basin and Rocky Mountains, easternmost California east to the Black Hills of South Dakota and south to southern Arizona and southern New Mexico. A few overwinter in the Southwest.

SIMILAR SPECIES: See Blue-headed Vireo and Cassin's Vireo.

Gray Vireo lacks the bold white spectacles and wing bars, and is usually found in undergrowth in semiarid habitat.

CONSERVATION: Plumbeous Vireo is still widespread and common despite a gradual decline during the past several decades. Recent surveys have shown a possible reversal of this downward trend.

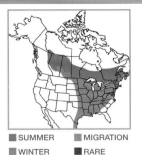

- ■ SUMMER ■ MIGRATION
- ■ WINTER ■ RARE
- ■ RESIDENT

Because this vireo was first described by John Cassin in 1842 from a specimen collected near Philadelphia, both its common and Latin names refer to Philadelphia, but it is by no means confined to that area. It is easily overlooked in spring since it does not sing much on migration; in addition, it tends to arrive later in the spring when the foliage is already dense.

DESCRIPTION: 6" (15 cm). This sparrow-sized vireo is olive above and yellowish below, with a pale eyebrow, a dark line through the eye to the base of the bill, and no wing bars. It has a yellow throat that is brightest in the center. Fall immatures are usually the most richly colored. Its tail is short.

VOICE: Similar to that of the Red-eyed Vireo but higher and slower: *See-me? Here-I-am! Up-here. See-me?*

NESTING: Lays 4 brown-spotted, white eggs in a cup of bark strips, grasses, and mosses lined with bits of lichen and thistledown.

HABITAT: Open second-growth woodlands (often aspens), old clearings and burned-over areas, and thickets along streams and lakes.

RANGE: Breeds in southern Canada and the northernmost United States. Winters in the American tropics.

SIMILAR SPECIES: See Warbling and Red-eyed vireos, Tennessee Warbler, and Black-throated Blue Warbler.

CONSERVATION: Philadelphia Vireo is generally uncommon, but its numbers are increasing.

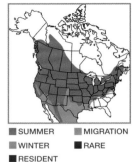

■ SUMMER　■ MIGRATION
■ WINTER　■ RARE
■ RESIDENT

The best place to look for this modestly plumaged vireo is in a grove of tall shade trees on the bank of a stream. Here, in the breeding season, one may hear its rambling song and, after a careful search, spot it moving deliberately through the foliage in pursuit of insects. In migration, it sometimes occurs with the Philadelphia Vireo.

DESCRIPTION: 5–6" (13–15 cm). A sparrow-sized bird similar to Red-eyed Vireo—it is olive-green above, whitish below, with no wing bars—but it lacks the bold face pattern, having only a narrow white eyebrow. The underparts, including the throat, are whitish, often washed with yellow or greenish-yellow on the sides and flanks, particularly in young birds in later summer and early fall. Birds in juvenal plumage may exhibit a single, faint buff wing bar. The Philadelphia Vireo is also similar, but has a yellow tinge to the underparts and a dark spot between the eye and the base of the bill.

VOICE: A drowsy, rambling warble, like the song of a Purple Finch but slower; it ends on a rising note.

NESTING: Lays 3 or 4 brown-spotted white eggs in a well-made pendant cup of bark strips and plant down fastened to a forked twig, usually near the top of a tall tree.

HABITAT: Deciduous woodlands, especially near streams; in isolated groves and shade trees.

RANGE: Breeds from British Columbia, southern Mackenzie, Manitoba, and New Brunswick south to northern Mexico, Louisiana, and Virginia. It winters in the tropics.

SUBSPECIES: This species has two distinct subpopulations in the east and the west. Eastern birds (subsp. *gilvus*) sing more musically in long, clear, melodious phrases. Western birds (subsp. *swainsoni*) average slightly smaller with a darker crown and drabber flanks; they sing less musically—choppier, buzzier, and in a higher pitch. Some contend that the eastern and western populations may represent two distinct species.

SIMILAR SPECIES: Philadelphia Vireo has pale yellow underparts and dusky lores; its song is different. Red-eyed Vireo has a gray crown, an olive-green back, and a black-bordered straight white eyebrow. Tennessee Warbler is greener above, with a tiny, pointed bill.

CONSERVATION: ![LC]
Warbling Vireo is common and its population is increasing. These birds favor open woods and edges created by forest clearings, but decline where streamside habitat is degraded and where insecticides and herbicides are heavily used. Because the entire global population of Warbling Vireos crowds into a relatively small winter range from Mexico to Nicaragua, habitat conservation in this region is especially important.

■ SUMMER ■ MIGRATION
■ WINTER ■ RARE
■ RESIDENT

This vireo is one of the more abundant birds in eastern forests during the summer. A persistent singer during the breeding season, the Red-eyed Vireo utters its constant series of short phrases from dawn till dusk, even on the hottest days when other birds are silent, and may even sing while grappling with the large insects it captures. The Red-eyed Vireo is a fierce fighter around its nest and can intimidate even the large Pileated Woodpecker. Its horizontal posture and slow movement through the understory of broad-leaved woods make it an easy bird to observe.

DESCRIPTION: 5½–6½" (14–17 cm). Sparrow-sized. It is olive green above, whitish below, with a narrow white eyebrow bordered above with black. It has a gray crown, a red eye (dark in immatures), and no wing bars.

VOICE: A series of short, musical, robin-like phrases persistently repeated all day; like that of Blue-headed Vireo but faster and not so musical.

NESTING: Lays 3 or 4 white eggs, sparsely marked with dark brown, in a thin-walled pendant cup of bark strips and plant fibers, decorated with lichen and attached to a forked twig.

HABITAT: Broad-leaved forests; shade trees in residential areas.

RANGE: Breeds from British Columbia, Ontario, and the Gulf of Saint Lawrence south to Oregon, Colorado, the Gulf Coast, and Florida. Winters in the tropics.

SIMILAR SPECIES: See Warbling and Black-whiskered vireos. Warbling Vireo is similar, but lacks the gray crown and black border over its bold white eyebrow.

Philadelphia Vireo is smaller, duller above and more yellow below, with no strong eyebrow stripe.

CONSERVATION: Red-eyed Vireo numbers are gradually increasing despite some local declines, particularly in the West and Great Plains. Forest clearing and fragmentation reduce available habitat for these birds, and also leaves them more vulnerable to Brown-headed Cowbird parasitism, which occurs more frequently near forest edges.

SUMMER ◼ MIGRATION
WINTER ◼ RARE
◼ RESIDENT

Yellow-green Vireo is a rare summer visitor to southern Texas that may also appear casually in fall in coastal California or in spring on the upper Gulf Coast. This species is one of the tropical members of the group of vireos that includes our familiar Red-eyed Vireo. Like the Red-eyed, this bird obtains its food by searching rather carefully in the foliage of trees, without the more active motions of warblers. Its song is repeated monotonously throughout the day.

DESCRIPTION: 6–7" (15–18 cm). This sparrow-sized tropical vireo is olive-green above, paler below, with a strong yellowish tinge on the back, flanks, and undertail coverts. It has a dull gray crown, a whitish eyebrow, and red eyes.

VOICE: A series of deliberate, musical phrases, more widely spaced than in the song of Red-eyed Vireo.

NESTING: Lays 3 or 4 white eggs lightly spotted with brown in a pendant cup of plant fibers and bark strips, bound together with spiderweb and suspended from a forked branch in a bush or small sapling.

HABITAT: Streamside thickets and woodlands.

RANGE: Breeds from Rio Grande Valley of Texas southward. Winters in the tropics.

SIMILAR SPECIES: Similar to Red-eyed Vireo, but it is much yellower below, and has more indistinct markings on the head.

CONSERVATION: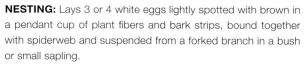
The North American population, at the northernmost edge of this species' native range, can fluctuate. Overall the population is stable throughout its primary range of Mexico and Central America, where this bird is widespread and common.

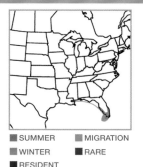

■ SUMMER   ■ MIGRATION
■ WINTER   ■ RARE
■ RESIDENT

These vireos are not shy and come regularly into gardens and shade trees in Key West. They may also be seen in the dense scrub and tropical hammocks in the Upper Keys and occasionally in coconut palms and mangroves around Miami. They eat insects and, rarely, berries and other soft fruits.

DESCRIPTION: 5½" (14 cm). Similar to the Red-eyed Vireo—olive green above, white below—but with a dusky throat streak below the eye that gives bird its name. The streak is often hard to see, however, and bird is best identified by voice.

VOICE: Similar to that of Red-eyed Vireo but distinctly more abrupt, and uttered in one- to four-note phrases, sometimes described as *Whip-Tom-Kelly*.

NESTING: Lays 2 or 3 white eggs, with a few small scattered spots, in a nest of grass, leaves, and rootlets in the fork of a branch, usually in mangroves.

HABITAT: Mangroves, thick scrub, and shade trees.

RANGE: Breeds in southern Florida and West Indies. Winters in the tropics.

SIMILAR SPECIES: Red-eyed Vireo lacks whiskers; its range generally overlaps with Black-whiskered only in migration.

CONSERVATION:

The Black-whiskered Vireo population is thought to be stable, although its numbers in North America were severely reduced in the 1980s after several harsh winters destroyed much prime mangrove habitat in western Florida. The species has also been affected by the spread of cowbirds into Florida, which often parasitize this species as they do other vireos.

SUMMER █ MIGRATION
WINTER █ RARE
█ RESIDENT

Anyone who has camped in the western mountains or the northern forests is familiar with this bird, formerly called Gray Jay and popularly known as "Whiskey Jack" or "Camp Robber." This bird is bold and curious, and is often attracted to campsites and cabins, from which it is known to steal food. These omnivorous birds will eat almost anything they can find, including seeds, fruits, insects, fungi, small mammals, and carrion. It stores excess food by gluing scraps into balls with its saliva and hiding them among bark crevices and pine needles.

DESCRIPTION: 10–13" (25–33 cm). This bold jay is gray above and pale gray to whitish below. Its forehead and throat are white; its nape and stripe through the eye are dull black. It has a small bill and no crest. Immatures are sooty-gray with a faint, pale "mustache."

VOICE: *Whee-ah, chuck-chuck*; also scolds, screams, and whistles.

NESTING: Lays 3–5 gray-green eggs spotted with dark olive-brown in a solid bowl of twigs and bark strips lined with feathers and fur and placed near the trunk of a dense conifer.

HABITAT: Coniferous forests.

RANGE: Resident from Alaska east across Canada to Labrador and south to northern California, New Mexico, northern New York, and northern New England.

SUBSPECIES: Three distinguishable subspecies groups exist. The nominate Boreal/Taiga group (subsp. *canadensis*) has a white collar and forehead with a dark gray crown and nape. Birds of the southern Rocky Mountains (subsp. *capitalis*) have more white on the head extending over the crown, making its head appear mostly white. Pacific/Northwest birds (subsp. *obscurus*) are darker overall and have a larger, darker cap, and a more whitish belly. All three groups are connected by intermediate populations.

SIMILAR SPECIES: See Clark's Nutcracker and Northern Shrike—the only other gray, black, and white birds in Canada Jay's range with which it might be confused.

CONSERVATION:
Canada Jay is common. Its wide range in the Far North makes monitoring its population difficult, but these birds are believed to have experienced a slight decline, mainly due to the clearcutting of northern forests.

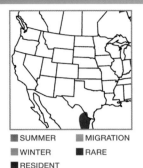

■ SUMMER   ■ MIGRATION
■ WINTER   ■ RARE
■ RESIDENT

The largest North American jay, this species has only recently colonized the lower Rio Grande Valley, where it travels in noisy flocks. It is uncommon to rare and local in southern Texas. The birds have deep, slow wingbeats and pump their long tails as they fly.

DESCRIPTION: 14–18" (36–46 cm). This crow-sized jay is large and long-tailed. It is dusky brown above with a darker brown head; it is paler on the breast and whitish on the belly and flanks. Its thick bill is black in adults and yellow in immatures.

VOICE: A shrill *pow!* or *kreeow!*

NESTING: Lays 3–5 blue-gray eggs marked with brown in a cup of twigs, usually on a branch far out from the trunk.

HABITAT: Dense streamside woodlands and thickets.

RANGE: Rare resident in extreme southern Texas. Also found in the American tropics.

SIMILAR SPECIES: American Crow lacks the pale underside and is black rather than sooty brown.

Black-billed Magpie has white on the wings and shoulders.

CONSERVATION:

Brown Jay is widespread and common in Mexico and Central America. Its population is increasing across its range and expanding into southern Texas, although it remains relatively uncommon north of the border.

GREEN JAY *Cyanocorax yncas*

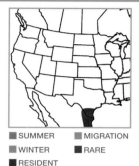

These brilliantly colored tropical birds are locally common residents in southern Texas. In winter months and when not nesting, these inhabitants of dense thickets visit more open country, even near ranches and smaller towns. Like most jays, they are omnivorous, eating fruits, seeds, insects, and even corn. At times they may visit populated areas in search of food. They tend to be gregarious and are often found in small groups that call frequently to one another.

DESCRIPTION: 12" (30 cm). Strikingly colored, with a bright green body and green tail with yellow on the sides. It has a brilliant blue crown and cheeks; the rest of the head, throat, and breast are black. Juveniles are similar but drabber.

VOICE: Gives a wide variety of rattling calls. Also *shink, shink, shink*.

NESTING: Lays 4 brown-spotted, grayish eggs in a loosely made stick nest of thorns, lined with rootlets or grass and placed in a bush or small tree.

HABITAT: Dry thickets and open forest with thick undergrowth; sometimes in more open country around ranch houses.

RANGE: Resident in southernmost Texas (Rio Grande Valley) southward. Also found in the American tropics.

SIMILAR SPECIES: Other jays have a similar body structure, but Green Jay's vivid coloration is unmistakable.

CONSERVATION: LC

The Green Jay population is increasing in southern Texas and throughout its range in the tropics. The species relies heavily on native Tamaulipan brushland habitat in northeast Mexico and southern Texas.

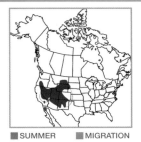

■ SUMMER ■ MIGRATION
■ WINTER ■ RARE
■ RESIDENT

Although they sometimes pull up earthworms from lawns in the fashion of robins, Pinyon Jays feed principally on pine nuts, which they store in fall and consume during winter and spring. The birds' local population varies from year to year with the success of the nut crop. They nest early after a good harvest; in poor years they delay breeding until August.

DESCRIPTION: 9–11¾" (23–30 cm). A stocky, short-tailed jay. Its long, slender bill gives it a resemblance to Clark's Nutcracker. It is gray-blue, darkest on the head, with white streaking on the throat. It is crow-like in its flight and flocking habits.

VOICE: A high-pitched *caaa*, often quavering at the end and resembling a laughing *haa-a-a-a*.

NESTING: Lays 3 or 4 speckled, greenish-white eggs in a twiggy cup nest. Nests in loose colonies.

HABITAT: Ponderosa pine, pinyon-juniper, and forests of mixed pine and oak.

RANGE: Resident from central Oregon and Montana southward to central Arizona, New Mexico, and extreme northwestern Oklahoma.

SIMILAR SPECIES: See Clark's Nutcracker.

CONSERVATION:

Although natural fluctuation in Pinyon Jay numbers make assessing trends challenging, surveys suggest the species is in substantial decline throughout its range. Uncontrolled fires, drought, and the converting of pinyon-juniper forest to grazing land have reduced available habitat.

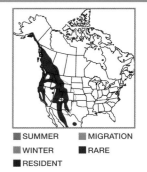

■ SUMMER ■ MIGRATION
■ WINTER ■ RARE
■ RESIDENT

Somewhat more reticent than the Canada Jay, Steller's never-theless quickly becomes accustomed to campsites and human providers. It is often seen sitting quietly in treetops, surveying the surroundings. Near its nest site, it is silent and shy.

DESCRIPTION: 12–13½" (30–34 cm). The only western jay with a crest. The front half of this bird is sooty black, and the rear half is dark blue-gray, with tight black cross-barring on the secondaries and tail. Its lightly streaked eyebrow, chin, and forehead markings vary considerably.

VOICE: A harsh *shack-shack-shack-shack* or *chook-chook-chook* call reveals its presence. It may also mimic the screams of hawks.

NESTING: Lays 3–5 spotted, greenish eggs in a neat twiggy bowl lined with small roots and fibers, well hidden in a shady conifer.

HABITAT: Coniferous forests: pine and oak woods in the southern part of its range, small groves and stands of mixed oak and redwood in northern California.

RANGE: Largely resident from coastal southern Alaska east to the Rocky Mountains and southward into Central America.

SUBSPECIES: The nominate birds of the Pacific Coast (subsp. *stelleri*) are dark blue and tend to become darker farther north and paler in the south. Birds in the central and southern Rockies (subsp. *macrolopha*) have a longer crest with white marks on the forehead and paler backs. On Haida Gwaii (formerly Queen Charlotte Islands) off the coast of British Columbia, the resident Steller's Jays (subsp. *carlottae*) are the largest and darkest of these birds, and are almost entirely black above.

SIMILAR SPECIES: Blue Jay, typically an eastern species, is paler blue, without the black head, breast, and back; it has white spots on the wings and tail and whitish underparts with a black breast band; its crest is shorter than in most Steller's Jays.

Scrub-jays and Mexican Jay are paler overall and lack a crest.

Pinyon Jay is stockier, shorter-tailed, and longer-billed; it lacks a crest.

CONSERVATION:  Widespread and common, Steller's Jay numbers are stable to slightly increasing.

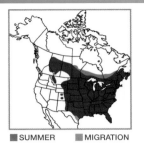

- ■ SUMMER
- ■ WINTER
- ■ RESIDENT
- ■ MIGRATION
- ■ RARE

Although sometimes disliked because they chase smaller birds away from feeders, Blue Jays are among the handsomest of birds. They often bury seeds and acorns, and because many of these caches are never retrieved, Blue Jays act as tree planters, in effect. They regularly mob predators; when they do, their raucous cries make it easy to locate a hawk or a roosting owl nearby. Although seen all year, they are migratory and travel in large, loose flocks in spring and fall. Birds from farther north replace local populations in winter.

DESCRIPTION: 12" (30 cm). This jay is bright blue above with much white and black in the wings and tail; it is dingy white below. It has black facial markings and a prominent blue crest.

VOICE: A raucous *jay-jay*, harsh cries, and a rich variety of other calls. One is almost identical to the scream of the Red-shouldered Hawk and the calls of Broad-winged Hawk. It also gives a musical *queedle-queedle*.

NESTING: Lays 4–6 brown-spotted, greenish eggs in a coarsely built nest of sticks, lined with grass and well concealed in a crotch or forked branch of a tree, often a conifer.

HABITAT: Chiefly oak forest, but now also city parks and suburban yards, especially where oak trees predominate.

RANGE: Resident east of the Rockies, from southern Canada to the Gulf of Mexico. Slowly encroaching westward, especially in southern Canada and the northern United States.

SIMILAR SPECIES: Scrub-jays lack a crest, and do not have the bold white bars and black necklace. The ranges of most scrub-jays usually don't overlap with Blue Jay, except for Florida Scrub-Jay in central Florida.

Steller's Jays are similar in shape, but they have black heads and no white on the wings or underside.

CONSERVATION: This jay species has become common and familiar as it has adapted to nesting in residential areas. Its numbers are stable following a gradual decline throughout the 19th and 20th centuries as eastern forests were cleared for development.

FLORIDA SCRUB-JAY *Aphelocoma coerulescens*

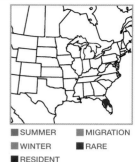

■ SUMMER ■ MIGRATION
■ WINTER ■ RARE
■ RESIDENT

The Florida Scrub-Jay is separated from any other scrub-jay species by a distance of 1000 miles (1600 km). Like all jays, this species may be secretive and silent around its nest or while perching in a treetop in early morning but is frequently noisy and conspicuous. Scrub-jays often eat the eggs or young of other birds, but in summer they are mainly insectivorous. They also eat acorns and bury many more acorns than they consume, helping to regenerate oak forests that have been destroyed by fire or drought.

DESCRIPTION: 11" (28 cm). This jay is robin-sized, but its large, strong bill and long tail make it appear larger. Its head, wings, and tail are blue (conspicuous when it glides in a long, undulating flight). Its back is a pale gray-brown; its underparts are pale with faint brown streaks. It has a black mask over the eyes, a whitish forehead, and no crest. Its white throat is offset by a blue necklace.

VOICE: Its song includes trills and high warbles. Its main call is a loud, harsh *shreep*.

NESTING: Lays 3–6 eggs, spotted on a darker, greenish or reddish base, in a twiggy nest well hidden in a tree or dense shrub. Young of the previous year help their parents to raise the next year's brood.

HABITAT: Scrub oak, pine scrub, and sandhills.

RANGE: Resident in peninsular Florida south to the northern edge of the Everglades. It is the only bird species found exclusively in Florida.

SIMILAR SPECIES: Mexican Jay is stouter, and usually shows less contrast and duller coloring; its mask is paler; it lacks a white eyebrow, white on the throat, and a bluish necklace. Immature Mexican Jay is stouter, with a shorter, less rounded tail. The calls and habitats of the two species are different.

CONSERVATION: VU

The Florida Scrub-Jay is on the U.S. Endangered Species List. It is classified as threatened throughout its range in Florida. Its total global population is estimated to be less than 10,000 individuals.

Habitat loss and fragmentation from heavy development is the primary threat to this species, which continues to decline. The Florida Scrub Jay is reliant on fire-thinned oak scrub habitat; human fire control measures have reduced the frequency of low-intensity fires sparked by lightning strikes that were once common in Florida, inadvertently further reducing the available habitat for this species. Without these naturally occurring fires, older-growth oak scrub communities become too dense for these specialist scrub-jays to use.

Aphelocoma insularis **ISLAND SCRUB-JAY**

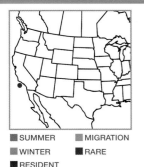

■ SUMMER   ■ MIGRATION
■ WINTER   ■ RARE
■ RESIDENT

Island Scrub-Jays are endemic to Santa Cruz Island, California, where California Scrub-Jays found on the adjacent mainland have never been recorded. Year-to-year population fluctuations are likely influenced by acorn availability. Unlike Florida Scrub-Jay and Mexican Jay, this species breeds in isolated pairs rather than in cooperative flocks.

DESCRIPTION: 13" (33 cm). Although similar in overall appearance to the closely related California Scrub-Jay, the Island Scrub-Jay is approximately 15 percent larger with a darker blue head, wings, and tail. Its back is dark brown; its black cheeks are set off from the blue of its head by a narrow white eyebrow. Its white throat is delineated by a blue breast band from its dusky breast and belly; its undertail coverts are bluish.

VOICE: No advertising song; its vocalizations are similar to those of other western scrub-jays, although generally louder and harsher than among mainland species. Its most common calls are a harsh *shek-shek-shek* or rising *shreeenk*.

NESTING: Lays 3–4 light bluish green eggs with faint olive spots in a large bulky cup nest of twigs, usually placed 7–10' (2–3 m) high in dense bush or tree. Its average clutch size (3.7 eggs) is slightly smaller than that of California Scrub-Jay populations on the adjacent mainland (4.1 eggs).

HABITAT: Oak woodlands, chaparral, dry scrub and pine forests, similar to California Scrub-Jay on the mainland.

RANGE: Endemic to Santa Cruz Island, approximately 25 miles (40 km) south of Santa Barbara, California. The island is the largest—about 100 square miles (250 km²)—and most topographically diverse of California's Channel Islands.

SIMILAR SPECIES: California Scrub-Jay on the California mainland is closely related but is smaller, less brightly colored, and has a somewhat smaller bill. Despite their proximity, the ranges of the two species are not known to overlap.

CONSERVATION: VU

This species is vulnerable due to its extremely limited range and small, concentrated population, last estimated at roughly 2300 individuals. The removal of feral sheep and pigs from Santa Cruz Island from the 1980s through the early 2000s has helped the island's overgrazed scrub habitat to recover, which has benefited the scrub-jays.

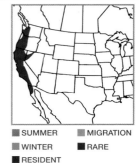

■ SUMMER ■ MIGRATION
■ WINTER ■ RARE
■ RESIDENT

This common Pacific Coast scrub-jay is often bold, noisy, and conspicuous. Scrub-jays are omnivorous and will readily come to backyard bird feeders, but in summer they are mainly insectivorous. These birds also eat acorns and have been described as "uphill planters," counter-balancing the tendency of acorns to bounce or roll downhill. The jays bury many more acorns than they consume and help to regenerate oak forests following fires or drought. This species and its interior cousin, Woodhouse's Scrub-Jay, were formerly considered a single species called Western Scrub-Jay.

DESCRIPTION: 11–13" (28–33 cm). This colorful jay is robin-sized, but its large, strong bill and long tail make it appear larger. Its head, wings, and tail are blue and conspicuous when it glides in its long, undulating flight. Its back is dull brown and its underparts are light gray. It has no crest and a dusky face mask. Its white throat is offset by an incomplete blue necklace.

VOICE: Call is loud, throaty *jayy?* or *jree?* In flight, it gives a long series of *check-check-check* notes.

NESTING: Lays 3–6 eggs, spotted on darker, greenish or reddish base, in a twiggy nest well hidden in a tree or dense shrub.

HABITAT: Scrub oak, woodlands, and chaparral, but does not breed in low scrub because it needs watch posts; also inhabits suburban gardens.

RANGE: Resident in California, Oregon, and Washington and south to extreme northwestern Mexico and Baja California.

SUBSPECIES: Several geographic subpopulations are recognized, showing subtle differences in size, bill shape, and coloration. The taxonomy of scrub-jays is complex and our understanding of the relationships among the subgroups continues to evolve.

SIMILAR SPECIES: All of our scrub-jays are closely related and look similar. See Woodhouse's Scrub-Jay. Island Scrub-Jay is endemic to Santa Cruz Island.

Also see Mexican Jay.

CONSERVATION: [LC] California Scrub-Jay's population appears to be healthy and stable, possibly increasing in the northern part of its range.

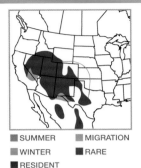

■ SUMMER ■ MIGRATION
■ WINTER ■ RARE
■ RESIDENT

This interior scrub-jay species tends to be more secretive and inconspicuous than its coastal kin. It is more uncommon and sparsely populated, although it does visit backyard feeders in some western towns. Aside from seeds, peanuts, and fruit, scrub-jays will eat a variety of fare including caterpillars, small lizards, and nestlings of other birds; in summer they are mainly insectivorous. This species and its coastal cousin, California Scrub-Jay, were formerly considered a single species called Western Scrub-Jay.

DESCRIPTION: 11–13" (28–33 cm). This is a robin-sized scrub-jay with a large bill (thinner and straighter than California Scrub-Jay) and a long tail. It has a paler blue head, wings, and tail than in California Scrub-Jay. Its back is dull gray-blue and its underparts are gray. It has a dusky face mask and lacks a crest. It has a white throat ending in a faint or almost entirely absent blue breast band.

VOICE: Call is loud, throaty *jayy?* or *jree?* In flight it gives a long series of *check-check-check* notes. Its voice is raspier than that of California Scrub-Jay.

NESTING: Lays 3–6 eggs, spotted on darker, greenish or reddish base, in a twiggy nest well hidden in a tree or dense shrub.

HABITAT: Sparse pinyon-juniper and oak-pinyon forests in arid foothills; also inhabits suburban areas.

RANGE: Resident from Nevada, Idaho, Wyoming, and Colorado south to interior Mexico.

SUBSPECIES: Several geographic subpopulations are recognized, showing subtle differences in size, bill shape, and coloration. The taxonomy of scrub-jays is complex and our understanding of the relationships among the subgroups continues to evolve.

SIMILAR SPECIES: See California Scrub-Jay and Mexican Jay.

CONSERVATION: Although still widespread, this species has shown declines in some regions in recent years. Further study is needed to determine this species' status since its split from California Scrub-Jay; most prior surveys included the two species lumped together.

MEXICAN JAY *Aphelocoma wollweberi*

■ SUMMER ■ MIGRATION
■ WINTER ■ RARE
■ RESIDENT

Nesting territories of Mexican Jays are small and adjacent; when a predator approaches, an entire colony moves to the defense, scolding loudly from a safe distance. Acorns are their staple diet, but they also glean insects and rob eggs and young from nests of other birds. This species was formerly known as the Gray-breasted Jay.

DESCRIPTION: 11½–13" (29–33 cm). Mexican Jays are similar to scrub-jays but larger and more muted, without the white markings on the throat or above the eyes. It has a dull blue head, rump, wings, and tail; a gray back; and a dusky ear patch. Juveniles have a pale bill.

VOICE: A loud *shrink?* or *wenk?*, often repeated.

NESTING: Lays 4 or 5 green eggs in a twig bowl lined with horsehair and placed low in a tree.

HABITAT: Oak forests and wooded canyons. These birds prefer open oak forests in Arizona and oak-pine woods in Texas.

RANGE: Resident from southern Arizona, New Mexico, and western Texas southward.

SUBSPECIES: Texas birds (subsp. *couchii*) have a richer blue head. Arizona birds (subsp. *arizonae*) are paler; juvenile birds take up to two years to lose the pale color on the bill.

SIMILAR SPECIES: See California and Woodhouse's scrub-jays.

CONSERVATION: Mexican Jays are numerous but may be decreasing slightly. Although data about Mexican Jay population trends is limited, they are locally common in their limited U.S. range.

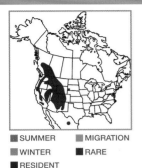

- ■ SUMMER
- ■ WINTER
- ■ RESIDENT
- ■ MIGRATION
- ■ RARE

These birds use their long, sharp, sturdy bills to crack open closed, unripe pine cones and remove seeds from the cone scales. Periodic irruptions of Clark's Nutcrackers every 10 to 20 years, which may bring the birds all the way to the Pacific Coast, are related to failures of the pine nut crop. This erratic winter wanderer may appear near camps and picnic sites, where it seems unwary of humans and often takes food scraps. It can hold several nuts in a special cheek pouch under the tongue in addition to those it holds in its bill.

DESCRIPTION: 12–13" (30–33 cm). A pigeon-sized corvid with a striking black, white, and gray pattern. Its body is light gray overall, with a dark eye and a long, sharply pointed bill. It has black wings with white wing patches at the trailing edge. From above, its tail is black with white outer tail feathers; the tail is almost entirely white underneath. The face is white from the forehead to the chin in adults, and almost entirely gray in juveniles. It has a crow-like flight.

VOICE: A drawn-out, grating, guttural *kraaaa*.

NESTING: Lays 2–6 spotted green eggs in a deep bowl nest of sticks in a coniferous tree. Nests very early.

HABITAT: Stands of juniper and ponderosa pine or of whitebark pine and larch on high mountain ranges, near the tree line.

RANGE: Resident in southern British Columbia and Alberta south throughout the pine-clad western mountains to California and Colorado.

SIMILAR SPECIES: Canada Jay, Northern Mockingbird, and shrikes have similar coloration, but are smaller, longer-tailed, and shorter-billed.

Pinyon Jay is similar in shape, but is smaller and essentially all blue.

CONSERVATION: The Clark's Nutcracker population is stable throughout its range. It is not subject to much human interference due to its habitat in the high mountains away from population centers. These fragile subalpine mountaintop ecosystems, however, may be especially vulnerable to the effects of climate change.

BLACK-BILLED MAGPIE *Pica hudsonia*

■ SUMMER ■ MIGRATION
■ WINTER ■ RARE
■ RESIDENT

Black-billed Magpies are a widespread, familiar bird found in open woodlands and thickets and along watercourses throughout the West. Magpies generally nest individually but can sometimes be found in loose colonies; they are social when feeding or after the breeding season. Because insects and small rodents factor heavily in their omnivorous diets, these birds are more beneficial than destructive to agriculture. These birds frequently associate with deer, moose, and domestic cattle and sheep, perching on the backs of these mammals and picking off ticks and flies.

DESCRIPTION: 17½–22" (44–56 cm). A large black and white bird with a long tail and dark bill. Its bill, head, breast, and underparts are black. The bird's wings and tail appear dark but have a green iridescence. It has a white belly and shoulders; its white primaries are conspicuous as large white wing patches in flight.

VOICE: A rapid, nasal *mag? mag? mag?* or *yak yak yak*.

NESTING: Lays 6–9 blotched, greenish eggs in a neat cup nest within a large, bulky, domed structure of strong, often thorny twigs, with a double entrance, in a tree or bush.

HABITAT: Open woodlands, savannas, brush-covered country, and streamside growth.

RANGE: Resident from Alaska and western Canada south to east-central California and east to the Great Plains.

SIMILAR SPECIES: See Yellow-billed Magpie.

CONVERSATION:

The Black-billed Magpie population is stable throughout its range. Although farmers and ranchers killed many of these birds as pests before the mid-20th century, these magpies remain widespread and common.

■ SUMMER ■ MIGRATION
■ WINTER ■ RARE
■ RESIDENT

Normally a bird of open country in California's central valleys, this adaptable magpie has increasingly moved into vacant city lots and weedy storage yards in response to the loss of its natural habitat to intensive agriculture and urban development. Even where it has become a city bird, it keeps away from places where people gather. A colony of Yellow-billed Magpies lives communally year-round, feeding, socializing, and collectively mobbing predators.

DESCRIPTION: 16–18" (41–46 cm). A slightly smaller relative of Black-billed Magpie, its coloration is similar but with a yellow bill and a bare yellow area of skin behind the eye. It has large white wing patches and a long, wedge-shaped, iridescent greenish-black tail. Juveniles may have a grayish-yellow bill.

VOICE: A raucous *qua-qua-qua* and a querulous *quack*.

NESTING: Lays 5–8 blotched, olive green eggs in a large, domed stick nest. It breeds in colonies in tall trees usually so overgrown with mistletoe that it is often hard to detect the nests.

HABITAT: Oak savannas, oak woods, riverside growth, ranches, and suburbs.

RANGE: Resident in California's Central Valley and adjacent foothills.

SIMILAR SPECIES: Black-billed Magpie is closely related but lacks the yellow bill and yellow skin around the eye; the ranges of the two species generally don't overlap except for occasional strays.

CONSERVATION: Its limited range and specialized habitat leave this species more vulnerable to urban and agricultural development and climate stressors. An outbreak of West Nile virus led to sharp population declines in the early 21st century. It has disappeared from many areas that it once inhabited, but its numbers appear to have stabilized.

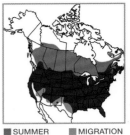

SUMMER MIGRATION
WINTER RARE
RESIDENT

Intelligent, wary, omnivorous, adaptable, and with a high reproductive capacity, the American Crow is undoubtedly much more numerous than it was before the arrival of European settlers. An opportunist in its feeding, the American Crow consumes a great variety of plant and animal food: seeds, fruits, refuse, insects, fish, and mice. American Crows are social and sometimes form large communal roosts in winter with thousands of individuals.

They are aggressive and will often mob and chase away larger birds such as owls and hawks.

DESCRIPTION: 17–21" (43–53 cm). A familiar, stocky, all-black bird with a stout bill and a fan-shaped tail. Its feathers have a slight purplish gloss.

VOICE: Familiar *caw-caw* or *caa-caa*.

NESTING: Lays 4–6 dull green eggs, spotted with dark brown, in a large mass of twigs and sticks lined with feathers, grass, and rootlets, and placed in a tree.

HABITAT: Deciduous growth along rivers and streams; orchards and city parks. It is also found in mixed and coniferous woods, but it avoids closed coniferous forests and desert expanses.

RANGE: Breeds from British Columbia, central interior Canada, and Newfoundland south to southern California, the Gulf Coast, and Florida. Winters north to southern Canada.

SIMILAR SPECIES: See Chihuahuan and Common ravens. American Crows vary considerably in size, but they average smaller than ravens, and their bills are noticeably smaller than those of ravens. Ravens have a wedge-shaped tail.

Also see other crows; Northwestern and Fish crows are smaller and best distinguished by range and voice.

CONSERVATION:

American Crows are abundant and widespread throughout North America, and their numbers continue to increase. American Crows are highly susceptible to West Nile virus, however, suffering a high mortality rate where outbreaks occur; most crows that contract the disease die within one week of infection. Severe crow die-offs can signal the emergence of West Nile virus in an area.

- ■ SUMMER
- ■ WINTER
- ■ RESIDENT
- ■ MIGRATION
- ■ RARE

This is the common crow of the Northwest Coast; on the coast of British Columbia and Alaska, it is the only crow one may expect to see. It usually acts as a scavenger along the shore, often raiding bird nests. In tidal marshes Red-winged Blackbirds attack these crows, just as inland blackbirds harass the American Crow to discourage their habitual plundering of nests. At cormorant or gull colonies, however, crows walk all day among incubating and brooding birds and snatch any eggs or hatchlings left exposed.

DESCRIPTION: 16–17" (41–43 cm). Like other crows, this species is all black with a slight purplish gloss to the feathers. It is slightly smaller and more slender than American Crow, but otherwise identical; it is best distinguished by range.

VOICE: Calls resemble those of the American Crow, but are somewhat more hoarse.

NESTING: Lays 4–6 brown-spotted, greenish eggs in a bowl-shaped stick nest in a tree, bush, or rarely on the ground.

HABITAT: Shorelines, tidewater areas, edges of coastal forest.

RANGE: Resident from coastal southern Alaska to Puget Sound in Washington.

SIMILAR SPECIES: American Crow is slightly larger, has a slower wingbeat and different voice; it overlaps only in parts of lower Washington state and British Columbia, mostly in late fall and winter.

CONSERVATION: These birds are fairly common in their limited range, and their numbers are stable or increasing slightly.

TAMAULIPAS CROW   *Corvus imparatus*

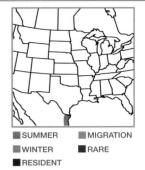

■ SUMMER   ■ MIGRATION
■ WINTER   ■ RARE
■ RESIDENT

This relatively little-known species occurs only in a limited range in northeastern Mexico. It first appeared north of the U.S.-Mexico border in the 1960s scavenging at a landfill around Brownsville, Texas. After the 1960s it became a regular visitor to the area, mainly in winter, and was also known to nest there, but in recent years it has become more scarce. Like most crows, these birds occur in flocks and feed on a great variety of items, including seeds, grains, fruits, meat, carrion, and insects.

DESCRIPTION: 15" (38 cm). A small, glossy crow, these birds are all black, including the bill and feet. It is smaller than other crows or ravens and has a distinctive voice.

VOICE: A soft, low-pitched croaking *gar-lic*, quite different from the familiar *caw-caw* of American Crow.

NESTING: Lays 4 or 5 greenish eggs blotched with brown in a stick nest lined with leaves, grasses, or reeds, and set in a low bush or tree.

HABITAT: Arid open country, but with thickets and brush such as mesquite; also found on ranches and farms, as well as along woodland streams.

RANGE: A rare but regular visitor to extreme southern Texas (Brownsville area) from Mexico.

SIMILAR SPECIES: American Crow is accidental in its range; it has a different voice.

Chihuahuan Raven is larger and has a heavier bill, a more wedge-shaped tail, and a different call.

Compare to an adult male Great-tailed Grackle in molt.

CONSERVATION: LC

Although Tamaulipas Crow's population is stable and it is not considered a species of special concern, the species inhabits a limited range that could make it vulnerable to habitat loss or other events. Its numbers occurring in North America have declined sharply in recent years.

■ SUMMER ■ MIGRATION
■ WINTER ■ RARE
■ RESIDENT

Many coastal heronries have attendant Fish Crows, ever ready to plunder the heron nests for eggs. Omnivorous feeders, like all crows, these birds also consume corn, insects, lizards, wild and cultivated fruits, and often refuse, carrion, and dead fish—hence the name. These birds are usually associated with water and don't often occur inland except near rivers, lakes, or swamps.

DESCRIPTION: 17" (43 cm). This bird is all black, somewhat smaller than American Crow with a smaller bill and feet and with somewhat more pointed wings. Size and proportions can be deceptive in the field, however; the species is best distinguished from American Crow by voice.

VOICE: This species has two calls, both distinct from the American Crow's familiar *caw*: a nasal *kwok* and a nasal, two-noted *ah-ah*. In breeding season, young American Crows have a similar *kwok* call.

NESTING: Lays 4 or 5 greenish eggs with brown blotches in a stick nest lined with pine needles, grass, hair, or bark flakes and placed in an evergreen or deciduous tree.

HABITAT: Low coastal country, near tidewater and pine barrens in the North; in the South, also found near lakes, rivers, and swamps far inland.

RANGE: Resident on the Atlantic Coast from Massachusetts and extreme southern New England south to Florida, and along the Gulf Coast west to Texas; also inland along larger rivers north to Illinois. Some northern birds migrate south in winter.

SIMILAR SPECIES: American Crow is only reliably distinguishable by its less nasal voice.

CONSERVATION: This species' population is healthy and increasing, and its range is spreading northward and farther inland along major river systems, especially up the Mississippi River Valley and on the Atlantic coastal plain.

CHIHUAHUAN RAVEN *Corvus cryptoleucus*

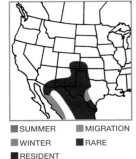

■ SUMMER ■ MIGRATION
■ WINTER   ■ RARE
■ RESIDENT

The Chihuahuan Raven replaces the Common Raven at lower elevations in the dry grasslands of the Southwest, and in the United States portion of its range it is the only raven likely to be seen. More gregarious than its widespread relative, it gathers in noisy and conspicuous roosts, soaring high in the air in group displays. During the breeding season, however, these birds are not social, with pairs nesting in widely spaced territories.

A scarcity of trees may have originally led to this bird's habit of using the same nest year after year. Chihuahuan Ravens feed in groups on grasshoppers or other insects as well as carrion, and often scavenge at landfills.

DESCRIPTION: 19–21" (48–53 cm). This all-black bird is similar to Common Raven, but somewhat smaller—it is closer to the size of American Crow. White bases on the feathers of its neck are seldom seen. It is best distinguished by voice.

VOICE: A harsh *kraak*, higher pitched than Common Raven's.

NESTING: Lays 5–7 dull green eggs spotted and streaked with brown and purple in a loose mass of thorny sticks lined with grass, moss, and bark strips, placed in an exposed tree or on a utility pole.

HABITAT: Arid grasslands and mesquite; plains and deserts.

RANGE: Breeds from southern Arizona, southeastern Colorado, and western Kansas southward into Mexico. It winters in the southern part of its breeding range.

SIMILAR SPECIES: Common Raven is nearly identical; the differences between the two species are subtle and difficult to detect. In general, Common Raven is larger, lacks white feathers in the neck, and has a larger bill and larger tail with a more clearly wedge-shaped outline. Common Raven also has a slightly longer wingspread relative to its body length; it flies with slightly slower wingbeats. These birds are best distinguished by calls: Common Raven's a low, hoarse croak, accompanied by other, higher-pitched calls; Chihuahuan's call is never as low and lacks variation. Chihuahuan prefers flatter, more open, grassy areas; Common Raven is more often found in rockier desert and mountain canyons, as well as more heavily forested habitat.

American Crow is square-tailed, with a thinner bill and different call; rarely overlaps in range and prefers different habitat.

CONSERVATION:

Chihuahuan Raven numbers are stable, although they are less numerous than they once were in the northern part of their range, in the rest of their range they remain quite common. Various interactions with human objects threaten these birds, including poisoning from pesticides and herbicides as well as electrocution related to their habit of nesting on utility poles and collecting wire for nest building.

■ SUMMER   ■ MIGRATION
■ WINTER   ■ RARE
■ RESIDENT

In most of its range, the Common Raven is common only in wilderness areas; despite its large size, adaptability, and note-worthy intelligence, it is sensitive to human persecution and was long ago driven out of settled areas by shooting and poisoning. These birds disappeared almost entirely from the eastern and midwestern United States before the 20th century, but now they are slowly reclaiming parts of their former range in the northeast and the Appalachian Mountains. Ravens are both predators and scavengers, eating almost anything but mostly animal prey and carrion. Around towns in the North they compete with gulls for refuse. They also raid seabird colonies, consuming many eggs and young. They regularly ride on rising air currents and fre-quently engage in aerial displays, with mock fighting, tumbling, and other forms of acrobatics.

DESCRIPTION: 21–27" (53–69 cm). Our largest passerine bird, the size of a hawk. This huge, all-black bird is similar to the American Crow but larger, with a heavier bill and a wedge-shaped tail. At rest, its throat appears shaggy because of long, lance-shaped feathers. It often soars like a hawk on its broad, black wings.

VOICE: Deep, varied, guttural croaking; a hollow *wonk-wonk*.

NESTING: Lays 4–7 dull green eggs spotted with brown in a large mass of sticks containing a cup lined with fur, moss, and lichens, and placed on a cliff or in the top of a conifer.

HABITAT: Coniferous forests and rocky coasts; in the West it is also found in deserts and arid mountains.

RANGE: Resident from the Aleutians, northern Alaska, and northern Canada south throughout the western United States and to Minnesota, the Great Lakes, and northern New England; in the Appalachians to northwestern Georgia. Also in found Eur-asia and North Africa.

SIMILAR SPECIES: See Chihuahuan Raven.

American Crow is much smaller, with a rela-tively smaller bill; a shorter, squared tail; and a different call. Crows fly on rather continuous, relatively faster, rolling wingbeats.

CONSERVATION: LC

Common Ravens are widespread and common, and their population is increasing. They are most numerous in the western and northern parts of their range. This species is slowly reclaiming parts of their range in the northeastern U.S. and in the Appalachian Mountains from which they were driven out by human persecution in the 19th century.

EURASIAN SKYLARK *Alauda arvensis*

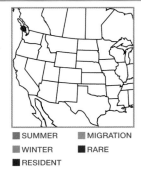

■ SUMMER ■ MIGRATION
■ WINTER ■ RARE
■ RESIDENT

The dense rainforest habitat of much of the Northwest prevents the Eurasian Skylark (often called simply "Sky Lark," especially in Europe) from spreading far from Vancouver Island, where a few pairs were introduced early in the 20th century; it briefly colonized the grassy slopes of the neighboring San Juan Islands, but this population is now extirpated. This bird's most notable feature is its clear, trilling, often canary-like song. Rising in arcs ever higher until almost out of sight, the songster flutters and sings continuously for three or four minutes, then folds its wings and falls like a stone toward the center of its territory.

DESCRIPTION: 7–7½" (18–19 cm). These songbirds are light earth-brown above with heavy, dark streaking on the back; it is buffy white below, with lighter streaking. Its outer tail feathers and belly are white. It has elongated crown feathers that are sometimes raised in a small, rounded crest.

VOICE: Utters a beautiful, trilling song high in the sky that may last for several minutes. Its calls are *trly* or *prrit*. It also mimics other birds.

NESTING: Lays 3 or 4 brown-spotted, whitish eggs in a grass nest in a ground scrape.

HABITAT: Grasslands and fields.

RANGE: Native to Eurasia and northern Africa. Introduced to southern Vancouver Island in British Columbia and San Juan Islands of Washington.

SUBSPECIES: The population introduced to North America belongs to the widespread nominate subspecies (*A. a. arvensis*). A highly migratory Asian subspecies (*A. a. pekinensis*) is a rare visitor to the western Alaskan islands.

SIMILAR SPECIES: American Pipit lacks the elongated crown feathers and crest. It is gray on the back and buff underneath with broken, dark brown streaks.

CONSERVATION: ![LC]
The introduced population of Eurasian Skylarks in North America is gradually declining. It remains as a resident only in southern Vancouver Island in British Columbia and in Hawaii. The native populations across Eurasia—although abundant from Ireland to eastern Russia—is also decreasing, especially in the southern part of its range in North Africa and the Indian subcontinent.

■ SUMMER ■ MIGRATION
■ WINTER ■ RARE
■ RESIDENT

The only true lark native to the New World, Horned Lark is one of our earliest nesting birds, and it may raise as many as three broods each year. This bird is philopatric, or faithful to its birthplace, where it returns after every migration. Consequently, each local population adapts to the color of its habitat; 15 distinct subspecies have been described in the West alone. The Horned Lark moves in an erratic pattern when feeding, and walks or runs instead of hopping. On its breeding territory and when in flocks during winter, it feeds on seeds and ground insects.

DESCRIPTION: 7–8" (18–20 cm). This variable lark is larger than a sparrow. It is brown above with a bold, black stripe below the eye and a white or yellowish stripe above the eye. It has a black crescent on the breast and black "horns" (not always visible) atop the head. The coloration of the face of breeding males in summer ranges from bright yellow in some populations to white in others. It walks rather than hops. In flight, its tail is black with white edges.

VOICE: A soft *ti-ti*. The song delivered in flight is a high-pitched series of tinkling notes.

NESTING: Lays 3–5 brown-spotted, gray eggs in a hollow in the ground lined with fine grass.

HABITAT: Plains, fields, airports, and beaches.

RANGE: Breeds in Alaska and the Canadian Arctic, coastal Canada, and south throughout all of the United States except the Southeast. Winters from southern Canada southward. Also widespread in the Old World in the northern hemisphere.

SUBSPECIES: This species shows tremendous, complex geographical variation, and dozens of subspecies are recognized. The differences mainly involve plumage color and are most evident in breeding males, including the color of the back, the amount and intensity of yellow on the face, and the presence and darkness of streaks on the breast. The differences among population groups is clinal with many intermediates. All subspecies show the distinctive facial pattern.

SIMILAR SPECIES: Similar-looking pipits have brown tails and lack the distinctive face pattern. Longspurs may share habitat with Horned Lark, but they also lack the distinctive facial pattern.

CONSERVATION: 🐦 LC
The Horned Lark population is declining in North America. The reasons for this are not fully known, although loss of open field habitat to human encroachment, reforestation, and development may be a factor. They remain common in North America and also widespread across Europe, Asia, and northern Africa.

■ SUMMER ■ MIGRATION
■ WINTER ■ RARE
■ RESIDENT

Bank Swallows originally nested only in steep, sandy riverbanks, but—like other swallows—they have adapted to humans and now nest in the sides of artificial sites such as gravel and sand piles at construction or industrial sites. They breed in colonies of from two or three pairs to a few thousand. Most lay their eggs at the same time and forage together for flying insects to feed their young. The scientific name *riparia* is from the Latin word for "riverbank."

DESCRIPTION: 4¾–5½" (12–14 cm). Our smallest swallow, this sparrow-sized bird is brown above (darkest on the wings and tail) and dull white below. Its breast is crossed by a distinct brown band that can be hard to see during the bird's agile, darting flight. Its tail is notched.

VOICE: Sharp, unmusical *pret* or *trit-trit*.

NESTING: Lays 4–6 white eggs in a grass and feather nest in a chamber at the end of a deep tunnel, which it digs near the top of a steep bank. Because it breeds in large colonies, nesting banks may sometimes appear riddled with holes.

HABITAT: Banks of rivers, creeks, and lakes; seashores.

RANGE: Breeds from Alaska across northern Canada south to California, Texas, and Virginia. Winters in the tropics. Also widespread in the Old World.

SIMILAR SPECIES: Northern Rough-winged Swallow is warmer brown, with a dusky throat and without a brown breast band. Also see Tree Swallow.

CONSERVATION: 🐦 LC

Although numerous, Bank Swallow is a common bird in a steep decline due to loss of habitat suitable for colony sites. These birds prefer steep banks along marshlands and rivers, which are negatively impacted by measures to control erosion and flooding, as well as by road projects. Construction sites that create large piles of gravel, sand, or dirt can attract a nesting colony of Bank Swallows, which will be destroyed if these piles are moved before the nesting season ends. Flying insects, which are these birds' primary food source, are also in broad decline.

- ■ SUMMER
- ■ WINTER
- ■ RESIDENT
- ■ MIGRATION
- ■ RARE

This bird's habit of feeding on bayberries (as well as other berries) enables it to winter farther north than other swallows that are more heavily reliant on insects. It is the first of our swallows to reappear in the spring. Hole-nesters such as the Tree Swallow often face a housing shortage and must fight to get into, or keep, old woodpecker holes and other sought-after cavity nest sites. Artificial nest boxes may help increase the numbers of these birds. The Tree Swallow almost invariably nests in the immediate vicinity of water. Tree Swallows often enjoy playing with a feather, which they drop and then retrieve as it floats in the air. They gather in enormous flocks along the coast in fall, where they circle in big eddies like leaves caught in a whirlwind.

DESCRIPTION: 5–6¼" (13–16 cm). A handsome, sparrow-sized swallow. It is metallic blue or blue-green above and pure white below. The immature is dull gray-brown above but may be distinguished from Bank and Northern Rough-winged swallows by its pale grayish breast band.

VOICE: A cheerful series of liquid twitters.

NESTING: Lays 4–6 white eggs in a feather-lined cup of grass placed in a hole in a tree or in a nest box.

HABITAT: Lakeshores, flooded meadows, marshes, and streams.

RANGE: Breeds from Alaska east through northern Manitoba to Newfoundland and south to California, Colorado, Nebraska, and Maryland. Winters north to southern California, the Gulf Coast, and the Carolinas; it occasionally lingers farther north.

SIMILAR SPECIES: Violet-green Swallow is smaller, glides less, and flaps its wings more quickly. The white on its face extends above the eye, and it shows conspicuous white patches on the sides of the rump.

Bank and Northern Rough-winged swallows resemble a juvenile Tree Swallow but are smaller; Bank Swallow has a distinct breast band; Rough-winged Swallow is dusky on the throat. Both lack the clean-cut, capped look.

Also see Purple Martin.

CONSERVATION:

Widespread and common across most of North America in spring and fall, the Tree Swallow population remains stable. They prefer wetlands, where the insects on which they feed are abundant. Pesticides and pollutants not only negatively impact their food supply availability, but also accumulate in these birds' systems and lead to poisoning. Forest clearing depletes natural areas in which they prefer to nest. They are also sensitive to climate change, as warmer springs can induce earlier egg laying and early heat waves can endanger young birds in the nest.

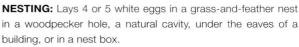

■ SUMMER   ■ MIGRATION
■ WINTER   ■ RARE
■ RESIDENT

This bird of western forests, woodlands, and steep-walled canyons forages at great heights and sails twittering through the trees. Like many other swallows, the Violet-green lives in colonies, basically because of its feeding needs. Where one finds food there is usually enough for all, and when feeding communally these birds can more readily detect and defend themselves from hawks.

DESCRIPTION: 5–5½" (13–14 cm). This swallow has dark, metallic bronze-green upperparts, an iridescent violet rump and tail that is slightly forked, and white underparts. Its white cheeks extending above the eyes and white on the sides of its rump distinguish it from Tree Swallow.

VOICE: A high *dee-chip* given in flight. Also a series of varying *tweet* notes.

NESTING: Lays 4 or 5 white eggs in a grass-and-feather nest in a woodpecker hole, a natural cavity, under the eaves of a building, or in a nest box.

HABITAT: Breeds in forests, wooded foothills, mountains, and suburban areas.

RANGE: Breeds from Alaska east to South Dakota, south to southern California and Texas. Winters mainly south of the U.S.-Mexico border, but a few winter in southern California.

SIMILAR SPECIES: See Tree Swallow, White-throated Swift, and Purple Martin.

CONSERVATION:

Violet-green Swallows are common and their numbers are increasing. Their biggest threat is competition with House Sparrows and European Starlings for nest sites; the species benefits from artificial nest boxes in some areas. Because these swallows feed almost entirely on insects, pesticides and pollutants can impact their food supply.

Stelgidopteryx serripennis NORTHERN ROUGH-WINGED SWALLOW

■ SUMMER ■ MIGRATION
■ WINTER ■ RARE
■ RESIDENT

A light brown, rather solitary bird, the Northern Rough-winged Swallow is widespread and fairly common, partial to stream banks, road cuts, gravel pits, dams, and bridges. Its flight is a helpful aid to identification; it is slower and more fluid than that of the smaller Bank Swallow, and the wing tips appear to be pulled back after each downstroke in a manner oddly evocative of the Solitary Sandpiper's flight. Unlike the Bank Swallow, Rough-wings do not usually dig their own nesting burrows but use ready-made nesting sites along streams. Thus they do not nest in large colonies, although occasionally a few pairs may be found close together. The name "Rough-winged" comes from tiny hooks (not visible in the field) on the outermost wing feathers.

DESCRIPTION: 5–5¾" (13–15 cm). This swallow is pale brown above and white below, with a dingy brown throat. Bank Swallow is similar but smaller, and has a white throat and brown breast band. Northern Rough-winged Swallows are more solitary, usually seen singly or in small groups.

VOICE: A low, unmusical *br-r-ret*, more drawn out than the call of a Bank Swallow and often doubled.

NESTING: Lays 4–8 white eggs in a burrow or cavity; it will use ready-made cavities in bridges, culverts, or other streamside masonry. It is not highly colonial and often nests singly.

HABITAT: Riverbanks. It prefers drier sites than the Bank Swallow.

RANGE: Breeds from southeastern Alaska and southern Canada southward throughout the United States. Winters north to southern California, the Gulf Coast, and southern Florida.

SIMILAR SPECIES: Bank Swallow is smaller and compact, with faster wingbeats and more direct flight. It has a clear brown breast band (difficult to see at a distance) contrasting with a white throat and upper breast, and it is slightly darker brown above. Bank Swallow breeds in colonies.

Young Tree Swallows are easily confused with Rough-wingeds because they often have dull grayish breasts, but usually they also have white throats and darker, grayer backs; they are commonly seen with masses of other Tree Swallows.

Calls of these three species are all subtly different.

CONSERVATION:
The Northern Rough-winged Swallow is widespread and fairly common but its numbers are gradually decreasing. Artificial nest sites have benefited this species. Because they eat insects almost exclusively, pesticides, pollutants, and climate change can adversely impact their food supply.

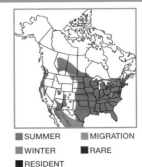

■ SUMMER   ■ MIGRATION
■ WINTER   ■ RARE
■ RESIDENT

Native American tribes began the custom of erecting a martin house to attract these beneficial birds, hanging clusters of hollow gourds in trees near their gardens—a practice which early European settlers also adopted. Martins consumed many insect pests, and the commotion of an alarmed colony could indicate an approaching threat. In wilderness areas, the species nested in tall dead trees riddled with woodpecker holes, but these original colonies never reached the size—as many as 200 pairs—of colonies found in large martin houses today. Most Purple Martins in the East now rely on artificial nesting sites. In the West, it tends not to occupy martin houses, preferring natural cavities (mostly old woodpecker holes) in trees or in giant cacti in the Southwest.

DESCRIPTION: 7–8½" (18–22 cm). Our largest swallow. The adult male is dark steel-blue to glossy purplish-black. Female and immature male are duller above and pale gray below. Overhead it appears similar in shape to European Starling, but its flight is more buoyant and gliding.

VOICE: A liquid, gurgling warble. Also a penetrating *tee-tee-tee*.

NESTING: Lays 4 or 5 white eggs in a mass of grass and other plant material placed in a cavity—sometimes a hole in a tree or a martin house with many separate compartments, where the birds nest in a colony. Birds in the East are more likely to use artificial nest boxes than those in the West.

HABITAT: Open woodlands, residential areas, and agricultural land.

RANGE: Breeds from British Columbia, central interior Canada, and Nova Scotia southward, but absent from the interior western mountains and Great Basin. It winters in the tropics.

SUBSPECIES: The nominate Eastern form (subsp. *subis*) is found in the eastern and midwestern North America; these birds are mostly reliant on artificial nest boxes. Females and imma-

tures of Western birds (subsp. *arboricola*) average paler; this population is less attracted to artificial housing and prefers natural tree cavities. A Southwestern population (subsp. *hesperia*) is similar to Western birds but nests in cavities in saguaro cactus. Males of all three populations look similar.

SIMILAR SPECIES: Nearly unmistakable.

European Starling has more obviously triangular wings; a square tail, not forked; and a longer bill.

Tree Swallow has a bluish back; Violet-green Swallow has a glossy green back. Both are smaller, with clean white underparts.

CONSERVATION: LC

The Purple Martin population is currently stable, although it has declined seriously in parts of the West. The prime threat is invasions of nest sites by introduced House Sparrows and European Starlings, which kill Purple Martin nestlings and destroy eggs in their attempts to overtake a nest cavity. Logging in the West has also diminished their habitats there. Martins are also susceptible to cold temperatures; unseasonable cold snaps can kill martins directly and can reduce their insect food supply.

■ SUMMER ■ MIGRATION
■ WINTER ■ RARE
■ RESIDENT

Common, gregarious, and extremely vocal, the familiar Barn Swallow occurs almost worldwide. The great majority of these birds now nest on or in buildings, building their mud nests on any structure offering overhead protection, but originally they used caves and rocky ledges over streams. Barn Swallows perform long migrations; some that breed in North America winter as far south as Argentina. Like other swallows, they migrate by day, often feeding as they travel. They are swift and graceful fliers, covering many miles each day in search of food for their young.

DESCRIPTION: 5¾–7¾" (15–20 cm). A familiar, sparrow-sized swallow with a deeply forked tail. Its upperparts are dark steel-blue, its underparts are usually cinnamon or buffy, and its throat and forehead are rusty reddish-brown. Juveniles have pale underparts.

VOICE: Constant liquid twittering and chattering.

NESTING: Lays 4–6 brown-spotted white eggs in a solid cup of mud reinforced with grass, lined with feathers and soft plant material, and placed on a rafter in an open building, or on a sheltered ledge, bridge, dock, or other structure.

HABITAT: Agricultural land, suburban areas, marshes, and lakeshores.

RANGE: Breeds from Alaska east across Canada to Newfoundland and south through all of the United States, although less common in southern Texas, the Gulf Coast, and peninsular Florida. Winters in the tropics. Also widespread in the Old World.

SUBSPECIES: North American Barn Swallows (described above) belong to the subspecies *erythrogaster*. Two Eurasian subspecies have been recorded regularly in western and northern Alaska and more rarely farther south along the Pacific Coast to Washington: The nominate Eurasian subspecies *rustica* has a white belly with a solid dark breast band, and the east Asian subspecies *gutteralis* has a white belly with an incomplete breast band.

SIMILAR SPECIES: Under good viewing conditions, Barn Swallow is nearly unmistakable thanks to its bold colors and long, deeply forked tail.

Cliff Swallow has a similar color pattern, but has a pale rump, a pale buff mark above the bill, and a square tail; its call notes are different and sound scratchy.

Cave Swallow has a pale rusty throat and a short, square tail.

CONSERVATION: Barn Swallows are widespread and abundant but decreasing slightly. They have greatly expanded their range and numbers following the path of human development, and benefit from artificial nesting sites in rural and urban areas. Introduced House Sparrows compete with Barn Swallows for nest sites, however, and more modern farms include fewer nest sites and insect food resources for these birds.

CLIFF SWALLOW *Petrochelidon pyrrhonota*

■ SUMMER ■ MIGRATION
■ WINTER ■ RARE
■ RESIDENT

The Cliff Swallow is a chunky bird with a square-tipped tail that forages over water or open country, usually in flocks. It soars and circles on flattened wings, interspersing more and longer bursts of gliding into its normal foraging flight than do most swallows. As its name implies, this swallow originally nested on cliffs. Cliff Swallows nest colonially, building juglike mud nests against vertical or overhanging surfaces. At one time, this habit restricted these birds to the vicinity of cliffs and cliff banks; but today, nesting on buildings and under bridges, they are locally fairly common in the East and especially common in the West. In California these swallows often return in early spring to ancestral colonial breeding sites, including their much publicized annual return to Mission San Juan Capistrano.

DESCRIPTION: 5–6" (13–15 cm). A stocky, sparrow-sized, square-tailed swallow with dull steel-blue upperparts, buff-white underparts, a dark chestnut throat, and a pale buff rump. In most adult Cliff Swallows, the forehead is white or pale buff. (Southwestern birds have dark chestnut foreheads.) Juveniles resemble adults, but may have a darker or duller forehead and, often, white feathers mixed into the chestnut throat.

VOICE: Constant squeaky chattering and twittering. Its calls include a low *chrrr* and a nasal *nyew*. Its song, often given in flight, is a harsh series of squeaking and grating notes.

NESTING: Lays 4–6 white eggs in a gourd-shaped structure of mud lined with feathers and placed on a sheltered cliff face or under eaves. Nests in colonies.

HABITAT: Open country near buildings or cliffs; lakeshores and marshes on migration.

RANGE: Breeds from Alaska, Ontario, and Nova Scotia southward through most of the United States except the Southeast. Winters in the tropics.

SUBSPECIES: A Southwestern/Mexican subpopulation (subsp. *melanogaster*) has a dark cinnamon-colored forehead more like a Cave Swallow.

SIMILAR SPECIES: Cave Swallows in Texas and the Southwest are similar but smaller, with a darker rump and a pale buff throat. A juvenile Cliff Swallow might be confused with a Cave Swallow, but Cave Swallow always has the appearance of a sharply defined black cap above a pale throat; it has a medium rufous-buff rump, a shade darker than that of a Cliff Swallow.

Also see Barn Swallow.

CONSERVATION: LC

Widespread across North America, Cliff Swallows are increasing and continuing to spread in the East. The introduction of House Sparrows to North America was a disaster for these birds because the sparrows usurp their nests and often cause the swallows to abandon a colony. Competition with House Sparrows caused serious regional declines in the 20th century. Long, cold, rainy spells while the young are in the nest also cause widespread mortality since the adults are unable to obtain enough insects.

■ SUMMER ■ MIGRATION
■ WINTER ■ RARE
■ RESIDENT

Once rare and local north of the Mexican border, these birds have adapted to using artificial nest sites and have since become fairly common breeders in Texas and southern New Mexico. Most natural nest sites are in inaccessible places, plastered to walls far inside remote caves and crevices; recently colonies of these birds have begun using bridges and culverts as sites on which to build their mud nests. Like all swallows, Cave Swallows catch their insect prey on the wing. Bird watchers have increasingly noted late fall incursions northward along the Atlantic seacoast as far north as Nova Scotia and inland along Lake Champlain.

DESCRIPTION: 5½" (14 cm). A stocky swallow with a square tail, steel-blue upperparts, a buff throat and rump, and a chestnut forehead. It is similar to Cliff Swallow in shape and color pattern, but its forehead is rufous-chestnut and its throat is pale buff, often forming a collar around the nape. Juveniles are duller, sometimes with small dark spots on the nape.

VOICE: Series of squeaks, twitters, and warbles.

NESTING: Lays 4 brown-spotted, pinkish eggs in a mud nest lined with grass, roots, and feathers, attached to a cliff wall, cave, or to a bridge or old building.

HABITAT: Chiefly open country near caves and cliffs.

RANGE: Breeds in southern Texas, southeastern New Mexico, and rarely in southern Arizona. Wanderers in fall casually appear far from their breeding range on both coasts and in the interior of the continent. Winters in the tropics.

SUBSPECIES: A Caribbean population (subsp. *fulva*) is a local breeder in southern Florida. These birds are smaller and average darker than the main Mexican population (subsp. *pelodoma*) that extends into southwestern U.S.

SIMILAR SPECIES: The more widespread Cliff Swallow is similar but has a dark chestnut throat. In most of North America, Cliff Swallow has a white forehead, but the Southwestern population has a chestnut forehead similar to Cave Swallow.

CONSERVATION: 🐦 LC

Cave Swallows are increasing as they expand their range in the rocky areas of the southwestern U.S., Mexico, and the Caribbean. These birds benefit from increased irrigated agriculture in these areas, which provides a reliable food source.

■ SUMMER ■ MIGRATION
■ WINTER ■ RARE
■ RESIDENT

Carolina Chickadee is a common, familiar visitor to backyard feeders and a regular member of the mixed flocks of small birds that roam the winter woods. So similar are the Carolina and Black-capped Chickadees that they were believed to be the same species for more than a century. The two species have much the same needs, and thus compete and generally don't coexist in a given range; instead, they replace each other geographically. Where the two species do come into contact, they often hybridize with one another and learn each other's songs.

DESCRIPTION: 4–5" (10–13 cm). A small songbird with a black cap and bib; its bib has a sharply defined lower edge. It has gray upperparts and a short gray tail. It has large white areas on the cheeks and is white below with pale buff sides and flanks. Gray feather edgings on the middle of its folded wing are less well defined than in the closely related Black-capped Chickadee.

VOICE: A buzzy *chickadee-dee-dee-dee*, higher pitched and faster than that of the Black-capped Chickadee; song has four whistled notes, *see-dee, see-dee*, with a downward inflection, rather than the two- or three-noted song of the Black-capped.

NESTING: Lays 6–8 white eggs lightly speckled with brown, placed in a cavity in a rotten stub or birdhouse lined with feathers, grass, and plant down.

HABITAT: Deciduous woodlands and residential areas.

RANGE: Resident from southeastern Kansas and central New Jersey south to Texas, the Gulf Coast, and central Florida.

SUBSPECIES: This species shows clinal geographical variation, with northeastern populations being brightest and more westerly populations becoming paler.

SIMILAR SPECIES: Similar to the more northern Black-capped Chickadee, but the feathers of its folded wing usually show less white edging; the lower edge of its black bib is more sharply defined than that of Black-capped. It is best identified by voice and range.

CONSERVATION: LC
Carolina Chickadee is common and its population is stable.

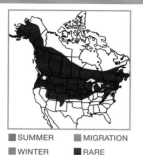

■ SUMMER ■ MIGRATION
■ WINTER ■ RARE
■ RESIDENT

These birds are constantly active—hopping, often feeding upside down, clinging to the underside of twigs and branches in their search for insect eggs and larvae. Flocks of this familiar and inquisitive bird spend the winter making the rounds of feeders in a neighborhood, often appearing at each feeder with striking regularity. Chickadees form the nucleus of mixed flocks of woodpeckers, nuthatches, creepers, and kinglets that move through the winter woods. In spring, chickadees disband into the woods to nest. Black-capped Chickadees usually prepare their own nesting hole in soft, rotting tree stumps. They may also use nest boxes that are filled with sawdust or wood shavings, which the birds will "excavate" by carrying away bit by bit.

DESCRIPTION: 4¾–5¾" (12–15 cm). These small songbirds have a black cap and throat, white cheeks, a gray back, and dull white underparts. Their wing feathers are narrowly and indistinctly edged with white. This species is difficult to separate from Carolina Chickadee. Black-capped has bolder white edges on the secondaries and a mostly white nape.

VOICE: A buzzy *chick-a-dee-dee-dee* or a clear, whistled *fee-bee*, with the second note lower and often doubled. In the overlap zone with Carolina Chickadee, voice may not be helpful for identification because each species can learn the other's song.

NESTING: Lays 6–8 brown-speckled, white eggs in a cup of grass, fur, plant down, feathers, and moss, placed in a hole in a rotten tree stub excavated by the birds, or in a natural cavity or artificial nest box.

HABITAT: Deciduous and mixed forests and open woodlands; suburban areas in winter.

RANGE: Largely resident from Alaska east across Canada to Newfoundland, south to northern California, northern New Mexico, Missouri, and northern New Jersey. Winters south to Maryland and Texas.

SUBSPECIES: Nine subspecies are recognized, each showing clinal geographical variation. Eastern birds (subsp. *atricapillus*) are brightest and Pacific Northwest birds (subsp. *occidentalis*) are darker; Rocky Mountain birds (subsp. *garrinus*) are larger and paler, and Great Basin birds (subsp. *nevadensis*) are the palest.

SIMILAR SPECIES: See Carolina and Mountain chickadees.

CONSERVATION: Black-capped Chickadees are widespread, common, and increasing. These birds benefit from the increase in edge habitat associated with forest clearing, and especially flourish if some dead trees are left standing. Bird feeders and nest boxes provided by humans may also marginally help these birds, offering supplemental food resources and nesting sites.

SUMMER   MIGRATION
WINTER   RARE
RESIDENT

A constantly moving insect-gleaner of the mountain forest, the Mountain Chickadee frequently descends into the lowlands in winter. In November an occasional flock can be found near sea level in desert oases containing planted conifers, while other flocks forage at 8500 feet (2600 meters) in the subalpine forests of nearby mountains.

DESCRIPTION: 5–5¾" (13–15 cm). This active bird is similar to Black-capped Chickadee, but with pale gray flanks and a bold white eyebrow that contrasts with its black cap. Like many familiar chickadees, it has a black throat and white underparts. Its back, sides, and flanks are generally gray but show geographical variation.

VOICE: A hoarse *chick-a-zee-zee, zee*. Its spring song is similar to that of the Black-capped Chickadee, but three-noted: *fee-bee-bee*, the *bee* notes at a lower pitch.

NESTING: Lays 7–9 white, sometimes spotted eggs in a hair- or fur-lined natural cavity or woodpecker hole; like other chickadees, it sometimes excavates a hole in soft, rotten wood.

HABITAT: High-altitude coniferous forests.

RANGE: Resident from interior British Columbia south through Rocky Mountain and Cascade-Sierra chains to southern California and western Texas.

SUBSPECIES: This species shows clinal variation and the various populations integrade, making the lines between subspecies blurry and not fully resolved. Birds of the Great Basin (subsp. *inyoensis*) are pale with more buff; birds from farther west (subsp. *baileyae*) are grayer; and birds of the Rockies (subsp. *gambeli*) have a browner back, and cinnamon sides and flanks.

SIMILAR SPECIES: Black-capped Chickadee does not usually overlap; its gray back is paler than its sides.

CONSERVATION: LC
Mountain Chickadees are common in their range, and their numbers have remained stable overall during the past several decades. Although they have declined in some areas, bird feeders and nest boxes have helped to bolster their numbers.

■ SUMMER   ■ MIGRATION
■ WINTER   ■ RARE
■ RESIDENT

This is the only chickadee found within a limited area of Arizona and New Mexico. In the Chiricahua Mountains in Arizona, this species can be found in almost any habitat with conifers, even where these trees are sparse, such as in pine-oak areas. In the summer, it is generally found in higher coniferous forests. This bird feeds along the outer tree canopy, often hanging upside down to pluck small insects from conifer needles. Like other chickadees, it has an ingenious arrangement of leg tendons that enables it to pull close to a branch while upside down. Vireos, warblers, and kinglets must hover above branches, and are unable to reach the undersides, so the chickadees can exploit this feeding opportunity without competition.

DESCRIPTION: 5" (13 cm). A predominantly gray chickadee with a black cap, a black bib extending onto the upper breast, and gray flanks. Its cheeks and mid-breast are white.

VOICE: A husky *chick-a-dee-dee-dee*, huskier and lazier than that of the Mountain Chickadee.

NESTING: Lays 5–8 whitish eggs, frequently with reddish-brown spotting, in a fiber nest lined with grass, feathers, or fur placed in an excavated hole in a dead branch.

HABITAT: Coniferous or pine-oak forests at high altitudes.

RANGE: Resident in extreme southeastern Arizona and southwestern New Mexico. Also found in Mexico.

SIMILAR SPECIES: Resembles Black-capped and Carolina chickadees, but its range does not overlap.

CONSERVATION: Mexican Chickadee numbers are believed to be stable in their limited U.S. range, but are decreasing in Mexico due to the loss of mountain fir forests and shrubland habitat.

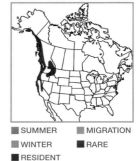

■ SUMMER ■ MIGRATION
■ WINTER ■ RARE
■ RESIDENT

This small, dark chickadee species prefers coniferous forests near the Pacific Coast, but it is also found in coastal riparian or eucalyptus groves of California. In the coastal forests of the Northwest, where the Chestnut-backed and Black-capped chickadees overlap, the former prefers the top half of conifers, while the latter feeds in the lower half of trees, frequently oaks. Thus they do not compete for space or food even within the same area.

DESCRIPTION: 4½–5" (11–13 cm). A small, sooty brown-capped, and black-bibbed chickadee with reddish-brown or chestnut flanks and back. It is white below with a black throat, and its wings and tail are dark gray.

VOICE: A squeaky *chick-a-dee*, somewhat shriller and faster than that of other chickadees. It often simply utters a thin *tsee-deee* and thin lisping notes.

NESTING: Lays 5–8 creamy-white, lightly spotted eggs in a natural cavity or woodpecker hole; much like the Black-capped Chickadee, it often excavates rotten stumps and then builds a nest of moss and hair.

HABITAT: Pacific rain forest; moist areas containing conifers.

RANGE: Resident from coastal Alaska south to central California; also in western ranges of the Rocky Mountains in southern British Columbia, southern Alberta, and western Montana.

SUBSPECIES: A subspecies that lives in central coastal California (subsp. *barlowi*), from Marin County southward, has pale gray flanks and shows almost no chestnut below.

SIMILAR SPECIES: Boreal Chickadee has duller white cheeks, and a duller back and flanks.

CONSERVATION:

Although still common in its range, Chestnut-backed Chickadee numbers have declined in recent decades due to loss of habitat. Their numbers may be starting to recover, but these birds remain vulnerable to forest management practices that eliminate dead limbs and trees where these cavity-nesters breed.

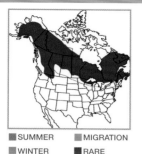

■ SUMMER   ■ MIGRATION
■ WINTER   ■ RARE
■ RESIDENT

Boreal Chickadees are primarily found in remote sections of northern Canada into Alaska where they live in conifer forests. They occasionally wander southward in winter. Unlike the Black-capped Chickadee, this species spends most of its time in the cover of dense spruces, coming less readily to the tips of branches, and so it is much less easily observed. During late summer and early fall, when there is an abundance of caterpillars and seeds, Boreal Chickadees store food for winter among needles or under the bark of branches at a height that will be above the winter snow cover.

DESCRIPTION: 5–5½" (13–14 cm). Similar to Black-capped Chickadee, but its crown and back are brown, and its flanks are pinkish-brown.

VOICE: A husky *chick-a-dee-dee*, lazier and more nasal than call of Black-capped.

NESTING: Lays 5–7 white eggs lightly speckled with red-brown in a cup of plant down, feathers, and moss in a natural cavity, often only a few feet (about a meter) from the ground.

HABITAT: Coniferous forests.

RANGE: Breeds from northern Alaska east to Labrador and Newfoundland, south to the northern edge of the United States. it occasionally wanders southward in winter.

SIMILAR SPECIES: See Gray-headed Chickadee and Chestnut-backed Chickadee.

CONSERVATION: Although widespread and still thought to be numerous, Boreal Chickadees may have declined in recent decades. Their vast, mostly remote habitat and secretive nature make the population difficult to survey accurately.

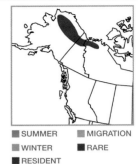

■ SUMMER　■ MIGRATION
■ WINTER　■ RARE
■ RESIDENT

Gray-headed Chickadee is the only member of its family that occurs in both the Old and New Worlds. Although the rarest of North America's chickadees, many aspects of its biology are better known than other widespread species because of extensive studies in Scandinavia and in Russia, where it is called Siberian Tit. Gray-headed Chickadee closely resembles Boreal Chickadee in morphology, behavior, ecology, and vocalizations.

DESCRIPTION: 4½–5" (11–13 cm). This far-northern chickadee has a grayish-brown cap, white cheeks, and a black bib; its upperparts are grayish-brown, showing little contrast with the nape and crown; its breast and belly are whitish, and its flanks are pale buff. Gray-headed Chickadee appears more robust, long tailed, and fluffy than other American chickadees. In northern Europe, the species has a browner crown, more contrast between the nape and back, and brighter buff on the flanks.

VOICE: A rapid set of hoarse *cheeow* calls. Its calls include an insistent, nasal *cheer* or *deer*, more forceful than Boreal Chickadee, and a quick, hoarse *schik-a-day*.

NESTING: Clutch size is variable, typically 6–10 white eggs marked with speckles or spots, most densely marked at the large end. It uses natural cavities and woodpecker holes, and also nest boxes. Its nest is formed of moss and rabbit fur.

HABITAT: Open coniferous and hardwood forest; in Alaska, it is often found in tracts of willow or low spruce located in river valleys or along mountain bases. In the Old World, populations are decreasing due to logging pressures.

RANGE: Subarctic, nearly circumpolar. Rare and local in Alaska and western Arctic Canada.

SIMILAR SPECIES: Boreal Chickadee has less extensive white on the cheeks and darker flanks; the calls of the two species are different.

CONSERVATION: Globally the species is numerous and widespread, although decreases in numbers of Gray-headed Chickadees and range contraction have been recorded in recent years. The species is also believed to be declining in northern Europe. Forest management practices and climate change are suspected to be behind the population changes.

■ SUMMER ■ MIGRATION
■ WINTER ■ RARE
■ RESIDENT

This small, distinctively marked titmouse is common in riparian and oak woodlands of central Arizona. The range of the Bridled Titmouse overlaps that of the Mountain Chickadee, but the unique face pattern and crest distinguish this species. It accepts nesting holes made or used by other species and may settle in artificial nest boxes.

DESCRIPTION: 4½–5" (11–13 cm). Warbler-sized. It is gray above and whitish below with a gray crest bordered with black. A "bridled" pattern on its face joins its eye line and throat patch.

VOICE: Vocalizations are similar to calls of other chickadees and titmice, but more rapid and on a somewhat higher pitch. The song is a two-syllable phrase, repeated several times. One of its common calls is a variant of the familiar *chick-a-dee*.

NESTING: Lays 5–7 white eggs in a tree hole or similar cavity.

HABITAT: Deciduous and mixed woods in the mountains.

RANGE: Resident from central Arizona and southwestern New Mexico southward. About 90% of the global population lives in Mexico.

SIMILAR SPECIES: Juniper Titmouse is larger and lacks the black face pattern. Mountain Chickadee lacks a crest.

CONSERVATION: Bridled Titmouse is quite common and its numbers are stable in its limited range in North America.

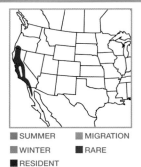

■ SUMMER ■ MIGRATION
■ WINTER ■ RARE
■ RESIDENT

Whereas chickadees gather in winter flocks, the related Oak Titmouse is usually found singly or in pairs. This bird is conspicuous, for it calls often as it feeds among bushes or high in the spring growth of freshly sprouted oaks. It also frequents gardens in suburbs of towns adjacent to its native habitat. Oak Titmouse was formerly lumped with Juniper Titmouse as a single species, called Plain Titmouse.

DESCRIPTION: 5–5½" (13–14 cm). Sparrow-sized. It is plain gray with paler underparts. It has a small crest, usually held erect.

VOICE: A harsh, fussy *see-dee-dee* or *chick-a-dee-dee*.

NESTING: Lays 5–8 white eggs with brown spotting in tree cavities, fence-post holes, or crevices of old buildings. The cavity nest is composed of grasses, fur, and some feathers.

HABITAT: Live oaks and deciduous growth of all kinds: oak woodlands, streamside cottonwoods, forest edges, and oak-juniper woodlands.

RANGE: Resident from southern Oregon south to Baja California.

SIMILAR SPECIES: See Juniper Titmouse, and Hutton's and Gray vireos.

CONSERVATION:

The Oak Titmouse is common in its limited range and its population is believed to be stable. Human population growth in California, especially along the coast, has reduced the state's old-growth oak woodlands and left most of this species' remaining habitat under private land ownership.

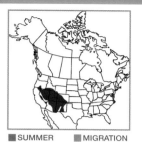

■ SUMMER   ■ MIGRATION
■ WINTER   ■ RARE
■ RESIDENT

This uncommon titmouse inhabits western pinyon-juniper forests. This acrobatic feeder eats nuts, seeds, and insects, calling often as it plucks food from trees and bushes. It was formerly lumped with Oak Titmouse as a single species called Plain Titmouse, but these species use different habitats and have different calls.

DESCRIPTION: 5¾" (15 cm). It is plain gray above, paler gray below, and has a prominent gray crest. Its tail is relatively long. Juniper Titmouse is larger, paler, and grayer than the closely related Oak Titmouse.

VOICE: A harsh *see-dee-dee*. It also gives a rapid, clipped trill that's faster than an Oak Titmouse call.

NESTING: Lays 5–8 white eggs, with brown spotting, in tree cavities, fence-post holes, or crevices. The cavity nest is composed of grasses, fur, and some feathers.

HABITAT: Pinyon-juniper woods.

RANGE: Resident from southeastern Oregon and central Colorado south to southeastern California, Arizona, and extreme western Texas.

SIMILAR SPECIES: See Oak Titmouse and Bridled Titmouse.

CONSERVATION: Uncommon to locally common in the Great Basin and Grand Canyon region of the U.S., the Juniper Titmouse population is stable. The greatest threat to the species is the loss of juniper woodlands.

SUMMER • MIGRATION
WINTER • RARE
RESIDENT

Titmice are active, social birds and, especially in winter, join with small mixed flocks of chickadees, nuthatches, kinglets, creepers, and the smaller woodpeckers. Although a frequent visitor at feeders, the titmouse is not as bold as a chickadee. It often clings to the bark of trees and turns upside down to pick spiders and insects from the underside of a twig or leaf. The closely related Black-crested Titmouse, found from southwestern Oklahoma and northern Texas south into Mexico, was once considered a subspecies of Tufted Titmouse.

DESCRIPTION: 6" (15 cm). Sparrow-sized. This familiar titmouse is gray above and whitish below, with rust-colored sides. It has a conspicuous gray crest and a small black area on the forehead just above the base of the bill.

VOICE: A whistled series of four to eight notes sounding like *Peter-Peter*, repeated persistently.

NESTING: Lays 5 or 6 brown-dotted white eggs in a tree cavity or bird box stuffed with leaves and moss.

HABITAT: Swampy or moist woodlands, and shade trees in villages and city parks; in winter, at feeders.

RANGE: Resident from eastern Nebraska, southern Michigan, and Maine south to Texas, the Gulf Coast, and central Florida.

SIMILAR SPECIES: The Black-crested Titmouse found in southwestern Oklahoma and Texas is similar but has a black crest and a pale forehead. Black-crested and Tufted titmice frequently hybridize where their ranges meet in central Texas; hybrids often have a dark gray crest and chestnut brown forehead.

CONSERVATION: LC

Tufted Titmouse numbers are increasing as the species expands its range northward across the eastern half of the continent. These birds are finding habitats in parks with older trees, farmlands that have been reverted to forests, as well as suburban areas in which backyard feeders are a food source.

■ SUMMER   ■ MIGRATION
■ WINTER   ■ RARE
■ RESIDENT

Black-crested Titmouse is closely related to the Tufted Titmouse, and formerly considered conspecific with it due to frequent hybridization in central Texas and southwestern Oklahoma. Although once again split into two full species, Black-crested is similar to Tufted Titmouse in most aspects of its ecology, demography, and behavior. The range of Black-crested Titmouse may have expanded into parts of southwest Oklahoma and northern Texas as a result of European settlement and the associated invasion of the region by mesquite.

DESCRIPTION: 6" (15 cm). A medium-sized crested tit. Its upperparts are gray, and its underparts are pale grayish with tawny flanks. Its prominent crest is black in adult males and dark gray in females and immatures, with a contrasting pale grayish forehead.

VOICE: Its song is similar to that of a Tufted Titmouse: *peter-peter-peter*. A one-noted song is more common in Black-crested than in Tufted Titmouse.

NESTING: Lays 4–7 white or pinkish-white eggs with small, evenly-dispersed reddish-brown speckles. Nests are typically placed 3–23' (1–7 m) high in abandoned woodpecker holes in living trees, stumps, and posts.

HABITAT: Broadleaf forests and woodlands, particularly oak and mesquite. It is also found in orchards, parks, and suburban areas as well as temperate brushlands and montane forests. Its preferred habitats contain tall vegetation, numerous tree species, and dense canopy; in Texas, high densities occur in riparian and open forest in the Rio Grande Valley and in pinyon-juniper-oak and cypress-pine-oak woodlands in the Chisos Mountains.

RANGE: Oklahoma and Texas south through northeastern Mexico.

SIMILAR SPECIES: See Tufted Titmouse.

CONSERVATION: LC
Black-crested Titmouse is common in its limited North American range, and its population appears stable.

■ SUMMER ■ MIGRATION
■ WINTER ■ RARE
■ RESIDENT

These tiny desert birds are thought to obtain moisture from insects, seeds, and berries—they are rarely seen drinking. A Verdin's nest is a globular mass of thorny twigs lined with feathers or soft grass. The thorny protection around most nests discourages predators, and the insulation protects the eggs and young from the intense heat. The species' small clutch size may be an adaptation to assure sufficient food in an area of climatic extremes.

DESCRIPTION: 4–4½" (10–11 cm). Verdin is smaller than a chickadee, a little larger than a Bushtit. It is gray with a yellow head and throat, a chestnut patch at the bend of the wing, and white underparts. Juveniles lack both the yellow and chestnut coloration of adults and are best distinguished from Bushtit by their shorter tail.

VOICE: A sharp *seep!* or *tsilip!*, frequently repeated. Its infrequent song is a three-note *kleep-er-zee!* with the final note highest in pitch.

NESTING: Lays 3–5 spotted greenish eggs in a hanging nest with an entrance hole in the side, built among the prickliest branches of a cholla cactus or in a crotch of a mesquite tree.

HABITAT: Low desert containing brush and taller shrubs.

RANGE: Resident from California, Utah, and south-central Texas southward to northern Mexico.

SIMILAR SPECIES: Bushtit lives in higher-elevation oak woodlands, scrub oak, pinyon-juniper, and chaparral; it is only rarely found in Verdin habitat. Bushtit is longer-tailed than immature Verdins, with a tiny chickadee-like bill. Its call notes are much different.

See Northern Beardless-Tyrannulet.

CONSERVATION: LC

A common bird in a variety of woodlands, Verdin numbers appear to be decreasing despite becoming adapted to urban areas. Loss of habitat related to housing development seems to be a primary contributor to a steady decline in the Verdin population during the past several decades.

■ SUMMER **■** MIGRATION
■ WINTER **■** RARE
■ RESIDENT

Bushtits flock in small bands, flitting nervously through trees and bushes, hanging, prying, picking, and gleaning, and keeping contact through a constant banter of soft chirps. They pervade a small area, then vanish, and reappear a couple of hundred yards away.

DESCRIPTION: 3¾–4" (10 cm). Bushtit is gray above with light underparts. It has a small bill and a relatively long tail. The subspecies (described below) show considerable geographic variation: they have a brown or gray crown, and a color patch on the cheek ("ears") ranging from pale to brown to black. Black-eared variants are most common in juveniles (more common in adults in Mexico). Interior birds are paler and grayer overall than Pacific Coast birds.

VOICE: Contact calls are light *tsip* and *pit* notes, constantly uttered. Its alarm call is a high trill.

NESTING: Lays 5–15 white eggs in a hanging gourd-shaped nest with a side entrance near the top. Made of soft plant wool and lichens, the nest is suspended in a bush or tree.

HABITAT: Varied. Often found in deciduous growth, usually streamside. In the coastal forest, it lives in second-growth alder thickets or in edges of coniferous forests composed of maple, dogwood, and birch; it is also found in oak woodland, chaparral, and juniper brush.

RANGE: Resident from extreme southwestern British Columbia, southern Idaho, southwestern Wyoming, and the Oklahoma panhandle southward.

SUBSPECIES: Pacific Coast birds (subsp. *minimus*) have a brown crown and pale ear patch; Interior/Rocky Mountain birds (subsp. *plumbeus*) have a gray crown and brown ear patch. Some adult males in the mountains near the Mexican border have a black ear patch; these "Black-eared Bushtits" were once considered a separate species.

SIMILAR SPECIES: Flocks of Bushtits may be accompanied by other small species: Ruby-crowned Kinglet has wing bars and eye rings; Blue-gray and Black-tailed gnatcatchers have longer, dark tails and eye rings; *Oreothlypis* warblers have larger, longer bills.

Juvenile Verdin has a much shorter tail; the adult has yellow on the head and a shorter tail. It is rarely found in the same habitat with Bushtit.

CONSERVATION: Bushtits are widespread and common, and their numbers are stable. They seem to adapt well to suburban settings where woodland habitat is degraded.

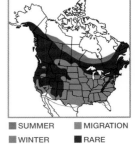

■ SUMMER   ■ MIGRATION
■ WINTER   ■ RARE
■ RESIDENT

Nuthatches are small, short-tailed, tree-creeping birds that often proceed head-downward as they seek food in the crevices of twigs, branches, and tree trunks. This species is primarily a denizen of coniferous forests, where it often gives calls that sound like a toy horn as it forages high overhead. Nuthatches hoard excess food and will transport seeds from a tree heavily laden with mature cones to their distant larders. In years of bad harvest, they migrate in large numbers to more southerly forests. They also feed on bark insects, maneuvering with agility around the tips of small, outer branches or in treetops.

DESCRIPTION: 4½–4¾" (11–12 cm). Smaller than a sparrow. The male has blue-gray upperparts, pale rust-colored underparts, a black crown and line through the eye, and white eyebrows. The female is similar, but the crown is gray.

VOICE: A tinny *yank-yank*, higher pitched and more nasal than the call of the White-breasted Nuthatch.

NESTING: Lays 5 or 6 white eggs spotted with red-brown in a cup of twigs and grass lined with softer material and placed in a tree cavity. The entrance is usually smeared with pitch, presumably to discourage predators; the pitch often gets on the birds' feathers giving them a messy appearance.

HABITAT: Coniferous forests; more widespread during migration and in winter.

RANGE: Breeds across Canada from southeastern Alaska, Manitoba, and Newfoundland south to southern California, Arizona, the Great Lakes region, and northern New England, and south in the Appalachians to North Carolina. Its winter range varies considerably from year to year, especially in the East; it winters in the breeding range and irregularly south to the Gulf Coast and northern Florida.

SIMILAR SPECIES: Other nuthatches have white underparts and lack the white eyebrow stripe.

CONSERVATION: LC

Red-breasted Nuthatches are common and they have extended their range farther east and south where ornamental conifers have been planted. Their numbers and winter range vary considerably from year to year, but overall they are increasing.

SUMMER ■ MIGRATION
WINTER ■ RARE
RESIDENT

The habit of creeping headfirst down a tree trunk is characteristic of nuthatches. The White-breasted is an inquisitive, acrobatic bird, pausing occasionally to hang and hammer at a crack. Essentially nonmigratory, during the fall it stores food for winter in crevices behind loose tree bark. Pairs seem to remain together year-round; the species may be found in twos even in the dead of winter. Although they often join mixed flocks of chickadees, woodpeckers, and kinglets roaming the winter woods, they tend to remain in their territories. They are familiar visitors to bird feeders; they often select items from a feeder and dart off with an undulating flight to eat on a nearby perch or to cache the food for later.

DESCRIPTION: 5–6" (13–15 cm). This sparrow-sized nuthatch is blue-gray above. It has white underparts and a white face with a black crown. It is usually seen creeping on tree trunks with its head facing downward, stopping to look around by raising its head at an angle in a characteristic nuthatch pose.

VOICE: A nasal *yank-yank*. Its song is a series of low whistled notes.

NESTING: Lays 5 or 6 white eggs, lightly speckled with red-brown, in a cup of twigs and grass lined with feathers and hair in a natural cavity, bird box, or hole excavated by the birds.

HABITAT: Deciduous and mixed forests.

RANGE: Largely resident from British Columbia, Ontario, and Nova Scotia south to southern California, Arizona, the Gulf Coast, and central Florida. Absent from most of the Great Plains.

SUBSPECIES: Several subspecies categorized into three main population groups differ slightly from one another. Eastern birds (subsp. *carolinensis*) have thicker bills, paler gray on the back, and buffier flanks; their calls are lower pitched and hoarse. Birds in the Interior West (subsp. *nelsoni*) have darker backs and flanks and thinner bills; their calls are higher and often given in short, repeating bursts. Pacific birds (subspp. *aculeata* along the coast and *tenuissima* in the Cascade Range) have bills similar to Interior West birds but are not as dark on the back and flanks; their calls are the highest and most nasal.

SIMILAR SPECIES: See other nuthatches. Chickadees have black bibs.

CONSERVATION: White-breasted Nuthatch is common and widespread, and its numbers are increasing. Like all cavity nesting birds, these nuthatches benefit from forest management practices that leave dead and dying stands of trees; these birds only occasionally use human-provided nest boxes. They readily accept food from backyard feeders, especially sunflower seeds and suet in winter.

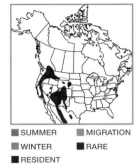

■ SUMMER   ■ MIGRATION
■ WINTER   ■ RARE
■ RESIDENT

These energetic, tiny nuthatches forage in small, talkative flocks high in tall pines. Common where it occurs, it has a patchy, mainly mountainous distribution. The three nuthatch species in the West live in separate wooded habitats. The Pygmy Nuthatch keeps mostly to pine woodlands. The White-breasted is found mainly in the lowland oaks and riparian forests through the foothills into mixed woods, though it also extends into the mountaintop pine forests. The Red-breasted Nuthatch is found in the firs of the subalpine forests. All feed on bark and twig insects, as well as stored nuts, seeds, eggs, and hibernating larvae in winter.

DESCRIPTION: 3¾–4½" (10–11 cm). This small nuthatch is bluish gray above with a gray-brown cap terminated by an indistinct black eyeline. It has a faint white smudge at the base of the nape. It is creamy white below. These gregarious nuthatches usually occur in flocks of 5–15 birds who wander together and roost communally, sometimes with more than a dozen birds sharing a single tree cavity.

VOICE: A monotonous *peep, peep-peep*.

NESTING: Lays 5–9 white eggs with reddish-brown speckles in a nest made of a quantity of soft material, often vegetable down, amassed in the cavity of a dead pine or stump approximately 15' (5 m) from the ground. Pygmy Nuthatches breed in extended-family groups, with nonbreeders helping parents bring food to the young.

HABITAT: Primarily ponderosa pine forests with undergrowth of bunchgrass. It is less common in stands of other pines, Douglas fir, and western larch.

RANGE: Resident locally from southern British Columbia, eastward to the Black Hills of South Dakota (rare), and southward into Mexico.

SIMILAR SPECIES: Other nuthatches have different calls, lack the pale nape patch, have different face patterns, and tend not to flock.

CONSERVATION: Common in its patchy range, Pygmy Nuthatch numbers appear stable to increasing, although these energetic birds' tendency to move around in large, active groups makes their population trends difficult to survey accurately. The loss of mature ponderosa pine forests has put some pressure on these birds, which need aging and dead trees for nest cavities and foraging habitat.

■ SUMMER ■ MIGRATION
■ WINTER ■ RARE
■ RESIDENT

Brown-headed Nuthatch is a fairly common and characteristic species of pine woodlands along the coastal plain of the Southeast; it is virtually never found outside this habitat and region. The smallest of the eastern nuthatches, this species spends more time than the other nuthatches among terminal branches and twigs of trees. After breeding, these birds gather in flocks of a dozen or more and move through the woods along with woodpeckers and chickadees. They are quite agile and restless, flitting from one cluster of pine needles to another.

DESCRIPTION: 4–5" (10–13 cm). Smaller than a sparrow, this tiny nuthatch has dull blue-gray upperparts and whitish underparts. Its crown is dull brown, with a whitish spot on the nape. A dark brown eyeline often contrasts with the paler brown crown.

VOICE: A series of high-pitched piping notes, unlike the calls of other eastern nuthatches.

NESTING: Lays 5 or 6 white eggs heavily speckled with red-brown in a cup of bark, grass, and feathers placed in a cavity in a dead tree or fence post, or under loose bark.

HABITAT: Coniferous and mixed forests.

RANGE: Resident from Delaware, Missouri, and eastern Texas south to the Gulf Coast and central Florida.

SIMILAR SPECIES: See Red-breasted, Pygmy, and White-breasted nuthatches.

CONSERVATION:
Brown-headed Nuthatch is still common in intact southern pine forests, but its population has been declining in the Southeast due to habitat loss. Logging and fire suppression efforts can alter mature pine forests to make them less suitable for these cavity-nesting birds, which require standing dead or decaying trees.

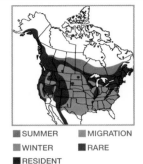

■ SUMMER ■ MIGRATION
■ WINTER ■ RARE
■ RESIDENT

This inconspicuous, supremely camouflaged bird is most often detected by its soft, lisping call as it works its way up a tree trunk, probing the bark for insects. This bird moves in an upward direction, circling tree trunks in spirals, pulling itself up in jerky motions and propping itself with its stiff tail. As it flies from the top of one tree to the base of another, it displays a buff-colored wing patch. In late winter and spring, one may sometimes hear its song—a thin, musical warble.

DESCRIPTION: 5–5¾" (13–15 cm). This well-camouflaged treecreeper is smaller than a sparrow. It is a slender, streaked, brown bird, tinged with buff on the flanks. It is usually seen creeping up tree trunks, using its long, stiff tail for support.

VOICE: A high-pitched, lisping *tsee*; its song is a tinkling, descending warble.

NESTING: Lays 6 or 7 white eggs lightly speckled with brown in a cup of bark shreds, feathers, sticks, and moss, usually placed against a tree trunk behind a peeling slab of bark.

HABITAT: Deciduous and mixed woodlands.

RANGE: Breeds from Alaska, Ontario, and Newfoundland southward throughout the western mountains, the Great Lakes region, North Carolina, and New England. Winters in the breeding range and south to the Gulf Coast and Florida.

SIMILAR SPECIES: Nuthatches are a similar size but have noticeably different coloration and shape. They work their way down a tree trunk rather than upward.

CONSERVATION:
Brown Creepers are locally common in the north and west but declined in the eastern United States due to loss of its mature-forest habitat. Dead and dying trees with loosening bark make ideal nest sites; additionally they require large, live trees for foraging. Overall their numbers appear stable, and they may be recovering in the East.

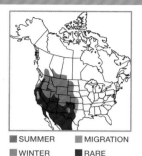

■ SUMMER ■ MIGRATION
■ WINTER ■ RARE
■ RESIDENT

This western wren species is found in much the same habitat as its relative the Canyon Wren but is more partial to rocky slopes, while the Canyon Wren favors sheer cliffs. A stocky, terrestrial bird, the partially migratory Rock Wren lives in open, rocky, often arid regions of western North America; it shows no preference for areas with water. The Rock Wren has the unusual habit of laying down a path of small pebbles in front of its nest; this little "pavement" often simplifies an observer's effort to locate nests.

DESCRIPTION: 5–6½" (13–17 cm). This is a sparrow-sized wren; it is pale grayish brown with fine speckles above, and with a finely streaked breast. Its outer tail feathers have whitish or pale buff tips. Its rump is cinnamon-colored, and its rounded tail is brown above, barred with black, and tipped with buff on the corners. It has an indistinct pale eyebrow.

VOICE: Gives a dry trill; also gives a rhythmic series of musical notes: *chewee, chewee, chewee, chewee*.

NESTING: Lays 4–6 white eggs lightly speckled with pale brown in a shallow nest of plant fibers and roots, lined with feathers and placed in a crevice among rocks or in a hollow stump.

HABITAT: Rock-strewn slopes, canyons, cliffs, and dams in arid country.

RANGE: Breeds from interior British Columbia, Saskatchewan, and North Dakota southward in the mountains. It winters from northern California to Oklahoma and south, throughout the southwestern United States and Mexico to Central America.

SIMILAR SPECIES: See Canyon Wren. Other wrens are smaller or darker and more strikingly marked.

CONSERVATION:

Still widespread in shrublands and rocky areas across the western half of North America, the Rock Wren population has somewhat decreased.

SUMMER ■ MIGRATION
WINTER ■ RARE
RESIDENT

This wren is found in remote, steep-walled canyons and on rocky mountainsides but has also adapted to using human structures such as stone buildings and rock walls. Like most wrens, this bird is quite secretive, and often when one can plainly hear its musical song reverberating from the walls of a canyon, it takes a long and patient search to spot the singer, perched high up on a ledge or quietly picking its way through a clump of brush.

DESCRIPTION: 5½–6" (14–15 cm). This sparrow-sized wren is dark, richly rust-colored above and below, with a conspicuous white throat and upper breast. The wings and the dark rusty tail are barred with black. The bill is long and slender, and it lacks a noticeable eyebrow.

VOICE: A high, clear series of descending notes: *tee-tee-tee-tee-tew-tew-tew-tew*.

NESTING: Lays 4–6 white eggs lightly speckled with reddish brown in a shallow cup of feathers, plant down, and moss placed in a crevice among rocks or, occasionally, on a building.

HABITAT: Rocky canyons and cliffs; it also uses old stone buildings.

RANGE: Resident from British Columbia, Montana, and western South Dakota southward.

SIMILAR SPECIES: Rock Wren has a dull white throat and breast blending into a cinnamon-to-buff belly, flanks, and under-tail coverts rather than contrasting sharply. Most other wrens have eyebrows.

CONSERVATION:
Although still common, the Canyon Wren population may be declining. The primary threat appears to be competition with introduced House Sparrows, which overtake their nests.

■ SUMMER ■ MIGRATION
■ WINTER ■ RARE
■ RESIDENT

The familiar House Wren is named for its tendency to live near human dwellings, often nesting in odd places such as mailboxes, flowerpots, shoes, and even the pockets of clothing left outside. House Wrens are territorial and aggressive when competing for nest sites with other cavity-nesting birds; a House Wren may throw out the nest, eggs, and even the young of its competitors. If House Wrens return in spring to find an old nest still in place, they usually remove it stick by stick, then proceed to rebuild, often using the very material they've just discarded. Outside the breeding season, House Wrens are shy and much less conspicuous than when they are singing during the breeding season.

DESCRIPTION: 4½–5¼" (11–13 cm). A tiny bird with a short tail, often held cocked over the back. Its upperparts are dull, unstreaked grayish-brown with dusky bars on the wings and tail. There is a thin, light eye ring and an indistinct, narrow grayish eyebrow stripe. The underparts are dull grayish white, lightest on the throat and breast, tinged with buff-gray and with faint dusky barring.

VOICE: A gurgling, bubbling, exuberant song, first rising, then falling.

NESTING: Lays 5–8 white eggs thickly speckled with brown in a cup lined with feathers and other soft material contained within a mass of sticks and grass, placed in a natural cavity or bird box. Before egg laying begins, the males build several incomplete "dummy" nests in various cavities in their territory; the female chooses one of these to complete by adding lining.

HABITAT: Residential areas, city parks, farmlands, and woodland edges.

RANGE: Breeds from British Columbia east across Canada to New Brunswick, and south to southeastern Arizona, northern Texas, Tennessee, and northern Georgia. Winters north to southern California, the Gulf Coast states, and Virginia. Also found throughout Central and South America.

SUBSPECIES: This species is highly variable, with as many as 30 subspecies recognized. In general, western House Wrens are grayer on average and have more contrasting rufous flanks and tail coverts than their eastern kin. The "Brown-throated" Wren (*T. a. brunneicollis*), a subspecies of the mountains of northeastern Arizona, has rustier upperparts, a buff throat, breast, and eyebrow stripe, and more prominent barring on the sides and flanks.

SIMILAR SPECIES: Winter Wren is similar but smaller and darker, with a shorter tail and a pale eyebrow; it has heavier barring on flanks. Other wrens have either prominent eyebrow stripes, back stripes, or tail spots.

CONSERVATION: LC
House Wren is widespread, common, and increasing. Its numbers declined in some areas following the introduction of the House Sparrow, with which it competes for nest sites.

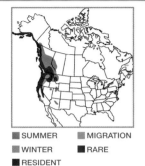

■ SUMMER   ■ MIGRATION
■ WINTER   ■ RARE
■ RESIDENT

This small, dark wren moves like a mouse, creeping through the low, dense tangle of branches covering the forest floor. Its nest is among the hardest to find, even when an observer has narrowed the search to a few square feet, so cleverly is the nest concealed. The Pacific Wren's song is rich and complex; a singing bird's entire body seems to shake while it produces a song that sounds like it must be coming from a much larger bird. The Pacific Wren was once considered a subspecies of Winter Wren; indeed the two species are similar.

DESCRIPTION: 4–4½" (10–11cm). A tiny, dark brown bird with a short tail, narrow pale eyebrow, and heavily banded flanks and belly. The throat area is similar in color to the breast and belly, often more rufous than in Winter Wren.

VOICE: A high-pitched, varied, and rapid series of buzzy trills and chatters; its call note is an explosive *kit!* or *kit-kit!*

NESTING: Lays 5–7 brown-speckled, white eggs in a bulky mass of twigs and moss, with an entrance on the side, lined with softer material and often concealed among the upturned roots of a fallen tree.

HABITAT: Dense tangles and thickets in coniferous and mixed forests.

RANGE: Breeds from the Aleutian Islands and Alaska south along the Pacific coast of North America to central California, inland to Alberta, Utah, Idaho, and Arizona. Many populations are year-round residents throughout much of the breeding range. Migratory birds winter in inland Oregon and Washington, and on the southern California coast. Care is needed in Alberta and throughout the Rocky Mountain region due to the risk of confusion with the similar Winter Wren. Vagrants of either species are possible in the Rockies.

SUBSPECIES: A resident subpopulation on Alaska's Aleutian Islands is larger and paler brown than mainland Pacific Wrens.

SIMILAR SPECIES: See Winter Wren and House Wren.

CONSERVATION:
Pacific Wren is common and its numbers appear to be stable. It is vulnerable to habitat destruction in the Northwest, where logging destroys the old-growth forests that it favors.

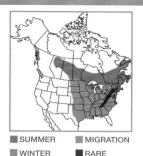

- ■ SUMMER   ■ MIGRATION
- ■ WINTER   ■ RARE
- ■ RESIDENT

In most seasons, Winter Wrens are inconspicuous and difficult to find, staying close to the ground and creeping through the dense undergrowth of the forest floor. In the northern woods in springtime, males fly to high, prominent perches to belt out a beautiful song of long-running musical trills. The Winter Wren's song, when recorded and played back at half- or quarter-speed, reveals a remarkable blend of halftones and overtones all sung at the same time.

DESCRIPTION: 4–4½" (10–11cm). A tiny, dark brown bird with a short tail, narrow pale eyebrow, and heavily banded flanks and belly.

VOICE: A high-pitched, varied series of musical trills and chatters; its call note is an explosive *kit!* or *kit-kit!*, distinctly lower and softer than those of Pacific Wren.

NESTING: Lays 5–7 brown-speckled, white eggs in a bulky mass of twigs and moss, with an entrance on the side, lined with softer material and often concealed among the upturned roots of a fallen tree.

HABITAT: Dense tangles and thickets in coniferous and mixed forests.

RANGE: Breeds from Alberta east to Newfoundland, south through the eastern Plains and Great Lakes region, and southern New England; also in the Appalachian Mountains to northern Georgia. It winters across much of the southern United States south to east Texas, the Gulf Coast, and Florida. Care is needed in Alberta and throughout the Rocky Mountain region due to the risk of confusion with the similar Pacific Wren. Vagrants of either species are possible in the Rockies.

SIMILAR SPECIES: See Pacific Wren and House Wren.

CONSERVATION:  Winter Wren is common and widespread, and its numbers appear to be stable.

SEDGE WREN *Cistothorus platensis*

■ SUMMER   ■ MIGRATION
■ WINTER   ■ RARE
■ RESIDENT

The Sedge Wren is most often seen as it is flushed from grass and flies off, only to drop from view a few feet (about a meter) away. Its flight is distinctive, the wings vibrating stiffly as the bird seems to float over the ground. Like other wrens, it builds "dummy" nests, often hidden in dense marsh grass.

DESCRIPTION: 4–4½" (10–11 cm). A tiny, secretive wren of grassy marshes. It is buff-colored with a finely streaked crown and back. It is best distinguished from other wrens by voice and habitat.

VOICE: A series of harsh notes, sounding like two pebbles tapping together; it is often heard at night.

NESTING: Lays 5–7 white eggs in a globular mass of marsh grass with a side entrance. The nest is lined with feathers and hair that has been woven into the top of a dense stand of grass or sedge.

HABITAT: Grassy freshwater marshes and sedges; it is also found in brackish marshes and wet meadows in winter.

RANGE: Breeds from Saskatchewan, Manitoba, and New Brunswick south to Kansas, Missouri, and Delaware. It winters north to southern Illinois and Virginia. It occurs quite locally and its numbers in an area often fluctuate.

SIMILAR SPECIES: See Marsh Wren.

CONSERVATION:

Sedge Wrens are widespread and common in grassland areas. Local numbers vary from year to year; its overall population trends are unclear but probably fairly stable.

■ SUMMER　■ MIGRATION
■ WINTER　■ RARE
■ RESIDENT

This wren feeds entirely on insects it takes from plants as well as the surface of water. It is a secretive bird; even the singing territorial male remains well hidden, briefly climbing a cattail for a look at an intruder. The male has a number of mates, each of which builds a nest of her own. The male may also build up to half a dozen "dummy" nests, often incomplete, one of which may be used as a roost. Thus a marsh frequented by these birds often contains many nests in various stages of completion, some of which will never be used to raise young.

DESCRIPTION: 4–5½" (10–14 cm). This small wren is smaller than a sparrow. It is brown above, pale buff below, with a bold white eyebrow and a white-streaked back.

VOICE: A liquid gurgling song ending in a mechanical chatter that sounds like a sewing machine.

NESTING: Lays 5 or 6 pale brown eggs, speckled with dark brown, in a globular nest of reeds and cattails with a side entrance. Nest is lined with feathers and cattail down and anchored to reeds.

HABITAT: Freshwater and brackish marshes with cattails, reeds, bulrushes, or sedges.

RANGE: Breeds from British Columbia, central interior Canada, Manitoba, and Nova Scotia south to Mexico, the Gulf Coast, and Florida. It winters across the southern tier of the U.S., north to Washington on the West Coast and in the East to New Jersey.

SUBSPECIES: More than a dozen subspecies can be categorized into two groups. Western subspecies average paler and sing a more rattling song that often begins with a few *tik* notes. Eastern populations tend to be darker rufous, and their songs are more musical and begin with a nasal *gran* note. Several distinctive local populations occur along the southern U.S. coasts, which complicates identification.

SIMILAR SPECIES: Sedge Wren is plain, lacking an obvious white eyestripe; its white back stripes do not contrast with the scapulars and lower back. Its crown is streaked, and its bill is shorter.

Carolina Wren is larger with a conspicuous white eyestripe and an unmarked brown back.

CONSERVATION: Marsh Wren is widespread and locally common. As marsh dwellers, they are vulnerable to the loss of freshwater habitat. Their numbers declined with the loss of wetlands until the early 20th century and have strongly rebounded in recent decades.

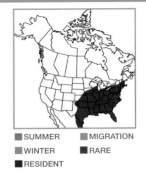

■ SUMMER ■ MIGRATION
■ WINTER ■ RARE
■ RESIDENT

The largest eastern wren, this lively, loud, familiar bird lives in the concealing undergrowth of thickets and swamps among honey-suckle, greenbrier, and brush piles. These wrens do not migrate. At the northern edge of their range they increase in mild years, but a severe cold season with heavy snows will often decimate their numbers and drive them back south. They occasionally visit bird feeders.

DESCRIPTION: 5½" (14 cm). This stubby bird has bright rust-buff underparts and rufous upperparts. There is a conspicuous, thick, long white eye-brow stripe, and a longish tail that is often cocked or switched back and forth. The rather long bill is somewhat decurved and there is some dark barring on the wings and tail. The flight is buzzy and jerking.

VOICE: Loud, whistled *tweedle-tweedle-tweedle* or *tea-kettle, tea-kettle, tea-kettle tea*, sung all day long in all seasons.

NESTING: Lays 5 brown-spotted, whitish eggs in a feather-lined, domed stick nest with an entrance on the side. The nest is placed in stone walls, hollow tree stumps, tin cans, mail boxes, birdhouses, and even coat pockets on clotheslines.

HABITAT: Woodland thickets, ravines, and rocky slopes covered with brush.

RANGE: Resident in the southeastern United States, north to Wisconsin and Michigan, southern Ontario, New York, and southern New England.

SIMILAR SPECIES: Bewick's Wren lacks the warm rufous coloring; it is grayer above and pale gray to dingy whitish below, and it has white tail borders.

Marsh Wren also has a white eyebrow stripe but is smaller, has small white stripes on the back, appears less reddish-brown, and is rarely found in the same habitat.

CONSERVATION:

Carolina Wren numbers are increasing and its range is expanding farther north. These birds tend to thrive in shrubby habitats and will source food from backyard feeders, especially in winter. Carolina Wren numbers can fluctuate following harsh winters, especially in the northern part of its range.

■ SUMMER ■ MIGRATION
■ WINTER ■ RARE
■ RESIDENT

Bewick's Wren uses its long, narrow, slightly down-curved bill for scavenging on the ground and picking in crevices for insects and spiders. Searching for food, it may venture into hollow trunks, rock crevices, or barns. This wren is found in brushy clearings, thick undergrowth, suburban areas, and scrubby woods throughout much of the United States and in southwestern Canada. It often fans and flicks its long tail sideways. John James Audubon named Bewick's Wren for Thomas Bewick (1753–1828), the English naturalist and engraver.

DESCRIPTION: 5½" (14 cm). This sparrow-size, slender wren has a conspicuous white eyebrow stripe, whitish underparts, and a long, limber tail with white outer tail feathers. It is reddish-brown to gray-brown above, with geographic variation.

VOICE: A loud, melodious song with the usual bubbly, wren-like warble, also reminiscent of a Song Sparrow.

NESTING: Lays 5–7 brown-spotted, white eggs in a stick nest lined with leaves, grass, and feathers, and placed in almost any available cavity, including woodpecker holes, coat pockets or sleeves, baskets, tool sheds, and brush piles.

HABITAT: Thickets, brush piles, and hedgerows in farming country; also open woodlands and scrubby areas, often near streams.

RANGE: Resident locally from southern British Columbia, Nebraska, southern Ontario, and southwestern Pennsylvania south to Mexico, Arkansas, and the northern Gulf States. Eastern birds winter south to the Gulf Coast.

SUBSPECIES: Bewick's Wren includes about 20 subspecies that show clinal regional variation in color and song complexity. Pacific coastal birds are browner and become darker brown farther north. A widespread Southwestern/interior population (subsp. *eremophilus*) is the grayest, and the nominate Eastern population (subsp. *bewickii*) is the most reddish. Eastern and Pacific birds have more complex songs than the duller and grayer populations in the western interior.

SIMILAR SPECIES: Although this species resembles the somewhat larger Carolina Wren, it has an entirely different song and, at close range, shows white in the outer tail feathers.

CONVERSATION:

Bewick's Wren is widespread and common in the West, and uncommon and local in the Great Plains. Once common across the eastern U.S., it is now almost completely absent east of the Mississippi River. Competition with increasing population of House Wrens for nesting sites is believed to be the main cause—House Wrens share the same nest site preferences and aggressively destroy nests and eggs of competing birds.

■ SUMMER　　■ MIGRATION
■ WINTER　　■ RARE
■ RESIDENT

Cactus Wrens forage for food methodically, searching under leaves and other ground litter. It is easy to spot an area inhabited by Cactus Wrens because, like other members of the family, they build many "dummy" nests, which are never used for breeding but serve as roosting places. These nests, built amid cacti, are usually so well guarded by sharp spines that it is difficult to understand how the birds can use them without being impaled. They are late sleepers and an early birdwatcher may surprise them still dozing in the snug nest. Although their grating song is hardly musical, it is a most evocative sound for those who love the desert.

DESCRIPTION: 7–8¼" (18–21 cm). A starling-sized wren with spotted underparts, white eyebrows, a rusty crown and flanks, and white spots on the outer tail feathers.

VOICE: A rapid, mechanical *chug-chug-chug-chug-chug*.

NESTING: Lays 4 or 5 buff eggs heavily speckled with brown. The nest, a mass of fine grass and straw with a side entrance, is lined with feathers and hair and placed in the top of a thorny desert shrub or spiny cactus.

HABITAT: Desert thickets and cacti.

RANGE: Resident from southern California, southern Nevada, Utah, and western Texas southward.

SUBSPECIES: More than a half dozen subspecies are recognized, each showing slight variations in pattern. Interior populations have dark, dense spots on the breast; California coastal plain populations show more widely spaced, rounder black spots and paler flanks.

SIMILAR SPECIES: Thrashers are slightly larger; they lack striped upperparts, the barred tail, and the bold eyebrow.

CONSERVATION:

Although still numerous and common in most of its range, recent surveys of Cactus Wrens suggest they are in decline. Residential and agricultural expansion threaten Cactus Wren habitats by removing cacti and desert shrubs. Local populations in parts of Texas and southern California may be threatened.

Polioptila caerulea BLUE-GRAY GNATCATCHER

■ SUMMER　■ MIGRATION
■ WINTER　■ RARE
■ RESIDENT

Several species of gnatcatchers are found throughout the warmer parts of the Americas. All of them build exquisite nests, which are exceedingly difficult to find unless the adults are feeding their young; the parents are quite noisy and conspicuous, and seem to ignore intruders. These gnatcatchers are lively birds, constantly flicking their conspicuous long tails upward while gathering insects from the branches of trees or bushes.

DESCRIPTION: 4½–5" (11–13 cm). Smaller than a sparrow, this gnatcatcher is a tiny, slender, long-tailed bird, blue-gray above and white below, with a white eye ring and broad white borders on its black tail. Its coloration resembles a miniature mockingbird.

VOICE: Its song is a thin, musical warble. Its call note is a distinctive, whining *pzzzz*, with a nasal quality. It also may mimic snippets of other bird sounds.

NESTING: Lays 4 or 5 brown-spotted, pale blue eggs in a small, beautifully made cup of plant down and spider webs, decorated with flakes of lichen and fastened to a horizontal branch at almost any height above ground.

HABITAT: Deciduous woodlands, streamside thickets, live oaks, pinyon-juniper, and chaparral.

RANGE: Breeds from northern California, Colorado, the southern Great Lakes region, southern Ontario, and New Hampshire southward. Winters north to southern California, the Gulf Coast, and Carolinas.

SUBSPECIES: The Eastern population (subsp. *amoenissima*) averages more white on the tail. Western birds (subsp. *caerulea*) are more drab overall with more gray tones. The subspecies use different habitats: Eastern birds prefer open woods and brushy edges; Western birds frequent chaparral, scrub-oak, and pinyon-juniper habitats.

SIMILAR SPECIES: See Black-tailed Gnatcatcher and California Gnatcatcher.

CONSERVATION:

Blue-gray Gnatcatchers are increasing and expanding their breeding range farther north, especially in the West. Gnatcatcher nests are particularly vulnerable to cowbird parasitism.

CALIFORNIA GNATCATCHER *Polioptila californica*

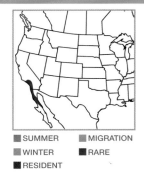

■ SUMMER ■ MIGRATION
■ WINTER ■ RARE
■ RESIDENT

This species is similar to the Black-tailed Gnatcatcher, but the ranges of the two do not overlap. The two were considered a single species until the late 1980s. When California Gnatcatcher became a full species, it immediately became recognized as threatened in California, as the remaining coastal sage scrub habitat in southern California was dwindling and severely fragmented.

DESCRIPTION: 4½–5" (11–13 cm). A tiny bird, it is gray above and paler below. The male has a black crown during summer that extends below the eyes. It has a long, black tail, with little white on the outermost feathers. Nonbreeding males, females, and juveniles are duller.

VOICE: Similar to the calls of Blue-gray Gnatcatcher (not the Black-tailed), but more prolonged and cat-like.

NESTING: Lays 3 or 4 pale blue, spotted eggs in a small, smooth cup nest placed in mesquite or other desert bush or a low tree.

HABITAT: Deserts and arid country; dry washes in the low desert.

RANGE: Resident in extreme southwestern California.

SUBSPECIES: The Coastal California Gnatcatcher (*P. c. californica*) is the subspecies that lives in the United States; the other two subspecies live in Baja California, Mexico.

SIMILAR SPECIES: Similar to Black-tailed Gnatcatcher but its underparts are grayer, and it has much less white in the tail. These two species are best distinguished by voice and range.

CONSERVATION: 🐦 LC
California Gnatcatcher numbers are declining globally. The Coastal California Gnatcatcher, the subspecies that occurs in the United States, is on the U.S. Endangered Species List and is classified as threatened in California.

Polioptila melanura BLACK-TAILED GNATCATCHER

■ SUMMER ■ MIGRATION
■ WINTER ■ RARE
■ RESIDENT

Similar to the Blue-gray Gnatcatcher in shape and behavior, the Black-tailed inhabits lower elevations of the Southwest. It is found in thorny scrub, especially in arroyos and washes, and in riparian underbrush in desert regions—primarily arid, coastal scrub of southwestern California. During the winter, Black-taileds can occur with Blue-gray Gnatcatchers, especially in riparian areas.

DESCRIPTION: 4½–5" (11–13 cm). A tiny bird similar to Blue-gray Gnatcatcher. It is gray above and whitish below. The male has black crown during summer that extends to the eyes. It has a long, black tail with narrow white edges and white tips on the outermost feathers. Nonbreeding males, females, and juveniles are duller.

VOICE: The common call is a harsh, two- or three-note, wren-like scold: *chee chee chee*.

NESTING: Lays 3 or 4 pale blue, spotted eggs in a small, smooth cup nest placed in mesquite or other desert bush or a low tree.

HABITAT: Deserts and arid country; dry washes in the low desert.

RANGE: Resident in southeastern California, Nevada, Arizona, New Mexico, and Texas, southward into Mexico.

SIMILAR SPECIES: Identification of gnatcatchers can be difficult, particularly in the Southwest, where there are four species: the Blue-gray, Black-tailed, California, and Black-capped. The amount of white in the tail, the range, and small differences in the voice offer the best means of separating them.

CONSERVATION:

Black-tailed Gnatcatchers are numerous but declining due to habitat loss and fragmentation. They rely on native vegetation and are much less common in areas with introduced and exotic plants or in residential areas. Additionally, Black-tailed Gnatcatcher is one of about 200 species of songbirds that fall victim to nest parasitism by Brown-headed Cowbirds.

■ SUMMER ■ MIGRATION
■ WINTER ■ RARE
■ RESIDENT

Black-capped Gnatcatcher is a Mexican species that has occurred in southeastern Arizona sporadically since 1971, and its appearances include a number of nesting records. It prefers moister environments than the Black-tailed Gnatcatcher, inhabiting scrubby riparian areas and dense thorn scrub on hillsides, in washes, and in canyons.

DESCRIPTION: 4½–5" (11–13 cm). A tiny, slender bird, the Black-capped Gnatcatcher is gray above and whitish below. Males in breeding plumage have an extensive black cap that covers the head and most or all of the nape, and extends downward on each side in a distinctive V shape.

VOICE: Buzzy and whining calls like those of Blue-gray Gnatcatcher.

NESTING: Lays 3 or 4 pale blue, spotted eggs in a small, smooth cup nest placed in mesquite or other desert bush or a low tree.

HABITAT: Streamside thickets.

RANGE: Western Mexico. In the United States, it is found only irregularly in several canyons in southeastern Arizona.

SIMILAR SPECIES: Similar to Black-tailed Gnatcatcher, but the black cap of the adult male is more extensive; its two outer tail feathers are wholly white.

CONSERVATION: Black-capped Gnatcatcher is decreasing due to habitat destruction in Mexico. Visitors to southern Arizona have not established permanent residency there.

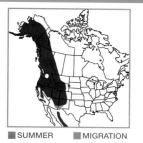

■ SUMMER   ■ MIGRATION
■ WINTER   ■ RARE
■ RESIDENT

This aquatic songbird, known colloquially as the "Water Ouzel," feeds on the insect life of streams. Where water is shallow and runs over gravel, the dipper appears to water ski on the surface. At deeper points it dives into the water and runs along the bottom with half-open wings. American Dipper molts its wing and tail feathers all at once in the late summer, much like a duck, becoming temporarily flightless during this time.

DESCRIPTION: 7–8½" (18–22 cm). American Dipper is a uniformly slate-gray, wren-shaped bird with a stubby tail and yellowish feet. It is usually solitary, and almost always found near (or in) rushing water.

VOICE: A loud, bubbling song that carries over the noise of rapids. Its call is a sharp *zeet*.

NESTING: Lays 3–6 white eggs in a relatively large, insulated nest of moss, with a side entrance. The nest is built under roots, in a rock crevice, or on the bank of a stream.

HABITAT: Near clear, fast mountain streams with rapids.

RANGE: Resident from northern Alaska south throughout mountains of the West. It may move to lowlands in winter.

SIMILAR SPECIES: Unmistakable; this is North America's only aquatic songbird.

CONSERVATION: 🐦 LC

American Dippers are uncommon but widespread in the West, and their numbers are mostly stable. Water quality and the availability of insect prey determine the local dipper population; the absence or disappearance of American Dippers in an area often indicates poor water quality and can signal pollutants in the water. Pollution from logging, mining, and agriculture has caused these birds to disappear from some locations.

RED-WHISKERED BULBUL *Pycnonotus jocosus*

■ SUMMER ■ MIGRATION
■ WINTER ■ RARE
■ RESIDENT

This species has long been adapted to living in the vicinity of towns and villages in Southeast Asia. After a small number escaped from a Miami aviary in the 1960s, these birds quickly became established in the area, taking advantage of the exotic plants grown in orchards and suburban yards. Bulbuls are noisy, gregarious birds, usually traveling in flocks in pursuit of insects and fruit.

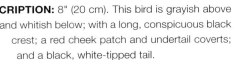

DESCRIPTION: 8" (20 cm). This bird is grayish above and whitish below; with a long, conspicuous black crest; a red cheek patch and undertail coverts; and a black, white-tipped tail.

VOICE: Various chattering notes; a whistled *queekey!*

NESTING: Lays 2–4 pinkish-white eggs spotted with reddish brown in a cup of dead leaves and grass that is lined with fine roots and hair and placed in a bush or small tree.

HABITAT: Residential areas, parks, and gardens.

RANGE: Native to Southeast Asia. Introduced and established in the region around Miami, Florida.

SIMILAR SPECIES: Cedar Waxwing is lighter tan and gray on the back and has a different face pattern; its crest is tan-brown rather than black, smaller, and not usually held erect.

CONSERVATION: Red-whiskered Bulbuls are declining globally. The small population in southern Florida doesn't seem to be spreading beyond the Miami suburbs and doesn't appear to be seriously competing with native birds there.

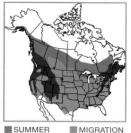

■ SUMMER ■ MIGRATION
■ WINTER ■ RARE
■ RESIDENT

Outside the breeding season, these tiny, insectivorous, energetic birds are frequently seen in the company of Ruby-crowned Kinglets, creepers, nuthatches, and chickadees. These feeding flocks move as a group through the trees, searching out the greatest abundance of hibernating insects and larvae.

DESCRIPTION: 3½–4" (9–10 cm). This tiny, active bird is olive green above and paler below, with two dull-white wing bars. It has a prominent white eyebrow and a colorful crown—orange bordered with yellow in adult males, or solid yellow in females and young birds. A narrow black line separates the crown patch from the white eyebrow.

VOICE: Thin, wiry, ascending *ti-ti-ti*, followed by tumbling chatter.

NESTING: Lays 8 or 9 cream-colored eggs speckled with brown in a large mass of moss, lichens, and plant down, with a small feather-lined cup at the top. Its nest is suspended between several twigs in a densely needled conifer, less than 60' (18 m) above the ground.

HABITAT: Dense, old conifer stands; also found in deciduous forests and thickets in winter.

RANGE: Breeds from Alaska to Alberta and from Manitoba to Newfoundland, and south to southern California and Southwest, and to Michigan, Massachusetts, and in mountains to North Carolina. It winters from southern Canada south to southern California, Arizona, the Gulf Coast, and northern Florida.

SIMILAR SPECIES: Ruby-crowned Kinglet is similar but has a plain face pattern; its crown is red (but usually concealed).

CONSERVATION: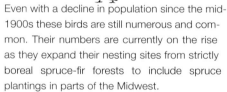

Even with a decline in population since the mid-1900s these birds are still numerous and common. Their numbers are currently on the rise as they expand their nesting sites from strictly boreal spruce-fir forests to include spruce plantings in parts of the Midwest.

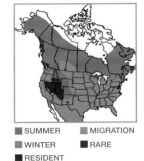

■ SUMMER ■ MIGRATION
■ WINTER ■ RARE
■ RESIDENT

Because kinglets weigh little, they are able to feed on the tips of conifer branches. The Ruby-crowned feeds lower in the canopy than the Golden-crowned and characteristically hovers above a twig looking for caterpillars, aphids, and other insects. The Ruby-crowned is not as social in its winter range as the Golden-crowned and occurs singly more often than in flocks. It takes a sharp eye to see the male's red crown patch, which is usually erected for a few seconds at a time when the bird is displaying aggressively. It has a characteristic habit of nervously flicking its wings.

DESCRIPTION: 3¾–4½" (10–11 cm). A tiny bird, similar to a Golden-crowned Kinglet but greener, with no distinct facial pattern except for a narrow white eye ring. It has two white wing bars with a dark area beyond the second. Males have a tuft of red feathers on the crown, kept concealed unless the bird is excited or agitated (typically in response to a potential mate, a rival, or a predator).

VOICE: Its song is an excited musical chattering.

NESTING: Lays 6–9 cream-colored eggs lightly speckled with brown in a large mass of moss, lichens, and plant down with a small feather-lined cup at the top.

HABITAT: Coniferous forests in summer; also deciduous forests and thickets in winter.

RANGE: Breeds from Alaska east across Canada to Newfoundland, south to southern California and New Mexico in the West, and to the Great Lakes region and northern New England in the East. It winters south from southern British Columbia and California across the southern tier of states to southern New England.

SIMILAR SPECIES: Golden-crowned Kinglet has a conspicuous face pattern; its crown is yellow to orange.

Hutton's Vireo is larger, with a thicker bill, a larger head, and no dark area beyond the second wing bar.

CONSERVATION: Ruby-crowned Kinglet numbers have been stable to increasing overall, although severe winters often take a heavy toll on the population. These birds are able to adapt to human development and forest fragmentation reasonably well, but are driven away where timber overharvesting or wildfires create more severe habitat destruction.

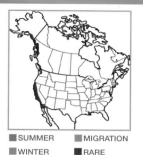

■ SUMMER　■ MIGRATION
■ WINTER　■ RARE
■ RESIDENT

This Siberian species is an irregular visitor to Alaska's offshore islands, chiefly in fall, and has also visited California as a fall vagrant at least a dozen times. A shy bird, it is usually located by its call note as it forages for insects in thickets and low, rank vegetation, flicking its wings.

DESCRIPTION: 5¼" (13 cm) with a wingspan averaging 7¼" (18 cm). Adults have dusky brown or olive-brown underparts, creamy white underparts with a buffy wash on the flank and undertail coverts, and a pale supercilium. It has a short, thin bill and dark legs. Unlike the Arctic Warbler, this bird has no wing bars; its wings are plain and have rather short primary projections.

VOICE: Its call is a sharp *shtek*, often compared to the call of a Lincoln's Sparrow.

NESTING: Lays 5–6 eggs in a nest built low in a bush.

HABITAT: Rank weedy vegetation in taiga bogs and wet meadows.

RANGE: Casual on the islands off western Alaska and along the Pacific Coast to California in fall. Widespread in Asia.

SIMILAR SPECIES: Arctic Warbler has more greenish upperparts, pale legs, and no wing bars.

CONSERVATION: Dusky Warbler is common in Asia, where its population is stable.

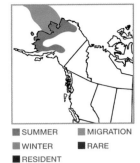

■ SUMMER   ■ MIGRATION
■ WINTER   ■ RARE
■ RESIDENT

This bird is the only North American pioneer from a large genus of similarly colored Old World warblers. It breeds in streamside willow thickets of the Alaskan tundra.

DESCRIPTION: 4¾" (12 cm). Breeding adults are olive green above, with a dark line through the eye and a light greenish-yellow eyebrow. It has a whitish throat and belly, olive-gray sides, and an indistinct single whitish wing bar. It has pale legs. Its bill is hooked at the tip. Juveniles brighter green above with bright yellow below, on the eyebrow, and on the wing bar.

VOICE: A quick trill, introduced by *zick* or *zick-zick-zick*. The call is also *zick* or *zirrup*.

NESTING: Lays 5–7 pink-speckled white eggs in a domed cup nest placed in grass on the ground.

HABITAT: Birch woods and willow thickets.

RANGE: Breeds in western and northern Alaska. Also in northern Eurasia.

SUBSPECIES: The Arctic Warblers native to the Alaskan mainland belong to the subspecies *kennicotti*. Larger Asian subspecies (subspp. *borealis* and *xanthrodyas*) with larger bills occur on the western Aleutian Islands.

SIMILAR SPECIES: See Tennessee Warbler; its range does not overlap.

CONSERVATION: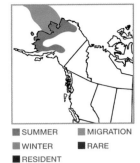
Arctic Warbler's remote breeding area in North America leaves it largely unaffected by human disturbance. Its small population in Alaska is stable; these birds are abundant and increasing in northern Eurasia.

■ SUMMER ■ MIGRATION
■ WINTER ■ RARE
■ RESIDENT

The Wrentit spends all of its adult life within the territory chosen in its first year. Individuals hesitate to cross open spaces of even 30 to 40 feet (9 to 12 meters), and it is believed that the wide Columbia River effectively stops the species from entering Washington, even though both sides of the river offer suitable habitat.

DESCRIPTION: 6–6½" (15–17 cm). This elusive bird is uniformly brown, with a faintly streaked breast and conspicuous pale eyes. Its name is apt: its head, bill, and eyes resemble those of a tit, whereas the long, cocked tail and secretive habits are reminiscent of a wren.

VOICE: An accelerating series of musical notes running together into a trill and dropping slightly in pitch toward the end: *peep peep peep-pee-pee-peepeepepeprrrr.* Its call is a prolonged, dry "growling" note. This species is far more often heard than seen.

NESTING: Lays 3–5 greenish-blue eggs in a neat cup nest of bark fiber, held together by cobwebs and hidden in a low bush.

HABITAT: Chaparral, shrubs, and brush.

RANGE: Resident from the Columbia River on the northern border of Oregon southward along coastal chaparral into Baja California and in the Sierra Nevada foothills of California.

SUBSPECIES: Wrentits can be divided into several geographical subspecies, each showing clinal variation in color. Northern and coastal birds in wetter climates are darker and more red, whereas southern and inland birds in drier areas are paler and grayer.

SIMILAR SPECIES: Compare to wrens and titmice.

CONSERVATION: Wrentits are common and their numbers are generally stable within a restricted range. The coastal areas it prefers are prime real estate locations, and the loss of scrub and chaparral habitat to commercial and residential development decreases their numbers and creates isolated populations.

BLUETHROAT *Cyanecula svecica*

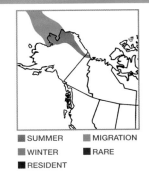

SUMMER ■ MIGRATION
■ WINTER ■ RARE
■ RESIDENT

Bluethroat is one of the most recent arrivals among North American breeding birds. As Siberian populations of this handsome songster have increased with the recent warming climate, the species has been able to spread across the Bering Strait into Alaska. A small breeding population is now established in northern Alaska and northern Yukon. Its remote habitat and secretive, skulking nature make seeing this elusive chat a prize for intrepid bird watchers.

DESCRIPTION: 4¾" (12 cm). This small bird is brown above and white below. The male has a striking blue throat and breast with a rusty red "star" in the middle; it has black, white, and red bands across the breast, and a white neck stripe and eyebrow. Females and juveniles have a light buff throat bordered with dark brown feathers. All plumages have a rusty red patch at the base of its brown tail (similar to that of American Redstart) displayed during nervous tail-flicking.

VOICE: Its song is loud, varied, and introduced by a repeated *dip, dip, dip*. It sometimes mimics the songs of other birds. Its alarm call is *huyt-tock*.

NESTING: Lays 4–7 brown-dotted, green eggs in a cup nest well hidden on the ground.

HABITAT: Shrubby tundra in the breeding season.

RANGE: Breeds in northern Alaska and northern Yukon. Also widespread in the Old World.

SIMILAR SPECIES: Breeding males with blue and rufous breast bands are unmistakable. See Northern Wheatear.

CONSERVATION: LC
Bluethroats are a relatively new addition to the North American landscape; their breeding habitats are fairly remote, making long-term population trends difficult to estimate. Their numbers are thought to be stable worldwide; the small population in North America is stable or possibly increasing.

NORTHERN WHEATEAR
Oenanthe oenanthe

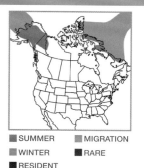

■ SUMMER ■ MIGRATION
■ WINTER ■ RARE
■ RESIDENT

Two geographically separate populations of Northern Wheatears breed in North America. In fall the western population migrates southwestward and the eastern population migrates southeastward, both wintering in Africa with as many as 22 other species of wheatears. Thus the New World has been colonized by Northern Wheatears from both East and West; they maintain their ancestral distinction by continuing to follow separate migratory routes. The scientific name *Oenanthe* is from the ancient Greek and means "wine-flower," alluding to the fact that these birds return to Greece in the spring just as the vineyards blossom.

DESCRIPTION: 5½–6" (14–15 cm). A very rare, sparrow-sized bird of open ground. It is warm brown above and buff-pink below. The bold white rump and sides of its tail contrast with a black center and tip of the tail, which form an inverted T.

VOICE: Harsh *chak-chak!* Its song is a jumble of warbling notes.

NESTING: Lays 5–7 pale green eggs in a fur-lined cup of grass concealed under a rock, in a rabbit burrow, or in a crevice in a wall.

HABITAT: Nests in rocky tundra; barren pastures and beaches in winter.

RANGE: Breeds in Alaska and extreme northern Canada, appearing very rarely farther south especially along the Atlantic Coast in fall. Most winter in North Africa with some wintering in Eurasia; stragglers are casual in North America in winter.

SUBSPECIES: Eastern birds (subsp. *leucorhea*) average larger and richer buff underneath; western birds (subsp. *oenanthe*) are whiter below with a subtle buff tinge.

SIMILAR SPECIES: See Bluethroat.

CONSERVATION: Northern Wheatear numbers are stable, with the northeastern Canada population possibly increasing.

EASTERN BLUEBIRD *Sialia sialis*

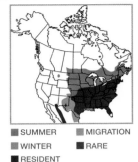

■ SUMMER   ■ MIGRATION
■ WINTER   ■ RARE
■ RESIDENT

Many people await this beautiful, bright blue bird in the spring after a long winter. Eastern Bluebirds are found in open woodlands, orchards, and farmlands. In places where bluebird nest boxes are erected and European Starlings and House Sparrows are controlled, up to six pairs of bluebirds will nest on as many acres. All bluebirds nest in cavities. They occur in flocks in the nonbreeding season, often feeding on berries.

DESCRIPTION: 7" (17 cm). This bird is bright blue above and on the wings and tail. It has a chestnut throat and breast and a white belly and undertail coverts. The female is similar but duller, and with whitish eye rings. Juveniles are duller and strongly spotted.

VOICE: Its call is a liquid and musical *turee* or *queedle*. Its song is a soft, melodious warble.

NESTING: Lays 4–6 pale blue eggs in a loose cup of grasses and plant stems in natural tree cavities, old woodpecker holes, fence posts, and bird boxes.

HABITAT: Open woodlands and farmlands with scattered trees.

RANGE: Breeds east of the Rockies from southeastern Canada to the Gulf of Mexico; also in the mountains of southeastern Arizona and southwestern New Mexico. It winters in the southern part of its breeding range. Also found in Mexico.

SUBSPECIES: The subpopulation in southeastern Arizona (subsp. *fulva*) is somewhat paler overall and nonmigratory.

SIMILAR SPECIES: See Western and Mountain bluebirds.

CONSERVATION: LC

Eastern Bluebird numbers have increased in recent decades, recovering from a 20th century decline after bluebird trails and specially designed nest boxes relieved competition for nesting sites with introduced European Starlings and House Sparrows.

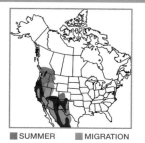

■ SUMMER ■ MIGRATION
■ WINTER ■ RARE
■ RESIDENT

Western Bluebird is found around forest edges, in orchards, and in open hardwood and conifer forests and woodlands. Except during the nesting season, Western Bluebirds travel in flocks, feeding on berries and fruiting shrubs, in addition to the insects they take throughout the year. In the winter, these flocks may move from forest and woodland areas into more open country nearby. This species is the western counterpart of the Eastern Bluebird; the ranges of the two overlap only in the Southwest. Females are attracted by the vivid blue of the male and by the availability of nesting holes, which are often in short supply. Upon securing a nesting hole, the male entices the female with a colorful display that also serves to repel rivals. Its rusty breast, like that of the American Robin, is used to signal aggression toward other males.

DESCRIPTION: 6–7" (15–18 cm). A long-winged, rather short-tailed bird. The male has a deep blue hood and upperparts, a rusty red breast and crescent mark across the upper back, and a white belly. The female is sooty gray above, with dull blue wings and tail. Juveniles resemble females but are grayer, with speckled underparts.

VOICE: Soft calls sound like *phew* and *chuck*. Its song is a short, subdued *cheer, cheer-lee, churr*.

NESTING: Lays 4–6 pale blue eggs in a grass nest placed in a tree cavity or woodpecker hole.

HABITAT: Open woodlands and pastures where old trees provide nest sites.

RANGE: Breeds from southern British Columbia and western Alberta south to Baja California and east throughout the mountains of the West to eastern New Mexico and extreme western Texas. It winters throughout most of the breeding range, although the northernmost populations usually withdraw slightly southward.

SIMILAR SPECIES: See Eastern and Mountain bluebirds. The female Eastern Bluebird is similar to the female Western, but usually has a pale rusty (not grayish) throat.

CONSERVATION:
Western Bluebirds have declined in some areas with the loss of habitat, but the species' numbers are stable overall. Habitat loss is the biggest threat to these birds, followed by competition for nesting sites with introduced European Starlings and House Sparrows in the breeding habitat that remains.

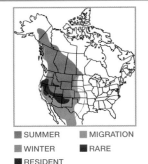

■ SUMMER   ■ MIGRATION
■ WINTER   ■ RARE
■ RESIDENT

This sky-blue bird frequents open western sagebrush plains, mountain meadows, and timberline areas. This species has longer wings and a more graceful, swallow-like flight than the Eastern Bluebird. They frequently hover low over the ground and drop down to catch insects, or dart out from a branch, flycatcher fashion, and then return to another perch. Mountain Bluebirds are highly migratory and usually travel in small flocks in winter.

DESCRIPTION: 7" (18 cm). The male is pure sky-blue above, and paler blue below with a white abdomen. The female is similar, but duller and grayer; the throat and breast may have a rusty tinge in fresh fall plumage.

VOICE: Soft warbling notes: *tru-lee*.

NESTING: Lays 5 or 6 pale blue eggs in a nest of grass and plant fibers built in a natural cavity or bird box.

HABITAT: Breeds in high mountain meadows with scattered trees and bushes; in winter descends to lower elevations, where it occurs on plains and grasslands.

RANGE: Breeds from southern Alaska, Mackenzie, and Manitoba south to western Nebraska, New Mexico, Arizona, and southern California. It winters from British Columbia and Montana south through the western United States.

SIMILAR SPECIES: See Eastern and Western bluebirds. Mountain Bluebird lacks the deep chestnut breast of both of these relatives.

CONSERVATION: LC

Mountain Bluebird numbers are slightly increasing. Their higher-elevation nesting sites face less intense competition from introduced European Starlings and House Sparrows than those of other bluebirds.

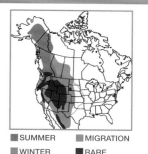

■ SUMMER ■ MIGRATION
■ WINTER ■ RARE
■ RESIDENT

This is the northernmost of a number of mountain-forest thrushes (the solitaires) of the New World and the only species north of Mexico. Like other thrushes, it forages on the ground for berries and insects; in winter it descends to lower elevations and may even occur in desert oases.

DESCRIPTION: 8–9½" (20–24 cm). A slender bird, resembling a mockingbird. It is gray overall, unstreaked, slightly darker above, with a thin white eye ring and white outer tail feathers. It has a pale rusty wing patch. Juveniles are mottled gray and white. It sits upright, usually high on a branch.

VOICE: Its song is made up of loud, melodious, fluty rising and falling phrases. Its call is a squeaky *eeek*.

NESTING: Lays 3 or 4 grayish-white eggs, with light brown spots concentrated at the large end, in a large, loosely built nest of weeds, lined with rootlets, placed on the ground, in a hole, among roots, in a road cut, in an old mine shaft, or among rocks on talus slopes.

HABITAT: Open coniferous forests, edges, or burns with single standing trees in the mountains.

RANGE: Breeds from central Alaska, western Alberta, and the Black Hills of South Dakota south to central California and central New Mexico. Its winters throughout the western United States north to British Columbia and the Black Hills.

SIMILAR SPECIES: A female Mountain Bluebird is similar but usually has detectable blue tones in the wings and tail; it lacks the bold, buffy wing patches.

CONSERVATION:
Townsend's Solitaire is common and its population is stable to increasing. These birds may benefit from limited logging and development activities that thin forests, creating ideal breeding areas for these birds.

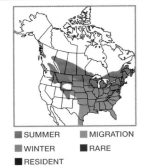

SUMMER ■ MIGRATION
WINTER ■ RARE
■ RESIDENT

The secretive Veery lives in dense shade. Its beautiful song sounds best at dusk, as it echoes through the deepening gloom of the forest. Its diet is evenly divided between insects obtained on the ground and fruit. It migrates at night, the flock keeping together in dark skies by means of a contact call characteristic of the species. Studies of other thrushes show that their vision in shade or twilight is better than that of most other birds.

DESCRIPTION: 6½–7¼" (16–18 cm). Smaller than a robin, this thrush is uniform cinnamon-brown or rufous-olive above, with faint spotting on the upper breast. It has a clean, white belly; other thrushes in the genus *Catharus* are more heavily spotted below.

VOICE: Its song is a rich downward spiral with an ethereal quality; its call note is a descending *whew*.

NESTING: Lays 4 blue-green eggs in a bulky cup of moss, plant fibers, and leaves, placed on the ground in a clump of grass or ferns or a few feet (about a meter) off the ground in a shrub.

HABITAT: Moist deciduous woodlands; willow thickets along streams in the West.

RANGE: Breeds from southern British Columbia east to Newfoundland and south to Arizona, South Dakota, Minnesota, New Jersey, and in the mountains to Georgia. Winters in the tropics.

SUBSPECIES: Eastern birds (subsp. *fuscescens*) are brighter reddish above and weakly spotted. Western birds (subsp. *salicicola*), sometimes called "Willow Thrush," have duller upperparts and a more heavily spotted breast. Newfoundland birds (subsp. *fuliginosus*) resemble the Western population.

SIMILAR SPECIES: Western birds may be difficult to distinguish from Pacific "Russet-backed" Swainson's Thrush; Swainson's has an off-white belly sometimes smudged with pale rufous.

Wood Thrush and Hermit Thrush have darker spots on the breast.

CONSERVATION:
Although still common, Veery numbers have experienced a slow, steady decline. Fragmented breeding areas in North America have meant fewer nest sites and more extensive cowbird parasitism in edge habitats. The bird's wintering habitat in South America is also threatened as forests are converted to agricultural land.

- ■ SUMMER
- ■ WINTER
- ■ RESIDENT
- ■ MIGRATION
- ■ RARE

A reticent bird, the Gray-cheeked Thrush keeps mostly under cover, searching for food on the ground. This thrush is one of the few American birds that have spread to northeastern Siberia in the scrub tundra but migrate back through North America to the American tropics.

DESCRIPTION: 6½–8" (17–20 cm). This bird is dull olive-brown with pale, spotted underparts and no rust color in the plumage; the sides of the face are tinged with gray, and it has no eye ring. Its lower mandible is flesh colored.

VOICE: A series of thin, reedy notes inflected downward at the end.

NESTING: Lays 3–5 pale blue-green eggs finely speckled with brown in a solidly built cup of grass reinforced with mud and placed in a low conifer.

HABITAT: Nests in coniferous forests, especially in dense stands of stunted spruce and balsam; widespread on migration.

RANGE: Breeds from northern Alaska across northern Canada to Newfoundland, south to northern British Columbia, northern Ontario, and central Quebec. Throughout much of eastern North America on migration.

SUBSPECIES: The Newfoundland population (subsp. *minimus*) tends to be warmer brown above, more like Bicknell's Thrush.

SIMILAR SPECIES: Swainson's Thrush is similar, but has a buff eye ring and buff (not gray) cheeks. Other spotted thrushes show rust color on the upperparts or tail. See Bicknell's Thrush.

CONSERVATION: Although still common in its breeding range in spruce woods, the remoteness of its breeding areas makes it difficult to assess the population trends of this species. It may be declining, especially in the southern part of its breeding range.

■ SUMMER ■ MIGRATION
■ WINTER ■ RARE
■ RESIDENT

A crepuscular bird, Bicknell's Thrush keeps mostly hidden in dense forest. Summering in the mountains of northeastern North America, it migrates to the Caribbean for the winter, and may be seen throughout the East while on migration. Extremely similar to the Gray-cheeked Thrush, Bicknell's Thrush was recognized as a distinct species in 1995. It is estimated that the entire population is less than 100,000 birds.

DESCRIPTION: 7½" (19 cm). This thrush's back, head, and wings are grayish brown. It has dark brown spots on its pale buffy throat and chest, and a white belly. Its tail is often rusty reddish, contrasting with an olive-brown back reminiscent of a Hermit Thrush. Its cheeks are gray and it has a thin, pale eye ring. The inner half of its lower mandible is yellow, compared to the pale tan of a Gray-cheeked Thrush.

VOICE: Its song is nasal, rising at the end: *whee-wheeoo-ti-ti-whee*. Its call is a down-slurred *whee-ah*.

NESTING: Lays 3–4 pale blue eggs, finely speckled with brown, in a bulky cup built of moss and twigs and lined with fine stalks of Horsehair Fungus and usually placed in a low conifer. Females of the species may mate with more than one male, and several males may help tend the same nest, a behavior not seen in other thrushes.

HABITAT: High elevation evergreen forests and less commonly in cool maritime evergreen forests.

RANGE: Breeds from southern Quebec and the Maritimes south to northern New England and northern New York. Winters in the Caribbean.

SIMILAR SPECIES: Bicknell's Thrush was once considered a subspecies of Gray-cheeked Thrush, to which it is nearly identical but is usually best distinguished by voice. Also see Swainson's Thrush.

CONSERVATION: Complete population data for Bicknell's Thrush only goes back to the mid-1990s, but surveys since that time show a clear declining trend. Development, pollution, and climate change are reducing this species' high-elevation forest habitat. Development for agriculture and industry threaten its wintering habitat in the West Indies.

SUMMER   MIGRATION
WINTER   RARE
RESIDENT

This bird is named after the English naturalist William Swainson (1789–1855). Like the Hermit Thrush, it is a furtive, ground-dwelling bird of the northern forests. Its song, while perhaps not as beautiful as that of the Hermit Thrush, is better known to most birdwatchers because the species sings more frequently during migration. Because each bird's territory is small and the species is abundant, one may hear a chorus of male Swainson's Thrushes sing briefly every morning and evening. This species sings, feeds, and breeds in shady thickets; migrants fly at night, feeding and resting during the day.

DESCRIPTION: 6½–7¾" (17–20 cm). This thrush is uniformly dull olive-brown or olive-russet above, spotted below, with a buff eye ring and cheeks. The breast is washed with buff and has heavy, rounded black spots that become wedge-shaped at the sides of the throat. Juveniles are darker olive above and have buff streaks on the back.

VOICE: Its song is a series of reedy, spiraling notes inflected upward.

NESTING: Lays 3 or 4 pale green-blue eggs finely spotted with light brown in a well-built cup of moss and lichen lined and strengthened with twigs, leaves, and grass. The nest is generally concealed in a small forest shrub or tree.

HABITAT: Coniferous forests and willow thickets.

RANGE: Breeds from Alaska east across Canada to Newfoundland, south to British Columbia, Michigan, and northern New England, and in the mountains to southern California, Colorado, and West Virginia. Winters in the tropics.

SUBSPECIES: Pacific-region "Russet-backed" Swainson's Thrush (subsp. *ustulatus*) has a rufous-tinged back and flanks, and may resemble a drab Veery. The remainder of the Swainson's Thrush population in the taiga and Interior West is of the "Olive-backed" variety with colder olive-gray upperparts and olive tinged flanks.

SIMILAR SPECIES: The Gray-cheeked Thrush is similar, but has grayish cheeks and lacks the conspicuous eye ring.

CONSERVATION: Swainson's Thrush is common and its population is thought to be fairly stable. In migration, these birds are highly vulnerable to collisions with windows, communication towers, and tall buildings. Studies have shown this species to be among the most frequent building-collision casualties; light pollution and lighted buildings at night may confuse these and many other nighttime migrants into such fatal collisions.

■ SUMMER ■ MIGRATION
■ WINTER ■ RARE
■ RESIDENT

To many, the song of the Hermit Thrush, the Vermont state bird, is the most beautiful of any North American bird. Outside the breeding range it may occasionally be heard late in spring, before the birds head north to nest. This is the only one of our spotted thrushes that winters in some northern states, subsisting on berries and buds. During the warm months, however, it feeds largely on insects taken from the ground, most of the time under dense cover, hopping around and then watching in an upright position like a robin.

DESCRIPTION: 6½–7½" (17–19 cm). This thrush is smaller than a robin, olive-brown above with a reddish tail. Its face is gray-brown with a thin whitish eye ring. It is whitish below with a pale buff cast; large spots on the breast form narrow streaks on the sides of the throat and flanks. It frequently flicks its tail.

VOICE: A series of clear, musical phrases, each on a different pitch, consisting of a piping introductory note and a reedy tremolo. Its call note is a low *tuck*.

NESTING: Lays 4 blue-green eggs in a well-made cup of moss, leaves, and rootlets concealed on the ground or in a low bush in the forest.

HABITAT: Coniferous and mixed forests; deciduous woodlands and thickets on migration and in winter.

RANGE: Breeds from central Alaska east to Newfoundland and south to southern California, northern New Mexico, Wisconsin, and Virginia. It winters from Washington and southern New England southward.

SUBSPECIES: Three groups of intergrading subspecies are recognized. Pacific birds (subsp. *guttatus*) are smaller and darker with thinner bills. Birds of the mountains in the Interior West (subsp. *auduboni*) are larger and paler, with gray-brown backs and gray flanks. Eastern and northern birds are medium-sized and brightly colored, with buff-brown flanks and thicker bills.

SIMILAR SPECIES: See other brown, spotted thrushes; Hermit Thrush's dull brown upperparts and a strongly contrasting rusty tail can distinguish it from related thrushes in the genus *Catharus*. It is the most likely to be seen in winter in North America.

CONSERVATION: 🐦 LC
Hermit Thrush is fairly common but inconspicuous, and its numbers are stable to increasing. Their winter habitats are farther north than other thrushes, with most remaining in North America and Mexico, making them less susceptible to loss of habitat due to the shrinking tropical forests.

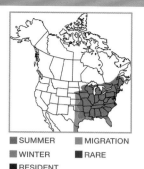

■ SUMMER ■ MIGRATION
■ WINTER ■ RARE
■ RESIDENT

This familiar forest bird of the East is the only one of our spotted brown thrushes that nests regularly in residential areas. The Wood Thrush has one of the most beautiful songs of any North American bird. Thoreau wrote of it: "Whenever a man hears it he is young, and Nature is in her spring; wherever he hears it, it is a new world and a free country, and the gates of heaven are not shut against him." Its numbers are declining, however, especially in the heart of its range in New England and along the Atlantic Coast, earning the attention of conservationists.

DESCRIPTION: 8" (20 cm). This starling-sized thrush is brown above, bright rusty colored on the head, and white below with large, blackish spots. It has a narrow white eye ring, and the ear coverts are streaked with white and dusky coloring. The cheeks are grayish. Juveniles are similar to adults but have tawny-olive or buff spots on the head and upperparts, and faint buff spots on the wing coverts that may form one or two indistinct wing bars.

VOICE: Its song is a series of rich, melodious, flute-like phrases; its call is a sharp *pit-pit-pit-pit*.

NESTING: Lays 4 greenish-blue eggs in a cup of grass and twigs, reinforced with mud and lined with fine grass and rootlets, placed in a bush or sapling.

HABITAT: Moist, deciduous woodlands with a thick understory; also well-planted parks and gardens.

RANGE: Breeds from Manitoba, Ontario, and Nova Scotia south to Florida and the Gulf of Mexico. Winters in the American tropics.

SIMILAR SPECIES: Other brown thrushes have finer spotting on the breast. Brown Thrasher is streaked below and has a longer tail and a longer, decurved bill.

CONSERVATION: The Wood Thrush is a common forest bird in steep decline. In the last several decades, it is estimated that this bird's numbers have dropped by more than half. Much of the loss can be attributed to forest fragmentation, which leaves these birds exposed to predators and Brown-headed Cowbirds. Cowbirds thrive where unbroken forests have been reduced to smaller fragments with more edges, and they lay many eggs in Wood Thrush nests; the thrushes often raise broods of cowbirds, with few young of their own surviving.

This widespread European and Asian species has been sighted several times in eastern North America. Most North American sightings are from Canada, but they have been found as far south as Pennsylvania. The nearest regular breeding population to our area is in Iceland.

DESCRIPTION: 8–10" (20–24 cm). This European and Asian species is slightly smaller than its close relative the American Robin. It is generally brown above and white to tan below, with lines of dark spots reaching from the throat to the belly. It has a prominent buffy to whitish eyebrow. The name Redwing comes from the distinctive red patches on the flanks and underwing, which distinguish the Redwing from any native spotted thrush.

VOICE: Its song is a descending warble composed of simple notes, with many different dialects. It has a wide variety of calls, from a buzzy *dsssi* to *chip* notes.

NESTING: In Eurasia, this bird lays 4–6 eggs in a neat nest on the ground or in a shrub.

HABITAT: Mix of forest or shrubland and open country. It occupies orchards and other cultivated open woodland area, often seen on grassy fields near wooded areas.

RANGE: Casual to Newfoundland in winter, accidental elsewhere in North America. Breeds across northern Europe and Asia, from Iceland and the Faroe Islands through much of Siberia, although not reaching the Pacific Coast. It winters across Western Europe and parts of the Middle East, generally south of the breeding range.

SIMILAR SPECIES: American Robin is slightly larger and has distinctive chestnut to brick red underparts and no eyebrow. Other brown, spotted native thrushes lack the bold eyebrow and rusty red flanks.

CONSERVATION: NT
Although still numerous and widespread across Eurasia, global Redwing populations are declining at an alarming pace, approaching 30 percent in 15 years (three generations)—enough for this common species to become listed as Near Threatened by the IUCN Red List.

SUMMER ▪ MIGRATION
WINTER ▪ RARE
RESIDENT

The Clay-colored Thrush is a scarce but regular vagrant to the lower Rio Grande Valley in Texas, where it occasionally breeds. Most sightings occur in winter. In Panama, this species elects to breed in the dry season, despite limited food availability, presumably because the danger from predation is less. It was formerly called Clay-colored Robin.

DESCRIPTION: 9–10½" (23–27 cm). This thrush resembles a pale, tawny-beige American Robin. Its head and upperparts are grayish to tawny brown, its throat is pale with dusky streaking, and its underparts are buff. It has a yellow bill and pale legs. The juvenile's upperparts are cinnamon-flecked, and its underparts are mottled and spotted brown.

VOICE: Its song is a series of rich, variable phrases; likened to a sweet call of an American Robin but slower and clearer. It also makes clucking call notes and a thin, high-pitched flight call.

NESTING: Lays 2–4 pale blue-toned eggs in heavy cup nest of mud, moss, and grasses.

HABITAT: Open or semi-open areas, usually with associated trees; it also uses forest edges, gardens, and suburban lots. It tends to forage on the ground or in low- or mid-level shrubs, singly or in pairs. The exception is at fruiting trees, where groups may feed in the canopy.

RANGE: Resident from eastern Mexico to Columbia; it occurs rarely but regularly in the lower Rio Grande Valley in Texas.

SIMILAR SPECIES: Resembles an Ameican Robin, but its coloration makes it distinctive.

CONSERVATION:
The Clay-colored Thrush is quite common in its range, and its numbers are increasing.

RUFOUS-BACKED ROBIN *Turdus rufopalliatus*

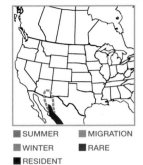

■ SUMMER   ■ MIGRATION
■ WINTER   ■ RARE
■ RESIDENT

This handsome thrush occasionally turns up as a winter vagrant in the Southwest. It is more retiring than American Robin, keeping to dense foliage of trees and thickets. It feeds on berries but, unlike Clay-colored Thrush, it does not frequent feeding stations. Like American Robin, Rufous-backed calls and sings mostly early in the day, often before dawn.

DESCRIPTION: 9¾" (24 cm) with an average wingspan of 16" (41 cm). Males have chestnut coverts and back and auburn underparts. The throat is strongly streaked to the upper breast. Females are paler than males. Both sexes have dark lores and lack eye rings (unlike American Robin).

VOICE: Song a series of rich, burry, warbled phrases, reminiscent of American Robin. Calls include a loud, descending, sibilant *sssiiuu*, a low *tuk* note (often in series), and a high, thin, lispy *si* in flight.

NESTING: Lays 3 whitish eggs with heavy spotting in a cup nest in woods or dense thickets.

HABITAT: Found in areas of dense vegetation, often near water and fruiting trees.

RANGE: Native to west Mexico. It is rare in winter to southern and central Arizona. It has been recorded in west and south Texas and southern California.

SIMILAR SPECIES: See American Robin and, in southern Texas, Clay-colored Robin.

CONSERVATION:
Rufous-backed Robin is fairly common to uncommon in its range, although its population size hasn't been officially quantified. Its numbers are believed to be stable.

- ■ SUMMER
- ■ MIGRATION
- ■ WINTER
- ■ RARE
- ■ RESIDENT

Robins originally nested in forests; where they still do so, they are much shyer than the robins of the dooryard. They breed only rarely in the Deep South, where they prefer large shade trees on lawns. Although considered a harbinger of spring, robins often winter in the northern states, where they frequent cedar bogs and swamps and are not usually noticed by a casual observer except for when they gather in large roosts, often containing thousands of birds. Earthworms are a staple of the American Robin's diet; the bird hunts on lawns, standing stock-still with its head cocked to one side as it scans for its prey.

DESCRIPTION: 9–11" (23–28 cm). This familiar bird is dark gray above and brick red below. The head and tail are black in males and dull gray in females. Most have white corners on the tail. It has a yellow bill and a broken white eye ring. Young birds are heavily spotted.

VOICE: Its song is a series of rich caroling notes, rising and falling in pitch: *cheer-up, cheerily, cheer-up, cheerily.*

NESTING: Lays 3–5 blue-green eggs in a well-made cup of mud reinforced with grass and twigs, lined with softer grasses, and placed in a tree or on a ledge or windowsill. Robins usually have two broods a season.

HABITAT: Towns, gardens, open woodlands, and agricultural land.

RANGE: Breeds from Alaska east across continent to Newfoundland and south to California, Texas, Arkansas, and South Carolina. It winters north to British Columbia and Newfoundland.

SUBSPECIES: Most western individuals are paler and duller than eastern birds; a northwestern population that breeds north to southeastern Alaska (subsp. *caurinus*) lacks white corners on the tail.

SIMILAR SPECIES: Eastern and Spotted towhees have similar color patterns but different foraging habits. Their eyes and bills are different and they have much more white on the belly and in the wings.

Varied Thrush has boldly patterned wings, a dusky breast band, an unmarked throat, and an orange eyebrow and wing bars.

CONSERVATION: American Robins are abundant and increasing. American Robins forage in short grass environments, making them especially well-adapted to life in suburban areas. When these birds go missing from an area, it can indicate an environmental problem such as pollution or the overuse of pesticides.

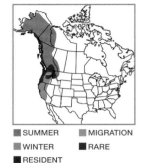

■ SUMMER ■ MIGRATION
■ WINTER ■ RARE
■ RESIDENT

This thrush lives on the shaded floor of coniferous forests. Like the American Robin, it feeds on earthworms and insects in open, bare areas. In winter it migrates to lowlands or flies south to California parks—habitats it shares with robins.

DESCRIPTION: 9–10" (23–25 cm). Superficially similar to American Robin but with bold color patterns. It has slate gray upperparts, a rusty orange throat and breast interrupted by a broad slate-colored or black breast band, two orange wing bars, and an off-white belly. The female is similar but paler; the breast band may be gray or absent. A young bird's breast band is incomplete, frequently with orange and dusky speckles. Its flight is more undulating than American Robin's.

VOICE: Its song is two or three buzzy whistles, each drawn out until it fades away, followed by a short silence. Its call is a low *took*.

NESTING: Lays 3–5 pale blue, spotted eggs in a moss-lined twig cup built in a small tree, sapling, or bush.

HABITAT: Dense coniferous or deciduous forests with abundant water.

RANGE: Breeds from Alaska and Yukon south to Oregon, California, Idaho, and Montana. It winters from coastal Alaska southward.

SIMILAR SPECIES: See American Robin.

CONSERVATION: Although still common, Varied Thrushes are declining significantly due to habitat loss. They require large, unbroken old-growth forests for nesting and feeding, and as cover during migration and winter. Logging and development have fragmented swaths of mature forests, decreasing the nesting and wintering sites suitable for these birds.

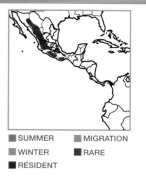

■ SUMMER ■ MIGRATION
■ WINTER   ■ RARE
■ RESIDENT

This uncommon Mexican thrush is a rare and irregular vagrant to the southwestern U.S. from Texas to Arizona. In irruption years, as many as 20 birds will find their way north in a fairly small area, where these normally solitary birds will gather at good food sources. They are most often seen in the mountains and canyons near the Mexican border in southeast Arizona, especially in late summer, but do not occur there every year.

DESCRIPTION: 8½–9½" (21.5–24 cm). This beautiful thrush is larger than a Wood Thrush but smaller than an American Robin. The striking pattern of blacks, browns, and whites on the folded wing of both males and females is unique to this species. Males have a dark head, back, and throat, whereas females are browner.

VOICE: A whining *wheerr*, given both as call and (louder, repeated) as a song.

NESTING: Lays 3–6 pale-blue eggs in a cup-shaped nest made of grass and moss.

HABITAT: Humid montane forest from 5800–11,000' (1800–3500 m).

RANGE: Mountains of Central and Western Mexico. Rare in southeastern Arizona and casual along the Mexican border to Texas.

SIMILAR SPECIES: Juvenile Spotted Towhee has a thicker bill and a different wing and tail pattern.

CONSERVATION: Aztec Thrush may number fewer than 50,000 individuals in the world, and its numbers are declining due to ongoing destruction and fragmentation of its forest habitat in Mexico.

This beautiful Mexican mockingbird is an accidental visitor across the southwestern U.S. from Texas to California. It is a popular cage bird in Mexico, so there are questions of origin surrounding some sightings, but at least some appear to be wild vagrants.

DESCRIPTION: 9½–11" (24–27 cm). Approximately the size of the familiar Northern Mockingbird, the Blue Mockingbird is almost entirely blue. Because the color is produced by feather structure rather than pigments, the bird can appear slaty blue-gray to a rich indigo, depending on the light. It has a black eyepatch running from the bill across much of the face and surrounding its reddish eyes.

VOICE: A complex song of varied notes, including many melodic, but occasional harsh notes. It has a wide variety of calls.

NESTING: Lays 2–6 pale blue or greenish white eggs splotched with red or brown in a cup nest made of twigs and rootlets.

HABITAT: Shrublands, brush, and forests; it prefers riparian areas when in arid habitats. Sea level to 10,000' (3000 m).

RANGE: Southern Mexico, extending north along both the Atlantic and Pacific Coasts. Closest approach to the United States is in central Sonora.

SIMILAR SPECIES: Gray Catbird is dark gray and has a black cap; it lacks the thick black eyepatch.

CONSERVATION:
Blue Mockingbirds are numerous in their native range but declining due to ongoing forest habitat destruction and fragmentation.

■ SUMMER ■ MIGRATION
■ WINTER ■ RARE
■ RESIDENT

This bird is often seen in suburban gardens. It forages mainly on the ground, gleaning insects from litter and low bushes and eats fallen berries during late summer and fall. It does not uncover litter with its feet like a sparrow but pokes with its bill, turning leaves and twigs to find the food underneath. This common bird inhabits undergrowth, brush, and gardens, and usually stays near dense cover. It often announces its presence by a harsh, cat-like whine issued from a dense tangle of vegetation. It has a musical song and a varied repertoire. When giving its cat-like call, it often flicks its tail. It was formerly known simply as the "Catbird."

DESCRIPTION: 8–9¼" (20–23 cm). This talkative bird is smaller than a robin. It is a slender, long-tailed, dark gray bird with a black cap and rusty undertail coverts.

VOICE: A long, irregular succession of musical and mechanical notes and phrases; it also gives a cat-like mewing. It sometimes mimics other birds.

NESTING: Lays 4 or 5 glossy blue-green eggs in a bulky mass of twigs, stems, and leaves, lined with finer plant material and concealed in a dense bush or in a tangle of vines.

HABITAT: Thickets and brush, residential areas and gardens.

RANGE: Breeds from British Columbia, Manitoba, and Nova Scotia south to Washington, Texas, and Georgia. It winters from the Carolinas and the Gulf Coast southward; small numbers occur regularly in winter along the Atlantic Coast to southern New England.

SIMILAR SPECIES: Northern Mockingbird is slightly larger with whitish underparts and distinctive white wing patches visible in flight. Gray Catbird typically lacks white in its plumage.

CONSERVATION:
Gray Catbird populations are stable, with its numbers increasing in some areas in the East. Coastal development along the Atlantic and Gulf coasts can threaten its wintering habitat.

CURVE-BILLED THRASHER *Toxostoma curvirostre*

SUMMER ■ MIGRATION
WINTER ■ RARE
■ RESIDENT

The most characteristic dawn sound in the Texas brush country—or indeed wherever this bird occurs—is its sharp call, which sounds much like a human whistling to attract attention. Like the Cactus Wren, it builds nests that are conspicuous but hard to reach because they are placed in the center of dense, thorny desert vegetation. The Curve-billed Thrasher forages on the ground, tossing aside litter in search of insects with its prominently down-curved bill.

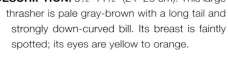

DESCRIPTION: 9½–11½" (24–29 cm). This large thrasher is pale gray-brown with a long tail and strongly down-curved bill. Its breast is faintly spotted; its eyes are yellow to orange.

VOICE: Its song is a rapid series of musical notes and phrases. Its call is a sharp, whistled *whit-wheet!*

NESTING: Lays 4 pale blue-green eggs finely speckled with brown in a bulky cup of twigs and rootlets placed in a dense thorny desert shrub or in a branching clump of cactus.

HABITAT: Desert brush and cactus.

RANGE: Resident from northwestern and central Arizona, southeastern Colorado, and western Oklahoma southward.

SUBSPECIES: The westernmost Sonoran population (subsp. *palmeri*) has overall plainer plumage than the Chihuahuan population (subsp. *oberholseri*) that occurs along the Mexican border to Texas. Sonoran birds have indistinct spotting below, faint tail spots, and weak wing bars; Chihuahuan birds have more distinct wing bars and defined tail spots, and have darker spots more concentrated on the breast.

SIMILAR SPECIES: See Bendire's Thrasher. Other large thrashers have strong face patterns and lack spots on the breast.

CONVENTION:
Curve-billed Thrasher is common, especially in the western part of its range. Slight declines in its population in recent decades can be traced to urban and agricultural development in the Sonoran Desert and south Texas.

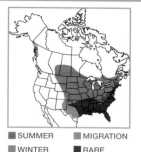

■ SUMMER ■ MIGRATION
■ WINTER ■ RARE
■ RESIDENT

Brown Thrashers may be confused with thrushes but are larger, have longer tails, and are streaked (not spotted) below. They belong to the same family as the Northern Mockingbird but, unlike that species, are retiring and secretive. They often feed on the ground, scattering dead leaves with their long, curved bills as they search for insects.

DESCRIPTION: 11½" (29 cm). This thrasher is bright rufous-brown above. The underparts are whitish, washed with buff on the breast and sides, with thin, dark brown streaks. It has a slightly curved bill, a long tail, and yellow eyes.

VOICE: A variety of musical phrases, each repeated twice. Its call is a sharp *smack!*

NESTING: Lays 4 or 5 pale blue, brown-dotted eggs in a large, coarsely built nest of twigs, leaves, and rootlets lined with grass. The nest is usually near the ground in a dense, often thorny bush.

HABITAT: Thickets, fields with scrub, and woodland borders.

RANGE: Breeds from southeastern Alberta, Manitoba, Ontario, and northern New England south to the Gulf Coast and Florida. It winters in the southern part of its breeding range.

SUBSPECIES: Western populations are paler than eastern birds on average, with thinner streaking below. Western birds also average slightly larger.

SIMILAR SPECIES: May be confused with Wood Thrush in the East. Wood Thrush has a shorter tail and is spotted below, not streaked.

See Long-billed Thrasher.

CONSERVATION:  Although still widespread and common in most areas, Brown Thrasher numbers are declining. The shrubby habitat in which they thrive in is disappearing from the eastern U.S. as land usage changes. They face competition in some areas with Northern Mockingbirds, and are vulnerable to collisions with telecommunication towers and cars, as well as to pesticide poisoning.

LONG-BILLED THRASHER *Toxostoma longirostre*

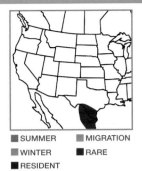

☐ SUMMER ☐ MIGRATION
☐ WINTER ■ RARE
■ RESIDENT

Resident in eastern Mexico north to south Texas, this close relative of the Brown Thrasher is equally at home in dense mesquite thickets in the driest regions and in heavy bottomland forests near the Rio Grande. This tropical species closely resembles the Brown Thrasher in its voice, appearance, and habits. They feed extensively on insects, supplemented by fruits.

DESCRIPTION: 11" (28 cm). This jay-sized thrasher is brown to gray-brown above and white below with black streaks. It has a curved bill and a long tail. It is similar to Brown Thrasher, but darker and grayer on the head and face, with a longer bill, and with orange (not yellow) eyes.

VOICE: Its song is a varied series of paired phrases similar to those of the Brown Thrasher; its call is a low *chuck*.

NESTING: Lays 3 or 4 pale blue, brown-dotted eggs in a nest of twigs and leaves, lined with rootlets and placed in a dense thorn bush or cactus.

HABITAT: Dense tangles and thickets in both open country and wooded areas and in both moist and dry regions.

RANGE: Resident in south-central Texas and nearby northeastern Mexico.

SIMILAR SPECIES: Similar to Brown Thrasher in habits and appearance, but the two can usually be distinguished by range. Brown Thrasher has off-white underparts (not as white) and a brighter rufous-brown back.

CONSERVATION: 🐦 LC

Long-billed Thrashers are common in their range and increasing. Clearing of brushland and river woods for agriculture causes local declines.

■ SUMMER ■ MIGRATION
■ WINTER ■ RARE
■ RESIDENT

Bendire's Thrashers are uncommon and local, found in deserts with scrub and cactus. This thrasher flies from bush to bush, whereas other desert thrashers almost never fly. However, it does most of its feeding on the ground.

DESCRIPTION: 9–11" (23–28 cm). A grayish-brown, short-billed thrasher of desert thickets, this robin-sized bird is rather small and short-tailed for a thrasher. It is similar to a young Curve-billed Thrasher with a short bill, but smaller, with a shorter tail and more triangular spots on its breast. Its eyes are yellow.

VOICE: Its song is a clear, melodious warble with some repetition, and continuing at length. Its call is a low *chuck*.

NESTING: Lays 3 or 4 pale greenish eggs, with buff spots, in a stick nest lined with fine, soft material and hidden in a bush or cactus.

HABITAT: Desert scrub.

RANGE: Breeds in southeastern California, southern Nevada, Arizona, and western New Mexico. It winters from southern Arizona southward into northwestern Mexico.

SIMILAR SPECIES: Curve-billed Thrasher is similar but has a longer, more curved bill and round spots on the breast. Curve-billed generally uses different habitats (including suburban areas and parks), and only overlaps in desert scrub.

CONSERVATION: VU Bendire's Thrasher numbers continue to fall due to degradation and conversion of habitat. Populations have declined substantially since the middle of the 20th century. They are more common in protected areas of undisturbed desert and in some types of open farmland, but ongoing land development efforts further reduce the amount of habitat available for these birds.

CALIFORNIA THRASHER *Toxostoma redivivum*

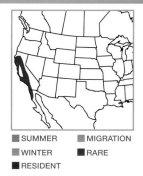

■ SUMMER ■ MIGRATION
■ WINTER ■ RARE
■ RESIDENT

The active California Thrasher inhabits chaparral and feeds on the ground under the shelter of bushes, using its heavy, curved bill to turn over leaf litter in search of food. It spends most of its time on the ground; its wings are shorter than those of the desert thrashers and it often escapes by scurrying rather than flying.

DESCRIPTION: 11–13" (28–33 cm). A large, slender thrasher with a long, deeply curved bill. It is dark brown above with a lighter gray-brown breast. It has buff-brown undertail coverts. Its eyes are dark brown. It has an indistinct light brown eyebrow and a dark "mustache."

VOICE: Its song recalls that of a Northern Mockingbird but harsher, more halting, and less repetitious. Both males and females of this species sing exuberantly, sometimes duetting. This thrasher is also an expert mimic. Its calls include a low, harsh *chuck* and a throaty *quip*.

NESTING: Lays 2–4 pale blue-green, speckled eggs in a bowl-shaped nest of sticks and roots lined with finer materials and placed in a shrub.

HABITAT: Chaparral, foothills, and dense shrubs in parks or gardens.

RANGE: Resident in California west of the Sierra Nevada.

SIMILAR SPECIES: See other large thrashers; these do not overlap with California Thrasher's coastal range. Crissal Thrasher is paler and grayer overall and has a light yellowish iris. LeConte's Thrasher is much paler and prefers arid habitat with sparse vegetation.

CONSERVATION: 🐦 LC
California Thrashers are still common in many areas, but they have disappeared from urbanized coastal areas and are declining overall. The main threat to these birds is the loss of chaparral habitat to clearing, development, and agriculture. These birds require large territories; smaller, fragmented habitats cannot support them.

Toxostoma lecontei LECONTE'S THRASHER

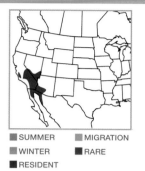

SUMMER ■ MIGRATION
WINTER ■ RARE
RESIDENT

This thrasher is a permanent resident in the Southwest. Like most other desert thrashers, it prefers to escape by scurrying away through the sparse vegetation but will fly if pressed. It feeds mostly in the early morning or just before dark, when insects are most active, and seeks shade in the midday heat.

DESCRIPTION: 10–11" (25–28 cm). The palest of the thrashers. It is the color of light sand, with lighter, unstreaked underparts and a darker tail. It has a dark bill, dark eyes, and dark eyeline. Freshly molted (fall) birds have tawny undertail coverts.

VOICE: Its song is a loud, rich melody recalling that of a California Thrasher, but less harsh and with infrequent repetition of phrases. Its calls are a rising *whit* and *tu-weep*.

NESTING: Lays 2–4 light blue-green eggs speckled with brown in a bulky twig nest covered with coarse grasses and lined with fine stems and feathers, placed in a cholla cactus or low thorny bush.

HABITAT: Deserts with scant vegetation (mostly cholla and creosote bush), where the bird blends with the light-colored, sandy soil.

RANGE: Resident in southeastern California, southern Nevada, southwestern Utah, and western and central Arizona.

SIMILAR SPECIES: California Thrasher is darker—brown overall with buffy underparts.

CONSERVATION:
LeConte's Thrasher is still common in appropriate habitat and its numbers appear to be stable to slightly declining. LeConte's Thrasher has lost extensive habitat to development in some parts of its limited range; irrigated lawns, farmland, and fields do not support this desert specialist.

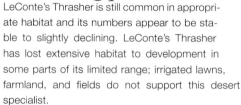

CRISSAL THRASHER *Toxostoma crissale*

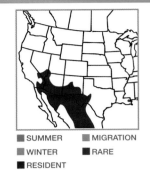

■ SUMMER　　■ MIGRATION
■ WINTER　　　■ RARE
■ RESIDENT

The Crissal Thrasher inhabits the more heavily vegetated areas of southern deserts. It is common at lower elevations in dense mesquite and similar riparian vegetation, and where underground water supports thickets, becoming uncommon in other habitats. The Crissal Thrasher seldom flies in the open, but moves furtively among streamside mesquite thickets, willows, and other tangles. Except during the hottest months and briefly after molting, it delivers its loud melodious song year-round.

DESCRIPTION: 10½–12½" (27–32 cm). A large, dark thrasher with a deeply curved bill. It is brown above with lighter gray-brown, unstreaked underparts. It has a dark "mustache" line and yellowish eyes. Its undertail coverts are chestnut brown.

VOICE: Its call is a rolling *chorilee, chorilee*. Its song consists of loud, repeated phrases.

NESTING: Lays 2–4 pale blue-green eggs in a rather large twiggy nest well hidden in dense mesquite or other thick desert vegetation.

HABITAT: Found in dense underbrush near desert streams, and at the edges of canyon chaparral in the hot, low desert.

RANGE: Resident in southeastern California, southern Nevada, southwestern Utah, and western Texas southward.

SIMILAR SPECIES: This bird resembles the California Thrasher in its appearance and its habit of gathering food by hacking the ground with its heavy curved bill, but the ranges of the two species do not overlap.

CONSERVATION:
Crissal Thrashers are secretive and difficult to survey, but their numbers appear to be stable. Some populations may face threats from agricultural or urban development.

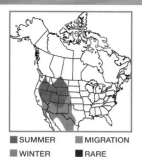

■ SUMMER ■ MIGRATION
■ WINTER ■ RARE
■ RESIDENT

Sage Thrasher inhabits open country year-round, occurring in summer in the sage and scrub of basin and range country; in winter it frequents a variety of more southerly deserts. This highly migratory bird flies swiftly with rapid wingbeats. When singing from a conspicuous perch or in flight, the Sage Thrasher is a less repetitious mimic than the Northern Mockingbird. The flicking of its tail and its general appearance would suggest a mockingbird except with streaked underparts; its generally terrestrial habits—particularly its habit of diving into a bush for cover when alarmed—are characteristic of a thrasher. It feasts on fruits and vegetables in gardens of desert towns, but also eats many damaging insects in alfalfa fields near its sagebrush nesting area.

DESCRIPTION: 8½" (22 cm). This small thrasher is brown-gray above and buff below with conspicuous black streaks that become fainter with wear by the end of summer. Its bill is short for a thrasher and strongly curved. Its tail is also relatively short with white patches in the corners. It has two white wing bars that are often worn away by spring.

VOICE: A continuous, sweet warble without the broken-up phrases of the more familiar Brown Thrasher. The common call note is a deep *chuck*.

NESTING: Lays 4 or 5 brown-blotched, blue-green eggs in a stick nest lined with rootlets and grass, and often with fur or feathers, and placed in a bush, usually with thorns.

HABITAT: Dry sagebrush plains and arid areas such as the floors of rocky canyons; winters in dense thickets and lowland scrub.

RANGE: Breeds from southern interior British Columbia, central Idaho, and southern Montana south to southern inland California, southern Nevada, New Mexico, and western Oklahoma; it also occurs in an isolated area in southwestern Saskatchewan. It winters chiefly in the southwestern states, southern Texas, and northern Mexico.

SIMILAR SPECIES: In worn birds in late summer, the streaking on the underside may become extremely faint. In this condition, Sage Thrasher can be difficult to distinguish from Bendire's Thrasher.

CONSERVATION: Sage Thrasher populations have declined during the past few decades, mainly due to habitat loss. Heavy livestock grazing, urban and agricultural development, fire suppression efforts, and herbicide and pesticide use have heavily impacted the sagebrush steppe areas favored by these birds.

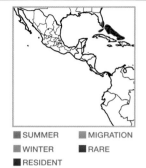

The Bahama Mockingbird is a casual visitor to south Florida. Populations restricted to islands often evolve independently of the widespread parent species, leading to a closely related, but distinct island endemic. The Bahama Mockingbird may be an island version of the widespread Northern Mockingbird.

DESCRIPTION: 11" (28 cm). A large mockingbird, somewhat larger than the familiar Northern Mockingbird. Its plumage is more brownish, especially on the upperparts, and it has streaking on the head, back, and flanks that is entirely absent in Northern. It lacks the Northern Mockingbird's extensive white wing patches; the white in the wings is restricted to the covert edgings.

VOICE: Song of varied notes and phrases. Does not mimic other species.

NESTING: Lays 2–6 creamy-white to pink eggs in a nest made of sticks, stems, dried leaves, and various fibers, lined with finer materials, and placed in a tree or shrub.

HABITAT: Scrub and shrub habitats. It is shyer than Northern Mockingbird and less willing to use human-cleared habitats.

RANGE: Native to the Bahamas, Turks and Caicos Islands, southern Jamaica, and a few small islands off the Cuban coast. It is casual to south Florida.

SIMILAR SPECIES: Similar to the Northern Mockingbird but somewhat larger. Bahama Mockingbird is browner and more streaked, especially on the breast and belly.

CONSERVATION: 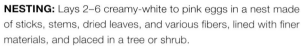 Native to islands in the western Caribbean, the Bahama Mockingbird population has not been officially quantified, and although they are said to be fairly common, their numbers are declining.

■ SUMMER ■ MIGRATION
■ WINTER ■ RARE
■ RESIDENT

This bird's beautiful song is richest on warm, moonlit nights in spring, when the bird may spend hours giving amazing imitations of other birds—sometimes dozens of other species. Birds in the western part of the species' range have less musical songs and are less imitative. Mockingbirds are strongly territorial and, like a number of other birds, will attack their reflection in a window, hubcap, or mirror. At mating time, the male Northern Mockingbird becomes increasingly exuberant, flashing its wings as it flies up in an aerial display, or singing while flying from one song post to another. After breeding, each parent establishes and vigorously defends its own winter territory. Mockingbirds require open grassy areas for their feeding; thick, thorny, or coniferous shrubs for hiding the nest; and high perches where the male can sing and defend its territory.

DESCRIPTION: 9–11" (23–28 cm). A robin-sized mimic, the Northern Mockingbird is a slender, long-tailed gray bird with white patches on the wings and tail. Two large, white wing patches that seem to flash in flight are diagnostic. Its tail is long, rounded, and mostly black, with several white outer feathers. Juveniles are similar but with faint spotting on the breast.

VOICE: A long series of musical and grating phrases, each repeated several times; it often imitates many other birds in succession, and it regularly sings at night. Its call is a harsh *chack*.

NESTING: Lays 3–5 blue-green eggs, spotted with brown, in a bulky cup of sticks and weed stems in a bush or low tree.

HABITAT: Found in residential areas, city parks, farmlands, open country with thickets, and desert brush.

RANGE: Breeds from northern California, eastern Nebraska, southern Ontario, and Maritime Canada southward. It winters in the southern part of its breeding range.

SIMILAR SPECIES: See Northern and Loggerhead shrikes. Townsend's Solitaire is darker gray and has a different posture; it has buff wing bars instead of large white wing patches.

CONSERVATION:  Northern Mockingbirds are common and widespread, and their numbers are stable. The species has been expanding its range northward in recent decades, especially in the East. These birds have recovered from declines in the 19th century caused by their extensive capture for the pet trade, a practice which has since been outlawed.

■ SUMMER ■ MIGRATION
■ WINTER ■ RARE
■ RESIDENT

Conditioned by centuries of living in settled areas in Europe, this species easily adapted to American cities after 100 birds were liberated in Central Park, New York City, in 1890. Since then it has spread over most of the continent. Its large roosts, often located on buildings, may contain tens of thousands of birds. Hordes of these birds create much noise, damage vegetable or fruit crops, and do considerable damage around feedlots, consuming and fouling the feed of domestic cattle, and have proved difficult to drive away. Starlings compete with native hole-nesters for woodpecker holes and natural cavities. Although often considered an invasive pest, these birds are undeniably adaptable, intelligent, and excellent mimics.

DESCRIPTION: 7½–8½" (19–22 cm). European Starling is a short-tailed, chunky, iridescent black bird that's smaller than a robin. Its long, pointed bill is yellow in summer and dark in fall and early winter. Its plumage is flecked with white in winter. The juvenile is uniform dull gray with a dark bill.

VOICE: A series of discordant, musical, squeaky, and rasping notes; often imitates other birds. Its call is a descending *whee-ee*.

NESTING: Lays 4–6 pale blue eggs in a mass of twigs, grass, and trash lined with finer plant material and feathers, and placed in a tree or building cavity.

HABITAT: Cities, suburban areas, farmlands, and ranches.

RANGE: Occurs from Alaska and Quebec south throughout the continent to the Gulf Coast and northern Mexico. It is native to Eurasia and widely introduced around the world.

SIMILAR SPECIES: Compare to blackbirds and grackles. The starling's purplish-green iridescent plumage; pinkish legs; and long, slender yellow bill distinguish it from other iridescent black songbirds.

Gray juvenile starlings can be confused with juvenile waxwings, which have a different bill shape, vertical streaking on the breast and flanks, and yellow tail tips.

CONSERVATION:
Starlings have become widespread and abundant in North America, competing with many cavity-nesting native songbirds, including bluebirds and woodpeckers. Their numbers are decreasing, however, both in North America and in Eurasia.

■ SUMMER ■ MIGRATION
■ WINTER ■ RARE
■ RESIDENT

This Asian species was first recorded in Florida in 1983, presumably as escaped cage birds; feral birds have now established populations from Key West to Orlando as well as many other sites around the world. Escaped captives are thought to have nested in southern California, but did not become established there.

DESCRIPTION: 9–10" (23–26 cm). A stocky, mostly dark-brown bird. Its head is glossy black; its legs, bill, and bare orbital region are yellow. A large white patch is visible in flight and at rest. Its tail is brown and tipped with white.

VOICE: A wide assortment of high-pitched chattering notes; a loud, scolding *radio-radio-radio*.

NESTING: Lays 3–5 blue eggs without markings. Both sexes incubate the eggs. These birds will nest in any place that will hold a large pile of leaves, twigs, paper, etc., including tree cavities, crevices in walls of houses, ventilators between ceiling and roof of buildings, utility poles, drain pipes, air conditioners, and traffic lights.

HABITAT: Open country, forest edges, agricultural areas, residential gardens, city streets, and suburbs; it avoids dense forest. It is especially fond of open areas such as airstrips and large parking lots.

RANGE: This bird's native range is south and central Asia east through the Indian subcontinent and much of southeast Asia; it is introduced in many other parts of the world. In the U.S., resident populations are established in Florida and Hawaii.

SIMILAR SPECIES: European Starling is smaller and has iridescent black body feathers and pinkish legs.

CONSERVATION:
Common Myna numbers are increasing in Asia and in introduced populations throughout the world, especially in cities and suburbs.

BOHEMIAN WAXWING *Bombycilla garrulus*

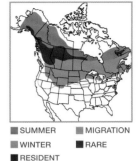

■ SUMMER ■ MIGRATION
■ WINTER ■ RARE
■ RESIDENT

Common in winter in Canada's prairie provinces, this species forms large winter flocks in the northern United States about once a decade. Its occasional erratic movements southward in winter are thought to be caused by food shortages in the North. When it appears, it feeds on berries. One hundred or more of these birds perched in the top of a leafless tree in midwinter, calling shrilly, is an unforgettable event. Highly social, Bohemian Waxwings usually move about in tight formations, descending en masse on a clump of bushes and quickly stripping them of fruit.

DESCRIPTION: 7½–8½" (19–22 cm). A sleek, gray-brown, crested bird with a yellow-tipped tail and black mask and throat markings. Seen in good light and from the side or below, this large waxwing is best identified by the distinct dark rusty undertail coverts. Bohemians also have white and (usually) yellow wing spots. Like adults, juvenile Bohemians have pale rust-colored undertail coverts and white marks on the wings, but are not as gray and have diffuse streaking below.

VOICE: A high-pitched, lisping *seeee*, harsher and more grating than the call of Cedar Waxwing.

NESTING: Lays 4–6 pale blue eggs, heavily spotted and scrawled with black, in a loose, flat saucer of twigs, lichens, and grass in a conifer.

HABITAT: Open coniferous forests.

RANGE: Breeds from Alaska, Yukon, Mackenzie, Saskatchewan, and Manitoba south to central Washington, northern Idaho, and northwestern Montana. It wanders irregularly farther south and east during winter. Also found in Eurasia.

SIMILAR SPECIES: Similar to Cedar Waxwing but larger, grayer, and with conspicuous white wing patches and rusty (not white) undertail coverts.

CONSERVATION: Bohemian Waxwings are common and increasing. They breed in the Far North away from heavily populated areas and are known to adapt to disturbed habitats. Vehicle strikes and collisions with windows are common as these birds feed on fruiting plants near buildings and roads. They are also susceptible to poisoning by ingesting road salt and pesticides used on fruits they eat.

■ SUMMER ■ MIGRATION
■ WINTER ■ RARE
■ RESIDENT

Waxwings spend most of the year in flocks whose movements may be quite erratic. Hundreds will suddenly appear in an area to exploit a crop of berries, only to vanish when that crop is exhausted. Since the young are fed insects and small fruits to some extent, waxwings tend to nest late in the summer when there is a good supply of both. Adults store food for the young in the crop, a pouch located in the throat, and regurgitate into the gaping mouths of the nestlings. In summer these birds take insects, hawking for them like flycatchers. These social birds have the amusing habit of passing berries or even apple blossoms from one bird to the next down a long row sitting on a branch, until one bird eats the food.

DESCRIPTION: 6½–8" (17–20 cm). Smaller than a robin, Cedar Waxwing is a sleek, crested, brown bird with a black mask and a pale yellow belly. It has yellow tips on the tail feathers (sometimes orange or reddish due to diet) and hard, red, wax-like tips on the secondary wing feathers. It is almost always seen in flocks. Juveniles tend to be grayer overall; they are diffusely streaked, especially on the underparts, and have little or no black around the eye and throat.

VOICE: A thin lisp: *tseee*.

NESTING: Lays 4–6 blue-gray eggs, spotted with dark brown and black, in a bulky cup of twigs and grass placed in a tree in the open.

HABITAT: Open woodlands, orchards, and residential areas.

RANGE: Breeds from southeastern Alaska east to Newfoundland and south to California, Illinois, and Virginia. It winters from British Columbia, the Great Lakes region, and New England southward.

SIMILAR SPECIES: See Bohemian Waxwing.

CONSERVATION:
Cedar Waxwings are widespread and common, and their numbers are increasing as agricultural fields are converted back to forests and shrublands, and as more berry trees are used in landscaping. Local numbers may vary widely in response to food availability.

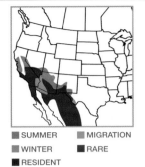

- ■ SUMMER   ■ MIGRATION
- ■ WINTER   ■ RARE
- ■ RESIDENT

The Phainopepla is the northernmost of a group of tropical birds that feed on mistletoe. In the Southwest the berries are seasonal, so it supplements them with insects, which it takes from the air in long sallies, like a typical flycatcher.

DESCRIPTION: 7–7¾" (18–20 cm). Larger than a sparrow, Phainopepla is a slender, elegant bird with a conspicuous crest, longish tail, and upright posture. The male is glossy black, with two white wing patches that show only in flight. Females and juveniles are plain gray with pale wing patches.

VOICE: Its common calls include an up-slurred, whistled *hoooeet* and a low *quirk*. Its short warbled song is rarely heard.

NESTING: Lays 2–4 pale greenish, speckled eggs in a simple shallow nest placed in a mistletoe-bearing desert tree, such as the mesquite along washes, or in a tall tree bordering a river.

HABITAT: Desert scrub, but does not have strong preference for desert; it favors hot country with single, tall trees, preferably with mistletoe or other berries available when flying insects are scarce.

RANGE: Breeds in northern interior California, southern Nevada, southern Utah, and southern New Mexico southward into Mexico. It winters in the southern part of its breeding range.

SIMILAR SPECIES: Juvenile Cedar Waxwings are streaked below and lighter grayish than a female or juvenile Phainopepla.

Northern Mockingbird is also much lighter gray, has a white belly, and does not have a crest.

CONSERVATION: LC
The Phainopepla population appears to be stable, although their numbers vary from year to year. The conversion of riparian desert to agricultural land has reduced available breeding and wintering habitat.

■ SUMMER   ■ MIGRATION
■ WINTER   ■ RARE
■ RESIDENT

The Olive Warbler has no close relatives among the warblers, and indeed may not really be a warbler at all. It is currently placed in its own family, Peucedramidae. This southwestern bird lives in mountainous open pine, pine-oak, and fir forests. It often forages in the tops of coniferous trees, revealing its presence year-round with a loud, descending whistled call. They fly from the interior or top of one tree to another, only occasionally feeding from the outside or lower branches. In the nonbreeding season they often flock together and forage on the understory of deciduous trees or even on the ground.

DESCRIPTION: 4½–5" (11–13 cm). This bird has a tawny orange head, nape, and breast. A broad black mask extends from the bill to behind the ear. It is gray above, white below, with dark wings and tail, and broad white wing bars. The female has an olive-gray crown, nape, and ear patch; the eyestripe, throat, and upper breast have a dingy yellowish wash. Its plumage is duller in fall; young males resemble females.

VOICE: Its song is a whistled, titmouse-like series of phrases: *peter-peter-peter*. Its call is a down-slurred *kew*.

NESTING: Lays 3 or 4 grayish-white or bluish eggs heavily speckled with black in a neat cup of fine rootlets, grass, moss, and lichens, placed high in a conifer near the end of a horizontal branch.

HABITAT: High-altitude pine and subalpine fir belts in mountains.

RANGE: Breeds in central and southeastern Arizona and southwestern New Mexico. it winters mainly south of U.S.-Mexico border.

SIMILAR SPECIES: Except for immature Hermit and Pine warblers, other similar warblers have streaking above or below and lack the long, tapering, decurved bill and large, flat head.

Pine Warbler lacks bold edgings to the flight feathers; it is not recorded within the range of Olive Warbler in the United States.

Immature Hermit Warbler is smaller, with a shorter, straighter bill and a greener back. It usually shows streaking around the throat and upper sides, and its call note is different. The dark area behind the eye is lighter and smaller; the yellow coloration is duller when present.

CONSERVATION: LC
Common in Mexico, the Olive Warbler is uncommon in the U.S., where its range is limited. The species is declining slightly, vulnerable to habitat loss from deforestation.

SUMMER ■ MIGRATION
WINTER ■ RARE
RESIDENT

Now ubiquitous throughout most of North America, this Eurasian native was first released in New York City in 1851. These birds found an unoccupied niche—the many towns and farms of the settled parts of the country—and quickly multiplied. Because House Sparrows compete aggressively for food and nest sites, some native species have suffered. Within a short time after their introduction, these sparrows adapted to the local environment. Thus the sparrows of the rainy climate of Vancouver, British Columbia, are plump, dark birds, whereas those inhabiting Death Valley, California, are slim, pale, sand-colored birds. These changes took less than 60 years, and influence our ideas about the speed of evolutionary change in birds.

DESCRIPTION: 5–6½" (13–17 cm). The male has a black throat, white cheeks, and a chestnut nape; it has a gray crown and rump. Females and immatures are streaked dull brown above and dingy white below, with a pale eyebrow.

VOICE: Shrill, monotonous, noisy chirping.

NESTING: Lays 5 or 6 white eggs lightly speckled with brown in a loose mass of grass, feathers, strips of paper, string, and similar debris placed in a man-made or natural cavity. It may raise two or three broods in a season. It sometimes builds a globular nest in a tree.

HABITAT: Cities, towns, and agricultural areas.

RANGE: Introduced and resident throughout temperate North America. It is native to Eurasia and North Africa, and introduced on every continent except Antarctica, as well as on many islands.

SIMILAR SPECIES: The male is distinctive and could only be confused at first glance. Plain females and young could be confused with several of the "plain" western sparrows, but habits, habitats, and voice separate true western sparrows from this Old World sparrow.

See Eurasian Tree Sparrow and Dickcissel.

CONVERVATION: House Sparrows are abundant in populated areas across North America. Their numbers in North America likely peaked around 1900 and have been gradually declining since, but they remain one of the most abundant birds on the planet. They are highly aggressive, fiercely competing with native birds for food and nest sites, especially cavity nests.

■ SUMMER ■ MIGRATION
■ WINTER ■ RARE
■ RESIDENT

This introduced species differs from its relative, the House Sparrow, in that the sexes are alike. It is much less aggressive and quarrelsome, and it is more gregarious, often assembling in larger flocks. Altogether, the Eurasian Tree Sparrow is a more attractive bird, both in appearance and behavior. These birds sometimes visit grainfields and feed on corn, oats, and wheat, but they also consume many injurious weed seeds and, to a lesser extent, insects.

DESCRIPTION: 6" (15 cm). This sparrow is streaked brown above and dull white below. It has a chocolate brown crown, a black throat, and a white cheek with a prominent black spot. Both sexes are alike. It is smaller and thinner than a House Sparrow.

VOICE: Loud chirping, similar to that of House Sparrow.

NESTING: Lays 5 brown-spotted, buff eggs in a tree cavity, bird box, or hole in a wall.

HABITAT: City parks, suburban areas, and farmland.

RANGE: Introduced around St. Louis, Missouri, in 1870. The population in North America is nonmigratory and resides in an area that includes eastern Missouri, western Illinois, and southeastern Iowa. Native to Europe and much of Asia.

SIMILAR SPECIES: Male House Sparrow is similar, but has a gray crown and lacks a black spot on cheek.

CONSERVATION:

The Eurasian Tree Sparrow population in North America is small, all descending from the original 12 birds released in 1870, and its numbers appear stable. The species is still numerous but declining in its native range across Eurasia.

EASTERN YELLOW WAGTAIL *Motacilla tschutschensis*

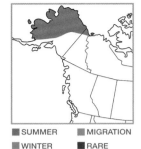

■ SUMMER ■ MIGRATION
■ WINTER ■ RARE
■ RESIDENT

Although its range in North America is limited, the Yellow Wagtail is easy to locate during its short Arctic breeding season. When a ground predator or a human appears, several males gather, fly up, and circle the intruder.

DESCRIPTION: 6½" (17 cm). The tail of this small bird makes up half its total length. The adult is olive-gray above and bright yellow below. It has a white eyestripe, wing bars, and outer tail feathers, which seem to flash in flight. Immatures are olive-gray above, with buff underparts and eyestripe, and a dusky throat collar. This species bobs its tail constantly.

VOICE: This bird rarely sings, but often utters a call: *tsweep*. Its alarm note sounds like *ple-ple-ple*.

NESTING: Lays 4–7 buff or greenish eggs, heavily mottled and spotted, usually hidden in a sheltered place on the ground.

HABITAT: Willow tundra.

RANGE: Breeds in northern and western Alaska and the Aleutians. Winters in the Old World.

SIMILAR SPECIES: See American Pipit.

CONSERVATION:

The Eastern Yellow Wagtail population appears to be stable.

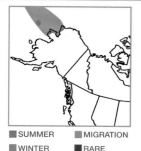

- ■ SUMMER
- ■ WINTER
- ■ RESIDENT
- ■ MIGRATION
- ■ RARE

White Wagtail is a lively ground bird that bobs its head in dove-like fashion and walks rather than hops. It flies in uneven arcs, calling as it flies. This shy, slender bird of open habitats near water reaches North America only in coastal western Alaska, where it is a rare annual breeder. Except when breeding, it is quite social.

DESCRIPTION: 7" (18 cm). This is a slim, small-bodied bird with a long, slender tail that wags constantly and is half its total length. In summer, it has a black crown, nape, and extensive bib; a white face and underparts; and a black back, wings, and tail, with a large white wing patch and white outer tail feathers. In fall, the adult's black areas mute to grays. Immatures have an olive-gray head and back, with a dark throat band and white eyestripe, underparts, wing bars, and outer tail feathers.

VOICE: Its call, constantly uttered in flight, is a two-tone *tschiz-zik* or *tzilip*. Its warning call is *zipp*.

NESTING: Lays 5 or 6 grayish-white eggs finely speckled with blackish-brown, especially around the larger end, in a nest of grasses, rootlets, and leaves. The nest is placed near or on the ground in an earthen bank, rock crevice, stone wall, or niche of an old building.

HABITAT: Open country with short vegetation; frequently found near water—streamsides, riverbanks and seacoasts. Also seen near towns and villages.

RANGE: Breeds in western Alaska and on neighboring islands. Winters in Old World. Casual strays can occur along both coasts

SUBSPECIES: "Black-backed Wagtail" (*M. a. lugens*), formerly considered a separate species, is an annual visitor to Attu in spring, where it has bred several times. It is also known to visit the coast of the Alaskan mainland on a more or less regular basis (has bred on the mainland once), and has even been seen as far south as California. The male Black-backed Wagtail has a jet-black back, a black stripe through the eye, and a black throat patch that touches the black on the back. Other similar wagtails do not have all three of these characteristics. Accidental strays on the Atlantic Coast may be the nominate subspecies *alba*, which breeds in Greenland and Iceland.

SIMILAR SPECIES: Snow Bunting has a much thicker bill and lacks the distinctive black bib.

CONSERVATION: Widespread and abundant in the Old World, the White Wagtail population is stable. The population in Alaska is small but stable.

OLIVE-BACKED PIPIT *Anthus hodgsoni*

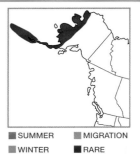

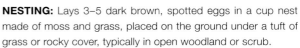

This shy Eurasian species has reached Alaska's Bering Sea islands and Aleutian Islands and even California and Nevada during migration. Unlike other American pipits, it readily perches in bushes and trees and when flushed often flies to a perch or flies off some distance.

DESCRIPTION: 6" (15 cm) with an average wingspan of 10" (25 cm). This bird has finely streaked, olive-green upperparts and white underparts. It has a white spot and a black spot at the rear of the auriculars. It has a distinct buffy loral spot, and its white supercilium has a black upper border.

VOICE: Its call, often given when flushed, is a high, rough *speez*, much lower than Red-throated Pipit.

NESTING: Lays 3–5 dark brown, spotted eggs in a cup nest made of moss and grass, placed on the ground under a tuft of grass or rocky cover, typically in open woodland or scrub.

HABITAT: Open country, woodlands, and scrub.

RANGE: This Asian species occurs as a rare migrant in western Alaska, mostly in the outer Aleutian Islands. It has occurred as an accidental stray to Nevada and California.

SIMILAR SPECIES: See American Pipit.

CONSERVATION: The Olive-backed Pipit population is considered stable in its native range.

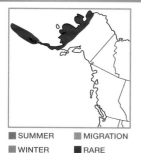

■ SUMMER ■ MIGRATION
■ WINTER ■ RARE
■ RESIDENT

Pechora Pipit, which breeds in Siberia and winters in Southeast Asia, has been recorded in North America only rarely on western Alaskan islands, mostly in the fall. Pechora Pipit skulks mouse-like through low vegetation.

DESCRIPTION: 5½" (14 cm) with an average wingspan of 9½" (24 cm). This bird is heavily streaked with dark brown upper-parts. Its breast, sides, and flanks are washed yellow with heavy black streaks. Primaries visible beyond tertials (unlike Red-throated Pipit). Unlike in similar pipits, the bold, streaked pattern on the back extends onto this bird's nape.

VOICE: Call a short, wiry *tdzip*, seldom heard, even from flushed birds.

NESTING: Lays 4–5 eggs in a ground nest.

HABITAT: Damp tundra, open forests, and marshlands.

RANGE: Widespread in northern and eastern Asia.

SIMILAR SPECIES: See American Pipit. Red-throated Pipit of western Alaska has an unpatterned nape; breeding males have a distinctive pinkish-red head and throat.

CONVERSATION:
Pechora Pipit's numbers are stable in their native range.

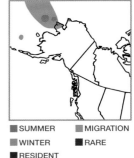

■ SUMMER ■ MIGRATION
■ WINTER ■ RARE
■ RESIDENT

The Red-throated Pipit is found on short tundra in the breeding season; during winter and migration it inhabits damp grassy areas near marshes and in river valleys. It sings from an elevated perch or while in flight and pumps its tail occasionally.

DESCRIPTION: 6" (15 cm). This sparrow-sized bird is a slim, long-legged ground bird with an erect stance. It is light brown above, with dark streaking on the mantle and indistinct white wing bars. In winter, it is buff-white below and heavily streaked on the sides of the neck and breast, extending to the flanks. In summer, its face, throat, and breast are washed with wine-red or pink.

VOICE: Its call is a sharp *seeep*, or *see-eep*.

NESTING: Lays 5–7 bluish eggs spotted with brown in a grass nest lined with fine material, on the ground sheltered by a tussock.

HABITAT: Shrubby tundra or open areas of forest tundra; in winter, it uses fallow agricultural fields, meadows, or beaches.

RANGE: Breeds in western Alaska and throughout northern Eurasia. It winters in the Old World, but a few turn up along the Pacific Coast in fall and winter.

SIMILAR SPECIES: See American Pipit.

CONSERVATION:
The Red-throated Pipit is numerous in the Old World, and its population is thought to be stable.

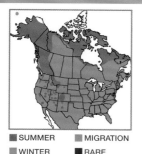

SUMMER   MIGRATION
WINTER   RARE
RESIDENT

In winter and migration, American Pipit inhabits shores and fields with little or no vegetation; during the breeding season it is found on tundra. It walks in the open, often pumping its tail down and up; it almost never perches in trees. It is normally found in pairs or in winter flocks. In the North the American Pipit feeds on the countless insects on the edges of tundra puddles. Insects and their larvae make up most of this pipit's diet; migrants in marine areas may also take marine worms and small crustaceans. Inland in fall and winter, it also eats the seeds of grasses and weeds. The American Pipit was formerly considered a form of the Water Pipit of the Old World.

DESCRIPTION: 6–7" (15–18 cm). A sparrow-sized, slender brown bird of open country. Its crown and upperparts are uniform brown; its underparts are buff with streaks. Its outer tail feathers are white and its legs are usually black. It often bobs its tail and usually walks rather than hops.

VOICE: Its flight song is a weak and tinkling trill. Its call is a paired, high-pitched *pip-pip*.

NESTING: Lays 4 or 5 gray eggs, thickly spotted with brown and streaked with black, in a cup of grass and twigs built on the ground in the shelter of a rock or tussock.

HABITAT: Arctic and alpine tundra; during migration and winter, it may be found on beaches, barren fields, agricultural land, and golf courses.

RANGE: Breeds from northern Alaska, Mackenzie, the Canadian Arctic islands, and Newfoundland, south in the mountains to California, New Mexico, and northern New Hampshire on Mount Washington. It winters across the southern United States and north to British Columbia and southern New England.

SUBSPECIES: Breeders in the Rocky Mountains (subsp. *alticola*) are paler, buffy and unstreaked below. Arctic breeders (subsp. *rubescens*) are darker and more heavily streaked. Asian birds (subsp. *japonica*) are rare but regular in western Alaska and casual in fall to California; these birds are boldly streaked below, with pale legs.

SIMILAR SPECIES: Sprague's Pipit has a streaked back and yellow legs, and seldom bobs its tail.

CONSERVATION: American Pipit is still common, but it is declining. It is vulnerable to changes in wetlands used in migration and winter, and in the Arctic and alpine habitats it uses for breeding. These habitats are all affected by development, deforestation, and climate change.

SPRAGUE'S PIPIT *Anthus spragueii*

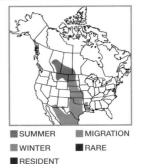

■ SUMMER   ■ MIGRATION
■ WINTER   ■ RARE
■ RESIDENT

Sprague's Pipit is an uncommon and inconspicuous bird, more secretive and solitary than the American Pipit. It does not run in the open when disturbed but tries to hide in dense grass; when flushed, it flies low for a short distance and then drops down. It is usually seen on its breeding grounds in the northern Great Plains, where the males put on a display that involves delivering its lovely, descending flight song while hovering high in the air, often for several minutes. John James Audubon named this species for Isaac Sprague (1811–1895), an artist who accompanied him on his trip up the Missouri River.

DESCRIPTION: 6¼–7" (16–18 cm). This sparrow-sized pipit is a slender-billed, streaked bird with white outer tail feathers and yellow legs. The adult's upperparts are heavily streaked overall with blackish and buff to buff-brown. It has a "necklace" of fine streaks on the upper breast and two white wing bars. It rarely bobs its tail. Juveniles resemble adults, but the back is black with narrow buff streaks and fine white scales.

VOICE: Its flight song, performed high in the air, is a descending series of tinkling double notes. Its call is a series of sharp *pips*.

NESTING: Lays 4 or 5 gray eggs spotted with purple and brown in a cup of grass, concealed in a tussock on the ground, and usually covered by an arch of bent grass stems.

HABITAT: Short-grass plains and plowed fields.

RANGE: Breeds from Alberta and Manitoba south to Minnesota and Montana. It winters from the southern Great Plains east to the Mississippi and in the Southwest.

SIMILAR SPECIES: American Pipit is similar, but has darker legs and an unstreaked back; it constantly bobs its tail.

CONSERVATION: VU
Sprague's Pipit numbers are vulnerable and decreasing. These birds have disappeared as breeders from large sections of northern Canada as prairie has been converted for agriculture. Conservation of native grasslands and replanting of grasslands with native species will help to protect this species.

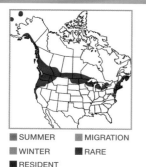

SUMMER ■ MIGRATION
WINTER ■ RARE
RESIDENT

Fairly common in Eurasia, especially during irruptive periods, Brambling is a rare vagrant in North America. Migrant flocks as large as 50 individuals are sometimes observed in the western Aleutians, but scattered individuals are more typical. Wanderers may appear at bird feeders.

DESCRIPTION: 5¾–6" (14.5–15.5 cm). The breeding male has a black head and back, a tawny-orange breast and shoulders, spotted flanks, and a white belly; in fresh fall plumage, the head, back, and chest are flecked with buff. Juveniles and females have a plain gray face, a mottled crown, a striped nape, and tawny shoulders and breast.

VOICE: An extended, wheezy song; it also makes a nasal flight call: *sweep*.

NESTING: Lays 5–7 greenish or brownish eggs with dark brown spots, in a woven cup nest of grasses and fibers trimmed with lichens or bark and lined with hair or feathers. Nests in northern Eurasian forests and arctic scrub; there are no North American breeding records.

HABITAT: Taiga in summer, especially northern birch forests. Outside of the breeding season, it flocks in agricultural fields and woodlands (especially beech), where it feeds on grain and nut mast; it is also found in parks and gardens.

RANGE: A Eurasian species, fairly common but irregular as a migrant in the Bering Sea region, including the Aleutians; it is casual in fall and winter in southern Alaska; accidental south to Canada and the northwestern U.S.

SIMILAR SPECIES: Black-headed Grosbeak has a much larger bill and a different pattern on the face and wings.

CONSERVATION:
Brambling is widespread and common in Eurasia; its numbers are declining slightly.

EVENING GROSBEAK *Coccothraustes vespertinus*

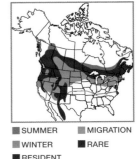

■ SUMMER ■ MIGRATION
■ WINTER ■ RARE
■ RESIDENT

This grosbeak formerly bred no farther east than Minnesota, but expanded its range eastward in the late 19th and early 20th century, only for the eastern population to decline again in recent decades. Like most of the northern finches, however, these birds are more numerous in some years than in others. In winter they feed in flocks, mainly on the seeds of box elder or on sunflower seeds at bird feeders. In spring the outer coating of the bill peels off, exposing the blue-green color beneath.

DESCRIPTION: 7½–8½" (19–22 cm). A starling-sized, stocky finch with a large, pale greenish or yellowish conical bill. The male has a brown head shading to yellow on the lower back, rump, and underparts. It has a bright yellow forehead and eyebrow, and bold white wing patches. The female is similar but grayer.

VOICE: Its song is a series of short, musical whistles. Its call note is similar to the chirp of the House Sparrow but louder and more ringing.

NESTING: Lays 3 or 4 pale blue-green eggs, lightly speckled with dark brown, gray, and olive, in a shallow, loose cup of twigs lined with rootlets and placed in a conifer.

HABITAT: Nests in coniferous forests; it visits deciduous woodlands and suburban areas in winter.

RANGE: Breeds from British Columbia east to Nova Scotia and south to northern New England, Minnesota, Mexico (in the mountains), and California. It winters south to southern California, Texas, and South Carolina.

SUBSPECIES: Regional vocal variations exist between eastern populations (east of the Rocky Mountains), a complex of western types, and the Mexican populations found in southeastern Arizona.

SIMILAR SPECIES: American Goldfinch is much smaller, with a tiny bill and no white wing patches.

CONGCONSERVATION:
Evening Grosbeaks are widespread and numerous, but their populations are in serious decline, especially in the East. The reasons for this decline are not fully known, although deforestation due to development is one possible factor, as is insecticide use to control spruce budworms and other forest insects that these birds eat. Outbreaks of diseases such as salmonella, West Nile virus, and House Finch eye disease may also factor into their reduced numbers.

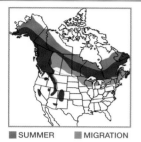

■ SUMMER ■ MIGRATION
■ WINTER ■ RARE
■ RESIDENT

The largest of the northern finches, Pine Grosbeak is less common than Pine Siskin or the redpolls. When these birds appear, their preference for the seeds and fruit of trees such as mountain ash and cedar makes them more conspicuous than their smaller relatives. They are slow moving and slow to flush, often sitting motionless in the presence of a human observer. During snowy winters these grosbeaks can be located in scattered open forests by the feeble calls that keep the flock together. They settle in a tree and feed, snapping off buds or seeking the pits in fruit, until sated or disturbed. When food is scarce, they may descend from the mountains into woods at sea level.

DESCRIPTION: 8–10" (20–25 cm). A large, plump finch with a stubby, strongly curved black bill. The male has a dull rose-red body, with dark streaking on the back, dark wings with two white wing bars, and a dusky, notched tail. A juvenile male is dull pinkish red on the head and rump, with a gray body. Females are similar to first-year males in pattern, mostly gray overall with a dull mustard-yellow head and rump.

VOICE: Quiet, low calls: *pui pui pui*. Its flight calls vary geographically: Taiga populations give a three-note whistle similar to that of Greater Yellowlegs, Pacific and Interior West populations give more complex, harsher notes that resemble a Western Tanager.

NESTING: Lays 2–5 pale blue-green, blotched eggs in a bulky nest of grasses, rootlets, and moss lined with hair; its nest is placed low in a coniferous tree, usually no more than about 10–12' (3–4 m) from the ground.

HABITAT: Coniferous forests.

RANGE: Breeds from Alaska east to Newfoundland and Nova Scotia, and south in the western mountains to California and Arizona. It winters south to the Dakotas and New York, and occasionally farther. Also found in Eurasia.

SUBSPECIES: Voice, size, and male plumage has some regional variation. Pacific males are darker with extensive red on the underparts; Interior West males are duller red with much more gray on the breast; Taiga populations show an intermediate amount of pinkish-red on the underparts.

SIMILAR SPECIES: Male White-winged Crossbill is also bright pinkish with dark wings and white wing bars, but it is smaller and has a distinctive bill shape.

Bohemian Waxwing (also found in flocks in mountain ash) has a different shape, with a crest and a thinner bill; it has a shorter, yellow-tipped tail.

The bill of Pine Grosbeak is stubbier than that of any other winter finch.

CONSERVATION: LC
Pine Grosbeaks are widespread and common, but their vast, far-northern breeding range is difficult to survey accurately. Their numbers are believed to be decreasing based on estimates by the North American Breeding Bird Survey and by the results of recent Christmas Bird Counts.

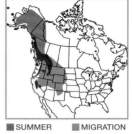

■ SUMMER ■ MIGRATION
■ WINTER ■ RARE
■ RESIDENT

This species feeds mainly on minute alpine plant seeds and insects wind-borne from lower elevations. The Gray-crowned Rosy-Finch is found farther to the west than the similar Brown-capped Rosy-Finch and Black Rosy-Finch, and is the most widespread of these related species. The ancestors of the rosy-finches came from Asia. The mosaic distribution of rosy-finch forms in the West may result from the splitting of one population during glacial periods, or from multiple prehistoric invasions from Asia.

DESCRIPTION: 5¾–6¾" (15–17 cm). These birds have a dark brown back and underparts, a black forehead, and a gray nape and crown. The shoulders, flanks, and rump are washed with pink. The face is gray in coastal birds and brown in interior populations. Females are similar but paler.

VOICE: Flying flocks give harsh *cheep, cheep* notes.

NESTING: Lays 3–5 white eggs in a bulky nest placed in a rock cavity.

HABITAT: Alpine tundra and high snowfields; it winters in nearby lowlands.

RANGE: Breeds from Alaska to California. It descends to lower elevations near breeding areas in winter.

SUBSPECIES: Three distinct populations of this species differ in head pattern, size, and body color. Birds that are resident on the islands around the Bering Sea (subspp. *umbrina* and *griseonucha*) average larger than other populations, are darker chocolate brown on the breast, and show more gray on the face.

Coastal birds (subsp. *littoralis*), sometimes called "Hepburn's Rosy-Finch" or "Gray-cheeked Rosy-Finch," also show extensive gray on the face but are a warm cinnamon brown on the breast.

Birds that breed in the Rocky Mountains and interior ranges from Alaska to Montana (subsp. *tephrocotis*), or "Gray-crowned Rosy-Finch," have a well defined gray crown and brown on the face.

SIMILAR SPECIES: Similar to the other rosy-finches, Black Rosy-Finch and Brown-capped Rosy-Finch; all three were once considered a single species called "Rosy Finch."

CONSERVATION: LC
Gray-crowned Rosy-Finch is fairly common locally in appropriate habitat, and its numbers are stable. Most of its breeding range is remote from human disturbance.

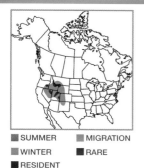

■ SUMMER   ■ MIGRATION
■ WINTER   ■ RARE
■ RESIDENT

These uncommon birds reside in the high mountains of the northern Great Basin. In winter, when mixed flocks of rosy-finches roam the highlands of the Great Basin, Blacks and Gray-crowns are seen roosting together in caves or abandoned mine shafts, in barns, or under bridges.

DESCRIPTION: 5½–6½" (14–17 cm). The male is dark blackish-brown with a conspicuous gray cap, black forehead, and much pink on the belly, rump, wings, and tail. The female is browner, showing some pink, and may not have a gray cap. In both sexes, the bill is black during breeding season and yellowish outside of the breeding season.

VOICE: A variety of low *cheep* notes are used in various situations: as a contact call in flight and in proclaiming an occupied nesting territory.

NESTING: Lays 3–5 white eggs in a cup nest placed in a hole in a vertical cliff.

HABITAT: Alpine tundra and meadows; winters in nearby lowlands.

RANGE: Breeds in the Rocky Mountains of southwestern Montana, Idaho, Wyoming, northeastern Nevada, and northern Utah. It winters south to northern Arizona and New Mexico.

SIMILAR SPECIES: See Gray-crowned Rosy-Finch; hybrid Gray-crowned x Black Rosy-Finches occur in a few locations along the border of Idaho and Montana.

CONSERVATION:

Black Rosy-Finch is uncommon and local, and its numbers are declining. This bird has a small population of perhaps 15,000 individuals, and inhabits only a limited range. Its mountaintop habitats are especially vulnerable to the effects of climate change; this species may lose its entire habitat as warmer temperatures reach higher elevations and reshape alpine tundra ecosystems.

BROWN-CAPPED ROSY-FINCH *Leucosticte australis*

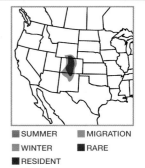

■ SUMMER ■ MIGRATION
■ WINTER ■ RARE
■ RESIDENT

Winter flocks are noisy with the sound of twittering; upon alighting, these finches hop over the ground looking for seeds. These birds of inaccessible high mountains are largely unwary of humans. When they move to lower elevations in winter, closer to populated areas, they will come to bird feeders.

DESCRIPTION: 5¾–6½" (15–17 cm). These birds are mostly light brown, without the gray crown patch of the closely related Gray-crowned Rosy-Finch and Black Rosy-Finch. The male's rump, wings, and belly are extensively pinkish-rose. The female is chiefly brown. Both sexes have blackish bills during the breeding season and yellow bills outside of the breeding season.

VOICE: A series of low *cheep* notes are uttered to maintain contact in the flock. In the mating season the male gives a similar song during a long, circular, undulating flight.

NESTING: Lays 3–5 white eggs in a cup nest in a rock crevice or on a hidden, covered ledge.

HABITAT: Alpine tundra and meadows; it winters in nearby lowlands.

RANGE: Resident in the southern Rocky Mountains from southeastern Wyoming to northern New Mexico. It descends to lower elevations near the breeding areas in winter.

SIMILAR SPECIES: See Gray-crowned Rosy-Finch and Black Rosy-Finch.

CONSERVATION: EN
Brown-capped Rosy-Finch is uncommon and local, and its numbers are declining. This bird has a small population and inhabits an extremely limited range at high elevations in the southern Rocky Mountains. These high alpine tundra habitats are especially vulnerable to the effects of climate change, and may disappear entirely as warmer temperatures reach higher elevations.

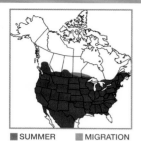

■ SUMMER   ■ MIGRATION
■ WINTER   ■ RARE
■ RESIDENT

The House Finch is abundant in areas inhabited by humans and is often one of the most common birds in suburban areas of the West. In 1940, pet store owners released a small number of captive House Finches after illegally attempting to sell "Hollywood Finches" as cage birds; these birds quickly became established and have spread throughout the East. House Finches are omnivorous, gleaning insect pests and, in winter, grass and weed seeds; it feeds from the treetops to the ground but avoids heavy undergrowth and tall grass. It is highly gregarious; a flock of 25 or more House Finches perched in the top of a cottonwood is a characteristic sight. At feeding stations, the House Finch lands hesitatingly, jerking its tail, and departs twittering. Its musical song and bright colors add a cheerful touch to many a backyard.

DESCRIPTION: 5–6" (13–15 cm). A sparrow-sized finch, most adult males are bright red on the crown, breast, and rump, but less extensively so than male Cassin's and Purple finches. The female has a plain, unstriped head and heavy streaking on a light gray-brown underside. Immature males are less highly colored and are often orangish or yellowish on the head and breast.

VOICE: Makes a *chirp* call like that of a young House Sparrow. Its song is an extensive series of warbling notes ending in a *zeee*, canary-like but without the musical trills and rolls. It sings from a high tree, antenna, or similar post for prolonged periods.

NESTING: Lays 3–5 bluish, lightly streaked or spotted eggs, with each pair breeding 2–4 times per summer; it builds a tightly woven, compact nest in a bush, thicket, natural cavity, or on a building.

HABITAT: In the East, it thrives in cities and residential areas; in the West, it inhabits chaparral, deserts, and orchards, as well as coastal valleys that were formerly forested with redwood, cedar, or Douglas fir but have now become suburban.

RANGE: Resident throughout the West, from southern Canada to southern Mexico, and east to Nebraska. Introduced and now widespread in eastern North America.

SIMILAR SPECIES: See Purple and Cassin's finches, Pine Siskin, and Common Redpoll.

CONSERVATION:
House Finch is abundant and increasing. They may compete with Purple Finches in the East. House Finches suffered a steep decline beginning in the mid-1990s with an outbreak of mycoplasmal conjunctivitis, also called House Finch eye disease, which causes their eyes to swell shut and also produces respiratory problems; this bacterial infection spreads locally from bird to bird through feeding stations, and hit the eastern population especially hard.

PURPLE FINCH *Haemorhous purpureus*

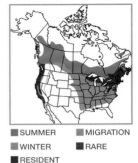

■ SUMMER　■ MIGRATION
■ WINTER　■ RARE
■ RESIDENT

Purple Finches are numerous and conspicuous during spring migration; pairs are territorial, the brightly colored male displaying in front of the female with a rich, spirited, warbling song. After the clutch is raised, they may be seen in large flocks visiting orchards, parks, and other woodlands. In winter they visit feeding stations in large numbers, showing a fondness for sunflower seeds.

DESCRIPTION: 5½–6½" (14–17 cm). This finch is larger and stockier than a House Finch but smaller than a Cassin's, and darker than both. The dusky rose-red of the male—more raspberry than purple—extends from the upperparts to the breast and flanks, and is brightest at the crown and rump. It is off-white below, its mantle is streaked with brown, and its wings and notched tail are brown. The female has a pronounced light stripe behind the eye, a dark stripe on the jaw, and a more heavily streaked breast than female House or Cassin's finches.

VOICE: A rich, musical warble. Its call is a distinctive *tick* given in flight.

NESTING: Lays 4 or 5 blue-green eggs spotted at the larger end with dark brown in a well-made cup of grasses and twigs, often lined with hair, placed in a conifer.

HABITAT: Mixed and coniferous woodlands, and ornamental conifers in gardens.

RANGE: Breeds from British Columbia east to Newfoundland, southward in the western mountains to California, and from eastern Minnesota east to West Virginia. It winters south to the U.S.-Mexico border.

SUBSPECIES: In the Pacific population (subsp. *californicus*), the underparts of the males are washed with dingy brown and the rump is dark red; females are greenish above and are washed with yellowish below with blurry streaks. In the Eastern population (subsp. *purpureus*) the males are brighter than Pacific males; the females are more brownish above and whiter below with shorter and darker streaks.

SIMILAR SPECIES: A male Cassin's Finch has much greater contrast between its red crown and brown nape or back, which have only a trace of reddish color; the throat and breast of a male Cassin's also appear paler and rosier. A female Cassin's Finch lacks strongly contrasting cheeks and mustache; it has narrower, sharper breast streaks; is pure whitish below without buff-yellowish tone; and its undertail coverts are almost always streaked. In both sexes of Purple Finch, overall body size is smaller than that of Cassin's Finch; its bill is shorter and stubbier-looking, and its flight calls are different.

Also see House Finch and Pine Siskin.

CONSERVATION:
Purple Finches are uncommon and their numbers are declining slightly, especially in the Northeast where they face competition with an increasing population of introduced House Finches.

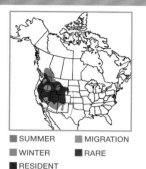

SUMMER ■ MIGRATION
WINTER ■ RARE
RESIDENT

The closely related Cassin's, House, and Purple finches are each found in different altitudes and habitats; thus there is no competition among them. Cassin's Finch is found in montane, coniferous forests of the West that are higher and drier than those favored by the Purple Finch. This species' behavior is similar to that of the Purple Finch, but Cassin's is much more restricted to conifers, primarily pines. The shiny, red crown of the male Cassin's Finch is often slightly elevated, making the bird appear to have a short crest.

DESCRIPTION: 6–6½" (15–17 cm). Cassin's Finch is larger than both House and Purple finches. The male's breast coloration is paler rose-red than that of Purple Finch. Its brown-streaked nape and mantle make its rosy crown and rump appear more brilliant. It has unstreaked flanks and a pale pink to whitish belly. The female resembles a female Purple Finch but is more finely streaked above and below, with a less distinct eyeline and malar stripe.

VOICE: Its song is a series of warbles, similar to the Purple Finch's but flutier and more varied. Its call note, a high *pwee-de-lip*, is diagnostic.

NESTING: Lays 4 or 5 bluish-green eggs with dark brownish spots in a cup nest of twigs and rootlets, in a conifer.

HABITAT: Open conifer stands at high elevations.

RANGE: Breeds from southwestern Canada south to southern California, Arizona, and New Mexico. It visits lowlands during winter.

SIMILAR SPECIES: See Purple Finch, House Finch, and Pine Siskin. House Finch is smaller and slimmer; the male is redder with a brown-streaked belly. Female House, Purple, and Cassin's finches differ from streaked sparrows in being less conspicuously marked on the face and back; they are less terrestrial and have richer, more variable call notes; their flight is slower and more undulating.

CONSERVATION: NT
Cassin's Finch is common but declining for reasons that are poorly understood. The species seems to prefer open forest habitat, so selective logging and small-scale forest clearing do not seem to affect this species as severely as they do many other songbirds. More study is needed to determine the cause of this species' declines.

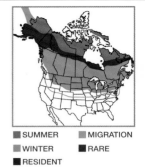

■ SUMMER ■ MIGRATION
■ WINTER ■ RARE
■ RESIDENT

These are lively birds, extremely social and constantly moving; even when resting at night, members of the flock fidget and twitter. A stand of winter weeds visited by a flock is a scene of feverish activity as they tear dried flower stalks apart and rush to the ground to pick up the seeds. During the long Arctic night, redpolls sleep in snow tunnels to keep warm. They are able to hang upside down like chickadees and pry the birch seed from hanging catkins. They are somewhat nomadic; where the birch supply is good, they settle in numbers, but they may move away with their fledglings and attempt a second brood elsewhere if they find another area with ample food supply.

DESCRIPTION: 5–5½" (13–14 cm). Smaller than a sparrow, these active winter finches are pale and brown-streaked, with bright red cap and black chin. The male has a pink breast, with the pink often extending down the flanks and onto the rump. Females and juveniles are more heavily streaked.

VOICE: A twittering trill; its call is a soft rattle.

NESTING: Lays 4–6 pale green eggs, spotted with red-brown, in a well-made cup of grass, moss, and twigs lined with plant down and placed in a low willow or birch.

HABITAT: Tundra and dwarf arctic birch in summer; brushy pastures, open thickets, and weedy fields in winter.

RANGE: Breeds from Alaska and northern Quebec south to British Columbia, Newfoundland, and Magdalen Islands. Winters irregularly south to California, Oklahoma, and the Carolinas. Also found in Eurasia.

SUBSPECIES: Greenland (or Greater) Redpoll (*A. f. rostrata*) is a larger, darker, heavier-billed subspecies with an extensive black throat that breeds on Baffin Island and Greenland; it is rare farther south in winter.

SIMILAR SPECIES: Hoary Redpoll is essentially identical. Paler Common Redpolls look much like Hoary Redpolls and may be impossible to distinguish in the field. Commons tend to look frostier when perched in a tree and seen from below, but on the ground they appear distinctly darker. Male Commons often look frostier than females, but a bird with extensive pink on the breast is nevertheless a Common, since male Hoaries normally have only a pale pinkish cast to the breast.

House Finch may be unfamiliar to beginning birders in the East; it has been misidentified as Common Redpoll. In the West, see also Cassin's Finch, which has similar red cap.

CONSERVATION: LC
Common Redpoll is common across the Northern Hemisphere but decreasing globally. It is nomadic and its numbers vary from year to year.

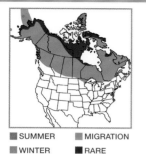

■ SUMMER ■ MIGRATION
■ WINTER ■ RARE
■ RESIDENT

The Hoary Redpoll generally breeds and winters farther north and on more open tundra than the related Common Redpoll, only occasionally reaching the northern United States. In areas where their ranges overlap in parts of Canada and Alaska, Hoary tends to nest on the more barren upland tundra. In winter flocks it often mingles with Common Redpolls; when seen together, Hoary Redpolls appear in small numbers as the paler, "frostier" birds in the group. This species is known as Arctic Redpoll in Europe.

DESCRIPTION: 4½–5½" (11–14 cm). Smaller than a sparrow, these birds are extremely similar to the Common Redpoll but slightly paler, with a smaller bill and an unstreaked rump and undertail coverts.

VOICE: A series of metallic *chips* given in flight; it gives soft twittering calls when feeding on the ground. Its calls are sharper than those of Common Redpoll.

NESTING: Lays 5 or 6 pale blue eggs lightly spotted with brown in a feather-lined cup of grass and shreds of bark, concealed under a rock or a clump of tundra vegetation.

HABITAT: Weedy pastures and roadsides in winter, tundra in summer.

RANGE: Breeds along Arctic coasts, wandering southward in winter to much of Canada and irruptively to the northernmost United States.

SUBSPECIES: The Greenland (or Hornemann's) form (subsp. *hornemanni*) is larger and paler than the more widespread "southern" population (subsp. *exilipes*).

SIMILAR SPECIES: Paler Common Redpolls and darker Hoary Redpolls are not always distinguishable; both have whitish rumps, but Common's is completely or mostly streaked, while Hoary's is at least partly unstreaked. They can be equally frosty above; however, male Common Redpoll has a deeper pink breast. The presence or absence of streaking on the undertail coverts is usually difficult to discern. Darker Hoary Redpolls can be heavily streaked on the sides. The bill of the Hoary Redpoll does not always appear stubbier.

CONSERVATION: 🐦 LC

Due to the extreme remoteness of its breeding habitat, little is known about this species' population size or trends. They are uncommon and irregular in their winter range. Climate change could threaten this bird's high Arctic habitat.

RED CROSSBILL *Loxia curvirostra*

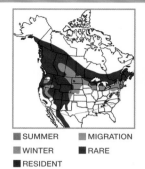

■ SUMMER ■ MIGRATION
■ WINTER ■ RARE
■ RESIDENT

The crossed mandibles of the bill of these unusual birds are specialized for opening pine cones. Holding the cone with one foot, the bird inserts its closed bill between the cone and the scales, pries the scales apart by opening its bill, and extracts the seed with its flexible tongue. Because of its dependence on pine seeds, the Red Crossbill is an erratic and nomadic species, appearing in large numbers, then not appearing for several years. When the cone supply fails, these birds gather in flocks and may wander far from their normal haunts. They may breed almost anywhere, and, because their chosen food is available in winter, they commonly begin nesting as early as January, but have been found nesting in every month of the year.

DESCRIPTION: 5¼–6½" (13–17 cm). This sparrow-sized bird has an unusual bill, with its upper and lower mandibles crossed at the tips. The typical male is dusky brick red but may be darker or paler, or even mostly yellow. The female is gray tinged with dull green, brightest on the rump.

VOICE: Its song is *chipa-chipa-chipa, chee-chee-chee-chee*; it also gives a sharp *kip-kip-kip*.

NESTING: Lays 3 or 4 pale blue-green eggs, lightly spotted with brown, in a shallow saucer of bark strips, grass, and roots lined with moss and plant down, placed near the end of a conifer branch.

HABITAT: Coniferous forests; visits ornamental evergreens in winter.

RANGE: Breeds from southern Alaska, Manitoba, Quebec, and Newfoundland, south in the West to northern Nicaragua, in the eastern United States to Wisconsin and North Carolina (in the mountains). It winters irregularly south to the Gulf Coast. Also found in Eurasia.

SUBSPECIES: A puzzling complex of subspecies can be found throughout North America, most of which wander outside of their core range. Subspecies vary widely in size, vocalizations, and bill size.

SIMILAR SPECIES: White-winged Crossbill has two broad, white wing bars.

Pine Siskin is somewhat similar to immature Red Crossbill, but is smaller and has a thinner bill.

CONSERVATION:
Red Crossbills are uncommon and irregular in most areas, but they are widespread and their numbers appear to be stable. Some subpopulations may be threatened by habitat loss. These birds are attracted to salt and may visit salted roads in winter, where they become vulnerable to vehicle collisions and poisoning from chemicals used to treat icy roads.

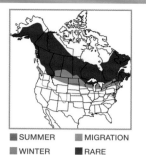

■ SUMMER ■ MIGRATION
■ WINTER ■ RARE
■ RESIDENT

With its smaller, slimmer bill, the White-winged Crossbill is more dependent upon spruce cones than pines, but like the Red Crossbill, it wanders widely and irregularly in search of cones and may breed at any month of the year. In years when seeds are abundant in the northern forests, the birds tend to remain there. When the supply fails they come south in large numbers and may often be seen in quiet flocks, clinging to clusters of cones like little parrots. Their travels sometimes take them far to the south of their breeding range. This species is known as Two-barred Crossbill in Eurasia, named for its pair of prominent, white wing bars.

DESCRIPTION: 6–6½" (15–17 cm). This crossbill is the size of a largish sparrow. Its mandibles are crossed at the tips. The male is raspberry-pink; females are grayer, without pink. Both sexes have two bold white wing bars.

VOICE: Its call resembles that of the Red Crossbill, but is a softer *chiff-chiff-chiff*. Its song is a series of sweet canary-like warbles and trills.

NESTING: Lays 2–4 pale blue eggs spotted with dark brown in a shallow saucer of bark strips, grass, and roots lined with moss and plant down, placed near the end of a conifer branch.

HABITAT: Coniferous forests.

RANGE: Breeds from Alaska and northern Quebec south to Newfoundland and British Columbia. In winter, it occurs south to the Carolinas and Oregon. Also found in Eurasia.

SIMILAR SPECIES: In all plumages, Red Crossbill can be distinguished from White-winged by its lack of wing bars. Red Crossbill's call is harder and flatter, with a downward inflection. Also see Pine Grosbeak.

CONSERVATION:

Although its numbers are difficult to estimate because of its erratic wandering, White-winged Crossbills are believed to be declining. They may be affected by habitat fragmentation and also by shorter rotation cycles for logging, especially of spruce trees, which produce more cones if allowed to mature to about 60 years old.

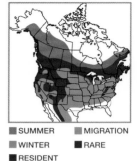

■ SUMMER ■ MIGRATION
■ WINTER ■ RARE
■ RESIDENT

Pine Siskins are small, nondescript, noisy finches whose diagnostic yellow markings can be quite inconspicuous. Like other winter finches, they typically occur in erratic flocks. They prefer feeders and coniferous trees and can be found in a variety of habitats. The Pine Siskin's winter wanderings occur mainly in years when the seed crop has failed in the boreal forests. In some years large flocks may appear as far south as Florida. Their principal foods are the seeds of hemlocks, alders, birches, and cedars. Like most northern finches, they are also fond of salt, and can be found along highways that have been salted to melt snow. They almost always occur in flocks, sometimes alongside goldfinches.

DESCRIPTION: 4½–5" (11–13 cm). The smallest of the winter finches, the Pine Siskin is usually heavily and uniformly streaked with brown. It has diagnostic yellow patches along the base of the flight feathers and on the sides of the base of its notched tail, which are conspicuous in flight but concealed and difficult to see in perched birds. It has a thin, pointed bill. They are usually seen in flocks, which have a distinctive flight pattern: the birds alternately bunch up and then disperse in undulating flight.

VOICE: A distinctive, rising *bzzzzzt*. Its song is like a hoarse goldfinch.

NESTING: Lays 3 or 4 pale green eggs, lightly speckled with dark brown and black, in a shallow saucer of bark, twigs, and moss lined with plant down and feathers and placed in a conifer.

HABITAT: Coniferous and mixed woodlands, alder thickets, and brushy pastures.

RANGE: Breeds from southern Alaska, Mackenzie, Quebec, and Newfoundland south to California, Arizona, New Mexico, Texas, the Great Lakes region, and northern New England. In winter, it wanders southward throughout the United States.

SIMILAR SPECIES: See immature Red Crossbill. It also resembles juvenile redpolls and the female House Finch; these have thicker bills and lack the siskin's yellow wing and tail patches (but these may be concealed and difficult to see).

CONSERVATION:
Pine Siskins are widespread and common, but their numbers and population trends are difficult to determine because of their nomadic movements. Their numbers vary from year to year but are believed to be stable overall. Dense flocks of siskins may be vulnerable to diseases that are transmitted at bird feeders, such as salmonella. Forest fragmentation can leave these birds and their nests more vulnerable to cowbird parasitism and to predation by domestic cats, squirrels, and other birds.

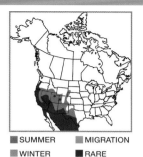

■ SUMMER ■ MIGRATION
■ WINTER ■ RARE
■ RESIDENT

Lesser Goldfinches feed on dandelion seeds and raise their young on soft, unripe seeds. They adjust the time and place of their breeding to the presence of this staple food. At lower elevations, small flocks of Lesser Goldfinches can be found in open, brushy country with scattered trees and weedy stream borders. The flocks remain together when flushed, flying around the grassy ditches or hillsides, then gradually reassembling to feed on dry seeds. Plaintive calls, white wing patches, yellow underparts, and undulating flight distinguish a flock of Lesser Goldfinches. This bird appropriates the songs and calls of other birds; the males sing incessantly all year except during the molt period.

DESCRIPTION: 3½–4" (9–10 cm). Male Lesser Goldfinches occur in two forms: a black-backed form in the southern part of its range, and a green-backed form in the western part. Both forms have a black crown, large white patches on its black wings and tail, and bright yellow underparts. Nonbreeding black-backed males turn greenish, but both races retain a black cap. The female is similar to an American Goldfinch but is smaller, with a dark rump. The immature is similar to the female, but with greener underparts.

VOICE: Its song is a rapid medley of twittering notes. Its calls include a plaintive *tee-yee?* or *cheeo?*

NESTING: Lays 4–5 pale blue eggs in a twiggy nest in a bush or low tree.

HABITAT: Oak savannas, woodlands, suburban gardens.

RANGE: Resident from Washington, Oregon, and northern Nevada east to northern Colorado and Texas, and south to beyond U.S.-Mexico border. Black-backed males are found from northern Colorado southward through Texas and westward to Utah and Arizona. Green-backed birds occur from Utah westward to Columbia River and southward into Mexico.

SUBSPECIES: There are two subspecies of Lesser Goldfinches in North America. Almost all of the population in southern Texas is the black-backed form (subsp. *psaltria*). The frequency of the green-backed form (subsp. *hesperophila*) increases farther north and west; nearly all Lesser Goldfinches west of New Mexico and Colorado are green-backed.

SIMILAR SPECIES: American Goldfinch is not greenish—it is either all bright yellow (spring male) or brownish-yellow—and it lacks the large white wing patches.

CONVERSATION:
Lesser Goldfinch is common and widespread in the West and in tropical America. The species' population increased steadily in the late 20th century as human development created favorable habitat for these birds; they are now declining slightly but still numerous.

LAWRENCE'S GOLDFINCH *Spinus lawrencei*

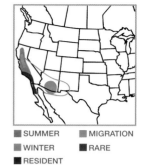

■ SUMMER   ■ MIGRATION
■ WINTER   ■ RARE
■ RESIDENT

Goldfinches are late nesters, waiting until plants and weeds have grown, bloomed, and gone to seed so the soft, fresh seeds can be fed to the young. Lawrence's Goldfinch nests late in May. It breeds erratically; one year many may be found in an area; the next, if the seed crop fails, few may be seen. After breeding, they feed in flocks on the abundant chamise chaparral. They appear even in the driest washes and slopes, as long as they have access to water.

DESCRIPTION: 4–4½" (10–11 cm). The male has a black cap and face; a pale, pink bill; a gray nape, cheek, and mantle; a yellow breast, lower back, and rump; and white undersides and belly. The female lacks black facial markings. Both sexes have dark wings and tails with bright yellow wing bars. In winter, the blacks and yellows are paler. Juveniles are streaked with buff or light brown on the back.

VOICE: Its song is a hurried jumble of melodious and scratchy notes, often incorporating both its own call notes and those of other species. Its flight note, often revealing the bird's presence high overhead, is a high tinkle, with the first note higher.

NESTING: Lays 4 or 5 bluish-white eggs in a tightly woven cup nest in a low tree or bush.

HABITAT: Dry grassy slopes with weed patches, chaparral, and open woodlands.

RANGE: Breeds in central and southern California, west of the Sierra Nevada and south into Baja California. It winters south and east to extreme western Texas.

SIMILAR SPECIES: See Pine Siskin and American and Lesser goldfinches.

CONSERVATION:  LC
Lawrence's Goldfinch is uncommon and local. Its numbers are difficult to track because they are highly nomadic, but they are thought to be declining due to habitat lost to development and invasive plants.

SUMMER MIGRATION
WINTER RARE
RESIDENT

The American Goldfinch is a widespread and relatively common bird that regularly graces residential areas with its bright colors and cheerful song. This species prefers to feed on plants bearing many seeds, like thistles; deciduous trees and weedy fields are also used, especially by wintering flocks. American Goldfinches need trees for nesting and, except in winter, avoid treeless plains and thick forests. In California and the Southwest, these birds are associated with riparian areas, particularly where there are willows along streams and ditches. Over most of its breeding range this species is a late nester (July through August), but birds of California and the Southwest have an early nesting period (April through May) that is carefully timed to avoid the summer drought. They migrate in compact flocks with an erratic, "roller coaster" flight.

DESCRIPTION: 4½–5" (11–13 cm). American Goldfinch is smaller than a sparrow. The breeding male is bright yellow with a white rump, black forehead, white edges on its black wings and tail, and yellow at the bend of the wing. The female and winter male are duller and grayer with black wings and tail, and white wing bars. This bird almost always travels in flocks; it has an undulating flight.

VOICE: A bright *per-chick-o-ree*, also rendered as *potato-chips*, delivered in flight and coinciding with each undulation.

NESTING: Lays 4 or 5 pale blue eggs in a well-made cup of grass, bark strips, and plant down, placed in the upright fork of a small sapling or a shrub.

HABITAT: Brushy thickets, weedy grasslands, and nearby trees.

RANGE: Breeds from southern British Columbia east to Newfoundland and south to California, Utah, southern Colorado, central Oklahoma, Arkansas, and Carolinas. Winters in much of the United States.

SIMILAR SPECIES: See Lesser Goldfinch. Immature Indigo Bunting is also rich cinnamon-buff, but it is browner and streaked below, with thinner buff wing bars.

CONSERVATION: Common and widespread, these familiar songbirds are increasing across North America.

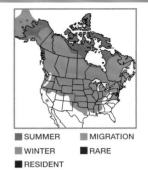

SUMMER ■ MIGRATION
WINTER ■ RARE
■ RESIDENT

In the Far North, the Lapland Longspur is the most common small bird in the vast expanses of sedgy, moist tundra. It has a long hind toenail, which may aid it in walking—these birds run or walk rather than hop as other finches normally do. Like other longspurs, it is almost invisible on the ground; often a whole flock will dart into the air at an observer's feet, only to disappear again when they land on bare ground a few hundred yards away. Lapland Longspur is bold in its breeding territories, but wintering flocks are wary. This species is the only one of four longspurs that is found in both hemispheres.

DESCRIPTION: 6–7" (15–18 cm). This sparrow-sized bird is the only longspur in most of the East. The breeding male has a black face, crown, and upper breast and a chestnut nape. It is streaked above and white below, with streaked flanks. The female and winter male are dull and without the bold pattern; these are best identified by their largely black tail with white outermost feathers.

VOICE: A rattling call. Its flight song is sweet and bubbling.

NESTING: Lays 4 or 5 pale, olive green eggs, heavily spotted with brown and purple, in a grass-lined hollow in the ground, concealed under a clump of grass or a dwarf birch.

HABITAT: Arctic tundra; winters in open windswept fields and on grassy coastal dunes.

RANGE: Breeds from Aleutians, Alaska, and Arctic islands to northern Quebec. Winters regularly throughout northern states to California, Texas, and New York. Also in northern Eurasia.

SIMILAR SPECIES: Several other field birds have white in the tail, but Horned Larks and pipits are thin-billed, Vesper Sparrow is heavily streaked below, and Thick-billed and Chestnut-collared longspurs have much more white in the tail.

Smith's Longspur has a similar tail, but is always buff above and below and usually shows a small white wing patch. It has more clean-cut white outer tail feathers, never has black smudging on the neck, and lacks obvious rufous on the nape and wings. Its flight call is recognizably different.

CONSERVATION: Lapland Longspurs are abundant and increasing. Their breeding range is remote and generally unaffected by human development, although their Far-North habitat is threatened by the effects of climate change.

■ SUMMER ■ MIGRATION
■ WINTER ■ RARE
■ RESIDENT

The upland prairies the Chestnut-collared Longspur favors for nesting have been extensively planted with wheat, so these birds are much less numerous than in the past. They need only a small area, however, and often several pairs will crowd into a patch of land or even the narrow strips of unplowed grassland along highways. Here the males can be seen singing from the tops of fence posts, rocks, or tall weed stalks.

DESCRIPTION: 5½–6½" (14–17 cm). This sparrow-sized bird is similar to Lapland Longspur, but the breeding male has wholly black underparts and some white on its face. The tail of the female and the winter male are similar to that of Lapland Longspur but with more white at the sides.

VOICE: Its song is soft, sweet, and tumbling, somewhat like that of the Western Meadowlark; it also gives a hard *ji-jiv* in flight.

NESTING: Lays 3–5 pale green eggs, spotted with brown and lavender, in a grass-lined hollow under a clump of grass.

HABITAT: Dry elevated prairies and short-grass plains.

RANGE: Breeds from Alberta and Manitoba south to Minnesota and Wyoming. It winters from Colorado and Kansas south to Texas and northern Mexico.

SIMILAR SPECIES: Winter birds can be confused with Smith's Longspur because of buff underparts and the occasional presence of a white shoulder mark, but Chestnut-collared is paler above with much more white in the tail.

Thick-billed Longspur is sometimes claimed to be sighted among Chestnut-collared flocks on the basis of rattle calls and tail patterns, which may be difficult to discern in the field. Thick-billed is noticeably larger and paler; it has a much larger bill that appears somewhat swollen at the base of the lower mandible. Most winter Thick-billed have at least a trace of rufous or tawny on the shoulder. In flight, Thick-billed appears to have broad-based wings, emphasizing its short tail. Flight calls are helpful in distinguishing species.

CONSERVATION: VU

Locally common to uncommon, Chestnut-collared Longspurs have declined during the past half-century and are still decreasing. These birds are adapted to living on grazed prairie land, and were heavily impacted by European settlement and the ensuing decline of native grazers like the American bison. Conservation efforts to protect prairie habitat for other grassland birds also benefit this species.

SMITH'S LONGSPUR *Calcarius pictus*

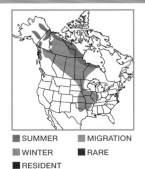

☐ SUMMER ☐ MIGRATION
☐ WINTER ☐ RARE
☐ RESIDENT

Longspur identification is difficult in the Midwest, where all four species winter. This species, clad in warm buff year-round, can be distinguished at a glance. At times they are found in huge flocks moving over the dry winter grasslands in search of seeds, uttering a distinctive clinking call. A beautiful bird, the Smith's Longspur breeds at the treeline and does not have a flight song, instead marking its territory by singing from the top of a small tree or hillock.

DESCRIPTION: 5¾–6½" (15–17 cm). The breeding male is streaked dark brown and buff above, and is clear warm buff below. It has a bold black-and-white head pattern. Its small white wing patch is most evident in flight. Its tail is black with white outer feathers. Females and winter males are duller and lack the black-and-white head pattern, but are always more buff-colored than other longspurs.

VOICE: A dry rattle, like a finger running along the teeth of a comb.

NESTING: Lays 3–5 pale brown eggs spotted with darker brown in a grass-walled hollow lined with plant down and feathers and concealed under a clump of grass or a dwarf willow.

HABITAT: Arctic tundra and forest edges; it winters on open grassy plains.

RANGE: Breeds from northern Alaska across northern Canada to Hudson Bay. It winters from Nebraska south to Texas.

SIMILAR SPECIES: See Lapland and Chestnut-collared longspurs. Other field birds have clean-cut white outer tail feathers, but pipits and Horned Larks have thin bills. Vesper Sparrow has a strongly streaked breast.

CONSERVATION: LC

Smith's Longspur is uncommon and local. Its breeding grounds are remote, and rarely impacted by human activity; its population is believed to be stable.

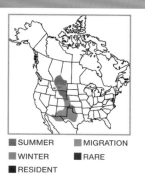

SUMMER
MIGRATION
WINTER
RARE
RESIDENT

This longspur nests in higher and more arid short-grass plains than does the Chestnut-collared Longspur, and so it has been less affected by the plowing of the prairies. These birds so dislike moisture that in wet seasons they may abandon areas in which they normally are abundant. In summer they feed chiefly on grasshoppers, but in fall and winter, when they gather in large flocks with other longspurs and with Horned Larks, they prefer seeds. In winter plumage they can be difficult to distinguish from the other longspurs, but close up they are easily identified by their stouter bill.

DESCRIPTION: 5¾–6" (15 cm). The breeding male is streaked above, with a black crown, a whitish face, and a black "mustache." It is gray below with a bold black band across the breast. The female and winter male are duller and more streaked; they are best identified by tail pattern, which is largely white with a central pair of black tail feathers and with a narrow black band at the tip forming a black T shape.

VOICE: A dry rattle; it also gives a clear, sweet warble during a fluttering flight with its wings raised high over the back.

NESTING: Lays 3 or 4 pale green eggs spotted with dark brown and black in a hollow scrape lined with fine grass and hair, on open ground.

HABITAT: Arid plains.

RANGE: Breeds from Alberta and southwestern Manitoba south to the Dakotas, Wyoming, and Colorado. It winters from Nebraska and Colorado southward.

SIMILAR SPECIES: Lapland and Smith's longspurs have less white in the tail. Also see Chestnut-collared Longspur. All three other longspurs have smaller bills.

CONSERVATION:
Uncommon and local, Thick-billed Longspur has undergone a small decline in recent years. It is far less numerous today than it was a century ago, likely due to loss of habitat.

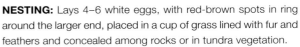

SUMMER   MIGRATION
WINTER   RARE
RESIDENT

This circumpolar bird, often called the "Snowflake," breeds farther north than almost any other land bird. In severe winters large flocks descend to southern Canada and the northern United States, where they favor the most barren places. They occasionally can be found at beach parking lots in the dead of winter searching for weed seeds.

DESCRIPTION: 6–7¼" (15–18 cm). A sparrow-sized bird, the breeding male has a black back with extensive white on the head, underparts, wings, and tail. The female is similar but duller. Winter birds have brown on the crown and upperparts, and have duller underparts, but still show much white in the wings.

VOICE: A clear whistle or a soft, buzzy note. Its song is a sweet warble.

NESTING: Lays 4–6 white eggs, with red-brown spots in ring around the larger end, placed in a cup of grass lined with fur and feathers and concealed among rocks or in tundra vegetation.

HABITAT: Arctic tundra. It winters on windswept grasslands and beaches.

RANGE: Breeds from the Aleutians, northern Alaska, and the Arctic islands south to northern Quebec. It winters regularly across southern Canada and the upper tier of the U.S. to Oregon and Pennsylvania. Also found in Eurasia.

SIMILAR SPECIES: See McKay's Bunting. Beware of confusion with albino and partial albino individuals of any similar species.

CONSERVATION:
The breeding areas for Snow Buntings are so remote that they are rarely impacted directly by human activity, and their populations are difficult to survey. They are still widespread and common but have declined in recent decades.

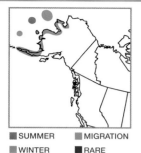

■ SUMMER ■ MIGRATION
■ WINTER ■ RARE
■ RESIDENT

McKay's Buntings may represent the last survivors of a population of large white buntings that lived north of the ice sheet of the last Ice Age. The more common Snow Bunting occupies adjacent breeding territory on all surrounding Arctic mainlands, but McKay's seems to hold its ground on its tiny, remote nesting islands of the Bering Sea.

DESCRIPTION: 7" (18 cm). Similar to, but whiter than, the widespread Snow Bunting. The breeding male is snow white except for a dark bill, black tips of the primaries, and the tips of the central tail feathers. The female has darkish areas on the back but a pure white head. In winter, both sexes have light brown areas on the head and back, more so on the female. Immatures are similar, but the head, back, and rump are mottled with a highly variable amount of rusty-beige feather edging, and the bill is straw-colored.

VOICE: A loud warbling song reminiscent of that of the goldfinch. Its call is a musical rattle.

NESTING: Lays 3 or 4 light green, brown-dotted eggs in a grass-lined scrape on the ground in a rock crevice.

HABITAT: Tundra; coastal shores in winter.

RANGE: Breeds on Hall and St. Matthew islands in the Bering Sea. It winters east to the coast of western Alaska and Nunivak Island.

SIMILAR SPECIES: A summer male Snow Bunting has a black back; the female has much more extensive mottling in the back than a female McKay's. In all seasons, both sexes of Snow Bunting have much more black in the tail and in the flight feathers. Both species have a black bill in summer and a straw-colored bill in winter.

CONSERVATION:

McKay's Bunting is uncommon to rare, and it breeds and winters in an extremely limited range in western Alaska and Bering Sea islands. Although it is increasing and its nesting islands are remote from human interference, its total population is estimated to be only around 25,000–35,000 birds.

LITTLE BUNTING *Emberiza pusilla*

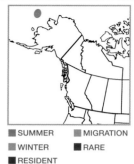

■ SUMMER ■ MIGRATION
■ WINTER ■ RARE
■ RESIDENT

Little Bunting is widespread in northern Eurasia in summer, and strays have been recorded in fall on Bering Sea islands and a couple of times in California. This species forages on the ground in open field and edge habitats, where its cryptic plumage and small size make it easily overlooked.

DESCRIPTION: 5" (13 cm). This bird has a heavily streaked brown back and white underparts with dark streaking. Its chin, face, and central crown stripe are rust-brown. Its crown and malar are black. These birds have a neat, white eye ring and black-bordered auriculars.

VOICE: Its song is a rollicking but short, goldfinch-like warble of modulated trills and high, sweet notes. Its call is a quick *tsit* or *tsik*.

NESTING: Lays 4–6 eggs in a tree nest. It is not known to nest in North America.

HABITAT: Found in open and edge habitats.

RANGE: Widespread in northern Eurasia from Scandinavia to Siberia. Winters in southeast Asia.

SIMILAR SPECIES: Other *Emberiza* species recorded rarely in Alaska include Pine, Yellow-breasted, Gray, Pallas's, and Reed buntings.

CONSERVATION: LC

The population of this widespread Eurasian species is large and stable.

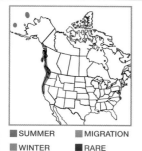

■ SUMMER ■ MIGRATION
■ WINTER ■ RARE
■ RESIDENT

Rustic Bunting is one of many Eurasian *Emberiza* buntings that have been found in the Aleutian and other Alaskan islands as an uncommon spring and rare fall visitor. It is also a fall vagrant along the West Coast, found in brushy areas. Fall birds recall sparrows, but most show some rusty color in the rump and nape.

DESCRIPTION: 6" (15 cm). This bird has bright chestnut-brown upperparts streaked with black on the back. It has a rusty nape with rich rusty streaks on the sides. It has a black cheek and crown that contrasts with a white throat and supercilium.

VOICE: Its song is a sweet, fluting warble recalling a longspur but more pure-toned. Its call is a sharp, short, high *tsic* or *tic*.

NESTING: Lays 4–6 eggs in a nest built in a bush or on the ground.

HABITAT: Found in brushy areas. It breeds in wet coniferous woodlands.

RANGE: Native to northern Europe and Asia. It is a rare but somewhat regular migrant on the western Aleutian Islands and occasionally elsewhere in western Alaska, usually in spring. It is accidental along the Pacific Coast south to California in fall and winter.

SIMILAR SPECIES: Several related Asian bunting species stray rarely into Alaska. See Little Bunting.

CONSERVATION:
The European Red List of Birds notes a significant decline in Rustic Bunting numbers in northern Europe and Russia. Although it is still numerous, its sharp declines make it a vulnerable species. Habitat destruction associated with forest logging and draining of swamps is blamed for the declines.

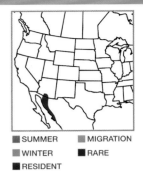

■ SUMMER   ■ MIGRATION
■ WINTER   ■ RARE
■ RESIDENT

An important habitat requirement for this geographically restricted species seems to be tall sacaton grass. Its range was formerly more widespread in Arizona, but areas heavily grazed by cattle have seriously reduced its habitat and it has all but disappeared from these places. It lives in small, scattered populations in isolated areas, and expert guidance is usually necessary to locate it.

DESCRIPTION: 5–5½" (13–14 cm). This bird resembles Rufous-crowned Sparrow, but is lighter, with finer streaking on the back and two pronounced "whisker" marks (instead of one). It has a rufous crown divided by a gray median stripe, and a rufous eyeline and shoulder patch. It is unstreaked whitish below, with light wing bars and a rounded tail. Juveniles lack rufous markings and wing bars but display double "whiskers" and a finely streaked, light brown upper breast and sides.

VOICE: Its characteristic call is a sharp *seep*. Its song is variable but always ends in a trill of rapid *chip*s.

NESTING: Lays 4 or 5 light bluish-white eggs in a cup of coarse grass lined with finer grasses, placed low in a bush, young mesquite, or cactus, not well hidden. It nests at the end of summer when rains come.

HABITAT: Grasslands mixed with thorn bushes, mesquite trees, or cholla patches.

RANGE: Resident in south-central Arizona and northwestern Mexico.

SIMILAR SPECIES: Differs from *Spizella* sparrows in its shape, with a noticeably larger head and bill (often bicolored), longer but relatively heavy body, and long, wider, and more rounded tail. *Spizella* species have a dark eyeline; immatures show a marked contrast between the ear covert region and the rest of the head and neck.

Rufous-crowned Sparrow is much darker, has darker gray on the head and underparts, and lacks light edgings to the wings; it has a single, thicker, black whisker mark and conspicuous white eye ring; it is found at higher elevations and has an entirely different song.

CONSERVATION:

These birds are uncommon and local. They are locally more common in areas where good desert grass habitat remains. Their numbers are undoubtedly smaller than they were historically, but the population has been stable over the past several decades. It is vulnerable to the loss of its remaining habitat to cattle grazing, especially in Mexico.

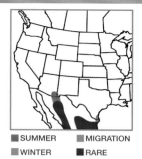

SUMMER ■ MIGRATION
WINTER ■ RARE
RESIDENT

Botteri's Sparrow is an entirely terrestrial bird that lives and feeds on the ground and hides in thick vegetation. This solitary, secretive bird of the Southwest is associated with dense, tall grass. Usually heard before it is seen, it is best distinguished from the similar Cassin's Sparrow by its song and its more limited range.

DESCRIPTION: 5¼–6¼" (13–16 cm). Similar to Cassin's Sparrow but more slender, Botteri's Sparrow is browner and less boldly streaked on the upperparts, with a more conspicuous eyebrow and a slightly less conical bill. It is plain buff below, and its brownish wings and tail are often tinted rust.

VOICE: Its song consists of several short trills often introduced by a couple of *clips* and *che-licks*, but is variable.

NESTING: Lays 2–5 white eggs. Apparently builds its nest on the ground, but little else is known about its breeding habits.

HABITAT: Open arid country such as grasslands, savannas, or desert-scrub areas.

RANGE: Breeds in southeastern Arizona and southern Texas. Winters south of U.S.-Mexico border.

SUBSPECIES: The Arizona population (subsp. *arizonae*) averages redder and darker above than the Texas population (subsp. *texana*), which tends to be pale grayer above.

SIMILAR SPECIES: See Cassin's and Bachman's sparrows.

CONSERVATION:
The Arizona and Texas populations of Botteri's Sparrow are stable, aided by the fact that their remaining habitat in both states is protected. The Texas population was reduced by habitat loss and is now rare and local. The species' biggest threat is the degradation of coastal prairie habitats in the core of its range in Mexico.

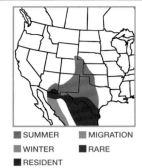

■ SUMMER ■ MIGRATION
■ WINTER ■ RARE
■ RESIDENT

This bird is extremely secretive except when the male is on its breeding grounds; there it steadily proclaims its territory with its lark-like flight song. After summer rains finally drench the normally arid southwestern grasslands, these areas may suddenly come alive with singing, skylarking Cassin's Sparrows. Rival males often hold song duels from atop grass stalks just 20 feet (6 meters) apart. This species is relatively erratic in numbers and distribution. The Great Plains population is believed to migrate southwestward after breeding into the grassy deserts of Arizona and Mexico.

DESCRIPTION: 5¼–5¾" (13–15 cm). This sparrow has fine brown streaking on a grayish-brown head and back. It has dingy buff, unstreaked underparts, with faint streaking on the lower flanks occasionally visible. Both sexes look alike. The young are streaked on the breast as well.

VOICE: Its song consists of four loud, melodious, clear whistles, uttered from the tops of tall grass stalks and also in flight. The second note is prolonged and quavering; the third note is lowest.

NESTING: Lays 3 or 4 white eggs in a deep, almost tunnel-like cup placed on the ground or at the base of a bush or cactus.

HABITAT: Semidesert; arid uplands such as those with yuccas and tall grass.

RANGE: Breeds from southern Arizona and southwestern Kansas south to southern New Mexico and western and southern Texas; also in Mexico. It winters in the southern part of its breeding range, along the U.S.-Mexico border and south.

SIMILAR SPECIES: The song and skylarking behavior of Cassin's Sparrow is distinctive. Botteri's Sparrow is somewhat less stocky, generally browner, and less conspicuously streaked on the upperparts; it has a more conspicuous eyebrow and slightly less conical bill. Its wings and tail are often rust-tinted, and it has more buff on the eyebrow, face, and underparts. Botteri's also lacks streaks on the flanks and the diagnostic heavy cross-barring on its central tail feathers.

CONSERVATION:
Cassin's Sparrow is common but irregular in appropriate habitat. The natural variation in its numbers make trends difficult to assess, but its numbers seem to have been mostly stable (perhaps slightly decreasing) during the past several decades. Habitat loss to development, agriculture, and grazing remain the greatest threat to these birds.

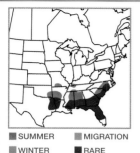

■ SUMMER ■ MIGRATION
■ WINTER ■ RARE
■ RESIDENT

In the southern parts of this bird's range, its former name, "Pine-woods Sparrow," seems appropriate because it dwells in open stretches of pines with grass and scattered shrubs for ground cover. Farther north it is also found in abandoned, overgrown fields and pastures. Bachman's Sparrow spends much of the time feeding on the ground, where it is hard to see except when it mounts a bush or weed stalk to sing. Like many other sparrows, it feeds on insects such as crickets and beetles, and on seeds of grasses and sedges. John James Audubon named this bird for his close friend Dr. John Bachman (1790–1874), who discovered the species in South Carolina.

DESCRIPTION: 6" (15 cm). A dull-colored, nondescript bird, it is streaked above and plain below with a buff breast. It is virtually identical to Botteri's Sparrow (not found in the same range), but usually more reddish above, especially west of the Mississippi.

VOICE: A clear, sweet whistle followed by a trill on a different pitch.

NESTING: Lays 4 white eggs in a domed nest made of plant fibers and placed on the ground in a grass clump or at the base of a bush or palmetto; nest has entrance on the side.

HABITAT: Dry, open pine or oak woods with a scattering of scrub; overgrown weedy fields and pastures.

RANGE: Found in the southeastern United States, breeding north to Missouri, Kentucky, and North Carolina; rarely to Illinois, Indiana, Ohio, and Pennsylvania, but very local. It winters chiefly in the southern Atlantic and Gulf Coast states.

SUBSPECIES: The population west of the Mississippi River (subsp. *illinoensis*) is brighter and reddish with few or no black streaks above. The birds farther east (subsp. *bachmani* and especially subsp. *aestivalis* in South Carolina, Georgia, and Florida) have stronger black streaking on the back and are drabber overall.

SIMILAR SPECIES: See Botteri's, Grasshopper, and Swamp sparrows.

CONSERVATION: NT

Bachman's Sparrow has declined significantly during the past few decades. The species is now absent from most of the northern part of its historical range, and is uncommon to rare in the southern part. Timber harvesting practices, fire suppression, and fragmentation of suitable habitat have all contributed to the declines. In particular, careful management of pine woodlands is critical to protecting this species. In their natural state, fires thin these habitats every 3–5 years, creating openings in the understory that Bachman's Sparrow uses to nest. Controlled burning, mechanical thinning, and herbicide treatments of pine forests can create habitat conditions that support Bachman's Sparrows as well as the endangered Red-cockaded Woodpecker.

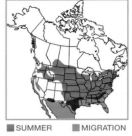

■ SUMMER ■ MIGRATION
■ WINTER ■ RARE
■ RESIDENT

The Grasshopper Sparrow is found in grain fields, prairie grasslands, and weedy fields, usually in drier, upland grasses. This elusive sparrow—named for its buzzy song—is sensitive to subtle changes in its habitat. As soon as a weedy field becomes overgrown or trees have filled in an abandoned pasture, the Grasshopper Sparrow no longer uses the site for breeding. Less of a seed-eater than our other grass sparrows, it feeds largely on insects. Its flight is usually short and weak, with rapid, buzzy wingbeats; when flushed, this sparrow flies a short distance and drops out of sight into tall grass.

DESCRIPTION: 4½–5" (11–13 cm). A small, chunky grassland sparrow with clear buff breast and scaly-looking, dark rufous upperparts. Grasshopper Sparrows have a conspicuously unmarked buff face, with plain buff ear coverts and no whisker marks; its "beady" black eyes are prominent and obvious. It has a pale central stripe on the crown and a short, pointed tail.

VOICE: A high-pitched, insect-like *kip-kip-kip, zeeee*, usually uttered from the top of a weed stalk.

NESTING: Lays 4 or 5 white eggs, speckled with red-brown, in a cup of grass, often domed, lined with rootlets and hair and placed on the ground.

HABITAT: Open grassy and weedy meadows, pastures, and plains.

RANGE: Breeds from British Columbia, Manitoba, and New Hampshire south to Florida (rare), the West Indies, and Mexico. It winters north to California, Texas, and North Carolina.

SUBSPECIES: Several subspecies are poorly differentiated and vary subtly in overall color. The Eastern population (subsp. *pratensis*) is somewhat more richly colored than the Western population (subsp. *perpallidus*). The seriously endangered subspecies found in Florida (subsp. *floridanus*) is distinctly darker above and paler below.

SIMILAR SPECIES: Adult Henslow's Sparrow is similar to immature Grasshopper Sparrow but darker overall, with dark spots on the ear coverts, whisker marks, an olive head, and rust wings; its breast streaks are more sharply defined. Immature Henslow's is similar to an adult Grasshopper Sparrow, but Grasshopper is paler and more buff-colored overall; it has an unmarked face and lacks the dingy olive head and rust-colored wings of Henslow's. Adult LeConte's Sparrow has a triangular gray patch on the ear coverts, more extensive orange-buff on the face, a bluish gray bill, and streaked sides and flanks. Immature LeConte's resembles immature Grasshopper—both are streaked on the breast—but has streaked sides and flanks and the triangular gray ear patch, like the adult. See Baird's Sparrow.

CONSERVATION:  LC
Uncommon and local in large expanses of suitable habitat, Grasshopper Sparrows are declining continent-wide due to habitat loss through fragmentation and degradation of native prairie. The Florida Grasshopper Sparrow is on the U.S. Endangered Species List; it is classified as state-endangered in Florida and has continued to decline rapidly despite an intensive recovery plan.

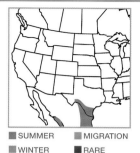

■ SUMMER ■ MIGRATION
■ WINTER ■ RARE
■ RESIDENT

Flitting from shrub to shrub and skulking about the undergrowth, this unobtrusive, drab little bird is seldom seen out in the open. Nevertheless, it may be readily observed when it sings from an exposed perch or engages in nesting activities. It feeds on seeds, small larvae, and grubs.

DESCRIPTION: 5¾" (15 cm). An unstreaked, dull olive green sparrow that is brighter yellow-olive on the wings and tail and has no wing bars. Its head is pale brownish gray with two bold brown crown stripes and a narrow dark eyeline. Its throat and belly are whitish; the chest and flanks are dull brownish gray. The immature is duller and browner above, more buff-colored below, with faint wing bars. It resembles a smaller version of a Green-tailed Towhee.

VOICE: A series of musical *chip*s, becoming more rapid at the end.

NESTING: Lays 4 white eggs in a domed nest made of twigs, grass, and leaves, placed low in a shrub or cactus.

HABITAT: Brushy areas, woodland borders and clearings, and overgrown fields.

RANGE: Resident in lower Rio Grande Valley of Texas.

SIMILAR SPECIES: See Green-tailed Towhee.

CONSERVATION:

After a decline in the 1930s caused by extensive land clearing for agriculture, and another decline in the 1980s, Olive Sparrow populations have stabilized and begun to recover. The bird is still common in what remains of its habitat and its numbers are increasing again.

FIVE-STRIPED SPARROW   *Amphispiza quinquestriata*

■ SUMMER   ■ MIGRATION
■ WINTER   ■ RARE
■ RESIDENT

This Mexican species was first found in the United States south of Tucson in 1957, and was seen north of the border occasionally, sometimes feeding newly fledged young. It took many years before it was confirmed to be a rare and local nesting bird in several canyons in southern Arizona, but it remains unclear whether it is a recent arrival north of the border or if this secretive and hard-to-see bird was simply overlooked in the past.

Five-striped Sparrow is found on steep, arid, rocky hills with dense brush.

DESCRIPTION: 5½" (14 cm). A dark sparrow with five white stripes on the face: above and below the eyes, and in the center of the throat. It has a bold, triangular black "whisker" mark. It is rich, dark brownish gray above, and rustier on the back. Its breast is dark gray with dark central spot. The sides and flanks are dark gray and its belly is whitish. The juvenile resembles a young Black-throated Sparrow but lacks bib streaking.

VOICE: Its song is variable but similar to that of Black-throated Sparrow.

NESTING: Lays 2–4 bluish eggs speckled with brown in a loose cup of grass and twigs hidden deep in the base of a shrub.

HABITAT: Arid rocky hills with dense brush.

RANGE: Possibly resident in southeastern Arizona, but it has been recorded in winter there only a few times, suggesting that much of the population may move south after breeding. It is also found year-round in western Mexico.

SIMILAR SPECIES: Black-throated Sparrow is solidly black on the throat, paler on the breast, and lacks a central breast spot.

CONSERVATION:
Rare and local in North America, found only at a few sites in Arizona. Its population is believed to be stable.

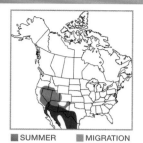

■ SUMMER ■ MIGRATION
■ WINTER ■ RARE
■ RESIDENT

This handsome sparrow of the arid Southwest is well named. Its former name, "Desert Sparrow," is also apt, for despite its vivid markings, it is often difficult to detect among the rocks and scrub, especially when not moving. However, it may be observed when it mounts a bush or rock to sing its pleasant song. Black-throated Sparrow is well adapted to the extremes of its habitat. Studies have shown that it has a great tolerance for heat and drought. During the hot months of late summer and early fall it maintains itself on dry seeds and drinks regularly at water holes. After the rains, these sparrows scatter into small flocks and feed on vegetation and insects, from which they derive all the moisture they need. They raise their young in the dry upland desert.

DESCRIPTION: 5¼" (13 cm). This sparrow is gray above, white below, with a striking black throat and breast. It has two conspicuous white stripes on the sides of the head: one above and one below the eye. It has whitish spots on the outer tail feathers. Both sexes are alike. Juveniles are similar but usually much browner, especially on the back, and have a breast band of indistinct streaks; it lacks black on the throat, and the rest of the adult face pattern is present but often paler.

VOICE: Two clear notes followed by a buzzy trill.

NESTING: Lays 4 white eggs in a loosely built nest of bark strips, grass, and stems, lined with wool, hair, or feathers, and placed in a thorny bush.

HABITAT: Found in deserts with cactus, mesquite, and creosote bush, and also in sagebrush habitat. It is partial to rocky places.

RANGE: Breeds from northeastern California, southwestern Wyoming, and southeastern Colorado southward. It winters north to the desert regions of the southern United States.

SUBSPECIES: Populations farthest west (subsp. *deserticola*) are slightly larger and paler with less prominent white spots on the outer tail feathers compared to the populations in west and south Texas (subspp. *opuntia* and *bilineata*).

SIMILAR SPECIES: Juveniles are similar to an adult Sage Sparrow, but any dusky streaking below is usually diffuse and confined to the bib area, unlike the well-defined streaking on Sage Sparrow's sides (both can show a central breast spot), or fine streaking on the back. Sage Sparrow has a complete whitish eye ring—much bolder than in Black-throated—and more conspicuous whitish wing bars. Sage Sparrows run on the ground with their tail carried high; frequent flicking of the tail in perched birds is more indicative of Sage. Their calls are nearly identical.

CONSERVATION:
Black-throated Sparrow is still common in suitable habitat, but its numbers are declining. It seems less adaptable to suburban environments than many other sparrows. Drought, cowbird parasitism, and habitat loss due to urbanization, fire suppression, and invasive grasses are all threats to these birds.

■ SUMMER ■ MIGRATION
■ WINTER ■ RARE
■ RESIDENT

The easiest way to find Lark Sparrows is to drive through grasslands and watch for the birds to fly up into trees along the road. The Lark Sparrow frequents open areas sparsely vegetated with scattered trees and shrubs. These birds are also found around agricultural areas, pastures, and ranchlands, and in adjacent open residential areas. They are often seen perched on fences or utility lines along roadsides in open country. Its strong flight is punctuated by long, shallow glides. A male Lark Sparrow may be monogamous or may have two females with nests close together, and it will fiercely defend its nests but not a large territory. Lark Sparrows are highly social, crowding together for feeding even during the nesting season.

DESCRIPTION: 5½–6½" (14–17 cm). This distinctive sparrow's head is boldly patterned with black, chestnut, and white. It is streaked above, white below with a black spot in the center of the breast; and its tail is black with white edges. Juveniles have a streaked brown crown, a lightly streaked breast, and lack the black breast spot; the adult head pattern is present but less distinct.

VOICE: Alternating buzzes and melodious trills.

NESTING: Lays 3–5 white eggs heavily spotted with dark brown and black in a well-made cup of grass and plant stems on the ground or in a bush.

HABITAT: Grasslands with scattered bushes and trees; open country generally in winter.

RANGE: Breeds from British Columbia, Saskatchewan, and northern Minnesota, south to California, northern Mexico, Louisiana, and Alabama. It winters from southern California to Florida and southward.

SIMILAR SPECIES: Adults are unmistakable. Vesper Sparrow also shows white in the tail, but is more heavily streaked and lacks the distinct head pattern.

CONSERVATION: 🐦 LC

Lark Sparrows are fairly common and widespread west of the Mississippi; it formerly bred in the East but is now rare there due to forest clearing. Its numbers are declining, possibly due to habitat loss to urbanization or to the spread of invasive grass species.

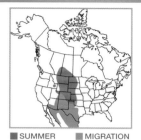

■ SUMMER ■ MIGRATION
■ WINTER ■ RARE
■ RESIDENT

Lark Buntings are usually seen in large flocks feeding along roadsides. On the breeding grounds they are quite gregarious, with several pairs crowding into a few acres of suitable habitat. Because there are few elevated song perches in their grassland breeding area, the spectacular black-and-white male advertises its presence with a conspicuous song flight, in which it rises almost vertically, then drops back to its original perch. Often one can see several singing males in the air at one time, providing watchers an easy way to locate a nesting colony. Like many seed-eating birds, they supplement their summer diet with insects.

DESCRIPTION: 6–7½" (15–19 cm). The breeding male is black overall with large, white wing patches. Females, immatures, and winter males are streaked sandy-buff above and white below, with a white eyeline, a faint "mustache" stripe, and a white wing patch (not always visible). Adults of both sexes have rounded, white-tipped tail feathers.

VOICE: A canary-like song with loud bubbling sequences and trills interspersed with harsher notes. Its call is a two-note whistle.

NESTING: Lays 4 or 5 light blue eggs in a loose grass nest placed in a scrape with rim flush with the ground; often protected by weedy patch.

HABITAT: Dry plains and prairies; open sagebrush.

RANGE: Breeds on the prairies of south-central Canada and the central United States. It winters in the Southwest and into Mexico.

SIMILAR SPECIES: A breeding-plumage male Bobolink has white patches on the back, a buff nape, and a whitish rump.

Females, juveniles, and winter males resemble other streaked sparrows but are larger and have a brown cheek patch, a larger bill, a hint of the white wing patch, and a more rounded tail with white corners.

CONSERVATION:

As North American prairies, shrub-steppes, and desert grasslands change or become converted to agricultural land, the Lark Bunting faces the loss of both breeding and wintering habitat. The fact that its numbers vary widely from year to year in many areas makes it difficult to monitor population trends. It is still common, although populations have decreased substantially in recent decades.

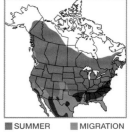

■ SUMMER ■ MIGRATION
■ WINTER ■ RARE
■ RESIDENT

The Chipping Sparrow is a familiar and common summer resident of gardens, woodlands, and forest edges in the East and open woodlands and mountain meadows in the West. It mixes loosely with other sparrows during migration. Somewhat more arboreal than most sparrows, the Chipping Sparrow typically sings from an elevated perch and often takes cover in trees. It generally forages on the ground in open meadows or lawn-like areas. Its diet consists mainly of seeds, but in summer the adults and the young feed on insects.

DESCRIPTION: 5–5½" (13–14 cm). A small sparrow. Its upperparts are brown and streaked with black; its underparts, the sides of the face, and the rump are gray. The adult has a chestnut crown and a white eyebrow with a thin black line through the eye. Young birds have a streaked crown, a buff eyebrow, and duller underparts.

VOICE: Thin musical trill, all on one note like the whir of a sewing machine.

NESTING: Lays 3–5 pale blue eggs lightly spotted with brown in a solid cup of grass and stems, almost always lined with hair, placed in shrubbery or in a tangle of vines.

HABITAT: Grassy woodland edges, gardens, city parks, brushy pastures, and lawns.

RANGE: Breeds throughout most of the continent from Yukon, Manitoba, and Newfoundland south to California, Texas, and northern Florida; also in Mexico. Winters across the southern United States southward into Mexico.

SIMILAR SPECIES: Breeding adults differ from all other "rufous-capped" sparrows and from Green-tailed Towhee by their prominent white eyebrow and strong black eyeline. Non-breeding adults and immatures are easily identified as *Spizella* sparrows by their small size, slim build, notched tail, and wing bars. Tree and Field sparrows have unstreaked crowns and rufous in the back and crown. Brewer's Sparrow is smaller, relatively longer tailed, paler, and more finely streaked; it has pale lores, a faint eye ring, and a brownish rump (but juvenile Chipping Sparrow has a brown rump, too). Juveniles are best identified by their characteristic *Spizella* shape; Savannah Sparrow is most similar, but has a shorter tail, heavier breast streaks, a more distinct median crown stripe, yellowish color around the eyebrow and face, and brighter legs. See Clay-colored Sparrow.

CONCONSERVATION: 🐦 LC

Widespread and common throughout North America, Chipping Sparrows nest in open, tree-filled spaces typical of suburbs and parks, so their numbers are increasing alongside residential development.

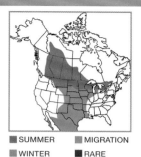

SUMMER MIGRATION
WINTER RARE
RESIDENT

The plowing of the prairies reduced the habitat of the Clay-colored Sparrow, but with the clearing of forests it has extended its range northeastward and now breeds in the eastern Great Lakes region. Each spring and fall a few individuals, most of them immatures, appear on the Eastern Seaboard, where they can be difficult to distinguish from immature Chipping and Brewer's sparrows, with which they often associate. Most migrate through a narrow corridor through the Great Plains, where they can be quite common.

DESCRIPTION: 5–5½" (13–14 cm). A small sparrow with a streaked crown and buffy upperparts with a clear gray breast. It is similar to an immature Chipping Sparrow but brighter, with a brownish buff rump instead of lead gray, gray sides of the neck, and a buff cheek patch bordered above and below with black.

VOICE: A series of four or five toneless, insect-like buzzes.

NESTING: Lays 3–5 pale blue eggs spotted with dark brown in a bulky cup of hair-lined grass placed in a bush or clump of weeds up to 6' (2 m) above the ground.

HABITAT: Brushy grasslands and prairies.

RANGE: Breeds from north-central Canada and the Great Lakes region south to Colorado and Michigan. It winters north to southern Texas.

SIMILAR SPECIES: Adults in breeding plumage are fairly distinctive, but may be confused with Brewer's Sparrow. Immature Chipping and Brewer's sparrows are similar to fall adult and immature Clay-colored Sparrows, but are generally less buff-colored with less contrast in the head pattern and with a grayer breast that contrasts less with the malar stripe. The best field mark is the medium gray on the side of the neck and nape; although this is present to some extent on both Chipping and Brewer's, it does not contrast as strongly with the rest of the plumage as in Clay-colored. Chipping Sparrow is also larger and has a bold outline only above the cheek patch, not above

and below; it has dark lores and a grayish rump except in juvenal plumage. Brewer's Sparrow has a much less prominent (or absent) median crown stripe; a faint eye ring; a longer tail; and paler, grayish-brown, more finely streaked upperparts.

Also see Grasshopper Sparrow, which has buff underparts.

CONSERVATION:

Clay-colored Sparrows are common but have declined slightly in recent decades. Their nests are commonly parasitized by Brown-headed Cowbirds, and their habitat has been affected by various agricultural activities. The species has expanded its range to the north and east, readily occupying reclaimed land recovering from logging and grazing.

SUMMER ▪ MIGRATION
WINTER ▪ RARE
RESIDENT

Very little is known about the habits of this sparrow. Singing males are conspicuous when they sit on top of high bushes; their song carries well through the narrow, brushy canyons they inhabit, but in general the species is shy and secretive.

DESCRIPTION: 5–5½" (13–14 cm). A gray sparrow with a black chin and an eye smudge, a pink bill, a chestnut-streaked mantle, and a white belly. It has thin white wing bars. Females and juveniles lack black facial markings.

VOICE: The beautiful song is a series of slurred notes, either *swee? swee?* or *chew chew chew*, running together into a rapid canary-like trill.

NESTING: Lays 3 or 4 pale blue, plain or spotted eggs in a grass-lined cup well concealed in a low bush.

HABITAT: Low, dense chaparral on arid mountain slopes; sagebrush.

RANGE: Breeds from central California, southern Nevada, southern Utah, Arizona, southern New Mexico, and western Texas southward. Winters along Mexican border.

SIMILAR SPECIES: Juncos are stockier, more rotund, with relatively large heads and much more white in the outer tail feathers; they lack streaking on the back.

CONSERVATION: LC

Black-chinned Sparrows are still fairly common in appropriate habitat, but their numbers have declined significantly in recent decades. These birds are sensitive to changes in climate and rainfall patterns—too much rain or drought can affect nesting success or delay breeding. Much of this bird's habitat has also been degraded by overgrazing. They are quick to reoccupy brushlands after fires.

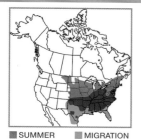

■ SUMMER ■ MIGRATION
■ WINTER ■ RARE
■ RESIDENT

When farms and pastures become overgrown with weeds and bushes, birds such as Field Sparrows and Indigo Buntings move in and nest. Although shyer than its close relative the Chipping Sparrow — and thus more difficult to observe — the Field Sparrow may be studied at leisure when it sings its sweet plaintive song from a conspicuous perch atop a bush or fence post. During fall migration it may be seen among mixed flocks of sparrows.

DESCRIPTION: 5¼" (13 cm). Adults have stout, bright pink bills. The crown is warm rust-orange, and the gray face is set off by a broad whitish eye ring and rust eyeline and ear coverts. The gray-white underparts have a buff wash across the breast and flanks. The breast lacks a central spot but the side of the breast is bright rust-orange.

VOICE: A series of soft, plaintive notes, all on the same pitch, accelerating to a trill at the end.

NESTING: Lays 4 brown-spotted pale green eggs in a woven cup-shaped nest of grass, lined with rootlets or fine grass and set on or near the ground.

HABITAT: Abandoned fields and pastures overgrown with weeds, scattered bushes, and small saplings.

RANGE: Breeds from northern North Dakota, central Minnesota, northern Wisconsin, and central New England south to Georgia, Mississippi, Louisiana, central Texas, and western Colorado. It winters south to the Gulf of Mexico and northeastern Mexico.

SUBSPECIES: Western populations (subsp. *arenacea*) average paler and grayer than Eastern birds (subsp. *pusilla*), but individual variation can be found in all populations.

SIMILAR SPECIES: The combination of a bright pink bill, a rufous cap, a white eye ring, and an unstreaked buff breast distinguishes this from other sparrows.

Tree Sparrows are larger with a dusky upper mandible, yellow lower mandible, and a dark breast spot.

Adult Chipping Sparrow has a black bill, a white eyestripe, a black eyeline, and plain gray underparts.

CONSERVATION:
Field Sparrows are widespread and common but declining. Although they thrive in open areas such as those created by clearing of forests, these birds tend not to nest near human activity, avoiding tilled agricultural fields and suburbs. Field Sparrow habitat is best maintained by allowing limited woody vegetation in unused fields undergoing succession, and by creating openings in forested habitat by thinning the shrubs and saplings in the underbrush.

■ SUMMER ■ MIGRATION
■ WINTER ■ RARE
■ RESIDENT

This common sparrow is the dominant summer land bird of the great sagebrush flats and dry, brushy mountain meadows of the Great Basin and northern Rocky Mountain region. In winter, it mixes with other sparrows, particularly other *Spizella* species, in brushy desert scrub. This sparrow is unusual in having two distinct nesting populations, one in the alpine meadows of the Rocky Mountains of the Yukon and the other in the sagebrush deserts of the western United States.

DESCRIPTION: 5" (13 cm). This somewhat nondescript bird has light brown upperparts with fine, black streaks; an unstreaked, dingy gray-brown breast; and unmarked, pale underparts. It resembles a Clay-colored Sparrow but has a brown crown, finely streaked with black. It has a well-defined darker ear patch bordered by a fine black eyeline and two parallel "whisker" marks.

VOICE: Alternating trills, musical or buzzy, often quite prolonged. Its call note is a soft *seep*, most often given in flight.

NESTING: Lays 3–5 brown-spotted, bluish eggs in a grass nest on or near the ground.

HABITAT: Sagebrush and alpine meadows.

RANGE: Breeds in the northern Rocky Mountains of Yukon and British Columbia, and in the Great Basin south to southern California and New Mexico. It winters in the southwestern United States but is absent from the Pacific Coast.

SUBSPECIES: The Northern subspecies in the alpine zone of the Canadian Rockies to east-central Alaska (subsp. *taverneri*), sometimes called "Timberline Sparrow," is slightly larger and darker overall; has a different song; and has a darker, longer bill than the nominate Southern race.

SIMILAR SPECIES: See Chipping and Clay-colored sparrows. Brewer's can be distinguished from other clear-breasted sparrows by its characteristic *Spizella* shape, the lack of either a rufous cap or strong head markings, and its generally nondescript plumage.

CONSERVATION: 🐦 LC

Brewer's Sparrow is common in mountain meadows and sagebrush flats, but its numbers are declining. Like other species dependent on sagebrush ecosystems, threats to these birds include livestock grazing, housing and industrial development, conversion of habitat to agriculture, and invasive grass species such as cheatgrass.

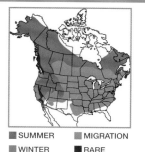

- **SUMMER**
- **MIGRATION**
- **WINTER**
- **RARE**
- **RESIDENT**

Away from the breeding grounds, Fox Sparrows are most conspicuous during spring migration, when one frequently hears their rich, melodious song coming from brushy thickets and roadsides. They scratch in leaves for insects and seeds and often make so much noise that one expects to find a larger animal. Western birds tend to be more dusky brown or slate-colored, and they bear little resemblance to the "fox-colored" eastern birds.

DESCRIPTION: 6–7½" (15–19 cm). This chubby, large, and variable sparrow is either rich rufous-and-gray in the East, or dusky brown or slate-colored in the West, often so dark that no back pattern can be discerned. Heavy streaking of the underparts converges at mid-breast into a large brown spot. It has a heavy, usually yellow bill with a lighter-colored lower mandible, a slightly notched rust-colored tail, and a rounded head outline. It is heavier than a House Sparrow.

VOICE: A lively song that opens with one or more clear whistles followed by several short trills or churrs. Its call is a sharp *chink*.

NESTING: Lays 4 or 5 pale green eggs densely spotted with red-brown in a thick-walled cup of leaves in grass and moss, concealed in vegetation on or near the ground.

HABITAT: Thickets and edges of coniferous, mixed, or second-growth forests or chaparral. In winter, particularly in the East, weedy pastures and brushy roadsides.

RANGE: Breeds from the Aleutians and mainland Alaska east to northern Quebec and the Maritimes and south to southern California and Colorado. It winters south from British Columbia and across the southern United States, and locally farther north.

SUBSPECIES: Fox Sparrows include many recognized subspecies, categorized into four subspecies groups that are sometimes considered separate species. All of these populations interbreed where their ranges overlap, producing many intergrades. *(continued on next page)*

Taiga breeders in the Far North (*iliaca* group, "Red Fox Sparrow") are the brightest, with a distinctly rufous-and-gray streaked pattern on the head and back; these birds have a gray rump and a relatively short tail. This group is the most widespread across the eastern two-thirds of North America.

Rocky Mountain/Interior West birds (*schistacea* group, "Slate-colored Fox Sparrow") have a plain grayish head and back that contrast with rufous-red wings and a relatively long, reddish tail. This group has large, blackish spots on the underparts that become brownish on the flanks.

California breeders (*megarhyncha* group, "Thick-billed Fox Sparrow") have a noticeably thicker, grayish bill. They are drab gray on the back with reddish wings and tail, showing less contrast than in the Slate-colored group.

Pacific coastal birds (*unalaschcensis* group, "Sooty Fox Sparrow") are uniformly brown above, with large brown spots underneath, a brown rump and tail, and dark flanks. Birds that breed the farthest north are paler, while those that breed farther south are the darkest; some individuals are slightly redder on the wings and tail.

SIMILAR SPECIES: In the East, Hermit Thrush is more olive-brown on the back and has a thinner bill. In the West, all brown thrushes are thin-billed and spotted on the breast, not streaked; most thrushes have an eye ring.

CONSERVATION: LC

Fox Sparrows are numerous and widespread; their populations are stable. These birds thrive in the thickening regrowth that follows logging or forest fires, and their remote nesting grounds leave them free from most human disturbance.

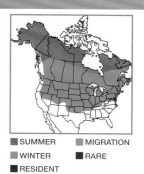

■ SUMMER ■ MIGRATION
■ WINTER ■ RARE
■ RESIDENT

This northern species occurs as a migrant through much of Canada and as a winter visitor to the continental United States. Unlike northern finches such as Pine Siskins and crossbills, its numbers seem to depend on weather, not on the food supply—American Tree Sparrows are less numerous in mild winters. These birds can tolerate subzero temperatures if they get sufficient calories from their seed diet; thus they are able to winter in open country where snow does not entirely cover the weeds and grasses. They are more commonly seen in brushy pastures at the edges of fields and woods. They roam the snow-covered landscape in flocks, uttering tinkling calls and often visiting feeders.

DESCRIPTION: 5½–6½" (14–17 cm). This sparrow has a gray head with a rufous crown and ear stripe. It is streaked brown above and has two prominent wing bars. It is plain gray below, with a dark spot in the center of the breast. It is similar to Field Sparrow, but larger and without the white eye ring or pink bill.

VOICE: Gives one or two clear notes followed by a sweet, rapid warble. Its winter feeding call is a silvery *tsee-ler*.

NESTING: Lays 4 or 5 pale blue eggs speckled with brown in a bulky, well-insulated cup of bark strips and weed stems lined with feathers and hair, concealed in low tundra vegetation.

HABITAT: Arctic willow and birch thickets; fields, weedy woodland edges, and roadside thickets in winter.

RANGE: Breeds from Alaska, northern Saskatchewan, northern Manitoba, and northern Quebec south to northern British Columbia, central Quebec, and Newfoundland. It winters regularly across most of the United States south to California, Arkansas, and the Carolinas.

SUBSPECIES: The Eastern population (subsp. *arborea*) averages slightly smaller and darker overall than Western birds (subsp. *ochracea*).

SIMILAR SPECIES: Field Sparrow is smaller, has a bright pink bill, a conspicuous white eye ring, and lacks a dark breast spot. Also see Chipping Sparrow.

CONSERVATION:  American Tree Sparrows are numerous and widespread but may be slightly declining; they are generally less common west of the Rocky Mountains. They breed north of the treeline, leaving them largely remote from direct human disturbance, and these birds seem able to adapt to disturbed habitats and human settlements at other seasons, often flocking around backyard feeders. Climate change, however, severely threatens the Arctic ecosystems that support these familiar birds.

DARK-EYED JUNCO   *Junco hyemalis*

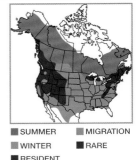

SUMMER   MIGRATION
WINTER   RARE
RESIDENT

Juncos are conspicuous, unstreaked, and somewhat chunky sparrows that forage on the ground. Unlike many other sparrows, they do not scratch in the leaf litter, but instead pick exposed seeds and insects from the surface. In spring and summer, they are common to abundant breeding birds in northern or mountain forests of conifers, birches, and aspen, where they prefer edges and openings rather than the deep interior of the forest. They hop among the leaves on the forest floor, flying up into trees when disturbed, showing their white outer tail feathers and giving alarm notes. During the fall and winter, they gather in flocks and forage in fields, along woodland edges, and in brushy areas, and are frequent and familiar visitors to feeding stations throughout most of the United States and southern Canada.

DESCRIPTION: 5–6¼" (13–16 cm). This species shows much geographic variation in color. Dark-eyed Juncos of all subspecies have pink bills, white outer tail feathers, white bellies, and dark eyes. The rest of the plumage varies geographically (see below). Females of all forms resemble their male counterparts but may be paler. Juveniles of all forms are similar—streaked brown above with a streaked breast and flanks fading to a white belly.

VOICE: A ringing metallic trill on the same pitch. Members of a flock may spread out widely, keeping in contact by constantly calling *tsick* or *tchet*. They also give a soft, buzzy trill in flight.

NESTING: Lays 3–6 pale bluish or greenish eggs with variegated blotches concentrated at the larger end in a deep, compact nest of rootlets, shreds of bark, twigs, and mosses. The nest is lined with grasses and hair and placed on or near the ground, protected by a rock ledge, a mud bank, tufts of weeds, or a fallen log.

HABITAT: Openings and edges of coniferous and mixed woods; in winter, it occurs in fields, parks, and suburban gardens.

RANGE: Breeds from Alaska east across Canada to Newfoundland, south to the mountains in Mexico and Georgia. It winters south to the Gulf Coast and northern Mexico.

SUBSPECIES: The Dark-eyed Junco includes several rather distinct populations that were formerly considered to be separate species but, because they interbreed freely where their ranges come into contact, are all now treated as a single species that is geographically highly variable.

"Slate-colored Junco" (*hyemalis* group) is the most widespread group, nesting throughout Canada and the northern and eastern United States; in winter this population can occur almost anywhere in the United States. This form is dark slate-gray on the head, upper breast, flanks, and upperparts, with a white lower breast and belly. Its dark gray tail with white outer tail feathers is conspicuous in flight.

"Oregon Junco" (*oreganus* group) breeds along the Pacific Coast and in the northwest of the Rocky Mountains. It has a black hood, a chestnut mantle, and white underparts with buff sides. Like Slate-colored, its dark gray tail with white outer tail feathers is conspicuous in flight.

"Pink-sided Junco" (*mearnsi* group) breeds in the mountains from eastern Idaho to southeastern Alberta and southwestern Saskatchewan (Cypress Hills) south to northern Utah and southern Wyoming. It has a pale blue-gray hood, black lores, a pale grayish throat, and extensive pinkish flanks.

"White-winged Junco" (*aikeni* group) is an isolated population in the pine forests of the Black Hills in western South Dakota and eastern Montana. It is similar to the eastern "Slate-colored" form but with two white wing bars and extensive white outer tail feathers.

"Gray-headed Juncos" (*caniceps* group) are birds of the Southwest. They are gray overall with black lores, a pale gray throat, and a well defined, reddish-brown back.

SIMILAR SPECIES: Winter Lapland Longspur resembles an immature Dark-eyed Junco in pattern, but has a shorter tail, a sharply defined ear patch, and white on the outer tail feathers; it lives in barren, open fields.

CONSERVATION:
Dark-eyed Junco is widespread and abundant, and its numbers are stable.

SUMMER   MIGRATION
WINTER   RARE
RESIDENT

Found near the Mexican border, this ground-dwelling junco is slower and more deliberate in its movements than the Dark-eyed Junco; it walks rather than hops on the forest floor. It is a resident of pine and boreal forests at elevations above 7000 feet (2100 meters). In winter, they do not wander widely and are not usually found in mixed flocks with other juncos.

DESCRIPTION: 5½–6½" (14–17 cm). This sparrow has a unique, bright yellow-orange eye and black lores. Its bicolored bill has a dark upper mandible and a pale lower mandible. The bird is gray above, with a bright rusty mantle and white outer tail feathers. Its underparts are lighter.

VOICE: Its song is more highly patterned than that of the Dark-eyed Junco. One representation is *chip-chip, seedle-seedle, chee-chee-chee*, although it is variable.

NESTING: Lays 3 or 4 bluish-white, spotted eggs in a slight cup nest of small rootlets and fine grass lined with horsehair, on the ground under the protection of a log, a stump, or grass tufts, or in a low tree.

HABITAT: Coniferous forests; pine-oak woods.

RANGE: Resident in mountains of southeastern Arizona and southwestern New Mexico.

SIMILAR SPECIES: The "Gray-headed" form of Dark-eyed Junco is similar, but it has dark eyes and an all-pink bill; it regularly hops along the ground.

CONSERVATION:

Yellow-eyed Junco is common in suitable habitat, and its numbers are stable in its limited U.S. range. In Mexico, the species has declined in recent decades.

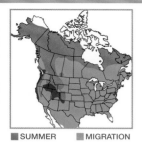

SUMMER   MIGRATION
WINTER   RARE
RESIDENT

The handsome White-crowned Sparrow is a favorite of bird-watchers; it is common in much of the North, especially in western regions, and often nests in residential areas. The White-crowned Sparrow breeds in a variety of shrubby habitats. Much of their feeding is done on the ground. There are several different populations that have distinctive plumage differences and song dialects. In the Arctic, where the sun does not set during the breeding season, these sparrows sing all night long; however, White-crowns farther south, in the Pacific Northwest, also sing frequently during the dark May nights. In the East, these birds are much less numerous than White-throated Sparrows, but flocks of White-throats often contain a few of these slender, elegant birds.

DESCRIPTION: 6–7½" (15–19 cm). This bird is similar to White-throated Sparrow, but is more slender, without the white throat, and generally with a more erect posture. Its crown has bold black and white stripes. Its upperparts are streaked, and its underparts are clean, pearly gray. It has a pink bill. Young birds are similar, but the crown stripes are buff and dark brown, and the underparts are washed with dull buff.

VOICE: A short series of clear whistles followed by buzzy notes. Its song varies regionally.

NESTING: Lays 3–5 pale green eggs thickly spotted with brown in a bulky cup of bark strips, grass, and twigs, lined with grass and hair, on or near the ground.

HABITAT: This bird nests in dense brush, especially near open grasslands; it winters in open woods and gardens.

RANGE: Breeds from Alaska and Manitoba east to Labrador and Newfoundland, and south in the western mountains to northern New Mexico and central California. It winters north to southern Alaska, Idaho, Kansas, Kentucky, and Maryland.

SUBSPECIES: The northern, northwestern, and mountain subspecies of White-crowned Sparrows have slightly different head patterns and songs. Song dialects vary locally as well.

SIMILAR SPECIES: Golden-crowned Sparrow is larger, with a darker bill; it is duskier overall and darker below; the immature lacks well-defined head striping and has a faint tinge of yellow on the forecrown.

CONSERVATION:
White-crowned Sparrow is widespread and common, and its population is stable.

SUMMER · MIGRATION
WINTER · RARE
RESIDENT

The Golden-crowned Sparrow is a dark, handsome western bird that breeds at the timberline in mountains and, in Alaska, in shrub thickets along the seacoast. One or two of these sparrows often join winter flocks of White-crowned Sparrows. They live with the flock but feed more in the shelter of bushes and visit open lawns less often.

DESCRIPTION: 6–7" (15–18 cm). This bird is similar to White-crowned Sparrow. The male's gold crown is bordered by a wide black cap. It has a dusky bill. It is brown above with an unstreaked gray breast, cheek, and collar; and two white wing bars. Fall immatures have two dark brown crown stripes with a dusky yellowish central area and a trace of a "mustache" stripe.

VOICE: Its song consists of three descending plaintive notes sounding like *oh, dear me*. Its calls are *tseet* and *chink*.

NESTING: Lays 4 or 5 bluish, speckled eggs in a neat cup nest well hidden in a dense weed clump or bush.

HABITAT: Alpine meadows and coniferous forest clearings; it winters in coastal brushland and chaparral.

RANGE: Breeds from western Alaska south through Yukon Territory to northwestern Washington. Winters from Kodiak Island and coastal Alaska south to Baja California.

SIMILAR SPECIES: See White-crowned Sparrow.

CONSERVATION:

This bird breeds in such remote locations that exact population trends are difficult to determine. Their population is estimated to have risen slightly in the last few decades.

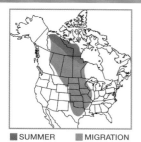

■ SUMMER ■ MIGRATION
■ WINTER ■ RARE
■ RESIDENT

These large, handsome sparrows rarely stray far from their normal Midwestern range. They vigorously scratch in the leaves and soil for food, and eat weed seeds, flower buds and blossoms, small fruits such as berries, and a great variety of insects, spiders, and snails. In winter, Harris's Sparrows mix with and generally dominate flocks of the more numerous White-crowned and Golden-crowned sparrows. When a flock is disturbed it often flies up to the top of a nearby bush. This sparrow is shyer and warier in its northern breeding territory. John James Audubon named this species for Edward Harris (1799–1863), who accompanied him on his western trip in 1843.

DESCRIPTION: 7½" (19 cm). Our largest sparrow, the adult has a black crown, throat, and chest; a pink bill; a gray face; and a brown back, wings, and tail. It has a white abdomen with spotted or streaked sides. Immatures have buff faces and lack the solid black crown, throat, and breast.

VOICE: A series of clear, high notes followed by another series, each on a different pitch.

NESTING: Lays 3–5 pale green, brown-blotched eggs in a plant-fiber and leaf nest, lined with grass and placed on the ground at the base of a bush or in a stunted spruce tree.

HABITAT: Breeds in mossy bogs and scrub forests. It migrates through the prairie regions and winters in dense riverside thickets, woodland borders, clearings, and brush piles.

RANGE: Breeds in northern Canada west of Hudson Bay south to northern Manitoba. It winters in the interior from Iowa and Nebraska south to Texas and Louisiana. Stragglers reach the Pacific Coast nearly every year.

SIMILAR SPECIES: Winter Lapland Longspur resembles the immature in pattern but has a shorter tail, a sharply defined ear patch, and white on the outer tail feathers; it lives in barren, open fields.

CONSERVATION: ![NT]

Harris's Sparrow is declining for reasons that aren't well understood, but may be related to habitat loss to urbanization and agriculture. Climate change has a greater impact on the forest-tundra margins at high latitudes where these birds breed, seriously threatening their nesting grounds.

WHITE-THROATED SPARROW *Zonotrichia albicollis*

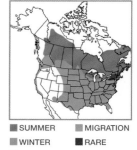

■ SUMMER   ■ MIGRATION
■ WINTER   ■ RARE
■ RESIDENT

This common sparrow breeds across most of Canada and is known in the United States primarily as a migrant or winter visitor. During the colder months, every hedgerow and thicket seems to be filled with White-throateds, and on warm days one can readily hear their plaintive song. When evening comes and they gather to roost in dense thickets, their silvery flocking call is almost as evocative as their song.

DESCRIPTION: 6–7" (15–18 cm). This familiar sparrow has streaked upperparts and clear gray underparts. There are two color forms: one with black and white head stripes, the other with dark brown and tan head stripes. Both have a sharply defined white throat patch and a dark bill. Females and young birds are duller.

VOICE: Song a clear, whistled *Poor Sam Peabody, Peabody, Peabody*, or *Sweet Sweet Canada, Canada, Canada*.

NESTING: Lays 4 or 5 pale green eggs, heavily spotted with brown, in a cup of grass, rootlets, and moss on or near the ground in forest undergrowth.

HABITAT: Brushy undergrowth in coniferous woodlands. It winters in brushy woodlands, pastures, and suburban areas.

RANGE: Breeds from Mackenzie, central Quebec, and Newfoundland south to North Dakota, Wisconsin, and Pennsylvania. Winters in much of the eastern United States and in small numbers in the southwestern U.S. and along the Pacific Coast.

SIMILAR SPECIES: White-crowned Sparrow is similar but lacks the white throat patch, is slimmer, and has a pink bill.

Immature Swamp Sparrow is similar to young White-throated Sparrow but is smaller and darker, with a rounded, not notched, tail; it has a gray collar and lacks head striping.

CONSERVATION: White-throated Sparrow is widespread and common, and its population is stable.

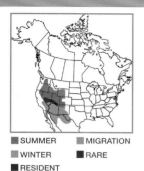

■ SUMMER   ■ MIGRATION
■ WINTER   ■ RARE
■ RESIDENT

Sagebrush Sparrow is a common, elegant sparrow found in the open shrubby flats of the intermountain West, including the sagebrush plains of the Great Basin. These mostly gray sparrows live among sagebrush and other shrubs, where they forage mostly on the ground for insects and seeds by running, often with their longish tails held high. In early summer, males sing a short, lively song from the shrub tops, where it often flicks and waves its tail like a phoebe. This species and Bell's Sparrow were formerly considered a single species, called "Sage Sparrow."

DESCRIPTION: 5–6" (13–15 cm). This sparrow has a mostly gray head with white malars, white "eyebrows," a pronounced white eye ring, and black lores. It has white underparts with a dark spot on the chest. The sides and flanks are light buffy gray, with dusky streaking. The back is brown with dark streaks. Its wings are lighter with buff-colored feather edges, and it has two wing bars. The outer wing feathers are widely edged with white. Both sexes are identical. Immatures are browner with a white throat and fine dark streaking on a buff breast and belly.

VOICE: Only males sing. Its song is a series of short, musical buzzes and whistles rising and falling in various frequencies. Both sexes give a short, musical *tink* call.

NESTING: Lays 3 or 4 bluish-white, speckled eggs in a loose cup built of sagebrush pieces, lined with fur, and well hidden in sagebrush or other scrub.

HABITAT: This species prefers big sagebrush areas in the breeding range; it is rarely found in mixed sagebrush-juniper. It usually breeds below 5500' (1700 m), but can be found higher. During wet years it may breed in creosote bush. During winter it can be found in a variety of arid habitats including desert washes, big sagebrush, creosote bush, sparse cactus scrub, arid grasslands, and arboreal yucca mixed with greasewood.

RANGE: Breeds from eastern Washington and southern Idaho and Montana south throughout the Great Basin to northern New Mexico and Arizona. It winters in small flocks in the low desert of southern California, Arizona, New Mexico, and western Texas, south into Mexico.

SIMILAR SPECIES: The interior subspecies of Bell's Sparrow (*A. b. canescens*) appears most similar in coloration to Sagebrush Sparrow, but it breeds in the Mojave Desert region of southern Nevada and southeastern California, and shows limited migration. Sagebrush Sparrow breeds throughout the Great Basin and migrates southward, overlapping the winter range of *canescens* during October-March.

CONSERVATION: The Sagebrush Sparrow population is generally stable, showing only a small decline during the past several decades. These birds abandon habitat that is degraded by fragmentation, overgrazing, or the spread of invasive cheatgrass.

BELL'S SPARROW   *Artemisiospiza belli*

■ SUMMER   ■ MIGRATION
■ WINTER   ■ RARE
■ RESIDENT

Bell's Sparrow is often secretive, except during the spring breeding season when males sing from a perch to announce their territory. It has a habit of flicking its tail while hopping around on the ground. Most populations are non-migratory. The inland subspecies *canescens* moves up-slope after breeding in early spring, and in late summer and fall moves south and east toward wintering grounds. This species and Sagebrush Sparrow were formerly considered a single species, called "Sage Sparrow."

DESCRIPTION: 4–5½" (10–13 cm). This sparrow has a dark gray head with white malars, white "eyebrows," a pronounced white eye ring, and black lores. It has thick black streaks at the sides of the throat, and white underparts with a dark chest spot. Its back is dark brown with obscure dark streaking. The wings are dark gray-brown with the outermost feathers edged in deep beige. Immatures are browner and have a white throat and fine dark streaking on a buffy breast and underparts. The sexes are identical.

VOICE: Only the males sing. Its song is a jumbled series of upslurred and downslurred notes on different pitches, mostly lacking trills or buzzes of the closely related Sagebrush Sparrow. Intermediate songs between the two species can be found in interior regions. Both sexes give a short, musical *tink* call.

NESTING: Lays 3 or 4 bluish-white, speckled eggs in a loose cup built of brush pieces, lined with fur, and well hidden in scrub patches.

HABITAT: Dry chaparral and coastal sage scrub along coastal lowlands, inland valleys, and in lower foothills in California. Found in big sagebrush at higher elevations in southern mountains. Inland it prefers low desert scrub.

RANGE: From northern California to Baja California.

SUBSPECIES: The nominate Pacific population (subsp. *belli*) is uncommon and local in dense chaparral along the California coast and foothills.

The inland subspecies (subsp. *canescens*), sometimes called "Saltbush Sparrow," is found in flat expanses of arid sagebrush and saltbush plains. It most resembles the closely related Sagebrush Sparrow in coloration.

The endangered "San Clemente Sage Sparrow" (subsp. *clementeae*) is found only on San Clemente Island off the coast of southern California; it is a locally common resident in maritime desert scrub slopes on the island.

SIMILAR SPECIES: See Sagebrush Sparrow.

CONSERVATION:

Bell's Sparrow has been listed as a Species of Special Concern in California. As with many species along the densely populated California coast, it faces habitat loss due to development and urbanization. The San Clemente Island subspecies (*A. b. clementeae*) has been listed as Threatened by the U.S. Fish and Wildlife Service since 1977.

■ SUMMER ■ MIGRATION
■ WINTER ■ RARE
■ RESIDENT

The rich, musical song of this sparrow is a most distinctive sound on rolling farmlands. Long known as the "Bay-winged Bunting" because of its bright chestnut wing patch, the naturalist John Burroughs gave this bird the name Vesper Sparrow because he thought the song sounded more melodious in the evening. The bird is usually found on the ground but often mounts an exposed perch to deliver its song.

DESCRIPTION: 5–6½" (13–17 cm). A grayish, streaked sparrow with white outer tail feathers, a narrow white eye ring, and a small patch of chestnut on the bend of the wing. It has pale gray-brown upperparts with dark brown streaks. The dull gray-white underparts have thin, dark brown stripes on the throat, breast, sides, and flanks. The breast lacks a dark central spot and may be tinged with a buff wash.

VOICE: Its song is a slow series of four clear musical notes, the last two higher, ending in a descending series of trills— sometimes rendered as *come-come-where-where-all-together-down-the-hill*.

NESTING: Lays 4–6 white eggs heavily spotted with brown in a well-made cup of grass and rootlets concealed in grass on the ground.

HABITAT: Fields, pastures, and roadsides in farming country.

RANGE: Breeds from British Columbia, Ontario, and Nova Scotia south to central California, Texas, Tennessee, and western North Carolina. It winters north to central California, Oklahoma, New Jersey, and Long Island.

SUBSPECIES: The more common and widespread Western population (subsp. *confinis*) is slightly paler than the nominate Eastern population (subsp. *gramineus*), which is uncommon and declining.

SIMILAR SPECIES: Water Pipit and Sprague's Pipit have thin bills and walk rather than hop. Savannah Sparrow usually has yellow lores and shorter tail without obvious white feathers. Female Lark Bunting is larger and has an obvious white wing patch and a larger, silver-blue bill.

CONSERVATION:
Vesper Sparrow remains widespread and numerous overall; it is common in the West and uncommon in the East. Its numbers are declining, especially in the East, due to grassland habitat loss and changing agricultural practices such as earlier harvesting, more frequent mowing, and reversion of unused farmland to forests. It is listed as endangered, threatened, or of special conservation concern in several U.S. states.

LECONTE'S SPARROW   *Ammospiza leconteii*

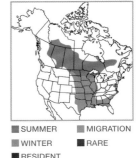

■ SUMMER   ■ MIGRATION
■ WINTER   ■ RARE
■ RESIDENT

This elusive bird keeps to the thick grass like all grass-loving sparrows except when it mounts an exposed perch to sing. It is almost impossible to flush, for it prefers running to flying. Common in the prairie regions of west-central Canada, it inhabits the drier grass borders of rush-grown marshes. The species is named for Major John LeConte of Georgia, an early American naturalist (1818–1891).

DESCRIPTION: 5" (13 cm). LeConte's is a relatively colorful sparrow, with a buff or pale orange face and breast, gray ear coverts, a white median crown stripe, and a bluish bill. The sides are streaked; at close range dull pinkish streaks are visible on the nape. Juvenile LeConte's also have a buff-and-gray face pattern, but are paler buff overall, with light streaking across the breast and a tinge of rust in the wings.

VOICE: Two thin, insect-like hisses.

NESTING: Lays 4 brown-spotted whitish eggs in a grass cup lined with hair and set on the ground, usually in a grass clump.

HABITAT: Moist grasslands and boggy meadows; also dry fields in winter.

RANGE: Breeds from Mackenzie and central Quebec south to northern Montana, Minnesota, and northern Michigan. It winters in the southeastern United States.

SIMILAR SPECIES: LeConte's face can be as orange as that of the interior population of Nelson's Sparrow, but Nelson's lacks the white median crown stripe; it has a wide reddish collar on the nape and upper back.

Grasshopper Sparrow lacks the distinct dark streaks on the flanks; the immature has a buff breast but lacks the gray ear coverts of an immature LeConte's.

See Baird's Sparrow and Henslow's Sparrow.

CONCERVATION:

LeConte's Sparrow is relatively common but secretive. Its population is believed to have undergone a slight decline in recent decades, following a more significant decline in the latter half of the 20th century. As damp fields have been converted to farmland, their available nesting area has decreased, and housing developments have affected coastal nesting grounds as well.

■ SUMMER ■ MIGRATION
■ WINTER ■ RARE
■ RESIDENT

This is literally a seaside bird; few other sparrows have so restricted a habitat. Favoring the wetter sections of salt marshes, it feeds much less on seeds than other sparrows do, but eats tiny young crabs, snails, and other small marine animals along the tidal creeks of salt meadows. Like all birds living near the ground in grass, the Seaside Sparrow is difficult to detect until it is almost underfoot, whereupon it flushes, flies for a short distance, drops down into the thick grass, and runs along like a mouse. The best opportunity to view one is when it is singing atop a grass stem or small shrub.

DESCRIPTION: 6" (15 cm). A dark, gray-streaked salt-marsh sparrow with a dull yellow "mustache" and a dull yellow spot in front of the eye. Adults are olive-gray above with indistinct light grayish stripes on the back. They lack wing bars and have a bright yellow edge at the bend in the wing. The throat and underparts are whitish with blurry grayish stripes on the breast, sides, and flanks. Plumage in this species is variable geographically.

VOICE: Gives two short, sharp notes followed by a buzzy *zeeee*.

NESTING: Lays 4 or 5 white eggs with brown blotches in a woven grass nest placed in a grass tussock above the high-tide line.

HABITAT: Exclusively grassy salt marshes, favoring the wetter portions.

RANGE: Breeds in salt marshes of the Atlantic and Gulf coasts from southern New England to Florida and Texas. It winters in the southern portions of this range.

SUBSPECIES: Seven extant subspecies are recognized, which vary in plumage, range, and song. Gulf Coast populations have more distinct streaks and longer bills; Atlantic Coast populations are somewhat drabber gray with blurry, indistinct streaks above and below. "Cape Sable Seaside Sparrow" (subsp. *mirabilis*), which inhabits a small area in southwestern Florida, is

brighter olive-green above and whiter underneath with distinct dark streaks.

SIMILAR SPECIES: Nelson's Sparrow is smaller and browner, except for the Atlantic *subvirgatus* subspecies, which is grayish, with sharper back streaks and an ochre face pattern.

CONSERVATION:

Seaside Sparrow is generally common, and most populations are stable, but its numbers are declining due to the destruction of coastal marshes. Some localized populations are highly vulnerable; the Cape Sable Seaside Sparrow is on the U.S. Endangered Species List and is classified as endangered in Florida.

"Dusky Seaside Sparrow" (*A. m. nigrescens*), a subspecies formerly found near Titusville, Florida, became extinct in 1987 due to habitat destruction.

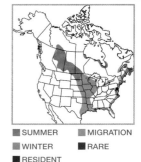

■ SUMMER ■ MIGRATION
■ WINTER ■ RARE
■ RESIDENT

Nelson's Sparrow can be frustratingly difficult to glimpse in the marsh grasses they prefer to inhabit year-round. The birds often run among the short grasses, looking for all the world like marsh-dwelling mice, and then launch themselves into the air for a short flight before diving back down into cover. Eventually, though, one or more will usually perch in the open. Patience is the key. This species was formerly called "Nelson's Sharp-tailed Sparrow"; it and Saltmarsh Sparrow were once considered a single species ("Sharp-tailed Sparrow").

DESCRIPTION: 5" (13 cm). This marsh bird has a short tail, a gray crown, a well-defined white belly, no streaks on the nape, and an orange triangle on the face. Three geographically distinct populations have variable plumage. Inland birds are the richest buff below, with vague breast streaks and bold white streaks on the back. Atlantic coastal forms range in color from grayish above with indistinct breast streaking to dark above with sharply defined streaks both above and below.

VOICE: Its song is an unmusical, dry, staticky *tschyyy-drrr*, with the second part lower, often likened to water hitting a hot skillet. Its call is a dry, hard *stik*.

NESTING: Lays 4 or 5 brown-dotted, pale blue eggs in an open grass cup, sometimes built up on the sides to form partial covering.

HABITAT: Edges of freshwater marshes and in wet meadows of interior North America, and in salt marshes along the northern Atlantic Coast.

RANGE: Breed in marshes on the Atlantic coast of Canada and Maine, central Canada (the Canadian Prairies region and a coastal strip on the south of Hudson Bay), and the north central United States.

SUBSPECIES: Three subspecies breed in disjunct regions: *subvirgatus*, in coastal marshes of New England and Southeastern Canada; *alterus*, in sedge bogs with dwarf willow and birch of the Hudson Bay coast; and the nominate *nelsoni*, in freshwater marshes of the northern prairies.

SIMILAR SPECIES: See Saltmarsh Sparrow.

LeConte's Sparrow is similar but has streaks on the nape and lacks the gray crown stripe. Nelson's Sparrow generally uses wetter habitats.

CONSERVATION: Nelson's Sparrows are relatively common and their numbers are stable.

■ SUMMER   ■ MIGRATION
■ WINTER   ■ RARE
■ RESIDENT

Saltmarsh Sparrows can be quite difficult to see because they are often on the ground in tall grasses, occasionally flying up to a perch on a stem, only to return almost immediately to the ground. If the observer waits long enough, one will eventually perch on top of a grass stem, providing a better look. One of the most beautiful sparrows in fresh plumage (September and October), it is quite drab in worn plumage at the end of the breeding season in July and August. This species was formerly called "Saltmarsh Sharp-tailed Sparrow"; it and Nelson's Sparrow were once considered a single species ("Sharp-tailed Sparrow").

DESCRIPTION: 5½" (14 cm). The combination of a dark cap, a gray ear patch, a bright orange-buff triangular area on the face, and white streaks on the back distinguishes the Saltmarsh Sparrow from all other sparrows except for the closely related Nelson's Sparrow.

VOICE: A complex but quiet song, with a wheezy or whispered quality. The syllables of this complex song include trills and accented syllables, with each syllable differing from those preceding and following. Only the male sings. The male can continue with a single uninterrupted song from one perch, through a short flight, to another perch.

NESTING: Lays 4 or 5 brown-dotted, light greenish or bluish eggs in a nest both constructed from and set among marsh grasses above the high-tide line.

HABITAT: In saltmarsh grasses, although using a somewhat wider variety of habitats during migration.

RANGE: Breeds in coastal marshes from southern Maine to North Carolina. It winters along the Atlantic Coast from Long Island, New York, to Florida.

SIMILAR SPECIES: Range is the most important way of separating Saltmarsh and Nelson's Sparrows—this species is entirely coastal, whereas Nelson's is found much farther north, and primarily in inland marshes, although also along the coasts of Maine and Atlantic Canada. There is some range overlap in Maine, where Nelson's Sparrow reaches the coast and Saltmarsh Sparrow reaches the northern extent of its range. There is also significant overlap in winter range. In areas of overlapping range, the Saltmarsh Sparrow is larger than Nelson's, and is distinctly streaked with brown on the flanks and breast (Nelson's Sparrows in this range have blurry grayish streaks).

See LeConte's and Seaside sparrows. Savannah Sparrow, which can occur in salt marshes, has a white crown stripe, yellow lores, a notched tail, and a more zigzagging flight.

CONSERVATION: EN
Saltmarsh Sparrows are endangered and decreasing. Rising sea levels present their most pressing danger; the birds nest in vegetation that generally sits only inches above water. Higher tides have begun immersing nests for short periods of time. Also, further saltmarsh habitat loss is being caused by coastal development, pollution, and invasive plant species.

BAIRD'S SPARROW *Centronyx bairdii*

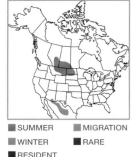

■ SUMMER ■ MIGRATION
■ WINTER ■ RARE
■ RESIDENT

Among bird watchers, Baird's Sparrow is a highly sought-after bird of the northern plains. Males in the breeding season can be easily identified by their distinctive song despite their subtle plumage characteristics. Of all grassland sparrows, Baird's is the most reluctant to fly, and when flushed, it slips through the grass like a mouse. The total population of Baird's Sparrows is small, and once they leave the breeding grounds they are difficult to find. Even on the breeding grounds, one must search hard for the habitat that suits them, but a few singing males usually can be found there, often perched on the tips of weed stalks. John James Audubon first described this elegant sparrow in 1844, naming it after Spencer F. Baird, a 19th-century ornithologist and Secretary of the Smithsonian Institution.

DESCRIPTION: 5–5½" (13–14 cm). This pale, streaked sparrow is whitish below, and its breast is crossed by a band of narrow black streaks. It has a bright buffy to ocher crown stripe.

VOICE: Three short notes followed by a musical trill on a lower pitch.

NESTING: Lays 3–5 white eggs, blotched and scrawled with dark brown, in a cup of weed stems and grass, concealed in grass or weeds on the ground.

HABITAT: Dry upland prairies.

RANGE: Breeds from Saskatchewan and Manitoba south to Montana and Minnesota. It winters in Texas, Arizona, and northern Mexico.

SIMILAR SPECIES: Adult Henslow's and juvenile Grasshopper and LeConte's sparrows have well-defined necklaces of streaks across the breast, have shorter tails, and a flat-headed and larger-billed profile.

CONSERVATION:
Once quite common but diminished by the conversion of native prairie to agriculture, Baird's Sparrow is uncommon and local. Fire suppression practices also affect this species—Baird's Sparrows are more numerous where controlled burning is used to maintain successional habitat; unburned areas that become gradually dominated by woody shrubs do not support these birds.

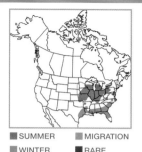

■ SUMMER   ■ MIGRATION
■ WINTER   ■ RARE
■ RESIDENT

This sparrow is secretive and mouse-like, skulking low in the grass. It relies on running rather than flying, and is seldom observed unless perched atop a weed stalk uttering its insect-like "song." These birds are sometimes found in loose colonies of up to a dozen pairs, but one to three pairs are more common. Curiously, Henslow's Sparrows may be present in a certain locality and absent from a seemingly similar habitat not far away. The bird is named for John Henslow, a prominent early 19th-century English botanist.

DESCRIPTION: 5" (13 cm). In addition to its distinctive profile, Henslow's unique olive-colored head makes this bird relatively easy to identify. The wings are dull rust, and there are sharply defined streaks on the buff breast and sides. Two whisker marks are present, as well as a dark smudge toward the back of the ear coverts. Juveniles are unstreaked, with extensive buff below, but they typically have an olive head and rust-colored wings like the adults.

VOICE: A high, insect-like two-note burst, *tsi-lick*, sometimes characterized as a "sneeze" or "hiccup."

NESTING: Lays 4 brown-spotted, whitish eggs in a woven grass nest on the ground, usually in a grass clump.

HABITAT: Moist or dry grasslands with scattered weeds and small shrubs.

RANGE: Breeds (locally) from Minnesota, southern Ontario, and central New York (rarely to New England) south to Kansas, Illinois, and North Carolina. It winters in the Gulf Coast states, northern Florida, and along the Atlantic Coast to South Carolina.

SIMILAR SPECIES: Immature LeConte's Sparrow has breast streaking and some rust in the wing, like an adult Henslow's, but is paler and more buff-colored like a Grasshopper Sparrow. It lacks Henslow's olive head and has gray ear coverts.

See Baird's Sparrow, which also has whisker marks and a smudge on the ear coverts.

CONSERVATION:

Henslow's Sparrows have declined seriously in much of their former range, but thanks to conservation efforts their numbers have begun to climb again. The species is listed as endangered in Canada, and as endangered, threatened, or of special concern in more than a dozen U.S. states. The IUCN Red List upgraded Henslow's Sparrow from Near Threatened to Least Concern in 2018 thanks to an increasing population trend. Grassland conservation efforts and the federal Conservation Reserve Program—a U.S. Department of Agriculture initiative that assists farmers in setting aside ideal swaths of land for conservation purposes—can be credited with reversing long-term declines of this uncommon species.

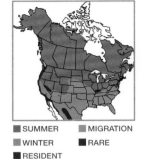

■ SUMMER ■ MIGRATION
■ WINTER ■ RARE
■ RESIDENT

The common Savannah Sparrow inhabits open, wet grasslands such as tundra, mountain meadows, marshes, streamsides, and grassy dunes. Dense cover is essential to this bird. It flies a short distance when flushed, quickly dropping out of sight into weedy cover. The Savannah Sparrow exhibits a fair degree of variation, especially between the different habitats it occupies. Savannah Sparrows are able runners; once discovered, they drop into the grass and dart away. In the fall they migrate southward in huge numbers and may then be found almost anywhere, even in city parks. The species is named for Savannah, Georgia, where 19th century ornithologist Alexander Wilson encountered this bird.

DESCRIPTION: 4½–6" (11–15 cm). This variable sparrow is pale and streaked, with a yellowish eyebrow and pinkish legs. Its tail is notched; other grassland sparrows have shorter, more pointed tails.

VOICE: High-pitched, buzzy *tsip-tsip-tsip-se-e-e-srr*.

NESTING: Lays 4–6 pale blue-green eggs, variably spotted and speckled with dark brown, in a cup of grass lined with finer plant material and hair, placed on the ground.

HABITAT: Fields, prairies, salt marshes, and grassy dunes.

RANGE: Breeds from Alaska east to Labrador and south to New Jersey, Missouri, and northern Mexico. It winters regularly north to southeastern Alaska and Massachusetts.

SUBSPECIES: The Savannah Sparrow subspecies complex remains unresolved. As many as 16 or 17 subspecies have been recognized in the past, many of which have since been consolidated, invalidated, or proposed as distinct species. Each is slightly different in coloration and song. "Ipswich Sparrow" (subsp. *princeps*), a large and pale form that breeds at Sable Island, Nova Scotia, was formerly considered a separate species, but is now considered a subspecies of Savannah Sparrow again. "Belding's Savannah Sparrow" (subsp. *beldingi*) is resident in the salt marshes of southern California. "Large-billed Sparrow" (subsp. *rostratus*) appears in southern California as a post-breeding visitor from Mexico.

SIMILAR SPECIES: Vesper Sparrow has white outer tail feathers, evenly placed stripes on underparts, dark cheeks, a thin white eye ring, and no pale medial crown stripe.

Song Sparrow is longer with a rounded tail. It is grayer about the head and lacks yellow over the eye.

Lincoln's and Baird's sparrows are buff on the breast and head.

CONSERVATION:

Widespread and abundant, Savannah Sparrows were beneficiaries of the changes to the environment that occurred in the early 20th century. As forests were cleared and tilled for pastureland, populations boomed. Urbanization and shifting agricultural practices that focused on intensive row-cropping versus dairy farming and hayfields brought numbers to their current levels, which are stable overall.

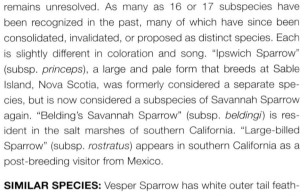

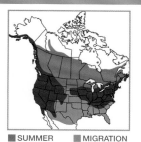

- ■ SUMMER
- ■ WINTER
- ■ RESIDENT
- ■ MIGRATION
- ■ RARE

The Song Sparrow is one of the most widespread, diverse, and geographically variable of North American birds. This common bird is a permanent resident in many areas, while in others it arrives early in the spring and often departs late in the fall. It usually prefers thickets, woodland edges, hedgerows, pond margins, and weedy fields with adjacent brush for cover. It has a peculiar way of pumping its longish, rounded tail as it flies.

DESCRIPTION: 5–7" (13–18 cm). This bird has heavy brown streaking on white underparts, with a prominent central breast spot (sometimes lacking in juveniles). Subspecies show considerable variations in size and colors, ranging from pale sandy to dark brown (see below). It pumps its relatively long, rounded tail in flight.

VOICE: Its song consists of three short notes followed by a varied trill, sometimes interpreted as *Madge-Madge-Madge, put-on-your-tea-kettle-ettle-ettle*.

NESTING: Lays 3–6 pale greenish-white, heavily marked eggs in a neat, well-hidden grassy cup nest often lined with hair, placed in a bush or on the ground. Lays up to 3 clutches in a season.

HABITAT: Forest edges, clearings, thickets, and marshes with open grassy feeding areas; undergrowth in gardens, and city parks. It uses low, dense scrub for nesting, and tall vantage points for singing.

RANGE: Breeds from the Aleutians and mainland Alaska east to Newfoundland and south to California, North Dakota, and the Carolinas. It winters from southern Canada throughout the United States to the Gulf Coast and Mexico.

SUBSPECIES: More than two dozen subspecies are recognized; these range from large, dark-colored, large-billed birds on the rocky beaches of the humid Aleutian Islands to small, sandy, short-billed birds in scrub desert areas in the lower Colorado River valley. Other subspecies are found in coastal salt marshes, freshwater marshes, humid coastal belts, and dry, sagebrush-covered regions. Variation is most prominent in overall coloration and the color and thickness of the streaks on the underparts.

SIMILAR SPECIES: Savannah Sparrow has a short, notched tail, a white crown stripe, yellow in front of the eye, sharp breast streaks that do not usually form a spot, and pinker legs.

Swamp Sparrow has a grayish breast with finer streaks, grayer cheeks and collar, and a grayer eyebrow. It is slightly smaller overall, with broad black streaks on the back; its call is different.

See Lincoln's Sparrow.

CONSERVATION:

Song Sparrows are widespread and abundant. Some local populations are vulnerable to habitat loss, especially those that live in coastal marshes, but the species overall has a large and stable population.

■ SUMMER ■ MIGRATION
■ WINTER ■ RARE
■ RESIDENT

This unobtrusive bird of the northern bogs is wary and secretive when not singing. Although not uncommon during migration, Lincoln's Sparrow is seldom noticed because of its shyness and its resemblance to a Song Sparrow and several other common sparrows. In the West, Lincoln's is more common and comparatively easy to see, especially in winter. John James Audubon named the bird in 1834 for Robert Lincoln, a companion on his trip to Labrador.

DESCRIPTION: 5–6" (13–15 cm). This bird's crown has two rusty stripes, and it has a gray eyebrow. There is usually a narrow, distinct white eye ring. The throat and underparts are white; a broad band of buff across the breast extends down to the sides and flanks. Within the buff areas there are thin black streaks that occasionally converge into a central spot. Juveniles in late summer resemble juvenile Song and Swamp sparrows but usually have a spotted chin and throat.

VOICE: A rich, gurgling, wren-like song rising in the middle and dropping abruptly at the end.

NESTING: Lays 4 or 5 pale green eggs, heavily spotted with brown, in a cup of grass well concealed in forest undergrowth.

HABITAT: Brushy bogs and willow or alder thickets; it winters in woodland thickets and brushy pastures.

RANGE: Breeds from Alaska, northern Quebec, Labrador, and Newfoundland south to California, northern New Mexico, and northern New England. It winters across the southern tier of the United States.

SIMILAR SPECIES: Lincoln's Sparrow is similar to Song Sparrow, but is more finely streaked and shyer. It often pumps its tail like a Song Sparrow, although without the same energy.

Chipping Sparrow has a longer tail, a whiter eyebrow stripe, and different habitat.

Tree and Field sparrows have conspicuous wing bars.

See immature Song and White-throated sparrows.

CONSERVATION:
Lincoln's Sparrow is widespread and common, although less common in the East, and often inconspicuous and secretive. Its numbers are stable.

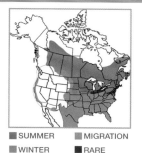

■ SUMMER ■ MIGRATION
■ WINTER ■ RARE
■ RESIDENT

A bird of the wetlands during the breeding season, the Swamp Sparrow appears in a variety of other habitats during migration and in winter. It is rather shy, but responds readily to any squeaking noise, and can usually be lured into view by a patient observer. It is never seen in large flocks like the White-throated and White-crowned sparrows, but is usually found singly, foraging on the ground in rather dense cover.

DESCRIPTION: 5" (13 cm). A chunky, dark sparrow with unstreaked underparts, a bright rufous cap, and rusty wings. It has a dark brown back and tail, a gray face and breast, and a white throat.

VOICE: A sweet, musical trill, all on one note.

NESTING: Lays 4 or 5 blue-green eggs, with brown blotches, in a grassy cup on the ground, well hidden in dense tussocks or marsh vegetation.

HABITAT: Freshwater marshes and open wooded swamps; during migration with other sparrows, weedy fields, parks, and brush piles.

RANGE: Breeds from Mackenzie east to Newfoundland, and south to northern Missouri, Ohio, Maryland, and Delaware. It winters north to Nebraska, the southern Great Lakes region, and southern New England.

SIMILAR SPECIES: White-throated Sparrow has a striped crown and a whiter throat, and lacks rusty coloration on the wings.

CONSERVATION:
Swamp Sparrow is widespread and common in good habitat. Localized populations are hurt by the loss of marsh and salt marsh habitat, but overall this species' population is increasing.

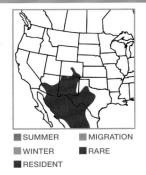

■ SUMMER ■ MIGRATION
■ WINTER ■ RARE
■ RESIDENT

The Canyon Towhee is found in scrubby, rocky hills and mountainous areas in the arid Southwest. It usually feeds alone or in pairs on seeds, fruit, and insects in relatively open areas with patches of brush, including yards and parks. The California and Canyon towhees were long considered the same species, called the "Brown Towhee," although they have different songs and calls and their ranges do not overlap.

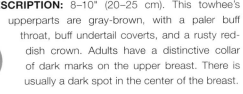

DESCRIPTION: 8–10" (20–25 cm). This towhee's upperparts are gray-brown, with a paler buff throat, buff undertail coverts, and a rusty reddish crown. Adults have a distinctive collar of dark marks on the upper breast. There is usually a dark spot in the center of the breast.

VOICE: Its song is a musical *chili-chili-chili-chili*. Its call is a clear *chud-up*.

NESTING: Lays 3 or 4 bluish-green eggs, lightly spotted or scrawled with blackish-brown markings, in a cup nest placed low in a bush or young tree.

HABITAT: Brushy and rocky hills in arid country.

RANGE: Resident from western and central Arizona, northern New Mexico, southeastern Colorado, and west-central Texas southward.

SIMILAR SPECIES: California Towhee is similar in habits and appearance, but its range does not overlap with Canyon Towhee.

See Abert's Towhee; the two species can usually be distinguished by habitat, and their calls are different.

CONSERVATION:
Canyon Towhees are common and their numbers appear to be stable. Residential development along rivers in the Southwest have removed habitats, but these birds have adjusted to living at the edges of neighborhoods and agricultural fields. Near human populations, these birds are vulnerable to predation by domestic and feral cats.

SUMMER | MIGRATION
WINTER | RARE
RESIDENT

These birds are common in desert valleys, especially around riparian areas with cottonwood, willow, mesquite, and salt cedar. Although related to and closely resembling California and Canyon towhees, this bird is paler, more secretive, and has a different song.

DESCRIPTION: 8–9" (20–23 cm). This towhee is grayish-brown above with slightly paler underparts, a buffy belly, and a tawny undertail. A black facial patch surrounds its pale bill.

VOICE: Its call is a single, bell-like note. Its song resembles a rapid series of call notes.

NESTING: Lays 3 or 4 pale blue-green eggs with brown scrawlings mostly at the wide end in a cup nest close to the ground in a bush or tree.

HABITAT: Along arroyos in desert thickets; associated with cottonwood, willow, and mesquite, although it is also found around farms, orchards, and urban areas.

RANGE: Resident in southern and western Arizona, parts of neighboring Utah, New Mexico, and California, southward into Baja California and Sonora in Mexico.

SIMILAR SPECIES: See California and Canyon towhees.

CONSERVATION:
Abert's Towhee is common in its limited range, and its numbers are increasing. Although vulnerable to the loss of streamside habitat, the species readily adapts to suburban habitats and invasive saltcedar (tamarisk) stands. Abert's Towhee also benefits from conservation efforts aimed at protecting several other species that share its native desert riparian habitat.

CALIFORNIA TOWHEE *Melozone crissalis*

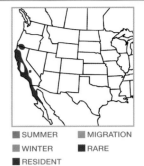

■ SUMMER ■ MIGRATION
■ WINTER ■ RARE
■ RESIDENT

The California Towhee is easily overlooked because it often forages quietly among chaparral bushes or garden cover. Although its range in the chaparral overlaps during winter with that of the Spotted Towhee, this bird lives in low scrub, whereas the Spotted keeps to scrub oaks and other taller forest-edge areas.

DESCRIPTION: 8–10" (20–25 cm). This towhee is uniform gray-brown above and below, with buff or rust-colored undertail coverts. It lacks a dark central spot on the breast. Some birds may be paler and grayer in more arid regions, and average darker brown in humid environments.

VOICE: Its song is a series of squeaky *chip*s on the same pitch, accelerating into a rapid trill. The pattern varies according to the geographical area. The call is a sharp *chink* and thin *tseeee*.

NESTING: Lays 3 or 4 bluish-green eggs, lightly spotted or scrawled with blackish-brown markings, in a cup nest placed low in a bush or young tree.

HABITAT: Shady underbrush, open woods, pinyon-juniper woodlands, and suburban gardens.

RANGE: Resident in coastal and foothill chaparral from Oregon to southern Baja California.

SUBSPECIES: The regional variation in populations is clinal and quite subtle. A small, isolated subpopulation found in the Argus Range in Inyo County, California (subsp. *eremophila*), is considered threatened.

SIMILAR SPECIES: See Canyon Towhee.

CONSERVATION: Although still common, California Towhee has declined locally due to increasing development and urbanization along the California coast, and overgrazing by livestock. The Inyo California Towhee is on the U.S. Endangered Species List and classified as threatened in California, numbering perhaps 200 birds.

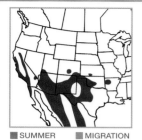

- ■ SUMMER ■ MIGRATION
- ■ WINTER ■ RARE
- ■ RESIDENT

The Rufous-crowned Sparrow is a bird of rocky, brushy, relatively arid hillsides. A secretive bird, the male sings in the early morning from the tops of boulders in spring, but otherwise it is usually on the ground. If disturbed, it will fly to a nearby rock for a short survey, then return to the grass.

DESCRIPTION: 5–6" (13–15 cm). This bird has a rufous crown with a darker rufous eyestripe on a gray head; it has a conspicuous black "whisker" mark. The mantle is gray with rufous-brown streaks, and the underparts are unstreaked gray. Juveniles have a buff-colored breast with faint streaking and little, if any, rufous marking.

VOICE: Its song is a rapid, pleasing jumble of notes, recalling that of the House Wren, but huskier and less gurgling. Its distinctive call is a down-slurred *dear dear dear* and a thin, plaintive *tseeee*.

NESTING: Lays 3–5 white or slightly bluish eggs in a neat nest of plant fiber and grasses on or near the ground.

HABITAT: Open oak woodlands; treeless dry uplands with grassy vegetation and bushes, often near rocky outcrops.

RANGE: Mainly resident from California, southern Arizona, and southern New Mexico east to Texas and central Oklahoma.

SUBSPECIES: A dozen and a half subspecies vary in overall color. The Pacific coastal populations average smaller and darker; the widespread eastern interior subspecies *eremoeca* is paler and grayer. A Southwestern subspecies, *scottii*, is pale and more reddish.

SIMILAR SPECIES: Chipping Sparrow is smaller; with a thinner, notched, *Spizella*-like tail; and a black eyeline. Adults lack the conspicuous malar stripe.

Adult Field Sparrow also has *Spizella* characteristics; it lacks the whisker mark, and has a pink bill and a richly colored back. Also see Rufous-winged Sparrow.

CONSERVATION: Rufous-crowned Sparrows are still common but decreasing. As habitat specialists, they are especially vulnerable to changes in their hillside habitat, which is often degraded or fragmented by residential or agricultural development.

SUMMER ■ MIGRATION
WINTER ■ RARE
RESIDENT

The highly migratory Green-tailed Towhee breeds in relatively unforested, dense shrub cover at higher elevations in the western United States. This shy bird hops and scratches for food under low cover, flicking its tail and raising its rufous cap into a crest. It prefers low scrub and occurs in brushy openings in boreal forests on western mountains, as well as in sagebrush habitats.

DESCRIPTION: 6¼–7" (16–18 cm). This is a ground-dwelling species, smaller than the other towhees. It is olive green above with a rufous cap, a white throat and belly, and a gray breast. On the face it has white lores and a dark "mustache" stripe. It has yellow wing linings. Both sexes are similar. Juveniles lack the crown patch, show brown streaks above and below, and have two olive-buff wing bars (a plumage not seen in migration).

VOICE: Its song is a loud, lively series of slurred notes and short, buzzy trills. Its call is a short, nasal *mew*.

NESTING: Lays 4 heavily spotted white eggs in a rather loosely built nest on the ground or in low, protected sites such as chaparral, juniper, or yucca.

HABITAT: Sagebrush, mountain chaparral, pinyon-juniper stands, and thickets bordering alpine meadows.

RANGE: Breeds from central Oregon south through the mountains to southern California and the Great Basin to southeastern New Mexico. It winters at lower elevations and south to southern Arizona and central and southern Texas. Also found in Mexico.

SIMILAR SPECIES: Olive Sparrow is smaller and has a shorter tail, dark eyeline, and striped crown.

CONSERVATION:
Green-tailed Towhees are common and their numbers are stable. Their habitat in the sagebrush steppes of the Interior West has undergone degradation by grazing, farming, and changes in fire management practices.

■ SUMMER ■ MIGRATION
■ WINTER ■ RARE
■ RESIDENT

This species was formerly combined with the Eastern Towhee as a single species, the "Rufous-sided Towhee." They are now considered distinct species and vary considerably in voice and appearance. The two species are known to interbreed where they come in contact in the northern Great Plains. Towhees often feed on the ground and are usually detected by their noisy scratching through the dry leaves; like other towhees, this bird scratches up seeds and insects from the ground by kicking both feet backward.

DESCRIPTION: 7–8½" (17–22 cm). The male's head, chest, rump, and tail are black; the back and wings are also black, with many white spots. Its sides are rufous and the mid-belly is white. In the female, brown replaces areas of black on the male. Both sexes have red eyes and white tail corners and outer feathers. Juveniles are brownish and streaked all over.

VOICE: The song varies—a long, buzzy *cheweeeee*. Its call is an inquisitive *meewww?*

NESTING: Lays 3–6 white eggs, with reddish-brown and lilac spots, in a loose cup nest built in a dense bush, close to or on the ground if sheltered by tall planting.

HABITAT: Forest edges, thickets, woodlands, gardens, and shrubby park areas.

RANGE: Breeds from British Columbia south to California and the Southwest, east to central Dakotas and western Texas. Winters from British Columbia, Nevada, Utah, Colorado, and Nebraska south to Baja California and east to Oklahoma and south-central Texas.

SUBSPECIES: About a dozen subspecies occur in North America; these differ in the amount of white spots above and the extent of white on the tail. Great Plains birds (subsp. *arcticus*) show the most white. Great Basin and Rocky Mountain birds (subsp. *montanus*) show less white. Birds in the Pacific Northwest (subsp. *oregonus*) are the darkest and show the least white; populations farther south to southern California (subsp. *megalonyx*) and the Central Valley region (subsp. *falcinellus*) show increasingly more white. The songs and calls of the subspecies also vary considerably.

SIMILAR SPECIES: See Eastern Towhee.

CONSERVATION: LC

Spotted Towhees are common and widespread, and their numbers are stable. They thrive in the open, shrubby habitats created by residential development, although proximity to residential areas makes them vulnerable to predation by domestic and feral cats.

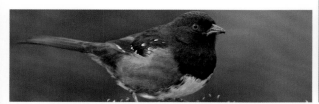

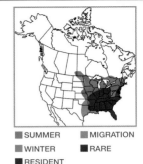

■ SUMMER   ■ MIGRATION
■ WINTER   ■ RARE
■ RESIDENT

The name "Towhee," an imitation of this bird's call note, was given in 1731 by the naturalist and bird artist Mark Catesby, who encountered it in the Carolinas. These towhees often feed on the ground, scratching noisily in the dry leaves. Their distinctive, memorable song is often transcribed *drink-your-tea*. Sometimes also called the Red-eyed Towhee, this species was formerly combined with the western Spotted Towhee as a single species, the "Rufous-sided Towhee."

DESCRIPTION: 7–8½" (17–22 cm). The male has a black hood, back, and wings. The tail is black with white edging on the outer feathers; the breast and belly are white with bright rufous sides. The female has the same pattern but is dark brown where the male is black. Both sexes have red eyes except in the Southeast, where white-eyed individuals occur. Juveniles are brownish and streaked all over.

VOICE: The song varies, often with a few introductory notes and usually ending with a long trill, such as *drink-your-teeaaa* or *to-wheeeee*. Call is an inquisitive *meewww?*

NESTING: Lays 3–6 white eggs, with reddish-brown and lilac spots, in a loose cup nest built in a dense bush, close to or on the ground if sheltered by tall planting.

HABITAT: Forest edges, thickets, woodlands, gardens, and shrubby park areas.

RANGE: Breeds from southern Saskatchewan east to Maine and south to the Gulf Coast and Florida. It winters across much of the eastern United States north to Nebraska and southern New England.

SUBSPECIES: "White-eyed Towhee" (subsp. *alleni*) occurs in Florida. Its eyes are white instead of red, it has less white on the tail, and its call is an upslurred *zwink*; its song is more variable than the nominate "Red-eyed Towhee" populations farther north.

SIMILAR SPECIES: See Spotted Towhee.

CONSERVATION: LC

Eastern Towhees are common and widespread, and their numbers are stable except in the Northeast, where they have declined seriously in recent decades. The species increased as eastern farming began to wane, and farmlands began returning to shrublands and thickets. Over time, abandoned farms and fields left to grow back into successional forest—or converted to residential housing or other forms of development—are less suitable habitat for towhees.

■ SUMMER   ■ MIGRATION
■ WINTER   ■ RARE
■ RESIDENT

The Western Spindalis is considered an aberrant tanager of uncertain taxonomic affinities. It is a common West Indian species that occurs irregularly in southern Florida. This bird was first recorded in the United States in 1961 on the Florida Keys. It is found in heavily landscaped gardens, dense shrubs and thickets, and West Indian hardwood hammocks; this species is highly coastal and generally does not range more than 3 miles (5 km) from the ocean. It was formerly called "Stripe-headed Tanager."

DESCRIPTION: 6–7" (15–18 cm). A small tanager with a relatively long tail and a small bill. It has distinctive black and white stripes on the head and face; a rufous-orange collar, breast, and rump; a grayish belly; and a black tail with white outer feathers. Its back is variable from black to greenish-black; it has large white patches on blackish wings. There is a broad white wing bar (secondary coverts) and a small square white spot on the edge of the wing at the base of the primaries. The female is plain olive-gray, darker above, with a small, square white spot on the edge of the wing.

VOICE: Varied, high thin calls, including some that are reminiscent of Black-and-white Warbler song, transitioning to buzzier phrases.

NESTING: Lays 2–4 light blue eggs with brown patches around the large end. Its cup-shaped nests are constructed of various plant materials.

HABITAT: Tropical montane and lowland evergreen forests, second-growth forest, and scrub. In the U.S., it is found in open or brushy woods or suburban neighborhoods, often at flowering or fruiting trees.

RANGE: Resident in the Bahamas, Cayman Islands, Cuba, Mexico, Turks and Caicos Islands; it is a rare visitor to southern Florida, and has nested in Everglades National Park.

SIMILAR SPECIES: The male is unmistakable.

Female Brown-headed Cowbird, Indigo and Painted buntings, and Summer and Scarlet tanagers have no white on the wings. Female House Sparrow is brown with streaks on the back and a buff eyebrow stripe.

CONSERVATION:

Western Spindalis populations are believed to be stable in the core of their range. Most U.S. records have been of single birds in winter, but sightings of small groups in spring suggest that the species may nest in Florida occasionally.

YELLOW-BREASTED CHAT *Icteria virens*

- ■ SUMMER
- ■ WINTER
- ■ RESIDENT
- ■ MIGRATION
- ■ RARE

The Yellow-breasted Chat is an atypical wood warbler. Its large size and stout bill, long tail, and distinctive display flight—hovering with slow, deep-flapping wings and dangling feet—make it seem more like one of the mockingbirds or thrashers. Because it prefers brushy tangles and is relatively shy, it is more often heard than seen.

DESCRIPTION: 6½–7½" (17–19 cm). Our largest warbler, the size of a large sparrow, this bird is olive green above, with a bright yellow breast and white abdomen. It has a stout, black bill; a long tail; a black face mask bordered above and below with white; and white "spectacles."

VOICE: A series of widely spaced croaks, whistles, and short repeated phrases, unlike a typical warbler's song. It often sings at night. At times it performs a musical display flight, flopping awkwardly up and down with its legs dangling while singing.

NESTING: Lays 4 or 5 brown-spotted, white eggs in a bulky mass of bark, grass, and leaves, lined with finer grass and concealed in a dense bush.

HABITAT: Dense thickets and brush, often with thorns; streamside tangles and dry brushy hillsides.

RANGE: Breeds from British Columbia, Ontario, and (rarely) Massachusetts south to California, the Gulf Coast, and Florida. Winters in the tropics.

SUBSPECIES: Western populations (subsp. *auricollis*) average grayer with a deeper yellow-orange throat and breast and a slightly longer tail compared to Eastern populations (subsp. *virens*).

SIMILAR SPECIES: Its large size, long tail, odd song, olive-gray head, bright yellow throat, and white spectacles and mustache stripe make this species distinctive from typical warblers.

CONSERVATION: Yellow-breasted Chats are widespread and common throughout North America, and their numbers are stable overall despite some local declines in the Southwest and in some provinces and states on the edge of its range.

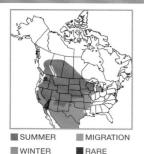

■ SUMMER ■ MIGRATION
■ WINTER ■ RARE
■ RESIDENT

In spring, visiting a Yellow-headed Blackbird colony in a marsh or slough is an exciting experience. The surrounding water provides safety but often limits the nesting habitat; crowding is thus inevitable. Some males are always in display flight, with head stooped, feet and tail drooped, and wings beating in a slow, accentuated way. Some quarrel with neighbors over boundaries while others fly out to feed. Approaching predators are mobbed by clouds of Yellow-headed and neighboring Red-winged blackbirds, which nest in the drier stands of cattails.

DESCRIPTION: 8–11" (20–28 cm). A robin-sized blackbird; the male is much larger than the female. The male is bright yellow on the head, neck, and upper breast, and is blackish elsewhere, with conspicuous white markings on the wings. The female is duller and lighter; yellow on the chest, throat, and face; and has no white wing marks.

VOICE: Harsh, incessant *oka-wee-wee* and *kruck* calls, coming from many individuals in a colony, blend into a loud, wavering chorus.

NESTING: Lays 3–5 brown-speckled, whitish eggs in a basket woven around several strong stalks. Nests in colonies.

HABITAT: Freshwater marshes.

RANGE: Breeds from central British Columbia, northern Alberta, and Wisconsin south to southern California, northern New Mexico, and Illinois. It winters mainly in the Southwest and Mexico.

SIMILAR SPECIES: Female Red-winged Blackbirds are more heavily streaked than female Yellow-headed.

CONSERVATION: LC
Yellow-headed Blackbird is widespread and common. Wetland drainage projects have impacted its breeding habitat, but its overall numbers are increasing. This may be due to new food sources created by fields of corn, sunflower, and small grains being planted in increasing numbers near their natural habitats.

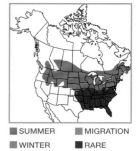

■ SUMMER ■ MIGRATION
■ WINTER ■ RARE
■ RESIDENT

The male Bobolink is a familiar sight as it flutters over hay fields, delivering its bubbling song. Like the Red-winged Blackbird, the male uses its song to attract several females to its territory. A polygamous bird, the male Bobolink courts with the basic blackbird stance: head down, neck feathers ruffled, tail fanned, and wings arched downward, displaying prominent white shoulder patches. Bobolinks prefer lush fields with tall grasses, alfalfa, clover, and grain crops. In the Southwest, they have extended their range as cropland has been irrigated, but their numbers seem to have decreased in the Northeast as agriculture has declined. Each fall, migrant Bobolinks gather in large numbers in southern rice fields, where their habit of eating grain has earned them the name "Ricebird."

DESCRIPTION: 6–8" (15–20 cm). The breeding male is largely black with a white rump and back, and a dull yellow-buff nape. It is solid black underneath. The female and winter male are rich buff-yellow and streaked on the back and crown. It has a short, finch-like bill.

VOICE: Its flight song is a series of joyous, bubbling, tumbling, gurgling phrases with each note on a different pitch. Its call is a soft *pink*, often heard on migration.

NESTING: Lays 4–7 gray eggs spotted with red-brown and purple in a poorly made but well-concealed cup of grass, stems, and rootlets, placed on the ground in a field.

HABITAT: Prairies and meadows; marshes during migration.

RANGE: Breeds from British Columbia, Manitoba, and Newfoundland south to northern California, Colorado, and Pennsylvania. It winters in southern South America.

SIMILAR SPECIES: A female Red-winged Blackbird is darker, less buffy, and has a longer bill.

Savannah Sparrow has streaks across the breast.

CONSERVATION: LC

Originally the Bobolink was probably confined to the central grasslands, but with the settling of the Northeast it quickly spread into New England. Now, with farms abandoned and the land returning to forest, the species is declining. Bobolinks are adaptable and still numerous, but loss of habitat—especially the loss of meadows, hay fields, and natural prairie—has put pressure on these birds. Conservationists suggest that mowing fields once annually (after the nestlings have fledged) maintains ideal Bobolink breeding habitat.

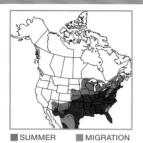

SUMMER ■ MIGRATION
WINTER ■ RARE
RESIDENT

A common bird of American farmlands, the Eastern Meadowlark usually delivers its bright song from a conspicuous perch. The Eastern and Western meadowlarks are so similar that at a distance only their songs and calls distinguish them. Moreover, the two may even learn each other's song where their ranges overlap. Meadowlarks are often polygamous; more than one female may be found nesting in the territory of a single male. Because the birds often breed in hay fields, their nests may be destroyed by mowing; unless the season is well advanced, they normally nest again. During migration and winter Eastern Meadowlarks band together in groups of up to a dozen birds and can be found in almost any open grassy area. In flight they keep their wings stiff, typically fluttering them a few times and then sailing.

DESCRIPTION: 9–11" (23–28 cm). A stocky, robin-sized, brown-streaked bird with a white-edged tail, a bright yellow throat and breast, and a black V crossing the breast. The upperparts and flanks are cryptically patterned with buff, brown, and black, making it difficult to spot birds on the ground. The head is broadly striped with buff and dark brown. Its straight, pointed bill is about as long as the head, and its tail is relatively short. Populations from the Southwest are significantly duller than those from the East, and more closely resemble the Western Meadowlark.

VOICE: A clear, mellow whistle: *see-you, see-yeeeer*. It also gives a loud, rattling alarm note.

NESTING: Lays 3–7 white eggs spotted with brown and dull lavender in a partly domed structure of grass concealed in a depression in a meadow.

HABITAT: Meadows, pastures, and prairies; generally in open country during migration.

RANGE: Breeds from southeastern Canada south throughout the eastern United States, west to Nebraska, Texas, and Arizona. It winters in most of its breeding range.

SUBSPECIES: Four subspecies are recognized in North America. The Northern population (subsp. *magna*) is the most typical and widespread of these. Southeastern birds (subsp. *argutula*) are smaller and darker, especially in Florida. The South Texas population (subsp. *hoopesi*) is slightly paler and limited to extreme southeastern Texas. The distinct population of the arid Southwest, also called "Lilian's Meadowlark" (subsp. *lilianae*) is paler overall and more closely resembles Western Meadowlark; its song is lower pitched than other Eastern Meadowlarks.

SIMILAR SPECIES: Western Meadowlark is extremely similar but paler above; the yellow of the throat extends onto the cheeks. It is best distinguished by voice.

CONSERVATION: NT

Once much more abundant, Eastern Meadowlarks have declined during the past several decades because of their disappearing grassland habitats. Prairie, meadows, and small family farms of the eastern U.S., which once hosted these songbirds in droves, have gradually been replaced by row-cropping operations, livestock farms, or housing developments. Although still numerous, Eastern Meadowlarks are undergoing a steep decline in North America.

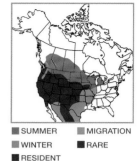

■ SUMMER   ■ MIGRATION
■ WINTER   ■ RARE
■ RESIDENT

Its bright colors, fearless behavior, abundance, and above all its loud, cheerful song make the Western Meadowlark one of the best known of western birds. The song is often heard on movie soundtracks even when the setting is far from the bird's range. This bird is virtually identical to the Eastern Meadowlark in both appearance and habits; where their ranges overlap in the north-central states, Western Meadowlarks prefer drier grasslands in uplands, while Eastern Meadowlarks favor wetter, more poorly drained meadows in river valleys. In the Desert Southwest their habitat preferences are more variable. The two species are among the most difficult of North American birds to distinguish by plumage alone; they are so similar that it was not until 1844 that John James Audubon noticed the difference, and named the western bird *neglecta* because it had been overlooked for so long.

DESCRIPTION: 8½–11" (22–28 cm). A robin-sized bird, streaked brown above and bright yellow below, with a bold, black V on the breast. Visually it is almost identical to Eastern Meadowlark, but the upperparts are paler, and the yellow of the throat extends onto the cheeks. The two species are best distinguished by voice.

VOICE: A rich, flute-like jumble of gurgling notes, usually descending the scale; quite different from Eastern Meadowlark's series of simple, plaintive whistles.

NESTING: Lays 3–7 white eggs with dark brown and purple spots in a domed cup of grass and weed stems concealed in grass or weeds.

HABITAT: Meadows, plains, and prairies.

RANGE: Breeds from British Columbia, Manitoba, northern Michigan, and northwestern Ohio south to Missouri, central Texas, and northern Mexico. It has spread eastward in recent years but remains most common in the West. It winters in much of the breeding range north to southern British Columbia, Utah, and Arkansas.

SIMILAR SPECIES: Eastern Meadowlark is slightly darker; the yellow on the throat does not extend as far on the cheek. It tends to have more white in the tail feathers (at least in birds of the Southwest); more eastern populations of Eastern Meadowlark have a blacker crown than Western. Plumage differences are subtle; identification is difficult if not impossible without recourse to voice.

CONSERVATION: Western Meadowlarks are widespread and common, but have shown a gradual decline over several decades. Factors contributing to the decline are thought to include conversion of habitats to housing and agricultural uses, pesticide use, and grassland degradation by invasive plant species.

This species is common in its range, but a very rare visitor to the far southern United States from Texas to Arizona. Several vagrants over the years have remained in the United States for a period of months, allowing many birders to see them. The amount of black on this species is distinctive, but compare Scott's Oriole, which breeds in some of the areas where the Black-vented has been seen.

DESCRIPTION: 8.5–9" (22–23 cm). One of the larger orioles, the Black-vented is midway between a Baltimore Oriole and an American Robin in size. It has more black than any oriole native to North America, being entirely black on the head, back, and tail, and almost entirely black on the wings. Most of the underside is bright yellow, but the black hood extends down the neck onto the upper breast.

VOICE: A weak *nyah*.

NESTING: Lays 2–6 white to pale-blue eggs heavily marked with brown and black in a shallow hammock-shaped nest constructed from plant fibers and lined with finer materials. The nest is placed low in a bush or tree.

HABITAT: Tropical dry and moist forests.

RANGE: Native resident from Mexico to Nicaragua; individuals rarely stray to southern Arizona and Texas.

SIMILAR SPECIES: Scott's Oriole is brighter lemon-yellow and has substantial white in the wings.

CONSERVATION:  Black-vented Oriole populations are stable throughout Mexico and Central America.

ORCHARD ORIOLE *Icterus spurius*

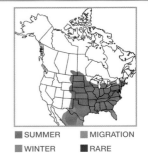

■ SUMMER   ■ MIGRATION
■ WINTER   ■ RARE
■ RESIDENT

The Orchard Oriole is a widespread, locally common songbird of eastern North America. Unlike the brilliant yellows and oranges typical of most orioles, the males of this species are a rich chestnut color underneath, almost like an American Robin. It is found in orchards, shade trees, and woodland edges, and prefers open country with a few scattered trees. Like other orioles, these birds have a loud, musical song; the male often sings in flight and from favorite perches. Orchard Orioles eat insects and small fruits. The nest is a tightly woven, shallow suspended cup constructed mostly of grasses. This species migrates in the early autumn.

DESCRIPTION: 7" (18 cm). A bluebird-sized oriole. The sexes are strikingly different. The adult male has a chestnut body and black head, back, wings, and tail. The female is olive-green above and greenish-yellow to bright yellow below, with two white wing bars. The immature male is similar to the female, but has a black throat.

VOICE: A rapid musical warble, somewhat like that of Purple Finch, but not as rich in quality.

NESTING: Lays 4–6 whitish eggs with purple scrawls in a woven, pouch-shaped nest of vegetable fibers and grass, suspended from the forked branch of a tree or bush.

HABITAT: Orchards, shade trees in parks and gardens, and scattered trees along lakes and streams.

RANGE: Breeds from Manitoba, Wisconsin, Michigan, Ontario, New York, and central New England south to the southern United States and west to the Dakotas, Nebraska, Colorado, and Texas. It winters in the tropics.

SIMILAR SPECIES: Female and immature male Baltimore Orioles are larger, have longer bill and darker upperparts, do not appear greenish, and have orange-yellow underparts. See female Hooded Oriole.

Female Scarlet and Summer tanagers lack wing bars; they have a different bill shape and a different overall profile.

CONSERVATION: 🐦 LC

Orchard Orioles are widespread but have declined slightly since the middle of the 20th century. Declines in the southeastern and central United States have been offset by increases in the western and northern parts of the bird's range. Habitat loss and degradation, particularly to riverside habitat, tend to drive local numbers down.

- ■ SUMMER
- ■ WINTER
- ■ RESIDENT
- ■ MIGRATION
- ■ RARE

This bird's long, thin, slightly decurved bill, slender body, and long, thin tail distinguish it from other North American orioles. Its call note—a high, nasal, slightly metallic *wheenk* or *wheet*—is also distinctive. Because these birds frequently nest in dense palm fronds, often in tall trees, their calls may be the only indication of their presence. These birds often visit ranches and suburban areas for food; they are largely insectivorous but take fruit when it is available.

DESCRIPTION: 7–7¾" (18–20 cm). The male is yellow to orange, with a black tail, black throat and upper breast, and black wings crossed with two white bars. Its bill is thin and curved; its tail is long and graduated. The female is olive-gray above and olive-yellow below, with two white wing bars. The yearling male looks like a female but has a black throat.

VOICE: A series of whistles, chatters, and warbles.

NESTING: Lays 3–5 white eggs blotched with dark brown and purple in a basket of plant fibers with the entrance at the top, hanging from palm fronds or the branches of eucalyptus or other trees.

HABITAT: This bird originally preferred streamside growth, but it has adapted to tree plantations, city parks, and suburban areas with palm or eucalyptus trees and shrubbery.

RANGE: Breeds from central California, Nevada, central Arizona, southern New Mexico, and southern Texas southward. A few winter in southern California and southern Texas.

SUBSPECIES: The nominate eastern population in Texas (subsp. *cucullatus*) tends to be more orange, whereas the western population (subsp. *nelsoni*) is yellower.

SIMILAR SPECIES: Altamira Oriole is much larger and heavier, with a relatively large, deep bill.

Female and immature Bullock's Orioles are stockier, with contrasting paler bellies; Hooded Orioles have uniformly colored underparts.

Female and immature Orchard Orioles are difficult to distinguish from Hooded, especially young birds. Orchard Oriole has a short tail, often flicked sideways in quick, jerky manner; it has a shorter, less decurved bill than most Hoodeds (except for very young Hooded). Orchard gives a diagnostic low *chuck* note.

Also see Scott's and Streak-backed orioles.

CONSERVATION:

Hooded Orioles are fairly common and their populations have increased in the southwestern United States. Its range is expanding northward in conjunction with the proliferation of backyard gardens, feeding stations, and ornamental palms. Numbers in the lower Rio Grande Valley have declined, however, likely due to extensive cowbird parasitism; this species is heavily parasitized by Brown-headed and Bronzed cowbirds, and most Hooded Oriole nests contain one or more cowbird eggs.

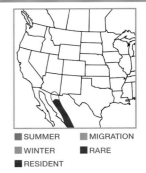

■ SUMMER ■ MIGRATION
■ WINTER ■ RARE
■ RESIDENT

Of the neotropical orioles that may be seen in the southern United States, this is one of the scarcest. It is a rare visitor from Mexico, with annual strays occuring in the Southwest. It has not established a permanent foothold, as have the Hooded, Altamira, Scott's, and Audubon's orioles. Most past records were winter visitors, but a few pairs in recent years have nested in Arizona through the summer.

DESCRIPTION: 7½–9" (19–23 cm). This species is similar to Hooded Oriole, in whose range it may occur. The upper back is streaked lengthwise in all plumages (not barred side-to-side, as in a winter male Hooded). Its bill is thicker and straighter. The head of the male Streak-backed is deeper red-orange than a male Hooded's. The female and immature are duller than the male, and are yellow-orange on the head; the immature lacks the black lores and bib present in adults.

VOICE: Its song is generally similar to Bullock's Oriole; it includes an unmelodious warble and dry chattering. It also makes a series of clear *wheet* call notes, softer than the call of a Hooded Oriole.

NESTING: Its nest is a pendulous woven net, 10–16" (25–40 cm) long, placed mid-level in an often thorny tree or shrub. It commonly nests in proximity to other orioles.

HABITAT: Arid and semi-arid scrubby open areas and brushy woodland; also plantations.

RANGE: Resident from northwestern Mexico to northern Costa Rica; a casual visitor (usually fall or winter) to southeastern Arizona and southern California.

SIMILAR SPECIES: Bullock's Orioles are similar to an immature female Streak-backed but lack streaking on the back and have a more curved upper mandible.

Hooded Oriole is much slimmer; in fresh winter plumage, it can show black scalloping or spotting on its olive-tinted back (the back becomes entirely black by breeding season); it shows more contrast between the back and its paler head; it has a narrow, slightly decurved bill. Streak-backed has a straight upper mandible and a black lower mandible with a deep, contrasting bluish base.

Young and females of other orioles do not show a bright forehead contrasting sharply with the rest of the head; they lack bright malar areas and their calls differ.

CONSERVATION:
Streak-backed Oriole numbers are believed to be stable in its native range.

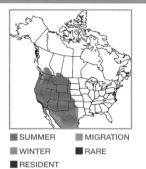

■ SUMMER ■ MIGRATION
■ WINTER ■ RARE
■ RESIDENT

Bullock's Oriole is a common summer bird in the West, where it frequents forest edges, open woodlands, farmland, and suburbs with plenty of trees. It is the western counterpart to the Baltimore Oriole; the two species were formerly considered the same species, known as "Northern Oriole." The habits of these two species are quite similar, and they are known to hybridize freely where their ranges overlap in the Midwest.

DESCRIPTION: 7–8½" (18–22 cm). The male's crown, eyeline, throat stripe, back, wings, and central tail are black. It has a large white wing patch. Much of the head, eyebrow, underparts, and outer tail feathers are orange. The female is olive above, has a pale orange chest, a white belly, and two white wing bars. The bird's bill is slender and pointed, and its tail is rounded.

VOICE: Clear and flute-like, whistled single or double notes in short, distinct phrases with much individual variation. Also gives a rapid chatter.

NESTING: Lays 4–6 grayish eggs, spotted and scrawled with dark brown and black. The nest is a well-woven pendant bag of plant fibers, bark, and string, suspended from the tip of a branch.

HABITAT: Deciduous woodlands, shade trees, riparian woodlands, parks, and towns, to 8000' (2400 m) elevation.

RANGE: Breeds from British Columbia and southern Alberta south to southern California and Mexico and east to the Dakotas and Texas. Winters in the tropics.

SIMILAR SPECIES: See Baltimore Oriole.

Hooded Oriole is slimmer, with a longer tail, and a slimmer and more decurved bill; it gives a whistled *wheet* call in addition to a chatter. The male has an orange crown and lacks the white wing patch; the female and first-winter male have more uniform and deeper yellow underparts.

Female and first-winter male Orchard Orioles are smaller, shorter billed, brighter yellow below, and more greenish above; they give a *chuck* call.

Female Scott's Oriole is deeper greenish-yellow below, including the belly, and has a gray back with distinct dark streaking, as well as a broader-based bill; it gives a *shack* call.

Also see Streak-backed Oriole.

CONSERVATION:

Bullock's Orioles are common and widespread in the West, and their numbers are stable.

■ SUMMER ■ MIGRATION
■ WINTER ■ RARE
■ RESIDENT

This handsome tropical oriole was first reported in the Miami area in 1949, where it was probably originated from escaped captives. It has since been found in Florida from Homestead to Fort Lauderdale.

DESCRIPTION: 8" (20 cm). This tropical oriole is bright orange with a black throat, wings, and tail. It has white patches on the wings and prominent black spots on the sides of the breast. Unlike many orioles, males and females have similar plumage. Juveniles are yellower and lack black on the head and throat.

VOICE: Like that of other orioles—loud, varied, and continuous.

NESTING: Lays 4 whitish eggs with black scrawls in a woven basket nest of palm fibers or other vegetable matter.

HABITAT: Open country with scattered trees, orchards, gardens, and parks.

RANGE: Resident from southern Mexico to northern Costa Rica. Introduced around Miami, Florida, and established in several southeastern Florida counties.

SIMILAR SPECIES: Baltimore Oriole averages smaller and has a clean upper breast; Spot-breasted has a heavier bill and dark spots on the upper breast.

CONSERVATION:
Spot-breasted Oriole has become established and numerous locally in several counties across southeastern Florida. A string of cold winters sharply reduced the Florida population in the late 1970s and early 1980s, and their numbers have only partially recovered since. Information about this species' global population trend is incomplete, but their numbers may be declining.

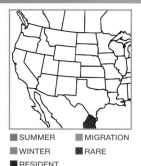

■ SUMMER ■ MIGRATION
■ WINTER ■ RARE
■ RESIDENT

Altamira Oriole is one of the specialty birds of the lush Rio Grande Valley in southern Texas. The best places to see this local species north of the Mexican border are the Brownsville region and the Santa Ana Wildlife Refuge, where these brilliant birds may visit feeding stations, and often sing from tall trees near water in the spring and summer. Although mainly found in the dense foliage of tall forest trees, the Altamira Oriole builds a conspicuous nest suspended far out on a slender, drooping limb, safe from most predators. It varies a diet of insects and spiders with fruits such as figs and berries.

DESCRIPTION: 9" (23 cm). A robin-sized, bright orange-yellow oriole with a black face, throat, upper back, wings, and tail. It is similar to Hooded Oriole but larger, with a heavier bill and orange-yellow shoulders. The male and female look alike.

VOICE: A series of loud whistles and harsh chatters.

NESTING: Lays 3 or 4 purple-streaked, whitish eggs, often in a cylindrical or bag-shaped nest up to 2' (about 60 cm) long, woven of tough fibers and suspended from a branch.

HABITAT: Forest and scattered groves of tall trees, especially near water.

RANGE: Resident in the Rio Grande Valley of extreme southern Texas.

SIMILAR SPECIES: Adults resemble adult male Hooded Orioles (now less common in southern Texas), but are larger, with a proportionately thicker bill. Their wing patterns differ: Hooded has two white wing bars, with the upper bar broad and conspicuous; Altimira lacks an upper wing bar, and has yellow-orange lesser coverts and a more conspicuous white crescent formed by broad white edgings at the bases of the outer primaries. Immature Altimira is larger than other Texas orioles, and usually has traces of the adult wing pattern; it is brighter yellow than an immature Audubon's Oriole.

CONSERVATION:
Altamira Oriole populations have increased in the past half-century. They have always been plentiful in their Central American habitat, while numbers in Texas have seen steady growth. Its unique nest design may help to discourage cowbirds, notorious for parasitizing nests of most other oriole species.

AUDUBON'S ORIOLE   *Icterus graduacauda*

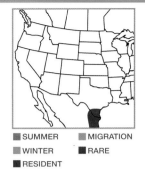

■ SUMMER   ■ MIGRATION
■ WINTER   ■ RARE
■ RESIDENT

This tropical oriole is uncommon and local within a limited range in southern Texas. More secretive than other orioles, its retiring habits make it difficult to locate; it keeps well within foliage or under the forest canopy. It feeds extensively on wild fruits, especially hackberries. In Texas and Mexico these birds travel in pairs, even outside the nesting season.

DESCRIPTION: 9" (23 cm). A robin-sized oriole. The male is greenish yellow with a black head, wings, and tail. Females are slightly duller and smaller. Immatures lack black on the head.

VOICE: A three-syllable warble—one of the sweetest, most melodious songs of any oriole.

NESTING: Lays 4 whitish eggs, with black scrawls, in a woven and partly hanging nest made of fresh green grass. Nests are often found in mesquite; less often in hackberry, ebony, persimmon, and other trees.

HABITAT: Wet thickets in woodlands, forest openings, and tangles near water.

RANGE: Resident from southern Texas to northern Guatemala.

SIMILAR SPECIES: No other oriole has a yellow back and a black head. The immature can be distinguished by its size, greenish-yellow cast, and dark wings and tail.

CONSERVATION: LC

Audubon's Oriole numbers have declined in recent decades, particularly in Texas. They have been impacted by habitat loss and forest fragmentation, which interferes with nesting sites and makes them vulnerable to parasitism by cowbirds.

■ SUMMER ■ MIGRATION
■ WINTER ■ RARE
■ RESIDENT

Baltimore Oriole is a well-known bird in the East, where it inhabits a variety of shade trees in open deciduous woodland and residential neighborhoods. It is the only bright orange bird in most of its range. This species and the western Bullock's Oriole were once considered a single species called "Northern Oriole." The two often hybridize where their ranges meet in a limited area of the Midwest.

DESCRIPTION: 7–8½" (18–22 cm). The male has a black head, back, wings, and tail; and an orange breast, rump, and shoulder patch. The female is olive-brown, with dull yellow-orange underparts and two dull white wing bars.

VOICE: Gives clear, flute-like, whistled single or double notes in short, distinct phrases with much individual variation.

NESTING: Lays 4–6 grayish eggs spotted and scrawled with dark brown and black. Its nest is a well-woven pendant bag of plant fibers, bark, and string, suspended from the tip of a branch.

HABITAT: Deciduous woodlands and shade trees. Before the tree's decline, the American elm was a favorite nesting site for the eastern bird.

RANGE: Breeds from Saskatchewan and Nova Scotia south through the Dakotas to eastern Texas, Louisiana, and Virginia. It winters in Florida and the southern Atlantic Coast.

SIMILAR SPECIES: Male Bullock's Oriole has an orange cheek and eyebrow, and a large white wing patch. Female Bullock's resembles a paler female Baltimore but is always paler yellow overall; it is paler gray above with less bold wing bars, usually a more extensive whitish belly, and a yellowish eyebrow. Chatter calls given by the two species are distinguishable with practice.

Orchard Oriole is smaller, shorter billed, and gives a *chuck* call; the male is chestnut brown and black; most females and first-winter males are bright yellow below; its call is an ascending, whistled *wheet* and chatter notes.

In southern Florida, see Spot-breasted Oriole.

CONSERVATION:
Baltimore Orioles are widespread and common with a stable population. Dutch Elm Disease was responsible for the loss of many of this bird's favored nesting trees in the mid-1900s, which reduced oriole numbers. The species remains vulnerable to habitat loss on its wintering grounds in Central and South America.

■ SUMMER ■ MIGRATION
■ WINTER ■ RARE
■ RESIDENT

Besides gleaning insects, this fine songster of the Southwest feeds on available fruits, including those of cacti, and has been observed taking nectar—a habit practiced by many tropical orioles. Like most orioles, it skillfully climbs drooping branches and twigs as well as delicate yucca flowers.

DESCRIPTION: 7½–8¼" (19–21 cm). The male has a black head, mantle, throat, and central breast area; and bright lemon-yellow underparts, rump, and outer tail feathers. Its wings, central tail feathers, and wide terminal tail band are also black. The male has one slender, white wing bar. The female is lime-yellow with dusky streaks on the back, and has two wing bars. A first-year male resembles a female, but with a small, fainter black area on the throat and bib.

VOICE: The song, a series of rising and falling flute-like notes, resembles that of a Western Meadowlark. Its call is a harsh *chuck*.

NESTING: Lays 3–5 bluish-white, irregularly spotted eggs in a grassy hanging pouch nest, often skillfully hidden among dry yucca fronds, pines, or live oaks.

HABITAT: Breeds in the pinyon-juniper woodlands of semi-desert areas; in yucca trees or palms in deserts; or in sycamores or cottonwoods in canyons.

RANGE: Breeds in southern California, southern Nevada, Utah, Arizona, New Mexico, and western Texas. It winters mainly south of the U.S.-Mexico border.

SIMILAR SPECIES: Black-headed Oriole is larger, with a green back and a solid black tail.

Similar female orioles (except for Streak-backed) lack vertical streaking on the back; their bills are usually thinner and shorter. Other orioles are lighter, more yellow or orange, and have different call notes.

CONSERVATION:
Scott's Oriole has expanded its breeding range into western Colorado since the 1970s. Local populations may fluctuate, but on the whole the species' numbers are stable or increasing. Habitat destruction and degradation are the leading causes of local population declines.

■ SUMMER   ■ MIGRATION
■ WINTER   ■ RARE
■ RESIDENT

Although primarily a marsh bird, the Red-winged Blackbird will nest near virtually any body of water and occasionally breeds in upland pastures. Each pair raises two or three broods a season, building a new nest for each clutch. After the breeding season, the birds gather with other blackbirds in flocks, sometimes numbering in the hundreds of thousands. Although blackbirds are often considered pests because they consume grain in cultivated fields, farmers benefit because the birds consume harmful insects during the nesting season.

DESCRIPTION: 7–9½" (18–24 cm). A familiar blackbird, smaller than a robin. The male is black with bright red shoulder patches tipped with buffy below (although the buffy tips may be concealed or absent). The female and young are heavily streaked with dusky brown.

VOICE: A rich, musical *o-ka-leeee!*

NESTING: Lays 3–5 pale blue eggs spotted and scrawled with dark brown and purple in a well-made cup of marsh grass or reeds, attached to growing marsh vegetation or built in a bush in a marsh.

HABITAT: Marshes, swamps, and wet and dry meadows; pastures.

RANGE: Breeds from Alaska east across Canada to Newfoundland and south to northern Baja California, central Mexico, the Gulf Coast, and Florida. It winters regularly across the United States north to British Columbia, the Great Lakes, and Pennsylvania.

SUBSPECIES: Almost two dozen subspecies are recognized, most showing minimal, indistinct variation. The exceptions are the populations known as "Bicolored Blackbirds," which are resident in California's Central Valley and central coast region—these males nearly or completely lack the buffy band bordering the red shoulder patches.

SIMILAR SPECIES: Females and immatures are distinguished from other blackbirds (except Tricolored) by their streaking below. Juvenile Brown-headed Cowbirds are also streaked below but are slightly smaller overall, stockier, and paler with shorter, more conical bills.

Tricolored blackbird is similar; its range is restricted to California and southern Oregon. Male Tricolored is slightly slimmer than Red-winged and glossier blue-black overall; its bill is also slimmer. Tricolored has a deeper red shoulder patch with a white border; it gives more raspy and nasal calls and songs. The female Tricolored closely resembles a female Red-winged but is darker overall, particularly on the belly, which shows little distinct streaking.

CONSERVATION: LC
Widespread and among the most abundant North American songbirds, Red-winged Blackbirds are a species of least conservation concern. Their population size continues to show a small decline each year.

TRICOLORED BLACKBIRD *Agelaius tricolor*

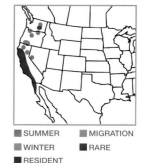

■ SUMMER ■ MIGRATION
■ WINTER ■ RARE
■ RESIDENT

This close relative of the Red-winged Blackbird is largely restricted to California west of the Sierra Nevada. During the late-summer drought, grasshoppers abound and support the wandering hordes of Tricolored Blackbirds; in winter rice fields and marshes provide food. It breeds in large, localized colonies among cattails and bulrushes in freshwater marshes; it forages in marshes, fields, and livestock pens. This endangered blackbird has undergone a long-term and rapid decline. In the past, some colonies were estimated to contain one to two million birds; today the total population is down to about 300,000 individuals due to the loss of wetland habitat.

DESCRIPTION: 7½–9" (19–23 cm). Similar to Red-winged Blackbird; the male is black but with dark red "epaulets" with broad white margins. The female is much darker than the brownish-dusky female Red-winged Blackbird and lacks streaks on the rump and belly.

VOICE: Its calls are rather similar to those of the Red-winged Blackbird, but the song is more nasal and less musical.

NESTING: Lays 3 or 4 greenish eggs, covered with brown scrawls, in a nest woven onto reed stems or blackberry brambles. It is more colonial than the Red-winged Blackbird, and its territories are crowded, with nests often less than 5 or 6' (1½ or 2 m) apart. Colonies in California's Central Valley may contain thousands of birds.

HABITAT: Cattail marshes, marshy meadows, and rangelands.

RANGE: Breeds from southern Oregon southward throughout most of California. It winters north to northern California.

SIMILAR SPECIES: Male Red-winged Blackbirds are stouter and have a slightly thicker bill. They are not as glossy and have a more orange-red shoulder patch, usually with a buff (or no) border. The female Red-winged has a lighter brown belly. Its song also differs.

CONSERVATION: EN

Loss of wetland habitats pushed the Tricolored Blackbird into agricultural areas, where their breeding and growth cycles came into conflict with farming practices. This, combined with the habit of nesting in dense colonies, has led the Tricolored Blackbird population into steep decline. Conservation efforts aimed at protecting this endangered species include working with farmers to alter their harvesting schedules to allow young birds to fledge, and improving natural nesting areas on public lands such as National Wildlife Refuges.

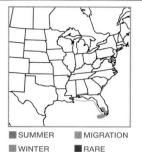

■ SUMMER ■ MIGRATION
■ WINTER ■ RARE
■ RESIDENT

During the 20th century, the Shiny Cowbird began to spread from South America through the West Indies, and now seems poised to add at least the southeastern states to its range. The species was first recorded in Florida in 1985 and by the 1990s had become resident in much of the southern tip of the state. As it spreads, this brood parasite poses an additional threat to our native songbirds.

DESCRIPTION: 7–8" (18–20 cm). The male is purplish black glossed with blue above, and shiny purplish black below. The female is grayish brown and paler below. It has a large, conical, black bill and dark eyes.

VOICE: Its song is a melodious warble. It also gives a variety of harsh, metallic call notes.

NESTING: Lays 1–3 heavily spotted white eggs, deposited in the nests of other species and left for the host parents to brood.

HABITAT: Open country and farmlands.

RANGE: A recent invader from West Indies. Has been recorded in a number of southeastern states and is now firmly established in southern Florida.

SIMILAR SPECIES: Brown-headed Cowbird has a shorter tail on average and a thinner bill.

CONSERVATION:

Shiny Cowbirds are increasing, both globally and in North America. Their spread is being monitored by conservationists for their parasitic impact on other species. Shiny Cowbirds have played a role in the decline of other birds native to Puerto Rico and may similarly disrupt native songbirds in the Southeast.

BRONZED COWBIRD *Molothrus aeneus*

■ SUMMER ■ MIGRATION
■ WINTER ■ RARE
■ RESIDENT

In their limited range in the southern United States, Bronzed or "Red-eyed" Cowbirds are found in a variety of relatively open areas at lower elevations. There they are common on lawns in well-watered residential areas, in agricultural areas, and at feedlots. Like their close relatives the Brown-headed Cowbirds, these birds follow livestock, especially cattle, snapping up insects flushed from the grass. They alight on the backs and necks of livestock to feed on ticks. Cowbirds also feed extensively on seeds and grain. During courtship, both sexes, but especially males, erect their neck feathers into a ruff. The males bow and jump up and down, whistling unmusical, squeaky calls. During the colder months these birds form enormous flocks and move around the countryside with other species of blackbirds.

DESCRIPTION: 8½" (22 cm). The male is bronze-black with glossy bluish-black wings and tail. It has a thick ruff on the neck. Its prominent red eye can be seen at close range. The female is similar but duller.

VOICE: Wheezy and guttural whistling notes and various squeaks and squeals.

NESTING: Lays 1–3 blue-green eggs, deposited in other birds' nests, particularly nests of orioles, tanagers, flycatchers, buntings, and grosbeaks, and more rarely thrashers and thrushes.

HABITAT: Pastures, roadside thickets, ranches, and open country generally; also parks and orchards.

RANGE: Breeds in southern Arizona, New Mexico, and south-central Texas. It withdraws southward from much of Arizona during the winter.

SUBSPECIES: Eastern and Western populations differ mainly in female and juvenal plumage. In Eastern birds (subsp. *aeneus*), females and juveniles are dark blackish-brown, rather similar to the male. In Western birds (subsp. *loyei*), females and juveniles are paler gray-brown.

SIMILAR SPECIES: Its deep red eye is diagnostic. Brown-headed Cowbird is smaller with a distinctive and rounder brown head. It is less elongated; has a shorter, more conical bill; and lacks the ruff.

CONSERVATION: LC
Bronzed Cowbird numbers are stable and the species has expanded its range northward in recent decades. The cowbird's success leads to increased parasitism on other species and can be linked to the declining populations of other birds such as Audubon's Oriole in Texas.

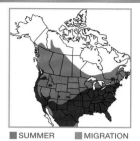

- ■ SUMMER ■ MIGRATION
- ■ WINTER ■ RARE
- ■ RESIDENT

Cowbirds are brood parasites and promiscuous; they form no pair bonds and build no nests. In late spring the female cowbird and several suitors move into the woods. The males sit upright on treetops, uttering sharp whistles, while the female searches for nests in which to lay eggs. Upon choosing a nest, the female cowbird removes one egg of the host's clutch, and deposits one of her own in its place. Unlike parasitic Old World cuckoos, which lay eggs closely resembling those of a host species, cowbirds lay eggs in the nests of more than 200 other species, most smaller than themselves. Some host species eject the unwanted egg, others lay down a new nest lining over it, but most rear the young cowbird as one of their own. The young cowbird grows quickly at the expense of the young of the host, pushing them out of the nest or taking most of the food.

DESCRIPTION: 6–8" (15–20 cm). The male is black with a glossy brown head; the female is plain gray-brown. Both have a stout, finch-like bill.

VOICE: A squeaky gurgle. Its call is *check* or a rattle.

NESTING: Lays 4 or 5 white eggs, lightly speckled with brown, laid one at a time in the nests of other songbirds. The female cowbird removes an egg from the host's clutch and replaces it with her own, leaving the host parent to raise the cowbird chick.

HABITAT: Agricultural land, fields, woodland edges, and suburban areas.

RANGE: Breeds from British Columbia, central Saskatchewan, central Ontario, Quebec, and Newfoundland southward throughout the United States. It winters in the central and southern parts of its breeding range.

SIMILAR SPECIES: All other blackbirds have longer, more pointed bills. Bronzed Cowbird is similar to the female. Bronzed Cowbird has a heavier bill; a more elongated, slightly ruffled appearance; and a diagnostic deep red eye.

CONSERVATION:
Although Brown-headed Cowbird populations have declined slightly in recent decades, they are still far more abundant and widespread today than they were historically. Once a small population tied to the bison herds of the Great Plains, these birds spread east as the bison disappeared and the forests were cleared. Their numbers ballooned in the 19th century to the detriment of other songbirds whose nests the cowbirds parasitize. Cowbird control programs have been enacted to try to protect several endangered species threatened by extensive cowbird parasitism, notably Kirtland's Warbler and Black-capped Vireo.

RUSTY BLACKBIRD *Euphagus carolinus*

■ SUMMER   ■ MIGRATION
■ WINTER   ■ RARE
■ RESIDENT

The Rusty Blackbird is almost always found near water. It breeds in boggy spruce woods in the Far North and winters around swamps, riversides, and lakes. In the breeding season, this is the only blackbird in most of its range and is easily identified. Typically it forages by wading in shallow water, but it also ventures into pastures and agricultural fields. In fall, the rusty tinge to the mantle and light eyes of both sexes distinguish this species from the similar Brewer's Blackbird, which is abundant in most of the West.

DESCRIPTION: 9" (23 cm). In spring, the males are black with a bluish and greenish iridescence; females are dark gray. In fall, they are much more rust-brown, especially on the head, breast, and back. Both sexes have conspicuous pale yellow eyes.

VOICE: Like the squeaks of a rusty gate. Its call note is a sharp *check*.

NESTING: Lays 4 or 5 blue-green eggs with brown blotches in a bulky stick nest lined with grass, moss, and lichens set in a dense shrub or low tree near or over water.

HABITAT: Boreal bogs in the breeding season; wooded swamps and damp woods with pools during migration.

RANGE: Breeds from Alaska and across northern Canada to southern Canada, northern New York, and northern New England. It winters from southeastern South Dakota and southern New England south to the Gulf Coast.

SIMILAR SPECIES: Common Grackle is larger and more iridescent with a longer, wedge-shaped tail.

Some Brewer's Blackbirds in winter plumage may have pale bars on the back and chest as well as a pale eyebrow, but these areas are dull gray or brownish-gray rather than rust-brown or buff.

CONSERVATION:  VU

Rusty Blackbirds have undergone one of the most dramatic declines of any North American songbird in recent decades. The causes of the decline aren't fully understood, and the bird's low population concentrations and remote breeding habitat make it hard to study them. Several causes are suspected, including the loss, degradation, clearcutting, and pollution of their boreal wetland habitats.

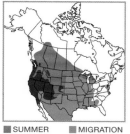

■ SUMMER   ■ MIGRATION
■ WINTER   ■ RARE
■ RESIDENT

This blackbird, named for 19th-century ornithologist Thomas M. Brewer of Boston, is best known as a visitor to stockyards and farms—especially in winter—where it feeds on spilled grain. It also takes insects stirred up by livestock and plows. Brewer's Blackbirds nest in hay fields, but the young are usually fledged before the hay is harvested. During breeding season, the male has an elaborate display that includes fluffing out the feathers, making the wing quiver, cocking the tail, and pointing the bill upward. A highly social species, it is usually found in small flocks.

DESCRIPTION: 8–10" (20–25 cm). A robin-sized blackbird, the male is solid black with a purplish-blue iridescent head and yellow eyes. The female is gray with dark eyes. It has a square tail and jerks its head forward as it walks.

VOICE: Gurgles, squawks, and whistles.

NESTING: Lays 3–5 gray eggs, with dark brown spots, in a nest of coarse grass and twigs reinforced with mud and lined with fine grass and hair, placed on the ground or in a tree. Nests in loose colonies of up to 30 pairs.

HABITAT: Prairies, fields, and farmyards.

RANGE: Breeds from British Columbia, Manitoba, and Ontario south to southern California, New Mexico, and Texas. Winters north to British Columbia and Carolinas.

SIMILAR SPECIES: See Common Grackle.

In flight overhead, Red-winged Blackbird has a discernibly shorter tail.

Rusty Blackbird is extremely similar in some plumages. Brewer's looks noticeably small-headed with a straight, conical bill; Rusty is more bulky-headed, usually with a longer, acutely pointed bill that sometimes appears slightly decurved. Rusty is slightly bulkier overall and has a slightly shorter tail; the breeding male is usually dull black without noticeable iridescence, but rarely has a conspicuous green gloss on the wings and tail. Rusty's eyes are usually dull medium-yellow (Brewer's is usually more whitish).

CONSERVATION: LC

Brewer's Blackbird is common and widespread, although its population has declined steadily during the past 50 years. Human settlements and agriculture have increased available habitat and feeding opportunities for these birds. Their large flocks are seen as a threat to agricultural yields; as a result, these birds are sometimes persecuted in attempts to protect crops.

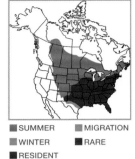

■ SUMMER ■ MIGRATION
■ WINTER ■ RARE
■ RESIDENT

The Common Grackle is a common and familiar blackbird in eastern North America, where it frequents parks, residential areas, woods and groves of trees along rivers, and croplands. It is also expanding its range into northwestern North America. It nests in small, loose colonies, usually in conifers. This bird is an opportunistic feeder, varying an insect and grain diet with crayfish, frogs, mice, and both the eggs and the young of small birds. During courtship it jerks its body; lowers its wings, tail, and head; and squeals. It also exhibits its long, conspicuous tail in a display flight. In some northern areas it congregates by the thousands during migration as well as in winter roosts.

DESCRIPTION: 12" (30 cm). A dark, jay-sized bird. It has a long, wedge-shaped tail displaying a longitudinal ridge or keel when in flight. It appears all black at a distance but is actually highly iridescent, with colors varying from blue to purple to green to bronze, depending on the light. It has bright yellow eyes. The female is duller and somewhat smaller than the male. Juveniles are sooty brown with brown eyes.

VOICE: Clucks; also makes a high-pitched rising screech that sounds like a rusty hinge.

NESTING: Lays 5 pale blue eggs with black scrawls in a bulky stick nest lined with grass, placed anywhere from low in a bush to high in a tree. Nests partly in colonies, most often in tall evergreens.

HABITAT: Lawns, parks, fields, and open woodlands.

RANGE: Breeds from northern Alberta, central Ontario, and Newfoundland south to the Gulf Coast states east of the Rockies, but expanding into Idaho and Washington in the Northwest. It winters north to Kansas, the southern Great Lakes region, and New England.

SUBSPECIES: The most widespread population, found in New England and west of the Appalachian Mountains, is sometimes called "Bronzed Grackle" (subsp. *versicolor*). These birds have a bronze-colored back, a dark blue head, and a purplish tail. A smaller subpopulation in the southeastern United States, sometimes called "Purple Grackle" (subsp. *quiscula*), has a dark green back, purple head, and blue tail. Mid-Atlantic birds (subsp. *stonei*) are intermediate between these, usually showing a purplish back with variable bands of other iridescent colors.

SIMILAR SPECIES: Blackbirds, cowbirds, and starlings are smaller and stockier, with shorter fan-like tails and proportionately shorter bills. All have a more rounded head in profile. Great-tailed and Boat-tailed are larger, with longer tails, less metallic gloss, and very different voices.

CONSERVATION: NT
Although still widespread and abundant, Common Grackle populations have been in a steady, severe decline for several decades. At the same time, the species continues to expand its range westward throughout North America.

- ■ SUMMER
- ■ WINTER
- ■ RESIDENT
- ■ MIGRATION
- ■ RARE

A close relative of the Great-tailed Grackle, the somewhat smaller Boat-tailed Grackle is common along the Atlantic and Gulf coasts, where it is found mainly in marshes, farmland, and city parks. Male Boat-tailed Grackles often fluff their head feathers during spring and summer, and thus appear thick-headed compared to the sleek Great-tail.

DESCRIPTION: Males average 16–17" (41–43 cm) long; females average 12–13" (30–33 cm). This grackle's tail is long and keel-shaped. The male appears black, with iridescent blue on the back and breast; it has yellow or brown eyes. The female is brown with a paler breast and is noticeably smaller.

VOICE: A harsh *jeeb-jeeb-jeeb-jeeb*, unlike the whistles and clucks of the Great-tailed Grackle.

NESTING: Lays 3 or 4 pale blue eggs, spotted and scrawled with brown and purple, in a bulky cup of grass, mud, and decayed vegetation placed from 2 to 10' (60 cm to 3 m) up in marsh grass or bushes.

HABITAT: Marshes along the coast; in Florida, it is also found on farmlands.

RANGE: Resident along coasts from New Jersey south and west to Louisiana; also inland in peninsular Florida.

SUBSPECIES: Populations differ most notably in eye color. Atlantic Coast birds (subsp. *torreyi*) have a yellow iris. Birds of the western Gulf Coast in Texas and Louisiana (subsp. *major*) have dark brown eyes. In the populations from coastal Mississippi to western Florida (subsp. *alabamensis*) and in peninsular Florida (subsp. *westoni*), most birds have dark eyes, but some individuals have pale eyes.

SIMILAR SPECIES: A Great-tailed Grackle in western Louisiana and Texas is larger, has an iridescent purple back and breast, and has clear yellow eyes; if the eye is not absolutely clear yellow, the bird is probably a paler-eyed variant of Boat-tailed Grackle. Male Great-tailed has a thin-headed profile. Its voice is different.

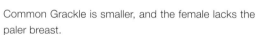

Common Grackle is smaller, and the female lacks the paler breast.

CONSERVATION:  The Boat-tailed Grackle is common and increasing in its range, which has expanded northward along the Atlantic Coast. The species' reliance on coastal marsh habitat makes these birds vulnerable to coastal development. Some consider their large flocks a nuisance and try to deter them.

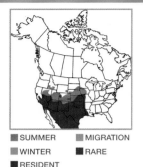

■ SUMMER ■ MIGRATION
■ WINTER ■ RARE
■ RESIDENT

In the Southwest and southern Great Plains, these noisy and conspicuous birds are familiar residents of city parks, towns, ranch lands, and occasionally marshes, where they form huge nesting colonies in isolated groves. With their long keel-shaped tails, piercing yellow eyes, and distinctly odd songs and calls, the males are among our more conspicuous native birds. At all seasons these grackles have a sleek, thin-headed profile. Where Great-tailed and Boat-tailed grackles occur together, the Great-tailed tends to avoid salt marshes, the chief habitat of the Boat-tailed. Like magpies, these noisy, opportunistic birds feed on a great variety of food: fruits, grain, insects, garbage, and offal. They are usually bold but become cautious and wary when in danger.

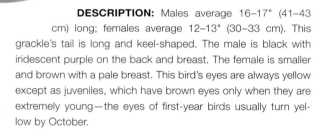

DESCRIPTION: Males average 16–17" (41–43 cm) long; females average 12–13" (30–33 cm). This grackle's tail is long and keel-shaped. The male is black with iridescent purple on the back and breast. The female is smaller and brown with a pale breast. This bird's eyes are always yellow except as juveniles, which have brown eyes only when they are extremely young—the eyes of first-year birds usually turn yellow by October.

VOICE: A variety of whistles, clucks, and hissing notes.

NESTING: Lays 3 or 4 pale blue eggs, spotted and scrawled with brown and purple, placed in a bulky nest of sticks, grass, and mud in a tree. Nests in loose colonies.

HABITAT: Farmlands with scattered trees and thickets.

RANGE: Resident from California, Colorado, Kansas, and western Louisiana southward.

SUBSPECIES: The Western population (subsp. *nelsoni*) averages smaller and paler, with a relatively short tail and longer bill than the "Eastern" populations east of central Arizona.

SIMILAR SPECIES: Crows have heavier bills and proportionately shorter, fan-shaped tails.

Other blackbirds are much smaller, also with fan-shaped tails.

Other grackles are most easily distinguished by call. Common Grackle is smaller; the female lacks the pale breast.

Boat-tailed Grackle is quite similar, but males are iridescent blue or blue-green and often have brown eyes; it prefers salt marshes. In Florida, yellow-eyed grackles are usually wintering Boat-tailed Grackles from the Atlantic Coast.

CONSERVATION:
Great-tailed Grackle populations are growing along with their range. These birds thrive in human-altered landscapes, spreading rapidly through agricultural and urban areas alike. They can be crop pests and prey upon the eggs and young of other bird species.

■ SUMMER   ■ MIGRATION
■ WINTER   ■ RARE
■ RESIDENT

This warbler gets its name from its peculiar ground nest, which resembles a miniature Dutch oven. The Ovenbird breeds abundantly throughout eastern North America in open, dry deciduous woods devoid of thick brush and tangles. It will also accept wet swampy conditions and, in the north, nests in jack pine or spruce forests. Ovenbirds and waterthrushes, primarily ground-feeders, are notable because they walk rather than hop.

DESCRIPTION: 6" (15 cm). A terrestrial, thrush-like warbler. It is olive green above and white below with dark streaks. It has a conspicuous eye ring and an orange-brown crown bordered with black stripes. It has pinkish legs.

VOICE: A loud, staccato song—*teacher, teacher, teacher*—with geographical variation in emphasis. Its flight song, often given at night, is a bubbling and exuberant series of jumbled notes ending with the familiar *teacher, teacher*.

NESTING: Lays 4 or 5 brown-spotted, white eggs in a domed or oven-shaped nest of dead leaves and plant fibers, lined with grass. The nest is placed on the ground, with a side entrance.

HABITAT: Mature, dry forests with little undergrowth.

RANGE: Breeds from west-central Canada east to the Maritimes, and south to the northern Gulf Coast states, and South Carolina. Winters from the Gulf Coast and Florida to South America.

SIMILAR SPECIES: Louisiana and Northern waterthrushes have prominent white or buff eyestripes and brown upperparts; they often wag their tails.

Thrushes are larger and lack the orange-and-brown striped crown; they hop rather than walk.

CONSERVATION: These birds are generally uncommon but their numbers appear to be stable. Ovenbirds experience frequent parasitism from cowbirds in fragmented woodlands; they require large, undisturbed mature broadleaf and mixed forests to establish territories and successfully breed.

■ SUMMER ■ MIGRATION
■ WINTER ■ RARE
■ RESIDENT

The Worm-eating Warbler spends much of its time on or near the ground, quietly searching for its insect prey in leaf litter and low vegetation. A singing male, however, often perches rather high up in a forest tree, where its habit of sitting motionless for long periods of time makes it very difficult to spot. The name "Worm-eating" reflects the bird's fondness for smooth caterpillars and grubs, not earthworms.

DESCRIPTION: 5½" (14 cm). This sparrow-sized warbler is plain brownish above and below, with conspicuous dark and light crown stripes. It has two black stripes on the crown and one through each eye. Its back, wings, and tail are dull olive; it is buff below. Its bill is thick and light brown; its legs are yellowish-pink. Both sexes look alike.

VOICE: Its song is like that of a Chipping Sparrow, but faster, buzzy, and more insect-like.

NESTING: Lays 4 or 5 brown-spotted, white eggs in a ground nest of dead leaves lined with moss.

HABITAT: Chiefly dry wooded hillsides.

RANGE: Breeds from southeastern Iowa, Ohio, New York, and southern New England south to northeastern Texas, the central Gulf Coast states, and eastern North Carolina. Winters in the tropics.

SIMILAR SPECIES: Swainson's Warbler lacks bold head stripes and has a rufous crown.

CONSERVATION:
Although Worm-eating Warblers have lost some habitat to deforestation, their numbers have remained stable or slightly increased over several decades. These birds depend on large swaths of mature forest for their nesting grounds. Forest fragmentation reduces suitable breeding habitat and simultaneously makes Worm-eating Warbler nests more vulnerable to cowbird parasitism.

■ SUMMER ■ MIGRATION
■ WINTER ■ RARE
■ RESIDENT

The elusive Louisiana Waterthrush is the southern breeding counterpart of the Northern Waterthrush over much of the eastern United States. The two species are extremely similar and confused early American ornithologists, who at one time thought there were three species. During spring migration, this species arrives much earlier than the Northern. Where the two species breed together, the Northern prefers bogs and swamps, while the Louisiana prefers rushing streams and clear brooks.

DESCRIPTION: 6½" (17 cm). This terrestrial, thrush-like warbler is dark olive-brown above, and white and streaked below. It frequently bobs its tail. It is similar to Northern Waterthrush, but its throat is unstreaked and its eyebrow stripe is longer, broader, and whiter.

VOICE: Its song is three clear notes followed by a descending jumble.

NESTING: Lays 5 brown-blotched, white eggs in a grass-lined nest of dead leaves and moss set under the overhang of a stream bank, in a stump cavity, or among exposed tree roots.

HABITAT: Swift-moving brooks on hillsides; where Northern Waterthrush is absent, it occurs in river swamps and along sluggish streams.

RANGE: Breeds from Minnesota, southern Ontario, and central New England south to Texas and Georgia. Winters in the tropics.

SIMILAR SPECIES: Northern Waterthrush has a narrower yellow or buff eyebrow stripe; its throat is yellowish or off-white; its underparts have sharp, heavy spots that sometimes form a necklace.

CONSERVATION:
Louisiana Waterthrush is uncommon in its range, but its numbers are increasing slightly. They are sensitive to both forest fragmentation and water pollution. Poor water quality caused by human activity limits the insect and small vertebrate prey available for these birds.

SUMMER / MIGRATION / WINTER / RARE / RESIDENT

Waterthrushes are aberrant, ground-dwelling warblers that teeter and bob as they walk. The Northern Waterthrush is common, but shy and retiring; it chooses cool, dark wooded swamps, brushy bogs, and lake shores for breeding and is particularly fond of areas with standing water. Like its relative the Ovenbird, it walks rather than hops. This species is among the first to move south during the fall migration, and southern migrants are regularly reported by the middle of July or earlier. Ornithologist E. H. Forbush's 1929 observation about the Northern Waterthrush still applies: "It is a large wood warbler disguised as a thrush and exhibiting an extreme fondness for water."

DESCRIPTION: 6" (15 cm). A terrestrial, thrush-like warbler. It is olive-brown above and pale yellowish below with black streaks. It has a narrow, yellowish-white eyebrow and a streaked yellowish throat. It frequently bobs its tail.

VOICE: Its song is *chee-chee-chee, chip-chip-chip-chew-chew-chew*, loud and ringing, speeding up at the end. Its call is a sharp *chink*.

NESTING: Lays 4 or 5 creamy-white eggs with brown blotches in a nest of moss set in a bank, at the base of a trunk, or among the roots of an overturned tree.

HABITAT: Lakeshores, wooded swamps, and cool bogs in the breeding season; it uses almost any wooded habitat during migration.

RANGE: Breeds from Alaska and much of Canada south to the northern United States. Winters in the tropics.

SIMILAR SPECIES: See Louisiana Waterthrush.

CONSERVATION: LC

Northern Waterthrush numbers are stable. These birds are numerous, and many fall victim to predation by domestic and feral cats; these birds are also frequent victims of collisions with buildings or communication towers. The biggest threats to the species may be habitat loss, especially on its wintering grounds, as rising sea levels threaten the mangrove forests along the world's tropical oceans.

■ SUMMER   ■ MIGRATION
■ WINTER   ■ RARE
■ RESIDENT

The Golden-winged Warbler is a strikingly patterned species of open deciduous woods, second-growth woods, and overgrown pastures. It generally occupies higher and drier areas than the Blue-winged Warbler, although the two species overlap broadly in habitat. Where these breeding ranges overlap, the two frequently hybridize; the offspring of these crosses show various combinations of the characteristics of the parent species and have been called "Brewster's Warbler" and "Lawrence's Warbler." The fact that these two species interbreed shows that they are closely related and suggests that the striking differences between them have evolved only during the last few tens of thousands of years.

DESCRIPTION: 4½" (11 cm). The male is gray above and white below, with a black mask and throat; it has a white eyebrow and "mustache," and a yellow crown and wing patch. The female is similar but has a gray mask and throat.

VOICE: A slow, drawled, insect-like song resembling that of Blue-winged but longer: *seee-bzzz, bzzz*, with the first note higher.

NESTING: Lays 5 purplish-spotted, white eggs in a cup of dead leaves and fibers set on or near the ground in thick vegetation.

HABITAT: Abandoned fields and pastures grown to saplings, usually in drier situations than Blue-winged.

RANGE: Breeds from southern Manitoba and New Hampshire south to New Jersey and Iowa, and in the mountains to Georgia. It winters from southern Mexico to northern South America.

SIMILAR SPECIES: See Blue-winged Warbler.

Blue-winged and Golden-winged warblers frequently hybridize; the first generation offspring, called "Brewster's" Warbler, show the dominant traits of the parent species: a black eye line, a whitish throat, and yellow wing bars. Hybrids are fertile and freely cross with one another or backcross with either parent species, creating a confusing array of variants. Rare backcrossed hybrids that resemble Blue-winged Warblers but showing the Golden-winged's recessive black throat and mask pattern are called "Lawrence's" Warbler.

CONSERVATION: Golden-winged Warblers are in serious decline, especially in the southern part of their breeding range. Extensive interbreeding with and competition from Blue-winged Warblers have driven Golden-winged numbers lower, as have habitat loss and nest parasitism from cowbirds. These birds are also losing open forest habitat on their wintering grounds in Central America; conservation efforts promoting bird-friendly or shade-grown coffee and cacao plantations can help preserve good habitat for this and many other species.

■ SUMMER   ■ MIGRATION
■ WINTER   ■ RARE
■ RESIDENT

The Blue-winged Warbler is an inhabitant of overgrown fields with scattered trees, second-growth woods, and brushy hillsides. It is usually seen in undergrowth or on the lower branches of trees, although males may sing from treetops. This warbler perches motionless for minutes at a time when uttering its song. It frequently hybridizes with its close relative the Golden-winged Warbler. Where the ranges of the two species overlap, the Blue-winged is crowding out the Golden-winged.

DESCRIPTION: 4½" (11 cm). Both sexes are similar—mostly bright yellow with blue-gray wings, two narrow white or yellowish wing bars, and a black line through the eye. It has a greenish back and tail. It is bright yellow below with white undertail coverts; it flicks open its tail, showing the white coverts.

VOICE: An insect-like buzzy song, which sounds like a tired sigh: *seee-bzzz*, with the *bzzz* pitched lower.

NESTING: Lays 5 brown-dotted, white eggs in a grass-lined cup of dead leaves and fibers, placed on or near the ground in thick undergrowth.

HABITAT: Abandoned fields and pastures grown up to saplings; forest clearings and edges with clumps of catbrier, blackberry, and various bushes and young trees.

RANGE: Breeds from Nebraska, central Iowa, southern Wisconsin, southern Ontario, and central New England south through east-central and Atlantic Coast states to northern Georgia. Winters in tropics.

SIMILAR SPECIES: See Golden-winged Warbler and the discussion on Blue-winged x Golden-winged hybrids.

Immature Chestnut-sided Warbler may lack chestnut on the flanks; it is greenish on the back with a somewhat yellower crown, white underparts, and yellowish wing bars. It may look somewhat like "Brewster's" Warbler but has a brighter green back, usually with at least faint streaking, and lacks a black eyeline.

CONSERVATION: LC

Blue-winged Warbler is uncommon in the eastern United States but may be common locally. Its numbers have declined slightly due to habitat loss and cowbird parasitism. Its range began shifting northward in the late 1800s with changing land usage, bringing this species into more frequent contact with Golden-winged Warblers. Where the two species occur together, Blue-winged Warblers hybridize with and outcompete Golden-winged Warblers, to the detriment of the latter.

Mniotilta varia **BLACK-AND-WHITE WARBLER**

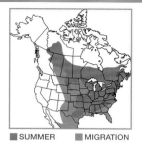

- ■ SUMMER
- ■ MIGRATION
- ■ WINTER
- ■ RARE
- ■ RESIDENT

This conspicuous warbler arrives in the North early in spring, usually by mid- to late April. It is known for its habit of creeping around tree trunks and along larger branches in search of insect food in crevices in or under the bark—hence its former name, "Black-and-white Creeper." Unlike the Brown Creeper, which only moves up a tree, this species may climb in any direction. This bark-gleaning feeding behavior has freed this species from the need for a green canopy overhead, allowing Black-and-white Warblers to migrate north well before the foliage has emerged.

DESCRIPTION: 5" (13 cm). A distinctive warbler with bold black and white stripes, including on the crown. The male has a black throat; the female's throat is white. Immatures resemble females, but often have more heavily streaked sides. This bird typically creeps on tree trunks and branches.

VOICE: A thin, high-pitched, monotonous *weesy-weesy-weesy-weesy*, like a squeaky wheel.

NESTING: Lays 4 or 5 purple-spotted, white eggs in a ground nest composed of leaves, grass, and rootlets, and lined with hair and plant down. The nest is found at the base of a tree, stump, or rock.

HABITAT: Primary and secondary forests, chiefly deciduous. During migration it occurs in parks, gardens, and lawn areas with trees and shrubs.

RANGE: Breeds from southern Mackenzie, northern Alberta, and central Manitoba east to Newfoundland, and south to the southern United States east of the Rockies. It winters from the southern parts of the Gulf Coast states southward.

SIMILAR SPECIES: Male Blackpoll Warbler has a solid black crown and pure white undertail coverts; it lacks a white eyestripe.

CONSERVATION:
Although still common, the Black-and-white Warbler population is decreasing, especially in the Southwest and Midwest. Their main threats are loss of habitat due to forest fragmentation and collisions with buildings and communication towers.

■ SUMMER ■ MIGRATION
■ WINTER ■ RARE
■ RESIDENT

This is one of the characteristic birds of the southern swamplands, where its bright plumage is conspicuous in the gloomy, cypress-lined bayous. It is unusual among warblers in that it nests in holes in trees; this may be an adaptation to a habitat where such holes are numerous but dense bushes—typical warbler nesting sites—are scarce.

DESCRIPTION: 5½" (14 cm). The male is golden-orange with blue-gray wings with no wing bars, and it has large white spots in the tail. The back is olive and the undertail coverts are white. The female is similar but duller. Its black eye and the long bill are both prominent.

VOICE: Its song is a ringing *sweet-sweet-sweet-sweet-sweet-sweet-sweet*; it also has a canary-like flight song. Its call is a loud, metallic *chip*.

NESTING: Lays 6 creamy-white, purple-spotted eggs in a tree cavity, hole in a stump, birdhouse, or other man-made structure, such as a mailbox. The hole is stuffed with mosses to form a nest cup.

HABITAT: Wooded swamps, flooded bottomland forests, and streams with dead trees.

RANGE: Breeds mainly in southeastern states north to Minnesota, Michigan, and New York. Winters in the American tropics.

SIMILAR SPECIES: Blue-winged Warbler has a somewhat similar color pattern, but its blue-gray wings have conspicuous white wing bars; it has a black eyeline but lacks an orange cast.

Yellow Warbler has yellowish wings, a greenish-yellow back, and much yellow instead of white in the tail.

CONSERVATION:
The Prothonotary Warbler population is decreasing as southern swamp forests, their primary habitat, are cleared for development. This species requires swampland with sufficient depth to construct its nests and avoid raccoons, which are natural predators to their eggs. Conservationists are installing nest boxes with predator guards and restoring forested wetlands in an attempt to increase the Prothonotary Warbler population. Depletion of mangrove trees due to coastal development and aquaculture also threatens this bird's winter habitat in the American tropics.

■ SUMMER   ■ MIGRATION
■ WINTER   ■ RARE
■ RESIDENT

Swainson's Warbler is an uncommon, local bird of the Southeast that spends most of its time on or near the ground. This dull-colored warbler is shy and retiring, dwelling in remote, often impenetrable swamps and cane thickets. If not for its song—like that of a Louisiana Waterthrush—it would frequently be overlooked. It is named after William Swainson, an early 19th century British naturalist.

DESCRIPTION: 5" (13 cm). A plain warbler, olive-brown above and whitish beneath, with a rufous cap and a whitish line over the eye. Its bill is large, thicker at the base and tapering to a sharp point. The immature is similar to the adult.

VOICE: Gives three or four clear notes followed by several rapid descending notes, described as *whee-whee-whee-whip-poor-will*; similar to the song of Louisiana Waterthrush.

NESTING: Lays 3 bluish-white eggs in a loose, bulky nest of vegetable fibers, rootlets, and dead leaves, placed in a dense bush or vine.

HABITAT: Wooded swamps and southern canebrakes; also rhododendron thickets in the mountains.

RANGE: Breeds from northeastern Oklahoma, southern Illinois, southern Virginia, and southern Delaware south to the southeastern United States. Winters in the tropics.

SIMILAR SPECIES: Worm-eating Warbler has a black-and-buff striped head.

CONSERVATION:
Swainson's Warbler is increasing. They are vulnerable to habitat destruction of the mature southern forests, whether by human hands or by hurricane damage. A common cause of mortality for these birds is collision with lighted structures—especially lighthouses and communication towers—during their nocturnal migration, especially in inclement weather.

CRESCENT-CHESTED WARBLER *Oreothlypis superciliosa*

■ SUMMER ■ MIGRATION
■ WINTER ■ RARE
■ RESIDENT

Crescent-chested Warbler—a Central American species related to parulas and to *Vermivora* warblers—has strayed several times to pine-oak woodlands in Arizona and western Texas. It forages much like Northern Parula, although often more slowly, methodically, and reclusively inside deep vegetation, often probing leaf clusters.

DESCRIPTION: 4¼" (11 cm) long with an average wingspan of 6" (15 cm). Adults have olive backs, and bluish-gray crowns and napes with darker grayish auriculars. Its supercilium is strikingly white and the breast is bright yellow, with a chestnut crescent below the throat.

VOICE: Its song is a unique short, dry, electric buzz: *zzzzzzz*. Its call is a high, short *tsic*.

NESTING: Lays 3 plain white eggs in a nest built from moss, grass, and conifer needles and lined with finer materials. There are no nesting records in North America.

HABITAT: Mountain pine forests.

RANGE: Native to Mexico and northern Central America; it has strayed several times to southeastern Arizona and possibly to Texas.

SIMILAR SPECIES: Northern Parula has two white wing bars and lacks the prominent white eyebrow; in males, the breast includes reddish and black bands.

CONSERVATION: Crescent-chested Warbler is decreasing in its native range, but it remains widespread and common in Mexican mountain pine forests.

SUMMER MIGRATION
WINTER RARE
RESIDENT

The relatively common Tennessee Warbler breeds in northern coniferous and deciduous woodland, and is found in a wide variety of wooded habitats during migration. Its numbers fluctuate greatly from year to year in response to outbreaks of the spruce budworm, a forest insect that periodically undergoes population explosions. In years following budworm outbreaks this warbler is quite numerous, and a dozen or more may be observed in a single tree, while in other years few are seen. This warbler was discovered in 1811 by the noted ornithologist Alexander Wilson, who chose its common name because he first saw it in Tennessee.

DESCRIPTION: 5" (13 cm). In spring, the male is greenish above, white below, with a gray cap, a white line over the eye, and a dusky line through the eye. In fall, it is olive above and yellowish below. The female has a greener crown; the eyebrow may be washed with yellow, and the throat or upper breast may be lightly washed with yellow. Immatures have unmarked lime-green upperparts; there is a yellow eyebrow and usually a faint wing bar.

VOICE: A sharp, staccato *di-dit-di-dit-swit-swit-swit-chip-chip-chip-chip-chip*, fastest at the end; its song is often comprised of three distinct parts.

NESTING: Lays 5 or 6 brown-spotted, white eggs in a nest lined with fine grasses, placed on the ground, and usually well hidden under a shrub or in a moss clump under a tussock.

HABITAT: Open mixed woodlands in the breeding season; in trees and bushes during migration.

RANGE: Breeds from Yukon, Manitoba, and Labrador south to British Columbia, Wisconsin, southern Ontario, and Maine. It winters in the American tropics.

SIMILAR SPECIES: The brightly colored Orange-crowned Warbler is deeper olive green above. It has a thin, broken eye ring; yellow undertail coverts; a less white belly; and often dusky streaking on breast. Its voice also is different.

Philadelphia and Warbling vireos are stouter, with thicker bills; their behavior is more sluggish. Warbling Vireo is much less green above. Most immature Philadelphia Vireos have yellow undertail coverts.

In Alaska, Arctic Warbler may appear similar but is slightly larger, with a stouter bill.

CONSERVATION: Tennessee Warblers are common and their numbers are stable. Local populations can fluctuate in response to spruce budworm outbreaks.

ORANGE-CROWNED WARBLER *Leiothlypis celata*

■ SUMMER ■ MIGRATION
■ WINTER ■ RARE
■ RESIDENT

The Orange-crowned Warbler is one of the most common western warblers and an uncommon migrant in the East. Its lack of conspicuous field marks is an aid to its identification. Like other birds with concealed crown patches, this warbler displays the crown only during courtship or when alarmed.

DESCRIPTION: 4½–5½" (11–14 cm). This plain warbler is olive green above with orange crown feathers that usually remain hidden. It has drab olive-yellow underparts with faint breast streaking. It has no eye ring or wing bars. Its bill is thin and slightly downcurved.

VOICE: Its song is a simple trill going up or down the scale toward the end. Its call is a sharp *stik*.

NESTING: Lays 4–6 white eggs, with reddish or lavender spots often concentrated around the large end, in a rather large nest of grass and other plant fibers that is lined with fur or feathers. Its nest is usually placed on the ground or in a low shrub.

HABITAT: Forest edges, especially in low deciduous growth, burns, clearings, and thickets. On migration, it is often seen in riverside willows and in scrub oak chaparral.

RANGE: Breeds from Alaska east to Quebec and Labrador and south to California, Arizona, and New Mexico. It winters from the southern United States into the tropics.

SUBSPECIES: Four populations differ slightly in plumage and song. The subspecies *lutescens* of the West Coast is the brightest yellow below and the greenest above. Subspecies *sorilida*, which is restricted to southwestern California and particularly the Channel Islands, is darker and somewhat duller. Subspecies *orestera* breeds in the Great Basin and Rocky Mountains; it is duller yellow below than *lutescens* and has a gray head. The nominate subspecies, *celata*, breeds across Canada from Alaska to Quebec and occurs throughout the East. It is the dullest

plumaged of the different forms, particularly the immature, which may appear quite grayish overall with yellow undertail coverts. Many individuals of all forms show a narrow, pale yellowish-white area along the leading edge of the shoulder at the bend of the wing. The orange crown patch is almost never seen.

SIMILAR SPECIES: See Tennessee Warbler.

A bright Orange-crowned may be confused with a female Yellow Warbler or Wilson's Warbler. Yellow Warbler has a beady-eyed look, lacks dusky breast streaking, and has yellow edgings to the primaries and secondaries; it also has yellow tail spots and a shorter tail. Wilson's Warbler also has beady eyes and lacks dusky streaking on the breast; it usually has the suggestion of a darker forecrown. Both species have different call notes.

In Alaska, Arctic Warbler is darker with some brown above; it is dull whitish below with no streaking and has a whitish eyebrow and wing bar.

CONSERVATION:
Orange-crowned Warblers are abundant and their numbers appear stable. They tend to thrive more in areas with dense shrub growth, which means they are less impacted by logging that opens up forest canopies. However, loss or degradation of shrub layers or wooded stream corridors reduce suitable habitat for these birds.

■ SUMMER ■ MIGRATION
■ WINTER ■ RARE
■ RESIDENT

This Mexican warbler reaches North America only in Big Bend National Park in western Texas, in the Chisos Mountains, where it lives at about 6000 feet (1800 meters) in low oak, pinyon-juniper, maple, and Arizona cypress. Rare and local, Colima Warbler has one of the most restricted ranges in North America, comparable to that of the similarly local Kirtland's Warbler (*Dendroica kirtlandii*), which breeds only in central Michigan. However, because of its high mountain home, this warbler is not as well known. It is a rather slow-moving warbler that feeds in the low canopy of bushes or scrub oaks, although the male sings its territorial song from a high perch.

DESCRIPTION: 5" (13 cm). This warbler is gray above with a chestnut crown patch and an olive-yellow rump. It is whitish below with a yellow-orange undertail patch. It has a narrow, complete eye ring and no wing bars. It is larger than Virginia's Warbler and lacks yellow on the breast.

VOICE: Its song is a musical *seedle-seedle-seedle, sweet, sweet*, like that of Virginia's Warbler. Its call is a sharp *plisk*.

NESTING: Lays 4 creamy-white, spotted and splashed eggs in a cup nest built on the ground.

HABITAT: Deciduous and mixed montane forests.

RANGE: Breeds in Chisos Mountains of western Texas and adjacent Mexico. It winters in Mexico.

SIMILAR SPECIES: See Virginia's Warbler. Virginia's and Nashville warblers bob their tails much more frequently.

CONSERVATION: ![LC]

The Colima Warbler population is decreasing. The numbers of Colima Warblers reaching Texas vary from year to year but are never more than a few hundred individuals. These birds are still more common in northern Mexico. Grazing by livestock such as goats and sheep, predation by feral cats and dogs, and nest parasitism by Brown-headed Cowbirds are the most significant threats to this warbler in Mexico.

LUCY'S WARBLER *Leiothlypis luciae*

SUMMER MIGRATION
WINTER RARE
RESIDENT

The only desert warbler, Lucy's is characterized by a flicking tail, rapid motions, and a rich song. This active bird is an early migrant and quite common in summer in parts of the Southwest. It frequents riparian areas, washes, ponds, and well-vegetated deserts, becoming restricted to riparian areas at higher elevations. It flicks its tail often, its wings less frequently, and flies with weak, jerky wingbeats.

DESCRIPTION: 4" (10 cm). A small, plain warbler with a white eye ring. Both sexes are gray above, creamy white below, with a bright chestnut rump. Its chestnut crown feathers are usually concealed, except in display. In fall, the underside is buff but the undertail coverts are white. Immatures have a buff rump.

VOICE: Its song is reminiscent of that of Yellow Warbler: *chit chit chit chit sweeta che-che-che*. Its call is a soft *plenk*, often run into a series.

NESTING: Lays 4 or 5 white, speckled eggs in a well-lined cup nest in a tree, placed under loose bark or in a hole—a rare nest site among warblers.

HABITAT: Southwestern deserts, especially among cottonwoods and streamside trees and mesquite in washes or canyons.

RANGE: Breeds from California, Nevada, and Utah south to southern Arizona and New Mexico. It winters south of the U.S.-Mexico border.

SIMILAR SPECIES: Bell's Vireo in the arid Southwest is rather gray but larger and stockier; it has a much heavier, decurved bill with a slightly hooked upper mandible; and its calls are different.

Immature Virginia's and Nashville warblers have a brighter eye ring, and a yellow rump and undertail coverts.

A grayish Orange-crowned Warbler (typically a migrant and winter visitor) has a dry call note like a Chipping Sparrow's, a heavier bill, a bolder eyebrow, and usually some greenish or yellowish on the undertail coverts.

CONSERVATION:

Lucy's Warbler is still rather common in suitable habitat, and its population is stable. The loss of streamside groves and clearing of mesquite woods in the Southwest has decreased its numbers from historical levels.

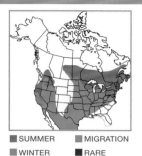

■ SUMMER ■ MIGRATION
■ WINTER ■ RARE
■ RESIDENT

Aspen and birch are often good indicators of the Nashville Warbler's habitat, and the species' persistent song will readily lead the observer to the bird. Despite its ground-nesting habit, the Nashville Warbler regularly forages in the tree tops. This warbler benefited from the arrival of settlers and the clearing of forests. It breeds most successfully in brushy, overgrown pastures, a habitat that has become more widespread with the decline of farming in the Northeast. As these pastures become second-growth woodland and the ground loses its cover of brush, the Nashville Warbler may become less abundant.

DESCRIPTION: 4–5" (10–13 cm). This small warbler is olive green above and bright yellow below, with gray on the top and sides of the head, a narrow white eye ring, and an inconspicuous patch of rust on the crown. It differs from Mourning Warbler and MacGillivray's Warbler in having a yellow throat—not gray or black—and a complete white eye ring. The adult Nashville Warbler has greener upperparts and more extensive yellow on the underparts; fall birds are also extensively yellow below with a white vent.

VOICE: A loud, ringing *teebit-teebit-teebit, chipper-chipper-chipper-chipper*; the song usually has two distinct segments.

NESTING: Lays 4 or 5 white eggs speckled with brown in a cup of grasses, leaves, and roots, lined with pine needles and fine grass and concealed on the ground in the base of a bush or a tussock of grass.

HABITAT: Woodland edges; thickets in open mixed forests or brushy borders of swamps.

RANGE: Breeds from British Columbia and northwestern Montana south to central California and central Idaho; and from Manitoba, Quebec, and Nova Scotia, south to Minnesota, northern West Virginia, and western Maryland. It winters south of the U.S.-Mexico border.

SUBSPECIES: The Rocky Mountains and the prairies form a barrier between the western and eastern forms of this species. The two populations show minor differences in color but have similar habits. The eastern form (subsp. *ruficapilla*) sings a lower and richer song. The western form (subsp. *ridgwayi*) was once called the "Calaveras Warbler"; these birds average grayer on the back with a brighter rump than in the eastern population.

SIMILAR SPECIES: See Virginia's Warbler. Western Nashville Warblers have reduced yellow on the underparts, especially in immatures; the back color in young birds can be similar to a young Virginia's Warbler, even showing a contrasting yellowish rump. Immature Nashvilles show more yellow on the breast and throat than immature Virginia's, and lack neutral gray upperparts.

CONSERVATION: LC
Nashville Warbler is fairly common and its population is increasing. Because they prefer second-growth forest habitats, the clearing of forested land provided additional habitat for these birds. Interestingly, this species seems less susceptible than other warblers to cowbird parasitism.

VIRGINIA'S WARBLER *Leiothlypis virginiae*

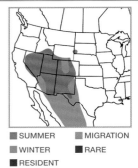

■ SUMMER   ■ MIGRATION
■ WINTER   ■ RARE
■ RESIDENT

In the Rockies and other arid mountains of the interior Southwest, Virginia's Warbler prefers scrubby brush interspersed with pinyon-juniper and yellow pine. At high elevations, this bird is found in fir and spruce as well as riparian willow and alder thickets. This warbler forages for insects and spiders in scrub oaks near the ground. Although males occasionally use a song post such as the top of a juniper, they also sing while feeding in the middle of the chaparral. The range of Virginia's Warbler overlaps with three other closely related warblers: Nashville, Lucy's, and the rare Colima. Virginia's is similar to the Nashville Warbler in its calls and behavior, but twitches its tail more conspicuously.

DESCRIPTION: 4–4¼" (10–11 cm). The male is gray above with a yellow breast, rump, and undertail coverts. Its throat and belly are white. It has a chestnut crown patch and a white eye ring visible at close range. The female is similar but duller overall.

VOICE: Its song a musical *seedle-seedle-seedle, sweet, sweet*. Its call is a sharp *plink*.

NESTING: Lays 3–5 white, finely speckled eggs in a loosely built cup nest on the ground.

HABITAT: Scrub oak and other chaparral, pinyon-juniper brushland, and pine and oak woodlands.

RANGE: Breeds from southeastern California, southern Idaho, and northern Colorado south to Arizona, New Mexico, and western Texas. It winters south of the U.S.-Mexico border.

SIMILAR SPECIES: Lucy's Warbler lacks a conspicuous white eye ring and has no yellow in the plumage.

Virginia's passes through Big Bend as an uncommon spring migrant and may overlap with the superficially similar Colima Warbler; but Colima is larger, less active, and has a stouter bill; it has a grayer throat and belly, with only a faint greenish-yellow wash on the breast (not bright yellow spot as in Virginia's). Colima's rump and undertail coverts are slightly deeper yellow.

Also see Nashville Warbler.

CONSERVATION:
Virginia's Warbler is uncommon and has been undergoing a slow, steady decline for many decades for reasons that are not well understood. Habitat loss due to climate change or forest management practices are possible culprits; this species is also heavily victimized by Brown-headed Cowbirds in parts of its range where these brood parasites are abundant.

■ SUMMER ■ MIGRATION
■ WINTER   ■ RARE
■ RESIDENT

Connecticut Warbler is a fairly robust wood warbler character-ized by long pinkish legs, a rather heavy bill, a short tail, long undertail coverts, and a lack of wing bars. It breeds locally in spruce and tamarack bogs and open poplar or jack pine woodland. It walks on the ground with a peculiar mincing gait, bobbing head, and elevated tail, in a fashion reminiscent of an Ovenbird. The bird is seldom seen except by observers who know where to look. During spring migration, it feeds close to the ground in dense, swampy woods; in the fall, it occurs most often in woodland edges where the growth is rank. Named for its place of discovery, this species is only an uncommon migrant in Connecticut.

DESCRIPTION: 5½" (14 cm). This large warbler is olive green above and dull yellow below. The head, throat, and upper breast are gray in males and dull brownish in females. It has a conspic-uous, unbroken white eye ring and no wing bars.

VOICE: A loud, ringing *beecher-beecher-beecher-beecher* or *chippy-chipper-chippy-chipper.*

NESTING: Lays 4 or 5 whitish eggs, blotched with brown, in a nest of grass concealed in a clump of moss.

HABITAT: Open larch-spruce bogs; during migration, it uses low, wet woods and damp thickets.

RANGE: Breeds from eastern British Columbia east through central Canada to western Quebec, and south to northern Min-nesota, Wisconsin, and Michigan. It winters in the tropics.

SIMILAR SPECIES: MacGillivray's Warbler has an incomplete eye ring.

Most Mourning Warblers either lack an eye ring or have an inter-rupted one, but occasionally females or immatures appear to have a complete eye ring. Mourning Warbler with a complete eye ring can be distinguished, with care, from Connecticut Warbler by its smaller size and shorter undertail coverts, lack of peculiar walking gait, a less prominent and less uni-form eye ring, and brighter, yellow underparts. An immature Mourning Warbler has a less exten-sive and less brownish hood, and a yellow or yellow-tinged throat.

The much smaller, more arboreal Nashville Warbler is superficially like a male Connecticut but always has a bright yellow throat and shorter legs.

A dull female Yellow Warbler or Common Yellowthroat with a complete eye ring could possibly be mistaken for Connecticut, but both are smaller and have a yellow or yellowish throat.

CONSERVATION: 🐦 **LC**
Connecticut Warblers are uncommon, and are generally secre-tive and difficult to find. It is believed that its numbers are decreasing, mainly due to habitat loss. Forest fragmentation associated with logging, oil and gas development, corridors for power lines, and agriculture reduce quality habitat available for these birds. Habitat loss on the wintering grounds may also be a problem, although it is little studied.

GRAY-CROWNED YELLOWTHROAT *Geothlypis poliocephala*

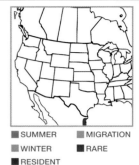

- ■ SUMMER
- ■ MIGRATION
- ■ WINTER
- ■ RARE
- ■ RESIDENT

Gray-crowned Yellowthroat is most closely related to Common Yellowthroat, but its heavier bill, longer tail, and dark lores suggest a chat (it was once called "Ground Chat"). It is a rare year-round visitor to southern Texas, where it was once resident and nested in grassy areas with scattered trees and shrubs. It feeds on insects and other invertebrates. It forages by gleaning low in scrub and grass, sometimes on the ground, and sometimes flycatching.

DESCRIPTION: 5½" (14 cm) long with an average wingspan of 8¼" (21 cm). The male is larger than a Common Yellowthroat, and has a graduated tail that is longer. It has a broken eye ring and black lores. Its heavy, bicolored bill is black on the culmen, and the rest of the bill is pale. The female is similar to the adult male, but the lores are dusky (not blackish).

VOICE: Its songs include a garbled warble similar to a Passerina bunting and a cascade of sweet notes similar to a Canyon Wren. Its call is a sweet, nasal *cheedleet*.

NESTING: Lays 2 to 4 eggs in a deep cup of grasses lined with finer grass and hair, placed on the ground or in low, dense vegetation. This species no longer nests in North America.

HABITAT: Subtropical or tropical moist shrubland.

RANGE: Resident in Mexico and Central America. It is a rare stray to Texas, with only a few accepted records since the 1950s.

SIMILAR SPECIES: Common Yellowthroat has a much more extensive black mask, no eye ring, and a straight black bill.

CONSERVATION: The Gray-crowned Yellowthroat population is stable in its native range.

SUMMER • MIGRATION
WINTER • RARE
RESIDENT

MacGillivray's is a fairly common western warbler found in the dense understory of open montane forests and brushy mountain hillsides and in shrubby mountain riparian locations. This bird flies in a somewhat hesitant fashion and typically shows a bit of tail "pumping," much like a Common Yellowthroat. It is closely related to the Mourning Warbler, a similarly hooded warbler east of the Rockies. These species doubtlessly have a common "hooded warbler" ancestor predating the most recent Ice Age, when the forests expanded during warm interglacial periods, only to be split again when the cold grip of the glaciers returned.

DESCRIPTION: 4¾–5½" (12–14 cm). This warbler has a slate gray hood extending to the upper breast, where it darkens to black. It is olive green above, yellow below; the female is slightly paler. Both sexes have a broken white eye ring. In fall, the hood becomes lighter, and the broken eye ring is less distinct.

VOICE: Its song is a chanting *tree tree tree tree sweet sweet!* Its call is a loud *tik*, sharper than the calls of most other western warblers.

NESTING: Lays 3–5 white eggs with brown spotting in a grassy cup nest close to the ground in a bush or tall weeds.

HABITAT: Coniferous forest edges, burns, brushy cuts, or second-growth alder thickets and streamside growth.

RANGE: Breeds from Alaska and Yukon south to California and central New Mexico. Winters in the tropics.

SIMILAR SPECIES: See Connecticut Warbler.

Mourning Warbler is extremely similar but often lacks an eye ring and has a relatively shorter tail that is rarely pumped in flight. Adult male Mourning Warbler generally has paler lores and more black on the upper breast. An adult female Mourning with a broken eye ring may be impossible to distinguish from MacGillivray's, but usually has a fainter eye ring that is narrower and

more nearly complete (especially in the back). Under careful scrutiny, an immature Mourning is seen to differ from MacGillivray's in these features and usually has some yellow on the throat, has a less hooded appearance (especially across center of breast), and has stronger spectacles or eyebrows.

Female Common Yellowthroat lacks a hooded appearance, and has a yellowish throat and a whitish or dull yellowish abdomen.

The smaller Nashville Warbler has a complete eye ring, a bright yellow throat, and shorter legs.

Certain grayish races of Orange-crowned Warbler are superficially similar (with a vague hooded appearance, a grayish throat, and a broken white eye ring) but are smaller, with shorter legs; they have at least a faint eyebrow and are vaguely streaked below.

CONSERVATION:
MacGillivray's Warblers are fairly common to uncommon; their numbers are decreasing for unknown reasons. These birds seem to prefer new growth in logged or burned areas (especially those with dead and fallen trees). Pine plantations introduced to replace native forests harvested for timber do not create sufficient understory to support these birds.

MOURNING WARBLER *Geothlypis philadelphia*

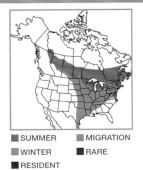

■ SUMMER ■ MIGRATION
■ WINTER ■ RARE
■ RESIDENT

The Mourning Warbler is often heard before it is seen, inhabiting the shrubby undergrowth of woodland and forest edges as well as shrubby burned-over land, young second growth, and the edges of swamps and bogs. This warbler supposedly gets its vernacular name from the black crepe-like patch on the breast of the male, which suggests a symbol of mourning. The scientific species name, *philadelphia*, derives from the city where Alexander Wilson discovered the bird in 1810. It is actually less common in Philadelphia than in many other places.

DESCRIPTION: 5½" (14 cm). This warbler is olive above and bright yellow below with a gray hood; it usually has no eye ring. The male has a black patch below the throat; the female has a gray throat. Immatures usually have a faint, broken eye ring.

VOICE: A loud, ringing, musical song, *teedle-teedle, turtle-turtle*, with the last pair of notes lower.

NESTING: Lays 4 brown-spotted, white eggs in a nest of fibers and leaves, lined with grass and hair, on or near the ground.

HABITAT: Dense thickets of blackberries and briars in forest clearings; it is also found in wet woods with thick undergrowth.

RANGE: Breeds from Alberta to Newfoundland and south to North Dakota and northern New England, and in the mountains to Virginia. It winters in the tropics.

SIMILAR SPECIES: See MacGillivray's and Connecticut warblers; their different calls are useful for distinguishing species.

CONSERVATION:
Fairly common to uncommon but difficult to see, Mourning Warbler numbers are decreasing slightly. Its preference for shrubby second growth in both summer and winter makes it less vulnerable to habitat disruption and fragmentation than some other warblers. This species, however, is a frequent victim of collisions with lighted buildings during its nocturnal migrations.

■ SUMMER   ■ MIGRATION
■ WINTER   ■ RARE
■ RESIDENT

This small, fairly common yellow songbird inhabits moist, shaded deciduous and mixed woodlands with well-developed ground cover in bottomlands, ravines, and swamp borders. It spends most of its time on the ground but sings from lower limbs of trees. This bird is a persistent singer and feeds mainly on insects. Usually heard before it is seen, the rather secretive Kentucky Warbler remains hidden, especially in ravines with thick vegetation and running streams. Alexander Wilson, considered the father of American ornithology, named this species for the state in which it was discovered in 1811, but this bird is no more common in Kentucky than elsewhere in its range.

DESCRIPTION: 5½" (14 cm). This relatively large and short-tailed warbler is olive green above and bright yellow below. It has a black forecrown, lores, and sides of the throat resembling "sideburns"; it also has bright yellow "spectacles." It has no wing bars. Both sexes are similar. The immature is similar to the adult but slightly more brownish above; the black sideburns are often reduced or absent.

VOICE: A loud, penetrating, rich *tur-dle, tur-dle, tur-dle, tur-dle*, reminiscent of the song of a Carolina Wren.

NESTING: Lays 4 or 5 brown-spotted, white eggs in a nest of dead leaves lined with grass, hair, and rootlets, placed on or near the ground.

HABITAT: Low, moist, rich woodlands with luxuriant undergrowth; it is often found in ravines.

RANGE: Breeds from Iowa and Indiana east to New Jersey, and south to the southeastern United States. It winters in the tropics.

SIMILAR SPECIES: Male Hooded Warbler has a black crown and throat. Females and immature Hooded warblers have a cleaner yellow face with no black sideburns or mottling.

Canada Warblers have a necklace of dark marks on the breast and a prominent eye ring.

Common Yellowthroat has an extensive black mask and a whitish belly, not bright yellow.

CONSERVATION: LC
Kentucky Warblers are declining. They face many of the same threats as other warblers—forest fragmentation leading to increased cowbird parasitism, loss of mature deciduous forest habitat in its breeding range in the eastern U.S., and habitat loss on the wintering grounds.

COMMON YELLOWTHROAT *Geothlypis trichas*

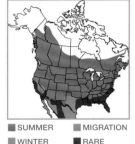

- ■ SUMMER ■ MIGRATION
- ■ WINTER ■ RARE
- ■ RESIDENT

A small bird with a yellow throat skulking in the grass or weeds of a marshy spot is almost certainly a Common Yellowthroat, whose cheerful song is well known. At the height of the breeding season, the males perform an attractive flight display, mounting into the air while uttering a jumble of high-pitched notes, then bouncing back into the grass while giving the usual song. To foil predators, parents drop down into the thick of the grasses or weeds, secretly approach their well-hidden nest, deliver the food, and depart by another route. The bird is the northernmost member of a group of yellowthroat species that occurs as far south as Argentina.

DESCRIPTION: 4½–6" (11–15 cm). This small, stocky bird is olive-brown above, with bright yellow on the throat and upper breast. The male has bold a black mask, bordered above with white. Females and young males lack the face mask, but may be recognized by their bright yellow throat and wren-like behavior.

VOICE: A loud, fast *witchity-witchity-witchity-witchity-wit* or *which-is-it, which-is-it, which-is-it*. Its call is a sharp *chip*.

NESTING: Lays 3–5 white eggs with brown and black spots in a loose mass of grass, sedge, and bark, lined with rootlets, hair, and fine grass, and concealed on or near the ground in a dense clump of weeds or grass.

HABITAT: Moist thickets and grassy marshes.

RANGE: Breeds from Alaska, Ontario, and Newfoundland south throughout the United States. It winters in the southern states and in the tropics.

SUBSPECIES: Several subpopulations differ geographically in the extent of the yellow on the underside and the shade of the pale border around the facial mask. Eastern birds have a medium amount of yellow on the breast and a grayish facial border. Interior West populations have yellow limited to the throat and a whitish facial border. Pacific birds are darker overall, with extensive yellow below and a whitish facial border. The Southwestern population is brighter olive overall with an almost entirely yellow underside and a white facial border, sometimes with hints of yellow.

SIMILAR SPECIES: Adult males are distinct.

Kentucky Warbler is similar to an immature male Yellowthroat but always has distinct yellow spectacles and completely yellow underparts.

The female Nashville Warbler resembles a female Yellowthroat but has a blue-gray crown, a distinct white eye ring, and yellow flanks.

CONSERVATION: Widespread and common, the Common Yellowthroat population is stable. Their primary threats are loss of habitat and food sources as wetlands are converted for agricultural and urban uses. Habitat loss has driven some subpopulations in coastal California and southern Texas into steep decline. Polluted waters and pesticides impact the insect population on which these birds feed.

- ■ SUMMER
- ■ WINTER
- ■ RESIDENT
- ■ MIGRATION
- ■ RARE

The male Hooded Warbler is one of the most handsome in the warbler family and, unlike many others, it has a loud, penetrating, and melodious song. The female, although less strikingly patterned and colored, also commands attention by raising and fanning its long tail when moving about, flashing conspicuous white tail spots. This species usually ranges at a low level, rarely 10 feet (3 meters) above the ground. Like most members of the family, it is adept at flycatching.

DESCRIPTION: 5½" (14 cm). This brightly colored warbler is olive above and yellow below. The male has a yellow face, a black hood, and a black throat. The female lacks the hood or has only a trace of it. Both sexes have white tail spots.

VOICE: A clear, ringing *tawee-tawee-tawee-tee-o*.

NESTING: Lays 3 or 4 creamy-white, brown-spotted eggs in a grass-lined nest of dead leaves and plant fibers, placed low in a small tree or shrub.

HABITAT: Mature, moist forests with luxuriant undergrowth, especially in ravines; also found in wooded swamps.

RANGE: Breeds from Iowa, Michigan, and southern New England south to the Gulf Coast and northern Florida. Winters in the tropics.

SIMILAR SPECIES: The male is distinctive.

Female Wilson's Warbler is closely similar to a female Hooded but lacks olive around the sides of the neck and white tail spots. Wilson's does not spread its tail, is smaller, has a different call, and breeds in the Far North.

Fall Nashville and Canada warblers have distinct eye rings, are grayer above, and lack white tail spots.

CONSERVATION: Hooded Warblers are common, and although their population is increasing, these birds are vulnerable to brood parasitism from cowbirds and to the loss of their favored tropical forest undergrowth habitat on the wintering grounds.

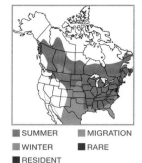

■ SUMMER ■ MIGRATION
■ WINTER ■ RARE
■ RESIDENT

American Redstart is widespread and common; its favored habitat, second-growth woodland, covers extensive areas of the continent. The American Redstart has a distinctive habit of dropping down suddenly in pursuit of a flying insect, then fanning its brightly marked tail from side to side. Only after a full year do males acquire the black-and-orange adult plumage, so it is not unusual to find what appears to be a female singing and displaying like a male.

DESCRIPTION: 4½–5½" (11–14 cm). The male is black with bright orange patches on the wings and tail, and has a white belly. Females and young birds are dull olive-brown above, white below, with yellow wing and tail patches. Immature males have a darker tail and some irregular patches of black on the head and body. These birds often fan their tails and wings when perched.

VOICE: Gives five or six high-pitched notes or two-note phrases, ending with an upward or downward inflection: *chewy-chewy-chewy, chew-chew-chew*.

NESTING: Lays 4 dull-white eggs speckled with brown in a neat, well-made cup of grass, bark shreds, plant fibers, and spiderweb lined with fine grass and hair, and placed in a fork in a sapling or next to the trunk of a tree.

HABITAT: Second-growth woodlands; thickets with saplings.

RANGE: Breeds from southeastern Alaska east to central Manitoba, Quebec, and Newfoundland, and south to northern California, Colorado, Oklahoma, northern Louisiana, and South Carolina. It winters in California, Texas, Florida, and in the tropics.

SIMILAR SPECIES: Baltimore Orioles have colors that resemble American Redstarts, but orioles are larger and have longer bills. The belly is bright orange (males) or yellow-orange (females) rather than mostly white.

CONSERVATION:

American Redstarts are widespread and common but their numbers are decreasing slightly. Like many other nocturnal migrants, American Redstarts frequently fall victim to collisions with buildings such as skyscrapers, communication towers, and wind turbines.

■ SUMMER ■ MIGRATION
■ WINTER ■ RARE
■ RESIDENT

This federally endangered warbler is noted for its extremely limited range. During the breeding season it is confined to dense stands of young jack pines that spring up after forest fires. Once such stands reach about 20 feet (6 meters), the birds abandon them. Even in winter Kirtland's Warbler inhabits low scrub, although not always pines.

DESCRIPTION: 6" (15 cm). This large warbler is gray above with black streaks, and yellow below with black streaks on the sides. It has black cheeks with a conspicuous white eye ring. The female is similar but duller. This bird often bobs its tail.

VOICE: Low-pitched, loud, bubbling, and rising at the end.

NESTING: Lays 4 brown-dotted white eggs in a nest composed of bark strips and vegetable fibers, lined with grass and pine needles and sunk in the ground.

HABITAT: Dense stands of young jack pines; in winter, it is also found in other low scrub.

RANGE: It nests in just a few counties in Michigan's northern Lower and Upper peninsulas, in Wisconsin, and in Ontario. It winters in the Bahamas.

SIMILAR SPECIES: Prairie and Palm warblers also bob their tails, but both have yellowish or pale faces in all plumages.

Fall Magnolia Warbler has yellow on the rump and prominent white marks in the tail.

CONSERVATION: **NT**

The Kirtland's Warbler is on the U.S. Endangered Species List, with an estimated total population of less than 5000 mature birds. The species is the subject of intensive conservation efforts and its numbers are gradually increasing. (Only about 200 singing males were recorded in most years during the 1970s and 80s.) This warbler nests only in young jack pines, the cones of which need fire in order to open up and release their seeds. Controlled fires are needed to replenish the jack pine forests with younger trees suitable for these birds' nests. Brown-headed Cowbirds also parasitize this species, so cowbird control measures are employed in prime Kirtland's Warbler habitat.

CAPE MAY WARBLER *Setophaga tigrina*

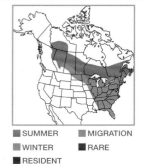

■ SUMMER ■ MIGRATION
■ WINTER ■ RARE
■ RESIDENT

These birds are uncommon warblers in the mature spruce woods of eastern Canada, but, like the Bay-breasted Warbler, they occasionally undergo local population explosions in areas heavily infested with spruce budworms. Much of their summer foraging and singing is confined to the upper branches of spruce and fir trees; during migration, however, they may occur in a variety of situations, often seeming to prefer pines, where they methodically explore dense clusters of needles or hover momentarily at the tips of branches. This warbler gets its name from the fact that the first specimen was collected at Cape May, New Jersey, where it is sometimes a common migrant.

DESCRIPTION: 5" (13 cm). In breeding plumage, the male is yellow below with a conspicuous chestnut cheek patch, a yellow neck patch, a white wing patch, a yellow rump, and heavy black streaks on the underparts. The female is much duller, with a greenish-yellow patch on the neck.

VOICE: Its song is four or more high, thin notes without change in pitch or volume: *seet-seet-seet-seet.*

NESTING: Lays 4 brown-spotted, white eggs in a bulky, compact, twig-and-moss nest lined with grass, fur, and feathers.

HABITAT: Open spruce forests; during migration, evergreen or deciduous woodlands and often parks or suburban yards.

RANGE: Breeds from southern Mackenzie, Manitoba, Ontario, and Quebec south to North Dakota, Michigan, northern New York, Maine, and Nova Scotia. It winters in southern Florida and the West Indies.

SIMILAR SPECIES: Immature Yellow-rumped Warbler also has a yellow rump but is larger, lacks the yellow neck patch, and has a different note.

Palm Warbler in fall wags its tail; it is usually found close to the ground.

CONSERVATION:

The Cape May Warbler population is stable, although its numbers tend to fluctuate in conjunction with the population of spruce budworm and other prey insects in the northern forests. Logging of mature forests, especially in western Canada, and the use of insecticides to control spruce budworms may impact this species. Like many other warblers, these birds are highly susceptible to collisions with buildings during their nocturnal migration.

■ SUMMER ■ MIGRATION
■ WINTER ■ RARE
■ RESIDENT

This rather local, uncommon, small warbler of the East has a discontinuous range, occurring here and there in rather loose colonies. They favor mature, open deciduous forests in bottomland swamps and wooded hillsides along streams. They build their nests high in hardwoods and well out from the trunk, and can be difficult to see well because of their preference for the tops of big trees.

DESCRIPTION: 4½" (11 cm). The male has a sky-blue head and back, and a black band across its white breast. The female is dull blue-gray above and whitish below, and lacks a breast band. The immature is similar to the female.

VOICE: A series of short buzzy notes, followed by a higher-pitched *buzz*.

NESTING: Lays 4 brown-spotted, whitish eggs in a nest of plant fibers lined with grass, moss, and hair, and placed high in a deciduous tree, generally near the end of a branch.

HABITAT: Open woodlands, often near streams and rivers.

RANGE: Breeds from southeastern Minnesota, southern Ontario, and western New England south to Texas, Louisiana, and the northern Gulf Coast states. It winters in South America.

SIMILAR SPECIES: Black-throated Blue Warbler has a black throat; the female lacks wing bars.

Northern and Tropical parulas have bluish backs but also have true yellow on some of the underparts.

A spring Tennessee Warbler is slightly similar to a female Cerulean, but lacks wing bars.

The spring female Blackpoll Warbler is heavily streaked, appearing much more black-and-white. A fall Blackpoll Warbler is similar to a female Cerulean but is greener above, has streaks on the back, and has a less prominent eyebrow.

CONSERVATION: VU
The Cerulean Warbler is of conservation concern because of its small total population size and significant declines. The primary threat to these birds is habitat loss and degradation, and conservation efforts to protect the species focus on promoting forestry practices such as long-rotation timber harvesting and selective logging. Cowbird parasitism also affects the nesting success of these small warblers.

■ SUMMER ■ MIGRATION
■ WINTER   ■ RARE
■ RESIDENT

This species is almost entirely dependent upon either Spanish moss or "beard moss" for nest sites. Although they breed mostly in coniferous forests in the North, during migration Northern Parulas also frequent deciduous trees and shrubs. In spring they are commonly seen in trees along roadsides, and in parks, yards, orchards, and gardens as well as woods.

DESCRIPTION: 4½" (11 cm). A small warbler; it is blue above with a yellow-green "saddle" across its back, a yellow throat and breast, and a white belly. It has two white wing bars. The adult male has an orange-brown chest band. Adult females are duller and lack the chest band. Immatures may be quite dull but have the same general color pattern as the adults.

VOICE: One or more rising, buzzy notes dropping abruptly at the end: *bzzzzz-zip* or *bz-bz-bz-zip*.

NESTING: Lays 4 or 5 brown-spotted, white eggs in a woven basket-shaped nest of grass, bark, and vegetable fibers—neatly hidden in Spanish moss in the South, and in "beard moss" (*Usnea* lichens) in the North.

HABITAT: Breeds in wet, chiefly coniferous woods, in swamps, and along lakes and ponds; it is more widespread during migration.

RANGE: Breeds from southeastern Canada to the Gulf Coast. It winters from southern Florida southward into the tropics.

SIMILAR SPECIES: Nashville and immature Mourning warblers may have roughly similar face patterns, but are larger and lack wing bars.

The two parulas must be carefully distinguished. The adult male Northern Parula has a broken white eye ring and a distinct chest band; Tropical Parula lacks these and has black on the face. Females and immature Northerns have a broken eye ring, which Tropicals usually lack (but may be faint). The extent of yellow below is a good field mark: the malar tract of feathers (extending back from the base of the lower mandible) is blue-gray in Northern, continuous with the side of the head; in Tropical this area is yellow, the same color as the throat—this detail is hard to discern but makes the yellow throat area appear wider on Tropical Parula. The yellow below on the Tropical extends to the belly; it ends at mid-breast on the Northern.

CONSERVATION: LC
Northern Parulas are common and increasing. Clearcutting, wetland drainage, and poor air quality can reduce the availability of the lichen species used for nesting in the North.

■ SUMMER ■ MIGRATION
■ WINTER ■ RARE
■ RESIDENT

This species has disappeared from areas along the Rio Grande—the only part of the United States in which it has been known to nest—due to parasitism by cowbirds, the disappearance of Spanish moss, and the use of pesticides. During a period in the 1960s it was not recorded nesting north of the U.S.-Mexico border at all, but now a few pairs breed annually in certain tracts of river-bottom woods in southern Texas.

DESCRIPTION: 4–5" (10–13 cm). A small, bluish-backed warbler with bright yellow underparts, two white wing bars, and a patch of olive green in the middle of the back. The male has an orange wash on the breast. Northern Parula is closely similar, but the male has an orange-brown breast band.

VOICE: A buzzy, ascending trill: *zzzzzzzzzz-up*.

NESTING: Lays 3 or 4 white eggs spotted with brown in a cup built into a mass of hanging moss, usually along a stream.

HABITAT: River-bottom woodlands and thickets.

RANGE: Breeds in Rio Grande Valley of Texas. A few winter in Texas, but most winter in Mexico and in the American tropics.

SIMILAR SPECIES: See Northern Parula. Occasional sightings of birds that resemble a Tropical Parula but with a pale, broken eye ring are believed to be Tropical x Northern parula hybrids.

CONSERVATION: Tropical Parula is widespread and common in the tropics but has almost disappeared from North America. Its global numbers are increasing.

MAGNOLIA WARBLER *Setophaga magnolia*

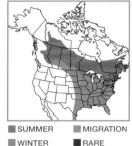

■ SUMMER   ■ MIGRATION
■ WINTER   ■ RARE
■ RESIDENT

The active and colorful Magnolia is a common nesting warbler in open stands of young spruce and fir, particularly along woodland roads or in old, neglected pastures. It regularly forages near the ground in low bushes. These warblers frequently fan their tails, revealing a white median band. This attractive warbler got its name from the first specimen obtained by the famous ornithologist Alexander Wilson among some magnolia trees in Mississippi in the early 1800s. It actually breeds in conifers in the North, but the name has persisted.

DESCRIPTION: 5" (13 cm). The male is bright yellow below with heavy black streaks, a black facial patch, a large white wing patch, and a yellow rump. Female and immature birds are similar but duller. It has broad white patches on the sides of the tail in all plumages.

VOICE: Its song is transcribed *weeta-weeta-weeteo*. Its call note is a *tslip*.

NESTING: Lays 4 brown-spotted, white eggs in a shallow twig-and-grass nest lined with rootlets.

HABITAT: Breeds in open stands of young spruce and fir. On migration, it can be found in almost any place with shrubbery or trees.

RANGE: Breeds from British Columbia across central Canada to the northeastern United States, and in the Appalachian Mountains south to Virginia. It is a rare visitor to the West Coast. It winters in the tropics.

SIMILAR SPECIES: Yellow-rumped Warbler has a white breast.

Cape May Warbler male has chestnut cheeks and lacks a white median tail band.

Immature Prairie Warbler wags its tail, lacks a tail band, and has a dusky jaw stripe.

CONSERVATION: 🐦 LC

Magnolia Warblers are common and increasing. They are an adaptable species, able to thrive in second-growth woods and cut-over areas that do not support many other wood warblers.

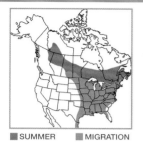

- ■ SUMMER
- ■ MIGRATION
- ■ WINTER
- ■ RARE
- ■ RESIDENT

The Bay-breasted Warbler requires spruce and fir—often in secondary growth or with lots of edge—for breeding, and it tends to forage at about the middle of the tree. This warbler, like the Cape May and Tennessee warblers, increases in numbers during years of spruce budworm outbreaks in its breeding areas; the excess of food means the warblers are able to produce more young. A handsome bird, it is eagerly sought by enthusiasts during the warbler migrations in middle and late May. A rather rapid but late spring migrant, the Bay-breasted is among the earliest warblers to go south in the fall; it often moves in August, a full month ahead of the main flight of the Blackpoll Warbler, which it closely resembles at that season.

DESCRIPTION: 5½" (14 cm). In breeding plumage, the male has a chestnut cap, throat, and sides; a blackish face; and a conspicuous pale buff patch on the side of the neck. Its upperparts are streaked. Females, fall males, and immatures are olive above, with two white wing bars; they are similar to fall Blackpoll Warblers, but with dark legs, buffy undertail coverts and flanks, and sometimes a trace of rust color on the flanks.

VOICE: A high, thin *teesi-teesi-teesi-teesi*, without change in pitch or volume.

NESTING: Lays 5 white eggs, with brown markings, in a loosely built, hair-lined nest of twigs, grass, and needles set in a conifer as much as 50' (15 m) above ground.

HABITAT: Breeds in open spruce forests. During migration, frequents deciduous trees as well.

RANGE: Breeds from northeastern British Columbia east to Maritime Provinces and south to the northern Great Lakes region and northern New England. Winters in the tropics.

SIMILAR SPECIES: Chestnut-sided Warbler in spring has a yellow crown; fall birds lack the colorful crown patch.

See Blackpoll Warbler.

CONSERVATION:

The Bay-breasted Warbler is an uncommon bird that breeds in remote habitat that makes them difficult to track. Overall it is probably slightly declining, and its population fluctuates based on outbreaks of spruce budworms and other prey insects. Pesticide spraying to control budworms and the loss or fragmentation of mature forests decreases their numbers. Like many warblers, these nighttime migrants are susceptible to fatal collisions with buildings and communication towers.

BLACKBURNIAN WARBLER *Setophaga fusca*

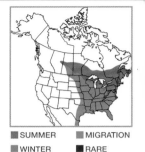

■ SUMMER ■ MIGRATION
■ WINTER ■ RARE
■ RESIDENT

Blackburnian Warblers are usually found high in trees, even during migration, and are not readily noticed in the dense foliage unless their high-pitched song announces their presence. At times they may be detected at the ends of branches, picking among leaves for bugs or caterpillars.

DESCRIPTION: 5" (13 cm). The breeding male is black and white with a vivid orange throat, crown patch, and eyebrow; it has a large white wing patch. The female is similar but has a yellow throat. The back of both sexes is boldly striped. The immature male resembles an adult female.

VOICE: A thin and wiry song, increasing in speed and rising to the limit of hearing: *sleet-sleet-sleet-sleet-sleetee-sleeeee*. It also sings *tiddly-tiddly-tiddly-tiddly*, delivered at the same speed and pitch.

NESTING: Lays 4 brown-spotted, white eggs in a twig nest lined with lichens, mosses, and hair, usually placed high in a large conifer.

HABITAT: Most numerous in mixed forests of hemlock, spruce, and various hardwoods, usually ranging high in trees.

RANGE: Breeds from Saskatchewan east to Nova Scotia, south to the Great Lakes, southern New England, and in the mountains to northern Georgia. It winters in the tropics.

SIMILAR SPECIES: Yellow-throated Warbler has an unstreaked gray back and white above the eye.

The female Townsend's Warbler lacks pale back stripes and median crown stripes, and has a different call.

CONSERVATION:

Blackburnian Warbler is common and increasing slightly. Deforestation is the biggest threat to these birds, as their mature woodland habitat is being lost to logging on both the breeding and wintering grounds. The loss of Fraser firs in the Applachians to Balsam woolly adelgids, invasive insects from Europe, has led to these birds' disappearance from the southernmost part of its breeding range.

- ■ SUMMER   ■ MIGRATION
- ■ WINTER   ■ RARE
- ■ RESIDENT

This is one of the most widespread North American warblers, showing great geographical variation. In the tropical parts of its breeding range this bird nests mainly in mangrove swamps, and there it may have a chestnut head or crown patch. In temperate North America the Yellow Warbler is one of the principal victims of the cowbird, which lays its eggs in the nests of other birds. A cowbird lays only one egg per host nest, but may lay eggs in four or five nests in a short time, thus jeopardizing many broods. If the female Yellow Warbler discovers a cowbird parasitizing its nest, it quickly covers the intruder's egg with a new foundation and lays another clutch. Yellow Warbler nests can come to include several layers, each containing one cowbird egg.

DESCRIPTION: 4½–5" (11–13 cm). This warbler is bright yellow with a light olive green tinge on back. The male has fine rusty streaks on the breast. It is the only largely yellow warbler with yellow spots in the tail (not white).

VOICE: Song a bright, musical *sweet-sweet-sweet, sweeter-than-sweet*. Its call is a sharp *chip*.

NESTING: Lays 4 or 5 pale blue eggs thickly spotted with brown in a well-made cup of bark, plant fibers, and down, placed in an upright fork in a small sapling.

HABITAT: Moist thickets, especially along streams and in swampy areas; gardens.

RANGE: Breeds from Alaska east across Canada to Newfoundland and south to southern California, northern Oklahoma, and northern Georgia; local in southern Florida. Winters in the tropics. *(continued on next page)*

SUBSPECIES: More than 40 subspecies are recognized; these can be categorized into three groups in North America. The "Northern" group is characteristic of Yellow Warblers on most of the continent; geographic variation is weak and clinal, with birds farther north and west generally becoming more drab (except much paler in subsp. *sonorana* of the desert Southwest). Southmost Florida hosts a resident population of birds (subsp. *gundlachi*) belonging to the "Golden" Caribbean group, which sports a darker olive crown; broader reddish streaks on the underparts; and a thinner, slightly decurved bill. The "Mangrove" group, found from Mexico and farther south, may nest in southernmost Texas and occasionally appears in Arizona and southern California; males of this group have a distinct rufous head; females and immatures show some rufous on the head.

SIMILAR SPECIES: Female and immature Wilson's Warbler are olive-green above and lemon-yellow below; they each have a dark tail that lacks yellow spots, and a yellow face sharply framed with olive-green along the crown and nape. All Wilson's lack yellow wing bars and wing edges, and have a flatter-looking crown.

A drabber Yellow Warbler's pale legs and plain face pattern can distinguish them from Orange-crowned, Nashville, and other similar wood warblers.

CONSERVATION:

Yellow Warbler is common and widespread; its population is large and stable. Grazing in the western U.S. can degrade habitat, but these warblers are less vulnerable to habitat loss because they prefer second-growth forest and edges that don't support many other warblers. They are highly vulnerable to cowbird parasitism in these habitats, however; although this species can sometimes recognize cowbird eggs in its nest, the females must expend extra energy rebuilding parasitized nests and relaying clutches of eggs. Yellow Warblers are also nocturnal migrants and are vulnerable to collisions with lighted structures such as buildings and communication towers.

■ SUMMER ■ MIGRATION
■ WINTER ■ RARE
■ RESIDENT

This attractive bird was rare in the days of John James Audubon and Wilson, who seldom saw it and knew little about its habits. It has increased tremendously as abandoned pastures in the northern states have grown into dense thickets, a vast new habitat unavailable when the land was covered with virgin forest. The colorful males can often be seen drooping their wings and cocking their tails as they pour forth their loud, clear, emphatic song.

DESCRIPTION: 5" (13 cm). Both sexes of this colorful warbler are similar: a yellow-green crown, long chestnut lines on the sides, white underparts, and a streaked back. Nonbreeding adults and immatures are uniform yellow-green above and dull whitish below, with a white eye ring and yellow wing bars.

VOICE: A rich and musical song with an emphatic ending, sometimes interpreted as *very very pleased to meet cha!*

NESTING: Lays 4 brown-spotted, white eggs in a grass-and-bark nest lined with hair and rootlets, a few feet (about a meter) off the ground in a small tree or bush.

HABITAT: Young, open, second-growth woodlands and scrub.

RANGE: Breeds from south-central Canada, east to Nova Scotia, south to the east-central United States and in the Appalachian Mountains. It winters in the tropics.

SIMILAR SPECIES: Ruby-crowned Kinglet resembles an immature Chestnut-sided but has white wing bars; it is smaller, duller, and more energetic.

The immature Bay-breasted Warbler has white wing bars and a different face pattern. It has dull yellowish-buff underparts and also is larger than Chestnut-sided Warbler.

CONSERVATION:

Far more common today than a century ago, Chestnut-sided Warblers are gradually declining. Probably more than any other wood warbler in eastern North America, the Chestnut-sided Warbler benefited from the changing land use brought about by the development and subsequent decline of agriculture. As farming diminished in the Northeast, abandoned pastures and fields became overgrown with shrubs and vines. Similarly, the brushy regrowth of clear-cut forests provided excellent habitat for Chestnut-sided Warblers. This habitat is gradually "lost" to these warblers as regrowing eastern forests mature.

BLACKPOLL WARBLER *Setophaga striata*

■ SUMMER ■ MIGRATION
■ WINTER ■ RARE
■ RESIDENT

The Blackpoll is one of the most common warblers in the East during migration and has an enormous breeding range in the northern part of the continent. During migration in late May, and again in September and early October, dozens may be seen in a single day. It is rarely seen west of the Rockies in spring; however, in fall small numbers of mostly young birds occur regularly along the Pacific Coast. Like all wood warblers, these birds migrate at night.

DESCRIPTION: 5½" (14 cm). The breeding male is gray streaked above, with a black cap, white cheeks and underparts, and blackish streaks on the sides. The female and nonbreeding male are greenish above with vague streaking, and yellowish green below. Its feet usually are pinkish.

VOICE: A rapid series of high lisping notes all on one pitch, increasing and then decreasing in volume: *seet-seet-seet-seet-seet-seet-seet-seet*.

NESTING: Lays 4 or 5 brown-spotted, white eggs in a twig-and-grass nest, often lined with feathers and usually placed in a small evergreen tree.

HABITAT: Breeds in coniferous forests. During migration it is found chiefly in tall trees.

RANGE: Breeds from Alaska and northern Canada to southern Canada and northern New England. Winters in the tropics.

SIMILAR SPECIES: Black-and-white Warbler has a striped crown.

Black-throated Gray Warbler has a black cheek patch.

Immature Pine Warbler has dark legs and an unstreaked gray or brownish back, a larger bill, and darker ear coverts.

See Bay-breasted Warbler. Immature Bay-breasted is plumper, more yellow-green above, unstreaked buff or buff-white below and on the undertail coverts, often has a rufous wash on the flanks, and has dark legs and feet.

CONSERVATION: NT
Although still quite numerous, Blackpoll Warblers are undergoing a population crash and are in steep decline. The primary threat is habitat loss due to logging and extractive industries, especially on the wintering grounds but increasingly in the boreal forest breeding range. Their high-elevation conifer habitat is also threatened by climate change and could disappear entirely according to some models. Sometimes large numbers of these nocturnal migrants—attracted to bright lights on overcast or stormy nights—fatally collide with structures such as lighthouses, communication towers, and skyscrapers.

Setophaga caerulescens **BLACK-THROATED BLUE WARBLER**

- ■ SUMMER
- ■ WINTER
- ■ RESIDENT
- ■ MIGRATION
- ■ RARE

The male Black-throated Blue Warbler is one of the easier warblers to identify because it retains its strikingly patterned plumage year-round. The husky song of the Black-throated Blue Warbler is a familiar summer sound on the beech- and maple-covered slopes of the northern hardwood forests of eastern Canada and the northeastern United States. In the southern Appalachians, the species is often associated with dense mountain laurel thickets; farther north, it prefers hardwood sprout growth with an understory of shrubs, especially American yew. Northern populations tend to winter in western Caribbean and Central America, while southern populations tend to winter in eastern Greater Antilles. This is the only warbler that sometimes flashes a white wing stripe in flight.

DESCRIPTION: 5" (13 cm). The male is dark blue-gray above and bright white below with a black face, throat, and sides. Males have a prominent white wing patch at the base of the primaries. The female is dull olive green with a narrow white eyebrow and a small, square, white wing patch (absent in first-year females). Males in the southern portion of the range have variable black streaks on the back. Immatures resemble the adults.

VOICE: Its song is a husky, rising *zwee-zwee-zwee*.

NESTING: Lays 4 brown-spotted, white eggs in a nest made of leaves and grass, lined with cobwebs and hair and placed near the ground in a shrub or a young tree.

HABITAT: Mixed deciduous and evergreen woodlands with thick undergrowth, especially mountain laurel in southern portion of its range and hobblebush in the north.

RANGE: Breeds from western Ontario east to southern Quebec and Nova Scotia; south to Minnesota, the Great Lakes, and Connecticut; and in the mountains to northern Georgia. Winters in the Gulf Coast states (irregularly) and the Greater Antilles.

SUBSPECIES: Males that nest in the Appalachian Mountains (subsp. *cairnsi*) are darker above and usually have black streaks on the back.

SIMILAR SPECIES: Tennessee Warbler in fall is greener above and lacks dark cheek patches and white wing spots.

The female Cerulean Warbler has two white wing bars.

Philadelphia Vireo lacks a wing spot and has paler cheeks and a stouter bill.

CONSERVATION:
Black-throated Blue Warblers are common and increasing from historic lows that followed the widespread clearcutting of forests in the 18th and 19th centuries. Climate change may have adverse effects on breeding, wintering, and migratory stopover habitats.

PALM WARBLER   *Setophaga palmarum*

■ SUMMER ■ MIGRATION
■ WINTER ■ RARE
■ RESIDENT

The Palm Warbler is one of the first warblers to arrive in the spring, and at this season is commonly found feeding quietly on the ground, sometimes with flocks of sparrows. It is unusual among warblers for its habit of walking along the ground wagging its tail—a behavior that helps to identify it in any season.

DESCRIPTION: 5½" (14 cm). An olive-drab, streaked, ground-feeding warbler with a bright olive rump, bright yellow under-tail coverts, and a distinctive habit of wagging its tail. Its underparts vary from yellow to whitish buff, depending on age and geography. Adults in spring have a rufous cap.

VOICE: A weak, dry trill, like that of a Chipping Sparrow but slower.

NESTING: Lays 4 or 5 brown-speckled, white eggs in a grass nest fashioned with shreds of bark and lined with feathers and rootlets. Nest is placed on the ground in a grass clump, often at the base of a small tree or bush.

HABITAT: In summer, it is found in bogs in the North; during migration, it uses open places, especially weedy fields and borders of marshes.

RANGE: Breeds from west-central Canada east to Labrador and Newfoundland, and south to the extreme northern portions of the United States. It winters from the southeastern United States southward.

SUBSPECIES: The nominate Western population (subsp. *palmarum*) has a pale buff to whitish belly; the Eastern population (subsp. *hypochrysea*) has bright yellow underparts.

SIMILAR SPECIES: Prairie Warbler also wags its tail but lacks a crown patch and has a dusky jaw stripe and ventral stripes on the sides.

Yellow-rumped Warbler has a bright yellow rump.

CONSERVATION: LC

The Palm Warbler population is increasing. Its primary breeding grounds in the boreal forest of Canada are vast and remote, but are increasingly threatened by extractive industries (timber, peat, tar sands oil) and climate change. This nocturnal migrant is also highly vulnerable to collisions with lighted structures.

■ SUMMER ■ MIGRATION
■ WINTER ■ RARE
■ RESIDENT

As its name implies, Pine Warbler is closely associated with pines—it spends most of its life in pine trees, nests in pines exclusively, and tends to stay in the tops of these trees. Only during migration is it found in other habitats, such as shrubbery or the deciduous growth of parks and gardens. The Pine Warbler feeds in a creeping manner on insects from the ground to the tree tops, and in winter takes seeds and small fruits. It will sometimes alight on the trunks of pine trees in the manner of nuthatches or creepers. The Pine Warbler's song is pleasant and not loud; it occasionally sings in winter. It is one of the few North American wood warblers whose winter range includes much of its breeding area.

DESCRIPTION: 5½" (14 cm). This relatively long-tailed warbler is unstreaked olive above with a yellow throat and breast, blurry streaking below, a white belly, an inconspicuous eyestripe, and two white wing bars. The female and immature are similar but duller; they often lack the yellowish color on the breast.

VOICE: Musical and somewhat melancholy; a soft, sweet version of the trill of the Chipping Sparrow.

NESTING: Lays 4 brown-spotted, white eggs in a compact nest well concealed among pine needles near the tip of a horizontal branch, usually higher than 20' (6 m).

HABITAT: Pine forests.

RANGE: Breeds from southeastern Manitoba, southern Ontario, and Maine south to eastern Texas, Gulf Coast, and Florida. Winters in southern states, occasionally north to New England.

SIMILAR SPECIES: Yellow-throated Vireo has a heavier bill, no streaks on the underparts, and yellow spectacles.

Immature Blackburnian, Bay-breasted, and Blackpoll warblers have streaked backs; Blackpoll has pale feet and usually pale legs.

The immature Cape May Warbler has a pale neck spot; a subdued yellowish rump; and a streaked breast, sides, and flanks.

Blue-winged Warbler has a black eyeline and unstreaked yellow flanks.

CONSERVATION:
Pine Warblers are common and their numbers are increasing. Although some native pine forest habitat has been lost, these birds are able to relocate to areas in which pines have been introduced into deciduous forests.

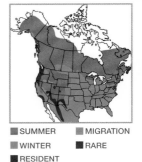

■ SUMMER ■ MIGRATION
■ WINTER ■ RARE
■ RESIDENT

Yellow-rumped Warblers are vivid and conspicuous birds that search for food both high and low in Douglas firs or pines. They most often sing from the high canopy of trees. During winter they disperse in loose flocks, and usually two or three birds at most are observed at a time. The birds constantly chirp a "contact call" that keeps the flock together. The eastern and western populations were once considered two distinct species, respectively the "Myrtle Warbler" and "Audubon's Warbler." However, the birds hybridize freely in the narrow zone where the ranges of the two come together. In the East, the "Myrtle Warbler" is an abundant migrant, and the only warbler that regularly spends the winter in the northern states.

DESCRIPTION: 5–6" (13–15 cm). The breeding male is dull bluish above, streaked with black; its breast and flanks are blackish. The rump, crown, and a small area at the sides of the breast are yellow. Western ("Audubon's Warbler") male has a yellow throat and a large white patch in the folded wing. Eastern ("Myrtle Warbler") male has a white throat and two white wing bars. Females, fall males, and young are streaked gray-brown but always have a yellow rump and white spots in the tail.

VOICE: A colorless, buzzy warble; also gives a sharp *chek!*

NESTING: Lays 4 or 5 white eggs, spotted and blotched with brown, in a bulky nest of twigs, rootlets, and grass, lined with hair and feathers and placed in a conifer.

HABITAT: Coniferous and mixed forests; it is widespread during migration and in winter.

RANGE: Breeds from northern Alaska, northern Manitoba, central Quebec, and Newfoundland south in the West to northern Mexico and in the East to Michigan, northern New York, Massachusetts, and Maine. It winters from the southern part of its breeding range southward into the tropics.

SUBSPECIES: The Western population known as "Audubon's Warbler" can be distinguished from the Taiga-breeding population known as "Myrtle Warbler" by differences in their calls and plumage. "Audubon's" has a bright yellow throat and a gray face. "Myrtle" has a sharply contrasting white throat that wraps around the sides of the neck, darker cheeks, a pale eyebrow, and less black at the tips of the tail feathers. The two forms overlap and interbreed frequently in the Canadian Rockies, producing "mismatched" features—especially in the face pattern—on a single individual.

SIMILAR SPECIES: Magnolia, Palm, and Cape May warblers can all show a yellow rump. Magnolia Warbler is yellow below. Palm Warbler has a strong cap and eyebrow, and it wags its tail. Some immature Cape May Warblers are similar to the dullest "Myrtles" but have shorter tails, finer bills, and usually pale neck spots.

Not all Yellow-rumpeds can be assigned to either "Myrtle" or "Audubon's" because they interbreed regularly; the area of contact is small, so intergrades make up only a small percentage of the population.

CONSERVATION: 🐦 LC

Yellow-rumped Warbler is abundant and widespread; its numbers are believed to be stable. Like many other warblers that migrate at night, this species is a frequent victim of fatal collisions with lighted structures.

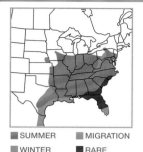

- ■ SUMMER
- ■ MIGRATION
- ■ WINTER
- ■ RARE
- ■ RESIDENT

This attractive warbler is usually found in live oaks draped with Spanish moss or in longleaf pines. It often creeps over the branches of the trunk like a Black-and-white Warbler. Occasionally it may stray, and even breed, as far north of its usual range as New York and southern New England.

DESCRIPTION: 5" (13 cm). This boldly patterned warbler is gray with unstreaked upperparts, a bright yellow throat, a white belly, a black-and-white facial pattern, and heavy black streaks on the sides. Both sexes are alike.

VOICE: A series of clear, ringing notes descending in pitch and increasing in speed, rising abruptly at the end: *teeew-teeew-teeew-teeew-tew-tew-twi.*

NESTING: Lays 4 purple-spotted, greenish eggs in a nest of grass and bark strips lined with hair and feathers, often set in clumps of Spanish moss or among pine needles.

HABITAT: Forests of pine, cypress, sycamore, and oak, in both swampy places and dry uplands.

RANGE: Breeds from Illinois, Ohio, and New Jersey south to Missouri, Texas, the Gulf Coast, and northern Florida. It winters from the Gulf Coast states southward.

SIMILAR SPECIES: Grace's Warbler has a different face pattern, a yellow eyebrow, and a different range.

CONSERVATION:
Yellow-throated Warblers are common and increasing. These birds declined at the northern edge of their range in southern Michigan and northern Ohio for unknown reasons, but appear to be recovering and expanding their range northward.

PRAIRIE WARBLER *Setophaga discolor*

■ SUMMER   ■ MIGRATION
■ WINTER   ■ RARE
■ RESIDENT

The misnamed Prairie Warbler is an eastern bird that prefers dry, scrubby areas, old fields, barrens, and low, semi-open second growth, especially with scrub oak, cedars, and pines. In Florida it also inhabits mangroves. This species avoids thick woods and has benefited greatly from the cutting and burning of the forests, which favors the younger seedlings and smaller bushes that sprout after fires. Like the Palm Warbler, it forages in low undergrowth, rarely ascending higher than 10 feet (3 meters).

DESCRIPTION: 5" (13 cm). This small, long-tailed warbler is olive above and bright yellow below, with black spots and streaks along the sides. The male has chestnut streaks on the back. Females and immatures have fewer streaks. This bird bobs its tail vigorously.

VOICE: A buzzy *zee-zee-zee*, up to 10 rapidly ascending notes.

NESTING: Lays 4 brown-spotted, white eggs in a nest of grass and leaves lined with hair and feathers, usually set low in a bush or small tree.

HABITAT: Not found on prairies. In the North, it uses mixed pine-oak barrens, old pastures, and hillsides with scattered red cedars; in the South, it prefers open scrub; in extreme southern Florida, it uses mangrove swamps.

RANGE: Breeds from eastern Nebraska, central Wisconsin, southern Ontario, and central New England south to Oklahoma, the Gulf Coast, and Florida; it is local in many areas. It winters in southern Florida and in the tropics.

SIMILAR SPECIES: Palm Warbler also bobs its tail but is usually less yellowish (especially below), has more extensive streaking and a brownish cap; and is more commonly encountered in open areas (except on the breeding grounds).

Pine Warbler is duller, less uniformly yellow below, and has more prominent white wing bars. It is bigger, chunkier, and has a larger bill; it often stays higher up in the trees.

Also see Magnolia Warbler.

CONSERVATION: LC

Prairie Warblers are common but declining, primarily due to the loss of habitat as many shrubby or brushy areas are lost either to the maturation of the forest or to development. Cowbird parasitism also impacts this species' numbers.

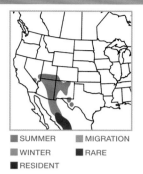

■ SUMMER　■ MIGRATION
■ WINTER　　■ RARE
■ RESIDENT

Because this small bird lives high up in pine trees and is difficult to observe, little is known of its life history. It moves from treetop to treetop with a quick erratic flight, darting out of the canopy to catch prey in midair. During migration it prefers mountain forests similar to those in which it breeds, but in winter, in Central America, it also frequents lowland pine savannas and stands of tall pines.

DESCRIPTION: 4½–5" (11–13 cm). This slender warbler has a bright yellow eyestripe, chin, throat, and breast. Its upperparts are gray streaked with black; its underparts are white with black striping on the sides; and its wings and tail are dark, with two white wing bars and whitish outer tail feathers. The sexes are similar, although females and juveniles may be paler than adult males.

VOICE: Its song is a short musical trill, faster toward the end: *che che che che che-che-che-che*. Its call is a soft *chip*.

NESTING: Lays 3 or 4 white or cream-colored eggs finely spotted with reddish brown in a small cup nest of rootlets and bark shreds lined with hair or feathers, well concealed in a conifer, some 20–60' (6–18 m) above the ground.

HABITAT: Forests of pine or mixed pine and oak.

RANGE: Breeds from southern Nevada, Utah, and Colorado southward along the mountains of the Southwest. It winters south of the U.S.-Mexico border.

SIMILAR SPECIES: See Townsend's, Yellow-throated, and Blackburnian warblers.

CONVERSATION:
Grace's Warbler is still common in its limited range, but it is declining. Its biggest threat is habitat loss, especially on its wintering grounds in the mountains of Mexico and Central America.

■ SUMMER ■ MIGRATION
■ WINTER ■ RARE
■ RESIDENT

This bird resembles Townsend's Warbler in every respect except that it lacks green and yellow colors. Whereas the bright plumage of Townsend's blends well with the bright green of the spruces and pines of the coastal forest, the drab appearance of the Black-throated Gray is a good adaptation to the bluish gray-green of western junipers. It has no yellow in its plumage other than a tiny spot on the lores. Its range overlaps those of the Hermit and Townsend's warblers, but it prefers dry forests in warm climates. It often breeds in areas where the trees are widely spaced with much intervening brush. Oak woodland is the preferred habitat, although the pinyon-juniper woodland runs a close second; some pine and fir communities are also used, generally in the north and particularly if oaks are present. This species is common throughout most of its range.

DESCRIPTION: 4½–5" (11–13 cm). This warbler's head is striped black and white, and it has a black bib on the throat. It is white below, with black stripes on the sides. It has a gray back with black striping, two white wing bars, and white outer tail feathers. It shows a small yellow spot between the bill and eyes. Winter males, females, and juveniles lack the black bib.

VOICE: Its song is a series of buzzes, rising in pitch and intensity, then falling: *zee zee zee zee bzz bzz*. Its call is a dull *tup*.

NESTING: Lays 3–5 creamy-white eggs splashed with brown in a tightly woven plant-fiber cup in a bush or tree, usually not higher than 10' (3 m).

HABITAT: Shrubby openings in coniferous forests or mixed woods, dry scrub oak, pinyon and juniper, chaparral, and other low brushy areas; also found in forests.

RANGE: Breeds from southern British Columbia (except Vancouver Island), Washington, Idaho, and Colorado southward. It winters in the Southwest and in Mexico.

SIMILAR SPECIES: Closely related to Townsend's, Hermit, Black-throated Green, and Golden-cheeked warblers. These four other warblers have similar patterns but all show yellow on the face, which Black-throated Gray lacks.

Black-and-white Warbler has a white stripe down the center of the crown and white streaks on the back; it behaves like a creeper.

Various chickadees have all-white cheeks and no wing bars.

CONSERVATION: Black-throated Gray Warblers are common and widespread in the West. Their population is thought to be stable.

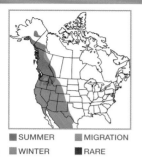

■ SUMMER ■ MIGRATION
■ WINTER ■ RARE
■ RESIDENT

Coniferous forest is the habitat of the Townsend's Warbler for most of the year. It breeds in the Pacific Northwest, where it may spend most of the summer singing, feeding, and nesting at dizzyingly high levels of the trees. In winter it occupies conifers of a curiously disjunct range: in coastal Oregon and California, and from central Mexico south to Nicaragua. It is a widespread migrant in the West, occurring in the lowlands and in a variety of habitats. Active insect-eaters, Townsend's Warblers may be found by themselves, in small groups, or mixed in with other warblers foraging from high to low in trees; in migration, they are frequently found in chaparral and desert scrub. This warbler is a darker counterpart of the Black-throated Green Warbler, which breeds east of the Rocky Mountains. The pattern of Townsend's plumage is similar to that of the Hermit, Black-throated Gray, and Golden-cheeked warblers; all these warblers are believed to have developed from one common ancestor.

DESCRIPTION: 4¼–5" (11–13 cm). The adult male has a black crown, nape, ear patch, throat, and bib; and an olive green back. Its face and breast are bright yellow, its sides are heavily streaked with black, and it has a white belly. The wings and tail are dusky, with two white wing bars and white outer tail feathers. In females and immatures, the black bib is replaced by dark streaking, and the black areas on the face and head are replaced by dusky olive.

VOICE: A rising series of notes, usually with two phrases, the first repeated three or four times, the second once or twice: *weazy weazy weazy weazy twea* or *dee dee dee-de de*. Its call is a soft *chip*.

NESTING: Lays 3–5 white eggs, wreathed and speckled with brownish markings, in a well-concealed shallow cup in a conifer.

HABITAT: Coniferous forests; in old stands of Douglas firs, where it forages in the upper canopy.

RANGE: Breeds from Alaska and British Columbia to northern Washington, Idaho, Montana, and Wyoming. It winters from southwestern California southward.

SIMILAR SPECIES: Hermit Warbler has an entirely golden cheek, no yellow on the breast, few or no streaks on the side, and a primarily gray back. Hybrids of Townsend's and Hermit warblers are uncommon but encountered annually in Washington and Oregon. These most closely resemble Black-throated Green Warblers, which occur as vagrants along the Pacific Coast with roughly the same frequency as hybrids, making identification difficult.

Black-throated Gray Warbler has paler cheeks and lacks yellow on the breast.

CONVERSATION:
Townsend's Warbler is common and its population is stable. Fragmentation of mature forests reduces available habitat and exposes these birds to predators, both on the breeding and wintering grounds. Like many warblers that migrate at night, they are prone to fatal collisions with lighted structures such as buildings and communication towers.

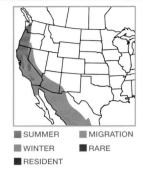

SUMMER ■ MIGRATION
WINTER ■ RARE
■ RESIDENT

The Hermit Warbler is fairly common within its narrow range along the Pacific Coast. This species lives high in the canopy of the tallest redwoods and Douglas firs and is therefore difficult to observe. Occasionally it has been found to hybridize with Townsend's Warbler. The zone of overlap is narrow, and nesting Hermit Warblers tend to occupy well-forested areas that are higher and drier than those of Townsend's. The similarity in the songs of the two species suggests that they are close relatives.

DESCRIPTION: 4½" (11 cm). This warbler has a clean yellow head, a black chin and throat, a gray back, and white underparts with black-streaked flanks. It has a gray tail with white outer tail feathers, and gray wings with white wing bars. Females and immatures have little or no dark on the throat; the gray of the back extends to the top of the crown. No other western warbler is as clean white underneath.

VOICE: A series of high notes, somewhat less buzzy than the song of a Townsend's Warbler; the song recalls a Yellow Warbler song in pattern but is less emphatic. Its call is a soft *chup*.

NESTING: Lays 3–5 creamy-white eggs, speckled and wreathed with light brown markings, in a neat shallow cup nest of rootlets, bark, and pine needles, "saddled" on a conifer branch, usually 20–40' (6–12 m) high, but occasionally near the ground.

HABITAT: Mature coniferous forests.

RANGE: Breeds from Washington to northern California and the Sierra Nevada. It winters south of the U.S.-Mexico border.

SIMILAR SPECIES: See Townsend's Warbler.

CONSERVATION: LC

The Hermit Warbler population is considered stable. Although common in its range, it occupies a specialized habitat in a limited area, making it potentially vulnerable to the loss of northwestern forests to logging or other alterations. Townsend's Warbler may be displacing this species in some areas where their ranges overlap.

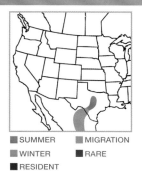

■ SUMMER ■ MIGRATION
■ WINTER ■ RARE
■ RESIDENT

This relative of the Black-throated Green Warbler of the East breeds only in Texas in juniper woodlands on the Edwards Plateau and in a small area near Dallas. Even in this restricted range, these birds are localized, and the small population is being steadily reduced by habitat loss and heavy cowbird parasitism.

DESCRIPTION: 4½–5" (11–13 cm). The male is black with two white wing bars, a white belly, and a conspicuous yellow face. Females are similar but have an olive green back with dark streaks.

VOICE: A buzzy *zee, zoo, zeedee, zeep*.

NESTING: Lays 4 white eggs, finely dotted with brown, in a cup of bark strips, grass, and cobwebs, placed in a juniper.

HABITAT: Rocky hillsides covered with juniper.

RANGE: Breeds in a limited area in south-central Texas. It winters south of the U.S.-Mexico border.

SIMILAR SPECIES: Female and immature are similar to Black-throated Green Warbler (a migrant through central Texas). Golden-cheeked usually has at least some black on the back (virtually always lacking on Black-throated Green, except in the adult male); the lower belly is pure white (faintly washed with yellow in Black-throated Green); and it has some indication of a dark eyeline. Hybrids of Townsend's and Hermit warblers might duplicate these characteristics, so all except for adult male Golden-cheekeds are probably not safely identified outside of their normal range.

CONSERVATION: ![EN]

The Golden-cheeked Warbler is on the U.S. Endangered Species List and is classified as endangered in Texas. It is uncommon, local, and declining, with an estimated total population under 10,000. Its breeding habitat is old-growth and mature second-growth juniper-oak woodlands, which may take decades to recover from disturbance, if they ever regenerate. This habitat has been subject to clearing for land development, ranching, and agriculture, and has also been impacted by recent drought and floods. Fragmentation of this habitat has made these warblers vulnerable to nest predators and to cowbirds, which heavily parasitize this species. It is also losing habitat on its wintering grounds.

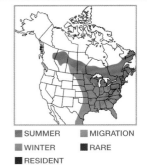

■ SUMMER   ■ MIGRATION
■ WINTER   ■ RARE
■ RESIDENT

The Black-throated Green Warbler is a common bird in coniferous and mixed forests, especially where birch and aspen are prevalent in the North and where cypress is dominant in southern swamps. As with a number of canopy-dwelling warblers, this species is often first detected by its distinctive, lazy song that comes from high in a tree. The Black-throated Green is one of the most commonly seen warblers during migration; at this season it feeds at any height above the ground, but where the trees are tall it spends most of its time among the highest branches.

DESCRIPTION: 5" (13 cm). Males in breeding plumage have upperparts that are yellowish-green, sometimes lightly spotted with black, two broad white wing bars, and white outer tail feathers. The forehead, face, and sides of the neck are yellow, contrasting with a black throat and upper breast; there is a faint olive line through the eye and bordering the ear coverts. The lower breast and belly are white with black side streaks. The female is similar but duller.

VOICE: A thin, buzzy, lazy *zeer, zeer, zeer, zeer, zee?* or faster *zee-zee-zee-zoo-zee.*

NESTING: Lays 4 or 5 brown-spotted, white eggs in a cup of grass, moss, and plant fibers, lined with hair and feathers and placed in the branches of a conifer.

HABITAT: Open stands of hemlock or pine; during migration, it uses a variety of habitats.

RANGE: Breeds from eastern British Columbia, Ontario, and Newfoundland south to Alberta, Minnesota, Ohio, northern New Jersey, and in the mountains to Georgia. It winters from Florida and Texas southward.

SIMILAR SPECIES: See Golden-cheeked and Townsend's Warblers.

CONSERVATION: LC

The Black-throated Green Warbler is widespread and common but decreasing, especially in the Northeast. The primary threat to these birds is habitat degradation, fragmentation, and loss. Invasive woolly adelgids have caused serious habitat loss in parts of this bird's range, and winter habitat has been lost to deforestation in the tropics.

SUMMER   MIGRATION
WINTER   RARE
RESIDENT

Fan-tailed Warbler, a tropical species native to Mexico and Central America, is recorded rarely in the mountains and canyons of extreme southeastern Arizona in spring. It forages like a redstart and engages in tail flipping and spreading reminiscent of American Redstarts.

DESCRIPTION: 5¾" (15 cm). Adults have yellow underparts that become almost orange on the breast. Its crown patch is yellow and black-bordered. It has white loral spots and eye arcs. Its long, broad tail—often raised and fanned—is graduated and tipped with white.

VOICE: Its song is a clear, whistled *tyew tyew tyew tyew whee-ta-wee*, falling then rising. Its call is a distinctive, descending *tseeoo*.

NESTING: Lays 2 to 4 white eggs with gray and reddish brown flecks in a ground nest.

HABITAT: Dense woodlands.

RANGE: Native to Mexico and Central America. Rarely, individual strays have occurred in the canyons of Arizona just north of the Mexican border, usually in late spring. Records of single vagrants exist in New Mexico and Texas.

SIMILAR SPECIES: Yellow-breasted Chat is larger and has a distinctive malar stripe. It tends to be more olive green than a Fan-tailed Warbler, which is slaty gray above.

Golden-crowned Warbler is drabber yellow-olive underneath and has dark crown stripes.

CONSERVATION: LC
Fan-tailed Warbler is believed to be declining in its native range due to ongoing habitat destruction.

RUFOUS-CAPPED WARBLER *Basileuterus rufifrons*

■ SUMMER ■ MIGRATION
■ WINTER ■ RARE
■ RESIDENT

This rare visitor from Mexico has a longish tail that is often held high or flipped about expressively. It mostly stays low in heavy undergrowth along ravines, canyon edges, or streams. Strays have been recorded in southeastern Arizona and southern and western Texas, sometimes staying for several weeks. This species has nested in Arizona.

DESCRIPTION: 5" (13 cm). This tropical warbler has a bright yellow throat and breast; its belly and undertail coverts are white. It has a distinctive facial pattern comprised of a rufous cap, white superciliary, a dark eyeline, a rufous cheek, and a white malar marking. Its upperparts are plain olive; it has no wing bars or tail spots. Its bill is rather stout for a warbler, and its relatively long tail is often cocked at a high angle and flicked sideways.

VOICE: Its song is an accelerating, chippy trill, mostly on one pitch, sometimes ending with accented notes or a complex flourish. Its call is a staccato but soft *tsic*.

NESTING: Lays 3–4 white eggs with brownish flecks and splotches in a domed nest with a side entrance made of grass and plant fibers, built on the side of a steep bank, rock, or log. Both sexes incubate.

HABITAT: Tropical deciduous forest, pine-oak forest, arid montane scrub. North American sightings are usually in canyon bottoms where oak woodlands are located near running water.

RANGE: Mexico (northern Sonora, western Chihuahua) south to northern Colombia and northwestern Venezuela; rare in southeastern Arizona and western and southern Texas.

SIMILAR SPECIES: Yellow-breasted Chat is larger and lacks the rufous crown and cheeks.

CONSERVATION: LC
The Rufous-capped Warbler population is considered stable in its native range.

GOLDEN-CROWNED WARBLER

Basileuterus culicivorus

■ SUMMER ■ MIGRATION
■ WINTER ■ RARE
■ RESIDENT

Golden-crowned Warbler has visited Texas and New Mexico rarely, mostly in fall and winter. It forages in low scrub and riparian thickets, sometimes in mixed foraging flocks with other songbirds. The Mexican and Central American population is sometimes called "Stripe-crowned Warbler" to distinguish it from the South American population, which may be a separate species.

DESCRIPTION: 5" (13 cm). Adults have a yellow or gold-orange crown stripe with black borders, unlike other warblers, but similar to a Golden-crowned Kinglet. Its underparts are deep yellow. The upperwings are unpatterned; it has no wing bars or tail spots.

VOICE: Song a set of distinct, rich *wee* and *chew* whistles, simple but varied, with an upslurred ending. Its calls include insect-like ticking and other calls that resemble a wren or Ruby-crowned Kinglet.

NESTING: Lays 2 to 4 white eggs with reddish-brown marks toward the large end in a domed nest made of grass, rootlets, stems, and other plant fibers. It does not nest in North America.

HABITAT: Low, brushy vegetation, often near wet areas with dense grass.

RANGE: Resident in the American tropics.

SIMILAR SPECIES: Golden-crowned Kinglet also has a yellow-orange crown stripe, but also has a distinct black-and-white face pattern and bold barring across the wings.

CONSERVATION: The population trends for this species are poorly studied, but it is widespread in the tropics.

CANADA WARBLER *Cardellina canadensis*

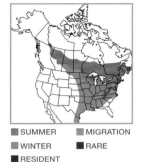

SUMMER ■ MIGRATION
WINTER ■ RARE
RESIDENT

This warbler received its name from its discovery in Canada, although it is certainly not confined to Canada, even in the breeding season. It is at home in the luxuriant, moist undergrowth of mature northern and eastern woodlands, ordinarily seen at low levels, usually from the ground to 6 feet (nearly 2 meters) up. Like several other warblers, it is adept at flycatching, conspicuously flitting from bush to bush. Flying insects form a great portion of its diet, but it also captures spiders and insect larvae.

DESCRIPTION: 5" (13 cm). This warbler is solid gray above, without wing bars, and yellow below. It has yellow "spectacles" around the eyes and a black-spotted "necklace" on the breast. The female is similar but duller, with only a trace of a necklace.

VOICE: A rapid, sputtering warble.

NESTING: Lays 4 brown-spotted, white eggs in a nest of dried leaves and grass, on or near the ground at the base of a stump or in a fern clump.

HABITAT: Cool, moist woodlands that are nearly mature and have much undergrowth.

RANGE: Breeds from southern Canada to the northern United States east of the Rockies, and in the mountains to northern Georgia. It winters in the tropics.

SIMILAR SPECIES: Kentucky Warbler has a similar face pattern but lacks the black necklace and gray upperparts.

CONSERVATION:  LC
Canada Warblers are uncommon and declining due to changes in forest structure. These warblers require the shrubby and mossy undergrowth of mature woodlands for breeding and feeding sites during migration. Logging, forest management practices, and heavy browsing by white-tailed deer have degraded or eliminated much of the understory in many mature woodlands.

- ■ SUMMER
- ■ WINTER
- ■ RESIDENT
- ■ MIGRATION
- ■ RARE

Wilson's Warbler is a common species, especially from the Rocky Mountains and westward, that most often occurs in willow and alder thickets and tangles near water. It is easy to observe this warbler because it seldom ventures more than 10 feet (3 meters) off the ground, and it searches the outsides of leafy branches. It is an active, flycatching warbler, often engaging in aerial cartwheels that are punctuated by a sharp snap of the bill. This species frequently twitches its longish, unspotted tail in a circular motion and flicks its wings like a kinglet. During early summer, the foraging male utters long bursts of vivid song. The species is named for Scottish-American ornithologist and artist Alexander Wilson (1766–1813).

DESCRIPTION: 4½–5" (11–13 cm). A small, active warbler, the adult male is olive green above and yellow below, with a black crown patch. Most females and all young birds lack the black crown and may be distinguished from other olive green warblers with yellow underparts by their lack of wing bars, streaks, tail spots, or other markings.

VOICE: A rapid, staccato series of *chips*, which drop in pitch at the end.

NESTING: Lays 4 or 5 brown-spotted, white eggs in a bulky mass of leaves, rootlets, and moss, lined with hair and fine plant materials, concealed on the ground in a dense clump of weeds or sedge.

HABITAT: Moist thickets in woodlands and along streams; alder and willow thickets and bogs.

RANGE: Breeds from Alaska eastward to Newfoundland and south to southern California, New Mexico, central Ontario, and Nova Scotia. Winters in the tropics.

SUBSPECIES: Western birds (subsp. *chryseola*) have a brighter yellow face, forehead, and breast. Taiga/Eastern breeders (subsp. *pusilla*) are paler lemon-yellow with a darker forehead and crown. Birds of the Interior West (subsp. *pileolata*) are intermediate

between these and difficult to distinguish in the field. There also are subtle vocal differences among these subpopulations.

SIMILAR SPECIES: Yellow Warbler has yellow wing bars and tail spots, and a shorter tail.

Female and immature Hooded Warblers are larger, with flashing white tail spots and a different head pattern.

CONSERVATION: Wilson's Warbler is still common in the West, and generally uncommon in the East. Its numbers are declining, especially in the West, due to habitat loss on the breeding grounds, along its migration routes, and on its wintering grounds in Mexico and Central America. The species is also parasitized by Brown-headed Cowbirds, especially where forest fragmentation gives the brood parasites easier access to nests.

RED-FACED WARBLER *Cardellina rubrifrons*

■ SUMMER ■ MIGRATION
■ WINTER ■ RARE
■ RESIDENT

Red-faced Warbler is an uncommon breeder in streamside canyons and open mountain forests in the Southwest, and is most easily seen from early to mid-spring. Active and energetic like most warblers, the Red-faced keeps to the outside canopy of tall trees. This warbler has the characteristic habit of flicking its tail sideways.

DESCRIPTION: 5¼" (13 cm). These long, slender warblers are gray above and white below, with a distinctive red-and-black head. It has a bright red forehead, throat, and breast; a black crown and ear patch; and a white nape patch and rump. Immatures resemble faded versions of the adults. Its tail is long and often flicked.

VOICE: Its song is a series of rich notes: *sweet-sweet-sweet-weeta-see-see-see,* similar to that of the Yellow Warbler. Its call is a loud *chup*.

NESTING: Lays 3 or 4 white, marked eggs in a loosely assembled ground nest of rootlets and grasses, sheltered by a log, rock, or patch of weeds.

HABITAT: Montane coniferous forests.

RANGE: Breeds in southeastern Arizona and southwestern New Mexico. Winters in the tropics.

SIMILAR SPECIES: The unique plumage on the head and face makes Red-faced Warbler unmistakable.

CONSERVATION:

The Red-faced Warbler population is declining slightly, however since it is a challenge to specify the population trends of this species, a true level of concern is difficult to ascertain. Partners in Flight estimates the current breeding population at 700,000. The global breeding population spends some of the year in the U.S. but spends most of the year in Mexico, where loss of forest habitat is a threat. Climate change also has an impact on these birds, driving their nesting range northward.

The Painted Redstart is one of the flashiest birds in North America. Both sexes are glossy jet-black on the upperparts with a scarlet breast and pure white wing and tail patches. These highland birds of the Southwest are common breeders in evergreen oak woods, primarily those mixed with other trees. They are especially common in moist mountain canyons and somewhat concentrated along flowing streams. Painted Redstart often flits energetically, drooping its wings and fanning its tail in typical redstart fashion. It catches flying insects, much as the American Redstart does. The two birds are not closely related but have evolved in a similar way and fill the same ecological niche in the forest.

DESCRIPTION: 5" (13 cm). This distinctive, attractive bird has a black hood and upperparts accentuated by a large white wing patch and outer tail feathers. It has an unmistakable bright red breast and white belly. The sexes are alike.

VOICE: Its song is a rich, chanting *cheery cheery cheery chew*. Its call is a *cheereo*, different from the calls of other warblers.

NESTING: Lays 3 or 4 creamy-white, finely speckled eggs in a grass nest with fine grass or hair lining, placed in a ground hollow.

HABITAT: Pine or pine-oak woods, oak canyons, pinyon- and juniper-covered high slopes.

RANGE: Breeds in southern Arizona, New Mexico, and western Texas. A few remain through the winter, but most winter south of the U.S.-Mexico border. It is a permanent resident in much of its range in Mexico and Central America.

SIMILAR SPECIES: Slate-throated Redstart, an extremely rare visitor from Mexico, has no white around the eye, a red cap, and dark wings with no white patches.

CONSERVATION: Painted Redstarts are common in their range and increasing. Most of these birds winter in the tropics, where habitat loss due to deforestation could affect their numbers.

SUMMER ■ MIGRATION
WINTER ■ RARE
RESIDENT

Slate-throated Redstart, a widespread warbler in the Neotropics, has strayed a few times to the shady mountain canyons of Arizona, New Mexico, and Texas. Warblers in the tropical genus *Myioborus* are often called whitestarts.

DESCRIPTION: 5¼" (13 cm). Adults are gray above, rose-red below, with a blackish throat and a crimson central crown. Their large tails with extensive white are often fanned.

VOICE: Its song is a variable, usually loose set of sweet notes, sometimes falling or rising in pitch or with accented ending. Its call is a sweet, quick *tik*.

NESTING: Lays 3 white, speckled eggs in a bulky, enclosed nest with a side entrance, usually built against a bank or steep slope.

HABITAT: Montane pine-oak forests.

RANGE: Resident across much of the American tropics. Wanderers into North America have been recorded in the Southwest on a handful of occasions, mostly in the spring.

SIMILAR SPECIES: This bird resembles Painted Redstart in plumage and behavior, but lacks white in the wing. Its upperparts are more gray and its underparts more orange, compared to the black and red of Painted Redstart.

CONSERVATION: LC
The Slate-throated Redstart is still seen widely throughout the American tropics with an extensive range; its numbers are stable.

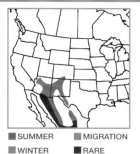

■ SUMMER ■ MIGRATION
■ WINTER ■ RARE
■ RESIDENT

Hepatic Tanagers are found in pine-oak and oak woodlands in the Southwest; they are fairly common in more monotypic pine, oak, and pinyon-juniper woodlands near streams. They are occasionally seen flycatching or singing from an exposed perch. Although insect feeders during the nesting period, these tanagers eat figs, ripe guavas, and other fruits on their wintering grounds in the tropics.

DESCRIPTION: 7–8" (18–20 cm). A large, stocky tanager. The male is a subdued orange-brick color, darker than a Summer Tanager. Both sexes have a dark bill and ear patch. The female is olive green above and deep yellow below, with more orange tint to the throat than other female tanagers.

VOICE: Strong short phrases, whistled vireo-fashion at even intervals; each phrase may rise, fall, or remain on the same tone. Its call notes are a low *chup* and an inquisitive *wheet?*

NESTING: Lays 3–5 bluish eggs with fairly heavy overall blotches in a shallow nest of rootlets and weeds on a low horizontal branch.

HABITAT: Coniferous mountain forests; live oaks.

RANGE: Breeds from northwestern Arizona, New Mexico, southern Nevada, southeastern California, and Texas, south to Mexico; also from Costa Rica to South America. It winters south of the U.S.-Mexico border.

SIMILAR SPECIES: Western Tanager has a prominent, short wing bar near the shoulder and a second, thinner whitish wing bar below. It lacks a dark ear patch and has a smaller, paler, unhooked bill. Its yellow rump and dark back contrast strongly.

Female and immature Scarlet Tanagers have smaller bills and much greener upperparts, and lack a dark cheek patch.

The male Summer Tanager is brighter, richer red all over; both males and females lack a dark ear patch and usually have a paler bill. Their songs and calls are different.

CONSERVATION: Hepatic Tanager is fairly common and increasing. Drought, fire, grazing, and timber extraction threaten its limited breeding habitat in the Southwest, and this species is often the victim of cowbird parasitism. Its winter habitat in the tropics may also be threatened by deforestation.

SUMMER ■ MIGRATION
WINTER ■ RARE
RESIDENT

Summer Tanager is a common bird of oak and pine-oak wood-lands and riparian forests, especially cottonwood-willow; it favors the dry oak and mixed forests of the southern United States. Despite their bright colors, the males are difficult to detect because they tend to remain concealed high in dense foliage. On their breeding grounds the birds are most easily located by their calls, which they utter persistently throughout the day. A major part of the diet during the summer consists of flying insects captured in the air.

DESCRIPTION: 7–8" (18–20 cm). The adult male is solid rose-red. Females and imma-tures are pale olive green above and dull yel-low below; young males in their first spring are usually blotched with variable red patches. Both sexes have large bills that are pale in the breed-ing season but darker (especially in immatures) at other times of the year.

VOICE: Its song is like an American Robin's, but softer and sweeter. It also gives a distinctive rattling *chick-tucky-tuck*.

NESTING: Lays 3 or 4 blue-green eggs spotted with brown in a shallow, flimsy cup near the end of a horizontal branch, 10–20' (3–6 m) above the ground.

HABITAT: Open woodlands and shade trees.

RANGE: Breeds from southern California, Nevada, Nebraska, and New Jersey, south to the Gulf Coast and northern Mexico. It winters in the tropics.

SUBSPECIES: Summer Tanagers west of central Texas (subsp. *cooperi*) are slightly paler about the back and neck, and have a slightly longer bill than Eastern birds (subsp. *rubra*). The song of the Eastern population is slightly faster and higher-pitched.

SIMILAR SPECIES: See Hepatic, Scarlet, and Western tana-gers. All North American tanagers except Summer Tanager have a sharp, fairly conspicuous "tooth" midway along the upper mandible.

Male Northern Cardinal has a black face, a conical red bill, and a prominent crest.

CONSERVATION: Summer Tanagers are common and their numbers are stable. Some local populations, such as those along the lower Colo-rado River, have experienced a sharp decline due to the conver-sion of riverside forests to agriculture and other uses.

■ SUMMER   ■ MIGRATION
■ WINTER   ■ RARE
■ RESIDENT

The brilliantly colored male Scarlet Tanager gleams in the sunlight but is often difficult to see in thick foliage, especially if the bird is motionless or moving slowly from branch to branch high up in the tree canopy. It is conspicuous only when perched on a dead tree limb or when feeding on the ground during a cold, rainy spell. During late summer or early autumn, some of the males may show a patchwork plumage of red and green as they undergo a molt to olive green, except for their wings and tails, which remain black throughout the winter.

DESCRIPTION: 7½" (19 cm). In breeding plumage, the adult male is brilliant scarlet with solid black wings and tail. In non-breeding plumage, both the female and male are olive green; the male has black wings while the female's are dark gray-brown. Juvenile birds resemble females but are more variable; some have bright yellow wing bars, which may cause them to be confused with the Western Tanager.

VOICE: Its song is a hurried, burry, repetitive warble, somewhat like that of a robin. Its call note is an emphatic, nasal *chip-bang*.

NESTING: Lays 3 or 4 brown-spotted, greenish eggs in a shallow nest of twigs and stems lined with grass and placed on a horizontal branch.

HABITAT: Chiefly mature woodlands, especially oak and pine.

RANGE: Breeds from extreme southeastern Canada to the east-central United States. It winters in the tropics.

SIMILAR SPECIES: Summer Tanager's bill is more massive, deeper, longer, and usually paler; the tooth on the upper mandible is less obvious. The female Summer Tanager has generally paler wings; its body plumage, although variable, is typically a warmer orange-yellow.

Western Tanager has two obvious wing bars; the median coverts form a short, broad yellow wing bar and the greater coverts form a thinner, yellow-white wing bar.

CONSERVATION: LC
Scarlet Tanagers are fairly common, and their numbers are stable. They are vulnerable to habitat loss and fragmentation on both the breeding and wintering grounds. Forest fragmentation in their breeding range leaves Scarlet Tanager nests more vulnerable to cowbird parasitism and nest predators. This species does best in large areas of unbroken, mature forest.

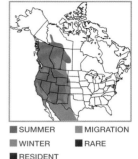

- ■ SUMMER
- ■ WINTER
- ■ RESIDENT
- ■ MIGRATION
- ■ RARE

The Western Tanager's casual song is a characteristic sound of western forests. Despite the male's bright yellow-and-black plumage, this bird can be difficult to see—it is often located by following its song, because the male stays for some time on an exposed perch while singing. In late spring and early summer the Western Tanager feeds on insects, often like a flycatcher, from the high canopy. Later it feeds on berries and other small fruits. This species was first described to Western science after being discovered on the Lewis and Clark expedition (1803–1806).

DESCRIPTION: 6–7½" (15–19 cm). The adult male has a brilliant red head and a bright yellow body with black back, wings, and tail. It has two wing bars; the smaller, uppermost bar is yellow and the lower one is white. The female is yellow-green above and yellow below, with wing bars similar to the male's.

VOICE: Its song is robin-like in its short, fluty phrases, rendered with a pause in between. The quality is much hoarser, however. Its call is a dry *pit-r-ick*.

NESTING: Lays 3–5 bluish-green, speckled eggs in a frail, shallow saucer nest of woven rootlets, weed stalks, and bark strips, "saddled" in the fork of a horizontal branch of Douglas fir, spruce, pine, or occasionally oak, usually at a low elevation.

HABITAT: Open coniferous forests.

RANGE: Breeds from southern Alaska and Mackenzie southward. Winters in the tropics.

SIMILAR SPECIES: Wing bars and contrasting grayish back distinguish Western Tanager from all other tanagers. Orioles may appear somewhat similar but can be distinguished at a glance by their long, pointed, conical bills.

CONSERVATION: Western Tanagers are widespread and common, and their populations are increasing. Because they do not require large blocks of forest and their habitat is along forest edges, they are less vulnerable to forest fragmentation than other species. They are, however, closely associated with Douglas-firs, making the proper management of Douglas-fir forests in the Interior West of high importance for this species.

Piranga bidentata # FLAME-COLORED TANAGER

■ SUMMER　■ MIGRATION
■ WINTER　■ RARE
■ RESIDENT

Flame-colored Tanager is a casual but fairly regular summer visitor to southeast Arizona. It occasionally visits pine-oak forests of the southeastern Arizona mountains, where it has nested on rare occasions and has hybridized with Western Tanager. Like other tanagers, Flame-colored tends to stay concealed in the foliage of larger trees while foraging or singing. Unknown in the U.S. until 1985, since then several sightings of these birds have occurred in Arizona and southern Texas.

DESCRIPTION: 7¾" (20 cm). This well-named tanager is bright orange-yellow overall, brightest on the head, which is orange to reddish. It has black wings with two wing bars and large white spots on the tertials. Its back is streaked from crown to rump and its tail is black with white corners.

VOICE: Its song is similar to Western Tanager but burrier and more hesitant. Its common call, also similar to Western Tanager, is a low *prrrlek*.

NESTING: Lays 2–5 greenish-blue eggs with darker speckles in a cup nest placed on a tree branch 15–50 ft (4.5–15 m) high.

HABITAT: Humid coniferous, oak, and pine-oak forests in mountains.

RANGE: Resident in the mountainous regions of Mexico south through Central America to western Panama. In the U.S., it rarely visits the mountains of southwest Texas and southeastern Arizona.

SUBSPECIES: North American visitors are of the nominate subspecies, which nests in the mountains of western Mexico.

SIMILAR SPECIES: See Western Tanager—the two species are closely related and occasionally hybridize.

CONSERVATION: The Flame-colored Tanager population is thought to be stable in its native range.

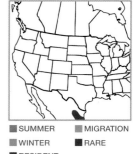

■ SUMMER   ■ MIGRATION
■ WINTER   ■ RARE
■ RESIDENT

An unusual grosbeak endemic to brushlands of northeastern Mexico, Crimson-collared Grosbeak has strayed on rare occasions to southernmost Texas, mostly in winter. It is a shy bird that forages in thickets and thorn scrub, rarely perching for long in the open. This species is more closely related to cardinals and the saltators of tropical America than to other so-called "grosbeaks."

DESCRIPTION: 8¾" (22 cm). The male has black plumage and a black head surrounded by dark red "collar." The mature female's head and breast are like males, but with greenish upperparts and yellowish underparts. The bills of both sexes have a distinctive curved culmen.

VOICE: Its song is a sweet, modulated warbling, rising at the end. Its call is a loud, slurred *psseuu*.

NESTING: Lays 2 or 3 pale blue-gray eggs with brown markings in a bulky cup nest made of grass and twigs, usually placed in a bush.

HABITAT: Dense woods, usually in brushy cover.

RANGE: Endemic to a small area in northeastern Mexico; it occurs in southern Texas as a rare stray.

SIMILAR SPECIES: See Black-headed Grosbeak.

CONSERVATION:
Population trends for the Crimson-collared Grosbeak are not well known, but it is estimated that the global population of this species includes fewer than 50,000 birds.

- ■ SUMMER   ■ MIGRATION
- ■ WINTER   ■ RARE
- ■ RESIDENT

This species, named after the red robes worn by Roman Catholic cardinals, has extended its range northward into southern Canada in recent decades. Cardinals are aggressive birds that occupy territories year-round. Both sexes are accomplished songsters and may be heard at any time of year, rather than just in the spring when most other birds are singing. Seeds form a main part of the diet, although insects are eaten in the breeding season. These birds often come to feeders in winter.

DESCRIPTION: 8–9" (20–23 cm). The male is bright red overall with a crest atop the head, a black face, and a stout red bill. The female is buff-brown tinged with red on the crest, wings, and tail.

VOICE: A rich *what-cheer, cheer, cheer; purty-purty-purty-purty*; or *sweet-sweet-sweet-sweet*. It also gives a metallic *chip*.

NESTING: Lays 3 or 4 pale green eggs spotted with red-brown in a deep cup of twigs, leaves, and plant fibers concealed in a thicket.

HABITAT: Woodland edges, thickets, brushy swamps, and gardens.

RANGE: Resident in eastern United States and southern Canada (locally) south to Gulf Coast, and from southern California, Arizona, and southern Texas southward.

SUBSPECIES: Southwestern populations (mostly in Arizona) have a slightly larger bill with a more downcurved culmen. These birds have a larger, shaggier crest and less black on the forehead.

SIMILAR SPECIES: A male Pyrrhuloxia is gray with bright pink patches on the face, crown, underparts, wings, and tail; its bill is bright yellow. An adult female is usually much grayer, less buff-brown, than a female Northern Cardinal, but individual color varies considerably. Juvenile and first-year birds of both species are similar. A young Pyrrhuloxia is usually grayer, and a young Northern Cardinal is usually browner; call notes and bill shape are the best field marks, and immatures tend to associate with adults of the same species.

CONSERVATION:
Northern Cardinals are widespread and abundant. With a population estimated around 120 million breeding Northern Cardinals in North America, according to Partners in Flight, the species has increased both its numbers and range since the 1960s; today its numbers are stable. The expansion of suburban habitat and feeding stations across eastern North America has been particularly beneficial to these common backyard birds.

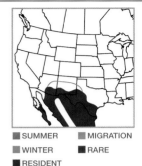

■ SUMMER ■ MIGRATION
■ WINTER ■ RARE
■ RESIDENT

Pyrrhuloxias feed on seeds and insects and benefit cotton fields by consuming great numbers of cotton worms and weevils. Partial to mesquite thickets, these birds use their strong bills to crush the mesquite beans. Although shy and difficult to detect in their dense habitat, when flushed, a pair will fly up to a high watch post, erect their crests, and sound a loud alarm. The name Pyrrhuloxia comes from Latin and Greek words meaning "bullfinch with a crooked bill." Also called the "Gray Cardinal," the Pyrrhuloxia is similar to the Northern Cardinal in most respects except that it is often found in flocks after the breeding season.

DESCRIPTION: 7½–8½" (19–22 cm). The male is gray with a rose-red breast, crest, wings, and tail. The female is similar but paler, and lacks red on the breast. It has a stubby, rounded, parrot-like bill. In adults, the bill is usually yellow, although it can be darkish in winter. Immatures are similar to females and have a dark bill.

VOICE: A series of whistled notes, similar to those of Northern Cardinal, but thinner and shorter.

NESTING: Lays 3 or 4 white eggs, lightly speckled with brown, in a loosely built cup of grass, twigs, and bark strips concealed in dense, thorny bush.

HABITAT: Desert brush, especially along streambeds.

RANGE: Resident from Arizona, southern New Mexico, and southern Texas southward.

SIMILAR SPECIES: See Northern Cardinal.

CONSERVATION: LC

Although still common in their range in the desert Southwest and through much of Mexico, the Pyrrhuloxia is declining. Loss of its desert scrubland habitat due to clearing for urbanization and agriculture has contributed to the decline. A good portion of its remaining habitat in the U.S. is protected within national wildlife refuges and parks.

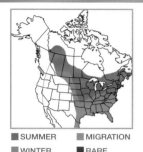

- ■ SUMMER
- ■ WINTER
- ■ RESIDENT
- ■ MIGRATION
- ■ RARE

This handsome grosbeak is one of the most conspicuous birds before the foliage comes into full leaf in early May. It is beneficial to farmers, consuming many potato beetles and larvae as well as weed seeds, wild fruits, and buds. The Rose-breasted Grosbeak seems to require a combination of large trees and open areas and thick shrubs or brush—a habitat that occurs regularly along streams, ponds, marsh borders, and roadsides, and in overgrown pastures or even residential areas. The striking male is one of the forest's most fluent vocalists; its clear, rich, rolling song rivals those of the thrushes in its beauty.

DESCRIPTION: 8" (20 cm). A starling-sized bird with a heavy, pinkish-white, arched bill. The male is black on the head, throat, and back, and white below with a conspicuous rose-red patch on the breast and underwings. The female is white above and below with heavy brown streaking, a prominent white eyebrow, and yellow wing linings.

VOICE: Its distinctive call note is a sharp, penetrating, metallic *eek-eek*. Its song is like that of an American Robin, but softer and more melodious.

NESTING: Lays 4 or 5 purple-spotted, whitish eggs in a loosely made nest of twigs, grass, and plant fibers set in a low branch of a tree.

HABITAT: Moist woodlands adjacent to open fields with tall shrubs; also old and overgrown orchards.

RANGE: Breeds from northeastern British Columbia, southern Manitoba, and Nova Scotia south to southern Alberta, central North Dakota, central Oklahoma, and New Jersey, and in the mountains as far south as northern Georgia. It appears regularly on the West Coast. It winters from central Mexico through Central America and into northern South America.

SIMILAR SPECIES: A female Purple Finch is much smaller and more heavily streaked below; it has a plain crown and wings.

Female Black-headed Grosbeak has a warm buff to orange-buff breast; its finer dark stripes are generally restricted to the sides and flanks. The wing linings of female Black-headed are lemon-yellow rather than saffron-yellow. Black-headed's call note is not as high or squeaky.

CONSERVATION:
Rose-breasted Grosbeaks are common but their numbers have gradually declined since the mid-20th century. Because the species nests in saplings, the maturation of forests in the eastern U.S. may be contributing to the decline. Illegal capture of Rose-breasted Grosbeaks for sale as pets in their wintering range in Mexico and Central America may also contribute to the decline of their numbers in the wild.

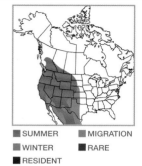

■ SUMMER ■ MIGRATION
■ WINTER ■ RARE
■ RESIDENT

The Black-headed Grosbeak is a rather still and secretive bird throughout the summer; it breeds in a broad range of habitats with diverse vegetation and open edges. Like its eastern counterpart, the Rose-breasted Grosbeak, the males of this species share incubation duties with the females. The brightest coloration is on the breast and belly, which is concealed as they incubate. Black-headed Grosbeaks have a varied diet; they can easily crack open seeds with their huge bills, and they also take fruit and consume many insects harmful to crops. Black-headed Grosbeak hybridizes with Rose-breasted Grosbeak along their mutual boundary. Such opportunities to mingle arose when the treeless prairies, which once formed a barrier between the two species, became dotted with towns and homesteads, providing suitable habitats for both species.

DESCRIPTION: 7½" (19 cm). A starling-sized bird with a heavy, bicolored bill. The male has a black head, a tawny-orange breast, a yellow belly, a tawny back with black streaking, and black wings and tail with conspicuous white patches. The female has white eyebrows and pale buff underparts; brown streaks on the breast may be rather fine or absent. Adults show a large, lemon-yellow patch on the underwing in flight. Young birds resemble females.

VOICE: A rich warble similar to that of a robin but softer, sweeter, and faster. Its call note is an emphatic, sharp *tick*, slightly metallic in tone.

NESTING: Lays 3 or 4 greenish eggs spotted with brown in a loosely built stick nest lined with rootlets, grasses, and leaves, and placed among the dense foliage of an outer tree limb.

HABITAT: Open, deciduous woodlands near water, such as river bottoms, lakeshores, and swampy places with a mixture of trees and shrubs.

RANGE: Breeds from southwestern Canada east to western North Dakota and Nebraska and south to the mountains of Mexico. It winters in Mexico.

SIMILAR SPECIES: See Rose-breasted Grosbeak.

CONSERVATION:

Black-headed Grosbeaks are widespread and common, and their numbers are stable to increasing. Since Black-headed Grosbeaks can live in disturbed landscapes and can adapt to many breeding environments and nesting habitats, they have fared well despite deforestation. They are also flexible in their diet, relying on a mix of plant and insect sources.

■ SUMMER   ■ MIGRATION
■ WINTER   ■ RARE
■ RESIDENT

The Blue Bunting is a scarce visitor to extreme southern Texas and is much sought-after by birders when it appears. Vagrancy patterns in this and other Mexican passerines may be affected by habitat destruction in northern Mexico near the U.S. border; the possibility of escaped cagebirds also must be considered in assessing individual vagrants.

DESCRIPTION: 5–5½" (13–14 cm). The male is dark blue-black overall, somewhat paler on the crown, rump, and shoulders. The female is richer brown than a female Indigo and lacks streaking on the underparts. This bird has a short, thick bill.

VOICE: Its call note is a hard *click*. Its song is a variable warble, sweet but slightly melancholy, *swee slee lee*.

NESTING: Lays 2 unmarked, bluish white eggs. There are no North American breeding records.

HABITAT: Brushy fields and forests, woodland edges, and scrubby thickets. It typically forages low in the forest understory.

RANGE: A Mexican endemic; it is a rare vagrant to the lower Rio Grande Valley in Texas.

SIMILAR SPECIES: See Indigo Bunting and Blue Grosbeak. The coloration of the male Indigo Bunting, by comparison, is relatively uniform, shading to darker on the head. Female Indigo Buntings have a contrasting white throat and are finely streaked below.

CONSERVATION: The Blue Bunting is a fairly common resident in Mexico and Central America. Its population trends are not well documented.

- ■ SUMMER
- ■ WINTER
- ■ RESIDENT
- ■ MIGRATION
- ■ RARE

The Blue Grosbeak is a fairly common bird of the southern United States, and has expanded into the more northerly states in recent decades. It is found along hedgerows and roadsides, in thickets, shrubby areas, and farmlands, and near woodland borders and stream and ditch banks. It frequently perches on utility wires and fences; the male may sit motionless for long periods, singing from a favorite perch. After breeding, small flocks of Blue Grosbeaks feed together or mix with other seed-eating birds such as sparrows. They also search out insects, especially grasshoppers, that live in the grassy vegetation of open fields. The Blue Grosbeak has a tendency to flick its tail occasionally.

DESCRIPTION: 6–7½" (15–19 cm). Slightly larger than a House Sparrow. The male is dark blue with two chestnut wing bars and a stout, dark bill. The female is dark buff-brown with two buff wing bars. The immature male resembles the female but has a variable mixture of blue and brown plumage.

VOICE: A sweet, jumbled warble. Also gives a metallic *klink*.

NESTING: Lays 3 or 4 pale blue eggs in a loose cup of grass, weed stems, and leaves concealed in a clump of weeds.

HABITAT: Brushy moist pastures and roadside thickets.

RANGE: Breeds from California, Colorado, Missouri, Illinois, and New Jersey southward. It winters in the tropics.

SIMILAR SPECIES: Indigo Bunting is found in the same types of habitats but is smaller with a smaller bill; it lacks wing bars.

Female and juvenile Brown-headed Cowbirds are paler brown, lack wing bars, have a different call, and do not flick the tail.

CONSERVATION: LC

Blue Grosbeaks are widespread across the southern tier of the United States, and their range is expanding northward. The species is historically uncommon and is known to live in sparse, low-density populations, but its numbers may be slowly increasing. This species prefers to avoid suburban habitats, occurring more frequently on abandoned agricultural land, the longleaf pine forests of Florida, and the loblolly-shortleaf pine forests of eastern Texas.

■ SUMMER   ■ MIGRATION
■ WINTER   ■ RARE
■ RESIDENT

The Lazuli Bunting nests in weedy areas with scattered shrubs near streams or springs. The Lazuli sings from exposed branches of bushes or low trees. A diligent songster, the male patrols the perimeter of its territory, spending much time on its song perches. The Lazuli hybridizes with its eastern counterpart, the Indigo Bunting, where their ranges overlap on the Great Plains. In fall, these migratory birds are often found with sparrows and finches.

DESCRIPTION: 5–5½" (13–14 cm). A sparrow-sized bunting, the male is bright blue with a pale cinnamon breast, and a white belly and wing bars. The female is dull brown, lighter below, with two pale wing bars. Both sexes are warm buffy to a rich orange-brown across the breast and partway down the flanks; beneath these areas it is pure white.

VOICE: A high-pitched, excited series of warbled phrases, the first notes usually repeated, descending the scale and ascending again at the end; similar to the song of Indigo Bunting, but the phrases are less distinct and only the first phrases are repeated. It accompanies its nervous tail-flicking with a hard *pit* note.

NESTING: Lays 3 or 4 pale blue eggs in a loose cup of grass and rootlets in a bush.

HABITAT: Dry, brushy ravines and slopes; cleared areas and weedy pastures.

RANGE: Breeds from British Columbia, Saskatchewan, and North Dakota south through the western United States to southern California, northern New Mexico, western Oklahoma, and eastern Nebraska. It winters south of the U.S.-Mexico border.

SIMILAR SPECIES: Female and immature Indigo Buntings are richer brown to cinnamon overall, with underparts more uniformly buff to the belly and with faint streaks on the sides; their thinner wing bars are usually cinnamon buff.

The female Varied Bunting lacks the buff wash across the breast, is grayish-brown overall, lacks wing bars, and has a stubbier bill; the upper mandible is more convexly curved than Lazuli's (visible at close range).

CONSERVATION: The Lazuli Bunting is widespread and common, and its population is stable to increasing. Their nests are frequently parasitized by Brown-headed Cowbirds but their population overall appears able to weather the threat.

■ SUMMER ■ MIGRATION
■ WINTER ■ RARE
■ RESIDENT

Indigo Buntings have no blue pigment; they are actually black, but the diffraction of light through the structure of the feathers makes them appear blue. Indigo Buntings nest in patches of dense, brushy ground cover where there are tall singing perches nearby. Old overgrown pastures, forest edges, and damp shrubs near water provide such a habitat. These attractive birds are also found in rural roadside thickets and other areas where woodlands meet open spaces. They are beneficial to farmers and fruit growers, consuming many insect pests and weed seeds.

DESCRIPTION: 5½" (14 cm). A sparrow-sized bunting. In bright sunlight, the male is brilliant turquoise blue, otherwise it looks black; its wings and tail are darker. The female is drab brown, and paler beneath. It has a stout, conical bill with an obviously curved upper mandible. Immature birds closely resemble females but are usually more obviously streaked on the breast; first-spring males may have irregular blue patches.

VOICE: A rapid, excited warble, each note or phrase given twice.

NESTING: Lays 3 or 4 pale blue eggs in a compact woven cup of leaves and grass placed in a sapling or bush in relatively thick vegetation and within a few feet (a meter) of the ground.

HABITAT: Brushy slopes, abandoned farmland, old pastures and fields grown to scrub, woodland clearings, and forest edges adjacent to fields.

RANGE: Breeds from southeastern Saskatchewan east to New Brunswick, and south to central Arizona, central Texas, the Gulf Coast, and northern Florida. It winters in southern Florida and in the tropics.

SIMILAR SPECIES: Blue Grosbeak is larger with a much heavier bill.

Female and immature Lazuli Buntings have an unstreaked, warm buff-colored breast and obvious buff-white wing bars.

Female and immature Varied Buntings are browner and unstreaked below, with a stubbier, more sharply curved bill.

Also see Blue Bunting.

CONSERVATION: ![LC]
Although Indigo Buntings are still abundant, their numbers have steadily declined in recent decades. Due to their preference for shrubby, weedy habitat along roadsides, frequent mowing of roadsides and fields and vehicle collisions kill many Indigo Buntings. Many also die during migration because of collisions with buildings and communication towers. Reforestation, urbanization, and intensive agriculture limit available brushy habitat. Due to the attractiveness of the males, they are often illegally trapped for sale as pets in their Mexican range. Climate change may be pushing their range northward.

SUMMER MIGRATION
WINTER RARE
RESIDENT

This primarily Mexican species reaches the southernmost parts of the United States. It is unevenly distributed and inconspicuous, keeping mainly to uninviting dense, thorny habitat. The birds spend most of their time concealed in dense desert brush, coming into view only when the male sings from the top of a bush. The females are generally the only brownish, unstreaked buntings in the thorn scrub habitats in summer. These birds probably feed primarily on weed seeds and insects, but their diet is little known.

DESCRIPTION: 4½–5½" (11–14 cm). A sparrow-sized bunting, the male is dark purple-blue with a dull red patch on the nape; it looks all black at a distance. Females and immatures are dull gray-brown with slightly darker wings and tail; they lack streaking or conspicuous wing bars. The bill is conical, stubby even for a bunting, with a strongly curved upper mandible and a wide lower mandible.

VOICE: A series of sweet notes, each note or phrase repeated.

NESTING: Lays 3 or 4 pale blue eggs in a deep cup of grass, twigs, and bark strips placed in a dense thicket.

HABITAT: Dense desert brush, especially along streambeds.

RANGE: Resident in southern Arizona, southern New Mexico, and southern Texas.

SIMILAR SPECIES: See Indigo Bunting. The female Indigo Bunting is browner, with the suggestion of wing bars.

CONSERVATION:
Varied Buntings are locally common in the Southwest and numerous in Mexico. With little known about the population of Varied Buntings in Mexico, overall trends are hard to determine, although they may be slightly declining. Several factors impact their numbers, including habitat degradation caused by livestock overgrazing, mining, and urbanization. These buntings also are captured for sale as cage birds in Mexico.

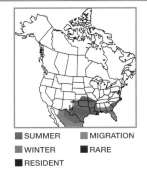

SUMMER · MIGRATION
WINTER · RARE
RESIDENT

This gaudy bird is one of the most beautiful in North America. Its brilliant plumage made it a popular cage bird until it came under federal protection; it is still captured and sold illegally in the tropics. Despite its vivid coloration, however, it is often difficult to see as it skulks among dense thickets, although in Florida, at least, it often comes to feeding stations. Its other well-known name is "Nonpareil," meaning "without equal." This species, common in parts of the Deep South, raises as many as three broods each year. The female is the only plain, bright green songbird in North America.

DESCRIPTION: 5½" (14 cm). A colorful, sparrow-sized bunting, the male has bright red underparts and rump, a green back, a blue head, and a red eye ring. The female is bright green all over, darker above and lighter yellow below. The immature female is lime-green above, dull grayish below, with a slight yellow wash to the sides and flanks.

VOICE: Loud, clear, and variable song consisting of a series of high-pitched musical notes. Its call is a sharp, metallic *tsick*.

NESTING: Lays 3 or 4 white eggs, marked with reddish-brown dots, in a cup of compactly woven grass stems, rootlets, and bark strips, lined with moss and hair, placed near the ground in the fork of a bush or small tree.

HABITAT: Brushy tangles, hedgerows, briar patches, woodland edges, and swampy thickets.

RANGE: Breeds from Missouri and North Carolina south to the southeastern states and west to New Mexico and Oklahoma. Winters from Gulf Coast states southward.

SIMILAR SPECIES: The adult plumages of both sexes are unmistakable; Indigo Buntings have similar shapes and habits but are easy to distinguish by color.

CONSERVATION:

Uncommon and local, Painted Bunting numbers declined markedly in the late 20th century, but they appear to have stabilized. Habitat loss in riverside thickets and molt staging habitats in northwestern Mexico and Arizona, plus woodland edges and swampy thickets in the eastern U.S., all impact this species; they are also illegally captured and sold as pets in the tropics.

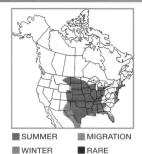

■ SUMMER ■ MIGRATION
■ WINTER ■ RARE
■ RESIDENT

Formerly common in farming regions of the eastern states, especially on the Atlantic coastal plain, the Dickcissel disappeared from that region by the middle of the last century and is now most numerous in the Midwest. It appears in small numbers on the East Coast during the fall migration and rarely but regularly in winter at feeders, often with House Sparrows.

DESCRIPTION: 6" (15 cm). The male is patterned like a miniature meadowlark—a yellow breast with a black V—but has a heavy bill and chestnut wing patch. The female is much like a female House Sparrow, but with narrow streaks along the sides, and a yellowish throat and breast.

VOICE: Its song sounds like *dick-dick-cissel*, the first two notes being sharp sounds followed by a buzzy, almost hissed *cissel*; repeated over and over again from a conspicuous perch on a fence, bush, or weed. Its call is a distinctive buzzy note, often given in flight.

NESTING: Lays 4 or 5 pale blue eggs in a cup of plant stems and grass set on or near the ground, often in alfalfa and clover fields.

HABITAT: Open country in grain or hay fields and in weed patches.

RANGE: Breeds from eastern Montana and the Great Lakes region south to Texas and the Gulf Coast, and locally farther east. It winters mainly in the tropics.

SIMILAR SPECIES: House Sparrow has a shorter, black bill and lacks yellow on the face and breast.

CONSERVATION:

Dickcissels are common but their numbers declined in the late 20th century before stabilizing in recent years. They were historically more common along the Atlantic seaboard, nearly disappeared in the East in the 19th century, and have since reappeared in the eastern U.S. in small numbers. Several factors threaten their global population, including illegal poisoning in their wintering grounds in Venezuela, where large flocks are seen as pests to grain crops. In North America, many former grasslands are being converted to large-scale agriculture. While these birds often nest in fallow lands and hayfields, they often have not fledged their young before the fields are mowed.

BANANAQUIT *Coereba flaveola*

■ SUMMER ■ MIGRATION
■ WINTER ■ RARE
■ RESIDENT

This brightly colored songbird, related to tropical honeycreepers, is a signature species in much of the neotropics, where it is common and widespread in the West Indies and Central and South America; North American strays occur irregularly in southern Florida. A nectar feeder, the Bananaquit is attracted to flowering trees and shrubs as well as hummingbird feeders; it also consumes small insects, spiders, and fruit. Most strays to southeastern Florida and the Keys are of Bahamian origin.

DESCRIPTION: 4–5" (10–12.5 cm). A small, warbler-like bird with a thin, decurved bill. The adult has black upperparts, a white throat and belly, a conspicuous white eyestripe, and a white wing patch at the base of the primaries. It has yellow on the upper breast and rump, and a small red mark at the base of the bill. Immatures are duller with gray-brown upperparts, and a less prominent yellow eyebrow and rump.

VOICE: A repeated series of high-pitched, buzzy, disorganized trills; its call note is a sharp *quit*.

NESTING: Lays 2 whitish eggs with thick brown speckling in a globe nest of plant fibers and mosses. The nest opening faces down.

HABITAT: Variable habitats, including moist forests and edge, plantations, second growth, and gardens; it often forages for insects or takes nectar at flowering trees and shrubs. It is relatively adaptable in disturbed habitats.

RANGE: A familiar resident of the New World tropics, it occurs from Mexico and the Caribbean to Peru and northern Argentina; it is found in the U.S. as a rare stray from the Bahamas to southeastern Florida and the Keys.

SIMILAR SPECIES: The female Black-throated Blue Warbler has a straighter bill, a much thinner white eyebrow, and a drab olive color overall; it lacks a white throat.

CONSERVATION:
Common and widespread throughout the American tropics, Bananaquit numbers are stable.

SUMMER ■ MIGRATION
■ WINTER ■ RARE
■ RESIDENT

This tropical species is a casual visitor to southern Florida. The grassquits were long considered sparrows, but recent genetic studies have placed them in the tanagers, closely related to Darwin's "finches."

DESCRIPTION: 4½" (10 cm). The male of this tiny species (smaller than a chickadee) is distinctive because of its entirely dark coloration. The male's head is black, with olive wings and back, and gray underparts. The female lacks most of the black on the head and is a nondescript, lighter olive-brown in overall color. Both sexes have a relatively large, black bill.

VOICE: *Tik-zeee* or *tik-zeee-zeee*.

NESTING: Lays 2 or 3 whitish eggs blotched with reddish brown in a domed grass nest lined with finer grasses. Both sexes build the nest, which is typically placed low in a bush or on a bank.

HABITAT: Open and semi-open areas, in long grass or bushes.

RANGE: Common in many areas throughout the Caribbean (although apparently not on Cuba), and the northern coasts of Colombia and Venezuela.

SIMILAR SPECIES: The female Painted Bunting is greener; the female Indigo Bunting is browner.

CONSERVATION: These birds are widespread in the Caribbean and common in the Bahamas, and their numbers appear to be increasing.

■ SUMMER   ■ MIGRATION
■ WINTER   ■ RARE
■ RESIDENT

Although the Morelet's Seedeater was once fairly common in southern Texas, it has become increasingly rare in recent decades. A highly variable species, its plumages appear quite different in different parts of its range.

DESCRIPTION: 4" (10 cm). A tiny, large-billed, round-tailed, drab-colored bird of the Rio Grande Valley. Breeding males in Texas are olive-brown above and unstreaked buffy below; the head is blackish with a white crescent below the eye; it has an incomplete buffy collar on the hindneck; and its wings are dark with two white wing bars and a white patch at the base of the flight feathers. Females and immatures are paler and buffier overall, lack the cap and collar, and have buffy wing bars.

VOICE: Its song is a variable *twee twee twee, chew chew*; it also gives a high *tik-it*.

NESTING: Lays 2–3 pale blue eggs speckled with brown in cup-like nest of grasses and horsehair placed in crotch of weed, vine, or shrub.

HABITAT: Rank weedy areas and brushy fields.

RANGE: Northern Mexico to Panama; it is a rare visitor to the Texas borderlands.

SIMILAR SPECIES: Goldfinches are slightly larger and do not have the seedeater's stubby, rounded bill. Lesser Goldfinch is always more yellow; American Goldfinch has a white rump and undertail coverts; both have shorter, notched tails with some white on the inner webs of the tail feathers.

CONSERVATION:
Widespread and common in its range south of the U.S.-Mexico border, where its numbers are thought to be increasing.

Anatidae — Duck, Geese, and Swans

Ducks, geese, and swans make up the family Anatidae, commonly known as waterfowl. They are medium-sized birds with stocky bodies, webbed feet, usually short tails, and often flat bills. Most show pronounced sexual dimorphism in plumage for most of the year, with males more strikingly colored and patterned. (Males of most species molt for a brief time after mating into a duller eclipse plumage.) All ducks live in or near aquatic habitats, where they forage for aquatic vegetation, fish, insect larvae, and crustaceans. A few species also venture into cultivated lands to eat grain. Most ducks nest in remote northern lakes and marshes and migrate southward for the winter; they are highly gregarious, sometimes forming winter flocks in the thousands. Courtship, usually occurring through winter and into spring, involves calling, exaggerated head movements, and flight displays by males or by both sexes.

BARROW'S GOLDENEYE

Cracidae — Curassows and Guans

The tropical American family Cracidae has just one species in the United States, Plain Chachalaca, whose range barely crosses the border into southernmost Texas. Plain Chachalaca is a talented tree climber and has a long hind toe adapted for arboreal life.

Odontophoridae — New World Quail

The gallinaceous (chicken-like) birds in the order Galliformes are represented in North America by three families; in the family Odontophoridae are the quail, including Northern Bobwhite. Galliforms are largely ground-dwelling birds that peck at the ground for food much in the manner of chickens. They feed mostly on plant matter, especially seeds and buds, and also eat insects and other invertebrates. Most are compact and sturdy, with strong feet for walking and scraping the ground; some have long tails, but most are short-tailed and short-legged. Although galliforms are capable of flight, most run rather than flush.

Phasianidae — Partridges, Grouse, Turkeys, and Old World Quail

This family contains grouse, sage-grouse, prairie-chickens, ptarmigan, and Wild Turkey, as well as the introduced Old World pheasants, peafowl, partridges (including Chukar), and Himalayan Snowcock. They have stocky bodies; thick, short legs; large toes that are adapted for walking and scratching; and short, blunt bills that are well suited for crushing seeds and feeding on a variety of insects and other small creatures. In North America these birds can be divided into three groups: the introduced pheasants and partridges; the grouse, which have feathered legs and feet; and the turkeys. New World quail (family Odontophoridae) are close relatives and were formerly considered part of this group.

GUNNISON SAGE-GROUSE

Phoenicopteridae — Flamingos

The United States has few wild flamingos, at most a few dozen in Florida's Everglades, but flamingos may turn up in southern states, both escapees from captivity (and these include other species such as Lesser, Chilean, and Greater Flamingos) and wild wanderers from their West Indian range. Flamingos have highly specialized, angular bills with lamellae, or filters, which allow them to sift through mud and water to feed on tiny insects, crustaceans, algae, and other food. They usually forage by lowering the bill into shallow water while standing, although their webbed feet also make them good swimmers. Flamingos display in tight groups, turning their bills back and forth, stretching their legs, and raising their wings to reveal black remiges. Their nests are muddy mounds built on the ground.

Podicipedidae — Grebes

Grebes are members of a group of birds that probably arose in South America millions of years ago. They share qualities with both waterfowl and loons, but they have toes that are lobed rather than webbed; tails so tiny as to be almost invisible; and fluffy, almost fur-like plumage on the flanks and undertail. The bills of grebes also differ from those of other diving birds, varying from blunt and pointed in the Pied-billed Grebe to stiletto-like in Clark's and Western grebes. Grebe bodies are well adapted to hunting underwater for fish, crustaceans, and other aquatic prey; smaller species can regulate their buoyancy and submerge without diving by compressing the body plumage.

Grebes nest on freshwater lakes and ponds. Their courtship displays involve bobbing and bowing, and pairs of some species engage in an almost ballet-like footrace across the water's surface. In fall grebes in northern areas leave the nesting grounds for coastal and inland wintering grounds to the south. Some grebe populations have declined in recent decades. Horned Grebes have disappeared from the northern prairie pothole country, and at Mono Lake, California, the flocks of Eared Grebes that once numbered more than a million are lately reduced to less than 200,000.

Columbidae — Pigeons and Doves

Pigeons and doves are represented in North America by 12 breeding species, three of which are not native, and six vagrants from Eurasia or tropical America. Most columbids are medium-sized, stocky birds with small heads, short, thin bills, medium-long tails, and short legs. Most North American columbids have rather plain plumage that is countershaded gray or brown above and paler below. The dark tropical Red-billed and White-crowned Pigeons are exceptions, and many species have pink or green tints or iridescent colors in the nape. Rock Pigeons, those urban dwellers known to most people as simply "pigeons," show a wide variety of plumage types that are derived from many centuries of captive breeding. Many individuals seen in North America, however, exhibit the species' ancestral phenotype—that is, the way wild Rock Pigeons still look today on the cliffs of Scotland.

Pigeons and doves are found mostly in open habitats, from deserts to prairies to city parks; a few thrive in forested habitats. They forage on the ground and in trees for seeds, fruits, and nuts. Perhaps because of their high-fiber diet, most species consume large amounts of water; they drink by siphoning, as through a straw, continuously (other birds dip the bill and let gravity deliver the water to the stomach). In North America, columbids court and breed through much of the year, and courting males are easy to observe as they strut, bow, coo, and make display flights over the nesting area. All species build sloppy-looking stick nests in trees or bushes in which they lay just one or two eggs. After the breeding season, some species gather in rather large flocks, and at least four species are migratory—Mourning and White-winged doves and White-crowned and Band-tailed pigeons.

RUDDY GROUND DOVE

Cuculidae — Cuckoos, Roadrunners, and Anis

Cuckoos, roadrunners, and anis are members of the family Cuculidae, an ancient group of birds with no close relatives among other bird families. Cuculids are long-tailed, medium-sized birds; with their relatively short legs and zygodactyl feet (two toes point forward, two backward), they are best suited for perching, although Greater Roadrunner is terrestrial. Most cuculids are found in warmer climes, even in deserts; Black-billed Cuckoo ranges well north into Canada to the edge of the boreal forest. In addition to the six regular nesting species found in North America, Oriental and Common cuckoos (of Eurasia) have occasionally turned up on Alaskan islands.

In plumage, cuculids show remarkable diversity, from the coal black simplicity of the anis, to the countershaded plumage and patterned tails of cuckoos, to the streaky camouflage of roadrunners. They generally have curved, short bills, although the bills of anis are extremely deep and those of roadrunners are rather long. Their bills suit their diets well: cuckoos forage on caterpillars, including large, hairy caterpillars few other birds eat; anis eat a wide variety of seeds, fruits, insects, and reptiles; and roadrunners take prey as large as adult rattlesnakes, kangaroo rats, and sparrows. Anis and cuckoos are stolid foragers, peering around slowly while perched and then making a swift sally out to snare prey. Roadrunners are sometimes stealthy when hunting but also use direct pursuit; when running down lizards they can achieve speeds of up to 25 miles per hour (40 km per hour). Roadrunners sometimes capture prey by teamwork; for example, when confronting a poisonous snake, one bird distracts the snake while the other strikes. When taking live prey, cuculids tend to dispatch the prey and then soften it by beating it against a branch or, in the case of roadrunners, a stone.

Caprimulgidae — Nightjars

Nighthawks and nightjars are members of a large family found across the world in tropical and temperate regions. Most are familiar only in their voices, which ring out on spring evenings, or as a set of glowing orange-red eyes seen in the headlights on country roads at night. Their colloquial name, goatsuckers, derives from the (erroneous) folk belief that some species drink the milk of goats. Caprimulgids are medium-sized, slender birds, usually with rather long wings and tails, short but broad bills, and extremely short legs. Their plumages have complex patterns of dark browns, black, and white, which help them blend into their environment and escape detection by predators. Their cryptic coloration and nocturnal habits recall owls, which are their nearest relatives. Owls, however, have much larger, stronger feet and heavier bills—even those species that eat mostly flying insects, the chief food of caprimulgids.

Apodidae — Swifts

Swifts are mostly dark, highly aerial birds with slender bodies; long wings; short, stiff tails; and small bills. They have extremely small legs and feet suited to clinging rather than perching; the family name Apodidae is derived from the Greek word *apodos*, meaning "without feet." Swifts forage much like swallows, but their closest relatives are hummingbirds. Few birds are as suited as swifts to a life in the open air. They rarely rest during the day—stopping mainly at the nest to feed their young—and spend most of their time high in the air, foraging at rapid speeds for aerial insects and floating spiders. Their ability to flap their wings independently of one another increases their aerial agility, already considerable due to their long, slim wings that provide both lift and maneuverability. Swifts inhabit most environments except open desert and tundra. Their paired courtship flights, always accompanied by twittering calls (and sometimes by mid-air copulation), are familiar signs of spring. They nest mostly in hidden recesses; nests of the smallest species are half-cups of twigs cemented together and affixed with saliva to a vertical surface; Black Swift makes a horizontal nest of moss and lichen. All North American swifts migrate southward in fall, and most winter in the tropics.

Trochilidae — Hummingbirds

This strictly American family is most numerous in South America, especially in the Andes. Only 14 species breed regularly in North America, of which only the Ruby-throated is widespread in the East. Hummingbirds are extraordinary creatures: They are the smallest of birds, with the smallest of eggs; they are the only birds able to fly backward, and their wings beat faster than any other bird—up to 30 beats per second. All hummingbirds have slender bodies, wings, and bills and tiny feet adapted only for perching.

Male hummingbirds have throat patches (gorgets) of iridescent colors to which ornithologists have given vivid labels—ruby, amethyst, and sapphire. These colors are generated by complex feather structures that reflect certain wavelengths of light but not others. Males use their jewel-like gorgets (and crowns in some species) in courtship displays and territorial clashes; adult females and young males lack full gorgets and are usually more subtly plumaged than adult males.

Hummingbirds forage on flower nectar, using their long, grooved tongues to wick the fluid directly to the throat. Many species are attracted to red flowers that are tubular in structure; manufactured hummingbird feeders that imitate this shape and color attract one or more species almost instantly, whether set out in desert washes or alpine meadows. As a hummingbird sips nectar, it often collects the flower's pollen on its head; cross-pollination occurs as the bird moves from flower to flower. In addition to nectar, hummingbirds eat a great variety of insects and other invertebrates, some spotted from a perch and caught on the wing, others gleaned from foliage, still others picked from the ground or from emerging swarms. Some hummingbirds take tiny insects trapped in sap wells made by sapsuckers.

Male hummingbirds perform dazzling courtship displays: they make steep dives from high in the air, often following up with an aerial dance of side-to-side flying or other acrobatics and much calling and flashing of the gorget. Hummingbird males are promiscuous, mating with as many females as possible within their territory (and even outside it). The males leave the females to construct the nest and raise the young alone. They lay two white eggs in a soft, compact nest made of down.

Many hummingbird species are strongly migratory. Ruby-throated Hummingbird, which breeds as far north as Canada, migrates across the Gulf of Mexico to the Yucatán Peninsula; Rufous Hummingbirds from Alaska may travel as far as the mountains of Mexico. Other species wander widely; at least seven have made their way from the tropics into the United States. In some cases, western species have begun to spend the winter season in the Southeast instead of tropical areas, apparently sustained by feeding stations. Despite their extraordinary popularity, hummingbirds are some of the least understood of North America's birds from the standpoint of conservation. A few range-restricted species, such as Allen's and Buff-bellied hummingbirds, are apparently declining because of habitat loss. The population sizes and dynamics of most other species are either unstudied or poorly known.

RUBY-THROATED HUMMINGBIRD

Rallidae — Rails, Gallinules, and Coots

The family Rallidae is represented in North America by seven breeding species of rail (including Sora), two species of gallinule, and one species each of swamphen and coot. These small to medium-sized birds somewhat resemble chickens, having rotund bodies, chicken-like feet, and a strutting gait, but they are most closely related to cranes and Limpkin and are classed with them in the order Gruiformes. Rallids are generally secretive, retiring birds with complex plumage patterns that make them difficult to see in the dense marshes most inhabit; the species that tend to forage more often in the open—such as American Coot and Common Gallinule—lack such cryptic coloration. In structure, rails may appear plump, but they are able to compress their bodies laterally and thus run quickly through dense vegetation. All rallids swim well; coots have specialized lobed

toes with flanges that help them swim and dive nearly as well as a duck, and they are the only North American rallid species apt to be found in flocks like ducks. Purple Gallinules have exceedingly long toes that enable them to walk on floating vegetation.

Rails and their relatives forage in aquatic habitats by picking and probing for small invertebrates and vertebrates; most species also incorporate plant matter in their diet. Like the smaller rails (often referred to as crakes), coots and gallinules have short, blunt bills best suited for picking up small prey or taking seeds and aquatic vegetation; the longer-billed species are better at probing into mud for small crabs or similar prey.

In courtship, the males of most rallid species strut and show off wings, flank patterns, and undertail coverts to the females. Although courting rallids are seldom observed, they are quite often heard. Their calls serve to keep a pair in touch with one another and to maintain territories. Nests are constructed of plant material and are usually well hidden within a marsh. Rail chicks are semi-precocial and are usually blackish (and thus confused with adult Black Rails on occasion). They follow their parents until they fledge, roosting at night in the nest in which they were hatched or in a nursery nest constructed by the parents. After breeding, most rallids in temperate areas migrate southward for the winter. Some are hunted as game birds.

When seen flushing from a marsh, a rallid may seem to have hectic, sloppy wing beats that barely keep it airborne before it drops back into the vegetation. This impression is misleading: rallids are strong fliers, and they have colonized remote oceanic islands reached by few other birds. Their strong flight makes them capable of remarkable feats of vagrancy; several species that have been recorded extralimitally in the United States and Canada include Spotted Rail and Paint-billed Crake from the American tropics and Eurasian Coot, Baillon's Crake, and Corn Crake from Eurasia.

VIRGINIA RAIL

Aramidae — Limpkins

Restricted to tropical America, and breeding as far north as southern Georgia, Limpkins are the lone extant representative of the family Aramidae. This is a swamp-loving, secretive, rail-like bird. It feeds exclusively on aquatic snails, which it extracts without breaking the shell. It lays up to eight eggs in a nest in reeds. A Limpkin might be mistaken for a bittern or young night-heron, but its decurved bill is a clue that it is related to rails. A closer look at the bill—with its right-hand curve and a twist at the mandible tip—reveals its specialized purpose: to extract the aquatic apple snail (the mainstay of this species' diet) from its shell. Nesting Limpkins tend to defend territories as rails do, but they sometimes form loose colonies. Limpkins wander north-ward on rare occasions, possibly in response to drought.

LIMPKIN

Gruidae — Cranes

Globally the 15 species in the crane family are fairly widespread, but they are absent in South America. Two species breed in North America. One, the endangered Whooping Crane, is strictly protected; the other, the Sandhill Crane, is more numer-ous and has a fairly wide range. Cranes superficially resemble herons but are not related to them. Unlike herons, cranes fly with the neck outstretched and with the upstroke faster than the down stroke. They are among the tallest birds in the world and inhabit open country, where they nest on the ground and lay only two eggs. Their colors run to black, white, and gray; most of them have a bare patch on the head. Cranes have

inspired humans for millennia with their extraordinary courtship displays: they perform exuberant dances that involve leaps, bows, dips, and wing movements and are accompanied by roll-ing, bugling cries. Cranes forage by walking slowly with the bill near the ground and pecking and probing for a variety of prey and vegetable material. They nest solitarily, often in large terri-tories in bogs or marshes. Young cranes stay with their parents through their first winter and spring, learning migration routes and foraging techniques.

Recurvirostridae — Stilts and Avocets

Stilts and avocets are fairly widespread in warmer regions, and two species breed in North America. Avocets and stilts are ele-gant and flashy shorebirds with vivid patterns of black, white, tan, and pink. Both are long-legged and long-necked with long, slender bills; the bills are upturned in avocets and straight in stilts. The upwardly curved bills of avocets are adapted for sweeping insect larvae and other small organisms from the water. Avocets have partially webbed feet, presumably as an aid in swimming in deeper water than most waders attempt.

BLACK-NECKED STILT

Haematopodidae — Oystercatchers

The oystercatchers are husky birds with powerful bills designed to crack open mollusks. They are large and boldly patterned in black or in black and white, with reddish bills and legs. They inhabit seacoasts and, less often, inland rivers, where they feed on shellfish, crustaceans, and sandworms. Oystercatchers are conspicuous birds whether feeding on mud banks or nesting in the sand, where they lay from two to five eggs. Two species breed in North America.

Charadriidae — Lapwings and Plovers

Plovers are small to medium-sized shorebirds with short bills slightly swollen at the tip. As a rule, plovers have shorter, thicker bills than similarly sized sandpipers, and they tend to forage more in the manner of American Robins: running for short distances, then pausing, looking, and listening before extracting small invertebrate prey from the substrate. These birds run along the sand or mud, suddenly stop and probe for food in the soft ooze, and snatch worms, snails, small crustaceans, and insects from the ground. Most of the species have characteristic black or brown breast bands on a white background.

SEMIPALMATED SANDPIPER

AMERICAN GOLDEN-PLOVER

Jacanidae — Jacanas

Jacanas occur worldwide in the tropics; one species is an occasional breeder in North America. Jacanas have long toes and claws, and are adapted for walking on lily pads and other floating marsh vegetation. They are aggressive birds, several species being armed with spurs with which they defend their territories. In their exposed habitat, they have no need for cryptic coloration; most species are boldly patterned, and several have brilliantly colored frontal shields.

Scolopacidae — Sandpipers, Phalaropes, and Allies

Nearly 40 species of sandpiper breed in North America. This family includes curlews, godwits, snipes, woodcocks, turnstones, phalaropes, dowitchers, yellowlegs, and the "peeps"— the smallest sandpipers of the genus *Calidris*. The members of this family that frequent our waters range in size from the large Long-billed Curlew to one of the smallest, the Least Sandpiper. They are wading birds that are found on seacoasts and on inland lakes and rivers, and most of them nest on the Arctic tundra. Many perform tremendous migrations to the Southern Hemisphere in fall and back north again in the spring. Sandpipers show extraordinary diversity in size and shape. They are usually brown, white, and rust, although some are more dapper. In phalaropes, females are more brightly colored than males, a reverse sexual dimorphism that is rare among birds; the more cryptically plumaged males incubate the eggs and tend the young. Sandpipers rely on touch and smell when foraging. The smaller species pick around in open habitats for tiny invertebrate prey, while larger species probe more deeply into mud or sand to extract much larger prey. Many shorebird species feed near one another on mudflats or pond margins. Phalaropes often forage on lakes and ponds by spinning in circles to create a vortex that brings tiny prey items to the surface.

Stercorariidae — Skuas and Jaegers

Formerly classified alongside gulls and terns in the family Laridae, the mostly dark-plumaged jaegers and skuas recall birds of prey. Jaegers, with their pointed wings and swift flight, resemble falcons; skuas, with their heavy bodies and bills and aggressive manner, recall hawks. Jaegers and skuas derive much of their food in the manner of raptors, either through direct predation of small mammals and birds or by stealing food from other birds. Like gulls, jaegers and skuas are omnivores. Unlike most larids that nest in colonies, jaegers and skuas often nest solitarily and defend large territories.

Alcidae — Auks, Murres, and Puffins

Members of the family Alcidae—commonly called alcids— are marine birds with relatively short wings, webbed feet, and well-insulated, compact bodies. Perfectly suited to a life spent in cold, rough seas, alcids are awkward, almost penguin-like, on land and come to shore mostly to nest or when ailing. This family shows great diversity in bill structure and in size, ranging from the petite Least Auklet, the world's smallest alcid (3 oz or 85 g), to the extinct, flightless Great Auk (11 lbs or 5 kg). Alcids have countershaded plumages that help them escape notice of both aerial and marine predators. Some species show different plumages in summer and winter; puffins and auklets sport head plumes and brightly colored bills in breeding dress, which they shed after nesting. Birds in this group can be confused with ducks, grebes, and loons at a distance, but their shape and distinctive manner of flight—low to the water, with rapid wing beats—quickly distinguish them from other water birds. Alcids dive for their prey, using both their wings and feet for propulsion and steering, appearing to "fly" under water.

LAUGHING GULL

Laridae — Gulls, Terns, and Skimmers

All larids are small to medium-sized water birds with webbed feet and relatively long wings. The group includes familiar birds, such as the gulls that wheel around the seashore or above fast food franchises, as well as pelagic species rarely observed on land in North America. The so-called "seagull" is represented on this continent by no fewer than 30 species, from the world's largest, the goose-sized Great Black-backed Gull, to the world's smallest, the dove-sized Little Gull. Bill size and shape in gulls is strongly tied to body size: larger species have heavier, deeper bills, while the smallest gulls have rather thin, tern-like bills. Terns are less adaptable than gulls in most respects, and they also show relatively less diversity in structure and plumage. Black Skimmer differs markedly from other larids (and all other birds) in its outsized bill, with mandible longer than maxilla.

Larids show a remarkable range of foraging techniques. Most gulls are adapted to seizing fish or other prey from the water's surface; others pick fruit on the wing, flycatch, dig for grubs and worms, and even drop shellfish onto rocks to break them open. Few birds are better adapted to human-altered environments than gulls, which forage in an astonishing array of places: city parks and streets, landfills, sewage treatment plants, agricultural fields, and hydroelectric plants, to name only a few. Most terns forage by diving, but some also fly-catch insects or pick prey from the water's surface. Skimmers forage by lowering the mandible into the water when flying and snapping the bill shut upon sensing prey.

Most larids nest in colonies, sometimes extremely large ones, though the larger gulls often nest solitarily and defend large territories. Most species nest on the ground or on sea-cliffs, with little in the way of a true nest; a few, such as noddies and Bonaparte's Gull, nest in trees. Courtship usually consists of ritualized posturing, parading, and calling; some species make offerings of small fish or other items. Gulls, particularly the larger species, have long calls that they use in a variety of contexts, including pair-bonding. Both parents feed their young. Gull populations are mostly stable or increasing. Terns and Black Skimmers, however, are vulnerable to a variety of disturbances at nesting colonies, and productivity in several species of terns is considered low.

Phaethontidae — Tropicbirds

Tropicbirds are creatures of the tropical and subtropical oceans of the world. These birds resemble huge terns with long tail streamers. They are locally numerous and easy to see near their nesting colonies on oceanic islands, but outside the breeding season they roam widely over the ocean and are usually solitary. They spend most of their lives over the open ocean, diving from great heights in the air to seize fish, squid, and cuttlefish. Formerly considered part of the order Pelecaniformes, tropicbirds are smaller than pelicans, with wingspans of a mere 38" (1 m).

Gaviidae — Loons

Loons are members of the ancient family Gaviidae, fossils of which date back tens of millions of years. They are heavyset diving birds with dagger-like bills that they use to spear fish, crustaceans, and other aquatic prey. They have solid bones to reduce their buoyancy and aid diving after prey. Like grebes, loons have feet set far back on the body, an adaptation for agile pursuit of prey underwater. The larger species may spend more

PACIFIC LOON

than a minute below the water's surface and dive to depths of several hundred feet. Loons nest on remote lakes or sheltered coastlines in Canada and Alaska; Common Loon also nests in the northern United States. Their elaborate courtship displays involve synchronized swimming, chasing, and bill movements; males and females also give a variety of yodeling, quacking, and whinnying calls. In fall loons migrate southward to winter on large lakes and ocean coasts, where they can sometimes be observed in large, loose flocks; Yellow-billed Loon is usually seen singly, especially in the lower 48 states. Common Loon, which nests on boreal lakes farther south than other loons, faces a host of conservation problems: acidification of the lakes, development (resulting in pollution of the lakes and disturbance by recreational boaters), and poisoning by ingestion of lead sinkers used in fishing tackle.

Diomedeidae — Albatrosses

Albatrosses are found mostly in the oceans of the Southern Hemisphere; all are distinctly migratory, and three species visit North America when not breeding. These seabirds are goose-sized or larger, with a powerful bill that is hooded at the tip; tube-like nostrils; and exceptionally long, narrow wings that allow them to glide effortlessly over the waves, picking live squid or floating edibles from the ocean. They lay one egg in a scrape or mound on the beach, mainly on islands but also on remote coasts.

Oceanitidae — Southern Storm-Petrels

Southern storm-petrels occur worldwide in tropical and temperate oceans, and although they normally breed in the Southern Hemisphere, a few species sometimes migrate north of the equator and can be seen off of North American shores. These small birds flutter over the surface of the water, where they feed on small crustaceans, fish, and plankton. Like the shearwaters, they have tubular nostrils on top of the bill. Most species are black, and some have white on the rump, but a few are gray. Because they are small and usually seen from the dock of a pitching boat, they can be difficult to identify. Flight characteristics, rather than color and pattern, are often the best clues. Storm-petrels nest in burrows on offshore islands and isolated coasts, which they visit only at night.

Hydrobatidae — Northern Storm-Petrels

Northern storm-petrels occur worldwide in tropical and temperate oceans—predominantly in the Northern Hemisphere—and four species breed in North America. These small birds flutter over the surface of the water, where they feed on small crustaceans, fish, and plankton. Like the shearwaters, they have tubular nostrils on top of the bill. Most species are black, and some have white on the rump, but a few are gray. Like southern storm-petrels, they can be difficult to identify by color or pattern; flight characteristics are often the best identification clues. Storm-petrels nest in burrows on offshore islands and isolated coasts, which they visit only at night.

Procellariidae — Shearwaters and Petrels

Members of this family, mainly oceanic in the nonbreeding season, nest in burrows on islands and along coasts, where they are chiefly nocturnal. Only three species breed in North America, but many winter here. These birds have tubular nostrils, webbed feet, and long pointed wings that are held stiffly during prolonged effortless glides low over the waves. As in the closely related storm-petrels, the nostrils are enclosed in horny tubes on top of the bill. Most species feed on fish, squid, crustaceans, or plankton. Among North American species shearwaters tend to be larger than petrels.

Ciconiidae — Storks

Storks are large, long-legged, long-necked, and long-billed birds that live chiefly in open marshy country. They nest either singly or in colonies in trees and bushes, often with herons and ibises. They feed on all sorts of animal matter and a few species eat carrion. Wood Stork and the enormous Jabiru, a vagrant from Central America, are the only storks found in the United States. Like spoonbills, they have unfeathered heads and feed by touch in shallow water. To hunt, they lower the bill into the water and snap it shut upon sensing prey (mostly fish); their reaction time can be remarkably fast, with Wood Stork measured at 0.03 seconds. Like other wading birds, storks sometimes appear far out of range in summer and fall; some will remain for weeks in an area, especially where drying ponds concentrate fish.

Fregatidae — Frigatebirds

Frigatebirds are denizens of the tropical oceans of the world. In North America, one species breeds in extreme southern Florida on the Marquesas Keys off Key West. These are large, extremely long-winged birds with long, deeply forked tails, hooded bills, and webbed feet. Males have inflatable throat patches. Nesting chiefly on oceanic islands, they rob other seabirds, forcing them to disgorge the fish they have caught. The courtship display of Magnificent Frigatebird is spectacular: the male inflates an enormous, cherry red gular sac like a great balloon and clatters his long bill as the female looks on.

Sulidae — Boobies and Gannets

Members of this family occur nearly worldwide on islands and coasts. Only one species breeds in North America. Boobies and gannets are large birds with long pointed bills, webbed feet, and pointed wings, adapted for plunge diving for fish from great heights into the ocean. They nest on steep cliffs and rocky islands, and sometimes in trees. Boobies, especially the smaller species, can be distinguished from gannets by their narrower wing shape and their style of diving for prey: Boobies often dive at shallow angles, whereas gannets usually dive from directly above prey.

NORTHERN GANNET

Phalacrocoracidae — Cormorants

Six species of cormorants breed in North America. These are large birds, usually black, with long necks, long hooked bills, and webbed feet. The feet of these expert divers are located far back on the body to give them forward thrust under water; on land cormorants stand upright, often with their wings partially extended to dry. In the air, they fly in long lines or wedge shaped formations. Cormorants swim on the surface, diving under to seize fish and crustaceans much like loons, plunging headfirst. Great and Pelagic cormorants often leap upward, almost clearing the water before submerging; Double-crested Cormorant dives without the leap. Overall size and shape of head and neck help distinguish these species from other birds on the water or in flight.

Anhingidae — Darters

Darters occupy tropical or subtropical regions of the world. One species in this family, Anhinga, breeds in North America. These large, web-footed birds have long, slender necks and pointed spear-like bills with which they impale fish. They inhabit inland freshwater lakes, streams, and marshes, and nest in trees and bushes.

Pelecanidae — Pelicans

Pelicans are huge birds with webbed feet, long bills, and enormous gular (throat) pouches. The American White Pelican inhabits inland waters and coastal lagoons, catching fish at the surface, while the Brown Pelican is exclusively coastal and plunge-dives from the air to catch its prey. Flocks of both species fly in long lines, alternately flapping and gliding, or occasionally soaring high in the sky.

Ardeidae — Bitterns, Herons, and Allies

Some of these large to medium-sized, long-legged wading birds have long necks that they fold over their backs in flight. Bitterns and herons have long bills for catching prey, and their toes are unwebbed. Many species nest in colonies in trees and bushes. Some species have elaborate plumes during the breeding season. Herons and egrets are the most familiar members of the family Ardeidae. These birds are often seen posed elegantly at the edge of a pond or stream, watching for fish and frogs. They spear prey with lightning quick jabs propelled by strong muscles in their long necks. Cattle Egret is exceptional among ardeids in that it forages mostly in fields, following livestock or tractors that stir up insects, its chief prey. Bitterns nest in freshwater or brackish marshes, where they often stay hidden in reed beds and are hard to find. Night-herons forage extensively at night, as their name implies, but are still usually easier to detect than the bitterns.

GREAT EGRET

Threskiornithidae — Ibises and Spoonbills

Ibises and spoonbills are found chiefly in tropical regions of the world. Four species breed in North America, including the colorful Roseate Spoonbill. The bills of ibises are long and curved downward; those of spoonbills are straight and spatulate. They are aquatic birds that feed on fish, frogs, insects, and other small animals in the water. They nest in colonies in trees and bushes, often with herons. Ibises and spoonbills are specialized foragers, as their unusual bill shapes indicate. They usually sweep their bills from side to side in shallow water, creating currents that dislodge aquatic prey. Ibises also forage by touch in mud or soft soil, using their long, curved bills to extract worms, crayfish, small fish, and amphibians. Both spoonbills and ibises have been found wandering far from their typical ranges, especially in recent years.

Cathartidae — New World Vultures

Vultures are large, mostly blackish birds with broad wings and bare heads. California Condor and the two vultures found north of Mexico are sometimes considered honorary raptors, as they forage and migrate in the skies much like raptors; however, their evolutionary relationships with raptors are unclear and they seldom take live prey. These scavengers feed on carrion and refuse. Their claws are blunt instead of sharp talons like those of hawks. Vultures and condors have strong legs and bills for gaining access to carcasses of dead animals, which form almost their entire diet. Their naked heads are an adaptation for feeding on carrion, which would quickly soil feathers and spread disease. Vultures possess keen senses of smell and vision that allow them to locate dead animals. They nest in tree cavities or on the ground.

Pandionidae — Ospreys

The family Pandionidae contains only a single species, the Osprey. These birds are related to hawks and eagles, and together they are part of the taxonomic order Accipitriformes, which has undergone recent reorganization due to emerging genetic research. The Osprey is a specialized predator whose diet is composed almost entirely of fish. Ospreys are found throughout the world, on every continent except Antarctica, wherever there are fish populations it can feed on. They hunt by hovering over a body of water, spotting a shallow-swimming fish with their acute eyesight, then diving powerfully and pulling the fish from the water in their talons. The Osprey was one of the bird species most severely affected by DDT poisoning, but has experienced a remarkable recovery in North America since DDT was banned in the 1970s. Ospreys nest on trees or any other tall object near a body of water where they can feed, and have shown great adaptability to artificial nesting surfaces.

Accipitridae — Hawks, Kites, Eagles, and Allies

Diurnal raptors, usually recognized by casual observers as hawks or eagles, are birds of prey with hooked bills and talons adapted for killing prey and tearing into flesh. Their speed and skill when hunting have been a source of wonder for humans since our earliest written history. Some species of diurnal raptors supplement their diet with carrion, especially under adverse conditions or when prey is scarce. Members of the family Accipitridae, often called accipitrids or accipiters, range greatly in size—from the tiny Sharp-shinned Hawk, with a wingspan of less than 20" (50 cm), to the mighty Steller's Sea-Eagle (a

GOLDEN EAGLE

vagrant in North America), our largest eagle with an 88" (2.5 m) wingspan. Because accipitrids have evolved to exploit different prey resources, they differ greatly in shape as well as size.

Tytonidae — Barn Owls

Although members of this family occur worldwide, only one species, the Barn Owl, occurs in North America. These long-legged, densely plumaged owls have conspicuous heart-shaped facial disks and dark eyes. They are found mostly in forests, but several species in the Old World tropics are adapted to open grasslands.

Strigidae — Typical Owls

Also called "typical owls" or "true owls," more than 200 members of the family Strigidae occur worldwide, and 18 species breed in North America. Members of this well-known family range from the huge Great Horned Owl and Great Gray Owl to the diminutive Elf Owl of the arid Southwest. Nearly all of the species are nocturnal, but some, such as the beautiful Snowy Owl of the Arctic, also hunt in the daytime. Owls do not build their own nests but use abandoned nests of other birds, such as stick nests in trees. They also nest in hollow trees, and more rarely, on cliffs or on the ground. During the cold months, many of these birds roost in dense evergreens. Although, like hawks, they have sharp talons and hooked bills for killing their prey, they are not related to hawks.

Owls vary greatly in size, but all have strong, hooked bills and talons suited for capturing, killing, and eating live prey; eyes adapted for foraging at night; and broad, usually rounded wings.

Ecologically, owls are rather like hawks: They are widespread and found in virtually every habitat, even heavily urbanized areas; the smallest species prey on large insects, the largest on small mammals. Their plumages are composed mostly of browns, rusts, black, and white.

Owls, however, have several morphological differences from hawks that are related to their nocturnal activities. They have a round facial disc that focuses sound waves to their highly sensitive ear openings. The ear openings of some species, such as Great Gray Owl, are strongly asymmetrical, which permits them to pinpoint the location of rodents tunneling under deep snow or hidden beneath grasses on moonless nights. Many species have "horns" (ear tufts) that, along with cryptic plumages, help camouflage them as they roost by day. Like hawks, owls have keen vision, but the eyes of most owls are specially adapted for gathering light in order to hunt at night. Night-hunting owls also have tiny serrations in the edges of the outer primaries, which make their flight almost inaudible. They hunt by stealth in flight, usually taking prey on the ground; many species are adroit hunters in thick cover, particularly those that eat birds, such as pygmy-owls.

Owls usually swallow prey items whole, later regurgitating a pellet of the bones, fur, and other indigestible parts. Owl pellets found in the daytime are good indicators of the presence of a local population of owls.

Many owls time their breeding to coincide with peak abundance of prey. Larger species make bulky stick nests in trees or on cliffs (Barn Owl also nests in barns and other structures), while smaller owls nest in cavities. Some species take readily to nest boxes, which they also use for daytime roosting. Flammulated and Elf owls are Neotropical migrants, and Short-eared Owls regularly leave northern parts of their breeding range; most species, however, are sedentary or irrupt southward in "flight years," mostly when prey is scarce in the breeding range.

GREAT HORNED OWL

Trogonidae — Trogons

The family of trogons and quetzals includes 39 species found throughout the tropical areas of America, Asia, and Africa. Trogons are long-tailed, medium-sized birds with short legs and short, rather heavy bills. Plumage patterns of males and females are similar, although males are more brightly colored. When foraging, trogons and quetzals sit almost motionless, peering around slowly much like cuckoos. Upon spotting a large insect or small lizard, they fly swiftly to pluck it from a branch. Both trogons and quetzals also readily forage on berries; they nest in old woodpecker cavities. Most members of this family inhabit the deep tropics, but the mountains and canyons of southeastern Arizona host a small number of Elegant Trogons and Eared Quetzals.

Alcedinidae — Kingfishers

Kingfishers are heavyset birds with heavy bills and heads but small feet and short tails. Their structure reflects an adaptation for fishing, specifically for plunge-diving from a perch or a hovering position. North American species are blue or green above and white below, with a rufous breast or belly in all but the male Belted Kingfisher and female Green Kingfisher. They eat fish, aquatic crustaceans, and amphibians. Many tropical species also catch insects and lizards on land. Courtship consists of aerial chases and feeding. All North American species nest in burrows excavated in earthen banks where they lay their white eggs.

Picidae — Woodpeckers and Allies

The woodpecker family includes more than 200 species worldwide and 22 species that breed in North America. Woodpeckers live wherever there are trees or large cacti. They specialize in foraging on trees, usually by removing bark or drilling holes to take insects and their larvae. Some species also eat acorns, which they may store in granary trees for later consumption. Woodpeckers have chisel-like bills suited to scaling bark or creating foraging pits in trees. They have strong feet, with toes usually in a zygodactyl arrangement (two toes pointing forward and two backward), and stiff tails to brace against as they cling to or hitch up trees in small vertical leaps. Built to extract prey from tight spaces, woodpeckers' tongues are barbed and quite long (up to 5" or 13 cm). Most species use rapid-fire, loud drumming to mark territory and to attract and keep in contact with mates. Many species also communicate with descending fuss or whinny calls. Woodpecker courtship is ostentatious: most species call rapidly, raise the crown feathers, spread the wings while clinging to a tree, and bob rhythmically together. All woodpeckers excavate cavities for nesting; some accept artificial cavities. Many species mate for life.

RED-BELLIED WOODPECKER

Falconidae — Caracaras and Falcons

This family includes true falcons (genus *Falco*) and also the caracaras, which are larger and often feed on carrion, as vultures do. True falcons have long pointed wings and long tails, and are among the fastest flying birds in the world. They mainly inhabit open country and many pursue birds on the wing. Unlike other birds of prey, true falcons do not build nests of their own but utilize other birds' nests or lay eggs in hollow trees, on cliffs or on the ground. Falcons are renowned for their speed and grace in the air, which many feel are unrivaled in the world of birds. True falcons range in size from the petite American Kestrel to the stocky Gyrfalcon, but all are somewhat similar in shape. Their long, pointed wings and moderately long tails are adapted for rapid acceleration and maximum maneuverability when pursuing prey, whether aerial insects, shorebirds, or ptarmigan. Crested Caracara, a distinctively patterned relative of falcons, is quite different in shape, its long legs and heavy, deep bill suited for flexible foraging strategies that include walking on the ground to scavenge carrion. Caracaras build nests like other birds of prey.

Psittacidae — Parakeets, Macaws, and Parrots

Parrots and parakeets (and macaws) are members of the family Psittacidae, which includes about 360 species worldwide. While psittacids vary in body shape—from the slender, long-tailed parakeets to the stout-bodied, short-tailed parrots—all have strong, curved maxillas for opening fruits, seeds, and nuts. They typically are highly social, nest in cavities, and have loud, far-carrying calls. Most New World species have green plumages with other colors in the wings and head.

The only native representative from temperate North America, Carolina Parakeet, is now extinct. The southern United States is home to many exotic psittacids (more than 90 species recorded), nearly all of which are escapees from pet owners. Many *Amazona* species are resident nesters in Florida and California. In addition, psittacids from Africa and Australasia, such as Budgerigar, Cockatiel, and various lovebirds and cockatoos, are also often observed. North America lacks the natural habitats in which most exotic psittacids evolved, and the birds depend on urban and suburban environments to provide their food—mostly from exotic fruit and nut trees—and nesting and roosting areas. Unlike the tropical species, Monk Parakeets are adapted to living in temperate climates and can be observed year-round in many large cities, even as far north as Chicago.

Because they are found mainly in developed environments, parrots and parakeets tend not to displace native birds from their niches, as some other introduced birds have done (European Starling, for instance). Conservationists, however, are concerned about the potential spread of avian diseases by parrots to native birds in North America, and about the damage to native populations of parrots in the tropics posed by the caged bird trade. Many species of psittacids worldwide have become endangered, and several even extinct, because of this trade.

Tityridae — Becards, Tityras, and Allies

This primarily tropical family contains birds formerly classified in several different families including the Tyrant Flycatchers. Only one representative, the Rose-throated Becard, is found in North America north of Mexico.

Tyrannidae — Tyrant Flycatchers

Tyrant flycatchers in North America are part of the enormous family Tyrannidae, which contains more than 400 species; 35 species in 10 genera nest in the United States and Canada, from deserts to boreal forests, and another 10 have been seen as vagrants north of Mexico and the Caribbean. Tyrant flycatchers evolved in the New World tropics, and their diversity there is remarkable. Tyrannidae is the only family of suboscine passerines (a tropical American group that includes cotingas, woodcreepers, and antbirds) that extends northward across the Mexican border. Birds in this group, unlike all other North American passerines, do not learn their songs; rather, their songs are innate.

HAMMOND'S FLYCATCHER

Flycatchers are upright-perching, small to medium-sized passerines with typically broad-based bills surrounded by rictal bristles. Their rather long, pointed wings are typical of long-distance migrants (temperate-zone nesters generally migrate to the tropics in winter). Most species are brown, gray, or greenish above and a paler whitish or yellowish below, and many have wing bars. Although some tropical species are strikingly patterned, most flycatchers are subtly plumaged and quite similar to each other.

Flycatchers take mostly insect prey, primarily flying insects; fruit forms an important part of the diet in migration and on the wintering grounds for some of the larger species. Larger flycatchers and the pewees, including Olive-sided Flycatcher, usually sit on a conspicuous perch and watch for passing insects, which they fly out and capture with the bill in midair, returning to the same perch. Smaller species tend to show less fidelity to one perch. A few species, especially the phoebes and the larger flycatchers, also take prey from the ground, including spiders, small lizards, and even small birds such as hummingbirds.

Most tyrannids sing to attract mates and mark territory; a few, notably the kingbirds and Vermilion Flycatcher, have striking aerial displays as well. Many species have dawn songs that differ from their daytime vocalizations. Temperate zone flycatchers make cup-shaped nests, placing them in the fork of a tree or along a limb; Yellow-bellied and Cordilleran flycatchers sometimes nest on or near the ground. *Myiarchus* species nest in cavities, as does Sulphur-bellied Flycatcher. Several other tropical species, notably kiskadees, make larger spherical nests with side entrances.

Populations of tyrant flycatchers have declined in many areas.

Laniidae — Shrikes

Shrikes are medium-sized passerines of open-country habitats. These birds recall a small jay in overall shape. Both North American shrike species are plumaged in gray, black, and white; younger birds show browner tones above and faint barring below. Northern Shrike, the larger species, nests in boreal forests and muskeg and is seen regularly only south to the northernmost United States in winter; Loggerhead Shrike nests mostly south of Canada and ranges southward into the deserts of Mexico. Both are regularly confused with Northern Mockingbird, which has much more white in the wings and tail, a more slender bill, and a different flight style that lacks the rapid wing beats and often undulating path of the shrikes. The black mask of shrikes (absent in mockingbirds) probably functions, like a falcon's mask, to absorb glare in the well-lit habitats shrikes occupy.

Shrikes are unique among passerines in that they feed like birds of prey, taking birds, rodents, and large insects in swift, direct capture much as kestrels do. Their short but powerful bills have a hooked maxilla with a small tomial notch (a tiny, toothlike serration), as in a falcon's bill, which they use to dispatch prey quickly, often with a bite to the neck. Although shrikes lack the talons of a raptor, having simple perching feet like other passerines, they can tear into prey using their heavy bills. Like owls, shrikes regurgitate pellets of indigestible material. Shrikes cache what they catch, using barbed wire or thorn trees to display prey items; this larder presumably functions both to impress potential mates and to indicate occupied territories. Because they rely on sites where they can impale prey and find hunting perches, shrikes shun grasslands that lack trees, unless artificial features such as utility poles are available.

Vireonidae — Vireos

The vireo family includes 51 species in the New World, mostly in tropical and subtropical climes. Twelve species breed in North America, all in the genus *Vireo* (a Latin word whose root means "green").

Vireos are small land birds that resemble warblers but have heavier bills and heads. Once assumed to be close relatives of warblers, vireos are now thought to be most closely related to shrikes (the tomial notch near the tip of the maxilla perhaps hints at this relationship) and also to corvids. Vireos have heavier legs than warblers, often with a bluish tone; this can be helpful for identification. In plumage, vireos are plainer than warblers

YELLOW-GREEN VIREO

overall: mostly olive or gray above and paler below, with touches of yellowish in some species. Most have distinctive markings around the eyes—either "spectacles" or a supercilium—and most have wing bars in fresh plumage.

Like most warblers, vireos forage by gleaning prey from vegetation, from low scrub up through the canopy; they eat insects and their larvae and also, especially during the nonbreeding season, small fruits. While foraging, vireos often seem less animated and more methodical than warblers, scanning from a perch before moving to the next branch; however, smaller vireos, such as Black-capped and White-eyed, seem to be in constant, nervous motion when foraging. Hutton's Vireo closely resembles Ruby-crowned Kinglet and often flicks its wings like a kinglet, while Bell's and Gray vireos use distinctive tail movements while foraging. These actions of wings and tail probably serve to startle prey. Some vireos make short sallies from a perch to pick insects, much as a flycatcher does.

Male vireos sing to advertise territories and occasionally engage in song flights; unlike most passerines, males of some species sing from the nest. Vireo songs are often quite similar, as between Plumbeous and Yellow-throated or Philadelphia and Red-eyed. Philadelphia may actually imitate a Red-eyed's song to keep that species away from its territory. The calls of most vireos are quite similar and in some cases indistinguishable among species—a descending, raspy, nasal set of scolding calls with a cat-like quality. Both sexes guard their territory against intruders. Most vireos make cup-shaped nests that hang on the fork of a small branch; only Gray Vireo regularly nests on top of a branch. All species except Hutton's Vireo migrate southward in winter.

Populations of most vireos are relatively stable across the continent.

Corvidae — Jays and Crows

Ravens, crows, jays, magpies, and nutcrackers compose this diverse group of medium-sized to large passerines with sturdy legs and bills, rounded wings, and often long tails. Their plumages can be simple shades of blue or black or quite stunning, as with the strikingly patterned magpies or the multicolored Green Jay. Corvids are found in every major habitat on the continent; Common Raven, the world's largest passerine, remains year-round even in northern Nunavut, enduring the brutal, dark winters. Much of a corvid's success in difficult environments can be credited to its ingenuity in finding food and its ability to adapt to human-modified landscapes. Its gregariousness appears to be another advantage; birds of this group are quick to share new foraging techniques, whether raiding campsites and picnic baskets, dropping nuts on asphalt roads, or following toddlers for dropped food. Corvids are also among the few birds that appear to use tools, and experiments have shown that they are able to count, to remember the location of thousands of sites of cached nuts, and to find solutions to obstacles in procuring food. Most are omnivores, taking carrion, small animals, nestling birds and eggs, fruit, aquatic vertebrates and invertebrates, worms, waste grain, and other foods. Smaller corvids, especially jays, eat mostly seeds and nuts as well as insects and other arthropods. Pinyon Jay feeds on pine nuts; flocks of this species and of Clark's Nutcracker travel widely in search of good cone crops.

Alaudidae — Larks

This almost exclusively Old World family is represented in North America by one native species, the Horned Lark, and by the Eurasian Skylark introduced in British Columbia. Distant relatives of wagtails and pipits (family Motacillidae), they share habitat preferences, foraging strategies, and some structural and behavioral features. All are small to medium-sized, rather slim passerines that walk through shortgrass fields and other open habitats, often in groups, to feed on insects and seeds.

Hirundinidae — Swallows

Swallows, unlike swifts, are passerines (perching birds), and they are regularly seen resting on utility wires, fences, and clotheslines—something that swifts cannot do because of their tiny feet. Swallows are more robust of body and wing than swifts, with larger bills and feet (although both are still relatively small);

CLIFF SWALLOW

they also have more colorful plumages, often electric blue, green, or purple above and sometimes with rufous accents. Except for the sexually dimorphic Purple Martin, males and females are similar, although females are often noticeably less colorful. Like swifts, swallows forage by chasing aerial insects on the wing, but their flight appears less erratic. Although most forage at lower altitudes than swifts, several swallow species are known to forage high in the atmosphere. Swallows are often found in open terrain near water. Like swifts, they often sip water or even bathe while flying, skimming and splashing low over a lake or river. They nest in recesses including old woodpecker cavities and nest boxes, cavities in riverbanks, and spaces in old wharves and farm buildings. Many swallow species nest in colonies. Most North American swallows are long-distance Neotropical migrants.

Paridae — Chickadees and Titmice

Chickadees and titmice are small, agile, animated passerines of diverse woodlands—from dwarf willow fens of northern Alaska, to juniper-clad foothills of the Great Basin, to the suburban East. A dozen species occur in North America. In structure, chickadees and titmice share some attributes: relatively compact bodies; short, conical bills; and fairly long tails. Chickadees usually have a pale cheek set off by a dark cap and bib. Titmice are larger on average and gray overall with crests and few other adornments; the exception is Bridled Titmouse, which has a more intricate head pattern.

Parids eat a variety of insect matter, seeds, and berries. They often cache food for later consumption; this behavior can sometimes be observed at bird-feeding stations, although usually the birds retrieve a seed from the feeder and fly a short distance

MOUNTAIN CHICKADEE

away to open and eat it. Parids and their allies do not have elaborate courtship displays. Males sing and feed females, and both sexes investigate potential nest cavities, where they make cup-shaped nests. Many species readily accept nest boxes. They have a monogamous breeding system; some apparently mate for life. Away from feeders, nonbreeding parids forage in family groups or in company with nuthatches, kinglets, small woodpeckers, Brown Creeper, vireos, and warblers. In these groups parids lead the flocks, often announcing the presence of a predator—such as an owl, snake, or hawk—with noisy scolding. Although harassing a predator at close range would seem to be a risky affair, mobbing serves to draw the attention of numerous small birds to the location of the predator and probably teaches young birds to recognize potentially dangerous animals.

Remizidae — Verdins

One species from this Old World family of penduline tits, Verdin, breeds in North America. Verdins are small birds with short wings, relatively long tails, and sharply pointed bills. A few species undertake short migrations, but most are nonmigratory. All make elaborate nests. Verdin most resembles parids—especially chickadees—in structure, with its fine, conical, pointed bill and rotund body and head. Instead of a chickadee-like bib and cap, however, the adult Verdin has a yellow head and thus can be confused with warblers. This species forages by gleaning and, like parids, readily hangs upside down to reach the tips of light branches. It makes a spherical twig nest with a side entrance and apparently builds separate roosting nests as well.

Aegithalidae — Bushtits

These are tiny, active, mainly insectivorous birds with small, somewhat conical bills, short rounded wings, and long tails. Bushtits are social birds, most often seen traveling in large groups comprised of several families that hold large communal territories, but they also regularly travel with foraging flocks of other passerines, including parids and warblers. They are noted for their pendant, bag-shaped nests, often attached to mistletoe.

Sittidae — Nuthatches

Four species of nuthatch breed in North America. Nuthatches frequent much the same woodland habitats as parids, but their structure is quite different. They are stocky birds with long, pointed bills; short tails; and strong, sizable feet with which they cling to tree bark. Both nuthatches and woodpeckers are scansorial birds, adapted to climbing; but unlike woodpeckers, which mostly move upward around a tree, nuthatches move all around the trunk and limbs. Like parids, nuthatches nest in cavities and are not predictably migratory. Red-breasted Nuthatch does stage large-scale fall irruptions from montane and boreal habitats in years when food is scarce.

Certhiidae — Creepers

The Brown Creeper is North America's sole representative of family Certhiidae. A resident in many sorts of mature forests, it is reminiscent of a tiny woodpecker. Creepers forage up trees with quick, hitching motions made possible by their stiff tails and strong legs. Their thin, decurved bills are weaker than the bills of woodpeckers and are suited for prying tiny prey from bark crevices. Creepers make nests behind loose strips of bark and, like nuthatches, sometimes roost communally in a cavity during cold weather.

Troglodytidae — Wrens

The wren family is predominantly found in the Western Hemisphere; one wide-ranging species, the Eurasian Wren, also occurs in Eurasia. Ten species breed in North America. Wrens are small, mostly brown passerines with thin, decurved bills and often long tails that they hold cocked above the back. They occupy a wide array of habitats, from border deserts to the rocky Aleutian Islands, and spend most of their time near the ground. To many suburban dwellers, wrens are familiar visitors to backyard brambles, brush heaps, and feeding stations; several species readily accept nest boxes and will nest even in old boots, automobiles, or sheds. Wrens are probably relatives of the gnatcatchers (and the tropical gnatwrens), which are most closely related to Old World warblers, but their relationships and phylogenetic placement have yet to be clearly determined.

Although this group's family name derives from the Latin for "cave-dweller," most of the species that breed in North America never enter caves. Wrens are expert foragers in tight spaces, including thickets, tangles, tree falls, and rocky crevices—any site that supports an abundance of insects, millipedes, spiders, and their eggs, which are a wren's chief foods. Some species also eat seeds and small fruits, especially in the cooler months, and a few eat snails, small frogs, lizards, or other small vertebrates. Their long, thin bills allow them to deftly pluck prey from crannies.

Wrens sing to attract mates and defend territories; they are among the most musical of American birds. Their repertoires are variable among species: Cactus Wren seems to sing the same chugging song year after year, whereas Marsh Wren may sing more than 150 song types over the breeding season. Females sometimes counter-sing or duet with the males, especially in Carolina Wren, although their vocalizations are less varied and musical. Wrens build cup-shaped or spherical nests mostly in bushes or reeds, but some nest in crevices or cacti. Most of the wrens that nest in northern North America migrate southward in fall or at least withdraw from the northern parts of their range.

CACTUS WREN

Polioptilidae — Gnatcatchers and Gnatwrens

Gnatcatchers, with their long tails and active foraging habits, remind many observers of tiny mockingbirds. These slender, tiny-billed birds chase insects in the air like flycatchers but move through the vegetation more rapidly, more like a kinglet, constantly flipping the tail to flush prey. Although distinctive, gnatcatchers can be confused with the even shorter-billed Bushtit, which travels in flocks most of the year. Pale females of the western gnatcatchers might also be taken for flycatchers but for their different foraging behaviors and thin bills.

Cinclidae — Dippers

Members of this family are found in temperate zones of the Old World and the Americas. One species, American Dipper, breeds in North America, where it is largely nonmigratory. American Dipper is a gray, heavyset bird, about the size of a thrush. Dippers have short tails and pointed bills; their powerful legs and feet are adapted for doing something no other passerine does: swimming and walking underwater, where they forage for invertebrates. Dippers make round nests of mosses and various plants, placing them near streams, usually on a ledge, cliff, or underside of a bridge.

Pycnonotidae — Bulbuls

Bulbuls include 137 species found in the Old World tropics. One species, Red-whiskered Bulbul, has been introduced into North America where it has established colonies restricted to small areas in southern California and Florida. Bulbuls are generally rather dull-colored birds that travel in flocks and eat fruit or insects. Some are noisy and conspicuous, while others are retiring and difficult to detect.

Regulidae — Kinglets

Kinglets are truly tiny birds with the smallest of bills. They forage almost continuously, moving actively through the trees, and can hover at the tips of branches to glean tiny insect larvae. Although superficially similar to warblers, vireos, and flycatchers, kinglets have even thinner bills, thinner legs, and shorter tails.

GOLDEN-CROWNED KINGLET

Phylloscopidae — Leaf Warblers

This family is a product of a recent split in the Old World Warblers, and most of this family's species are Eurasian. One species in this family breeds in Alaska, and another is a rare vagrant to the West Coast.

Sylviidae — Sylviid Warblers

These Old World warblers are small passerines with thin, pointed bills, active foraging habits, and usually colorful plumages, par-

ticularly in breeding adult males. This family used to contain hundreds of species, although never many in North America. Recent studies have shown that the old Sylviidae contained several families, some only distantly related. The only North American species in the current, much reduced, Sylviidae family is the Wrentit.

Muscicapidae — Old World Flycatchers

This is a large Old World family with only a few species that breed in the northernmost reaches of North America. These flycatchers historically were considered allies of chickadees and titmice (family Paridae) and often were treated as part of the same group. The evolutionary relationships between creepers, nuthatches, and parids are not well understood, and their placement together is based more on their shared habitat and association in the nonbreeding season than on similarities in plumage and structure.

Turdidae — Thrushes

Thrushes occur worldwide except in Antarctica; the family consists of 310 species, 13 of which breed in North America. Thrushes are medium-sized, usually plump-looking passerines found in a great diversity of habitats, from bleak, stony tundra to Pacific coastal rainforests to inner city ball fields. Thrushes have sturdy, slim bills; rather long wings; and strong, moderately long legs that are well suited for their mostly terrestrial foraging

VARIED THRUSH

CURVE-BILLED THRASHER

habits. The larger American thrushes are usually found in woodlands, whereas the bluebirds and Townsend's Solitaire prefer open country with scattered trees.

Most thrushes hop on the ground looking for insects and other arthropods, which they capture with a quick pounce. The open-country species also flycatch or make quick sallies from a perch to the ground. Virtually all thrushes take fruit at some point during the year, usually in fall and winter. In the nonbreeding season some species, such as American Robin, form large, roving flocks that quickly strip trees of berries before moving on. Thrushes are famous for their sublime songs, Hermit Thrush and Varied Thrush in particular. Male thrushes arrive on the breeding grounds earlier than females and sing to mark and defend their territories. After nesting, spotted thrushes migrate to the American tropics.

Mimidae — Mockingbirds and Thrashers

Mockingbirds, catbirds, and thrashers are reminiscent of thrushes in overall build, but they have longer tails, shorter and less pointed wings, and bills that are either longer and decurved (most thrashers) or shorter and thinner. Like thrushes, mimids are fine songsters; in some cases, they imitate other birds' songs (hence the family name, which means "mimics"). Most mimids are terrestrial foragers that lurk in thickets, kicking back leaf litter in search of insects and the like; all species eat fruit as well. Most mimids appear to be in a pattern of long-term decline, probably related to the fragmentation of habitat, which permits cowbirds and predators better access to nests, to deforestation in the tropics, and to acid rain, which may reduce the abundance of arthropods, snails, and other prey items.

Sturnidae — Starlings and Mynas

Members of this family are found in tropical and temperate regions of the Old World. A few species have been introduced into North America. Members of this family are medium-sized songbirds with large feet and strong bills, often with brilliantly glossy black plumage. They are mainly birds of open country, although a few are adapted for living in forests. Most species are gregarious and some form huge flocks outside the breeding season. European Starling is an introduced species in North America and has become one of the continent's most numerous bird species.

Bombycillidae — Waxwings

These handsome, sleek, crested birds are named for the unique red, wax-like tips on the wing feathers of the adults. Waxwings

BOHEMIAN WAXWING

are gregarious and often form large flocks, except in the nesting season, which is usually in late summer. They feed on insects, berries, and fruits.

Ptiliogonatidae — Silky-flycatchers

Silky-flycatchers are mostly Central American, and only one species (Phainopepla) from this family reaches the southwestern United States. Silky-flycatchers are slender, crested, short-winged, towhee-sized birds. They feed by catching flies or gleaning insects. They also take berries. Phainopepla is a silky-flycatcher found in the arid Southwest, usually near mistletoe or other small fruit; it makes seasonal movements but is apparently only a short-distance migrant.

Peucedramidae — Olive Warblers

Olive warblers are small passerines with thin, pointed bills, active foraging habits, and usually colorful plumages, particularly in breeding adult males. Olive Warbler was until recently thought to be a parulid and grouped with the family of New World warblers, but it now belongs to its own family, of which it is the only member. Studies suggest a possible close relationship to finches (family Fringillidae). The nests of Olive Warblers are recognizable by their edges, which are covered with the feces of the nestlings long after the young have fledged; this phenomenon is shared by both finches and Olive Warblers, and is not seen in any other passerines.

Passeridae — Old World Sparrows

This family is widespread in the Old World, especially in Africa. Passerids, or Old World sparrows, are represented in North America by only two species, both of them introduced. Passerids are generally colonial when nesting; males perform animated courtship displays, hopping around with cocked tail and drooped wings like windup toys. Passerids usually nest in cavities; they will accept virtually any cranny available (often in buildings), constructing a round nest of twigs and grasses within the cavity.

Motacillidae — Wagtails and Pipits

Wagtails and pipits are small to medium-sized, rather slim passerines that walk through shortgrass fields and other open habitats, often in groups, to feed on insects and seeds. They have strong legs, sometimes with elongated hind claws. All are ground-nesters, monogamous, and highly migratory. Motacillidae is a mainly Old World family; only four motacillids breed on this continent. Wagtails are larger than pipits and have longer tails, which they constantly wag, and striking plumages. They are conspicuous, active foragers, chasing insects on the ground, flycatching, and even taking invertebrates in streams. Pipits forage less actively, usually walking erratically through fields.

WHITE WAGTAIL

Fringillidae — Fringilline and Cardueline Finches and Allies

Finches are small passerines that are sometimes confused with sparrows or buntings; this is particularly the case with the smaller species, which—like the other small, seed-eating passerines—have short, conical bills adapted for feeding on seeds. Finches, however, differ from sparrows in many ways. Most have shorter tails that show a distinct, shallow fork. Finches are usually sexually dimorphic: males are usually brightly colored (brighter than sparrows) in reds, yellows, and rusts, and females and young of the smaller species are often mousy brown above and sometimes streaked below. Finches are more arboreal than sparrows, although most frequent open woodlands and edges rather than closed forests. Larger finches have heavy, powerful bills. In the crossbills, the maxilla and mandible cross, like misaligned pincers—an adaptation for foraging on pine and spruce seeds.

WHITE-WINGED CROSSBILL

Calcariidae — Longspurs and Snow Buntings

These are short-legged, plump sparrows of open habitats such as tundra, shortgrass prairies, and beaches. Longspurs, named for the elongated nail on the hind toe, are rather heavy-billed for their size. Members of this family have white in the outer tail feathers (rectrices). Like larks and pipits, members of this family frequent farm fields in the nonbreeding season to forage for seeds, sometimes in mixed flocks.

Emberizidae — Emberizids

This family used to include most of the sparrows in North America, but now family Emberizidae is reserved for Old World buntings, which occur in North America only as vagrants. The native North American sparrows now belong to family Passerellidae.

Passerellidae — Towhees and Sparrows

New World sparrows are small, mostly brown birds with short, conical bills and moderately long tails. They typically have a straight-edged culmen (upper edge of the maxilla), whereas the Old World sparrows (family Passeridae) have a distinctly curved culmen, especially in males.

With a few exceptions, sparrows are birds of thickets and open brushy or marshy environments, where both seeds and insects, the mainstays of their diet, abound. A few species are found in open forests. Bill size differs subtly but importantly among sparrows and is a good clue as to the size of seed the species is likely to eat. Towhees and sparrows scratch both feet backward in rapid motion to move leaf litter and other material quickly, exposing insects and other arthropods as well as seeds.

Most sparrows have monogamous mating systems, with males singing to defend a territory and mate. Some are polygynous, notably Lark Bunting and Savannah Sparrow. Sparrows maintain rather small territories (they may seem almost colonial when habitat is optimal) or show little interest in territorial defense. Most sparrows build a cup-shaped nest of grasses on the ground or in a small tree or bush; a few species cover the cup with a dome of grasses for added concealment.

Conservation concerns for native sparrows abound in North America, largely because their habitats—fields, grasslands, and salt marshes in particular—have been heavily developed and modified for centuries.

Spindalidae — Spindalises

This is a small family containing a single genus of nonmigratory birds endemic to the Greater Antilles that can sometimes be found in southern Florida. They were once considered to be aberrant tanagers (Thraupidae) but are now considered a distinct family.

Icteriidae — Yellow-breasted Chats

Yellow-breasted Chats were formerly classified as an odd member of the family of wood warblers (New World warblers). This

SPOTTED TOWHEE

classification was (and is) contested, because the species is twice as large as any other member of the family, and its body structure, vocalizations, and even behaviors are unlike those of typical wood warblers. The taxonomic status of Yellow-breasted Chats has proven so problematic that they have been designated their own family, of which they are the only member.

Icteridae — Blackbirds

Blackbirds and their kin are medium-sized passerines with straight, pointed bills (shorter and more conical on cowbirds and Bobolink) and relatively long, thick legs that are equally well adapted for perching and walking on the ground. Some species, such as Yellow-headed Blackbird, have large feet that help them balance on aquatic vegetation or mud. The plumages of icterids are often striking and colorful, ranging from brilliant orange and yellow in the long-tailed orioles and the short-tailed meadowlarks to glossy purple, green, and bronze in the grackles, cowbirds, and blackbirds. In most species, females are less gaudily colored or less iridescent and often have brown rather than black tones. Many species of icterids, especially the blackbirds, have adapted well to human-modified landscapes. Collectively, their breeding habitats extend from the tundra of eastern Alaska, where Red-winged Blackbirds sing from marshy swales, to the strip malls of southernmost Texas, where gangs of Great-tailed Grackles patrol parking lots for french fries.

Parulidae — Wood-Warblers

Also called New World warblers, members of this family are small passerines with thin, pointed bills, active foraging habits, and usually colorful plumages, particularly in breeding adult males. Warblers and their allies are tenacious, adaptable, hardy birds that have radiated into habitats as diverse as their jewel-like colors: from marshes and muskeg to thorn scrub and mangrove forests. Most species fare poorly, however, in developed urban and modern agricultural environments, which have too little in the way of insect life, nest sites, or both. Some warblers specialize to a greater degree than others in their choice of habitat: Kirtland's Warbler, for instance, nests almost entirely in young jack pine forests found in Michigan, and Golden-winged Warbler selects recently disturbed and early successional habitats, which are ephemeral and increasingly scarce in most parts of its range. Bachman's Warbler, probably extinct, was a species of southeastern swampwoods, apparently around stands of native cane; these habitats disappeared as flood regimes of many rivers were altered, although it is not known

if this was a cause of the species' disappearance. Populations of many warbler species have declined across large parts of North America as a result of clearcutting, development, and fragmentation of many types of forest. The same activities, however, have often produced local increases in species that use disturbed and regenerating habitats, such as Prairie Warbler and Common Yellowthroat. Conservationists are currently most concerned about localized species with small populations (Kirtland's, Golden-cheeked, Lucy's, Hermit, and Colima warblers) and about widespread species whose declines are well-documented and appear to be steady (Cerulean, Golden-winged, and Prothonotary warblers).

MAGNOLIA WARBLER

Cardinalidae — Cardinals, Piranga Tanagers, and Allies

Cardinals and their relatives in North America include Northern Cardinal and Pyrrhuloxia (genus *Cardinalis*), the *Piranga* tanagers, the *Passerina* buntings, the *Pheucticus* grosbeaks, and Dickcissel (genus *Spiza*). Vagrants from Mexico, Crimson-collared Grosbeak and Blue Bunting, are also recorded in Texas on occasion. All cardinalids are small to medium-sized passerines. Breeding adult males often have dazzlingly colorful plumages, while females and young birds are cryptic and plain. Northern Cardinal and Pyrrhuloxia are long-tailed, crested, slender birds with heavy, short bills. The smaller *Passerina* buntings have more sparrow-like bills and shorter tails. The large Blue Grosbeak, while now considered a *Passerina*, has a much heavier bill, closer to those of the larger, heavyset *Pheucticus* grosbeaks. Dickcissel differs from the more typical cardinalids in its plumage and breeding system. Adult male Scarlet and Western tanagers, two of the more distinctive and attractive passerines in North America, are easy to identify. Male Hepatic and Summer tanagers are sometimes confused with one another. Female tanagers are much more difficult to identify than males.

Most cardinalids inhabit weedy fields, thickets, and edge habitats for at least some time during the year; they eat seeds, insects, fruit, flowers, and buds, and most are readily attracted to feeding stations stocked with seeds. The *Pheucticus* grosbeaks nest in mature forests but can often be found in brambles during migration. Courtship among cardinalids consists of energetic singing, feeding, and some posturing on the part of males. Unusual among songbirds, female Black-headed Grosbeaks and female Northern Cardinals sing fully developed songs during the breeding season. Tanagers in the genus *Piranga* form seasonally monogamous pairs and defend territories, and females in some species sing.

Despite the monogamous mating system of birds in this group, extra-pair copulation is not uncommon. Where ranges meet, hybridization, especially between Indigo and Lazuli buntings and Rose-breasted and Black-headed grosbeaks, is common. Most cardinalids are long-distance migrants to the tropics.

NORTHERN CARDINAL

A

Accidental – A species that has appeared in a given area a very few times only and whose normal range is in another area.

Allopatric – Occupying separate, non-overlapping geographic ranges. Cf. Sympatric.

Alula – A small, feathered projection attached to a bird's wrist and extending outward along the leading edge of the wing; the alula can be moved independently and used to affect air flow over the wing during flight.

Anterior – Toward the head.

Auriculars – See Ear coverts.

Axillars – The long, innermost feathers of the underwing, covering the area where the wing joins the body. Cf. Scapulars.

B

Back – The portion of the upperparts located behind the nape and between the wings.

Barred – Having stripes across the feathers.

Basal – Toward or at the base of a structure. Cf. Distal.

Belly – The portion of the underparts between the breast and the undertail coverts.

Bib – An area of contrasting color on the chin, throat, upper breast, or all three of these.

Boreal – Northern, specifically referring to the tundra and coniferous forest habitats.

Breast – The area of the underparts between the foreneck and the belly.

Breastband – A band of contrasting color that runs across the breast.

Breeding plumage – A coat of feathers worn by an adult bird during the breeding season, usually acquired by partial spring molt, feather wear, or both; the male's breeding plumage is often more brightly colored than its winter plumage or than the adult female's breeding plumage.

Breeding range – The geographic area in which a species nests.

C

Call – A brief vocalization with a relatively simple acoustical structure, usually given year-round by both sexes. Cf. Song.

Cap – An area of contrasting color on the top of the head.

Carpal joint – See Wrist.

Casual – Occurring infrequently in a given geographic area but more often than an accidental.

Cere – A bare, fleshy area at the base of the upper mandible that surrounds the nostrils; swollen and distinctively colored in some birds.

Cheek – The side of the face.

Chin – The area immediately below the base of the lower mandible.

Collar – A band of contrasting color that runs across the foreneck, hindneck, or both.

Colonial – Nesting in groups or colonies rather than in isolated pairs.

Color morph – One of two or more distinct color types within a species, occurring independently of age, sex, or season.

Conspecific – Belonging to the same species.

Cosmopolitan – Occurring on all continents except Antarctica; worldwide.

Coverts – Small feathers that cover the bases of other, usually larger, feathers and provide a smooth, aerodynamic surface.

Crepuscular – Active at twilight.

Crest – A group of elongated feathers on the top of a bird's head.

Crissum – The undertail coverts, especially when these are distinctively colored.

Crown – The upper surface of the head, between the eyebrows.

Cryptic – Serving to conceal by camouflage, either by coloring or by form.

Culmen – The midline ridge along the top of a bird's upper mandible.

D

Dimorphic – Having two distinct forms within a population, differing in size, form, or color.

Distal – Away from the center of the body. Cf. Proximal, Basal.

Diurnal – Active during the day.

Dorsal – Pertaining to the upper surface of the body.

E

Ear coverts – Small, loose-webbed feathers on the side of the face behind and below the eye, covering the ear region.

Ear patch – An area of contrasting color on the ear coverts.

Ear tuft – A group of elongated feathers above the eyes that resemble ears; characteristic of some owl and grebe species, and the Horned Lark.

Escape – A bird that has escaped from captivity rather than arriving in an area by natural means.

Exotic – Not native to an area, and coming from outside North America.

Eyebrow – A stripe on the side of the head immediately above the eye.

Eyeline – A straight, thin, horizontal stripe on the side of the face, running through the eye.

Eye plate – A small, horny plate adjacent to the eye.

Eye ring – A fleshy or feathered ring around the eye, often distinctively colored.

Eyestripe – A stripe that runs horizontally from the base of the bill through the eye; usually broader than an eyeline.

F

Face – The front of the head, generally including the cheeks, forehead, and lores, and sometimes the chin or crown.

Facial disk – The feathers that encircle the eyes of some birds, especially owls.

Facial frame – A color pattern that borders or encircles the face, as in many owls.

Field mark – A characteristic of color, pattern, or structure useful in identifying a species in the field.

Filoplume – A hair-like or bristle-like feather that consists of a shaft, few side branches, and no vanes.

Flank – The rear portion of the side of a bird's body.

Flight feathers – The long, firm feathers of the wings and tail used during flight. The flight feathers of the wings are the primaries, secondaries, and tertials; those of the tail are called rectrices.

Forecrown – The portion of the crown just behind the forehead.

Forehead – The area of the head just above the base of the upper mandible.

Foreneck – The front or underside of the neck.

Frontal shield – A fleshy, featherless, and often brightly colored area on the forehead.

G

Gape – The angle between the upper and lower mandibles when the bill is open; the opening between the upper and lower mandibles.

Gonys – The prominent midline ridge along the lower surface of the lower mandible.

Gorget – In hummingbirds, a throat patch composed of iridescent feathers.

Greater wing coverts – A row of short feathers that covers the bases of the secondaries; also called greater secondary coverts.

H

Hallux – The innermost toe of a bird's foot; it usually extends backward, is sometimes reduced or absent, and sometimes raised above the level of other toes.

Hindcrown – The rear portion of the crown.

Hindneck – The rear or upper surface of the neck; the nape.

Hind toe – See Hallux.

Hood – A distinctively colored area usually covering most or all of the head.

Hybrid – The offspring of a pair made up of two different species. In certain cases (e.g., Brewster's and Lawrence's warblers), hybrids may have their own names.

I

Immature – A bird that has not yet begun to breed, and often has not yet acquired adult plumage.

Inner wing – The part of the wing between the body and the wrist.

Introduced – Established by humans in an area outside the natural range.

Irruption – A large-scale movement into an area by a species that does not regularly occur there.

J

Juvenal plumage – The first covering of true feathers, usually of a somewhat looser texture than later plumages; the juvenal plumage, often brown and streaked, is usually replaced during the bird's first summer or fall.

Juvenile – A bird in juvenal plumage.

L

Lateral – Toward or at the side of the body.

Leading edge – The forward edge of the wing, composed of the lesser coverts, the alula, and the edge of the outermost primary; in flight, the surface that first meets the air.

Lesser wing coverts – The short feathers on the shoulder of the wing that are arranged in several irregular rows and cover the base of the median wing coverts.

Local – Of restricted occurrence within a larger, discontinuous range; birds with local distributions are often dependent on some uncommon habitat type.

Lore – The area between the eye and the base of the bill; sometimes distinctively colored.

Lower mandible – The lower of the two parts of a bird's bill.

M

Malar streak – See Mustache.

Mantle – The upper back and occasionally the scapulars and upperwing coverts when these are the same color as the upper back.

Mask – An area of contrasting color on the front of the face and around the eyes.

Maxilla – See Upper mandible.

Median – Situated in the middle or on the central axis.

Median crown stripe – A stripe of contrasting color along the center of the crown.

Median wing coverts – The row of short feathers that covers the bases of the greater wing coverts.

Melanistic – Having an excess of black pigment; melanistic birds are usually rare, but certain species have a high percentage of dark-morph individuals. See Color morph.

Migrant – A bird in the process of migrating between its breeding area and its winter range.

Migration – A regular, periodic movement between two regions, usually a breeding area and a wintering area.

Mirror – A translucent area on the extended wing of some birds, usually at the base of the primaries; in gulls, small white spots at or near the tips of the dark primaries.

Molt – The periodic loss and replacement of feathers; most species have regular patterns and schedules of molt.

Morph – See Color morph.

Morphology – The form and structure of an animal or plant.

Mustache – A colored streak running from the base of the bill back along the side of the throat.

N

Nape – The back of the head, including the hindneck.

Nares – The external nostrils; usually located near the base of the upper mandible; singular, naris.

Necklace – A band of spots or streaks across the breast or around the neck.

Neck ruff – Feathers of the neck that are enlarged or otherwise modified for display.

Nocturnal – Active during the night.

O

Outer wing – The part of the wing between the wrist and the tip.

GLOSSARY

P

Patagium – A membrane extending from the body to the wrist along the front of the wing, supporting many of the wing coverts.

Pectinate – Having short, narrow projections, like those of a comb.

Pelagic – Of or inhabiting the open ocean.

Permanent resident – A bird that remains in one area throughout the year; nonmigratory.

Phase – See Color morph.

Pinnae – See Ear tuft.

Plumage – Generally, the feathers worn by a bird at any given time. Specifically, all the feathers grown during a single molt; in this sense, a bird may have elements of more than one plumage at a time.

Plume – An elongated, ornamental feather, often used in displays.

Polyandrous – Mating with more than one male.

Polymorphic – Having two or more distinct types within a population, usually differing in size, form, or color.

Posterior – Toward the tail.

Postocular stripe – A stripe extending back from the eye, above the ear coverts and below the eyebrow.

Preen – To clean and smooth the plumage with the bill.

Primaries – The outermost and longest flight feathers on a bird's wing, forming the wing tip and part of the outer trailing edge; there are usually nine to twelve primaries on each wing, attached to the wing distal to the wrist.

Primary coverts – The small feathers of the wing that overlie the bases of the primaries.

Proximal – Toward the body. Cf. Distal.

R

Race – See Subspecies.

Rectrices – The long flight feathers of the tail; singular, rectrix.

Resident – Remaining in one place all year; nonmigratory.

Riparian – Pertaining to the banks of streams, rivers, ponds, lakes, or moist bottomlands.

Rump – The lower back just above the tail; may also include the uppertail coverts.

S

Scaly – Finely barred; the bars often formed by feather edgings of a different color.

Scapulars – The feathers of the upperparts at the side of the back that cover the area where the wing joins the body.

Secondaries – The large flight feathers of the inner wing, attached to the inner wing proximal to the wrist.

Sexual dimorphism – A difference between the sexes in size, form, or color.

Shaft – The stiff central axis of a feather.

Shoulder – The bend of the wing, or wrist, including the lesser wing coverts.

Side – The lateral part of the breast and belly.

Song – A specific and often complex pattern of notes, usually given only by the male during the breeding season. Cf. Call.

Spatulate – Spoon-shaped or shovel-shaped.

Spectacles – A color pattern formed by the lores and eye rings.

Spishing – A squeaking or swishing noise made by some bird watchers to attract birds into view.

Stray – A migrant found outside of its normal range.

Streaked – Having a pattern of vertical or longitudinal stripes, as opposed to horizontal bars; often formed by feather shafts that contrast with the rest of the feathers.

Subadult – A bird that has not yet acquired adult plumage.

Subspecies – A geographical subdivision of a species differing from other subdivisions in size, form, color, song, or several of these in combination; also called a race.

Subterminal – Before or short of the end or tip.

Summer resident – A bird that remains in an area during the summer but winters elsewhere.

Sympatric – Having overlapping ranges. Cf. Allopatric.

T

Talon – One of the long, sharp, curved claws of a bird of prey.

Tarsus – The lower, usually featherless, part of a bird's leg, often called simply the "leg."

Terminal – At the end or tip.

Territory – An area defended against other members of the same species, and usually containing a nest or food resource or both.

Tertials – The innermost secondaries (usually three), often with a different shape, pattern, and molt schedule from the other secondaries, and sometimes considered distinct from them; also called tertiaries.

Throat – The area of the underparts between the chin and the breast.

Trailing edge – The posterior edge of the extended wing, consisting of the tips of the primaries and secondaries.

Transient – A bird that occurs at a location only during migration between its winter and breeding ranges.

U

Underparts – The lower surface of the body, including the chin, throat, breast, belly, sides and flanks, and undertail coverts, and sometimes including the underwing surface and the under surface of the tail.

Undertail coverts – The small feathers that lie beneath and cover the bases of the tail feathers; sometimes referred to as the crissum.

Upper mandible – The uppermost of the two parts of a bird's bill; also called the maxilla.

Upperparts – The upper surface of the body, including the crown, nape, back, scapulars, rump, and uppertail coverts, and sometimes including the upperwing surface and the upper surface of the tail.

Uppertail coverts – The small feathers that lie over the bases of the tail feathers.

V

Vagrant – A bird occurring outside of its normal range, usually during or following migration.

Vane – One of the two broad, thin, flexible portions of a feather, separated by the shaft and composed of a row of barbs that are connected along the shaft; also called a web.

Ventral – Pertaining to the lower surface of the body.

Vermiculated – Marked by fine lines.

W

Web – The fleshy membrane that unites the toes of some water birds. See also Vane.

Window – A translucent area on the wing of certain birds that is visible from below on a bird in flight.

Wing bar – A stripe or bar of contrasting color on the upper surface of the wing, formed by the tips of one of the rows of wing coverts.

Wing lining – A collective term for the coverts of the underwing.

Wing stripe – A conspicuous lengthwise stripe on the upper surface of the extended wing, often formed by the pale bases of the primaries and secondaries.

Winter plumage – The plumage worn by a bird during the non-breeding season; often duller than the breeding plumage and usually acquired by a complete molt in the fall.

Winter range – The geographic area occupied by a species during the winter or nonbreeding season.

Wrist – The forward-projecting angle or bend of the wing; also called the carpal joint.

This glossary was prepared by Peter F. Cannell.

PHOTOGRAPHY CREDITS

Photography credits for each page are listed in top to bottom and left to right order.

VIREO (Visual Resources for Ornithology) is the fore-most global collection of bird photographs taxonomically curated at the Academy of Natural Sciences of Drexel University.

4: © Bob Steele/VIREO; © Glenn Bartley/VIREO.

5: © Brian E. Small/VIREO.

6: © Brian E. Small/VIREO; © Garth McElroy/VIREO.

7: © Glenn Bartley/VIREO; © Johann Schumacher/VIREO.

8: © Robert Goodell/VIREO; © Laure W. Neish/VIREO.

9: © Dustin Huntington/VIREO.

10: © Joe Fuhrman/VIREO; © Jari Peltomaki/VIREO.

11: © Bob de Lange/VIREO.

12: U.S. Fish and Wildlife Service.

13: © Glenn Bartley/VIREO.

14: © Rolf Nussbaumer/VIREO.

15: © Rick and Nora Bowers/VIREO; © Rob Curtis/VIREO.

16: © Joe Fuhrman/VIREO.

17: © Paul Bannick/VIREO.

18: © Brian E. Small/VIREO.

19: © Greg Lasley/VIREO; © Kevin Schafer/VIREO.

20: © Brian E. Small/VIREO.

21: © Rob Curtis/VIREO.

22: © Glenn Bartley/VIREO; © Rick and Nora Bowers/VIREO.

24: © Arthur Morris/VIREO.

25: © Joe Fuhrman/VIREO.

26: © Glenn Bartley/VIREO; © Arthur Morris/VIREO.

27: © Rob Curtis/VIREO.

28: © Glenn Bartley/VIREO.

29: © Rob Curtis/VIREO.

30: Charles J. Sharp, Sharp Photography; © Joe Fuhrman/VIREO; Carly & Art; © Joe Fuhrman/VIREO; © Dr. Joseph Turner/VIREO.

31: Dick Daniels; © Glenn Bartley/VIREO; nnc.banzai; © Tom Friedel/VIREO; jerryoldenettel.

32: U.S. Fish and Wildlife Service Headquarters; D. Dewhurst - National Digital Library of the U.S. Fish and Wildlife Service; U.S. Fish and Wildlife Service; Andy Roberts; Tim Bowman, U.S. Fish and Wildlife Service.

33: © Jukka Jantunen/VIREO; © Arthur Morris/VIREO; © Arthur Morris/VIREO.

34: © Brian E. Small/VIREO; © Rob Curtis/VIREO; © Arthur Morris/VIREO; © Rob Curtis/VIREO; © Kevin Smith/VIREO.

35: © Jukka Jantunen/VIREO; © Brian E. Small/VIREO.

36: © Jens Eriksen/VIREO; © Jens Eriksen/VIREO; © Jens Eriksen/VIREO; © Steve Young/VIREO.

37: © Johann Schumacher/VIREO; © Joe Fuhrman/VIREO.

38: Andreas Weith; © Jari Peltomaki/VIREO; © Dustin Huntington/VIREO.

39: Dominic Sherony.

40: © Rob Curtis/VIREO; © Laure W. Neish/VIREO.

41: © Steve Young/VIREO; © John Cancalosi/VIREO; © John Cancalosi/VIREO; © Doug Wechsler/VIREO.

42: © Jukka Jantunen/VIREO; © Glenn Bartley/VIREO; © Rob Curtis/VIREO.

43: © Jim Culbertson/VIREO; © Gerrit Vyn/VIREO; © Peter LaTourrette/VIREO.

44: © Arthur Morris/VIREO; © Jari Peltomaki/VIREO; © David Tipling/VIREO; © Arthur Morris/VIREO; © Jens Eriksen/VIREO.

45: © Glenn Bartley/VIREO; © Joe Fuhrman/VIREO; © Nate and Angie Chappell/VIREO; © Joe Fuhrman/VIREO.

46: © Rob Curtis/VIREO; © Rob Curtis/VIREO; © Rob Curtis/VIREO; © Arthur Morris/VIREO; © Rob Curtis/VIREO.

47: © Flights of Fancy Adventures, Inc./VIREO; © Harold Stiver/VIREO; © Harold Stiver/VIREO; Pallav Pranjal Baikal; Dick Daniels.

48: © Jari Peltomaki/VIREO; Frankie Chu; Stefan Berndtsson; © Jari Peltomaki/VIREO.

49: Dominic Sherony; © Laure W. Neish/VIREO; © Rob Curtis/VIREO.

50: © Joe Fuhrman/VIREO; © Rob Curtis/VIREO; © Joe Fuhrman/VIREO; © Peter LaTourrette/VIREO.

51: © Martin Hale/VIREO; © Johann Schumacher/VIREO; Judy Gallagher; © Rob Curtis/VIREO; © Johann Schumacher/VIREO.

52: © Greg Lasley/VIREO; © David Tipling/VIREO; Becky Matsubara; © Rob Curtis/VIREO; © Joe Fuhrman/VIREO.

53: Francis C. Franklin; © Harold Stiver/VIREO; © Harold Stiver/VIREO.

54: Imran Shah; © Jari Peltomaki/VIREO; © Julian R. Hough/VIREO; © Jari Peltomaki/VIREO.

55: © Nate and Angie Chappell/VIREO; © Glenn Bartley/VIREO; © Rick and Nora Bowers/VIREO; © Arthur Morris/VIREO; © Arthur Morris/VIREO.

56: Laitche; Kuribo; Francesco Veronesi; Dick Daniels.

57: © Johann Schumacher/VIREO; © Danny Brown/VIREO; © Marcus Robertson/VIREO; © Rob Curtis/VIREO; © John Verm Sherman/VIREO.

58: © G. Schneider/VIREO; © Harold Stiver/VIREO; © Glenn Bartley/VIREO; © Marvin R. Hyett, M.D./VIREO; © Jukka Jantunen/VIREO.

59: © Adrian & Jane Binns/VIREO; © Tom Friedel/VIREO; © Brian E. Small/VIREO; © Greg Lasley/VIREO.

60: © Nate and Angie Chappell/VIREO; Dominik Hofer; © Glenn Bartley/VIREO; jerryoldenettel; © Steve Mlodinow/VIREO; © Claude Nadeau/VIREO; © Harold Stiver/VIREO.

61: © Arthur Morris/VIREO; © Jukka Jantunen/VIREO; © Glenn Bartley/VIREO; © Glenn Bartley/VIREO.

62: © Arthur Morris/VIREO; © David Tipling/VIREO; © Arthur Morris/VIREO; © Lee Trott/VIREO.

63: © Geoff Malosh/VIREO; © Rob Curtis/VIREO; © Joe Fuhrman/VIREO; © Glenn Bartley/VIREO; © Rob Curtis/VIREO.

64: © Rob Curtis/VIREO; © Rick and Nora Bowers/VIREO; © Rob Curtis/VIREO; © Rob Curtis/VIREO.

65: © Geoff Malosh/VIREO; © Fred Truslow/VIREO; © Tom Vezo/VIREO; © Arthur Morris/VIREO; © Nate and Angie Chappell/VIREO; © Rob Curtis/VIREO.

66: © Martin Hale/VIREO; © Peter LaTourrette/VIREO; © Steve Young/VIREO; © Jari Peltomaki/VIREO; © Glenn Bartley/VIREO.

67: © Garth McElroy/VIREO; © Blake Shaw/VIREO; © Richard Crossley/VIREO; © Joe Fuhrman/VIREO.

68: © Arthur Morris/VIREO; © Glenn Bartley/VIREO; © Glenn Bartley/VIREO.

69: © Jari Peltomaki/VIREO; © Jari Peltomaki/VIREO; © Joe Fuhrman/VIREO; © Jari Peltomaki/VIREO; © Jari Peltomaki/VIREO.

70: © Brian E. Small/VIREO; © Brian E. Small/VIREO; © B. Gadsby/VIREO; © Brian E. Small/VIREO.

71: © Joe Fuhrman/VIREO; © Jari Peltomaki/VIREO; © Joe Fuhrman/VIREO.

72: © Glenn Bartley/VIREO; © Barry Miller/VIREO; © Glenn Bartley/VIREO; © John Cancalosi/VIREO.

73: © Joe Fuhrman/VIREO; © Glenn Bartley/VIREO; © Johann Schumacher/VIREO; © Richard Crossley/VIREO; © Johann Schumacher/VIREO.

74: © Claude Nadeau/VIREO; © Richard Crossley/VIREO; © Jukka Jantunen/VIREO; © Richard Crossley/VIREO; © Greg Lasley/VIREO.

75: © Jukka Jantunen/VIREO; © Harold Stiver/VIREO.

76: © Richard Crossley/VIREO; © George L. Armistead/VIREO; © Richard Crossley/VIREO; © Glenn Bartley/VIREO.

77: © Jari Peltomaki/VIREO; © Jari Peltomaki/VIREO; © Joe Fuhrman/VIREO; © Jari Peltomaki/VIREO; © Jari Peltomaki/VIREO.

78: © Laure W. Neish/VIREO; © Jukka Jantunen/VIREO; © Glenn Bartley/VIREO; © Laure W. Neish/VIREO.

79: © Glenn Bartley/VIREO; © Rob Curtis/VIREO; © Claude Nadeau/VIREO.

80: © Peter LaTourrette/VIREO; © Laure W. Neish/VIREO; © Laure W. Neish/VIREO; © Laure W. Neish/VIREO.

81: Dick Daniels; Keven Law; © Bob de Lange/VIREO; Dick Daniels; © Jari Peltomaki/VIREO.

82: © Glenn Bartley/VIREO; © Rob Curtis/VIREO; © Garth McElroy/VIREO.

83: © Laure W. Neish/VIREO; © Rob Curtis/VIREO; © Danny Brown/VIREO; © Arthur Morris/VIREO.

84: © Brian E. Small/VIREO; © Rob Curtis/VIREO; © Rob Curtis/VIREO; © Rob Curtis/VIREO; © Rob Curtis/VIREO.

85: © Tom Vezo/VIREO; Felix Uribe; © Dr. Robert Ridgely/VIREO; Felix Uribe.

86: © Glenn Bartley/VIREO; © Greg Lasley/VIREO; © Arthur Morris/VIREO; © Arthur Morris/VIREO.

87: © Steven Holt/VIREO; © Arthur Morris/VIREO; © Rick and Nora Bowers/VIREO; © Joe Fuhrman/VIREO; © Brian E. Small/VIREO.

88: © Garth McElroy/VIREO; © Arthur Morris/VIREO; © Joe Fuhrman/VIREO.

89: © Greg Lasley/VIREO; © Nate and Angie Chappell/VIREO; © Nate and Angie Chappell/VIREO.

90: © Greg Lasley/VIREO; © Patricio Robles Gil/VIREO; © Greg Lasley/VIREO; © Tom Vezo/VIREO.

91: © Laure W. Neish/VIREO; © Laure W. Neish/VIREO; © Laure W. Neish/VIREO; © Brian E. Small/VIREO; © Mathew Tekulsky/VIREO; © Laure W. Neish/VIREO.

92: © Rick and Nora Bowers/VIREO; © Greg Lasley/VIREO; © Greg Lasley/VIREO; © Nate and Angie Chappell/VIREO; © Rolf Nussbaumer/VIREO.

93: Alan Schmierer; © Brian E. Small/VIREO; © Dale Zimmerman/VIREO; Alan Schmierer; © Brian E. Small/VIREO.

94: Imran Shah; © Arthur Morris/VIREO; © Laure W. Neish/VIREO; © Glenn Bartley/VIREO.

95: Shashank Shekhar; Quartl; Koshy Koshy.

96: Imran Shah; © James D. Bland/VIREO; Oivin F Madsen.

97: © Jari Peltomaki/VIREO; © Jari Peltomaki/VIREO; © Bob de Lange/VIREO.

98: © Laura C. Williams/VIREO; © Steven Holt/VIREO; © Rick and Nora Bowers/VIREO; © Kevin Smith/VIREO; © David Tipling/VIREO.

99: © Rick and Nora Bowers/VIREO; © Glenn Bartley/VIREO.

100: © Bob Steele/VIREO; © Bob Steele/VIREO; Christian Hagenlocher; © Nate and Angie Chappell/VIREO.

101: Alan Schmierer; © Lance Beeny/VIREO.

102: © Steven Holt/VIREO; © Jukka Jantunen/VIREO; © Kevin Schafer/VIREO.

103: © Tom Vezo/VIREO; © Claude Nadeau/VIREO; © David Tipling/VIREO; © David Tipling/VIREO; © Glenn Bartley/VIREO; © Glenn Bartley/VIREO.

104: © Jari Peltomaki/VIREO; © Brian E. Small/VIREO; © Brian E. Small/VIREO; © Glenn Bartley/VIREO; © Jukka Jantunen/VIREO.

105: © Adrian & Jane Binns/VIREO; © Paul Bannick/VIREO; © Bob Steele/VIREO; © Joe Fuhrman/VIREO; © Bob Steele/VIREO.

106: © Laure W. Neish/VIREO; © Laure W. Neish/VIREO; Paul Asman and Jill Lenoble; © Brian E. Small/VIREO.

107: © Glenn Bartley/VIREO; © Glenn Bartley/VIREO; © Bob de Lange/VIREO; © Greg Lasley/VIREO; © Bob Steele/VIREO.

108: Rick Bohn Sharp; © John Cancalosi/VIREO; Alan Schmierer; © Glenn Bartley/VIREO.

109: © Greg Lasley/VIREO; © Greg Lasley/VIREO; © Adrian & Jane Binns/VIREO; © Greg Lasley/VIREO.

110: © Dustin Huntington/VIREO; © Brian E. Small/VIREO; © Rick and Nora Bowers/VIREO; © Brian E. Small/VIREO.

111: © Andy Papadatos/VIREO; Andy Reago & Chrissy McClarren; © Arthur Morris/VIREO; © Greg Lasley/VIREO.

112: © Patricio Robles Gil/VIREO; Andrea Westmoreland; Robert Claypool; © Claude Nadeau/VIREO.

113: © Joe Fuhrman/VIREO; © Joe Fuhrman/VIREO; © Greg Lasley/VIREO; © Rolf Nussbaumer/VIREO; © Greg Lasley/VIREO.

114: © Nate and Angie Chappell/VIREO; © Rob Curtis/VIREO; © Arthur Morris/VIREO.

115: © Glenn Bartley/VIREO; © Glenn Bartley/VIREO; © Greg Lasley/VIREO; © Laure W. Neish/VIREO.

116: © Glenn Bartley/VIREO; © Arthur Morris/VIREO; © Laure W. Neish/VIREO; © Laure W. Neish/VIREO; © Jukka Jantunen/VIREO.

117: © Bob de Lange/VIREO; © Greg Lasley/VIREO; © Glenn Bartley/VIREO; © Laure W. Neish/VIREO.

118: © Laure W. Neish/VIREO; © Joe Fuhrman/VIREO; © Brian E. Small/VIREO; © Arthur Morris/VIREO; © Rob Curtis/VIREO.

119: © Blake Shaw/VIREO; © Joe Fuhrman/VIREO; © Rob Curtis/VIREO; U.S. Fish and Wildlife Service Headquarters.

120: © Laure W. Neish/VIREO; © Claude Nadeau/VIREO; © Claude Nadeau/VIREO.

121: © Paula Cannon/VIREO; © Paula Cannon/VIREO; © Paula Cannon/VIREO; © Paula Cannon/VIREO; © Paula Cannon/VIREO.

122: © Joe Fuhrman/VIREO; © Rick and Nora Bowers/VIREO; © Rick and Nora Bowers/VIREO; © Glenn Bartley/VIREO.

123: © Joe Fuhrman/VIREO; © Dale Zimmerman/VIREO; Becky Matsubara; © Hugh P. Smith, Jr. & Susan C. Smith/VIREO; Becky Matsubara.

124: © Martin Hale/VIREO; Mike Prince; © Martin Hale/VIREO; Lip Kee Yap; © John Grahame Holmes/VIREO.

125: © Greg Lasley/VIREO; © Jens Eriksen/VIREO; © Jens Eriksen/VIREO; © Jari Peltomaki/VIREO.

126: David Vraju; Charles J Sharp; Dr. Raju Kasambe; Manoj K; Mike Prince; Nrik Kiran.

127: © Greg Lasley/VIREO; © Barth Schorre/VIREO; © George M. Jett/VIREO; © Greg Lasley/VIREO.

128: © Joe Fuhrman/VIREO; © Nate and Angie Chappell/VIREO; © John Cancalosi/VIREO; © John Dunning/VIREO.

129: © Joe Fuhrman/VIREO; © Tom Friedel/VIREO.

130: © John Dunning/VIREO; Félix Uribe; © Doug Wechsler/VIREO.

131: © Doug Wechsler/VIREO; © Doug Wechsler/VIREO; Charles J Sharp.

132: © Greg Lasley/VIREO; Tony Castro; © Greg Lasley/VIREO; © Greg Lasley/VIREO; © Nate and Angie Chappell/VIREO.

133: © Adrian & Jane Binns/VIREO; © Nate and Angie Chappell/VIREO; © Brian E. Small/VIREO; © Tom Vezo/VIREO; © Arthur Morris/VIREO.

134: © Doug Wechsler/VIREO; Gail Hampshire; © Doug Wechsler/VIREO.

135: © Alan & Sandy Carey/VIREO; © Rick and Nora Bowers/VIREO; © Rob Curtis/VIREO; © Laure W. Neish/VIREO.

136: © Marvin R. Hyett, M.D./VIREO; © Paula Cannon/VIREO; © Glenn Bartley/VIREO; © Bill Gozansky/VIREO.

137: © Rick and Nora Bowers/VIREO; © Tom Friedel/VIREO; © Rick and Nora Bowers/VIREO; © Rick and Nora Bowers/VIREO.

138: © Tom Vezo/VIREO; © Laure W. Neish/VIREO; Rolf Dietrich; Jessie Eastland.

139: © Steve Young/VIREO; © Jari Peltomaki/VIREO; © Jari Peltomaki/VIREO.

140: © Brian E. Small/VIREO; © Glenn Bartley/VIREO; © Doug Wechsler/VIREO; © Richard & Susan Day/VIREO; © Joe Fuhrman/VIREO.

141: © Manuel Grosselet/VIREO; © George L. Armistead/VIREO; Gail Hamshire; © Marvin R. Hyett, M.D./VIREO.

142: © Tom J. Ulrich/VIREO; Dominic Sheroni; Wolfgang Wander; Bettina Arrigoni.

143: © Glenn Bartley/VIREO; © Rolf Nussbaumer/VIREO; © Brian E. Small/VIREO; © Rob Curtis/VIREO; © Joe Fuhrman/VIREO.

144: © Nate and Angie Chappell/VIREO; © Paul Bannick/VIREO; © Rob Curtis/VIREO; © Glenn Bartley/VIREO; © Rob Curtis/VIREO.

145: © Michael P. Gage/VIREO; © Paula Cannon/VIREO; © Paula Cannon/VIREO.

146: Danita Delmont; Andy Morffew; Andy Morffew.

147: Rolf Nussbaumer; Rachel Portwood; Rachel Portwood.

148: © Rob & Ann Simpson/VIREO; © Dr. Joseph Turner/VIREO; Dick Daniels.

149: © Rick and Nora Bowers/VIREO; © Rick and Nora Bowers/VIREO; © Rick and Nora Bowers/VIREO.

150: Frode Jacobsen; © Rob Curtis/VIREO; Farjana Run Nesa.

151: © Glenn Bartley/VIREO; © Rick and Nora Bowers/VIREO; © Rick and Nora Bowers/VIREO; © Glenn Bartley/VIREO.

152: © Manuel Marin/VIREO; © Steve Mlodinow/VIREO; © Steve Mlodinow/VIREO.

153: © Jesper Bay Jacobsen/VIREO; © Tom Friedel/VIREO; © Tom Friedel/VIREO.

154: © Rob Curtis/VIREO; © George L. Armistead/VIREO; © Rob Curtis/VIREO; © Rob Curtis/VIREO.

155: Annette Teng; © Glenn Bartley/VIREO; © Laure W. Neish/VIREO.

156: © Glenn Bartley/VIREO; © Glenn Bartley/VIREO; © Glenn Bartley/VIREO.

157: © Robert Goodell/VIREO; © Glenn Bartley/VIREO; © Tom Friedel/VIREO; © Glenn Bartley/VIREO; © Greg Lasley/VIREO.

158: © Glenn Bartley/VIREO; © Glenn Bartley/VIREO; © Marvin R. Hyett, M.D./VIREO; © Glenn Bartley/VIREO; © Glenn Bartley/VIREO.

159: © Rick and Nora Bowers/VIREO; © Rick and Nora Bowers/VIREO; Alan Schmierer; © Glenn Bartley/VIREO.

160: © Jesper Bay Jacobsen/VIREO.

161: © Rick and Nora Bowers/VIREO; © Sid & Shirley Rucker/VIREO; © Arthur Morris/VIREO; © Rick and Nora Bowers/VIREO.

162: © Rick and Nora Bowers/VIREO; © Rick and Nora Bowers/VIREO; © John Hoffman/VIREO; © Rick and Nora Bowers/VIREO.

163: © Richard & Susan Day/VIREO; © Glenn Bartley/VIREO; © Rob Curtis/VIREO; © Rob Curtis/VIREO; © Garth McElroy/VIREO.

164: © Rolf Nussbaumer/VIREO; © Brian E. Small/VIREO; © Greg Lasley/VIREO; © Rick and Nora Bowers/VIREO.

165: Matt MacGillivray; © John Henry Dick/VIREO; New Jersey Birds/Calliphlox Evelynae.

166: © Glenn Bartley/VIREO; © Paul Bannick/VIREO; © Joe Fuhrman/VIREO; © Glenn Bartley/VIREO.

167: © Greg Lasley/VIREO; © Rolf Nussbaumer/VIREO; © Laure W. Neish/VIREO; © Rick and Nora Bowers/VIREO.

168: © Dale Zimmerman/VIREO; © Joe Fuhrman/VIREO; © Joe Fuhrman/VIREO; © Rick and Nora Bowers/VIREO; © Dale Zimmerman/VIREO.

169: © Sid & Shirley Rucker/VIREO; © Greg Lasley/VIREO; © Greg Lasley/VIREO.

170: © Joe Fuhrman/VIREO; © Glenn Bartley/VIREO; © Laure W. Neish/VIREO; © Greg Lasley/VIREO; © Laure W. Neish/VIREO.

171: © Dr. Joseph Turner/VIREO; © Brian E. Small/VIREO; © Joe Fuhrman/VIREO; © Joe Fuhrman/VIREO.

172: © Rick and Nora Bowers/VIREO; © Laure W. Neish/VIREO; © Laure W. Neish/VIREO; © Glenn Bartley/VIREO; © Dr. Joseph Turner/VIREO.

173: © Glenn Bartley/VIREO; © Glenn Bartley/VIREO; © Rolf Nussbaumer/VIREO; © Manuel Grosselet/VIREO; © Sid & Shirley Rucker/VIREO.

174: © Jesper Bay Jacobsen/VIREO; © Rick and Nora Bowers/VIREO; Amado Demesa.

175: © Jim Culbertson/VIREO; © Flights of Fancy Adventures, Inc./VIREO; © Greg Lasley/VIREO; © Sid & Shirley Rucker/VIREO; © Dr. Joseph Turner/VIREO.

176: © Marvin R. Hyett, M.D./VIREO; Amado Demesa; © Brian E. Small/VIREO; © Bob Steele/VIREO.

177: © Rick and Nora Bowers/VIREO; © Rick and Nora Bowers/VIREO; © Brian E. Small/VIREO; © Herbert Clarke/VIREO.

178: © Joe Fuhrman/VIREO; © Steve Mlodinow/VIREO; © Steve Mlodinow/VIREO; © Laure W. Neish/VIREO.

179: © Matt White/VIREO; © Rick and Nora Bowers/VIREO; © Richard Day/VIREO.

180: U.S. Fish and Wildlife; © Brian E. Small/VIREO; © Brian E. Small/VIREO.

181: © David Tipling/VIREO; Ron Knight; © Jari Peltomaki/VIREO.

182: Mike's Birds; Mike's Birds; Mike's Birds; Mike's Birds; Mike's Birds.

183: © Doug Wechsler/VIREO; © Doug Wechsler/VIREO; © Arthur Morris/VIREO; © Joe Fuhrman/VIREO; © Fred Truslow/VIREO.

184: © Greg Lasley/VIREO; © Brian E. Small/VIREO; © Rick and Nora Bowers/VIREO; © Brian E. Small/VIREO.

185: © Rick and Nora Bowers/VIREO; © Rob Curtis/VIREO; © Bob Steele/VIREO; © Rob Curtis/VIREO; © Geoff Malosh/VIREO.

186: © Rick and Nora Bowers/VIREO; © Rob Curtis/VIREO; © Rob Curtis/VIREO.

187: © Arthur Morris/VIREO; © Rick and Nora Bowers/VIREO; © Joe Fuhrman/VIREO; © Richard Crossley/VIREO; © Arthur Morris/VIREO.

188: Pavel Kirillov; U.S. Fish and Wildlife Service; Dario Sanches; Hans Hillewaert.

189: © Greg Lasley/VIREO; © Jukka Jantunen/VIREO; © Arthur Morris/VIREO; © Rob Curtis/VIREO; © Greg Lasley/VIREO.

190: © Arthur Morris/VIREO; © Arthur Morris/VIREO; © Tom Friedel/VIREO.

191: © Tom Vezo/VIREO; © Arthur Morris/VIREO; © Arthur Morris/VIREO; © Arthur Morris/VIREO.

192: © Jorge Sierra/VIREO; © David Tipling/VIREO; © Rob Curtis/VIREO; © Jorge Sierra/VIREO; © Jorge Sierra/VIREO.

193: © Kevin Smith/VIREO; © Joanne Williams/VIREO; © Joanne Williams/VIREO; © Arthur Morris/VIREO; © Rob Curtis/VIREO.

194: © Richard Crossley/VIREO; © Claude Nadeau/VIREO; © Greg Lasley/VIREO.

195: © Glenn Bartley/VIREO; © Arthur Morris/VIREO; © Arthur Morris/VIREO; © Joe Fuhrman/VIREO.

196: © Lloyd Spitalnik/VIREO; © Johann Schumacher/VIREO; © Richard Crossley/VIREO; © Johann Schumacher/VIREO; © Doug Wechsler/VIREO.

197: © Martin Meyers/VIREO; © Arthur Morris/VIREO; © Rick and Nora Bowers/VIREO; © Glenn Bartley/VIREO.

198: © David Tipling/VIREO; © John Cancalosi/VIREO; © David Tipling/VIREO; © David Tipling/VIREO.

199: © Richard Crossley/VIREO; © Arthur Morris/VIREO; © Glenn Bartley/VIREO; © Richard Crossley/VIREO.

200: © Arthur Morris/VIREO; © Glenn Bartley/VIREO; © Richard Crossley/VIREO; © Joe Fuhrman/VIREO.

201: © John Grahame Holmes/VIREO; © Martin Meyers/VIREO; © Arthur Morris/VIREO; © Arthur Morris/VIREO.

202: © Jari Peltomaki/VIREO; © David Tipling/VIREO; Frank Vassen; © Jens Eriksen/VIREO.

203: © Rob Curtis/VIREO; © Richard & Susan Day/VIREO; © John Cancalosi/VIREO; © Richard & Susan Day/VIREO; © Richard Crossley/VIREO.

204: © David Tipling/VIREO; © Joe Fuhrman/VIREO; © David Tipling/VIREO; © David Tipling/VIREO; © David Tipling/VIREO.

205: © Doug Wechsler/VIREO; © Doug Wechsler/VIREO; © Rob Curtis/VIREO; © Arthur Morris/VIREO; © Johann Schumacher/VIREO.

206: © Garth McElroy/VIREO; © Tom Vezo/VIREO; © Greg Lasley/VIREO; © Greg Lasley/VIREO; © Johann Schumacher/VIREO.

207: © Martin Hale/VIREO; © Jens Eriksen/VIREO; © Christian Artuso/VIREO; © K K Hui/VIREO.

208: © Richard Crossley/VIREO; © Richard Crossley/VIREO; © Greg Lasley/VIREO; © Geoff Malosh/VIREO.

209: © Bob Steele/VIREO; © John Cancalosi/VIREO; © Brian E. Small/VIREO.

210: © James M. Wedge/VIREO; © Arthur Morris/VIREO; © Arthur Morris/VIREO; © Martin Hale/VIREO.

211: © Glenn Bartley/VIREO; © Glenn Bartley/VIREO; © Brian E. Small/VIREO.

212: © Richard Crossley/VIREO; © Greg Lasley/VIREO; © George L. Armistead/VIREO; © G. Schneider/VIREO.

213: © Bob Steele/VIREO; © Mark J. Rauzon/VIREO; © Joe Fuhrman/VIREO; © Bob Steele/VIREO.

214: © Nate and Angie Chappell/VIREO; © Adrian & Jane Binns/VIREO; © Tadao Shimba/VIREO; © Geoff Malosh/VIREO.

215: © Arthur Morris/VIREO; © Arthur Morris/VIREO; © Rick and Nora Bowers/VIREO; © Arthur Morris/VIREO; © Joe Fuhrman/VIREO; © Richard Crossley/VIREO.

216: © John Grahame Holmes/VIREO; © John Grahame Holmes/VIREO; © David Tipling/VIREO; © John Grahame Holmes/VIREO; © George L. Armistead/VIREO.

217: © Geoff Malosh/VIREO; © Jari Peltomaki/VIREO; © John Grahame Holmes/VIREO; © John Grahame Holmes/VIREO.

218: © Brian Chudleigh/VIREO; © George L. Armistead/VIREO; © Bob de Lange/VIREO; © Jens Eriksen/VIREO; © David Tipling/VIREO.

219: © Geoff Malosh/VIREO; © Glenn Bartley/VIREO; © Glenn Bartley/VIREO; © Geoff Malosh/VIREO.

220: © Arthur Morris/VIREO; © Arthur Morris/VIREO; © Nate and Angie Chappell/VIREO; © Glen Tepke/VIREO; © James M. Wedge/VIREO.

221: © David Tipling/VIREO; © Glenn Bartley/VIREO; © Rob Curtis/VIREO; © Richard Crossley/VIREO.

222: © Jukka Jantunen/VIREO; © Glenn Bartley/VIREO; © Joe Fuhrman/VIREO; © Laure W. Neish/VIREO.

223: © Arthur Morris/VIREO; © Rob Curtis/VIREO; © Rob Curtis/VIREO.

224: © Kevin Smith/VIREO; © Arthur Morris/VIREO; © Martin Meyers/VIREO.

225: Alpsdake; Alpsdake; Jerzy Strzelecki; Fars News Agency; Ken Billington.

226: © Martin Hale/VIREO; © Tadao Shimba/VIREO; © John Grahame Holmes/VIREO; © John Grahame Holmes/VIREO; © Eric Skrzypczak/VIREO.

227: © Bill Gozansky/VIREO; © Glenn Bartley/VIREO; © Rob Curtis/VIREO; © Richard Crossley/VIREO; © Geoff Malosh/VIREO; © Kevin Smith/VIREO.

228: © Martin Hale/VIREO; © John Grahame Holmes/VIREO; © Dr. Warwick Tarboton/VIREO; © Martin Hale/VIREO; © John Grahame Holmes/VIREO.

229: © Jari Peltomaki/VIREO; © Amit Thakurta/VIREO; © Jari Peltomaki/VIREO; © Jari Peltomaki/VIREO; © Jari Peltomaki/VIREO.

230: © Martin Hale/VIREO; © Brian Chudleigh/VIREO; © Martin Hale/VIREO; © Martin Hale/VIREO.

231: © Richard Crossley/VIREO; © Rob Curtis/VIREO; © Joe Fuhrman/VIREO; © Rob Curtis/VIREO; © Arthur Morris/VIREO.

232: © Richard Crossley/VIREO; © Arthur Morris/VIREO; © Steve Young/VIREO; © Doug Wechsler/VIREO.

233: © Rick and Nora Bowers/VIREO; © Marvin R. Hyett, M.D./VIREO; © Steve Mlodinow/VIREO; © Steve Mlodinow/VIREO; © Steve Mlodinow/VIREO.

234: © Garth McElroy/VIREO; © Jari Peltomaki/VIREO; © David Tipling/VIREO; © Marcus Robertson/VIREO.

235: © Joe Fuhrman/VIREO; © Rob Curtis/VIREO; © Brian E. Small/VIREO.

236: © David Tipling/VIREO; © Steve Young/VIREO; © John Grahame Holmes/VIREO; © Arthur Morris/VIREO.

237: © Arthur Morris/VIREO; © Glenn Bartley/VIREO; © Rob Curtis/VIREO; © Johann Schumacher/VIREO; © Rob Curtis/VIREO; © Glenn Bartley/VIREO; © Claude Nadeau/VIREO.

238: © Garth McElroy/VIREO; © Rob Curtis/VIREO; © Richard Crossley/VIREO; © Claude Nadeau/VIREO.

239: © Brian E. Small/VIREO; © Jukka Jantunen/VIREO; © Brian E. Small/VIREO; © Rob Curtis/VIREO.

240: © Arthur Morris/VIREO; © Brian E. Small/VIREO; © Dr. Michael Stubblefield/VIREO; © Arthur Morris/VIREO.

241: © Claude Nadeau/VIREO; © Arthur Morris/VIREO; © James M. Wedge/VIREO; © Nate and Angie Chappell/VIREO.

242: © Bob Steele/VIREO; © Richard Crossley/VIREO; © Jukka Jantunen/VIREO.

243: © Richard Crossley/VIREO; © Glenn Bartley/VIREO; © Flights of Fancy Adventures, Inc./VIREO; © Arthur Morris/VIREO; © Geoff Malosh/VIREO; © Arthur Morris/VIREO.

244: © Richard Crossley/VIREO; © Richard Crossley/VIREO; © Garth McElroy/VIREO; © Rick and Nora Bowers/VIREO.

245: © Garth McElroy/VIREO; © Lloyd Spitalnik/VIREO; © Richard Crossley/VIREO.

246: © Garth McElroy/VIREO; © Robert A. "Spike" Baker/VIREO; © Nate and Angie Chappell/VIREO; © Garth McElroy/VIREO; © Laure W. Neish/VIREO.

247: © Martin Hale/VIREO; © George L. Armistead/VIREO; © John Grahame Holmes/VIREO; © John Grahame Holmes/VIREO.

248: © Jens Eriksen/VIREO; © Steve Young/VIREO; © Jari Peltomaki/VIREO; © John Grahame Holmes/VIREO; © Jens Eriksen/VIREO.

249: © Rob Curtis/VIREO; © Rob Curtis/VIREO; © Johann Schumacher/VIREO; © Rob Curtis/VIREO.

250: © Richard Crossley/VIREO; © Jukka Jantunen/VIREO; © Richard Crossley/VIREO.

251: © Tadao Shimba/VIREO; © Martin Hale/VIREO; © John Grahame Holmes/VIREO; © Tadao Shimba/VIREO.

252: © Joe Fuhrman/VIREO; © George L. Armistead/VIREO; © Glenn Bartley/VIREO.

253: © Johann Schumacher/VIREO; © Johann Schumacher/VIREO; © Johann Schumacher/VIREO; © Jukka Jantunen/VIREO.

254: © Kevin Smith/VIREO; © Flights of Fancy Adventures, Inc./VIREO; © Arthur Morris/VIREO; © Brian E. Small/VIREO.

255: © Jens Eriksen/VIREO; © David Tipling/VIREO; © Jens Eriksen/VIREO; © Jari Peltomaki/VIREO.

256: © John Grahame Holmes/VIREO; © David Tipling/VIREO; © John Grahame Holmes/VIREO; © Jari Peltomaki/VIREO; © George L. Armistead/VIREO.

257: © Johann Schumacher/VIREO; © Glenn Bartley/VIREO; © Nate and Angie Chappell/VIREO; © Geoff Malosh/VIREO.

258: © Jens Eriksen/VIREO; © Jari Peltomaki/VIREO; © Arthur Morris/VIREO; © Jari Peltomaki/VIREO.

259: © Dustin Huntington/VIREO; © Greg Lasley/VIREO; © Arthur Morris/VIREO; © Brian E. Small/VIREO.

260: © David Tipling/VIREO; © Jukka Jantunen/VIREO; © Brian E. Small/VIREO; © Geoff Malosh/VIREO; © Glenn Bartley/VIREO.

261: © Jens Eriksen/VIREO; © Arthur Morris/VIREO; © Rob Curtis/VIREO; © Brian E. Small/VIREO.

262: © Arthur Morris/VIREO; © David Tipling/VIREO; © David Tipling/VIREO; © Jens Eriksen/VIREO; © Joe Fuhrman/VIREO.

263: © Jeff Poklen/VIREO; © Arthur Morris/VIREO; © Santiago Imberti/VIREO; © Santiago Imberti/VIREO; © Santiago Imberti/VIREO.

264: © Joe Fuhrman/VIREO; © Bill Schmoker/VIREO; © Dr. Yuri Artukhin/VIREO.

265: © Glenn Bartley/VIREO; © Glenn Bartley/VIREO; © Arthur Morris/VIREO; © Arthur Morris/VIREO; © Jeff Poklen/VIREO.

266: © Joe Fuhrman/VIREO; © Joe Fuhrman/VIREO; © Arthur Morris/VIREO; © Jari Peltomaki/VIREO; © Arthur Morris/VIREO.

267: © Joe Fuhrman/VIREO; © Jens Eriksen/VIREO; © Jens Eriksen/VIREO; © Dan Roby & Karen Brink/VIREO; © Jens Eriksen/VIREO.

268: © Glenn Bartley/VIREO; © David Tipling/VIREO; © David Tipling/VIREO; © Steven Holt/VIREO; © John Cancalosi/VIREO.

269: © Arthur Morris/VIREO; © Rick and Nora Bowers/VIREO; © Jens Eriksen/VIREO; © John Grahame Holmes/VIREO.

270: © David Tipling/VIREO; © Arthur Morris/VIREO; © Joe Fuhrman/VIREO; © Rob Curtis/VIREO.

271: © Jari Peltomaki/VIREO; © David Tipling/VIREO; © Jari Peltomaki/VIREO; © Jari Peltomaki/VIREO.

272: © Glenn Bartley/VIREO; © Joe Fuhrman/VIREO; © Glenn Bartley/VIREO; © Dr. Yuri Artukhin/VIREO.

273: Richard Crossley; Richard Crossley; © Stuart Elsom/VIREO.

274: © Martin Meyers/VIREO; © Glenn Bartley/VIREO; Marin Raphael.

275: © Tim Zurowski/VIREO; © Glen Tepke/VIREO; © Robert H. Day/VIREO; © Glen Tepke/VIREO.

276: Greg Schechter; National Park Service Scripps; © Glen Tepke/VIREO; © Robert L. Pitman/VIREO.

277: David Pereksta; David Pereksta, Pacific Southwest Region U.S. Fish And Wildlife Service; © Brian E. Small/VIREO.

278: © Joe Fuhrman/VIREO; © Glen Tepke/VIREO; © Patricio Robles Gil/VIREO; © Joe Fuhrman/VIREO.

279: © Tom Middleton/VIREO; © Glenn Bartley/VIREO; © Glenn Bartley/VIREO; © Glenn Bartley/VIREO.

280: © Glen Tepke/VIREO; © Brian E. Small/VIREO; © Glen Tepke/VIREO; © Robert L. Pitman/VIREO.

281: © Martin Hale/VIREO; © Tom Vezo/VIREO; © Joe Fuhrman/VIREO; © Arthur Morris/VIREO; © Arthur Morris/VIREO.

282: © Martin Meyers/VIREO; © Mark J. Rauzon/VIREO; © Greg Lasley/VIREO; © George L. Armistead/VIREO; © Arthur Morris/VIREO.

283: © Dr. Yuri Artukhin/VIREO; © John Grahame Holmes/VIREO; © John Grahame Holmes/VIREO; © Dr. Yuri Artukhin/VIREO; © Steve Mlodinow/VIREO; © Dr. Yuri Artukhin/VIREO.

284: © John Grahame Holmes/VIREO; © Kevin Schafer/VIREO; © Kevin Schafer/VIREO; © John Grahame Holmes/VIREO; © John Grahame Holmes/VIREO; © Arthur Morris/VIREO.

285: © Glenn Bartley/VIREO; © Tom Middleton/VIREO; Dick Daniels; Dick Daniels; © George L. Armistead/VIREO.

286: © Patricio Robles Gil/VIREO; © David Tipling/VIREO; © David Tipling/VIREO; © Greg Lasley/VIREO; © David Tipling/VIREO.

287: © Mark J. Rauzon/VIREO; © Arthur Morris/VIREO; © Arthur Morris/VIREO; © Arthur Morris/VIREO.

288: © George L. Armistead/VIREO; © Arthur Morris/VIREO; © Arthur Morris/VIREO; © Arthur Morris/VIREO.

289: © Tom Vezo/VIREO; © Dr. Yuri Artukhin/VIREO; © Marvin R. Hyett, M.D./VIREO; © Martin Hale/VIREO; © Arthur Morris/VIREO; © Martin Hale/VIREO.

290: © Arthur Morris/VIREO; © Dr. Yuri Artukhin/VIREO; © David Tipling/VIREO; © Dr. Yuri Artukhin/VIREO; © Jeff Poklen/VIREO; © John Grahame Holmes/VIREO.

291: © Bob Steele/VIREO; © Geoff Malosh/VIREO; © Joe Fuhrman/VIREO; © Cindy Creighton/VIREO.

292: © Glenn Bartley/VIREO; © Bob Steele/VIREO; © Steve Young/VIREO; © Peter LaTourrette/VIREO; © Steve Young/VIREO.

293: © Arthur Morris/VIREO; © Rob Curtis/VIREO; © Greg Lasley/VIREO; © Geoff Malosh/VIREO; © Jukka Jantunen/VIREO; © Jukka Jantunen/VIREO.

294: © Claude Nadeau/VIREO; © Arthur Morris/VIREO; © David Tipling/VIREO; © Arthur Morris/VIREO; © David Tipling/VIREO.

295: © Jari Peltomaki/VIREO; © David Tipling/VIREO; © Jari Peltomaki/VIREO; © Garth McElroy/VIREO; © Steve Young/VIREO; © Steve Young/VIREO.

296: © Steve Young/VIREO; © Steve Young/VIREO; © Steve Young/VIREO; © Steve Young/VIREO; © Laure W. Neish/VIREO.

297: © Joe Fuhrman/VIREO; © Doug Wechsler/VIREO; © Doug Wechsler/VIREO; © Arthur Morris/VIREO; © Arthur Morris/VIREO.

298: © Rob Curtis/VIREO; © Martin Hale/VIREO; © Geoff Malosh/VIREO; © Rob Curtis/VIREO; © Manuel Grosselet/VIREO; © Geoff Malosh/VIREO.

299: © Claude Nadeau/VIREO; © Tom Friedel/VIREO; Mosmas Larus.

300: © Geoff Malosh/VIREO; © Geoff Malosh/VIREO; E Bamse.

301: © Jukka Jantunen/VIREO; © Jeff Poklen/VIREO; © Glenn Bartley/VIREO; © Arthur Morris/VIREO; © Glenn Bartley/VIREO; © Jeff Poklen/VIREO.

302: © Jukka Jantunen/VIREO; © Arthur Morris/VIREO; © Arthur Morris/VIREO; © Arthur Morris/VIREO; © Arthur Morris/VIREO.

PHOTOGRAPHY CREDITS

344: © Dr. Yuri Artukhin/VIREO; © Joe Fuhrman/VIREO; © Arthur Morris/VIREO; © Steve Mlodinow/VIREO; © Dr. Yuri Artukhin/VIREO; © Joe Fuhrman/VIREO.

345: © Joe Fuhrman/VIREO; © Laure W. Neish/VIREO; © Joe Fuhrman/VIREO; © Joe Fuhrman/VIREO; © Joe Fuhrman/VIREO.

346: © Glen Tepke/VIREO; © Glen Tepke/VIREO; © Harold Stiver/VIREO.

347: Ed Dunens; Christopher Watson; Christopher Watson.

348: © Laure W. Neish/VIREO; © Kevin Schafer/VIREO; © John Grahame Holmes/VIREO.

349: © Steve Young/VIREO; © Steve Young/VIREO; © Steve Young/VIREO.

350: © Herbert Clarke/VIREO; © Peter LaTourrette/VIREO; © Glen Tepke/VIREO.

351: © Adrian & Jane Binns/VIREO; USFWS Pacific Region; Kim Starr.

352: © Robert L. Pitman/VIREO; © Adrian & Jane Binns/VIREO; © Adrian & Jane Binns/VIREO.

353: © Ronald M. Saldino/VIREO; © Robert L. Pitman/VIREO; © Ronald M. Saldino/VIREO.

354: © John Hoffman/VIREO; © Harold Stiver/VIREO; © Brian Sullivan/VIREO.

355: © Adrian & Jane Binns/VIREO; © Arthur Morris/VIREO; © Harold Stiver/VIREO; © Harold Stiver/VIREO; © John Grahame Holmes/VIREO.

356: © Martin Hale/VIREO; © Martin Hale/VIREO; © Martin Hale/VIREO; Angela K. Kepler.

357: © Greg Lasley/VIREO; © George L. Armistead/VIREO; © Greg Lasley/VIREO.

358: © John Brian Patrick Patteson/VIREO; © Claude Nadeau/VIREO; © Harold Stiver/VIREO.

359: © Martin Meyers/VIREO; © Tony Palliser/VIREO; © Tadao Shimba/VIREO.

360: © Geoff Malosh/VIREO; © Geoff Malosh/VIREO; Jardim Botanico; Richard Crossley.

361: © Dr. Peter Stettenheim/VIREO; © Mark J. Rauzon/VIREO; © Robert L. Pitman/VIREO; © Tony Palliser/VIREO.

362: © Tadao Shimba/VIREO; © Jeff Poklen/VIREO; Greg Schechter; Gregory "Slobirdr" Smith.

363: © John Grahame Holmes/VIREO; © John Grahame Holmes/VIREO; Ed Dunens; JJ Harrison.

364: © Joe Fuhrman/VIREO; © Joe Fuhrman/VIREO; © Joe Fuhrman/VIREO; © Glenn Bartley/VIREO; © David Tipling/VIREO.

365: © Harold Stiver/VIREO; © Joe Fuhrman/VIREO; © Andrea Angel & Ross Wanless/VIREO; © Glen Tepke/VIREO.

366: © Glenn Bartley/VIREO; © Joe Fuhrman/VIREO; © Peter LaTourrette/VIREO; © Martin Hale/VIREO; Bill Bouton.

367: © Ian Hutton/VIREO; © Ian Hutton/VIREO; © Ian Hutton/VIREO.

368: © Martin Meyers/VIREO; © Brian Sullivan/VIREO; © Brian Sullivan/VIREO.

369: © Glen Tepke/VIREO; © Rick and Nora Bowers/VIREO; Cato Neimoidia; Caleb Putnam; © Glen Tepke/VIREO.

370: © Adrian & Jane Binns/VIREO; © George L. Armistead/VIREO; © Adrian & Jane Binns/VIREO; © Adrian & Jane Binns/VIREO.

371: © Barry Miller/VIREO; © Kevin Schafer/VIREO; © Barry Miller/VIREO; © Barry Miller/VIREO.

372: © Rolf Nussbaumer/VIREO; © Arthur Morris/VIREO; © Joe Fuhrman/VIREO; © Arthur Morris/VIREO; © Arthur Morris/VIREO.

373: © Marvin R. Hyett, M.D./VIREO; © Bill Gozansky/VIREO; © Adrian & Jane Binns/VIREO; © Arthur Morris/VIREO; © Arthur Morris/VIREO.

374: © Jens Eriksen/VIREO; © Robert L. Pitman/VIREO; © Ian Hutton/VIREO; © Ian Hutton/VIREO.

375: © Greg Lasley/VIREO; © Joe Fuhrman/VIREO; © Arthur Morris/VIREO; © Arthur Morris/VIREO; © Greg Lasley/VIREO.

376: © Peter LaTourrette/VIREO; © Kevin Schafer/VIREO; © Jesper Bay Jacobsen/VIREO; © Patricio Robles Gil/VIREO.

377: © Bob Steele/VIREO; © Arthur Morris/VIREO; © Greg Lasley/VIREO; © Arthur Morris/VIREO; © Joe Fuhrman/VIREO; © Joe Fuhrman/VIREO.

378: © Rob Curtis/VIREO; © Stuart Elsom/VIREO; © Kevin Schafer/VIREO; © Claude Nadeau/VIREO.

379: © Arthur Morris/VIREO; © Arthur Morris/VIREO; © Joe Fuhrman/VIREO; © Joe Fuhrman/VIREO.

380: © Arthur Morris/VIREO; © Rob Curtis/VIREO; © Greg Lasley/VIREO; © Kevin Schafer/VIREO; © Rob Curtis/VIREO.

381: © Rick and Nora Bowers/VIREO; © Loren P. Schisler/VIREO; © Arthur Morris/VIREO; © Dr. Michael Stubblefield/VIREO.

382: © Jukka Jantunen/VIREO; © Garth McElroy/VIREO; © Martin Hale/VIREO; © Steve Young/VIREO; © John Grahame Holmes/VIREO.

383: © John Grahame Holmes/VIREO; © Arthur Morris/VIREO; © Arthur Morris/VIREO; © Art L. Sowls/VIREO.

384: © John Grahame Holmes/VIREO; © Bob Steele/VIREO; © Joe Fuhrman/VIREO; © Brian Sullivan/VIREO; © Robert L. Pitman/VIREO; © Rob Curtis/VIREO.

385: © Arthur Morris/VIREO; Charles J Sharp; A Stewart; © Greg Lasley/VIREO; Hans Hillewaert.

386: © Martin Meyers/VIREO; © Arthur Morris/VIREO; © Arthur Morris/VIREO; © Rob Curtis/VIREO.

387: © Arthur Morris/VIREO; © Arthur Morris/VIREO; © Joe Fuhrman/VIREO; © Arthur Morris/VIREO; © Joe Fuhrman/VIREO.

388: © Dr. Michael Stubblefield/VIREO; © Tom Vezo/VIREO; © Laure W. Neish/VIREO.

389: © Bill Gozansky/VIREO; © Glenn Bartley/VIREO; © Kevin Smith/VIREO; © Flights of Fancy Adventures, Inc./VIREO.

390: © Arthur Morris/VIREO; © Greg Lasley/VIREO; © Arthur Morris/VIREO; © Rob Curtis/VIREO.

391: © John Cancalosi/VIREO; © Arthur Morris/VIREO; © Doug Wechsler/VIREO; © Dr. Joseph Turner/VIREO.

392: © Jens Eriksen/VIREO; © Dr. Warwick Tarboton/VIREO; © Martin Hale/VIREO; © John Grahame Holmes/VIREO.

393: © Jens Eriksen/VIREO; © Jens Eriksen/VIREO; © Jens Eriksen/VIREO; Francesco Veronesi; © Lloyd Spitalnik/VIREO.

394: © Arthur Morris/VIREO; © Arthur Morris/VIREO; © Arthur Morris/VIREO; © Arthur Morris/VIREO.

395: © Arthur Morris/VIREO; © Joanne Williams/VIREO; © Arthur Morris/VIREO; © Arthur Morris/VIREO; © Arthur Morris/VIREO.

396: © Tom Vezo/VIREO; © Bill Gozansky/VIREO; © Arthur Morris/VIREO.

397: © Arthur Morris/VIREO; © Richard Crossley/VIREO; © Fred Truslow/VIREO; © Laure W. Neish/VIREO; © Arthur Morris/VIREO; © Rob Curtis/VIREO.

398: © David Tipling/VIREO; © Arthur Morris/VIREO; © Arthur Morris/VIREO; © Brian Pfeiffer/VIREO; © Arthur Morris/VIREO.

399: © Joe Fuhrman/VIREO; © Arthur Morris/VIREO; © Rob Curtis/VIREO; © Rob Curtis/VIREO; © Laure W. Neish/VIREO.

400: © Rob Curtis/VIREO; © John Grahame Holmes/VIREO; © Arthur Morris/VIREO; © Dr. Warwick Tarboton/VIREO.

401: © Arthur Morris/VIREO; © Rob Curtis/VIREO; © Danny Brown/VIREO; © Arthur Morris/VIREO; © Bill Gozansky/VIREO; © Blake Shaw/VIREO.

402: © Doug Wechsler/VIREO; © Arthur Morris/VIREO; © Joe Fuhrman/VIREO.

403: © Don Grall/VIREO; © Johann Schumacher/VIREO; © Arthur Morris/VIREO; © Arthur Morris/VIREO.

404: © Joe Fuhrman/VIREO; © Rick and Nora Bowers/VIREO; © Nate and Angie Chappell/VIREO; © Glenn Bartley/VIREO; © Nate and Angie Chappell/VIREO.

405: © Arthur Morris/VIREO; © Richard Stade/VIREO; © Brian E. Small/VIREO; © Doug Wechsler/VIREO; © Arthur Morris/VIREO.

406: © Christian Artuso/VIREO; © Rick and Nora Bowers/VIREO; © Arthur Morris/VIREO; © Joe Fuhrman/VIREO; © Arthur Morris/VIREO.

407: © Joe Fuhrman/VIREO; © Paula Cannon/VIREO; © Neal G. Smith/VIREO; © Joe Fuhrman/VIREO; © Tom Vezo/VIREO.

408: © Rick and Nora Bowers/VIREO; © Marvin R. Hyett, M.D./VIREO; © Fred Truslow/VIREO; © Steven Holt/VIREO; © Christie Van Cleve/VIREO.

409: © Steve Young/VIREO; © Arthur Morris/VIREO; © Susan Liddle/VIREO; © John McKean/VIREO; © Joe Fuhrman/VIREO.

410: © Joe Fuhrman/VIREO; © Joe Fuhrman/VIREO; © Brian E. Small/VIREO; © Brian E. Small/VIREO.

411: © Tom Friedel/VIREO; © Tom Friedel/VIREO; © Brian K. Wheeler/VIREO; © Jim Culbertson/VIREO.

412: © Brian E. Small/VIREO; © James M. Wedge/VIREO; © Fred Truslow/VIREO; © Glenn Bartley/VIREO; © Marvin R. Hyett, M.D./VIREO.

413: © David Tipling/VIREO; © Kevin Smith/VIREO; © Kevin Smith/VIREO.

414: © Garth McElroy/VIREO; © Harold Stiver/VIREO; © Geoff Malosh/VIREO; © Bob Steele/VIREO.

415: © Johann Schumacher/VIREO; © Johann Schumacher/VIREO; © John Heidecker/VIREO; © Manuel Grosselet/VIREO.

416: © Lloyd Spitalnik/VIREO; © Richard Crossley/VIREO; © Rick and Nora Bowers/VIREO; © Glenn Bartley/VIREO; © Brian K. Wheeler/VIREO.

417: © Richard Crossley/VIREO; © Brian K. Wheeler/VIREO; © Paul Bannick/VIREO; © Richard Crossley/VIREO.

418: © Arthur Morris/VIREO; © Rob Curtis/VIREO; © Rob Curtis/VIREO; © Rob Curtis/VIREO; © Joe Fuhrman/VIREO; © Jon Hunter/VIREO.

419: © Stuart Elsom/VIREO; © Stuart Elsom/VIREO; © John Grahame Holmes/VIREO; © Stuart Elsom/VIREO.

420: © Brian K. Wheeler/VIREO; © Arthur Morris/VIREO; © Brian K. Wheeler/VIREO; © Richard Stade/VIREO.

421: © Arthur Morris/VIREO; © Brian E. Small/VIREO; © Brian E. Small/VIREO; © Greg Lasley/VIREO; © Dr. Joseph Turner/VIREO.

422: © Greg Lasley/VIREO; © Greg Lasley/VIREO; © Greg Lasley/VIREO; © Greg Lasley/VIREO; © Rick and Nora Bowers/VIREO.

423: © Joe Fuhrman/VIREO; © Rick and Nora Bowers/VIREO; © John Cancalosi/VIREO; © Joe Fuhrman/VIREO.

424: © Brian K. Wheeler/VIREO; © Paul Bannick/VIREO; © Kevin Schafer/VIREO; © Brian K. Wheeler/VIREO; © Kevin Schafer/VIREO.

425: © Joe Fuhrman/VIREO; © Joe Fuhrman/VIREO; Tony Castro; © Joe Fuhrman/VIREO.

426: © John McKean/VIREO; © Arthur Morris/VIREO; © Owen Deutsch/VIREO; © Greg Lasley/VIREO; © Richard Crossley/VIREO.

427: Michael Furtman; Michael Furtman; Michael Furtman; Michael Furtman; Michael Furtman; Michael Furtman.

428: © Brian K. Wheeler/VIREO; © Paula Cannon/VIREO; © Paula Cannon/VIREO; © Paula Cannon/VIREO; © Paula Cannon/VIREO.

429: © Greg Lasley/VIREO; © Blake Shaw/VIREO; © Nate and Angie Chappell/VIREO; © Arthur Morris/VIREO; © Arthur Morris/VIREO; © Greg Lasley/VIREO.

430: © Brian E. Small/VIREO; Greg Schechter; Alan Schmierer; Dominic Sherony.

431: © Marcus Robertson/VIREO; © Ron Austing/VIREO; © Rob Curtis/VIREO.

432: © Rob Curtis/VIREO; © John Cancalosi/VIREO; Mark Bohn of the U.S. Fish and Wildlife Service.

433: © G. Schneider/VIREO; © Peter LaTourrette/VIREO; © Paul Bannick/VIREO; © Nate and Angie Chappell/VIREO; © Laure W. Neish/VIREO; © Rob Curtis/VIREO.

434: © Rick and Nora Bowers/VIREO; © Paul Bannick/VIREO; © Rick and Nora Bowers/VIREO; © Bob Steele/VIREO.

435: © David Tipling/VIREO; © Martin Meyers/VIREO; © Steve Greer/VIREO; © Rick and Nora Bowers/VIREO.

436: © Paul Bannick/VIREO; © Paul Bannick/VIREO; © Laure W. Neish/VIREO; © Laure W. Neish/VIREO.

437: © John Cancalosi/VIREO; © Jukka Jantunen/VIREO; © Jukka Jantunen/VIREO, © Jukka Jantunen/VIREO.

438: © Helen Cruickshank/VIREO; © Rob & Ann Simpson/VIREO; © Tom Vezo/VIREO.

439: Bettina Arrigoni; Julio Mulero; Julio Mulero.

440: Yellowstone National Park; Becky Matsubara; William H. Majoros.

441: © Paul Bannick/VIREO; © Ron Austing/VIREO; © Rob Curtis/VIREO.

442: © Richard Crossley/VIREO; © Paul Bannick/VIREO; © G. Schneider/VIREO; © Rob Curtis/VIREO.

443: © Paul Bannick/VIREO; © Manuel Grosselet/VIREO; © Laure W. Neish/VIREO; © Glenn Bartley/VIREO.

444: © Joe Fuhrman/VIREO; © Paul Bannick/VIREO; © Rolf Nussbaumer/VIREO; © Brian E. Small/VIREO; © Robert A. "Spike" Baker/VIREO.

445: RoSy76; Susan E. Viera; © Rick and Nora Bowers/VIREO.

446: © Greg Lasley/VIREO; © Blake Shaw/VIREO; © Glenn Bartley/VIREO; © Arthur Morris/VIREO; © Paul Bannick/VIREO.

447: © Rick and Nora Bowers/VIREO; © John Cancalosi/VIREO; © Rick and Nora Bowers/VIREO.

448: © Paul Bannick/VIREO; © Rob Curtis/VIREO; Matthew Paulson; © Arthur Morris/VIREO; Marianna Scarr.

449: © Richard Crossley/VIREO; © Richard Crossley/VIREO; © Rob Curtis/VIREO; © Paul Bannick/VIREO; © Harold Stiver/VIREO.

450: © Brian E. Small/VIREO; © Brian E. Small/VIREO; © John McKean/VIREO.

451: © Paul Bannick/VIREO; © Tony Beck/VIREO; © Laura C. Williams/VIREO; © Paul Bannick/VIREO.

452: © Brad Bolduan/VIREO; © Paul Bannick/VIREO; © Paul Bannick/VIREO; © Jari Peltomaki/VIREO; © John Grahame Holmes/VIREO.

453: © Laure W. Neish/VIREO; © Bob Steele/VIREO; © Paul Bannick/VIREO.

454: © Rick and Nora Bowers/VIREO; © Rick and Nora Bowers/VIREO; © Rick and Nora Bowers/VIREO; © Joe Fuhrman/VIREO; © Rick and Nora Bowers/VIREO.

455: © Rick and Nora Bowers/VIREO; © Brian E. Small/VIREO; Dominic Sherony; © Joe Fuhrman/VIREO.

456: © Joe Fuhrman/VIREO; © George L. Armistead/VIREO; © Barry Miller/VIREO; © Tom J. Ulrich/VIREO; © Glenn Bartley/VIREO; © Rob Curtis/VIREO.

457: © Arthur Morris/VIREO; © Scott Linstead/VIREO; © John Heidecker/VIREO; © Laure W. Neish/VIREO; © Tom Vezo/VIREO.

458: © Scott Linstead/VIREO; © Glenn Bartley/VIREO; © Glenn Bartley/VIREO; © John Dunning/VIREO.

459: © Glenn Bartley/VIREO; © Glenn Bartley/VIREO; © Joe Fuhrman/VIREO; © Laure W. Neish/VIREO.

460: © Rob Curtis/VIREO; © Paul Bannick/VIREO; © Rob Curtis/VIREO; © Arthur Morris/VIREO.

461: © Paul Bannick/VIREO; © Rick and Nora Bowers/VIREO; © Paul Bannick/VIREO; © Paul Bannick/VIREO; © George M. Jett/VIREO.

462: © Paul Bannick/VIREO; © Nate and Angie Chappell/VIREO; © Rick and Nora Bowers/VIREO; © Rick and Nora Bowers/VIREO.

463: © Joe Fuhrman/VIREO; © Paul Bannick/VIREO; © Nate and Angie Chappell/VIREO; © Joe Fuhrman/VIREO; © Greg Lasley/VIREO.

464: © Johann Schumacher/VIREO; © Philip D. Moylan/VIREO; © Rick and Nora Bowers/VIREO.

465: © Paul Bannick/VIREO; © Glenn Bartley/VIREO; © Glenn Bartley/VIREO; © Glenn Bartley/VIREO; © Glenn Bartley/VIREO.

466: © Rick and Nora Bowers/VIREO; © Rob Curtis/VIREO; © Glenn Bartley/VIREO; © Rob Curtis/VIREO.

467: © Greg Lasley/VIREO; © Laure W. Neish/VIREO; © Laure W. Neish/VIREO; © Paul Bannick/VIREO.

468: © Bob Steele/VIREO; © Glenn Bartley/VIREO; © Glenn Bartley/VIREO; © Laure W. Neish/VIREO.

469: © Glenn Bartley/VIREO; © Glenn Bartley/VIREO; © Garth McElroy/VIREO; © Brian E. Small/VIREO; © Jukka Jantunen/VIREO.

470: © Joe Fuhrman/VIREO; © Glenn Bartley/VIREO; © Garth McElroy/VIREO; © Garth McElroy/VIREO; © Claude Nadeau/VIREO.

471: © Glenn Bartley/VIREO; © Rick and Nora Bowers/VIREO; © Rick and Nora Bowers/VIREO; © Kevin Smith/VIREO; © Adrian & Jane Binns/VIREO.

472: © Glenn Bartley/VIREO; © Marcus Robertson/VIREO; © Rolf Nussbaumer/VIREO; © Paul Bannick/VIREO.

473: © Joe Fuhrman/VIREO; © Paul Bannick/VIREO; © Hugh P. Smith, Jr. & Susan C. Smith/VIREO; © Joe Fuhrman/VIREO.

474: © Flights of Fancy Adventures, Inc./VIREO; © Paul Bannick/VIREO; © Rick and Nora Bowers/VIREO; © Rolf Nussbaumer/VIREO; © Bob Steele/VIREO; © Rolf Nussbaumer/VIREO.

475: © Greg Lasley/VIREO; © Greg Lasley/VIREO; © Rick and Nora Bowers/VIREO; © Stephen G. Maka/VIREO.

476: © Paul Bannick/VIREO; © Glenn Bartley/VIREO; © Martin Meyers/VIREO; © Glenn Bartley/VIREO.

477: © Glenn Bartley/VIREO; © Rob Curtis/VIREO; © Glenn Bartley/VIREO; © Rob Curtis/VIREO.

478: © Paul Bannick/VIREO; © Brian E. Small/VIREO; © Brian E. Small/VIREO; © Kevin Smith/VIREO.

479: © Paul Bannick/VIREO; © Brian E. Small/VIREO; © Rob Curtis/VIREO; © Brian E. Small/VIREO.

480: © Fred Truslow/VIREO; © Glenn Bartley/VIREO; © Paul Bannick/VIREO; © John McKean/VIREO.

481: © Geoff LeBaron/VIREO; U.S. Fish and Wildlife Service; © John Cancalosi/VIREO.

482: © Greg Lasley/VIREO; © Nate and Angie Chappell/VIREO; © Arthur Morris/VIREO; © Arthur Morris/VIREO; © Joe Fuhrman/VIREO; © Joe Fuhrman/VIREO.

483: © Steve Young/VIREO; © Steve Young/VIREO; © William S. Clark/VIREO; © John Grahame Holmes/VIREO; © Tom Vezo/VIREO.

484: © Bob Steele/VIREO; © Lloyd Spitalnik/VIREO; © Jim Culbertson/VIREO; © Glenn Bartley/VIREO; © Richard Crossley/VIREO.

485: © Brian K. Wheeler/VIREO; © Richard Crossley/VIREO; © Rob Curtis/VIREO; © John Heidecker/VIREO; © Johann Schumacher/VIREO.

486: © David Tipling/VIREO; © David Tipling/VIREO; © David Tipling/VIREO; © Stuart Elsom/VIREO.

487: © Greg Lasley/VIREO; © Greg Lasley/VIREO; © Tom Vezo/VIREO; © Joanne Williams/VIREO; © Nate and Angie Chappell/VIREO.

488: © Jens Eriksen/VIREO; © Bill Gozansky/VIREO; © Richard & Susan Day/VIREO; © Jens Eriksen/VIREO; © Jens Eriksen/VIREO.

489: © Marcus Robertson/VIREO; © Marcus Robertson/VIREO; © Arthur Morris/VIREO; © Doug Wechsler/VIREO.

490: © Tom Vezo/VIREO; © Rick and Nora Bowers/VIREO; © Tom Vezo/VIREO.

491: © Rob Curtis/VIREO; © Glenn Bartley/VIREO; © Rob Curtis/VIREO; © Rob Curtis/VIREO; © Glenn Bartley/VIREO.

492: © Greg Lasley/VIREO; © Arthur Morris/VIREO; © Greg Lasley/VIREO; © Greg Lasley/VIREO.

493: © Glenn Bartley/VIREO; © Adrian & Jane Binns/VIREO; © Glenn Bartley/VIREO.

494: © Marvin R. Hyett, M.D./VIREO; © Rick and Nora Bowers/VIREO; Ltshears.

495: © Adrian & Jane Binns/VIREO; © Tom Friedel/VIREO; © John H. Boyd III/VIREO; © Adrian & Jane Binns/VIREO.

496: © Patricio Robles Gil/VIREO; © Rick and Nora Bowers/VIREO; © Adrian & Jane Binns/VIREO; © Rick and Nora Bowers/VIREO; © Rick and Nora Bowers/VIREO; © Joe Fuhrman/VIREO.

497: © Brian E. Small/VIREO; © Steven Holt/VIREO; © Joe Fuhrman/VIREO; © Joe Fuhrman/VIREO.

498: © Joe Fuhrman/VIREO; © Blake Shaw/VIREO; © Rick and Nora Bowers/VIREO; © Rob Curtis/VIREO.

499: © Joe Fuhrman/VIREO; © Kevin Schafer/VIREO; © Marvin R. Hyett, M.D./VIREO.

500: © Bill Gozansky/VIREO; © David Tipling/VIREO; © Glenn Bartley/VIREO; © Jorge Sierra/VIREO.

501: © Jorge Sierra/VIREO; © Jorge Sierra/VIREO; © Tom J. Ulrich/VIREO; © Jorge Sierra/VIREO.

502: © Jens Eriksen/VIREO; © Bob Steele/VIREO; © Bob de Lange/VIREO; © David Tipling/VIREO.

503: © Tadao Shimba/VIREO; © Jim Culbertson/VIREO; © Crawford H. Greenewalt/VIREO.

504: © Greg Lasley/VIREO; © Brian E. Small/VIREO; © Greg Lasley/VIREO; © Greg Lasley/VIREO.

505: © Brian E. Small/VIREO; © Rick and Nora Bowers/VIREO; © Manuel Grosselet/VIREO; © Brian E. Small/VIREO.

506: © Rick and Nora Bowers/VIREO; © Joe Fuhrman/VIREO; © Tom Friedel/VIREO; © Brian E. Small/VIREO.

507: © Greg Lasley/VIREO; © Rolf Nussbaumer/VIREO; © Rick and Nora Bowers/VIREO.

508: © Bob Steele/VIREO; © Bob Steele/VIREO; © Joe Fuhrman/VIREO; © Joe Fuhrman/VIREO.

509: © Greg Lasley/VIREO; © Tom Vezo/VIREO; © Rob Curtis/VIREO; © Rob Curtis/VIREO.

510: © Rick and Nora Bowers/VIREO; © Paul Bannick/VIREO; © Bob Steele/VIREO; © Joe Fuhrman/VIREO.

511: © Doug Wechsler/VIREO; © Tom Friedel/VIREO; © Claude Nadeau/VIREO.

512: © Frank Schleicher/VIREO; © Jens Eriksen/VIREO; Andy Reago & Chrissy McClarren; © Tom Vezo/VIREO.

513: © Joe Fuhrman/VIREO; © Joe Fuhrman/VIREO; © Rick and Nora Bowers/VIREO; © Brian E. Small/VIREO.

514: © Glenn Bartley/VIREO; © Glenn Bartley/VIREO; © Glenn Bartley/VIREO.

515: © Tony Beck/VIREO; © Adrian & Jane Binns/VIREO; © Tony Beck/VIREO.

516: © Tom Friedel/VIREO; © George M. Jett/VIREO; © Stuart Elsom/VIREO; © Glenn Bartley/VIREO; © Manuel Grosselet/VIREO.

517: © Rob Curtis/VIREO; © Greg Lasley/VIREO; © Greg Lasley/VIREO; © Rick and Nora Bowers/VIREO.

518: © George L. Armistead/VIREO; © Greg Lasley/VIREO; © Brian E. Small/VIREO; © Brian E. Small/VIREO.

519: © Brian E. Small/VIREO; © Joe Fuhrman/VIREO; © Rick and Nora Bowers/VIREO; © Brian E. Small/VIREO.

520: © Laure W. Neish/VIREO; © Rob Curtis/VIREO; © Kevin Smith/VIREO.

521: © Rob Curtis/VIREO; © Jukka Jantunen/VIREO; © Glenn Bartley/VIREO; © Joe Fuhrman/VIREO; © Laure W. Neish/VIREO.

522: © Geoff Malosh/VIREO; © Adrian & Jane Binns/VIREO; Photochem_PA; Don Faulkner.

523: © Doug Wechsler/VIREO; © Claude Nadeau/VIREO; © Doug Wechsler/VIREO; © Claude Nadeau/VIREO.

524: © Hugh P. Smith, Jr. & Susan C. Smith/VIREO; © Rick and Nora Bowers/VIREO; © Joe Fuhrman/VIREO; © Greg Lasley/VIREO.

525: © George L. Armistead/VIREO; © Lloyd Spitalnik/VIREO; © Christian Artuso/VIREO; © Glenn Bartley/VIREO; © Adrian & Jane Binns/VIREO.

526: © Brian E. Small/VIREO; © Garth McElroy/VIREO; © Glenn Bartley/VIREO; © Garth McElroy/VIREO.

527: © Rick and Nora Bowers/VIREO; © Bob Steele/VIREO; © Brian E. Small/VIREO.

528: © Hugh P. Smith, Jr. & Susan C. Smith/VIREO; © Glenn Bartley/VIREO; © Peter LaTourrette/VIREO; © Laure W. Neish/VIREO.

529: © Rob Curtis/VIREO; © Brian E. Small/VIREO; © Rick and Nora Bowers/VIREO; © Glenn Bartley/VIREO; © Brian E. Small/VIREO.

530: Ekaterina Chernetsova; Charles J. Sharp; Laura Gooch; Laura Gooch; Matt MacGillivray.

531: © Glenn Bartley/VIREO; © Rob Curtis/VIREO; © Rob Curtis/VIREO; © Arthur Morris/VIREO.

532: © Greg Lasley/VIREO; © Greg Lasley/VIREO; © Greg Lasley/VIREO; © Doug Wechsler/VIREO; © Brian E. Small/VIREO.

533: © Thomas McNish M./VIREO; © Brian E. Small/VIREO; © Greg Lasley/VIREO; © Rick and Nora Bowers/VIREO.

534: © Bob Steele/VIREO; © Laure W. Neish/VIREO; © Joe Fuhrman/VIREO; © Brian E. Small/VIREO.

535: © Philip D. Moylan/VIREO; © Dr. Edgar T. Jones/VIREO; © Rick and Nora Bowers/VIREO; © Rob Curtis/VIREO; © Garth McElroy/VIREO.

536: Gablaj Hammond; © Glenn Bartley/VIREO; © Glenn Bartley/VIREO; Andy Reago & Chrissy McClarren; © Laure W. Neish/VIREO.

537: © Brian E. Small/VIREO; © Greg Lasley/VIREO; © Glenn Bartley/VIREO; © Glenn Bartley/VIREO.

538: © Bob Steele/VIREO; © Glenn Bartley/VIREO; © Joe Fuhrman/VIREO; © Kevin Smith/VIREO.

539: © Peter LaTourrette/VIREO; © Rick and Nora Bowers/VIREO; © Glenn Bartley/VIREO; © Rick and Nora Bowers/VIREO.

540: © Joe Fuhrman/VIREO; © Joe Fuhrman/VIREO; © Manuel Grosselet/VIREO; © Glenn Bartley/VIREO.

541: © Glenn Bartley/VIREO; © Brian E. Small/VIREO; © Manuel Grosselet/VIREO; © Brian E. Small/VIREO.

542: © Alan David Walther/VIREO; © Hugh P. Smith, Jr. & Susan C. Smith/VIREO; © Blake Shaw/VIREO; © Alan David Walther/VIREO; © Laure W. Neish/VIREO.

543: © Greg Lasley/VIREO; © Lee Trott/VIREO; © Johann Schumacher/VIREO; © Rob Curtis/VIREO.

544: © Geoff Malosh/VIREO; © Joe Fuhrman/VIREO; © Glenn Bartley/VIREO; © Laure W. Neish/VIREO.

545: © Rob Curtis/VIREO; © Glenn Bartley/VIREO; © Bob Steele/VIREO; © Geoff Malosh/VIREO; © Greg Lasley/VIREO.

546: © Adrian & Jane Binns/VIREO; © Gerard Bailey/VIREO; © Arthur Morris/VIREO; © Rob Curtis/VIREO.

547: © Joe Fuhrman/VIREO; © Geoff Malosh/VIREO; © Glenn Bartley/VIREO; © Jari Peltomaki/VIREO; © Jari Peltomaki/VIREO.

548: © Greg Lasley/VIREO; © Greg Lasley/VIREO; © Brian E. Small/VIREO; © Greg Lasley/VIREO.

549: © Brian E. Small/VIREO; © Greg Lasley/VIREO; © Brian E. Small/VIREO; © Greg Lasley/VIREO; © Greg Lasley/VIREO.

550: © Bob Steele/VIREO; © Greg Lasley/VIREO; © Greg Lasley/VIREO; © Glenn Bartley/VIREO; © Bob Steele/VIREO.

551: © Brian E. Small/VIREO; © Brian E. Small/VIREO; © Rick and Nora Bowers/VIREO.

552: © Rick and Nora Bowers/VIREO; © Bob Steele/VIREO; © Bob Steele/VIREO; © Glenn Bartley/VIREO.

553: © Greg Lasley/VIREO; © Martin Meyers/VIREO; © Richard Crossley/VIREO; © Joe Fuhrman/VIREO; © Rob Curtis/VIREO; © Martin Meyers/VIREO.

554: © Brian E. Small/VIREO; © Laure W. Neish/VIREO; © Kevin Smith/VIREO; © Glenn Bartley/VIREO.

555: © Rick and Nora Bowers/VIREO; © Greg Lasley/VIREO; © Brian E. Small/VIREO; © Manuel Grosselet/VIREO; © Brian E. Small/VIREO.

556: © Greg Lasley/VIREO; © Bob Steele/VIREO; © Glenn Bartley/VIREO; © Brian E. Small/VIREO; © Rick and Nora Bowers/VIREO.

557: © Rob Curtis/VIREO; © Rob Curtis/VIREO; © Rob Curtis/VIREO; © Rob Curtis/VIREO.

558: © Martin Meyers/VIREO; © Rob Curtis/VIREO; © Gerard Bailey/VIREO; © Rob Curtis/VIREO.

559: © Glenn Bartley/VIREO; © Arthur Morris/VIREO; © Greg Lasley/VIREO.

560: © Peter LaTourrette/VIREO; © Doug Wechsler/VIREO; © Manuel Grosselet/VIREO; © Doug Wechsler/VIREO.

561: © Adrian & Jane Binns/VIREO; © Martin Meyers/VIREO; © Tom Friedel/VIREO; © John Dunning/VIREO.

562: © Adrian & Jane Binns/VIREO; © Garth McElroy/VIREO; © Garth McElroy/VIREO; © Garth McElroy/VIREO; © Adrian & Jane Binns/VIREO; © Glenn Bartley/VIREO.

563: © Greg Lasley/VIREO; © Joe Fuhrman/VIREO; © Don Grall/VIREO; © Greg Lasley/VIREO; © Joe Fuhrman/VIREO.

564: © Greg Lasley/VIREO; © Scott Linstead/VIREO; © Glenn Bartley/VIREO; © Kevin Smith/VIREO; © Greg Lasley/VIREO; © Tom Friedel/VIREO.

565: © Glenn Bartley/VIREO; © Kevin Smith/VIREO; © Joe Fuhrman/VIREO; © Dale Zimmerman/VIREO; © Dale Zimmerman/VIREO.

566: Andy Reago & Chrissy McClarren; Mike's Birds; Andy Reago & Chrissy McClarren; VJ Anderson; Eric Ellingson.

567: © Garth McElroy/VIREO; © Rick and Nora Bowers/VIREO; © Arthur Morris/VIREO; © Rob Curtis/VIREO; © Glenn Bartley/VIREO.

568: © John Verm Sherman/VIREO; © Brian E. Small/VIREO; © Arthur Morris/VIREO; © Brian E. Small/VIREO.

569: Ben Smegelsky; © Joe Fuhrman/VIREO; © Joe Fuhrman/VIREO; Pacific Southwest Region; Glenn Benson.

570: © Garth McElroy/VIREO; © Mathew Tekulsky/VIREO; © Arthur Morris/VIREO; © Kevin Smith/VIREO; © Hugh P. Smith, Jr. & Susan C. Smith/VIREO; © Garth McElroy/VIREO.

571: © Brian E. Small/VIREO; © Rolf Nussbaumer/VIREO; © Brian E. Small/VIREO; © Rolf Nussbaumer/VIREO; © Brian E. Small/VIREO; © Rolf Nussbaumer/VIREO.

572: © Joe Fuhrman/VIREO; © Brian E. Small/VIREO; © Sid & Shirley Rucker/VIREO; © Joe Fuhrman/VIREO.

573: © Jukka Jantunen/VIREO; © Paul Bannick/VIREO; © Doug Wechsler/VIREO; © Jukka Jantunen/VIREO; © Doug Wechsler/VIREO.

574: © Rick and Nora Bowers/VIREO; © Rob Curtis/VIREO; © Glenn Bartley/VIREO; © Martin Meyers/VIREO.

575: © Hugh P. Smith, Jr. & Susan C. Smith/VIREO; © Hugh P. Smith, Jr. & Susan C. Smith/VIREO; Steve Voght; © Joe Fuhrman/VIREO.

576: © Bob Steele/VIREO; © Dustin Huntington/VIREO; © Rick and Nora Bowers/VIREO; © Joe Fuhrman/VIREO; © Johann Schumacher/VIREO.

577: © Rick and Nora Bowers/VIREO; © Rick and Nora Bowers/VIREO; © Greg Lasley/VIREO; © Glenn Bartley/VIREO.

578: © Joe Fuhrman/VIREO; © Greg Lasley/VIREO; © Serge LaFrance/VIREO.

579: © Johann Schumacher/VIREO; © Marvin R. Hyett, M.D./VIREO; © Johann Schumacher/VIREO; Chuck Homler; © Johann Schumacher/VIREO.

580: © Dale Zimmerman/VIREO; © Rick and Nora Bowers/VIREO; © Rick and Nora Bowers/VIREO; © Rick and Nora Bowers/VIREO.

581: © Marvin R. Hyett, M.D./VIREO; © Arthur Morris/VIREO; © Arthur Morris/VIREO; © Laure W. Neish/VIREO.

582: © Stuart Elsom/VIREO; © Stuart Elsom/VIREO; © David Tipling/VIREO; © David Tipling/VIREO.

583: © Joe Fuhrman/VIREO; © Brian E. Small/VIREO; © Claude Nadeau/VIREO; © Rick and Nora Bowers/VIREO.

584: © Glenn Bartley/VIREO; © Laure W. Neish/VIREO; © Arthur Morris/VIREO; © Glenn Bartley/VIREO; © Rob Curtis/VIREO.

585: © Glenn Bartley/VIREO; © Arthur Morris/VIREO; © Rob Curtis/VIREO; © Flights of Fancy Adventures, Inc./VIREO.

586: © Glenn Bartley/VIREO; © Laure W. Neish/VIREO; © Brian K. Wheeler/VIREO; © Laure W. Neish/VIREO; © Laure W. Neish/VIREO.

587: © Manuel Grosselet/VIREO; © Rob Curtis/VIREO; © Gerard Bailey/VIREO; © Rob Curtis/VIREO.

588: © Dr. Michael Stubblefield/VIREO; © Glenn Bartley/VIREO; © Rob Curtis/VIREO; © Rob Curtis/VIREO.

589: © Dr. Warwick Tarboton/VIREO; © Arthur Morris/VIREO; © Rob Curtis/VIREO; © Rob Curtis/VIREO; © Sidney W. Dunkle/VIREO.

590: © Joe Fuhrman/VIREO; © Arthur Morris/VIREO; © Greg Lasley/VIREO; © Greg Lasley/VIREO.

591: © Rick and Nora Bowers/VIREO; © Rick and Nora Bowers/VIREO; © Rick and Nora Bowers/VIREO.

592: © Brian E. Small/VIREO; © Rick and Nora Bowers/VIREO; © Joe Fuhrman/VIREO.

593: © Rolf Nussbaumer/VIREO; © Rob Curtis/VIREO; © Paul Bannick/VIREO; © Garth McElroy/VIREO; © Rick and Nora Bowers/VIREO.

594: © Bob Steele/VIREO; © Paul Bannick/VIREO; © Glenn Bartley/VIREO; © Dustin Huntington/VIREO; © Tom Middleton/VIREO; © Brian E. Small/VIREO.

595: © Joe Fuhrman/VIREO; © Brian E. Small/VIREO; © Joe Fuhrman/VIREO.

596: © Glenn Bartley/VIREO; © Glenn Bartley/VIREO; © Arthur Morris/VIREO; © Paul Bannick/VIREO; © Tom J. Ulrich/VIREO.

597: © Bahrt Inc./VIREO; © Paul Bannick/VIREO; © Garth McElroy/VIREO; © Brian E. Small/VIREO.

598: © Jari Peltomaki/VIREO; © Jari Peltomaki/VIREO; © Aaron Lang/VIREO; © Aaron Lang/VIREO.

599: © Brian E. Small/VIREO; © Bob Steele/VIREO; © Rolf Nussbaumer/VIREO; © Sid & Shirley Rucker/VIREO; © Rick and Nora Bowers/VIREO.

600: © Joe Fuhrman/VIREO; © Hugh P. Smith, Jr. & Susan C. Smith/VIREO; © Bob Steele/VIREO; © Bob Steele/VIREO; © Joe Fuhrman/VIREO.

601: © Dustin Huntington/VIREO; © Brian E. Small/VIREO; © Dustin Huntington/VIREO; © Brian E. Small/VIREO.

602: © Garth McElroy/VIREO; © Arthur Morris/VIREO; © Arthur Morris/VIREO; © Steve Greer/VIREO.

603: © Joe Fuhrman/VIREO; © Brian E. Small/VIREO; © Glenn Bartley/VIREO; © Rolf Nussbaumer/VIREO.

604: © Brian E. Small/VIREO; © Bob Steele/VIREO; © Greg Lasley/VIREO; © Joe Fuhrman/VIREO; © Rick and Nora Bowers/VIREO.

605: © Glenn Bartley/VIREO; © Joe Fuhrman/VIREO; © Brian E. Small/VIREO; © Joe Fuhrman/VIREO.

606: © Glenn Bartley/VIREO; © Joe Fuhrman/VIREO; © Brian E. Small/VIREO; © Garth McElroy/VIREO.

607: © Glenn Bartley/VIREO; © Rick and Nora Bowers/VIREO; © Philip D. Moylan/VIREO; © Garth McElroy/VIREO.

608: © Greg Lasley/VIREO; © Glenn Bartley/VIREO; © Kevin Smith/VIREO; © Laure W. Neish/VIREO.

609: © Brian E. Small/VIREO; © Greg Lasley/VIREO; © Brian E. Small/VIREO; © Brian E. Small/VIREO.

610: © Rob Curtis/VIREO; © Glenn Bartley/VIREO; © Garth McElroy/VIREO; © Dr. Edgar T. Jones/VIREO.

611: © Rick and Nora Bowers/VIREO; © Glenn Bartley/VIREO; © Jukka Jantunen/VIREO; © Rick and Nora Bowers/VIREO; © Brian E. Small/VIREO.

612: © Garth McElroy/VIREO; © Brian E. Small/VIREO; © Greg Lasley/VIREO; © Garth McElroy/VIREO; © Bob Steele/VIREO.

613: © Santiago Imberti/VIREO; © Glenn Bartley/VIREO; © Martin Meyers/VIREO; © Laure W. Neish/VIREO; © Glenn Bartley/VIREO.

614: © Glenn Bartley/VIREO; © Glenn Bartley/VIREO; © Bob Steele/VIREO; © Glenn Bartley/VIREO.

615: © Garth McElroy/VIREO; © David Tipling/VIREO; © Garth McElroy/VIREO; © David Tipling/VIREO; © David Tipling/VIREO; © Garth McElroy/VIREO.

616: © Rob Curtis/VIREO; © Rick and Nora Bowers/VIREO; © Edson Endrigo/VIREO; © Rick and Nora Bowers/VIREO.

617: © Bob Steele/VIREO; © Dr. Edgar T. Jones/VIREO; © Doug Wechsler/VIREO; © Greg Lasley/VIREO.

618: © Dr. Michael Stubblefield/VIREO; © Rob Curtis/VIREO; © Brian E. Small/VIREO; © Rob Curtis/VIREO; © Glenn Bartley/VIREO.

619: © Joe Fuhrman/VIREO; © Joe Fuhrman/VIREO; © Bill Gozansky/VIREO; © Rick and Nora Bowers/VIREO.

620: © Rick and Nora Bowers/VIREO; © Joe Fuhrman/VIREO; © Greg Lasley/VIREO; © Brian E. Small/VIREO.

621: © Greg Lasley/VIREO; © Joe Fuhrman/VIREO; © Dr. Joseph Turner/VIREO; © Gerard Bailey/VIREO.

622: © Brian E. Small/VIREO; © Bob Steele/VIREO; © Joe Fuhrman/VIREO; © Bob Steele/VIREO; © Brian E. Small/VIREO; © Joe Fuhrman/VIREO.

623: © Rick and Nora Bowers/VIREO; © Rick and Nora Bowers/VIREO; © Rick and Nora Bowers/VIREO; © Bob Steele/VIREO; © Bob Steele/VIREO; © Bob Steele/VIREO.

624: © Bob Steele/VIREO; Andy Reago & Chrissy McClarren; © Christian Artuso/VIREO; Andy Reago & Chrissy McClarren.

625: © Bob Steele/VIREO; © Greg Lasley/VIREO; © Joe Fuhrman/VIREO; © Glenn Bartley/VIREO; © Glenn Bartley/VIREO.

626: © Martin Hale/VIREO; © Jens Eriksen/VIREO; © John Grahame Holmes/VIREO; © Martin Hale/VIREO; © Jens Eriksen/VIREO.

627: © Brian E. Small/VIREO; © Brian E. Small/VIREO; © Rob Curtis/VIREO; © Rob Curtis/VIREO; © Brian E. Small/VIREO.

628: © Brian E. Small/VIREO; © Rob Curtis/VIREO; © Garth McElroy/VIREO; © Greg Lasley/VIREO; © Bob Steele/VIREO.

629: © Amit Thakurta/VIREO; © Martin Hale/VIREO; © Martin Hale/VIREO; © John Grahame Holmes/VIREO.

630: © Joe Fuhrman/VIREO; © Brian E. Small/VIREO; © Martin Hale/VIREO; © Brian E. Small/VIREO.

631: © Brian E. Small/VIREO; © Joe Fuhrman/VIREO; © Joe Fuhrman/VIREO; © Joe Fuhrman/VIREO; © Martin Meyers/VIREO.

674: © Martin Hale/VIREO; © Jens Eriksen/VIREO; © Martin Hale/VIREO; © Martin Hale/VIREO.

675: © Greg Lasley/VIREO; © Rob Curtis/VIREO; © Marcus Robertson/VIREO; © Glenn Bartley/VIREO.

676: © Glenn Bartley/VIREO; © Brian E. Small/VIREO; © Glenn Bartley/VIREO; © Brian E. Small/VIREO.

677: © Jari Peltomaki/VIREO; © Laure W. Neish/VIREO; © Jari Peltomaki/VIREO; © Jari Peltomaki/VIREO.

678: © Laure W. Neish/VIREO; © Glenn Bartley/VIREO; © Glenn Bartley/VIREO; © Glenn Bartley/VIREO; © Martin Meyers/VIREO.

679: © Garth McElroy/VIREO; © Glenn Bartley/VIREO; © Garth McElroy/VIREO; © Stuart Elsom/VIREO.

680: © Rick and Nora Bowers/VIREO; © Paul Bannick/VIREO; © Paul Bannick/VIREO; © Bob Steele/VIREO.

681: © Brian E. Small/VIREO; © Paul Bannick/VIREO; Tony Castro; Gregory "Slobidr" Smith; Tony Castro.

682: © Glenn Bartley/VIREO; © Brian E. Small/VIREO; © Brian E. Small/VIREO; © Geoff Malosh/VIREO; © Glenn Bartley/VIREO.

683: © Rick and Nora Bowers/VIREO; © Nate and Angie Chappell/VIREO; © Rolf Nussbaumer/VIREO; © Bob Steele/VIREO; © Greg Lasley/VIREO.

684: © Garth McElroy/VIREO; © Rick and Nora Bowers/VIREO; © Garth McElroy/VIREO; © Garth McElroy/VIREO.

685: © Glenn Bartley/VIREO; © Arthur Morris/VIREO; © Joe Fuhrman/VIREO; © Rick and Nora Bowers/VIREO.

686: © Claude Nadeau/VIREO; © Glenn Bartley/VIREO; © Rob Curtis/VIREO; © Richard Crossley/VIREO.

687: © Brian E. Small/VIREO; © Rob Curtis/VIREO; © Brian E. Small/VIREO; © Claude Nadeau/VIREO; © Robin Chittenden/VIREO.

688: © Robin Chittenden/VIREO; © Joe Fuhrman/VIREO; © Glenn Bartley/VIREO; © Glenn Bartley/VIREO; © Jukka Jantunen/VIREO.

689: © Garth McElroy/VIREO; © Garth McElroy/VIREO; © Garth McElroy/VIREO; © Garth McElroy/VIREO; © Garth McElroy/VIREO.

690: © Glenn Bartley/VIREO; © Laure W. Neish/VIREO; © Greg Lasley/VIREO; © Martin Meyers/VIREO.

691: © Greg Lasley/VIREO; © Hugh P. Smith, Jr. & Susan C. Smith/VIREO; © Brian E. Small/VIREO; © Kevin Smith/VIREO; © Greg Lasley/VIREO.

692: © Bob Steele/VIREO; © Rick and Nora Bowers/VIREO; © Rick and Nora Bowers/VIREO; © Hugh P. Smith, Jr. & Susan C. Smith/VIREO; © Brian E. Small/VIREO.

693: © Rick and Nora Bowers/VIREO; © Steve Greer/VIREO; © Bob Steele/VIREO; © Hugh P. Smith, Jr. & Susan C. Smith/VIREO.

694: © Glenn Bartley/VIREO; © Glenn Bartley/VIREO; © Brian E. Small/VIREO; © Robert Royse/VIREO.

695: © Greg Lasley/VIREO; © Greg Lasley/VIREO; © Bob Steele/VIREO; © Greg Lasley/VIREO.

696: © Glenn Bartley/VIREO; © Glenn Bartley/VIREO; © Glenn Bartley/VIREO; © Glenn Bartley/VIREO.

697: © Glenn Bartley/VIREO; © Greg Lasley/VIREO; © Greg Lasley/VIREO; © Rob Curtis/VIREO.

698: © Lloyd Spitalnik/VIREO; © Brian E. Small/VIREO; © Rob Curtis/VIREO; © Rob Curtis/VIREO; © Lloyd Spitalnik/VIREO.

699: © Paul Bannick/VIREO; Alan Schmierer; © Bob Steele/VIREO; © Paul Bannick/VIREO.

700: Imran Shah; © Steve Young/VIREO; © Aurélien Audevard/VIREO; Dibyendu Ash.

701: © Jari Peltomaki/VIREO; Kjetil Hansen; © David Tipling/VIREO; © Jari Peltomaki/VIREO; © Tadao Shimba/VIREO.

702: © Rick and Nora Bowers/VIREO; © Rick and Nora Bowers/VIREO; © Brian E. Small/VIREO; © Bob Steele/VIREO.

703: © Rick and Nora Bowers/VIREO; © Brian E. Small/VIREO; © Brian E. Small/VIREO; © Rick and Nora Bowers/VIREO.

704: © Joe Fuhrman/VIREO; © Greg Lasley/VIREO; © Joe Fuhrman/VIREO; © Greg Lasley/VIREO.

705: © Brian E. Small/VIREO; © Brian E. Small/VIREO; © Brian E. Small/VIREO; © Greg Lasley/VIREO.

706: © Joe Fuhrman/VIREO; © Gerard Bailey/VIREO; © Bob Steele/VIREO.

707: © Greg Lasley/VIREO; © Joe Fuhrman/VIREO; © Greg Lasley/VIREO; © Greg Lasley/VIREO; © Greg Lasley/VIREO.

708: © Rick and Nora Bowers/VIREO; © Brian E. Small/VIREO; © Joe Fuhrman/VIREO; © Joe Fuhrman/VIREO; © Brian E. Small/VIREO.

709: © Brian E. Small/VIREO; © Rick and Nora Bowers/VIREO; © Greg Lasley/VIREO; © Rick and Nora Bowers/VIREO.

710: © Joe Fuhrman/VIREO; © Glenn Bartley/VIREO; © Joe Fuhrman/VIREO; © Greg Lasley/VIREO; © Rolf Nussbaumer/VIREO.

711: © Rob Curtis/VIREO; © Greg Lasley/VIREO; © Greg Lasley/VIREO; © Brian E. Small/VIREO.

712: © Glenn Bartley/VIREO; © Marcus Robertson/VIREO; © Garth McElroy/VIREO; © Glenn Bartley/VIREO; © Rick and Nora Bowers/VIREO; © Claude Nadeau/VIREO.

713: © Claude Nadeau/VIREO; © Rick and Nora Bowers/VIREO; © Rick and Nora Bowers/VIREO; © Steve Mlodinow/VIREO.

714: © Brian E. Small/VIREO; © Joe Fuhrman/VIREO; © Brian E. Small/VIREO; © Bob Steele/VIREO; © Brian E. Small/VIREO.

715: © Greg Lasley/VIREO; © Gerard Bailey/VIREO; © Rick and Nora Bowers/VIREO; © John Heidecker/VIREO.

716: © Arthur Morris/VIREO; © Glenn Bartley/VIREO; © Glenn Bartley/VIREO; © Rick and Nora Bowers/VIREO; © Steve Mlodinow/VIREO.

717: © Dr. Michael Stubblefield/VIREO; © Bob Steele/VIREO; © Adrian & Jane Binns/VIREO.

718: © Glenn Bartley/VIREO; © Joe Fuhrman/VIREO; © Dr. Edgar T. Jones/VIREO; © Garth McElroy/VIREO.

719: © Johann Schumacher/VIREO; © Johann Schumacher/VIREO; © Garth McElroy/VIREO; © Johann Schumacher/VIREO; © Brian E. Small/VIREO.

720: © Glenn Bartley/VIREO; © Garth McElroy/VIREO; © Garth McElroy/VIREO.

721: © Paul Bannick/VIREO; © Bob Steele/VIREO; © Dustin Huntington/VIREO.

722: © Greg Lasley/VIREO; © Adrian & Jane Binns/VIREO; © Greg Lasley/VIREO; © Greg Lasley/VIREO; © Glenn Bartley/VIREO.

723: © Greg Lasley/VIREO; © Laure W. Neish/VIREO; © Rick and Nora Bowers/VIREO; © Laure W. Neish/VIREO; © Rick and Nora Bowers/VIREO; © Greg Lasley/VIREO.

724: © Brian E. Small/VIREO; © Glenn Bartley/VIREO; © Paul Bannick/VIREO; © Glenn Bartley/VIREO; © Arthur Morris/VIREO.

725: © Greg Lasley/VIREO; © Greg Lasley/VIREO; © Rob Curtis/VIREO; © Rob Curtis/VIREO; © Rob Curtis/VIREO.

726: © Claude Nadeau/VIREO; © Johann Schumacher/VIREO; © Brian E. Small/VIREO; © Garth McElroy/VIREO; © Garth McElroy/VIREO.

727: © Brian E. Small/VIREO; Becky Matsubara; Dominic Sherony.

728: Becky Matsubara; Becky Matsubara; Alan Schimierer; Alan Schimierer; Alan Schimierer.

729: © Brian E. Small/VIREO; © Glenn Bartley/VIREO; © Garth McElroy/VIREO; © Greg Lasley/VIREO.

730: © Kevin Karlson/VIREO; © Greg Lasley/VIREO; © Brian E. Small/VIREO; © Brian E. Small/VIREO.

731: © Richard Crossley/VIREO; © Joe Fuhrman/VIREO; © Greg Lasley/VIREO; © Joe Fuhrman/VIREO.

732: © Bob Steele/VIREO; Dawn Beattie ; Melissa McMasters; Andrew C.

733: © Gerard Bailey/VIREO; © Brian E. Small/VIREO; © Gerard Bailey/VIREO; © Arthur Morris/VIREO.

734: © Brian E. Small/VIREO; © Greg Lasley/VIREO; © Greg Lasley/VIREO.

735: © Rob Curtis/VIREO; © Rick and Nora Bowers/VIREO; © Robert Royse/VIREO; © Joe Fuhrman/VIREO.

736: © Rick and Nora Bowers/VIREO; © Joe Fuhrman/VIREO; © Gerard Bailey/VIREO; © Laure W. Neish/VIREO; © Rob Curtis/VIREO.

737: © Doug Wechsler/VIREO; © Jukka Jantunen/VIREO; © Rick and Nora Bowers/VIREO; © Garth McElroy/VIREO.

738: © Glenn Bartley/VIREO; © Laure W. Neish/VIREO; © Garth McElroy/VIREO.

739: © Rob Curtis/VIREO; © Garth McElroy/VIREO; © Johann Schumacher/VIREO; © Rob Curtis/VIREO; © Rob Curtis/VIREO.

740: © Greg Lasley/VIREO; © Glenn Bartley/VIREO; © Steven Holt/VIREO; © Rick and Nora Bowers/VIREO; © Rick and Nora Bowers/VIREO; © Bob Steele/VIREO.

741: © Rick and Nora Bowers/VIREO; © Bob Steele/VIREO; © Rick and Nora Bowers/VIREO; © Brian E. Small/VIREO.

742: © Joe Fuhrman/VIREO; © Brian E. Small/VIREO; © Mathew Tekulsky/VIREO; © Rick and Nora Bowers/VIREO; © Laure W. Neish/VIREO.

743: © Greg Lasley/VIREO; © Bob Steele/VIREO; © Rick and Nora Bowers/VIREO; © Rick and Nora Bowers/VIREO.

744: © Rick and Nora Bowers/VIREO; © Brian E. Small/VIREO; © Rick and Nora Bowers/VIREO.

745: © Brian E. Small/VIREO; © Glenn Bartley/VIREO; © Brian E. Small/VIREO; © Kevin Smith/VIREO; © Joe Fuhrman/VIREO.

746: © Doug Wechsler/VIREO; © Garth McElroy/VIREO; © Greg Lasley/VIREO; © Rick and Nora Bowers/VIREO; © Johann Schumacher/VIREO; © Johann Schumacher/VIREO.

747: © Doug Wechsler/VIREO; © Claude Nadeau/VIREO; © John Dunning/VIREO.

748: © Brian E. Small/VIREO; © Joe Fuhrman/VIREO; © Brian E. Small/VIREO.

749: © Greg Lasley/VIREO; © Arthur Morris/VIREO; © Rob Curtis/VIREO; © Greg Lasley/VIREO; © Arthur Morris/VIREO.

750: © Rob Curtis/VIREO; © Joe Fuhrman/VIREO; © Rick and Nora Bowers/VIREO; © Brian E. Small/VIREO.

751: © Rob Curtis/VIREO; © Teresa Hedden/VIREO; © Rick and Nora Bowers/VIREO.

752: © Arthur Morris/VIREO; © Doug Wechsler/VIREO; © Manuel Grosselet/VIREO; © Greg Lasley/VIREO; © Doug Wechsler/VIREO.

753: © Knut Eisermann/VIREO; Ron Knight; © Joe Fuhrman/VIREO.

754: © Brian E. Small/VIREO; © Brian E. Small/VIREO; © Brian E. Small/VIREO; © Brian E. Small/VIREO; © Brian E. Small/VIREO.

755: © Joe Fuhrman/VIREO; © Bob Steele/VIREO; © Bob Steele/VIREO; © Hugh P. Smith, Jr. & Susan C. Smith/VIREO; © Bob Steele/VIREO.

756: © Joe Fuhrman/VIREO; © Rick and Nora Bowers/VIREO; © Rick and Nora Bowers/VIREO; © Joe Fuhrman/VIREO.

757: © Brian E. Small/VIREO; © Marvin R. Hyett, M.D./VIREO; © Bob Steele/VIREO; © Bob Steele/VIREO.

758: © Adrian & Jane Binns/VIREO; © Joe Fuhrman/VIREO; © Joe Fuhrman/VIREO.

759: © Glenn Bartley/VIREO; © Rob Curtis/VIREO; © Glenn Bartley/VIREO.

760: © Greg Lasley/VIREO; © Joe Fuhrman/VIREO; © Glenn Bartley/VIREO; © Brian E. Small/VIREO; © Joe Fuhrman/VIREO.

761: © Brian E. Small/VIREO; © Johann Schumacher/VIREO; © Brian E. Small/VIREO; © Johann Schumacher/VIREO; © Arthur Morris/VIREO; © Johann Schumacher/VIREO.

762: © Bob Steele/VIREO; © Bob Steele/VIREO; © Rick and Nora Bowers/VIREO; © Rick and Nora Bowers/VIREO.

763: © Rick and Nora Bowers/VIREO; © Garth McElroy/VIREO; © Johann Schumacher/VIREO; © Rick and Nora Bowers/VIREO.

764: © Hugh P. Smith, Jr. & Susan C. Smith/VIREO; © Garth McElroy/VIREO; © Bob Steele/VIREO; © Bob Steele/VIREO.

765: © Joe Fuhrman/VIREO; Tim Sackton; © Tom J. Ulrich/VIREO.

766: © Greg Lasley/VIREO; © Arthur Morris/VIREO; © Robert Shantz/VIREO; © Joe Fuhrman/VIREO; © Joe Fuhrman/VIREO.

767: © Rob & Ann Simpson/VIREO; © Arthur Morris/VIREO; © Brian E. Small/VIREO; © Rick and Nora Bowers/VIREO.

768: © Johann Schumacher/VIREO; © Brian E. Small/VIREO; © Brian E. Small/VIREO; © Rick and Nora Bowers/VIREO.

769: © Glenn Bartley/VIREO; © Jukka Jantunen/VIREO; © Brian E. Small/VIREO; © Marvin R. Hyett, M.D./VIREO; © Brian E. Small/VIREO.

770: © Rob Curtis/VIREO; © Michael Patrikeev/VIREO; © Rob Curtis/VIREO; © Rob Curtis/VIREO; © Tom Vezo/VIREO.

771: © Doug Wechsler/VIREO; © Arthur Morris/VIREO; © Doug Wechsler/VIREO; © Brian E. Small/VIREO.

772: © Joe Fuhrman/VIREO; © Glenn Bartley/VIREO; © Brian Sullivan/VIREO; © Kevin Smith/VIREO.

773: © Glenn Bartley/VIREO; © Joe Fuhrman/VIREO; © Marcus Robertson/VIREO; © Brian E. Small/VIREO; © Tom Friedel/VIREO.

774: © Brian E. Small/VIREO; © Brian E. Small/VIREO; © Brian E. Small/VIREO.

775: © Brian E. Small/VIREO; © Brian E. Small/VIREO; © Brian E. Small/VIREO; © Garth McElroy/VIREO; © Rob Curtis/VIREO.

776: © Brian E. Small/VIREO; © Joe Fuhrman/VIREO; © Garth McElroy/VIREO; © Garth McElroy/VIREO.

777: © Glenn Bartley/VIREO; © Brian E. Small/VIREO; © Lloyd Spitalnik/VIREO; © Brian E. Small/VIREO.

778: © Glenn Bartley/VIREO; © Johann Schumacher/VIREO; © Rob Curtis/VIREO; © Garth McElroy/VIREO; © Dr. Joseph Turner/VIREO.

779: © Brian E. Small/VIREO; © Rob Curtis/VIREO; © Brian E. Small/VIREO; © Glenn Bartley/VIREO; © Brian E. Small/VIREO.

780: © Greg Lasley/VIREO; © Rick and Nora Bowers/VIREO; © John McKean/VIREO; © Rick and Nora Bowers/VIREO; © Brad Bolduan/VIREO.

781: © Doug Wechsler/VIREO; © Doug Wechsler/VIREO; © Brian E. Small/VIREO; © Brian E. Small/VIREO.

782: © Joe Fuhrman/VIREO; © Manuel Grosselet/VIREO; © Manuel Grosselet/VIREO.

783: © Glenn Bartley/VIREO; © Brian E. Small/VIREO; © Glenn Bartley/VIREO; © Glenn Bartley/VIREO.

784: © Brian E. Small/VIREO; © Paul Bannick/VIREO; © Laure W. Neish/VIREO.

785: © Greg Lasley/VIREO; © Rick and Nora Bowers/VIREO; © Rick and Nora Bowers/VIREO; © Rick and Nora Bowers/VIREO.

786: © Rick and Nora Bowers/VIREO; © Rob Curtis/VIREO; © Greg Lasley/VIREO; © Rick and Nora Bowers/VIREO.

787: © Brian E. Small/VIREO; © Dr. Joseph Turner/VIREO; © Laure W. Neish/VIREO.

788: © Bob Steele/VIREO; © Bob Steele/VIREO; © Bob Steele/VIREO; © Brian E. Small/VIREO.

789: © Glenn Bartley/VIREO; © Glenn Bartley/VIREO; © Robert Royse/VIREO; Alan Schmierer; © Dr. Joseph Turner/VIREO.

790: © Manuel Grosselet/VIREO; © Arthur Morris/VIREO; © Arthur Morris/VIREO.

791: © Joe Fuhrman/VIREO; © Glenn Bartley/VIREO.

792: © Rick and Nora Bowers/VIREO; © Garth McElroy/VIREO; © Brian E. Small/VIREO; © Brian E. Small/VIREO.

793: © Rob Curtis/VIREO; © James M. Wedge/VIREO; © Brian E. Small/VIREO.

794: © Greg Lasley/VIREO; © Greg Lasley/VIREO; © Garth McElroy/VIREO.

795: © Rob Curtis/VIREO; © Rob Curtis/VIREO; © Greg Lasley/VIREO; © Rob Curtis/VIREO.

796: © Dr. Joseph Turner/VIREO; © Brian E. Small/VIREO; © Joe Fuhrman/VIREO; © Brian E. Small/VIREO.

797: © Ron Austing/VIREO; © Ron Austing/VIREO; © Rob Curtis/VIREO.

798: © Garth McElroy/VIREO; © Rob Curtis/VIREO; © Arthur Morris/VIREO; © Rob Curtis/VIREO.

799: © Brian E. Small/VIREO; © Robert Royse/VIREO; © Glenn Bartley/VIREO.

800: © Arthur Morris/VIREO; © Robert Royse/VIREO; © Brian E. Small/VIREO; © Brian E. Small/VIREO.

801: © Glenn Bartley/VIREO; © Glenn Bartley/VIREO; © Rick and Nora Bowers/VIREO; © Greg Lasley/VIREO; © Nate and Angie Chappell/VIREO.

802: © Rob Curtis/VIREO; © Greg Lasley/VIREO; © Garth McElroy/VIREO.

803: © Garth McElroy/VIREO; © Garth McElroy/VIREO; © Rick and Nora Bowers/VIREO; © Garth McElroy/VIREO.

804: © Brian E. Small/VIREO; © Brian E. Small/VIREO; © Brian E. Small/VIREO; © Garth McElroy/VIREO; © Rick and Nora Bowers/VIREO.

805: © Garth McElroy/VIREO; © Arthur Morris/VIREO; © Greg Lasley/VIREO.

806: © Greg Lasley/VIREO; © Rick and Nora Bowers/VIREO; © Greg Lasley/VIREO.

807: © Paul Bannick/VIREO; © Rob Curtis/VIREO; © Glenn Bartley/VIREO; © Garth McElroy/VIREO.

808: © Tom Friedel/VIREO; © Glenn Bartley/VIREO; © Garth McElroy/VIREO; © Garth McElroy/VIREO.

809: © Glenn Bartley/VIREO; © Rob Curtis/VIREO; © Gerard Bailey/VIREO; © James M. Wedge/VIREO.

810: © Glenn Bartley/VIREO; © Garth McElroy/VIREO; © Rob Curtis/VIREO.

811: © G. Schneider/VIREO; © Gerard Bailey/VIREO; © Greg Lasley/VIREO.

812: © Glenn Bartley/VIREO; © Rob Curtis/VIREO; © Richard Crossley/VIREO.

813: © Brian E. Small/VIREO; © Greg Lasley/VIREO; © Greg Lasley/VIREO; © Jim Culbertson/VIREO; © Scott Elowitz/VIREO.

814: © Glenn Bartley/VIREO; © Glenn Bartley/VIREO; © Glenn Bartley/VIREO; © Garth McElroy/VIREO.

815: © Rick and Nora Bowers/VIREO; © Bob Steele/VIREO; © Glenn Bartley/VIREO; © Brian E. Small/VIREO.

816: © Glenn Bartley/VIREO; © Glenn Bartley/VIREO; © Joe Fuhrman/VIREO; © Glenn Bartley/VIREO.

817: © Glenn Bartley/VIREO; © Paul Bannick/VIREO; © Glenn Bartley/VIREO; © Glenn Bartley/VIREO.

818: © Brian E. Small/VIREO; © Brian E. Small/VIREO; © Joe Fuhrman/VIREO; © Brian E. Small/VIREO.

819: © Greg Lasley/VIREO; © Greg Lasley/VIREO; © Brian E. Small/VIREO.

820: © Garth McElroy/VIREO; © Arthur Morris/VIREO; © Rob Curtis/VIREO.

821: Rick and Nora Bowers/Alamy Stock Photo; Rick and Nora Bowers/Alamy Stock Photo; Francesco Verones.

822: © Rick and Nora Bowers/VIREO; © John Dunning/VIREO; © Rick and Nora Bowers/VIREO.

823: © Doug Wechsler/VIREO; © Doug Wechsler/VIREO; © John Dunning/VIREO.

824: © Garth McElroy/VIREO; © Bob Steele/VIREO; © Bob Steele/VIREO; © Bob Steele/VIREO; © Glenn Bartley/VIREO.

825: © Glenn Bartley/VIREO; © Brian E. Small/VIREO; © Kevin Smith/VIREO; © Garth McElroy/VIREO.

826: © Glenn Bartley/VIREO; © Greg Lasley/VIREO; © Glenn Bartley/VIREO.

827: © Glenn Bartley/VIREO; © Geoff Malosh/VIREO; © Brian E. Small/VIREO; © Glenn Bartley/VIREO.

828: © Glenn Bartley/VIREO; © Joe Fuhrman/VIREO; © Joe Fuhrman/VIREO; © John Dunning/VIREO.

829: © Tom Friedel/VIREO; © Tom Friedel/VIREO; © Tom Friedel/VIREO; © Rick and Nora Bowers/VIREO.

830: © Rob Curtis/VIREO; © Brian E. Small/VIREO; © Nate and Angie Chappell/VIREO; © Rob Curtis/VIREO; © Joe Fuhrman/VIREO.

831: © Brian E. Small/VIREO; © Rob Curtis/VIREO; © Brian E. Small/VIREO; © Glenn Bartley/VIREO.

832: © Laure W. Neish/VIREO; © Glenn Bartley/VIREO; © Brian E. Small/VIREO; © Bob Steele/VIREO; © Paul Bannick/VIREO.

833: © Glenn Bartley/VIREO; © Joe Fuhrman/VIREO; © Glenn Bartley/VIREO; © Robert A. "Spike" Baker/VIREO; © Glenn Bartley/VIREO.

834: Joseph Fuhrman; Joseph Fuhrman; © Mark Lockwood/VIREO.

835: © Johann Schumacher/VIREO; © Rick and Nora Bowers/VIREO; © Johann Schumacher/VIREO; © Joe Fuhrman/VIREO; © Nate and Angie Chappell/VIREO.

836: © Nate and Angie Chappell/VIREO; © Joe Fuhrman/VIREO; © Glenn Bartley/VIREO; © Greg Lasley/VIREO; © Brian E. Small/VIREO.

837: © Brian E. Small/VIREO; © Claude Nadeau/VIREO; © Rob Curtis/VIREO; © Rob Curtis/VIREO; © Rob Curtis/VIREO.

838: © Glenn Bartley/VIREO; © Glenn Bartley/VIREO; © Rick and Nora Bowers/VIREO; © Nate and Angie Chappell/VIREO.

839: © Greg Lasley/VIREO; © Greg Lasley/VIREO; Dominic Sherony.

840: © Rob Curtis/VIREO; © Rob Curtis/VIREO; © Brian E. Small/VIREO.

841: © Joe Fuhrman/VIREO; © Brian E. Small/VIREO; © Brian E. Small/VIREO; © Peter LaTourrette/VIREO.

PHOTOGRAPHY CREDITS

842: © Joe Fuhrman/VIREO; © Brian E. Small/VIREO; © Rob Curtis/VIREO; © Glenn Bartley/VIREO; © Dr. Joseph Turner/VIREO.

843: © Joe Fuhrman/VIREO; © Greg Lasley/VIREO; © Greg Lasley/VIREO; © Rick and Nora Bowers/VIREO; © Joe Fuhrman/VIREO.

844: © Greg Lasley/VIREO; © Brian E. Small/VIREO; © Brian E. Small/VIREO; © Rolf Nussbaumer/VIREO; © Manuel Grosselet/VIREO; © Arthur Morris/VIREO.

845: © Brian E. Small/VIREO; © Greg Lasley/VIREO; © Rob Curtis/VIREO; © Rick and Nora Bowers/VIREO; © Rick and Nora Bowers/VIREO.

846: © Dr. Michael Stubblefield/VIREO; © Doug Wechsler/VIREO; © Arthur Morris/VIREO; © Doug Wechsler/VIREO.

847: © John Dunning/VIREO; © Steve Mlodinow/VIREO; © Flights of Fancy Adventures, Inc./VIREO; © Tom Friedel/VIREO.

848: © Greg Lasley/VIREO; © John Dunning/VIREO; © John Dunning/VIREO; © Antonio Hidalgo/VIREO.

850: © Jukka Jantunen/VIREO; Alan Schmierer.

851: © Glenn Bartley/VIREO.

852: Brian A. Wolf; Amanda Guercio.

853: © John Hoffman/VIREO; © Brian E. Small/VIREO.

854: © Joe Fuhrman/VIREO; © Steve Mlodinow/VIREO.

855: © Doug Wechsler/VIREO; © Glenn Bartley/VIREO.

856: © Arthur Morris/VIREO.

857: © Dan Roby & Karen Brink/VIREO.

858: © Fred Truslow/VIREO.

859: © Arthur Morris/VIREO.

860: © David Tipling/VIREO; U.S. Fish and Wildlife Service.

861: © Rob Curtis/VIREO.

862: © Brian E. Small/VIREO.

863: © John McKean/VIREO.

864: © Greg Lasley/VIREO.

865: © Dustin Huntington/VIREO.

866: © Bob Steele/VIREO.

867: © Johann Schumacher/VIREO; © Glenn Bartley/VIREO.

868: © Greg Lasley/VIREO; © Paul Bannick/VIREO.

869: © Robin Chittenden/VIREO; © Claude Nadeau/VIREO.

870: © Glenn Bartley/VIREO.

871: © Glenn Bartley/VIREO.

872: © Rick and Nora Bowers/VIREO.

Any work of this scope takes a dedicated team of talented experts, advisors, and editors to bring it to life. It also takes an inspirational spark, and for that, we want to thank the National Audubon Society, which since 1905 has championed the conservation of bird species and habitat throughout North America. **www.audubon.org**

The images used throughout this book reflect countless, patient hours in the field on the part of scores of photographers as well as the painstaking curation of those images. We thank Dan Thomas of VIREO, along with all of the photographers noted on pages 886–906, whose images bring these species to the printed page with immediacy, intimacy, and elegance.

We are grateful to the following collaborators whose expertise informed the bird biology discussions in the beginning of this book. We appreciate their work to further the cause of bird research, conservation, and education: Alan B. Bond, Ph.D., Emeritus Professor of Biological Sciences at the University of Nebraska-Lincoln; Luke Butler, Ph.D., Associate Professor of Biology at The College of New Jersey; Brian Cassie, author, dedicated naturalist, conservationist, and teacher; Judy Diamond, Ph.D., Professor and Curator at the University of Nebraska State Museum; Michael Goldman, Conservation and Outreach Manager at Grange Insurance Audubon Center; Jonathan T. Hagstrum, Ph.D., U.S. Geological Survey; John Marzluff, Ph.D., author and the James Ridgeway Professor of Forest Resources at the University of Washington.

Warm thanks to Jane Cirigliano for masterfully designing this book's pages, Heather Rowland of Add+Water for the book design concept, and Kirill Litvinov and Alexandra Kovernzieva for rendering the range map illustrations. Very special thanks to our publishing partners at Alfred A. Knopf for their ongoing encouragement, guidance, and support; most notably Andy Hughes and his editorial staff.

Lastly, at the core of this effort is the team at Fieldstone Publishing, whose devotion to this project imbues every page of this book:

Shyla Stewart, President and CEO

Andrew Stewart, Publisher Emeritus

Jim Cirigliano, Editor-In-Chief

Katy Savage, Production Coordinator

Heather Coon, Finance

Shavar Dawkins, Photo Editor / Research

Sophia Foster, Social Media Coordinator

We thank all of the Audubon experts who contributed their knowledge to ensure this book represents the organization's mission: Audubon's Marketing Division, including Jose Carbonell, Chief Marketing Officer; Julisa Colón, Senior Manager of Brand Marketing; Holly Mascaro, Manager of Brand Marketing; Audubon's Science Division, including Geoffrey S. LeBaron, Director of the Christmas Bird Count; Audubon's Content Division, including Jennifer Bogo, Vice President of Content; Kristina Deckert, Art Director; Sabine Meyer, Photography Director; Melanie Ryan, Assistant Art Director; Hannah Waters, Senior Editor, Climate; and Camilla Cerea, Photo Editor and Photographer.

THIS IS A BORZOI BOOK PUBLISHED BY ALFRED A. KNOPF

Copyright © 2021 by Fieldstone Publishing, Inc.

All rights reserved. Published in the United States by Alfred A. Knopf, a division of Penguin Random House LLC, New York, and distributed in Canada by Penguin Random House Canada Limited, Toronto.

www.aaknopf.com

Knopf, Borzoi Books, and the colophon are registered trademarks of Penguin Random House LLC.

Audubon™ is a licensed, registered trademark of the National Audubon Society. All rights reserved.

Based on *The Audubon Society Master Guide to Birding* (Alfred A. Knopf, 1983), *National Audubon Society Field Guide to North American Birds: Eastern Region* (Alfred A. Knopf, 1994), and *National Audubon Society Field Guide to North American Birds: Western Region* (Alfred A. Knopf, 1994).

For more information about Audubon, including how to become a member, visit www.audubon.org or call 1-844-428-3826.

Library of Congress Cataloging-in-Publication Data
Names: National Audubon Society, editor. | Cirigliano, Jim, 1981- editor.
Title: The National Audubon Society birds of North America / edited by Jim Cirigliano, editor in chief, Fieldstone Publishing, Inc.
Description: First edition. | New York: Alfred A. Knopf, 2021. | Includes index.
Identifiers: LCCN 2020026445 (print) | LCCN 2020026446 (ebook) | ISBN 9780525655671 (hardcover) | ISBN 9780525655688 (ebook)
Subjects: LCSH: Birds—North America—Identification.
Classification: LCC QL681 .N27 2021 (print) | LCC QL681 (ebook) | DDC 598.097—dc23
LC record available at https://lccn.loc.gov/2020026445
LC ebook record available at https://lccn.loc.gov/2020026446

Jacket photograph: Bohemian Waxwing (*Bombycilla garrulous*) © Paul Bannick
Jacket design by Linda Huang
Frontispiece by Tim Timmis / Audubon Photography Awards

Manufactured in China

First Edition